ISBN 978-1-5280-8711-7
PIBN 10925828

1 MONTH OF
FREE
READING

at
www.ForgottenBooks.com

By purchasing this book you are eligible for one month membership to ForgottenBooks.com, giving you unlimited access to our entire collection of over 1,000,000 titles via our web site and mobile apps.

To claim your free month visit:

www.forgottenbooks.com/free925828

English
Français
Deutsche
Italiano
Español
Português

www.forgottenbooks.com

Mythology Photography **Fiction**
Fishing Christianity **Art** Cooking
Essays Buddhism Freemasonry
Medicine **Biology** Music **Ancient**
Egypt Evolution Carpentry Physics
Dance Geology **Mathematics** Fitness
Shakespeare **Folklore** Yoga Marketing
Confidence Immortality Biographies
Poetry **Psychology** Witchcraft
Electronics Chemistry History **Law**
Accounting **Philosophy** Anthropology
Alchemy Drama Quantum Mechanics
Atheism Sexual Health **Ancient History**
Entrepreneurship Languages Sport
Paleontology Needlework Islam
Metaphysics Investment Archaeology
Parenting Statistics Criminology
Motivational

THE LIBRARY
OF
THE UNIVERSITY
OF CALIFORNIA
IRVINE

AMERICAN STATE REPORTS,

CONTAINING THE

CASES OF GENERAL VALUE AND AUTHORITY

SUBSEQUENT TO THOSE CONTAINED IN THE "AMERICAN
DECISIONS" AND THE "AMERICAN REPORTS,"

DECIDED IN THE

COURTS OF LAST RESORT

OF THE SEVERAL STATES.

SELECTED, REPORTED, AND ANNOTATED

BY A. C. FREEMAN,
AND THE ASSOCIATE EDITORS OF THE "AMERICAN DECISIONS."

VOL. LXII.

SAN FRANCISCO:
BANCROFT-WHITNEY COMPANY,
LAW PUBLISHERS AND LAW BOOKSELLERS.
1898.

SAN FRANCISCO:
THE FILMER-ROLLINS ELECTROTYPE COMPANY,
TYPOGRAPHERS AND STEREOTYPERS.

AMERICAN STATE REPORTS.

VOL. LXII.

SCHEDULE

showing the original volumes of reports in which the cases herein selected and re-reported may be found, and the pages of this volume devoted to each state.

SCHEDULE

SHOWING IN WHAT VOLUMES OF THIS SERIES THE CASES
REPORTED IN THE SEVERAL VOLUMES OF OFFICIAL
REPORTS MAY BE FOUND.

State reports are in parentheses, and the numbers of this series in bold-faced figures.

ALABAMA. — (83) **3**; (84) **5**; (85) **7**; (86) **11**; (87) **13**; (88) **16**; (89) **18**; (90,
91) **24**; (92) **25**; (93) **30**; (94) **33**; (95) **36**; (96, 97) **38**; (98) **39**; (99)
42; (100, 101) **46**; (102) **48**; (103) **49**; (104, 105) **53**; (106, 107, 108) **54**;
(109, 110) **55**; (111) **56**; (112) **57**; (113) **59**; (114) **62**.

ARKANSAS. — (48) **3**; (49) **4**; (50) **7**; (51) **14**; (52) **20**; (53) **22**; (54) **26**;
(55) **29**; (56) **35**; (57) **38**; (58) **41**; (59) **43**; (60) **46**; (61, 62) **54**;
(63) **58**; (64) **62**.

CALIFORNIA. — (72) **1**; (73) **2**; (74) **5**; (75) **7**; (76) **9**; (77) **11**; (78, 79) **12**; (80)
13; (81) **15**; (82) **16**; (83) **17**; (84) **18**; (85) **20**; (86) **21**; (87, 88) **22**;
(89) **23**; (90, 91) **25**; (92, 93) **27**; (94) **28**; (95) **29**; (96) **31**; (97) **33**;
(98) **35**; (99) **37**; (100) **38**; (101) **40** (102) **41**; (103) **42**; (104) **43**;
(105) **45**; (106) **46**; (107) **48**; (108) **49**; (109) **50**; (110, 111) **52**; (112)
53; (113) **54**; (114) **55**; (115) **56**; (116) **58**; (117) **59**; (118) **62**.

COLORADO. — (10) **3**; (11) **7**; (12) **13**; (13) **16**; (14) **20**; (15) **22**; (16) **25**;
(17) **31**; (18) **36**; (19) **41**; (20) **46**; (21) **52**; (22) **55**; (23) **58**.

CONNECTICUT. — (54) **1**; (55) **3**; (56) **7**; (57) **14**; (58) **18**; (59) **21**; (60) **25**;
(61) **29**; (62) **36**; (63) **38**; (64) **42**; (65) **48**; (66) **50**; (67) **52**; (68) **57**;
(69) **61**.

DELAWARE. — (5 Houst.) **1**; (6 Houst.) **22**; (7 Houst.) **40**; (9 Houst.) **43**.

FLORIDA. — (22) **1**; (23) **11**; (24) **12**; (25, 26) **23**; (27) **26**; (28) **29**; (29) **30**;
(30) **32**; (31) **34**; (32) **37**; (33) **39**; (34) **43**; (35) **48**; (30) **51**; (37) **53**;
(38) **56**.

GEORGIA. — (76) **2**; (77) **4**; (78) **6**; (79) **11**; (80, 81) **12**; (82) **14**; (83, 84) **20**;
(85) **21**; (86) **22**; (87) **27**; (88) **30**; (89) **32**; (90) **35**; (91, 92, 93) **44**;
(94) **47**; (95, 96) **51**; (97) **54**; (98) **58**; (99) **59**; (100) **62**.

IDAHO. — (2) **35**.

ILLINOIS. — (121) **2**; (122) **3**; (123) **5**; (124) **7**; (125) **8**; (126) **9**; (127) **11**;
(128) **15**; (129) **16**; (130) **17**; (131) **19**; (132) **22**; (133, 134) **23**; (135)
25; (136) **29**; (137) **31**; (138, 139) **32**; (140, 141) **33**; (142) **34**; (143,
144, 145) **36**; (146, 147) **37**; (148) **39**; (149, 150) **41**; (151) **42**; (152) **43**;
(154) **45**; (153, 155) **46**; (156) **47**; (157) **48**; (158) **49**; (159) **50**; (160,
161) **52**; (162) **53**; (163) **54**; (164, 165) **56**; (166) **57**; (167) **59**; (168, 169)
61; (170) **62**.

INDIANA. — (112) **2**; (113) **3**; (114) **5**; (115) **7**; (116) **9**; (117, 118) **10**; (119)
12; (120, 121) **16**; (122) **17**; (123) **18**; (124) **19**; (125) **21**; (126, 127) **22**;
(128) **25**; (129) **28**; (130) **30**; (131) **31**; (132) **32**; (133) **36**; (134) **39**;

(135) **41**; (136) **43**; (137) **45**; (138) **46**; (139) **47**; (140) **49**; (1, 2, 3, Ind. App.; 141) **50**; (4, 5, 6, Ind. App.; 142) **51**; (7, 8, Ind. App.; 143) **52**; (9, 10 Ind. App.) **53**; (11 Ind. App.) **54**; (13 Ind. App.; 144) **55**; (14 Ind. App.) **56**; (15 Ind. App.; 145) **57**; (146) **58**; (16 Ind. App.) **59**; (17 Ind. App.) **60**; (147, 148) **62**.

IOWA. — (72) **2**; (73) **5**; (74) **7**; (75) **9**; (76, 77) **14**; (78) **16**; (79) **18**; (80) **20**; (81) **25**; (82) **31**; (83) **32**; (84) **35**; (85) **39**; (86) **41**; (87) **43**; (88) **45**; (89, 90), **48**; (91) **51**; (92) **54**; (93) **57**; (94, 95) **58**; (96, 97) **59**; (98) **60**; (99) **61**; (100) **62**.

KANSAS. — (37) **1**; (38) **5**; (39) **7**; (40) **10**; (41) **13**; (42) **16**; (43) **19**; (44) **21**; (45) **23**; (46) **26**; (47) **27**; (48) **30**; (49) **33**; (50) **34**; (51) **37**; (52) **39**; (53) **42**; (54) **45**; (55) **49**; (56) **54**; (57) **57**; (58) **62**.

KENTUCKY. — (83, 84) **4**; (85) **7**; (86) **9**; (87) **12**; (88) **21**; (89) **25**; (90) **29**; (91) **34**; (92) **36**; (93) **40**; (94) **42**; (95) **44**; (96) **49**; (97) **53**; (98) **56**; (99) **59**.

LOUISIANA. — (39 La. Ann.) **4**; (40 La. Ann.) **8**; (41 La. Ann.) **17**; (42 La. Ann.) **21**; (43 La. Ann.) **26**; (44 La. Ann.) **32**; (45 La. Ann.) **40**; (46, 47 La. Ann.) **49**; (48 La. Ann.) **55**; (49 La. Ann.) **62**.

MAINE. — (79) **1**; (80) **6**; (81) **10**; (82) **17**; (83) **23**; (84) **30**; (85) **35**; (86) **41**; (87) **47**; (88) **51**; (89) **56**; (90) **60**.

MARYLAND. — (67) **1**; (68) **6**; (69) **9**; (70) **14**; (71) **17**; (72) **20**; (73) **25**; (74) **28**; (75) **32**; (76) **35**; (77) **39**; (78) **44**; (80) **45**; (79) **47**; (81) **48**; (82) **51**; (83) **55**; (84) **57**; (85) **60**.

MASSACHUSETTS. — (145) **1**; (146) **4**; (147) **9**; (148) **12**; (149) **14**; (150) **15**; (151) **21**; (152) **23**; (153) **25**; (154) **26**; (155) **31**; (156) **32**; (157) **34**; (158) **35**; (159) **38**; (160) **39**; (161) **42**; (162) **44**; (163) **47**; (164) **49**; (165) **52**; (166) **55**; (167) **57**; (168) **60**; (169) **61**.

MICHIGAN. — (60, 61) **1**; (62) **4**; (63) **6**; (64, 65) **8**; (66, 67) **11**; (68, 69, 75) **13**; (70) **14**; (71, 76) **15**; (72, 73, 74) **16**; (77, 78) **18**; (79) **19**; (80) **20**; (81, 82, 83) **21**; (84) **22**; (85, 86, 87) **24**; (88) **26**; (89) **28**; (90, 91) **30**; (92) **31**; (93) **32**; (94) **34**; (95, 96) **35**; (97) **37**; (98) **39**; (99) **41**; (100) **43**; (101) **45**; (102) **47**; (103) **50**; (104) **53**; (105) **55**; (106) **58**; (107) **61**; (108) **62**.

MINNESOTA. — (36) **1**; (37) **5**; (38) **8**; (39, 40) **12**; (41) **16**; (42) **18**; (43) **19**; (44) **20**; (45) **22**; (46) **24**; (47) **28**; (48) **31**; (49) **32**; (50) **36**; (51, 52) **38**; (53) **39**; (54) **40**; (55) **43**; (56) **45**; (57) **47**; (58) **49**; (59) **50**; (60) **51**; (61) **52**; (62) **54**; (63) **56**; (64) **58**; (65) **60**; (66) **61**.

MISSISSIPPI. — (65) **7**; (66) **14**; (67) **19**; (68) **24**; (69) **30**; (70) **35**; (71) **42**; (72) **48**; (73) **55**; (74) **60**.

MISSOURI. — (92) **1**; (93) **3**; (94) **4**; (95) **6**; (96) **9**; (97) **10**; (98) **14**; (99) **17**; (100) **18**; (101) **20**; (102) **22**; (103) **23**; (104, 105) **24**; (106) **27**; (107) **28**; (108, 109) **32**; (110, 111) **33**; (112) **34**; (113, 114) **35**; (115) **37**; (116, 117) **38**; (118) **40**; (119, 120) **41**; (121) **42**; (122) **43**; (123) **45**; (124, 125) **46**; (126) **47**; (127) **48**; (128) **49**; (129) **50**; (130) **51**; (131) **52**; (132) **53**; (133) **54**; (134) **56**; (135, 136) **58**; (137) **59**; (138) **60**; (139) **61**; (140) **62**.

MONTANA. — (9) **18**; (10) **24**; (11) **28**; (12) **33**; (13) **40**; (14) **43**; (15) **48**; (16) **50**; (17) **52**; (18) **56**; (19) **61**.

NEBRASKA. — (22) **3**; (23, 24) **8**; (25) **13**; (26) **18**; (27) **20**; (28, 29) **26**; (30) **27**; (31) **28**; (32, 33) **29**; (34) **33**; (35) **37**; (36) **38**; (37) **40**; (38) **41**; (39, 40) **42**; (41) **43**; (42, 43) **47**; (44) **48**; (45, 46) **50**; (47) **53**; (47, 48,

Nevada. — (19) 3; (20) 19; (21) 37; (22) 58; (23) 62.

New Hampshire. — (64) 10; (62) 13; (65) 23; (66) 49.

New Jersey. — (43 N. J. Eq.) 3; (44 N. J. Eq.) 6; (50 N. J. L.) 7; (51 N. J. L.; 45 N. J. Eq.) 14; (46 N. J. Eq.; 52 N. J. L.) 19; (47 N. J. Eq.) 24; (53 N. J. L.) 26; (48 N. J. Eq.) 27; (49 N. J. Eq.) 31; (54 N. J. L.) 33; (50 N. J. Eq.) 35; (55 N. J. L.) 39; (51 N. J. Eq.) 40; (56 N. J. L.) 44; (52 N. J. Eq.) 46; (57 N. J. L.; 53 N. J. Eq.) 51; (54 N. J. Eq.; 58 N. J. L.) 55; (59 N. J. L.) 59; (55 N. J. Eq.) 62.

New York. — (107) 1; (108) 2; (109) 4; (110) 6; (111) 7; (112) 8; (113) 10; (114) 11; (115) 12; (116, 117) 15; (118, 119) 16; (120) 17; (121) 18; (122) 19; (123) 20; (124, 125) 21; (126) 22; (127) 24; (128, 129) 26; (130, 131) 27; (132, 133) 28; (134) 30; (135) 31; (136) 32; (137) 33; (138) 34; (139) 36; (140) 37; (141) 38; (142) 40; (143) 42; (144) 43; (145) 45; (146) 48; (147) 49; (148) 51; (149) 52; (150) 55; (151) 56; (152) 57; (153) 60; (154) 61.

North Carolina. — (97, 98) 2; (99, 100) 6; (101) 9; (102) 11; (103) 14; (104) 17; (105) 18; (106) 19; (107) 22; (108) 23; (109) 26; (110) 28; (111) 32; (112) 34; (113) 37; (114) 41; (115) 44; (116) 47; (117) 53; (118) 54; (119) 56; (120) 58; (121) 61.

North Dakota. — (1) 26; (2) 33; (3) 44; (4) 50; (5) 57.

Ohio. — (45 Ohio St.) 4; (46 Ohio St.) 15; (47 Ohio St.) 21; (48 Ohio St.) 29; (49 Ohio St.) 34; (50 Ohio St.) 40; (51 Ohio St.) 46; (52 Ohio St.) 49; (53 Ohio St.) 53; (54 Ohio St.) 56; (55, 56 Ohio St.) 60.

Oregon. — (15) 3; (16) 8; (17) 11; (18) 17; (19) 20; (20) 23; (21) 28; (22) 29; (23) 37; (24) 41; (25) 42; (26) 46; (27) 50; (28) 52; (29) 54; (30) 60.

Pennsylvania. — (115, 116, 117 Pa. St.) 2; (118, 119 Pa. St.) 4; (120, 121 Pa. St.) 6; (122 Pa. St.) 9; (123, 124 Pa. St.) 10; (125 Pa. St.) 11; (126 Pa. St.) 12; (127 Pa. St.) 14; (128, 129 Pa. St.) 15; (130, 131 Pa. St.) 17; (132, 133, 134 Pa. St.) 19; (135, 136 Pa. St.) 20; (137, 138 Pa. St.) 21; (139, 140, 141 Pa. St.) 23; (142, 143 Pa. St.) 24; (144, 145 Pa. St.) 27; (146 Pa. St.) 28; (147, 150 Pa. St.) 30; (151 Pa. St.) 31; (148 Pa. St.) 33; (149, 152, 153 Pa. St.) 34; (154, 155 Pa. St.) 35; (156 Pa. St.) 36; (157 Pa. St.) 37; (158 Pa. St.) 38; (159 Pa. St.) 39; (160 Pa. St.) 40; (161 Pa. St.) 41; (162 Pa. St.) 42; (163 Pa. St.) 43; (164, 165 Pa. St.) 44; (166 Pa. St.) 45; (167 Pa. St.) 46; (168, 169 Pa. St.) 47; (170, 171 Pa. St.) 50; (172, 173 Pa. St.) 51; (174, 175 Pa. St.) 52; (176 Pa. St.) 53; (177 Pa. St.) 55; (178 Pa. St.) 56; (179, 180 Pa. St.) 57; (181 Pa. St.) 59; (182 Pa. St.) 61.

Rhode Island. — (15) 2; (16) 27; (17) 33; (18) 49; (19) 61.

South Carolina. — (26) 4; (27, 28, 29) 13; (30) 14; (31, 32) 17; (33) 26; (34) 27; (35) 28; (36) 31; (37) 34; (38) 37; (39) 39; (40) 42; (41) 44; (42) 46; (43) 49; (44) 51; (45) 55; (46) 57; (47) 58; (48) 59; (49) 61; (50) 62.

South Dakota. — (1) 36; (2) 39; (3) 44; (4) 46; (5) 49; (6) 55; (7) 58; (8) 59; (9) 62.

Tennessee. — (85) 4; (86) 6; 87) 10; (88) 17; (89) 24; (90) 25; (91) 30; (92) 36; (93) 42; (94) 45; (95) 49; (96) 54; (97) 56; (98) 60.

Texas. — (68) 2; (69; 24 Tex. App.) 5; (70; 25, 26 Tex. App.) 8; (71) 10; (27 Tex. App.) 11; (72) 13; (73, 74) 15; (75) 16; (76) 18; (77; 28 Tex. App.) 19; (78) 22; (79) 23; (29 Tex. App.) 25; (80, 81) 26; (82) 27;

(30 Tex. App.) **28**; (83) **29**; (84) **31**; (85) **34**; (31 Tex. Cr. Rep.; 86) **37**; (86; 32 Tex. Cr. Rep.) **40**; (87; 33 Tex. Cr. Rep.) **47**; (34 Tex. Cr. Rep.; 88) **53**; (89, 90) **59**; (35 Tex. Cr. Rep.) **60**; (36 Tex. Crim. Rep.) **61.**

UTAH.—(13) **57**; (14) **60**; (15) **62.**

VERMONT. — (60) **6**; (61) **15**; (62) **22**; (63) **25**; (64) **33**; (65) **36**; (66) **44**; (67) **48**; (68) **54**; (69) **60.**

VIRGINIA. — (82) **3**; (83) **5**; (84) **10**; (85) **17**; (86) **19**; (87) **24**; (88) **29**; (89) **37**; (90) **44**; (91) **50**; (92) **53**; (93) **57.**

WASHINGTON. — (1) **22**; (2) **26**; (3) **28**; (4) **31**; (5) **34**; (6) **36**; (7) **38**; (8) **40**; (9) **43**; (10) **45**; (11) **48**; (12) **50**; (13) **52**; (14) **53**; (15) **55**; (16) **58**; (17) **61.**

WEST VIRGINIA. — (29) **6**; (30) **8**; (31) **13**; (32, 33) **25**; (34) **26**; (35) **29**; (36) **32**; (37) **38**; (38, 39) **45**; (40) **52**; (41) **56**; (42) **57.**

WISCONSIN. — (69) **2**; (70, 71) **5**; (72) **7**; (73) **9**; (74, 75) **17**; (76, 77) **20**; (78) **23**; (79) **24**; (80) **27**; (81) **29**; (82) **33**; (83) **35**; (84) **36**; (85, 86) **39**; (87) **41**; (88) **43**; (89) **46**; (90) **48**; (91) **51**; (92) **53**; (93) **57**; (94) **59**; (95) **60.**

WYOMING. — (3) **31**; (4) **62.**

AMERICAN STATE REPORTS.

CASES REPORTED.

VOL. LXII.

AMERICAN STATE REPORTS.

VOL. LXII.

CASES

IN THE

SUPREME COURT

OF

WYOMING.

NUGENT v. POWELL.

[4 WYOMING, 173.]

PARENT AND CHILD—ADOPTION—PROCEEDINGS IN.—
A finding of fact by the district court in a case involving the validity of adoption proceedings, that a probate judge after full inquiry consented to the adoption, but did not enter the record thereof in the records of his office, but did write his consent and approval of the adoption upon a detached piece of paper and retained it among the papers in his office, is conclusive of the fact of application for, and consent to, the adoption and of an entry thereof upon the records, when it appears that such probate judge kept his records upon detached pieces of paper, and was not required by statute to keep them in any other manner.

EVIDENCE.—ADMISSIONS IN PLEADINGS are conclusive, even though evidence is admitted, and the court, jury, or referee finds otherwise.

PARENT AND CHILD.—ADOPTION IS purely a statutory matter and to give validity to proceedings relating thereto they must have been conducted in substantial conformity with the provisions of the statute; but the statute must be given a liberal construction in order to uphold the validity of proceedings under it.

PARENT AND CHILD—ADOPTION—CONSENT OF PARENT—NECESSITY FOR.—When, in adoption proceedings, a parent makes application to the court to relinquish all right to his or her child, the judge must make inquiry as to the right of the parent to make such relinquishment, and if, upon inquiry, it is ascertained that the other parent of the child is still living, and still possesses a right to the care, custody, or control of the child, the judge must refuse to approve such adoption unless the written consent of such absent parent is obtained and filed. But, if such parent, though living, has relinquished his or her right to the care, custody, or control of the child, his or her consent is not necessary to its adoption.

PARENT AND CHILD—RIGHT TO CUSTODY AND SERVICES OF CHILD.—All things being equal, the father has a better right to the custody and services of his child than has the mother, but he has no absolute vested right in such custody.

PARENT AND CHILD—FATHER'S RIGHT TO CUSTODY OF CHILD.—The right of a father with respect to his child is not an absolute paramount proprietary right or interest in or to its custody, but is in the nature of a trust reposed in him, which imposes upon him the reciprocal obligation to maintain, care for, and protect the child. The law secures him this right so long as, and no longer than, he shall discharge the correlative duties and obligations.

PARENT AND CHILD—ADOPTION.—ABANDONMENT OF A CHILD by its father constitutes a relinquishment on his part of his right to the custody and services of the child. Thereupon the mother becomes its natural guardian, and thereafter, in adoption proceedings, has the right to relinquish the custody and control of such child, and no rights of the father are affected thereby.

PARENT AND CHILD—ADOPTION—CONCLUSIVENESS OF AFTER ABANDONMENT OF CHILD.—Adoption proceedings instituted upon application of the mother without notice to the absent father, in which it is found that such father has abandoned the child adopted, are not subject to collateral attack by collateral heirs of the party adopting such child on the ground of the absence of notice to such father.

PARENT AND CHILD—ADOPTION—CONSTITUTIONAL LAW.—A statute which authorizes adoption without notice to, or the consent of, an abandoning parent of the child, and with the consent of the remaining parent only, is constitutional.

The three sections of the General Statutes of Wyoming referred to in the opinion as affecting the adoption proceedings are as follows: "Sec. 2274. Any parent willing to relinquish all right to his or her minor child to any other person willing to adopt the same, shall make application to the judge of probate of the county in which such parent resides; and if such judge of probate, after due investigation, shall be satisfied that the person making said application is entitled to make such relinquishment, and that the person proposing to adopt such child is a suitable person to assume the relation of parent, and that the consent of both parties to such adoption is natural [mutual] and voluntary, he shall enter of record in the records of his office, the fact of such application and consent, with his approval of such agreement and adoption. Sec. 2275. Any person may appear before the judge of probate of the county where he or she resides and offer to adopt any minor child as his or her own; provided, such minor and his or her parents, if living, or guardian, if any, or county commissioners, as hereafter provided, shall appear and consent to such adoption. Sec. 2279. In case the parent of any child is a nonresident of this territory, or shall have removed from the county in which his or her child may be at the time it is proposed to adopt the same as aforesaid, the written consent of such parent, properly acknowledged, shall be obtained and filed with said judge of probate, which shall have the same ef-

fect as if such parent were personally present and consented to
such adoption. And said judge of probate shall note the filings
of such written consent in his record of approval, and the like
proceedings shall be had as if such parent were present."

Brown & Arnold, for the plaintiff in error.

Lacey & Van Devanter, for the defendants in error.

[181] CLARK, J. This case comes before this court upon exceptions duly reserved, taken by plaintiffs in error to sundry rulings,
findings of fact, conclusions of law, and final decree made by the
district court of Laramie county in the matter of the final distribution of the estate of Michael Powell, deceased. The matter was
heard in the court below upon the petition for final distribution,
filed by the defendants in error, the answer of Emily Powell, by
Francis J. Nugent, her guardian, one of the plaintiffs in error, to
said petition, and the reply to said defendants in error thereto
and the evidence adduced in support of the issues presented by
said pleadings.

It appears from the record that on July 1, A. D. 1891, M. C.
Brown, one of the plaintiffs in error, was duly appointed guardian
ad litem of said child, Emily Powell, and qualified as such. From
the record these facts conclusively appear: That [182] the child
Emily Powell is the daughter of one John Leonard and Esther
Leonard, born in lawful wedlock in the month of November,
1877, at Hillsburgh in the state of California, while the said
father and mother were living together. In August, 1878, nine
months after the birth of said child, John Leonard, the husband
and father, left his family and went to San Francisco, California,
and has lived there ever since. The wife and four children, including the said child Emily, remained at Hillsburg until June,
1879, when they removed to Omaha, Nebraska, where they remained until May, 1880, in which month they removed to Cheyenne, Wyoming, where they have lived since.

At the time Leonard left his family in August, 1878, he left
them without money or means of support, and in circumstances
of extreme destitution, and from that time up to the time of the
adoption proceedings hereinafter mentioned he in no way whatever contributed to the support of his wife and children, except
the sum of twenty dollars furnished them while they were at Omaha, Nebraska, and before they came to Cheyenne, Wyoming, in May,
1880, and this notwithstanding the fact that during most of the
period he was earning reasonable wages and could have contrib-

uted to their support had he so desired, and also notwithstanding the fact that the wife and children frequently appealed to him for assistance and apprised him of their destitute condition.

Prior to the date of the adoption proceedings, John W. Leonard, in a court of competent jurisdiction of the state of California, obtained a decree of divorce from his said wife, and in said decree he was awarded the custody of the child Emily. On the fourth day of January, 1882, Esther Leonard, who was then living in Cheyenne, Wyoming, with her four children, appeared before the probate judge of Laramie county, Wyoming, made application to relinquish her child Emily, and consented that she might be adopted by Michael Powell, the son of Patrick and Margaret Powell and the brother of the full blood of the other six defendants in error. In this proceeding she filed in the office of said probate judge, as stated in the petition of defendants in error for distribution, [183] from which we quote, "a paper in writing, in the words and figures following, to-wit:

"In the Probate Court of Laramie County. Territory of Wyoming.

"To Isaac Bergman, Judge of Probate:

"The undersigned, Mrs. Esther Leonard, would respectfully represent that she is the mother of Emily Leonard, a minor female child of the age of four (4) years, and is willing to relinquish all right to the said Emily Leonard to Michael Powell and Elizabeth Powell, his wife, who have signified their willingness to adopt such child and to assume the relation of parent to her, and she further represents that she is a resident of Laramie county, territory of Wyoming.

"Mrs. ESTHER LEONARD.

"Sworn to and subscribed to before me this 4th day of January, A. D. 1882.   ISAAC BERGMAN, Judge of Probate.

—and thereupon the following order was entered by the said probate judge, to-wit:

"January 4, 1882.

"Matter of Adoption of Emily Leonard, a Minor.

"On this day came before me Mrs. Esther Leonard and Michael Powell, and the said Mrs. Esther Leonard made her application in writing to relinquish all her right to her minor child Emily Leonard, aged four (4) years, of which she is the mother, to the said Michael Powell and Elizabeth Powell, his wife, and the said

Michael Powell and Elizabeth Powell being willing to adopt
the said minor child, Emily Leonard, I hereby consent to and
allow such adoption to be made. Said child to be hereafter
known as Emily Powell. ,   ISAAC BERGMAN, Judge."

Upon the hearing before the probate judge evidence was introduced tending to show that the father was living, but [184] had
for a long time prior thereto wholly abandoned his wife and
said children.

Michael Powell died intestate at Laramie county, Wyoming,
February 24, 1888, owning real and personal property in said
county. He left surviving him neither wife nor children of his
body begotten.   His estate was fully adminstered upon, and being in condition for distribution this controversy arose between
the defendants in error and the said child Emily, concerning the
property left by the deceased.

In the said adoption proceedings no notice of any kind was
given to said John Leonard, nor did he in any manner consent
to said adoption of the said child, nor did he in any way appear
in said proceedings or in relation thereto.

Upon these facts the court found as conclusions of law that
John W. Leonard had abandoned the child Emily before and
at the time of said adoption proceedings; that Esther Leonard was not entitled to make any relinquishment of said child;
that said adoption proceedings were and are void and of none
effect, and that the defendants in error were the heirs and only
heirs at law of said Michael Powell, deceased, and entered up a
decree accordingly.

Motion for new trial was filed, and overruled, and the case
brought for review to this court.

Upon the argument of this cause these main questions were
presented to the court, viz: 1. Were the adoption proceedings
had before the probate judge of Laramie county, Wyoming, in
conformity with the provisions of the statute relating thereto?
2. Is the action of the probate judge in allowing and consenting
to the adoption of the child Emily by Michael Powell subject
to collateral attack in this proceeding? 3. Are the circumstances
surrounding the case such that Michael Powell would have been,
and consequently these defendants in error, his privies in blood
and in law, are estopped to deny the validity and legality of the
proceedings in adoption?

It is evident that if the first and third questions, or either of

[185] them, are answered in the affirmative, or the second in the negative, that the action of the court below must be reversed and the cause remanded. But before proceeding to the consideration of these questions, it may, perhaps, be well to dispose of one subsidiary proposition and get it out of the way.

The statutory provisions relating to the adoption of children in this state are to be found in sections 2274 to 2286, inclusive, of the Revised Statutes of 1887. Those which relate particularly to this controversy are as follows: 2274, 2275, 2276, 2277, 2278, 2279 and 2286.

It will be observed that section 2274 provides that, in cases of adoption, the probate judge "shall enter of record in the records of his office the fact of such application and consent with his approval of such agreement and adoption."

Upon the hearing below, the court found as a fact that the probate judge, after full inquiry, consented to the adoption of the child Emily, and we quote: "But did not enter of record in the records of his office any consent or approval of such adoption. The court further finds that the said judge of probate did write out his consent and approval of such adoption upon a detached piece of paper and retained the same in his office among the papers of his office, which said paper is in the words and figures following, to wit," and then is set forth the consent order, set forth in our statement of facts, supra.

Upon the argument, it was strongly urged that, inasmuch as the probate judge failed to enter the order as required by the statute, the adoption did not take place; that the entry of the order of consent was a condition precedent to the adoption.

There was no evidence upon the hearing tending to show that the said probate judge kept the records of his proceedings or the proceedings of his court in any other way than by writing them out upon sheets of paper; and inasmuch as there was no statute prescribing the manner in which the records should be kept, whether in bound books or upon pieces of paper, we know of no rule of law which would prohibit him from keeping his records in the way in which it seems he did in this case; he certainly had very ancient authority for so [186] doing, for at common law "a record signifies a roll of parchment upon which the proceedings and transactions of a court are entered or drawn up by its officers": 3 Stephen's Commentaries, 583. Substantially the same definition is given in 3 Blackstone's Commentaries, 24. But in the United States paper has

universally supplied the place of parchment as the material for
the records: 2 Burrill's Law Dictionary, tit. Record; Hahn v.
Kelly, 34 Cal. 422; 94 Am. Dec. 742. And hence we think that
the facts found by the court below show conclusively that the entry was made as required by statute. But even if this were not so
we are unable to see how in this case and in cases of this nature it
can be said that the failure of the probate judge to do his duty
should be held to work the destruction of the rights of others
who have done all that they were required to do in the matter:
Abney v. Deloach, 84 Ala. 394-402. But a conclusive answer
to the contention upon this proposition is to be found in the fact
that in the pleadings in this matter, as will appear from that
portion of the petition of defendants in error copied in the
statement of facts, it is expressly admitted that the order was
entered. The only reasonable construction that can be given to
the language of the petition is that the order was entered by the
probate judge in the records of his office. This admission having been made, there could be no finding of fact to the contrary,
for the reason that it is well settled that admissions in pleadings
are conclusive, even though evidence is admitted and the court,
jury, or referee find otherwise: 7 Bacon's Abridgment; Van
Dyke v. Maguire, 57 N. Y. 431; Ballou v. Parsons, 11 Hun, 602.
See, also, upon this question generally, Van Fleet on Collateral
Attack, sec. 688.

We now come to the main question in the case, viz: Were the
adoption proceedings had in conformity with the provisions of
our statute? The determination of this question demands an examination of the statute, and also of the general principles of
the law relating to the rights and duties of parents and children.
It must be admitted in the beginning that a proceeding in adoption was wholly unknown to the common law, and in our system
of jurisprudence it is purely a statutory matter; hence it follows
that, in order to give any validity [187] to such proceedings, they
must have been conducted in substantial conformity with the
provisions of the statute, and its requirements observed; but, notwithstanding this, it ought not to be overlooked in the examination of cases growing out of the exercise of this statutory right,
that the right is a beneficial one both to the public and to those
immediately concerned in its exercise. Since its incorporation
into our system (and the fact is such statutes have been adopted
in nearly every one of our states) the homes of many childless
parents have been brightened and made happier because the

law enabled them to bring into that home a child upon whom
their affections could center and develop. Many an orphan
child, and many a child whose parents were unable by misfortune or their own infirmities to care for, have by means of
this statutory right found good homes, loving and affectionate
parents, and thereby grown up to be good and valuable members of society, when otherwise they would have spent their
early years in ignorance and vice, and in such surroundings
have grown up to young manhood or young womanhood simply to swell the overflowing ranks of the vicious and criminal
classes of society; and hence it seems to me that, in cases of
this kind, it is not the duty of the courts to bring the judicial
microscope to bear upon the case in order that every slight
defect might be enlarged, and magnified, so that a reason might
be found for declaring invalid an act consummated years before;
but rather approach the case with the inclination to uphold such
acts, if it is found that there was a substantial compliance with
the statute: Van Fleet on Collateral Attack, sec. 1, p. 3. Several
cases were cited to us upon argument, in which collateral heirs
attacked proceedings of this nature, and in which the courts held
that the statute being in derogation of the common-law rights
of the natural heirs, it must be rigidly construed. I am unable
to perceive how the rights of the natural heirs were affected by
the act of adoption, because at the time of the act they had no
rights whatever under the law—no one is the heir of the living:
Sewall v. Roberts, 115 Mass. 277, 278.

From a careful and through examination of our statutes [188]
we are convinced that section 2274 is complete in itself and is
not in any manner qualified by sections 2275 or 2276. These
three sections provide for two different methods of adoption.
Under section 2274 any parent having the right to relinquish
his or her child may make application to the probate judge
for leave so to do. If the judge is, upon inquiry, satisfied of
the parents' right to relinquish, and that the persons proposing
to adopt are suitable persons, and that the consent of the
parent and of the persons adopting is mutual and voluntary,
he shall enter the fact of such application and consent with his
approval thereof. In proceeding under this section it is clear
that the initial step is to be taken by the parent. It is also
clear that, in proceeding under sections 2275 and 2276, the
initial step is to be taken by the parties proposing to adopt
the child. It is also clear to our minds, from the language used

in section 2276, that the legislature made and intended to make
a distinction between the two proceedings; that section provides
that in cases brought under section 2275 the probate judge,
after due investigation, if satisfied as provided in section 2271,
shall make a "like entry of record" as specified in section 2274.
The requirement that the proceedings authorized by sections
2275 and 2276 shall in certain respects be conducted in the same
manner as required by section 2274 necessarily implies different
proceedings. We are unable to perceive how we are to avoid
this construction, unless we refuse to give force and effect to the
plain words used in the statute. We think, also, that sections
2279 and 2274 qualify each other, and that the true construction of these two sections is as follows: When a parent makes
application to the probate judge to relinquish all right to his or
her child, it is, among other things, the duty of the probate
judge to make inquiry as to the right of the parent making the
application to make such relinquishment, and if upon such inquiry it should be ascertained that the other parent of the child
is still living, and still possesses a right to the care, custody, or
control of the child, it would be the duty of the judge to refuse
to approve such adoption unless the written consent of such
absent parent was obtained and filed. On the other hand, if the
judge should [189] find that the child had another parent living,
and also that that parent had relinquished his or her right to
the care, custody, or control of the child, it would not be necessary to have his or her consent; "the parent" referred to in
section 2279 is a parent who still possesses some right in or to
the custody over and control of the child which he or she can
relinquish. To give any other construction to the statute would
be tantamount to saying that the legislature intended that the
consent of a parent who had ceased to have any interest in the
child was still necessary to enable the other parent to transfer his or her interest in it: Van Fleet on Collateral Attack, sec.
408.

This brings us to the consideration of the question whether
or not the mother in this instance had the right to relinquish
the child, or to use the words of the statute, was "entitled to
make such relinquishment."

Upon the argument, it was strongly, forcibly, and eloquently
urged upon the court by the distinguished counsel for defendants in error, that even though the statute does not in terms
"require notice to the absent father, where proceedings were in-

stituted for the adoption of his child by a stranger, such a proceeding so materially affecting and invading his rights would be invalid and without jurisdiction unless upon due notice to him, that he might have the opportunity of defending and protecting his rights. That if the statute should be so construed as to authorize the adoption of a child with the consent of the mother but in the absence of the father, and without his consent and without notice to him, such construction would render the statute unconstitutional, and therefore any proceeding under it void. That if the expression 'the parent' or 'any parent,' as used in sections 2274, 2277, and 2279 is meant to give to a single parent, where both are living, the right to relinquish, then the father is the parent intended, because he it is who has under the law the right to the custody and services of the child and who is charged with its maintenance and nurture. That 'the fundamental principle of the common law was that the father possessed the paramount right to the custody and control of his minor [100] children and to superintend their education and nurture. The mother, as such, had little or no authority in the premises.' The father had in America the paramount right of custody of his minor child in the absence of statutes to the contrary. And in this state the common law of England has been directly and distinctly adopted, and hence the common-law rule, as above stated, must obtain here. That the statute provides for no forfeiture of his or her rights by any parent, so that the other shall succeed to all the rights; and without some statutory provision it is plain that there could be no such forfeiture; that the only case or cases in which one parent could be held to have forfeited to the other any right to their child would be the case or cases where such forfeiture is provided for by the statute itself. That in this case, if the probate judge decided anything on the question of abandonment, he assumed to hear and decide that question and thereby invade and materially affect the rights of the father, and this too without any averment of abandonment, without any statutory authority in him to hear that question, and without giving to the father by any kind of notice whatever any day in court; such a determination, in the light of reason and of the authorities, is absolutely void, whether the conclusion reached by the probate judge was true or otherwise. A judgment without notice to the defendant is utterly void, no matter whether the claim on which it is based is just or unjust."

Such, in brief, is the argument made by defendants in error;

we have stated it so fully because we desire to give the fullest
consideration to it. In the first place, it is to be remembered
that this entire argument in support of a father's alleged rights
is not made in a case in which a father is seeking to establish
those rights. The father is not before this court and is a stranger
to these proceedings; it is made in a case in which the collateral
heirs of Michael Powell are seeking to have declared invalid a
proceeding in which Michael Powell participated, and they base
their claim, not upon the fact that the legal rights of the person
under whom and through whom they claim have been invaded,
but upon the [191] fact that the rights of a stranger to this contest, who is not here complaining, have been infringed. Still,:
notwithstanding this fact, this court will fully admit that if the
propositions contended for by defendants in error have place in
the law, as applied to this case, then the consequences claimed
by them must follow.

But what are the rights of a father with respect to his child?
It is claimed in this case, and there are many sayings in the
books, that at common law the father has the paramount right
to the custody of his child, and, that, independently of statutes,
such is the prevailing rule in America. If this statement simply
means that inasmuch as the law has imposed upon the father the
duty of caring for and maintaining his minor child, and therefore
has given him the custody and control of it in order that he
might the better perform these duties, the statement may be
accepted as accurate; and, in a general way, it may be said that,
all things being equal, the father has a better right to the custody
and services of his child than has the mother, because the law
primarily imposes upon the father the duty of maintenance and
nurture. But it is, I think, well settled that the father has not an
absolute vested right in the custody of his child.

Judge Story, in the case of United States v. Green, 3 Mason,
485, states what I conceive to be the true rule as follows: "As to
the question of the right of the father to have the custody
of his infant child in a general sense it is true. But this is not
on account of any absolute right of the father, but for the benefit of the infant, the law presuming it to be for its interest to be
under the nurture and care of his natural protector both for
maintenance and education. . . . . It is an entire mistake to suppose the court is at all events bound to deliver over the infant
to his father or that the latter has an absolute right in the custody."

It may well be doubted whether the rule of the common law was other than as stated in the case above cited. From an examination of the authorities it will be found that prior [192] to 1804 the English courts entertained precisely the views expressed by Judge Story, and quoted above. In that year, the decisions in England took a direction in favor of establishing the paramount right of the father to the custody of his infant child, and continued in that direction until they culminated in the famous decision rendered in 1836 in the case of King v. Greenhill, 4 Ad. & E. 614, in which case three children, females, aged respectively five and a half, four and a half, and two and a half years, were in custody of the mother, a woman of un-blemished, reproachless character; upon application of the father, who was living in open adultery with another woman, the children were taken from the mother and delivered over to the custody of the father. These decisions led to the introduction of a bill in Parliament relating to the custody of infants, which finally, in 1838 or 1839, became a law and restored the mother to her natural rights and put her upon an equality with her husband in relation to the care and custody of her children within the age of nurture. In the debate upon the bill Lord Lynd-hurst, referring to the decision in King v. Greenhill, 4 Ad. & E. 614, said: "As the laws now stand, the father of a child born in lawful wedlock was entitled to the entire and absolute control and custody of that child, and to exclude from any share in that control and custody the mother of that child. The mother might be the most virtuous woman that ever lived, amiable in her manners, fond and attached to her children; the father, on the other hand, might be profligate in character, brutal in manner, living in adultery, and yet would have the right, under the existing law, to the custody of the children of his marriage, to the exclusion of even access to them of his wife, their mother."

Lord Denman, who was the chief justice of the king's bench, and who concurred in the decision in the above-cited case, in the course of the debate upon the bill referred to, said:

"In the case of Greenhill, which had been decided in 1836 before himself and the other judges of the king's bench, he believed that there was not one judge who had not felt [193] ashamed of the state of the law, and that it was such as to render it odious in the eyes of the country. The effect in that case was to enable the father to take his children from his young and blameless wife, and place them in charge of a woman with whom he then cohabited."

If such was the common law of England, it is not surprising that Lord Denman might say he was ashamed of it. But, as stated by Chief Justice Ranney in Gishwiler v. Dodez, 4 Ohio St. 622, I am strongly disposed to think that the learned chief justice of the king's bench mistook a judicial excrescence upon the law for the law itself, and that parliament did little more than restore it to its former condition. If, however, the English cases alluded to were fair expressions of the common law, it is safe to say that they have never found place in American jurisprudence; and I have no sort of doubt but that in American jurisprudence the right of a father to the custody of his child is not an absolute inalienable right, but that it is in all cases referable and subordinate to the interest and welfare of the child: Mercein v. People, 25 Wend. 67; 35 Am. Dec. 653.

It has been said that: "By the law of nature, the father has no paramount right to the custody of his child. By that law the wife and child are equal to the husband and father. . . . . There is no parental authority independent of the supreme power of the state. But the former is derived altogether from the latter. In the civil state there is no inequality between the father and the mother. Ordinarily, a child during infancy is entirely under the discipline of its mother; and very frequently wives discharge the duty of education of their children better than the husband: De Felice's Lectures on Natural Rights, lecture 30. It seems, then, by the law of nature, the father has no paramount, inalienable right to the custody of the child; and the civil or municipal law, in setting bounds to his parental authority, and in entirely or partially depriving him of it in cases where the interests and welfare of his child require it, does not come in conflict with or subvert any of the principles of natural law": Mercein v. People, 25 Wend. 103; 35 Am. Dec. 653.

[194] This right which is given by the municipal law to the father is, strictly speaking, more in the nature of a "trust" than anything else. As was said by Lord Redesdale in Wellesley v. Wellesley, 2 Bligh, N. S., 124: "Why is the parent intrusted with the care of his children? Because it is generally supposed that he will best execute the trust imposed in him, for that it is a trust of all trusts the most sacred none of your lordships can doubt": See, also, Ex parte Crouse, 4 Whart. 11.

The true doctrine was stated in In re Moore, 11 I. R. C. L., N. S., ˉ1, by Hayes, justice, as follows: "The dominion which a parent has over a child is a qualified one and given for the discharge of important trusts. He will be secured in it so long as, and no longer than, he discharges the correlative duties; and a failure in them, under circumstances and to an extent to bring on him the brand of 'unfitness,' amounts to a forfeiture of his right and warrants the interposition of the proper legal tribunal for the protection of the child by wresting from the parent the trust which he has abused, or which the court plainly sees he is unable or unwilling to perform."

The right to custody and services of the child and the obligation to support and educate are reciprocal rights and obligations; they are dependent upon each other; they do not exist apart. One may not and ought not to be permitted to deny the obligations, to refuse to perform them, and still claim the existence of the right.

In Chapsky v. Wood, 26 Kan. 652, 653, 40 Am. Rep. 321, Justice Brewer, in delivering the opinion of the court, says: "A child is not in any sense like a horse or any other chattel, subject matter for absolute and irrevocable gift or contract. The father cannot, by merely giving away his child, release himself from the obligation to support it nor be deprived of the right to its custody. In this it differs from the gift of any article which is only property. If to-day Morris Chapsky should give a horse to another party that gift is for all time irrevocable and the property never can be reclaimed; but he cannot, by simply giving away his child, relieve himself from [195] the obligation to support that child, nor deprive himself of the right to its custody.

"A parent's right to the custody of a child is not, like the right of property, an absolute and uncontrollable right. If it were, it would end this case and relieve us from all further difficulties. A mere right of property may be asserted by any man, no matter how bad, immoral, or unworthy he may be, but no case can be found in which the courts have given to the father who was a drunkard and a man of gross immoralities the custody of a minor child, especially when the child is a girl. The fact that in such cases the courts have always refused the father the custody of his child shows that he has not an absolute and uncontrollable right thereto."

In Hochheimer on Custody of Infants, at section 10, we find

this statement of the American rule: "The general result of the American cases may be characterized as an utter repudiation of the notion that there can be such a thing as a proprietary right or interest in or to the custody of an infant, or that a claim to such custody can be asserted merely as a claim, and the general drift of opinion is in the direction of treating the idea of trust as the controlling principle in all controversies in relation to such custody."

And hence, from a careful examination of the question, we come to the conclusion that the right of a father with respect to his child is not an absolute paramount proprietary right or interest in or to the custody of the infant, but is in the nature of a trust reposed in him, which imposes upon him the reciprocal obligation to maintain, care for, and protect the infant, and that the law secures him in this right so long and no longer than he shall discharge the correlative duties and obligations. The fact that by a mere gift of his child, or a contract with reference to its custody, the father may not divest himself of the right to the custody of his child to such an extent that he may not reclaim it does not militate against this conclusion. Such right to reclaim has its foundation in the regard which the courts have for the interest and [196] well-being of the child, and not out of regard to the rights of the father, and it may well be that though a gift of one's child to another may at the time appear to be for the best interests of the child, that afterward circumstances may arise which would render it imperative upon the father to revoke that gift and reclaim his child. But in cases of abandonment, such as is disclosed by this record, the court would hesitate a long time before it would restore the father to the custody of the child. It may be that even in such cases the law preserves a locus poenitentiae for the father, but proof of his repentance ought to be very convincing before he should be restored to his parental privileges.

And it follows from the foregoing that the contention of counsel for defendants in error that there can be no forfeiture of a father's right except by means of some statutory provision cannot be sustained. Take this case. The facts found by the court below upon this proposition are substantially as follows: "That nine months after the birth of the child the father left his wife, Esther Leonard, and their four children without means of support, and in circumstances of extreme destitution, and never thereafter up to the time of the adoption proceedings in

question (a period of three years and five months) contributed
to the support of his wife and children except the sum of twenty
dollars furnished them while in Omaha, and before said family
came to Wyoming in the month of May, 1880, and during all
that period had left the said child Emily to the sole support and
care of its mother, Esther Leonard; that the said John Leonard
during most of said period was earning reasonable wages and was
thereby enabled to contribute to the support of his said family
had he desired to do so."

And the court further expressly finds that these acts constitute an abandonment of the child by the father, and of this
there can be no sort of doubt in the mind of anyone who will
read the record.

In the face of these facts, how can it be said that this father
did not by his own acts forfeit and part with and lose all the
[197] rights which he possessed in and to the custody and control
and services of this infant child; not only did he forfeit all
of his rights, but so far as he was able to do, if he could by
any act of his make any transfer of such rights, he transferred
them to the mother. The finding of fact is, that he "during
all of that period had left the said child Emily to the sole support and care of its mother, Esther Leonard."

The father in this case parted with all of his rights. It did
not require any transfer on his part in order that the right
of custody, control, and services of the child might devolve
upon the mother. In such a case as this, in which a father
has cruelly deserted his family, and refused to recognize and
be bound by those obligations which not only the law but nature and the plainest instincts of humanity imposed upon him,
upon whom should devolve the care and custody of an infant
child nine months old, if not upon its mother? Is there a case
to be found in the books in which the lawfulness of the custody
and control of an infant child by its mother under such circumstances as appear in this case has been denied? If there be
such a case then it is a case, in which every principle of natural
law and common justice and right has been utterly and entirely
disregarded.

Our statute, section 2250 of the Revised Statutes, provides:
"The father is the natural guardian of the persons of his minor
children. If he dies or is incapable of acting, the mother becomes the guardian." This statute is but declaratory of the
general rule, and in that view we may consider it.

Is it to be said that the words "incapable of acting," when viewed in the light of the general principles of the law, are not broad enough by fair and reasonable intendment to cover and embrace this case. If the father had been convicted of a crime and imprisoned in the penitentiary, in such case he certainly would be "incapable of acting." Such would be the case if he should become insane, and such also, in my opinion, would be the case if he should become mentally weak to such "an extent as to bring on him the brand of unfitness." Such would be the case if he should become unable by reason of physical disabilities to perform the ordinary duties of a natural [198] guardian of the person of his child. Or if, by reason of physical infirmities, it became necessary to place a father in a hospital or sanitarium for a long period of time, in order that he might have the constant care of nurses and physicians. Would it not be a case within the spirit and meaning of the rule expressed in the statute? And certainly, when we consider that the object of the rule is to appoint or recognize someone who shall have and exercise personal supervision and control over the child for the benefit of the child, we cannot doubt that a father, who has separated from his child, willfully deserted and abandoned it, and continues to do so, has, within the fair meaning of this rule, by his own acts rendered himself "incapable of acting," and, such being the law, it follows that in this case the mother became the natural guardian of her child upon the father's abandonment.

In Clark v. Bayer, 32 Ohio, 310, 30 Am. Rep. 593, the court, after an exhaustive review of the authorities, say: "From authority and reason the following propositions may be stated generally: 1. As a general rule, the parents are entitled to the custody of their minor children. When the parents are living apart, the father is prima facie entitled to that custody, and when he is a suitable person, able and willing to support and care for them, his right is paramount to that of all other persons, except that of the mother in cases where the infant child is of such tender years as to require her present care; but in all cases of controverted right to custody the welfare of the minor is first to be considered. 2. The father's right, however, is not absolute under all circumstances. He may relinquish it by contract, forfeit it by abandonment, lose it by being in a condition of total inability to afford his minor children necessary care and support."

In Commonwealth v. Dougherty, 1 Pa. Leg. Gaz. 63, cited
at pages 376, 377 of 17 American and English Encyclopedia of
Law, the court held that: "A parent may relinquish the care,
custody, and control of his child, and, after having done so, his
right to claim it is [199] gone and will not be enforced by the
court. Second, such relinquishment by a parent of a child may
be either by a deed or other instrument in writing; or it may be
by parol, or by abandonment, or by turning it out of the house
and permitting it to go upon its own resources; and such relinquishment or abandonment may be presumed from the act
of the parties."

In Pennsylvania, a statute provided that justices of the peace
who performed the ceremony of marriage of minors without the
consent of the parents should be liable to the father in the sum
of fifty dollars, which might be recovered in an action.

In the case of Stansbury v. Bertrou, 7 Watts & S. 364, a
justice of the peace solemnized the marriage of plaintiff's minor
daughter, and plaintiff brought suit against the justice. The defense was, that the father was a drunkard, often intoxicated,
and when in that condition frequently turned the daughter
out of doors, and that he told her to go about her business and
do for herself. The supreme court speaking by Gibson, C. J.,
held this to be a good defense, saying: "But the father had
ceased to stand in the relation of a parent, or consequently of a
party who could be grieved. By turning his daughter loose on
the world to shift for herself, he relinquished his paternal right
in relation to her person, and absolved her from filial allegiance."

In Farrell v. Farrell, 3 Houst. 639, which was an action
brought by a son against a father to recover the amount of the
son's wages earned by him during his minority and collected by
the father, the court charged the jury: "If, therefore, the defendant neglected or refused to support and maintain his son,
or denied him a home or discarded or abandoned him so that
he was forced to labor abroad to procure a living for himself,
he is not, upon any principle of law or justice, entitled to the
earnings of his son; because, under such circumstances, the law
will imply that the father has emancipated or freed the son from
his service and conceded to him the right to enjoy the fruits
and profits of his own labor." [200] For other cases upon this
general doctrine, see Liberty v. Palermo, 79 Me. 473; McCarthy
v. Boston etc. R. R. Co., 148 Mass. 550.

From the foregoing we conclude that at the time of the adoption proceedings, and for a long time prior thereto, this father by his own acts had parted with and relinquished all right in and to the custody of the child; that under the circumstances of this case, the mother at said time was, and for a long time prior thereto had been, lawfully and exclusively in the custody and control of the child, and had the right to relinquish that custody and control, and no rights of the father were affected thereby, because, upon the conceded facts, he had no rights in the premises, having divested himself of them.

But it is contended that the probate judge had not the power, in the absence of the father and without notice to him, to determine the question of abandonment by him; and, further, that if the statute is to be so construed as that it confers upon the mother in such case as this the power to make such relinquishment without notice to or consent of the father, then the statute deprives the father of his sacred rights without due process of law, and is unconstitutional. We will examine these two contentions in their order.

What is abandonment? It is simply the evidentiary fact which proves the ultimate fact of relinquishment; in other words, the relinquishment of one's rights is the effect and result of one's abandonment of those rights. As we have seen, this relinquishment "may be either by a deed or other instrument in writing, or it may be by parol or by abandonment or by turning the child out of the house," etc: Commonwealth v. Dougherty, 1 Pa. Leg. Gaz. 63.

In this case it was by abandonment, which I conceive in cases of this kind to be the strongest possible kind of relinquishment; but suppose that, instead, it had been by deed executed by the father, and the mother had produced the deed, could it in such a case be successfully contended that in order to enable the judge to determine the due execution of the deed or its effect that notice to the father was necessary in [201] order that he might have the opportunity to come in and say whether or not it was obtained from him by duress or fraud? I apprehend not. Or suppose that the mother had brought with her to the judge the written consent of the father, would it then have been necessary for the judge to have given notice to the father before he proceeded to determine whether or not the paper purporting to be executed by him, in order that he might have opportunity to say that it was not executed by him, was so executed or was or was not procured from him by duress or fraud? I think not. And what is the difference in principle in the three cases? In either case the judge would be required to determine whether or not the act or deed was the act or deed of the father and the legal effect thereof. It might be that in either case the father might avoid the proceeding by showing perjury in the evidence establishing abandonment, or forgery in the execution of, or fraud or duress in the procurement of, the instrument of relinquishment or consent: but it does not follow that because the proceedings may be voidable they were also void and open to such collateral attack as it attempted here. Nay more, we may go still farther, and say that, notwithstanding these proceedings in adoption, the father might, at any time since they took place, have brought an action for the recovery of the possession or custody of the child, and no one will contend, or perhaps can successfully contend, that in such case these adoption proceedings would constitute a bar to the father's action, or that they were conclusive upon him. But it does not follow that because the adoption proceedings were not conclusive upon the father they were not conclusive upon the parties to the proceedings and their privies: Van Fleet on Collateral Attack, sec. 408; Barnard v. Barnard, 119 Ill. 93; Fridge v. State, 3 Gill & J. 112, 113; 20 Am. Dec. 463; Sewall v. Roberts, 115 Mass. 275, 276; Jenkins v. Peckinpaugh, 40 Ind. 133; Davis v. Greve, 32 La. Ann. 420; Plume v. Howard Sav. Inst., 46 N. J. L. 227; on the contrary, we think they are, and so hold.

As to the constitutionality of the statute when construed as we construe it, we have this to say: An examination of the 202 statutes of adoption in force in the United States will show that in several states the consent of and notice to abandoning parents is not required. It is enough if the fact of abandonment is made to appear, then the remaining parent may consent to the adoption. This is the case in Colorado, Illinois, Alabama, and perhaps other states. After careful search we have been unable to find any case in which the constitutionality of such statutes has been denied or questioned, and certainly we have not been referred to any.

Upon principle, I am unable to conceive of any valid constitutional objection to the statute as we construe it. Under the facts of this case, we are without doubt that the mother could lawfully exercise all the common-law rights of the parents without any express consent of the father; and no reason occurs to us why she could not also, under the circumstances of this case, exercise the statutory power of both parents with respect to the adoption of the child: Van Vleet on Collateral Attack, sec. 408; Sewall v. Roberts, 115 Mass. 277, 278.

The case of Furgeson v. Jones, 17 Or. 204, 11 Am. St. Rep. 808, was strongly urged upon us as being exactly in point with and decisive of this case. But from an examination of that case we are of opinion that except upon one minor proposition it substantially supports the views herein expressed. No attempt was made in that case to show that the father had abandoned the child, and there is a clear intimation in the original opinion and also in the opinion upon rehearing that, had such been the case, neither his consent or notice to him would have been necessary. It is true that the Oregon statute provides that in cases where the parent has abandoned his child the court may proceed as if he were dead, but in our opinion, this is the rule in the absence of a statute.

But little stress was laid at the argument upon the fact found by the court that the father had, prior to the adoption proceedings obtained a decree of divorce from the mother, in which he was awarded the custody of the child. It appears from the findings that he not only abandoned the child before the decree was obtained, but continued to abandon it even [203] after the decree and up to the time of the adoption. We do not consider this fact as of much consequence, nor as materially affecting the case.

Our conclusion upon the whole is, that Emily Powell, alias Emily Leonard, was the lawfully adopted child of the late Michael Powell, and that the district court of Laramie county erred in its decree.

The decree of that court is reversed and the cause remanded to it, with instructions to further proceed in this matter in accordance with the views herein expressed.

Groesbeck, C. J., and Conaway, J., concurred.

ADOPTION — STATUTES AUTHORIZING — CONSTRUCTION OF.—In order to effect an adoption there must be a substantial compliance with all of the essential requirements of the statute: Note to Cofer v. Scroggins, 39 Am. St. Rep. 58. The right of adoption was unknown to the common law and is repugnant to its principles. Such right being in derogation of common law is a special power conferred by statute, and the rule is that such statutes must be strictly construed: Furgeson v. Jones, 17 Or. 204: 11 Am. St. Rep. 808. and note. That a liberal construction should be given to such statute see Cofer v. Scroggins, 98 Ala. 342; 39 Am. St. Rep. 54.

ADOPTION — CONSENT OF PARENTS.—Consent lies at the foundation of statutes of adoption, and when it is required to be given and submitted to the court, the court cannot take jurisdiction of the subject matter without it: Furgeson v. Jones, 17 Or. 204; 11 Am. St. Rep. 809. But adoption without such consent on the part of the parents may be valid under some circumstances: Van Matre v. Sankey, 148 Ill. 536; 39 Am. St. Rep. 196, and monographic note. And a statute authorizing such an adoption may be valid: In re Williams, 102 Cal. 70; 41 Am. St. Rep. 163.

ADOPTION—COLLATERAL ATTACK.—If the proceeding for an adoption is judicial, and the officer or tribunal is acting as a court or judge, then, upon principle, the order of adoption partakes of the characteristics of a judgment, and if there is jurisdiction over the parties and over the subject matter, it cannot be avoided for errors or irregularities except upon appeal or by motion to vacate it, and is therefore exempt from collateral attack: Monographic note to Van Matre v. Sankey, 39 Am. St. Rep. 218, discussing the various questions relative to the adoption by one person of the children of another.

PARENT AND CHILD—FATHER'S RIGHT TO SERVICES OF CHILD.—During his lifetime a father is entitled to the services and earnings, and liable for the support of his minor children independent of statute or decree; but during such period the wife is not entitled to the services of, nor is she bound to support such child: Gilley v. Gilley, 79 Me. 292; 1 Am. St. Rep. 307, and note. See, Lawyer v. Fritcher, 130 N. Y. 239; 27 Am. St. Rep. 521. An infant owes reverence and respect to his mother, but she has no legal authority over him, nor any legal right to his services: Commonwealth v. Murray, 4 Binn. 487; 5 Am. Dec. 412; Fairmount Ry. Co. v. Stutler, 54 Pa. St. 375; 93 Am. Dec. 714.

CHADWICK v. HOPKINS.

[4 WYOMING, 379.]

JOINT LIABILITY—DEATH OF OBLIGOR—PRACTICE AT COMMON LAW.—At common law the estate of a deceased joint contractor was not liable to the obligee in the joint contract except in case of the insolvency of the surviving joint obligor. In the latter case the obligee had the right to proceed in equity against the administrators of the deceased joint obligor. Otherwise, he must proceed against the solvent surviving obligor at law.

JOINT LIABILITY—DEATH OF ONE OBLIGOR—PARTIES—PRACTICE UNDER CODES.—Under codes removing any objection to joining causes of action formerly distinguished as legal and equitable, the administrator or executor of a deceased co-obligor in a joint contract may, in an action thereon, be joined with the surviving obligor whether he is insolvent or not, and separate judgment may be entered against such defendants in such action.

JOINT LIABILITY—DEATH OF ONE OBLIGOR—PROPER PARTIES DEFENDANT.—In an action to recover on a joint contract after the death of one of the co-obligors, the personal representative of the latter should be joined with the surviving obligor as parties defendant, and their rights and liabilities determined in one action, under a statute removing any objection to joining causes of action, legal and equitable, and providing that "any person may be made a defendant who has or claims an interest in the controversy adverse to the plaintiff, or who is a necessary party to a complete determination or settlement of a question involved therein."

CONTRACTS FOR PURCHASE OF CORPORATION STOCK —REASONABLE TIME FOR PAYMENT.—A contract to repurchase capital stock in a corporation, and to pay therefor as soon and as fast as the purchasers are able financially to do so, without sacrificing their interests in, or the property of the corporation, does not contemplate that they can take all the time they may desire and that may be convenient for them to take, but implies that payment must be made within a reasonable time. The lapse of four years from the date of the contract is more than a reasonable time.

CONTRACTS FOR REPURCHASE OF CORPORATION STOCK—DEFENSES—BURDEN OF PROOF.—If, in an action to recover on a contract for the repurchase of capital stock in a corporation, the plaintiff alleges and proves a contract for repurchase, three years from the time of his original purchase of the stock, and denies a contract set up by the defendant to repurchase such stock and to pay therefor as soon and as fast as he was financially able to do so, financial ability to pay on the part of the defendant need not be shown by the plaintiff, and, if material, want of such ability must be shown as a defense.

TRIAL—VERDICT.—When two contracts are in issue in an action, and the amount of indebtedness is precisely the same under one as the other, it is immaterial upon which one the jury bases a verdict.

EXECUTORS AND ADMINISTRATORS — JUDGMENT AGAINST—FORM OF.—If the cause of action against administrators is a contract to which the decedent was a party, the judgment rendered against them should not be personal in its nature, but should be that they pay in due course of administration the amount ascertained to be due.

Lacey & Van Devanter, for the plaintiffs in error.

Potter & Burke, for the defendants in error.

887 CONAWAY, J. These two cases in error in this court arise from a single action in the district court. Edwin W. Hopkins brought his action in that court against Charles F. Fisher, and John M. Chadwick and Charles F. Fisher, administrators of the estate of Jehu J. Chadwick, deceased. He obtained judgment against them. Charles F. Fisher brings the cause to this court for review by his individual petition in error. John M. Chadwick and Charles F. Fisher, administrators of the estate of Jehu J. Chadwick, deceased, also bring the cause to this court for review by their separate petition in error.

The petition of plaintiff Hopkins filed in the trial court alleges a joint and several contract of Charles F. Fisher and Jehu J. Chadwick with himself. Before the commencement of this action Jehu J. Chadwick died, and the action is against his administrators and Charles F. Fisher as joint defendants. The administrators of the estate of Jehu J. Chadwick, deceased, demurred to this petition, on the ground that it does not state facts sufficient to constitute a cause of action against them in not alleging the insolvency of Charles F. Fisher, the surviving joint contract-

or; and that there is an improper joinder of causes of action
against Charles F. Fisher individually and against these administrators.

At common law, the rule was absolute that the estate of the
deceased joint contractor was not liable to the obligee in the
joint contract except in case of the insolvency of the surviving
joint obligor. If the survivor was solvent, there was a plain
and adequate remedy by action at law against him. In such
case, the liability of the estate of the deceased joint obligor was
to contribute to him after the debt was collected from or paid
by him. In case of his insolvency, the obligee in the joint contract could bring his action in equity against the administrators
of the deceased joint obligor. But the petition alleges a joint
and several contract. It is not claimed that these rules apply
or ever applied to such a contract.

But the same point is raised by an instruction to the jury [388]
requested by the defendant administrators and refused by the
trial court. This instruction is as follows: "The plaintiff cannot recover against the administrators of Jehu J. Chadwick, deceased, in this action, upon a joint agreement or contract jointly made, by Charles F. Fisher and Jehu J. Chadwick."

There is evidence in the record from which the jury might
have found that the contract in question was joint and not joint
and several as alleged. And there is no allegation in the petition of the insolvency of the survivor. Therefore, if the common-law rule prevails, the instruction should have been given,
and the refusal to give it was error which might have been very ·
prejudicial.

The question is thus fairly presented whether, under our code,
the common-law rule prevails that the administrators or executors of a deceased co-obligor in a joint contract are liable to
the obligee in an action on the contract only in case of the insolvency of the survivor. This is a question upon which our
American courts are in direct and hopeless conflict. It is a
question of first impression in this state, and it is our duty to endeavor to ascertain and adopt the view which is most in harmony with the provisions of our Code of Civil Procedure, and
best adapted to carry out those provisions in their true meaning and intent.

The one sufficient reason for the rule of the common law
that the surviving joint obligor and the representatives of the
estate of the deceased could not be joined as defendants in an

action at law was the inability of a court of law to render separate and different judgments in a single action against the survivor to be satisfied de . bonis propriis, and against the administrators of the estate of the deceased to be satisfied from such estate in due course of administration. From the same reason it followed that the survivor alone was liable in an action at law, and that if he were solvent and the action thus available for the collection of the debt, the plaintiff need go no further, and he was not permitted to do so.

In the code states this the only reason ₊for the rules of the common law upon this subject has entirely disappeared. There is no longer any objection to joining causes of action which were formerly distinguished as legal and equitable. Our courts are no longer hampered as to the form of the judgments they may render in one single form of action, called a civil action. But sometimes a rule of law survives after the reason for it is gone. This may be the case where the reason for the rule has been abolished by legislation, unless concurrent legislation also furnish a new rule.

With all due respect for the opinions of some eminent courts which seem to hold differently, we are of the opinion that codes such as ours, doing away with the reason of the common-law rule under consideration as to joinder of parties defendant, also furnish, in terms sufficiently clear, a new rule to be followed in its stead. As to parties defendant we have the following broad provision: "Any person may be made a defendant who has or claims an interest in the controversy adverse to the plaintiff, or who is a necessary party to a complete determination or settlement of a question involved therein": Rev. Stat., sec. 2395.

The defendants in the case at bar all deny any liability on their part to the plaintiff in the action. The primary question to be determined is whether they are so liable. If it be determined that they are liable, the next question is the amount of such liability. In both these questions the defendant administrators are interested in their representative capacity precisely to the same extent as their decedent would be interested were he alive. It is just as necessary for them to defend for the estate as it would be for him to defend for himself. If the action were against the survivor alone they would still be interested. It does not change the extent of their liability whether they are held to pay to the obligee in the joint contract or to the surviving obligor by way of contribution. To a complete determination or settlement of the questions involved they are necessary parties. Their interest in the amount of the judgment, whether the action be against the survivor alone or not, is direct. It is also adverse to the plaintiff. If the action were against the survivor alone, their liability to contribute could be no more than their proportion [390] of the judgment collected from him. If he succeeded in defeating the action, there would be no contribution. It seems evident that it is the true intent and meaning of this provision of the code, and, indeed, authorized by its express language, that all of these parties should be joined as defendants, and that their rights and liabilities should be determined in a single action. The evident policy of the legislation is to avoid a multiplicity of suits and to reach an end to litigation.

The English courts no longer follow the old common law rule making the solvent surviving joint obligor alone liable to the obligee in the joint contract. They permit the action to be brought against the administrators in the first instance, whether the survivor be solvent or not. Several of the American states hold with the English courts: See Pomeroy's Remedies and Remedial Rights, secs. 302-304; Bliss on Code Pleading, secs. 105, 106; Braxton v. State, 25 Ind. 82; Burgoyne v. Ohio Life Ins. Co., 5 Ohio St. 586; Trimmier v. Thompson, 10 S. C. 164.

A number of code states hold differently, but we think not with the better reason: See Voorhis v. Childs, 17 N. Y. 354; Sherman v. Kreul, 42 Wis. 33. We are of the opinion that the trial court did not err in overruling the demurrer nor in refusing the instruction quoted.

In order to discuss some further assignments of error it is necessary to have before us the issues made by the pleadings. The petition of plaintiff Hopkins sets up a contract as made on or before October 15, 1884. It alleges that as a consideration and inducement to him to purchase stock in the North Crow Land and Cattle Company Charles F. Fisher and Jehu J. Chadwick did jointly and severally agree to and with said plaintiff that if he would purchase stock in said company and pay cash therefor, if he became dissatisfied with such purchase, they would, at the end of three years from the purchase, take the stock back at his option, and pay him his money invested therein with ten per cent per annum interest from the time of investment. It is further alleged that on [391] October 15, 1884, **he** received one hundred and fifty shares of such stock, and paid to said Fisher and Chadwick twelve thousand dollars therefor; and that thereafter, on or before September 15, 1885, he became dissatisfied with his purchase and notified said Fisher and Chadwick that he would exercise his option of returning said stock to them and receiving from them therefor the said sum of twelve thousand dollars with interest thereon at the rate of ten per cent per annum from October 15, 1884. A payment of three thousand dollars of this sum on May 19, 1887, and another payment of two hundred dollars on September 23, 1888, is alleged, and it is further alleged that no other payments have been made. Charles F. Fisher in his separate answer, and John M. Chadwick and Charles F. Fisher, administrators of the estate of Jehu J. Chadwick, deceased, in their separate answer, deny that any such agreement was ever made, and deny that any payments were ever made on such an agreement. What they allege on these points they state in the following language:

"And for a second and further defense by said defendants to said cause of action set forth in said amended petition, the defendant alleges that on or about the tenth day of September, A. D. 1885, at the county aforesaid, the said plaintiff, being then and there the holder and owner of one hundred and fifty shares of the capital stock of the North Crow Land and Cattle Company, did then and there agree to and with said defendant Charles F. Fisher and said Jehu J. Chadwick to sell and deliver to them all of his said shares of the capital stock of said company, in consideration of the promises and agreements of the said defendant Charles F. Fisher and the said Jehu J. Chadwick then and there made to take the same and pay said plaintiff therefor the amount which he, the said plaintiff, had paid for the said shares of stock, together with interest thereon at the rate of ten per cent per annum from the date when he, the said plaintiff, had taken the said shares of stock and advanced the money to pay for the same, such payment to be made by said defendant and Jehu J. Chadwick as soon and fast as they were able financially to do so without sacrificing their interest in or the property of said North Crow Land and Cattle Company."

[302] The jury were instructed that such an agreement as this, if entered into by said Fisher and Chadwick, does not contemplate that they could take all the time that they may desire and that may be convenient for them to take, but that the law will imply that that means a reasonable time; "so that if you

further believe that a reasonable time for the disposition of the property has elapsed since the agreement of the said Chadwick and Fisher to purchase the stock of the plaintiff you must find for the plaintiff." This is assigned as error. We think this instruction is not erroneous. It is not a sacrifice of property to put it upon the market and sell it at the market price. All the time necessary to do this is a reasonable time. But it is urged that there is no proof that a reasonable time for the sale of the property had elapsed when this action was begun. The contract is alleged and testimony introduced tending to prove it as of date September 10, 1885. It is shown by uncontroverted testimony that this action was commenced about the 1st of October, 1889. Here is a lapse of a little more than four years—certainly ample time.

It was claimed in argument that, in order to recover on this contract, financial ability to pay on the part of the obligors should be shown, and that this instruction of the court to the jury does not require such a showing, and is therefore erroneous. It should be remembered that the plaintiff Hopkins in his pleadings and in his testimony denied the existence of such contract. He alleged and proved a contract for money to become due three years from the date of his purchase of the stock of the company. Defendants set up a different contract made at a subsequent time, fixing no certain time when any money should become due. It was incumbent on them to establish their defense.

Charles F. Fisher testifies that the time of the first payment under the contract was to be within two years from its date. Jehu J. Chadwick, in conversation with Mrs. Kate E. Hopkins and others, stated that the money on the contract was due in the fall of 1887. This is all inconsistent with the idea that payment was made conditional on the financial [393] ability of the parties. Really, the contract set up by the defendants would seem not to question but rather to assume the financial ability of the obligors to fulfill their contract. The evidence also shows that they had abundant means to do so. These means consisted of a large number of neat cattle and horses, a large quantity of land, forty miles of fence, ranch improvements, implements, etc. The obligors furnished all this property to the North Crow Land and Cattle Company. They continued in the control of the property and the business. The capital stock of the company was placed at one hundred thousand dollars.

Hopkins paid eighty cents on the dollar for his stock. This all bears on the question of their financial ability. The fact that they received twelve thousand dollars from Hopkins is very material in this connection. The testimony of defendant Fisher shows an entire misapprehension of the effect of such a contract as he alleges and attempts to prove. He seems to assume that it gave himself and Chadwick the right to carry on the business without contraction and without limit as to time, and that they were under no obligation to pay under the contract unless they could do so from the profits of the business. In answer to the question, "What was the agreement as to when the money should be obtained," he says: "By selling off company property. For instance, if we sold off a bunch of horses for ten thousand dollars, any amount that was needed out of that to pay running expenses or indebtedness was first to be deducted, and then the balance applied to him." This construction would destroy the essential elements of a contract. It would make it of no binding force. It would leave the obligors at liberty to sell or not and to pay or not at their option. It is simply a claim of the right to take the stock of Hopkins and pay for it if they should find it profitable or desirable to do so, otherwise not to take it or pay for it.

The inconsistency of the testimony of Fisher with the contract which he sets up in his pleading, and the inherent improbability that Chadwick would make such a losing contract as that alleged to have been made on September 10, 1885, would seem to leave the preponderance of the evidence [394] largely in favor of the contract alleged by plaintiff Hopkins. The record does not reveal upon which contract the jury based their verdict. Really it is not material. The amount of indebtedness is precisely the same under one as under the other. It is twelve thousand dollars with interest at ten per cent per annum from October 15, 1884, less the payment mentioned. The answers of defendants show their liability after the lapse of a reasonable time for the disposal of the necessary amount of property. They do not show the lapse of time nor the amount of the liability. If they did, the answers alone would sustain the verdict and the judgment. These particulars are supplied by uncontroverted evidence. There are some other assignments of error, but under these views they become immaterial.

The form of the judgment as to the administrators is objectionable. It is against John M. Chadwick and Charles F.

Fisher, administrators of the estate of Jehu J. Chadwick, deceased. This might be considered as a personal judgment against these administrators for waste, to be satisfied de bonis propriis. No such a cause of action or any personal cause of action against the administrators as such is alleged or proven. The cause of action against the administrators is the contract to which the decedent was a party. The judgment against the administrators should be reformed, and should be that the administrators pay in due course of administration the amount ascertained to be due: Sess. Laws 1890-91, sec. 13, p. 272. This section seems to be a legislative enactment of a pre-existing rule of law: See Rice v. Innskeep, 34 Cal. 224; Senescal v. Bolton, 7 N. Mex. 351, and cases cited.

These causes are remanded to the district court with directions to modify the judgment as to the administrators in accordance with this opinion. When so modified, the judgment of the district court will stand affirmed, each party to pay his own costs in this court.

Groesbeck, C. J., and Clark, J., concur.

JOINT LIABILITY—EFFECT OF DEATH OF ONE JOINT DEBTOR.—Upon the death of one joint debtor the survivor may be sued for the debt; and if he is insolvent, the estate of the deceased is chargeable in equity: Brown v. Benight, 3 Blackf. 39; 23 Am. Dec. 373. Accepting a confession of judgment by a survivor in a joint action against two obligors, where one has died pending the action, discharges the latter's estate: Finney v. Cochran, 1 Watts & S. 112; 37 Am. Dec. 450. See Ayer v. Wilson, 2 Mill. 319; 12 Am. Dec. 677.

CONTRACTS—TIME AS OF THE ESSENCE OF.—As to when time is considered of the essence of the contract, see the extended note to Jones v. Robbins, 50 Am. Dec. 597-600.

EXECUTORS AND ADMINISTRATORS—JUDGMENT AGAINST.—A judgment against an administrator in the form that "plaintiff have and recover from the defendant's administrator" the sum adjudged, is sufficient, although the better mode would be to have added the words "to be levied of the goods and chattels of his intestate in his hands to be administered": Guice v. Sellers, 43 Miss. 52; 5 Am. Rep. 476. See Ewing v. Handley, 4 Litt. 346; 14 Am. Dec. 140. A judgment against an administrator merely establishes the debt against the estate to be paid in due course of administration in Illinois, and no execution can issue thereon: Judy v. Kelly, 11 Ill. 211; 50 Am. Dec. 455; Ansley v. Baker, 14 Tex. 607; 65 Am. Dec. 136.

TRIAL—VERDICT—SUFFICIENCY OF.—The object of a verdict is to respond to and decide issues between the parties upon the evidence adduced, and to declare their respective rights as involved in the issue with certainty, so that the judgment can be entered with like certainty, and the ministerial officers can carry it into execution without determining additional facts: Stafford v. King, 30 Tex. 257; 94 Am. Dec. 304. See Trudo v. Anderson, 10 Mich. 357; 81 Am. Dec. 795, Barnett v. Caruth, 22 Tex. 173; 73 Am. Dec. 255.

KAHN *v.* TRADERS' INSURANCE COMPANY.

[4 WYOMING, 419.]

APPELLATE PRACTICE—FINAL ORDERS.—If, after an order is made by the district court vacating a verdict in favor of plaintiff and granting a new trial, the plaintiff elects to rely upon his exceptions thereto, and declines to further prosecute the action in that court, the court orders that the action be dismissed at plaintiff's costs, and that the defendant go hence without day and recover his costs from plaintiff, such order is final and may be reviewed on appeal.

APPELLATE PRACTICE—REVIEWABLE ORDERS.—An order setting aside a verdict and granting a new trial may be made the basis of a specification of error, and may be reviewed on appeal.

INSURANCE—ARBITRATION—INSTRUCTIONS.—If, in an action on a fire insurance policy, a defense based upon a failure to comply with an arbitration clause in the policy is not specially pleaded, it is error to submit to the jury an issue based upon such clause.

INSURANCE—ARBITRATION—NECESSITY OF PLEADING.—If a policy of fire insurance provides that the loss shall not be payable "until sixty days after the proofs, certificates, plans, and specifications, and award of appraisers herein required, shall have been rendered and examinations perfected by assured," an award by arbitrators or appraisers is not absolutely essential to a cause of action on the policy, nor is it necessary for the insured to plead either a submission of the amount of loss to appraisers and an award by them, or facts showing that the insurer has committed a breach of the agreement to arbitrate.

INSURANCE—ARBITRATION CLAUSE AS A DEFENSE.—Breach of a condition for arbitration in a fire insurance policy is not effective as a defense when the insurer asserts that the policy has become absolutely void, or denies the general right of the insured to recover anything under the policy.

INSURANCE—ARBITRATION AS COLLATERAL AGREEMENT.—If an insurance policy contains, first, an agreement to pay a loss within a certain time, and, secondly, an agreement to refer the loss to arbitration, the agreement to arbitrate is collateral to the agreement to pay.

INSTRUCTIONS—QUESTIONS OF LAW.—If the evidence of a fact is positive, and not disputed or questioned, it ought to be taken as an established fact by the court and the jury instructed accordingly.

INSURANCE—POWER OF AGENT—ADDITIONAL INSURANCE.—An insurance agent clothed with authority to make contracts of insurance, to issue policies and to receive premiums therefor, is the general agent of the insurer and authorized to consent to additional insurance. The insurer is bound not only by notice to such agent, but his knowledge of matters relating to the contract of insurance must be held to be the knowledge of the insurer.

INSURANCE—ADDITIONAL INSURANCE—WAIVER OF CONDITION.—If a general insurance agent who issues the policy in suit has knowledge of, and consents to, additional insurance, but fails to indorse it thereon, and through neglect fails to notify his company thereof, and its adjuster, after the loss and with knowledge of such additional insurance, and without objection thereto, seeks to adjust the loss, the company is estopped from insisting on a forfeiture of the policy on the ground that such additional insurance was procured by the insured without the consent of the company thereto being indorsed on the policy as required therein.

INSURANCE—NOTICE OF LOSS.—If the general agent of
the insurer on the day of a loss informs him by letter thereof, and
within a few days thereafter the insurer sends an adjuster with
power to investigate, adjust, and settle the loss, this is a compliance
with the requirement of immediate notice of loss contained in the
policy, and a waiver of proof of loss and magistrate's certificate.

WITNESSES—REFRESHING MEMORY.—In an action to re-
cover on a fire insurance policy one year after the loss, a witness
who was the bookkeeper for the assured up to the time of the fire
may refesh his memeory from a schedule of the property destroyed,
furnished by the insured to the insurer as a proof of loss and made
up from duplicate invoices, from recollection of the stock on hand,
from the insured's books and original invoices, and such witness may
read the schedule to the jury in response to a question as to the
amount of goods on hand at the time of the fire.

INSURANCE—EVIDENCE OF LOSS.—In an action to re-
cover on a fire insurance policy, a witness who was the bookkeeper
for the insured up to the time of the fire is competent to enumerate
and state the value of certain property destroyed by the fire, but not
included in the proofs of loss.

INSURANCE—EVIDENCE OF PROOFS OF LOSS.—An affi-
davit of loss and schedule of goods in stock at the time thereof furnished by the insured to the insurer, are competent evidence, in an
action to recover on a policy of fire insurance, to show a compliance,
or attempted compliance, with the requirement of the policy that
proofs of loss should be furnished.

INSURANCE—EVIDENCE OF OFFERS OF COMPROMISE.
If a claim for loss under a fire insurance policy is admitted by all
parties, and the only dispute between the adjuster of the insurer and
the insured is the amount of his claim, offers of settlement made by
such adjuster to the insured are admissible in evidence. They are
not only admissible, but they tend to show a waiver of additional
insurance without the consent of the insurer, and also a waiver of
proof of loss.

INSURANCE—CONDITION AGAINST FALSE SWEARING.
To constitute fraud or false swearing under a condition in a policy
of fire insurance avoiding it therefor, there must be false statements
willfully made, with respect to a material matter, with the intention
of thereby deceiving the insurer. An affidavit sent as proof of loss,
stating that the insured goods "were burned up and destroyed by
fire," when in fact most of them were destroyed by smoke and water,
so as to constitute a total loss, is not false swearing within the meaning of such a policy.

FRAUD—BURDEN OF PROOF.—One who alleges fraud must
clearly and distinctly prove it so as to satisfy the ordinary mind and
conscience of its existence as a fact.

Action on a fire insurance policy. Verdict for plaintiff. The
court on motion of defendant vacated the verdict and ordered a
new trial, and upon the refusal of the plaintiff to further prosecute the case in that court, and election to stand upon his exceptions to the orders of the court, the action was ordered dismissed at plaintiff's costs, and judgment rendered in favor of defendant for costs. Plaintiff prosecuted error to the supreme
court.

Defendant moved to vacate the verdict and for a new trial on the ground that the court erred in refusing instructions requested by the defendant, and numbered 1, 2, 3, and 4. These instructions so refused were, that the jury should find for the defendant, first, because the policy provided for arbitration as to the amount of the loss, and that though it was shown there was a disagreement as to such amount, there was no evidence of arbitration; second, because it was shown that the plaintiff had procured additional insurance in violation of the policy, without the consent of the defendant; third, because the plaintiff had not complied with the condition of the policy requiring him to furnish a particular account of the loss, subscribed and sworn to as in the policy directed; and, also, because the court erred in instructing the jury that the plaintiff could recover if the defendant had notice of the additional insurance, and in instructing that the evidence was such that the jury had a right to determine whether objections to the proofs of loss, or to the failure to make the same had not been waived by the defendant, and because the court erred in instructing the jury that it was not fatal to the plaintiff's right of recovery that the consent to the additional insurance was not indorsed on the policy, if the defendant had knowledge of such additional insurance, and thereafter, upon receipt of the notice of fire, sent an adjuster to investigate the circumstances and settle with the plaintiff therefor, and such adjuster, after such investigation and after examining the policy of insurance, continued further investigations and made propositions of settlement and proofs of loss, or did any act fairly showing an adjustment of the defendant's liability upon the policy after its knowledge of the additional insurance.

The defendant further urged as a ground for a new trial that the findings of the jury were contradictory and inconsistent; that the court erred in permitting Samuel Kahn, as a witness for the plaintiff, to refer to, and refresh his memory from, a schedule which was afterward introduced in evidence, and to enumerate and state therefrom the value of different articles alleged to have been lost; and because the court erred, at the trial, in permitting Mr. Baird, a witness on behalf of plaintiff, to testify concerning certain offers made by the adjuster of the defendant to the plaintiff.

W. R. Stoll, for the plaintiff in error.

Lacey & Van Devanter, for the defendant in error.

[440] CLARK, J. There are two principal questions presented by the record in this cause, viz: 1. Is the plaintiff in such position that he can lawfully. call upon the court to review the rulings of the trial court in setting aside and vacating the verdict rendered by the jury and in granting a new trial? 2. If he is in such position, are there apparent upon the record errors of such nature that this court should reverse the action of the court below?

As to the first question: The appellate jurisdiction of this court is limited by statute to the review of judgments and final orders. The final order which can be reviewed on proceedings in error is defined to be, "An order affecting a substantial right in an action, when such order in effect determines the action and prevents a judgment": Rev. Stats., sec. 3126.

In this case, the court ordered that the case be dismissed at plaintiff's costs, and rendered judgment for defendant that it go hence without day and recover its costs of plaintiff. It cannot be doubted that the effect of this action by the court was to finally determine the cause, and, while it may not be such a determination of the matters in controversy between the parties as to preclude the plaintiff from bringing another action based upon those matters, it cannot be questioned that, so far as this particular action is concerned, it was as completely disposed of by the final order entered herein as would have been the case had there been a judgment for defendant upon the merits.

But it is strongly urged upon us on behalf of the defendant that, inasmuch as the plaintiff refused to submit to the order vacating the verdict, and refused to proceed further in the court, that by such action it became necessary for the court below to make the order it did make, and therefore the plaintiff ought not to be heard to complain of it; that the order was not either necessarily or logically the result of any act or ruling of the court, and hence it is immaterial what proceedings [440] were had in court anterior thereto, and the appellate court should not review such anterior proceedings to determine whether there be error therein, for the reason that such error, if any, is not connected with the final determination, and cannot have contributed to or influenced the same, and is not prejudicial.

If this contention was sound, it would necessarily follow that in no case where a verdict had been rendered for the plaintiff and set aside by the trial court could the action of the court be

reviewed by the appellate court. It is, I think, well settled that
where a new trial is granted and the party in whose favor the
verdict was rendered submits and participates in the new trial
he cannot afterward be heard to complain of the order granting
a new trial, even though there be gross error in such order, otherwise he would be in a position to take his choice of the verdicts
upon the first and second trials. And, inasmuch as he cannot
be heard in the appellate court until there has been a final determination of the cause in the court below, and the action is
no longer pending there, it seems to me that he ought to be permitted to stand upon his exceptions and let the court make such
final determination of the cause as it deems proper.

I know that there are cases which hold that an order granting a new trial does not affect any substantial right of a party,
and may not be reviewed, and as well there are cases which
hold that such an order in effect does determine the action and
prevent a judgment and hence may be directly appealed from;
but these are extreme views in opposite directions, and I do not
feel inclined to be guided by them. I think a fair construction
of our statute does authorize the granting of a new trial to be
the basis of a specification of error. It can hardly be doubted
that an order setting aside the verdict of a jury does affect the
substantial rights of the party in whose favor it was rendered,
under our system of jurisprudence. From time immemorial it
has been one of the most cherished rights of the individual that
he should be permitted to have his matters in litigation submitted to a fair and impartial jury of his countrymen, and it
would seem to [441] need no argument to show that when he has
brought his cause to court, and at the expense of time and
money secured at the hands of such a jury their declaration in his
favor, he ought to have and enjoy the fruits of that declaration,
unless there be grave and weighty reasons to the contrary: Edwards v. O'Brien, 2 Wyo. 496. I do not mean to intimate that
trial courts ought not to exercise a wise and discreet supervision over all the proceedings in their courts, including the
action of juries, but only this, that when a verdict has been
rendered there ought to be sound, weighty, substantial reasons
for interfering with it; and, this being so, it would seem that
an order granting a new trial might be, in the language of our
statute, "material and prejudicial to the substantial rights of
the party excepting," and hence the subject of review: Rev.
Stats., sec. 2650. Section 2649 of the Revised Statutes provided

the method in which an exception to the opinion of the trial
court on a motion for a new trial may be preserved, and I can see
nothing in that section or in the entire chapter of our code on
exceptions which would indicate that it was the intention of
the legislature to limit the right to an exception to cases where
a new trial had been refused, but rather, on the contrary, the
intention was to permit the exception in either case. This being so, and the exception being allowed in such cases solely for
the purpose of reversing the question for review in the appellate
court, it follows that the action of the court in granting a new
trial may be reviewed. Owing to the fact that in this state the
Code of Civil Procedure was taken almost without change from
the state of Ohio, we have carefully examined the decisions of
that state upon this question, but have been unable to find any
case exactly in point, but, so far as the cases there do go, they
seem to support the contention of the plaintiff here.

In Beatty v. Hatcher, 13 Ohio St. 120, the court, in commenting upon a statute of that state which provided that
"either party shall have the right to except to the opinion of
the court in all cases of motion for new trial, ... so that
said case may be removed by petition in error," use the following language: "And while it is not necessary to [442] hold that
we will in no case employ this power apparently conferred by
the letter of the statute, we are free to say that it will require
a strong case to justify its exercise."

In Spafford v. Bradley, 20 Ohio, 74, the court, in referring
to the above mentioned statute, say that a party would, it seems,
be entitled to his writ of error as well in a case where a motion
for a new trial is sustained, as where it is refused. I feel convinced that our statute on exceptions as certainly confers the
right of exception upon either party in cases of motions for new
trials as does the Ohio statute above mentioned.

In Dean v. King, 22 Ohio St. 134, the court in discussing
the matter of new trials, etc., say: "Motions for new trials upon
the ground that the verdict is against the weight of evidence
are addressed to the sound discretion of the court, and, if
granted, the judgment will not be reversed on error, unless the
case is so strong as to show an abuse of discretion."

Our attention was called by counsel for defendant to the cases
of Concord v. Runnels, 23 Ohio St. 601, and Smith v. Board
of Education, 27 Ohio St. 44, in support of the proposition that
it had "long been held in Ohio that error will not lie from the

granting of a new trial even after final judgment." But in each of these cases there had been a new trial in which the complaining party participated, and the holding was, that under such circumstances the court would not review the proceedings upon the first trial, the reason therefor being stated in Andrews v. Youngstown, 35 Ohio St. 221, as follows: "Where a new trial has been awarded, and a party has voluntarily submitted to such trial, it seems to us but reasonable that he should be held to have waived the right to prosecute error to reverse the judgment of reversal." It would seem, then, that in Ohio an order granting a new trial would be subject to review. In Missouri, under a system of practice which prohibits the appellate court from entertaining proceedings in error until there has been a final determination of the case in the trial court, there is a long line of decisions commencing in the early days of the court and continuing down to the present time, which establish and uphold the [443] method of practice observed in this case. In Iron Mountain Bank v. Armstrong, 92 Mo. 277, in discussing the precise question we have here, the court say: "As to the first question presented by this record as hereinbefore stated, we are of opinion that under numerous decisions of this court it must be answered in the affirmative. While those authorities hold that a judgment setting aside a verdict and granting a new trial is not a final judgment, and will not, therefore, support an appeal or writ of error, still they all in effect hold that when the trial court improperly grants a new trial the party complaining may avail himself of the error by tendering his bill of exceptions and abandoning the case at that point, and that when a final judgment is then afterward rendered in said cause he may then, by excepting thereto, take and support an appeal, and in this way secure a review of errors committed, if any, in setting aside said verdict and granting said new trial. These authorities also hold that if such party participates in the new trial awarded he will not afterward be heard to complain of the errors committed in the first trial": Citing Hill v. Wilkins, 4 Mo. 87, 88; Davis v. Davis, 8 Mo. 56-58; Martin v. Henley, 13 Mo. 312, 313; Bowie v. Kansas City, 51 Mo. 459; Gilstrap v. Felts, 50 Mo. 431.

Coupling with the foregoing considerations the fact that in many of our sister states statutes have been enacted expressly authorizing by direct appeal a review of orders granting as well as refusing new trials, a fact which indicates a widespread belief that such is the just and proper rule, I am of opinion that the question must be answered in the affirmative.

The foregoing conclusion leads to the consideration of the second question as above stated, and the consideration of that question renders necessary a review of the evidence and instructions given at the trial as far as may be deemed material to a proper understanding and disposition of the cause.

The evidence shows substantially the following facts: On May 5, 1890, and continuously until the date of the fire on December 26, 1890, Frank A. Stitzer was the agent of the [444] defendant at Cheyenne, Wyoming. As such agent he was intrusted with blank policies of insurance bearing the signatures of the president and secretary of the company, and was authorized by the company to make contracts of insurance, and to countersign and issue policies, and to receive the premiums therefor. On that day, May 5th, the plaintiff, who was then and until the fire occurred a grocery merchant, engaged in business in Cheyenne, applied to said agent for insurance upon his stock of goods and store fixtures in the sum of twelve hundred dollars and three hundred dollars, respectively, paid to said agent the premiums, thirty dollars, and received the policy sued on in this action, which was countersigned by said Stitzer. Thereafter, on the thirteenth day of October, 1890, the plaintiff applied to said Stitzer for additional insurance upon his stock of goods in the sum of one thousand dollars and obtained it in the Hartford Fire Insurance Company, of which company said Stitzer was also the agent, with like authority as in the case of the defendant company. The policy issued by the Hartford Company bears the indorsement "twelve hundred dollars other concurrent insurance," and is countersigned by said Stitzer. This additional insurance was not indorsed upon the policy sued upon, and through oversight the agent, Stitzer, failed to notify the defendant of it.

Thereafter, on December 26, 1890, while both policies were in force, fire occurred, and the stock of goods and fixtures insured were burned and damaged by smoke and water, together with plaintiff's books of account.

On the morning after the fire, the agent, Stitzer (who testified that after loss he was merely authorized to report the loss and if there were any goods not destroyed to instruct the assured to take proper care of them until an adjuster arrived), was notified by plaintiff of the fire, and at once proceeded to the store and remained there three-quarters of an hour examining into the condition of matters there. He saw nothing of any consequence that could be saved. After visiting the scene of the

fire, and upon the same day, he reported by letter the fact of
the loss to the defendant company at Denver and Chicago.

Thereafter, and a short time prior to January 12, 1891, the
[445] defendant, through Cobb, Wilson & Benedict, of Denver,
Colorado, its general agents for the states of Colorado and
Wyoming, sent an adjuster, one Norton, to Cheyenne, with authority to adjust and settle plaintiff's loss. In the performance
of this duty the adjuster was engaged for two and perhaps three
days, and while so engaged he subjected plaintiff to a rigid
examination as to the quantity of goods he had, from whom he
purchased them, what he paid for them, the quantity thereof,
their value before and after the fire, etc., making extensive
memoranda of the facts elicited. He several times offered plaintiff
three hundred dollars in settlement of the loss and urged him
to take it, saying to him: "You cannot afford to fight this case;
we represent more capital than you do and you are a poor man
and had better compromise." The only difficulty in the way
of a settlement of the loss seems from the testimony to be owing to the fact that the plaintiff and the adjuster did not arrive at
an agreement as to the amount of the loss; no other reason of
any kind for delay was assigned by the adjuster than doubt as
to the amount of plaintiff's loss. After a few days spent in the
endeavor to make a settlement, the adjuster told plaintiff that
he had to go away and would be back again in a few days, and
he hoped the matter would be settled up, to which plaintiff replied, to quote his own language: "Mr. Norton, I don't know
anything about a fire; never had any experience about it; I want
you to tell me what I have to do. Mr. Baird said I have to
have some papers and I don't know what to do." He said:
"You don't need anything at all; don't need any papers. I have
got all the company needs in this book; that's all they want;
you don't need to make out any papers at all." At the commencement of these attempts at adjustment the plaintiff handed
both the policies to the adjuster, he representing both the defendant and the Hartford Fire Insurance Company. The adjuster left, and, not returning, the plaintiff in person and through
his attorney during the next two or three weeks had frequent
and repeated interviews with the agent, Stitzer, in the endeavor
to get the matter settled, and to ascertain what the defendant intended doing about it; but [446] all that Stitzer could say was
that he was constantly expecting another adjuster, and that the
matter would be speedily settled. Nothing further seems to

have been done until on February 7, 1891, the plaintiff, through
his attorney, sent by mail to the defendant at Chicago, Illinois
a schedule of the property destroyed, setting opposite the description of each item the cost price thereof; this was attached
to an affidavit of plaintiff in which he stated that he was the
person named in the policy sued on, that the insured property
was burned up and destroyed by fire on December 26, 1890; that
he believed the fire to have been of incendiary origin; that he
was the owner of the goods; that attached thereto was a statement of each article of property burned up and the cost price
thereof; that on October 13, 1890, he obtained through the
agency of Stitzer one thousand dollars additional insurance in
the Hartford Fire Insurance Company upon said stock of goods;
that Stitzer received immediate notice of the fire and at once
made an examination thereof; that Stitzer a few days thereafter
brought with him an adjuster of the defendant, and they together made several examinations of all things connected with
the fire; that Stitzer at several times represented that the adjuster would settle the matter, but he had failed to appear; that
the statement attached had been prepared for a long time for the
examination of the defendant's agents, but that inasmuch as they
had not appeared he, plaintiff, sent it direct to the company.

Accompanying this affidavit was a letter under date February 7, 1891, from plaintiff's attorney to defendant, in which
after reiterating some of the statements in the affidavit, it is
stated: "For the information of the adjuster the list hereto
attached has been made out and held in readiness. Mr. Kahn
has held himself in readiness to give such information as might
be desired at all times, and, owing to the failure of the adjuster
to be here in accordance with the information conveyed to us by
Mr. Stitzer, we have at last decided to send the list direct to the
company. Owing to the unsatisfactory status of the case, I hope
you will kindly respond and inform [147] us whether the insured
is going to be paid or not. If you wish any information in addition to what is contained in the inclosed it will be gladly furnished you."

This letter, with accompanying statement and affidavit, was
duly received by defendant and forwarded by it to its general
agents, Cobb, Wilson & Benedict, at Denver, Colorado, who,
on February 28, 1891, wrote to plaintiff acknowledging receipt,
and further saying; "These notices, we presume, are sent in compliance with the terms of your contract, in which it is covenanted

that, 'If a fire occur the assured shall give immediate notice of any loss thereby in writing to this company,' and they are accepted as such notice. We respectfully refer you to the conditions of your policies, wherein it states that you must first give immediate notice in writing to this company, and then give minute instructions as to your course in presenting the claim. We must insist upon a full and complete compliance in every particular with all the terms and conditions of your policy, which is the contract. Until a full and complete compliance on your part with all the conditions and requirements therein contained, we cannot give consideration to the questions which you present."

With respect to the foregoing facts there seems to be no sort of conflict in the evidence. All the evidence introduced upon the trial was on behalf of the plaintiff; the defendant offering none and contenting itself with the cross-examination of the plaintiff's witnesses.

1. It appears from the record that at the close of the examination of witnesses the defendant extracted from the testimony a defense additional to the five-distinct defenses set forth in its answer, viz., one based upon the arbitration clause in the policy; and requested the court to give to the jury five separate and distinct instructions and to submit four specific questions, based upon this clause; four of these instructions were given by the court to the jury, to each of which plaintiff objected and excepted to the ruling of the court. One of said instructions was refused by the court, and defendant preserved its exception thereto; the questions were [448] submitted to the jury, and to this plaintiff reserved his exception. The first, tenth, eleventh, twelfth, and thirteenth and one branch of the eighth and ninth grounds of defendant's motion for a new trial were based upon this clause in the policy and the testimony which was deemed to apply to it.

At the argument and in briefs of counsel this question was discussed from every conceivable point of view, and every phase of the law relating thereto exhaustively presented to the court; but from the view we take of the matter it is not necessary to enter upon any very extended consideration of this particular matter. It is sufficient to say that this defense was not pleaded by the defendant, and hence no question based upon this arbitration clause should have been submitted to the jury. Matter in defense cannot be availed of unless pleaded: 2 May on

Insurance, sec. 591; Dyer v. Piscataqua etc. Ins. Co., 53 Me. 119; New York Cent. Ins. Co. v. National Prot. Ins. Co., 20 Barb. 468; Cassacia v. Phoenix Ins. Co., 28 Cal. 629; Coburn v. Travelers' Ins. Co., 145 Mass. 226; Home Ins. Co. v. Curtis, 32 Mich. 403; Minnoch v. Eureka etc. Ins. Co., 90 Mich. 240; Sussex County Mut. Ins. Co. v. Woodruff, 26 N. J. L. 541; Northrup v. Mississippi etc. Ins. Co., 47 Mo. 435; 1 Am. Rep. 337; 2 Wood on Insurance, sec. 522, p. 1141, and cases cited.

But it is contended with very considerable force that the clause providing for arbitration, coupled with the additional clause that "until sixty days after the proofs, certificates, plans, and specifications and award of appraisers herein required shall have been rendered and examination perfected by assured the loss shall not be payable," makes an award by appraisers or arbitrators absolutely essential to plaintiff's cause of action, and that plaintiff should have either pleaded a submission of the amount of loss to appraisers and an award by them or else such facts as showed that the defendant committed a breach of the agreement to arbitrate.

I am unable to acquiesce in this view. Assuming for the purposes of this question that the agreement was not a mere collateral agreement to refer, but valid, and such a one as the courts will enforce. it is beyond question that it did not become ⁴⁴⁹ effective and in force at all events; by its terms it only became so upon the happening of a contingency, to wit, the failure of the insurer and the assured to mutually agree upon the amount of the loss, and hence until the happening of this contingency it was wholly without force or effect. And in the absence of some allegation in plaintiff's petition or defendant's answer to the effect that there had been, within the meaning of the language of the policy, a failure between plaintiff and defendant to agree upon the amount of the loss, how could the court say from the pleadings that a submission to and award of appraisers, or else some breach of the agreement on part of defendant, was an essential element of plaintiff's right to recover of defendant? In this case, the conditions of the policy were not set forth as they should have been in plaintiff's petition. But many of them were set forth in defendant's answer, and plaintiff's failure to comply therewith alleged as defenses. In plaintiff's reply facts tending to show a waiver of such conditions were alleged. Looking at all the pleadings, a complete

cause of action and defense thereto were stated, whatever may
have been the case looking only at plaintiff's petition. Yet in all
the pleadings there was no approach to an allegation with respect to the arbitration clause of the policy. And for the purpose of this case it must be treated as though there was no such
clause. But even though this defense had been set up by defendant with its other defenses, I am of opinion that it would
not have availed the defendant.

In this case the defendant denies its liability to pay any loss
whatever under this policy in suit; it asserts that the policy has
become absolutely void, and there is no provision in the policy
in suit that the arbitration shall be had regardless of the question of defendant's liability on other grounds; and I am of opinion that in such cases the condition for arbitration does not
have effect.

In Mentz v. Armenia Fire Ins. Co., 79 Pa. St. 478, 21 Am.
Rep. 80, the condition in the policy was very much more direct
and certain than in the policy sued on here. It provided as follows:

"In case any difference or dispute shall arise between the [450]
assured and this company touching the amount of any loss
or damage sustained by him, such difference shall be submitted to the judgment of arbitrators, one to be appointed by each
party with power to select a third in case of disagreement, whose
decision thereupon shall be final and conclusive; and no action,
suit, or proceedings at law or in equity shall be maintained on this
policy, unless the amount of loss or damage in case of difference
or dispute shall be first thus ascertained."

On the trial, the defendants moved for a nonsuit because
the section above requires the parties to the policy to submit
to a referee, etc. The motion for a nonsuit was allowed. Upon
error in the supreme court it was held that, in order that defendants might avail themselves of this defense, they must show
that they "admitted the validity of the policy and their liability
under it, and that the only question was as to the extent of the
loss." Other authorities holding that a condition for arbitration is
not effective in cases where the insurer denies the general right of
the assured to recover anything are Goldstone v. Osborne, 2 Car.
& P. 550; Robinson v. Georges Ins. Co., 17 Me. 131; 35 Am. Dec.
239; Phoenix Fire Ins. Co. v. Badger, 53 Wis. 283; Randall v.
American Fire Ins. Co., 10 Mont. 360; 24 Am. St. Rep. 50; Farnum v. Phoenix Ins. Co., 83 Cal. 247; 17 Am. St. Rep. 233;

Bailey v. Aetna Ins. Co., 77 Wis. 336; 2 Wood on Insurance, sec. 456.

In this case, it does not appear that the defendant ever at any time requested or suggested a submission of the amount of the loss to arbitration; in its pleadings it made no suggestion thereof, and, so far as the record discloses, no idea of arbitration was ever at any time suggested by anyone in any manner connected with this cause until after the plaintiff had closed his testimony, and I can conceive of no sort of reason why it (the defendant) should not be held to have conclusively waived the condition. Under such a provision as the one in question the defendant was the only party who could effectually demand and bring about arbitration or gain a defense by reason of the other party's failing to comply with such demand. If the assured fails to demand arbitration, [451] this deprives the insurer of no rights whatever. If the insurer is deprived of the right of arbitration, it can only be by his own laches, because he has only to demand it, and if the assured should refuse to accede to the demand without good substantial reason for such refusal, the courts will probably afford him no relief until he submits to arbitration. But, on the other hand, if the insurer is unwilling to arbitrate, he may without penalty ignore the request made by assured therefor. And inasmuch as, under the terms of the contract, it depends upon the will of the insurer alone as to whether he will have arbitration or not, why should he be permitted to complain in cases like this, when it not only appears that he never requested or suggested arbitration, but, on the contrary, everything leads to the belief that had the assured requested it the insurer would not have assented to such request: Cox v. Delmas, 99 Cal. 104.

But, again, the condition is that when personal property is damaged "the amount of sound value and of damage shall be determined by mutual agreement of the company and assured; or, failing to thus agree, the same shall be determined by appraisal of each article by two competent and disinterested appraisers," etc. The evidence discloses practically a total loss, and it would hardly seem that this provision was at all applicable to such a case. It is, however, clear from the evidence that the differences existing between plaintiff and defendant as to the amount of the loss were due in no sense whatever to any failure to agree as to the "amount of sound value and of damage," but to a different thing altogether, viz., as to the quantity of goods the plaintiff had on hand at the time of the fire, the defendant insisting that the quantity of goods at that time did not exceed one-fourth the quantity claimed by plaintiff. This was the real point of difference between the parties; and I am wholly unable to perceive or understand how it is possible to bring this particular question within the terms or fair meaning of the arbitration clause of the policy.

As to the question. which was exhaustively argued at the hearing and in briefs of counsel, as to whether the agreement [452] in this policy constituted a condition precedent or was simply a collateral agreement to refer, we have but little to say; we have assumed for the purpose of this case that in the event of failure to agree between the parties that it became a condition precedent to defendant's liability; but in view of the rule, well established, that the language of an insurance policy is to be most strongly construed against the insurer (Insurance Co. v. Wright, 1 Wall. 456; May on Insurance, sec. 175, and cases cited; 1 Wood on Insurance, sec. 58), it may well be doubted if it is anything more than an agreement to refer, collateral to the main contract set forth in the earlier portion of the policy, which provides that the loss or damage shall be "paid sixty days after the written notice and proofs as hereinafter required shall have been made by assured and delivered to the company in Chicago in accordance with the terms and conditions of the policy": Gibbs v. Continental Ins. Co., 13 Hun, 611; Phoenix Ins. Co. v. Badger, 53 Wis. 284; Canfield v. Watertown Fire Ins. Co., 55 Wis. 422; Hamilton v. Home Ins. Co., 137 U. S. 370; Liverpool etc. Ins. Co. v. Creighton, 51 Ga. 95; May on Insurance, sec. 494, and note 2; Richards on Insurance, sec. 168; 2 Wood on Insurance, secs. 456, 457.

In Hamilton v. Home Ins. Co., 137 U. S. 370, Justice Gray, in delivering the opinion of the supreme court of the United States, uses this language in deciding this question; "The rule of law upon the subject was well stated in Dawson v. Fitzgerald by Sir George Jessel, master of the rolls: 'There are two places where such a plea at the present is successful: 1. Where the action can only be brought for the sum named by the arbitration; 2. When it is agreed that no action shall be brought till there has been an arbitration, or that arbitration shall be a condition precedent to the right of action. In all other cases where there is, first, a covenant to pay, and, secondly, a covenant to refer, the covenants are distinct and collateral, and the plaintiff may sue on the first,

leaving the defendant to bring an action for not referring or
(under a modern [453] English statute) to stay the action till
there has been an arbitration'": L. R. 1 Ex. Div. 260.

Testing the arbitration clause in the policy by this rule, it
would seem that the agreement to arbitrate is collateral to the
agreement to pay.

On this branch of the case I am of opinion that the court
below erred in giving the four instructions referred to, which
were based upon the arbitration clause in the policy, and in submitting the general questions to the jury; that it did not err in
refusing the instruction assigned by defendant as its first cause
for a new trial and set forth in its motion therefor; and that the
first, tenth, eleventh, twelfth, and thirteenth, and so much of
the eighth and ninth grounds of defendant's motion for a new
trial as relates to this question of arbitration did not justify the
court in vacating the verdict and granting a new trial.

2. The second, third, fifth, and seventh grounds of defendant's motion for a new trial are all based upon the provision in
the policy providing that it should be void in the event that assured should procure additional assurance without defendant's
written consent being indorsed upon its policy.

There is no controversy between the parties as to the facts
relating to this particular matter, and it may be well to briefly
restate them. The only controversy between the parties is as to
the conclusion of law to be drawn from the facts.

Frank A. Stitzer, on the fifth day of May, 1890, and continuously until after the loss herein mentioned occurred, was
the agent of the defendant, and also of the Hartford Fire Insurance Company. As agent of the defendant he was authorized
to receive applications for insurance, moneys for premiums, and
to countersign, issue, and renew policies of insurance signed
by the president and attested by the secretary of the defendant company for the territory of Cheyenne and vicinity, etc.,
and for the purpose of carrying out such authority he was intrusted with blank policies of insurance signed by the president
and attested by the secretary. In the conduct of the business he
received applications for insurance, acted upon them without
consultation with any other officer or agent [454] of the company,
received the premium and made the contract of insurance—that
is, filled up, countersigned, and issued the policy. On the fifth
day of May, 1890, he issued the policy sued on. Thereafter, on
October 13, 1890, at request of plaintiff he issued a policy in the

Hartford Fire Insurance Company for additional insurance upon the stock of groceries, provisions, etc., covered by defendant's policy of May 5, 1890. The Hartford policy was indorsed by him thus: "$1,200 other concurrent insurance." He did not indorse upon defendant's policy consent to the additional insurance, nor did he notify the defendant thereof. He says that his failure to so notify defendant was through an oversight. Loss occurred December 26th following. Early in January, 1891, an adjuster representing defendant was sent to Cheyenne, with authority to adjust and settle this loss. He had interviews with plaintiff extending over two or three days in the attempt to make a mutual agreement as to the loss. At the first interview plaintiff handed him both policies, which he carefully examined. On February 7, 1891, plaintiff forwarded to defendant at Chicago an affidavit setting forth the loss and mentioning the additional insurance, to which was attached a schedule of the property burned. This affidavit and schedule was sent by the company to its general agents in Denver, and they, under date of February 28, 1891, acknowledged receipt to plaintiff, stating that they accepted it as notice of loss and calling upon plaintiff to fully and completely comply with all the conditions and requirements of the policy here sued on. At no time was any objection made to settlement or any complaint on account of the additional insurance until after suit was brought and it was interposed as a defense to this action.

The sole question, then, is, Does the fact of this additional insurance under the circumstances constitute a defense to this action? The determination of this question is purely a question of law, and the jury should have been peremptorily instructed either one way or the other, which way depending upon the answer given by the court to the question of law. The facts were plain, simple, and undisputed, and there was [455] no question of fact to be determined by the jury. When the evidence to a fact is positive and not disputed or questioned, it ought to be taken as an established fact, and the charge of the court should proceed upon this basis: Wintz v. Morrison, 17 Tex. 372; 67 Am. Dec. 658.

The fact that the agent Stitzer indorsed upon the Hartford policy the words "$1,200 other concurrent insurance" convinces me that at the time of issuing that policy there was then actually present in his mind the knowledge of the existence of the policy here sued on; the policy in suit being the only other policy

upon the property covered by the Hartford policy and being for
the sum of twelve hundred dollars. There is no room to doubt
that the indorsement referred to and was intended to refer to
the policy in suit. This being so, it must be assumed that the
agent Stitzer actually consented to the additional insurance;
otherwise, we would have to assume that he intended to perpetrate a fraud upon the plaintiff, and that assumption, of course,
ought not to be made if it can be avoided. But these facts of actual knowledge and consent seem to be conceded. The question to
be determined is by no means free from difficulty, and has been
determined in both ways by the courts of the different states of
the Union. By the great weight of authority it seems to me to
be reasonably clear that the agent Stitzer must be deemed to
be the general agent of the defendant, and not simply a local,
special agent with limited power. He was clothed with authority to make contracts of insurance, to issue policies, and to receive the premiums therefor, and, possessing such powers, he
stood toward the plaintiff in the stead of the company. In
short, he was the insurance company to the assured. The defendant was bound not only by notice to him, but his knowledge
of matters relating to the contract must be held to be the knowledge of his principal: May on Insurance, sec. 125; Rivara v.
Queen's Ins. Co., 62 Miss. 728; Phenix Ins. Co. v. Munger, 49
Kan. 178; 33 Am. St. Rep. 360; Insurance Co. v. Gray, 43 Kan.
497; 19 Am. St. Rep. 150; Walsh v. Hartford Fire Ins. Co., 73
N. Y. 5; Farnum v. Phoenix Ins. Co., 83 Cal. 246, 261; 17 Am.
St. Rep. 233; Walsh v. Hartford Fire Ins. Co., 9 Hun, 421.

[456] And there can be no question but that he had authority
to indorse the defendant's consent to additional insurance upon
the policy here sued on: Warner v. Peoria etc. Ins. Co., 14 Wis.
318; Walsh v. Hartford Fire Ins. Co., 73 N. Y. 5; 2 Wood on Insurance, sec. 382. This being so, it seems to me that, under the
facts of this case, the defendant ought not now to be heard to
complain because the consent to additional insurance was not indorsed upon its policy by its agent. In 2 May on Insurance,
section 370, in discussing this question the author says:
"But the courts have become more liberal in favor of the assured
in their construction of this sort of provision, whether it be contained in the charter or in the policy. While, as we have seen,
the old rule required the consent to be in writing and indorsed
on the policy, it is the decided tendency of the modern cases
to hold that if the notice of the additional insurance be duly given

to the company or its agent, and no objection is made, the company will be estopped from insisting on a forfeiture of the policy because their consent thereto was not indorsed, as literally required by the stipulation. ، . . . . An office which issues a subsequent policy will be presumed to have notice of the prior one, and where both policies are negotiated through the same person who is agent for both companies, his knowledge is the knowledge of both companies."

In New Orleans Ins. Assn. v. Griffin, 66 Tex. 235, in discussing this question, the court used this language: "The fact is that the majority of men contracting fire insurance know little of the contents of the policy, until a clause in fine print is presented as a defense in adjusting the loss. The agent, however, is generally familiar with all the conditions of the contract. For this reason the agent upon the commonest principles of honesty, encouraged and enforced by the courts as universally as practicable, is required to do what the policy prescribes shall be done to preserve the contract when notified of the facts. . . . . It would be unfair if the agent has not done his duty. It was the duty of the [457] agent to consent and make the indorsement or to refuse to do so if he was informed of the plaintiff's purpose."

In Von Bories v. United Life etc. Ins. Co., 8 Bush, 136, the facts were as here. The subsequent insurance was issued by the person who issued the prior policy—consent was not indorsed upon defendant's prior policy—nor did the agent give notice to his principal. The court held that the defendant had notice from the very moment its general agent issued the second policy, and that "good conscience and fair dealing required the company, in case it was intended to enforce the forfeiture, to take the necessary steps within a reasonable time after notice of the second insurance. . . . . Much stress is laid upon the fact that Moore did not notify the officers of the company of the second insurance. His failure to do so was a violation of his duty to his principal, which cannot and ought not to prejudice the rights of the insured."

In American Cent. Ins. Co. v. McCrea, 8 Lea, 513, 41 Am. Rep. 647, the policy provided that if the assured should procure additional insurance without the written consent of the insurer indorsed upon it it should become void, and also contained this condition: "The use of general terms, or anything less than a distinct, specific agreement clearly expressed and indorsed upon this

:policy, shall not be construed as a waiver of any printed or writ-
.ten condition or restriction."

In the case at bar, the provision is that: "Neither the agent
·who issued the policy nor any other person except its secretary
:in the city of Chicago has authority to waive, modify, or strike
:from the policy any of its terms and conditions."

I am of opinion that the language used in the case cited
.is, so far as it affects the question under consideration, viz., the
necessity of written consent to additional insurance, stronger
than in the policy here sued on, because that condition literally
taken provided that no one could waive it, while here it provides
that no one except the secretary could waive it: Gladding v. California etc. Ins. Assn., 66 Cal. 6. The rule of law with reference to
:this matter is so clearly stated in the case [458] just cited, from 8
Lea, that I quote from the opinion at pages 522, 523, and 524:
·"What acts or declarations, say the learned editors of 'American
Leading Cases,' will operate as waiver of the warranties or conditions, which play a large and important part in most modern
policies of insurance on life or against fire, is a question about
which the authorities differ too much to be easily reduced to order and method.   For while the courts have been desirous on
the one hand to carry out the general purpose of the contract
·as one of indemnity, they have been fettered on the other by stipulations introduced as safeguards against fraud or malpractice,
and the conflict has arisen between the general design and the
incongruity or unfitness of the means employed which has at all
periods formed one of the difficulties of the law: 2 American
Leading Cases, 5th ed., 911.   The struggle on the part of the
·courts has been to protect the innocent policy-holder from the
literal operation of conditions designed for one purpose and used
for another.   Each new decision has been met by a new condition, and the struggle recommenced.   Perhaps, it would have
been better to have left the parties to make their own contracts
in this as in other cases, subject to the ordinary rules of interpretation. . . . . Our duty is, however, to administer the law as
we find it. . . . . It was at first held by the courts, when these
requirements were inserted in policies, to be essential that these
requirements should be literally complied with, and that any-
·thing short of the prescribed formalities would work a forfeiture.
'But the weight of authority is now that if notice be duly given
·to the company or its agent of the additional insurance or in-
·creased risk, and no objection is made, the company will be es-

topped to insist upon a forfeiture of the policy because their consent was not indorsed as literally required by the stipulation. The authorities pro and con are collated in May on Insurance, secs. 369, 370; 2 American Leading Cases, 911; Wood on Insurance, secs. 496, 497."

In Carrugi v. Atlantic Fire Ins. Co., 40 [459] Ga. 140, 2 Am. Rep. 567, McCay, J., in delivering the opinion of the court, uses this language: "So, too, after the policy has issued, the assured desires additional insurance; he informs the agent of it; he approves and consents, and the assured, thinking all right, takes new risks, pays out his money, and, at the very time he feels that he has made himself doubly safe, he has only done that which makes his policy void. This is an every day occurrence, and arises from the introduction of this new clause only lately thought of in insurance policies. We have given this matter great consideration, and have come to the conclusion that if the agent be in fact informed and do in fact consent, and the insured, relying on that consent do in good faith pay out his money, it does not make the policy void. . . . . Consent to a prior or subsequent insurance is within the scope of 'the agent's authority,' as the every-day practice of the country proves, and if an agent does in fact so consent and the insured in good faith acts upon it, we think it is a fraud for the company to set up that they had stipulated this consent to be in writing. . . . . The only object of this clause, at least the only legitimate object, is to guard against the overinsurance of the property and the consequent temptation to crimes. But when it affirmatively appears that the consent was given, and that the assured had acted upon it, we think it would be but the perpetration of a fraud to permit the company to take advantage of its own wrong and escape liability because its agent has failed to do his duty to the assured."

In the case of Weed v. London etc. Fire Ins. Co., 116 N. Y. 106, a case cited by the defendant in error, it is stated in the opinion of the court at page 117: "Notwithstanding the provisions of the policy 'that anything less than a distinct, specific agreement clearly expressed and indorsed on the policy should not be considered as a waiver of any printed or written condition or restriction therein,' the court recognize and affirm the law as settled in this state that such condition can be dispensed with by the [460] company or its general agents by oral consent as well as by writing."

In National Fire Ins. Co. v. Crane, 16 Md. 260, 77 Am. Dec. 289, which was a case in equity brought for the purpose of reforming the instrument and recovery thereon, it is said at page 295 in the opinion of the court: "Whatever effect the want of such an indorsement may have at law, in an action on the policy, we think it cannot be urged in a court of equity in a case otherwise free from objection. The judge below has correctly stated the law on the subject. The indorsement could have been made only by the company. If it be omitted, who is to blame? Certainly not the assured. These policies contain many stipulations— some of them operating as conditions precedent—for the benefit of the company, and few for that of the assured. It is too common for application to be met and adjustment refused on frivolous and unjust pretenses in order to defeat fair claims, on contracts of which good faith is the very essence, and we think it would promote the interest of insurance companies, and tend to a higher state of morals in business transactions, if they would exhibit more readiness to settle demands upon them, than, as we discover from the numerous reported cases on the subject, appears to be usual with them," and then calling attention to the fact that it was the president of the company who negotiated the policy, the opinion proceeds: "In such a case we are called upon to say that the party is without remedy; on the contrary, we think it would be a reproach to the jurisprudence of the state if this company were discharged from their contract on any such ground."

In the case just cited, the defect complained of was that insurance existing at the time the policy sued on was issued was not noted upon that policy, although assured had given the agent who negotiated the subsequent insurance notice of it. I am aware that many courts have drawn a distinction in this respect between prior and subsequent insurance; but I am unable to perceive any substantial reason for the distinction. If the doctrine is entirely true, that the assured is bound [461] to know the conditions of his policy, and to that I shall hereinafter refer, it would seem that after receiving the policy it would be his duty to examine it within a reasonable time, and in such case he would observe that the clause related to prior as well as to subsequent insurance, and, if the prior insurance was not noted upon it, he should take it back to the company and have the correction made.

In Peck v. New London Mut. Ins. Co., 22 Conn. 575, the assured obtain additional insurance; the charter of the defendant company provided that in such case the policy should be void, unless consent to such additional insurance should be given by the board of directors of the defendant company and signified

by an indorsement on the back of the policy by the secretary of
the company, and by him subscribed in pursuance of an order to
that effect given and passed by said board of directors. Consent was given and indorsed by a local agent of the company.
Evidence was introduced tending to show that by the uses and
practice of the defendant the agent was authorized to grant
such license on all policies issued by him. The court held that
under such circumstances the policy did not become void. They
give as their reason that, under the circumstances, the local agent
might be deemed the secretary of the company for the purpose
of making such indorsement—a better reason, in my judgment,
would have been that, under the circumstances, the company
was estopped to set up such defense.

In Felkington v. National Ins. Co., 55 Mo. 176, the court say:
"The court, by its ruling in striking out the replication, virtually
decided that it was absolutely necessary to obtain the written
indorsement of the company's consent to the additional insurance
before any recovery could be had. There are cases which undoubtedly sustain this proposition, but the tendency of the modern decisions is to relax and modify this stringent doctrine. It is
emphatically averred that the agent was duly notified of the subsequent insurance and assented to the same. Notice to the agent
was notice to the principal, and the company was bound
by that notice. When the [462] assured has notified a company that he has procured additional insurance, it is the
duty of the company, if it does not intend to be further
bound or to continue the risk, to express its dissent and not allow
the party to repose in fancied security to be victimized in case of
loss. It is unconscientious to retain the premium and affirm the
validity of the contract whilst no risk is imminent, but the very
moment that a loss occurs to then repudiate all liability and claim
a forfeiture. If the indorsement is not made upon notice duly
given, a waiver will be presumed in the absence of any dissent.
If a party by his silence directly leads another to act to his injury,
he will not be permitted, after the injury has happened, to then
allege anything to the contrary, for he who will not speak when
he should will not be allowed to speak when he would."

The following authorities which we have examined seem to
be in accord with those from which we have so fully quoted:
Richmond v. Niagara Fire Ins. Co., 79 N. Y. 230; Farnum v.
Phoenix Ins. Co., 83 Cal. 246; 17 Am. St. Rep. 233; Viele v.
Germania Ins. Co., 26 Iowa, 9; 96 Am. Dec. 83; Morrison v. In-

surance Co., 69 Tex. 353; 5 Am. St. Rep. 63; Horwitz v. Equitable etc. Ins. Co., 40 Mo. 557; 93 Am. Dec. 321; Hayward v. National Ins. Co., 52 Mo. 181; 14 Am. Rep. 400; Thompson v. St. Louis etc. Ins. Co., 52 Mo. 473; Northeastern Fire etc. Ins. Co. v. Schittler, 38 Ill. 168; Russell v. State Ins. Co., 55 Mo. 585; Piedmont etc. Ins. Co. v. Young, 58 Ala. 476; 29 Am. Rep. 770; Westchester Fire Ins. Co. v. Earle, 33 Mich. 153; Pierce v. Nashua Ins. Co., 50 N. H. 297; 9 Am. Rep. 235; Gans v. St. Paul etc. Marine Ins. Cc., 43 Wis. 111; 28 Am. Rep. 535; Planters' etc. Ins. Co. v. Lyons, 38 Tex. 253; 2 Wood on Insurance, secs. 382, 392, 395.

The fact that the policy here contains the provision that neither the agent nor any other person except the defendant's secretary have the authority to waive, modify, or strike from the policy any of its terms and conditions does not, with respect to the matter under discussion, add much, if any, force to the provision set forth in the earlier portion of the policy, to the effect that if the assured should procure additional insurance without the written consent of defendant indorsed upon the policy, it, the policy, should become and be absolutely null and void. This latter provision is, in effect, but a [463] provision that the person who has the power to give the consent to additional insurance must evidence it in writing. The cases we have already cited show that consent not indorsed in writing on the policy, when established, will bind the company as effectually and as fully as would the written consent, when acted and relied upon by the assured. The ground upon which the company is held liable under policies like the one before us for the acts of its agent in the exercise of a lawful power, but not in the manner provided by the policy, is that the agent represents the company, and notice to him is notice to the company, and through him the company has knowledge of every fact relating to the matter of which the agent has knowledge, and, in failing to repudiate the acts of the agent, the company will be held to have ratified them, or, at least, having failed to speak when it should, it will not be permitted to speak when it would. It is not only by force of the fact that the agent consented to the additional insurance that the company is held bound, but as the law imputes the knowledge of the agent to the principal, it must be held to have ratified the consent given by him, though not in the manner specified by the policy. As said by the supreme court of Michigan in a similar case:

"The condition literally applied would prevent any unindorsed consent by the company itself by instruction of its board or by act of its officers as effectually as by anyone else. And the case seems to settle down to the simple question whether a person who has agreed that he will only contract by writing in a certain way precludes himself from making a parol bargain to change it. The answer is manifest. A written bargain is of no higher legal degree than a parol one. Either may vary or discharge the other, and there can be no more force in an agreement in writing not to agree by parol than in a parol agreement not to agree in writing. Every such agreement is ended by the new one which contradicts it": Westchester Fire Ins. Co. v. Earle, 33 Mich. 153; American Cent. Ins. Co. v. McCrea, 8 Lea, 524; 41 Am. Rep. 647. See, also, Farnum v. Phoenix Ins. Co., 83 Cal. 261; 17 Am. St. Rep. 233.

⁴⁶⁴ There is another matter in this connection to which I will briefly allude: In my opinion, it is not competent for the defendant company to so tie its own hands and those of its general agents as is attempted by the restrictive clause in this policy. The clause is broad enough to include not only every officer and agent of the company, excepting only its secretary, but even the company itself. In my opinion, such attempted restrictions are ineffectual, and ought not to be and will not be upheld.

The authorities already cited and quoted from, in effect, uphold this view of the matter; the following authorities state the proposition broadly: Renier v. Dwelling House Ins. Co., 74 Wis. 89; German Ins. Co. v. Gray, 43 Kan. 498; 19 Am. St. Rep. 150; Lamberton v. Connecticut Fire Ins. Co., 39 Minn. 129; Willcutts v. North Western etc. Ins. Co., 81 Ind. 300; Gans v. St. Paul etc. Ins. Co., 43 Wis. 108; 28 Am. Rep. 535; American Ins. Co. v. Gallatin, 48 Wis. 37; Phenix Ins. Co. v. Munger, 49 Kan. 178; 33 Am. St. Rep. 360.

Upon the argument and in their briefs counsel for defendant in error called our attention to many authorities unmistakably and emphatically holding that under the terms of a policy like the one in suit, unless the consent to additional insurance is indorsed upon the policy, it becomes void. It would be useless to attempt to reconcile these cases with the cases hereinbefore cited, the conflict between them is irreconcilable; in fact, it is by no means easy to reconcile all the cases of the same state; in many it would seem that the courts, in order to preserve consistency, have from the facts drawn distinctions more

fanciful than substantial. It would serve no useful purpose to
herein review all the cases cited to us by defendant in error;
the review of a few will answer our purpose.

In the case of Cleaver v. Traders' Ins. Co., 65 Mich. 527, 8
Am. St. Rep. 908, the policy substantially contained the conditions of the policy before us, with respect to additional insurance; such insurance was obtained through the assistance of
the company's agent, but was not indorsed upon the policy, and
no notice was given [465] by the agent to the company; it was
held that plaintiff could not recover, and a judgment in his
favor was reversed and the cause remanded. This case may,
perhaps, be distinguishable from the case before us, by reason
of the fact that there the evidence showed that the agent had
no authority to consent to additional insurance, while here I
have no doubt of such authority on the part of the agent. The
case was remanded, and on the second trial the court directed
the jury to find a verdict for defendant, and from the judgment
for defendant plaintiff on this occasion appealed, and the judgment reversed: Cleaver v. Traders' Ins. Co., 71 Mich. 414; 15
Am. St. Rep. 275. The reason given was that on the second
trial it was made to appear that on the day of the fire the company was notified of it, and a day or so afterward it was notified
of the additional insurance; that thereafter it sent an adjuster
to the place of fire to adjust and settle the loss; that in endeavoring to adjust the loss the plaintiff, at the request of the
adjuster, spent two days of his own time and the services of
another man, and say the court: "This information, time, and
labor asked by the company and furnished by the plaintiff was
wholly unnecessary under the defense made in this suit." Taking the whole case, both in 65 and 71 Michigan, I regard it
as authority for the plaintiff here, because, in this case, the plaintiff, after handing the two policies to the adjuster, gave two or
more days of his time to the adjuster in endeavoring to furnish him proper information, etc., but, notwithstanding this,
my judgment is that the case cited, when first before the court,
should have been affirmed upon the ground of notice to defendant through its agent, and no dissent, the company thereby
being estopped. Another strong case cited by defendant in
error: Walsh v. Hartford Fire Ins. Co., 73 N. Y. 5. In that case,
the condition was "that no officer, agent, or representative of
the company shall be held to have waived any of the terms and
conditions of the policy unless such waiver shall be indorsed

hereon in writing." And the court held the condition binding
and that it prescribed the only way in which the agent could
manifest his consent. It was also held that the plaintiff was
presumed to have known the conditions of the policy and was
bound by them. If it [466] be true that a policy-holder is bound
by all the conditions of his policy, and is presumed to know
what they are, that is to understand them, it seems to me that if
this idea is to be pushed to its limit, he, the policy-holder, who
is generally a layman, is charged with a rather heavy responsibility, in view of the fact that there is such a wide divergence
of opinion among lawyers and judges as to the meaning and
effect of these conditions, as the history of the case just cited
abundantly proves. In that case, the trial court held that the
agent could only consent by indorsement in writing, and defendant had judgment. On appeal to the general term of supreme court, fourth department, before a full bench of three
justices, it was unanimously held just the contrary: Walsh v.
Hartford Fire Ins. Co., 9 Hun, 421; and then on appeal to the
court of appeals four judges held that the trial court was right in
its understanding of the condition, and the supreme court
wrong, and three judges held that the supreme court was right
and the trial court wrong.

In this case it was admitted, both in the supreme court and
in the court of appeals, that the agent who gave consent but
did not indorse was a general agent of the company. Yet the
same court of appeals in Weed v. London etc. Fire Ins. Co., 116
N. Y. 117, say: "Notwithstanding the provisions of the policy
that anything less than a distinct. specific agreement clearly expressed and indorsed on the policy should not be considered as
a waiver of any printed or written condition or restriction therein,
the court recognize and affirm the law as settled in this state
that such condition can be dispensed with by the company
or its general agents by oral consent as well as by writing." The
conditions in both policies were substantially to the same effect.

We are also referred to Hankins v. Rockford Ins. Co., 70 Wis.
1, and to Knudson v. Hekla Fire Ins. Co., 75 Wis. 198. In the
first case, the condition was that if the property should become
encumbered without the consent of the defendant's secretary
indorsed upon it, it should become void; and also this clause:
"It is expressly provided that no officer, agent, or employé, or
any person or persons except the secretary, in [467] writing. can
in any manner waive either of the conditions of the policy

which is made and accepted upon the above express conditions." The case may be distinguished from the case before us from the fact that here the agent Stitzer had the right to consent to additional insurance. As to the condition above quoted, I have only this to say, that a substantially similar condition was in Renier v. Dwelling House Ins. Co., 74 Wis. 89, held to be ineffectual as a restriction upon the general officers and agents of the company. In the other case in 75 Wisconsin, there was no proof of loss, and under the facts no waiver. I am not inclined to think the case much in point. Of the cases from California cited, viz., Shuggart v. Lycoming Fire Ins. Co., 55 Cal. 408, is not clearly in point, and Gladding v. California etc. Ins. Assn., 66 Cal. 6, and Enos v. Sun Ins. Co., 67 Cal. 621, are, I think, clearly opposed to Farnum v. Phoenix Ins. Co., 83 Cal. 246; 17 Am. St. Rep. 233.

On the whole, I am of opinion that this matter did not constitute a defense to the action, and that the court should have so instructed the jury; and that the second, third, fifth, and seventh grounds of defendant's motion for a new trial afford no sufficient reason for vacating the verdict and granting a new trial. The instruction that "the defendant must show by a preponderance of the evidence that it has not waived its right," with respect to the additional insurance, was erroneous, but in our view of the case not prejudicial, because the matter should not have been submitted to the jury at all.

3. The fourth and sixth grounds of defendant's motion for a new trial were based upon the clause in the policy requiring proofs of loss to be furnished by assured. The clause is fully stated in the statement of facts hereto appended. The facts clearly established with reference to this matter are as follows: On the day of the fire, the agent of the company, being informed of the fire by plaintiff, by letter, notified the defendant both at Chicago and Denver of the loss. Within a few days thereafter the defendant sent an adjuster, Mr. Norton, to Cheyenne, to investigate the loss, and with power to adjust and settle it. This must be deemed a sufficient compliance with the requirement of immediate notice of loss; any notice that produces such a result is sufficient without reference to [468] its form: Insurance Co. of N. A. v. McDowell, 50 Ill. 129; 99 Am. Dec. 497. Thereafter the adjuster arrived and was engaged for two and perhaps three days in investigating the loss and endeavoring to adjust it with the plaintiff; being called away, he notified plaintiff of

his intended departure without completing the adjustment, and just before leaving plaintiff stated to him (quoting from the record), "Mr. Norton, I don't know anything about a fire, never had any experience about it; I want you to tell me what I have to do. Mr. Baird said I have to have some papers and I don't know what to do." He (the adjuster) said, "You don't need anything at all, don't need any papers; I have all the company need in this book, that's all they want; you don't need to make out any papers at all. He left, promised to come back again, he did not come."

There is no doubt whatever in my mind that under these facts it must be held that the entire provision of the policy with respect to proofs of loss, magistrate's certificate, was waved. I can conceive of no acts or declarations of the company or its agents which would more completely constitute a waiver than these. It will not do to say that the plaintiff had not the right to rely upon this parol waiver on the part of the adjusting agent, because the policy expressly denied his authority thereto. He was fully authorized and empowered to "adjust and settle the loss." And this general authority was wholly and entirely inconsistent with the restriction. An insurance company, and especially a foreign insurance company, in negotiating insurance, adjusting and settling losses, must act through its agents, if it acts at all. To hold that in such negotiations between such general agents, or agents possessing such general authority, and the assured, the latter is bound, but the company is not, because of having incapacitated itself and them by such restrictions is, in effect, to hold that there is no mutuality in such negotiations, and that the only power given to such general agents is to obtain the premiums and then defeat the enforcement of the policies upon which they were paid: Renier v. Dwelling House Ins. Co., 74 Wis. 99; Aetna Ins. Co. v. Shryer, 85 Ind. 362; East Texas Fire Ins. Co. v. [469] Dyches, 56 Tex. 571; Ligon v. Insurance Co., 87 Tenn. 341. But this is not all. After the adjuster left, though promising to return and complete the matter, he did not do so. And for four weeks the plaintiff, in person and through his attorney, was constantly importuning the agent, Mr. Stitzer, to know what he should do, and what the company intended to do about the loss, but received no satisfactory response. On the seventh day of February, 1891, he, the plaintiff, forwarded to the company at the city of Chicago, an affidavit and schedule of the property destroyed, which was accompanied

by a letter from plaintiff's attorney. This was duly received by
the company and referred to its general agents at Denver, and
they, on February 28th, acknowledged receipt to plaintiff. The
substance of this affidavit and the letter of plaintiff's attorney
and the general agent's letter are hereinbefore set forth, and
need not be here repeated. Subsequent to the agent's letter of
February 28th, nothing further was done until this suit was
commenced April 16, 1891. Under these facts, it is claimed, on
the one hand, that the affidavit and schedule were at least attempted proofs of loss, and, inasmuch as the defendant did not
specifically point out the defects therein, it is estopped to raise
the objections. On the other hand, it is contended that since
the affidavit and schedule did not comply with the terms of the
policy requiring proofs of loss therefor, the defendant rightly
treated them as notice of loss, and as there was no further correspondence between the parties, and plaintiff did not at any
time attempt to correct defendant in its belief and statement
that they were intended as notice of loss, plaintiff thereby acquiesced in what was done by defendant, and that it would be
unreasonable to allow him now to assert that he sent defective
proofs, and that, because defendant did not specifically object
thereto the defects were waived.

If there was anything in the facts of this case, or anything
in the affidavit of plaintiff and schedule of property attached
thereto, or in the accompanying letter of plaintiff's attorney, by
which any reasonable man would be justified in the fair belief
that they were sent in compliance with the provisions [470] of
the policy that "persons sustaining loss or damage by fire shall
forthwith give notice thereof to this company in writing," there
might be some foundation for defendant's contention. But there
is no such fact to be found in the entire record. On the contrary, the facts lead to the conclusion that they were intended
as proofs of loss, and nothing less, and I am wholly unable to
understand how any fairly intelligent man could have arrived at
any other conclusion. These identical agents who wrote the
letter stating that they "presumed" the affidavit, etc., were sent
as notice of loss, had six weeks prior thereto, upon being notified
of the fire by Mr. Stitzer, sent an adjuster from Denver to Cheyenne to adjust and settle the loss. Why, under such circumstances, should they imagine for a moment that plaintiff desired to
give further notice of the fire? What is there in the requirement
of the policy as to notice which would induce anyone to believe

that such an affidavit covering a page and a half or more of type written matter, attached to which was a schedule setting forth the description and the cost price of over two hundred items of property, was intended simply to be a notice of the fact that a fire had occurred and destroyed the insured property? A notification in fifteen or twenty words, not sworn to, would have been ample to fully comply with the requirement of the policy in this respect. I am not much impressed with defendant's claims on this proposition. On the contrary, it seems to me that the plaintiff may have very properly, on receipt of the letter from these general agents, come to the conclusion that defendant did not intend to deal fairly with him in the settlement of this matter, and that he would only recover the amount of his loss at the end of a lawsuit. Defendant has not in this case treated said affidavit and schedule as simply notice of loss. In its third defense it charges plaintiff with false swearing, and that such false swearing was done through this affidavit by plaintiff "knowingly and willfully, and for the purpose of misleading and deceiving this defendant in relation to the amount of loss by him sustained. . . . . And that the said plaintiff, for the purpose of carrying out said fraud so by him attempted to be perpetrated, furnished this [471] defendant the said false affidavits and oaths by him made as aforesaid." If they were intended and are to be regarded as simply notice of loss, and not as proofs of loss, how could the fraud charged be predicated upon them? It seems to me that defendant in this defense practically admits that they were intended to be proofs of loss upon which it was expected defendant would act in adjusting and settling the loss. The letter accompanying the proofs closed with these words: "If you wish any information in addition to what is contained in the enclosed it will be gladly furnished you." No response was made to this, no suggestion that additional information was desired, but rather the intimation that plaintiff had to pursue his own course without assistance or suggestion from the defendant. Most abundant good faith is the very essence of these contracts of insurance, and that requires perfect candor and openness on the part of each of the parties. Insurance companies are just as much bound as the assured to endeavor heartily and strenuously to bring about a fair and a just and equitable settlement of loss incurred, for which they have contracted to indemnify the assured, and they have no sort of right when such loss has occurred to stand aloof and cast obstacles in the way of rather than assist in bringing about such settlement.

It follows that there was nothing in the fourth and sixth grounds of defendant's motion for a new trial which would have justified the court in sustaining it: 2 May on Insurance, secs. 468, 469 b, 474, 475; Insurance Co. of N. A. v. Hope, 58 Ill. 78; 11 Am. Rep. 48; Jones v. Mechanics' Fire Ins. Co., 36 N. J. L. 29, 38; 13 Am. Rep. 405.

The fourteenth ground for defendant's motion for a new trial challenges as error the action of the trial court in permitting Samuel Kahn, a witness for plaintiff, to refresh his memory from the schedule of property destroyed furnished defendant by plaintiff. I think there was no error in this. The witness was the plaintiff's book-keeper up to the time of the fire. At the fire the plaintiff's books of account and invoices of purchases were destroyed. After the fire, for the purpose of enabling him to make up a list of the goods on hand at the time of the fire, the plaintiff obtained from the merchants from whom [472] he had purchased goods duplicate invoices thereof, and with these invoices and from recollection of what was on hand and of the condition of the stock of goods, the plaintiff and witness, within three weeks of the fire, made up this schedule. It certainly was desirable that such a schedule should have been made up, as much for the benefit of defendant as of plaintiff. The evidence in no manner whatever impeaches its integrity or casts any suspicion upon it. On the contrary, it appears to have been made fairly and in an honest desire to do the right thing in what seems to me, under the circumstances, the best possible way. Upon the trial, the witness was examined and re-examined, and again and again cross-examined about this matter, and the jury fully apprised of all the facts surrounding it. I am convinced the court was clearly right in permitting the witness testifying a year after the schedule was made, to refer to it, and refresh his memory from it: 1 Greenleaf on Evidence, secs. 436-439; see note to Insurance Co. v. Weide, 11 Wall. 438.

The fifteenth ground in the motion for a new trial alleges error on the part of the court in permitting said witness to read the said schedule to the jury in response to a question as to the amount of goods in the store at the time of the fire. For the reasons just stated in discussing the fourteenth ground of said motion, I perceive no error in this.

The sixteenth ground of said motion challenges as error the ruling of the court in permitting the said witness to enumerate and state the value of certain articles alleged to have been destroyed by the fire which were not included in the plaintiff's proofs of loss. There was no error in this. The defendant promised to indemnify the plaintiff to the extent of fifteen hundred dollars for loss upon his stock of goods, not merely those stated in the proofs of loss, but those which he had in his store at the time of the fire.

The seventeenth ground of said motion alleges error in permitting the affidavit and schedule offered as proofs of loss to be read to the jury. These papers were certainly not competent evidence of the facts therein stated, and the court very properly charged the jury that they were not to be considered as evidence [473] of the quantity and value of the property destroyed. They were, however, competent evidence to show compliance or attempted compliance with the requirement of the policy that proofs of loss should be furnished, and there was no error in permitting them to be read to the jury.

The eighteenth ground of said motion alleges error in permitting Mr. Baird, a witness for plaintiff, to testify respecting certain offers of settlement made by the adjuster to plaintiff. The rule with respect to offers of compromise as stated in 1 Greenleaf on Evidence, section 192, is, "that confidential overtures of pacification, and any other offers or propositions between litigating parties expressly stated to be made without prejudice are excluded on ground of public policy. An offer of a sum by way of compromise of a claim tacitly admitted is receivable, unless accompanied with a caution that the offer is confidential." Tested by this rule, there can be no question that the evidence was admissible. The adjuster was not here attempting to compromise a disputed claim; so far as can be gathered from anything he did or said the claim was at least tacitly admitted. The only controversy between him and the assured was as to the amount of the claim; and his offers of settlement did not come within or even approach the rule excluding offers of compromise. Besides this, what was said and done by the adjuster was clearly admissible as tending to show a waiver of the additional insurance (Cleaver v. Traders' Ins. Co., 71 Mich. 414; 15 Am. St. Rep. 275), and to show a waiver of the proofs of loss. There is nothing in the proposition that there was error in this matter.

It is further urged that the plaintiff was guilty of false swearing with respect to the quantity of goods destroyed and the amount of his loss. The condition of the policy is: "All

fraud or attempt at fraud by false swearing or otherwise shall
forfeit all claim under this policy." The rule is well settled
that, under such provision, to constitute fraud or false swearing there must be false statements willfully made with respect
to a material matter with the intention of thereby deceiving
the insurer: 7 Am. & Eng. Ency. of Law, 1047, and cases cited; .
2 May on Insurance, 3d ed., sec. 477. With especial [474] regard
to this matter of false swearing I have several times carefully
read the entire evidence given upon the trial, and have constantly
kept in mind the fact that the trial court saw the witnesses,
heard them testify, observed their manner, etc., and consequently
had much better opportunity of properly judging the evidence
and its effect than I could possibly have; but I have been unable
to find any facts in the entire record which raise a reasonable
doubt in my mind as to the good faith of the plaintiff or any
facts or circumstances which would or could have justified the
trial court in vacating the verdict upon this ground.

It is true that in the affidavit of plaintiff sent as proof of
loss to defendant it is stated that the stock of insured goods
"was burned up and destroyed by fire on the night of the 26th
of December, A. D. 1890," and also that the schedule attached
to the affidavit was "a statement of each article of property
burned up and opposite thereto the cost price thereof." And
it is also true that, literally speaking, the goods were not actually "burned up and destroyed by fire." In fact, the evidence clearly shows that most of the goods were destroyed by
smoke and water, and some few only damaged thereby, and it
may be that a few items of the property were only slightly
injured; but practically the entire stock of goods was destroyed.
A large quantity of the goods were in the cellar situate just beneath the storeroom. A large hole was burned in the floor of
the storeroom, so that the fire must have reached the goods in the
cellar; besides, the cellar was filled to overflowing with water
used by the fire department in endeavoring to extinguish the
fire. Under the circumstances with regard to the fire as disclosed by the evidence, it seems to me that it is altogether improbable that there could have been anything less than a total
loss to all practical intents and purposes of the goods in the
store. Mr. Stitzer, the defendant's agent, visited the place of
the fire within six or eight hours after it occurred, in the discharge of his duty, which required him to instruct the assured
to take proper care of articles not destroyed, and he testified

that at that time he "saw nothing of any consequence which could be saved." The plaintiff, testifying [475] in his own behalf, explained what he meant by the language used in his proofs of loss, viz., "burned up and destroyed by fire," etc., and in view of the fact that these proofs were made after the property destroyed and damaged, and all the circumstances of the fire had been fully examined and inquired into by Mr. Stitzer, the defendant's agent, and also by its adjuster, I can perceive no foundation in this matter upon which to base the charge of an attempt at fraud by false swearing or otherwise.

As to the claim that the total amount of loss as stated in the proof of loss was four times greater than it actually was, I can find nothing in the evidence to sustain it. On the contrary, the evidence showed that there were many articles of considerable value destroyed which were not included in the proofs. Indeed, defendant alleged as one of the grounds of its motion for a new trial the fact that the court permitted, over its objection, the introduction of testimony to that effect.

The defendant alleged this defense in its answer filed six months or more before the trial. The adjuster a year before the trial made the same objection to settling with plaintiff, viz., that plaintiff claimed to have lost more goods than he really had; yet upon the trial the defendant did not offer a scintilla of evidence in support of this, or any other of its defenses. It is incomprehensible that if the fact had been as alleged by defendant in its defense, that it could not at the trial have produced some evidence in support thereof.

As to the value of plaintiff's stock of goods at the time of the fire, the testimony was clear and positive that it was from three thousand three hundred dollars to three thousand five hundred dollars. It is impossible to gather from the evidence that the damaged goods' which remained over after the fire were worth more than one hundred dollars, or two hundred dollars at the outside, and this, too, by including damaged meat, butter, and lard, which some of the witnesses stated might be worth something for what they called "tanking purposes," and which the proof shows plaintiff threw away as utterly worthless, to his own damage, if the judgment of the witnesses was right.

It is true that plaintiff on cross-examination was not able without reference to his memorandum or list of goods which [476] he made soon after the fire, to state the quantity and value of the different classes of goods he had in stock. Had he been able to

do so, he would have exhibited a very remarkable memory, so
remarkable that it would be looked upon with some suspicion.
I can very readily understand how a man in the business plaintiff
was engaged in would have a very clear and correct idea of the
value of his entire stock of goods, and at the same time be wholly
unable to state from memory the number of cans of corn and
number of mousetraps, etc., which he had on hand. Had the
plaintiff in this case attempted to state from recollection the
exact number of cans of corn and the exact number of mousetraps, etc., he had on hand, I should be a good deal more disposed
to regard his testimony with suspicion than I am. Even if the
testimony upon this question had been evenly balanced, it would
have been insufficient to establish the defense. A man who alleges fraud must clearly and distinctly prove the fraud he alleges,
and the proof must be clear and sufficient to satisfy the mind and
conscience of the existence of the fraud. It cannot be pretended
that such was the case here.

In conclusion, I am satisfied, from a careful review of this
particular matter, that the court did not grant the motion for
a new trial upon this ground, and not only this, but if the court
had done so its action would have been erroneous and a clear
abuse of discretion: Edward v. O'Brien, 2 Wyo. 496.

I am of opinion that the final order entered by the court below
should be reversed, and that the cause should be remanded to
the district court of Laramie county, with directions to enter
up judgment upon the verdict, with interest from the date of
its rendition for plaintiff and against defendant, with costs.
Plaintiff to recover of defendant his costs in this court.

Groesbeck, C. J., and Conaway, J., concur.

APPEAL—WHAT ORDERS ARE APPEALABLE. — Judgments
or orders from which an appeal will lie are those which either terminate the action itself, or operate to divest some right in such a
manner as to put it out of the power of the court making the order
to place the parties in their original condition after the expiration of
the term: Harrison v. Lebanon Waterworks, 91 Ky. 255; 34 Am. St.
Rep. 180, and note. See Hawkins v. Lutton, 95 Wis. 492; 60 Am.
St. Rep. 131; Brown v. Cooper, 98 Iowa, 444; 60 Am. St. Rep. 190;
extended note to Davie v. Davie, 20 Am. St. Rep. 173, 174.

INSURANCE—POWER OF AGENT TO WAIVE CONDITIONS
IN POLICY.—An insurance agent whose powers are limited to making contracts of insurance and delivering policies, has no authority
after he has issued a policy to waive a clause therein expressly providing that additional insurance shall avoid the policy unless written, consent thereto should be indorsed thereon, and that no condition therein can be waived except in writing signed by the secretary. Additional insurance taken upon the authority of such at-

tempted waiver by such agent avoids the policy: Taylor v. State Ins. Co., 98 Iowa, 521; 60 Am. St. Rep. 210, and note. As to who is a general agent, and his power to waive conditions in policies, see Goode v. Georgia Home Ins. Co., 92 Va. 392; 53 Am. St. Rep. 817; American Employers' etc. Ins. Co. v. Fordyce, 62 Ark. 562; 54 Am. St. Rep. 305; Wood v. American Fire Ins. Co., 149 N. Y. 382; 52 Am. St. Rep. 733, and notes thereto.

INSURANCE—EFFECT OF CONDITION AS TO ARBITRATION.—If one clause in a fire insurance policy provides that, in case of loss, an estimate shall be made by the insured and the company, and another clause provides that in case they differ the subject shall be referred to appraisers selected as therein provided, the remedies are successive, and neither party can insist upon the second who has not shown himself willing and ready to enter upon the first: Moyer v. Sun Ins. Office, 176 Pa. St. 579; 53 Am. St. Rep. 690, and note. See Aetna Ins. Co. v. McLead, 57 Kan. 95; 57 Am. St. Rep. 320, and note.

INSURANCE—FIRE—WAIVER OF ARBITRATION.—The denial by an insurance company of its liability under a fire policy issued by it, upon the ground of a forfeiture by reason of a breach of warranty, is a waiver of its right to insist upon arbitration as a means for ascertaining the amount of the plaintiff's damage, although such means are provided for in the policy: Home Fire Ins. Co. v. Kennedy, 47 Neb. 138; 53 Am. St. Rep. 521, and note.

INSURANCE—PROOFS OF LOSS—WHEN IMMEDIATE.—Notice of loss is immediate within the meaning of a policy of insurance stipulating for immediate notice, when it is given to an agent of the insurer a day or so after the loss occurs, with a request that he notify his principal, and he at once complies with such request: Burlington Ins. Co. v. Lowery, 61 Ark. 108; 54 Am. St. Rep. 196, and note. See, also, Moyer v. Sun Ins. Office, 176 Pa. St. 579; 53 Am. St. Rep. 690, and note, as to when defects in such notice or proof are deemed waived by the insurer.

INSURANCE—FALSE SWEARING AS AVOIDING POLICY—WHAT CONSTITUTES.—"False swearing" is fraud and consists in knowingly and intentionally stating upon oath what is not true: Linscott v. Orient Ins. Co., 88 Me. 497; 51 Am. St. Rep. 435, and note.

FRAUD—BURDEN OF PROOF.—Fraud will not be presumed, but must be proved: Note to Flanders v. Cobb, 51 Am. St. Rep. 413. The burden of proof is upon the one who sets it up as a cause of action or defense: Beck & Pauli Lith. Co. v. Houppert, 104 Ala. 503; 53 Am. St. Rep. 77. It must be shown by a preponderance of the evidence, but he is not required to "establish it beyond any doubt": Baltimore etc. Ry. Co. v. Scholes, 14 Ind. App. 524; 56 Am. St. Rep. 307, and note.

CASES

IN THE

SUPREME COURT

OF

ALABAMA.

LOISEAU v. STATE.

[114 ALABAMA, 34.]

LOTTERIES. — TO CONSTITUTE A CRIMINAL lottery, there must be a consideration. When small amounts are hazarded to gain large amounts, the result of winning to be determined by the use of a contrivance of chance, in which neither choice nor skill can exert any effect, it is gambling by lot, or a prohibited lottery.

LOTTERIES—SLOT MACHINES.—If an owner of a slot machine is a party to an agreement between others, that each of the latter shall drop nickels and play the machine, and that the one whose play shall indicate the highest card hand shall have all the cigars purchased by the nickels thus dropped, and the owner of the machine furnishes a cigar for each nickel dropped into the machine, and delivers all of them to the player thus obtaining the high hand, such machine, thus used, is a lottery, within the meaning of a constitutional provision prohibiting lotteries; and neither a municipality nor the legislature of the state can authorize the licensing of slot machines to be thus used.

J. A. W. Smith and Tillman & Campbell, for the appellant.

W. C. Fitts, attorney general, for the state.

36 COLEMAN, J. The indictment against the defendant contains three counts, the first charging that defendant did unlawfully set up, carry on, or operate a device of chance, to wit, a slot machine; the second, that he did unlawfully sell chances in a device of chance, to wit, a slot machine; and the third, that defendant did set up, or was concerned in setting up or carrying on a lottery, to wit, a slot machine.

The defense is rested upon an ordinance of the city of Birmingham, which included in its schedules of licenses slot machines, and an act of the legislature (Acts 1896-97, p. 1099), which "ratified, approved, and confirmed" the schedule of licenses es-· tablished by the board of mayor and aldermen of the city of Birmingham.

Article 4, section 26, of the constitution of the state, reads as follows: "The general assembly shall have no power to authorize lotteries or gift enterprises for any purpose, and shall pass laws to prohibit the sale of lottery or gift enterprise tickets, or tickets in any scheme in the nature of a lottery in this state; and all acts or parts of acts heretofore passed by the general assembly of this state authorizing a lottery or lotteries, and all acts amendatory thereof, or supplemental thereto, are hereby avoided."

The defendant had set up a slot machine in his store, and it and its operation are described as follows: "It is a box-shaped arrangement, in the top of which was a slot, into which a nickel was dropped; there was a lever on the machine which was pressed down after the nickel was placed in the slot, and when the lever was released, [37] the machinery in the box or machine caused the cards to revolve on a cylinder, and when the revolution ceased the cards could be read by a bystander. That on the said occasion three certain parties went into said store, and each of them dropped five nickels in the slot, and pressed the lever after each nickel was dropped in. That the said parties agreed among themselves that the one after whose play the machine would indicate the highest card hand should have all the cigars which the said nickels purchased. That the said defendant had furnished from his stock of cigars a nickel cigar for each nickel which was put into the machine by said three parties, and when it was determined by working the lever, as aforesaid, which one of the three parties had made the highest score, as indicated by the cards on the machine, the defendant delivered to such party cigars to the amount and equal in value to the amount of nickels put into the machine." This is the substance of all the evidence.

That the parties were guilty of gambling, and were within the prohibition of the general law of the state, is not seriously controverted, but it is contended that the slot machine as operated was not a lottery, and that the legislature had authority to license such gambling. We are unable to assent to this conclusion. Calling it by name, a slot machine, instead of a lottery machine, does not vary its character; nor does the fact that parties agreed that the winner should receive the value of the money in cigars, instead of the money itself, exert any influence in determining the character of the winning chance to have been by lot. The three parties agreed between themselves, to which the defendant, the owner and setter up of the machine, was a party, that the highest cards to be determined by the revolving of the wheel should win the value of all the money in cigars to be furnished by the defendant, he taking the money. There have been many definitions of lottery by the decisions of the various courts, each generally made with reference to the particular case then under consideration; and as soon as rendered the ingenuity of the gambler has gone to work to invent some way to avoid the effect and compass of the precise words used in the particular case. There may be gambling which is not by lot, but in every prohibited lottery there is an element of gambling. The constitutional [38] provision is, "The general assembly shall have no power to authorize lotteries." "Lot" has been correctly defined to be "a contrivance to determine a question by chance, or without the action of man's choice or will." To be a criminal lottery there must be a consideration, and when small amounts are hazarded to gain large amounts, and the result of winning to be determined by the use of a contrivance of chance in which neither choice nor skill can exert any effect, it is gambling by lot, or a prohibited lottery. We could cite many cases in which principles have been declared which, if applied to the facts of the present case, would determine it to be a lottery.

We are unable to perceive any difference in principle in a machine which revolves the wheel laterally and one where it revolves vertically; in the former, the question of losing or winning being determined by the pointing of an arrow or paddle, and in the latter by the showing of cards. We think the case of Reeves v. State, 105 Ala. 120, is conclusive of the question. See, also, the following authorities: Chavannah v. State, 49 Ala. 396; Yellowstone Kit v. State, 88 Ala. 196; 16 Am. St. Rep. 388, and notes; State v. Shorts, 32 N. J. L. 398; 90 Am. Dec. 668; Cross v. People, 18 Colo. 321; 36 Am. St. Rep. 292; 13 Am. & Eng. Ency. of Law, 1178, and notes. The references in the extensive notes in these reports are full and satisfactory.

The legislature has no authority to authorize the licensing of slot machines to be used as the evidence shows it was used in the present case. We would not be understood as deciding that a slot machine is necessarily one of lot, within the prohibition of the law: nor do we hold that a wheel of fortune carries with it the legal import of a lottery. Whether it is so or not depends upon the use to which it is put in the particular case. Whatever may be the name or character of the machine or scheme, if in its use a consideration is paid, and there is gambling, the hazarding of small amounts to win larger, the result of winning or losing to be determined by chance in which neither the will nor skill of man can operate to influence the result, it is a determination by "lot," within the comprehensive word "lottery" used in the constitution of this state. If [39] there is anything to the contrary to be found in Buckalew v. State, 62 Ala. 334, 34 Am. Rep. 22, it must be regarded as modified so as to conform to what is herein declared. The case of Hewlett v. Camp, Ala., May 19, 1897, is also in point. We will not now undertake to decide the effect of the act of February 1, 1897 (Acts 1896-97, p. 901), and of February 5, 1897, in one of which the penalties are increased and in the other diminished, upon the acts of February 16, 1891 (Acts 1890-91, p. 757), and of February 26, 1889 (Acts 1888-89, p. 45), as the question is not involved in the case before us.

The indictment evidently was preferred under the act approved February 13, 1897 (Acts 1896-97, p. 901). The first section reads as follows:

"Section 1. Be it enacted by the general assembly of Alabama, that any person who sets up, carries on, or operates any wheel of fortune, slot machine, or any device of chance, or scheme of raffling, or any person who sells tickets or chances in such devices or scheme of raffling, shall be deemed guilty of a misdemeanor, and upon conviction shall be fined not less than ten nor more than fifty dollars."

The evidence in the case authorized a conviction under either the first or second count of the indictment, and we are not prepared to say that he might not have been properly convicted under the third count.

Affirmed.

LOTTERIES—WHAT ARE—SLOT MACHINES.—A lottery is a scheme by which, on one's paying money or some other thing of value, he obtains the contingent right to have something of greater value, if an appeal to chance, by lot or otherwise, under the direction of the manager of the scheme, should decide in his favor. A valuable consideration must be paid, directly or indirectly, for a chance to draw a prize by lot, to bring the transaction within the class of lotteries or gift enterprises that the law prohibits as criminal: Cross v. People, 18 Colo. 321; 36 Am. St. Rep. 292, and note. See extended note to Yellowstone Kit v. State, 16 Am. St. Rep. 43-48, as to what is a lottery. A slot machine has been held a gaming device and its operation unlawful under the Georgia statute against gaming: Kolshorn v. State, 97 Ga. 343.

McCaa v. Elam Drug Company.

[114 Alabama, 74.]

SALES OF ARTICLES FOR SPECIAL PURPOSE—IMPLIED WARRANTY.—If a manufacturer or a dealer contracts to supply an article he manufactures or produces or in which he deals, to be applied to a particular purpose, so that the buyer necessarily trusts to his judgment or skill, there is an implied warranty that the article sold and furnished shall be reasonably fit for the purpose to which it is to be applied.

SALES OF ARTICLES FOR SPECIAL PURPOSE—IMPLIED WARRANTY.—A dealer in paints and oils, by virtue of the fact that he is a dealer, is held to an implied warranty of the quality of paints and oils sold, when he knows the purpose for which they are intended, and the purchaser relies upon his judgment and skill.

SALES—IMPLIED WARRANTY.—If a manufacturer or dealer contracts to sell an article known and described to the buyer, although the former may know that the buyer intends it for a specific use, there is no implied warranty that when delivered it will be suitable for the specific use to which the purchaser intends applying it.

SALES—IMPLIED WARRANTY.—Every vendor, whether a dealer or not, is responsible for his representations or affirmations as to quality which are more than expressions of opinion, relied upon by the buyer, and upon which he has a right to rely.

SALES—IMPLIED WARRANTY.—If one buys an article for a particular purpose, made known to the seller at the time of the contract, and relies upon the skill or judgment of the seller to supply what is wanted, there is an implied warranty that the thing sold is fit for the desired purpose; aliter, if the buyer purchases on his own judgment.

SALES—PLEADINGS SHOWING BREACH OF CONTRACT AND NOT BREACH OF WARRANTY.—If, in an action by a buyer against a dealer in paints and oils, the complaint avers that such dealer agreed to furnish the plaintiff with paints and oils of a quality suitable to be used in painting his house, and this is followed by an averment of a breach of the agreement, stating wherein such paints and oils were defective, the complaint states a cause of action for a breach of the contract and not for a breach of an implied warranty, and an averment that the seller was a "dealer" in paints and oils adds nothing to the sufficiency of the complaint as an allegation of a breach of warranty, nor does it authorize a recovery on less evidence than if the seller had been other than a "dealer."

SALES—BREACH OF WARRANTY—PLEADING.—A warranty of quality by a vendor, whether expressed or implied, is collateral to the main contract of sale, and a cause of action based upon a breach of warranty is not the same as a cause of action based upon a breach of the contract itself.

Cassady, Blackwell & Keith, for the appellant.

J. B. Knox, for the appellee.

81 COLEMAN J. The plaintiff (appellant) purchased paints and oils from the defendant drug company, a dealer in such articles of merchandise, to be used by her in painting her dwelling-house, the defendant knowing the use for which said articles were purchased. The articles were delivered to plaintiff, paid for and used. Afterward the plaintiff discovered, as averred, that the [82] paints and oils were worthless and proved an injury to the building instead of a benefit. She sued to recover damages, claiming, as special damages, the purchase money paid for the oils and paints, the amount paid to workmen for painting the house, and damage done to the building by reason of the inferior material. The liability of the defendant as set up in the complaint was raised by demurrer.

There is no averment in either count of the complaint that the defendant manufactured the articles sold, or perpetrated a fraud in the sale of the articles, or knew that they were unsuitable for the purposes for which they were intended. There is an averment that the defendant was a dealer in paints and oils, and knew the purposes for which they were purchased, and "undertook and agreed to supply suitable paints and oils," which he failed to do. There is also an averment that plaintiff did not know before use the quality of the materials purchased, that it was impracticable to discover the quality, and she relied upon the judgment and skill of the defendant to furnish suitable articles for painting her building. In one count it is averred that defendant "undertook and agreed to supply 'pure linseed oil,' and that the oil furnished was not pure linseed oil." The complaint nowhere avers an express warranty as to the quality of the articles purchased, nor any distinct affirmation or representation of the quality of the paints and oils.

The cause of action is based upon the averment that the quality was inferior to that the defendant undertook and agreed to supply to plaintiff, and that they were unsuitable for the purposes intended. The liability of the defendants depends upon two questions. The first is, whether a vendor who is a dealer in certain articles of merchandise, by virtue of the fact that he is a dealer, is held to an implied warranty of the quality of the article sold, when he knows the purposes for which it is intended, and the purchaser relies upon his judgment and skill? and if not, does the common-law doctrine of "caveat emptor" apply to a purchaser who fails to exact an express warranty, but relies upon the agreement of the vendor to supply articles suitable for certain purposes for which he knows they are purchased, under the facts averred in the complaint? Upon this last proposition, [83] we think it clear that where a vendor agrees to furnish articles of a certain kind and quality, the purchaser may refuse to receive

and pay for any which do not correspond with those agreed to be
furnished; but if he actually receives them and uses them, so that
they cannot be returned, there being no express warranty, will
the law imply a warranty, or allow the purchaser after using
them to repudiate the contract? Action for breach of covenant
is not an avoidance of the contract, and the suit is maintainable
only upon the ground that it is founded upon the breach of a
valid contract. The rule of the civil law is, "caveat venditor,"
while that of the common law is "caveat emptor." Under the
civil law, unless the seller stipulated against a warranty, he was
bound by an implied warranty of the quality of the article sold.
Under the common law, to hold a seller bound for the quality of
the goods sold, it was necessary to require of him a warranty. It
is much easier to apply the doctrine of the civil law as construed
by the courts than that of the common law as interpreted and
applied in many courts, both in the United States and England.
A very extended discussion, with many citations, may be found
in 10 American and English Encyclopedia of Law, under subject
of Implied Warranty, and in volume 28 of same work, under
subject of Warranty generally. In the case of Barnett v. Stanton, 2 Ala. 181, it was declared that a purchaser cannot recover for a defect in the quality of the property sold, except
under special circumstances, unless he show the seller warranted
the things sold, or concealed or fraudulently represented its qualities. This principle was reaffirmed in Armstrong v. Bufford,
51 Ala. 410, and in the case of Farrow v. Andrews, 69 Ala. 96,
it was declared "that, in the sale of goods by one who was not
shown to be a manufacturer, there was no implied warranty—
that it was reasonably adapted to the purposes for which it was
purchased. In such a sale, like that of any other merchandise,
the law exacts from the seller only good faith and fair dealing."
It is fairly inferable from the facts of the case as reported that
the plaintiffs were dealers. There is an entire absence of evidence reported in the case, to show that the purchaser informed
the seller of the purposes for which the goods were intended.
In Perry v. Johnston, 59 Ala. 648, the law is stated as follows:
"It is doubtless true, as a general [84] rule, that on a sale of an
existing thing, which is present and open to the inspection and
examination of the purchaser, there is no implied warranty of
its fitness for any particular use: Deming v. Foster, 42 N. H.
174. But if the vendor is informed the vendee is purchasing the
thing for a particular use, and its fitness for that use is the
element of value to the purchaser, a representation by him of its·

fitness is an implied, if not an express, warranty." In this case
the sale was that of a Jersey bull, bought for breeding purposes.
It does not appear that the seller was a dealer, and the principle
announced held the vendor responsible upon a warranty because
of the representation made of its suitableness, without reference
to the question of fraud or deceit.

In the case of Gachet v. Warren, 72 Ala. 288, the appellant
sold to the plaintiff two hundred and fifty bushels of "rust proof
oats." The oats were delivered and paid for. The defendant
seems to have been a dealer in the sale of oats, and knew the
purposes for which they were purchased. The plaintiff's crop
of oats failed because of rust, and he sued to recover damages
upon an implied warranty. This case with others is relied upon
by appellee to sustain the action of the court in sustaining his
demurrer to the plaintiff's complaint. The jury found from the
evidence that the defendant agreed to sell "rust proof oats," and
that the oats sold and delivered to the plaintiff were "rust proof
oats." This court held, that if the defendant agreed to sell to
the plaintiff a species or kind of oats known as "rust proof oats,"
and did sell such, there was no breach of the warranty. The
effect of the decision was, that a sale of "rust proof oats" could
not imply more than a warranty on the part of the dealer that
they were of the species known as "rust proof oats," and not a
warranty of quality. The law is thus stated: "Where a manufacturer, or a dealer, contracts to supply an article he manufactures or produces, or in which he deals, to be applied to a particular purpose, so that the buyer necessarily trusts to the judgment or skill of the manufacturer or dealer, there is, in that
case, an implied term of warranty that it shall be reasonably
fit for the purpose to which it is to be applied: Pacific Guano
Co. v. Mullen, 66 Ala. 582; Benjamin on Sales, sec. 157.
But if a manufacturer, or dealer, contracts to sell a known
and described thing, [85] although he may know the purchaser
intends it for a specific use, if he delivers the thing sold, there
is no implied warranty that it will answer or is suitable for
the specific use to which the purchaser intends applying it.
Chanter v. Hopkins, 4 Mees. & W. 399; Hoe v. Sanborn, 21 N. Y.
552; 78 Am. Dec. 163; Bartlett v. Hoppock, 34 N. Y. 118; 88
Am. Dec. 428; Dounce v. Dow, 64 N. Y. 411; Port Carbon
Iron Co. v. Groves, 68 Pa. St. 149; Gossler v. Eagle Sugar Re-
finery, 103 Mass. 331; 1 Parsons on Contracts, 586." The word
"dealer" is contained in the quotation from Benjamin, section
157, but the word "dealer" is not in the Alabama case (Pacific

Guano Co. v. Mullen, 66 Ala. 582) cited, but only "manufacturer."

In the case of Englehardt v. Clanton, 83 Ala. 336, after stating the rule applicable to manufacturers, it is said: "The same rule extends to dealers in articles sold for a special use or purpose": Citing 2 Benjamin on Sales, secs. 988, 995; Perry v. Johnston, 59 Ala. 648. Says the opinion: "The circumstances to an implied warranty in such cases are, that the seller shall be a manufacturer or dealer, shall have information of the particular use for which the article is intended, and the purchaser trust to the skill of the manufacturer or dealer from necessity, or other sufficient cause, and not on his own judgment."

In volume 28 of American and English Encyclopedia of Law, page 757, the law is stated as follows: "If the vendee buys an article for a particular use, which is known to the vendor at the time, and he assures the vendee that the 'article is all right,' or uses equivalent language, his assurance or representation amounts to a warranty that the article is reasonably fit for the use for which the vendee desires it; the vendee would naturally so understand it, and the vendor must be presumed to have intended it so. But when the vendor delivers goods of the character and quality represented, the vendee cannot defend upon the ground that they are unsuitable for the purposes for which he desired them."

The principle that a manufacturer is held to an implied warranty of quality is based upon the fact that he must know the "make-up" of the article sold by him. The law does not presume that a mere dealer is possessed of the same information as a manufacturer, and the same reason for the rule does not exist as to a mere dealer.

There may be apparent exceptions in some cases, as [so] druggists, etc. Every vendor, whether he be a dealer or not, is responsible for his representation or affirmation as to quality, which are more than expressions of opinion and which are relied upon, and upon which the party purchasing has the right to rely. Says Mr. Benjamin (Benjamin on Sales, 485): "If a man buy an article for a particular purpose, made known to the seller at the time of the contract, and rely upon the skill or judgment of the seller to supply what is wanted, there is an implied warranty that the thing sold will be fit for the desired purpose; aliter, if the buyer purchases on his own judgment." This principle does not depend upon the fact that the vendor is a dealer, but the warranty may arise from the character of the article and

circumstances of the contracting parties, whether the seller be
a dealer or not. The purchaser may have had no opportunity
to examine the article, or, if subject to examination and in fact
examined, he may not possess the requisite information to enable him to determine. In such a case, if the vendor affirms or
represents the quality of the goods as a fact, he is bound by
such representation or affirmation; or if, under such circumstances, knowing the use intended, he undertakes and agrees to
furnish an article, not merely in kind, but such as may be suitable for the purposes intended, he will be bound by such undertaking, whether he be a dealer or merely a seller. But if the
purchaser exercises and relies upon his own judgment in the
selection of the articles, and purchases accordingly, there is no
warranty. The complaint in the case at bar avers that the seller
was a dealer in paints and oils. The complaint does not merely
aver an undertaking on the part of the defendant to supply
her with paints and oils, but avers that it undertook and agreed
to supply paints and oils of certain qualities, to wit, such as were
suitable to be used in painting her house, and this is followed
by an averment of a breach of the agreement, stating wherein
they were defective. A warranty of quality by a vendor, whether
expressed or implied, is collateral to the main contract. A cause
of action based upon the breach of the warranty is not the same
as the cause of action founded upon the breach of the
contract of sale itself. If the vendor does not deliver the
article he undertook and agreed to furnish, he is guilty
of a breach of his [87] contract, and the purchaser need
not receive it; or, if delivered and used, when sued, the purchaser
may set up breach of contract, unless he has waived his right
of action for the breach; or if the article delivered, used, and
paid for, was of such a character, that the purchaser did not
detect that it did not correspond with the article purchased, and
the vendor undertook and agreed to deliver, he may then sue
for breach of contract. As we have seen in the case of the
"rust proof oats," where the purchase is of a kind or species, a
delivery of the species is a correspondence or compliance with
the contract; and in the case of the Jersey bull, the species was
delivered, but there was no correspondence in the quality affirmed, the defect being of such a character that it could not
be detected except by the use. The complaint in the present
action is so framed that, to entitle the plaintiff to recover, she
must prove the contract as laid, and the breach thereof. She
cannot recover on an implied warranty. The averment that the

defendant was a "dealer" adds nothing to its sufficiency, nor will this averment and proof of it authorize a recovery on less evidence, than if the vendor had been other than a "dealer." The complaint is for a breach of the contract of sale, and not for a breach of warranty collateral to the contract.

The second and third counts contain a statement of facts from which it may be that an implied warranty might arise, but each of the counts specially avers a contract of sale and purchase, and the breach of the contract, as distinguished from an implied warranty, is counted on as the cause of action. We construe the counts according to their legal effect, without reference to the purpose of the pleader.

The ground of demurrer that the damages sought to be recovered are too remote apply to all the damages sued for. Some of them clearly are not remote. We are of opinion the court erred in sustaining the demurrer to the complaint.

Reversed and remanded.

SALES—GOODS TO BE MANUFACTURED—IMPLIED WARRANTY.—If an article is purchased to be manufactured or produced for a specific purpose or use, there is an implied warranty that it is reasonably fit or suitable for the purpose or use for which it was ordered: Merchants' etc. Sav. Bank v. Fraze, 9 Ind. App. 161; 53 Am. St. Rep. 341, and note. A dealer contracting to sell an article in which he deals to be applied to a particular purpose, the buyer necessarily trusting to the judgment of the dealer, impliedly warrants that it is for the purpose to which it is to be applied: Edwards v. Dillon, 147 Ill. 14; 37 Am. St. Rep. 199, and note. But where a known, described, and defined article is ordered of a manufacturer, and the exact thing bargained for is supplied, there is no implied warranty of its fitness for the use intended by the purchaser, although it may have been stated by him that it was required for a particular purpose: Milwaukee Boiler Co. v. Duncan, 87 Wis. 120; 41 Am. St. Rep. 33, and note; Jarecki Mfg. Co. v. Kerr, 165 Pa. St. 529; 44 Am. St. Rep. 674; Wisconsin etc. Brick Co. v. Hood, 60 Minn. 401; 51 Am. St. Rep. 539.

SALES—WARRANTIES—NATURE OF.—A warranty is an express or implied statement of something which the party undertakes shall be a part of the contract, and, though part of the contract, collateral to the express object of the contract: Fairbank Canning Co. v. Metzger, 118 N. Y. 260; 16 Am. St. Rep. 753, and note.

City Council of Montgomery v. Parker.
[114 Alabama, 118.]

HIGHWAYS AND STREETS—DEDICATION—RIGHT TO CONTROL.—When part of a freehold becomes in fact a public highway or public street of a city, whether affected by dedication or conveyance of the owner, the state has full police power to regulate the actions of all persons in their use of it not inconsistent with its use as a street or highway, and to make such alterations from time to time as the state may deem proper. Subsequent to such dedication or conveyance, the dedicator or grantor has no greater right or interest in the use of such street or highway, as such, than any other person.

MUNICIPAL CORPORATIONS—STREETS—DELEGATION OF RIGHT TO CONTROL.—A state may delegate the supervision and control over streets of a city to the municipality in which they are located.

MUNICIPAL CORPORATIONS—ORDINANCES REGULATING USE OF STREETS.—A municipal ordinance providing that a portion of a certain street in front of a designated hotel shall be "established as a stand for two hacks," and prescribing a punishment for a violation of the ordinance, if within the power conferred by the city charter and not shown to be unreasonable, may be enforced, and the fact that a hack driver who violates such ordinance by attempting to occupy such stand with his hack, when it is already occupied by two others, is employed by the proprietor of·such hotel, who runs a hack line, and owns the fee in the street subject to the easement of the public, does not give the violator of the ordinance immunity from punishment.

MUNICIPAL ORDINANCES—STREETS—USE OF BY ADJOINING OWNER.—The proprietor of a hotel, who owns the fee in the street subject to the easement of the public, has no more right to permanently occupy the street adjacent to the sidewalk in front of the hotel with his hacks, in violation of a city ordinance, than has any other person, nor are his guests entitled to any greater consideration in the use of the sidewalks and streets of the city, because they are guests.

MUNICIPAL CORPORATIONS — STREETS—RIGHT OF ABUTTING OWNER TO INJUNCTION.—The proprietor of a hotel abutting on the street has the right to enjoin the use of the street in such manner as prevents and obstructs him and the guests of the hotel in the reasonable access to and egress therefrom and in the transportation of baggage to their great inconvenience and his injury, and to restrain the occupancy of the street in front of his hotel in a manner prohibited by a city ordinance.

Graham & Steiner, for the appellant.

G. McDonald and T. G. & C. P. Jones, for the appellees.

124 COLEMAN, J.   There is one question involved in each of these cases, the disposition of which determines the former, and may have a material bearing in the other. For this reason but one opinion will be delivered in the two cases.

The city council of Montgomery adopted two ordinances, the first of which reads as follows: "Be it ordained by the city council of Montgomery as follows: That the west side of Commerce street in front of the Exchange Hotel is hereby established as a stand for two [125] hacks." The second ordinance provided for "the punishment of anyone guilty of a violation of the ordinance by a fine," etc.

The facts show without conflict that the defendant, Will Parker, violated the above ordinance. The evidence on the part of the defendant showed that, at the time of the alleged violation, he, with others, was in the employment, as hack-drivers, or common carriers of persons, of the proprietor of the Exchange Hotel, then open and conducted as a public hotel, and that his hacks were kept for the use of his guests as well as for the public use.

In the second case, D. P. West, proprietor of the Exchange Hotel, filed a bill in equity for the purpose of having respondents enjoined "from keeping or allowing their servants to keep their carriages, hacks, and other vehicles on said street and along the sidewalk in front of complainant's hotel, in the manner above mentioned." We will state, substantially, the facts averred in the bill, upon which appellant bases the prayer for the injunction. First, that he is the owner in fee of the land to the center of the street: that for the purpose of carrying on his business, he is compelled to run a number of carriages and baggage wagons to carry his guests, the traveling public, and their baggage to and from the hotel, and that respondents have kept and continue to keep "their various hacks, carriages, or many of them, on said Commerce street, along the edge of the sidewalk, in front of complainant's hotel, as a usual and customary stand for them to await employment, to the great loss and annoyance of appellant in his said business, preventing and obstructing him and the guests of his said hotel in their reasonable access to and egress from said hotel, and obstructing and preventing the transportation of the baggage of said guests to and from the said hotel, and crowding and keeping carriages and baggage wagons away from the front of said hotel, where it is necessary for the comfort and convenience of complainant's guests the said carriages and wagons should be kept; . . . . and by reason of the wrongful conduct of respondents he is greatly hindered, hampered, harassed, and injured in his business of running his said hotel." A temporary injunction issued. Some of the respondents (appellees) answered the bill, and by [126] consent of parties the cause was set down for hearing upon motion to dissolve the injunction. At the hearing, the chancellor decreed a dissolution of the injunction, from which decree the complainant appealed, and here assigns the decree dissolving the injunction for error.

The wrong complained of by complainant in his bill, and for which he seeks redress and relief principally, is one which affects his personal business. The provisions of the city ordinances are within the terms of the power conferred by the legislature in the city charter. We declare the law to be, that when a part of a freehold becomes in fact a public highway or public street of a city, whether effected by dedication or conveyance of the owner, the state, in its sovereignty over all public highways and public places, has full police power to regulate the actions of all persons in their use of them, and the manner of their use, not inconsistent with their use as public streets or highways, and to make such alterations from time to time as the state may deem proper; and we further hold that the dedicator or grantor has no greater right or interest in the use of a street or public highway, as such, and the manner of its use, than any other person of the public: Perry v. New Orleans etc. R. R. Co., 55 Ala. 413; 28 Am. Rep. 740, and authorities; Elliott on Roads and Streets, 662.

It has been frequently decided, and we hold correctly decided, that the state may confer or delegate the same supervision and control over streets of a city to the municipality itself in which they are located: Authorities, supra: Brook v. Horton, 68 Cal. 554; Polack v. Trustees, etc., 48 Cal. 490; McCain v. State, 62 Ala. 138.

We find nothing in these ordinances of the city in question which show that the city council, by their adoption, exceeded the power conferred in its charter by the legislature, nor is there any provision contained in the ordinance, nor is there any evidence in the record of the case of City Council v. Will Parker which would authorize the conclusion that the ordinances are unreasonable It follows from the principles of law declared to be applicable that the defendant, Will Parker, prosecuted for a violation of the ordinance, and the complainant in the injunction suit, cannot claim any immunity, nor derive any special privilege or benefit, from the fact that the proprietor of the hotel owns the fee in the street, subject [127] only to the easement. Their right must be determined without regard to this fact. It is not seriously controverted that Will Parker violated the ordinance of the city. He should have been convicted under the evidence.

The proprietor of the Exchange Hotel has no more right to permanently occupy the street adjacent to the sidewalk in front of the hotel with his hacks than any other person, nor are his guests entitled to any greater consideration in the use of the sidewalks and streets of the city, because they are guests. The public, in these respects, are upon an equal footing. The complainant's bill, however, charges facts which, if true, show that the respondents occupy the street in front of the hotel in a manner not authorized by the city ordinances, but in a way the city ordinance, no doubt, was intended to prevent, and thereby "prevents and obstructs him and the guests of the hotel in the reasonable access to and egress from the hotel, and in the transportation of baggage, to their great inconvenience and to his injury." These averments, and there may be others of a similar character, in our opinion, gave the bill equity, and, if proven, would entitle the complainant to relief. The answer of the respondents positively and explicitly denies every allegation of fact made by the complainant, which gives equity to the bill, and which must be established to entitle complainant to relief.

There are affirmative averments in the answer of respondents, and which are discussed in the brief of counsel. We do not consider these, in reviewing the decree of the court dissolving the injunction upon the answer: Birmingham Mineral R. R. Co. v. Bessemer, 98 Ala. 277, and cases cited.

We are of opinion the decree is fully sustained upon the general rule stated in the foregoing authority.

The first case, that of City Council v. Will Parker, is reversed and remanded.

The second case, West v. Brown et al., is affirmed.

HIGHWAYS—CONTROL OF STATE—DELEGATION OF CONTROL TO MUNICIPAL CORPORATIONS.—The subject of highways, bridges, etc., is under the control of the state in its sovereign capacity as represented by the legislature: Wellington, Petitioners, 16 Pick. 87; 26 Am. Dec. 631. A municipal corporation has no authority to appropriate streets or to narrow or widen them, unless vested with such power expressly by its charter, or as an incident to an express delegation of power: State v. Mobile, 5 Port. 279; 30 Am. Dec. 564. Streets of an incorporated town are public highways and the regulation thereof given to the corporation for corporate purposes is subject to the paramount right of the state to provide for a more general and extended use of them: Case of Philadelphia etc. R. R. Co., 6 Whart. 25; 36 Am. Dec. 202, and note. See People v. Walsh, 96 Ill. 232; 36 Am. Rep. 135.

HIGHWAYS—RIGHTS OF ABUTTING OWNERS—INJUNCTION.—An abutting owner of lands fronting on a public street is entitled to every right and advantage in that part of the street in which he owns the fee, not required by the public: White v. Northwestern etc. Ry. Co., 113 N. C. 610; 37 Am. St. Rep. 639; Theobald v. Louisville etc. Ry. Co., 66 Miss. 279; 14 Am. St. Rep. 564; Kincald v. Indianapolis Nat. Gas Co., 124 Ind. 577; 19 Am. St. Rep. 113, and note. He may enjoin the use of the street for purposes inconsistent with those uses to which streets should be, or ordinarily have been, subjected, unless just compensation is made: Buffalo v. Pratt, 131 N. Y. 293; 27 Am. St. Rep. 592, and note.

MUNICIPAL CORPORATIONS—ORDINANCES—PUBLIC VEHICLES.—Concerning the power of municipal corporations to regulate the use of hacks and public vehicles in the public streets, see Commonwealth v. Stodder, 2 Cush. 562; 48 Am. Dec. 679; Veneman v. Jones, 118 Ind. 41; 10 Am. St. Rep. 100; Lindsay v. Mayor etc. of Anniston, 104 Ala. 257; 53 Am. St. Rep. 44. A hackney-coach stand on a public street, interfering with access to the premises of an adjoining proprietor, is a nuisance, and is not justified by a city ordinance permitting its establishment: Branahan v. Hotel Co., 39 Ohio St. 333; 48 Am. Rep. 457.

WATT v. GANS.

[114 ALABAMA, 264.]

BANKS AND BANKING—CHECKS—PRESENTMENT.—The holder of a bank check must present it for payment within a reasonable time. depending upon the facts in each case. In the absence of exceptional circumstances, such reasonable time is the shortest period within which, consistently with the ordinary employments and duties of commercial business, the duty of presentment and demand can be performed.

BANKS AND BANKING—CHECKS—PRESENTMENT.—The payee who receives a check from the drawer in a place distant from the place of payment must, in the absence of exceptional circumstances, forward it by the post to some person at the latter place on the next secular day after it is received, and the person to whom it is forwarded is not bound to present it for payment until the day after it has reached him by due course of the post. If payment is not thus regularly demanded, and the bank should fail before the check is presented, the loss falls on the holder, who thus makes the check his own by his laches.

BANKS AND BANKING—CHECKS—PRESENTMENT.—A bank check is intended for payment, not circulation, and, as between the original parties, the time allowed for its presentation cannot be enlarged by successive transfers.

BANKS AND BANKING—CHECKS—DELAY IN PRESENTMENT—BURDEN OF PROOF.—Checks are presumably drawn upon or against a deposit of funds, and if the drawer establishes negligence or undue delay in the presentation of his check, and the failure of the drawee bank, after the expiration of the period within which, with due diligence, the check should have been presented for payment, the presumption of injury to the drawer arises, casting upon the holder the burden of proof to show that the drawer has suffered no loss or damage by the delay.

BANKS AND BANKING—CHECKS—DELAY IN PRESENTMENT—PRESUMPTION OF LOSS AND REBUTTAL THEREOF. The presumption of loss to the drawer arising out of want of diligence in the presentation of his check and the intervening failure of the drawee may be rebutted by proof that the drawer had no available funds with the drawee to meet the check, or that he withdrew them before the failure, but, if such presumption remains unrebutted, the loss must fall upon the holder to whose want of diligence in presentation it is attributable.

BANKS AND BANKING—CHECKS—DELAY IN PRESENTATION, WHEN OPERATES AS PAYMENT.—While, in the absence of agreement, a check received for a debt is merely conditional payment, its acceptance implies an undertaking of due diligence in presenting it for payment; and if the party from whom it is thus received sustains loss by want of such diligence, it must be held to operate as actual payment.

BANKS AND BANKING—CHECKS—DELAY IN PRESENTATION—PLEA OF PAYMENT.—In an action upon an original debt, in payment of which a check has been given, the failure of the plaintiff to present such check for payment within a reasonable time, resulting in loss to the drawer, is available as a defense under the plea of payment.

C. Wilkinson, for the appellant.

Farnham, Crum & Weil, for the appellees.

²⁶⁹ HEAD, J. In general terms, it may be said that the law imposes upon the holder of a bank check the duty of presenting it for payment within a reasonable time; and, if he fail to present the check seasonably, the delay is at his own peril. What is a reasonable time will depend upon the facts in each case; yet, in the absence of exceptional circumstances, such reasonable time has been fixed. Thus it has been defined to be "the shortest period, within which, consistently with the ordinary employments and duties of commercial business, the duty of presentment and demand could be performed": Boone on Banking, 173; Story on Promissory Notes, 497.

In the case of Industrial Trust etc. Co. v. Weakley, 103 Ala. 458, 49 Am. St. Rep. 45, this court recognized and applied the rule which requires the holder of a check, receiving it at the same place in which the drawee transacts business, to present it for payment within banking hours on the day it is received, or the following secular day.

In the case now before us, a check drawn on a bank, at Greenville, Alabama, by the appellant, a debtor, was sent by him to the appellees, his creditors, at Philadelphia, Pennsylvania, and hence we are required to determine what diligence the appellees ought to have exercised in the collection of the check, which they received and accepted at a place remote from the location of the bank upon which it was drawn.

Speaking of the duty of a holder of a check, under the circumstances stated, Judge Story says: "Where he receives the check from the drawer in a place distant from the place of payment, it will be sufficient for him to forward it by the post to some person at the latter place on the next secular day after it is received; and the person to whom it is thus forwarded will not be bound to present it for payment until the day after it has reached him by the course of the post. If the payment is not thus regularly demanded, and the bank or bankers should fail before the check is presented, the loss will be the loss of the holder, who will have made the [270] check his own by his laches": Story on Promissory Notes, 493.

A check is intended for payment, not circulation; and, as between the original parties to it, the time allowed for its presentation will not be enlarged by successive transfers.

These principles seem to be well established and to be recognized by the standard text-writers: 2 Daniel on Negotiable Instruments, sec. 1592; Boone on Banking, 173; 2 Morse on Banks nd Banking, sec. 421; Tiedeman on Commercial Paper, sec. 443; Randolph on Commercial Paper, sec. 1106; Byles on Bills, sec. .0; Chitty on Bills, 13th Am. ed., 436.

Undoubtedly, cases may be found, some of which are cited by council for appellees, where a longer time than that above stated was, under exceptional and peculiar circumstances, allowed for presentation of a check. Here, no extraordinary or unusual circumstances calling for a relaxation of the settled rule are presented; and hence the simple and definite requirement, imposing the duty of sending the check to a person, bank, or other collecting agency at Greenville for presentation, without the selection of a circuitous route or the intervention of intermediate and successive collecting banks, whereby of necessity the presentation would be unduly delayed, must be applied.

The appellees having received the check of the appellant on December 12, 1893, at Philadelphia, it was their duty to forward it to Greenville, Alabama, at the latest, on the following day. This duty they could perform in person, or they might intrust it to a local bank.

The latter course they pursued, by depositing the check on December 13, 1893, with the Union National Bank of Philadelphia for collection. This, however, did not enlarge the time for transmitting the instrument to the place of payment; and in the collection of the check the bank acted as the agent of the holders.

In sending the check to Charleston, South Carolina, whence it went, first to Montgomery, Alabama, and hence to Greenvile, Alabama, the place of payment, whereby presentation and

demand was delayed until December 19, 1893, after the failure
of the drawee bank, there was negligence, imposing upon the
appellees whatever loss the appellant suffered from the laches:
Gifford v. Hardell, 88 Wis. [271] 538; 43 Am. St. Rep. 925; First
National Bank v. Miller, 37 Neb. 500; 40 Am. St. Rep. 499.
There is nothing in the evidence from which it can be inferred
that the method pursued was within the contemplation or expectation of the appellant, nor that it was according to any previous course of dealing between the parties, or that he expressly
or impliedly assented to the delay. Neither can we judicially
know that any custom existed in Philadelphia whereby checks
received for collection on Greenville, Alabama, were sent by way
of Charleston, South Carolina, for presentation, nor, if such a
practice prevailed, that it was known to the appellant. If any
one of these things, or all combined, would authorize the inference that he assented to the intervening delay, or could justify a
holding that he could not complain of a delay—questions we do
not now consider—it was incumbent upon the appellees to introduce into the record evidence of the existence of such facts. It
is satisfactorily established, by letters incorporated in the bill of
exceptions, and from the postmarks on the envelopes, admitted
to be the true dates on which the letters were mailed at Philadelphia and received at Greenville, that by due course of mail a
letter posted at the former place, on December 13, 1893, at any
time up to 7:30 o'clock P. M. would have reached the latter
point not later than 10 o'clock P. M. on the 15th of the same
month, or within forty-eight hours. Thus, the original envelope
sent up for our inspection shows that the letter, inclosing a receipt for the check, mailed at 7:30 o'clock P. M. on December 12th
at Philadelphia, arrived at Greenville at 1 o'clock P. M. on December 14th, or in less than two days. Hence, if the check had
been forwarded directly to Greenville on December 13th, when it
was sent to Charleston, it would, with the diligence the law requires, have been presented to the bank upon which it was drawn
on Saturday, December 16th, and of consequence prior to the
failure on Monday, the 18th.

It may be that the appellees, or their local bank, had no corres-
pondent at Greenville, although as to this the evidence does not
inform us; or it may not have been convenient to pursue the
course the law directs. If such was the case, they could easily
have declined to accept the check; they were not bound to receive
it; but having done so, and having undertaken its collection [272]
they must bear all the burdens, and exercise all the diligence
imposed by law.

At this point, the appellees invoke the well-recognized rule, which declares that the drawer of a check has no cause to complain of its delay in its presentation if he has thereby suffered no loss or damage; and, they contend that the appellant must show affirmatively that he had funds from which the check would have been paid in the hands of the drawee during the period within which, by the exercise of due diligence upon the part of the holders, the check would have been presented. The contention is rested upon the fourth paragraph of the agreed statement of facts, which recites merely that the appellant had the amount of the check to his credit with the drawees at the time of the assignment and failure. As the fact is thus presented, a question is raised as to the burden of proof. In most cases of this kind to be found in the books, there is positive evidence that the drawer had or had not funds to meet the check when drawn, or during the interval before the failure or that he had or had not withdrawn his funds. In this case, the parties have not advised us by affirmative testimony, or by agreement as to the state of appellant's accounts with his bankers anterior to the time of their failure; and hence the refusal must turn upon legal presumptions, arising out of the facts which are stated in the agreement of the parties, constituting the evidence in the case. The important inquiry is, Where rests the burden of proof? Without entering upon any prolonged discussion, it will be sufficient to say that the authorities are quite uniform in holding that checks are presumably drawn upon or against a deposit of funds, and where the drawer establishes negligence or undue delay in the presentation of his check, and the failure of the drawee bank, after the expiration of the period within which, with due diligence, the check would have been presented, the presumption of injury arises, casting upon the holder the burden of proving the drawer has suffered no loss or damage by the delay: Stevens v. Park, 73 Ill. 387; Willetts v. Paine, 43 Ill. 433; Anderson v. Rodgers, 53 Kan. 542; Little v. Phenix Bank, 2 Hill, 427; Planters' Bank v. Merritt, 7 Heisk. 177; 2 Morse on Banks and Banking, sec. 421; Daniel on Negotiable Instruments, sec. 1588; Story on Promissory Notes, sec. 498; Edwards on Bills, 398; 3 [273] Randolph on Commercial Paper, sec. 1106, p. 94. As Kent, J., said in Cruger v. Armstrong, 3 Johns. Cas. 5, 2 Am. Dec. 126, "the presumption is, that the check would have been paid if diligently presented."

The presumption of loss arising out of want of diligence in the presentation of a check, and the intervening failure of the drawee, may be rebutted by proof that the drawer had no available funds with the drawee to meet the check, or that he withdrew them before the failure. No such proof was produced in this case; on the contrary, it is admitted that the necessary amount, presumably in the bank wherewith to pay the check, remained to the credit of the appellant with his bankers when the failure occurred, and it is further admitted that the proprietors of the bank were still insolvent at the time of the trial. In this state of evidence, the appellees failed to meet the burden resting upon them; the presumption of damage to the appellant stands unrebutted and the loss must fall upon the appellees, to whose want of diligence it is attributable.

The suit was brought upon the original debt, in settlement of which the check was given, and the appellant, who was defendant in the circuit court, interposed the plea of payment. It is contended by the appellees that the defense arising out of the failure to present the check, whereby loss resulted, is not available under that plea. With this view we do not agree. The correct rule is thus stated by Sterritt, J., in Kirkpatrick v. Home Building etc. Assn., 119 Pa. St. 30: "It is well-settled that, in the absence of an agreement to the contrary, a check or promissory note of either the debtor or a third person, received for debt, is merely conditional payment, that is, satisfaction of the debt if and when paid; but that acceptance of such note or check implies an undertaking of due diligence in presenting it for payment, etc.; and, if the party from whom it is received sustains loss by want of such diligence, it will be held to operate as actual payment."

By failure of appellees to exercise proper diligence in the collection of the check, whereby the appellant, if held upon the original debt, would suffer loss, they made the check their own, and turned what was at first only a conditional payment into an absolute discharge of the debt for which the check was given: Boone on Banks [274] and Banking, sec. 181; Industrial Trust etc. Co. v. Weakley, 103 Ala. 458; 49 Am. St. Rep. 45; Middlesex v. Thomas, 20 N. J. Eq. 39; Kahn v. Walton, 46 Ohio St. 195.

The plaintiff's were not entitled to recover, and the circuit court erred in giving the affirmative charge in their behalf.

As the facts were agreed upon by the parties, and as no inferences entitling the plaintiff to recover were deducible therefrom, the court might well, upon request, without hypothesis, have directed the jury that upon the agreed evidence the defendant was entitled to a verdict.

Let the judgment be reversed and the cause remanded.

CHECKS — PRESENTMENT — REASONABLE TIME.—A bank check should be presented for payment within a reasonable time. Otherwise the delay is at the peril of the payee: Industrial Trust etc. Co. v. Weakley, 103 Ala. 458; 49 Am. St. Rep. 45, and note. If a check is received at a place distant from the place where the bank upon which it is drawn is situated, and is forwarded by due course of mail to a person in the latter place for presentment, the person to whom it is thus forwarded has until the close of banking hours on the next secular day after he has received it to present it for payment, unless there are special circumstances which require him to act more promptly: Comer v. Dufour, 95 Ga. 376; 51 Am. St. Rep. 89, and note.

CHECKS—PRESENTMENT.—Ordinary checks are not designed for circulation, but for immediate presentment for payment: First Nat. Bank v. Miller, 37 Neb. 500; 40 Am. St. Rep. 499. And if not thus presented within a reasonable time according to the circumstances, the maker or indorser is released from liability: Scroggin v. McClelland, 37 Neb. 644; 40 Am. St. Rep. 520.

CHECKS—DELAY IN PRESENTMENT—WHEN RELEASES DRAWER.—Delay in presenting a check is immaterial unless it injures the drawer: Note to Anderson v. Gill, 47 Am. St. 'Rep. 414. Such presentment is unnecessary when the drawer has no funds in the bank to meet the check: Extended note to Holmes v. Briggs, 17 Am. St. Rep. 810; Industrial Trust etc. Co. v. Weakley, 103 Ala. 458; 49 Am. St. Rep. 45. But the burden of proof is on the holder of the check to show that no loss or injury has resulted to the maker through the delay in making presentment and giving notice: Note to Holmes v. Briggs, 17 Am. St. Rep. 810.

ANDERSON *v.* TIMBERLAKE.

[114 ALABAMA, 877.]

PRINCIPAL AND AGENT—LIABILITY TO THIRD PERSON.—If one known to be an agent deals or contracts within the scope of his authority, the presumption is, that credit is extended to the principal alone and that the act or contract is his engagement as if he were personally present and acting or contracting. This presumption prevails, in the absence of evidence that credit was given to the agent exclusively, and the burden of proof is upon the party seeking to charge such agent exclusively.

PRINCIPAL AND AGENT—CONSTRUCTION OF CONTRACT.—If a contract made with a known agent, acting within the scope of his authority, is in writing, its construction and effect are ordinarily questions of law to be decided by the court, but, if the contract is verbal, the question whether credit was given to the agent alone is one of fact to be determined by the jury from a consideration of all the facts and circumstances attending the transaction.

PRINCIPAL AND AGENT—LIABILITY TO THIRD PERSON.—If a contract is made with a known agent acting within the scope of his authority for a disclosed principal, the contract is that of the principal alone, unless credit was given expressly and exclusively to the agent, and it appears that it was clearly his intention to assume the obligation as a personal liability and he was informed that credit was extended to him alone.

PRINCIPAL AND AGENT—LIABILITY TO THIRD PERSON—QUESTION FOR JURY.—If a known agent contracts an ac-

count within the scope of his authority, the fact that at the beginning of the transactions he directed the account to be charged to him
is not conclusive that he intended to become sole debtor to the exclusion of all liability on the part of his principal, nor is it conclusive of the fact that credit was not extended to the principal. These
questions are for the consideration and determination of the jury, to
be taken in connection with all the circumstances attending the
dealings between the parties in ascertaining whether exclusive credit
was extended to the agent, and whether, with knowledge of that fact,
he intended to assume individual responsibility.

PRINCIPAL AND AGENT—SUBSEQUENT PROMISE TO
PAY BY AGENT—CONSIDERATION.—If a known agent contracts
an account for his principal, a subsequent promise of payment by
such agent is void for want of consideration.

PRINCIPAL AND AGENT—PROMISE TO PAY BY AGENT.
If a known agent, acting within the scope of his authority, contracts
an account for his principal, his promise to pay, made at the time,
is, prima facie, the promise of the principal, not involving the agent
in personal liability, and, in an action to charge him therewith, evidence of such promise is admissible to show whether credit was extended to the agent solely, and whether it was his intention to bind
himself and not his principal, and such evidence cannot be considered
by the jury by itself, but may be considered in connection with all
the circumstances attending the transactions between the parties.

NOTICE.—A PARTY TO A WRITING, the genuineness of
which is not disputed, is charged with notice of its contents and the
effect thereof.

INSTRUCTIONS WITHDRAWING FROM CONSIDERA-
TION BY THE JURY any evidence, however weak, tending to establish material facts, are calculated to mislead, and therefore improper.

NEGOTIABLE INSTRUMENTS—ASSIGNMENT OF AS COL-
LATERAL—LACHES OF HOLDER—DISCHARGE OF ASSIGNOR.
A creditor accepting a transfer of negotiable paper by mere delivery,
and without indorsement, as a conditional payment or as collateral
security, is bound to the use of due diligence in rendering it available,
but his laches in this respect does not of itself operate to discharge
the transferror, and to have this effect it must appear that such
laches caused loss or damage to the latter.

NEGOTIABLE INSTRUMENTS.—DISCOUNT signifies the interest allowed in advancing upon negotiable instruments, and is, in
effect, buying such instruments for a less sum than that which upon
their face is payable.

Action to recover on an account. It was not disputed that
the defendant was a mere agent, on a salary, of the North Alabama Lumber and Manufacturing Company during the time
that the indebtedness was contracted, in running a sawmill which
he was operating as agent. The plaintiff insisted that the account was contracted by the defendant on his own responsibility, that he credited him personally, and that he knew no
other person in the transaction. The defendant insisted that
he never authorized the plaintiff to charge the account to him,
and never agreed to become personally bound for its payment.
The company for which the defendant was agent was insolvent
at the time this action was commenced. Judgment for plaintiff, and the defendant appealed.

Martin & Bouldin, for the appellant.

J. E. Brown, for the appellee.

386 BRICKELL, C. J. The legal presumption is, when a known agent deals or contracts within the scope of his authority, that credit is extended to the principal and not to the agent; and that the dealing is the act, or the contract is the engagement, of the principal alone, as if he were personally present and acting or contracting. This presumption prevails in the absence of evidence that credit was given to the agent exclusively, and the burden of proof rests upon the party seeking to charge him personally. If the contract or promise is in writing, its construction and effect are, ordinarily, questions of law for the decision of the court. But when the contract or promise is verbal, the question whether the credit was given to the agent in exclusion of the credit of the principal is a question of fact for the determination of the jury, to be ascertained from a consideration of all the circumstances attending the transaction: Mechem on Agency, sec. 558; 1 Am. & Eng. Ency. of Law, 2d ed., 1119, 1120; Whitney v. Wyman, 101 U. S. 392. In 1 Am. Leading Cases, fifth edition, page 764, speaking in reference to verbal contracts made by or through an agent, it is said: "That when the relation of principal and agent exists in reference to a contract, and is known to the other party to exist, and the principal is disclosed at the time as such, the contract is the contract of the principal, and the agent is not bound, unless credit has been given to him expressly and exclusively, and it was clearly his intention to assume a personal responsibility; but, if credit was given to him exclusively, and he intended to give his own personal engagement, he will be bound; and this, upon sufficient evidence, is a question for the jury on all the circumstances of the case." In the recent case, Humes v. Decatur Land Imp. etc. Co., 98 Ala. 461, it was said by Coleman, J: "To hold an agent personally liable in cases in which he discloses his principal, and that the services to be rendered are for the sole benefit of the principal, and the contract is within the scope of his authority, it must be shown that the credit was given exclusively to the agent, and that the agent was informed of that fact."

Applying this well-settled principle, the instructions **387** to the jury given at the instance of the plaintiff, numbered 1, 2, and 4, are essentially erroneous. They proceed, manifestly, on the theory, that the principal, the North Alabama Lumber and Manufacturing Company, and the defendant as agent, were, or could be bound, jointly or severally, by the same contract or engagement; or, that the promise of the one could be collateral to the promise of the other. While the true inquiry, an inquiry to be solved by the jury upon a consideration of the course of dealing between the parties, and all the attendant facts and circumstances, was, whether any credit was given to the principal, or whether it was given exclusively to the defendant, and it was his intention to become the sole debtor to the plaintiff. The fact that the defendant, at the commencement of the transaction from which the account originated, may have directed the accounts, as created, to be charged to him, or to himself and Kilpatrick, to which so much of prominence is given by the instructions, is far from being decisive that he intended to become the sole debtor, or a debtor jointly with Kilpatrick, to the exclusion of all liability on the part of the North Alabama Lumber and Manufacturing Company; nor is it decisive that the plaintiff did not extend any credit whatever to that company. The purpose of the direction may have been only to separate and distinguish the accounts the defendant was creating as agent from the individual dealings he was having, or might have, with the plaintiff. As a fact, the direction is for the consideration of the jury, to be taken in connection with all other facts and circumstances attending the dealings between the parties, in ascertaining whether exclusive credit was extended to the defendant, and whether, with knowledge of that fact, he intended to assume individual responsibility.

There was evidence having a tendency to show that, prior and subsequent to the creation of the accounts, the defendant promised to pay them. Whether the instructions were intended to direct the attention of the jury to the prior or to the subsequent promises, or, without distinguishing between them, were intended to embrace the whole, is not clear and certain. In this respect the instructions may have a tendency to mislead and confuse the jury, and for this reason could have been properly [388] refused. But we are not prepared to say the error is cause for reversal; the defendant should have avoided whatever of injury may have been apprehended by a request for additional or explanatory instructions. A promise of payment by the defendant, subsequent to the creation of the accounts, would be void for want of all consideration. The debt had been contracted, and if it was the debt of the principal, the promise of the defendant to pay it was a mere undertaking or engagement upon a consideration past and executed: Jackson v. Jackson, 7 Ala. 791. A promise to pay at the time of the creation of the accounts, prima

facie, would be the promise of the principal, not involving the
defendant in personal liability. Evidence of these promises is
admissible upon the pivotal inquiry whether credit was extended
to the defendant solely, and whether it was his intention to bind
himself and not the principal; they are circumstances attending
the transaction between the parties, not to be disconnected from
other facts and circumstances, and of themselves are not fitting
elements of an instruction to the jury.

It does not clearly appear that the agency of the defendant for
the North Alabama Lumber and Manufacturing Company was a
disputed fact. If it was whether the plaintiff had knowledge,
or was charged with knowledge of the fact, depended in a
degree upon oral testimony, and the inferences drawn from it
by the jury. In such case, an instruction not referring to the
jury the credibility of the testimony is an invasion of their province. For this reason, the first instruction requested by the defendant was properly refused: 1 Brickell's Digest, sec. 8, p. 366.
The second and third are general instructions on the effect of
the evidence, which are not proper, when there is any conflict in
the evidence, as to any material fact or point involved in the
determination of the case. The seventh instruction should have
been given. The writing to which it refers, in the execution of
which plaintiff joined, plainly contemplates the operation of the
mill by the North Alabama Lumber and Manufacturing Company; and of that fact the plaintiff, being a party to the writing,
was charged with notice. This is the legal effect of the writing
as a matter of evidence, which it was the province and duty of the
court to declare without hypothesis, the genuineness of the [389]
writing not being controverted: Knox v. Fair, 17 Ala. 503; Rigby
v. Norwood, 34 Ala. 129. The sixth instruction was properly refused. It withdrew from the consideration of the jury the evidence having a tendency to show that the acounts were created
by the defendant on his own credit solely, in exclusion of the
credit of the lumber company. An instruction withdrawing from
the consideration of the jury any evidence, however weak, tending to establish material facts, is calculated to mislead them, and
is improper: 1 Brickell's Digest, sec. 135, p. 344; Brown v.
Newman, 66 Ala. 275.

The fourth and fifth instructions proceed on the proposition
that laches on the part of the plaintiff in causing the drafts on
Kilpatrick & Co. to be presented for payment and in giving the
defendant notice of their dishonor, discharged him from liability.
Without discussing the truth of the proposition, if the defendant

had been a party to the drafts—if he had indorsed them, or guaranteed their payment—they were transferred by delivery merely, if in the transfer the defendant had any agency. A creditor accepting a transfer of paper by mere delivery, as a conditional payment, or as collateral security, is bound to the use of due diligence in rendering it available. But the laches of the creditor in this respect does not of itself, operate to discharge the transferror; the laches must have caused loss or damage: 2 Daniel on Negotiable Instruments, sec. 1278; Story on Bills, secs. 109, 305; Russell v. Hester, 10 Ala. 535; Powell v. Henry, 27 Ala. 612. The instructions pretermit the material inquiry whether the laches imputed to the plaintiff worked injury to the defendant, and were properly refused: Wood v. Brewer, 66 Ala. 570.

The eighth instruction properly defined a discount, and should have been given: Youngblood v. Birmingham Trust etc. Co., 95 Ala. 521; 36 Am. St. Rep. 245; Saltmarsh v. P. & M. Bank, 14 Ala. 668. The ninth instruction is subject to the objection that it was calculated to mislead the jury by diverting their attention from the consideration of the testimony that the drafts were by agreement of the parties taken only as conditional payment.

For the errors pointed out, let the judgment be reversed and the cause remanded.

***

AGENCY—WHEN AGENT IS PERSONALLY LIABLE.—An agent acting within the scope of his authority, and not concealing his agency, is not liable on a contract made for the benefit of his principal: Hall v. Huntoon, 17 Vt. 244; 44 Am. Dec. 332, and note; Ogden v. Raymond, 22 Conn. 379; 58 Am. Dec. 429, and note; Piercy v. Hedrick, 2 W. Va. 458; 98 Am. Dec. 774. He is personally liable on contracts which show an intention to bind himself personally: Simonds v. Heard, 23 Pick. 120; 34 Am. Dec. 41; or where he fails to disclose his agency to the person with whom he is dealing; Argersinger v. Macnaughton, 114 N. Y. 535; 11 Am. St. Rep. 687. But if an agent says that he will pay a bill or will see it paid, such promise binds his principals, though he does not mention them, if he was acting in their business, and what he said was in their behalf: Cannon v. Henry, 78 Wis. 167; 23 Am. St. Rep. 399. See Cream City Glass Co. v. Friedlander, 84 Wis. 53; 36 Am. St. Rep. 895; Johnson v. Armstrong, 83 Tex. 325; 29 Am. St. Rep. 648, and notes thereto.

NOTICE—WHAT CONSTITUTES.—Notice may be inferred from circumstances, and by reasonable inferences therefrom: Connecticut etc. Ins. Co. v. Smith, 117 Mo. 261; 38 Am. St. Rep. 656. See extended note to Lodge v. Simonton, 23 Am. Dec. 47-53; National Bank v. Morris, 114 Mo. 255; 35 Am. St. Rep. 754; Backer v. Pyne, 130 Ind. 288; 30 Am. St. Rep. 231, and note.

DISCOUNT—DEFINITION OF.—A discount by a bank means a deduction or drawback made upon its advances or loans of money

upon negotiable paper, or other evidences of debt payable at a future
day which are transferred to the bank. In other words, discount
is the interest reserved from the amount loaned at the time the
loan is made: Youngblood v. Birmingham etc. Co., 95 Ala. 521; 36
Am. St. Rep. 245.

NEGOTIABLE INSTRUMENTS—TRANSFER AS COLLATERAL
SECURITY—DUTY OF TRANSFEREE.—A contract whereby collateral security is given for the performance of an obligation carries
with it the implication that the security shall be made available
to discharge the obligation. If the collateral security is a negotiable
instrument, and measures are necessary to charge any party thereon, then there is no doubt that the holder of such security owes to
the pledgor the duty of taking the measures necessary to preserve
the liability of all the parties to the instrument: Monographic note
to Griggs v. Day, 32 Am. St. Rep. 718, 719.

BOYLSTON V. RANKIN.

[114 ALABAMA, 408.]

EXEMPTIONS—TIME FOR FILING CLAIM.—Under a stat-
ute providing that a claim of exemption must be filed after levy of
process upon the property claimed as exempt from sale, such claim
may be filed at any time before the sale under the levy.

EXEMPTIONS.—RIGHT OF EXEMPTION OF PERSONAL
PROPERTY coexists and is coextensive with the right of the creditor to reach the subject, except in cases specially saved from the
operation of the exemption.

ESTOPPEL.—CONDUCT OR STATEMENTS of a party do
not operate as an estoppel in favor of another party, who was not
influenced by them, and who would not suffer injury if there was a
contradiction of them.

EXEMPTIONS—ESTOPPEL TO CLAIM—WHAT IS NOT.—
If, after levy of an execution upon property as that of the execution
defendant, a third party institutes a statutory trial of the right
thereto, and such defendant testifies therein that the property under
levy is not his, but belongs to such claimant, he is not thereby
estopped, upon judgment subjecting the property to the satisfaction of such execution, from claiming the property as exempt at
any time prior to the execution sale.

EXEMPTIONS — ESTOPPEL TO CLAIM — JUDGMENT,
WHEN IS NOT.—If, after levy of execution upon property as that
of the execution defendant, a third party institutes a statutory trial
of the right thereto, judgment therein subjecting the property to
the satisfaction of such execution is not conclusive upon, and does
not estop, the execution defendant, who is not a party to the claim
suit, to claim his right of exemption at any time before the execution sale.

Rankin & Co. recovered judgment against Boylston, and execution thereunder was levied upon ten shares of stock in the
Sheffield and Tuscumbia Street Railway Company standing on
its books in the name of Boylston, and on which no certificates
of stock had been issued. W. S. White then interposed a claim

to and trial of right to the property, claiming that Boylston
had subscribed for the stock for him in payment of a debt.
On the claim trial, Boylston testified as White claimed and that
he regarded the property as belonging to the latter. The court
in the claim suit rendered judgment subjecting the stock to
the satisfaction of the execution already levied, and that judgment was affirmed on appeal. A few days before the stock was
to be sold under such execution Boylston interposed a claim of
exemption. Rankin & Co. then filed a contest of this claim of
exemption and obtained judgment dismissing such claim. Said
claimant thereupon appealed.

Kirk & Almon, for the appellant.

J. B. Moore and J. Jackson, for the appellees.

411 BRICKELL, C. J. This was a claim of exemption from
liability to sale under execution of ten shares of the capital stock
of the Sheffield & Tuscumbia Railway Company, in which the
appellant was the claimant, and the appellees were the contest-
ants. The trial was had in the court below, by consent of the
parties, without the intervention of a jury.

The causes of contest assigned by the appellees are drawn
to an unusual, if not unnecessary, length, but when analyzed,
and read in connection with the argument of counsel in support
of them. they are readily resolvable into three separate, distinctive causes. it is convenient to consider in the order in which we
enumerate them. The first is, that as more than three years
intervened after the levy of the original execution before the
claim of exemption was interposed, the claim came too late, and
must be regarded as having been waived. The second is, that the
appellant is estopped from asserting the claim; the estoppel arising from the fact, that on a trial of the right of the property in
and to the stock, had by and between the appellees as execution
creditors, and one White as claimant, the appellant, as a witness
for the claimant, had testified that though the stock on the books
of the company was standing in his name as the sole owner
thereof, his title was but nominal; the real beneficial interest
residing in the claimant. The third is, that the judgment rendered on the trial of the right of property, declaring the stock
was liable to the satisfaction of the execution, is a bar to the claim
of exemption.

1. The statutes under which the proceedings were had in express terms limit the time within which the claim of exemption,

and the contest of the validity of the claim must be filed. The claim must be filed after the levy, and thereafter may be filed at any time before the [412] sale: Code 1886, secs. 2520, 2521. There was no other provision which would have been in accord with the constitution, for it is the right or privilege of exemption not from levy, but "from sale on execution, or other process of any court," the constitution creates and confers. The shares of stock in a private corporation the statutes subject to levy and sale under execution or attachment against the shareholder as if they were visible, tangible chattels. When the levy of the original execution was made, and White made affidavit and gave bond for the trial of the right of property, the sheriff lost all custody and control of the stock; it passed into the custody of the court in which the trial of the right of property was pending, and until the trial, or the proceedings for the trial were determined, there could not be a sale, or the issue of any process for the sale of the stock: Dollins v. Lindsey, 89 Ala. 217; Williams v. Dismukes, 106 Ala. 402. Until there was the issue of such process by which a sale could have been effected, the claim of exemption could not be interposed. Having been interposed before a sale, the claim was not too late; it was within the limitation of time the statute prescribes.

2. An error pervading the second ground of contest lies in the theory that the contest involves an inquiry into the nature of the title or ownership the claimant may have in the property on which the levy is made. The levy of the process was an admission, an assertion by the plaintiff therein, that the defendant had in the property an ownership or interest, the subject of levy and sale. This is the foundation fact on which the legality of the levy and all of right plaintiff could assert depends; and he could not be heard to gainsay it: Leinkauff v. Munter, 76 Ala. 194; Kolsky v. Loveman, 97 Ala. 543; Kennedy v. First Nat. Bank, 107 Ala. 170. Nor is there soundness in the theory outlined, rather than distinctly expressed, in the argument of counsel for the appellees, that a debtor may have a right or interest in personal property a creditor can reach and subject, and yet not a right or interest from which the debtor is entitled to claim exemption. The right of exemption of personal property coexists and is coextensive with the right of the creditor to reach and subject, except in cases specially saved from the [413] operation of the exemption. The two are conjoined, and there can be no separation of them: Sannoner v. King, 49 Ark. 299; 4 Am. St. Rep. 49.

Nor is there any room for the application of the doctrine of
estoppel as to the appellant. The statements or conduct of a
party do not operate an estoppel in favor of another party, who
was not influenced by them, and who would not suffer injury if
there was contradiction of them: Leinkauff v. Munter, 76 Ala.
194. There was no action of the appellees induced by the testimony given by the appellant on the trial of the right of property.
The trial had its origin in the levy on the stock as the property
of the appellant—the levy being induced by the fact that on the
books of the company the stock was standing in his name as
owner. When on the trial he disavowed ownership, and testified
that the real beneficial ownership resided in White, the appellee
disregarded the disavowal and testimony, and proceeded in the
prosecution of the trial. True, if they had not notice, prior to
the levy, of the equity asserted to reside in White, under the
statute, they acquired rights which were entitled to precedence
of that equity. But this does not tend to show any element of
estoppel in the statements, representations, or acts of the appellant, nor reliance upon them by the appellee. When reduced to
its last analysis, the logic of the situation is, that whatever of
estoppel is to be applied must be applied not to the appellant, but
to the appellees. They are asserting, and in this proceeding can
assert, no other right or title than that which is consequential, or
derivative from a legal title to the stock, residing in the appellant; and for their own uses, for their own benefit uno flatu, they
cannot be heard to claim that title, and to impeach it, so far as
the appellant is entitled to corresponding and resultant rights and
benefits. In the terse language of Stone, C. J., in Leinkauff v.
Munter, 76 Ala. 194, if this were not true, we would have the
anomalous situation "of one estopped from denying the fundamental fact on which his claim rests; his adversary, from asserting the truth of the same fundamental fact." The stock, the
property of the appellant for the purpose of making it liable for
his debts, but not his property to enable him to claim exemption
therein. Suppose there was inconsistency between the testimony
given by the [414] appellant on the trial of the right of property,
and the claim of exemption—suppose that fraud, actual fraud on
his creditors could be imputed (and in view of the facts found in
the record, inconsistency or fraud cannot be imputed, unless it
can be imputed to any and every embarrassed debtor who, in the
course of transacting business, comes into the possession and
control of personal property, impressed with a trust for the use
of another), every fact remains entitling the appellant to claim

the exemption. He was a resident of the state when the transaction occurred, and the residence was continuous to the trial in the court below; and residence is the only personal qualification the constitution declares and prescribes. In Pinkus v. Bamberger, 99 Ala. 266, where there was much of evidence having a tendency to show that Pinkus, the claimant of the exemption, had perpetrated frauds on his creditors, it was said by Stone, C. J: "We hold, however, that on the issue presented by this record such inquiry was wholly immaterial, except to the extent, if any, it showed that Pinkus had moneys or other effects, which he failed to discover in his inventory. No matter how fraudulent his conduct and intentions may have been, if he was a resident of Alabama, he was entitled to have set apart to him, as exempt from his debts, one thousand dollars in value of his personal property, to be selected by him."

3. The affirmative allegation the statute required the appellees to propound on the trial of the right of property was that the stock was the property of the appellant and liable to the satisfaction of the execution: Code 1886, sec. 3005. The allegation involved a negation of the claim White asserted, as well as the assertion of title in the appellant, from which resulted liability to the satisfaction of the execution. This was an issue between the appellees and White, to which the appellant was not a party, and on the trial of which he could not have intervened to assert a claim of exemption. The judgment of condemnation rendered on the trial of the issue was conclusive, as between White and the appellees, that the stock was the property of the appellant, subject or liable to the satisfaction of the execution. But, as to the appellant, it had in it no element of conclusiveness, because he was not a party to the suit in which it was rendered, and in no event a bar to a claim [415] of exemption. Not a bar, because in that proceeding the claim could not have been asserted; not a bar, because the statutes and constitution contemplate that the claim of exemption may be interposed at any time before a sale of the property.

The result of the foregoing views is, that the causes of contest were not well assigned, and the court below erred in refusing to strike them out, on the motion of the appellant. The bill of exceptions purports to contain all the evidence: the uncontroverted evidence supports the claim of exemption, and the judgment of the court below, disallowing it, is erroneous.

The judgment of the court below must be reversed, a judgment here rendered allowing the claim of exemption, and the appellees must pay the costs in this court and in the court below.

ESTOPPEL—WHO MAY SET UP.—Estoppel in pais can be set up and relied upon only by a party who has been actually misled to his injury: Union Bank v. Mechanics' Bank, 80 Md. 371; 45 Am. St. Rep. 350, and note. An estoppel must be mutual. It must bind both parties, and one who is not bound by it cannot take advantage of it: First Nat. Bank v. Northwestern Bank, 152 Ill. 296; 43 Am. St. Rep. 247.

EXECUTION—EXEMPTIONS—NECESSITY FOR CLAIMING—WAIVER.—Personal property may be claimed as exempt up to the time of sale when it is taken by virtue of an execution upon a general personal judgment against the defendant: Note to Eltzroth v. Webster, 77 Am. Dec. 79. See Harrington v. Smith, 14 Colo. 376; 20 Am. St. Rep. 272. In Iowa it has been held that such claim must be made at the time of the levy, else the right of exemption, which is purely personal, will be considered waived. Extended note to Brown v. Leitch, 31 Am. Rep. 44. One who sees his exempt property levied on and makes no objection, but, being advised of his right, permits it to be taken, waives his right, and is estopped from asserting it afterward: Angell v. Johnson, 51 Iowa. 625; 33 Am. Rep. 152. See contra, Vanderhorst v. Bacon, 38 Mich. 669; 31 Am. Rep. 328.

LOUISVILLE AND NASHVILLE RAILROAD COMPANY
v. ANCHORS.
[114 ALABAMA, 492.]

NEGLIGENCE, WANTON—WILLFUL INJURY, WHAT CONSTITUTES.—To constitute willful injury there must be design, purpose, and intent to do wrong and inflict the injury; while to constitute wanton negligence, the party doing the act or failing to act must be conscious of his conduct, and, though having no intent to injure, must be conscious, from his knowledge of surrounding circumstances and existing conditions, that his conduct will naturally or probably result in injury.

NEGLIGENCE, WANTON—WILLFUL INJURY.—In an action against a railroad company to recover for the death of an employé a count in the complaint averring that defendant's engineer "wrongfully and willfully failed to blow the whistle or ring the bell," as required by law and "because of such willfulness or wantonness the passenger train of the defendant ran into and against a passenger-car of" another road, thus causing the injury complained of, is defective as a count charging willful injury, because it does not show that the purpose of the defendant, in failing to ring the bell or blow the whistle, was to run into or against such car, nor is such count good as charging wanton negligence, because it does not aver a state of facts from which knowledge can be imputed to the defendant that the natural and probable result of his conduct would result in a collision and the injury complained of.

NEGLIGENCE CAUSING DEATH—PLEADING.—In an action against a railroad company to recover for the death of an employé, a count in the complaint averring that the "engineer negligently permitted and suffered the said locomotive and train to run into and against a passenger-car." thus causing the injury, is sufficient as a count for simple negligence.

NEGLIGENCE, WANTON—WILLFUL INJURY—INSUFFICIENT PLEADING.—In an action against a railroad company to

recover for the death of an employé, a count in the complaint averring that the injury sued for resulted by reason of the willful running of the train at a high rate of speed, but not averring that the
intention or purpose of so running the train was to inflict the injury,
nor that the defendant knew that the probable result of his act
would be to inflict the injury, is insufficient as an averment of willful injury or wanton negligence, although it is also averred that
the defendant willfully caused the train to run into and against a
passenger-car, thus causing the injury complained of.

NEGLIGENCE.—The word "reckless." when applied to negligence, has no legal significance per se which imports other than
simple negligence or a want of due care; but the use of the word
"reckless," in connection with averments of facts to which it refers
and explains, may imply more than mere heedlessness or negligence.

RAILROADS.—AN ELECTRIC CAR-LINE running within
and beyond the limits of a city is a railroad within the meaning of
a statute regulating the duties of railroads whose tracks cross each
other, and requiring them to observe precautionary measures at
crossings.

J. B. Knox, for the appellant.

Carthell & Agee, for the appellee.

498 COLEMAN, J. The defendant in error, as administratrix sued to recover damages for an unlawful injury to J. F. Anchors, which resulted in his death. Each of the ten counts of
the complaint were demurred to by the defendant, and there
were several grounds of each of **499** the demurrers. The demurrer to the second, sixth, and tenth counts raise the question
as to whether these counts charge that the injury was willfully
inflicted, or resulted from such wanton negligence as to be the
equivalent of a willful wrong. The court overruled the demurrer which challenged the sufficiency of these counts in this
respect. We are of opinion the pleader and the trial court mis-
apprehended the nature of a willful injury or wanton negligence
as defined by this court. In the case of Georgia Pac. Ry. Co. v.
Lee, 92 Ala. 262, it was said: "Willful and intentional wrong, a
willingness to inflict injury, cannot be imputed to one who is
without consciousness, from whatever cause, that his conduct
will inevitably or probably lead to wrong and injury." In the
case of Birmingham Ry. etc. Co. v. Bowers, 110 Ala. 328, we said:
"To constitute willful injury, there must be design, purpose, intent to do wrong and inflict the injury." "In wanton negligence,
the party doing the act, or failing to act, is conscious of his conduct, and without having the intent to injure, is conscious, from
his knowledge of existing circumstances and conditions, that his
conduct will naturally or probably result in injury": Louisville
etc. R. R. Co. v. Webb, 97 Ala. 308; Stringer v. Alabama etc. R.
R. Co., 99 Ala. 397; Richmond etc. R. R. Co. v. Vance, 93 Ala.

149; 30 Am. St. Rep. 41; Louisville etc. R. R. Co. v. Richards, 100 Ala. 365.

Apply these principles to the tenth count of the complaint. It avers that "defendant's engineer, Robert Wallace, who had control of the running of the locomotive that propelled said train, wantonly or willfully failed to blow the whistle or ring the bell at least one-fourth of a mile before reaching the regular station or stopping place at Anniston, and said engineer wantonly or willfully failed to continue to ring the bell or blow the whistle at short intervals until he had reached the said stopping place, and *because of such* willfulness or wantonness, the said passenger train of the defendant ran into and against a passenger-car of the Oxford Lake Line at its crossing," etc.   Italics ours. Everything averred in this count might be true, and yet not show that the purpose of the defendant, in failing to ring the bell or blow the whistle, was to run into and against the passenger-car of the Oxford Lake Line.   As a count for willful injury it is defective.   Nor does the count aver a ^{500} state of facts from which a knowledge could be imputed to defendant, that the natural and probable consequences of his conduct would result in a collision.   If the count had averred that defendant willfully failed or refused to blow the whistle or ring the bell with the intent to commit the injury, or willfully refused to ring the bell, having a knowledge that probably the Oxford Lake train at the time was at the crossing, and the natural or probable result of the willful omission would be to collide, the count would have been sufficient.   It may be true that the injury resulted "because of such willfulness" in failing to ring the bell, "or by reason of such speed" as averred in the sixth count, or "whereby" as averred in the second count, and yet the result may not have been within the design or purpose of the engineer of the defendant, nor done or omitted under such circumstances and conditions, which would charge him with a knowledge that the natural or probable consequences of his conduct would be to inflict injury.   We would call attention to the use of the word "reckless" in the second count.   In the case of Kansas City etc. R. R. Co. v. Crocker, 95 Ala. 412, 433, we considered and declared the distinction between the words "willful" and "reckless," and in the case of Stringer v. Alabama Min. R. R. Co., 99 Ala. 397, we declared that the words "gross," "reckless" per se, "when applied to negligence, have no legal significance which import other than simple negligence or a want of due care."   The use of the word "reckless," in connection with averments of facts to which it refers and explains, may imply more than mere heedlessness or negligence. The fourth count charges, that Robert Wallace "negligently .... permitted and suffered the said locomotive and train to run into and against a passenger-car." This averment is sufficient as a count for simple negligence. The legal effect would not be different, if the word "recklessly" had been substituted for the word "negligently" in this count: Alabama etc. R. R. Co. v. Hall, 105 Ala. 599.

Construing the sixth count, our opinion is, the latter clause gives meaning and controls the preceding averments, and, construed as a whole, charges no more than that the death of plaintiff's intestate resulted "by reason of" the willful running of said train at a high rate of speed, but does not aver that the intention or purpose [501] in running the train was to inflict the injury, nor does it aver facts which show that defendant knew that the probable result of such conduct would be to inflict injury: Alabama etc. R. R. Co. v. Hall, 105 Ala. 599. The demurrer to the sixth and tenth counts should have been sustained. The second count charges that the defendant "willfully caused the locomotive and train to run into and against a passenger-car," etc. A similar averment was held sufficient to show a willful injury in the case of Birmingham etc. R. R. Co. v. Jacobs, 92 Ala. 187. It may be that this count is objectionable in that it unites averments of simple negligence with averments showing a willful injury, but no objection was raised on this account, and the demurrer to it was properly overruled: Louisville etc. R. R. Co. v. Markee, 103 Ala. 160; 49 Am. St. Rep. 21.

Section 1145 of the code of 1886 provides as follows: "When the tracks of two railroads cross each other, engineers and conductors must cause the trains of which they are in charge to come to a full stop within one hundred feet of such crossing, and not proceed until they know the way to be clear; the train on the railroad having the older right of way being entitled to cross first." The demurrer raises the question as to whether "the railroad of the Oxford Lake Line, an electric railroad running from Anniston to a point beyond the corporate limits of the city, upon which the plaintiff's intestate was conductor," is a railroad within the meaning of said section 1145.

In the case of the Birmingham etc. R. R. Co. v. Jacobs, 92 Ala. 199, we had occasion to consider sections 1145 and 1173. The question in that case was, whether railroads using dummy engines and operated beyond city limits are subject to these provisions. After careful deliberation, this court reached the conclusion that railroad corporations organized under and by virtue of sections 1918 and 1921 of the code of 1886, as amended by act of February 25, 1887 (Acts 1886-87, p. 144), were not strictly street railways, as contemplated in the statute providing for the organization and operation of street railroads (Code 1886, secs. 1603-1612), and that railroads organized under the act of February 25th, supra, using dummy engines, were subject to said statutory provisions. The question now is, whether a railroad upon which electricity is used as the moving power, [502] is a railroad within the provisions of the statute. The statute itself makes no distinction, and in considering the purposes intended in the adoption of these regulations, we are unable to see any good reason why persons traveling upon electric cars are not entitled to the same protection as those traveling upon cars propelled by steam. Public necessities, even within city limits, demand increased facilities for travel over the horse-car, and many decisions of courts applicable to street railways operated by horses could not be applied without manifest injustice to trains operated by steam or electricity. The speed, economy, and convenience afforded by electricity commend its use even for commercial purposes as well as travel, as superior in some respects to any other motive power thus far applied. A railroad, within the provisions of the statute, does not cease to be such railroad because it may discontinue the use of steam, and substitute that of electricity. The change in the motor power may relieve it from some provisions of the statute, but those which are needful for the protection of life and property continue in force: Birmingham etc. R. R. Co. v. Jacobs, 92 Ala. 199, and authorities cited; Birmingham Ry. etc. Co. v. Baylor, 101 Ala. 498.

Reversed and remanded.

NEGLIGENCE—PLEADING.—An allegation specifying the act, the doing of which caused an injury, and averring generally that it was negligently done, states a cause of action, though it is not apparent from the complaint how the injury resulted from the negligence alleged: Railroad Co. v. Mackey, 53 Ohio St. 370; 53 Am. St. Rep. 641, and note; Louisville etc. R. R. Co. v. Markee, 103 Ala. 160; 49 Am. St. Rep. 21.

NEGLIGENCE — WANTON — PLEADING.— Under a complaint averring simple negligence, the plaintiff should not be permitted to prove willful injury or wanton negligence: Louisville etc. R. R. Co. v. Markee, 103 Ala. 160; 49 Am. St. Rep. 21.

RAILROAD—WHAT IS, WITHIN MEANING OF STATUTE.— The word "railroad" in its broadest signification includes a street railroad, although it extends over the streets of a single city, and is wholly located within the limits of a single county: Bloxham v. Consumers' etc. R. R. Co., 36 Fla. 519; 51 Am. St. Rep. 44, and note.

ALABAMA MINERAL RAILROAD COMPANY v. JONES.

[114 ALABAMA, 519.]

NEGLIGENCE CAUSING DEATH—EVIDENCE OF COLLECTIVE FACT.—In an action to recover for the death of a railroad section hand, alleged to have been caused by negligence in the sudden stopping, under direction of a foreman, of a hand-car immediately in front of another hand-car upon which the deceased was riding, evidence that the place where the accident occurred was a dangerous place to stop is a statement of a collective fact and admissible in evidence.

EVIDENCE.—EXPERT TESTIMONY as to a matter within the common knowledge of the jury is inadmissible.

EVIDENCE—IMPROPER QUESTION—ERROR.—The admission of improper evidence is not reversible error, if it is favorable to the party objecting.

NEGLIGENCE CAUSING DEATH—MEASURE OF DAMAGES—EVIDENCE.—If, in an action to recover for the death of a railroad employé caused by negligence, the evidence is circumstantial as to what proportion of his earnings were consumed in his own support, and hence what amount of pecuniary benefit his dependents enjoyed from such earnings, evidence to show how many and what dependents there were is admissible to aid in determining the pecuniary loss sustained by his death.

NEGLIGENCE CAUSING DEATH—MEASURE OF DAMAGES.—In an action to recover for negligence causing the death of a person leaving a dependent family enjoying support from his earnings and also surplus accumulations, the recovery is not confined to the amount of injury sustained by the loss of such support, but the entire present value of the accumulations may be recovered as well.

NEGLIGENCE CAUSING DEATH — EXPECTANCY OF LIFE—ERRONEOUS INSTRUCTIONS.—In an action to recover for death caused by negligence, the jury must, in assessing damages, take into consideration all the circumstances bearing upon the subject, as disclosed by the evidence, and ascertain what the duration of the party's natural life would have been. Hence, for the court to instruct as to the period of expectancy of life of the deceased as fixed by mortuary tables, is an invasion of the province of the jury and erroneous.

NEGLIGENCE CAUSING DEATH—MEASURE OF DAMAGES.—In an action to recover for a death caused by negligence, recovery may be had in "an amount equal to the present cash value of the decedent's' life to his family dependent upon him, during his expectancy of life."

NEGLIGENCE CAUSING DEATH—MEASURE OF DAMAGES.—In an action to recover for a death caused by negligence, the recovery, if any may be had, may be for an amount equal to the decedent's pecuniary worth to his family, who were dependent upon him, from the time of his death to the time of the trial, added to the present cash value of his pecuniary aid to his family during the balance of- his expectancy of life.

NEGLIGENCE CAUSING DEATH—PROOF AUTHORIZING RECOVERY.—In an action against a railroad company to recover for the death of a section hand by being thrown from a hand-car, where the complaint requires proof that the foreman on a car stopped it suddenly while it was in front of another car on which deceased was riding, while both cars were going at a high rate of

speed, without first ordering the rear car to stop, "or" without notifying those upon it of his intention to stop the car he was on,
proof of either of the alternatives may authorize a recovery, and
proof of both is not necessarily required.

NEGLIGENCE—QUESTION FOR JURY.—In an action to re-
cover for a death caused by negligence in a collision of hand-cars,
it is a question for the jury to determine whether it was negligence
for the foreman of such cars to run them closely following each
other at a high rate of speed over a river bridge.

NEGLIGENCE CAUSING DEATH—IMPROPER INSTRUC-
TIONS.—In an action against a railroad company to recover for the
death of a section hand, caused by being thrown from a hand-car
through the alleged negligence of the section foreman in suddenly
stopping another car in front of the car on which the deceased was
riding while both cars were going at a high rate of speed, when the
evidence shows that such foreman caused the brakes to be suddenly
applied on his car, without signaling those on the rear car to slacken
their speed, charges which instruct the jury under what circumstances the acts of the men on the rear car would authorize a verdict for the defendant, but which ignore the negligence of such foreman taken in connection with such acts, are properly refused. .

Action by Mary A. Jones, as administratrix of the estate of
John Jones against the Alabama Midland Railroad Company,
to recover damages for his death, caused by the alleged negligence of the defendant. Judgment for plaintiff, and the defendant appealed. The following instructions were given at
the request of plaintiff: 1. "If the jury believe from the evidence
that Scott, the section boss of the defendant, ordered the section hands to run the two hand-cars across the bridge, and that
said section hands, in compliance with said order, started across
the bridge with said hand-cars, one following fifteen or twenty
feet behind the other, and that while on the trestle after crossing
the bridge, said Scott, who was on the front car, made a sign
for the hands on said hand-car to stop or check up, without
first ordering the rear car to check up or giving those on said
rear car sufficient notice of his intention to check up the front
car, and that immediately, as soon as those on the rear car
discovered the checking of the front car, one of the hands on the
rear car suddenly put on the brake of said car, and that this
was the best thing to do under the circumstances in order to
avoid a collision between the two cars, and that plaintiff's intestate, John Jones, was on said rear car at the time, and that
he was at his post in discharge of his duty beside one of the
handles of the lever, with his hands upon the same, working
it in order to propel the car, and that said putting on of the
brake snatched the handle out of his hands, and that before he
was able to recover it, the rear car ran into the front car, and
thereby threw the said John Jones to the ground, and killed

him, then they must find for the plaintiff." 2. "If the jury believe from the evidence that Scott, the section boss of defendant, ordered the section hands to run the hand-cars across the bridge, and that said section hands, in compliance with said order, started across the bridge with said hand-cars, one following the other fifteen to twenty-five feet behind the other, and that while on the trestle, after crossing the bridge, the said Scott, who was on the front car, made a sign to the hands on that car to put on the brake and check up, without first ordering the rear car to check up, or giving those on said rear car sufficient notice of his intentions to check the front car, and that immediately, as soon as those on the rear car discovered the checking of the front car, one of the hands on the rear car suddenly put on the brake of said car and that that was the best thing to do under the circumstances in order to avoid a collision of the front car, and that plaintiff's intestate, John Jones, was on said rear car at the time, and that he was at his post of duty, beside one of the handles of the lever, with his hands upon the same, working it in order to propel the car, and that said putting on of the brakes snatched the handles out of his hands, and that before he was able to recover it the rear car ran into the front car and thereby threw said John Jones to the ground and killed him, then they must find for the plaintiff." 3. "If the jury believe from the evidence that John Jones came to his death by reason of section foreman Scott's negligently and carelessly causing his car to be checked up without sufficient notice to those on the rear car, and that by reason of this the rear car collided with the front car, and that said John Jones was thrown out of said rear car and killed, and that he did nothing that contributed proximately to his death, then the jury must find for the plaintiff." 4. "The court charges the jury that if they believe from the evidence that the plaintiff is entitled to recover in this cause, she is entitled to recover an amount equal to the present cost value or pecuniary value of John Jones' life to his family dependent on him during his expectancy of life." 5. "The court charges the jury that if they believe from the evidence that John Jones, at the time of his death, was in good health and of sober habits, and was forty-eight years of age, that his expectancy of life was as much as eighteen years." 6. "If the jury believe from the evidence that the plaintiff is entitled to recover, she is entitled to recover an amount equal to John Jones' pecuniary worth to his family, who were dependent upon him from the time of his death to this time, added to the cash value of his pecuniary worth to his said family during the balance of his expectancy of life." 7. "If there is a conflict in the evidence, then the jury may look to the opportunities and means of knowledge of the various witnesses in determining which of them they will believe." 8. "If the jury believe from the evidence that Bill Scott was section boss, and that John Jones was one of the hands in the employ of said Bill Scott, and that said Bill Scott had control of the running of the two hand-cars spoken of by witnesses, and that while crossing the bridge over the Coosa river, in accordance with his orders at a great rate of speed, and that said hand-cars were running in about fifteen or twenty feet apart, and that just after the two cars had crossed the iron part of the bridge, he gave a signal to the hands on the front car to check up, without first giving warning to those on the rear car, and if they further believe from the evidence that the time said Bill Scott gave a signal to those on the front car, Woods put his foot on the brake and checked it up, and if they further believe from the evidence that the checking of the front car caused Guy to put his foot on the brakes of the second car, and that the handle of the lever was jerked out of John Jones' hands by the putting on of the brake by Guy, and that said rear car ran into the front car and threw John Jones to the ground and killed him, the jury must find for the plaintiff." 9. "If the jury believe from the evidence that at the time John Jones was killed he was in the employ of the Alabama Mineral Railroad Company, and that said Bill Scott was the foreman or section boss, and that deceased was on a hand-car at the time of the accident, and if they further believe that said hand-cars were operated under the direction of said Bill Scott, and that said Bill Scott told the deceased and the other hands to go over the Coosa River bridge as fast as they could, and that in compliance with said orders the hands started across the bridge at a great rate of speed, and that they were running about fifteen or twenty feet apart, and that just after they passed the iron part of the bridge the said Bill Scott waved his hand to those on the front car to slow up, and that John Woods at once placed his foot on the brake of the front car and checked it up, and if they further believe that Lee Benson as soon as John Woods put his foot on the brake, waved to the hindmost car to check up, and that Guy at once placed his foot on the brake, and if they further believe that the placing of Guy's foot on the brake suddenly checked the speed of the car, jerked the handle of the lever out of John Jones' hand; and if they further believe that before he could recover and get hold of the handle, the hindmost car ran into the front car, and threw John Jones off and he was killed, then the plaintiff is entitled to damages." 11. "The jury may look to the opportunities of the witnesses for observing and knowing the facts which they may testify about in determining which witnesses they will believe." The court refused to give the following instructions requested by the defendant. 1. "If the jury believe the evidence, they will find for the defendant." 2. "If the jury believe from the evidence that said front car, upon which said W. A. Scott was riding, was not stopped, or its speed checked suddenly while crossing the Coosa River bridge without notifying those on the car behind of its intention to stop, then they must find for the defendant." 3. "If the jury believe from the evidence that said cars were not run over said river at said time and at a great rate of speed, and that said front car was not stopped suddenly or its speed checked while both cars were going at a high rate of speed and without first ordering the hindmost car to stop, and without notifying those on the hindmost car of the intention to stop, then they must find for the defendant." 4. "If the jury believe from the evidence that Scott before or at the time of checking the speed of the front car, notified those on the rear car to check their speed also, and gave them the usual and customary signal for that purpose, then they must find for the defendant." 5. "The court charges the jury that it was not negligence in the said Scott to run two hand-cars at the same time in the manner in which these cars are shown to have been run across the Coosa River bridge, and if they further find from the evidence that said cars were following one another, and that said Scott who was in charge of both of said cars gave the signal for both to slow up at the same time, that they must find for the defendant." 6. "The court charges the jury that even if they believe from the evidence that John Jones was holding the handle and was thrown loose from the same by the sudden putting on of the brake by John Guy, that then they must find for the defendant." 7. "If the jury believe from the evidence that the other section hands riding on the car with John Jones jerked the handle or lever in front, and caused him to loose his hold of the handle, that then they must find for the defendant." 8. "The court charges the jury that if the evidence leaves them in doubt as to what threw John Jones from said car, that then they must find for the defendant." 10. "The court charges the jury that if they believe from the evidence that the said John Jones was riding along on said car, having only hold of the handle with one hand, that this was not the proper way for the said John Jones to ride, and they must find for the defendant." 12. "The court charges the jury that they may look to the fact, if they find it to be a fact, that no one else fell off of said car, in connection with all the other facts in the case in determining whether or not said Jones was grasping the handle in a manner to properly protect his own safety." 14. "The court charges the jury that it was not negligence to run said cars over said bridge at the rate of speed as shown by the evidence in this case." 15. "The court charges the jury that there is no evidence that W. A. Scott gave any order or signal which required anyone to put on the brake suddenly on either car." 18. "The court charges the jury that if Scott was sitting in a position where his signal could be seen by those riding on the rear car, that then it was not negligence for him not to look back to ascertain whether the same had been seen or not." 19. "The court charges the jury that if they believe from the evidence that Guy promptly obeyed the signal given by Scott, and that he saw it when Scott gave it, and applied the brake in the usual and customary manner, and that this was all the appliance for checking the speed of said cars, that then they must find for the defendant." 20. "If the jury believe that John Woods put on the brake too suddenly, and in an improper manner, and checked the speed of said front car too rapidly, and that that caused the accident, then the plaintiff cannot recover." 24. "The court charges the jury that if they believe from the evidence that the signal was given by Scott for both hand-cars to check their speed at the same time, and that it was known by those on the rear car, and that Guy properly applied the brake in the usual and customary way, that then they must find for the defendant." 25. "The court charges the jury that the plaintiff can only recover nominal damages, if she is entitled to recover at all." 26. "If the jury believe from the evidence that the death of John Jones was caused by accident such as was naturally incident to his employment, then they must find for the defendant."

T. G. Jones, for the appellant.

Browne & Leeper and Longshore & Beavers, for the appellee.

530 HEAD, J.   The leading facts of this case may be found in the report of the former appeal: Jones v. Alabama etc. R. R. Co., 107 Ala. 400.   New questions upon the admission of evidence, and very many instructions given and refused, are predicated for assignments of error on the present appeal.

The cause of action, as stated in the first count of the complaint, was that Scott, section foreman and superintendent of road repairs, in the exercise of such superintendence, negligently ordered and directed plaintiff's intestate and the other section hands to take the two lever cars over the river at once, and at a great rate of speed, and negligently stopped his car suddenly while it was in front of the other car, while both were going at a **531** high rate of speed, and without first ordering the rear car to stop, or notifying those on it of his intention to stop the car he was on, causing the rear car to run into the front car, whereby plaintiff's intestate was knocked off the rear car and killed.

That stated in the second count is, that Scott, the defendant's section foreman, in charge of the two lever cars, the one running closely behind the other, at a high rate of speed, negligently stopped the front car suddenly, without notifying those on the car behind, by reason of which the rear car ran into the front car, whereby plaintiff's intestate was knocked off the rear car and killed.

These allegations were put in issue by the general denial; and the defendant further defended upon a plea of contributory negligence on the part of the intestate, the gravamen of which was that he failed to grasp or hold to the lever or handle of the car on which he was riding (the rear car), as it was his duty to do, but stood at the rear end of the car, and was negligently looking up and down the river over which the cars were passing, or was looking backward without holding onto any part of the car, or the handle thereof, which was an unsafe and dangerous way of crossing said river and trestle on a moving hand-car.   Issue was joined on this plea.   There was evidence tending to support both the complaint and pleas.

Smith Peoples, one of the section hands on the car with the deceased, was permitted to testify that the place where the injury occurred—on the abutting trestle of a river bridge—was a dangerous place to stop.   The defendant's objection to the question calling out the testimony was, that it was illegal, and called for incompetent, inadmissible, and illegal testimony.   The question called for the statement of a collective fact, and answer to it is not reversible error.

The section foreman, expert in the operation of hand-cars, was asked by the defendant to state whether or not the danger of riding on one of the hand-cars while in motion is obvious and patent to a man—whether any man of common sense would know that to be dangerous? A general objection to the question was sustained. We think there was no error in this ruling. It is common knowledge that danger attends riding on a moving hand-car and that this danger is patent and obvious to a man [532] of common sense. If the witness had answered the question affirmatively, the answer would have been declaratory merely of what the jury already knew.

There was no reversible error in allowing the question to be asked the foreman by the plaintiff: "Is it always necessary when four of the hands are on the lever car for all four hands to have hold of the handles, all the time, in order to propel the car at a safe rate of speed?" for the reason, if no other, that the answer of the witness was, "Yes, they should hold to it." The answer was favorable to the defendant.

Witness, Guy, one of the section hands, was asked by defendant, how a person operating the car should grasp the handle The court sustained an objection to the question, but it is shown that the witness, immediately, without objection, explained fully how the handle should be grasped, rendering harmless the error, if any, in the court's ruling.

The evidence was circumstantial as to what proportion of the earnings of deceased were consumed in his own support, and hence what amount of pecuniary benefit the dependent next of kin enjoyed from such earnings. As a circumstance, aiding the solution of this question, it was competent to show how many and what dependents there were, and their ages. Particularly, in view of the cautionary instructions given the jury by the court, in reference to this proof, there was no error in the ruling. The authorities hereafter cited, touching the measure of damages, make a distinction between cases where the entire earnings are consumed in the support of the family and where a portion only is so consumed, leaving a surplus for accumulation, though it seems that in cases where there are dependent families, who are distributees, enjoying support from the earnings, and also surplus accumulations, the plaintiff, administrator, is not confined in his recovery to the amount of injury sustained by the loss of their support, but may recover the entire present value of the accumulations as well. The present record raises no question calling for any further explanation of this distinc-

tion or how it operates, than is stated in Louisville etc. R. R. Co.
v. Trammell, 93 Ala. 350, which gives the dependent family annual benefits.   The writer's own views are that under the statute, which gives the right of action to the administrator for [533]
the benefit of all distributees alike, the measure of damages is
the same in all cases, whether some or all of the distributees
were dependent or not.

The court, at the request of the plaintiff, instructed the jury
that if deceased was, at the time of his death, in good health and
of sober habits, and was forty-eight years of age, his expectancy
of life was as much as eighteen years.   This charge was an invasion of the province of the jury.   In assessing damages, in
cases like this, it devolves upon the jury, upon consideration of
all the circumstances bearing upon the subject, as disclosed by
the evidence, to ascertain what the duration of the party's natural life would have been.   There is no method of ascertaining
it as a positive fact.   The period fixed, in any case, is necessarily
an inference drawn from many conditions and circumstances.
In the same case, different minds of equal intelligence, might
reach different conclusions.   The tables of mortality, computed
upon the experience of life insurance companies, which, being
of such universal recognition, courts will judicially notice, are
not conclusive that the life expectancy of any particular person,
though in good health and of sober habits, should be declared
to be the period they estimate.   It may be stated as a fact generally known that in the system of insurance many conditions
enter as factors in the determination of the hazards and duration of a person's life.   Though good health and sober habits
at the time prevail, there may be other physical infirmities creating extraordinary hazard; such, for instance, as heritable dis-
eases in ancestors, undue relation of height to weight, and the
like.   Again, the occupation the party pursues is of weighty
consideration—whether or not involving extraordinary risk and
danger.   These may all be matters of evidence before the jury
in a given case, and it is for that body to draw the proper inference as to the real duration of the party's natural life.   In the
present case, not only the age, good health, and sober habits of
the deceased were shown in evidence, but he was pursuing an
occupation attended with unusual dangers.   The charge was
bad, in that it withdrew that fact from the consideration of the
jury, as well as because it made the court to draw the inference
which it was alone the province of the jury to draw.

When the case was formerly before us, we held that [534] the two charges requested by the plaintiff and numbered 8 and 9 in the present record ought to have been given. On the trial from which this appeal comes, a question was prominently raised by evidence and is now argued before us, whether or not the deceased, though he may have had hold of the lever or handle, held it with the firmness and care which was reasonably necessary to his safety. The plea, it will be remembered, on both trials, specially, made no complaint of the manner in which the lever was grasped. Its sole complaint was, that deceased did not grasp it at all, but stood at the rear end of the car and was negligently looking up and down the river, over which the cars were passing, or looking backward without holding onto any part of the car or the handle thereof; and there was a special replication, on which issue was joined, which alleged that he was holding to the handles of the car, and continued to so hold until he was knocked loose by the sudden putting on of the brake, etc., without saying anything as to the firmness or careful manner of the grasp. The charges referred to do not submit this question, as to the manner of the grasp, to the jury, but are so framed as to instruct that legal requirements on that point were satisfied if deceased had the handles of the lever in his hands. We will not now determine whether the plea and replication, and the evidence adduced on the last trial, legally raise the question. It may be that they do. It will be safer, on another trial, to so frame the instructions as to submit the question to the jury.

The foregoing remarks apply alike to charges 1 and 2 given for the plaintiff.

The measure of damages, in cases of this character, viz., where the next of kin were dependents and all earnings were consumed in the support of the family, will be understood by consulting the following authorities: Louisville etc. R. R. Co. v. Trammell, 93 Ala. 350; McAdory v. Louisville etc. R. R. Co., 94 Ala. 272; Bromley v. Birmingham etc. R. R. Co., 95 Ala. 397; Louisville etc. R. R. Co. v. Markee, 103 Ala. 160; 49 Am. St. Rep. 21; Alabama etc. R. R. Co v. Hall, 105 Ala. 599. Charge 4 given for the plaintiff seems to come within the rule, except that it omits, in one of its alternatives, to confine the recovery to the present pecuniary value, etc. It authorizes the recovery of the "present cash value, or the pecuniary value," etc.

[535] The defendant cannot complain of the basis of computation authorized by charge 6, given for the plaintiff. Though

charges 7 and 11 given for plaintiff might have been properly refused there was no error in giving them.

Counsel did not insist, in argument, upon the error assigned upon the giving of charge 3 for the plaintiff. We notice, however, that the clause herein, "and that said John Jones was thrown out of said rear car and killed," should have inserted therein before the word, "thrown," the word "thereby," or some change made of similar effect.

The allegations of the first count of the complaint requires proof that the foreman, Scott, stopped his car suddenly while it was in front of the other car, while both cars were going at a high rate of speed, either without first ordering the rear car to stop, or without notifying those on it of his intention to stop the car he was on. Both these alternatives are not required to be proven. The second charge requested by the defendant requires proof of the second alternative, though the first might have been proven. It was properly refused. The third charge requires proof of both alternatives, and hence is bad.

If the defendant's fourth charge meets one of the above-mentioned alternatives, it does not the other. Nor does it meet the averment of the second count. It was properly refused.

It was a question for the jury whether or not it was negligent for Scott to run two hand-cars at the same time in the manner in which these cars are shown to have been run across the bridge. The defendant's fifth charge was, therefore, properly refused.

If the injury was caused by the sudden putting on of the brake by John Guy, we cannot say, as a matter of law, that the act of Guy was negligent or wrongful and was not rendered reasonably necessary by the negligence of the foreman. That question was for the jury. The sixth charge was, therefore, properly refused. The same as to charge 7. Charge 8 states an incorrect measure of proof. Nor are we able to declare as matter of law, as charge 10 does, that it was negligent in deceased to have hold of the handle with one hand only. Charge 12 singles out a particular fact for the special attention [536] of the jury, which justified its refusal. Charges 14, 15, and 18 invaded the province of the jury.

Charge 19 ignores the question whether the order or signal given by the foreman, under all the circumstances, involved negligence on his part. So charge 20 ignores the question whether the acts of John Woods therein stated were superinduced by a negligent order of the foreman.

We think it cannot be stated, as a legal proposition, that if the foreman gave the signal for both the cars to check their speed at the same time, and that it was known by those on the rear car, and that Guy properly applied the brake in the usual and customary way, there was, necessarily, no negligence upon which a recovery for plaintiff might be based. Whether these facts, in view of other circumstances, involve sufficient notification to those on the rear car of the intention to stop, within the meaning of the second count of the complaint, and whether there was no negligence in the fact of giving such a signal, under such circumstances, were for the jury to determine. Charge 24 was, therefore, properly refused.

Charges 25 and 26 as well as the general charge were obviously improper.

Reversed and remanded.

***

NEGLIGENCE CAUSING DEATH—MEASURE OF DAMAGES.—Damages which a widow may recover for the negligent killing of her husband should not be measured by the wealth or poverty of the recipient or giver, but by his earnings, care, health, beneficient and pecuniary contributions given, or in reasonable expectation of being given, to the widow and children as shown by the proof and judged from all the circumstances of the case to be just, but measured by a pecuniary standard: English v. Southern Pac. Co., 13 Utah, 407; 57 Am. St. Rep. 772, and note. The measure of damages for the loss of human life resulting from negligence is the present value of the net income, ascertained by deducting the cost of living and expenditures from the gross income: and no more can be allowed than the present value of accumulation arising from such net income, based upon the expectancy of life: Pickett v. Wilmington etc. R. R. Co., 117 N. C. 616; 53 Am. St. Rep. 611, and note. See Louisville etc. R. R. Co. v. Markee, 103 Ala. 160; 49 Am. St. Rep. 21; Mattise v. Consumers' Ice Mfg. Co., 46 La. Ann. 1535; 49 Am. St. Rep. 356, and note.

NEGLIGENCE—WHEN A QUESTION FOR JURY.—Negligence is a question for the jury where the facts are disputed, or where, from the undisputed facts, different minds may reasonably draw different conclusions as to the existence of negligence: Brotherton v. Manhattan Beach Imp. Co., 48 Neb. 563; 58 Am. St. Rep. 709, and note; Lowe v. Salt Lake City, 13 Utah, 91; 57 Am. St. Rep. 708, and note.

APPEAL—ADMISSION OF IMPROPER EVIDENCE—WHEN NOT REVERSIBLE ERROR.—The admission of inadmissible evidence if harmless is not ground for reversal of judgment: Stewart v. State, 35 Tex. Crim. Rep. 134; 60 Am. St. Rep. 35, and note; St. Louis etc. Ry. Co. v. Hackett, 58 Ark. 381; 41 Am. St. Rep. 105.

WITNESSES—TESTIMONY OF EXPERTS—WHEN NOT ADMISSIBLE.—Expert evidence is incompetent if the facts proposed to be proved are within the common experience of mankind: Mulry v. Mohawk Valley Ins. Co., 5 Gray, 541; 66 Am. Dec. 380; and is not admissible upon a question which the court or jury can decide from the facts; Stumore v. Shaw, 68 Md. 11; 6 Am. St. Rep. 412; monographic note to Hammond v. Woodman, 66 Am. Dec. 229.

ADLER v. VAN KIRK LAND AND CONSTRUCTION CO.

[114 ALABAMA, 551.]

BILLS OF REVIEW—NEWLY DISCOVERED EVIDENCE.— To maintain a bill of review upon newly discovered evidence, the matter must not only be ascertained or discovered after the court has passed its decree, but it must also affirmatively appear, by appropriate averments and evidence, that the party complaining, by the use of reasonable diligence, could not, prior to the decree, have ascertained or discovered it.

BILLS OF REVIEW—DECREE OF FORECLOSURE—NEWLY DISCOVERED EVIDENCE.—If a decree foreclosing a mortgage rendered by consent is based upon a settlement made by the parties eight months prior thereto, the mortgagor cannot, one year after the rendition of such decree, maintain a bill to review it upon the ground of newly discovered evidence, consisting in the fact that such settlement and consent to the decree were induced by false and fraudulent representations made by the mortgagee, the falsity of which was not known to the mortgagor until just prior to the filing of the bill, when it does not appear therefrom that the complainant, prior to the rendition of the decree made any effort to ascertain the truthfulness of the representations upon which the settlement was based or that such effort, if made, would have been unavailing, while it does appear from the bill that the falsity of such representations could have been ascertained by reasonable diligence at the time of the settlement, or at any time prior to the rendition of the decree, or thereafter.

BILLS OF REVIEW—NEWLY DISCOVERED EVIDENCE—MORTGAGE FORECLOSURE.—The relation between mortgagor and mortgagee is not confidential in character but simply that of debtor and creditor, and does not, of itself, relieve the mortgagor, in a settlement with the mortgagee and a consent to a decree foreclosing the mortgage, from his laches in failing to discover the falsity of facts inducing the settlement and subsequently relied upon by him as the basis for a bill of review of the foreclosure decree, on the ground of newly discovered evidence.

JUDGMENTS RENDERED DURING VACATION—VALIDITY.—A decree in equity rendered in vacation, as authorized by statute and in compliance with court rules, has the same validity as if rendered in term time.

JUDGMENTS BY CONSENT—CONCLUSIVENESS.—As between parties sui juris, not standing in confidential relations to each other, and in the absence of fraud in its procurement, a judgment or decree of a court having jurisdiction of the subject matter, and rendered by consent of the parties, though without any ascertainment by the court of the truth of the facts averred, is as binding and conclusive between the parties and their privies as if the suit had been an adversary one, and the conclusions embodied in the decree had been rendered upon controverted facts and due consideration thereof by the court.

JUDGMENTS BY CONSENT—REVIEW OF.—Consent to the rendition of a decree in foreclosure is a waiver of error precluding a review upon appeal, and, as a general rule, by bill of review.

JUDGMENTS BY CONSENT—BILL OF REVIEW.—To maintain a bill of review to impeach for fraud a decree rendered by consent, it must be averred and proved that the decree, or the consent upon which it was based, was procured by fraud practiced in

the act of obtaining it, as distinguished from fraud which vitiates
the cause of action and can be interposed only as a defense thereto.

J. P. Tillman and J. B. Knox, for the appellants.

G. Macdonald, for the appellee.

556 BRICKELL, C. J.   On the twenty-fourth day of March,
1894, by consent of parties, a decree was entered by the chancery court of Escambia county, in vacation, upon a submission
duly made by the parties under the statute and rule 80a of chancery practice, for a final decree in vacation, in favor of Morris
Adler against the Van Kirk Land and Construction Company,
foreclosing a mortgage upon a large body of lands executed by
that company to Worthington, Elliott & De Bardeleben, and by
them assigned, together with the demands thereby secured, to
said Adler.   After the register, proceeding to the execution of
the decree, had advertised the lands for sale, on the ninth day
of February, 1895, the land and construction company filed the
bill in this cause, seeking to review the proceedings had, and the
decree rendered in the foreclosure suit, and to vacate and set
aside the decree, and for an accounting, and, as an incident to
the main relief, prayed an order temporarily restraining the
sale under the decree.

The bill is essentially a bill of review, based upon alleged
newly discovered evidence, which, it is the theory of the bill,
shows that, by false and fraudulent representations made several months prior to the rendition of the consent decree, upon
an accounting and settlement then had between the parties
touching the demands secured by the mortgage, the land and
construction company, relying upon such representations and
believing them to be true, had been induced to admit and to
bind itself to pay an amount largely in excess of what was in
fact owing by it upon those demands, which amount, by the
consent decree, the company was ordered. to pay in redemption
of the mortgage.   The chancellor overruled a motion interposed by the defendants, the appellants here, to dismiss the bill
for want of equity: and that ruling is the only error assigned.

The argument in support of the motion and against the ruling of the chancellor is, that while in the bill it is averred that
the fraud alleged was not discovered by **557** the complainant
until after the consent decree was entered, the bill is wholly
wanting in averments showing the exercise of any diligence
whatever by the complainant, its officers or agents, to ascertain
the facts out of which the fraud arose, or the evidence relied

upon to establish it, or that such facts or evidence, by the use of
reasonable diligence, could not have been discovered prior to
the rendition of the decree or the execution of the agreement
upon which it was based. '

The doctrine is now too well settled to admit of controversy,
and is upheld by a sound and conservative public policy, that
to maintain a bill of review upon newly discovered evidence the
matter must not only be new, that is, ascertained or discovered
after the court has passed its decree, but it must also affirmatively appear, by appropriate averments and by proof, that the
party complaining, by the use of reasonable diligence, could
not have, prior to the decree, ascertained or discovered it. If
such matter was known to him before decree entered, and he
failed to avail himself of it, or if unknown, but by the exercise
of proper diligence he could have known it, the court will not
afford him relief. A wrong may have been inflicted, rather
than a right enforced, by the decree; yet, according to the uniformly declared policy of the court, it is better that such wrong
should go unredressed, than that the solemn decree of the court
should be set aside at the suit of a party who, having had his
day in court, failed, by reason of his own negligence or laches,
to timely present the matter of his defense for adjudication.
Diligence in this respect is of the essence of the equity of the
bill; laches or negligence is as fatal to relief as the actual absence of a matter of defense. In Young v. Keighley, 16 Ves.
348, Lord Eldon says: "The question always is, not what the
plaintiff knew, but what, using reasonable diligence, he might
have known"; and this court, in Banks v. Long, 79 Ala. 219,
speaking through Chief Justice Stone, said: "The equity of a
bill of review for newly discovered testimony, is the fact that it
is newly discovered. and that, with the other testimony, it entitles the complaint to a decree different—beneficially different—
from that rendered in the cause. It must be newly discovered;
for, if known before the trial, or if with proper diligence it
would have been known, this is a complete bar to such
relief." This principle is uniformly [558] recognized and upheld by the text-writers and adjudged cases: Story's Equity
Pleading, sec. 414; 2 Daniell's Chancery Pleading and Practice,
5th ed.. 1578; 2 Beach's Modern Equity Practice, sec. 862: Dexter
v. Arnold, 5 Mason, 312, 321; Wiser v. Blachly, 2 Johns. Ch. 488;
Traphagen v. Voorhees, 45 N. J. Eq. 41; Davis etc. Co. v. Dunbar, 29 W. Va. 617; Murrell v. Smith, 51 Ala. 301; Randall v.
Payne, 1 Tenn. Ch. 142. Considering a similar question, in

Waring v. Lewis, 53 Ala. 625, the court said: "There must be an end to litigation; and without offending principles of public policy, endangering the order and peace of society, and deranging the whole structure of our judicial system, a court of equity cannot intervene against the decree or judgment of a court of competent jurisdiction, because of facts known, or capable of discovery by reasonable inquiry, at the time of its rendition. Fraudulent practices or concealments may be resorted to by an unscrupulous suitor; witnesses may be corrupted, or evidence suppressed, and an unjust, unconscientious judgment wrested from the court; these must have been unknown, and reasonable diligence not sufficient to have guarded against them; the judgment must stand, or the conservatism of the law will be violated: Freeman on Judgments, secs. 493-506."

Turning to the bill, an examination of its averments leaves it free from doubt that it wholly fails to show that the complainant made any effort whatever, prior to the rendition of the consent decree, to ascertain for itself the true status of the accounts between it and Worthington, Elliott & De Bardeleben, secured by the mortgage, or to ascertain whether the representations made upon the settlement were true or false; nor does the bill contain any averment that shows or even tends to show that such effort, if made, would have been unavailing and fruitless. The settlement was effected in July, 1893, more than eight months before the agreement was made for the consent decree, and before that decree was entered and payment of the amount then agreed upon as due from the company to Worthington, Elliott & De Bardeleben, was extended until the twenty-seventh day of December, 1893, the company executed to them its several promissory notes in evidence of the indebtedness. Not only is this true, but it is fair to presume from the averments of the bill and the exhibits thereto, that, prior to the [550] settlement, the company had several months in which to ascertain the extent of its liability upon the secured demands. It was not until Adler was proceeding to have his decree executed by a sale, nearly one year after its rendition, that the company, for the first time, so far as disclosed by the bill, took any steps to ascertain whether the representations made upon the settlement were true or false. So far as disclosed by the bill, it then did what it could easily have done before; it caused estimates to be made of the embankment and excavation done by Worthington, Elliott & De Bardeleben under the contract with the Mobile & Girard Railroad Company, and inquiries to be made as to payments made on the

indorsed note by Worthington, Elliott & De Bardeleben; and
upon information thus and for the first time obtained, it files
its bill, seeking to have the consent decree vacated and set aside,
and the account between the parties reopened. It is a clear inference from the averments of the bill that the complainant was as
fully possessed of the facilities for prosecuting its inquiries before as it was after the consent decree was entered; that it then
knew of the location of the railroad upon which the work was
done, and of the holder and owner of the indorsed note, and its
place of business. Manifestly, such conduct constitutes negligence or laches that bars relief in cases involving the principle
under consideration. However much the court might desire to
relieve against the decree, it is powerless to grant any relief
consistently with well-settled principles and a true regard to a
sound and conservative public policy.

The only pretense of an excuse offered in the bill for this
remarkable supineness is, that the complainant, its officers and
agents, relied implicitly on the representations, which are alleged to have been made by a member of the firm of Worthington, Elliott & De Bardeleben, believing them to be true, and not
having any reason to suspect that they were untrue. The only
relation shown by the bill to have existed between the complainant and Worthington, Elliott & De Bardeleben is that of
mortgagor and mortgagee. Such relation is, so far as the question under consideration is concerned, one merely of debtor and
creditor, the creditor holding the mortgage as security for his
debt; this relation is not one of a confidential character: Pauling
v. Creagh, 54 Ala. **560** 657; O'Bear Jewelry Co. v. Volfer, 106
Ala. 205; 54 Am. St. Rep. 31. In Otis v. Dargan, 53 Ala. 178,
legatees sought to excuse their laches by asserting confidence
reposed by them in the executor of the testator, in a case involving a like principle with the one under consideration; but
the court held the excuse insufficient, saying: "They reposed
confidence in the appellee, it is alleged; but there is no evidence
that it was in any other degree than such confidence as is usually
extended from one person to another in the ordinary transactions
of life. The confidence, the trust, which, when abused, will invoke the aid of a court of equity is not shown to have existed,
except so far as it may be deduced from the relation of executor
and legatee in every case."

Whether the relation of trust and confidence, if it had existed
between the complainant and Worthington, Elliott & De Bardeleben would have relieved the complainant from its laches, it

is not material here to consider; for no such relation existed between them, and the complainant, in relying with implicit confidence upon the representations made to it, did so at its peril. To admit of such an excuse would be, in effect, to destroy the principles so well established and so essential to the conservatism of the law.

It is disclosed by the bill that the decree complained of was rendered in vacation upon a submission had in vacation. The code authorizes the rendition of final decrees at any time, whether in term time or vacation, by consent of parties or their counsel: Code 1886, sec. 3593. The bill shows that the decree was rendered by consent of parties, and the copy of the decree exhibited with the bill, shows that rule 80 a of chancery practice was strictly complied with. The decree was, therefore, of the same validity as if it had been rendered in term time.

It is averred in the bill that the decree in the foreclosure suit was "solely upon the consent of the parties to said cause, and that no judicial ascertainment of the facts stated in the bill filed in said cause was ever had"; and that "said consent decree does not and did not constitute an adjudication of said cause." The purpose of the pleader in making this averment was, doubtless, to state as a fact that the decree was merely a consent decree, a decree agreed upon by the parties, and upon [561] such consent rendered by the court, without an ascertainment of the truth of the facts averred in the bill, or of the rights .of the parties therein asserted; and, as a conclusion of law flowing from these facts, that the decree does not operate an adjudication against the land and construction company of the matters embraced in the lis pendens of the foreclosure suit; and the argument is, that the decree is not an estoppel of record against the company as to the amount by the decree declared to be owing upon the demands secured by the mortgage.

Whatever effect such a conclusion, if logically deducible from the premises stated, would have upon the rights of the parties in this cause, under the averments contained in the bill, it is not necessary to consider; and this because the conclusion is a non sequitur. In the absence of fraud in its procurement, and between parties sui juris, who are competent to make the consent not standing in confidential relations to each other, a judgment or decree of a court having jurisdiction of the subject matter, rendered by consent of parties, though without any ascertainment by the court of the truth of the facts averred, is, according to the great weight of American authority, as binding and conclusive between the parties and their privies as if the suit had been an adversary one, and the conclusions embodied in the decree had been rendered upon controverted issues of fact and a due consideration thereof by the court: Freeman on Judgments, sec. 330; 2 Black on Judgments, sec. 705; Gifford v. Thorn, 9 N. J. Eq. 722; French v. Shotwell, 5 Johns. Ch. 568; Walsh v. Walsh, 116 Mass. 383; 17 Am. Rep. 162; Dunman v. Hartwell, 9 Tex. 495; 60 Am. Dec. 177; Nashville etc. Ry. Co. v. United States, 113 U. S. 261; Curry v. Peebles, 83 Ala. 228; Rogers v. Prattville Mfg. Co., 81 Ala. 483; 60 Am. Rep. 171; Patillo v. Taylor, 83 Ala. 233.

The fact that the decree in the foreclosure suit was rendered by consent of parties does not, therefore, detract from its dignity, or lessen its conclusiveness, as an adjudication between the parties. Not only is such its effect, but its consent is a waiver of error, precluding a review of the decree upon appeal and, as a general rule, upon a bill of review: Thompson v. Maxwell, 95 U. S. 391; Nashville etc. Ry. Co. v. United States, 113 U. S. 266; 2 Daniell's Chancery Pleading and Practice, 5th Am. ed., 1576; ⁵⁰² Dunman v. Hartwell, 9 Tex. 495; 60 Am. Dec. 176; Curry v. Peebles, 83 Ala. 227.

As an original bill, or as an original bill in the nature of a bill of review seeking to impeach the consent decree for fraud it is equally without equity, for the reason that the fraud charged does not relate to the procurement of the decree, or of the consent upon which it was based, but to the accounting and settlement had between the parties in July, 1893, and to the consideration of the notes which were executed in pursuance of the accounting and settlement. If the allegations of the bill charging the fraud were all true, they would have constituted pro tanto a defense to any suit brought for the collection of the notes or of the debts evidenced thereby, and, therefore, any suit brought to foreclose the mortgage. As a legal question, the fraud charged was no more than any other defense the complainant might have had to the foreclosure suit; and to allow relief to be granted in this case upon such allegations would open the doors of a court of equity to every defendant who has, by negligent failure to interpose his defense, suffered an unjust judgment or decree to be rendered against him. As we have seen, this would be contrary to the well-settled rules of that court. To give equity to such a bill it must be clearly shown that the decree or the consent upon which it was based, was procured by fraud; that the fraud was practiced in the act of ob-

taining the decree or the consent therefor. The principle is too
well settled to admit of controversy. In Stratton v. Allen, 16
N. J. Eq. 231, the chancellor says: "It seems to be conclusively
settled that a judgment can only be impeached in a court of
equity for fraud in its concoction"; and in United States v.
Throckmorton, 98 U. S. 61, it is said: "The acts for which a
court of equity will, on account of fraud, set aside or annul a
judgment or decree between the same parties, rendered by a
court of competent jurisdiction, have relation to frauds, extrinsic or collateral to the matter tried by the first court, and not
a fraud in the matter on which the decree was rendered." The
principle is thus clearly expressed by Mr. Freeman in his work
on Judgments, section 489: "It must be borne in mind that it
is not fraud in the cause of action, but fraud in its management,
which entitles a party to relief. The fraud for which a [563] judgment may be vacated or enjoined in equity must be in the procurement of judgment. If the cause of action is vitiated by
fraud, this is a defense which must be interposed, and unless
its interposition is prevented by fraud, it cannot be asserted
against the judgment; for judgments are impeachable for those
frauds only which are extrinsic to the merits of the case, and
by which the court has been imposed upon or misled into a
false judgment. They are not impeachable for frauds relating
to the merits between the parties." The principle has been
frequently declared by this court: Watts v. Frazer, 80 Ala. 188;
Humphreys v. Burleson, 72 Ala. 1; Noble v. Moses, 74 Ala. 604;
Cromelin v. McCauley, 67 Ala. 542; Curry v. Peebles, 83 Ala. 227.

In any aspect in which the bill may be considered, it is without equity, and the chancellor should have sustained appellant's
motion and dismissed the bill.

The statute under which this appeal is taken provides that
"if the decree of the chancellor be reversed, the court shall
render such decree as should have been rendered by the chancellor." It is, therefore, mandatory upon this court, to render
a decree, reversing the decree of the chancellor and dismissing
the bill for want of equity.

Reversed and rendered. ————

BILLS OF REVIEW FOR NEWLY DISCOVERED MATTER.—
Newly discovered matter, to warrant a bill of review, must be so
material as to entitle the petitioner to a decree, or to render a decree
in his favor very probable; and the petitioner must show not only
that it came to his knowledge after the fit time for using it, but
also that with reasonable diligence he could not have known of it in
time: Simpson v. Watts, 6 Rich. Eq. 364; 62 Am. Dec. 392; monographic note to Brewer v. Bowman, 20 Am. Dec. 168.

BILLS OF REVIEW.—For an exhaustive treatment of bills of review, their nature, scope, and use, see the monographic note to Brewer v. Bowman, 20 Am. Dec. 160-175.

JUDGMENTS BY CONSENT of the parties, or upon their stipulation, should be accorded the same force as other judgments: Short v. Taylor, 137 Mo. 517; 59 Am. St. Rep. 508, and note.

JUDGMENTS—RENDITION IN VACATION.—A judgment rendered in vacation and entered as of the preceding term is valid, if such entry was in accordance with the agreement of the parties entered in open court: King v. Green, 2 Stew. 133; 19 Am. Dec. 46. But, generally, judgments rendered in vacation are without jurisdiction and void: Davis v. Fish, 1 G. Greene, 406; 48 Am. Dec. 387; In re Terrill, 52 Kan. 29; 39 Am. St. Rep. 327.

MORTGAGE — RELATIONS BETWEEN MORTGAGOR AND MORTGAGEE.—The relation of mortgagor and mortgagee is peculiar, and the decisions touching the rights and interests of each are not entirely harmonious: Extended note to Cotton v. Carlisle, 7 Am. St. Rep. 31. This confusion is due largely to the difference between the equitable and common-law views of mortgages, and to the general adoption in the United States of the equitable conception of a mortgage: Monographic note to Bradbury v. Davenport, 55 Am. St. Rep. 101. Ordinarily, the relation between the parties to a mortgage is not one of trust: Extended note to King v. Cushman, 89 Am. Dec. 372. It is not fiduciary where the mortgage does not convey the legal title nor give the mortgagee any control over the estate: De Martin v. Phelan, 115 Cal, 538; 56 Am. St. Rep. 115, and see the note thereto criticising the case to which it is appended.

Hall *v.* Henderson.

[114 Alabama, 601.]

CORPORATIONS—CREDITOR'S BILLS AGAINST.—A judgment creditor of an insolvent corporation, with a return of execution "no property found," may maintain a bill in equity on behalf of himself alone, to subject the equitable assets of such corporation to the payment of his debt.

EQUITY PLEADING—MULTIFARIOUSNESS.—A bill in equity may be framed in a double aspect, embracing alternative averments for relief, provided each aspect entitles the complainant to substantially the same relief, and the same defenses are applicable to each.

CORPORATIONS—CREDITOR'S BILL AGAINST—MULTIFARIOUSNESS.—A bill by a judgment creditor of an insolvent corporation, with a return of execution "no property found," against a stockholder in such corporation to reach his unpaid subscription to the extent of the judgment, is not multifarious or inconsistent because it seeks in the alternative, if the subscription has been paid, to reach for the same purpose property of the corporation which such subscriber has received from its officers with their knowledge that the corporation has received no consideration therefor.

Tompkins & Troy and Gunter & Gunter, for the appellants.

J. M. & P. W. White and R. L. Harmon, for the appellee.

⁶⁰⁶ HARALSON, J. This bill was filed, not to administer the assets of an insolvent corporation for the benefit of all its creditors, on the theory, no longer obtaining in this court, that the stock and other property of a corporation is deemed a trust fund for the payment of the debts of the corporation, but it is one by appellants, a single judgment creditor of the corporation, with a return of execution "no property found," to reach equitable assets of the corporation in satisfaction of their judgment at law, and filed for such purpose on two theories, in reference to the same transaction.

1. The defendant, Henderson, as is shown, subscribed to the capital stock of the Alabama Terminal & Improvement Company, a corporation under the laws of this state, the sum of thirty thousand dollars, which, by the terms of subscription, became due and payable. He was a director and the treasurer of said corporation, and co-operated with J. W. Woolfolk, who was president and general manager, and who, as such, had the entire control and management of the business of said corporation, as said Henderson well knew. A. C. Saportas was also a director, who, it is alleged, was entirely under the control and management of said Woolfolk, in reference to the management of the business of said terminal company. It is alleged, as presenting Henderson's claim, that he asserts that he has paid his said subscription of stock in full, and that afterward he sold and transferred the same to said J. W. Woolfolk and A. C. Saportas— to one or both of them, and that they, or the one buying his stock, agreed to pay him thirty thousand dollars therefor.

The bill avers, touching this transaction, that if said sale and assignment were made to said Woolfolk and Saportas, as claimed by Henderson, it was merely colorable, and was in fact a sale of said stock to the said terminal company; that said Henderson was of ample ability to pay and satisfy his said debt and liability to ⁶⁰⁷ said company, but was anxious and desirous to escape therefrom; and that he knew that said Woolfolk was largely indebted to said company for his own subscription of stock and otherwise, and said company was also largely indebted, and hastening to insolvency. It is also averred that said Henderson well knew that said Woolfolk was, at the time, carrying out a scheme for withdrawing a very large amount of the assets of said company from its treasury, by buying up at par, in the name of the company, large amounts of the stock of the subscribers to its capital stock, and paying for the same with the assets of the company without any authority whatever—

the persons thus favored by said Woolfolk being the brothers
and relations, partners and neighbors of said Henderson; that
said Woolfolk, as president and general manager, having incurred large debts for the company, and being unable to use
to advantage the assets in his hands belonging to the company,
owing to the financial depression in the country, proposed to a
number of subscribers for stock of said company residing at
Troy, Alabama, among whom were the said Henderson and his
brothers, relatives, partners, and acquaintances, that they could
get rid of their stock and avoid all liability therefor, and at
the same time provide for his present need of money, by paying
in cash their subscriptions for stock, and by his buying the stock
thus paid for, in the name of and for the company, and paying
for the same in assets of the company in his hands at a certain
price, generally, in bonds of the Alabama Midland Railroad
Company, belonging to the said improvement company, at
eighty-five cents on the dollar; and this plan was carried out
with a number of said subscribers, of all of which said Henderson was informed.

But, as to said Henderson and in his case, it is averred, that
on account of his relation to said company, or for some other
reason, for his supposed security it was arranged, that he should
pay up his stock subscription of thirty thousand dollars in full,
and that said Woolfolk and Saportas should buy his stock and
execute to him their three notes, each for ten thousand dollars,
payable, respectively, in thirty, forty-five, and sixty days from
date, the said Henderson retaining the stock as collateral for
securing their payment; and that these notes should be charged
up to and paid by said company, as a purchase by it of said
stock, and this plan [608] was carried into effect between them;
that said notes, on the 5th of January, 1891, were entered on the
books of the company on bills payable account, as debtor, in
the sum of thirty thousand dollars, and a corresponding entry
on the credit side of the cash-book of said company, was made
in these words: "Investment Acct. Dr. Bought of Fox Henderson 300 shares capital stock of A. T. & I. Co. In suspense.
$30.000"; that said notes were renewed from time to time, and
continued on the books of the company as its obligations, and
were paid in part, from time to time, out of the funds of said
company, of all of which said Henderson had full knowledge;
that at the time of such payments, said Henderson had good
reasons to know that said company was largely indebted, if not
wholly insolvent, and that the use of said company's money and

assets in the payment and discharge of said notes was a fraud upon complainants and the creditors of said company, and said Henderson received of the money and assets of said company, in the manner aforesaid, after the fifth day of January, 1891— the date of the entry of said transaction on the books of the company—the sum of, to wit, twenty-five thousand dollars.

It is again averred, in this connection, that said Henderson never, in fact, paid up his said subscription in full; that the said Woolfolk, in making the settlement with him, allowed him credits for fifteen thousand dollars, or other large sum, to which he was not legally entitled, and that such amount, with interest, in addition to said sum received by him from the assets of said company, since the 5th of January, 1891, is still due and unpaid upon said subscription to the capital stock of said company; so that, as complainants aver, the said Henderson has never, in fact, made any bona fide payment of his said subscription to the capital stock of said company, but that he still owes the same.

The foregoing presents the case as made by the bill in its first aspect. If its averments are true, one of two things is certain, either that Henderson has made no valid payment at all on his stock, and still owes the same, or that, if he has made any payment, he still owes a large amount of money thereon; and, in either event, by the alleged fraudulent devices resorted to by defendant, Woolfolk, and Saportas, to cover up and shield the stock, the right of complainants at law to subject the property to their judgment is obstructed, entitling them, therefore, to the aid of a court of equity to remove the obstructions which prevent them from so doing, and to subject equitable assets to the payment of said judgment: Allen v. Montgomery R. R. Co., 11 Ala. 447.

The act of February 18, 1895 (Acts 1894-95, p. 881), amending section 2972 of the code, provides that "a judgment creditor of a corporation, having an execution returned 'no property found,' may by garnishment subject the unpaid subscription of any stockholder in such corporation to the payment of his debts without giving bond or security, and without regard to whether the corporation can maintain suit against such stockholder for such unpaid subscription or not; or such creditor may proceed in equity against any one or more of such stockholders, and subject such unpaid subscription without joining the other subscribers, or stockholders, and without regard to whether the corporation has called for such unpaid subscriptions and could maintain suit therefor, or not." The act, in terms, expressly authorizes a single judgment creditor to proceed in equity to subject unpaid subscriptions to his debts. A decree in any case of the kind, therefore, would necessarily be a money decree for the amount of unpaid subscription, if the creditor's debt is equal thereto, or for so much thereof as would equal his debt: Hatch v. Dana, 101 U. S. 205. It is clear, then, that should the court ascertain that Henderson has not paid up his subscription to the stock of the said company, as is averred in the bill, in its first aspect, it would, after ascertaining the amount due by him, whether in whole as subscribed or only as a balance due thereon, render a money decree against him within the limits of the complainants' judgment, for the amount so ascertained to be owing by him. It would look through the alleged fraudulent devices resorted to to shield defendant from liability, and subject the unpaid stock as an equitable asset to the payment of the judgment, which an execution on the judgment cannot now reach. There is nothing in O'Bear Jewelry Co. v. Volfer, 106 Ala. 205, 54 Am. St. Rep. 31, opposed to what is here said.

2. The second or alternative aspect in which the bill is filed is presented in the following language, the pertinency of which is dependent in large measure upon the preceding averments as above recited: "But [610] if orators are mistaken in the foregoing averment as to the subscription of the capital stock of said company not having been paid, they aver that subsequent to the 5th of January, 1891, the said Fox Henderson being a director and treasurer of said company, received assets of said company amounting to thirty thousand dollars, or other large sum knowingly, and without proper or legal consideration to said company, which he is liable for, with interest." This averment is stated following and in connection with the ones before referred to, to the effect that said Henderson had received of the money and assets of said company large sums of money and other assets to which he was not entitled, the receipt of which was a fraud upon complainants and the creditors of the company. In this aspect, the object and prayer of the bill is, that said Henderson may be decreed to pay such money and assets of said improvement company, which were improperly received and converted by him, and that complainants' debt may be paid out of the same.

The demurrer to the bill, in the ground mainly relied on, is, that it is filed in the alternative, or in a double aspect, presenting inconsistent and repugnant claims for relief; the relief that could be granted in one aspect being materially variant from the relief that could be granted in the other. The court overruled this ground of demurrer. We have deemed it important, however, to fully consider it, for the purpose of another trial, and to settle the main contention on demurrer.

The rule on that subject, as settled in this court, is, that a bill in equity may be framed in a double aspect, embracing alternate averments for relief, provided each aspect entitles the complainant to substantially the same relief, and the same defenses are applicable to each. If the causes of action presented are so distinct as to require inconsistent and repugnant reliefs, and different defenses, the bill is demurrable on the grounds of multifariousness: Adams v. Sayre, 70 Ala. 318; Bolman v. Lohman, 74 Ala. 510; Globe etc. Co. v. Thacher, 87 Ala. 464.

When the purpose of a bill is single in seeking satisfaction of the complainant's demand out of the debtor's property, which is alleged to have been fraudulently conveyed, or attempted to be placed beyond the reach of execution, it is not multifarious, as we have held, [611] although it is exhibited against several fraudulent grantors. Where fraud permeates the whole transaction, it imparts to the suit a singleness of object and purpose: Handley v. Heflin, 84 Ala. 604; Hinds v. Hinds, 80 Ala. 227. In Allen v. Montgomery R. R. Co., 11 Ala. 437, referred to above, judgment creditors of the railroad company were suing to obtain payment of their judgments by proceedings against the stockholders, for their unpaid shares of stock, and against its vendee for the proceeds of the property alleged to have been fraudulently conveyed to him, and the bill was held not to be subject to the objection of multifariousness. The court said: "The object of the bill is to reach the equitable assets of the corporation in satisfaction of the complainant's judgment at law. These assets, it seems, are supposed to be of two sorts: 1. Those arising from the right of the corporation to call in its unpaid stock; and 2. Those which may be produced by setting aside the alleged illegal conveyance. Now, if this is true, the stockholders have no concern with the allegations which affect the deed; but, supposing the unpaid subscriptions and the property conveyed to be assets of the company, the creditor has the right to pursue them as such, and is entitled to the aid of a court of equity to remove the obstructions which prevent him from doing so. In Brinkerhoff v. Brown, 6 Johns. Ch. 139, the object of the bill, as it is here, was to set aside conveyances as well as to compel payment from defaulting stockholders."

The case before us is stronger than the one just quoted from, for here the same person, Henderson, is the alleged defaulting stockholder, and the party to whom it is alleged the assets of the corporation have been fraudulently transferred, in order to defeat complainants' judgment.

It will not be denied that a debtor cannot give away his property as against his creditors, and that one who acquires it from a donee, with notice, is in no better attitude, as to the creditor, than the donee. Woolfolk and Saportas had no right, as officers of the corporation, to appropriate its assets toward the payment of their own obligations, even if authorized by the company to do so, and if Henderson is the holder of money or property of the said company, which passed out of the company without consideration, as it is alleged, and he knew [612] that fact, he holds in fraud of the company's creditors, and in trust for them: Wait on Fraudulent Conveyances, secs. 383-385. To the extent of such a holding a decree would be rendered against him for the satisfaction of a judgment creditor of the company.

Each aspect of the case entitles the complainants to substantially the same relief, and the same defenses are applicable to each. There is no inconsistency or repugnancy of relief. The decree of the court is flexible and adjustable to reach the equities of the case. The fraud alleged in the transaction is the same in either alternative, entitling the complainants to the same character of relief in either case.

The court sustained the demurrer on the first, eleventh, twelfth, and thirteenth grounds, and overruled it as to the others. The bill was amended to meet the objection raised by the first ground. The eleventh, twelfth and thirteenth raised the objection in different forms, but the same in substance, that the bill was not a general creditors' bill, filed for the benefit of all the creditors of the corporation. In this there was error. We find no fault with the decree otherwise. It is reversed, and one will be here rendered overruling the demurrer. The defendant is allowed thirty days in which to answer.

Reversed, rendered, and remanded.

Brickell, C. J., not sitting.

CREDITORS' SUIT—USE AND OBJECT—PREREQUISITES.—
The nature, purpose, or scope of a creditor's bill is merely to bring into exercise the equitable powers of the court to enforce the satisfaction of a judgment by means of an equitable execution, because execution at law cannot be had: Pierstoff v. Jorges, 86 Wis. 128; 39 Am. St. Rep. 881. An execution must have issued and been re-

turned unsatisfied: Herrlich v. Kaufman, 99 Cal. 271; 37 Am. St.
Rep. 50, and note; Gilbert v. Stockman, 81 Wis. 602; 29 Am. St. Rep.
922, and note. See the monographic note to Massey v. Gorton, 90 Am.
Dec. 288-301.

CREDITORS' SUIT TO RECOVER UNPAID STOCK SUBSCRIP-
TIONS.—In equity a creditor's bill may be maintained by the creditors of a corporation against the stockholders who have not paid up
their stock subscriptions: Savings Bank v. Butchers' etc. Bank, 107
Mo. 133; 28 Am. St. Rep. 405. See monographic note to Thompson v.
Reno Sav. Bank, 3 Am. St. Rep. 812, 815; monographic note to Massey
v. Gorton, 90 Am. Dec. 295.

PLEADING IN EQUITY—MULTIFARIOUSNESS.—No general
principle in regard to multifariousness can be extracted from the
cases; on the one hand, multiplicity of actions is to be avoided, and
on the other hand, the blending in one suit of distinct and incon-
gruous claims and liabilities: Johnson v. Brown, 2 Humph. 327; 37
Am. Dec. 556. The objection of multifariousness is discouraged by
the courts where it would defeat, instead of promote, the ends of
justice: Marshall v. Means, 12 Ga. 61; 56 Am. Dec. 444. As to when
a bill is not multifarious, see Varick v. Smith, 5 Paige, 137; 28 Am.
Dec. 417, and note; Ruhey v. Barnett, 12 Mo. 3; 49 Am. Dec. 112.
As to when it is multifarious and demurrable, see Stuart v. Coalter,
4 Rand. 74; 15 Am. Dec. 731; Ohio etc. Co. v. Merchants' etc. Co., 11
Humph. 1; 53 Am. Dec. 742.

CASES

IN THE

SUPREME COURT

OF

ARKANSAS.

CLEMENTS v. CRAWFORD COUNTY BANK.

[64 ARKANSAS, 7.]

HOMESTEAD.—WHERE TWO PARCELS OF LAND COR-
NER WITH EACH OTHER, they are contiguous, and there is nothing unreasonable or unjust in holding that they may be selected and
held as a homestead where they do not exceed the legal area or
value.

HOMESTEAD.—THE PLATTING OF PART OF A HOME-
STEAD INTO LOTS and naming it as a village, and the filing of
the plat and the selling of part of the lots do not create a town or
village, so as to confine and limit a homestead to a village homestead, nor as to constitute an abandonment of the homestead right
in the part so platted but remaining unsold.

An execution having been levied on certain real property, it
was claimed as a homestead. It consisted of two parcels touching only at one corner, and of a parcel which had been platted
into lots and streets and given the name of Dora, the plat
of which had been filed in the office of the county recorder. A
supersedeas issued forbidding the sale of the tract so claimed,
but on motion to quash the supersedeas, the motion was denied
as to the part designated on the plat as Dora, but granted as to
a parcel of land which touched the residue of the homestead at
one corner only. The homestead claimant appealed, and the
execution creditor prosecuted a cross-appeal.

Miles & Miles, for the homestead claimants.

Jessie Turner, for the creditors.

⁕ HUGHES, J. Where a person entitled to claim a homestead
exemption owns two parcels of land which corner, and who has

his dwelling and resides upon one of them, and they together do not exceed one hundred and sixty acres in quantity, nor two thousand five hundred dollars in value, can he legally claim as a part of his homestead the parcel other than that upon which his dwelling-house is, exempt from execution?

Section 3711 of Sandel and Hill's Digest provides that: "The homestead, outside any city, town, or village, owned and occupied as a residence, shall consist of not exceeding one hundred and sixty acres of land, with the improvements thereon, to be selected by the owner, etc."

This court has heretofore defined a homestead to be "the place of a home or house—that part of a man's landed property which is about and contiguous to his dwelling-house": Tumlinson v. Swinney, 22 Ark. 400; 76 Am. Dec. 432. As defined in Webster's Unabridged Dictionary "contiguous" means "in actual or close contact; touching; adjacent; near; lying adjoining." In McCrosky v. Walker, 55 Ark. 303, it is held that a homestead [10] cannot consist of two noncontinguous tracts. In that case the two pieces of land claimed to constitute the homestead were one mile apart, the dwelling of the owner being on one parcel, and the other being used in connection with it to supply fuel. In the case at bar the two parcels touch, adjoin; i. e., corner with each other.

A homestead cannot be laid off in an arbitrary, capricious, and unreasonable shape, where it is practical to do it otherwise: Sparks v. Day, 61 Ark. 570; 54 Am. St. Rep. 279. In Jaffrey v. McGough, 88 Ala. 651, Judge Somerville humorously says: "A homestead, if we could suppose such a case, fenced in the shape of an animal, a bird, a flower garden, or other fantastic shape, would not cease to be exempt from execution on this account, provided it be of lawful area and value, and the entire tract owned was in this particular form. Although it is manifest that a selection in these quaint forms, made from a large tract of land, would be unreasonable and capricious, and not allowable." In the case at bar, the appellants owned no land in any shape other than that claimed as a homestead, and as this did not exceed in quantity one hundred and sixty acres, nor in value two thousand five hundred dollars, they were entitled to claim the same as a homestead exempt from execution.

Where two parcels of land corner with each other, they are contiguous, they touch; and there can be nothing unreasonable or unjust in allowing the two pieces to be selected and claimed as a homestead, where they constitute all the land the claimant owns, and do not exceed the legal area and value. Unless this could be done in this case, the appellants would be deprived of a part of the land allowed them by law as a homestead. The homestead law should be liberally construed to effect its benign purposes. The judgment of the court sustaining the motion to quash the supersedeas as to the east half of the northwest quarter of the southwest quarter, and the northeast quarter of the southwest quarter, of section 20, in township 9 north, range 32 west, is reversed and remanded, with directions to overrule the same.

The only other question in the case is, Is the judgment of the court overruling the motion to quash the supersedeas as to the land laid off into lots, and platted, and called "Dora," correct? The contention of the appellant in the cross-appeal is [11] that, the land having been platted as laid off into lots, blocks, and streets, and the plat having been filed in the clerk's office, it was dedicated to public use, and became a village. It was not incorporated. It does not appear that there was any collection of houses there for residence or business, and it only appears that there was a postoffice there. There was no acceptance of the dedication, if dedication was intended. Does this constitute a town or village, so as to confine and limit the homestead to not more than one acre, which is the limit to the area which a homestead may cover in "any city, town, or village," as provided in section 3712 of Sandel and Hill's Digest? We think not. In Murray v. Menefee, 20 Ark. 561, this court, through Judge Compton, said: "In this country, there seems to be no precise legal definition of the term 'town,' and we suppose it was used in the statute in its popular sense. . . . . There was at 'Cadron' one store, which did business to the amount of about four thousand dollars per annum; dwelling-house for two families, and outhouses; the population consisted of two families, numbering in all six persons; one warehouse, from which in 1855 produce to the value of two hundred dollars was shipped. . . . . In 1854, which was a favorable year, the exports amounted to the value of fifteen hundred dollars. To call this a town, in any sense, would be an obvious misapplication of the term." It is evident that "Cadron" was more nearly a town than Dora was, which, according to this case, was neither a town or a village.

We are of the opinion that the part of the land known as "Dora" had not been segregated and abandoned as part of appellants' homestead, so as to avoid the claim of it as part of the homestead. Wherefore the judgment of the court overruling the motion to quash the supersedeas as to this, and allowing appellants to claim the same as part of their homestead, is affirmed.

HOMESTEAD—OCCUPANCY AS AN ESSENTIAL.—It is generally held that there must be both possession and occupancy of the premises in order to stamp them with the character of a homestead, but upon this question there is a decided conflict of authority: Note to Mason v. Columbia Finance Co., 59 Am. St. Rep. 452. In Linn County Bank etc. v. Hopkins, 47 Kan. 580, 27 Am. St. Rep. 309, it was held that a homestead must consist of one body of land, and where the claimant owns two tracts within the homestead limit, but which touch only at a common corner, he cannot claim them both as exempt, and is entitled to a homestead only in the tract on which he resides: See note to Turner v. Turner, 54 Am. St. Rep. 114.

HOMESTEAD—URBAN—PLATTING INTO LOTS.—If blocks in the platted and laid out part of an incorporated city are generally subdivided on the plat into lots of various sizes, the owner of a part of one block which has not been thus subdivided, and which is urban in character, is entitled to hold only a tract equal in area to the average size of platted lots in that part of the city: Heidel v. Benedict, 61 Minn. 170; 52 Am. St. Rep. 592, and note. See, also, Klewert v. Anderson, 65 Minn. 491; 60 Am. St. Rep. 487, and note.

WILKERSON v. CRESCENT INSURANCE COMPANY.

[64 ARKANSAS, 80.]

PRINCIPAL AND SURETY — DEFAULT OF WHICH SURETY WAS NOT NOTIFIED.—The fact that an agent, for the performance of whose duties a bond with sureties was given, has, to the knowledge of his principal, been delinquent for more than three years in making payments of moneys collected by him, during which time he has been continued in his employment without notice to the surety of such delinquency, does not release the latter. The surety is bound to inquire for himself, and cannot complain that the creditor has not notified him of the state of the accounts for which he is answerable.

Action by the insurance company against Wilkerson as surety on a bond given for the performance of the duties of S. L. Ingalls as agent for the company. It was admitted that there had been a breach of the condition of the bond, that Ingalls should properly account for, and pay over, all moneys collected by him as agent for the company, but it was insisted, as a defense, that his delinquency had become known to the company some three years before the bringing of this action, and that it had continued him in his agency without giving notice to his surety of his default until he had finally become insolvent, that the defendant had notice, when he executed the bond, that the agent was required to make a report every thirty days of the moneys collected by him and to pay them over to the insurance company. Such appeared to have been the course of business until October, 1891, when the agent got behind with his monthly payments. The company became aware of the delinquency, but continued Ingalls in its employment until January, 1894, he, in the mean time, making some payments, but never fully settling his accounts. The instruction of the court was, that the facts thus relied upon constituted no defense, and the jury, therefore, returned a verdict in favor of the plaintiff for two hundred and fifty dollars, for which sum judgment was entered.

P. R. Andrews and N. W. Norton, for the appellant.

J. C. Hawthorne, for the appellee.

[82] RIDDICK, J. The question presented for our consideration is thus stated by counsel for appellant: "Can the appellee recover from the surety, after having had knowledge of the principal's delinquencies for about three years, during which time the appellee failed to advise the surety that his principal was in default"? The answer to this question must be in the affirmative, for the failure of the insurance company to notify the surety of such default does not, in our opinion, discharge the surety. To discharge the surety the act of the creditor must be injurious to the legal rights of the surety. An agreement with the principal debtor extending time for payment or in any manner changing the contract will have that effect, but mere indulgence is not sufficient: Clark v. Sickler, 64 N. Y. 231; 21 Am. Rep. 606; Grisard v. Hinson, 50 Ark. 229.

The inaction of the creditor will not discharge the surety, unless it amounts to fraud or concealment, for the surety is bound to inquire for himself, and cannot complain that the creditor does not notify him of the state of the accounts of his agent for which the surety is liable: Watertown Fire Ins. Co. v. Simmons, 131 Mass. 85; 41 Am. Rep. 196; Atlantic etc. Tel. Co. v. Barnes, 64 N. Y. 385; 21 Am. St. Rep. 621.

This very question was considered in the case of Watertown Fire Ins. Co. v. Simmons, 131 Mass. 85; 41 Am. Rep. 196. It was there held, under circumstances very similar to those in this case, that the law imposed no duty upon the insurance company either to dismiss its agent or to modify the surety of his default. "It is," said the court, "the business of the surety to see that his principal performs the duty which he has guaranteed, and not that of the creditor."

In this case the amount for which the agent was in arrears was not large, and it seems reasonable to believe that the insurance company kept him in its employ with the expectation that eventually he would settle his accounts by paying the balance due. The company was not called on by the surety for information concerning the state of the agent's account, and there seems to have been nothing done by the company that amounted to either fraud or concealment. We therefore conclude that the judgment of the circuit court was right, and it is affirmed.

SURETYSHIP—KNOWLEDGE OF PRINCIPAL'S DISHONESTY —DISCHARGE OF SURETY.—In case of a continuing suretyship for the honesty of a servant, if the master discovers that the servant has been guilty of dishonesty in the service, and if, instead of dismissing him, he continues him in his employ without the consent of the surety, express or implied, the latter is not liable for any loss arising from the dishonesty of the servant during the subsequent service. This rule applies as well to a private corporation as an employer, as to an individual, when its agent, in the discharge of his duties discovers the dishonesty of the servant, and having authority, fails to give notice of such dishonesty to the surety, and the corporation thereafter retains the servant in its employ: Saint v. Wheeler etc. Mfg. Co., 95 Ala. 362; 36 Am. St. Rep. 210, and note. See Fidelity etc. Co. v. Gate City Nat. Bank, 97 Ga. 634; 54 Am. St. Rep. 440: Chew v. Ellingwood. 86 Mo. 230; 56 Am. Rep. 429; Home Ins. Co. v. Holway, 55 Iowa, 571; 39 Am. Rep. 179.

St. Louis, Iron Mountain & Southern Railway Company v. Paul.

[64 Arkansas, 83.]

CORPORATIONS, PROPERTY RIGHTS OF.—Though the constitution of a state declares that the legislature has power to alter, revoke, or amend any charter of incorporation, the property which corporations acquire in the exercise of the capacities conferred upon them they hold subject to the same guaranties which protect the property of individuals from spoliation.

CORPORATIONS—PENALTIES FOR NOT PAYING EMPLOYES WHEN DISCHARGED.—A statute requiring all railway corporations, upon discharging any employé, whether with or without cause, to on that day pay him his wages earned by him according to the contract rate, and, on default in such payment, that such wages shall continue at the same rate until paid, provided such wages shall not continue more than sixty days unless action therefor shall be commenced within that time, is not unconstitutional. The penalty thus imposed for the failure to discharge the obligation due to the employé is not unreasonable,

CONSTITUTIONAL LAW — STATUTES, REPEAL OR AMENDMENT WITHOUT RE-ENACTMENT AT LENGTH.—If a statute conflicts with a previously enacted statute, the latter is to that extent repealed or amended, whether expressly mentioned or not, although the constitution of the state declares that no law shall be revised, amended, or the provisions thereof extended or conferred by reference to its title only, but so much thereof as is revised, modified, extended, or conferred shall be enacted and published at length.

Dodge & Johnson, Wallace Pratt, and Olden & Orr, for the appellants.

[85] BATTLE, J. The appellees, Charles Paul, John Boland, and Fritz Whiddick were day laborers in the employment, respectively, of the appellants, the St. Louis, Iron Mountain & Southern Railway Company, and the Kansas City, Fort Scott & Memphis Railroad Company; one earning one dollar and twenty-five cents a day, and each of the other two one dollar and thirty-five cents. Their employers discharged them without paying the wages they had, respectively, earned; and each brought a suit against his debtor for the amount due him, and the damages allowed by the act of the general assembly of the state of Arkansas, entitled, "An act to provide for the protection of servants and employés of railroads," approved March 25, 1889. The defendants did not deny that the wages claimed were due them, but resisted the recovery of the damages on the ground that the act under which they were claimed was in violation of the fourteenth amendment of the constitution of the United States, and of the constitution of the state of Arkansas.

The first section of the act in question, to the extent it was sustained in Leep v. St. Louis etc. Ry. Co., 58 Ark. 407, 41 Am. St. Rep. 109, is as follows: "Whenever any corporation engaged in the business of operating or constructing any railroad or railroad bridge shall discharge with or without cause, or refuse to further employ, any servant or employé thereof, the unpaid wages of any such servant and employé then earned at the contract rate, without abatement or deduction, shall be and become due and payable on the day of such discharge or refusal to longer employ; and if the sum be not paid on such day, then, as a penalty for such nonpayment, the wages of such servant or employé shall continue at the same rate until paid. Provided, such wages shall not continue more than sixty days, unless an action therefor shall be commenced within that time." In sustaining it, the court held that the words "without abatement or deduction," as used in the act, mean "that the unpaid wages earned at the contract rate, at the time of the discharge, shall be paid without discount on account of the payment thereof before they were payable according to the terms of the contract of employment."

The railroad companies contend that they are "persons," within the meaning of that word as used in the fourteenth [80] amendment of the constitution of the United States; and that the act in question, as sustained and construed in Leep v. St. Louis etc. Ry. Co., 58 Ark. 407, 41 Am. St. Rep. 109, is in violation of the amendment in this, that it denies to them the "equal protection of the law." If it be conceded that they are persons, as contended, it would not follow that they are entitled to all the rights of natural persons. They possess only those rights, powers, or properties which the charters of their creation confer upon them, either expressly or as incidental to their existence. The same is true of all other corporations. All of them are creatures of the legislature. In their creation the legislature could and did divide them into classes, and give to each class such rights, capacities, and powers as it saw fit. Neither has the right to complain of a discrimination in favor of one agent against the other, or that all or any of the rights of natural persons have not been given to it.

The powers conferred upon them by their charters may be modified or diminished by amendment, or extinguished by the repeal of the charters. The constitution of this state ordains: "The general assembly shall have the power to alter, revoke, or amend any charter of incorporation now existing and revocable at the adoption of this constitution, or any that may hereafter be created, whenever, in their opinion, it may be injurious to the citizens of this state; in such manner, however, that no injustice shall be done to the corporators": Const. 1874, art. 12, sec. 6. The railroad companies in this case do not deny, but tacitly concede, that their charters are subject to alteration under this provision of the constitution. The question is, Did the legislature have the power to do so in the manner and to the extent it undertook by the act in question?

In commenting upon such a power to amend, which was reserved by the state of California, Mr. Justice Field, in delivering the opinion of the court in the Railroad Tax cases, 13 Fed. Rep. 754, said:"It [the state] may confer, by its general laws, upon corporations certain capacities of doing business, and of having perpetual succession in their members. It may make its grant in these respects revocable at pleasure; it may make the grant subject to modifications, and impose conditions upon its use, and reserve the right to change these at will. But [87] whatever property the corporations acquire in the exercise of the capacities conferred they hold under the same guaranties which protect

the property of individuals from spoliation. It cannot be taken
for public use without compensation. It cannot be taken
without due process of law, nor can it be subjected to burdens
different from those laid hpon the property of individuals under
like circumstances. The state grants to railroad corporations
formed under its laws a franchise, and over it retains control,
and may withdraw or modify it. By the reservation clause it
retains power only over that which it grants; it does not grant
the rails on the road; it does not grant the depots alongside of
it; it does not grant the cars on the track, nor the engines which
move them, and over them it can exercise no power except such
as may be exercised through its control over the franchise, and
such as may be exercised with reference to all property used by
carriers for the public. The reservation of power over the franchise—that is, over that which is granted—makes its grant a
conditional or revocable contract, whose obligation is not impaired by its revocation or change."

In the Sinking-Fund case, 99 U. S. 700, the question was
whether Congress had the constitutional power to enact a law
compelling the Union Pacific and Central Pacific Railroad Companies to set aside a portion of their current earnings as a sinking fund for the purpose of meeting a very large indebtedness
secured by mortgage upon the roads, and payable at a future
day. The majority of the court held that the legislation was
valid as an exercise of the general legislative powers of the government, and also because the right to alter or amend the charters of the companies had been expressly reserved to Congress.
In commenting on the reserved power to amend or repeal the
charters of corporations in that case, Chief Justice Waite, in delivering the opinion of the court, said: "All agree that it cannot be used to take away property already acquired under the
operations of the charter, or to deprive the corporation of the
fruits actually reduced to possession of contracts lawfully made;
but, as was said by this court, through Mr. Justice Clifford, in
Miller v. State, 15 Wall. 498, 'it may safely be affirmed that the
reserved power may be exercised, and to almost any extent, to
carry into effect the original [ss] purposes of the grant, or to secure the due administration of its affairs, so as to protect the
rights of stockholders and of creditors, and for the proper disposition of its assets'; and again, in Holyoke Co. v. Lyman, 15 Wall.
519, 'to protect the rights of the public and of the corporators,
or to promote the due administration of the affairs of the corporation.' Mr. Justice Field, also speaking for the court, was

even more explicit when, in Tomlinson v. Jessup, 15 Wall. 459, he said: 'The reservation affects the entire relation between the state and the corporation, and places under legislative control all rights, privileges, and immunities derived by its charter drectly from the state'; and again, as late as Railroad Co. v. Maine, 96 U. S. 510, 'by the reservation . . . . the state retained the power to alter it [the charter] in all particulars constituting the grant to the new company, formed under it, of corporate rights, privileges, and immunities.' Mr. Justice Swayne, in Shields v. Ohio, 95 U. S. 324, says, by way of limitation, 'the alterations must be reasonable; they must be in good faith, and be consistent with the object and scope of the act of incorporation. Sheer oppression and wrong cannot be inflicted under the guise of amendment or alteration.' The rules, as here laid down, are fully sustained by authority. . . . . Giving full effect to the principles which have thus been authoritatively stated, we think it safe to say that whatever rules Congress might have prescribed in the original charter for the government of the corporation in the administration of its affairs, it retained the power to establish by amendment. In so doing it cannot undo what has already been done, and it cannot unmake contracts that have already been made, but it may provide for what shall be done in the future, and may direct what preparations shall be made for the due performance of contracts already entered into. It might originally have prohibited the borrowing of money on mortgage, or it might have said that no bonded debt should be created without ample provision by sinking fund to meet it at maturity. Not having done so at first, it cannot now by direct legislation vacate mortgages already made under the powers originally granted, nor release debts already contracted. A prohibition [89] now against contracting debts will not avoid debts already incurred."

The act of March 25, 1889, does not interfere with the disposition or control of the property of railroad companies, with their vested rights, or with contracts already made. All it requires them to do is to pay the wages earned by their servants or employés under contract entered into after its enactment, at the time they discharge them or refuse to give them further employment. The effect of this requirement is to make the wages payable at the time of the discharge or refusal to employ, and to limit the right to contract. But this right was derived from the laws under which the railroad companies were organized, and, according to the cases cited, was subject to be limited,

· regulated, and controlled by the general assembly, under the
constitution of this state, whenever, in its opinion, it may be
beneficial to the public, in such manner as may be just to the corporators.   Consequently, no right of the railroad companies was
violated by the act in limiting the right to contract: Leep v. St.
Louis etc. Ry. Co., 58 Ark. 407; 41 Am. St. Rep. 109.

In the Sinking Fund cases, 99 U. S. 700, the act of Congress
required the railroad companies to provide for the payment of
certain debts by a sinking fund before their maturity, virtually
to pay debts before they were due.   The act of March 25th requires the wages of the laborer to be paid when he leaves the employment of the company.   One applies to past, the other to
future transactions; one to secured debts, the other to the wages
of the laborer.   The object of each is the enforcement of a
duty—the payment of debts.   If the former act is constitutional,
how can the latter be unconstitutional?

But an act of the legislature is not necessarily unconstitutional, in the absence of a reservation of the power to alter or
revoke charters, and does not deny the equal protection of the
law, because it imposes certain duties and liabilities upon only
one class of corporations, and upon no others.   In Missouri Pac.
Ry. Co. v. Mackey, 127 U. S. 205, a statute of Kansas provided
that every railroad company organized or doing business in that
state "shall be liable for all damages done to any employé of such
company in consequence of any negligence of its agents, or by
any mismanagement of its 90 engineers, or other employés, to
any person sustaining such damage."   Mr. Justice Field, in
delivering the opinion of the court said: "Such legislation does
not infringe upon the clause of the Fourteenth Amendment requiring equal protection of the laws, because it is special in its
character; if in conflict at all with that clause, it must be on other
grounds.   And when legislation applies to particular bodies or
associations, imposing upon them additional liabilities, it is not
open to the objection that it denies to them the equal protection
of the laws, if all persons brought under its influence are treated
alike under the same conditions.   A law giving to mechanics
a lien on buildings constructed or repaired by them, for the
amount of their work, and a law requiring railroad corporations
to erect and maintain fences along their roads, separating them
from lands of adjoining proprietors, so as to keep cattle off their
tracks, are instances of this kind.   Such legislation is not obnoxious to the last clause of the Fourteenth Amendment, if all persons subject to it are treated alike under similar circumstances

and conditions in respect to both of the privileges conferred and the liabilities imposed. It is conceded that corporations are persons within the meaning of the amendment. . . . . But the hazardous character of the business of operating a railway would seem to call for special legislation with respect to railroad corporations, having for its object the protection of their employés as well as the safety of the public. The business of other corporations is not subject to similar dangers to their employés, and no objections, therefore, can be made to the legislation on the ground of its making an unjust discrimination. It meets a particular necessity, and all railroad corporations are without distinction made subject to the same liabilities. As said by the court below, it is simply a question of legislative discretion whether the same liabilities shall be applied to carriers by canal and stagecoaches and to persons and corporations using steam in manufactories."

In the last case cited, the protection of the employés of railroad companies, as in this case, was the object of the act in question. The act in that case, as in this, applies to only one class of corporations, and to no others. But the act of March 25th is not dependent on the same power to legislate. The constitution [91] of this state, as before stated, expressly provides that the general assembly shall have the power to alter, revoke, or annul any charter of incorporation now existing and revocable at the adoption of the constitution, or any that may thereafter be created, whenever, in their opinion, it may be injurious to the citizens of this state; in such manner, however, that no injustice shall be done to the corporators. In Leep v. St. Louis etc. Ry. Co., 58 Ark. 407, 41 Am. St. Rep. 109, we held that the legislature had the power to pass the act of March 25th by virtue of this provision of the constitution. In justifying it, however, we based it, as in the case cited, upon the peculiar character of the business of railroads, and the particular benefits to be derived therefrom by the public. We said: "Whenever the charters of railroad companies become obstacles in the way of the legislature so regulating their roads as to make them subserve the public interest to the fullest extent practicable, their charters are, in that respect, injurious to the citizens of the state, and can be amended as to defects in such manner as will be just to the corporators. For they are organized for a public purpose, and their roads are declared by the constitution to be public highways and they are made common carriers. They are clothed with a public trust, and in many respects are expressly subjected by the constitution to the control of the legislature. There is no enterprise in which the public is so largely interested as it is in the successful and efficient operation of railroads. With the trust with which they are clothed is imposed the duty to serve the public as common carriers in the most efficient manner practicable. For this reason the legislature may impose on them such duties as may be reasonably calculated to secure such results. Being created by statute, the legislature may so change them by amendment as to make them subserve the purpose for which they were created. If the legislature, in its wisdom, seeing that their employés are and will be persons dependent on their labor for a livelihood, and unable to work on a credit, should find that better servants and service could be secured by the prompt payment of their wages on the termination of their employment, and that the purpose of their creation would thereby be more nearly accomplished, it might require them to pay for the labor of their employés when the [92] same is fully performed at the end of their employment," and might require them to do so for the purpose of preventing that discontent produced by the nonpayment of wages upon discharge which may lead to "strikes," and consequent injury to the interest of the public.

Another evidence of the validity of the act in question may be adduced: The legislature has the power to limit the right of railroad companies to contract by fixing the maximum of charges for the transportation of persons and property over their roads for the protection of passengers and shippers. When the rates of charges allowed are sufficient to yield a reasonable profit, the statute by which they are fixed is within the limits of the power. So, in this case, the act in question is an exercise of, and is within the limits of, the same power. It does not seriously impair the right of corporations to contract, but leaves them to contract with their employés on profitable terms; and, in view of the public interest thereby subserved, is just to the corporators: Leep v. St. Louis etc. Ry. Co., 58 Ark. 407; 41 Am. St. Rep. 109.

The validity of the act of March 25th is assailed upon the ground that the exemplary damages allowed for the nonpayment of wages are excessive and unreasonable. The same complaint was made of a statute of Iowa, which is as follows: "Any corporation operating a railway that fails to fence the same against livestock running at large at all points where such right to fence exists, shall be liable to the owner of any such stock injured or killed by reason of the want of such fence for the value of the property or damage caused, unless the same was occasioned by the willful act of the owner, or his agent. . . . . And if such corporation neglects to pay the value of or damage done to such stock within thirty days after notice in writing, accompanied by an affidavit of such injury or destruction, has been served on any officer, station, or ticket agent employed in the management of the business of the corporation in the county where the injury complained of was committed, such owner shall be entitled to recover double the value of the stock killed or damage caused thereto." The penalty in that act is imposed on account of the nonpayment of damages within the thirty days. The validity of the statute was contested in Minneapolis etc. Ry. Co. v. Beckwith, 129 U. S. 26. [93] Mr. Justice Field, speaking for the court, said: "As it is the duty of the railway company to keep its track free from animals, its neglect to do so by adopting the most reasonable means for that purpose, the fencing of its roadway as indicated by the statute of Iowa, justly subjects it, as already stated, to punitive damages, where injuries are committed by reason of such neglect. The imposition of punitive or exemplary damages in such cases cannot be opposed as in conflict with the prohibition against the deprivation of property without due process of law. It is only one mode of imposing a penalty for the violation of duty, and its propriety and legality have been recognized, as stated in Day v. Woodworth, 13 How. 363, 371, by repeated judicial decisions for more than a century. Its authorization by the law in question to the extent of doubling the value of the property destroyed, or of the damage caused, upon refusal of the railway company, for thirty days after notice of the injury committed, to pay the actual value of the property or actual damage cannot therefore be justly assailed as infringing upon the fourteenth amendment of the constitution of the United States."

So in the act of March 25th, it is made the duty of railroad corporations to pay the wages of an employé at the end of his employment. To enforce the performance of this duty, exemplary or punitive damages are imposed upon them for the failure to do so; that is, the liability to pay the wages at the contract rate until the wages earned on the day of the discharge or refusal to longer employ are paid. They are not necessarily more unreasonable, then, or as much so, as those allowed by the Iowa statute. The railroad company can stop them by the payment or tender of payment of the amount due the employé for wages actually earned. No other amount need be tendered for that purpose. But, if it does not adopt this course, the damages will not accrue for more than sixty days, "unless an action therefor

shall be commenced within that time." The bringing of the
action calls its attention to the demands of the employé, and
continues the wages (damages) beyond the sixty days, unless the
company pays, or offers to pay, the wages earned at an earlier
day. If it then fails to pay, the continuance of the penalty is
due to its own fault. But it can [34] only continue up to the trial,
when the cause of action is merged in the judgment. The law
which prohibits the dividing a cause of action, and the bringing
of a separate action upon each part (Reynolds v. Jones, 63 Ark.
259), and merges the cause of action into the judgment, is not
changed by the act, which is not inconsistent with the rule in
such cases.

The damages imposed by the act in question for a violation
of the duty enjoined are commensurate with the violation, and
are within the limits of the discretion of the legislature. Like
the penalty imposed by the act which was sustained by the court
in State ex rel. Barton Co. v. Kansas City etc. Ry. Co., 32 Fed.
Rep. 722, they are large or small as the delay to pay is of long
or short duration.

Our attention has been called to Gulf etc. Ry. Co. v. Ellis,
165 U. S. 150. The statute involved in that case provided that
railroad companies failing to pay claims for labor, damages,
overcharges on freight, or for stock killed or injured by trains,
amounting to less than fifty dollars, within thirty days after presentation thereof, and to reduce the same in a suit thereon, shall
be liable for an attorney's fee not exceeding ten dollars. This
penalty was not imposed because of the violation of any duty
rightfully imposed upon railroad companies. but merely for the
failure to defeat the recovery of the full amount of the claim
sued on. It was not an amendment, or in the nature of an
amendment, of the charters of railroad corporations; and, if
it was, it does not appear to have been made by virtue of any
power reserved to the legislature. The court held that it was
unconstitutional because it arbitrarily imposed a penalty upon a
class of corporations which is not imposed upon others guilty of
a like delinquency, and because it punishes a railroad company
for defending a suit brought against it, if it fails to defeat the
recovery of the full amount sued for. The act was like that held
by this court, in St. Louis etc. Ry. Co. v. Williams, 49 Ark. 492,
to be unconstitutional. The act in question in that case provided
for the appointment of a board to assess damages, and that if
either party refused to abide by the assessment of the board. and
a suit was brought, the party refusing should be taxed with an

attorney's fee, in the event the judgment of [95] the court should not be more favorable to him than the award of the board. This court held that the act was unconstitutional, because the legislature had no power to substitute boards of arbitration for the courts without the consent of the parties; that the courts, organized under the constitution, had exclusive jurisdiction to hear and determine all controversies referred to in the act, and could not be deprived of it by the legislature. But the act of March 25th is not subject to the same objections as the act involved in Gulf etc. Ry. Co. v. Ellis, 165 U. S. 150. It does not arbitrarily impose a penalty, but it rightfully enjoins a duty and imposes a penalty for the failure to discharge the duty. It was enacted by the legislature in the exercise of the power to regulate railroad companies for the advancement of the interest of the public, and for the protection of their employés against the unnecessary withholding of their earnings and consequent injuries.

Appellants deny that the legislature has the power to amend their charters, except by enacting and publishing at length so much thereof as is amended. This contention is based on a section of the constitution which provides that "no law shall be revived, amended or the provisions thereof extended or conferred by reference to its title only; but so much thereof as is revived, amended, or extended or conferred, shall be enacted and published at length." But it is not correct. It is well settled in this and other states where such constitutional limitations are in force, that a statute repeals, or operates as an amendment of, a prior law on the same subject, to the extent that they are in conflict, although the latter is not mentioned in the former: Scales v. State, 47 Ark. 481; 58 Am. Rep. 768; Churchill v. Hill, 59 Ark. 54, 64; Leep v. St. Louis etc. Ry. Co., 58 Ark. 407; 41 Am. St. Rep. 109; People v. Mahaney, 13 Mich. 481, 496, 497; Lehman v. McBride, 15 Ohio St. 573; Shields v. Bennett, 8 W. Va. 74, 87; Baum v. Raphael, 57 Cal. 361; Denver Circle Ry. Co. v. Nestor, 10 Colo. 405; Evernham v. Hulit, 45 N. J. L. 53; Sheridan v. Salem, 14 Or. 328, 337; Davis v. State, 7 Md. 151; 61 Am. Dec. 331; Cooley's Constitutional Limitations, 6th ed., 182; 1 Thompson on Corporations, sec. 94, and cases cited.

We therefore conclude that the act of March 25th, so far as it affects corporations, does not violate the fourteenth amendment [96] of the constitution of the United States, nor the constitution of the state of Arkansas, and to that extent is a valid act.

The judgments appealed from are affirmed.

CORPORATIONS—PROPERTY OF—DUE PROCESS OF LAW.—
A law singling out persons, corporations, or associations engaged
in any particular business, and depriving them of the right to contract as persons, corporations, or associations engaged in other business may lawfully do, is unconstitutional and void: Braceville Coal
Co. v. People, 147 Ill. 66; 37 Am. St. Rep. 206. A general law concerning persons may include artificial as well as natural persons, and
every corporation is a legal person: Louisville v. Commonwealth, 1
Duvall. 295; 85 Am. Dec. 624.

STATUTES—REPEAL BY IMPLICATION.—A repeal by implication does not exist unless there is a positive repugnancy between
the provisions of the new law and those of the old, and even then
the law is repealed by implication only pro tanto to the extent of the
repugnancy: State v. Walbridge, 119 Mo. 383; 41 Am. St. Rep. 663,
and note. Such repeals are not favored unless there is a strong and
clear inconsistency between enactments: Note to Winona v. School
Dist., 12 Am. St. Rep. 695. See extended note to Towle v. Marrett, 14
Am. Dec. 209, 210. If a new law is amendatory of an old law, the
sections of the old law not amended will stand: Taylor v. Dahu, 6
Ind. App. 672; 51 Am. St. Rep. 312.

Of the Protection of Corporations from Special and Hostile Legislation.

Altering or Repealing Charters of Incorporation.—It was at an early
day determined that the grant by a state to a corporation of a charter, followed by its acceptance by such corporation, in effect constituted a contract between it and the corporation, which was protected from substantial impairment by the provisions of the constitution of the United States declaring that no state shall pass any law
impairing the obligation of a contract: Dartmouth College v. Woodward, 4 Wheat. 518; Commonwealth v. Cullen, 13 Pa. St. 133; 53 Am.
Dec. 450, and note. Partly to avoid the effect of these decisions,
many of the states subsequently enacted statutes reserving the right
to alter, amend, or repeal charters of incorporation granted by them:
Miners' Bank v. United States, Morris, 482; 43 Am. Dec. 115, and note;
Griffin v. Kentucky etc. Co., 3 Bush, 592; 96 Am. Dec. 259; Story v.
Jersey City etc. Co., 16 N. J. Eq. 13; 84 Am. Dec. 134; Zabriskie v.
Hackensacker R. R. Co., 18 N. J. Eq. 178; 90 Am. Dec. 617; State v.
Mayor, 31 N. J. L. 575; 86 Am. Dec. 240; State v. Miller, 30 N. J. L.
368; 86 Am. Dec. 188. "Cases often arise where the legislature, in
granting an act of incorporation for a private purpose, either makes
the duration of the charter conditional or reserves to the state the
power to alter, modify, or repeal the same at pleasure. Where such
a provision is incorporated in the charter, it is clear that it qualifies
the grant, and that the subsequent exercise of that reserved power
cannot be regarded as an act within the prohibition of the constitution. Such a power, also, that is, the power to alter, modify, or
repeal an act of incorporation, is frequently reserved to the state by
a general law applicable to all acts of incorporation, or to certain
classes of the same, as the case may be, in which case it is equally
clear that the power may be exercised whenever it appears that the
act of incorporation is one which falls within the reservation, and
that the charter was granted subsequent to the passage of the general law, even though the charter contains no such condition nor

any allusion to such a reservation. Reservations in such a charter, it is admitted, may be made, and it is also conceded that where they exist, the exercise of the power reserved by a subsequent legislature does not impair the obligation of the contract created by the original act of incorporation. Subsequent legislation altering or modifying the provisions of such a charcter, where there is no such reservation, is certainly unathorized if it is prejudicial, to the rights of the corporators, and was passed without their assent, but the converse of the proposition is also true, that if the new provisions repealing or modifying the charter were passed with the assent of the corporation and they were duly accepted by a corporate vote as amendments to the original charter, they cannot be regarded as impairing the obligation of the contract created by the original charter. Private charters, or such as are granted for the private benefit of the corporators, are held to be contracts, because they are based for their consideration on the liabilities and duties which the corporators assume by accepting the terms therein specified, and the grant of the franchise on that account can no more be resumed by the legislature or its benefits diminished or impaired without the assent of the corporators than any other grant of property or legal estate, unless the right to do so is reserved in the act of incorporation or in some general law of the state which was in operation at the time the charter was granted": Pennsylvania College cases, 13 Wall. 213.

It is not our purpose to enter into a discussion of the Dartmouth College case or upon a general discussion of statutory enactments questioned as being in conflict with it, nor do we intend to examine in detail statutes enacted as professed repeals, alterations, or amendments of charters of corporations under powers reserved to a state to alter, amend, or repeal such charters. Our purpose is the more restricted one of inquiring whether legislation applying some special rule to a corporation may be adjudged unconstitutional as infringing its rights as a person or as a citizen of the state, for it must now be conceded that, though a state has reserved this right, a corporation organized after the reservation is made has rights which the legislature is bound to respect. As was said by Justice Field in the Railroad Tax cases, 13 Fed. Rep. 755, though a state may make a charter granted by it revocable by it at pleasure, and subject it to modifications, and may impose conditions upon its use, and reserve the right to change these at will, "whatever property the corporations acquire in the exercise of the capacities conferred, they hold under the same guaranties which protect the property of individuals from spoliation. It cannot be taken for public use without compensation. It cannot be taken without due process of law, nor can it be subjected to burdens different from those laid upon the property of individuals under like circumstances."

Citizenship, Rights of.—With respect to guaranties under the constitution and laws of the United States of the rights of citizenship, corporations are for some purposes deemed citizens and for others not. Thus with respect to the jurisdiction of the national courts and the right to sue or be sued therein and to remove suits thereto in proper cases, a corporation is deemed a citizen only of that state in which and by whose laws it was organized: Louisville etc. R. R. v. Letson, 2 How. 497; Steamship Co. v. Tugman, 106 U. S. 118; Southern Pac. Co. v. Denton, 146 U. S. 202. On the other hand, a corporation is not a citizen "within the meaning of that clause of the federal constitution which declares that the citizens of each state shall be entitled to all the privileges and immunities of citizens in the several states"; Thompson on Corporations, sec. 7876; Pembina etc. Co. v. Pennsylvania, 125 U. S. 187; Paul v. Virginia, 8 Wall. 168; Ducat v. Chicago, 48 Ill. 172; 95 Am. Dec. 529; Phoenix etc. Co. v. Commonwealth, 5 Bush, 68; 96 Am. Dec. 331; Daggs v. Orient etc. Co., 136 Mo. 382; 58 Am. St. Rep. 638; Commonwealth v. New York etc. R. R. Co., 129 Pa. St. 463; 15 Am. St. Rep. 724; and hence is not entitled, beyond the state in which it was organized, to exercise privileges or functions conferred by its charter, and, in so far as it does so, acts only by the comity and consent of the state wherein such acts take place and of which it is not a citizen nor resident.

The Protection of the Fourteenth Amendment. — The fourteenth amendment to the constitution of the United States declares that "all persons born or naturalized in the United States and subject to the jurisdiction thereof are citizens of the United States and of the state wherein they reside. No state shall make or enforce any law which shall abridge the privileges or immunities of citizens of the United States; nor shall any state deprive any person of life, liberty, or property without due process of law, nor deny to any person within its jurisdiction the equal protection of the laws." It will be seen that this amendment, while it declares certain persons to be citizens of the United States and of the state wherein they reside and forbids any state to make or enforce any law abridging the privileges of citizens, is not confined in its effect to citizens either of a state or of the United States, but includes within its ample protection all persons within a state, whether citizens or not, and forbids any state to deprive any person, irrespective of citizenship, of life or property, or to deny to any person within its jurisdiction the equal protection of the law. It is not at all probable that any state, or the people thereof, in giving assent to the adoption of this amendment had in view artificial persons or their protection. On the contrary, the persons particularly in view were natural persons, born within the United States, but against whom it was feared some of the states might enact hostile legislation because of their color and previous condition of servitude. When the claim, however, was finally made that corporations were persons within the meaning of this amendment, it was conceded by the supreme court of the United States, by whose decisions upon this subject all other courts within the United States are necessarily controlled. The first case in which the question was presented and decided by that court, so far as we are aware, was Santa Clara County v. Southern Pac. Ry. Co., 118 U. S. 394, in which it was claimed that a provision of the constitution of California respecting the assessment of property for the purposes of taxation, and which declared that a mortgage, deed of trust, or other obligation by which a debt was secured should, for the pur-

poses of assessment and taxation, be treated as an interest in the
property affected thereby, and that, except as to railroad and other
quasi public corporations, the value of the property affected by such
mortgage, deed of trust, or other obligation less the value of the
security should be assessed and taxed to the owner of the property,
and the value of the security assessed and taxed to the owner thereof, was invalid in that it subjected corporations to a mode of taxation not applicable to natural persons, and thereby imposed burdens
upon railway corporations forbidden by the Fourteenth Amendment.
In the course of the argument, Mr. Justice Waite said: "The court
does not wish to hear argument on the question whether the provision in the fourteenth amendment to the constitution, which forbids
a state to deny to any person within its jurisdiction the equal protection of the laws, applies to these corporations. We are all of
opinion that it does." The next case in which this amendment was
spoken of in its relation to corporations was that of Pembina etc.
Co. v. Pennsylvania, 125 U. S. 188, where the court said: "The inhibition of the amendment, that no state shall deprive any person
within its jurisdiction of the equal protection of the laws, was designed to prevent any person or class of persons from being singled
out as a special subject for discriminating and hostile legislation.
Under the designation of 'person' there is no doubt that a private corporation is included. Such corporations are merely associations of
individuals united for a special purpose, and permitted to do business under a particular name, and have a succession of members
without dissolution." A similar concession was made in Missouri
etc. Co. v. Mackey, 127 U. S. 205, and in Minneapolis Ry. Co. v.
Beckwith, 129 U. S. 28. It was said in Covington etc. Co. v. Sandford, 164 U. S. 592: "It is now settled that corporations are persons
within the meaning of the constitutional provisions forbidding the
deprivation of property without due process of law, as well as a
denial of the equal protection of the laws"; and this statement is
substantially reiterated in Smythe v. Ames, 169 U. S. 522. It is
somewhat remarkable that a question of such paramount importance should have been determined by the supreme court of the
United States without any statement on its part of the reasoning
influencing its decisions, and, we believe, also, without permitting
any discussion on the part of counsel, for in the case in which, so far
as we are aware, the question was first presented, the court declined
to hear counsel upon this subject, upon the ground that all its members had already reached a unanimous conclusion thereon.

Special Legislation, Extent to Which may be the Subject of.—Neither
by the decision in the Dartmouth College case nor by later decisions
bringing corporations within the operation of the Fourteenth Amendment by declaring them to be persons are they exempted from special legislation nor from such regulations as the legislature may,
from time to time, provide, though subsequent to the grant of their
charters and whether the right to repeal or amend has been reserved
or not. The Fourteenth Amendment, though it declares no person
shall by any state be deprived of life, liberty, or property without
due process of law, nor shall it deny to any person within its jurisdic-

tion the equal protection of the law, does not undertake to define the
rights which persons have to life, liberty, or property, nor to prescribe the limits which may be imposed upon those rights, nor the
offenses on account of which they may be deemed forfeited. Furthermore, every rule of law, whether statutory or constitutional,
must be considered in connection with other rules of equal dignity
and which may be regarded, as to some extent, limiting or modifying them. Thus it is well settled that the Fourteenth Amendment
does not destroy or impair the police power of the states, and that
such statutes as may be lawfully enacted in the exercise of that
power may be made applicable to corporations as well as to natural
persons, though they may impose obligations or create liabilities not
existing when their charters were granted: Note to State v. Goodwill,
25 Am. St. Rep. 870-890; Virginia etc. Co. v. Crozer etc. Co., 90 Va.
126; 44 Am. St. Rep. 893; New York etc. R. R. Co. v. Bristol, 151 U.
S. 556, 567; Missouri Pac. R. R. Co. v. Mackey, 127 U. S. 205; Slaugh-
ter-House cases, 16 Wall. 36; Barbier v. Connolly, 113 U. S. 27; Missouri Pac. R. R. v. Humes, 115 U. S. 512. A corporation is not necessarily denied the equal protection of the laws by a statute, "if all
persons under its influence are treated alike under the same conditions": Missouri Pac. Ry. Co. v. Mackey, 127 U. S. 205. It hence follows that legislation may be directed to a particular class of corporations, and may impose upon them liabilities not imposed on any other
person or corporation, if the conditions applicable to them do not
apply to all others, or if there is some special reason why they
should be subjected to the particular restraint or liability imposed.

Railways may be subjected to liabilities and penalties not imposed
on other corporations or persons, if the statutes imposing them may
fairly be regarded as an exercise, in good faith, of the police powers
of the state: Burdick v. People, 149 Ill. 600; 41 Am. St. Rep. 329.
Thus their trains, if not operated with the utmost care, might inflict
great injury upon persons and property, and, for the purpose of compelling the exercise of this care, special regulations may be imposed
on the company by holding it answerable for an injury inflicted
through the want of such care, for which another person or corporation is not subject to liability, and in some instances, by holding the
railway answerable whether it is shown to have been in fault or not.
Hence a statute may impose a liability upon railways for the death
of a human being, caused by their negligence or that of their servants, though in other cases no personal liability exists for so causing
such death: Schoolcraft v. Louisville etc. Co., 92 Ky. 233; and may
even fix the amount of damages to be awarded: Carroll v. Missouri
Pac. Ry. Co., 88 Mo. 239; 57 Am. Rep. 382; or may create a liability
against such railways in favor of their employés injured through the
negligence of a fellow-servant: Georgia etc. Co. v. Miller, 90 Ga. 571.
Liability may be imposed for an injury suffered by a passenger during his transportation over a railroad in all cases, except those in
which the injury done arose from the criminal negligence of the
passenger or from his violation of some express rule or regulation of
the railway, brought to his notice: Union R. R. Co. v. Porter, 38 Neb.
226. This statute is extreme in character, and the decision sustain-

ing it can hardly be deemed to have conclusively established its validity. Perhaps it is defensible on the ground that it is with difficulty
that a passenger injured on a train can establish the cause of his
injury, and that, from such injury, in the absence of proof of his
negligence in contributing to it, negligence on the part of the railway
or its servants is fairly inferable, and that due regard to the perils
to which the traveling public is exposed may require that railways
be made insurers of their safety when not themselves guilty of gross
negligence. A statute, however, imposing liability for the death of
a human being not due to any act or negligence of the railway or
at all attributable to the operation of its trains cannot be defended
as an exercise, in good faith, of the police power of the state. Therefore, a railway cannot be made liable "for all expenses of the coro-
ner and of his inquest and of the burial of all persons who may die in
cars, or may be killed by collision or other accident occuring to such
cars or otherwise": Ohio etc. Co. v. Lackey, 78 Ill. 55; 20 Am. Rep.
259.

For the Purpose of Protecting Livestock which might otherwise
stray or be upon their tracks railways have, by statute, been compelled to fence them and to maintain cattle guards: Toledo etc. Co.
v. Jacksonville, 67 Ill. 37; 16 Am. Rep. 611; Norris v. Androscoggin
etc. Co., 39 Me. 273; 63 Am. Dec. 621; Wilder v. Maine etc. Co., 65
Me. 332; 20 Am. Rep. 698; Pennsylvania etc. Co. v. Riblet, 66 Pa. 164;
5 Am. Rep. 360; Nelson v. Vermont etc. Co., 26 Vt. 717; 62 Am. Dec.
614; and such statute may provide that, when stock is injured by a
train and the statute has not been complied with, the railway shall
be absolutely liable therefor: Quackenbush v. Wisconsin etc. Co., 71
Wis. 472; and may, as a penalty, provide for the awarding of damages to the owner of the stock double those actually sustained by
him: Humes v. Missouri etc. Co., 82 Mo. 221; 52 Am. Rep. 369; Beck-
stead v. Montana etc. Co., 19 Mont. 147; Missouri Pac. Ry. Co. v.
Humes, 115 U. S. 512; Minneapolis etc. Co. v. Beckwith, 129 U. S. 26.
Statutes of this character are defensible as exercises of the police
power, for they may reasonably tend to the prevention of injury to
persons upon the train, as well as lessen the destruction of livestock.
Where, however, a railway is not shown to have been guilty of any
negligence or of the violation of any statutory regulation, it cannot
be made liable for livestock killed through the operation of its trains:
Zeigler v. Southern etc. Co., 58 Ala. 594; Birmingham etc. Co. v. Parsons, 100 Ala. 662; 46 Am. St. Rep. 92; Wadsworth v. Union Pac. Co.,
18 Colo. 600; 36 Am. St. Rep. 209; Cateril v. Union Pac. Ry. Co., 2
Idaho, 540; Bielenberg v. Montana etc. Co., 8 Mont. 271; Atchison etc.
Ry. Co. v. Baty, 6 Neb. 37; 29 Am. Rep. 356; State v. Divine, 98 N. C.
778; Jensen v. Union Pac. Ry. Co., 6 Utah, 253; Schenck v. Union
Pac. Ry. Co., 5 Wyo. 430. In some instances, where a statute undertook to impose a liability for the killing of stock when the track
was not fenced, thus apparently discriminating between fenced and
unfenced tracks, it was construed as impliedly imposing the obligation upon railways to fence their tracks, and therefore the liability
for the killing of stock on unfenced tracks was sustained as being in
the nature of a penalty imposed on the corporation for its implied dis-

regard of the mandate of the statute: Dacres v. Oregon etc. Ry. Co., 1 Wash. 525; contra, Oregon etc. Co. v. Smalley, 1 Wash. 206; 22 Am. St. Rep. 143. Nor can a railway company, while it has not been guilty of any negligence or any violation of law, be subjected to liability for the killing of the stock on the ground that its engineer and fireman, did not, within forty-eight hours, report the accident to the division superintendent of the road, nor did the division superintendent transmit the report to the owner of the stock, if known, and if not, cause the report to be filed with the agent of the company nearest the place of the accident, to be by him put up in his office for the inspection of the public: Jolliffe v. Brown, 14 Wash. 155; 53 Am. St. Rep. 868.

Fire, Liability for.—Statutes may be enacted making the communication of fire by railway locomotives prima facie evidence of negligence on the part of the corporation or its agents: Augusta etc. Co. v. Randall, 79 Ga. 304; Missouri Pac. Ry. Co. v. Martin, 40 Kan. 404. But the liability of a railway for fires communicated by its locomotives may be made absolute and not dependent upon any question of negligence. It is said that, by the common law, one who starts a fire becomes answerable for the consequences, and, in effect, is an insurer that the property of another shall not be damaged thereby. At all events, it is now well settled that a state may by statute impose an absolute liability upon railway corporations for damages caused to the property of others from fire communicated from locomotives, irrespective of the question of negligence and of the precautions which may have been taken by the railway to avoid injuries of that character: Union Pac. Ry. Co. v. De Busk, 12 Colo. 294; 13 Am. St. Rep. 221; Simmonds v. New York etc. Co., 52 Conn. 264; 52 Am. Rep. 587; Regan v. New York etc. Co., 60 Conn. 124; 25 Am. St. Rep. 306; Grissell v. Housatonic etc. R. R., 54 Conn. 447; 1 Am. St. Rep. 138; Rodemacker v. Milwaukee etc. Co., 41 Iowa, 297; 20 Am. Rep. 592; Chapman v. Atlantic etc. Co., 37 Me. 92; Thatcher v. Maine Cent. etc. Co., 85 Me. 502; Sherman v. Maine Cent. etc. Co., 86 Me. 422; Mathews v. St. Louis etc. Ry. Co., 121 Mo. 298; Rowell v. Railroad, 57 N. H. 132; 24 Am. Rep. 59; Smith v. Boston etc. Ry. Co., 63 N. H. 225; McCandless v. Richmond etc. Co., 38 S. C. 103; Grand Trunk Ry. Co. v. Richardson, 91 U. S. 454; St. Louis etc. Ry. Co. v. Mathews, 165 U. S. 1; Hartford Ins. Co. v. Chicago etc. Ry. Co., 62 Fed. Rep. 904.

Railway corporations may also be required to make changes in the construction of their road or in the method of operating it, where the object of such changes is, or may fairly be inferred to be, the greater protection of human life or the accomplishment of any other object which the state may rightfully seek in the exercise of its police power: Illinois etc. R. R. v. Willenborg, 117 Ill. 203; 57 Am. Rep. 862; Portland etc. R. R. v. Inhabitants, 78 Me. 67; 57 Am. Rep. 784. Thus, though the crossings have been constructed at a height and in a form approved at the time of their construction, they may, by statute subsequently enacted, be required to be changed at the expense of the railway corporations affected by such change or required to make it: Woodruff v. Catlin, 54 Conn. 277, 295; New York etc. Co. v.

Bristol. 151 U. S. 556. In referring to legislation of this class, the
supreme court of the United States in the case last cited said: "It
is likewise thoroughly established in this court that the inhibitions
of the constitution of the United States upon the impairment of the
obligation of contracts, or of the deprivation of property without
due process or of the equal protection of the laws, by the states,
are not violated by the legitimate exercise of legislative power in
securing the public safety, health, and morals. The governmental
power of self-protection cannot be contracted away, nor can the
exercise of rights granted, nor the use of property, be withdrawn
from the implied liability to governmental regulation in particulars
essential to the preservation of the community from injury: Beer Co.
v. Massachusetts, 97 U. S. 25; Fertilizing Co. v. Hyde Park, 97 U. S.
659; Barbier v. Connolly, 113 U. S. 27; New Orleans etc. Co. v. Louisiana Light Co., 115 U. S. 650; Mugler v. Kansas, 123 U. S. 623; Budd
v. New York, 143 U. S. 517. And also that 'a power reserved to the
legislature to alter, amend, or repeal a charter authorizes it to make
any alteration or amendment of a charter granted subject to it, which
wil not defeat or substantially impair the object of the grant, or any
rights vested under it, and which the legislature may deem necessary
to secure either that object or any other public right': Close v. Green-
wood Cemetery, 107 U. S. 466, 476; Spring Valley Water Works v.
Schottler, 110 U. S. 347; Pennsylvania College cases, 13 Wall. 190;
Tomlinson v. Jessup, 15 Wall. 454."

Railway corporations may also, by statute, be required to observe
precautions intended to better secure the safety either of their patrons, employés, or of the general public, such as the giving of signals
at crossings and the restricting the speed of trains in cities and
other densely populated places, and the failure to observe such
precautions may doubtless be made prima facie or conclusive evidence of negligence, or any other reasonable penalty may be imposed therefor: Kaminitsky v. Northeastern Ry. Co., 25 S. C. 53.
Penalties may also be imposed for delay in the delivery of freight:
Branch v. Wilmington etc. Co., 77 N. C. 347. In truth, it would be
difficult, if not impossible, to prescribe any limit to the power of
the legislature to impose penalties, provided they apply to all corporations and persons similarly situated, and may fairly be held
to tend to promote the general welfare or the public health and
safety or that of the employés of corporations or any other considerable class of the community, unless the imposition of such
penalties conflicts with constitutional provisions other than those
here under consideration. The penalty must not be arbitrarily
imposed, but must follow an act which has been made unlawful; and the legislature cannot make an act unlawful and subject the doer of it to a penalty if other persons doing the same
act under the same circumstances are not deemed to act unlawfully
and do not subject themselves to any penalty.

Imposing Liability for Attorney's Fees.—The question of the imposition of special penalties has arisen quite frequently in connection
with statutes authorizing the plaintiffs in special classes of actions
to recover attorneys' fees. There could be no valid objection to a

statute giving attorneys' fees to all successful litigants, but, if a statute authorizes the award of such fees to some litigants and withholds them from others, it must be justified by special circumstances or declared invalid. "Before a distinction can be made between debtors, and one be punished for the failure to pay his debts and another is permitted to become in like manner delinquent without any punishment, there must be some difference in the obligation to pay, some reason why the duty of payment is more imperative in the one instance than in the other": Gulf etc. Ry. v. Ellis, 165 U. S. 157. Decisions of various state courts have been pronounced sustaining statutes imposing liability upon corporations for attorneys' fees when sued to recover wages due their employés: Hawthorne v. People, 109 Ill. 302; 50 Am. Rep. 610; Vogel v. Pekoc, 157 Ill. 339; or for damages sustained from the killing of stock: Perkins v. St. Louis etc. Co., 103 Mo. 52; Missouri Pac. Ry. Co. v. Abney, 30 Kan. 41; or for the value of lands of which they have taken possession without first compensating the owner: Cameron v. Chicago etc. Ry. Co., 63 Minn. 384. Where, however, attorneys' fees have not been imposed in favor of all successful litigants, but in favor of some only, and their allowance is not based upon contract, they are generally regarded as in the nature of a penalty exacted of the successful litigant for some wrong done by him. There can be no arbitrary classification of litigants imposing attorneys' fees on some and exempting others equally guilty or equally guiltless. If a statutory rule has been violated, a penalty for its violation may be imposed and may consist of subjecting the wrongdoer to an attorney's fee when judgment is recovered against him in favor of one whom he has wronged, and hence a railway corporation which, in violation of such a statute, has made an overcharge may be compelled, in a suit to recover the amount thereof, to pay an attorney's fee to the plaintiff: Dow v. Beidelman, 49 Ark. 455; Burlington etc. Ry. Co. v. Dey, 82 Iowa, 312; 31 Am. St. Rep. 477. Where, however, the act complained of is not a tort and has not been made unlawful by statute, and when the defendant has been guilty of no wrong further than that implied in not paying without suit the sum which, after suit, is adjudged to be due from him, whether his liability is founded upon contract or not, he cannot be subjected to a penalty in the nature of liability for the attorneys' fees of his adversary, unless all other persons, natural and artificial, are also liable to such attorneys' fees if judgment is recovered against them upon a demand of like character: Southern etc. Ry. Co. v. Morris, 65 Ala. 193; St. Louis etc. Co. v. Williams, 49 Ark. 492; Braceville etc. Co. v. People, 147 Ill. 66; 37 Am. St. Rep. 206; Wilder v. Chicago etc. Ry. Co., 70 Mich. 382; Lafferty v. Chicago etc. Ry. Co., 71 Mich. 35; Chicago etc. Ry. Co. v. Moss, 60 Miss. 641; Coal Co. v. Rosser, 53 Ohio St. 12; 53 Am. St. Rep. 624; Jolliffe v. Brown, 14 Wash. 155; 53 Am. St. Rep. 868. But in those cases in which the cause of action is the commission of a tort or the violation of a statute upon the part of the defendant, we apprehend that he cannot be subjected to an attorneys' fee unless other persons or corporations guilty of the same wrong, under substantially the same circumstances, are also subjected to a like penalty. In declaring the uncon-

stitutionality of a statute imposing a liability on railway corporations
for attorneys' fees in suits brought against them for stock killed by
their trains, the supreme court of the United States said: "The supreme court of the state considered this statute as a whole and held
it valid, and as such it is presented to us for consideration. Considered as such, it is simply a statute imposing a penalty upon railroad corporations for failure to pay certain debts. No individuals
are thus punished, and no other corporations. The act singles out a
certain class of debtors and punishes them when, for like delinquencies, it punishes no others. They are not treated as other debtors,
or equally with other debtors. They cannot appeal to the courts as
other litigants under like conditions and with like protection. If litigation terminates adversely to them, they are mulcted in the attorneys' fees of the successful plaintiff; if it terminates in their favor,
they recover no attorneys' fees. It is no sufficient answer to say that
they are punished only when adjudged to be in the wrong. They do
not enter the courts upon equal terms. They must pay attorneys'
fees if wrong; they do not recover any if right; while their adversa-
ries recover if right, and pay nothing if wrong. In the suits, therefore, to which they are parties they are discriminated against, and
not treated as others. They do not stand equal before the law. They
do not receive its equal protection. All this is obvious from a mere
inspection of the statute": Gulf etc. Ry. v. Ellis, 165 U. S. 153.

The illustrations which we have given have been chiefly of statutes applicable to railway corporations, not because there is, in principle, any difference between these and other corporations, but because their business is such as to involve and justify special legislation. It is the business, however, and not the corporate capacity of
the associations transacting it, which justifies this legislation, and it
must have been declared unconstitutional if, by its terms, it had been
made inapplicable to natural persons conducting the same business
under the same circumstances. Neither special duties nor penalties
can be imposed on a corporation as such irrespective of the business
in which it is engaged. Some justification must be found for them
in that they tend to promote the public welfare or to accomplish some
other object which the legislature is entitled to seek, and even where
this is so, it does not justify the making of any arbitrary classification thereby subjecting one corporation or class of corporations to a
duty or penalty and exempting others therefrom, when it is clear that
no reason exists for including the one and exempting the other.
It is true that, to some extent, the states have the power of classification, and that, as a general rule, "if the law deals alike with all of
a certain class, it is not obnoxious to the charge of a denial of equal
protection. While, as a general proposition, this is undeniably true,
yet it is equally true that such classification cannot be made arbitrarily. The statute may not say that all white men shall be subject to the payment of attorneys' fees of parties successfully suing
them, and all black men may not. It may not say that all men
beyond a certain age shall be alone thus subject, or all men possessed
of a certain wealth. These are distinctions which do not furnish
any proper basis for the attempted classification. They must always

rest upon some difference which bears a reasonable and just relation to the act in respect to which the classification is proposed, and can never be made arbitrarily and without any such basis": Gulf etc. Ry. v. Ellis, 165 U. S. 155. Hence, whenever a special charge or duty has been enjoined or penalty imposed by statute upon a special class of persons or corporations from which others are exempt, the inquiry must be, Is there any reason for the classification or discrimination? In many instances there may be a reasonable difference of opinion respecting the answer, or, in other words, the courts may not be able to judicially notice or declare that the classification made is purely arbitrary, and may, therefore, regard the question as a proper one for legislative consideration and determination, and hence may not interpose to declare the legislative discretion has been abused. If, however, the legislature has singled out any class of persons or corporations and imposed upon them restrictions or penalties from which others are exempt, and there is no reason why the former should be subject to the restriction and the latter not, the statute must be pronounced unconstitutional: In re Eight Hour Law, 21 Colo. 29; Braceville Coal Co. v. People, 147 Ill. 66; 37 Am. St. Rep. 206; Chicago etc. Ry. Co. v. Moss, 60 Miss. 641; State v. Loomis, 115 Mo. 307.

Taxation.—The classification of property within a state for the purposes of taxation therein is a matter to be determined by the state acting by its legislative department, subject to the limitations imposed thereon by the state constitution. Courts will not undertake to revise its judgment, or to denounce or annul a system of taxation, or any part thereof, on the ground that the classification therein is arbitrary or not founded upon just reason. Hence a state is at liberty, not only to provide a mode of assessing corporations or some classes thereof different from that provided for the assessment of the property of natural persons or of other classes of corporations (Cleveland etc. Co. v. Backus, 133 Ind. 513; Grundy County v. Tennessee etc. Co,. 94 Tenn. 295; Pullman's etc. Co. v. Pennsylvania, 141 U. S. 18; Western Union Tel. Co. v Massachusetts, 125 U. S. 530), but to so tax corporations or any class thereof that they shall bear a greater burden of taxation than other persons or corporations upon property of equal value: Phoenix Ins. Co. v. Commonwealth, 5 Bush, 68; 98 Am. Dec. 331, and note; Western Union Tel. Co. v. Norman, 77 Fed. Rep. 13; State Railway Tax cases, 92 U. S. 575; Singer etc. Co. v. Wright, 33 Fed. Rep. 121; Pacific Exp. Co. v. Seibert, 142 U. S. 339; Home Ins. Co. v. New York, 134 U. S. 594; Marion Co. v. Coler, 23 U. S. App. 699; Sanford v. Poe, 37 U. S. App. 378; Pullman's etc. Co. v. Pennsylvania, 141 U. S. 18; Western Union Tel. Co. v. Taggart, 163 U. S. I. The legislature may also impose a special penalty upon corporations for not paying, when due, the taxes levied upon their property, if, in its opinion, the difference between the corporations subjected to such penalties and other taxpayers justifies the "placing them in a class by themselves and subjecting them to the particular method of effecting collection by means of penalties and suit for recovery of judgment for the delinquent taxes and penalties added": Western Union Tel. Co. v. Indiana, 165 U. S. 304. "It is not enough to justify the overthrow, by judicial decision, of a state law

imposing taxation, simply to show that such law operates unjustly":
Erie R. R. v. Pennsylvania, 153 U. S. 641.

As the principle justifying the imposition of special duties, burdens, and penalties upon corporations and others is now well settled,
the apparent divergence of judicial opinion upon this subject, so far
as it still exists, arises not from any doubt or uncertainty in the
principle, but in the differences of opinion which may reasonably be
expected in its application to existing controversies. In other words,
a classification which to one judge seems clearly arbitrary, to another may seem reasonable, or, at least, not so clearly unreasonable
that he can affirm that the legislature has acted beyond its authority
in making it. In Alabama, the jurisdiction of justices of the peace
in cases of tort was limited to fifty dollars, except in actions for injury to, or destruction of, livestock by locomotives or cars of railroads, in which it was extended to one hundred dollars. This exception was declared unconstitutional on the ground that the constitution
did not permit the legislature to discriminate between railway corporations and other persons, natural or artificial, in the matter of the
jurisdiction of inferior tribunals: Brown v. Alabama etc. Co., 87 Ala.
370. In Virginia, a statute giving liens to conductors, brakemen,
engine drivers, firemen, captains, stewards, pilots, clerks, depot or
office agents, storekeepers, mechanics, laborers, and all persons furnishing railroad iron, engines, cars, fuel, and all other supplies necessary to the operation of any railway, canal, or other transportation
company, or of any mining or manufacturing company doing business
in the state on the franchises, gross earnings, and on all the real
and personal property of the corporation, and awarding such liens
precedence over mortgages, trust deeds, and other hypothecations,
was upheld: Virginia etc. Co. v. Crozer etc. Co., 90 Va. 126; 44 Am.
St. Rep. 803.

Employés, Special Statutes Respecting.—Special statutes enacted for
the purpose of regulating the relations of corporations and their
employés have been assailed as forbidden class legislation with varied results. If employés in the discharge of their duties are subjected to special perils and hardships, legislation having for its object
their diminution is defensible. Hence, street railway corporations
may be compelled to provide screens in front of motormen in charge
of electric and other street-cars, to protect them from wind and
rain: State v. Nelson, 52 Ohio St. 88. Statutes regulating the time or
mode of the payment of wages due to employés of specified corporations, or undertaking to impose penalties if payment is not made at
such time or in such manner are more questionable. These are matters proper for regulation by contracts, express or implied, between
the corporations and their employés, and unless it may be reasonably
inferred that there is some reason for interposing for the protection
of employés of the class of persons or corporations designated in the
statute, not existing in the case of other employers and employés,
the statutes seem subject to assault both as class legislation and as
denying the parties the right to contract. The statute sustained in
the principal case and in a prior decision in the same state was directed against railway corporations only, and required them either

to pay their employés at the time of their discharge, or to be subject
to the penalty of having the employé deemed to remain in their employment at the same rate of wages as before his discharge, provided such wages should not continue more than sixty days unless
action therefor should be commenced within that time: Leep v. St.
Louis etc. Co., 58 Ark. 407; 41 Am. St. Rep. 109; St. Louis etc. Co. v.
Paul, 64 Ark. 83; ante, p. 154. It seems to us that both the spirit and
the result of these decisions are not susceptible of harmonization
with the decision of the supreme court of the United States declaring
that corporations are persons within the meaning of the Fourteenth
Amendment, and that a state may not, by arbitrary classification, discriminate against any person or corporation when no reason can be
suggested for the classification. Statutes requiring employés of a
designated class of corporations to be paid weekly or at other stated
times have been sustained by some of the state courts: Hancock v.
Yaden, 121 Ind. 366; 16 Am. St. Rep. 396; Opinion of Justices, 163.
Mass. 589; State v. Brown etc. Co., 18 R. I. 16; and overthrown by
others: Braceville Coal Co. v. People, 147 Ill. 66; 37 Am. St. Rep. 206,.
and note. It would doubtless be within the power of the legislature
to fix a time or mode of payment in the absence of any contract.
between the parties, but, as the time and mode of the performance of
a contract are substantial parts of it, to deny effect to the stipulations
of the parties upon these subjects is either to impair the obligation
of their contract or to deny that they have a right to contract respecting these matters. Neither of these results seems permissible
in a government having a constitution forbidding the impairment of
the obligations of contracts, securing to all persons the equal protection of the laws, and assuring to each the right to life, liberty,
and property, unless deprived thereof by due process of law. Of
course, we must concede that the right to contract is not so absolute
that it may not, in some instances, be subject to state legislation,
and that there may be classes of persons such as infants, lunatics,
adjudicated spendthrifts, and the like in whose favor the legislature
may interpose by denying them the right to contract, or, at least,
by denying persons contracting with them the right to enforce the
contract when it is manifestly unconscionable; but it can hardly be
assumed that reasons justifying an action of this character can be
applicable to whóle classes of employés or can be more applicable
to one class than to another, when it does not appear that the class
to which it is applied is specially incompetent to protect itself.
While these questions have not yet been decided by the national
courts, we judge those decisions of the state courts which have refused to enforce statutes restricting the right of corporations of desiguated classes to contract with their employés for the time and mode
of their payment and the hours during which they will work to be
more sustainable upon principle than the decisions indicating a contrary view. Under the assumption that persons or corporations engaged in mining or manufacturing made undue profits by reason of
compelling their employés to purchase supplies of them, statutes
have been enacted either forbidding such corporations or persons

from being interested in stores or schemes for the furnishing of supplies, or prohibiting them from issuing any script or other evidenco of indebtedness to their employés payable in anything except money. These statutes have been generally (Frorer v. People, 141 Ill. 171; State v. Loomis, 115 Mo. 307; Godcharles v. Wigeman, 113 Pa. St. 431; State v. Goodwill, 33 W. Va. 179; 25 Am. St. Rep. 863; State v. Fire Creek etc. Co., 33 W. Va. 188; 25 Am. St. Rep. 891), but not universally (Hancock v. Yaden, 121 Ind. 366; 16 Am. St. Rep. 396; State v. Peel etc. Co., 36 W. Va. 802), condemned as unconstitutional. A statute undertaking to provide the place where coal taken from a mine should be weighed, and that it should be unlawful for any person whose miners were paid upon the basis of the quantity of coal which each mined and delivered to his employer, to take any portion of the same by any process of screening or by any other device without accounting for and crediting the same to the miner from whose output such portion was screened or taken, was adjudged unconstitutional, because it attempted "to take from both employer and employé engaged in the mining business the right and power of fixing by contract the amount of wages the employé is to receive and the mode in which such wages are to be ascertained": Millett v. People, 117 Ill. 294; 57 Am. Rep. 869; Ramsey v. People, 142 Ill. 380; Harding v. People, 160 Ill. 459; 52 Am. St. Rep. 344; In re House Bill No. 203, 21 Colo. 27; contra, State v. Peel etc. Co., 36 W. Va. 802. A statute providing that no railway company, insurance company, or association of other persons shall demand, exact, require, or enter into any contract, agreement, or stipulation with any person about to enter or in the employment of any railway company whereby such person agrees and stipulates to surrender or waive any right to damages against any railway corporation, thereafter arising from personal injuries or death, or whereby he agrees to surrender or waive in case he asserts the same, or any other right whatsoever, and that all such agreements or stipulations should be void, was held unconstitutional in Shaver v. Pennsylvania Co., 71 Fed. Rep. 931. In Nebraska, a statute was enacted providing that for all mechanics, servants, and laborers, except those engaged in farm or domestic labor, a day's work should not exceed eight hours, and that for working any employé over the prescribed time, the employer should pay extra compensation in increasing geometrical progression for the excess over eight hours. This statute was declared void, because it discriminated against farm and domestic laborers and interfered with the right of parties to contract with reference to compensation for their services. It was said that "to forbid an individual or a class the right to the acquisition and enjoyment of property in such manner as should be permitted to the community at large would be to deprive them of liberty in particulars of primary importance to their pursuit of happiness; and those who shall claim a right to do so ought to be able to show specific authority therefor, instead of calling upon others to show how and where the authority is negatived": Low v. Rees etc. Co., 41 Neb. 127; 43 Am. St. Rep. 670; In re Eight Hour Bill, 21 Colo. 29. In Massachusetts, a statute declar-

ing that no employer should impose a fine or withhold the wages, or
any part of the wages, of an employé engaged in weaving for any
imperfection which might arise during the progress of weaving was
held void, because it conflicted with that part of the constitution enu-
merating as one of the inalienable rights of man that of acquiring,
possessing, and protecting property: Commonwealth v. Perry, 155
Mass. 117; 31 Am. St. Rep. 533.

The court of appeals of West Virginia, after having declared
unconstitutional a statute prohibiting all persons engaged in mining
or manufacturing from issuing for the payment of labor any order
or paper unless the same purported to be redeemable at its face value
in lawful money, bearing interest at the legal rate, payable to the
employé or bearer within thirty days, and also another statute declaring it to be unlawful for any person, firm, or corporation engaged in mining and manufacturing and interested in merchandis-
ing to knowingly sell any merchandise or supplies to any employé
at a greater per cent of profit than when selling merchandise or
supplies of like character, quality, and quantity to other customers
paying therefor in cash, on the ground that such statutes were
class legislation and unjust interferences with the rights, privileges,
and property both of employer and employé (State v. Goodwill, 33
W. Va. 179; 25 Am. St. Rep. 863; State v. Fire Creek etc. Co., 33
W. Va. 188; 25 Am. St. Rep. 891), some three years later affirmed,
by an equal division of its judges, the judgment of a subordinate
court sustaining a statute prohibiting any corporation, firm, or person engaged in any trade or business from issuing, selling, or delivering in payment of wages due to its employés any script, token,
draft, or other evidence of indebtedness payable or redeemable otherwise than in lawful money, and also another statute providing for
the weighing and measuring of coal at the place where mined before
it was screened, and that those mining for such coal should be paid
for their services computed upon its weight before screening. It
will be observed that both of these statutes were free from the objection that they were specially directed against corporations or
were class legislation, for they were applicable to all persons,
whether natural or artificial, engaged in any business. They were,
however, unquestionably interferences with the right of employers
and employés to so contract as to regulate the terms upon which
payments for their services should be made. The decision was justified largely on the ground, however, that the statutes were assailed
by corporations which had been granted peculiar privileges by the
state, from which peculiar responsibilities supervened, requiring
special legislation to be enacted. The judges affirming the constitutionality of the statutes recited the legislation of the state bestowing
extraordinary privileges on mining corporations and requiring every
corporation chartered under the laws of the state to take out a
license before doing any business, and also relied upon the general
provisions of the code reserving to the legislature the power to alter
and amend all charters of incorporation. The statutes were also
assailed as in conflict with the constitution of the state affirming

that "all men are by nature equally free and independent, and have
certain inherent rights, of which, when they enter into a state of
society, they cannot, by any compact, deprive or divest their pos-
terity, namely, the enjoyment of life and liberty, with the means
of acquiring and possessing property, and of pursuing and obtaining
happiness and safety." The conclusions leading to the sustaining
of the statute were summed up as follows: "Upon the whole, therefore, we are not able to say that the legislature has transcended its
power to make reasonable police regulations, or that it has violated
the article of the constitution of this state above quoted. We base
this decision in this case: 1. Upon the ground that the defendant is a
corporation in the enjoyment of unusual and extraordinary privileges, which enables it and similar associations to surround themselves with a vast retinue of laborers, who need to be protected
against all fraudulent or suspicious devices in the weighing of coal
and in the payment of labor; 2. The defendant is a licensee, pursuing a vocation which the state has taken under its general supervision for the purpose of securing the safety of employés, by ventila-
tion, inspection, and governmental report, and the defendant, therefore must submit to such regulations as the sovereign thinks conducive to public health, public morals, or public security. We do not
base this decision so much upon the ground that the business is affected by the public use, but upon the still higher ground, that the
public tranquility and the good and safety of society demand, where
the number of employés is such that specific contracts with each
laborer would be improbable, if not impossible, that in general contracts justice shall prevail between operator and miner; and, in the
company's dealing with the multitude of laborers with whom the
state has by special legislation enabled the owners and operators to
surround themselves, that all opportunities for fraud shall be removed": State v. Peel etc. Co., 36 W. Va. 802, 819. This decision was
by a court whose members were equally divided in opinion, two affirming and two denying the constitutionality of the statute in question, the decision of the trial court in favor of their constitutionality
being thereby affirmed. The judges thus sustaining these statutes
did not assume to overrule or otherwise question the previous decisions of the same court. Perhaps there was no unavoidable conflict
between the cases reported in 33 West Virginia, and that reported in
36 West Virginia, for the statutes overthrown by the former were
directed to certain employments only, and might hence have been
declared forbidden as class legislation, while the statutes sustained
in the latter were applicable to all persons and corporations and to
every business and trade in which the relation of employer and employé might exist. But when we examine the opinions of those
members of the court affirming the constitutionality of the later
statutes we find them founded not upon the ground that the legislation was general, but rather upon the ground that it was intended to
be special, or, in other words, to reach certain corporations which,
through receiving special benefits from the state, had acquired great
property and power and had come into contract relations with a

multitude of employés, and brought into being a peculiar class of
circumstances entitling the state to interpose for the protection of
such employés. The statutes were, however, on their face as applicable to natural persons as to corporations, and to persons employing
a single assistant or servant in their trade or business for a single
day as to corporations of the class by which their constitutionality
was questioned. In so far as the statutes were attempted to be defended as mere alterations or amendments of charters of incorporation which the legislature had reserved the power to make, the court
seems to have discovered a secret purpose of the legislature nowhere
suggested by the statutes themselves, for they were not directed
against corporations, except to the same extent as against natural
persons. Statutes of similar import were elsewhere sustained as
mere amendments of corporate charters: Shaffer v. Union etc. Co.,
55 Md. 74. We do not, however, understand that the reservation
of the right to amend or alter corporate charters involves the power
to deal with matters not usually germane to a charter, and hence we
cannot concede that it gives the legislature power to deprive corporations of rights assured to them as persons by the constitution of the
United States.

Female Employés.—The legislature of the state of Illinois enacted
that no female should be employed in any factory or workshop more
than eight hours in any one day or forty-eight hours in any one week.
and defined a factory, workshop, or manufacturing establishment,
to mean any place where goods or products are manufactured, repaired, cleaned, or sorted in whole or in part, for sale or for wages,
and provided that any firm or corporation violating the act should
be guilty of a misdemeanor, and on conviction, fined a sum not more
nor less than that designated in the statute. This statute was assailed on the ground that it was unconstitutional as imposing an unwarranted restriction upon the right to contract, and was defended
on the claim that it was a sanitary provision justifiable as an exercise of the police power of the state. The statute was declared to
be in conflict with section 2 of article 2 of the constitution of Illinois,
declaring that no person shall be deprived of life, liberty, or property
without due process of law, and it was said: "The legislature has
no right to deprive one class of persons of privileges allowed to
other persons under like conditions. The man who is forbidden to
acquire and enjoy property in the same manner in which the rest
of the community is permitted to acquire and enjoy it is deprived
of liberty in particulars of primary importance to his pursuit of
happiness. If one man is denied the right to contract as he has hitherto done under the law, and as others are still allowed to do by the
law, he is deprived of both liberty and property to the extent to
which he is thus deprived of such right." The court said it was
not unmindful that the right to contract might be subject to limitation "growing out of the duties which the individual owes to society,
to the public or to the government. These limitations are sometimes
imposed by the obligation to so use one's own as not to injure another, by the character of property as affected with a public interest

or devoted to a public use, by the demands of public policy, or the
necessity of protecting the public from fraud or injury, by want of
capacity, by the needs of the necessitous borrower as against the
demands of the extortionate lender. But the power of the legislature
to thus limit the right to contract must rest upon some reasonable
basis, and cannot be arbitrarily exercised. It has been said that such
power is based in every case upon some condition, but not on the
absolute right to control. Where legislative enactments, which
operate upon classes of individuals only, have been held to be valid,
it has been where the classification was reasonable, and not arbitrary." The court further denounced the act as partial and discriminating in its character, and as "a purely arbitrary restriction upon
the fundamental right of the citizen to control his or her own time
and faculties. It substitutes the judgment of the legislature for the
judgment of the employer and employé in a matter about which they
are competent to agree with each other. It assumes to dictate to
what extent the capacity to labor may be exercised by the employé,
and takes away the right of private judgment as to the amount and
duration of the labor to be put forth in a specified period. When the
legislature thus undertakes to impose an unreasonable and unjust
burden upon any citizen or class of citizens, it transcends the authority intrusted to it by the constitution, even though it imposes the
same burden upon all other citizens or classes of citizens. General
laws may be as tyrannical as partial laws": Ritchie v. People, 155
Ill. 98; 46 Am. St. Rep. 315, 321, 322. In California, a municipal ordinance forbidding any contractor employed under a contract with
the city to employ any person to work for more than eight hours a
day, or to employ Chinese labor, was held to be void, because it was
"simply an attempt to prevent certain parties from employing others in a lawful business and paying them for their services, and is
a direct infringement of the rights of such persons to make and enforce their contracts": Ex parte Kuback, 85 Cal. 274; 20 Am. St. Rep.
226.

Corporations are also protected by the constitution of the United
States, though they are subject to state regulation, from any action
of the state, whether by its legislature or otherwise, the result of
which may be to compel them to render services without reasonable
compensation therefor. The further consideration of this branch of
our subject will be found in the note to San Diego Water Co. v.
San Diego, post, p. 261.

Nebraska Meal Mills v. St. Louis Southwestern Railway Company.

[64 Arkansas, 169.]

RAILWAYS—BILLS OF LADING, DELIVERY OF GOODS WITHOUT EXACTING SURRENDER OF, LIABILITY FOR.—A railway corporation delivering goods to the consignee in accordance with the terms of the bill of lading, but without requiring the presentation or surrender thereof, is not answerable to the consignor, though he had forwarded such bill with a draft attached thereto to a bank for collection, thus showing an intention that the consignee should not have the goods without first paying therefor, the corporation having no knowledge of such intention.

BILLS OF LADING AND WAREHOUSE RECEIPTS, EFFECT OF STATUTES CONCERNING NEGOTIABILITY OF.—A statute providing that warehouse receipts and bills of lading shall be negotiable by written indorsement, and that persons to whom they may be transferred shall be deemed to be the owners of the property therein described, so far as to give validity to any pledge, lien, or transfer, and that the property described in such bills of lading or receipts shall not be delivered except on surrender and cancellation thereof, does not affect the right of the carrier to deliver the property to the consignee, where the bill of lading has not been transferred, though it is held by the consignor who does not intend that the property shall be delivered until he has been paid therefor, the carrier having no notice of this intention.

Action against the defendant railway corporation for delivering to E. D. Russell a carload of meal shipped him by the plaintiff, it having retained the bill of lading and sent it with a sight draft attached thereto to a bank, intending it to collect such draft before delivering the bill of lading. The defendant, having no notice of the draft, delivered the meal to the consignee without making any inquiry concerning the bill of lading, and the plaintiff, as a consequence, lost the money due it as the purchase price of the meal. Judgment for the defendant. The plaintiff appealed.

Bridges & Wooldridge, for the appellant.

Sam H. West, J. M. & J. G. Taylor, and Dodge & Johnson, for the appellees.

[171] RIDDICK, J. The bill of lading under which the meal was forwarded by defendant railway company stipulated that it was to be transported to Altheimer, Arkansas, and there delivered to the consignee, E. D. Russell. It is admitted that the railway company performed its contract in strict accordance with its terms. But it is said that the consignee, Russell, had not paid for the meal; that the consignor had drawn upon him for the price of the meal, and had forwarded the draft, with the bill of

lading attached thereto, to a bank for collection, thus showing an intention that Russell should not have the meal without first paying for it. The answer to this argument is, that if it be true that the consignor did not intend that the meal should be delivered until the payment of the purchase price, yet it is also true that the railway company had no notice of such intention. The meal was billed "straight" to the consignee, and, as the railway company had no notice of the intention of the consignor to retain the ownership and control of the property, it was justified in presuming that the consignee was the owner thereof, and was discharged by a delivery to him at the place specified in the bill of lading: Sweet v. Barney, 23 N. Y. 335; O'Dougherty v. Boston etc. R. R. Co., 1 Thomp. & C. 477; Lawrence v. Minturn, 17 How. 100; McEwen v. Jeffersonville etc. R. R. Co., 33 Ind. 368; 5 Am. Rep. 216; Hutchinson on Carriers, sec. 130; Elliott on Railroads, sec. 1426.

It is argued for appellant that the railway carrier had no right to deliver to the consignee except upon a production of the bill of lading. To this argument we reply that the carrier must deliver in accordance with the bill of lading, and if it delivers without requiring the production of the bill of lading, it assumes the consequence of a wrong delivery. But in this case the delivery was made strictly in accordance with the requirement of the bill of lading, which evidenced the contract made with plaintiff, and he therefore has no right to complain.

Counsel for appellant have cited Furman v. Union Pac. R. R. Co., 106 N. Y. 579, and Merchants' Despatch etc. Co. v. Merriam, 111 Ind. 6, as sustaining the contention that under the circumstances here the railway company [172] was guilty of negligence in making the delivery without requiring a production of the bill of lading. But a broad distinction between those cases and the one at bar is that in neither of those cases were the goods billed "straight," and in neither of them were the goods delivered to the person to whom the bill of lading stipulated the delivery should be made. In both of those cases it was said that the carrier was guilty of negligence in not requiring the production of the bill of lading before delivery of the goods, for the reason that such bill would have shown that the person to whom delivery was made was not the consignee. In each of those cases the carrier failed to deliver the goods in accordance with the terms of the bill of lading. The delivery was made to a person not named as consignee in the bill of lading, and the carrier was held liable for a wrong delivery.

But those cases can be no authority for holding a carrier liable for a delivery made to the person named as consignee in the bill of lading, and in exact accordance with its terms.

It is further said that; apart from the common law, the railway company is liable under the provisions of our statute: Sandel and Hill's Digest, secs. 509, 510. These sections provide that warehouse receipts and bills of lading given for goods, wares, merchandise, cotton, grain, and other commodity shall be negotiable by written indorsement, and that "any and all persons to whom the same may be transferred shall be deemed and held to be the owner of such goods, wares, merchandise, cotton, grain, flour, or other produce or commodity, so far as to give validity to any pledge, lien, or transfer given, made or created thereby, or on the faith thereof, and no property . . . . specified in such bills of lading or receipts shall be delivered except on surrender and cancellation of such receipts and bills of lading; provided that all such receipts and bills of lading which shall have the words 'Not negotiable' plainly written or stamped on the face thereof shall be exempt from the provisions of this act." But we are of the opinion that this act does not affect the right of the carrier to deliver, except in those cases where the bill of lading has been transferred. Bills of lading are frequently transferred as security for loans and advances, and the purpose of this statute was to protect those who make advances upon the faith of such transfers. The case of Colgate v. Pennsylvania [173] Co., 102 N. Y. 120, cited by counsel for appellant, arose under a statute similar to our statute. But in that case the bill of lading had been transferred by the consignee named therein, and, as it was issued without the words "Not negotiable" upon it, the court said that the carrier was bound to know that it "may have passed into other hands and become the property of others than the consignee." The carrier was held liable because by an assignment of the bill of lading the title of the property had been transferred from the consignee to the plaintiff in that case. The case thus came squarely within the scope of the statute which, to protect purchasers and others advancing money upon bills of lading, required the carrier to deliver only upon surrender of such bills of lading. But in this case the bill of lading was not transferred, the rights of no third party are involved and neither the statute nor the decision just referred to has any bearing upon the question to be determined. And so without discussing them, we may say, of the other cases cited by counsel for appellant, they do not in our opinion sus-

tain the contention that the railway company is liable under
the facts of this case.

If, as counsel for appellant contends, the bill of lading represented the meal, and the ownership of the meal was in appellant so long as it held the bill of lading, still, as such owner,
it unconditionally directed the carrier to deliver the meal to
Russell. It would seem unreasonable to believe that the legislature intended to impose a liability upon the carrier in favor
of the consignor for obeying and carrying out the directions
of such consignor in regard to the delivery of the consigned
property, for such intention would be contrary to common principles of reason and justice. To justify the court in arriving
at such a conclusion, the language of the act to that effect should
be so plain and direct that it would not be reasonable to give it a
different meaning. The language of this act does not, in our
opinion, justify any such conclusion. On the contrary, the purpose of it, as before stated, was to protect persons not parties
to the bill of lading originally, but who for a valuable consideration acquired an interest in the property represented by it
through the transfer of the bill of lading to them. There was
certainly no occasion for an act of this kind to protect [174] the
rights of the consignor, for he is a party to the contract of
shipment, and can protect himself by stipulations therein. In
this case the appellant could have protected itself against the
failure of the consignee to pay for the meal by making the consignment to its own order, or, after the meal had been consigned
to Russell, it might, upon discovery of his insolvency, have effected the same purpose by stoppage in transitu and notice to
the railway company not to deliver until payment of the draft
to which the bill of lading had been attached. But the appellant failed to do this, and the railway company in good faith
delivered the meal in accordance with its contract and the directions of appellant, as shown by the bill of lading. Under
such circumstances, it seems to us, notwithstanding the able
argument of counsel for appellant, that this claim for damages
has neither the letter of the law nor any principle of justice to
sustain it.

Judgment affirmed.

Battle, J., dissents.

———

BILLS OF LADING—MISDELIVERY OF GOODS BY CAR-
RIER.—The delivery of goods by a common carrier to a consignee
is made at the peril of the carrier, unless, when made, the consignee
surrenders the bill of lading either made or indorsed to himself;

Union Pac. Ry. Co. v. Johnson, 45 Neb. 57; 50 Am. St. Rep. 540, and
note. See Ratzer v. Burlington etc. R. R. Co., 64 Minn. 245; 58 Am.
St. Rep. 530. A railroad company, bound by a bill of lading to deliver
goods on payment of freight and "presentation of a duplicate" bill, is
responsible if it makes delivery without such presentation. Such
clause is for the benefit of the consignor: McEwen v. Jeffersonville
etc. R. R. Co., 33 Ind. 368; 5 Am. Rep. 216. See extended note to
Bolling v. Kirby, 24 Am. St. Rep. 816; also, monographic note to
Chandler v. Sprague, 38 Am. Dec. 407-426, on bills of lading; and extended note to Weyand v. Atchison etc. Ry. Co., 9 Am. St. Rep. 512-
514.

BILLS OF LADING—NEGOTIABILITY—STATUTES IN RE-
GARD THERETO.—A bill of lading does not possess such characteristics of negotiable instruments as do bills of exchange: Douglas v.
People's Bank, 86 Ky. 176; 9 Am. St. Rep. 276; Weyand v. Atchison
etc. Ry. Co., 75 Iowa, 573; 9 Am. St. Rep. 504. It is said rather to be
quasi negotiable: Monographic note to Chandler v. Sprague, 38 Am.
Dec. 420. Statutes in different states have made bills of lading
negotiable, but such statutes are construed as not putting them on
the footing of bills of exchange: Monographic note to Chandler v.
Sprague, 38 Am. Dec. 423; but merely as making the transfer and delivery of these symbols of property, in the mode therein prescribed,
equivalent, for certain purposes, to an actual transfer and delivery
of the property itself: National Bank of Commerce v. Chicago etc.
R. R. Co., 44 Minn. 224; 20 Am. St. Rep. 566; note to Bank of Roches-
ter v. Jones, 55 Am. Dec. 299, 300.

Cox v. Harris.

[64 Arkansas, 213]

MORTGAGE, WAIVER OF.—One who, having a mortgage on
personal property, sues out an attachment against the mortgagor
upon the mortgage debt and levies the writ upon the property mortgaged, thereby waives the mortgage lien thereon. This waiver cannot be avoided by proving that at the time of the attachment the
plaintiffs therein were not able to discover whether the property
attached was the same as that mortgaged, if they persisted in their
attachment until after the judgment therein, and desisted only when
the property was declared to be exempt from execution.

Replevin to recover possession of a mule. The plaintiffs
claimed under a mortgage executed by the defendant, Harris, to
the plaintiffs, Cox & Denton. They assigned the note secured
by the mortgage to Hill, Fontaine & Co., who brought suit
thereon, in which they procured the issuing of an attachment,
and caused it to be levied on the mule. After judgment was
recovered in the attachment suit, the defendant, Harris, filed a
schedule of his property, claiming the mule as exempt from execution. The claim was sustained, and this action was thereafter
brought to obtain possession under the mortgage. The court,
at the trial, instructed the jury that if the plaintiffs sued out the
writ of attachment and levied it on the mule in an effort to make

their debt secured by the mortgage, this would waive the lien held by the plaintiffs by virtue of such mortgage. Verdict and judgment for the defendants, the plaintiffs appealed.

Rose, Hemingway & Rose, for the appellants.

Carmichael & Seawell, J. C. Floyd, and S. W. Woods, for the appellees.

215 RIDDICK, J. The question to be determined in this case is, whether the appellants waived their mortgage lien by suing out an attachment against the mortgagor, and causing it to be levied upon the mortgaged property. It is a familiar principle of law that one is not, as a rule, allowed to avail himself of the advantages of inconsistent positions in a litigation concerning the same subject matter: Dyckman v. Sevatson, 39 Minn. 132.

The appellants in this case held the note of Harris, which was secured by a mortgage upon the mule in controversy. The note was past due, and appellants could have taken charge of the property, and sold it, under the power contained in the mortgage, but they elected, instead, to bring suit before a justice of the peace, and attach the property. Now, so long as the mortgage lien existed, the mortgagor, Harris, had no interest in the mule subject to attachment, for mortgaged personal property is not subject to execution or attachment for a debt to the mortgagor: Jennings v. McIlroy, 42 Ark. 236; 48 Am. Rep. 61. But appellants had the right to waive their mortgage lien and attach the property. The levy of the attachment amounted to an assertion by appellants that the property was subject to seizure and sale under the attachment. But, as this could not be true if the lien of the mortgage still existed, the levy of the attachment was the same as a denial on the part of appellants that the mortgage lien existed, and was in effect a waiver on their part of the lien created by the mortgage. In other words, having sued out an attachment, levied it upon the property in question, and prosecuted the attachment suit to judgment, they must be held to have waived rights which were inconsistent with such a course of procedure. The mortgage lien, being inconsistent with such attachment, was thereby waived, and appellants have nothing upon which to base their action of replevin: Evans v. Warren, 122 Mass. 303; Cochrane v. Rich, 142 Mass. 15; Whitney v. Farrar, 51 Me. 418; Haynes v. Sanborn, 45 N. H. 429; Dyckman v. Sevatson, 39 Minn. 132;

Jones on Chattel Mortgages, 2d ed., sec. 565; Pingrey on Chattel Mortgages, sec. 808; Cobbey on Chattel Mortgages, sec. 746.

The case of Whitmore v. Tatum, 54 Ark. 457, 26 Am. St. Rep. 56, cited by appellants, was a case where the mortgagee of real estate had [210] levied upon and sold the equity of redemption. In that respect there is a distinction between real and personal property, for the mortgagor's equity of redemption in real property may be sold under execution, but not so with his interest in mortgaged personal property. For this reason, neither of the cases cited by appellants conflict with the rule applied by the circuit court in this case: Jennings v. McIlroy, 42 Ark. 236; 48 Am. Rep. 61; Whitmore v. Tatum, 54 Ark. 457; 26 Am. St. Rep. 56; Rice v. Wilburn, 31 Ark. 109; 25 Am. Rep. 549.

We have not overlooked the contention of appellants that, at the time the attachment was begun, they were not able to find out which one of the mules owned by Harris was covered by the mortgage. The two mules were similar in appearance. Harris refused to say which mule was covered by the mortgage, and appellants claim that, in this dilemma, the attachment was sued out and levied on both mules, to prevent Harris from taking them out of the state before they could ascertain which one was mortgaged. But whatever cause may have led appellants to bring a suit by attachment, instead of one for the possession of the mule, the proof clearly shows that, having commenced it, they had no idea of abandoning or dismissing such suit. They commenced their action, and caused the mule to be seized under the writ of attachment on the 17th of March, and obtained judgment on the 28th of March. During all the time the mule was held under the writ of attachment, appellants, so far as the proof discloses, made no further effort to find out which mule was covered by the mortgage, but continued to prosecute their right under the attachment until they obtained judgment and an order of sale. They only desisted when the property was declared to be exempt from sale under the attachment, and taken from the officer by an order of the justice of the peace. Having all this time actively asserted that the attachment was valid, it is now too late to assume the inconsistent position of treating it as of no validity. As the determination of this question disposes of the case, we find it unnecessary to consider the other points discussed by counsel. Finding no error, the judgment is affirmed.

Absent, Wood, J.

ELECTION OF REMEDIES—WHEN IRREVOCABLE.—A man may not take two contradictory positions, and where he has a right to choose one of two modes of redress, and the two are so inconsistent that the assertion of one involves the negation or repudiation of the other, his deliberate choice of one, with knowledge or means of knowledge of such facts as would authorize a resort to each, will preclude him from going back and electing again: Kearney etc. Co. v. Union Pac. Ry. Co., 97 Iowa, 719; 59 Am. St. Rep. 434, and note. His failure to secure satisfaction by means of the remedy which he has adopted furnishes no legal reason for permitting him to resort to the other: Monographic note to Fowler v. Bowery Sav. Bank, 10 Am. St. Rep. 489. See extended note to Thomas v. Joslin, 1 Am. St. Rep. 626-629.

BATES *v.* DUNCAN.

[64 ARKANSAS, 339.]

LICENSE TO USE REAL PROPERTY, WHEN NOT ASSIGNABLE.—One who, in consideration of moneys furnished with which to assist in the erection of a building, is given the right to use and occupy the second story thereof, acquires a mere license which he cannot assign to another, and his attempt to assign terminates his license.

Action to recover possession of the second story of a building erected by the plaintiff, Bates, and others, upon a lot conveyed to them as trustees for the subscribers of a fund with which the lot was purchased. The trustees of the masonic lodge agreed to furnish moneys to construct the second story of the building and one-half of the roof, in pursuance of an understanding that the lodge might have, use, and occupy such second story. The first story was used as a schoolhouse of the Waldron school district. Four years after the construction of the building the trustees executed and acknowledged a writing as follows: "Know all men by these presents, that we, A. A. Sanford, T. G. Bates, John Rawlings, S. K. Duncan, Fred Malen, and J. K. Bell, trustees, recognizing the right of Waldron Lodge, No. 132, to the upper part of the Waldron Academy, which main building is twenty-eight by sixty feet, and is situated on the following described real estate, to wit, ... do hereby guarantee to said Waldron Lodge, No. 132, the exclusive right to use and occupy said room, together with the right of ingress and egress at any and all such times as said lodge or its representatives may designate. Given under our hands this 29th day of December." The lodge afterward, by an oral contract, sold and delivered to school district No. 15 all of its title, right and interest in the second story. The defendant, Duncan, was, at the commencement of the present action, in possession as teacher for that school district. Judgment in favor of the defendants. The plaintiffs appealed.

Miles & Miles and S. R. Cockrill, for the appellants.

A. G. Leming and Daniel Hon, for the appellee.

342 RIDDICK, J. This action was commenced by the appellants, T. G. Bates et al., trustees, to recover the possession of the second story of a schoolhouse situated in the town of Waldron. That portion of the building was in the possession of G. W. Duncan, who held it as teacher, employed by school district No. 15 of Scott county. He and said school district are the defendants in the action, but the school district is the real party in interest, and claims the right to the possession and control of the second story of the building by virtue of a purchase from the Masonic Lodge of Waldron. There are several interesting questions discussed by counsel in this case, but we will first consider and determine the nature and extent of the interest held by the Masonic Lodge of Waldron in the property in controversy.

The evidence in the case is not before us, except as the facts are stated in the findings of the circuit judge. On this point he found that, "by an arrangement and agreement entered into between the lodge and the appellant trustees, the lodge agreed to furnish the money and build a second story to said building, the floor for the same and one-half the roof, the said lodge to have, use, and occupy the said second story. It was understood that it was going to use the same as a lodge room, though no limitation of its use to that purpose, or of the right of the lodge to rent or sell the same, was entered into." We understand from this finding that the lodge paid nothing for the lots, and took no interest in them, but was permitted to build a second story upon the school building owned by the trustees, and to "have, use, and occupy the same."

Although there was no express limitation upon the power of **343** the lodge to sell, still we are of the opinion that, under the facts found by the court, the law itself affixed a limitation. In other words, we are of the opinion that the authority granted to the lodge to erect and to "have, use, and occupy" the second story was a personal right conferred upon the lodge, and not assignable. We are confirmed in this view by the instrument of writing which was afterward executed by the trustees, and delivered by them to the lodge. This instrument, which is set out in the statement of facts, guarantees to said lodge "the exclusive right to use and occupy said room, together with the right of ingress and egress at any and all such times as said lodge or its representatives may designate." The parol agreement did not convey any title to the lodge, and this written instrument does not pretend to convey any, but only grants the right to use and occupy. There is in it no mention of assignees, successors, or use of other words evincing an intent to extend the right to others beyond the members of the lodge or to give the lodge authority to assign their interest in the building. On the contrary, the understanding was that the lodge wanted it for a lodge room, and the grant of the right to use and occupy is to the lodge and its representatives, thus showing that the grant was a personal privilege to the lodge. Both the lodge and the school district seem to have recognized the fact that the lodge had no title or interest in the land, beyond the mere license to use and occupy this second story. The lodge took no conveyance from the trustees, but, in erecting this second story, acted upon a parol agreement, and afterward accepted a writing, which conveyed no title, but only gave the right to use and occupy. When the lodge sold to the school district, although it was a cash transaction, no deed or writing, such as is common in conveyances of land, was given, but the transfer was made by a parol agreement; thus evincing a tacit understanding that possession was all the lodge had to convey, and that it owned no interest in the land requiring a written conveyance.

These facts strengthen the conviction that the extent of the interest of the lodge in this property was only a license to use and occupy. But a license granted by the owner of land for another to erect a building thereon, with right to use and occupy it, and with privilege of ingress and egress, conveys
³⁴⁴ only a personal right to the grantee, and is not assignable: Jackson v. Babcock, 4 Johns. 418; Harris v. Gillingham, 6 N. H. 9; 23 Am. Dec. 701; Prince v. Case, 10 Conn. 375; 27 Am. Dec. 675; Jamieson v. Millemann, 3 Duer, 255; Dark v. Johnston, 55 Pa. St. 164; 93 Am. Dec. 732; Pearson v. Hartman, 100 Pa. St. 84; Washburn on Easements and Servitude, 4th ed., 17.

"A man," says Judge Strong, in Dark v. Johnston, 55 Pa. St. 164, 93 Am. Dec. 732, "may well accord a privilege upon his lands to one person which he would refuse to all others. Hence it is held that a personal license is not assignable, and that an assignment by a licensee determines his right. . . . . He may abandon or release. He cannot substitute another to his right." And in that case, although the licensee had expended money and

made such valuable improvements upon the faith of his license
that the court was of the opinion that the license as to him had
become irrevocable, still it held that his rights were terminated
by the sale, and that such sale conferred no rights in the property to his grantees.

We can conceive of many reasons why the trustees of this
property might be willing to extend this privilege to the lodge,
and not to other persons, but it is unnecessary to discuss that
question further.

Having, after some hesitation, concluded from the language
of the written instrument delivered by the trustees to the lodge,
and from the other facts stated in the findings of the court,
that this was a personal privilege conferred upon the lodge,
and not assignable, it follows that school district No. 15 took
nothing by the purchase from the lodge, and that the rights of
the lodge were terminated by such attempted sale.

It is true that the appellant trustees could have assented to
such sale, and could have extended the license to occupy the
second story to school district No. 15; but the findings of the
court do not show these facts. It is stated in the findings of
the court "that no objection was raised by the trustees or subscribers aforesaid, or anyone else, to the purchase from the Masonic lodge." But this does not show that the trustees assented
to the sale, nor is it sufficient to estop the trustees from asserting
their rights against the district. It is not shown that the trustees had notice of the purchase before it was consummated, or
[345] that their failure to object misled or affected in any way the
action of the school district.

The findings show that two of the appellant trustees were
in 1886 trustees also of school district No. 15, but it is not
shown that they were such in 1888 at the time of this purchase
from the Masonic lodge. As these trustees were residents within
school district No. 15 at the time of this purchase, we may suspect that they had notice of it, and assented to it; but the court
cannot base its judgment upon mere suspicion.

Our conclusion that the lodge had no assignable interest
in the property, and that such interest as it had was terminated
by its attempted sale thereof, makes it unnecessary to discuss the
question as to whether an unincorporated lodge, as such, could
take title to land, or, indeed, to notice any of the other points
raised. For the reasons given, the judgment of the circuit court
is reversed, and the cause remanded, with an order that judgment for the possession of said second story be entered in favor

of the appellants, T. G. Bates et al., as trustees. But so much
of the judgment as denied relief to the school district of Waldron
is affirmed.

LICENSE—ASSIGNABILITY OF.—A license is a bare authority to
do certain acts or series of acts upon another's land without possessing any estate therein, and is not assignable: Hazleton v. Putnam,
3 Pinney, 107; 3 Chand. 117; 54 Am. Dec. 158. It is a mere personal
privilege to the assignee and is not assignable: Extended note to
Lawrence v. Springer, 31 Am. St. Rep. 713; Cowles v. Kidder, 24 N.
H. 364; 57 Am. Dec. 287. See, however, Keystone Lumber Co. v.
Kolman, 94 Wis. 465; 59 Am. St. Rep. 905.

Hampton *v.* Cook.

[64 Arkansas, 353.]

JUDGMENT LIEN, EFFECT OF DEATH OF THE JUDG-
MENT DEBTOR.—By the statute of Arkansas, on the death of a
judgment debtor, his real property becomes subject to the exclusive
jurisdiction of the probate court, to be disposed of under its authority, notwithstanding existing judgment liens thereon.

HUSBAND AND WIFE—ESTATE BY THE CURTESY EX-
ISTS NOTWITHSTANDING STATUTES CONFERRING ADDI-
TIONAL RIGHTS ON MARRIED WOMEN.—A statute declaring
that the real and personal property of every married woman in the
state shall, so long as she may choose, be and remain her separate
estate and property, and may be devised, bequeathed, or conveyed
by her the same as if she were unmarried, and shall not be subject
to the debts of her husband, does not, in the event of her death
without conveying or making any other disposition of the property,
defeat her husband's rights as tenant by the curtesy.

HUSBAND AND WIFE—ESTATE BY CURTESY NOT SUB-
JECT TO WIFE'S LIABILITIES.—Though a judgment is recovered
against a wife, under which if a sale is made in her lifetime, the
title in fee will vest in the purchaser, yet, upon her death without
such sale, an estate vests in her husband as tenant by the curtesy
free from the lien of such judgment.

Fletcher Rolleson, for the appellants.

N. W. Norton and P. R. Andrews, for the appellees.

354 BATTLE, J. John J. Cook and Ella E. Cook were husband and wife. Issue of their marriage was born alive. The wife
carried on a mercantile business on her sole and separate account,
and during the course of the business acquired certain real estate,
consisting of farms and houses. Hampton, Reed & Co. sold goods
to her, and upon the debts thereby created obtained judgments
against her in the Woodruff circuit court. She mortgaged the
lands and houses to the bank of Newport. Thereafter, in 1892,
she died intestate, leaving her husband and children of their
marriage surviving. He became administrator of her estate,

and collected moneys for the rent of the lands accruing after
the death of his intestate. The judgment of Hampton, Reed
& Co. was allowed by the probate court against the estate in the
third class. After the collection of the rents by the administrator, the lands and houses were sold under the mortgage of
the Bank of Newport, in 1895. The administrator filed a settlement in the probate court, and failed to charge himself with
the rents. Hampton, Reed & Co. excepted to it on the ground
that he had failed to do so. The exception was sustained, and
the court ordered him to charge himself with the rents, which
he did, debiting himself with four hundred and twenty dollars
and fifty-two cents. The probate court thereupon ordered him
to pay that sum to Hampton, Reed & Co. on their judgment, it
being superior to all other claims allowed against the estate.
From this order the administrator appealed to the circuit court,
which reversed the order, holding that the administrator should
not be charged with the rents, because he, in his individual capacity, was entitled to hold them as tenant by the curtesy. From the
latter judgment, Hampton, Reed & Co. have appealed to this
court.

It is conceded that the only question presented by the latter appeal for our consideration is, Is Cook, as tenant by the
curtesy, entitled to the rents and profits in controversy? The
sufficiency of the estate of the wife in the land to support
tenancy by the curtesy is not denied. But appellants insist that
their right to the rents is superior to that of Cook as tenant by
the curtesy. They base this contention upon the facts that
they were judgment creditors of the deceased wife, with a lien
which they could have foreclosed by a sale of her lands in her
lifetime, and thereby extinguished the right to curtesy claimed
by Cook. Their claim is based solely on this foundation. Is
it tenable?

The judgment of the appellants was a general lien on the
lands of Mrs. Cook. When she died, the lien ceased to exist,
and her estate became subject to the exclusive jurisdiction of
the probate court, which was put in actual exercise by the grant
of letters of administration to her husband. Her entire estate,
real and personal, passed into the custody of the law, to be disposed of under the authority of the probate court, or until the
purposes for which it was placed there were or shall be fully
subserved. After that appellants could only enforce the payment of their judgment in that court. Their right to the
appropriation of any part of the property of the estate to the

payment of their claim, and the manner in which, as well as
the extent to which, it could be appropriated, were fixed by
the statutes of administration. Under these statutes they were,
upon proper proceedings, held entitled to an allowance of their
claim against the estate in the third class, and to be paid, after
the claims in the first and second classes were fully satisfied,
out of any moneys of the estate then remaining or thereafter
coming into the hands of the administrator, if there were or
should be sufficient to pay all claims in the third class, and, if
not, to receive in proportion to other creditors in the same class.
This was the extent to which they could enforce their judgment
against the estate: Branch v. Horner, 28 Ark. 341, 342; Powell
v. Macon, 40 Ark. 541, 544; Hornor v. Hanks, 22 Ark. 572, 584;
Meredith v. Scallion, 51 Ark. 361, 366.

³⁵⁶ Did the husband take curtesy in the lands of his deceased
wife subject to the claims of her creditors? To understand
fully the interest he took, it is necessary to consider the common law upon this subject. At common law, the husband, upon
the birth of a child of the marriage alive, became a tenant by
the curtesy of all the lands of his wife of which during coverture she was so seised as to support such an estate. He became
entitled to an estate for his own life, in his own right, as tenant
by the curtesy initiate, which became consummate upon the
death of the wife. The estate was not acquired by descent, but
vested in him by virtue of his marital rights, in the lifetime of
his wife, independently of all debts, and consequently did not
vest in him at her death subject to her debts, if any. In this
respect it was unlimited and without restrictions or conditions.

In this state, curtesy has not been the subject of legislation. The common law upon that subject prevails, except as
modified or changed by the statute, which provides: "The
property, both real and personal, which any married woman
now owns, or has had conveyed to her by any person in good
faith and without prejudice to existing creditors, or which she
may have acquired as her sole and separate property; that
which comes to her by gift, bequest, descent, grant, or conveyance from any person; that which she has acquired by her
trade, business, labor, or services carried on or performed on
her sole or separate account, that which a married woman in this
state holds or owns at the time of her marriage, and the rents,
issues, and proceeds of all such property shall, notwithstanding
her marriage, be and remain her sole and separate property, and
may be used, collected, and invested by her in her own name, and

shall not be subject to the interference or control of her husband or liable for his debts, except such debts as may have been contracted for the support of herself or her children by her as his agent" (Sandel and Hill's Digest, sec. 4945) and by the section of the constitution which declares: "The real and personal property of any feme covert in this state, acquired either before or after marriage, whether by gift, grant, devise, or otherwise, shall, so long as she may choose, be and remain her separate estate and property, and may be devised, bequeathed, or conveyed by her, the same as if she was a feme sole, and the same shall not be [357] subject to the debts of her husband": Const. 1874, art. 9, sec. 7.

In Neelly v. Lancaster, 47 Ark. 175, 58 Am. Rep. 752, this court held that the effect of the statute and constitution "upon the rights of the husband in her real estate was to exclude his marital rights during her life, and to secure to her the rights to use and dispose of it at will; but if she makes no disposal of it, and there be issue of the marriage born alive, his title by curtesy consummate attaches at her death as at common law." The effect of this decision is that the constitution and statutes of this state take away the husband's rights by the curtesy so far, and so far only, as their express words or plain implications affirmatively require. It follows that the estate by curtesy consummate which vests in the husband at the death of his wife in this state, in respect to creditors unsecured by specific liens on her lands, is as great as that vested in him at common law, and that he takes the estate independently of such creditors—not subject to the debts owing to them.

The judgment of the circuit court is affirmed.

CURTESY—EFFECT OF MARRIED WOMEN'S ACTS.—The Virginia married woman's act giving her the power to possess, enjoy, and devise her separate estate as if sole, destroys the tenancy by the curtesy initiate; but it seems that if a wife dies without having alienated the lands, the husband's curtesy attaches: Breeding v. Davis, 77 Va. 639; 46 Am. Rep. 740. The Arkansas statute giving married women the exclusive ownership and control of their real estate does not abolish the right of tenancy by curtesy: Neelly v. Lancaster, 47 Ark. 175; 58 Am. Rep. 752. Neither does the Illinois married woman's act of 1861; Freeman v. Hartman, 45 Ill. 57; 92 Am. Dec. 193; nor does the New Jersey statute of similar character: Johnson v. Cummins, 16 N. J. Eq. 97; 84 Am. Dec. 142.

JUDGMENT LIEN AFTER DEATH OF DEFENDANT.—A judgment obtained against a party in his lifetime creates a lien against all the real property held by him, and is not dissolved by his death, but may be satisfied out of his land in the hands of his heirs or devisees. Such lien continues and has preference over a debt in a fiduciary capacity as administrator, and the executor or administrator may be compelled to satisfy such lien in preference to an ordinary debt or specialty: Extended note to Kimball v. Jenkins, 89 Am. Dec. 242, 243. But such lien may be lost by laches: Union Bank v. Powell's Heirs, 8 Fla. 175; 52 Am. Dec. 367. It has been held that such lien is dissolved by the regularly ascertained insolvency of the judgment debtor's estate: Ray v. Thompson, 43 Ala. 434; 94 Am. Dec. 696. See, also, Jones v. Jones, 1 Bland, 443; 18 Am. Dec. 327.

KIES *v.* YOUNG.
[64 ARKANSAS, 381.]

A HUSBAND'S LIABILITY FOR THE ANTENUPTIAL DEBTS OF HIS WIFE is not affected by a statute providing that a married woman may bargain, sell, assign, and transfer her separate personal property, and carry on any trade or business and perform any labor or service on her sole and separate account, and she may alone sue or be sued in the courts of this state upon account of such property, business, or service.

Action by the plaintiff, Young, against J. H. Kies and wife to recover upon a judgment rendered against her while a widow and previous to her marriage with her codefendant. She had not at such marriage, or afterward, any property other than her wearing apparel. The trial court declared the husband to be liable for this antenuptial indebtedness, and gave judgment accordingly, and he appealed.

Joseph W. House, for the appellant.

Carmichael & Seawel, for the appellees.

[383] RIDDICK, J. The question presented in this case is, whether a husband is liable for the antenuptial debts of his wife. It is conceded that the husband was, [384] at common law, liable for such debts (Harrison v. Trader, 27 Ark. 288), but the contention is made that the effect of our statute, which excludes the marital rights of the husband in the wife's property during coverture, and confers upon married women power to acquire and hold property, is to abrogate this rule of the common law.

It is plain that this statute does not expressly change or affect the liability of the husband, but appellants argue that the reasons upon which the rule was based have, by virtue of such statute, ceased to exist, and that therefore the rule itself should cease. It will be admitted that if a rule of law be based upon certain specific reasons, which can be enumerated, and upon no others, and these reasons are all taken away, then the rule must fall; but if some of the reasons for the law remain, the law itself remains, and the courts must enforce it until changed by the legislature: 2 Bishop on Married Women, sec. 65. Now it is difficult to state precisely all the reasons upon which was based the rule of law making the husband responsible for the antenuptial debts of his wife. It is probably true, as stated by the supreme court of New York, that an inquiry into the reasons of such rule "involves the consideration of all the rights, obligations, duties, liabilities, and disabilities given by the common law to the marital relation. And, so far as observed, no writer has yet authentically furnished all the reasons which may have influenced the various conditions of coverture imposed by the common law": Fitzgerald v. Quann, 33 Hun, 652.

At common law, the husband and wife were regarded as one person; the wife's legal existence was merged in that of her husband. "Upon this principle of a union of person in husband and wife," says Blackstone, "depends almost all the legal rights, duties, and disabilities that either of them acquire by marriage": 1 Blackstone's Commentaries, 442. Among the duties imposed by the law upon the husband was the duty to pay the debts of the wife contracted dum sola, for, says the same learned author, "he has adopted her and her circumstances together": 1 Blackstone's Commentaries, 443.

But if the liability of the husband rested in any degree upon the legal unity of the husband and wife, that reason still [386] exists to some extent; for, notwithstanding the important changes wrought by our statute concerning the powers and rights of married women, many of the rules of law resting upon this unity of the husband and wife are still enforced by the courts of this state. This court, since the passage of the statute above referred to, has held that, by reason of such unity, the husband and wife cannot contract with each other: Pillow v. Wade, 31 Ark. 678; nor become partners in business: Gilkerson-Sloss etc. Co. v. Salinger, 56 Ark. 294; 35 Am. St. Rep. 105; nor sue each other in a court of law: Countz v. Markling, 30 Ark. 17. By reason of this legal unity, land in this state conveyed to the husband and wife jointly vests in them an estate by entirety so that the survivor takes the whole, whereas, but for this theory of legal unity, they would take as tenants in common: Robinson v. Eagle, 29 Ark. 202; Kline v. Ragland, 47 Ark. 116; Branch v. Polk, 61 Ark. 388; 54 Am St. Rep. 266. It will be seen, by reference to these and other decisions of this court, that the common-law unity of husband and wife still exists in this state, except so far as the legislative purpose to modify and change it has been expressed by statute.

But it is contended that the husband's liability rested upon the common-law principle, now abrogated by statute, that the personal property of the wife, the use of her real estate, the right to her labor and earnings, passed to the husband upon marriage. She was, it is said, by marriage deprived of the use and disposal of her property, and could acquire none by her industry; and it was, therefore, necessary at common law to impose upon the husband the duty of paying her debts, otherwise her creditors would be remediless.

It is true that at common law the creditor had, after marriage, no means of collecting his debt by action against the wife alone, so the common law solved the difficulty by requiring the husband to pay such debts. But the marriage of a feme sole may still place many obstructions in the way of her creditor who attempts to collect his debt by process of law. If there be issue of the marriage born alive, then, at the wife's death, the husband's title by curtesy attaches to her land as at common law, and this may result in postponing the rights of her [386] creditors until after the termination of such life estate, as was held in the recent case of Hampton v. Cook, 64 Ark. 353; ante, p. 194. The husband is still entitled to the benefit of her labor and services, except when "performed on her sole or separate account": Sandel and Hill's Digest, sec. 4995.

"The true construction of the statute," says the court of appeals of New York, "is that she may elect to labor on her own account, and thereby entitle herself to her earnings, but, in the absence of such an election, or of circumstances showing that she intended to avail herself of the privilege and protection conferred by the statute, the husband's common-law right to her earnings remains unaffected": Birkbeck v. Ackroyd, 74 N. Y. 356; 30 Am. Rep. 304.

Now while, under our statute, a married woman may acquire property by engaging in business, or by performing labor and services upon her sole and separate account, yet as the creditor has no means of compelling her to engage in such business, or to perform service upon "her sole and separate account," and as it is the rare exception that a married woman does engage in business or perform services for her separate account, we can easily see that marriage may still leave the creditor without a remedy unless the husband be held liable. The woman may be the earner of valuable wages, and may have been credited on that account; yet if, after marriage, she chooses to labor for her husband only, the creditor can do nothing as against her,

for, however valuable her earnings may be, they belong, under
such circumstances, not to her, but to her husband: Birkbeck
v. Ackroyd, 74 N. Y. 356; 30 Am. Rep. 304; 11 Hun, 365; Mc-
Cluskey v. Provident Inst., 103 Mass. 300, 304.

Again, it seems that the statute has made no provision for
an action against the wife alone upon her antenuptial contracts.
At common law, the wife could not be sued alone. This was
one reason for making the husband liable for the wife's antenuptial debts; and if the statute has made no change in the law in
this respect, it must follow that the husband is still liable for
such debts: 2 Bishop on Married Women, secs. 312, 322.

[387] The language of our statute is that "a married woman may
bargain, sell, assign, and transfer her separate personal property,
and carry on any trade or business, and perform any labor or
services, on her sole and separate account, ... and she may
alone sue or be sued in the courts of this state, on account of said
property, business or services": Sandel and Hill's Digest, sec.
4946. There are other sections of the statute providing that
the contracts of a married woman in reference to her sole and
separate estate or business shall not be binding upon her husband, and that judgments recovered against her may be enforced
by executions against her sole and separate property, etc., but
these and other sections of the statute relating to actions
against married women seem to refer to the actions mentioned
in the section above quoted; that is, to those on account of her
separate property, business, or services, or upon her contracts
in connection therewith. The reform undertaken by the legislature was to empower a married woman to hold property and
make contracts, and in effecting this purpose it provided that
she could be sued upon such contracts, and that her husband
should not be liable therefor. But the question of her antenuptial debts does not seem to have been considered by the
legislative mind, and there is in the statute nothing indicating
an intention to change the law in reference thereto, or to relieve
the husband of his liability therefor. Our statute under consideration was copied, or seems to have been copied, from the New
York statute, and the courts of that state hold that the statute
does not permit the wife to be sued alone in all cases, but simply
enacts that she may be sued alone in actions having reference
to her separate estate: Fitzgerald v. Quann, 109 N. Y. 441; 33
Hun, 652.

The legislature of New York, by act of 1853, relieved the
husband of liability for the antenuptial debts of his wife, but

previous to the passage of that act he was held to be liable for such debts, notwithstanding statutes there similar to our statute: Berley v. Rampacher, 5 Duer, 183.

The liability of the husband at common law for the torts of the wife not committed in his presence rests upon substantially the same reason as his liability for her antenuptial debts: Quann v. Fitzgerald, 33 Hun, 657; 2 Bishop on Married Women, secs. 254, 312. But the New York courts, under the [388] same statute that we have, hold that the husband is still liable for such torts, and base their decision upon the ground that the wife cannot be sued alone for such torts, and, further, that a statute should never be construed as abolishing a rule of common law, unless the intention to repeal is made known by express words or necessary implication: Fitzgerald v. Quann, 109 N. Y. 441.

The courts of many other states have arrived at the conclusion that these acts emancipating married women from the disabilities imposed by common law do not of themselves relieve the husband of his common-law liabilities, unless so expressed in the act. While some courts hold to the contrary, the weight of judicial opinion seems to be decidedly in favor of the view adopted by the New York courts, on the ground that the repeal of settled principles of law by mere implication should not be favored: Alexander v. Morgan, 31 Ohio St. 546; Platner v. Patchin, 19 Wis. 333; McElfresh v. Kirkendall, 36 Iowa, 224; Ferguson v. Brooks, 67 Me. 251; Morgan v. Kennedy, 62 Minn. 348; 54 Am. St. Rep. 647; Gill v. State, 39 W. Va. 479; 45 Am. St. Rep. 928; Seroka v. Kattenberg, 17 Q. B. Div. 177; Mangam v. Peck, 111 N. Y. 401; 9 Am. & Eng. Ency. of Law, 822.

The question as to whether the statute conferring enlarged powers upon married women has impliedly repealed the rule of law making the husband liable for the wife's antenuptial debts has never been decided by this court. That question was not involved in the case of Gill v. Kayser, 60 Ark. 266, for the debt there was contracted during marriage, and had reference to the wife's separate property. It came within the provision of the statute which exempted the husband, and did not stand on the same footing as her debts contracted dum sola. But in Stowell v. Grider, 48 Ark. 223, the question was incidentally referred to by Judge Smith, who said that the husband was still liable for such debts. The same learned judge in Kosminsky v. Goldberg, 44 Ark. 401, discussing the question of the liability of the husband for the torts of the wife, said that the husband was liable for such torts, although he was absent, and had no knowledge of the intended act; and he placed the husband's liability upon the ground [389] that the wife could not be sued alone. But there is no more reason for saying that a wife could be sued alone for her antenuptial debts than that she could be sued alone for her torts committed in the absence of her husband. If these two opinions by Judge Smith stood alone, we should attach no great importance to them, for the question as to the effect of the legislation giving enlarged powers to married women upon the common-law liability of the husband does not seem to have been raised in these cases. But these expressions of the learned judge are in harmony with many other expressions of opinion by this court, some of them quite recent, to the effect that the courts of this state will not move in advance of the clearly expressed legislative purpose to remove the disabilities, rights, and liabilities of coverture.

The rule of law making the husband liable for the debts of the wife contracted dum sola was well known, and had often been enforced by the courts of this state. As the legislature which enacted the married women's act did not, either by express words or by clear implication, express an intention to repeal such law, the presumption should be that they intended the rule should remain. Force is added to this argument when we consider that the act in question was copied from the New York law, but that our statute omits the provision found in the New York statute relieving the husband of the liability for his wife's antenuptial debts. Our conclusion is, that the husband should be joined with the wife in actions against her for debts contracted by her dum sola, and that he is still liable for such debts as at common law.

We admit that, as the husband has been deprived of the legal ownership and control of the wife's property during coverture, it would seem logically to follow that he should be relieved of some portion of his common-law liability for her antenuptial debts, but that is a question for the legislature, and not the courts. While, theoretically, the position of the husband is much worse now than at common law, still. as a matter of actual fact, this is not altogether true. The statute permits the wife to hold and use her property as her own, but the close relationship that exists between husband and wife, and the love of a wife for her husband, potent now as of old, generally results in placing at his [390] disposal all her worldly goods. The statute enabling married women to acquire and hold property does not, and no statute can, to any great extent, protect the wife's property against the aggressions of the husband, for it is generally her will that he should use such property as he pleases. But the statute does protect her property against the creditors of her husband. At the common law, if the husband became insolvent, the wife's personal property and the use of her real estate during his life could be seized by his creditors. If she acquired property by her earnings, that also could be seized, for it belonged to her husband. All this has been changed by the statute conferring upon married women power to acquire and hold property, and in this way these statutes frequently operate to the advantage of the husband. Many an insolvent husband has regained his financial footing by the use of his wife's property, protected against his creditors by the operation of such statutes.

It is, indeed, possible under our statute that a woman in debt, but with considerable money, should marry, and then hide away her money, and allow her creditors to force her husband to pay her debts. Yet, considering the nature of woman, we think the case would be rare when this would be done against the husband's will. But if the husband was exempt from liability, a woman in debt, but with money, might, upon marriage, bestow her money upon her husband, and he might squander or conceal it, and refuse to pay her creditors, and leave them with a very doubtful remedy. The worst effect of statutes enabling married women to acquire and hold property is that when the husband and wife are dishonest, they place the creditor at a great disadvantage. Mr. Bishop, who has given much thought to this question, says that under these statutes "husband and wife, if in due accord, and mutually inclined to defraud the rest of mankind, have it well in their power to live in wealth procured by lawful cheating from confiding creditors." If the debts are hers, the property can be shifted to him. If he be the one in debt, he can so arrange his affairs "that all the earnings shall be hers, and all the expenses his, whereby, in a short time his estate is indirectly, but effectually, transferred to her, while apparently it remains his": Bishop on Contracts, sec. 951.

Considerations of this kind furnish additional answer to [301] the argument that the courts should hold, as a matter of law, that all reason for the rule making the husband liable for the wife's antenuptial debts has passed away. Notwithstanding the statutes depriving the husband of his marital rights in the wife's property during coverture, it is still rare that a man marries a rich woman without receiving pecuniary benefit from her estate,

and he should at least be held liable to the extent of such
benefit; but these matters cannot be adjusted by the courts,
and should be left to the legislature, where they belong.
The hardship in this case is, not that the law allows the
wife to retain her separate property, but in the fact that she had
no property. The position of the husband here is not worse
than it would have been had the statute in question never been
passed. As such statute does not expressly or by clear implication relieve him of liability for the antenuptial debts of his
wife, we must hold that the judgment of the circuit court against
him is in accordance with the law, and it is therefore affirmed.

CHIEF JUSTICE BUNN dissented from the foregoing opinion on
the ground that the changes made by statute respecting the property
rights of married women rendered the reasons by which husbands
were, by the common law, declared liable for the antenuptial debts
of their wives no longer applicable. He insisted that the ground of
this common-law liability was, that the wife, by her marriage, was
entirely deprived of the use and disposal of her property, and could
acquire none by her industry, while her personal property passed
absolutely to her husband, together with the right to the use of her
real estate during coverture; that, in Arkansas, the wife was no
longer deprived in any degree of the use and disposal of her property
and retained the title thereto as absolutely as prior to her marriage,
and was further at liberty to acquire property by her industry as if
she remained unmarried; and that our more recent laws have shorn
the common-law rule, that the husband is liable for the antenuptial
debts and the antenuptial torts of the wife, of every particle of reason upon which it was based, therefore the husband should no longer
be held answerable for her antenuptial debts, and that the judgment
of the trial court should, therefore, have been reversed.

HUSBAND AND WIFE—HUSBAND'S LIABILITY FOR WIFE'S
ANTENUPTIAL DEBTS.—Upon the husband rests the duty of providing for his wife and family and of meeting their obligations, and
at the common law he was also answerable for her antenuptial debts:
Monographic note to Michigan Trust Co. v. Chapin, 58 Am. St. Rep.
493. The tendency of modern legislation has been to modify, if not
entirely to discharge, the liability of the husband for the antenuptial
debts of the wife; but the New York statute of 1848 giving to every
female who might thereafter marry, all the estate owned by her at
the time of the marriage as her sole and separate property, does not
repeal the common-law rule above referred to. The same has been
held of like statutes in other states: Monographic note to Cole v.
Seeley, 60 Am. Dec. 260, on the antenuptial debts of married women.

HELENA v. DWYER.

[64 Arkansas, 424.]

A MUNICIPAL ORDINANCE DECLARING THE SALE of fresh pork to be detrimental to the health of the citizens of the town, and making it unlawful to sell or offer it for sale therein between the first days of June and October in each year, is not authorized by a statute conferring power upon such town to prevent or regulate the carrying on of any trade, business, or vocation of a dangerous tendency to the morals, health, or safety, or calculated to promote dishonesty or crime. Such ordinance is unlawful, and therefore void.

R. W. Nichols, for the appellant.

Tappan & Porter, for the appellees.

425 BATTLE, J. The city council of Helena enacted the following ordinance:

"Whereas, the municipal board of health of Helena, Arkansas, at a regular meeting, held on the thirtieth day of April, 1880, declared the sale of fresh pork detrimental to the health of the citizens of Helena; therefore, be it ordained by the mayor and council of the city of Helena:

"Section 1. That it shall not be lawful for any person or persons to sell, or offer to sell, within the city any fresh pork, or sausage made thereof, between the first day of June and October in each year.

"Sec. 2. That any person or persons violating this ordinance shall be fined in a sum not less than five dollars nor more than twenty-five dollars," etc.

Is the ordinance valid? In determining the extent of the power of a city council to pass ordinances for the protection of the public health, much assistance can be derived from what has been held to be the limitations upon such power of the state, for it cannot be truthfully said that the state can grant to a municipal corporation greater power than it possesses.

The police power of the state is very broad and comprehensive, and can be exercised to promote the health, comfort, safety, and welfare of society. Its limits have not been definitely defined. It is not, however, without its limitations. In In re Jacobs, 98 N. Y. 110, 50 Am. Rep. 636, the court said: "If this were otherwise, the power of the legislature would be practically without limitation. In the assumed exercise of the police power in the interest of the health, the welfare, or the safety of the public, every right of the citizen might be invaded, and every constitutional barrier swept away. Generally, it is for the legisla-

ture to determine what laws and regulations are needed to protect the public health and secure the public comfort and safety,
and while its measures are calculated, intended, convenient, and
appropriate to accomplish these ends, the exercise of its discretion is not subject to review by the courts.   But they must have
some relation to these ends.   Under the mere guise of police
426 regulations, personal rights and private property cannot be
arbitrarily invaded, and the determination of the legislature is
not final or conclusive.   If it passes an act ostensibly for the
public health, and thereby destroys or takes away the property
of a citizen, or interferes with his personal liberty, then it is
for the courts to scrutinize the act, and see whether it relates to
and is convenient and appropriate to promote the public health.
It matters not that the legislature may, in the title to the act,
or in its body, declare that it is intended for the improvement
of the public health.   Such a declaration does not conclude the
courts, and they must yet determine the fact declared and
enforce the supreme law."

In Mugler v. Kansas, 123 U. S. 661, the court said: "The
courts are not bound by mere forms, nor are they to be misled
by mere pretenses.   They are at liberty—indeed, are under a
solemn duty—to look at the substance of things, whenever they
enter upon the inquiry whether the legislature has transcended
the limits of its authority.   If, therefore, a statute purporting
to have been enacted to protect the public health, the public
morals or the public safety, has no real or substantial relations
to those objects, or is a palpable invasion of rights secured by
the fundamental law, it is the duty of the courts to so adjudge,
and thereby give effect to the constitution."   To the same effect
other courts have held: Watertown v. Mayo, 109 Mass. 315;
12 Am. Rep. 694; Powell v. Pennsylvania, 127 U. S. 686.

The constitution of the state declares that "all men are created
free and independent, and have certain inherent and inalienable
rights, amongst which are those of enjoying and defending life
and liberty: of acquiring, possessing, and protecting property
and reputation, and of pursuing their own happiness": Const.,
art. 2, sec. 2.   In Powell v. Pennsylvania, 127 U. S. 692, Mr.
Justice Field said: "With the gift of life there necessarily goes
to everyone the right to do all such acts, and follow all such pursuits, not inconsistent with the equal rights of others, as may
support life and add to the happiness of its possessor.   The right
to pursue one's happiness is placed by the Declaration of Inde-
pendence among the inalienable rights of man, with which all

men are endowed, not by the grace of emperors or kings, or by
force of legislative **or** constitutional enactments, [427] but by
their Creator; and to secure them, not to grant them, governments are instituted among men. The right to procure healtby
and nutritious food, by which life may be preserved and enjoyed,
and to manufacture it, is among these inalienable rights, which,
in my judgment, no state can give and no state can take away
except in punishment for crime. It is involved in the right to
pursue one's happiness."

In People v. Marx, 99 N. Y. 386, 52 Am. Rep. 34, the court,
in speaking of the section of the constitution which declares that
"no state shall deprive any person of life, liberty, or property
without due process of law," said: "These constitutional safeguards have been so thoroughly discussed in recent cases that it
would be superfluous to do more than refer to the conclusions
which have been reached, bearing upon the question now under
consideration. Among these no proposition is now more firmly
settled than that it is one of the fundamental rights and privileges of every American citizen to adopt and follow such lawful
industrial pursuit, not injurious to the community, as he may see
fit. . . . . The term 'liberty,' as protected by the constitution,
is not cramped into a mere freedom from physical restraint of
the person of the citizen, as by incarceration, but is deemed to
embrace the right of man to be free in the employment of the
faculties with which he has been endowed by his Creator, subject
only to such restraints as are necessary for the common welfare.
In the language of Andrews, J., in Bertholf v. O'Reilly, 74 N. Y.
515, 30 Am. Rep. 323, the right to liberty embraces the right of
man 'to exercise his faculties and to follow a lawful avocation
for the support of life.'" Upon this doctrine the court held
that the provision of an act "prohibiting the manufacture or sale,
as an article of food, of any substitute for butter or cheese produced from pure, unadulterated milk or cream is unconstitutional, inasmuch as the prohibition is not limited to unwholesome or simulated substitutes, but absolutely prohibits the manufacture or sale of any compound designed to be used as a substitute for butter or cheese, however wholesome, valuable, or cheap
it may be, and however openly and fairly the character of the substitute may be avowed and published."

In Powell v. Pennsylvania, 127 U. S. 678, a statute of the
[428] state of Pennsylvania was involved. It provided: "No person, firm, or corporate body shall manufacture out of any oleag-
inous substance, or any compound of the same, other than that

produced from unadulterated milk or cream from the same, any article designed to take the place of butter or cheese produced from pure, unadulterated milk or cream from the same, or of any imitation or adulterated butter or cheese, nor shall sell or offer for sale, or have in his, her, or their possession, with intent to sell the same, as an article of food." The court, sustaining the statute, said: "It [the court] cannot adjudge that the defendant's rights of liberty and property . . . . have been infringed by the statute of Pennsylvania, without holding that, although it may have been enacted in good faith for the objects expressed in its title, namely, to protect the public health and to prevent the adulteration of dairy products and fraud in the sale thereof, it has, in fact, no real or substantial relation to those objects: Mugler v. Kansas, 123 U. S. 623, 661. The court is unable to affirm that this legislation has no real or substantial relation to such objects. . . . . Whether the manufacture of oleomargarine, or imitation butter, of the kind described in the statute, is, or may be, conducted in such a way, or with such skill and secrecy, as to baffle ordinary inspection, or whether it involves such danger to public health as to require, for the protection of the people, the entire suppression of the business, rather than its regulation in such manner as to permit the manufacture and sale of articles of that class that do not contain noxious ingredients, are questions of fact and of public policy, which belong to the legislative department to determine. And as it does not appear upon the face of the statute, or from any facts of which the court must take judicial cognizance, that it infringes rights secured by the fundamental law, the legislative determination of those questions is conclusive upon the courts."

But, fortunately, the ordinances of municipal corporations are not protected by conclusive presumptions in favor of their validity, as the statute was in Powell v. Pennsylvania, 127 U. S. 686. The city council is not the sole judge of their necessity, propriety, or reasonableness. Courts may inquire into their reasonableness when passed under powers granted in general or indefinite [420] terms, and, when found unreasonable, may set them aside: Haynes v. Cape May, 50 N. J. L. 55. Such corporations have none of the elements of sovereignty, and must exercise their powers in a reasonable manner; and, when necessary evidence may be adduced to show that they are unreasonable or oppressive: Corrigan v. Gage, 68 Mo. 541.

The statutes of this state confer upon cities of the first class powers "to prevent or regulate the carrying on of any trade, business, or vocation of a tendency dangerous to morals, health, or safety, or calculated to promote dishonesty or crime": Sandels and Hill's Digest, sec. 5313. Under this statute the city council of Helena undertook to prevent the sale of fresh pork "between the first day of June and October in each year." It obviously intended to prevent the eating of it in Helena during this time by prohibiting the sale of it. Was the ordinance passed for that purpose a reasonable or lawful exercise of the powers granted by the statute?

Fresh pork is an article of food of general consumption, and, when sound and free from disease, is useful and nutritious. Like all other food, it may become unwholesome when eaten to excess. The quantity eaten, under ordinary circumstances, produces the sickness, when it proves unwholesome. Any food is calculated to produce that effect when eaten in the same manner. The mere sale of it is not detrimental to the public health. The fact that individuals may be made sick by it, when imprudently eaten, does not justify a city council in prohibiting the sale of it. For the same reason it could prohibit the sale of any or all other food. The most delicious food, that which is most liable to be eaten to excess, would be subject to interdiction. If it be conceded that the city council may prohibit the sale of any article of food, the wrongful use of which will or may injure the health of the consumer, then they can prescribe what the citizen of the city shall eat by prohibiting the sale of all other food. The legislature or any of its creatures has no such power. The exercise of such power, we have seen, would be a violation of the inalienable right of man to procure healthy and nutritious food, by which life may be preserved and enjoyed. It would be an interference with the liberty of the citizen, which is not necessary to the protection [430] of others or the public health—would be an invasion of his personal rights.

Professor Tiedeman, in his work on the "Limitations of Police Powers," in elucidation of this doctrine, says: "A still stronger ground for the total prohibition of a trade or business is when the thing offered for sale is in some way injurious or unwholesome. It is not enough that the thing may become harmful, when put to a wrong use. It must be in itself harmful and incapable of a harmless use. Poisonous drugs are valuable, when properly used, but they may work serious injury by being improperly used, even to the extent of destroying life. Safeguards of every kind can be thrown around the sale of them, so that damage will not be sustained from an improper use of them, but that is the limit of the police control of the trade. Thus, for example, opium is a very harmful drug when improperly used, and it is all the more dangerous because the power of resistance diminishes rapidly in proportion to the growth of the habit of taking it as a stimulant and a miserable, degraded death is the usual end. . . . . But, on the other hand, opium is a very useful and indispensable drug. . . . . The sale of it can, of course, be prohibited to minors, and to all who may be suffering from some form of dementia, and to confirmed opium eaters. But it would seem to be taking away the free will of those who are under the law confessedly capable of taking care of themselves, if the law were to prohibit the sale of opium to adults in general. But where a thing may be put to a wrongful and injurious use, and yet may serve in some other way a useful purpose, the law may prohibit the sale of such things in any case where the vendor represents them as fit for a use that is injurious, or merely knows that the purchaser expects to apply them to the injurious purposes. Thus the sale of diseased or spoiled meats or other food, as food, intending or expecting that the purchaser is to make use of them as food, may be prohibited. So, also, the sale of milk which comes from cows fed in whole or in part upon still slops may be prohibited, if it is true that such milk is unwholesome as human food. In the same manner, a law was held to be constitutional which prohibited the sale of illuminating oil which ignited below a certain [431] heat. But it would be unconstitutional to prohibit altogether the sale of either of these things, if they could be employed in some other harmless and useful way. For example, the oil which was prohibited for illuminating purposes may be very valuable and more or less harmless while used for lubricating purposes": Tiedeman on Limitations of Police Power, 293-295. See, also, Des Plaines v. Poyer, 123 Ill. 348; 5 Am. St. Rep. 524; Babcock v. Buffalo, 56 N. Y. 268.

The legislature may enact such laws as may be necessary to protect the public against fraud, imposition, or deception in the sale of food, or any impurities, putridity, disease, or unsoundness in the same which renders it unwholesome, and may authorize municipal corporations to do so. The public is entitled to protection against imposition by the sale of impure or adulterated food, or of imitations as pure and genuine. In this respect it needs protection, and to this end the legislature may and can authorize city councils to pass laws. It has accordingly been held that an act is constitutional which prohibits the sale of "milk containing more than eighty-eight per centum of water fluids, or less than twelve per centum of milk solids, or less than two and one-half per centum of milk fats." In passing upon the validity of this act, in State v. Smyth, 14 R. I. 100, 51 Am. Rep. 344, the court said: "It is equally a fraud on the buyer, whether the milk which he buys was originally good and has been deteriorated by the addition of water, or whether in its natural state it is so poor that it contains the same proportion of water as that which has been adulterated. . . . . If a cow habitually gives milk of a quality so poor as to come within the statute, or, as the defendant puts it in his brief, so poor that as a commercial commodity it is valuable only for the purpose of irrigation, she is of no value as a milk producer and can have none as such to her owner, unless he can sell her milk to his unsuspecting neighbor for a price greatly in excess of its value, a species of fraud which ought not to be tolerated. The section is but a slight extension of the provision which prohibits the sale of adulterated milk, and, like that, was designed to protect the public against imposition": Commonwealth v. Waite, 11 Allen, 264; 87 Am. Dec. 711; People v. Cipperly, 101 N. Y. 634. Other examples might be given, but this, we think, is sufficient.

[432] The ordinance in question, for the reasons indicated, is unreasonable, invalid, and void, and the judgment of the circuit court so holding is affirmed.

MUNICIPAL CORPORATIONS—VALIDITY OF ORDINANCES. Municipal authorities cannot, under the claim of exercising the police power, substantially prohibit a lawful trade, unless it is so conducted as to be injurious or dangerous to the public health: State v. Taft, 118 N. C. 1190; 54 Am. St. Rep. 768, and note. Municipal ordinances regulating sales of commodities, enacted under legislative authority, must be consistent with general laws, reasonable in their provisions, and referable to the performance of some recognized governmental function: Ex parte Byrd, 84 Ala. 17; 5 Am. St. Rep. 328, and note. A municipal corporation has incidental power to enact sanitary regulations, but if an ordinance goes beyond or outside of this power, it cannot be sustained thereunder: Note to Walker v. Jameson, 49 Am. St. Rep. 231. See monographic note to Robinson v. Mayor, 34 Am. Dec. 627-643, as to the general limitations on the power of municipal corporations to pass ordinances.

CHESTNUT v. HARRIS.

[64 ARKANSAS, 580.]

TAX SALE.—A DESCRIPTION in an assessment and notice of sale for delinquent taxes of land as "NE, SE. sec. 24, township 13, R. 7, 40 acres," is sufficient.

Z. T. Wood, for the appellants.

Wells & Williamson, for the appellees.

⁵⁸⁰ BATTLE, J. An action was brought by appellant against appellees in the Drew circuit court to recover possession of the ⁵⁸¹ northeast quarter of the southeast quarter of section 24 in township 13 south and in range 7 west, containing forty acres. He claimed by virtue of a sale thereof by a collector of revenue for the taxes assessed against the same for the year 1891. Appellees disputed the validity of the sale on two grounds: 1. Because the description of the land in the assessment and in the notice of sale is insufficient; and 2. Because it was sold for too much cost.

The issues in the case were tried upon an agreed statement of facts. It was admitted that the land was described in the assessment list as follows:

	TOWNSHIP 13, RANGE 7.		
OWNER'S NAME	PARTS OF SEC.	SECTION	NO. OF ACRES
Bashie Harris	NE. SE.	24	40

and in the notice of the sale of delinquent lands as follows:

OWNER'S NAME	PARTS OF SEC.	SEC.	TOWNSHIP	R.	NO. OF ACRES
Bashie Harris	NE. SE.	24	13	7	40

It was also admitted that it was sold for the taxes of 1891 and penalty, and for sixty cents costs, which included a fee of ten cents of the county clerk for attending the sale and five cents for furnishing the printer with a description of it in the list of delinquent lands advertised for sale.

Upon this statement of facts, the court held that the sale was void because the description of the land in the assessment and in the notice of sale was insufficient; and rendered judgment in favor of the appellee. Did the court err?

The statutes of this state provide that each tract or lot of real property shall be so described in the assessment thereof for taxation as to identify and distinguish it from any other tracts or parts of tracts; and the same shall be described, if practicable, according to sections, or subdivisions thereof, and congressional townships. They recognize the survey of the United States, and the division of lands, according thereto, into townships and ranges, and sections and parts of sections, and that a description according to such survey will be good and ^{582} sufficient. For this reason it has been held that a description of land for assessment by the abbreviations commonly used to designate government subdivisions would be sufficient: Cooper v. Lee, 59 Ark. 460.

In the case at bar, the assessor attempted to assess forty acres in section 24, in township 13 and range 7, in Drew county, in this state. It was a legal subdivision of land—a fourth of a quarter of a section of land. As described, it was described as the NE. SE. of that section. The first is the abbreviation of northeast, and the last of southeast. In the order they are used, they could designate only one legal subdivision of a section into forty acres, and that is the northeast quarter of the southeast quarter. They are not reasonably susceptible of any other interpretation. We think the land was sufficiently described in the assessment and notice of sale.

We have not overlooked the ruling of the court in Cooper v. Lee, 59 Ark. 460. In that case the land in controversy was described as "N. NE. section 2, township 15, range 6, 87.19 acres." The section was not described as a fractional section, and 87.19 acres were not a legal subdivision, according to survey of the government, of a regular and complete section. There was nothing in the description in that case to show what was meant by the abbreviations, as in this. The "N" might have as reasonably been construed as meaning the north part as the north half. The description was not sufficiently certain to protect the interests of the owner.

The question we have decided is the only one presented by counsel in their briefs for our consideration. We decide no other.

Reversed and remanded for a new trial.

———

TAX SALES—SUFFICIENCY OF DESCRIPTION IN NOTICE.—
The notice of a tax sale must give a particular and certain description of land to be sold, so that the owner may know that it is his land, and bidders may ascertain its locality with a view to the regu-

lation of their bids: Bidwell v. Webb, 10 Minn. 59; 88 Am. Dec. 56,
and note. A notice containing no further description of the premises
than as "Roberts' and Randall's, lot 11, block 20, lot 12, block 20,"
and nowhere describing the addition or lots as being in any particular city or county is insufficient: Bidwell v. Webb, 10 Minn. 59; 88
Am. Dec. 56. See Alexander v. Walter, 8 Gill, 239; 50 Am. Dec. 688;
Knight v. Alexander, 38 Minn. 384; 8 Am. St. Rep. 675.

CASES

IN THE

SUPREME COURT

OF

CALIFORNIA.

Fox *v.* Oakland Consolidated Street Railway.

[118 California. 55.]

NEGLIGENCE—QUESTION FOR THE JURY.—It is only where the deduction to be drawn is inevitable that the court is authorized to withdraw the question of negligence from the jury. The absence of conflict in the evidence is not controlling, if differences of opinion as to the conclusions and inferences to be drawn therefrom may reasonably arise.

NEGLIGENCE IN LOOKING OUT FOR CHILDREN, WHEN A QUESTION FOR THE JURY.—Whether parents, in permitting their child of tender years to be out of their sight for fifteen or twenty minutes, during which time it went upon a street and was injured by a street-car, were, under all the circumstances, guilty of a want of ordinary care, is a question for the jury.

NEGLIGENCE, GROSS AND CONTRIBUTORY.—Though a person injured by a street-car was guilty of contributory negligence in placing himself in a situation of danger, he may recover for injuries there sustained, if the person inflicting them, or his servant or agent, was guilty of gross negligence.

NEGLIGENCE, CONTRIBUTORY, POVERTY AS AN EXCUSE.—WHERE A CHILD has been injured upon a public street, and it is claimed that his parents were guilty of contributory negligence in permitting him to go there unattended, evidence of their poverty and consequent inability to employ servants is not admissible as tending to aid the jury in determining the issue respecting contributory negligence. The question of the parents' negligence in any given case cannot be made to turn on the state of their finances.

JURY TRIAL—EXCESSIVE DAMAGES.—A verdict for six thousand dollars in an action by a parent to recover compensation for the death of his child, four and a half years of age, there being no averment or evidence of peculiar or special damages, or showing a right to exemplary damages, nor indicating that the value of the child's services would have been greater than that of an ordinary boy of his age, is so excessive as to show passion or prejudice by the jury in its verdict.

DAMAGES FOR THE DEATH OF A CHILD—OCCUPA-
TION OF PARENT, WHEN MAY BE TAKEN INTO CONSIDERA-
TION.—In determining what damages were sustained by a parent
from the death of his minor child, it is most reasonable, in judging
of the probable character of the occupation which the deceased
would have pursued, to regard, with other circumstances surrounding him, the calling of his father, since experience teaches that children do very frequently pursue the same general class of business
as that of their parents.

PLEADING — ELECTION BETWEEN AVERMENTS OF
DAMAGES.—Where a complaint in an action to recover compensation for the death of the plaintiff's minor child, through the alleged negligence of the defendants, avers that by such death the
plaintiff has been deprived of the society and companionship of his
child, to his damage in the sum of fifty thousand dollars, and of his
services and earnings of the reasonable value of eight thousand dollars, the trial court need not require plaintiff to elect upon which of
these separate averments of damages he will rely. They are not
properly the subjects of separate averments, being but elements in
estimating the value of services.

Chickering, Thomas & Gregory, and Fitzgerald & Abbott, for
the appellant.

Frederick E. Whitney and M. C. Chapman, for the respondent.

⁶⁰ VAN FLEET, J.   Action by the father to recover damages
resulting from the death of his infant son, alleged to have been
caused by the negligence of defendant in running over him with
one of its electric cars.

Judgment was for plaintiff, and defendant appeals therefrom
and from an order denying it a new trial.

1. Appellant devotes a considerable portion of its brief in an
effort to convince us that the evidence fails to show any negligence on the part of defendant. The task has proven fruitless.
An examination of the evidence discloses a substantial conflict
upon that issue, however much it may be said to preponderate in
defendant's favor. Much of counsel's argument in this behalf
is expended in endeavoring to demonstrate that the two witnesses
whose testimony tends to create the conflict were wholly unworthy
of credence, and that therefore the evidence, while apparently
conflicting, is not so in substance. But the credibility of witnesses is a question for the jury, so long as the testimony which
they give has a legal tendency to establish the fact, and where,
as here, there is nothing so inherently or otherwise manifestly
improbable in its character as to justify the court in ignoring it.

2. Appellant also contends that under the evidence the plaintiff was shown to have been guilty of contributory negligence in
permitting his child to expose himself unattended and unpro-

tected to the dangers of the street, and that that issue should have been withheld from the jury.

The evidence upon this question was in substance this: Plaintiff's dwelling fronted on Tenth street, in the city of Oakland, about one hundred feet from Franklin street, along which ran defendant's railway; his family consisted, at the time, of his wife, a daughter of about thirteen years, and the boy that was killed, aged four and one-half years. The father worked at his trade, and was away from home during the day; the daughter attended school, the little boy remaining at home with his mother, who did her own work. The boy was permitted to play on the sidewalk, there being no front yard, and sometimes with other boys on Tenth street in front of the dwelling, but he had been repeatedly admonished by his parents not to go to Franklin street where the cars ran, because they knew it was dangerous, and he [01] was not permitted to go there with their knowledge; he was an ordinarily obedient child, and generally, as admonished, played near his home, but would at times stray onto Franklin street without his mother's knowledge; on such occasions, when she discovered the fact, she would either go or send after him. Her daughter, when at home, generally looked after the boy, but when at school the mother had his sole care. To quote from the latter's testimony: "Of course, I couldn't watch him every minute; he could open the door and go out, but he was generally a very good child to mind—better than the average child. I tried to keep him in the best I could, anyway. It was not very often that I had occasion to call him away from Franklin street. If he was not in front of the house I would have some one go after him, or go after him myself and bring him back. He very seldom went away when I told him not to go."

On the occasion of the accident the mother was engaged in doing some washing on the back porch of the house. She testified: "I did not know for certain that the little boy was in the street at that time. He came in fifteen or twenty minutes before he was killed, and I told him not to go away. Then I went right on with my washing. I supposed he was in the house. I didn't go right to see, just exactly right away. . . . . There was no one in the house at the time the little boy came in, and I told him not to go out. The little girl, thirteen years old, at the time was helping me on the porch washing. I did not see the accident. There was no servant employed by myself or husband about the premises. The little boy was in the house about fifteen or twenty minutes before he was killed." The boy had gone to Franklin street, got on the defendant's railway in front of an advancing car, and was run over and killed.

This evidence is practically without controversy, and defendant's claim is that it establishes negligence per se which should preclude recovery.

If the term "negligence" signified an absolute quantity or thing to be measured in all cases in accordance with some precise standard, much of the difficulty which besets courts in the solution of this class of cases would be at once dissipated. But, unfortunately, it does not. Negligence is not absolute, but is a thing which is always relative to the particular circumstances of which [62] it is sought to be predicated. For this reason it is very rare that a set of circumstances is presented which enables a court to say as a matter of law that negligence has been shown. As a very general rule, it is a question of fact for the jury—an inference to be deduced from the circumstances; and it is only where the deduction to be drawn is inevitably that of negligence that the court is authorized to withdraw the question from the jury. The fact that the evidence may be without conflict is not controlling, nor even necessarily material. Conceded facts may as readily afford a difference of opinion as to the inferences and conclusions to be drawn therefrom as those which rest upon conflicting evidence; and, if there be room for such difference, the question must be left to the jury: Beach on Contributory Negligence, sec. 163; Schierhold v. North Beach etc. R. R. Co., 40 Cal. 447, 453; Van Praag v. Gale, 107 Cal. 438.

Within these principles the evidence in this case cannot be said to establish negligence per se. Parents are chargeable with the exercise of ordinary care in the protection of their minor children; and whether the conduct of the mother, for which plaintiff is to be held responsible, in permitting the deceased child to be out of her sight for a period of from fifteen to twenty minutes, without satisfying herself of his whereabouts, was, under all the circumstances, a want of ordinary care, was, we think, a fairly debatable question: Schierhold v. North Beach etc. R. R. Co., 40 Cal. 447, 453; Meeks v. Southern Pac. R. R. Co., 56 Cal. 513; 38 Am. Rep. 67; Birkett v. Knickerbocker Ice Co., 110 N. Y. 504.

But, were defendant's contention sustainable in this respect, it would not necessarily determine the plaintiff's right to recover. There was evidence tending to show that when the child went upon the railway track he was a sufficient distance in advance of the approaching car to have enabled those in charge thereof, by the exercise of ordinary care, to have stopped before striking him.

This evidence, if believed by the jury, and their verdict implies that it was, would tend to show gross negligence on the part of defendant's servants and justify a finding for plaintiff notwithstanding the negligence of the parents in permitting the child to be in the street. This is upon the principle, now firmly established in this state, that a party having an opportunity by the exercise of proper care to avoid injuring another must do so, [63] notwithstanding the latter has placed himself in the situation of danger by his own negligence or wrong: Schierhold v. North Beach etc. R. R. Co., 40 Cal. 447, 453; Needham v. San Francisco etc. R. R. Co., 37 Cal. 409; Meeks v. Southern Pac. R. R. Co., 56 Cal. 513; 38 Am. Rep. 67; Esrey v. Southern Pac. R. R. Co., 103 Cal. 541, 544; Cunningham v. Los Angeles Ry. Co., 115 Cal. 561.

3. Defendant complains of the action of the court in another respect affecting its defense of contributory negligence.

The court, against defendant's objection, permitted plaintiff to testify that he had no servants, and was too poor to employ any; and, in submitting the case to the jury, charged them that "the fact that plaintiff is a poor man, if that be true, constitutes no ground why he is entitled to a verdict, but is a matter to be considered by you in determining whether or not he has been guilty of contributory negligence." This action of the court is assigned as error, in that it submitted to the jury an element having no competent bearing upon the issue.

The question whether the poverty of the parents can be considered by the jury in such a case in determining the question of their negligence is one which has given rise to some contrariety of expression, both from courts and law-writers; but we think the better reasoning decidedly against its consideration. We are unable to perceive wherein the fact that a parent may or may not have the means to employ servants to look after his young children can have any relevant or competent bearing upon the question whether in any instance he has given them that degree of care which the law requires at his hands. Care, like its correlative, negligence, is a relative term, and is to be judged by the circumstances as they exist, not as they might have existed under other and different conditions; and the question, therefore, is, What, under the facts actually surrounding him at the time, and of which he had knowledge, could reasonably be demanded of the parent? This is a question which cannot be affected by a consideration of what he could or should have done under other circumstances. As suggested by the supreme court of Indiana in Mayhew v. Burns, 103 Ind. 339, 340, in holding the inadmissibility of such evidence: "Whether one was negligent or not in a given case must be determined by considering his or her conduct as it related to the particular circumstances of the occasion or affair out of which the case arises.

64 "It cannot be solved by showing their general pecuniary condition. Their ability to act, and what they did or omitted to do, with reference to the particular emergency, is all that is important. All that was necessary for the plaintiff to show in this case was the actual situation of his household, and that neither he nor those whom he had intrusted with his child were guilty of any act or omission in relation to the child and the excavation into which it fell. This was a question of conduct, not of property. The ability to comprehend and guard against the danger when comprehended, and the acts and omissions of the plaintiff and his housekeeper after the facts were known, were all the subjects material to the injury. His duty as it related to his child and the sources of danger were the same whether his household was managed as it was from choice or necessity. It would be monstrous to assume that the care or solicitude of a parent for the safety of a child in respect of danger to its person had any relation to his pecuniary condition."

And again by the same court in the later case of Indianapolis etc. Ry. Co. v. Pitzer, 109 Ind. 179, 190, 58 Am. Rep. 387, the doctrine is reaffirmed, and it is further suggested: "Any other rule would be impracticable as well as unsound in principle. If the pecuniary condition of the parent is accepted as the standard, all is uncertain, for no definite amount of pecuniary means can be taken as a guide, since it would be impossible to determine what a parent should be worth in order to impose upon him the duty of employing nurses or attendants for his children."

Judge Dillon, having occasion to consider this question, expresses his views thereon in this terse fashion: "Some of the cases seem to make the liability depend upon the means of the parents, and to countenance a distinction as to contributory negligence between parents able to employ nurses or attendants, and those who are not. This distinction may be doubted, for there is not in this country one rule of law for the rich and a different rule for the poor. It extends its protecting shield over all alike": Hagan's Petition, 5 Dill. 96.

And this court, in the very recent case of Cunningham v. Los Angeles Ry. Co., 115 Cal. 561, in considering an instruction bearing upon the same question, took occasion to say: "We think the court should have refrained from charging that the law does not require parents to keep an attendant with their young children; and that [65] they are not required to shut them up. While, abstractly speaking, these things are perfectly true, the question of whether such precautions are necessary under any given circumstances to constitute ordinary care for the safety of their children with which parents are charged, is one of fact for the jury, and not for the court to determine as matter of law."

The opposite doctrine would seem to have been largely built up from observations made by judges in discussing the general subject of the contributory negligence of parents in cases where the question of their pecuniary condition was not directly involved. In none of the cases cited by respondent does the question appear to have arisen upon the evidence or instructions, but was suggested in the course of reasoning pursued by the appellate court. Mr. Beach (Beach on Contributory Negligence, sec. 135) takes this side of the controversy; but the cases to which he refers are the same, with the exception of a recent one of the same type from Oregon (Hedin v. Suburban Ry. Co., 26 Or. 155), to which we are referred by respondent. Criticising these cases referred to by Beach, Mr. Patterson (Patterson's Railway Accident Law, sec. 81) says: "It has been held that poor parents of infant children are not contributorily negligent if they do not prevent their infant children from straying into the public streets or upon the lines of highways. The judgments in those cases seem to have been largely influenced by the sentimental reflections of the judges upon the poverty of the plaintiffs, and their consequent inability to employ servants to watch their children, and the hardship of requiring them to keep those children within doors when they could not safely go abroad; but those learned judges failed to give due weight to the consideration that the railway was not responsible for the acts of the parents in bringing the children into the world, nor for that degree of misfortune which retained those parents in a condition of more or less want, and that there is no rule of law nor principle of justice which compels railways to insure the public against the necessary incidents of poverty, nor which entitles people, either poor or rich, to make at the expense of railways profitable speculations out of the deaths of the children whom their own neglect of parental duty has exposed to peril."

In Mayhew v. Burns, 103 Ind. 339, 340, referring to this same line of cases, [66] it is said: "The cases relied on are cases where children escaped from the observation of persons in whose care they were left, and sustained injury by going on railway tracks. It is said in most of these cases that parents who are poor frequently find it necessary, while engaged by their duties, to leave their younger children in the custody of older sisters or brothers, who have attained to sufficient age and intelligence to guard them from danger, and that negligence should not be imputed to them if they escape their oversight and sustain injury. We should have no difficulty in saying as much, regardless of the pecuniary condition of the parents. We can conceive of no attendant who would be more solicitous for the welfare of an infant than its older sister or brother, who was of sufficient age and intelligence to be left as its guardian. It is idle to say that the propriety or impropriety of so leaving an infant is to be determined by an inquiry concerning the amount of property the parent owns. . . . . We can discover no principle upon which it can be determined whether negligence can be attributed to one in a given case by an inquiry into the state of his fortune."

After a careful review of the authorities, we are clearly of the opinion that the question of the parent's negligence in any given case cannot be made to turn upon the state of his finances, and that the rulings of the court below in this respect were erroneous.

Plaintiff contends that, if wrong, the rulings did not constitute prejudicial error, for the reason, suggested above, that there was evidence entitling plaintiff to recover notwithstanding any question of contributory negligence. Whether that be true or not we need not decide, since there must be a new trial upon another ground.

4. It is claimed that the verdict was so excessive as to show passion or prejudice by the jury in its verdict, and this contention must be sustained.

There was no averment or evidence of peculiar or special damages, nor of a right to exemplary or punitive damages, the plaintiff's cause of action resting solely upon his right to recover for the loss of the services of his child resulting from its death. The evidence simply tended to show that the boy was four and a half years old; was an ordinarily bright, healthy, affectionate, and obedient child; with an expectancy of life which, if realized, would have carried him considerably beyond the age of majority.

⁶⁷ The jury were properly instructed that they could award nothing in the way of penalty for his death, nor for sorrow or grief of his parents, but must confine their verdict to an amount which would justly compensate plaintiff for "the probable value of the services of the deceased until he had attained his majority, taking into consideration the cost of his support and maintenance during the early and helpless part of his life"; that while they could consider the fact that plaintiff had been deprived of the comfort, society, and protection of his son, this consideration could only go to affect the pecuniary value of his services to plaintiff.

Upon the evidence and these instructions the jury gave a verdict for six thousand dollars.

We think it quite manifest, upon its face, that the verdict was actuated by something other than a consideration of the evidence. Under no conceivable method or rule of compensation permissible under the evidence could such a result have been attained. There was nothing to indicate that the value of the child's services would have been greater than that of the ordinary boy of his age, assuming that such a fact would have been pertinent. He was a mere infant, and for many years at best, under ordinary conditions—and it is by such we must judge—he would have remained, however dear to their hearts, a subject of expense and outlay to his parents, without the ability to render pecuniary return. And common experience teaches further that, even after reaching an age of some usefulness, he yet would continue for the better part of his remaining years of minority more a source of outgo than of income. When we regard the probable number of years to be taken in his schooling, in this day of general desire and necessity for education and knowledge, comparatively little valuable time would be left to be devoted to the service of the parent.

But assuming that the deceased would have been set to useful and valuable employment of some appropriate character as early as ten years of age, which is unusual, at no average rate of income or wages which he could reasonably have earned would it be at all probable that in the time intervening his majority he could have earned, over and above the cost and expense of his maintenance, the very large sum given by the verdict.

⁶⁸ Under the circumstances of the case, it is solely by the probabilities that these things can be estimated. And while in no sense conclusive, we have the right, and it is most reasonable in

judging of the probable character of occupation the deceased would have pursued, to regard, with the other circumstances surrounding him, the calling of his father—since experience teaches that children do very frequently pursue the same general class of business as that of their parents: Walters v. Chicago etc. R. R. Co., 41 Iowa, 71, 73.

From these considerations we think it obvious, as contended, that the verdict was prompted by improper motives on the part of the jury. While it is the province of the latter to estimate the extent of the injury, the right is not arbitrary, but must be justly exercised within the evidence. And when it is apparent that the award "is obviously so disproportionate to the injury proved as to justify the conclusion that the verdict is not the result of the cool and dispassionate discretion of the jury," it will be set aside: Morgan v. Southern Pac. Co., 95 Cal. 510; 29 Am. St. Rep. 143; Tarbell v. Central Pac. R. R. Co., 34 Cal. 623; Sloane v. Southern Cal. Ry. Co., 111 Cal. 668, 687; St. Louis etc. Ry. Co. v. Robbins, 57 Ark. 377; Chicago etc. Ry. Co. v. Bayfield, 37 Mich. 205, 215; Potter v. Railroad Co., 22 Wis. 615.

5. The remaining points call for no extended notice.

We discover no material error in the refusal of the court to require plaintiff to elect upon which of the two separate averments of damage he would rely. They were not properly the subjects for separate averment, the loss of society, comfort, etc., being but an element in estimating the value of services. The objection to the manner of pleading might, perhaps, have been reached by a demurrer for uncertainty or ambiguity.

The instruction refused on the subject of exemplary or punitive damages was, we think, substantially covered in the charge of the court; the other instruction refused did not correctly state the law.

The judgment and order are reversed and the cause remanded for a new trial.

Harrison, J., and Beatty, C. J., concurred.

Hearing in Bank denied.

————

NEGLIGENCE—QUESTION FOR JURY WHEN.—Before the question of negligence becomes one of law for the court, the facts shown by the evidence must be such that all reasonable men must draw the same conclusions from them. If the facts proved are such that reasonable men may fairly differ as to whether or not there was negligence, the question is one for the jury to consider: Lowe v. Salt Lake City, 13 Utah, 91; 57 Am. St. Rep. 708, and note; Brotherton v. Manhattan Beach Imp. Co., 48 Neb. 563; 58 Am. St. Rep. 709,

and note. See Alabama etc. R. R. v. Jones, 114 Ala. 519; ante, p. 121.
The question as to parents' contributory negligence in allowing their
infant to go out in the street, where he was injured by a street-car,
is for the jury in a proper case: Evers v. Philadelphia Traction Co.,
176 Pa. St. 376; 53 Am. St. Rep. 674, and note.

NEGLIGENCE—CONTRIBUTORY—WHEN NOT A DEFENSE.—
The contributory negligence of the plaintiff does not preclude his
recovery, when the conduct of the defendant was wanton and willful,
or where it indicated that indifference to the rights of others which
must be justly characterized as recklessness: McDonald v. International etc. Ry. Co., 86 Tex. 1; 40 Am. St. Rep. 803, and note; Louisville etc. R. R. Co. v. Markee, 103 Ala. 160; 49 Am. St. Rep. 21; Hall
v. Ogden City etc. Ry. Co., 13 Utah, 243; 57 Am. St. Rep. 726, and
note; Brotherton v. Manhattan Beach Imp. Co., 48 Neb. 563; 58 Am.
St. Rep. 709.

DAMAGES RECOVERABLE FOR NEGLIGENT KILLING OF
MINOR CHILD.—In an action by a parent for the death of a minor
child, the main element of damages is in the probable value of the
services of the deceased until he would have attained his majority,
considering the cost of his support and maintenance during the early
and helpless part of his life: Morgan v. Southern Pac. Co., 95 Cal.
510; 29 Am. St. Rep. 143; Rockford etc. R. R. Co. v. Delaney, 82
Ill. 198; 25 Am. Rep. 308. See monographic note to Louisville etc.
Ry. Co. v. Goodykoontz, 12 Am. St. Rep. 381, 382. The jury must
not be allowed to base their estimate of damages recoverable upon
speculations upon contingencies too remote and uncertain: Cooper v.
Lake Shore etc. By. Co., 66 Mich. 261; 11 Am. St. Rep. 482. From
the facts proved and their own knowledge and experience the jury
may estimate the damages, and no proof of the value of prospective
services is necessary: Chicago v. Hessing, 83 Ill. 204; 25 Am. Rep.
378.

DAMAGES FOR DEATH OF MINOR CHILD—WHEN EXCES-
SIVE AND WHEN NOT.—A verdict of twenty thousand dollars, in
an action by a mother for the death of her daughter two years old,
will be set aside as excessive, especially where the complaint alleges no special damages, and no evidence whatever is introduced
upon the subject of damages: Morgan v. Southern Pac. Co., 95 Cal.
510; 29 Am. St. Rep. 143, and note. See Barnes v. Shreveport City
R. R. Co., 47 La. Ann. 1218; 49 Am. St. Rep. 400.

SCAMMAN *v.* BONSLETT.

[118 CALIFORNIA, 293.]

JUDGMENT, AMENDMENT OF, WHEN VOID.—Where a
decree foreclosing a mortgage gives no direction for the docketing of any judgment against the mortgagor for any deficiency
which may remain after the sale, and the complaint shows
that he has instituted proceedings in insolvency for his discharge
from his liabilities, a subsequent order made without notice to him
declaring him to be personally liable for the mortgage debt, and
directing judgment to be entered against him for any deficiency, is
void, though it is claimed that the mortgage debt was owing to a
nonresident of the state, and was, therefore, not subject to be discharged by the proceedings in insolvency.

INSOLVENT LAWS OF ONE STATE CANNOT DIS-
CHARGE THE CONTRACTS OF CITIZENS OF OTHER STATES,
because they have no extraterritorial operation, unless such citizens

voluntarily appear in the insolvency proceedings and become parties thereto.

JUDGMENT, AMENDMENT OF, WHEN UNAUTHORIZED. If an inspection of the record does not show an error of the clerk in entering the judgment, resort must be had to extrinsic evidence, and parties to be affected by a motion to amend the judgment must be given notice thereof and an opportunity to resist it.

JUDGMENT.—AN AMENDMENT OF A JUDGMENT CAN BE ALLOWED ONLY for the purpose of making the record speak the truth, and not for the purpose of revising or changing the judgment.

A JUDGMENT CANNOT BE AMENDED SO AS to include provisions or directions not proper to have been made at the date of its original entry upon the allegations of the pleadings.

AN EXECUTION MAY BE QUASHED on the ground that the amendment of the judgment by which the execution of the judgment was authorized was void.

INSOLVENCY—DEBTS DUE NONRESIDENTS, WHEN DISCHARGED BY.—If a debtor and creditor were residents of the same state at the date of a contract made and payable therein, a discharge granted under the insolvency law enacted before the making of the contract is a valid defense to an action thereon, notwithstanding the creditor subsequently and before the institution of the proceeding in insolvency became a resident of another state.

Freeman & Bates, for the appellant.

W. E. Duncan, Jr., and R. E. Robinson, for the respondent.

95 SEARLS, C. About November 20, 1894, Francesca B. Scamman, as executrix of the last will of Henry Scamman, deceased, brought an action in the superior court in and for the county of Butte to foreclose a mortgage executed by A. Bonslett, August 1, 1889, to secure the payment of his promissory note for eight thousand five hundred dollars of even date, payable five years after date, with interest made and payable in this state.

The complaint averred that the defendant, A. Bonslett, had been on the —— day of October, 1894, adjudged and declared to be an insolvent debtor upon his petition filed under the Insolvent Act of 1880, and that E. E. Biggs had been elected, etc., as the assignee of said insolvent, had qualified as such, and that all of the estate of the insolvent had been assigned to him.

That the mortgaged property was insufficient to satisfy the mortgage. The assignee, as well as Bonslett, were made defendants.

The complaint did not pray for a deficiency judgment against Bonslett in case there should be a deficiency after the sale of the mortgaged property.

L. L. Green was also made a defendant upon the ground that he had or claimed some interest in the mortgaged premises. He answered disclaiming any interest.

Defendants Bonslett and Biggs, as assignee, made default, and on January 19, 1895, a decree of foreclosure in the usual form was entered ordering a sale of the property and payment to plaintiff, out of the proceeds of such sale, of the sum of eleven thousand six hundred and eight dollars, besides costs, attorney's fees, etc. No provision was made in the decree for any deficiency which might remain after sale. The property was sold under the decree and a return made April 1, 1895, showing a deficiency of seventeen hundred and seventy-three dollars and sixty-five cents.

On the twenty-eighth day of October, 1895, defendant A. Bonslett was, by a decree of the superior court in the insolvency proceedings, discharged from all his debts existing against him on and prior to September 24, 1894, under and by virtue of the Insolvent Act of 1880, excepting only such debts, if any, as are by the said insolvent laws excepted from the operation of a discharge in insolvency.

⁹⁶ The petition and schedule in insolvency filed by said defendant described among his debts and liabilities the note and mortgage of Scamman.

On the seventeenth day of September, 1896, the superior court, on motion of plaintiff and without notice to defendant Bonslett, entered two orders in the case, viz:

1. An order amending the decree of foreclosure of January 19, 1895, by adding thereto the following, "and the defendant, A. Bonslett, is declared and adjudged to be the defendant who is personally liable for the sums in this judgment specified, to wit, said sum of eleven thousand six hundred and eight dollars, and interest and costs of suit."

2. An order directing the clerk of the court to docket a deficiency judgment against defendant Bonslett for seventeen hundred and seventy-three dollars and fifty cents, with interest, etc.

Thereafter two executions issued on said deficiency judgment, one to the sheriff of Butte county and the other to the sheriff of Yuba county.

Defendant Bonslett moved the court to set aside the amendments to the decree and for an order quashing the executions, etc., upon a variety of grounds, which we need not specify at length.

On the part of plaintiff, the affidavit of S. Davis was admitted, showing that from the year 1880 to the date of his death in 1893 Henry Scamman, the mortgagee, was a nonresident of the state of California and a resident and citizen of Saco, in the state of

Maine, at which last-named place his family, including the plaintiff herein, have at all times resided. The mortgage described said Henry Scamman as a resident of Downieville, county of Sierra, state of California. .'

It was admitted that plaintiff never presented any claim, and did not appear in the insolvency proceedings of A. Bonslett.

The court denied the motion to strike out the amendments to the judgment and the order to docket the deficiency judgment, and granted the motion to recall and quash the executions, from which order so recalling and quashing the executions plaintiff prosecutes this appeal.

1. "Insolvent laws of one state cannot discharge the contracts of citizens of other states, because they have no extraterritorial operation, and consequently the tribunal sitting under them, unless [97] in cases where a citizen of such other state voluntarily becomes a party to the proceeding, has no jurisdiction in the case. Legal notice cannot be given, and consequently there can be no legal obligation to appear and, of course, there can be no legal default": Baldwin v. Hale, 1 Wall. 223; Rhodes v. Borden, 67 Cal. 7; Bedell v. Scruton, 54 Vt. 493; Bean v. Loryea, 81 Cal. 151.

It follows that if plaintiff's testator was in fact a citizen of another state he was not bound by the insolvency proceedings under the statute of this state.

2. But, notwithstanding the foregoing well-settled proposition, we are at a loss to see upon what grounds the amendment to the decree of September 17, 1896, can be upheld.

If that amendment and the accompanying order directing the docketing of a deficiency judgment against defendant were void, the executions issued thereon should have been quashed, and if the court decided correctly, although basing its action upon erroneous reasoning, its action must be upheld.

A court may at any time render or amend a judgment where the record discloses that the entry on the minutes does not correctly give what was the judgment of the court: Morrison v. Dapman, 3 Cal. 255.

Any error or defect in a record occurring through acts of omission or commission of the clerk in entering or failing to properly enter of record the judgment or proceedings of the court—in short, what may be termed clerical misprisions—may, the record affording the evidence thereof, be corrected at any time by the court upon its own motion, or on motion of an interested party either with or without notice. Where, however, an inspection

of the record does not show the error, and resort must be had to
evidence aliunde, courts will require notice to be given of a motion to amend a judgment to the parties to be affected thereby, and
a motion for the amendment of a judgment in such last-mentioned case must, under section 473 of the Code of Civil Procedure, be made within six months, except in cases where personal
service of summons has not been had, in which case the court
may grant relief within one year after the entry of judgment:
People v. Greene, 74 Cal. 400; 5 Am. St. Rep. 448; Hegeler v.
Henckell, 27 Cal. 495; Bostwick v. McEvoy, 62 Cal. 502; Wharton v. Harlan, 68 Cal. 422.

[98] Again, amendments to judgments can only be allowed for
the purpose of making the record conform to the truth, not for
the purpose of revising and changing the judgment: Black on
Judgments, sec. 156. The same author adds: "If, on the other
hand, the proposed addition is a mere afterthought, and formed
no part of the judgment as originally intended and pronounced,
it cannot be brought in by any way of amendment."

We may add that, in the absence of express statutory authority
so to do, no court can amend its judgments so as to include in them
provisions which it could not have inserted at the date of the
original entry. How, then, stood the case at the date of the
amendment of the judgment?

Plaintiff had brought her action to foreclose, and not only had
not asked for any relief except the foreclosure and sale of the
mortgaged property, but by the affirmative allegations of her
complaint showed that defendant Bonslett had been declared an
insolvent, etc., and, having failed to aver that her testator was a
citizen of another state, she failed to make a case entitling her
to have the court, by its decree, declare said defendant "personally liable for the debt," as provided by section 726 of the Code
of Civil Procedure. A deficiency judgment may be docketed
by the clerk, when shown to be necessary by the return of the
sheriff, but it can only be so docketed against the defendant or
defendants declared personally liable by the decree. In a foreclosure suit, where judgment is taken by default, the decree can
give no relief beyond that which is demanded in the bill: Raun
v. Reynolds, 11 Cal. 15.

Had the plaintiff asked that defendant Bonslett be declared
personally liable, non constat, but that he would have answered
setting up the insolvency proceedings, and his immunity from
personal liability thereunder. But under the complaint it was
not necessary for him so to do, as no personal liability was sought

to be enforced against him. Had the court included the personal liability clause in the original decree, it would have been erroneous, but we are not prepared to say it would have been void: Blondeau v. Snyder, 95 Cal. 521.

But when the court waited for over seventeen months after the entry of the final decree, and then, without notice to defendant ᵘᵘ Bonslett, amended the decree, in matter of substance, granting relief different from that asked for or granted originally, we think the amendment was without jurisdiction and void.

Freeman, in his work on Judgments, at section 72 says: "If, however, an amendment is made to a judgment or decree in a matter of substance, whereby it is made to grant relief different from that granted when it was rendered, it is absolutely void as against a party having no notice of the application to thus amend it": Citing Swift v. Allen, 55 Ill. 303. The amendment being void was sufficient reason for quashing the executions: Chipman v. Bowman, 14 Cal. 157; Gates v. Lane, 49 Cal. 266; Buell v. Buell, 92 Cal. 393.

We cannot determine from the record precisely the ground upon which the court below discharged the writs.

The note secured by the mortgage was given and made payable at Gridley, in the state of California, and the mortgage recited, as before stated, that Scamman was a resident of this state.

Among the conclusive presumptions under section 1962 of the Code of Civil Procedure is the following: "The truth of the facts recited, from the recital in a written instrument between the parties thereto, or their successors in interest by a subsequent title; but this rule does not apply to the recital of a consideration."

The court below may have been of opinion that the debtor and creditor. having both been citizens of California at the date of the contract, which was made and payable in this state, in an action brought in the courts of this state to enforce such contract, a certificate of discharge of the debtor under the insolvent law of this state enacted before the indebtedness accrued is a valid defense to the action, even though the creditor had become a citizen of another state, after the making of the contract.

If this was the theory of the court, its conclusion is not without warrant in law: Freeman on Judgments, sec. 604, and cases there cited.

Again, as the question of the citizenship of Scamman was one of fact, the court may have concluded as a fact that he remained a citizen of the state of California.

We need not pursue, discuss, or decide these questions, as we are of opinion the amendment to the judgment was void; such **100** determination is conclusive of the case, and the order appealed from should be affirmed.

Haynes, C., and Chipman, C., concurred.

For the reasons given in the foregoing opinion the order appealed from is affirmed.

McFarland, J., Temple, J., Henshaw, J.

Hearing in Bank denied.

JUDGMENTS—AMENDMENTS OF.—A judgment may be amended whenever there is anything to amend by, as a clerical mistake in entering it, but it cannot be corrected when there is error of judgment in pronouncing it: Smith v. Hood, 25 Pa. St. 218; 64 Am. Dec. 692. Personal knowledge of the judge is not essential to the correction of a clerical error. The court may hear evidence and act on the proof: Hollister v. Judges, etc., 8 Ohio St. 201; 70 Am. Dec. 100. All parties to be affected by the amendment should be cited before the court: Whitwell v. Emory, 3 Mich. 84; 59 Am. Dec. 220; Hill v. Hoover, 5 Wis. 386; 68 Am. Dec. 70, and note. It has been held, however, that a merely clerical error of a clerk of court in making up a record may be corrected by the docket, by the order of the court, without notice to either party: Emery v. Berry, 28 N. H. 473; 61 Am. Dec. 622.

Insolvency, Effect of Discharge against Nonresidents. — In the principal case, it is suggested that the trial court may have been of the opinion that the debtor and creditor, having both been citizens of California at the date of the contract, a certificate of the discharge of the debtor under the insolvency law, enacted before the indebtedness accrued, was a valid defense to the action, even though the creditor had become a citizen of another state after the making of the contract, and it was said that, if such were the theory of the court, its conclusion is not without warrant in law, and Freeman on Judgments, section 604, was referred to as sustaining such conclusion. The section thus referred to is one treating of judgments of the courts of the Confederate States, and, it is scarcely necessary to add, has no relevancy to the subject under consideration, and cannot be the section intended to be cited by the court. The section intended to be referred to is 607, at which place it is, however, shown that the decisions of the supreme court of the United States necessarily affirm "that a bankruptcy or insolvency statute can have no extraterritorial operation, and that a citizen of one state cannot be required to appear in the courts of another, and to submit to their exercise of jurisdiction over him, or to their discharge of an obligation due him, though it was created or is to be performed in the state where such courts have jurisdiction." Later decisions upon the subject confirm these views: Pullen v. Hillman, 84 Me. 129; 30 Am. St. Rep. 340; Pattee v. Paige, 163 Mass. 352; 47 Am. St. Rep. 459; Chase v. Henry, 166 Mass. 577; 55 Am. St. Rep. 433; note to Murray v. Roberts, 15 Am. St. Rep. 212.

Amending Judgments. — In so far as the court held the amendment to the judgment made by the trial court in the principal case to be unauthorized, we think it but returned to the principles contended for by us in section 70 of our work on Judgments, namely, that "the law does not authorize the correction of judicial errors under the pretense of correcting clerical errors. To entitle a party to an order amending a judgment, order, or decree, he must establish that the entry as made does not conform to what the court ordered." It has, however, been insisted, especially in California, that we may look at a judgment-roll for the purpose of ascertaining therefrom what the court should have ordered from the conceded or established facts, and may regard the omission from the judgment of what should have been thus ordered as a mere clerical error, to be corrected by an amendment. This, we think, transforms a proceeding to amend the judgment entry into a correctory proceeding, for it by no means follows from the fact that the court ought to have rendered a particular judgment that it did in fact do so; for the frequency of reversal by appellate tribunals shows that error is by them often attributed to the subordinate courts. The California cases to which we shall here refer, and which we think are necessarily inconsistent with the principal case and ought to have been expressly overruled by it, are Leviston v. Swan, 33 Cal. 480, Bostwick v. McAvoy, 62 Cal. 496, and McNeil v. Ward, No. 8887, decided in the year 1883, and not officially reported, but the opinion in which may be found in 11 Pacific Coast Law Journal, 224. In the case first cited, a judgment in foreclosure was entered in 1864, which did not suggest that anyone was personally liable for the deficiency, should one be found after a sale of the property. More than three years subsequently an order of court was entered directing the docketing of a judgment for the deficiency. This order was affirmed, the court saying: "The judgment in this case, as first entered, was defective in not designating the defendants who were personally liable for the debt; but inasmuch as the record shows who they were, the court had the power to amend the judgment at any time by adding a clause designating the defendants who were personally liable. The more regular motion would have been to amend the judgment by supplying the omission which was apparent upon the face of the record, but we consider the course pursued as amounting substantially to the same thing." In the second case cited, judgments had been entered against administrators personally, instead of being made payable out of the estates of the decedents in due course of administration. Amendments were subsequently made, after the lapse of the term, correcting the judgments in question so as to free them from error. We may concede that in these cases it appeared from the record that the judgment ought to have been entered in the form in which it was made to read after the amendment thereto had been ordered, but there was certainly nothing in the case to show that the action of the clerk in entering the judgment, as he did, did not correctly represent the judgment as actually rendered by the court. In the unreported case, the action was to foreclose a mortgage, and the defendant pleaded the pendency of proceedings

In insolvency for his release. A judgment was, nevertheless, entered directing a sale of the mortgaged premises. The fact of the proceedings in insolvency was thus brought to the attention of the court, and neither the complaint nor the answer contained any averment respecting the place of the residence of the defendant. There was, however, a finding upon that subject, though it was not responsive to any allegation in the pleadings. No personal judgment having been entered against the defendant, the plaintiff, conceiving himself entitled to such a judgment, appealed to the supreme court, which held that the plaintiff's contention was correct, but that the judgment need not be reversed, because it was susceptible of amendment from the record, and the trial court was directed to make such amendment. This last case was surely in conflict with the principal case, and yet we do not doubt that the principal case was correctly decided, providing the court felt at liberty to disregard its prior adjudications. It should not, however, have passed them unnoticed, but should have expressly overruled them, in order that there might thereafter be no doubt of the principle controlling in this state upon this subject.

Los Angeles v. Young.

[118 California, 295.]

JURISDICTION.—NOTICE OF THE TIME WHEN A CAUSE IS SET FOR TRIAL is a prerequisite of the jurisdiction of a justice of the peace, if the statute requires such notice to be given.

JURISDICTION OF A JUSTICE OF THE PEACE, WHEN MUST APPEAR AFFIRMATIVELY.—If a statute requires a justice of the peace to give a party notice of the time when his cause is set for trial, such notice must be in writing and, upon certiorari, must appear by the return. Its existence is not proved by statements in the docket of the justice that the counsel for the adverse party stated that the notice of trial had been served on counsel for the defendant, and that he would produce the same.

CERTIORARI—EXTRINSIC EVIDENCE.—Upon certiorari, if it becomes necessary for the court of review to be put in possession of facts upon which the court below acted and which are not technically of record, the lower court may be required to certify such facts in its return to the writ, and a statement so made would then become a part of the record; and where a notice is indorsed "Served, H. H. Y." it is perhaps proper to receive evidence from a constable showing that the indorsement was made by him and that he served the notice in question.

CERTIORARI—EXTRINSIC EVIDENCE TO DISPROVE JURISDICTION.—Evidence dehors the record and contradicting it cannot be received in proceedings in certiorari for the purpose of proving that a statement made in a return or paper appearing by the record is false.

W. P. Hyatt, for the appellant.

W. E. Dunn, for the respondents.

²⁹⁶ HENSHAW, J. This is an appeal from the judgment of
the superior court upon a writ of review vacating and annulling
a judgment rendered in a justice's court.

One McCombs in the justice's court of the township of Los
Angeles had instituted a suit against the city of Los Angeles and
C. Compton. The defendants appeared in said action by their
attorney, W. E. Dunn, and interposed demurrers to the complaint. Thereafter the justice of the peace heard and passed
upon the demurrers, overruled them, and granted defendants
two days' time in which to answer. Defendants failed to answer, and judgment by default was entered for plaintiff. The
statutory period of thirty days during which an appeal could
have been taken to the superior court passed, and afterward the
defendants in that action obtained from the superior court of
the county a writ of review. After hearing upon this writ the
superior court annulled the judgment of the justice's court, and
this appeal followed.

The contention of petitioners in the superior court was that
neither they nor their attorney had been served with notice of
the time set for the trial; that service of such notice upon them
is, under section 850 of the Code of Civil Procedure, an imperative prerequisite to the jurisdiction of the justice of the peace to
try the cause; and that under the writ they were entitled to
show and did show to the satisfaction of the superior court, by
legal and competent evidence, that no notice had in fact been
served.

Respondent's contention that the service of notice of the time
set for trial is a jurisdictional prerequisite is supported by the
case of Jones v. Justice's Court, 97 Cal. 523. As appears by that
case, the entry in the justice's docket was to the effect merely
that at the time set for trial no one appeared for defendant, and
that counsel for the adverse party "stated that notice of trial
had been served on counsel for defendant, and that he would
produce the same." This was manifestly no proof of service of
the notice, and it was so held by this court. There was also an
affidavit of the service of the notice filed in that case, but this
affidavit was not embodied in the return of the justice to the
superior court, and this court further held in that regard that
the superior court was not required to accept the above ²⁹⁷
memorandum in the justice's docket as any evidence that the
affidavit contained proof that the notice had been given, it being
further said: "The return did not, moreover, purport to show
that the justice had given any notice, nor did it contain or refer

to the service of any notice given by him, and as all notices are
required to be in writing (Code Civ. Proc., sec. 1010), such notice, if it had existed, would have formed a part of the return
by the justice."

The case at bar differs in essential particulars from that of
Jones v. Justice's Court, 97 Cal. 523. Here the justice returned,
as by the writ he was commanded to do: 1. A transcript of his
docket entries, by which it appeared that on May 22d notice was
issued, and upon May 25th notice was returned and filed; and
2. The papers and files in the case, amongst which is a written
notice of the date set for the hearing of demurrer, addressed to
W. E. Dunn, attorney for defendants, dated May 22d, and notifying defendants' attorney that the demurrer had been set for
hearing upon the twenty-fifth day of May, 1896, at 1:30 o'clock
P. M. This notice bears the indorsement:

"Received copy of the within notice, ———, 1896.
                                        "W. E. DUNN,
                              "Attorneys for Defendant.
                                "Served H. H. Y."

Upon the hearing it was permitted to be shown that H. H. Y.
are the initials of H. H. Yonken, a constable, and that he served
the notice in question upon the twenty-third day of May, 1896,
by leaving a copy thereof with a man in the office of W. E. Dunn,
which man acknowledged service of the notice as above set
forth in the name of Dunn. This testimony, introduced by petitioners, was followed under objection of appellants by the testimony of the attorney, Dunn, who swore that he did not know
who signed his name to the notice; that it was not signed by
anyone authorized so to do; and that in fact he had never received notice of the time set for the hearing of the demurrer.

Upon certiorari, if it becomes necessary for the court of review to be put in possession of the facts upon which the court
below acted, and which are not technically of record, it is competent for that court to require the lower court to certify such
facts in its return to the writ, and this statement of facts would
then be a part of the record: 2 Spelling on Extraordinary
Relief, sec. 2020. Under this principle it was not, perhaps, improper for the trial court to admit the evidence of Youken, not
as contradicting the record of the justice, but as supplemental
thereto: People ex rel. Whitney v. San Francisco Fire Dept., 14
Cal. 479.

But it may be set down as a universal rule that, as the province of the writ of certiorari is to review a record of an inferior

court, board, or tribunal, and to determine from the record
whether such court, board, or tribunal has exceeded its jurisdiction, evidence dehors the record, and contradicting it, is never
permitted. The common-law writ of certiorari tried nothing
but the jurisdiction, and incidentally the regularity of the proceedings upon which the jurisdiction depends. In many cases,
therefore, under such writs, the evidence upon which the court
acted in determining its jurisdiction was made a part of the record
and reviewed under the writ, but the inquiry was always limited
to the evidence before the tribunal whose determination was
under review. If the jurisdiction of the inferior tribunal depended upon a question of fact, that fact was never tried de novo
upon its merits, but the inquiry thereupon was limited strictly
to the evidence upon which the inferior tribunal acted: People
ex rel. Whitney v. San Francisco Fire Dept., 14 Cal. 479.

In this essential feature, then, as above suggested, does this
case differ from the case of Jones v. Justice's Court, 97 Cal. 523.
In that case, the court, limiting its inquiry to the return, found
there had been no service of notice of the time set for trial. In
this case, the court reaches its conclusion by admitting and considering the parol testimony of the attorney, Dunn, to impeach
and contradict the record of the justice which in itself was legally sufficient to show jurisdiction. This may not be done.
The evidence of Dunn should not have been admitted.

Therefore, the judgment is reversed and the cause remanded.

Temple, J., and McFarland, J., concurred.

JUSTICE OF THE PEACE—JURISDICTION.—Ordinarily, noth-
ing is presumed in favor of the jurisdiction of a justice of the peace;
it must be affirmatively shown. This proposition has, however, not
been unquestioned: See Hambel v. Davis, 89 Tex. 256; 59 Am. St.
Rep. 46, and note. The jurisdiction and powers of justices of the
peace are derived from statutory provisions: Martin v. Fales, 18 Me.
23; 36 Am. Dec. 693; and must be measured strictly by statute law:
Firmstone v. Mack, 49 Pa. St. 387; 88 Am. Dec. 507. Proceedings in
justices' courts must show such facts as constitute a case within
their jurisdiction; otherwise, the law will regard such proceedings
as coram non judice and absolutely void: Levy v. Shurman, 6 Ark.
182; 42 Am. Dec. 690; Spear v. Carter, 1 Mich. 19; 48 Am. Dec. 688.

CERTIORARI—EXTRINSIC EVIDENCE.—Whether a court has
jurisdiction must be determined from the record taken as a whole:
Wulff v. Superior Court, 110 Cal. 215; 52 Am. St. Rep. 78. No questions can be presented for review upon certiorari other than those
which arise on the record, save and except that the court may sometimes hear evidence in support of the record for the purpose of showing that substantial justice has been done, or that for some reason
the discretion which the court has to deny relief by this writ ought
to be exercised and the petitioner left to such other means of redress

as he may have, but it is clear, in the absence of statutory authority, that the record cannot be contradicted by extrinsic evidence, and that the petitioner's cause must be determined on the record alone: Monographic note to Wulzen v. Board of Supervisors, 40 Am. St. Rep. 35.

CLOWDIS *v.* FRESNO FLUME AND IRRIGATION CO.

[118 CALIFORNIA, 315.]

ANIMALS, LIABILITY OF OWNER FOR INJURIES IN-FLICTED BY.—The owner of an animal not naturally vicious is not answerable for an injury done by it, unless it was in fact vicious, and the owner knew it. If an animal, being theretofore of a peaceable disposition, suddenly and unexpectedly, while in charge of its owner or of his servants, inflicts injury on another, neither is answerable, if at that time in the exercise of due care. If, on the other hand, the owner knew of the vicious propensity of the animal, he is answerable for injuries inflicted by it on the person or property of another who is free from fault.

MASTER AND SERVANT, KNOWLEDGE OF THE LATTER, WHEN IMPUTED TO THE FORMER.—If servants in charge of an animal become aware that it is of a vicious disposition, such knowledge must be imputed to their master, though there has been no opportunity to communicate with him, and he, in truth, has no knowledge thereof.

NEGLIGENCE OF SERVANT, WHEN IMPUTED TO HIS MASTER.—If servants are put in charge of a bull, to be driven from one place to another, and he develops a vicious disposition, attacking one or more human beings in their presence and to their knowledge, and they thereafter drive him along the public highway, where he attacks and injures another human being, it is a question of fact for the jury whether or not such servants exercised a proper degree of care in the management of the animal at the time of the last injury.

JURY TRIAL—INSTRUCTIONS MINGLING TWO CAUSES OF ACTION.—If, in an action to recover for injuries received from the defendant's bull, the court instructs the jury in one instruction that the defendant is liable for injuries resulting from the negligence of the defendant's employés in the performance of a given duty, and in another, that before plaintiff can recover, he must establish the fact that the bull at the time he inflicted the injury was vicious, and that the defendant had knowledge of such viciousness, will not be regarded as prejudicial or erroneous, if the complaint, though in one count, charges the defendant with negligence and also with keeping a bull known to him to be vicious and dangerous, and alleges injuries resulting to the plaintiff.

JURY TRIAL—VERDICT, WHEN NOT EXCESSIVE.—A verdict in favor of plaintiff for five thousand five hundred dollars for injuries suffered by him cannot be held excessive, when evidence showed that his coccyx was fractured, the muscles of the region atrophied, the sciatic nerve tender and painful to pressure, with other symptoms of spinal injury.

. L. L. Cory, for the appellant.

F. Laning and M. K. Harris, for the respondent.

318 HENSHAW, J.   Plaintiff recovered damages for injuries inflicted by a vicious bull, the property of defendant.   He averred that, prior to the attack upon him, the bull was of a vicious disposition and dangerous character, and that the fact was known to defendant, its agents, and employés.   He also averred that the injury was occasioned by the negligent conduct of defendant's servants engaged in driving the bull upon a public highway.   Defendant appeals from the judgment and from the order denying a new trial.

The facts disclosed by the evidence are as follows: In April, 1895, the defendant, which was engaged in the lumber business in the Sierra Nevada mountains, in Fresno county, sent two of its employés, John Lovelace and G. W. Treece, to a ranch on Kings river known as "The Grant," where its cattle had been pasturing during the winter, to bring them to the mountains. **319** There were some thirty-six head, consisting of bulls and steers.   The bull in question was wild, and the men had difficulty in yoking him.   On the second day after they started, this bull became tired and troublesome to drive and was allowed to remain temporarily at the ranch of Ben McCloskey, a place about four miles from Sanger, while the other cattle were driven on.   About noon, during the absence of the drivers, McCloskey and his neighbor, Martinez, went into the corral to look at the animal, and while they were walking around he charged upon Martinez, knocking him down, jumped the fence, and went out into the grainfield.   In the afternoon Treece and Lovelace returned for the bull, when McCloskey related to them what had taken place.   They asked why he had not corraled the animal.   McCloskey answered that he had only a single-barreled shotgun, and would not undertake to corral that bull with anything less than a Winchester rifle.   They secured the bull, and themselves on horseback drove him along the county road in the direction of the town of Sanger.   On the road they were overtaken by two men walking.   These men endeavored to pass the bull and walk ahead, when the bull turned as though he would charge them.   One of the drivers rode between them and the bull and warned them to look out, that the bull had already knocked one man down and would fight.   Proceeding down the road they approached a culvert, where several men were standing.   A short distance from this bridge the plaintiff was staking a horse on land adjoining the road, and which he had at that time leased and was in possession of.   As the drivers and the bull approached one of the drivers remarked: "We will see some fun," or "Watch these fellows scatter when we come up there with the bull." Something attracted the attention of the men, and, not liking the appearance of the bull, they made for an adjoining fence. Clowdis, who was a short distance away and behind his horse, did not observe the danger, but hearing a voice, he stepped out from behind his horse, and seeing the bull on the bridge asked if he would fight. The question was answered by the bull, which at once charged. Clowdis turned and ran for an outhouse some little distance off, but before he reached it he was overtaken, tossed in the air, and received the injuries complained of. During all of this time the bull was driven ahead of the men, [320] and was not secured in any way. He was six years old, and up to October, 1894, had been accustomed to run with a herd of dairy cows on the range in the mountains. In October, 1894, he was purchased by the defendant and broken to an ox team, and worked about six weeks and then placed upon pasture, where he remained until April, 1895. Witnesses for the defendant testified that during the six weeks when he worked he was a nervous and high-strung animal, but before this time had not displayed a disposition to attack.

Over these facts there is little or no dispute; but under them appellant contends that it is entitled to a reversal. Herein it is insisted that the evidence fails to show foreknowledge by defendant of the vicious disposition of the animal.

It is well settled in cases such as this that the owner of an animal, not naturally vicious, is not liable for an injury done by it, unless two propositions are established: 1. That the animal in fact was vicious; and 2. That the owner knew it: Finney v. Curtis, 78 Cal. 498. Thus, if an animal theretofore of peaceable disposition, while in charge of the master or of a servant, suddenly and unexpectedly, either through fear or rage, inflicts injury, neither is responsible, if at the time he was in the exercise of due care. But, conversely, the owner of such an animal knowing its vicious propensities is liable for injury inflicted by it upon property or upon the person of one who is free from fault: Laverone v. Mangianti, 41 Cal. 138; 10 Am. Rep. 269.

These propositions are accepted by appellant's counsel; but their contention in argument is, that the knowledge by defendant's servants of the viciousness was acquired at such time and under such circumstances that it could not be conveyed to the defendant, and, therefore, could not be imputed to it in law; and, further, that the men engaged in driving the bull were not agents of the corporation, but mere servants, not having general charge of the animal, but sent upon a limited mission with regard to it, and that for this additional reason their knowledge cannot be held to be the knowledge of their employer.

It is quite true that knowledge by or notice to a servant charged with no duty in the matter, of the vicious propensities of an animal owned by the master, is not notice to the master. The rule, however, is that a servant's knowledge, to whom an animal is intrusted, [321] of its ferocious disposition, is knowledge of the master sufficient to render the latter liable: Brice v. Bauer, 108 N. Y. 428; 2 Am. St. Rep. 454; Cooley on Torts, 406, and note.

In the present case Lovelace and Treece had been put in complete charge of the bull. It is a fundamental and most important principle of the law governing the responsibility of masters that whatever duty they owe to the public (or to their employés) must be performed, and a failure to perform, or improper performance, cannot be excused by a showing that execution was delegated to a servant even of approved carefulness, knowledge, or skill. It must further be shown that the servant in the particular matter exercised the full degree of care and showed the requisite amount of skill. And this is true, however subordinate or menial may be the rank of the servant. Whatever be his position, in that special employment he represents the master, and within its scope his knowledge is the master's knowledge, his acts the master's acts: Higgins v. Williams, 114 Cal. 176; Donnelly v. San Francisco Bridge Co., 117 Cal. 417. Everyone, whether acting individually or through agents, is bound to exercise ordinary care to prevent injury to the person or property of another: Civ. Code, secs. 1708, 1714, 2330, 2338. Therefore, when, as here, Lovelace and Treese had been sent upon an independent mission and put in complete charge of the animal, they stood in the performance of their task in the place of the defendant, and the question of defendant's responsibility will be answered as may be answered the inquiry: What would have been the master's responsibility and liability had he personally been in charge of the animal? To this there can be but one answer. He would have been liable. Twice before on that very day had the bull evinced its ugly disposition by attacks actual and threatened. Here was ample proof of the fact of viciousness and of the knowledge of that fact brought home to the master.

There is yet another and independent view of the matter which may be taken, and in this is eliminated all question of the master's knowledge. That view turns upon the master's liability for the negligent performance by a servant of a duty within the scope of his employment. The driving of the bull upon the highway was not only within the employment of Lovelace and Treece, [322] but it was their express task. In the performance of this duty, if injury was occasioned to one without fault by reason of their negligence, the master was liable. At the outset of the drive, when the men may be assumed to have believed that the beast was gentle, if it had suddenly and unexpectedly attacked and injured some person, it might well be argued that they were performing their task with due care, and that for the unexpected onslaught the master was not liable. But when thereafter, while engaged in this undertaking, they acquired knowledge of the animal's evil propensities, it became a question of fact for the jury whether or not they exercised the requisite degree of care in their subsequent management of it. The circumstance that the additional knowledge was acquired by them after the employment was undertaken, and was not known either to them or to their employer at the time it commenced, would not exonerate the latter. If the conductor of a passenger train should at any time during the journey discover a defective wheel and, continuing the trip, injury should thereby result, the company would not be exonerated because the knowledge was acquired after the train had started. Yet there is no difference in principle between the two cases, and what difference exists is merely in the degree of care exacted by law.

Precisely such a cause of action as the one which we have been considering was that of Ficken v. Jones, 28 Cal. 618; and another in which the question is considered with much elaboration is that in Barnum v. Terpenning, 75 Mich. 557.

This is unquestionably a distinct cause of action from that which would hold the master responsible by reason of his foreknowledge; but the complaint in this case sufficiently charges upon both causes of action. True, they are joined in one count, but no objection was made to the pleading upon this ground.

Appellant complains of the instructions given by the court as being contradictory and self-destructive. In one part of the charge the jury was instructed, in effect, that defendant was liable for injury resulting from the negligence of its employés in the performance of a given duty. In another part the jury was told that before plaintiff could recover he must establish the facts that the bull, at the time he inflicted injury, was vicious, and that defendant had knowledge of its vicious character.

323 But this grievance has its foundation in appearance rather than in substance. Undoubtedly, it would have been well founded had the pleading been confined to a charge that injury was occasioned by an animal which defendant knew to be vicious at the time. In such instances the owner is an insurer against the acts of the animal to one who is injured without fault, and the question of the owner's negligence is not in the case: Laverene v. Mangianti, 41 Cal. 138; 10 Am. Rep. 269. But the action at bar charged not only upon this but upon another and distinct cause of action, namely, an action for damages occasioned by the negligent performance upon the part of defendant's servants of an employment with which they were intrusted. Here, proof of negligence was essential to a recovery. It would certainly have been better if the instructions had more clearly recognized the distinctions between these two causes of action. But in and of themselves they were not wrong in point of law, nor, under a complaint charging upon both causes of action, were they contradictory. Both causes of action were here charged, though joined in one count; upon both issue was joined, and to both evidence was addressed sufficient to uphold the verdict of the jury upon either. The instructions could not then have injured appellant, and, if, by failing clearly to recognize the distinctions pointed out, they served to confuse the jury, that confusion must certainly have tended to defendant's advantage.

The jury rendered a verdict for plaintiff in the sum of five thousand five hundred dollars. There was, as is usual, much conflict in the testimony of the physicians over the nature and permanency of the injuries. But on the part of plaintiff it was shown that the coccyx was fractured, the muscles of the region atrophied, the sciatic nerve tender and painful to pressure, with other symptoms of spinal injury, upholding a finding that plaintiff's health was seriously impaired, if not positively wrecked. It may not be said under such a statement that the verdict was excessive.

The judgment and order appealed from are affirmed.

McFarland, J., and Temple, J., concurred.

————

ANIMALS—LIABILITY OF OWNER FOR INJURIES INFLICTED BY.—If domestic animals, such as oxen and horses, injure anyone in person or property when they are rightfully in the place where they do the mischief, the owner of such animals is not liable for such injury, unless he knows that they are accustomed to do mischief; and such knowledge must be alleged and proved: Reed v.

Southern Exp. Co., 95 Ga. 108; 51 Am. St. Rep. 62, and note; Strouse v. Leipf, 101 Ala. 433; 46 Am. St. Rep. 122.

ANIMALS—VICIOUSNESS OF—NOTICE OF—WHEN IMPUTED TO MASTER FROM NOTICE TO SERVANT.—An owner of premises who, having knowledge of the vicious and dangerous character of a dog owned by his agent, permits such dog to run at large is liable for any damage done by the dog to a passerby: Harris v. Fisher, 115 N. C. 318; 44 Am. St. Rep. 452. Knowledge of a servant or agent that a dog in his care is dangerous is equivalent to knowledge by his principal: Brice v. Bauer, 108 N. Y. 428; 2 Am. St. Rep. 454. But a servant's knowledge of the vicious character of a dog accustomed to follow him about in his master's business, but not put in his charge by the master, is not imputable to the master: Twigg v. Ryland, 62 Md. 380; 50 Am. Rep. 226, and note. See Harris v. Fisher, 115 N. C. 318; 44 Am. St. Rep. 452.

ESTATE OF MEADE.

[118 CALIFORNIA, 428.]

WILLS, WHAT ARE NOT.—A paper cannot be regarded as a will, unless the intention of the decedent that it should stand for a last will and testament is clearly apparent. The heirs at law are not to be disinherited when such intention is not expressed with legal certainty.

WILLS—TESTAMENTARY CHARACTER OF A PAPER, WHEN NOT APPARENT THEREFROM.—A letter directed to an undertaker, asking him, in the event of the writer's death, to cremate her body and to apprise her brother of such death, and adding that her brother would take charge of her estate and be sole administrator without bonds, to trade, sell, or occupy, as may seem fit to him, is not testamentary in character, and neither gives him her estate nor appoints him administrator thereof.

Charles Clark, for the appellant.

Nicholas Bowden, for the respondent.

[429] GAROUTTE, J. Appellant filed a petition asking that a certain document, olographic in character, be probated as the last will and testament of Euthanasia S. Meade, deceased. A copy of the purported document accompanied the petition. Upon demurrer it was held that the document was not a will, and upon this appeal the only question presented is, Was the paper testamentary in character?

The document under consideration was in the form of a letter addressed to an undertaker residing in the city of San José, and dated some sixteen months prior to the death of the writer. This letter is as follows:

"San José, June 30, 1894.

"Mr. Woodrow, Undertaker.

"Realizing the uncertainty of this life, and the surety of coming dissolution, and wishing the cremation of this my mortal

body, and also having a most absolute abhorrence of being put in
the ground to decay and rot, I hereby ask and empower you to
take my body to the nearest crematory and there have the same
reduced to ashes at the least possible expense, with no ostentation whatever. Money thrown away in useless parade of the
dead, in my opinion, might better be spent caring for the living
and making them comfortable and happy.

"In disposing of me use no unkindly care, neither make long
or expensive delays. I do not propose entering into detail; use
some judgment, and, above all, be simple, practical, expedient.

"The only person I care to have apprised of my death is my
brother, Porter Sherman, of Kansas City, Kansas, associated
430 with the Wyandotte First National Bank. A message sent
there will reach him, and perhaps he may be in Leipsic, Germany, where of late years he and his family have spent much
time.

"I intend at no distant day to write this in substance and send
to your address; but in case of accident or sudden demise this
may answer any purpose arising from such calamity.

"No, I have no fear of the hereafter. Oh, my Lord, teach me
to live right, then in dying there is no sting.

"My estate must pay all needful expenses accruing, but nothing for show or ostentation.

"My brother, Porter Sherman, will take charge of my estate,
and be the sole administrator, without bonds, to trade, sell, or
occupy, as may seem to him fit.

"I am very truly,

"EUTHANASIA SHERMAN MEADE.

"June 30, 1891."

The last paragraph of the writing is the one to which especial
importance is attached, as stamping the paper as of testamentary
character. It is claimed that by this clause the brother of deceased, Porter Sherman, was not only appointed executor of the
estate, but that a devise and bequest to him of all her property
is there declared. It is further claimed that, conceding there is
no disposition of her estate by the document, still there is an
appointment of an executor, and that such fact, standing alone,
makes the paper a will and entitled to probate. If the paper
appoints an executor, this contention is sound: In re Hickman,
101 Cal. 613.

The intention of the deceased that the paper should stand for
a last will and testament must be plainly apparent. The heirs

at law are not to be disinherited unless such intention is clearly manifested; and, in this case, the question coming to the court upon demurrer, we are confined to the face of the paper itself for a discovery of that intention. "Effect must be given to the intention of the testator, if that can be discovered, and is consistent with the rules of law. But the intention must be expressed and with legal certainty, otherwise the title of the heirs at law must prevail": Sutherland v. Sydnor, 84 Va. 880. "It must satisfactorily appear that he intended the very paper to be [431] his will. Unless it so appear the paper must be rejected": McBride v. McBride, 26 Gratt. 476. "It is not for courts to declare that to be a testamentary disposition of his estate when it does not clearly appear that such was the intention of the individual executing it": In re Richardson, 94 Cal. 65. Applying the principle of law just declared, we are not satisfied that the deceased intended the document above set out to be her last will and testament. It is not clearly apparent that it was written animo testandi. It is plain that the main question in the deceased's mind was the disposition of her body; and that she took her pen in hand to advise the undertaker upon that matter. Such being the principal purpose of the writing, it should certainly be made plain by apt words that incidentally she also intended the paper as her last will. It is evident that the lady was possessed of intelligence and education, and it is hardly conceivable that such a one should have so indistinctly and inappropriately expressed her wishes, if the making of a will was in her mind at the time. The language of the last paragraph of the writing is more consistent with the construction that she was referring to a will already made, or one thereafter to be made. As to the words of this paragraph possessing the importance of a devise to Porter Sherman of all her estate, it is entirely too weak and indefinite. In In re Richardson, 94 Cal. 65, we find in the letter there involved much stronger language; yet the court held that no devise was thereby made, and the paper was no will. In speaking of Porter Sherman as the administrator, and in speaking of his management of her estate, she wholly failed to use a word or words clearly expressing the intention contended for by appellant. It is an easy thing to do so. It was a probable thing for her to do. It is improbable that a woman like her would have used the language she used if she had intended the paper as a will.

Judgment and order affirmed.

Harrison, J., and Van Fleet, J., concurred.

Hearing in Bank denied.

___

WILL—WHAT MAY CONSTITUTE.—A will is an instrument by which a person makes a disposition of his property, to take effect after his decease: Barney v. Hayes, 11 Mont. 571; 28 Am. St. Rep. 495. The true test of the character of an instrument, as to whether it is a will, is not the testator's realization that it is a will, but his intention to create a revocable disposition of his property, to accrue and take effect only upon his death, and passing no present interest: Nichols v. Emery, 109 Cal. 323; 50 Am. St. Rep. 43, and note. To make a paper the last will and testament of a decedent at the time it is written, it must appear that such person possessed the animus testandi at the time: Boofter v. Rogers, 9 Gill, 44; 52 Am. Dec. 680. See Babb v. Harrison, 9 Rich. Eq. 111; 70 Am. Dec. 203; and extended note to Carlton v. Cameron, 38 Am. Rep. 621, 622.

___

BREON v. ROBRECHT.

[118 CALIFORNIA, 469.]

PRESCRIPTION.—ADVERSE POSSESSION PENDING AN ACTION OF EJECTMENT CANNOT CREATE A TITLE BY PRESCRIPTION in favor of the defendant, where judgment is rendered against him and a writ is issued thereon under which he is dispossessed, though before such writ is executed, he has been in the adverse possession of the property for a period sufficiently long to give him a prescriptive title but for the action against him. During the pendency of the action the defendant could not acquire any new right as against the plaintiff by merely remaining in possession.

A JUDGMENT IN FAVOR OF THE PLAINTIFF IN EJECTMENT in which the title of the parties or their right to the possession of the demanded premises is put in issue, tried, and determined, is conclusive as an estoppel against the defendant, to avoid which he must show some title or right to possession other than that which was available to him in the former action.

Scrivener & Schell, for the appellant.

Edward R. Taylor, for the respondent.

⁴⁷⁰ McFARLAND, J. This is an action to quiet title to certain lands. Judgment went for defendant—the court finding "that defendant is the owner and seised in fee of all the lands" in contest, and that "plaintiff was not at the time of the commencement of this action, and never was at any time, the owner in fee or otherwise, or at all," of said lands or any part thereof. The plaintiff appeals from the judgment upon a bill of exceptions which brings up only the judgment-roll and certain admitted facts.

Appellant has no ground for reversal unless this proposition be maintainable, namely: That although an action of ejectment be commenced within the statutory period of limitation, and although such action be prosecuted to a final judgment for plaintiff, and the defendant be evicted under a writ of possession issued under such judgment, still, if the defendant has remained in possession during the pendency of the action, and five years have elapsed from the time at which he first took possession until his eviction under the judgment, then he has acquired a new and independent title by prescription, which he can afterward enforce notwithstanding his eviction under the judgment in ejectment. If that be so, a successful plaintiff in ejectment, although he commenced his action within five years after the beginning of the adverse holding, gains nothing by his suit unless he can so control the machinery of the courts and the conduct of the defendant as to obtain a judgment and the execution of a writ of restitution within five years after the first unlawful entry of the defendant. But this proposition cannot be maintained.

It is true that the mere commencement of an action of ejectment which is afterward dismissed does not disturb an adverse possession. It is true, also, that a judgment in ejectment does not conclude a title acquired subsequently to its rendition; and perhaps it does not conclude a prior title which, owing to the peculiar character of the pleadings, findings, and judgment, is clearly not embraced in the decision—although the general rule is, that such a judgment concludes every right of possession which the defendant might have asserted under any title which he could have litigated in the action. Neither is it necessary, for the purposes of this case, to consider the effect of an unexecuted judgment [471] upon adverse possession—as in Carpenter v. Natoma Water etc. Co., 63 Cal. 616. An executed judgment for plaintiff in ejectment, where the suit had been commenced within the period of limitation, is conclusive against the defendant of any asserted right founded merely upon his possession either at the time of the commencement of the action or at the time of the judgment. During the pendency of the action he can acquire no new right as against the plaintiff by the mere fact that he remains in possession. During that period his right of possession is sub judice—"before the judge," awaiting judicial determination: Kirsch v. Kirsch, 113 Cal. 56; and a judgment against him judicially determines that down to the date of its rendition his possession, as against the plaintiff, has been wrongful. This principle is expressly recognized in one of the very authorities cited by appellant—Thrift v. Delaney, 69 Cal. 191—where the court say: "The bar of a judgment in such an action

is, however, limited to the rights of the parties as they existed
at the time when it was rendered, and neither the parties nor
their privies are precluded by the same from showing in a subsequent action any new matters accruing after its rendition which
gave the defeated party a title or right of possession." In Satterlee v. Bliss, 36 Cal. 514, the court say: "The judgment in the
case of Reese v. Mahoney et al. is binding and conclusive upon
the Mahoneys and all parties standing in privity with them, and
estops them from denying that Reese was entitled, as against
them, to the possession of the premises at the time of the rendition of the judgment."

The facts in the case at bar are, briefly, these: On April 23,
1885, one Reid went into the adverse possession of the lands in
contest, without title. Within five years thereafter the present
defendant, Robrecht, commenced an action (referred to by the
parties as "ejectment") against Reid and others claiming to be
his tenants, in which he averred that he was "the owner and entitled to the possession of" the said lands, and prayed for their
restitution. The defendants in that action denied Robrecht's
title, set up title in Reid, and also set up adverse possession;
judgment was rendered in that action in June, 1895, by which
it was found and decreed that Robrecht was the owner and entitled to possession of the lands and that Reid had no right, title,
or interest therein. There was also a finding against the alleged
adverse [472] possession, and Robrecht also recovered a certain
sum of money for rents, profits, etc., during the time Reid had
held possession. But in the same year, 1895, and shortly before
said judgment was entered, Reid, who had remained in possession of the lands pending the suit, conveyed his interest therein
to the present plaintiff, Breon, and put him in possession; Breon
commenced this present action to quiet title about a month before the rendition of the judgment in the ejectment suit. A
writ of restitution was issued on the judgment in the ejectment
suit, under which the present plaintiff, Breon, was evicted and
Robrecht placed in possession; and Robrecht was in possession
when this present action was tried. It is admitted that the present plaintiff knew all the facts, and occupies the same position
that Reid would have occupied if he had brought this action.

From the foregoing facts it is clear that title in the fullest
sense was involved in said action of ejectment, and that the
judgment in that action concluded every right which Reid had
to the lands at the time of its rendition: See Marshall v. Shafter,
32 Cal. 177; Mahoney v. Middleton, 41 Cal. 41, Satterlee v. Bliss,

36 Cal. 514, Byers **v.** Neal, 43 Cal. 210; Sampson **v.** Ohleyer, 22 Cal. 200, and cases there cited. In Marshall v. Shafter, 32 Cal. 177, it was declared—we quote for brevity from the syllabus—that "if the respective titles of the parties, or their right to the possession of the demanded premises, are put in issue and tried in ejectment, and the plaintiff recovers judgment for possession, the judgment is an estoppel, and the defendant, to avoid the estoppel in a subsequent action to recover the same premises, must show some other right of possession than he had when the judgment was entered." In Byers v. Neal, 43 Cal. 210, it was declared that "a judgment for plaintiff in ejectment, when the title has been brought directly in issue, concludes the defendant against setting up in a subsequent proceeding any mere legal defense which he might have made in such suit." But in the case at bar we are concerned only with the alleged right of appellant founded on the adverse possession of Reid, which was clearly concluded by the judgment in the ejectment suit. As was said in Marshall v. Shafter, 32 Cal. 177, speaking of ejectment: "The judgment for plaintiff determines that he was entitled to possession at the commencement of the [473] action and the rendition of the judgment." In Mann v. Rogers, 35 Cal. 318, the court said: "The judgment in ejectment precludes the plaintiff in this action from asserting in another action any legal title which he held or could have made available on the trial of the former action." If the present plaintiff can maintain this action upon the alleged adverse possession of Reid, then Reid could have defeated the ejectment by filing a supplemental answer averring that since the commencement of the action his continued adverse possession had ripened into title; and, therefore, such alleged right, even if any conceivable value could be attached to it, was under the authorities above cited concluded by the judgment in ejectment.

The order appealed from is affirmed.

Henshaw, J., concurred.

EJECTMENT—EFFECT OF JUDGMENT IN, UPON THE RUNNING OF STATUTE OF LIMITATIONS.—Judgment in ejectment, not followed by any writ nor by taking possession under it, does not suspend nor interrupt the running of the statute of limitations: Mabary v. Dollarhide, 98 Mo. 198; 14 Am. St. Rep. 639; Batterton v. Chiles, 12 B. Mon. 348; 54 Am. Dec. 539. But the adverse possession of a defendant in ejectment cannot, during the pendency of the suit, ripen into an absolute title under the operation of the statute of limitations: Extended note to Batterton v. Chiles, 54 Am. Dec. 545.

EJECTMENT—JUDGMENT IN, AS ESTOPPEL.—Judgment for the plaintiff in ejectment is conclusive against defendant on the question of title, from whatever source derived, and forever estops him from asserting a claim of title which existed at the time of its rendition: Hentig v. Redden, 46 Kan. 231; 26 Am. St. Rep. 91, and note. The defendant cannot recover the same premises in another action, unless he shows some other right of possession than that which he had when the judgment was rendered: Note to Batterton v. Chiles, 54 Am. Dec. 546.

JONES *v.* LAMONT.

[118 CALIFORNIA, 499.]

HUSBAND AND WIFE—SEPARATION, AGREEMENT OF, WHEN DOES NOT AFFECT HIS INTEREST IN HER ESTATE.—An agreement between a husband and wife entered into pending a suit for divorce, and for the disposition of their property, by which each is to receive a specific sum from their homestead and one-half of the net proceeds of their personal property, and is released from all obligations of every character for the future acts and debts of the other, does not affect his right to share in her estate upon her death intestate.

ATTORNEY FOR ADMINISTRATOR, WHEN NOT DISQUALIFIED TO ACT FOR AN HEIR.—An attorney for the administrator of the estate of a deceased person is not disqualified to act for one who claims to be entitled to a distributive share of the estate of the decedent, if such administrator does not claim to be an heir or otherwise entitled to any part of the estate.

C. H. Oatman, for the appellant.

James O. Prewett, for the respondent.

⁴⁹⁹ CHIPMAN, C. Appeal from decree of distribution. The controversy arises out of a certain contract of separation between deceased in her lifetime and her surviving husband, appellant. The court found that the husband had no interest in the wife's estate, she having died intestate. The court also found that shortly prior to May 29, 1884, the said deceased commenced an action against her said husband for divorce and division of the property; that a compromise was agreed to on said day last named, pursuant to which the agreement in question was entered into ⁵⁰⁰ and the suit for divorce and division of the property was dismissed; whereupon the parties separated, and so continued, holding no communication as husband and wife until her death, November 3, 1895. The appeal is on the judgment-roll presented by bill of exceptions.

The sole question presented by appellant is, "whether or not the separation agreement in question amounts to a waiver or release by appellant of his right to succeed to all or any portion of his wife's estate."

The agreement is as follows:

"This agreement, made the 29th day of May, 1884, between Cadwalader Jones, of Sutter county, California, the party of the first part, and Lavina Jones, his wife, of the same place, the party of the second part, witnesseth, that whereas differences have arisen between said parties, and they have agreed to live separate and apart from each other,

"Therefore it is agreed by said first party that said second party shall receive from the sale of the homestead of the parties hereto the sum of $2,850, and one-half of the net proceeds of all the personal property belonging to said parties, and one bay mare named Kittie, and that said second party shall be released from every and all obligations of every kind and character, and shall not be held liable for any of the debts of said first party.

"In consideration whereof, said second party agrees that she accepts in release and full payment from said first party the foregoing sum of money, for any and every demand, claim, obligation, debt, and liability, and does by these presents agree to release him, said first party, from all and any debt which she may now owe, or which may hereafter be contracted by her.

"And it is expressly understood and agreed by both parties hereto that each party is hereby released and absolved from all obligations and liability for the future acts and debts of each other, and that said first party shall retain and have one bay filly, Daisy, and that the remainder of said personal property shall be sold at auction within three weeks from this date, and that on the day of the sale the auctioneer shall divide the net proceeds of such sale equally between said first and second parties."

501 The agreement seems to be an attempt to make an equal division of the property, including the homestead. There is a mutual release "from all obligations and liability for the future acts and debts of each other"; there is also an individual release each to the other from the then existing debts and obligations of each. There is no release in terms, by either one, of claims upon the future acquisitions of the other, nor, in terms, any release by either one upon the estate of the other in case of death. In In re Davis, 106 Cal. 453, the agreement read that the wife "does relinquish and surrender forever all claims of any nature she may now or hereafter have against any property that said W. W. Davis may now have or may hereafter in any manner acquire." And it was held that "the wife contracted away her inheritable interest in her husband's property." Here were apt words importing an intention never to assert in any way any right to the property of the husband, present or future. No

such intention can be derived from the language of the contract
before us on the part of either one of the parties to it. It is
urged that this intention may be found in the situation of the
parties at the time; that a divorce suit was pending, in which a
division of the property was asked, and that the contract was the
result of a compromise of that suit; that the divorce, if granted,
might have given the wife all the property conveyed by the contract, free from all claim of the husband. While the law permits divorce, and also permits separation under articles affecting the property, it does not encourage the one more than the
other, nor, in fact, either. We cannot see that the dismissal of
the divorce suit affected the contractual relations of the parties
to the contract subsequently entered into. They may, upon
reflection, both have regarded that proceeding as a mistake and
ill advised, and without adequate cause; the contract is sufficiently clear to speak for itself; the divorce proceeding is not
referred to in the contract, and even the existence of unhappy
differences therein referred to was not essential to its validity:
Civ. Code, sec. 159. The contract in nowise affected the marriage status; the parties remained husband and wife. The utmost that the law permits is that they may agree to live apart,
and may make a valid contract as to their property, but this may
be terminated [502] at any moment by reconciliation which
"would avoid the contract—as to all features, at least, remaining executory": Sargent v. Sargent, 106 Cal. 541. We do not
think the courts should come to the aid of these contracts so as
to deprive either the husband or wife of the property rights
growing out of the married relation, except where there is a clear
and unmistakable intention to barter away such rights. Even
where "unhappy differences" exist, it is quite consistent with the
separation to so divide the property that in the event of death
the statute of succession and descents shall control its devolu-
tion. That there was an intention in this case to defeat the law
of inheritance, or to waive its beneficial provisions, we do not
think can be ascertained from anything in the contract, or from
any extrinsic facts before us.

If this contract is to be construed as an equitable assignment
of the husband's interest in the wife's estate, it falls short of accomplishing this object. To effect such result, "there must be
on the face of the instrument expressly, or collected from its
provisions by necessary implication, language of present transfer
applying directly to the future as well as the existing property,
or else language importing a present contract or agreement be-

tween the parties to sell or assign the future property": 3 Pomeroy's Equity Jurisprudence, sec. 1290.

We have examined the cases relied upon by respondents. They are Labbe v. Abat, 2 La. 553; 22 Am. Dec. 151; Bratton v. Massey, 15 S. C. 277; Dillinger's Appeal, 35 Pa. St. 357; Hitner's Appeal, 54 Pa. St. 110; Wallace v. Bassett, 41 Barb. 92; Rains v. Wheeler, 76 Tex. 390; Scott's Estate, 147 Pa. St. 102. We do not feel called upon to point out wherein the essential features of these cases, and the contracts under which they arose, are divergent from the case before us. Suffice to say that they are plainly distinguishable from this case. They apply to cases such as In re Davis, 106 Cal. 453, and to other cases cited from our own reports in the well-considered opinion of Mr. Justice Van Fleet filed in the Davis matter. But, rightly interpreted, they only emphasize the importance of holding strictly to the views we have endeavored to briefly present. In Scott's Estate, 147 Pa. St. 102, most relied upon by respondents, the language is, "forever discharge the said John Scott, his executors, administrators, etc., from all liability [503] to said Olivia R. Scott other than that assumed by him in this contract; and they also release, acquit, and discharge the said John Scott from all duties, liabilities, and obligations of every kind whatsoever, which otherwise she, the said Olivia, might or could claim under or by virtue of the marriage relation between her and the said John Scott." Here were apt words to show an intention to exclude Mrs. Scott from sharing in the distribution of the husband's estate, and to release her inheritable interest therein. But there is no approach to equivalent provisions in the contract involved in this controversy.

2. In their reply brief respondents raise the question that the attorney for appellant, Mr. C. H. Oatman, had no right to act as such, for the reason that he was previously, and is still, the attorney for the administrator.

We do not think the public administrator, making or having no claim upon the estate beyond his commissions, and not having filed the petition for distribution nor taken part at its hearing, was an adverse party within the meaning of this section: Senter v. De Bernal, 38 Cal. 637. Neither was he a necessary party to the appeal. It has been several times held that he cannot appeal from an order of distribution: Bates v. Ryberg, 40 Cal. 463; Estate of Wright, 49 Cal. 550; Estate of Marrey, 65 Cal. 287. He is not "an aggrieved party" who has the right of appeal under section 938 of the Code of Civil Procedure: Goldtree v. Thompson, 83 Cal. 420. He is there spoken of as an indifferent person between the real parties in interest: See, also, Estate of Welch, 106 Cal. 427. As to the relation of the administrator to the estate see Roach v. Coffey, 73 Cal. 281, and Rosenberg v. Frank, 58 Cal. 420. The reasons given why an administrator may not appeal from a decree of distribution are equally persuasive against his right to be heard, either voluntarily or involuntarily, as respondent, and also as to his being a necessary party to the appeal.

Whether an attorney, who is attorney for an administrator, may act for one of the heirs as against other heirs, in an adversary proceeding relating to the property of the estate, is a question which would depend upon the circumstances of the particular case. We can conceive of situations where it might be improper—for example, where the administrator is an heir at law—but in the case here no disqualifying relation is shown between 504 attorney and client. Furthermore, it does not appear that the administrator took any part or appeared by attorney or otherwise in the proceedings for distribution, and at that hearing no objection was made to Mr. Oatman's appearance in any capacity.

The judgment should be reversed.

Britt, C., and Haynes, C., concurred.

For the reasons given in the foregoing opinion the judgment is reversed.

Harrison, J., Van Fleet, J., Garoutte, J.

DESCENT—HUSBAND AND WIFE—EFFECT OF SEPARATION AGREEMENT.—Where a husband and wife have already ceased to live with each other as such, agreements entered into between them and a trustee, recognizing their inability to live together, and making provision for their property rights and interests, are very generally enforced unless inequitable; and doubtless, by such an agreement, duly executed, either spouse may relinquish his or her interest in the property of the other, both present and prospective: Monographic note to In re Ingram, 12 Am. St. Rep. 92. See extended note to Stephenson v. Osborne, 90 Am. Dec. 367-370.

AGENCY—ATTORNEY AND CLIENT—ADVERSE INTERESTS. It is an undisputed rule of law that, unless with the free and intelligent consent of his principal given after full knowledge of all the facts and circumstances, an agent cannot, in the same transaction, act both for the principal and the adverse party: Monographic note to Potter's Appeal, 7 Am. St. Rep. 280. The same rule applies to the relation of attorney and client, with some exceptions: See Jones v. Howard, 99 Ga. 451; 59 Am. St. Rep. 231, and note.

PEOPLE v. MAYNE.

[118 CALIFORNIA, 517.]

EVIDENCE.—AN ENTRY IN A FAMILY BIBLE is but a declaration made out of court, and not under the sanction of an oath. It is hearsay evidence, and is not admissible where the person making it is alive and capable of being examined as a witness in the cause. Hence, such an entry is not admissible in a prosecution for rape for the purpose of proving the age of the prosecutrix at the time of the alleged offense.

EVIDENCE—PEDIGREE.—A case is not necessarily one of pedigree because it involves questions of birth, paternity, age, or relationship, if these questions are merely incidental, and the judgment will simply establish a debt, or a person's liability on a contract, or his proper settlement as a pauper, or the commission of a crime.

EVIDENCE—SUPPORTING WITNESS BY HIS PRIOR DECLARATIONS.—A mother who has testified to the date of the birth of her child cannot be supported or corroborated by an entry of such date made by her in the family Bible.

JURISDICTION, LOSS OF BY APPEAL.—During the pendency of an appeal in a criminal case from an order denying a new trial, a motion to set aside such order cannot be heard in the trial court.

D. K. Trask, W. H. Shinn, J. L. Copeland, W. J. Murphy, and Van Sciever & Allen, for the appellant.

W. F. Fitzgerald, attorney general, and W. H. Anderson, assistant attorney general, for the respondent.

[517] HARRISON, J. The defendant was convicted of rape in having sexual intercourse with a female child under the age of fourteen years, and has appealed from the judgment of conviction and from an order denying a new trial.

There was sufficient evidence before the jury to authorize them to find the fact of sexual intercourse by the defendant with the child, and that she was at the time under fourteen years of age, and their verdict thereon is not open to review.

The crime is charged to have been committed March 30, 1895, and for the purpose of establishing the age of the girl at that date her mother testified that she was born June 14, 1881. The prosecution then offered in evidence a Bible, in which was entered the record of the birth of a girl named Elsie Shipton (the name [518] of the prosecuting witness) on the 14th of June, 1881. The court admitted the Bible in evidence against the objection of the defendant.

The mother testified that she made the entry of Elsie's birth some time after the girl was born, she thought at some time during that year. There were appearances on the face of the entry that the date had been changed by being written over after it had originally been written, but it does not appear that any other date was originally in the entry, and the mother testified that she had not changed it. Whether there had been a material alteration in the entry was to be determined by the court when it was offered and before it should be presented to the jury. In the absence of any showing to the contrary, we must assume that the court was satisfied that the alteration was immaterial. Like matters addressed to its discretion, its ruling in this respect is not open to review, unless it is made to appear that the discretion was abused.

It does not clearly appear that the book in which the entry was made was a family Bible. There was no direct evidence of this fact, and, although the mother testified that it came into her possession in 1876, it was not shown from whom she received it or in what manner it came into her possession. Nor was it shown that the other persons whose births and deaths were entered therein were members of her family, or that they had the same or similar names. We need not, however, determine whether the character of the book was sufficiently shown (see Jones v. Jones, 45 Md. 160), since the court erred upon other grounds in permitting the entry to be read in evidence.

An entry in a family Bible is a written declaration of a fact made out of court, not under the sanction of an oath, or with any opportunity to test its correctness by means of cross-examination. It is but a declaration by the person who made the entry, and is of the same character as any other declaration, whether written or oral. Being made in a book where entries of this nature are often made, it is entitled to greater weight by reason of its formality than would be a similar verbal declaration, but the principles upon which it is received in evidence are the same as govern verbal declarations of the same fact. It is hearsay evidence, and subject [510] to the general rule by which that class of evidence is governed, that the fact sought to be established cannot be otherwise shown. This rule was formulated by Chief Justice Marshall in Mima Queen v. Hepburn, 7 Cranch, 290, in the following terms: "Hearsay evidence is incompetent to establish any specific fact, which fact is in its nature susceptible of being proved by witnesses who speak from their own knowledge." Such evidence is admitted in matters of pedigree, but, as Mr. Greenleaf says (Greenleaf on Evidence, sec. 103): "The rule of admission is restricted to the declarations of deceased persons who were related by blood or marriage to the person." Taylor, in his treatise on Evidence, ninth edition, section 641, says: "Where, however, the declarant is himself alive and capable of being examined his declarations will be rejected"; and in the American notes to this edition it is said: "A familiar form of record is the family Bible. Declarations in such form of facts of pedigree, made by deceased members of the family, are competent evidence of the facts therein stated": See, also, Dupoyster v. Gagani, 84 Ky. 403; McCausland v. Fleming, 83 Pa. St. 36; Leggett v. Boyd, 3 Wend. 376; Greenleaf v. Dubuque etc. R. R. Co., 30 Iowa, 301; Campbell v. Wilson, 23 Tex. 252; 76 Am. Dec. 67; Robinson v. Blakely, 4 Rich. 586; 55 Am. Dec. 703. 1 Phillips on Evidence, *248, *250. These principles have been incorporated into the provisions relating to evidence in the statutes of this state. In part 4 of the Code of Civil Procedure, after declaring the general principles governing the admissibility of evidence, section 1870 declares: "In conformity with the preceding provisions evidence may be given at a trial of the following facts: . . . . 4. The act or declaration, verbal or written, of a deceased person in respect to the relationship, birth, marriage, or death of any person related by blood or marriage to such deceased person. . . . . 13. Monuments and inscriptions in public places as evidence of common reputation; and entries in family Bibles or other family books or charts, engravings on rings, family portraits, and the like, as evidence of pedigree."

By the preceding sections, which control the admission of evidence of the facts thus enumerated, and which merely declare the rules of evidence previously existing, the declaration or statement of a third person is admissible only in certain exceptional [520] cases. The provision in this section permitting evidence to be received of the written declaration of a deceased person in the instances there mentioned makes it evident that the declaration of a living person is not to be received. Neither does the section authorize the admission of a written declaration simply because it is made in a family Bible, unless it is otherwise admissible as a written declaration; and such entry, when admissible, is only to be received "as evidence of pedigree." Although the term "pedigree" includes the facts of birth, marriage, and death, and the times when these events happened (Greenleaf on Evidence, sec. 104), and evidence of these facts is pertinent for the purpose of establishing pedigree, the several facts, or either of them, do not of themselves constitute pedigree, and a case in which the age of an individual is the issue to be determined is not a case of pedigree. "A case is not necessarily a case of pedigree because it may involve questions of birth, parentage, age,

or relationship. Where these questions are merely incidental
and the judgment will simply establish a debt or a person's liability. on a contract, or his proper settlement as a pauper, and
things of that nature, the case is not one of pedigree, although
questions of marriage, legitimacy, death, or birth are incidentally inquired of": Eisenlord v. Clum, 126 N. Y. 566. See, also,
Haines v. Guthrie, L. R. 13 Q. B. Div. 818. In Leggett v. Boyd,
3 Wend. 376, the defense of infancy was made to an action upon
a promissory note, and in support of this defense the family Bible of the parents was offered in which the entry of his birth had
been made by his mother; and its exclusion was held upon the
ground that the person by whom it was made was in court and
could have been examined. Campbell v. Wilson, 23 Tex. 252,
76 Am. Dec. 67, was of the same character, and the evidence was
excluded because it was shown that the mother was within reach
of the process of the court. Greenleaf v. Dubuque etc. R. R. Co.,
30 Iowa, 301, was an action to recover damages for negligence
in causing the death of a person, and, for the purpose of establishing his age as an element in determining the amount of damages, the plaintiff was allowed to show the date of his birth from
an entry in the family Bible. This was held to be error, on the
ground that it was not shown that the person who made the entry
was dead. In Robinson v. Blakely, 4 Rich. 586, 55 Am. [521]
Dec. 703, the family register of births and deaths was held inadmissible to show the age of the plaintiff for the purpose of determining whether the action was barred by the statute of limitations, upon the ground that the father who made the entry
was still alive, the court saying: "These entries stand on no
higher footing than other declarations, and are entitled to no
higher consideration, except that if made at the time the fact
occurred they are more reliable." The admissibility in evidence
of these facts is limited by Mr. Greenleaf in the section above
referred to, to cases where they arise incidentally and in relation
to pedigree as follows: "Thus an entry by a deceased parent, or
other relative, made in a Bible, family missal, or any other book,
or in any document or paper, stating the fact or date of the birth,
marriage, or death of a child or other relative, is regarded as the
declaration of such parent or relative in a matter of pedigree."
Taylor says (Taylor on Evidence, 650): "Entries made by a parent or relation in Bibles, prayer-books, missals, almanacs, or, indeed, in any other book, or in any document or paper, stating
the fact and date of the birth, marriage, or death of a child or
other relation, are also evidence in pedigree cases as being writ-

ten declarations of the deceased persons who respectively made them."

The entry in the Bible in the present case was shown to have been made by Mrs. Shipton, and, as she was present in court and had testified to the date of the child's birth, it was not competent for the prosecution to introduce as a piece of substantive evidence in support of this issue her written declaration made several years previously. Nor can it be said that the error was harmless. The evidence was not cumulative, but was of an entirely different character from any other evidence in reference to the child's age, and the jury may well have given it a credit by reason of its formality and apparent authenticity which they would not grant to the living witness who testified respecting the age.

The motion for a new trial was denied, and judgment sentencing the defendant to imprisonment in the state prison rendered and entered November 23, 1895, and on the same day the present appeal was taken from this judgment and order. September 21, 1896, the defendant made a motion to set aside **522** the order denying his motion for a new trial, and offered to read several affidavits in support of the motion. The court refused to entertain the motion, or to hear or consider the affidavits. From the order thus refusing to hear his application the defendant has taken an appeal. The attorney general has moved to dismiss this appeal. By the appeal from the order denying a new trial the subject matter of that order was removed from the superior court, and while the appeal was pending that court had no jurisdiction to change the order. Besides, an order refusing to hear a motion to set aside a former order denying a new trial is not appealable.

The appeal from the order of September 21, 1896, is dismissed. The judgment and order denying a new trial are reversed, and a new trial ordered.

Van Fleet, J., and Beatty, C. J., concurred.

EVIDENCE—ENTRIES IN FAMILY RECORDS.—A register of births in the handwriting of a deceased father is admissible to prove the ages of his children: Woodard v. Spiller, 1 Dana, 180; 25 Am. Dec. 139. Entries in a family Bible are admissible to prove the date of a birth when primary evidence cannot be obtained. Such entries are secondary evidence and are excluded when better evidence is shown to be accessible. They come within the general rule which excludes secondary evidence when primary evidence can be obtained: Campbell v. Wilson, 23 Tex. 252; 76 Am. Dec. 67. Such an entry as to the birth of a child is admissible in an action brought by the father against a justice for unlawfully solemnizing a marriage with such child while a minor, and the testimony of the father is admissible to prove such entry: Carskadden v. Poorman, 10 Watts, 82; 36 Am. Dec. 145.

APPEAL—EFFECT WHILE PENDING.—The granting of an appeal and its subsequent perfection divest the court below of all jurisdiction, and it cannot afterward set aside the order from which an appeal has been taken: Planters' Bank v. Neely, 7 How. 80; 40 Am. Dec. 51; Helm v. Boone, 6 J. J. Marsh. 351; 22 Am. Dec. 75; Stewart v. Stringer, 41 Mo. 400; 97 Am. Dec. 278.

San Diego Water Company v. City of San Diego.

[118 California, 556.]

CONSTITUTIONAL LAW.—THE POWER OF THE STATE TO FIX AND REGULATE RATES OF COMPENSATION to be charged by persons and corporations in charge of certain public utilities is so limited by the constitution of the United States that it cannot be so exercised as to require the furnishing of property or services without reward.

CONSTITUTIONAL LAW—COURTS, POWER OF TO REVIEW THE FIXING OF RATES.—If rates are fixed by legislative power or otherwise than by appropriate judicial proceedings, in which full notice and an opportunity to be heard are given, it is within the province of the courts to review such action to the extent, at least, of determining whether the rates so fixed will furnish some reward for the property used and the services rendered. To fix rates which will not allow such reward is to take property for public use without compensation.

CONSTITUTIONAL LAW—FIXING RATES, TO WHAT EXTENT REVIEWABLE IN THE COURTS.—When it is claimed that the rates fixed by the common council of a municipality for the furnishing of water will deprive the corporation furnishing it of all reward, the courts may ascertain whether the power has been carried beyond constitutional limits, and, if so, declare the action void. The court is not limited to the evidence produced before the common council, or other body authorized to fix the rates, and may act without knowing what such evidence was. Whether the action of the council or other body was beyond the constitutional limits is a mixed question of law and fact, to be determined by the courts upon evidence produced before them.

CONSTITUTIONAL LAW—WATER RATES, POWER TO FIX.—The people of the state have power in and by its constitution to declare that all water not then reduced to private ownership shall thereafter remain public, and that every person thereafter undertaking to supply cities, towns, or their inhabitants with water shall do so upon the condition that the rates to be charged therefor shall be annually fixed by the city. Such a business is so far public in its nature that the state may lawfully forbid its exercise by a private individual, and, a fortiori, may impose such conditions and restrictions upon its exercise as may be thought proper.

CONSTITUTIONAL LAW—RESTRICTIONS, DUTY TO SUBMIT TO.—One engaged in the business of furnishing water to the inhabitants of towns or cities after the adoption of a constitution imposing certain restrictions upon such business is bound to submit to the restrictions so imposed.

CONSTITUTIONAL LAW — CONSTRUCTION OF STATE CONSTITUTION SO AS NOT TO CONFLICT WITH NATIONAL.—A provision of the constitution of a state requiring and authorizing the fixing by the board of supervisors of the county or the common council of a city of rates to be charged for water furnished to be used to the inhabitants thereof should so be construed as not to conflict with the constitution of the United States by depriving persons of property without compensation and without due process of law, and hence must be held to authorize the fixing of such rates by the exercise of judgment and discretion, and so as to allow just compensation.

CONSTITUTIONAL LAW—COMPENSATION TO BE PAID FOR WATER.—In determining the compensation to which a water company is entitled for supplying a municipality and its inhabitants with water, neither the sum for which the plant could be sold in the market, nor the cost of replacing it, is controlling. For the money which the company has reasonably expended for the public benefit in acquiring its property and constructing its works it is entitled to a reasonable reward. If the business appears to be honestly and prudently conducted, the rate which the company would be compelled to pay for borrowed money will furnish a safe, though not always a conclusive criterion of the rate of profit which will be deemed reasonable. [Per Van Fleet, Henshaw, and McFarland, JJ.]

PUBLIC UTILITIES—RATES OF CHARGES—BONDED INDEBTEDNESS.—The existence of a bonded indebtedness cannot be regarded as a material element in fixing the charges to be paid for the furnishing of water to a municipality and its inhabitants. No distinction can be made between corporations which have completed their works with their own money and those which have borrowed money for that purpose from others. In either case the money actually and reasonably invested is the basic criterion of the revenue to be allowed. [Per Van Fleet, Henshaw, and McFarland, JJ.]

PUBLIC UTILITIES—RATES OF CHARGES.—The fact that some reward or compensation is allowed to a water company for water furnished a municipality is not conclusive of the power of the court. The question of just compensation is a judicial question. to be determined in the ordinary course of judicial proceedings, and whenever the rates fixed by the common council of a municipality are grossly and palpably insufficient to furnish such revenue as will afford compensation. redress may be had in the courts. [Per Van Fleet, Henshaw, and McFarland, JJ.]

PUBLIC UTILITIES. RATES OF CHARGES—WHAT TO BE CHARGED AS EXPENSES.—In determining what a water company should be allowed as depreciation of its plant by use, ordinary repairs should be charged to current expenses, and substantial reconstruction or replacement should be charged to construction account, and depreciation should not be otherwise considered.

PUBLIC UTILITIES. RIGHT TO A HEARING WHEN CHARGES ARE TO BE FIXED.—The common council or other tribunal charged with the duty of fixing the rates to be charged by a corporation for water to be furnished to a municipality and its inhabitants should, if requested, give the corporation a reasonable opportunity to be heard, not merely for the purpose of presenting its own evidence, but also of explaining or overcoming, if it can, evidence presented by others. A refusal to permit it to be present when some of the evidence is given shows an unfairness in the investigation, and overcomes the presumption of the correctness of any decision which may be reached.

PUBLIC UTILITIES — BASIS UPON WHICH RATES SHOULD BE FIXED.—In determining what a corporation furnish-

Oct. 1897.] San Diego Water Co. v. City of San Diego. 263

ing water to a municipality and its inhabitants should be permitted to charge therefor, so as to realize a reasonable reward, the value of the plant is the basic element upon which the whole investigation rests. The original cost of construction is simply an item to be considered. [Per Garoutte, Temple, and Harrison, JJ.]

PUBLIC UTILITIES—RATES OF CHARGES, POWER OF COURTS TO REVIEW.—If the rates of charges fixed by a common council for the furnishing by a corporation of water to a municipality and its inhabitants are such as to give some compensation for the services rendered, the courts cannot inquire whether such compensation is proper or reasonable. That is a question of fact to be determined by such council, and is not subject to review by the courts. Rates which yield an income of more than three per cent of the value of the plant cannot be adjudged unreasonable by the courts. [Per Garoutte, Temple, and Harrison, JJ.]

PUBLIC UTILITIES, RATES WHICH SHOULD BE ALLOWED.—In fixing water rates the common council should provide for just and reasonable compensation to the water company. The rates ought to be, adjusted to the value of the services rendered, and this means that the company should be allowed to collect only a gross income sufficient to pay current expenses, maintain the necessary plant in a state of efficiency, and declare a dividend to stockholders equal to at least the current rates of interest, not on the par value of the stock, but on the actual value of the property necessarily used in providing and distributing the water to consumers. [Per Beatty, C. J.]

Suit to annul and enjoin the enforcement of an ordinance fixing the rates to be charged for furnishing water. Article 14 of the constitution of California, referred to by the judges in their respective opinions, is as follows: "Section 1. The use of all water now appropriated, or that may hereafter be appropriated, for sale, rental, or distribution, is hereby declared to be a public use, and subject to the regulation and control of the state, in the manner to be prescribed by law; provided, that the rates or compensation to be collected by any person, company, or corporation in this state for the use of water supplied to any city and county, or city or town, or the inhabitants thereof, shall be fixed, annually, by the board of supervisors, or city and county, or city or town council, or other governing body of such city and county, or city or town, by ordinance or otherwise, in the manner that other ordinances or legislative acts or resolutions are passed by such body, and shall continue in force for one year, and no longer. Such ordinances or resolutions shall be passed in the month of February of each year, and take effect on the first day of July thereafter. Any board or body failing to pass the necessary ordinances or resolutions fixing water rates, where necessary, within such time, shall be subject to peremptory process to compel action at the suit of any party interested, and shall be liable to such further processes and penalties as the legislature may prescribe. Any person, company, or corporation collecting water rates in any city and county, or city or town in this state, otherwise than as so established, shall forfeit the franchises and waterworks of such person, company, or corporation to the city and county, or city or town, where the same are collected, for the public use. Sec. 2. The right to collect rates or compensation for the use of water supplied to any county, city and county, or town, or the inhabitants thereof, is a franchise, and cannot be exercised except by authority of, and in the manner prescribed by, law."

William H. Fuller, Clarence L. Barber, H. E. Doolittle, and T. L. Lewis, for the appellants.

Works & Works, for the respondent.

John Garber and S. F. Lieb, amici curiae, for the respondent.

562 VAN FLEET, J. The plaintiff is a corporation engaged in the business of supplying water to the city of San Diego and its inhabitants. In February, 1890, the common council of the city passed an ordinance fixing the water rates for the year beginning July 1, 1890. In May, 1890, the plaintiff brought this action against the city, the common council, the mayor, and the individual members of the council, to annul this ordinance and enjoin its enforcement. The complaint alleged in substance that the entire revenue which plaintiff could receive during the year in question, under the rates so fixed, would be insufficient to pay its operating expenses and fixed charges for that year, and would, therefore, afford no reward whatever to plaintiff for furnishing the water, and that the ordinance would deprive plaintiff of its property without process of law and without compensation. It was also alleged that, by reason of certain fraudulent practices on the part of the council, the plaintiff was deprived of a fair opportunity to be heard before the council, and prevented from properly presenting its side of the case. The action was tried after the expiration of the year in question, and a judgment was entered declaring the ordinance to be void, and setting the same aside. From this judgment, and from an order denying their motion for a new trial, the defendants appealed.

The findings of the court were in substance: That the property **563** and plant of the plaintiff necessary to supply water to the city and its inhabitants actually cost $750,000; that the reasonable and necessary operating expenses of plaintiff for the year in question, and actually expended by it for that purpose, amounted to $40,000; that plaintiff was indebted upon its bonds for money borrowed, amounting to the sum of $1,000,000, bearing interest at the rate of five per cent per annum, of which amount $750,000 had been necessarily and properly expended for the construction of the plant; that the total receipts of plaintiff for the year in question derived from the rates fixed by said ordinance could not be and were not greater than $65,788.65; that the annual depreciation of the plant on account of natural decay and use amounted to three and one-third per cent of its value; that no dividends for the stockholders of plaintiff had been or could be earned from the rates fixed by said ordinance for said year; and that the rates so fixed were not just or reasonable.

The court also found certain facts concerning the proceedings of the common council and its committee in investigating the subject matter, which will be noticed hereafter.

These findings are assailed as being in some particulars unsupported by the evidence; and many questions of law have been ably argued by numerous counsel. Some of these questions, though highly interesting and important, are not necessarily involved in this appeal, and we shall therefore not notice them; but we will, so far as space will permit, consider each of the other points made.

1. It is contended by defendants that, under article 14 of the constitution of this state, a court has no power, in the absence of fraud, to hold such an ordinance invalid merely because the court finds the rates fixed thereby to be unjust and unreasonable.

We shall not attempt in this opinion to review the many cases on this subject. It is sufficient to say that the supreme court of the United States (whose decisions on this matter are controlling) has repeatedly decided that the power of the state to fix and regulate the rates of compensation to be charged by persons and corporations in charge of certain public utilities is so limited by the constitution of the United States that it cannot be exercised to such an extent as to require any such person or ⁵⁶⁴ corporation to furnish its property or services without reward, and that, if the rates are fixed by legislative power, or otherwise than by appropriate judicial proceedings in which full notice and opportunity to appear and defend are given, it is within the province of the courts to review such action, to the extent, at least, of ascertaining whether the rates so fixed will furnish some reward for the property used and services furnished. To fix rates that will allow no such reward is to take property for public use without just compensation. To this extent at least, then, the court was entitled to go in this case.

But appellants contend that in any event the court could do no more in reviewing the action of the common council than to say whether there was or was not evidence produced before that body sufficient to sustain its conclusions and that the court was not at liberty to determine the question upon other and perhaps new evidence not produced before the council, nor to substitute its judgment as to the reasonableness of the rates for the judgment of that body. In this contention we think that counsel entirely misconceives the nature of the functions respectively exercised under our constitution by the rate-fixing body and by the courts. Whether the fixing of rates by the council be called a legislative, a judicial, or an administrative act, it is certainly not an adversary judicial proceeding such as, under the constitution, will conclude private rights. It is a proceeding on the part of the government to which neither the water company nor the rate payers are parties, conducted without notice to them, and without any right on their part to effectually intervene. Such a proceeding cannot operate to divest private rights; and, though the supreme court of the United States holds it to be a legitimate exercise of governmental powers, that court also holds that when it is carried so far as to deprive anyone of his property without just compensation it is an unlawful exercise of such power, and simply void. The function of the courts is merely to ascertain whether the power has been carried beyond the constitutional limits so fixed; and, if such be found to be the case, to declare the acts of the council void. They do not sit as appellate tribunals to review the correctness of the council's determination, nor need they know anything about the evidence on which that body has acted. All that they have to consider is, whether, in a given case, the result of the council's action [565] will be to take the property of the complaining party without just compensation. That is a mixed question of fact and law, to be decided by the court upon the evidence produced before it.

2. On the other hand, the plaintiff contends that section 1 of article 14 of the constitution of this state is opposed to the constitution of the United States, and that it operates to deprive the water company of its property without due process of law. It is argued that no provision for the fixing of water rates by the tribunal thereby created can be valid without notice to those

whose rights are to be affected, and an opportunity to them to appear and defend, the right to which must be given by the constitution itself. That no such notice or hearing is provided for must be admitted; but the consequence contended for does not follow.

In the first place, there is nothing in the pleadings or evidence in this case to show that any water rights or property of plaintiff used in furnishing the water in question were acquired before the adoption of the present constitution. On the contrary, we think it substantially appears that they were all acquired since that time. We are unable to perceive why the people of this state in adopting that constitution had not the right to declare that all water not then reduced to private ownership should thereafter remain public, and that thereafter every person undertaking the business of supplying cities or towns or their inhabitants with water should do so upon the condition that the rates to be charged therefor should be conclusively fixed by the state. Such a business is so far public in its very nature that the state might lawfully forbid its exercise by any private individual, and, a fortiori, might impose such conditions and restrictions upon its exercise as might be thought proper. If, then, that section of the constitution could be construed as rendering the decision of the council absolutely final and conclusive, plaintiff, at least, could not be heard to complain. If it chose, with that section in force, to enter upon that business, it was bound to submit to the conditions thereby imposed.

But we think that the true construction of that section is such that it is not open to the constitutional objection urged, even if raised by one who at the time of its adoption was engaged in that business. It obviously was not the intention of ⁵⁰⁰ the framers of that provision to make any distinction between rights then existing and those to be thereafter acquired, nor can we attribute to them any intention of confiscating private property. The meaning of the section is, that the governing body of the municipality, upon a fair investigation, and with the exercise of judgment and discretion, shall fix reasonable rates and allow just compensation. If they attempt to act arbitrarily, without investigation, or without the exercise of judgment and discretion, or if they fix rates so palpably unreasonable and unjust as to amount to arbitrary action, they violate their duty and go beyond the powers conferred upon them. Such was the conclusion reached by this court in Spring Valley Water Works v. San Francisco, 82 Cal. 286, 16 Am. St. Rep. 116, to which conclusion we adhere. Although that case was decided without the light cast on the subject by later decisions of the supreme court of the United States, and contains some observations which perhaps may require modification, we are satisfied with the correctness of the conclusion there given to this section of the constitution.

According to this construction, the rules announced under the first head in this opinion are applicable. If the council has fixed rates so palpably unreasonable and unjust as to amount to a taking of plaintiff's property without just compensation, it has so far exceeded the powers conferred upon it, and the court is competent to afford redress.

3. This brings us, then, to the question whether the findings support the judgment. They show that the total receipts of the plaintiff from the rates fixed by the council would be and were insufficient to pay plaintiff's actual and necessary operating expenses, together with the interest on so much of its bonded indebtedness as was necessarily and properly expended by it in the construction of its plant, necessarily and actually used for the supplying of the water here in question—indeed, would fall short more than $11,000 of paying those charges. No circumstances requiring such a loss were found, and the finding that these actual charges were necessarily and properly incurred in the legitimate exercise of the business of furnishing water to the city negative the existence of any such circumstances. It is clear that under the rule laid down by the supreme court of the United States in Reagan v. Farmers' Loan [567] etc. Co., 154 U. S. 362, 412, that court would hold those rates to be so unreasonable and unjust as to require the court to set them aside. The decision in that case, however, is not in all respects satisfactory; and, after a careful examination of all the many cases on this subject, we are unable to discover that any consistent or adequate rules controlling the exercise of the governmental power of fixing rates have yet been judicially laid down. The subject is one of extreme complexity, and its inherent difficulties have been increased rather than diminished by the numerous decisions in which it has been discussed. We think, however, that a consideration of the real nature of the power conferred by our constitution will afford a sufficient solution of the question.

It is apparent that the water company does not own the water which it collects and supplies, or the plant which it uses to collect and distribute that water, in the same sense in which a man is said to own his house or his farm. By the very nature of the

use to which it is applied, the company has devoted that property
to a public use.   Having once undertaken to perform that public duty, it must continue to perform it, and must carry on its
business under the lawful regulations of the government.   In
effect, the state may be said to have appropriated the water and
the plant to public use.   For that appropriation it is bound to
make just compensation, and it has provided for such compensation by requiring the municipal authorities to fix just and reasonable rates at which the water is to be furnished to and re-·
ceived by the consumers.   Since the state has "taken" the use
of this property, it is bound to provide a just compensation for
that use, and article 14 of the constitution must be construed
as providing for that just compensation.

The question of what is just compensation in such a case is,
we think, in all respects analogous to the question which arises
in every case of appropriation under the power of eminent domain; and it may be reduced to the formula that the public must
pay the actual value of that which it appropriates to the public
use.   In determining such value, three, and we believe only
three, methods are possible: 1. Either by ascertaining what the
property could be sold for (its market value); or 2. By ascertaining what it would cost to replace it; or 3. By ascertaining the
revenue it is capable of producing.   In cases like the present,
568 however, neither the first nor the second method can be resorted to.   The judicial test of market value depends upon the
fact that the property in question is marketable at a given price,
which in turn depends upon the fact that sales of similar property have been and are being made at ascertainable prices.   But
such property as this is not so sold; at least, not often enough
to furnish a fair criterion; and the very fact of governmental
regulation would necessarily control the price.   Until the rates
are fixed, no one can say how much the property would sell for,
and therefore that price cannot be ascertained as a basis for fixing those rates.

The second method is entirely inapplicable to property of this
kind.   The construction of municipal waterworks is a matter of
growth.   It is necessary in common prudence, on the one hand,
to construct the works of such capacity as to satisfy the needs
of the growing city, not only at the moment, but within the
near future; and, on the other hand, not to extend them so
much as to cast an unnecessary burden on the stockholders, or
the present consumers.   As such works are a necessity to the
city, they must keep pace with, and to some extent anticipate,

its growth. When constructed, they stimulate to that extent the
progress of the city, and tend, like all conveniences, to lower
the general cost of production of all things. It results that at
least the first water system in any city occupies the position of
a pioneer. At any expense the works must be constructed, and
usually no reward can be realized by the constructors until some
time has elapsed. In the mean time, as the city grows, in part
by reason of this very supply of water, the facility of construct-
·ing works of all kinds is increased, and the cost of such construction diminished. It would, therefore, be highly unjust to
permit the consumers to avail themselves of the plea that at
the present time similar works could be constructed at a less
cost, as a pretext for reducing the rates to be paid for the water.
The reduced expense, if it be reduced, is due, in part at least,
to the very fact that the city has been provided at the cost of
the water company with increased facilities for doing business.

But it is said that those who enter upon any business enterprise undertake the risk of being undersold by those who, coming later into the field, have the advantage of a cheapening of
construction. But this is not an ordinary business enterprise.
569 Those who engage in it put their property entirely into the
hands of the public. Having once embarked it is beyond their
power to draw back. They must always be ready to supply the
public demand, and must take the risk of any falling off in that
demand. They cannot convert their property to any other use,
however unprofitable the public use may become. They have
expended their money for the benefit of others, and subjected
it to the control of others. That money has, in effect, been
taken by the public, and the public, while refusing to return
that money, cannot be heard to say that it no longer has need
for all of it.

Nor would it, on the other hand, be just to the consumers to
require them to pay an enhanced price for the water, on the
ground that it would now cost more to construct similar works.
Such a contingency may well happen; but to allow an increase
of rates for such reason would be to allow the water company
to make a profit, not as a reward for its expenditures and services, but for the fortuitous occurrence of a rise in the price
of materials or labor. The law does not intend that this business shall be a speculation in which the water company or the
consumers shall respectively win or lose upon the casting of
a die, or upon the equally unpredictable fluctuations of the markets. For the money which the company has expended for the

public benefit it is to receive a reasonable, and no more than
a reasonable, reward. It is to be paid according to what it has
done, and not according to what others might conceivably do.
In effect, the bargain between the company and the public was
made when the works were constructed; and this matter is to
be determined according to the state of things at that time.

We must then have recourse to the third standard of value—
the revenue which the property is capable of producing. At
the first blush, there might seem to be a difficulty in applying
this standard, for the revenue received by the company will be
absolutely controlled by the rates fixed, and no revenue can be
collected except upon rates so˙fixed. This difficulty has led one
of the counsel in this case, in a singularly able and ingenious
argument, to contend that the rates must be so fixed as to enable the company to obtain precisely the revenue which it would
realize if the rates were not regulated by the public at all. To
this proposition we cannot assent. The whole history of municipal [570] regulation conclusively shows that its principal purpose was always to diminish what were rightly or wrongly believed to be exorbitant charges. The theory of its application
has always been that it is necessary to restrain the proprietors
of what have been called "virtual monopolies" from imposing
extravagant and unreasonable tariffs for the use of their facilities. Whether the system be well conceived or not, whether it
accords with the theory of free government, are not questions
with which we have to do. It is sufficient that the law recognizes that there is a standard by which just compensation may
be measured, and that it is intended to prevent that measure
from being exceeded.

What that standard is, as applied to the present case, we think
not difficult of ascertainment. As we have said, it is not the
water or the distributing works which the company may be said
to own, and the value of which is to be ascertained. They
were acquired and contributed for the use of the public; the
public may be said to be the real owner, and the company only
the agent of the public to administer their use. What the company has parted with, what the public has acquired, is the money
reasonably and properly expended by the company in acquiring its property and constructing its works. The state has taken
the use of that money, and it is for that use that it must provide just compensation. What revenue money is capable of producing is a question of fact, and, theoretically at least, susceptible of more or less exact ascertainment. Regard must be

had to the nature of the investment, the risk attendant upon it, and the public demand for the product of the enterprise. It would not, of course, be reasonable to allow the company a profit equal to the greatest rate of interest realized upon any kind of investment, nor, on the other hand, to compel it to accept the lowest rate of remuneration which capital ever obtains. Comparison must be made between this business and other kinds of business involving a similar degree of risk, and all the surrounding circumstances must be considered. An important circumstance will always be the rate of interest at which money can be borrowed for investment in such a business; and where the business appears to be honestly and prudently conducted, the rate which the company would be compelled to pay for borrowed money will furnish a safe, though not always conclusive [571] criterion of the rate of profit which will be deemed reasonable. In ordinary cases, where the management is fair and economical, it would be unreasonable to fix the rates so low as to prevent the company from paying interest on borrowed money at the lowest market rate obtainable; and, even then, some allowance or margin should be made for any risk to which the company may be exposed, over and above the risk taken by a lender.

This being so, the existence of the bonded indebtedness on which so much stress has been laid, and which has seemed to present so difficult a problem in some of the cases, must be disregarded. That fact, indeed, it seems to us, can never be important, except as entitling the holders of the bonds, as parties in interest, to be heard in actions like the present. Evidently, no distinction can be made between those who construct the works with their own money and those who do so with money borrowed from others. In either case, the money actually invested is the basic criterion of the revenue to be allowed.

It follows that we cannot say that the finding of the court below, that the rates fixed by the city council were less than what was reasonable, is unsupported by the evidence. After deducting current expense for the year—$40,000—from the revenue received—$65,788.65—there would be left but $25,788.65 —or but little more than three and one-third per cent upon $750,000, the actual cost of the works; while the evidence shows that the company was compelled to pay a much higher rate upon money which it appears to have fairly borrowed. It is true that the evidence is not as full and satisfactory on this question as it should be, doubtless owing to the fact that the rules governing this inquiry were not clearly apprehended by the counsel who tried the case. But as no attempt was made to show that the rate of interest paid by the company was above the lowest market rate, and as the prudence and economy of the management were not successfully impeached, we cannot say that the court below was not justified in the conclusion to which it arrived on this question.

But it is contended that the power of the court is at most to inquire whether some reward will be provided by the rates fixed, and that if some reward, however small, is so provided, the court cannot interfere. We have been referred to dicta in some of the 572 cases which do support that contention but we are unable to agree with that conclusion. It is an elementary doctrine of constitutional law that the question of just compensation is a judicial question to be determined in the ordinary course of judicial proceedings; and, construing article XIV of our constitution with section 14 of article I (as we think we are bound to do), we find no difficulty in holding that whenever the rates fixed by the council are grossly and palpably insufficient to furnish such a revenue as will afford just compensation within the rules above declared, redress may be had in the courts. Of course, every slight or conjectural deficiency will not justify an appeal to the courts; nor, if the question be doubtful, will the court, in the absence of fraud or other special ground of equitable interference, substitute its judgment for that of the municipal body. But whenever it is clear and beyond question that the revenue which the company can possibly receive under the rates fixed will be wholly insufficient to allow it the compensation to which it is legally entitled, it is the duty of the court to declare the ordinance void. Such is the case under the findings here, and those findings must, therefore, be held to support the judgment.

It should, of course, be said that it does not follow that in every case the company will be entitled to credit for all of its current expenditures, or to receive a compensation based on the entire costs of its works. Reckless and unnecessary expenditures, not legitimately incurred in the actual collection and distribution of the water furnished, or in the acquisition, construction, or preservation of so much of the plant as is necessary for that purpose, cannot be allowed. Nor can the investment on which the company is entitled to base its compensation be held to include property not now actually employed in collecting or distributing the water now being supplied, however useful it may have been in the past, or may yet be in the future. It is the money reasonably and properly expended in each year in collecting and distributing the water which constitutes the current expenses which may be allowed; and it is the money reasonably and properly expended in the acquisition and construction of the works actually and properly in use for that purpose, which constitutes the investment on which the compensation is to be computed. The amounts stated in the findings in this case are found to be of that character.

573 4. But it is contended that the findings in several particulars are unsupported by the evidence.

It is claimed that the evidence does not justify the finding that $750,000 had been actually expended in the purchase and construction of the plant. On this subject the evidence is extremely unsatisfactory. Apart from estimates testified to by engineers, the only evidence of the cost was the books of the company, which placed the amount at $735,000. Of this sum defendants object to items amounting to about $127,000, viz., an alleged duplicate of the entry of $13,932, an alleged overcharge of $25,000 in the real estate account, and the sum of $88,000 alleged to be the cost of certain works abandoned and not in use. On these questions we have had little or no assistance from counsel for respondent, and our examination of the evidence has failed to satisfy us on any one of them. The books, or those portions of them brought up in the transcript, require much explanation, which has not been furnished us. In fact, the case appears to have been tried largely on a wrong theory, the greater portion of the evidence consisting of the testimony of expert witnesses as to the value of the property. This is at the best an unsatisfactory way of determining the question of actual cost (for which purpose only could it be admissible), and should not be resorted to when better evidence can be obtained. As against the company, at least, its books furnish better evidence on this subject, and cannot be disregarded. These books certainly show the cost to have been less than $750,000, though we are unable to determine the precise amount properly shown by them: and the evidence clearly discloses that portions of the plant included in that cost are not now in use, if, indeed, they have not been totally abandoned. We think, therefore, that this finding is not justified by the evidence. On this and kindred matters not only is the burden of proof on the plaintiff, but it is bound to establish them by the most clear and satisfactory evidence, in order to overcome the presumption of the correctness of the action of the city council.

The finding that the expenses of the company for the year in question were $40,000 is also attacked. The books of the company put the amount at $44,255.30. Of this amount appellants object to items of about $5,000 as unnecessary and improper, and object particularly to an item of $12,800, being an unpaid [574] bill which is disputed by plaintiff, and on which its liability is left doubtful. Counsel for respondents have not attempted to answer these points. As the evidence is presented to us in an unsatisfactory shape, we will say no more than that it does not support the finding. Whether all of the items complained of are proper or improper cannot be determined upon this record, but some of them are not shown to be proper. It will be the duty of the court on a retrial to allow no item of expenditure which is not satisfactorily shown to be an actual and proper charge in the actual conduct of the business of supplying water; and, when legal or other general expenses are claimed, they must be shown to have had a proper relation to that business. Of course, the items of expenses in the present action should be disregarded. The trial being had after the expiration of the year for which the rates in question were fixed, the amounts of revenue and expenses are capable of exact proof.

With regard to the question of the depreciation of the plant by use, it is sufficient to say that ordinary repairs should be charged to current expense, that substantial reconstruction or replacement should be charged to the construction account, and that depreciation should not otherwise be considered. It is doubtless difficult in many cases to properly discriminate between current and ordinary repairs and such repairs as amount in effect to new construction. Such difficulties, when they arise, must be solved by the application of the principles on which ordinary business enterprises are conducted.

It may be added that when, as appears to have been the case in this instance, portions of the company's expenses are specifically repaid by the consumers, such expenses should be climinated from the computation. This will apply at least to the "taps" put in for private consumers.

5. Among other things, the court below made the following finding:

"10· That the taking of evidence as to the value of the plaintiff's plant and the rates that should be fixed by the common council of said city, during the month of February, 1890, for the year commencing July 1, 1890, was by said common council delegated to a joint committee consisting of three members from the board of delegates and three members from the board of aldermen of said common council. That said joint committee [575] proceeded to and did take evidence from the plaintiff and its officers and other witnesses for a number of days, and that on the twenty-first day of February, 1890, the plaintiff then being before said committee by its attorney, said attorney inquired of said committee whether other evidence would be taken, and announced that, if other evidence would be taken, he, the said attorney, desired to be present, and especially that if evidence was given by members of the board of public works of said city, or estimates were taken from said members of the value or cost of the plaintiff's plant, that he, said attorney, desired to be present and examine said members of the board of public works as to the evidence given by them or the estimates furnished. That it was announced by one of said committee at that time, in the presence of the other members, that he did not know of any other evidence that was to be taken, which was not disputed by any other member of the committee. That there, at that time, and immediately following the demand of said attorney as aforesaid, the city engineer of said city, who was present, was privately and secretly informed that the committee desired to have him present at a meeting to be held the following day to give an estimate of the value of said plant. That on the following day said committee met secretly, and without notifying the water company or its said attorney, and took the testimony of said city engineer and one Schuyler, a member of the board of public works of said city, and took from them their estimates of the value and cost of every part of the distributing system, pumps, wells, and other property of the plaintiff, not including its water rights, rights of way, or real estate. That said meeting was held secretly in a back room of the office of the city attorney, while all of the other meetings of the committee had been held publicly in the room of the board of aldermen, was held on a legal holiday when the offices of the city in the City Hall were closed, and said meeting was held with the doors closed and locked. That the plaintiff had no notice or knowledge of said meeting or the taking of said evidence, and was not present either by its officers or its attorney or otherwise, and was given no opportunity to be present or investigate or cross-examine with reference to the evidence given and estimates furnished. That said estimates so furnished were largely less than the cost as proved or estimated by the evidence of the officers [576] of the plaintiff taken by said committee, and sworn statements furnished by its officers, and the estimates so furnished in the absence of the plaintiff were taken with but few exceptions, and as to small amounts, as the value and cost of said plant by said committee, and made the basis of their report, and of the rates fixed by them and subsequently adopted by the ordinance of the common council. That the report of said committee was made up and concluded on the twenty-fourth day of February, 1890, was presented to both houses of said common council on the evening of that day, and was then adopted by each of said bodies without change. That the attorney of the plaintiff appeared before each of said bodies and demanded that the plaintiff be allowed to offer evidence to said common council, with reference to the fixing of said rates, but his right to offer said evidence was denied, and no evidence was received or heard. That the evidence taken by the committee was taken down by a stenographer and transcribed, but was never read to or submitted to either board of said common council, but that the members of said committee, or some of them, stated their recollection of the evidence upon which their said report was based. That the ordinance mentioned in the complaint, fixing said rates, was passed and adopted by both of the bodies of said common council on the evening of the twenty-fifth day of February, 1890, without any further hearing, or opportunity to be heard, on the part of plaintiff."

It is claimed that this finding is not altogether in accord with the evidence; but, though we find some verbal inaccuracies, we think that in all material particulars it is sufficiently supported.

It is plain that these facts show so much of unfairness in the investigation had by the common council as to overcome the presumption of the correctness of its decision. It was clearly the duty of the council to give to the water company, at least when requested to do so, a reasonable opportunity to be heard, not merely for the purpose of presenting its own evidence, but also of explaining or overcoming, if it could, evidence presented by others. The company, of course, could not claim as a right to be heard at any time it chose; but it certainly was entitled, upon reasonable request for that purpose, to be present when evidence was being produced before the council or its committee, or to be otherwise informed of that evidence and allowed to 577 overcome it if possible. The action of the committee, for which no sufficient excuse was given, appears to have been taken for the very purpose of excluding the plaintiff when that evidence was received, and it therefore seriously impugns the fairness of the investigation. Indeed, such an investigation ought to be held publicly, and upon such reasonable public notice of the times and places of the meetings as will enable those interested to be present and a neglect of this precaution, when unexplained, must always give rise to injurious suspicions.

A number of other points have been discussed by counsel, but they are all either covered by what has been said, or have been thereby rendered unimportant.

For the reasons above set forth, the judgment and order appealed from are reversed, and the cause remanded for a new trial.

Henshaw, J., and McFarland, J., concurred.

GAROUTTE, J., concurring. The findings of fact made by the trial court which are deemed necessary to a consideration of the questions presented before us are as follows: 1. On the twenty-fourth day of February, 1890, and at the time the ordinance mentioned in plaintiff's complaint was enacted by the common council of said city, the water plant and system of the plaintiff was of the value of $750,000; 2. The necessary operating expenses of plaintiff in conducting its property from July, 1890, to July, 1891, and the sum actually expended, was $40,000; 3. Plaintiff was and is indebted upon its outstanding bonds regularly issued in the sum of $1,000,000, bearing interest at five per cent per annum, of which sum $750,000 was necessarily expended in the construction of the plant, and the interest upon which is $50,000 per annum; 4. The total receipts received under said ordinance from July 1, 1890, to July 1, 1891, amounted to $65,-788.95, and no more; 5. The annual depreciation of plaintiff's plant is three and one-third per cent per annum; 6. The rates as fixed by the ordinance for the year commencing July 1, 1890, were not just or reasonable, and were grossly oppressive, unjust, and unreasonable.

Owing to the fact that the case was not brought to trial in the lower court until the year had expired covered by the ordinance, [578] it will be observed that the court was enabled to find the actual receipts to the plaintiff from rate payers during that period. In the discussion of the questions presented by this appeal, we shall assume that the findings of the court, to the effect that the water plant of the plaintiff corporation was of the value of $750,000, and that its operating expenses for the year would be and were $40,000, have support in the evidence and stand as facts on the record.

In the fixing of water rates by a city, as contemplated by the constitution, it is evident that the valuation of the plant is the basic element upon which the whole investigation rests. The original cost of construction is simply an item to be considered in fixing the present valuation. It is a circumstance, strong or weak, entering into the final conclusion of the municipality upon the question. But as to the amount of the bonded indebtedness, or the amount of interest annually accruing thereon, we fail to see their materiality in determining the value of the plant, or the sum total of revenue to be raised from the sales of water. It is not a question in which rate payers are concerned, whether the water company has no outstanding indebtedness, or is floundering under a bonded debt which threatens to sink it at any moment. If the municipality is required to establish a scale of rates which will produce a revenue sufficient to pay interest upon outstanding bonds, this provision of the constitution would not only be a perpetual guaranty to the bondholders for the payment of their annual interest, but a constant incentive to additional issues of bonds. Such conditions were never contemplated by anybody. It is the duty of the municipality, when it has arrived at a determination as to the valuation of the plant, to determine the necessary outlay for the ensuing year; then to determine what would be a reasonable, just, and fair compensation to the company, based upon the valuation of the plant, and thereupon to fix a schedule of rates which will produce that sum of money. If there be outstanding bonds, the company may apply its income to the payment of interest thereon. If there be no outstanding bonds, this income may pass to the pockets of the stockholders in the shape of dividends declared. A municipality must fix a fair and just rate for the water, based upon the valuation of the plant, and when it has done this, its duty has been performed, and the revenue collected [579] under such rates is the property of the company, to do with as it seems best.

Under and pursuant to constitutional authority (Const., art. 14, secs. 1, 2), the legislature (Stats. 1881, p. 54) passed an act, by the terms of which it was made the duty of the board of supervisors, town council, board of aldermen, or other legislative body, of any city and county, city, or town, in the month of February of each year to fix the rates which shall be charged and collected by any person, association, company, or corporation for water furnished to any such city and county, or city or town, or the inhabitants thereof. It is now contended by appellant that the authority to fix water rates, coming directly from the constitution to the municipality, the rates fixed under such authority have the same binding force and effect, and occupy the same position as to the law and the courts, and should receive the same consideration as though fixed directly by the legislature, in the absence of the aforesaid constitutional provisions. Let it be conceded, still the claim is unsound that this action of the municipality is conclusive; it is neither above nor beyond the law, and a court of equity will reach out and review it whenever the facts so demand. The legislature itself has no right or power to legislate a man's property away from him, and, beyond doubt, courts are vested with jurisdiction to declare all such attempts void, and will exercise that jurisdiction whenever the occasion presents itself.

The legislature of the state of Minnesota enacted that the rates for freights and fares fixed by the railroad commission of that state should be conclusively presumed to be reasonable. In Chicago etc. Ry. Co. v. Minnesota, 134 U. S. 418, this enactment was declared void, as depriving a person of his property without due process of law, the court saying: "If the company is deprived of the power of charging reasonable rates for the use of its property, and such deprivation takes place in the absence of an investigation by judicial machinery, it is deprived of the lawful use of its property, and thus, in substance and effect, of the property itself, without due process of law, and in violation of the constitution of the United States; and, in so far as it is thus deprived, while other persons are permitted to receive reasonable profits upon their invested capital, the company is deprived of the equal protection of the law." Again, it is [580] said in Stone v. Farmers' Loan etc. Co., 116 U. S. 307: "From what has thus been said it is not to be inferred that this power or limitation or regulation is itself without limit. This power to regulate is not a power to destroy, and limitation is not the equivalent of confiscation. Under pretense of regulating freights and fares, the state cannot require a railroad corporation to carry persons or property without reward; neither can it do that which in law amounts to a taking of private property for public use, without just compensation or without due process of law." The same doctrine is also declared in Georgia etc. Banking Co. v. Smith, 128 U. S. 174; Budd v. New York, 143 U. S. 517; Reagan v. Farmers' Loan etc. Co., 154 U. S. 362; St. Louis etc. Ry. Co. v. Gill, 156 U. S. 649. As far as we are given light to see, from the consideration of the doctrine enunciated by the many cases

coming from the highest court of the land, it would appear
to be immaterial whether this power to fix a schedule of rates
is vested in the legislature, or delegated by the legislature to
some inferior board or tribunal, or given to such board or tribunal by direct grant from the constitution. Whether it be done
by the express act of the legislature, or by council or commission, under authority from a higher power, or whether the act
of such council or commission in fixing rates be judicial or legislative, are matters outside the question. If we understand the
doctrine declared by the highest judicial tribunal, it is that the
courts have no power to declare rates fixed by the body legally
authorized so to do unreasonable, unless those rates are so unreasonable and oppressive as to deprive a party of the equal protection of the law, and result in a practical confiscation of his
property. And when any attempt is made to despoil the owner
of his property, it is the highest duty of a court of equity under
the constitution to afford him shelter and protection.

In Spring Valley Water Works v. San Francisco, 82 Cal. 306,
16 Am. St. Rep. 116, an exact duplicate of the present question
was before this court, and it is there said: "But the courts cannot, after the board has fully and fairly investigated and acted
by fixing what it believes to be reasonable rates, step in and
say its action shall be set aside and nullified because the courts,
upon a similar investigation, have come to a different conclusion
as to the reasonableness of the rates fixed. There must be actual [581] fraud in fixing the rates, or they must be so palpably and
grossly unreasonable and unjust as to amount to the same thing."
Aside from any question of actual fraud, rates that are so unreasonable and unjust as to deprive the owner of any revenue whatever from his property would amount in law to fraud upon his
rights under the constitution. In disposing of appellant's contention that the schedule of rates fixed by the city council is
conclusive upon the court, we have also disposed of respondent's
contention that the law giving to the city the right to fix water
rates is violative of the constitution of the United States, as
depriving a man of his property without a hearing before a judicial tribunal. Both positions are equally erroneous.

This court is not here to declare what are reasonable rates.
The constitution has vested that power and duty in the council
of the city of San Diego, and the exercise of that power by the
council cannot be questioned by the courts unless constitutional
rights are violated. The question is not, What rate would this
court fix if the duty were cast upon it of fixing rates? but rather,

Will the owners of the plant be deprived of constitutional rights
by an enforcement of the order of the council fixing rates? If
the rate fixed by a municipal council was twice too large, I know
not what jurisdiction of this court could be invoked to right the
wrong. Hence, it is apparent that it is only in exceptional cases
that an order fixing rates may be set aside by judicial decree.

Taking the findings of fact as they stand, the schedule of rates
fixed by the city should not be disturbed. The valuation of the
plant is $750,000; the operating and current expenses are $40,-
000. The revenue from the sale of water under the schedule of
rates would be and actually was $65,000. This leaves a profit of
$25,000 upon the investment. To be sure it is small, when we
consider the amount of money invested. To be sure, it is not
enough, and possibly not one-half the sum that could be earned
if that amount of money was invested in other business undertakings, but with these things we have nothing to do. Those
are matters passed upon by the city in the exercise of a discretion granted by the constitution, and its decision as to the reasonableness of the amount of revenue to be derived by the company from the rates is conclusive upon the courts. While this
sum is not enough upon this character of investment, still it is
three and one-half per cent, and such return is a substantial
582 profit. We mean it is so substantial that a court of equity, in
view of the law of the land, cannot say that the rates are so
unreasonable as to be confiscatory in character, and thus violative of any principle of constitutional law.

Mr. Justice Brewer of the supreme court of the United States
has probably given this question more thought and investigation
than any other jurist in this country, and he says in Chicago
etc. Ry. Co. v. Dey, 35 Fed. Rep. 866: "Counsel for complainant
urge that the lowest rates the legislature may establish must
be such as will secure to the owners of the railroad property
a profit on their investment at least equal to the lowest current rate of interest, say three per cent. Decisions of the supreme court seem to forbid such a limit to the power of the
legislature in respect to that which they apparently recognize
as a right of the owners of the railroad property to some reward;
and the right of judicial interference exists only when the schedule of rates established will fail to secure to the owners of the
property some compensation or income from their investment.
As to the amount of such compensation, if some compensation
or reward is in fact secured, the legislature is the sole judge."
Subsequently, the same question was again presented to him

in Reagan v. Farmers' Loan etc. Co., 154 U. S. 362, and also in Ames v. Union Pac. Ry. Co., 64 Fed. Rep. 165, and in those cases neither he nor any other of the justices of the supreme court retreated or advanced from that position.

This balance of $25,000 is profit, unless it is swallowed up by the finding of the court that plaintiff's plant suffered an annual depreciation of three and one-half per cent, and the conclusion of law therefrom that a percentage upon the investment to that amount should be added to the operating expenses before the point is reached where profit begins. We are satisfied that this finding has no support in the evidence, even conceding the conclusion of law drawn therefrom sound. In the first place, the evidence develops that there can be no general depreciation of this plant as a whole. There are tunnels, wells, reservoirs, water rights and real estate, amounting to more than one-half of the valuation of the plant. There is no depreciation of these things; there is no wear and tear, no permanent and gradual destruction by use and age. Most of them stand as everlasting as the hills.

583 The theory of plaintiff in this regard seems to be that the life of a plant of this character may be approximated at thirty years, and that a sinking fund of one-thirtieth of its value should be collected from the rate payers annually and laid aside to be handed to the stockholders upon the sad occasion of its demise, as an alleviating salve to their sorrow. But such a thing is all wrong, for it results in the consumers of water buying the plant and paying for it in annual installments. Consumers of water cannot be charged with cost of construction. They are only to pay a fair interest upon such cost; and as we look at this matter, if this three and one-half per cent is not stowed away in the vaults as a sinking fund to make glad the hearts of the stockholders upon the expiration of the thirty years, which theory cannot be tolerated for a moment, then it must go into the plant as cost of construction, and, therefore, not chargeable against the consumers. The result of such expenditure is only to increase the valuation of the plant, and to thereby draw from the consumers an income upon the amount of the investment. If improvements are made in the plant, the cost of these improvements should be charged against the construction account. If repairs are made upon the plant as it stands, as, for example, a new pipe substituted for an old piece of the same size and quality, such charge should be considered operating expenses.

Upon an examination of the record we find these views fully

corroborated in the evidence of the water company, given by
one of its most important witnesses. He testified: "Where we
took up one pipe line or a portion of it on the street, and put
down another, if it was the same size pipe, to renew it we would
charge it to expenses. If it was a different size we would charge
the difference between them, the increased size, to construction.
Where we sell pipe that we take up, we credit that to construction. If we have to renew any portion of the same size pipe, we
charge it to expenses."

This question has arisen incidentally in Union Pac. R. R. Co.
v. United States, 99 U. S. 402, and also in Reagan v. Farmers'
Loan etc. Co., 154 U. S. 362, but neither case looks the other way
from the views we have expressed. When the question arises between the corporation upon the one side and its bondholders or
stockholders upon the other, or when it arises upon a construction of a contract with the government, as in one of the cases
just cited, [584] operating expenses, cost of construction, and net
earnings may stand upon a different footing. Those cases are
not this case. This is neither a question of bookkeeping nor
net earnings. The particular system pursued by corporations in
segregating and applying their gross receipts is likewise immaterial. The whole matter is a pure question of what is just and
right between all parties interested. The consumers of water
have rights, and possess equities which must be considered equally with those of the company. They are to be taxed to pay the
amount called for by the schedule of rates, and these rates, in
justice to them, should be fixed at the smallest possible amount,
taking into consideration what is just and equitable to the owners
of the property. In cases of the present character under the head
of operating expenses the company is entitled to charge for keeping the plant in its normal condition; and the sinking of new
wells, the building of new reservoirs, the erection of additional
buildings, and the substitution of larger and better pipe (to the
extent of the difference), do not come under the head of operating expenses, but should be charged to construction account.
If this were not so, a water plant inferior in all things in a few
years could be transformed into a water plant superior in everything, at the expense of the consumer. This would be an advantage to the owner and a burden to the rate payer neither
contemplated nor justified by the law.

For the foregoing reasons I think the judgment and order
should be reversed and the cause remanded.

TEMPLE, J., concurring. I agree generally in the views expressed by Mr. Justice Garoutte. I do not comprehend how in this case the exercise of the power to regulate charges or to fix compensation for furnishing water is a taking within the meaning of section 14, article I, of the constitution. The waterworks were all constructed subsequent to the adoption of the constitution of 1879. The city owns no waterworks. It is provided in section 19, article XI, of the constitution that any individual or company shall have the use of the streets, for laying down pipes and conduits and making connections therewith, so far as necessary for introducing into and supplying the city and the inhabitants with fresh water, "upon the condition that the municipal government shall have the right to regulate the charges **585** thereof." The corporation, therefore, constructed its works and invested every dollar of its capital upon this express condition. The privilege of distributing water for pay is a franchise which might have been withheld altogether. It is really a privilege granted to a private individual to perform a public service for pay. It is granted to all upon this express reservation of the right to regulate charges.

Article XIV is the complement to the section before quoted. It declares that the use of all water appropriated for sale or distribution is a public use, subject to the control of the state, and that in cities the "rates or compensation" shall be fixed annually by the governing body of such city, which rates shall continue in force for one year only, and, further, that any individual or company collecting water rates otherwise than as so established shall forfeit his or its franchise and works to the city.

There is here no taking under the power of eminent domain, nor in any other sense than is implied in every service rendered for hire.

There is, then, no obligation to remunerate water companies for investments made or to allow interest thereon, either upon first cost or present value. The obligation is to compensate for service rendered. What will constitute just compensation involves many considerations. Certainly, no allowance need be made for unnecessary expenditures, either in construction or management. Nor is the test always the cost to the companies. There is no limit to the number of companies which may bring water into a city. The franchise is freely offered to all in the constitution. If there are many companies, and thereby the cost of management is increased, this fact would not call for in-

creased rates. The service is worth no more when rendered by
ten companies than when one company furnishes all the water.
Incidentally to the inquiry as to what is a fair compensation for
the service, the governing board may well inquire into the cost
which the company whose rates are to be regulated have incurred
in bringing water to the city and in distributing it. But these
matters are merely incidental and never determinative of the
question.

All the elements entering into the question having been determined, opinions would still vary as to what would be fair compensation. The constitution has imposed upon the governing ^{586}
body of the city the duty of determining that question, and
granted the privilege of the streets and the franchise to distribute
water upon the express condition that such boards may determine the question. As already shown, the works have been constructed under this express agreement. The court cannot fix
the rates—is, in fact, expressly prohibited by the letter of the
constitution from so doing. The company will forfeit its franchise and property if it collects rates "otherwise than as so established." This prohibits them from collecting charges as fixed
by the courts. The only proper judicial question is, whether
compensating rates have been fixed. Whether they are too high
or too low is not a judicial question. The judge cannot substitute his judgment for that of the body to whom the discretion
is given by the constitution.

There is much learning upon this subject in the law books, and
a great variety of opinions, not to say contrariety, can be found.
I know of none which—the facts considered—need be deemed
adverse to these views. If there were no such constitutional provisions, the case might be different.

I notice that section 19, article 11, applies only to cities which
own no public works. Whether the privilege of using the streets
or the right to distribute and sell water exists or can exist in
cities which do own such works may be a question. If they do
exist, there can be no doubt of the application of article XIV to
persons or corporations selling water in such cities. In such
cases could the city be compelled to take and pay for other works
which only diminish the value of its own property?

HARRISON, J., concurring. I concur in the reversal of the
judgment and order of the superior court. In finding the value
as well as the cost of the plant the court included many items
which were not proper to be considered for that purpose, and

which are mentioned in the opinion of Mr. Justice Van Fleet as improperly constituting a part of the cost of the plant. While the cost of the plant may be properly considered as an element of evidence in ascertaining its value, I am clearly of opinion that it should not form the basis of estimating the revenue which the water company is entitled to receive. The value of the plant may change from year to year as materially as may the cost of operating the works, and there is good reason for holding that [587] the constitution requires the rates to be fixed each year, in order that they may be adjusted to this changing of value. It is not necessary here to lay down a rule which shall be applicable to all conceivable conditions, since the conditions governing in one municipality, or attending the supply of water to its inhabitants, will hardly ever be the same elsewhere, and it is only proper in the present case to consider the circumstances attending the water company and the municipality now before the court.

In designating the city council as the body to fix these rates the constitution has clearly indicated that they are not to be fixed by the courts. The water company has the right to protection by the judiciary from the enforcement of such rates as will deprive it of compensation for furnishing the water; but if the rates fixed by the council afford compensation to the water company, the question of the reasonableness of this compensation is a question of fact which is not open to review by the courts. If the courts are authorized to determine the amount of compensation which will be reasonable, the rates will be fixed by them, rather than by the city council; and, for the same reason, the city council, and not the courts, are authorized to determine whether the rates, to be reasonable, shall be fixed at such amount as will yield to the water company any definite rate of interest.

Even if it should be conceded that reasonable rates would be such as will yield to the water company a return equal to the lowest current rate of interest on the value of its property, it appears from the findings of the court that the rates fixed herein yielded a return of more than three per cent upon the value of the plant, and it is a matter of general notoriety that this is more than is on an average received by capitalists from permanent or fixed investments with the guaranty of the government as their security. What may be the lowest current rate of interest upon an investment depends upon so many circumstances that no particular rate can be predicated in advance of any particular investment, but it is in all instances a question of fact and

not of law, and is not to be determined by the judiciary. After
it has been determined by the city council, the judiciary are not
authorized to set aside its determination on the ground that in
its judgment it is too small, any more than it could set aside
[588] the rates on the ground that the income yielded thereby
would be too great.

BEATTY, C. J., dissenting. I think the judgment and order
appealed from should be affirmed. In fixing water rates, it is
the duty of the city council to provide for a just and reasonable
compensation to the water company. Anything short of that
is simple confiscation, and is not only a violation of constitutional rights, but is an extremely short-sighted policy. Rates
ought to be adjusted to the value of the service rendered, and this
means that the water companies should be allowed to collect annually a gross income sufficient to pay current expenses, maintain the necessary plant in a state of efficiency, and declare a
dividend to stockholders equal to at least the lowest current
rates of interest, not on the par or market value of the stock,
but on the actual value of the property necessarily used in providing and distributing the water to consumers.

To arrive at the actual value of the plant, water rights, real
estate, etc., cost is an element to be considered, but is not conclusive. The plant may have cost too much, it may have been
planned upon too liberal a scale, its construction may have been
extravagantly managed, the real estate and water rights may
have cost less or more than their present value, and, therefore,
cost will seldom represent the actual capital at present invested
in the works, but such present value is the true basis upon which
compensation, in the shape of dividends, is to be allowed.

As to current expenses, all operating expenses reasonably and
properly incurred should be allowed, taxes should be allowed,
and the cost of current repairs.

In addition to this, if there is any part of the plant, such as
main pipes, etc., which at the end of a term of years—twenty
years, for instance—will be so decayed and worn out as to require restoration, an annual allowance should be made for a
sinking fund sufficient to replace such part of the plant when it
is worn out.

In its findings and conclusions the superior court seems to have
conformed to these views, and, making every allowance for any
minor errors that may appear in the record, the evidence is

amply sufficient to sustain every material finding, and the findings [559] clearly sustain the conclusion that in this case the rates fixed were grossly and palpably unjust to the water company.

The judgment and order should be affirmed.

The Evolution and Diminution of Munn v. Illinois.

The decision in the principal case naturally presents the question of what remains of the law as declared in Munn v. Illinois, 94 U. S. 113, Chicago etc. R. R. v. Iowa, 94 U. S. 155, and Peik v. Chicago etc. R. R. Co., 94 U. S. 165, and the further, and, perhaps, more important question of how shall the courts apply the residuum to the controversies which may be presented to them? As that case was understood when decided, and for some years afterward, it was not regarded as second in importance to any ever determined by our courts, whether state or national, and was looked upon by one class of citizens as substantially destroying, or, at all events, as inviting the destruction of, property rights of almost incalculable value, and by another and more numerous class as affording a shield against unjust oppression and discrimination. Subsequent judicial history will show that the fears of the one class and the hopes of the other were unnecessarily and unduly excited. The essential elements of the decision as at first understood and as we should still understand it but for the explanations given by the court which pronounced it, were: 1. That "when private property is affected with a public interest, it ceases to be juris priviti"; 2. That it is "clothed with a public interest when used in a manner to make it of public consequence and affect the community at large," and that when "one devotes his property to a public use in which the public has an interest, he, in effect, grants to the public an interest in that use, and must submit to be controlled by the public for the common good to the extent of the interest thus granted"; 3. That while he may be entitled to a reasonable compensation for his property or services in such public use, the question of what is a reasonable compensation is one for the determination of the legislature or of such bodies as the authority to make the determination may be delegated to either by state constitutions or legislatures.

A little less than a quarter of a century has passed since these propositions were first judicially announced by the national courts. In that interval further judicial consideration has confirmed the first and second of them, while it has, we think, substantially impaired the third, and, by such impairment, has reduced the importance of the others to comparative insignificance. Hence it is that, in considering such questions as now arise involving the topics discussed in Munn v. Illinois, it is cited for the purpose of explaining and limiting its doctrines more frequently than of applying them rigidly to the case in hand, and in many of the decisions, and notably in the opinions of the judges in the principal case, the original and leading case upon the subject is not even mentioned.

Nothing decided since Munn v. Illinois has, however, tended to weaken the conclusions therein announced as to the classes of property which may be deemed affected by a public use, nor as to the authority of the state to regulate such use by preventing unjust discrimination nor by prescribing maximum rates of charges which may be collected for services rendered by persons or property employed in such use. Thus, in perhaps the most recent opinion upon this subject, it is said that "It cannot be doubted that the making of rates for transportation by railroad corporations along a public highway, between points wholly within the limits of a state, is a subject primarily within the control of the state. And it ought not to be supposed that Congress intended that, so long as it forbore to establish rates that the Union Pacific Railroad, the corporation itself, could fix such rates for transportation as it saw proper independently of the rights of the states through which the road was constructed to provide regulations for transportation beginning and ending within their respective limits": Smyth v. Ames, 169 U. S. 521; Budd v. New York, 143 U. S. 517; Spring Valley W. W. v. Schottler, 110 U. S. 347; Davis v. State, 68 Ala. 58; 44 Am. Rep. 128; Hockett v. State, 105 Ind. 250; 55 Am. Rep. 201; Central etc. Co. v. Bradbury, 106 Ind. 1; Central etc. Co. v. State, 118 Ind. 194; 10 Am. St. Rep. 114; Chesapeake etc. Co. v. Baltimore etc. Co., 66 Md. 399; 59 Am. Rep. 167; People v. Budd, 117 N. Y. 1; 15 Am. St. Rep. 460; Railway v. Railway, 30 Ohio St. 616; Zanesville v. Gas Light Co., 47 Ohio St. 1; Baker v. State, 54 Wis. 368.

As to the businesses which may be the subject of state regulation, because affected by a public use, we believe that the general rules stated in Munn v. Illinois have not been in any respect modified. Among these businesses are those of conducting grain elevators: Stewart v. Great Northern Ry., 65 Minn. 517; People v. Budd, 117 N. Y. 1; 15 Am. St. Rep. 460; street railways: Buffalo etc. Ry. Co. v. Buffalo etc. Ry. Co., 111 N. Y. 132; public warehouses: Nash v. Page, 80 Ky. 539; 44 Am. Rep. 490; Brass v. North Dakota, 153 U. S. 391; supplying patrons with or sending messages by telephones: Hackett v. State, 105 Ind. 250; 55 Am. Rep. 201; Central etc. Co. v. State, 118 Ind. 194; 10 Am. St. Rep. 114, and note; all classes of common carriers: Georgia R. R. Co. v. Smith, 128 U. S. 174; Railroad Co. v. Commissioners, 79 Me. 386; telegraph companies and corporations: Western Union Tel. Co. v. Pendleton, 95 Ind. 12; 48 Am. Rep. 692; gristmills: Burlington v. Beasley, 94 U. S. 310; Olmstead v. Camp, 33 Conn. 532; 89 Am. Dec. 221; State v. Edwards, 86 Me. 105; 41 Am. St. Rep. 528; hacks: Lindsay v. Mayor, 104 Ala. 261; 53 Am. St. Rep. 44; Veneman v. Jones, 118 Ind. 41; 10 Am. St. Rep. 100; public wharves: Chicago etc. Co. v. Garrity, 115 Ill. 155; Barrington v. Dock Co., 15 Wash. 175; hotels: Bostick v. State, 47 Ark. 126; theaters and other public places of amusement: Civil Rights cases, 109 U. S. 3; People v. King, 110 N. Y. 418; 6 Am. St. Rep. 389; companies formed for the purpose of supplying the public with gas: State v. Columbus etc. Co., 34 Ohio St. 572; 32 Am. Rep. 390; or water: Spring Valley W. W. v. Schottler, 110 U. S. 347; Wheeler v. Northern etc. Co., 10 Colo.

582; 3 Am. St. Rep. 603; White v. Canal Co., 22 Colo. 198; American
W. W. v. State, 46 Neb. 194; 50 Am. St. Rep. 610; and boards of trade
engaged in the business of collecting and furnishing to the public
reports and quotations of market prices: Stock Exchange v. Board
of Trade, 127 Ill. 153; 11 Am. St. Rep. 107; stockyard companies
receiving, yarding, and feeding livestock, and making sales thereof,
for the owners: Cotting v. Kansas City etc. Co., 82 Fed. Rep. 839.

In truth, it is only with respect to the right to conclusively fix
rates of charges and to enforce such regulations as may be held to
interfere with interstate commerce that the doctrine of Munn v.
Illinois has been substantially modified.   Under its influence, a great
mass of legislation has been enacted for the regulation of common
carriers and others engaged in businesses affected by a public use
for the purpose of preventing unjust discrimination and of compelling them to discharge their duties to the public with greater
promptness and efficiency, and to observe rules promulgated by the
state acting directly through its legislature or by some subordinate
body to which the legislative authority has been delegated, and intended, and reasonably designed, to promote the public welfare or
that of their employés or patrons or any other considerable class of
the community.   Legislation of this class has rarely been assailed,
and when assailed, has been generally, if not universally, sustained:
Louisville etc. Co. v. Hall, 87 Ala. 708; 13 Am. St. Rep. 84; Galena
etc. Co. v. Loomis, 13 Ill. 548; 56 Am. Dec. 471; Illinois etc. Co. v.
Slater, 129 Ill. 91; 16 Am. St. Rep. 242; Burdick v. People, 149 Ill.
600; 41 Am. St. Rep. 329; Central etc. Co. v. State, 118 Ind. 194; 10
Am. St. Rep. 114, and note; Louisville etc. Co..v. State, 66 Miss. 662;
14 Am. St. Rep. 599; Union etc. Co. v. Rasmussen, 25 Neb. 810; 13 Am.
St. Rep. 527; State v. Republican etc. R. R. Co., 17 Neb. 647; 52 Am.
Rep. 424; People v. Squires, 107 N. Y. 593; 1 Am. St. Rep. 893;
State v. Telephone Co., 36 Ohio St. 296; 38 Am. Rep. 583; Campbell
v. Cook, 86 Tex. 630; 40 Am. St. Rep. 878; Nashville etc. Co. v. Ala-
bama, 128 U. S. 96; Missouri etc. R. Co. v. Mackey, 127 U. S. 205;
New York etc. Co. v. Squire, 145 U. S. 175; New York etc. Co. v.
Bristol, 151 U. S. 556.

The authority which, according to the decision in Munn v. Illinois,
resides in the state to fix rates of charges need not be directly exercised by the state legislature.   It may be delegated by the state constitution or by general laws to some commission or to some local
board or tribunal, and when so delegated, the action of such commission, board, or tribunal is, as we understand the decisions, as
efficient and conclusive as if the action had been taken directly by
the legislature: Georgia R. R. v. Smith, 70 Ga. 694; 128 U. S. 174;
Chicago etc. R. R. v. Jones, 149 Ill. 380; 41 Am. St. Rep. 278; Railroad Commrs. v. Grocer Co., 53 Kan. 212; Clyde v. Richmond etc.
R. R., 57 Fed. Rep. 439; Railroad Commission cases, 116 U. S. 307.   It
is true that there are decisions from which the inference might
justly be drawn that there is a material difference between the action of a state legislature and that of some body to which had been
delegated the power and duty of fixing rates of charges; that the

rates fixed by the former might be made conclusive, while those fixed by the latter could be prima facie evidence only of·the reasonableness of charges authorized to be collected: Budd v. New York, 143 U. S. 517; Chicago etc. Co. v. Minnesota, 134 U. S. 418. We shall, however, hereafter show that the inconclusiveness thus attributed to the decision of a commission or other subordinate board or tribunal is equally attributable to the direct action of the state legislature.

The rule as at first applied respecting the authority of the state to fix rates of charges was explicit and of a terrible simplicity. It was in substance that, as to those businesses or employments affected by a public use, it was competent for the state, or some commission or board to which it had delegated its authority, to fix the maximum rates which might be charged for services rendered, and it was the duty of the persons carrying on the business or employment to render services for the rate so fixed, and the only escape from this duty was to abandon the business. Let us see what is said upon this subject in Munn v. Illinois, 94 U. S. 133, in response to the contention that the question of reasonableness was a judicial question to be determined by the courts: "As has already been shown, the practice has been otherwise. In countries where the common law prevails, it has been customary from time immemorial for the legislature to declare what shall be a reasonable compensation under such circumstances, or, perhaps more properly speaking, to fix a maximum beyond which any charge would be unreasonable. Undoubtedly, in mere private contracts, relating to matters in which the public has no interest, what is reasonable must be ascertained judicially. But this is because the legislature has no control over such a contract. So, too, in matters which do affect the public interest, and as to which legislative control may be exercised, if there are no statutory regulations upon the subject, the courts must determine what is reasonable. The controlling fact is the power to regulate at all. If that exists, the right to establish the maximum of charge, as one of the means of regulation, is implied. In fact, the common-law rule, which requires the charge to be reasonable, is itself a regulation as to price. Without it the owner could make his rates at will and compel the public to yield to his terms, or forego the use. But a mere common-law regulation of trade or business may be changed by statute. A person has no property, no vested interest, in any rule of the common law. That is only one of the forms of municipal law, and is no more sacred than any other. Rights of property which have been created by the common law cannot be taken away without due process; but the law itself, as a rule of conduct, may be changed at the will, or even at the whim, of the legislature, unless prevented by constitutional limitations. Indeed, the great office of statutes is to remedy defects in the common law as they are developed, and to adapt it to the changes of time and circumstances. To limit the rate of charges for services rendered in a public employment, or for the use of property in which the public has an interest, is only changing a regulation which existed before. It establishes no new principle in the law, but only gives a new effect to an old one. We know that this is a power which may be abused; but that is no argument against its existence. For protection against abuses by legislatures the people must resort to the polls, not to the courts." In the case of Peik v. Chicago etc. R. R. Co., 94 U. S. 178, the same court said: "As to the claim that courts must decide what is reasonable, and not the legislature. This is not new to this case. It has been fully considered in Munn v. Illinois. Where property has been clothed with a public interest, the legislature may fix a limit to that which shall in law be reasonable for its use. This limit binds the courts as well as the people. If it has been improperly fixed, the legislature, not the courts, must be appealed to for the change." Surely, in the face of this language, no other action could be anticipated by the subordinate courts, whether state or national, than that they should unhesitatingly affirm that the question of whether charges were reasonable or not was one committed to the legislature for decision, and that he who happened to be injured by its determination could not successfully claim that he had been deprived of his property without due process of law: Chicago etc. Co. v. Jones, 149 Ill. 361; 41 Am. St. Rep. 278; American Coal Co. v. Consolidated Coal Co., 46 Md. 15; Wellman v. Chicago etc. Co., 83 Mich. 592; Tilley v. Savannah Co., 4 Woods, 449; Tilley v. Savannah etc. R. R., 5 Fed. Rep. 641.

In still another respect the language of the court in the earlier opinions could hardly be otherwise than misunderstood if the court had in mind only what it has affirmed upon the subject in subsequent decisions. We refer to the question, whether the action of a state, in fixing rates of charges, could be applied to business involving interstate commerce. In Chicago etc. R. R. v. Iowa, 94 U. S. 155, 163, a state statute was assailed partly on the ground that it might be deemed applicable to such commerce, and amount to a regulation thereof, as the road seeking to escape from the statute was engaged in interstate as well as state commerce. The court answered: "The objection that the statute complained of is void because it amounts to a regulation of commerce among the states has been sufficiently considered in the case of Munn v. Illinois. This road, like the warehouse in that case, is situated within the limits of a single state. Its business is carried on there, and its regulation is a matter of domestic concern. It is employed in state as well as interstate commerce, and, until Congress acts, the state must be permitted to adopt such rules and regulations as may be necessary for the promotion of the general welfare of the people within its own jurisdiction, even though, in so doing, those without may be indirectly affected." At the same term the court, in an opinion written by the same judge, employed language still more emphatic, as follows: "As to the effect of the statute as a regulation of interstate commerce. The law is confined to state commerce, or such interstate commerce as directly affects the people of Wisconsin. Until Congress acts in reference to the relations of this company to interstate commerce, it is certainly within the power of Wisconsin to regulate its fares. etc., so far as they are of domestic concern. With the people of Wisconsin this company has domestic relations. Incidentally, these may reach beyond the state. But certainly, until Congress undertakes to legislate for those who are without the state, Wisconsin may provide for those within, even though it may indirectly affect those without": Peik v. Chicago etc. R. R. Co., 94 U. S. 177. Subsequently, however, it was explained that in the case in which this language had been used the question to which it had been addressed had not received adequate consideration; that the main question in those cases had been respecting "the right of the state to establish any limitation upon the power of railroad companies to fix the price at which they would carry passengers and freight"; that the importance of this question overshadowed all others and prevented them from receiving special or due consideration. When the question was again presented, it was not overshadowed by others. There may be doubt whether or not it was better or more thoroughly considered than in the preceding cases, but there can be no doubt that the conclusions reached were irreconcilable with those which the same court had a decade previously affirmed apparently after thorough argument and long deliberation. The new rule is, that as to transportation which does not begin and end in the same state, any regulation of it involves a regulation of interstate commerce, and further that such regulation by a state cannot be permitted, though Congress has not chosen to act. "When it is attempted to apply to transportation through an entire series of states a principle of this kind, and each one of the states shall attempt to establish its own rates of transportation, its own methods to prevent discrimination in rates, or to permit it, the deleterious influence upon the freedom of commerce among the states and upon the transit of goods through those states cannot be overestimated. That this species of regulation is one which must be, if established at all, of a general and national character, and cannot be safely and wisely remitted to local rules and local regulations, we think is clear from what has already been said. And if it be a regulation of commerce, as we think we have demonstrated it is, and as the Illinois court concedes it to be, it must be of that national character, and the regulation can only appropriately exist by general rules and principles, which demand that it should be done by the Congress of the United States under the commerce clause of the constitution": Wabash etc. Ry. v. Illinois, 118 U. S. 557, 577.

Whatever may have been the inference irresistibly arising from the language of the opinions in the earlier cases in the national courts affirming that the question of the reasonableness of rates charged was a legislative question, it is now well settled that this language must be understood in connection with limitations interposed by the national constitution, and especially the one denying the right of a state to deprive any person of property without due process of law. The states may still, by the action of their legislatures or of a commission or board given authority over the subject, fix maximum rates of charges. These rates are as applicable to corporations existing before as to those created after they were made. We doubt whether it is possible for a state by any charter granted by it to a corporation, or by any contract made by it, to deprive itself of its right to exercise this power. It is, at all events, certain that nothing short of the most explicit language will be construed as an agreement on its part not to exercise this sovereign right, and that no corporate charter has yet been presented for judicial consideration which has proved any adequate obstacle to such exercise: Dow v Beidelman, 49 Ark. 325; Georgia etc. R. R. v. Smith, 70 Ga. 694; 128 U. S. 174; Stock Exchange v. Board of Trade, 127 Ill. 153; 11 Am. St. Rep. 107; Rushville v. Rushville etc. Co., 132 Ind. 575; State v. Gas Co., 34 Ohio St. 572; 32 Am. Rep. 390; Chicago etc. R. R. v. Iowa, 94 U. S. 155; Winona etc. R. R. v. Blake, 94 U. S. 180; Louisville etc. R. R. v. Kentucky, 161 U. S. 695. Where a claim was made that the charter of a corporation exempted it from the authority of the state to fix maximum rates of charges for services rendered by such corporation, the court referred to the rules maintained by it when the claim was made that a state had granted exemption from taxation, among which was, that it was a "salutary rule of interpretation, founded upon obvious public policy, which regards such exemption as in derogation of the sovereign authority and of common right, and therefore not to be extended beyond the exact and explicit requirements of the grant construed strictissimus juris"; and added: "The same principles should be recognized when the claim is of immunity or exemption from the legislative control of tolls to be exacted by a corporation established by authority of law for the construction of a public highway. It is of the highest importance that such control should remain with the state, and it should never be implied that the legislative department intended to surrender it. Such an intention should not be imputed to the legislature, if it be possible to avoid doing so by any reasonable interpretation of its statutes. It is as vital that the state should retain its control of tolls upon the public highways as it is that it should not surrender or fetter its power of taxation": Covington etc. Co. v. Sandford, 164 U. S. 587.

Perhaps the conduct of a board authorized to fix rates of charges may be the subject of examination for the purpose of ascertaining whether its members have acted fraudulently or arbitrarily or with manifest intent to disregard the obligations imposed on them by their official station and to fix the rates in question irrespective of their reasonableness or unreasonableness, and where such conduct is established, perhaps it may furnish a sufficient reason for enjoining the proposed action or of refusing to give effect to action already taken: Spring Valley W. W. Co. v. San Francisco, 82 Cal. 286; 16 Am. St. Rep. 116; San Diego etc. Co. v. San Diego, 118 Cal. 556; ante, p. 261. Otherwise it still clear that the rates fixed must be regarded as prima facie reasonable, that the state may delegate to a commission or other body the power to establish rates which shall be deemed prima facie evidence of their own reasonableness: McWhorter v. Pensacola etc. Co., 24 Fla. 417; 12 Am. St. Rep. 220; Chicago etc. Co. v. Jones, 149 Ill. 361; 41 Am. St. Rep. 278; Burlington etc. Co. v. Dey, 82 Iowa, 312; 31 Am. St. Rep. 477; Chicago etc. Co. v. Dey, 35 Fed. Rep. 866;

and that a person or corporation resisting the action of the state legislature, or any other body having jurisdiction to act, must assume the burden of proving that the action complained of is so unreasonable that to give it effect will be to deprive the resistant of his property without due process of law: Pensacola etc. Co. v. State, 25 Fla. 310; Budd v. New York, 143 U. S. 517.

That a state may, by any means, so fix its rates of charges that its action shall be conclusive upon the persons and corporations subject thereto must now be denied.   Its authority is to fix reasonable rates, and it cannot enforce them if proved or admitted to be unjust or unreasonable: Wheeler v. Irrigation Co., 10 Colo. 582; 3 Am. St. Rep. 602; Chicago etc. R. R. v. Jones, 149 Ill. 374; 41 Am. St. Rep. 278; Telephone Co. v. Falley, 118 Ind. 194; 10 Am. St. Rep. 114; State v. Sioux City etc. R. R. Co., 46 Neb. 682; Lough v. Outerbridge, 143 N. Y. 277; 42 Am. St. Rep. 712; Laurel Fork etc. R. R. v. Transportation Co., 25 W. Va. 334; Ames v. Union etc. Co., 64 Fed. Rep. 165; Capitol City etc. Co. v. Des Moines, 72 Fed. Rep. 829; New Memphis etc. Co. v. Memphis, 72 Fed. Rep. 952; Reagan v. Farmers' etc. Co., 154 U. S. 362; nor can it determine this question for itself and assert its determination as anything more than prima facie evidence of its correctness or justness: Clyde v. Richmond etc. Co., 57 Fed. Rep. 436; New Memphis etc. Co. v. Memphis, 72 Fed. Rep. 952; Gas etc. Co. v. Cleveland, 71 Fed. Rep. 613; Southern etc. Co. v. Commissioners, 78 Fed. Rep. 261; Reagan v. Farmers' etc. Co., 154 U. S. 397; Interstate Com. Co. v. Railway Co., 167 U. S. 500; Chicago etc. Co. v. Minnesota, 134 U. S. 418.   There were, certainly, decisions, or, at least, judicial opinions, from which the inference might reasonably be drawn that this inconclusiveness did not attend direct legislative action, but was merely a limitation placed upon the power which might be granted to commissions and other bodies to which the subject of fixing rates of charges had been committed.   Thus Judge Blatchford, in his opinion in Budd v. New York, 143 U. S. 546, attempted to distinguish that case from Chicago etc. Co. v. Minnesota, 134 U. S. 418, by affirming that what was said in the opinion in the Minnesota case "had reference only to the case then before the court, and to charges fixed by a commission appointed under an act of the legislature, under a constitution of the state which provided that all corporations, being common carriers, should be bound to carry on 'equal and reasonable terms,' and under a statute which provided that all charges made by a common carrier for the transportation of passengers or property should be 'equal and reasonable.' What was said in the opinion in 134 U. S., as to the question of the reasonableness of the rate of charge being one for judicial investigation, had no reference to a case where the rates are prescribed directly by the legislature."   Manifestly, however, if the question is a judicial one, it cannot be conclusively determined by any other than a judicial tribunal, and the rank of the legislative or other nonjudicial authority undertaking to determine it cannot be material, provided it has been authorized to act either by the state constitution or any other competent authorization.   We cannot discover that the sugges-

tion thus made by Mr. Justice Blatchford that the decisions of the
supreme court of the United States were inapplicable when the
legislature of the state had acted directly in fixing rates of charges
has ever received any further attention from that court. It certainly would not have been deserving of any had it not been made
a part of an opinion of the court in which the majority of its members apparently wholly concurred. There are, however, several subsequent decisions of that court in which rates of charges fixed by
direct legislative action have been treated as dependent for their
validity upon their reasonableness, and hence we may affirm that
this is the controlling inquiry when the charges are imposed directly
by the legislature as well as when the action has been by a commission or some other subordinate body: St. Louis etc. Ry. v. Gill, 156
U. S. 649; Covington etc. Co. v. Sandford, 164 U. S. 578; Smyth v.
Ames, 169 U. S. 466.

The doctrine of Munn v. Illinois in its evolution in the quarter of
a century since its first announcement has surely undergone changes
of a radical character. First, it has been found to be wholly inapplicable to any business which the court may determine to constitute a part of the commerce between the states or with foreign
nations, or, more accurately speaking, it has been found that whatsoever authority exists as to such business rests in, and must be exercised by, Congress. Next, it is finally settled, after much controversy, that the authority of the state is substantially limited to the
enactment of a rule of evidence in so far as rates of charges are
concerned, for this is the net result of state action. It was always
the law that the rates of charges should be reasonable. Now, if the
state by any proper mode fixes rates, its action is presumed to be
just. Higher rates are presumed to be unreasonable, and persons,
whether natural or artificial, seeking to collect higher rates, must
satisfy judicial tribunals having the ultimate decision of this question that the action of the state is unreasonable.

In reaching the conclusion that the question of reasonableness is a
judicial question, the courts have discovered the threshold through
which they must necessarily pass and thence wander in search of
other landmarks to guide their future course. There are as yet no
beacon lights by which to distinguish the reasonable from the unreasonable, or, if any there are, they are so dim that little aid can be
given by them. This is clearly manifest from the opinions in the
principal case. Of the seven judges constituting the court five wrote
separate opinions, and this course was rendered necessary by the
fact that otherwise the views of each upon material questions involved could not have found expression. As the basis of judicial
interference is, that otherwise, persons, corporations being in this
connection included in that term, might be deprived of property
without due process of law by being deprived of the fruits or earnings thereof, it hence follows that rates of charges must always be
adjudged unreasonable when it is proved or admitted that therefrom the persons or property affected cannot, after paying necessary
expenses, acquire any profit from the use of their property. In

other words, service without compensation or reward cannot be compelled without violating the national constitution: Pensacola etc. Co. v. State, 25 Fla. 310; Chicago etc. Co. v. Becker, 35 Fla. 883; Indianapolis etc. Co. v. Indianapolis, 82 Fed. Rep. 245; Cleveland etc. Co. v. Cleveland, 71 Fed. Rep. 610; Chicago etc. R. R. v. Dey, 35 Fed. Rep. 866; Stone v. Farmers' etc. Co., 116 U. S. 307, 331; Chicago etc. R. R. v. Minnesota, 134 U. S. 418; Covington etc. Co. v. Sandford, 164 U. S. 578; St. Louis etc. Co. v. Gill, 156 U. S. 649, affirming 54 Ark. 101.

The rates of charges as fixed may afford some reward for the services rendered or the property used, so that something will remain after paying the necessary expenses, but what remains may be claimed to be an inadequate remuneration for the services rendered, or for the use of the property, and hence must arise the questions, Can the courts consider the question of inadequacy, and if so, upon what basis shall their calculations rest? Shall the value of the services rendered be considered, or only the cost of the property involved in rendering them, or both? If the cost or present value of the plant is to be taken as the basis, what amount of profits thereon must the rates of charges realize? Shall it be lawful interest, or the interest commonly paid in the community upon investments equally permanent in character, or shall it be all the traffic will bear? Shall the owners of this class of property, on the one hand, be protected from depreciations in value and from the consequences of the mistakes of themselves and their agents in not devising and carrying out their schemes in the most economical and efficient manner, and shall they, on the other hand, be excluded from the profits arising from appreciation in values and from the skill and good fortune of themselves and their agents in embarking upon the enterprise in question, and managing it with great prudence and foresight? From the opinions in the principal case it will be seen that a majority of the judges concluded that the constitution could not be satisfied by allowing mere nominal compensation, and strongly tended to the view that such compensation must be such profit as the capital employed would probably realize if invested in some other business involving a similar degree of risk, or, as the chief justice expressed it, the rates allowed "should be sufficient to pay current interest, maintain the necessary plant in a state of efficiency and declare dividend to stockholders equal to at least the lowest current rates of interest, not on the par value of the stock, but on the actual value of the property necessarily used in procuring and distributing the water to consumers." Others of the judges were manifestly of the opinion that if the rates fixed were such as to afford some net profit, its adequacy was rarely or never a subject for judicial consideration, that to authorize the interference of the courts, "there must be actual fraud in fixing the rates, or they must be so palpably unreasonable and unjust as to amount to the same thing," and perhaps if actual fraud were not shown, any rates which left the owner some net revenue from his property should not be adjudged unreasonable by the courts. In support of this view, it may be said that the

power to fix rates is primarily a legislative power, subject, like other
legislative powers, to the constitutional limitation that it shall
not be so exercised as to deprive persons of their property without
due process of law or to take it for a public use without just compensation, that there is no taking of the property while it remains intact and some net profit or revenue is derived therefrom,
and that, subject to the limitation that some net profit must be left,
the legislature, or such other bodies as have been given authority to
consider and determine the question, may conclusively settle the
amount or reasonableness of such profits. The following authorities
tend to sustain this conclusion: Spring Valley W. W. v. San Francisco, 82 Cal. 306; 16 Am. St. Rep. 116; People v. Budd, 117 N. Y. 125;
15 Am. St. Rep. 460. In the case last cited it was said: "It is purely
a question of legislative power. If the power to legislate exists, the
court has nothing to do with the policy or wisdom of the interference
in the particular case, or with the question of the adequacy or inadequacy of the compensation authorized."

If, however, it be conceded that the question of the reasonableness
of rates is a judicial question, and that there is, consequently, a
duty imposed upon the judiciary of protecting persons owning property clothed with a public use, and hence subject to state regulation,
from deprivation of reasonable compensation, this duty must result
in something more substantial than merely securing nominal compensation. Justice Brewer in Chicago etc. Ry. v. Dey, 35 Fed. Rep. 879,
after saying that, "As to the amount of such compensation, if some
compensation or reward is in fact secured—the legislature is the sole
judge"; to this sentence, added: "Compensation implies three things:
payment of cost of service, interest on bonds, and then some dividend. Cost of service implies skilled labor, the best appliances, keeping of the roadbed and the cars and machinery and other appliances
in perfect order and repair. The obligation of the carrier to the
passenger and shipper requires all these." The same judge in Ames
v. Union etc. Ry., 64 Fed. Rep. 176, said: "The value of the property
cannot be destroyed by legislation depriving the owner of adequate
compensation. The power which the legislature has is only to prescribe reasonable rates, not any rates." "It is obvious," said another judge, "that it must be held either that the right of judicial
interference exists only when the schedule of rates established will
fail to secure the owners of the property some compensation or income from their investment (however small), or else that the court
must adjudge, when properly called upon to do so, whether the rates
established by the municipal authorities are so manifestly unreasonable as to amount to the taking of property for a public use without
just compensation. Undoubtedly, every intendment is in favor of
the rates as established by the municipal authorities. But, as it is
firmly established that it is within the scope of judicial power, and
a part of the judicial duty, to inquire whether rates so established
operate to deprive the owner of his property without just compensation, it seems to me that it logically follows that, if the court finds

from the evidence produced that they are manifestly unreasonable,
it is its duty so to adjudge, and to annul them; for it is plain that if
they are manifestly unreasonable, they cannot be just"; San Diego
etc. Co. v. National City, 74 Fed. Rep. 83. In response to the contention that rates should be deemed reasonable if they produce any net
revenue, Judge McKenna, now a member of the supreme court of
the United States, in Southern Pacific Co. v. Board of Commrs., 78
Fed. Rep. 261, said: "This is claimed to be established by authority.
I do not think so. It seems to have been decided in Chicago etc.
Ry. v. Dey, 35 Fed. Rep. 866. But the same learned judge who
expressed that view in the Dey case retracted it in Ames v. Union
etc. Ry., 64 Fed. Rep. 165, and it has received no judicial sanction
since. This was inevitable when it came to be seen that the regulation of rates could not be an absolute legislative prerogative. When
the power of judicial review was asserted and entertained, the fourteenth amendment of the constitution was bound to be firmly and accurately applied. There could be no middle ground. Middle ground
would satisfy neither legislative prerogative nor judicial prerogative. That must apply justice as it is understood of men, and, in its
clear light, it was inevitable that it would come to be seen that the
fourteenth amendment of the constitution would be a composition of
delusive words if it forbade only the taking of the physical property,
while it permitted the taking of its value—if its guaranties of the
equal protection of the laws to all persons would be satisfied as to
railroads by leaving them a microscopical profit. If so, the pool of
Tantalus would lose its force to illustrate excited and disappointed
expectation when compared with the organic law of this great land.
We should keep in mind that a regulation of a railroad affects, in
reality, the natural persons who own it, not the insensible legal
artificiality and abstraction called 'a corporation.' For the natural
persons the protection of the constitution is intended, and would any
one say that justice is done them if their investment be allowed only
an infinitesimal fraction of one per cent, while all other investments
are expected to return, at least, legal interest, with freedom, besides,
of unlimited advantage?" In another case in which, however, the
question of adequacy of consideration was not necessarily involved,
the court said: "And the very use of the term 'regulation' implies
that an investigation shall be made; that an opportunity to present
the facts shall be furnished; that, when the facts are established,
they shall, by the regulating power, be given due consideration
and that such action as shall be taken in view of these facts,
thus ascertained, shall be just and reasonable, and such as enables the company to maintain its existence, to preserve the property
invested from destruction, and to receive, on the capital actually
and bona fide invested in the plant, a remuneration or dividend corresponding in amount to the ruling rates of interest. The company
has a right to such gross income from the sale of gas as will enable it to pay all legitimate operating expenses, pay interest on
valid fixed charges, so far as bonds or securities represent an expenditure actually made in good faith, and also to pay a reasonable

dividend on stock, so far as this represents an actual investment in the enterprise"; Memphis etc. Co. v. Memphis, 72 Fed. Rep. 955. The most recent decision in the supreme court of the nation upon this subject falling within our observation states the rule in this guarded language: "A state enactment, or regulations made under the authority of a state enactment, establishing rates for the transportation of persons or property by railroad that will not admit of the carrier earning such compensation as under all circumstances is just to it and the public, would deprive such carrier of its property without due process of law and deny to it the equal protection of the laws, and would, therefore, be repugnant to the fourteenth amendment of the constitution of the United States"; Smyth v. Ames, 169 U. S. 526. In this case it appeared by the testimony of a witness, whose general fairness, and competency to speak of the facts were not questioned, that the average reduction made by the statute on all the commodities at local rates was twenty-nine and a half per cent. From the computation made, it appeared that in the case of the Burlington road it had, prior to the fixing of these rates, earned one hundred dollars at the cost of seventy-six dollars and twenty-four cents, that if a reduction of twenty-nine and a half per cent was made, the operating expenses would exceed the earnings by more than five per cent, and that, by like calculation, it would appear that each of the railroad companies "would have conducted its local business at a loss during the periods stated, except that in the year ending June 30, 1891, and in the year ending June 30, 1893, the earnings of the Fremont Company, and in the years ending the 30th days of June, 1892, and 1893, respectively, the earnings of the Union Pacific Company, would have slightly exceeded their operating expenses," but that under the rates prescribed by the statute in question the costs of the respective companies of local business in Nebraska would have exceeded the earnings for the years ending June 30, 1891, 1892, 1893, in amounts ranging from four to thirty-three per cent. It hence appeared in these cases that the putting into effect of the schedule of rates in question would have substantially deprived the railway companies of all reward for the services rendered by them, over and above the expenses of the rendition, and hence this case cannot be regarded as an authority upon what amount of reward may be deemed reasonable.

Supposing, however, that the courts, in deciding whether rates of charges are reasonable, must further determine whether they are adequate, they are then met with the almost insuperable difficulty of formulating some test of reasonableness and adequacy. In the decisions which have heretofore been made, the cases have been deprived of great intrinsic difficulty by concessions made in the pleadings or otherwise, often presenting to the court a state of facts which we think it very unlikely the evidence, had it been taken, would have disclosed. In the case of Spring Valley W. W. v. San Francisco, 82 Cal. 286, 16 Am. St. Rep. 116, it was alleged that the order assailed was passed without affording the corporation an opportunity to show that it was unreasonable and unjust, and, in fact, after the refusal to hear any evidence upon this subject, that the rates were "fixed arbitrarily, at random, and by mere guesswork, or without any consideration of, or regard to, the right of the plaintiff to a reasonable compensation, or to a reasonable income, or any income, upon its investment, and without any consideration of, or regard to, the value of the plaintiff's works and property, or the amount of its interest bearing indebtedness and the annual interest charge thereon, or its operating expenses, or the amount of taxes which it would be required to pay, or the right of the plaintiff's stockholders to reasonable, or any, dividends upon their stock, and without any reference to, or consideration of, the actual cost of supplying water, but in total disregard of all such matters." No issue was taken upon any of these allegations, and the spectacle was presented of officers confessing the most gross omission and disregard of official duty, such as, if true, marked them as fit subjects of a penal colony. In the principal case, too, the officers whose action was questioned appeared before the court (p. 575) as having met secretly for the purpose of taking evidence without notice to, and in the absence of, the corporation to be affected, and, as basing their action on testimony taken at such secret meeting, which testimony the corporation was denied the right of controverting, though by it was developed the basis upon which the action of the officers in fixing their rates of charges rested. Hence in both of these cases the corporation assailing the charges was, by the action of public officers, or their attorneys, given the vantage ground of an assault upon proceedings confessedly attended with every indicia of unfairness. In Reagan v. Farmers' etc. Co., 154 U. S. 400, Covington etc. Co. v. Sandford, 164 U. S. 589, 592, Cleveland etc. Co. v. Cleveland, 71 Fed. Rep. 610, New Memphis etc. Co. v. Memphis, 72 Fed. Rep. 952, Indianapolis etc. Co. v. Indianapolis, 82 Fed. Rep. 245, and Smyth v. Ames, 169 U. S. 528, it appeared either by admissions or by testimony of witnesses, whom there was no attempt to contradict, that the charges assailed were not merely unreasonable, but that they were so extreme in character as to leave the corporations assailing them without any net profit for their services if such rates of charges were enforced. While we do not doubt that ultimately, when the question shall necessarily arise, that the courts will, to some extent, undertake to require that the charges be adequate as well as reasonable, the inherent difficulties in determining what charges must be deemed adequate are such that we can very rarely expect judicial interference against rates of charges where there is any substantial effort made to defend them. Even some of the general suggestions which have been made upon this subject must, we think, be abandoned. Thus in several of the decisions the amount of the bonded indebtedness of corporations was spoken of, and the court seemed inclined to the view that such indebtedness and the interest agreed to be paid thereon ought to be taken into consideration in fixing rates of charges, but we think this suggestion is sufficiently answered by the opinions in the principal case as well as in that of San Diego etc. Co. v. National City, 74 Fed. Rep. 87. It certainly cannot be material whether the corporation has used its own money or that which it has borrowed from others, nor can those who have loaned money be necessarily entitled to interest thereon if it has been injudiciously expended. To say, as is sometimes said, that the present value of the property should be taken as a basis for the adjustment of rates is but to reason in a circle, for it is clear that its value is dependent upon the rates established, and must be high or low according to such establishment. In the principal case, Mr. Justice Van Fleet suggests that the true basis is the actual cost of the property, supposing always that that cost has not been enhanced by corrupt means nor by gross mismanagement. It may, we think, be said of this test that it is neither more nor less liable to objection than the others which have been proposed. Its vice is that it places owners of this class of property, in one respect, in a favored position, in that they are guaranteed against losses arising from depreciation in general values or from their want of foresight in conducting their business operations and that impairment of values resulting from new improvements and inventions making necessary the discarding of old plans and appliances and the adoption of others in their place. We have already suggested that, though a basis of computation is agreed upon, there must still be difficulty in determining what interest or rate of profit shall be allowed. There may possibly be instances in which rates of charges cannot be found unreasonable, though no profit is realized therefrom. Thus it was said in Reagan v. Farmers' etc. Co., 154 U. S. 412: "It is not necessary to decide, and we do not wish to be understood as laying down as an absolute rule, that in every case a failure to produce some profit to those who have invested their money in the building of a road is conclusive that the tariff is unjust and unreasonable. And yet justice demands that everyone receive some compensation for the use of his money or property, if it be possible without prejudice to the rights of others. There may be circumstances which would justify such a tariff; there may have been extravagance and a needless expenditure of money; there may be waste in the management of the road, enormous salaries, unjust discrimination as between individual shippers, resulting in general loss. The construction may have been at a time when material and labor were at the highest price, so that the actual cost far exceeds the present value; the road may have been unwisely built, in localities where there is no sufficient business to sustain a road. Doubtless, too, there are many other matters affecting the rights of the community in which the road is built as well as those who have built the road." The difficulties of the subject are, to some extent, indicated by the following extract from the opinion of Judge Foster in Cotting v. Kansas etc. Co., 79 Fed. Rep. 684: "So it seems to be clearly established by most recent interpretations of the constitution that legislation which prevents a fair and reasonable return—the rights of the public considered—for capital engaged in legitimate business is obnoxious to the constitution; but how shall it be determined what is reasonable compensation? It is not every public

enterprise or investment, however unwisely undertaken or extravagantly managed, that can claim a fair return on its property. The
public have rights to be considered. If a company should build a
road across the Great Desert of Sahara, and carry but one passenger
or one car of freight a day, it would be absurd to say that its rates
should be fixed so as to make a fair return on the investment. Has
the income been dissipated by extravagant or bad management? or
has the property depreciated by a general decline in values? would
seem to be questions entering into the problem. And, after all, what
shall be the rule in determining if the compensation is reasonable? Is
it to be left to the unguided judgment or whim of the chancellor?
Doubtless, the rate fixed by law for interest on money furnishes a
test of which the investor cannot complain, although in many cases
it might be oppressive to the general public. It is apparent that if
the court is to form an intelligent judgment on the subject, and not
rely on mere conjecture, all the facts should be before it, such as
the cost, the present value of the property, receipts and expenditures,
the manner of its operation, etc." To say that the question is to
be left to the whim or the unguided judgment of the chancellor is
to give an offensive coloring to necessary judicial proceedings, and to
provoke hostile feeling and criticism respecting a department of the
government which merits support rather than stinging epithets. It is
not the fault of the judiciary that the question is difficult, and that
little aid for its solution can be found in tests already formulated
and judicially approved. The end will probably be that the courts
will receive evidence concerning an infinite variety of matters all
tending in some degree to satisfy the judicial mind as to what is
reasonable under the circumstances; and will reach their conclusion
without announcing, or themselves being conscious of, the precise
weight given to any one fact or circumstance. This course will be
more likely to reach substantial justice than the adoption and enforcement of any precise test requiring the value of the property to
be fixed according to its cost, or its market value, or the sum required to replace it if destroyed. One rule so far has not been
assailed with any degree of success. It is that the rates as established, unless fraud or wantonness on their establishment appears,
must be presumed to be reasonable, and those who assail them must
overcome this presumption. This presumption would seem sufficient
to protect the public, and to guarantee against overthrow by the
judiciary of any rates of charges fixed by the legislature or any other
competent body, not confessedly infected by fraud, or wanton disregard of the rights of the persons or corporations to be affected,
unless such charges clearly appear to be grossly inadequate.

WILCOX *v.* LUCO.

[1·8 CALIFORNIA, 639.]

CONSULS ARE NOT PUBLIC MINISTERS, and are not entitled, by the general law of nations, to the peculiar immunities of ambassadors. In civil and criminal cases they are subject to the local law in the same manner with other foreign residents owing a temporary allegiance to the state.

JURISDICTION—STATE AND NATIONAL TRIBUNALS.—Whenever judicial power is by the constitution of the United States vested in its courts, the jurisdiction may by Congress be made exclusive of state authority, but if Congress does not provide that jurisdiction of the national courts shall be exclusive, the state courts have concurrent jurisdiction.

CONSULS—JURISDICTION OF STATE COURTS OVER.—In the absence of any express declaration by Congress to the contrary, the state courts have jurisdiction over actions against consuls of foreign nations resident within the state, subject to the right of such consuls to have the judgment of the state tribunal reviewed by the supreme court of the United States, and the sufficiency of their defenses determined by that tribunal.

A JUDGMENT OF A STATE COURT AGAINST A FOREIGN CONSUL resident within the state, and served with process therein, is not void.

Orestes J. Orena and William Rix, for the appellant.

I. N. Thorne, for the respondent.

⁶⁴⁰ HARRISON, J. The defendant made his promissory note to the plaintiff for the sum of two thousand dollars, and in an action brought against him thereon in the superior court for San Francisco suffered default, and judgment was rendered against him and in favor of the plaintiff for the full amount of the note. Thereafter upon his motion, based upon his affidavit that at and prior to the commencement of the action and ever since he had been consul general of the republic of Chili, residing in San ⁶⁴¹ Francisco and engaged in performing the functions of his office, the court vacated and set aside this judgment and ordered the action dismissed upon the ground that by reason of his position as consul he was not subject to the jurisdiction of the courts of this state. From this order the plaintiff has appealed.

The correctness of the order appealed from is to be determined upon the construction to be given to the constitution of the United States and the legislation of Congress thereunder, and not upon any consideration of the rules of international law. The immunity of ambassadors and public ministers from suits in the courts of the country to which they are sent is not extended by any principles of international law to consuls. "Consuls are not public ministers. Whatever protection they may be entitled to in the discharge of their official duties, and whatever special privileges may be conferred upon them by the local laws and usages or by international compact, they are not entitled by the general law of nations to the peculiar immunities of ambassadors. In civil and criminal cases they are subject to the local law in the same manner with other foreign residents owing a temporary allegiance to the state": Wheaton's International Law, sec. 249; 1 Kent's Commentaries, 44; Story on the Constitution, sec. 1660; Giddings v. Crawford, Taney, 1.

Section 2 of article 3 of the constitution of the United States declares that: "The judicial power shall extend . . . . to all cases affecting ambassadors, other public ministers and consuls"; and, "In all cases affecting ambassadors, other public ministers and consuls, the supreme court shall have original jurisdiction. In all the other cases before mentioned, the supreme court shall have appellate jurisdiction, both as to law and fact, with such exceptions and under such regulations as the Congress shall make." It is held that the judicial power thus vested in the courts of the United States is to be exercised in accordance with such legislation as Congress may prescribe. Wherever the constitution does not make this jurisdiction exclusive of state authority, it may be made so by Congress, and Congress may also declare the extent to which the state courts may exercise concurrent jurisdiction, as well as at what stage of procedure the jurisdiction of the United States courts may attach in cases originally commenced in the state courts—either after 642 final judgment has been rendered therein, or at any period subsequent to the commencement of the action: Martin v. Hunter, 1 Wheat. 304; The Moses Taylor, 4 Wall. 411; Claflin v. Houseman, 93 U. S. 130. By the judiciary act of 1789, and afterward in the Revised Statutes, Congress distributed the exercise of this power between the courts of the United States and those of the several states, making it exclusive in the former in many instances, and in others giving to the state courts concurrent jurisdiction; and also provided for the removal to the United States courts in certain cases of causes commenced in the state courts, and for the exercise by the supreme court of an appellate jurisdiction over judgments of the state courts in causes of which those courts had original jurisdiction concurrent with the courts of the United States. Other statutes have since been enacted enlarging or changing this exclusive as well as concurrent jurisdiction.

Section 687 of the Revised Statutes of the United States,
which became the law on the subject from and after December
1, 1873, declares that the supreme court shall have "original, but
not exclusive jurisdiction' of all suits in which a consul or vice-
consul is a party." And by section 563 jurisdiction is given to
the district courts: . . . . "17. Of all suits against consuls or
vice-consuls," with the exception of certain offenses previously
named. It had been held in Giddings v. Crawford, Taney, 1, that
the provision in the constitution giving to the supreme court
"original" jurisdiction in all cases affecting consuls did not imply that that jurisdiction was to be exclusive, and in Bors v.
Preston, 111 U. S. 252, the supreme court approved this ruling
and held that Congress could confer upon the subordinate courts
of the United States concurrent original jurisdiction in cases affecting consuls. It was also held in Claflin v. Houseman, 93
U. S. 130, that the provision extending the judicial power of the
United States to "all cases" arising under the constitution and
laws of the United States does not imply that the jurisdiction of
the federal courts is necessarily exclusive.

Section 711 of the Revised Statutes, as originally enacted, declared: "The jurisdiction vested in the courts of the United
States, in the cases and proceedings hereinafter mentioned, shall
be exclusive of the courts of the several states. . . . . 8. Of all
suits or proceedings against ambassadors or other public ministers, [643] or against consuls or vice-consuls." By the act of February 8, 1875 (18 Stats., p. 316), entitled "An act to correct errors
and to supply omissions in the Revised Statutes of the United
States," section 711 was amended by striking out the above
subdivision 8, and since that date there has been no express declaration in the statutes of the United States that the jurisdiction
of its courts in actions against a consul is exclusive of the state
courts. It is 'very evident that prior to this amendment the
state courts had no jurisdiction in such cases: Davis v. Packard, 7 Pet. 276; Valarino v. Thompson, 7 N. Y. 576. We have
not been cited to any case since that date in which the question
appears to have been considered. The decision in Miller v. Van
Loben Sels, 66 Cal. 341, was made upon a consideration of the
judiciary act of 1789, and, although in the petition for rehearing the amendment to section 711 was called to the attention of
the court, the failure of the court to reconsider its opinion does
not authorize us to say that it held that the exclusive jurisdiction of the federal courts had not been changed: Kellogg v.
Cochran, 87 Cal. 192; San Francisco v. Pacific Bank, 89 Cal. 23.

We do not consider that the case of De Give v. Grand Rapids etc. Co., 94 Ga. 605, is entitled to any weight in determining the question before us, for the reason that the court in that case merely affirmed an order refusing to set aside a judgment against a consul without giving any opinion in support of its judgment. Claflin v. Houseman, 93 U. S. 130, cited by the appellant, was an action brought in a state court, prior to the enactment of the Revised Statutes, by an assignee in bankruptcy to recover the assets of the bankrupt's estate, and the jurisdiction of the state court was contested under the provision of the constitution that the judicial power of the United States shall extend to "all cases" arising under the constitution and laws of the United States. The supreme court, however, upheld the jurisdiction of the state court, upon the ground that the laws of the United States are operative within the states, and that wherever rights of property are created by virtue of these laws such rights may be enforced in state courts competent to decide rights of like character and class. This was a case, moreover, in which the assignee himself invoked the jurisdiction of the state court, and the court limits its decision to holding that he had authority to bring a suit in the state courts whenever those courts were invested [644] with appropriate jurisdiction suited to the nature of the case. The proposition thus determined is not, however, conclusive of the present appeal, since there is not here presented for determination any question of property rights or of personal liberty depending upon or arising under the constitution or any law of the United States. The defendant claims an exemption from the jurisdiction of the state courts as a right guaranteed to him by the constitution.

By the above amendment to section 711, removing from the statutes the express provision that the jurisdiction of the federal courts in suits or proceedings against consuls should be exclusive of the courts of the several states, Congress must have intended to declare that such jurisdiction should no longer be exclusive, unless it was made exclusive either by the constitution itself or by other existing legislation. There is, however, as above seen, no express declaration by Congress that such jurisdiction is exclusive, but it must be conceded that a consul who has been recognized by the President and admitted to the exercise of his official functions shall not, so long as he continues in the exercise of those functions, be deprived of the benefits of the provision in the constitution extending the judicial power of the United States to all cases in which he is affected, and that, un-

less there is some law by which he may invoke this judicial
power for the purpose either of removing the cause into the
courts of the United States before judgment, or to review the
judgment of the state court, a state court can have no jurisdiction to entertain an action in which he is a defendant. Under
this provision of the constitution, he is entitled to invoke the
exercise of that power in any case to which he may be a party
and, if Congress has made any provision by which he can avail
himself of this right, he is amply protected in the enjoyment
of this provision of the constitution. The constitution does not
declare that he shall be exempt from the jurisdiction of the
state courts, but that the judicial power of the United States
shall extend to all cases affecting him. It is for Congress to determine the mode and time at which he may invoke this jurisdiction, and, if that body has provided a means by which he
can avail himself of this judicial power, he is not deprived of
any right given him by the constitution. There is no provision
in the removal act of 1875, or in that of 1887, for removing to
645 the circuit court an action commenced in a state court against
a consul, but it is provided in section 709 of the Revised Statutes
that "A final judgment or decree in any suit in the highest court
of a state in which a decision in the suit could be had, where is
drawn in question the validity of a statute of or an authority
exercised under any state, on the ground of their being repugnant to the constitution, treaties, or laws of the United States,
and the decision is in favor of their validity, ... may be re-
examined and reversed or affirmed in the supreme court upon a
writ of error." Under this section that court has jurisdiction to
review the judgment of a state court whenever it appears from
the record that one of the questions mentioned in the section
was raised and presented to the state court, and decided by it
adversely to the claim asserted; and, if such decision is erroneous, that court will then examine the entire case, and affirm
or reverse the judgment according as it shall determine whether
the decision of the state court upon the other matters in the
record was correct or not: Murdock v. Memphis, 20 Wall. 590.
It is thus seen that, if a consul is sued in a state court, he can,
in addition to any defense he may have to the cause of action
set up against him, claim his right under the constitution to
have the matter determined by the courts of the United States;
and if judgment is rendered against him in the state court he
can have that judgment reviewed by the supreme court of the
United States and the sufficiency of his defense determined by

that tribunal, and thus fully enjoy the rights given him by the constitution. This right, however, may be waived by him, since he has the same right to rest content with the judgment of the state court, either by merely pleading his defense to the cause of action without invoking this provision of the constitution, or by suffering default, as he would have to invoke its jurisdiction as a plaintiff and, if so waived, he cannot, after judgment has been rendered against him, claim the right to a review of this judgment under a writ of error by the supreme court of the United States.

The superior court, therefore, had jurisdiction to entertain the action against the defendant, and as he did not appear in answer to the complaint, or in any mode present a defense to the action, the court properly rendered judgment against him, and [646] its subsequent order setting it aside and dismissing the action was erroneous.

The order is reversed.

Van Fleet, J., Garoutte, J., Henshaw, J., and Beatty, C. J., concurred.

———

THIS CASE WAS FIRST PRESENTED to Department Two which, in an opinion by Justice McFarland, filed July 16, 1896, affirmed the judgment of the trial court. To this opinion the judge writing it adhered after the hearing in Bank. He maintained that the question had been determined adversely to the contention of the appellant in Miller v. Van Loben Sels, 66 Cal. 341, and that this case ought to be regarded as conclusive authority, notwithstanding the alteration in the statutes of the United States by the amendment thereto made in February, 1875. He said that the attention of the court had been called to this change in the statute at the time of pronouncing the prior decision, and therefore such decision should be adhered to; that by the constitutional provision declaring that the judicial power of the United States should extend "to all cases affecting ambassadors, other public ministers, and consuls," the consuls were placed on the same footing as ambassadors, and the state courts could no more exercise jurisdiction over them than over such ambassadors; and he maintained that this view was sustained by the decision in Davis v. Packard, 7 Pet. 276.

JURISDICTION OF FEDERAL AND STATE COURTS—CONFLICT IN.—The only limitations upon a state in regard to questions cognizable in its courts are such as it may have itself created by the adoption of its constitution: State v. Bachelder, 5 Minn. 223; 80 Am. Dec. 410, and note. The unexercised jurisdiction of the United States courts over a question does not oust a state court of jurisdiction, when the question arises collaterally by way of a defense to an action in which the state has jurisdiction of the parties and the subject matter: Wilkinson v. Wait, 44 Vt. 508; 8 Am. St. Rep. 390. See Hines v. Rawson, 40 Ga. 356; 2 Am. Rep. 581; and extended note to Gilman v. Williams, 76 Am. Dec. 223.

JURISDICTION—AMBASSADORS AND FOREIGN MINISTERS—CONSULS.—The courts of a state have no jurisdiction over a foreign minister or ambassador. His person is inviolable, and his residence is regarded as a part of the territory of the state from which he is sent. Thus an indictment against a domestic servant of a foreign minister was quashed for want of jurisdiction. However, a consul who received money in a fiduciary capacity and failed to pay it over was held to bail on process of arrest: Monographic note to Molyneux v. Seymour, 76 Am. Dec. 668.

CASES

IN THE

SUPREME COURT

OF

GEORGIA.

SOUTHERN RAILWAY CO. *v.* COVENIA,

[100 GEORGIA, 46.]

EVIDENCE — JUDICIAL KNOWLEDGE — EARNING CA-
PACITY OF CHILD.—A court on demurrer, can take judicial cognizance of the fact that a child is of such tender years as to be
incapable of rendering services authorizing the parent to recover for
the loss thereof arising from its injury or death, and need not submit such question to the jury, although the declaration alleges an
earning capacity on the part of the child.

PLEADINGS.—DEMURRERS DO NOT ADMIT OPINIONS
OR CONCLUSIONS of the pleader, nor do they admit facts which
are in their nature improbable or impossible.

PLEADINGS.—DEMURRER CANNOT BE HELD TO ADMIT
impossible or improbable facts, so as to prevent the court from
passing upon the allegations which in their nature are contrary to
common experience and common knowledge as matter of law, and
to compel their submission to the jury.

DAMAGES—INJURY TO CHILD.—Although a parent cannot
recover damages for the death or injury of his child unless the child
is capable of rendering services, he can recover against the person
who inflicts the injury for his trouble and expense in caring for the
child, and, if it dies from such injury, he can recover his necessary
and reasonable expense in its burial, including compensation for his
loss of time.

Goodyear & Kay, for the plaintiff.

Symmes & Bennet and Johnson & Krauss, for the defendant
in error.

47 SIMMONS, C. J.   Whatever may be the rule in other jurisdictions, it is well settled in this state that the gist of an action
by a parent to recover damages for the death or injury of a
minor child is the loss of services: Shields v. Yonge, 15 Ga. 349;

60 Am. Dec. 698; Allen v. Atlanta Street R. R. Co., 54 Ga. 503. The loss of service being the cause of action, it follows that when the infant is incapable of rendering service at the time of its death or injury the parent cannot recover. This principle was recognized by the counsel of the plaintiff in the court below, for he alleged in the declaration that the child was capable of rendering service, and also specified what acts of service it did render and the value thereof per month; but in the same declaration it was alleged that the child was but one year, eight months, and ten days of age. One of the grounds of the demurrer was, that the plaintiff shows by his allegations in his petition that the child "was of such tender years as to be unable to have any earning capacity, and hence the defendant could not be held liable in damages for the killing of said child, even if negligently done." The question is, therefore, squarely made whether the court, on demurrer, can take judicial cognizance of the fact that a child of this tender age is incapable of rendering such service as would authorize the parent to recover, or whether in such a case the court is bound to submit the matter to the jury. In the case of Minnesota v. Barber, 136 U. S. 321, Mr. Justice Harlan said: "If a fact alleged to exist, upon which the rights of parties depend, is within common experience and knowledge, it is one of which the courts will take judicial notice." In Ah Kow v. Nunan, 5 Saw. 560, Mr. Justice Field said: "We cannot shut our eyes to matters of public notoriety and general cognizance. When we take our seats on the bench we are not struck with blindness, and forbidden to know as judges what we see as men." In the case of King v. Gallun, 109 U. S. 99, it was held that "the 48 court will take judicial notice of matters of common knowledge, and of things in common use." "Courts will take judicial notice of facts generally known as of uniform occurrence, or the invariable action of natural laws": 12 Am. & Eng. Ency. of Law, 196.

The fact that a child of less than two years of age cannot perform any services of value to its parent is a matter of common knowledge to all men. It is as well known to the judge as it is to the jury. It being so known to the judge, why should he not act upon it when he is called upon to do so by proper pleading? Why is he less qualified than the jury to declare a well-known fact? Why should he submit such a question to a jury, when, if they found contrary to this well-known fact, he would be compelled to set aside their verdict? Why should he go through the farce of a trial, at the expense of the country in time and money, in order to have a jury decide a fact which is already well known to everyone? There is no necessity for a jury trial when there is no issue of fact. In our opinion, there can be no issue of fact as to the ability of a child two years old to perform valuable services. Even if the parents should testify that a child of that age could render services of the value of two dollars per month, it would be so inconsistent with every person's knowledge of the incapacity of children of that age to render service, that such testimony would be unworthy of credit. In the case of Hall v. Hollonder, 10 Eng. Com. L. R. 746, 4 Barn. & C. 660, Bayley, J., in discussing an injury to a child two and a half years old, said: "It is manifest that the child was incapable of performing any service."

All courts of any respectability, so far as I know, decide as a matter of law that children of tender years cannot be guilty of contributory negligence. Upon what reason are these decisions made? Upon what theory do the courts hold this as a matter of law? The answer is apparent. Because reason, experience, and common sense teach that a [49] child of that age has not the sense or the capacity to contribute to an injury to itself. It cannot at that age be guilty of any negligence. If the courts can decide this as a matter of law, why can they not also decide as matter of law that such a child has no earning capacity? We see no reason why it cannot be done. But it is contended that by the demurrer in the court below it was admitted that the child was capable of rendering service, and that therefore the court was right in overruling the demurrer. The declaration enumerated certain services of the child which it alleged were worth two dollars per month. In passing upon a demurrer to a declaration, the court considers all the allegations therein. The demurrer admits all the facts well pleaded. If all the facts taken together show that the plaintiff is not entitled to recover, the court should sustain the demurrer although some of the facts alleged would show the measure and amount of the damages. If the major premise in the declaration shows no cause of action, the minor premise will not aid in sustaining it. The controlling fact alleged in this declaration was the age of the child, and consequently its incapacity to render service. We have shown that by reason of its tender age it could not perform service for the parent. Conceding, for the sake of the argument, that the fact alleged in the declaration that the child picked up chips, amused the baby, etc., was admitted by the demurrer, there was still no admission that these simple acts were of any value. The allegation in the declaration that they were valuable to the amount of two dollars per month was an opinion or conclusion of the pleader. It was necessarily an opinion or conclusion, because there was no standard by which services of this sort could be valued. We know as matter of fact that children of this age are not hired or employed. There can, therefore, be no criterion by which the value of such services could be estimated but that of an opinion. It is well settled that a demurrer does not admit opinions or conclusions [50] of the pleader. If a man, in his action for personal injuries, alleges that he was damaged ten thousand dollars, and there is a demurrer to the declaration, the demurrer does not admit the amount of damages claimed. Moreover, a demurrer does not admit facts which are in their nature improbable or impossible. In the case of Cole v. Maunder, 2 Bolle. Abr. 548, one person sued another for damages for throwing at and striking him with a stone. Defendant pleaded that he threw the stones at him molliter et molli manu and they fell upon him molliter, and it was held not a good justification, the judges saying that one cannot throw stones molliter although it were confessed by demurrer.

Suppose this child had been only six months old and these same allegations as to service and value had been made, it could not be held that a demurrer to the declaration admitted that the child six months old could render service. The allegation would have been improbable and impossible. Suppose that a boy five years old were indicted for the crime of rape, all the necessary allegations being made, certainly a demurrer to such an indictment would not admit that the boy did or could commit the offense charged. Suppose, again, that one female should sue another for the offense of seduction and the declaration contain all the necessary allegations, would it be held that a demurrer by the defendant would admit that she did commit the act necessary to constitute the crime? These illustrations are given for the purpose of showing that a demurrer to a declaration cannot be held to admit impossible or improbable allegations of fact, so as to prevent the court from passing upon the allegations which in their nature are contrary to common experience and common knowledge as matter of law, and to compel him to submit them to a jury. We think, therefore, that the court should have sustained the demurrer, in so far as to hold that the parent could not recover damages for the death of the child on account of loss of its services.

[51] 2. It is well settled that although a parent cannot recover

damages for the death or injury of his child unless the child was capable of rendering service, he can recover in an action against the person who inflicted the injury, for his trouble and expense in caring for the child, and if it dies from the injuries inflicted, he can recover his necessary and reasonable expenses in the burial, including compensation for the loss of such time on the parent's part as was needed for this purpose: See Dennis v. Clark, 2 Cush. 347, 48 Am. Dec. 671, where this subject is elaborately discussed by Metcalf, J. We therefore hold that while the father in this case cannot recover for the death of his child, he can recover for the expenses he incurred and the loss he sustained, rendered necessary by the conduct of the servants of the railroad company, and on this latter ground we affirm the judgment of the court below. If it is necessary, let this part of the declaration stand in order to try the amount of expenses necessarily incurred by the father.

Judgment affirmed, with direction.

PLEADING — DEMURRER — WHAT ADMITTED BY.—A demurrer admits only such facts as are well pleaded. It does not admit conclusions of law stated by the pleader, or the construction placed by him upon statutes: McPhail v. People, 160 Ill. 77; 52 Am. St. Rep. 306; American Water Works Co. v. State, 46 Neb. 194; 50 Am. St. Rep. 610. Whether an injury is remote and consequential is a conclusion of law upon the facts stated in the declaration: Tinsman v. Belvedere etc. R. R. Co., 26 N. J. L. 148; 60 Am. Dec. 565.

DAMAGES FOR NEGLIGENT KILLING OF MINOR CHILD.— Few cases will be found upholding the doctrine of the principal case, that where a child of such tender years as to have no earning capacity is negligently killed, the parent of such child is limited in an action for damages to a recovery for his trouble and expense in caring for, and burying it. The proper measure of damages in such a case is the probable value of the services of the deceased from the time of his death to the time he would have attained his majority, less the expense of his maintenance during the same time: Little Rock etc. Ry. Co. v. Barker, 33 Ark. 350; 34 Am. Rep. 44; Morgan v. Southern Pac. Co., 95 Cal. 510; 29 Am. St. Rep. 143. The jury is confined to pecuniary damages sustained by the parent: Agricultural etc. Assn. v. State, 71 Md. 86; 17 Am. St. Rep. 507; Fox v. Oakland etc. Co., 118 Cal. 55; ante, p. 216; and their allowance of damages should be in no sense a solatium for the parent's grief: Pierce v. Conners, 20 Colo. 178; 46 Am. St. Rep. 279. Except in very rare instances, however, it would be impracticable to furnish direct evidence of any specific loss occasioned by the death of a child of such tender years as that in the principal case, but it cannot be said, as a matter of law, that there is no pecuniary damage in such a case, or that the expense of maintaining and educating the child would necessarily exceed any pecuniary advantage which the parents could have derived from his services had he lived. The calculation is for the jury: Ihl v. Forty-second Street etc. R. R. Co., 47 N. Y. 317; 7 Am. Rep. 450; monographic note to Louisville etc. Ry. Co. v. Goodykoontz, 12 Am. St. Rep. 381.

Mutual Loan and Banking Co. v. Haas.
[100 Georgia, 111.]

MORTGAGES—POWER OF SALE—REVOCABILITY.—If a debtor executes a mortgage upon realty to secure a debt, the mortgage containing a power of sale to be exercised upon default of payment of the debt, such power becomes a part of the security, and is not revocable either by the mortgagor or by the rendition of a judgment against him in favor of another creditor, and if, on default in payment of the debt, the mortgagee exercises such power by selling the land, a bona fide purchaser at the sale obtains title free from the lien of judgments junior to the mortgage, though rendered before the exercise of the power.

MORTGAGES—POWER OF SALE—EFFECT ON JUDGMENT CREDITOR.—A creditor of a mortgagor, who obtains a judgment subsequently to the execution of a mortgage which contains a power of sale and has been duly recorded, takes it subject to the rights of the mortgagee; and the power of sale being a part of the security, he takes it subject to the exercise of that power, and his judgment attaches merely to the equity of redemption.

MORTGAGES—POWER OF SALE—RIGHT OF MORTGAGEE TO PURCHASE.—A mortgagee may purchase the mortgaged property at a sale by him under a power of sale contained in the mortgage, if by the terms thereof he is expressly authorized to do so. Though no such authority is given expressly, the sale, if made fairly and without fraud, is not void, but merely voidable.

Execution in favor of the Mutual Loan and Banking Company was levied upon realty claimed by J. Haas, M. Adler, and I. Liebman. It was agreed that the rulings of the court upon questions of law should control the result, and a verdict was directed for the claimants. Plaintiff excepted. On August 4, 1890, the defendant in execution, Mrs. S. J. Handy, executed a mortgage to Haas upon the property in dispute to secure the payment of her note and interest thereon at five years. The mortgage contained a power of sale to be exercised upon default in the payment of the note or an installment of interest thereon. Prior to May 1, 1894, Mrs. Handy defaulted in the payment of one or more installments of interest, and on that day, after complying with the terms of such power of sale, the property was sold by Haas thereunder, and purchased by himself and one Adler who had an interest in the mortgage. Haas made to himself and Adler a deed to the property as the attorney in fact of Mrs. Handy. Before May 15, 1894, Mrs. Handy delivered possession of the premises to Haas. On that day he and Adler conveyed to Liebman a one-third undivided interest in the same premises. Plaintiff's execution against Mrs. Handy was dated February 2, 1894, and was founded on a judgment rendered January 29, 1894. It was levied on the premises June 4, 1894.

Simmons & Corrigan, for the plaintiff.

Goodwin & Westmoreland, for the defendants.

[114] SIMMONS, C. J. 1. It was contended on the part of the judgment creditor that, the mortgagee not having the legal title and being merely an agent of the mortgagor in the sale of the land, a purchaser at the sale would take the land subject to the lien of judgments against the mortgagor existing at the time of the sale, just as he would if the land were sold by the mortgagor herself. We do not concur in this view. The mortgagee, in the exercise of the power of sale, was something more than a mere agent of the mortgagor. The mortgage, it is true, did not convey title, and therefore the mortgagee did not acquire such an interest in the mortgaged property as would prevent a revocation of the power of sale by the death of the mortgagor (Wilkins v. McGehee, 86 Ga. 766), but he did acquire such a vested right in the [115] power as could not be divested in the lifetime of the mortgagor, either by any act of revocation on her part, or by the rendition of a judgment against her in favor of a subsequent creditor: Calloway v. People's Bank, 54 Ga. 441; Ray v. Hemphill, 97 Ga. 564; and see Wilkins v. McGehee, 86 Ga. 766. In the present case, there was no stipulation that the power should be irrevocable, such as was contained in the mortgage dealt with in the case of Ray v. Hemphill, 97 Ga. 564; but we do not think such a stipulation is essential in order to give the power that effect; and in this view we are supported by the authorities cited in the opinion of the court in that case. See opinion of Marshall, C. J., in Hunt v. Rousmanier, 8 Wheat. 174; 1 American Leading Cases, Hare & Wallace ed., *578; 2 Story on Agency, 8th ed., sec. 477. Under these authorities a power of sale which is a part of a security is from its own nature and character, in contemplation of law, irrevocable, even though it be not made so in terms.

In Calloway v. People's Bank, 54 Ga. 441, a power of sale in a mortgage which contained no such stipulation was held irrevocable; and although in Wilkins v. McGehee, 86 Ga. 766, the reasoning of McCay, J., in so far as he treated the power as coupled with an interest in the land itself, was disapproved, and it was held that such a power would not survive the death of the mortgagor, we nevertheless said that under the facts of the case the decision was right, the mortgagor being in life at the time of the exercise of the power. In the Calloway case, as in the present case, the rights of a creditor holding a judgment junior to the mortgage were involved.

A creditor of a mortgagor, who obtains his judgment subsequently to the execution of a mortgage which has been duly registered,takes it subject to the rights of the mortgagee; and the power of sale being a part of the security, he takes it subject to the exercise of that power. His judgment attaches merely to the equity of redemption: Tarver v. Ellison, 57 Ga. 54. He stands in the shoes of the mortgagor, [116] and cannot defeat the exercise of the power any more than the mortgagor himself could.

"To permit the mortgagor to prevent the exercise of this power by subsequent grants, or to allow his creditors to defeat [it] by subsequent judgments, would be, in substance, a reservation of the power, and would render the security worthless, so far as its value depended on the power." Thompson, J., in Bancroft v. Ashhurst, 2 Grant Cas. 520. If a subsequent creditor could effect a revocation of the power by obtaining a judgment against the mortgagor, the mortgagor himself could at any time before the exercise of the power effect a revocation by contracting indebtedness to others, and permitting or procuring judgments to be taken against him; so that at last the right of the mortgagee to avail himself of the power which he had contracted for as a part of his security, would be dependent on the will of the mortgagor.

In Jones on Mortgages, it is said that the purchaser at a sale under a power of sale in a mortgage "takes the mortgagor's title divested of all encumbrances made since the creation of the power," and that "a sale regularly exercised under a power is equivalent to strict foreclosure by a court of equity properly pursued, or to a foreclosure and sale under a decree in equity, and cannot be defeated to the prejudice of one purchasing in good faith": 2 Jones on Mortgages, sec. 1897. See, also, sec. 1654. The same author further says: "Although in several states a mortgage is by statute or judicial interpretation declared to be a mere security for the payment of a debt, and not a conveyance of a legal title, yet this view of the nature of the security does not in any way interfere with or impair the doctrine of powers to sell": 2 Jones on Mortgages, sec. 1767.

2. It is well settled that a mortgagee may purchase the mortgaged property at a sale by him under a power of sale in the mortgage, if by the terms of the mortgage he is expressly authorized to do so: See 2 Jones on Mortgages, [117] sec. 1883. Even where no such authority is expressly given, the sale, if

made fairly and without fraud, would not be void, but merely voidable: Palmer v. Young, 96 Ga. 246; 51 Am. St. Rep. 136.
Judgment affirmed.

All the justices concurring.

MORTGAGE—POWER OF SALE IN—EFFECT OF.—A power to sell contained in a mortgage is a power appendant to the estate and coupled with an interest. It is irrevocable, and is deemed part of the mortgage security: Pardee v. Lindley, 31 Ill. 174; 83 Am. Dec. 219; Wilson v. Troup, 2 Cow. 195; 14 Am. Dec. 458. But see Johnson v. Johnson, 27 S. C. 309; 13 Am. St. Rep. 636.

MORTGAGES—FORECLOSURE—RIGHT OF MORTGAGEE TO PURCHASE.—An unauthorized purchase by a mortgagee of the mortgaged property at a sale thereof under a power contained in the mortgage, if made fairly and without fraud, is not void but merely voidable at the election of the mortgagor or his successor to redeem at any time before final judgment of eviction. Such a purchase is good for all purposes except that it does not bar the mortgagor's equity of redemption: Palmer v. Young, 96 Ga. 246; 51 Am. St. Rep. 136. See McCall v. Mash, 89 Ala. 487; 18 Am. St. Rep. 145. Perhaps it may be stated as a general rule that the mortgagee cannot purchase at his own sale under a power in the mortgage, in the absence of an agreement between the parties or of a statutory provision to that effect: Extended note to Wygal v. Bigelow, 16 Am. St. Rep. 499.

JUDGMENT AND MORTGAGE LIENS—PRIORITY BETWEEN.—The lien of an equitable mortgage is superior to that of subsequent judgments: Bank of Muskingum v. Carpenter, 7 Ohio, pt. I, 21; 28 Am. Dec. 616, and note. But the lien of a judgment takes priority over a prior unrecorded mortgage: Manufacturers' etc. Bank v. Bank of Pennsylvania, 7 Watts & S. 335; 42 Am. Dec. 240; and over a junior mortgage lien: Trapnall v. Richardson, 13 Ark. 543; 58 Am. Dec. 338. The right of a party founded solely on the lien of a judgment or attachment is subordinate to that of a purchaser in good faith: Shirk v. Thomas, 121 Ind. 147; 16 Am. St. Rep. 381, and note.

BEHRE v. NATIONAL CASH REGISTER COMPANY.

[100 Georgia, 213.]

CORPORATION—LIABILITY FOR SLANDER BY AGENT.—A corporation is not liable for a slander uttered by its agent or officer, even though he is acting honestly for the benefit of the company and within the scope of his authority, unless it is shown that the corporation expressly ordered and directed him to utter the very words in question.

LIBEL—SUFFICIENCY OF COMPLAINT.—A declaration alleging that defendant, a corporation, has caused to be published in a certain newspaper a statement concerning the plaintiff, who had been the agent of such company, that he was no longer connected with it, and that any contracts made by him for such company would be void, and also alleging that such publication was maliciously made with the motive and for the purpose of falsely holding the plaintiff out to the world as an impostor, seeking and undertaking to act as an agent for such company without authority, when in fact he was not so attempting, states a good cause of action for libel.

Hall & Hammond, T. B. Felder, and A. H. Davis, for the plaintiff.

T. W. Latham and Glenn & Roundtree, for the defendant.

[213] COBB, J.   Charles H. Behre brought his action against the National Cash Register Company, a corporation, alleging in his petition that he had sustained damage on account of certain slanderous words which had been uttered by the agent of the defendant while acting in and about the business of said corporation; and also by a libelous writing which the corporation had caused to be published in certain newspapers. On demurrer, the court dismissed the declaration, holding [214] that the same set forth no cause of action. To this ruling the plaintiff excepted.

1. The petition alleged that the defendant's agent went about from place to place and while in the conduct of the defendant's business uttered words in reference to plaintiff which were false and malicious. While it is distinctly alleged that the words complained of were uttered by the agent of defendant within the scope of the agency and in behalf of and for the interest of the defendant, it failed to allege that the defendant expressly directed or authorized the agent to speak the words in question. "A corporation will not be liable for any slander uttered by an officer, even though he be acting honestly for the benefit of the company and within the scope of his duties, unless it can be proved that the corporation expressly ordered and directed that officer to say those very words; for a slander is the voluntary and tortious act of the speaker": Odgers on Libel and Slander, 1st Am. ed., *368; Newell on Defamation, Slander, and Libel, 1st ed., 361. "As a corporation can act only by or through its agents, and as there can be no agency to slander, it follows that a corporation cannot be guilty of slander; it has not the capacity for committing that wrong. If an officer or an agent be guilty of slander, he is personally liable, and no liability results to the corporation": Townshend on Slander and Libel, 2d ed., sec. 265; Dodge v. Bradstreet Co., 59 How. Pr. 104.

2. "A corporation may make a libelous publication": Howe Machine Co. v. Souder, 58 Ga. 65. The remaining question to be determined in this case is, therefore, whether there is a cause of action as for a libel set forth in the declaration. The article complained of as libelous was as follows: "Mr. Chas. H. Behre

is no longer connected with the National Cash Register Company, and has not been since August, 1893. Any contracts made by him for the company will be void. [Signed] J. Block, Agent, National Cash Register Company."

[215] It was alleged that this notice was published in a newspaper in Albany, Georgia, and that a similar publication appeared in a newspaper in Atlanta, Georgia. It was further alleged, "that these publications were made for the purpose of injuring petitioner in his business by bringing him into discredit by making the public believe that he was undertaking to act as the agent of the said defendant, when in fact he was doing nothing of the kind, but was keeping as far aloof from them and their affairs as possible; and that the motive of the said defendant was to put him in a false attitude before the business public, by creating the impression that he was trying to act as their agent without authority, ... and was part of a general plan and purpose of said defendant to injure him in his business and bring him into disrepute; and that they were inspired and made by said defendant for that purpose." The words complained of may be literally true—the statement in the first sentence as a matter of fact, and the statement in the second sentence as a matter of law. If the words were published in good faith for the purpose of protecting the interest of the defendant, no liability would flow from their publication. They are not libelous per se; but the averment as to the intention with which the defendant caused them to be published and the effect which they have upon anyone reading them makes them libelous. The impression created upon the mind of anyone reading this notice is, that the plaintiff is seeking to impose himself upon the trading public as the agent of the defendant, and that through that means he is attempting to defraud the persons with whom he comes in contact in connection with the sale of the goods of the character sold by the defendant. The distinct allegation being that this was false and the words quoted above being, in effect, an allegation of malice, the petition sets forth a cause of action. In the case of Maynard v. Fireman's Fund Ins. Co., 47 Cal. 207, the words complained of were: "This company, for good and sufficient reasons, has resolved to dismiss D. D. [216] Maynard from its service." The court in the opinion say: "Words, which on their face appear to be entirely harmless, may, under certain circumstances, convey a covert meaning, wholly different from the ordinary and natural interpretation usually put upon them. To render such words actionable, it is necessary for the pleader to

aver that the author of the libel intended them to be understood, and that they were in fact understood by those who read them, in their covert sense." The definition of libel in the law of this state is as follows: "A libel is a false and malicious defamation of another, expressed in print, or writing, or pictures, or signs, tending to injure the reputation of an individual, and exposing him to public hatred, contempt, or ridicule": Civ. Code, sec. 3832. The plaintiff's petition showing that he was engaged in the business of selling cash registers, there can be no question but that the words complained of, when published with the intention alleged, tended to injure the reputation of the plaintiff, and also to expose him to the hatred, contempt, and ridicule of the business public.

There was no error in sustaining the demurrer to so much of the petition as attempted to set forth a cause of action for slander, but the demurrer should have been overruled as to the paragraphs referring to the libel complained of.

Judgment reversed.

All the justices concurring.

CORPORATIONS — LIABILITY FOR LIBEL — ACTS OF AGENTS.—It is well settled that a corporation may be held civilly liable for libel: Monographic note to Hoboken Printing etc. Co. v. Kahn, 59 Am. St. Rep. 594. A corporation is responsible in damages for the publication of a libel which is shown to have been made by its authority, or to have been ratified by it, or to have been made by a servant or agent in the due course of the business in which he was employed: Fogg v. Boston etc. R. R. Corp., 148 Mass. 513; 12 Am. St. Rep. 583; and if it publishes and circulates a libel by the aid and assistance of others, all are equally liable in a civil action, either jointly or severally: Belo v. Fuller, 84 Tex. 450; 31 Am. St. Rep. 75. But it is not liable for a libel by its agent, not in the course of his duty, nor authorized nor approved by the corporation: Southern Exp. Co. v. Fitzner, 59 Miss. 581; 42 Am. Rep. 379. See Missouri etc. Ry. Co. v. Richmond, 73 Tex. 568; 15 Am. St. Rep. 794.

GRAHAM v. SMITH.

[100 GEORGIA, 434.]

ANIMALS—DOGS—PROPERTY IN.—The owner of a dog has such a property right therein as enables him to maintain trover in case of its wrongful conversion.

W. D. Van Pelt, for the plaintiff in error.

S. F. Garlington, for the defendant in error.

[435] LITTLE, J. It is somewhat difficult to determine the status of the dog as property in this state; it is not difficult to

show that the owner has a property right in the animal, but it
is difficult to define the nature and extent of it. .This right
seems to be better defined at common law than it is by the construction which this court has put upon our statutes. Our constitution, article 7, section 2, paragraph 1, impliedly recognizes
dogs as property. It provides that the general assembly may impose a tax upon such domestic animals as from their nature and
habits are destructive of other property. It is true that this
power to tax partakes of the nature of a police regulation and is
made the exception to our uniform and ad valorem system of
taxation, but the constitution evidently intends to and does de-
note the dog as a domestic animal and by reference classes this
animal with other property. Section 3822 of the Civil Code
recognizes the ownership of dogs, in that it makes the owners
liable to suit for the recovery of damages for injuries inflicted
by their dogs under certain circumstances. Section 164 of the
Penal Code makes the dog eo nomine a subject of simple larceny.
The provision, however, does not seem to bring the dog as property to any high degree, because, in speaking of all other domestic animals, it is provided, "and also a dog" may be the subject of simple larceny; implying two things: that he was not
theretofore a subject of simple larceny, nor was he a domestic
animal. To one of us, at least, a possible reason why the dog
may not by common consent have been accorded a place among
domestic animals not more worthy and even less valuable, is suggested by a learned writer (Grotius) when he says, "The reason
why some creatures fly and avoid us is not the want of gentle-
ness and mildness on their part, but on ours." In Jemison v.
Southwestern R. R. Co., 75 Ga. 444, 58 Am. Rep. 476, which
was an action against a railroad [430] company for the negligent
and malicious killing of a dog by the operation of a train of cars,
it was held that a dog is property only in a qualified sense and
that such an action would not lie; and in the case of Patton v.
State, 93 Ga. 111, it was held that the willful and malicious killing of a dog was not an indictable offense under section 729 of
our Penal Code. In the latter case, however, the ruling was based
on the construction that the subjects of that particular statute
were inanimate property. In the case, however, of Manning v.
Mitcherson, 69 Ga. 447, 47 Am. Rep. 764, it was ruled that the
law of this state contemplated that to have property in animals
which are wild by nature, the owner must have them within his
actual possession, custody, or control, and this may be done by
taming, **domesticating, or confining them; and it was ruled also**

in that case that a possessory warrant would lie for the recovery
of a bird when so in possession; and animals by that decision
come under the same class. It is therefore apparent that an
owner has property in his dog, and that this property is sufficient
to support an action to recover possession of it when such has
been lost.

Dogs have been held to be property by the courts in the District of Columbia, in Kansas, Texas, Connecticut, Tennessee,
Michigan, Nebraska, Utah, and perhaps in other states. A contrary ruling has been made in several of the other states. His
status seems to be more clearly defined by the common law.
The compilers of the American and English Encyclopedia of Law,
volume 1, page 584, lay down the proposition that "at common
law the dog is considered a tame, harmless, and docile animal."
If this be true, and our investigation does not bear it out to its
full meaning, then the owner can have an absolute property in
such animals because "animals which are of a tame and domestic
nature are the subjects of absolute property": 1 Am. & Eng. Ency.
of Law, 572. The latter proposition is supported by reference to
a number of authorities. We, however, think that [437] Chancellor Kent more correctly lays down the common-law rule, that
"animals ferae naturae, so long as they are reclaimed by the art
and power of man, are also the subject of a qualified property,"
and that "while this qualified property continues, it is as much
under the protection of law as any other property, and every invasion of it is redressed in the same manner": 2 Kent's Commentaries, *348. Thus it has been held that trover lies for wild
geese which have been tamed, but which, without regaining their
natural liberty, have strayed away: Amory v. Flyn, 10 Johns. 102;
6 Am. Dec. 316. So also for domestic fowls: Leonard v. Belknap,
47 Vt. 603. Blackstone declares that the property in a dog is
base property, but that such property is sufficient to maintain a
civil action for its loss: 4 Blackstone's Commentaries, 236. Professor Schouler, in his treatise on the Law of Personal Property,
section 19, pronounces the dog to be a tame animal, from which
definition it would appear that an owner can acquire an absolute
property in the animal; and he distinguishes this animal from
such others as property can be acquired in only by possession. So
it will be seen that at the common law and under our statutes
the owner has property in his dog, and not only so, but such property right is sufficient to maintain a civil action to recover its
possession.

In the case now under consideration, the defendant in error

brought an action of trover in a justice's court to recover possession of his dog. A demurrer was filed to the proceeding in that
court, which was overruled by the magistrate, and the case taken
to the superior court by writ of certiorari; whereupon the judge
of the latter court held that the ruling of the magistrate was correct. So do we, on the authorities before referred to. The action
of trover, while changed with us in some respects, was originally
a special action on the case in favor of any person who had a general or special property in goods against any person who wrongfully withheld them from his possession. The special or qualified property which has been shown to exist in animals of this
character is sufficient to support the action. The action [438] lies
for every species of personal property, animate or inanimate: 6
Wait's Actions and Defenses, 128, 155. The question was expressly ruled in the state of Massachusetts, even though the courts
of that state had declared that the property right in a dog was
only a qualified one: See Cumming v. Perham, 1 Met. 555. The
question was likewise ruled in Binstead v. Buck, 2 W. Black.,
top p. 1117.

Judgment affirmed.

All the justices concurring.

ANIMALS—DOGS—PROPERTY IN.—Dogs have value and are
the property of the owner as much as any other animal which one
may have or keep: Ten Hopen v. Walker. 96 Mich. 236; 35 Am. St.
Rep. 599. and note: State v. McDuffie, 34 N. H. 523: 69 Am. Dec. 516.
See note to State v. Harriman, 46 Am. Rep. 425-428. A dog without
a collar is the subject of property, and trover may be maintained for
its conversion, even where a statute legalizes the killing of such dog:
State v. McDuffie, 34 N. H. 523; 69 Am. Dec. 516.

Temples v. Equitable Mortgage Company.

[100 Georgia, 503.]

MARRIED WOMEN—NOTE OF—PRESUMPTION.—If a mar-
ried woman gives her individual note, it is presumed that she gives
it on her own contract, for value, and to charge her separate estate.

MARRIED WOMEN—NOTE AND MORTGAGE OF—PLEA
AND PROOF NECESSARY TO DEFEAT.—If a married woman
gives her individual note and secures its payment by a mortgage
on her separate estate, and attaches an affidavit to the mortgage
stating that the money received is for her sole use and benefit,
and is not to be used in payment of any debt of her husband, nor in
any manner for his use and benefit, she cannot, in an action to

recover on the note. defend on the ground that it was given for a debt of her husband alone, unless she goes farther and alleges and proves that the holder of the note had notice of that fact.

MARRIED WOMEN—ESTOPPEL.—If a married woman gives her individual note and secures its payment by a mortgage on her separate estate, reciting that the loan received by her is for her sole use and benefit, and not to be used in the payment of any debt of her husband, nor in any manner for his use or benefit, she is estopped, in an action to recover on the note, from denying or contradicting the recitals contained in the mortgage.

MARRIED WOMEN—ESTOPPEL.—If a married woman borrows money, and by her conduct or representations induces the lender to suppose she is borrowing the money for her own use, when in fact her real purpose, unknown to him with whom she is dealing, is to obtain the money for her husband, she is estopped from denying that which she herself has induced the lender to believe.

JUDGMENTS—WHAT PROPERTY BINDS.—A court of general jurisdiction, having jurisdiction of the person of the defendant, can lawfully render a judgment against him binding his real property generally or specially, whether situated within the county in which the court was held or not.

Chambers & Polhill, for the plaintiff in error.

Dessau & Hodges and Payne & Tye, for the defendant in error.

503 LITTLE, J. The record shows that the plaintiff in error made an application in writing to the Georgia Security Investment Company to negotiate for her a loan of twelve hundred dollars, and proposed to secure the payment of that loan by a mortgage on certain real estate in Baldwin county. The application contained certain statements and representations concerning the nature and value of the land, made for the purpose of securing the loan. Among these were, that there were no judgments or other liens except a mortgage; that she had no indebtedness other than this; that she was the wife of John T. Temples. A written affidavit of the truth of the statements in the application was made by the **504** plaintiff in error, and attached. Accompanying these papers was also an agreement, constituting the investment company her agent to negotiate a loan of twelve hundred dollars on five years' time, bearing interest at six per cent per annum, and prescribing the nature of the note and mortgage to be executed by her. In this she agreed to pay the investment company two hundred and twenty-eight dollars as commissions to negotiate the loan. She also authorized her agent to pay off all liens on the property, which she recited to be one thousand dollars. These papers all bore date March 29, 1889. The record also contains copy of a promissory note for twelve hundred and ninety dollars principal, and coupons for interest made to the Equitable Mortgage Company, dated April 17, 1889, signed by

plaintiff in error; also, copy of a deed conveying title to the land
described in the application, to secure payment of the note; also
affidavit of the plaintiff in error, to the effect that the money received by her on the loan negotiated by the Georgia Security &
Investment Company is for her sole use and benefit, and is not to
be used in payment of her husband's debt. Copy of the check
for the money, payable to R. W. Roberts, agent of Sallie Temples,
follows: also a receipt for twelve hundred and ninety dollars, less commissions as agreed, from the Georgia Security &
Investment Company, signed by plaintiff in error. The evidence
showed that the loan was negotiated through the investment company with the Equitable Mortgage Company as the result of the
application made by plaintiff in error. The mortgage company
brought suit on the note, and prayed a general judgment against
the defendant and a special judgment against the land. The
plaintiff in error demurred to so much of the petition as prayed
for a special judgment against the land, on the ground that it was
situate in Baldwin county and the superior court of Bibb county
had no jurisdiction to grant a special lien thereon. The demurrer
was overruled, and exception pendente lite taken. Besides de-
murring to the petition, the plaintiff in error by answer denied
indebtedness, admitted 'the execution of the [505] note, and
averred that it was given to the plaintiff for the loan of
twelve hundred and ninety dollars to her hand; that she never
contracted for the loan of any sum in consideration of the note,
nor did she receive the money mentioned in the note from plaintiff or its agents, but the note was executed for money which her
husband said he had borrowed; that the deed was executed to secure an indebtedness of her husband; that no consideration
passed to her; that she never contracted any indebtedness to
plaintiff; that the land was her separate property; and prayed
the deed should be canceled. On the trial plaintiff introduced
the note and deed. Mrs. Temples testified for herself that she
executed the note and deed; was the wife of J. T. Temples at
that time; that she signed the application, agreement, affidavit,
etc., which were introduced by the plaintiff. Verdict was for
plaintiff. A motion for new trial was made on the general
grounds; because the court erred in overruling the demurrer;
because the court refused to permit Mrs. Temples while a witness
to testify as to the time, and the purpose she had in signing the
application for the loan; because the court erred in refusing to
allow Mrs. Temples to testify whether the loan was procured by
herself or her husband, her husband having died before the trial;

because the court erred in refusing to allow her to testify as to whether Roberts was her agent, or whether the money was loaned to her or her husband. The motion for new trial was overruled; defendant excepted.

In the argument here, the main ground of error insisted on was the refusal of the court to allow the plaintiff in error to testify as set out in the motion for new trial. In effect, the answer to the petition set up the defense that the loan for which the note was given was a debt of the husband, and that her separate estate was not liable therefor, notwithstanding she had signed the note, nor did the plaintiff take any title under the conveyance made by her to secure said note, because it was to secure such debt of the husband. The issue made, therefore, was whether the debt was the wife's, [?] who made the application and executed all the papers, or that of her husband.

It was not denied that the plaintiff in error signed the appiication for the loan, that the property described was her separate estate, that she made an agreement with the investment company to allow it a given commission to negotiate the loan applied for, and appointed a third person her agent to receive the money for her. And it appears from the record that on this application the company negotiated the loan for the plaintiff in error, and that she made affidavit that the loan was for her sole use, and not for the use or benefit of her husband; and she also executed the note payable to the defendant in error, and secured it by a convoyance of her real estate, according to the terms of the application. The answer to the petition fails to allege that the company lending the money had any notice, actual or constructive, that the money sought to be borrowed was for the husband.

It must be remembered that by the statute a married woman is vested with the powers of a feme sole as to her separate estate, with only certain named restrictions. She cannot bind such estate by any contract of suretyship, nor by any assumption of the debt of her husband; a sale of her separate estate to a creditor of her husband in payment of his debt is void. Other than as thus excepted, she has been vested with power to contract as to her separate estate. Notwithstanding the statute declares her acts within the prohibited limits absolutely void, this court has repeatedly held, in construing the statute, that in the hands of a bona fide holder for value, who purchased the same before due, without notice, her contract made within the forbidden limit is valid as to such purchaser, and binds her: Perkins v. Rowland, 69 Ga. 661; Strauss v. Friend, 73 Ga. 782. In Sutton v. Aiken,

62 Ga. 733, is an able argument on the rights of married women to contract with reference to the restrictions imposed by the statute. There, Bleckley, J., speaking for the court, says: "Our conclusion is, that a conveyance [507] amenable to section 1783 of the code [Civ. Code, sec. 2488] is absolutely void as between the maker and all persons affected with notice, but that a subsequent bona fide purchaser for value and without notice is protected."

When a married woman gives her individual note, the presumption of law is, that she gave it on her own contract and for value, to charge her separate property: Perkins v. Rowland, 69 Ga. 664. This being the legal presumption, it is not a sufficient defense to aver that it was given for the husband's debt. It may have been so given, and yet, as we have seen, if it for value, before due, go into the hands of one who is not charged with notice and who has no notice of its inherent defect, it is good in his hands. In the case at bar, the husband appears nowhere in the transaction; the wife has a separate estate; she made a written application to a third party to negotiate a loan for her, and agreed to pay a certain commission for his services. She made her individual note and secured its payment by a deed conveying title to her separate estate—all this she had a perfect legal right to do; she appointed an agent to receive the money for her; she attached an affidavit that the money was for her sole use and benefit, and was not to be used in payment of any debt of her husband or in any manner for his use and benefit. She gave her receipt for the money according to the terms of the contract. When suit to recover the amount of the note is instituted, her plea is made that it was given for a debt of the husband. This does not go far enough to set up a legal defense. If it were so, and the money were lent on the faith of her promise to pay, by one who had no knowledge that it was an assumption of a debt of the husband, she would be bound. On the face of the contract it is her debt, her paper. Prima facie it is a contract she can legally make. In order to successfully defend and avoid liability, she must go farther and charge notice on the holder of the note. "A plea to the effect that the note was given by the wife for the debt of the husband, but which did not [508] allege that the plaintiff had received the note after maturity or with notice, was fatally defective": Perkins v. Rowland, 69 Ga. 661.

Under the pleadings, proofs, and admissions as they stood at the trial, the purpose of the wife in signing the application—whether the loan was procured by her or her husband, whether it was loaned to herself or her husband, were inadmissible; so far as the face of the papers showed, it was her debt, and the loan made to her.   If the loan was procured by the husband, or for him, the plea must not only set out that fact, but charge the holder with notice, in order to overcome the legal presumption of the legality of her contract.

The evidence sought to be introduced, however, is inadmissible from another point of consideration.   The application, agreement, appointment of agent, affidavit that the loan was granted for her sole use, note, deed, and receipt for the money were all in writing, signed by the wife, and in evidence.   When the court refused to allow her to answer the questions propounded, these instruments spoke for themselves and were not ambiguous, and were all part of the contract.   Why was not the plaintiff in error estopped from denying the representations and terms of these instruments which she had executed and delivered?   Counsel for plaintiff in error insists that she is not estopped now from contradicting these written statements, and cites as authority the case of Dunbar v. Mize, 53 Ga. 435.   In that case William Mize and his wife executed a mortgage on land to secure a note given by William Mize, the husband, to Dunbar & Co.   The mortgage recited that the note was given in payment for merchandise which went to the use of Mize and wife.   On foreclosure proceedings, the wife set up as a defense that the note was the debt of the husband, that she derived no personal benefit from the consideration, and by the mortgage she was in effect giving a lien on her separate estate to secure his debt.   Plaintiff claimed that defendant **509** was estopped from denying recital in mortgage as to consideration of the note.   The court held she was not.   Without undertaking to review the decision in that case, it is sufficient to say that we are not prepared to hold it was wrong, nor irreconcilable with our construction of the law in the case at bar.   In the Mize case the husband gave his individual note to Dunbar & Co.   It was his debt.   Dunbar & Co knew the consideration, accepted the husband as the debtor.   Subsequent to the execution of the note, the husband and wife executed a mortgage to secure same note, on the separate estate of the wife, and placed in the mortgage a recitation that merchandise which went to the use of husband and wife was the consideration of the note.   It could not, however, be made to appear that Dunbar & Co. acted on the recitals in this mortgage, because the note was given antecedent to the execution of the mortgage.   No fraud could have been committed on the firm by recitation in the mortgage, because they were in no way hurt in their debt by taking the security; it was

their only security. The court held in that case that the wife
was not estopped by this recital from showing that the same was
untrue, and that the debt was wholly the husband's debt. It
also held: "If it had appeared that this recital misled the mortgagees, and that they acted to their hurt on the faith of it, there
might be some ground for an estoppel in pais, as a woman—even
a married one—cannot commit a fraud with impunity." The
principle here is different. The application, agreement, affidavit,
note, and mortgage were what the defendant in error acted on in
making the loan. If the evidence of the plaintiff in error was admissible, then it would appear that the lender acted to its hurt on
the faith of the representations, and here is made applicable the
doctrine of estoppel in pais. Herman, in the second volume of
his law of Estoppel and Res Judicata, page 1246, lays down the
rule that a married woman's estate may become bound by a participation in fraud, as where a mortgage is obtained upon [510]
property of the feme, on the false representation made by her
that she owned the absolute interest in the estate. . . . . "That
if a married woman, free from all constraint and with a full
knowledge of her rights, should represent that a certain tract of
land was not her homestead, and then cause a person to purchase
it, she would be concluded by her acts. . . . . These admissions,
whether of law or of fact, which have been acted on by others,
and which were calculated to influence a prudent man, and which
were the cause of another's actions, and which were deliberately
and knowingly made, are conclusive against the party making
them, in all cases between him and her, and the person whose
conduct was thus influenced"; and further, on page 1247, he
says: "Whatever may be the rule concerning the formalities
needed to bind married women, there is no doubt they may be estopped by their deliberate conduct, as well as anyone else": Citing Sharpe v. Foy, 4 Ch. App. 35; In re Lush's Trusts, 4 Ch. App.
591; and again on page 1248, same volume, he cites Bodine v.
Killeen, 53 N. Y. 93, and Lavasser v. Washburne, 50 Wis. 200,
for the doctrine that "married women, to the extent and in the
matter of business in which they are by law permitted to engage,
owe the same duty to those with whom they deal and may be
bound in the same manner as if unmarried."

Passing on the statute affecting the contract powers of married
women, the court, in the case of Sutton v. Aiken, 62 Ga. 733,
heretofore referred to, say: "If, trusting to the document which
she has signed, sealed, and delivered, any person should be honestly misled by it, why should she not abide the consequences?

If she has been taken at her werd, why should she not be required to make her word good, and be estopped from recalling or contradicting her own solemn utterance?"

When a married woman borrows money and by her conduct or representations induces the lender to suppose she is borrowing the money for her own use, when in fact her real purpose, unknown to the party with whom she is dealing, [511] is to obtain the money for her husband, she will be estopped from denying that which she herself had induced the lender to believe was true: Hibernia Sav. Inst. v. Luhn, 34 S. C. 175.

From any view which we take of this case, we are constrained to hold that there was no error in refusing the new trial by the court below. There was no error in sustaining the demurrer to that part of the petition which prayed for a special judgment against the land lying in Baldwin county. Title to the land was not affected by this prayer—the prayer was for a judgment against it. The superior court of Bibb county, having jurisdiction of the person of the defendant below, could properly and lawfully render a judgment against her, binding her property generally, or specially as prayed for in this case.

Judgment affirmed.

All the justices concurring.

MARRIED WOMEN—ESTOPPEL OF BY NOTE.—By signing a joint note with her husband a wife clothes the holder with evidence of her intention to charge her separate estate, and is estopped to deny such intention when an innocent holder has advanced money upon his faith in such intention: Nelson v. McDonald, 80 Wis. 606; 27 Am. St. Rep. 71. If she makes her note in terms referring to her separate estate, an innocent indorsee for value before maturity has the right to rely upon the statements made in the note and the maker is estopped to deny such statements unless she can prove that the holder of the note knew them to be untrue: Monographic note to Trimble v. State, 57 Am. St. Rep. 177, on estoppel against married women. See Deering v. Boyle, 8 Kan. 525; 12 Am. Rep. 480; Taddiken v. Cantrell, 60 N. Y. 597; 25 Am. Rep. 253; McVey v. Cantrell, 70 N. Y. 295; 26 Am. Rep. 605.

RYDER *v.* STATE.

[100 GEORGIA, 528.]

TRIAL—CONTINUANCE OF CRIMINAL CASE.—An application for continuance of a criminal case, on the ground of the absence of witnesses, should be granted when it appears that the proof which the accused expects to make by such witnesses is not only material upon the controlling issues, but is also such as he cannot fully and satisfactorily make by other witnesses.

TRIAL—CONTINUANCE OF CRIMINAL CASE.—An application for the continuance of a criminal case on the ground of the absence of witnesses should be granted, when it appears that the accused is indicted for murder and relies upon the defense of insanity alleged to have been produced by a chronic disease originating early in his life, and that the absent witnesses are persons who had exceptional opportunities for knowing him and his mental and physical condition at the time, although it appears by a counter showing that there are other witnesses, by whom many of the facts within the knowledge of the absent witnesses can be proved, and that none of the absent witnesses have actually seen the accused for a considerable period of time.

TRIAL—ORDER OF PROOF IN CRIMINAL CASE—ABSENCE OF WITNESS.—An accused in a criminal case has the right to be allowed to introduce his witnesses in the order in which he or his counsel think is to the best interests of his case, and the fact that a witness is compelled to leave the court for providential cause does not compel the accused to put him on the stand as a witness out of order and to his prejudice. The failure of the accused or his counsel to introduce the witness at a time which is inconsistent with the interest of the accused does not deprive him of his right to complain of the absence of such witness at a subsequent stage of the case, if that absence is in no way caused by the accused or his counsel.

INSANITY AS A DEFENSE.—To render the distinctive defense of insanity available, the burden is on the accused to show affirmatively by a preponderance of the evidence that he was insane at the time the act for which he is indicted was committed. Though this burden may not be successfully carried so as to authorize a verdict of not guilty on this particular ground, it is nevertheless the duty of the jury to consider the evidence touching the alleged insanity in connection with the other evidence in the case, and then, in view of it all, to determine whether or not a reasonable doubt of the guilt of the accused exists in their minds.

INSANITY AS A DEFENSE—EXPERT AND NONEXPERT TESTIMONY—INSTRUCTIONS.—If the defense of insanity is relied upon, and there is evidence of expert and nonexpert witnesses who testify as to the insanity of the accused, and who were "parties who associated with the defendant, lived with him, lived in the same community," it is error to charge the jury that the testimony of expert witnesses is entitled to great weight, and that the testimony of intimate associates of the accused should be given similar weight. The jury are the sole judges, and should be left untrammeled to pass upon the credibility of all witnesses.

EVIDENCE—OPINIONS.—If the question under examination and to be decided by the jury is one of opinion, any witness, whether expert or nonexpert, may state his opinion or belief, giving his reasons therefor, when authorized so to do, by statute.

JURY AND JURORS.—If a juror has qualified upon his voir
dire and has been accepted as a juror, the court, in the absence of
extrinsic evidence impeaching or attacking the juror's competency,
is not bound to investigate it, nor is the court bound to ask, or to
permit counsel to ask, the juror any question the answer to which
would tend to incriminate or disgrace him. The scope of such inquiry is largely within the discretion of the trial court.

HOMICIDE. — INSTRUCTIONS IN A HOMICIDE CASE
which intimate an opinion that the killing was done by the accused,
when the latter has not distinctly admitted that he committed the
homicide, are erroneous.

J. H. Worrill, A. A. Carson, Du Pont Guerry, J. J. Bull, and
C. J. Thornton, for the plaintiff in error.

J. M. Terrell, Attorney General, S. P. Gilbert, Solicitor General, and J. H. Martin, for the defendant in error.

531 COBB, J. W. L. Ryder was indicted for the offense of
murder. His defense was that he did not commit the homicide
charged in the indictment, and that if he did, he was insane at
the time the killing was done.

1, 2, 3. When the case of the accused was called for trial, he
made a motion for a continuance on account of the absence of
four witnesses. His motion complied strictly with the law regulating such matters: Pen. Code, sec. 962. And the only matters
about which there could be any question were whether the facts
sought to be proven by the absent witnesses were material to the
defense, and whether or not he could prove the same facts as well
by other witnesses. It was claimed that the accused was subject
to fits of insanity produced by a chronic disease of the ear which
originated at an early period of his life, and that when suffering
from the effects of this disease he was and had been at various
times in his life insane and irresponsible. Two of the absent witnesses were his brothers, who, according to the showing made, had
associated with him more intimately than his other relatives, and
his physical and mental condition was more peculiarly within
their knowledge than that of any other members of his family.
Another witness was one who had been acquainted with him from
his childhood, and who knew of his infirmity and of his periods
of alleged insanity and irresponsibility. The remaining witness
was a physician who had known the accused all his life, and was
professionally familiar with the nature of the alleged disease. It
further appeared in the showing for a continuance that all these
witnesses would swear to the insanity of the accused at times
when his disease was at its worst. In the showing the facts upon
which their testimony would be based appeared in detail. The
counter-showing disclosed that there were other relatives, mem-

bers of the immediate family of the accused, who were present at
the trial, and could be called as witnesses, but it did not appear
that any of these [532] would testify to the peculiar facts set out
in the motion for a continuance and upon which it was based. It
is proper, however, to add that the four absent witnesses did not
see the accused on the day of the homicide, or at any time immediately preceding that day. In a case like the present, where
there has been a shocking homicide, and where there can be
scarcely a doubt that the accused committed it, although he does
not expressly so admit in his plea, the defense mainly relied on
being that of insanity at the time of the killing, it was depriving
the accused of a very great right when he was forced to trial in the
absence of these four witnesses who knew the facts that were material to his defense, and whose presence was important to the
proper determination of the issue. It is especially so in the present case when the record shows that there was much evidence for
the state to show that the accused was sane. The large amount
of evidence for the state showing the sanity of the accused, instead of being a reason for overruling the motion for a new trial,
is a stronger reason for granting one. The refusal of the court
to continue his case deprived the accused of the benefit of the four
witnesses, who, above all others, were needed by him in his trial
to meet the mass of evidence showing sanity. The court should
have either continued the case for the term, or postponed the trial
until a later day in order that the accused might have secured the
attendance of these witnesses, in order that the jury might pass
upon the question of their credibility and the weight to be attached to their testimony.

4. The physician, who was the absent witness in the motion
above referred to, subsequently appeared at the trial, but was
compelled to leave the court for providential cause. Before leaving he requested counsel for the accused to allow him to go upon
the stand and testify, so as not to be required to return to the
court, to which request they declined to accede. We do not
think that the accused lost any of his rights to complain of the
subsequent absence of [533] this witness because his counsel failed
to interrupt and change the line of his defense and the manner in
which it was being conducted so as to place this witness upon the
stand in advance of the time when they had contemplated so doing. It is an important right of the accused to be allowed to introduce his witnesses in the order in which he or his counsel think
is to the best interest of his case, and witnesses should not be allowed to dictate to counsel as to when they should be put upon

the stand. The failure of counsel to introduce the witness at a time which was inconsistent with the interest of the accused should not generally deprive him of his right to complain of the absence of a witness at a subsequent stage of the case, if that absence is in no way occasioned by the accused or his counsel.

5. Following the decision of this court in the case of Carr v. State, 96 Ga. 285, and the cases there cited, the propositions stated in the fifth headnote are too well settled to need further discussion.

6. Where the defense of insanity is relied on, and there is evidence of expert and nonexpert witnesses who testify as to the sanity of the accused and who were "parties who associated with the defendant, lived with him, lived in the same community," it was error for the judge to charge the jury that the testimony of expert witnesses was entitled to great weight, and to add, in substance, that the testimony of intimate associates of the accused should be given similar weight. All this testimony is allowed for the purpose of informing the jury as to the truth of the issue, and the weight to be given to it is for them. The judge should not intimate in any way to them how they should deal with any particular class of witnesses, but under proper instructions leave the entire matter to them. It may be that in certain cases the testimony of nonexpert witnesses would, in the mind of an intelligent juror, outweigh the testimony of the alleged expert witnesses, and that in other cases the testimony of the expert would be given the greater weight; but [534] the jury are the sole judges of such things, and the judge should leave them untrammeled to pass upon the credibility of all witnesses, and give such weight to the testimony of each as they see proper.

7. "Where the question under examination, and to be decided by the jury, is one of opinion, any witness may swear to his opinion or belief, giving his reasons therefor": Pen. Code, sec. 1021. There seems to have been no violation of this well-settled rule in regard to the nonexpert witnesses in this case. Each witness examined was allowed to state his opinion, and no one did so without giving his reasons therefor. The opinion and the reasons go to the jury together. that the jury may determine what the opinion is worth. It may be that a particular reason given for an opinion is not really a good one, and such a reason would most probably in the mind of an intelligent juror destroy the opinion at once; but, nevertheless, the opinion and the reason ought to be considered, that the jury may give the opinion such weight as they think proper.

8. When a jury is about to be impaneled for the trial of a fel-ony case and the panel is "put upon the accused," and the names of the individual jurors are being called, it is competent for the state, or the accused, to make certain objections to each juror as he is called: Pen. Code, sec. 973. Upon such objections being made to a juror, it is the "duty of the court to hear immediately such evidence as may be submitted (the juror being a competent witness) in relation to the truth of these objections." On this issue the juror may be called as a witness, either by the party at-tacking his competency, or the party seeking to establish it. If, in this investigation, the juror is held to be competent, the next step is to place him upon his voir dire and ask him the questions prescribed in Penal Code, section 975. If he answers these ques-tions so as to qualify himself as a juror, the judge is not required, when the juror is placed upon him as a trior, to ask the juror any question in regard to his competency, nor to [533] permit counsel to do so; certainly neither the court nor counsel should ask any question which would involve a breach of the juror's privilege to refuse to answer on the ground that so doing would tend to in-criminate, or otherwise disgrace him; and neither the court itself should ask any question, nor should it permit counsel to ask any question of the juror until extrinsic evidence has been introduced tending to show that the juror has answered the questions or some of them falsely, thereby impeaching or attacking his competency. On this investigation the juror is not a competent witness in the broad sense in which the term is used when the challenge is for cause on one of the grounds stated in Penal Code, section 973. If the challenge for cause is overruled, and if the juror answers the statutory questions so as to qualify himself, he stands before the court as a competent juror, and he cannot be called upon to disqualify himself; and if placed upon the court as a trior, and his qualification is brought to the attention of the court by evi-dence other than that of the juror, then the court should deter-mine the question as to whether he is a competent juror or not, and ask him such questions only as he under the law would be compelled to answer if called as an ordinary witness, and then de-termine his competency from the extrinsic evidence, as well as the statement of the juror. No fixed rule can be laid down to be followed in all cases. The inquiry which the judge should make after the juror's competency is attacked by extrinsic evidence is to be left largely to the discretion of the trial judge according to the circumstances of each case.

9. While the accused mainly relied upon the defense of insan-

ity, still, as he did not expressly admit that he committed the
homicide, the court should not in its instructions to the jury have
referred to the homicide as "the act which the accused committed." But as counsel for the accused, in numerous requests
which were made to the judge to charge, used similar language,
this error on the part of the judge [536] would not have necessitated a new trial, even though the requests containing the language were not actually given by the judge. Counsel for the
accused should not, in their communications with the court in requests to charge, use language which would be calculated to mislead the court as to the contentions of the accused, and then
afterward complain that the language used, upon being subsequently adopted by the court, was calculated to prejudice the case
of the accused. Of course, if the requests containing the language had been given, there would be no question; but it seems to
us that where the requests gave to the judge language which he
used in his charge, independently of the requests, the language
ought not to be the subject of complaint at the instance of the accused. However, in cases where the accused does not expressly
admit that he committed the act, it is not good practice for the
judge to use such expressions as those above quoted.

10. The charge of the court was, in the main, correct and appropriate; and, considering it as a whole, except as herein criticised, was free from material error. The instructions as to the
law of insanity were in accord with the decisions of this court
cited above.

11. It is not necessary to decide in this case whether this court
has the power to review the decision of the judge of the superior
court upon a motion to change the venue in a criminal case under
the act of 1895: Acts 1895, pp. 70, 71. Even if this court has
the power to review such a decision, there is no present occasion
for exercising it, as the circumstances and surroundings of the
case when the accused is again put upon trial may, and probably
will be, essentially different from what they were at the time the
change of venue was requested.

12. We have dealt with all of the substantial errors committed
at the trial relating to any matter or question that is the least
likely to arise when the case is tried again; and [537] hence we do
not deal more specifically with the numerous grounds of the motion for a new trial.

Judgment reversed.

All the justices concurring.

TRIAL—CONTINUANCE FOR ABSENCE OF WITNESSES.—An application for a continuance on account of the absence of a witness should not be granted unless the application shows diligence to secure the attendance of the witness, and states definitely the facts expected to be proved by him: Miller v. State, 31 Tex. Crim. Rep. 609; 37 Am. St. Rep. 836, and note. See Reyons v. State, 33 Tex. Crim. Rep. 143; 47 Am. St. Rep. 25, and note; also the monographic note to Stevenson v. Sherwood, 74 Am. Dec. 144-149.

CRIMINAL LAW—INSANITY AS DEFENSE—DEGREE OF PROOF REQUIRED.—One charged with murder, and setting up his insanity as a defense, is bound to establish it, but he may do so by a bare preponderance of the evidence, and is not required to make any higher degree of proof: Kelch v. State, 55 Ohio St. 146; 60 Am. St. Rep. 680, and note.

INSTRUCTIONS—WEIGHT OF EVIDENCE—CREDIBILITY OF WITNESSES.—Instructions should avoid any statement of the evidence which may indicate the conclusions of the judge respecting the facts directly disputed on the trial: McShane v. Kenkle, 18 Mont. 208; 56 Am. St. Rep. 579. It is never the province of the court to tell the jury which class of conflicting testimony is entitled to the greater weight: West Chicago Street Ry. Co. v. Mueller, 165 Ill. 499; 56 Am. St. Rep. 263; McKeon v. Chicago etc. Ry. Co., 94 Wis. 477; 59 Am. St. Rep. 910, and note. The court cannot instruct upon the weight of evidence or the credibility of witnesses: Osborne v. Francis, 38 W. Va. 312; 45 Am. St. Rep. 855; Smith v. Milwaukee etc. Exchange, 91 Wis. 360; 51 Am. St. Rep. 912.

TRIAL BY JURY—VOIR DIRE EXAMINATION OF JURORS—DISCRETION OF COURT.—A court is invested with a certain degree of discretion in the selection of jurors, to be exercised by seeing that proper and competent men are selected: People v. Barker, 60 Mich. 277; 1 Am. St. Rep. 501, and extended note. See Pinder v. State, 27 Fla. 370; 26 Am. St. Rep. 75; also, extended note to State v. Crank, 23 Am. Dec. 128-131, on the examination of a juror on his voir dire. Only statutory questions respecting his competency should be propounded to a juror in a criminal case: Monday v. State, 32 Ga. 672; 79 Am. Dec. 314, and note.

SCOTT v. WILLIAMS.

[100 GEORGIA, 540.]

USURY—WHO MAY PLEAD.—While titles to property made as part of a usurious contract are void, yet the right to have them so declared rests only with the borrower, his personal representatives and privies, and a stranger to the transaction cannot set up the plea of usury in attacking such title.

USURY—TITLE VOID FOR—WHO MAY PLEAD.—If a borrower of money makes an absolute deed to realty to secure the payment of a debt tainted with usury, and then upon sufficient consideration procures the grantee to execute a bond for title in favor of a third person conditioned to convey the land to the obligee on payment of the original debt, the borrower thereby deprives himself of the right to redeem the land or to avoid the deed for usury, and his personal representative has no greater rights than his intestate had.

USURY—WHO MAY NOT PLEAD.—If a borrower of money exercises his personal privilege, and pays off a debt infected with usury without taking advantage of the plea of usury, neither his personal representatives nor privies can reopen the question or revise his act.

Busbee, Crum & Busbee, for the plaintiff.

Littlejohn & Thompson, for the defendant.

542 LITTLE, J. 1. The questions to be decided in this case arise on exceptions to the judgment of the court below in sustaining a demurrer to the declaration of the plaintiff, and involve the application of certain principles in the law of usury. Our Civil Code, section 2892, declares: "All titles to property made as part of an usurious contract, or to evade the laws against usury, are void." The record discloses that the title in question was made to secure a debt infected with usury; and the plaintiff, invoking this provision of our law, insists on a literal application of its precepts, while the defendant contends that such title is not ipso facto void. This is the question we have to decide.

Inasmuch as there is no qualification in the statute, we should consider first what is its effect; and we quote the language of an eminent writer, that "when the plain and unequivocal language of the law is rigidly followed, there are, to be sure, a few cases of hardship; but let it be once understood that statutes are not to be limited in their operation **543** by overrefined and artficial interpretations. Men are able to understand and govern themselves by the law of the land, and an incalculable amount of legal controversy is thus avoided." It may here be referred to that the statutes of the several states on the question of the effect of usury on contracts vary; in some instances, the statute declares that contracts founded in usury are void; in others, that such contracts are valid in the hands of a bona fide holder, etc. But it is unnecessary to pursue this branch of the investigation further, because our statute, when referring to titles infected with usury, declares the same void, and we construe these words to mean just what they say: they are void. When? A deed to a lot of land, though infected with usury, does not usually bear on its face any evidence that it is tainted with usury: it is prima facie a conveyance of such title as the grantor could convey; the defect in such deed is not patent; it does not rest on the terms of it, but must be shown by extrinsic proof, which goes to the consideration expressed. Therefore, on its face and as a natural effect of its terms, the deed conveys the title of the grantor to the premises described in the instrument, and such will be its effect until, on an examination of the consideration, it is ascertained that the consideration was usurious. Then, and not till then, will the court declare the apparent conveyance not to be a conveyance because of the vice in the consideration. Such conveyance is to be accredited good until the question is made and it is adjudicated to be bad.

Now, who can cause such or any other adjudication of that conveyance to be made? The answer is plain under the law: not a stranger to it, but only one who has an interest adverse to it. So that, deciding as we do that titles to property infected with usury are void, the practical effect of such decision is nugatory, until we further consider and determine who may have them so declared. The doctrine is well settled that the defense of usury can only be taken by the party to the usurious agreement, or persons representing [544] him as privies in blood or estate. A stranger cannot set up usury as a defense to an action: Tyler on Usury, 403. The plea of usury is a personal one, and no one can plead it but the borrower and his privies: Ryan v. American Freehold Mortgage Co., 96 Ga. 322; Zellner v. Mobley, 84 Ga. 749; 20 Am. St. Rep. 390. A title may be absolutely void between certain persons, and not void as between others: Zellner v. Mobley, 84 Ga. 749; 20 Am. St. Rep. 390. See, also, Jones on Mortgages, sec. 644. It may be said that in many cases where a transaction is declared void in terms of the common law, or even expressly by statute, where the obvious intent of the rule or statute is to secure and protect the rights of others, the construction of law is, that it is voidable so far that it shall not operate to defeat or impair those rights. A deed of this character is not a dead letter, but can be avoided by the injured person only, and at such time and in such manner as may be necessary to secure those rights; in other respects, it has its natural effects: Wait on Fraudulent Conveyances, sec. 445, et seq. Many other citations could be made, establishing these principles, but it is deemed unnecessary to further elaborate them. So that while we hold that titles to property made as part of an usurious contract are void, we further hold that the right to have the same so declared rests with the borrower, his personal representatives and privies. The case of Jaques v. Stewart, 81 Ga. 81, is not to be taken as an authority against the correctness of the principles here ruled, although a casual reading of that case would possibly lead to that conclusion. There, the record shows both parties claimed title from the same source, and the contest between the parties was, which particular bill

of sale made by Gordon, the one to Stewart, or the one to Jaques,
conveyed the title, and this court held that Jaques, when the
bill of sale made by Gordon to Stewart was offered as showing
title in the latter, might, in defense of the title conveyed to
him subsequently by Gordon, show that the first bill of sale was
infected with usury and therefore void; in other words, that
Gordon, the borrower, might [345] set up the fact of usury and
have the conveyance to Stewart declared void, and that Jaques
was his privy in estate, and, being such, the right to do so
inured to him.   These facts do not appear in the report of the
case, but are shown in the original record on file here, and formed
the basis for the opinion rendered: Zellner v. Mobley, 84 Ga.
750; 20 Am. St. Rep. 390.

2. It would seem conclusively to follow from the above reasoning that a stranger in law or in interest would not be heard
to attack a title as void because infected with an usurious consideration; indeed, we can conceive of circumstances where even
personal representatives, or privies in blood or estate, could not
do so.   This court held in the case of Zellner v. Mobley, 84 Ga.
746, 20 Am. St. Rep. 390, quoting from Mr. Tyler, that, referring to the borrower, "If for any reason—his desire to avoid
litigation, his pride of character, or his conscientious sense of
justice—he may be induced to waive his legal rights and to satisfy a demand, he is at liberty to do so, although it may be
obnoxious to the defense of usury." If a borrower may exercise his personal privilege and pay off a debt infected with usury,
or refuse to take advantage of this plea, preferring for such reasons as may actuate him to recognize and settle such usurious
contract, no one can deny him the right, and when he chooses
to do so and has done so, then neither his personal representatives nor privies can reopen the question or revise his act.   In
the case now under consideration, it is admitted that Perry,
the intestate, made to Lewis an absolute deed to real estate to
secure the payment of a debt infected with usury.   Under our
law, this title was void, and under any view of the law, Perry
would have the right to have it so declared; and if nothing more
appeared, the personal representative of Perry and his privies in
blood or estate would succeed to the same right.   But more does
appear.   At the time of the delivery of this deed, Perry, the intestate, made a contract with Lewis by which the latter executed
a bond conditioned to convey to [346] Mrs. S. A. T. Perry (wife
of the intestate) the land conveyed to him, on payment by her
or her assigns of the debt due by Perry.   Thus it appears that

Perry divested himself of the right to redeem the land and
placed such right in a third party. The record is silent as to
the consideration which moved this last agreement. The obligee,
however, being the wife of the debtor, the contract could be supported as a gift. In any event, Mrs. Perry accepted and held
the bond. We are not called on to decide whether Mrs. Perry
would have the right to set up usury in the deed to her obligor;
that question is not involved. After the death of Perry, Mrs.
Perry transferred and assigned her bond for titles to Williams,
who paid the debt of Perry to Lewis, received from the latter
a conveyance of the land and entered into possession. Now,
Scott, the administrator of Perry, files his petition, alleging the
facts; claiming that the deed from Perry to Lewis is infected
with usury and void, that Williams had notice of the usury before he took the conveyance from Lewis: and he prays damages
and judgment for the land and that title be vested in him as
administrator on payment of the original principal in the debt
owing by Perry to Lewis, with lawful interest thereon.

Under the view which we take of the case, the administrator
of Perry is not entitled to any of the relief prayed for by him;
nor in our opinion can he bring up the question of usury in the
original transaction between Perry and Lewis. When Perry
made the deed to Lewis, he procured the latter to make a bond
for titles to a third person, and the assignee of this third person
complied with the terms of the bond, paid the money, and received conveyance. Perry had a right to redeem. He chose,
however, for sufficient reasons, to part with his right, and when
he did so, he had no further right or interest in the land: Polhill
v. Brown, 84 Ga. 338; Shufelt v. Shufelt, 9 Paige, 137; 37 Am.
Dec. 381. If, after these transactions, Perry [547] could not open
the matter and recover the land, his personal representatives
could not.

Judgment affirmed.

All the justices concurring, except Fish, J., disqualified.

USURY AS DEFENSE—WHO MAY URGE—ESTOPPEL TO DO
SO.—Usury is a strictly personal defense, and the right to affirmative
relief is likewise personal and can only be taken advantage of by the
parties to the usurious agreement and their privies: Monographic
note to Davis v. Garr, 55 Am. Dec. 398. A stranger cannot set up
usury as a defense to an action: Zellner v. Mobley, 84 Ga. 746; 20 Am.
St. Rep. 390, and note; Hill v. Alliance Bldg. Co., 6 S. Dak. 160; 55
Am. St. Rep. 819, and note. Being a personal defense it may be
waived by a party entitled to set it up: Rock River Bank v. Sherwood, 10 Wis. 230; 78 Am. Dec. 669, or he may estop himself and
privies from setting it up, as where he borrows money on a mortgage,

covenanting that it is a valid lien, wholly unpaid and subject to no
defense: Union Dime Sav. Inst. v. Wilmot, 94 N. Y. 221; 46 Am. Rep.
137. See Ferguson v. Soden, 111 Mo. 208, 33 Am. St. Rep. 512; or permits judgment by default to be entered against him in which is included interest which ьe claims to be usurious: Ryan v. Southern
etc. Assn., 50 S. C. 185; post, p. 831.

TURNER *v.* LORILLARD COMPANY.

[100 GEORGIA, 645.]

STATUTE OF FRAUDS—CONTRACT, WHEN WITHIN.—A
contract for the purchase of goods "to the amount of fifty dollars or
more," though in writing, is within the statute of frauds, if it appears therefrom that it was the intention of the parties to contract
specifically as to the price to be paid, or if it appears from extrinsic evidence that such was the intention, and the writing neither
designates what the price was to be, nor otherwise states the actual
agreement of the parties with reference to the price in such manner
as to render its amount properly ascertainable by the aid of extrinsic
evidence.

STATUTE OF FRAUDS—STATEMENT OF PRICE WHEN
NOT NECESSARY.—If a verbal promise is made to pay what goods
are reasonably worth, or simply to pay for them, no definite or
fixed price need be stated in the subsequent written contract to satisfy the statute of frauds and parol evidence is admissible to fix
the reasonable worth of the goods.

STATUTE OF FRAUDS—STATEMENT OF PRICE, WHEN
NECESSARY.—If an intention is shown, either by the written contract itself or by extrinsic evidence, to agree specifically as to the
price to be paid for goods, the price becomes a part of the promise
and must be embraced in the writing, to meet the requirements of
the statute of frauds.

STATUTE OF FRAUDS—PAROL EVIDENCE.—If two writ-
ings are relied upon to satisfy the statute of frauds, and parol evidence is necessary to connect them with each other, they must fail
as a compliance with the statute, but if a writing refers to any other
writing, which can be completely identified by this reference, without the aid of parol evidence, then the two writings may constitute
a compliance with the statute.

STATUTE OF FRAUDS—STATEMENT OF PRICE WHEN
NECESSARY.—If an intention to contract specifically as to the price
to be paid for goods does not appear from the terms of the written
contract of purchase, but parol evidence makes it certain that such
intention existed at the time that the contract was made, the absence
of the statement of price from the contract as written renders it nugatory and within the statute of frauds.

T. B. West and L. D. Moore, for the plaintiff.

Dessau, Bartlett & Ellis and R. Hodges, for the defendant.

646 COBB, J. Turner sued Lorillard Company for damages
on account of an alleged failure on its part to deliver nine hun-

dred and sixty pounds of snuff at thirty-eight and three-quarter cents per pound, which Turner had previously ordered.

On the trial of the case, it appeared from the plaintiff's testimony that he had signed a written order for the snuff, which was accepted by Lorillard Company through its agent. Everything was stated in the writing to make it a complete contract, except the price, which was left blank after each item. It was sought to supply this defect by showing dealings between plaintiff and defendant, extending through a number of years, in which the article bargained for had always been sold at a stated price per pound, subject to the discounts which were stated in the writing. Bills for other goods ordered by the plaintiff from the defendant were introduced in evidence, and parol evidence was offered to show the dealings between these parties, in order to connect the writings and thereby complete the contract of sale. The court held that the contract was incomplete, that the price could not be supplied by parol evidence and granted a nonsuit in the case.

1. The fourth section of the statute of frauds provided that no action should be brought upon certain promises therein specified, "unless the agreement upon which such action shall be brought, or some memorandum or note thereof, shall be in writing and signed by the party to be charged therewith, or some other person thereunto by him lawfully authorized." The seventeenth section of the statute declared that "no contract for the sale of goods, wares, and merchandise, for the price of ten pounds sterling, or upward, shall be allowed to be good, except the buyer shall [447] accept part of the goods so sold, and actually receive the same, or give something in earnest to bind the bargain, or in part payment, or that some note or memorandum in writing of the said bargain be made and signed by the parties to be charged by such contract, or their agents thereunto lawfully authorized." It is to be noticed that in order to satisfy the fourth section the "agreement" must be in writing; and to satisfy the seventeenth section there must be some note or memorandum of the "bargain" in writing. This statute was embraced among those which are described in the act of February 25, 1784 (Cobb's Digest, 721), declaring what statute laws of England were of force in this state, and it remained the law of Georgia in the exact words above quoted until the adoption of the code of 1861.

In the case of Henderson v. Johnson, 6 Ga. 390, having under consideration the fourth section above quoted, the court says:

"By the word 'agreement' mentioned in the statute it must be understood the consideration for the promise, as well as the promise itself, and that if extrinsic parol evidence could be received to show the consideration of the written agreement, the very object of the statute would be defeated." This was the construction placed upon the section by the English courts in the case of Wain v. Warlters, 5 East, 10. In the case of Hargroves v. Cooke, 15 Ga. 321, the doctrine of Wain v. Warlters, 5 East, 10, is considered and questioned, but that it had been adopted by the court in the case cited supra is recognized. The decision in Wain v. Warlters, 5 East, 10, was made by Lord Ellenborough, in 1804, and was therefore not absolutely binding upon this court, and it seems that this was not the recognized construction placed upon the statute by the English courts. In Ex parte Gordom, 15 Ves. 286, Lord Eldon said: "Until that case (Wain v. Warlters, 5 East, 10) was decided some time ago, I had always taken the law to be clear that, if a man agreed in writing to pay the debt of another, it was necessary that the consideration should appear on the face [648] of the writing." In the case of Baker v. Herndon, 17 Ga. 568, the court having under consideration the act of January 19, 1852 (Acts 1851-52, p. 243), which provided that that part of the fourth section of the statute of frauds which relates to special promises to answer for the debt, default, or miscarriage of another person should be so construed that the agreement in writing would be sufficient, although no consideration was expressed therein, it was held that the act referred to was simply declaratory of the law of this state at the time of its passage. The court declined to follow the case of Wain v. Warlters, 5 East, 10, on the ground that it was decided in the year 1804, and was therefore not binding as authority; and the ruling in the case was to the effect that the proper construction of the fourth section of the statute of frauds was to give to the word "agreement" such a meaning as to make a writing which failed to disclose a consideration sufficient to satisfy the statute. The cases of Henderson v. Johnson, 6 Ga. 390, and Hargroves v. Cooke, 15 Ga. 321, cited supra, were not referred to in the opinion. The word "bargain," which occurs in the seventeenth section of the statute, does not seem to have been at any time under consideration by this court. We find, therefore, that up to the time that the code of 1861 went into effect, the meaning of the word "agreement" in the fourth section of the statute had been considered by this court in three decisions, which were not in harmony with each other.

The meaning of the word "bargain" has never been under consideration, and whether it was to be construed as synonymous with "agreement" was never determined. Section 1952 of the code of 1861 contained a provision that, to make "certain obligations binding on the promisor, the promise must be in writing, signed by the party to be charged therewith, or some person by him lawfully authorized." The promises enumerated in the section cited were eight in number, the first seven embracing those which were formerly embraced in the fourth section of the statute of frauds, and the eighth containing practically [649] what was embraced in the seventeenth section of the statute. The purpose of this section of the code was to place the contracts mentioned in the fourth and seventeenth sections of the statute of frauds under the same rules. The words "agreement" and "bargain" are entirely eliminated, and the statute declares that the writing shall contain the promise. The effect of this was to declare that a writing which contains the names of the parties, the subject matter of the agreement, and the promise to be enforced, signed by the party to be charged therewith, or some person by him lawfully authorized, would be sufficient to make the obligation binding, although no consideration for the promise was stated in the writing. The provisions of the code of 1861, quoted above, have been brought through the various editions of the code, and are now embraced in section 2693 of the Civil Code. It is therefore clear that our statute does not expressly require the consideration to be stated; and this being true, the validity of a contract for the sale of goods, wares, and merchandise, to the amount of fifty dollars, or more, is not necessarily affected by a failure to embrace in the writing a fixed price. If the verbal contract is silent as to price, it is not necessary that the price should be stated in the writing; for, "a contract for the sale of a commodity, in which the price is left unwritten, is in law a contract for what the goods shall be reasonably worth." If, however, the verbal contract entered into between the parties contains an agreement as to the price to be paid, the writing must state the price, as it is then of the essence of the contract: Wood on the Statute of Frauds, sec. 351. Where it is apparent from the writing which is relied on to satisfy the statute that it was the intention of the parties to contract specifically as to the price to be paid, or where it appears from extrinsic evidence that such was the intention, and the writing neither designated what the price was to be, nor otherwise stated the actual agreement of the parties with reference to price in such a manner as to show that the [650] parties were contracting with reference to a quantum valebat, then such an instrument would not be sufficient to satisfy the requirements of the statute. While the promise only is required to be in writing, still if the promise be to pay a certain amount, then that amount is an essential part of the writing. If the promise in terms, however, be to pay what the goods are reasonably worth, or if the promise be simply to pay for the goods, from which the law would infer a promise to pay their reasonable worth, then no definite or fixed price need be stated in the writing. In such cases the statute would be satisfied, and the admission of parol evidence to fix the reasonable worth of the articles which were the subject matter of the contract would not be violative of any rule of law, and would not in any way contravene the provisions of the statute either in its letter or its spirit. In other words, to satisfy the requirements of the section of the code which we have adopted in lieu of the statute of frauds, if an intention be shown, either by the writing itself or by extrinsic evidence, to contract specifically as to price, then the price is a part of the promise and must be embraced in the writing to meet the requirements of the section: Goodman v. Griffith, 1 Hurl. & N. 573; Ashcroft v. Butterworth, 136 Mass. 511; Waterman v. Megis, 4 Cush. 197; Stone v. Browning, 68 N. Y. 598; James v. Muir, 33 Mich. 223; Acebal v. Levy, 10 Bing. 170; Hanson v. Marsh, 40 Minn. 1; Elsmere v. Kingscote, 3 Bing. 594; Ide v. Stanton, 15 Vt. 685; 40 Am. Dec. 698.

2. It is not necessary that the writing provided for in the section quoted shall contain in itself all of the requirements which the statute embraces. The purpose of this law is to prevent the frauds and perjuries incident to the admission of parol testimony. If the writing, therefore, refer to any other writing which can be identified completely by this reference, without the aid of parol evidence, then the two or more writings may constitute a compliance with the statute. If, however, two writings are relied upon to satisfy [651] the statute, and parol evidence is necessary to connect them with each other, then they would fail as a compliance with the statute: North v. Mendel, 73 Ga. 400; 54 Am. Rep. 879. It would therefore follow that the effort made in this case to supply the defect in the writing relied on, by using other writings not referred to and which could only be connected with the writing relied on by the aid of parol testimony, was properly held to be insufficient to comply with the law.

3. If the writing relied on in this case was not sufficient to
show that the parties intended to contract specifically as to price,
and therefore make such writing insufficient under the statute
on account of the absence of such price from it, the parol evidence which the court admitted made it absolutely certain that
such was the intention of the parties. It clearly appeared from
this evidence that under the contract sought to be set up a
fixed price was intended to be agreed on, and that it was not
the intention of the parties to leave the price of the article
sold to be determined by what it was reasonably worth in the
market. Such being the prior verbal stipulation, the absence of
the price from the writing rendered it nugatory. Where the
writing might otherwise be construed to refer the price to a
quantum valebat, there seems to be no doubt that parol evidence would be admissible to show a prior verbal intention contrary to such presumption and thereby invalidate the writing.
While parol evidence will never be admitted in aid of a party
who has an incomplete writing, it will be admitted to defeat a
party who is attempting to impose upon the court a writing
which is not really a compliance with the statute: Wood on the
Statute of Frauds, sec. 391. There was no error in granting a
nonsuit.

Judgment affirmed.

All the justices concurring.

STATUTE OF FRAUDS—MEMORANDUM CONSISTING OF
DIFFERENT PAPERS.—Several papers signed at the same time by
the party sought to be charged may be considered and used together
to complete the memorandum required by the statute of frauds: Lee
v. Butler, 167 Mass. 426; 57 Am. St. Rep. 466, and note. A contract
binding under the statute of frauds, though signed by only one of the
parties thereto, may be gathered from letters between them relating
to the subject matter and so connected with one another as to fairly
constitute one paper: Hickey v. Dole, 66 N. H. 336; 49 Am. St. Rep.
614. See monographic note to Siemers v. Siemers, 60 Am. St. Rep.
437. Parol evidence may be introduced to show the situation of the
parties and the circumstances attending the transaction for the purpose of applying the contract to a subject matter and connecting the
memoranda with one another: Lee v. Butler, 167 Mass. 426; 57 Am.
St. Rep. 466.

STATUTE OF FRAUDS—EXPRESSION OF CONSIDERATION
IN MEMORANDUM.—The note or memorandum must express the
price upon which the sale was effected or it will be insufficient: Ide
v. Stanton, 15 Vt. 685; 40 Am. Dec. 698. The object of the memorandum is not merely to prove that there was a bargain, but to show
what the bargain was, at least the extent and entirety of the consideration for the promise: Peltier v. Collins, 3 Wend. 459; 20 Am. Dec.
711, and note. See Justice v. Lang, 42 N. Y. 493; 1 Am. Rep. 576;
also, extended note to Siemers v. Siemers, 60 Am. St. Rep. 433-441.

Rogers v. Georgia Railroad Company.

[100 Georgia, 699.]

RAILROADS—KILLING LIVESTOCK—DUTY TO LOOK OUT FOR.—If, in an action against a railroad company to recover for the killing of livestock, it appears that the engineer was at the place on the engine where his duty required him to be, that he was looking ahead when the stock were first seen on the track in a curve, that because thereof, and other obstructions to the view, the stock could not have been sooner seen, and that it was impossible to stop the train before striking them, and the only circumstance from which negligence can be inferred was that the fireman, at the time of the killing of the stock, was engaged in firing his engine, and was not on the lookout, such absence of the fireman from a position to look out, and the failure of the railroad company to place a third man on the engine to keep a lookout when the fireman was firing his engine, do not authorize a recovery against the company.

NEW TRIAL—ERROR IN RENDERING FINAL JUDG-MENT.—If it appears from the record that the trial judge would not have abused his discretion in ordering a new trial, and that the final determination of the case does not necessarily depend upon a controlling question of law, while there are issues of fact in the case which make it necessary for a new trial to be had, it is error to render a final judgment in the case instead of sending it back for a new trial.

H. Johnson and P. B. Johnson, for the plaintiff.

J. B. and B. Cumming, for the defendant.

⁷⁰⁰ COBB, J. Where it appears in a suit against a railroad company, for damage on account of the killing of livestock, that the engineer was at the place on the engine where his duty required him, that he was looking ahead when the animal was first seen in the middle of the track in a curve, that because of the curve, the boiler, smokestack, and sandbox, obstructing the view, the animal could not have been sooner seen, and that it was impossible to stop the train before striking the animal after it was seen, and the only circumstance from which negligence could be inferred was that the fireman, at the time of the killing of the animal, was engaged in supplying his engine with fuel, and was not on the lookout, such absence of the fireman from a position to look out, and the failure of the railroad company to place a third employé on the engine to take the fireman's place when he was supplying his engine with fuel, would not warrant a finding in favor of the plaintiff.

2. So far as what may be stated above may be in conflict with the decision rendered by this court in Northeastern R. R. Co. v. Martin, 78 Ga. 603, that case, after a review in accordance with the prescribed rules of this court, is overruled.

3. The jury in the justice's court having found in favor of the plaintiff, and there being some evidence to sustain the finding, but the preponderance of the evidence being against the finding, the judge of the superior court would not have abused his discretion if he had ordered a new trial in the justice's court; but as the record does not make a case where "the error complained of is an error of law which must finally govern the case," and as it is one involving a [701] question or questions of fact, which under the law made it "necessary to send the case back for a new hearing" before the justice's court, it was error in the judge of the superior court to render a final judgment in the case instead of sending it back for a new trial: Civ. Code, sec. 4652. This being true, direction is given that the judgment below be set aside, and in its stead that a judgment be entered sustaining the certiorari and ordering a new trial in the justice's court.

Judgment reversed, with direction.

All the justices concurring.

RAILROAD COMPANIES—LIABILITY FOR KILLING STOCK. The duty which a railroad company owes to the owner of stray stock upon its track is, that the engineer in charge of the train at the time shall use ordinary or reasonable care after the stock is discovered by him to prevent injury to it. It is not negligence for a railroad company to fail to keep a lookout for stock: Memphis etc. R. R. Co. v. Kerr, 52 Ark. 162; 20 Am. St. Rep. 159, and note. A railway company should not be adjudged guilty of negligence because its engineer and fireman in charge of a locomotive did not keep a lookout, and on that account failed to see an animal on the track, if they were prevented from keeping such lookout by giving their attention to other duties which it was at the time incumbent upon them to perform: Howard v. Louisville etc. Ry. Co., 67 Miss. 247; 19 Am. St. Rep. 302, and note. See Case v. Central Railroad Co., 59 N. J. L. 471; 59 Am. St. Rep. 617, and note.

NEW TRIAL—WHEN SHOULD BE GRANTED.—If the findings are contradictory, no judgment can be rendered on the verdict; and if one is entered a new trial must be ordered: Porter v. Western etc. R. R. Co., 97 N. C. 66; 2 Am. St. Rep. 272. A seeming preponderance of evidence against a verdict will not warrant the court in setting it aside, where the testimony is conflicting, involving a determination of the credibility of the witnesses: Douglass v. Tousey, 2 Wend. 352; 20 Am. Dec. 616, and note; Wilcoxson v. Burton, 27 Cal. 228; 87 Am. Dec. 66, and note.

STEWART *v.* COMER.

[100 GEORGIA, 754.]

CARRIERS—FREIGHT OVERCHARGES AND RECOVERY THEREOF.—If a bill of lading provides that if the goods shipped are transported in a box-car the rate shall be a certain amount per hundred pounds actual weight, and if transported on a flat-car, a certain rate per hundred pounds up to a certain limit, the goods shipped being far below this limit in weight, and the carrier transports part of the goods on flat-cars and part in box-cars, thus making the freight charges aggregate more than if the whole consignment had been transported on either kind of car alone, there is prima facie an overcharge, and the shipper having paid and the carrier having failed to show why the goods were so transported, the shipper is entitled to recover such overcharge, together with the penalty therefor prescribed by statute.

CARRIERS—BILLS OF LADING—OPTION IN MODE OF SHIPMENT—HOW EXERCISED.—If a contract for the transportation of goods gives the carrier an option between modes of transportation, this option must be exercised with regard to the interests of the shipper; and it is a breach of the contract to exercise it to his disadvantage, unless it is done in good faith and under circumstances which seem to demand it. The burden of proof is upon the carrier to show that it did exercise the option reasonably as demanded by the circumstances.

Goodwin & Westmoreland and C. Z. Blalock, for the plaintiff.

Dorsey, Brewster & Howell and H. M. Dorsey, for the defendants.

[756] SIMMONS, C. J. In issuing the bill of lading, the carrier reserved an option as to the mode of shipment, and the price was to [757] be controlled by the method of shipment adopted. If the plate glass was shipped in a box-car, the price for the freight was to be one dollar and fourteen cents per hundred pounds actual weight; if shipped upon a flat-car, the rate was to be seventy-three cents per hundred pounds for ten thousand pounds. Three plates of the glass were shipped on a flat-car, for which the carrier charged seventy-three dollars; and five plates were shipped in a box-car, for which the carrier charged fourteen dollars and thirty-one cents. It was not contemplated in this contract of affreightment that the glass should be divided and part shipped in a box-car and part on a flat-car. We think that the contract means that the eight plates of glass should all be shipped by one method either in a box-car or on a flat-car.

The weight of the eight plates of glass appears to have been fifteen hundred and fifty pounds. If all of them had been shipped in a box-car, the freight would have been seventeen dollars and sixty-seven cents; if all had been shipped on a flat-car, the freight would have been seventy-three dollars. The carrier charged eighty-seven dollars and thirty-one cents for the two shipments. This, without explanation on the part of the carrier, is an overcharge according to the contract. Section 2316 of the Civil Code provides, in substance, that where any common carrier shall demand and receive, for goods shipped from within or without this state to any point in this state, any overcharge or excess of freight over and beyond the proper or contract rate of freight, and a demand in writing for the return or repayment of such overcharge is made by the person paying the same, the common carrier shall refund said overcharge within thirty days from said demand; and if it shall fail or refuse to do so within thirty days, then it shall be liable to said person making the overpayment in an amount double the amount of the overpayment. This being prima facie an overcharge, the plaintiff having paid it and given the written notice required, and the common carrier having failed to refund it within the thirty days, the plaintiff was entitled under the code to recover it in an action brought for that [758] purpose and also to recover the penalty imposed. It will be observed that the penalty is not inflicted upon the common carrier for making the overcharge, but for its refusal to refund within thirty days after demand is made in writing. So it seems that where there is an overcharge of freight by a common carrier, and the person to whom the shipment is consigned pays it and makes demand in writing upon the carrier to refund such overcharge, and the carrier fails to do so within thirty days, as a matter of law such common carrier is liable both for the overcharge and the penalty.

It is contended that the common carrier, having reserved to itself in the contract an option like the one in the present case, has the right to exercise its option to advance its own interest, and not the interest of the shipper, and that inasmuch as this option was to ship the glass in either kind of car, it could divide the shipment as it did, if it was to its interest to do so. The rule, however, seems to be the contrary of this. It is laid down in Hutchinson on Carriers, section 313 a, as follows: "Where a contract for the transportation of goods gives the carrier an option between modes of transportation, this option must be exercised with regard for the interests of the shipper; and it is a breach of the contract to exercise it to his disadvantage, unless it is done in good faith and under circumstances which seem to demand it." See, also, Blitz v. Union Steamboat Co., 51 Mich. 558, decision by Judge Cooley. We think, therefore, that where a carrier has an option of this kind, he must exercise it reasonably, under the circumstances, to the best interests of the consignee or shipper; and it would be a breach of contract to exercise it to the disadvantage of the consignee or shipper, unless it be done in good faith and under circumstances which seem to require it. We think also that the burden is upon the carrier to show that it did exercise the option reasonably under the circumstances. If the carrier adopts a mode [759] of transportation which involves the payment of a higher rate of freight rather than a lower, it may show that it asked for and obtained direction from the shipper or consignee to employ the more expensive mode; or that, because of its inability to procure the means of shipment by the cheaper method, it was reasonably necessary, in view of the exigencies of the particular case and in order to complete the contract of carriage, to resort to the other and more expensive mode; or it may show other facts and circumstances which would justify it in exercising its option in a manner disadvantageous to the shipper or consignee.

Judgment reversed.

All the justices concurring.

CARRIERS—FREIGHT RATES-OVERCHARGES.—A common carrier is bound to carry for a reasonable remuneration: Johnson v. Pensacola etc. R. R. Co., 16 Fla. 623; 26 Am. Rep. 731; and an action lies after payment to recover back an overcharge by a carrier: Note to Cook v. Chicago etc. Ry. Co., 25 Am. St. Rep. 520; Chicago etc. R. R. Co. v. Wolcott, 141 Ind. 267; 50 Am. St. Rep. 320. For a discussion of the respective rights and liabilities of carrier and shipper as to the payment of freight, see monographic note to Crawford v. Williams, 60 Am. Dec. 149-154.

CASES

IN THE

SUPREME COURT

OF.

ILLINOIS.

MADISON *v.* LARMON.

[170 ILLINOIS, 65.]

A TENANT IN COMMON IS, as to his individual share, to be deemed the owner of an entire and separate estate.

THE RULE AGAINST PERPETUITIES IS, that no interest subject to a condition precedent is good, unless the condition must be fulfilled, if at all, within twenty-one years after some life in being at the creation of the interest.

PERPETUITIES CREATED BY WILLS.—The time of the testator's death is the true period at which to judge of the remote-ness of the provisions of his will. If it creates life estates and remainders, so that each remainder, however many estates there be, must take effect within twenty-one years after his death, it does not contravene the law against perpetuities.

PERPETUITIES.—THERE MAY BE GIFTS FOR LIFE OF UNBORN PERSONS IN SUCCESSION, provided their estate must vest within twenty-one years after some life in being.

PERPETUITIES.—A WILL GIVING LIFE ESTATES TO SEVENTEEN DEVISEES, constituting the children and grandchildren of the testator, with remainder over to the brothers and sisters, if any should die leaving no issue, is good.

WILLS—BROTHERS AND SISTERS, WHO MAY TAKE AS.—If a testator devises certain property for his life to his children, C. S. and M., and after their death to their children, naming them, but, if any of such children shall die leaving no issue, then his share shall be equally divided among his brothers and sisters, the brothers and sisters who may thus take are not limited to those named in the will, but include all brothers and sisters of the child so deceased, whether born in the lifetime of the testator or not.

WILLS—CONSTRUCTION OF WORDS IN.—If a testator uses the word "issue" in one part of his will as meaning children, it will be presumed that in using the same word in another part he intended it to have the same signification.

PERPETUITIES.—THE CONTINUANCE OF AN ESTATE FOR MORE THAN LIVES IN BEING AND TWENTY-ONE YEARS does not bring it within the rule against perpetuities, if it must all vest within that time.

PERPETUITIES — CONTINGENT REMAINDERS.—If the event upon which a contingent remainder is limited must happen, and the contingent become a vested remainder within the time allowed by the rule against perpetuities, the rule is not violated by the fact that the remainder so vested is not to be enjoyed until some future fixed time, or until the dropping out of an existing life estate.

REMAINDERS—CONTINGENT AND VESTED.—If a testator devises real property to seventeen persons, constituting his children and grandchildren, for their lives, and declares that after they shall all be dead, he devises his property to his grandchildren then living, share and share alike, and if any grandchild shall then be dead leaving issue, such issue shall take the share the parent would take if living, the interest last devised is a contingent remainder which does not vest until the death of the last surviving life tenant.

REMAINDERS.—WHERE A REMAINDER IS CONTINGENT, IT MUST VEST DURING the existence of the particular estate, or at the instant of its termination.

REMAINDERS—CONTINGENT WHICH NEVER BECOME VESTED, WHO TAKES THE PROPERTY.—If a life estate terminates before the contingent remainder limited thereon becomes vested, the property passes in reversion to the heirs at law of the testator at the time of the termination of such estate.

REMAINDERS—CONTINGENT WHERE THE PRECEDING ESTATE IS HELD IN COMMON.—Where the preceding estate upon which a contingent interest is limited is held in common, and as to each of the cotenants the particular estate terminates before the remainder can vest, it fails as to such share or shares and to that extent vests in the heirs at law of the testator.

WILLS—ESTOPPEL TO CONTEST.—Persons who are beneficiaries in a will and who have received property thereunder cannot maintain a bill, as heirs at law of the testator, to have it declared invalid.

J. Erb, D. J. Haynes, and Wilkins & Bradburn, for the plaintiffs in error.

Kerr & Barr, for the defendants in error.

[67] MAGRUDER, J. The circuit judge, before whom this cause was heard, sustained a demurrer to the bill and dismissed the bill for want of equity. The reasons given for the decree thus entered commend themselves to our judgment as being a proper disposition of the questions involved. We therefore [68] adopt such reasons as the opinion of this court. They are as follows:

"This is an action brought in this court on the equity side thereof, praying the partition and sale of certain premises known as No. 185 South Clark street, in the city of Chicago, county and state aforesaid, said premises having heretofore been devised by will of the late Henry Larmon, deceased, of Warren county, Kentucky, to certain of his children and grandchildren named

in the will. The fourth clause of his will contains the entire
terms, conditions, and limitations of the various devises of this
property, and is as follows, viz:

"'Fourth—I will and devise said house and lot, No. 185 South
Clark street, Chicago, Illinois, as follows: I divide it into twenty-
nine shares, which I bequeath as follows: To my son, Connelly,
two shares, for and during his life; to his children, Genie,
John, Euran, Clement, and Lucian, each one share, for and during their respective lives; to my daughter, Sardinia, six shares,
for and during her life; to her children, Monroe, Vernon, Charles,
and Sydney, each one share, for and during their respective lives;
to her children, Lilly, Jetta, Elizabeth, and Mary, each two shares,
for and during their respective lives; to said Katie Madison and
Arvilla Madison each two shares, for and during their respective
lives. If said Connelly shall die leaving any of his said children
alive, his two shares shall be divided equally among such of said
children as may be living, to be held by them, respectively, for
and during their lives. If said Sardinia shall die leaving any of
her said children alive, her six shares shall be divided equally
among such of said children as may be living, to be held by
them, respectively, for and during their lives. . If any of said
children of Connelly, Sardinia, or Mary shall die leaving no
issue alive at the date of such death, the share or shares of such
child so dying shall be equally divided among the brothers and
sisters, to be held by them, respectively, for and during their
lives; but if such child [69] dies leaving issue alive, such issue
shall have the parent's share in possession, to be held till my son,
Connelly, and his aforesaid children, my daughter and her aforesaid children, said Kate and Arvilla, shall all be dead; and when
they shall all be dead, I will and devise said house and lot to
all of my grandchildren then living, share and share alike, and
if any grandchild shall be then dead leaving issue alive, such
issue shall take the share the parent would have taken if living.
But it is my will that the share of the rent going to each of the
aforesaid children of my son, Connelly, shall go to him for his
own use till such child arrives at the age of twenty-one years,
and that likewise the share of the rent going to each of the
aforenamed children of my daughter, Sardinia, shall go to her
for her own use till such child arrive at the age of twenty-one
years; but this bequest of rents to Connelly and Sardinia is personal, and upon their respective deaths the rents shall go to
their respective children named, though infants. In order to
carry into effect this part of my will, my executor is directed to

rent and keep rented said house and lot and to distribute the
net proceeds according to this will. In his management of said
property he shall be governed by the majority of votes of those
entitled to rents at the time. The guardian of every infant entitled to rent shall have the right to vote for such infant. Such
renting and management shall continue till my son and daughter,
their aforenamed children, and said Katie and Arvilla, are all
dead, and after the death of my executor the proper court will
appoint an administrator with this will annexed for the purpose.'

"In construing this particular will, it will be necessary, in
the first place, to discuss the life estates created, before considering the remainder in fee.

"The seventeen named devisees for life (being the testator's
two children and fifteen grandchildren), each being given distinct shares in this Clark street house and lot, became, upon the
testator's death, tenants in common for [70] life. A tenant in common is, as to his own individual share, in the position of an
owner of an entire and separate estate. To illustrate what life
estates are provided for and are possible under this will, let us
take Connelly's two shares—his separate estate of two twenty-
ninths of the property. The first freehold or particular estate
is for the life of Connelly. Second, if Connelly dies, then his
(Connelly's) five named sons (grandchildren of testator), Genie,
John, Euran, Clement, and Lucian, take the two equal shares in
equal parts for life. Third, assuming that when the will speaks
of the 'brothers and sisters' taking the interests of a deceased
brother or sister (dying without 'issue alive') that only the
grandchildren, brothers and sisters named, are intended, then
upon Genie dying without issue alive, the other four named
brothers would take his interest in equal shares for their lives,
respectively. Fourth, if John should then die without issue
alive, the other three named brothers would take John's shares
or interests for their lives, respectively. Fifth, if Euran should
then die without issue, the other two named brothers would
take his interest for their lives, respectively. Sixth, if Clement
should then die without issue alive, Lucian, the last survivor,
would take Clement's interest for his life. Seventh, if Clement
should then die leaving issue alive, such issue would take his
interest for the life of the unspent lives of the seventeen life
devisees named in the will.

"Here are seven life estates in the two shares, or the two
twenty-ninths given to Connelly, which are possible before the

remainder in fee might vest. Is any known rule of law violated thereby? If any, it is the rule against perpetuities, which is defined to be, that 'no interest subject to a condition precedent is good unless the condition must be fulfilled, if at all, within twenty-one years after some life in being at the creation of the interest': Gray on Perpetuities, sec. 201. In Howe v. Hodge, 152 Ill. 252, our supreme court adopt this precise definition of the [71] rule as laid down by Gray, and adds that 'the true object of the rule is to prevent the creation of interests upon remote contingencies.' The question to be asked of any estate on condition precedent is, 'When must the contingency happen?' The time of the testator's death is the true period at which to judge of the remoteness of the provisions in his will: Vanderplank v. King, 3 Hare, 1; Lewis on Perpetuities, 53-57, and cases cited.

"Tested by these rules, and it will be seen that the contingency, to wit, the death of the prior life tenant as to all the six life remainders following Connelly's death, must in every case happen within a life in being at the death of the testator, except the last—i. e., the one to the children of the last surviving brother—and as to that, it would take effect on his death, to wit, within twenty-one years after a life in being at testator's death, so that all the successive life estates in remainder would happen within lives in being and twenty-one years thereafter, and would not violate the rule against perpetuities, which Gray says would be properly termed the rule against remoteness. The number of lives in being that are selected makes no difference, as any number of lives in esse are allowed: See Gray on Perpetuities, sec. 189. You cannot give successive remainders for life unless the contingency must occur within lives in being. The estate must vest within the required limits of lives in being and twenty-one years thereafter, and there can be a gift for life to unborn persons in succession, provided their estate must vest within the required limits: Gray on Perpetuities, sec. 206; Brudenell v. Elwes, 1 East, 442; Hodson v. Ball, 14 Sim. 558.

"The life estates given to the seventeen named devisees (children and grandchildren) are good, and took effect immediately upon testator's death. The remainder over for life to the 'brothers and sisters' of a grandchild who should die leaving no issue alive—is that good, and who are to take such remainder? That such a gift or remainder over for life is good, see Trickey v. Trickey, 3 Mylne & K. 560. [72] "What construction should be placed upon the provision that 'if any of said children of Con-

nelly, Sardinia, or Mary shall die leaving no issue alive at the
date of such death, then the shares of the child so dying shall
be equally divided among the brothers and sisters, to be held
by them, respectively, for and during their lives?' Does this
mean the brothers and sisters of the deceased who are theretofore named in the will, and who were in esse at testator's death,
or all the brothers and sisters, whether born before or after the
testator's death? I am of the opinion that it means the latter,
and that all the brothers and sisters living at the death of such
grandchild would share equally, for the reason that the testator,
in other parts of the will, appears careful to identify objects of
his bounty by the careful use of the words 'said,' 'aforesaid,'
'named' and 'aforenamed.' It also appears by the clause creating
the remainder in fee that he contemplated the existence of
grandchildren not named in his will; and I assume it to be a fact
that Kate Larmon (now Kate Stark), daughter of Connelly Larmon, was born prior to the date of testator's death, and as the
will speaks from his death, that he used the term 'the brothers
and sisters,' knowing that all the children of Connelly named
in the will were boys, intending to include her as capable of
sharing equally with her brothers upon the death of any one of
the brothers without issue him surviving.

"This construction is also based on the assumption that the
words 'leaving no issue alive at the date of such death' must
be construed to mean leaving no children alive, etc. It will be
observed that, when indicating to whom the remainder in fee
shall go, he declares that if any grandchild be then dead, 'leaving
issue alive, such issue shall take the share such parent would
have taken if living.' Where the word 'issue' is used with reference to the parent of such issue, as where the issue is to take
the shares of the deceased parent, it must mean his children—
that is, the word 'parent' confines the word 'issue' [73] to the
children of the taker: Fairchild v. Bushell, 32 Beav. 158; Sibley
v. Perry, 7 Ves. Jr. 522.

"It being clear that as to the remainder in fee he uses the
word 'issue' as meaning children, it will be inferred that he
used it in the same sense in other parts of the will, as it is a
rule that the court will not construe the same words used in
different parts of the will as having different meanings, if it is
possible to avoid doing so. The intention to use the words in
different senses must be clear and beyond question.

"It is contended by complainant that if the term 'the brothers and sisters' includes the brothers and sisters born after testator's death, then, as an after-born brother would have a share for life in the shares left by one of the grandchildren named in the will, as supposing one of ·Sardinia's named children should die without issue, leaving as his brother one who was born after the testator's death, that after-born brother would share equally with the other living brothers and sisters in the estate of the deceased brother, and such after-born brother, it is contended, might live for twenty-five years after all the seventeen named life devisees had died, and therefore the remainder in fee, as to the portion held by such after-born brother, would not vest in remainder during life or lives in being and twenty-one years thereafter, but would be postponed until the death of such after-born brother, which would be beyond the limited period and void as a perpetuity.

"In the case supposed, the life estate of the after-born brother would certainly vest within the rule against perpetuities, as he takes immediately upon the death of his brother, a named devisee living at the testator's death. That such life estate may continue beyond the time limited by the rule against perpetuities—i. e., beyond twenty-one years after his brother's death— does not invalidate the life estate. If it vests if it once commences, it will continue until the end of the life of the taker. 'An interest [74] is not obnoxious to the rule against perpetuities if it begins within lives in being and twenty-one years, although it may end beyond them. . . . . And an estate for life is good if it begins within the required limits': Gray on Perpetuities, sec. 232. Nor is it true that the remainder in fee would not vest until the termination of the life estate of such after-born brother. The event upon which a contingent remainder is limited may happen, and the contingent become a vested remainder, but not to be enjoyed in possession until some fixed time or until the dropping out of an existing estate for life. There is a difference between 'vesting' and 'the enjoyment of possession,' and it is sufficient if the contingent becomes a vested remainder within the time limited by the rule against perpetuities, although the enjoyment may be postponed beyond such time. 'If an estate is given to A for life and remainder to B's oldest son in fee, the remainder is contingent until the birth of A's first born son, and then vests': Gray on Perpetuities, sec. 9. The rule is, that the contingent remainder must become vested on or before the determination of the preceding vested estate:

Gray on Perpetuities, sec. 10. When a remainder becomes a vested remainder, the rule against perpetuities does not apply, as it cannot apply to vested interests.

"If any grandchild dies leaving issue (children) alive, what estate does such issue take? It will be observed that such issue (children) are 'to have the parent's share in possession until my son, Connelly, and his aforesaid children, my daughter and her aforesaid children, said Kate and Arvilla (the seventeen named devisees), shall all be dead.' This vests a life estate in such children on the death of the parent, subject to be divested by the death of the last of the seventeen named devisees. Strictly speaking, it is a life estate per autre vie for the life of the survivors of the said seventeen named devisees, all of whom were in being at the testator's death. That this is a good life estate, see Gray on Perpetuities, sections 225-227.

[75] "The only remaining question in this case is as to the devise of the remainder in fee. The testator declares: 'And when they' (i. e., Connelly and his aforesaid children), 'my daughter and her aforesaid children, said Kate and Arvilla' (the seventeen named devisees and first life tenants), 'shall all be dead, I will and devise said house and lot to all my grandchildren then living, share and share alike, and if any grandchild shall be then dead leaving issue alive, such issue shall take the share the parent would have taken if living.' It is contended on behalf of defendants that this provision creates a vested remainder in those who are to take under it, while complainants contend it is a contingent remainder.

"It will be observed that the testator divides the lot into twenty-nine shares, and divides these twenty-nine shares among the seventeen named devisees (children and grandchildren) for life, and, after carving out these life estates on the respective shares devised, he disposes in fee of the lot as a single property, as an entirety. Therefore, the vesting of the remainder in fee, as to any particular share, does not depend solely upon the death of the life tenant of that share, but also depends upon the death of the last of the seventeen life devisees named in the will, 'when they shall all be dead,' says the testator. The remainder in fee is a contingent remainder. The learned author, Fearne, states four kinds of contingent remainders: '3. Where the condition upon which the remainder is limited is certain in event, but the determination of particular estate may happen before it. . . . . 4. Where the person to whom the remainder is limited is not as yet ascertained or not yet in being.' This remainder would be a contingent remainder under either of these classifications. He also says the present capacity of taking effect in possession, if the possession becomes vacant, distinguishes the vested from the contingent remainder. The learned author says in illustration: 'So in case of a lease for life to A, and after the death of A and [76] M the remainder to be in fee, this is a contingent remainder for the particular estate. Being for the life of A, and the remainder not to commence until after the death of A and M, if A die before M the particular estate will end before the remainder commences': 1 Eearne on Contingent Remainders, 5, 7.

"The provisions of this will as to the remainder in fee are clearly within the illustration. The two grandchildren, Kate and Arvilla, are the children of Mary, a deceased daughter of the testator. These are given four shares, or two twenty-ninths each. If they both should die without issue before any of the other of the seventeen named life devisees, the remainder in fee of these four shares could not take effect in possession, for the reason the remaindermen take nothing until they, the seventeen life tenants, are 'all dead.' The remainder in fee is, therefore, clearly a contingent remainder. Is, therefore, the remainder in fee void? If not, what is its effect?

"If Kate should survive Arvilla, she would have four shares; and suppose she should live twenty-five years longer than any of the other fifteen named devisees of a life estate, then twenty-five twenty-ninths of the property would be without any remainder vested under the will for twenty-five years, and who would take the income thereof for that period of time? Would the remainder as to these twenty-five shares be void, as being obnoxious to the rule against perpetuities, or would the remainder over as to any shares be cut off by the dropping out of the life estate of such share?

"If all the interests held in severalty should determine at one time—that is, if all the seventeen named devisees should die at one and the same instant of time—then the remainder as to the several shares would vest at the same time. But it cannot be supposed that the testator contemplated such an almost impossible event. The difficulty as to the remainder arises from the fact that the shares held by the several life tenants are held in severalty, and the remainder is disposed of as one property [77] and a distinct entity. The remainder is to take effect upon the determination, not of the life estates carved out, but upon the extinguishment of the life of all the seventeen named devisees, children and grandchildren of the testator.

"A remainder over, to vest upon the death of a stranger to the estate, is a valid remainder. 'The contingency may be postponed for any number of lives, provided they are all in being when the contingent interest is created, and the persons whose lives are taken need have no interest in the estate,' is the rule as clearly laid down by Gray on Perpetuities, section 260. This rule was laid down in the leading case of Thelluson v. Woodford, 4 Ves. 227, 11 Ves. 112, where the testator directed the accumulation of the income during the lives of all his sons, grandsons, and grandsons' children who should be alive at his death, and then divided into three lots. The division was sustained by Lord Loughborough, whose decree was affirmed in the house of lords. In Cadwell v. Palmer, 1 Clark & F. 372, an executory devise to take effect upon the death of twenty-eight living persons, seven only of whom were to take interests under the devise, was sustained. At the death of the testator, Henry Larmon, these seventeen named devisees (children and grandchildren) were all alive, so that it is seen that the remainder in fee vests upon the determination of a life in being at the testator's death— i. e., upon the death of the survivor of the seventeen—and therefore does not contravene the law against perpetuities. 'All the candles are lighted at once, and therefore it was only the duration of one life.'

"What effect is to be given to this remainder in fee? In order to have a valid remainder there must always be a particular estate to support it. Where the remainder is a contingent remainder, the remainder must vest during the existence of the particular estate or at the instant of its determination. The rule is thus stated in Fearne: 'It has already been shown that a legal remainder must [78] vest either during the existence of the particular estate (in esse or in right of entry) or at the very instant of its determination, otherwise it will never take effect, consequently every such determination of the preceding estate as leaves no right of entry must effectually destroy such contingent remainder': Fearne on Contingent Remainders, sec. 316. And in section 310: 'Upon the principles here laid down that a contingent remainder must vest by the time the preceding estate determines, it follows that an estate limited on a contingency may fail as to one part and take effect as to another, wherever the preceding estate is in several persons in common or in severalty, for the particular tenant of one part may die before the contingency happens and the particular tenant of another part may survive it.' Unless a contingent remainder becomes vested on or before the determination of the preceding vested estate it can never come into possession—it has perished. It makes no difference whether the preceding estates have ended by reaching the limit originally imposed upon them, or whether they have been cut short by merger, forfeiture, or otherwise: Gray on Perpetuities, sec. 10.

"To illustrate the application of these rules to the case at bar, we will suppose that Katie Madison is the first of the seventeen devisees to die, and dies without issue. Her brother Arvilla takes her two shares for life. Arvilla then dies without issue, possessed of four shares. Having no brothers or sisters living, the life estates created by the will in the four shares, or four twenty-ninths, have determined with Arvilla's death. The remainder in fee as to the four shares has perished, because it did not vest by the time the preceding life estates determined, and could not vest under the will until all others of the seventeen devisees had deceased. The same thing might happen as to the life estates vested in Connelly and his five sons, and Sardinia and her named children. Connelly dying, all his sons might die without issue surviving; Sardinia and all her children might die without issue surviving; [79] Katie might also die without issue, leaving Arvilla the only named life tenant in existence. The remainder in fee as to all the shares held by Connelly and his children, Sardinia and her children, would have perished. There can be no interregnum as to a freehold, or between the ending of a life estate and the vesting of the remainder.

"It is, however, certain that the remainder in fee must vest as to some of the shares, but as to what particular shares or number of shares cannot be known until the death of the last survivor of the seventeen named children and grandchildren. The remaindermen will succeed to the ownership in fee of the shares held by such survivor at his death, but which one of the seventeen named life tenants will be such survivor cannot be determined until sixteen of them have died. If it should be Arvilla, the remaindermen in fee would take the four shares held by him. The life estates in the other shares (if Connelly and Sardinia die and their children should have deceased without issue) would all have determined and the remainders have perished. If any first-named life tenants, any of the seventeen, should die leaving issue (children) alive, and such issue should still be alive at the death of the last one of the seventeen, such issue would hold for life the shares which they took from their parents. The contingent remainder having become vested by the death of the last of the seventeen named devisees, it would be good to take effect in possession on the death of such last-named issue.

"As to the life estates that drop out before the remainder in-fee has vested, where is the fee as to the shares owned by such life tenants who have deceased?—as, for example, if Katie and Arvilla should both die without issue before the last of the seventeen. If a contingent remainder becomes impossible of vesting because of the determination of the life estate before the contingency upon which the remainder was limited has happened— so i. e., if the contingent remainder has perished—it is the same as if it never existed. Says Gray on Perpetuities, section 11: 'A future estate may be indirectly created by giving livery of seisin for one or more life estates without ultimate remainder in fee. The estate remaining in the former owner ready to come into possession on the termination of the life estate or estates is a reversion. The same result is reached when an ultimate remainder in fee is contingent. Until it vests there is a reversion to the feoffer and his heirs.' And in the note he says: 'When a conveyance is by way of use or devise, there is unquestionably, during the contingency of a remainder in fee, a reversion in the grantor or devisor, and his heirs.'

" 'If the devise of a future interest is void for remoteness, but the prior devise is for life only, or other limited period, ... the property, after the termination of the prior interest, goes to the person to whom the property which has been invalidly devised or bequeathed goes. This person is generally the heir in case of real estate, and the residuary legatee in case of personalty. There is no difference, in this respect, between a devise or bequest void for remoteness, and a devise or bequest void for any other reason': Gray on Perpetuities, sec. 248; Tongue v. Nutwell, 13 Md. 415; Deford v. Deford, 36 Md. 168. 'Void devises, like lapsed devises, go to the heir': 1 Jarman on Wills, 646; Van Kleck v. Reformed Dutch Church, 6 Paige, 604.

"Therefore, when any life estate drops out (i. e., where a life estate ceases, there being neither brother nor sister nor issue living to take for life under the will) before the last of the seventeen life devisees dies, the persons who would be the heirs at law of the testator at the time of such dropping out of the life estate would take the interest as to the shares held by such life

tenant at his decease. If any of the named grandchildren; who
are life tenants under the will, dies leaving issue (children) him
surviving, and any of such issue (children) dies before the last
of the seventeen named life devisees, then the remainder [81] as
to the interest held by such child, will go in reversion to the
then heirs at law of the testator.

"The only remaining question is as to who are the remaindermen in fee. When they (the seventeen named life tenants) shall
all be dead, 'I will and devise said house and lot to my grandchildren then living, share and share alike, and if any grandchild shall be then dead leaving issue alive, such issue shall take
the share the parent would have taken if living.' This carries
the fee, the property being required to be divided share and share
alike.

"In his will the testator names all the grandchildren living
at his death, except Kate Larmon, daughter of Connelly (now
Kate Stark), and gives them life estates, and when they shall
all be dead he gives to all his grandchildren—i. e., at the time
the last of the named seventeen devisees (children and grandchildren) shall die—the remainder in fee. This would include
Kate Stark, if living, and all grandchildren born after the testator's death and then living. But what does the testator mean
when he says, 'If any grandchild be then dead leaving issue
alive, such issue to take the share the parent would have taken
if living?' There does not appear upon the face of the will
any reason why he should discriminate among his great grandchildren. I am of the opinion that he did not intend to, and
that his intention was to place them upon an equality (per
stirpes) with the after-born (or not specifically named) grandchildren who might be living when the contingency happened
upon which the fee was to vest. He uses the most comprehensive words, 'If any grandchild shall be then dead leaving issue
alive, such issue to take.' He intended the living grandchildren
to take share and share alike, and the then living issue (which
we have seen means children) of any grandchild to take per
stirpes the interest (or share) which the parents would have
taken if the property had then been divided among all his grandchildren. The trust as to the [82] rents would cease as to any
interest in the property upon such interest being taken as 'heir
at law of the testator.'

"This bill is brought by complainants, as heirs at law, attacking the will as invalid and praying that it be so declared. The
complainants are Kate Stark and her husband, and Katie Kirby

(nee Madison) and her husband, and Arvilla Madison. The
bill cannot be maintained by Katie Kirby and her husband and
Arvilla Madison, because they are beneficiaries named in the will
and have taken their share of the rents. They cannot take under
the will as devisees and then contest it as heirs at law: Andrews
v. Andrews, 110 Ill. 223; Gorham v. Dodge, 122 Ill. 528.

"It follows that the demurrer in this case must be sustained,
and the motion for a receiver denied."

For the reasons above stated the decree of the circuit court of
Cook county is affirmed.

COTENANCY—INTEREST OF COTENANT.—The law regards an
undivided interest in lands a separate estate, just as much as a
divided one: People v. Treasurer, 8 Mich. 14; 77 Am. Dec. 433. Tenants in common have several and distinct titles and estates, independent of each other, so as to render the freehold several also.
They are separately seized, and there is no privity of estate between
them: Mobley v. Bruner, 59 Pa. St. 481; 98 Am. Dec. 360.

PERPETUITIES—RULE AGAINST.—The rule against perpetuities is that no interest subject to a condition precedent is good
unless the condition must be fulfilled, if at all, within twenty-one
years after some life in being at the creation of the interest. The
fulfillment of the condition must necessarily, and under any and
all circumstances, take place within the required time. With respect to the computation of time, in the case of a devise it is to
commence at the death of the testator, which is to say, when the
will becomes operative: Monographic note to In re Walkerly, 49
Am. St. Rep. 118, 119, thoroughly discussing the rule.

WILLS—CONSTRUCTION OF—THE WORD "ISSUE."—The word
"issue" in a will, if there is nothing to restrict the meaning of the
word to children, is a word of purchase and not of limitation, and
includes all descendants in being at the time the terms of the will
become operative: Pearce v. Rickard, 18 R. I. 142; 49 Am. St. Rep.
755, and note. The technical signification of words must yield to
the testator's intent as manifest from the whole will: Scott v. Nelson,
3 Port. 452; 29 Am. Dec. 266; though in the absence of a contrary intention being shown they are presumed to be used in their
technical sense: Sims v. Conger, 39 Miss. 231; 77 Am. Dec. 671.

ESTATES—REMAINDERS—WHEN CONTINGENT.—A contin-
gent remainder is one limited to take effect, either to a dubious or
uncertain person, or upon a dubious and uncertain event: Haward
v. Peavey, 128 Ill. 430; 15 Am. St. Rep. 120, and note; Chapin v.
Crow, 147 Ill. 219; 37 Am. St. Rep. 213, and note. See Watson v.
Smith, 110 N. C. 6; 28 Am. St. Rep. 665; Ducker v. Burnham, 146
Ill. 9; 37 Am. St. Rep. 135, and note.

WILLS—ESTOPPEL FROM CONTESTING.—One who receives a
legacy under a will is estopped from contesting its validity, without
repaying the amount of the legacy or bringing it into court: Holt
v. Rice, 54 N. H. 398; 20 Am. Rep. 138. See Ratliff v. Baldwin, 29
Ind. 16; 92 Am. Dec. 330.

ILLINOIS STEEL COMPANY *v.* MANN.

[170 ILLINOIS, 200.]

MASTER AND SERVANT—A SERVANT ASSUMES THE RISK OF DANGEROUS MACHINERY AND APPLIANCES, WHEN.—If a servant discovers that the service has become more dangerous than he anticipated, or that there are defects in machinery or appliances making it unsafe for him to continue in his employment, and notifies the master thereof, he has a right to rely, for a reasonable time, on the promise of the master that the defect will be repaired and the machinery made safe. If, however, the master does not repair the defect within a reasonable time, and the servant has full knowledge thereof and of the consequent danger, it is his duty to quit the service if he does not intend to take the risk, and if thereafter injured thereby, he cannot recover therefor of his master.

MASTER AND SERVANT.—REASONABLE TIME FOR THE SUPPLYING OF DEFECTS IN MACHINERY AND APPLIANCES by an employer after being notified by his employé and promising the latter to correct them is such time only as is reasonably necessary for such repairs; and if the servant continues in his employment after the lapse of that time, knowing that the defects have not been remedied, he assumes the risk of injury therefrom.

Action to recover for injuries received by the plaintiff while in the employ of the defendant from slipping and falling upon a very smooth floor. It had been in this condition about a year prior to the accident, to the plaintiff's knowledge. He several times complained of it, but insisted that the defendant or its agents had promised to repair, and that he continued in the service, relying upon such promise. Judgment for the plaintiff, and the defendant appealed.

E. Parmalee Prentice, for the appellant.

George B. Finch, for the appellee.

[204] PHILLIPS, C. J. Of the assignments of error made on this record and argued by appellant there is only one proper for this court to consider. The question of the negligence of appellant, and some other questions argued by counsel for appellant, are those of fact, which have been settled by the judgment of the appellate court.

Error is assigned by the appellant on the refusal of the trial court to give to the jury, on the trial of this cause, the following instruction: "The court instructs the jury that an employé who continues in the service of his employer after notice of a defect increasing the danger of the service assumes the risk as increased by the defect, unless the master promised to remedy the defect; and in the event that the master does so promise, the servant may, while relying upon such promise, remain in the

service of the master only for such a time thereafter as would
be reasonably sufficient to enable the master to remedy the defect, and that if the master does not, within a reasonable time
after such promise, remedy the defect, then and in such event,
if the servant continues still in the employ of the master, he assumes the risk as increased by the defect; and the court therefore instructs the jury that if they believe, from the [205] evidence
in this case, that the standing upon which the plaintiff worked
while in the employ of the defendant was defective, that the defendant promised to remedy the same but failed to do so within
a reasonable time after such promise, and that the plaintiff continued thereafter to work for the defendant knowing that the
defendant had failed to remedy the defect within a reasonable
time after such promise, then and in such event the court instructs the jury that the plaintiff assumed the additional risk
of the defect in the condition of the floor, and if the jury so
finds they will return their verdict for the defendant."

This instruction was refused by the trial court, and it is practically admitted that no other instruction involving the same
principle was given to the jury, for the reason, as counsel for
appellee insists, it does not contain a correct expression of the
law of this state. It is urged as an objection to this instruction
that it would inform the jury that the servant may, while relying upon the promises of the master to repair a defect, remain
in the service of the master only for such time thereafter as
would be reasonable and sufficient to enable the master to remedy
the defect, and that if the master does not, within a reasonable
time after such promise, remedy the defect, then and in such
event, if the servant still continues in the employ of the master,
he assumes the risk as increased by the defect of which he himself
had knowledge. The trial court not only refused this instruction, but, by another instruction requested by the plaintiff, told
the jury that if the defendant promised to repair the defect,
and he was led to believe and expect that the floor would soon
be repaired, and that he continued to remain in the employment of the defendant up to the time he was injured, irrespective of whether or not such time was a reasonable one in which
the defect might have been remedied, the plaintiff was entitled
to recover.

[206] It is a recognized rule that it is the duty of the master
to furnish to the servant reasonably safe machinery and appliances with which to perform his work, but when the servant discovers that the service has become more dangerous than

he anticipated when he entered the employment of the master, or when he discovers defects in the machinery or appliances which make it unsafe for him to longer continue in the employ of the master, or from any other cause he concludes there is danger in continuing further in the service, it is his duty to notify the master of such danger or of such defects in the machinery or appliances connected with his work, and, upon the master being notified, the servant has the right to continue in the employ of the master for a reasonable time awaiting the remedy of such defect. He has the right to rely for a reasonable time upon the promise of the master that such defect in the machinery, appliances, or other surroundings connected with his work will be repaired and the machinery made safe, and the right to expect that such promise so made by the master will be fulfilled. If such expectation on the part of the servant, however, is not fulfilled and the defect remedied by the master within a reasonable time, and the servant has full knowledge of the dangerous condition of his machinery, appliances, or surroundings, and that he is subjected at all times to prospective injury, it is his duty to quit the service of the master, and not subject himself to further danger.

In the case of District of Columbia v. McElligot, 117 U. S. 621, the cause arose out of personal injuries received by a laborer while at work upon a bank of gravel. The evidence tended to show he discovered the bank was in an unsafe condition and asked the supervisor for a man to watch it, whereupon he received assurance such would be done. No such assistance, however, was given, but the laborer continued to work for a half day thereafter, knowing the danger, when the bank fell and severely injured him. It was held by the court in that case it was the duty [207] of the laborer, having knowledge of the dangerous condition of the bank, to exercise diligence and care in protecting himself, without regard to any assurance which he might have received from his employer.

The rule in the above case is stronger than the rule in this state. As a general rule, courts will consider that the master who employs a servant has a better and more comprehensive knowledge of the machinery and materials to be used than the employé. The servant has the right to presume that the materials and appliances which are furnished to him in the performance of his duty are sufficient therefor. This rule, however, is not applicable to all cases, and where the servant has equal knowledge with the master and a full knowledge of all existing defects, and more especially in the performance of ordinary labor in which no intricate machinery is involved, the rule is not applicable. In Marsh v. Chickering, 101 N. Y. 400, this exception is recognized, and it is said that the facts that a laborer using ordinary tools and appliances notified the master of a defect of which the servant himself had full knowledge, and asked it to be remedied, and the master promised so to do, do not render the master responsible. The rule in this state is more liberal, however, and permits the servant to remain in the employ of the master for a reasonable time awaiting the remedy of such defects.

In Corcoran v. Milwaukee Gas Light Co., 81 Wis. 191, the plaintiff had been employed by the defendant in making general repairs about its building, and had occasionally been required to use a ladder. Upon his statement that the ladder was not safe, the foreman had promised to have a safe ladder provided. Relying upon such promise, the plaintiff continued in the employ of the defendant, but the foreman failed to provide such safe ladder. The plaintiff was ordered by the foreman to ascend the ladder and make certain repairs, and, the ladder being unsafe and the floor on which it rested being slippery, the plaintiff [208] was injured by the falling of the ladder while ascending it. The court in that case held no liability, saying it has been held by it that in a proper case the servant may rely upon such assurance to remedy defects for a reasonable time, but if he remains in such service after the expiration of such reasonable time he is thereby deemed to waive his objection and assume the risk. To the same effect, also, is Gowan v. Harley, 56 Fed. Rep. 974. In that case the court says: "The rule that the master is responsible for damages resulting to the servant from defects in machinery and appliances of which the servant has notified him and which he has promised to repair, governs cases in which machinery or tools that are used in the work are discovered to be dangerously defective while in use, and to cases in which tools and machinery are necessary for the safe performance of the work. It has no application to a case where the service rendered is simply manual labor, without tools and machinery, and where no such tools or appliances are necessary to the performance of the work with a reasonable degree of safety."

In Stephenson v. Duncan, 73 Wis. 404, 9 Am. St. Rep. 806, it was held that the servant has the right to abandon the service because it is dangerous, but that he may refrain for a reasonable time from so doing in consequence of assurances by the master that the danger shall be remedied, and he will not be held to

thereby assume -the risk.   But if he continues in the service for
a longer time than is reasonable to allow for the performance of
the master's promise, he will be deemed to have waived his
objection and assumed the risk.

In the case of Missouri Furnace Co. v. Abend, 107 Ill. 44, 47
Am. Rep. 425, this court said: "It is now uniformly stated by
text-writers, that where the master, on being notified by the servant of defects that render the service he is engaged to perform
more hazardous, expressly promises to make the needed repairs,
the servant may continue in the employment [209] a reasonable
time to permit the performance of a promise in that regard without being guilty of negligence, and if any injury results therefrom
he may recover, unless when the danger is so imminent that no
prudent person would undertake to perform the service. . . . . The
doctrine on this subject rests on sound principle, and it will be
found to be supported by English and American decisions.   The
reason upon which the rule is said to rest is, that the promise of
the master to repair defects relieves the servant from the charge
of negligence by continuing in the service after the discovery of
the extra perils to which he would be exposed."

In Counsel v. Hall, 145 Mass. 468, the plaintiff was employed
by the defendant to take charge of an engine and boiler, and
plaintiff complained to defendant that the glass water-gauge of
the boiler was defective and dangerous, and defendant promised
to get a new one.   About two weeks after, the gauge exploded,
injuring the plaintiff.   The court said: "If machinery upon
which a servant is employed has become dangerous, and the servant has complained of it and has been promised that it shall be
repaired, but is injured before the defect is remedied and while he
is reasonably expecting the promise to be performed, the promise
is a circumstance to be considered by the jury. . . . . If the time
for the performance has gone by before the accident, and, as must
have been, after the servant knows that the repairs have not been
made, there is very strong argument that the servant is no longer
relying upon the promise and has decided to take the risk."

In Anderson Pressed Brick Co. v. Sobkowiak, 148 Ill. 573, the
plaintiff was engaged in taking clay from the bank.   He had objected to go underneath on account of the dangerous condition
of the bank, and said that if it should go down he would be injured.   One Keily was foreman in charge, representing the defendant, and he insisted there was no danger and ordered the
plaintiff to go underneath [210] and perform his work.   Under
those circumstances, the court, in its opinion, held the plaintiff

was not on the same footing with the master, and that his primary duty was obedience, and while he believed it dangerous to go under the bank, and protested, yet where the master sought to allay his fears and induce obedience to his commands by declaring there was no danger, the servant, in such case, having such fears and relying upon such assurances, was entitled to recover. That case, however, presents various differences from the case at bar.

While it is true some cases hold the rule to be that the servant, after having informed the master of any defects in machinery, tools, appliances, or surroundings of his work, and the master having promised to repair and make safe such defects, has the right to rely upon such promise and continue in the employ of the master expecting such promise to be fulfilled, yet the rule in this state, and also in most other states, holds that such expectation on the part of the servant may continue only for a time reasonable for such repairs to be made or defects remedied, and if not so made within a reasonable time, the servant, having full knowledge of such defects, will be considered to have waived the same and subject himself to all the dangers incident thereto: Swift v. Madden, 165 Ill. 41. In the case at bar, the plaintiff says he had frequently gone to the foreman and told him that the standing where he was working was dangerous, and that the foreman would make an "offish" reply of some kind and say he would fix it. Plaintiff says he spoke to the foreman quite a number of times during the year prior to this accident, the last time being two or three weeks before the injury occurred. He also says, in substance, that he did not place much reliance upon the foreman's word, but supposed, however, the floor would be fixed.

It is apparent from this record the floor was in a dangerous condition. It is apparent, also, the plaintiff was fully aware of this dangerous condition, and had been so [211] for at least a year. It was his duty, being fully aware of the danger, to have notified the foreman or his employer, which he did. It was his right, also, under the law, having given such notice, to have continued in the work in which he was engaged for a reasonable time only, awaiting the fulfillment of this promise to remedy such dangerous condition. The jury should have been instructed that the law was as stated in the instruction which was refused. The instruction should have been given, and it was error to refuse it. For this error the judgment is reversed and the cause remanded to the circuit court.

JUSTICES CARTER, MAGRUDER, AND BOGGS dissented. They insisted that the judgment of the appellate court had finally

and conclusively settled the facts in favor of the appellee, and that
the instruction which the trial court refused to give to the jury
at the request of the defendant, and for which refusal the judgment
was now reversed, was itself erroneous; that it was not true that
a servant, relying on the promise of his master to repair, might remain in the service only for such a time after such promise as
would be reasonably sufficient to enable the master to remedy the
defect, and that, remaining longer, the servant assumed the increased risk. They insisted that "the reasonable time does not so
much relate to the time required to make the repairs as it does to
the time the servant is authorized, in the exercise of reason and
prudence, to rely upon the master's promise." They claimed that
the decision of the majority was in conflict with Weber Wagon
Co. v. Kehl, 139 Ill. 644, and that: "The true rule ought to be, and
is, that the assumption of the increased risk by the master and his
promise to repair, whereby the servant is induced to remain, will
continue until he fulfills his promise or notifies the servant of his
inability or unwillingness to do so, or until such a length of time has
lapsed as would, under all the attending circumstances, make it
unreasonable for the servant to longer rely upon the promise. Under
such a rule, the question would be whether the servant at the time
of the accident relied, or had reasonable ground to rely, upon the
promise of a master to repair, or had himself assumed the increased
risk of continuing in the service after he had ceased to rely upon
the master's promise."

MASTER AND SERVANT — DANGEROUS MACHINERY —
PROMISE TO REPAIR—ASSUMPTION OF RISKS.—When a mas-
ter or superior servant notified by an inferior servant of a defect in
the machinery, appliances, or premises furnished for his use, promises
to repair within a reasonable time, such servant by remaining in the
service a reasonable time thereafter, does not assume the risk, nor
waive his right to recover from the master if injured by reason of
the defect within such time: Breckenridge Co. v. Hicks, 94 Ky.
362; 42 Am. St. Rep. 361, and note; but if he continues his employment beyond the time within which he might reasonably expect
the master would keep his promise, he will be deemed to have
waived his objections, and assumed the risk: Stephenson v. Duncan,
73 Wis. 404; 9 Am. St. Rep. 806, and note; note to Cheeney v. Ocean
Steamship Co., 44 Am. St. Rep. 119. Under some circumstances,
where the danger arising from the defect complained of is obvious,
immediate, and constant, the servant may be held to have assumed
the risk of injury therefrom by remaining in the employment for
any time after his discovery of the danger, even though the master
has promised to repair: Erdman v. Illinois Steel Co., 95 Wis. 6; 60
Am. St. Rep. 66, and note.

PRAIRIE STATE LOAN & BUILDING ASSN. *v.* NUBLING.

[170 ILLINOIS, 240.]

BUILDING AND LOAN ASSOCIATION—STOCK IN, WHEN NOT CANCELED.—If a member of a building and loan association notifies its secretary that he wishes to withdraw, and delivers his stock and pass-book for that purpose, but, before the stock is canceled, informs the secretary that he desires to remain in the association, who answers, "All right," and payments of dues are subsequently made as required, his stock is not canceled, though the secretary fraudulently issues a warrant for the amount of withdrawal, and, without knowledge of the member, induces the association to cash it.

BUILDING AND LOAN ASSOCIATIONS—LIABILITY OF FOR ACTS OF THEIR SECRETARY.—If payments of his dues are made by a member of a building and loan association to its secretary, who fraudulently fails to report them, the association is bound by such payments, and must give the member credit therefor.

BUILDING AND LOAN ASSOCIATIONS—AUTHORITY OF SECRETARY.—Where the control and management of a building and loan association are vested, even tacitly, in its secretary, it is bound by his acts under such extended authority. If stock is handed in for cancellation, and the secretary procures a third person to purchase it and pay the amount due thereon, and the pass-book is delivered to him, and monthly payments are thereafter received from him by the secretary, who issues a warrant for the payment of such stock as canceled, and turns it over to the association as cash, the association, rather than the purchaser of the stock, must suffer from this fraud of the secretary.

BUILDING AND LOAN ASSOCIATION—MEMBERS, WHEN ENTITLED TO EXECUTION AGAINST.—Though the statute provides that only one-half of the funds in the treasury shall be applicable to the demands of withdrawing stockholders, yet, if the association denies that a member is such or has any right to withdraw, and he maintains a suit to enforce his rights, execution may properly issue in his favor for the whole sum found to be due him.

Williams & Kraft, for the appellant.

Samuel J. Howe, for the appellee.

243 PHILLIPS, C. J. The only questions necessary to be considered in the determination of the issues in this case are, whether there was such a cancellation of the stock of appellee in this association as amounted to a bar of his right to recover the money before then paid—a withdrawal of his membership from the association so that all payments of dues thereafter were unauthorized; and also whether or not the purchase by him from the secretary of this building association of stock presented by another party for cancellation gave him the right or title thereto.

In our view of the case, the master in chancery, the circuit court, and the appellate court have all reached the correct conclusions. The record in this case shows that the twenty shares of stock held by appellee were presented for cancellation at one time, but in fact never were canceled. The by-laws of appellant provide as [244] follows: "All members desiring to withdraw from the association, as provided by section 6 of the act under which this association is organized, shall be entitled to receive the amount of dues paid by them, less all fines and other charges, and also receive such shares of the profits then accrued as the board of directors may from time to time determine; provided, that no member withdrawing from the association within one year after having joined the same shall be entitled to any interest or profits." Appellee did not receive, after the presentation of his stock, all dues paid by him, together with any portion of the profits then accrued, but before any cancellation of his stock was made he notified the association, through its proper officer, the secretary, that he would not withdraw. He had a perfect right to do this at any time before the cancellation was actually consummated. The mere facts that about that time a fraudulent secretary caused a warrant to be drawn to appellee's order for the withdrawal value of this stock, and without procuring the indorsement of appellee was able to induce this association to cash the warrant, were not such facts as operated to cancel appellee's stock.

Common knowledge of the general conduct and management of associations known as building associations shows that in the majority of cases the secretary of such an association has largely the control of the details of its business. He generally possesses the confidence of its members and patrons, who largely rely on him. Many such associations, under our statute, transact a financial business far in excess of the ordinary bank. Its directors should certainly be held to an ordinary degree of diligence and watchfulness over the interests of the association and over those who handle its funds. There having been no withdrawal or cancellation of this stock, it follows that all payments of dues made to an officer of the association authorized to receive them created an additional liability from the appellant association to appellee. [245] The fact that the secretary of this association, either fraudulently or otherwise, did not report the collection of these monthly payments of dues to the association does not release the association. As long as he was secretary he was, under the by-laws, the proper officer to receive such payments, and payment to him was to the association.

It is contended that appellee acquired no title to the Marco stock. The Marco stock was not canceled, as the warrant for such purpose was never delivered to Marco, nor did he indorse it. It was a fraud on the part of the secretary to appropriate the amount of the warrant to himself. Appellee issued his check for the stock, and the proper representative of the appellant association, who also acted for Marco, received it and assigned the pass-book to appellee, who continued to make payments on this stock. In this association, as in many others of like class, great confidence seems to have been reposed in the secretary previous to his default. Endlich, in his work on Building Associations, paragraph 174, says that the secretary is often the general agent of the association, and often is, in point of fact, the manager of its entire business. Where such control and management are vested in him, even tacitly, the association will be bound by his acts under such extended authority.

Complaint is made that the decree of the superior court ordered execution against the association, when the statute provides that only one-half the funds in the treasury shall be applicable to the demands of withdrawing stockholders. There is no merit in this objection. Appellant denied that appellee was a member of its association or had any right to withdraw. After the decree appellee stood in the relation of a creditor, rather than a withdrawing member.

The judgment of the appellate court for the first district is affirmed.

BUILDING AND LOAN ASSOCIATIONS—POWERS OF OFFICERS.—The powers, duties, and liabilities of officers of building and loan associations are those which usually appertain to the officers of corporations: Monographic note to Robertson v. Homestead Assn., 69 Am. Dec. 156, on building and loan associations. See m n ap note to Lake v. Minnesota etc. Assn., 52 Am. St. Rep. 150. ogr hic

BUILDING AND LOAN ASSOCIATIONS—RIGHTS OF MEMBERS.—The important and peculiar rights of members of building and loan associations are their rights to loans and their rights of withdrawal. A member who complies with the constitution and by-laws of an association, and under their provisions withdraws, can recover the amount due him by assumpsit, using the common counts: Note to Robertson v. Homestead Assn., 69 Am. Dec. 156, containing an exhaustive discussion of the subject. See Eversmann v. Schmitt, 53 Ohio St. 174; 53 Am. St. Rep. 632.

YARNELL *v.* BROWN.

[170 ILLINOIS, 362.]

JUDGMENT, VACATION OF, WHO MAY COMPLAIN OF.—
If the only person whose rights are affected by the vacating of a
judgment or decree does not complain thereof, a third person will not
be heard to object that the method of obtaining relief was not proper.

A JUDGMENT IS NOT ASSIGNABLE under the common law
nor by the statutes of Illinois, so as to vest the legal title in the assignee. He obtains an equitable title only.

JUDGMENT.—THE ASSIGNEE OF A JUDGMENT TAKES
IT SUBJECT to all equities existing between the parties thereto, but
he is protected against the latent equities of third persons of which
he had no notice.

JUDGMENT.—THE LIEN OF AN ORDINARY JUDGMENT
is general, and not specific, against any particular thing. It exists
only in what the debtor really has, subject to the equities in it at the
date of the judgment.

JUDGMENT, ASSIGNMENT, CONFLICT BETWEEN AND
THE RIGHT TO REFORM A MORTGAGE.—If, after the levy of an
attachment and the rendition of a judgment, it is assigned and an execution sale made to the assignee of the land which the judgment
debtor had undertaken to mortgage, but which by mistake had not
been included in that instrument, the mortgagee is entitled, by a suit
in equity, to reform his mortgage so as to include all the property intended, after first paying such sums as had been advanced by the
assignee and such charges as had been incurred in his favor up to the
time when he had notice of the equities of the mortgagee.

W. L. Gross and E. S. Robinson, for the appellant.

G. Fred Rush and J. C. McBride, for the appellee.

[365] CARTWRIGHT, J. On September 1, 1876, James S.
Woolley owned and resided upon a farm of one hundred and
thirty-seven acres in Christian county, and on that day executed,
with his wife, a mortgage to the appellee, Lephia O. Brown, to
secure the payment of one thousand dollars borrowed money five
years after date, with interest to be paid annually, intending to
mortgage a forty acre tract of the farm which was situate in
range 1, east of the third principal meridian, but by mistake the
land was described as being in range 1, west. Woolley had also
given an unsecured note for six hundred dollars to one Spauld-
ing, who in 1889 gave that note to the appellant, Electa W. Yarnell, a daughter of Woolley. On July 22, 1889, Mrs. Yarnell began an attachment suit upon that six hundred dollar note against
her father, who had become a nonresident, and caused the attachment writ to be levied upon the forty acre tract which Woolley
and Mrs. Brown intended to be, and supposed was, included in the
mortgage. Woolley entered his appearance in the attachment
suit, and on June 6, 1890, a general judgment was rendered

against him in favor of Mrs. Yarnell for twelve hundred and
eighty-three dollars and twenty-one cents, which she on the same
day assigned to her attorney, William L. Gross, to secure him for
services [366] rendered and to be rendered for her as such attorney. Woolley paid the interest on his indebtedness to Mrs.
Brown up to September 1, 1889, but the interest due September
1, 1890, was not paid, and on November 7, 1890, the original bill
in this case was filed by Mrs. Brown for the foreclosure of her
mortgage. At the March term, 1891, the appearance of Woolley
was entered in writing in the foreclosure suit, his default was
taken, and the judge entered on his docket the usual order for a
decree of foreclosure and sale for eleven hundred and thirty-eight
dollars and thirty-five cents, with costs. Up to this time the mistake in the mortgage had never been detected, but it was discovered before the decree was entered by the clerk, and no decree was
ever entered at large upon the records. The entire entry of
record was a transcript of the judge's minutes, without the description of any property or any of the usual provisions. An execution having been issued on the judgment in the attachment
suit, the land in question was sold June 19, 1891, to Gross for
fourteen hundred and thirty-four dollars and twenty-four cents,
the amount due on the judgment with costs, and he received a
certificate of purchase. The error in the mortgage having been
discovered, the previous orders and decree in the cause were at
the August term, 1891, on the motion of Mrs. Brown, set aside,
with leave to amend the bill and make new parties. The bill was
amended, setting up the mistake and asking a correction, and
making Mrs. Yarnell and her husband and Gross defendants.
They were served for the November term, 1891, and answered the
amended bill. Their answers were afterward amended, and their
defense was, that the court had no right to set aside the former
decree, and that they had no notice of the mistake or of Mrs.
Brown's rights. Woolley answered admitting all the allegations
of the amended bill. Pending the litigation Gross obtained a
sheriff's deed, January 4, 1895. On a hearing a decree was entered finding that Mrs. Yarnell had notice of the equities of Mrs.
Brown; that her interest and that of Gross were subject to the
mortgage lien, and that the [367] husband, W. R. Yarnell, had no
interest in the premises. The decree corrected the mistake and
ordered a foreclosure and sale. Mrs. Yarnell and Gross appealed
to the appellate court, where the decree was reversed and the cause
remanded to the circuit court, with directions to ascertain the
amount due Gross from Mrs. Yarnell and make his claim the first

lien to that amount, to make the amount due Mrs. Brown a second lien and to order a sale accordingly. From that judgment Mrs. Yarnell has prosecuted this appeal, and Mrs. Brown has assigned cross-errors upon the record.

It is insisted on behalf of the appellant that the circuit court had no power, at the August term, 1891, to set aside its decree of the March term preceding, on the motion of appellee, but that appellee misconceived her remedy and should have proceeded by a bill of review. That decree was against James S. Woolley, and he was the only one whose rights were in any manner affected by the method employed to set aside the former decree. It is no concern of appellant that it was done by a motion, rather than upon an issue formed or by default upon a bill of review. The only party interested in that question has found no fault with the method but is content with the order, and appellant cannot be heard to object for him.

It is also claimed that appellant had no knowledge of the mortgage or of the land intended to be conveyed thereby; but we are well satisfied with the conclusion of the circuit and appellate courts that she had such knowledge and that her rights were subordinate to those of appellee.

The remaining question is whether the equities of William L. Gross are superior to those of appellee, and if so, to what extent. A judgment is not assignable, at common law or under our statute, so as to vest a legal title in the assignee, and the purchaser obtains only an equitable interest: McJilton v. Love, 13 Ill. 486; 54 Am. Dec. 449; Hughes [368] v. Trahern, 64 Ill. 48. The purchaser takes the judgment subject to all equities existing between the parties to it. It has been the rule in this state that the purchaser of certain things in action will be protected against the latent equities of third persons of whose rights he could know nothing. Thus, in the case of mortgages it has been repeatedly held that an assignee is so protected against such equities: Olds v. Cummings, 31 Ill. 188; Silverman v. Bullock, 98 Ill. 11; Himrod v. Gilman, 147 Ill. 293; Humble v. Curtis, 160 Ill. 193. But in order to make that rule applicable the equities must be equal. If the assignee is a mere donee, or the lien acquired is inferior in its nature to another equity, he will not be preferred. The lien of an ordinary judgment is general, and not specific against any particular thing. It only extends to what the debtor really has, subject to the equities in it at the date of the judgment. A mortgagee deals with particular property, and in this case appellee parted with her money upon the security of a particular tract of land which was misdescribed, so that her right was equitable only, but the equitable interest was in that particular tract. Such an equity would be regarded as superior to that of appellant, so far as her judgment was a general lien upon the property of her father, James S. Woolley. The appearance of Woolley was entered in the attachment suit, and a general judgment was rendered against him, and it is argued on behalf of appellee that the attachment was thereby abandoned and the lien of the attachment released, so that the lien of the judgment became a general one. We do not think that such is the effect of the judgment. It is true that execution might issue thereon, not only against the property attached but the other property of Woolley, and yet the lien as to the particular tract of land levied upon was preserved, and appellant was not put in a worse position by the appearance and general judgment than she would have been if Woolley had not appeared. It appears, therefore, that, 369 so far as the liens upon the land are concerned, the equities are such that the same rule applied in the assignment of mortgages should prevail, and the rights acquired by Gross without notice should be protected.

When the assignment was made to Gross he had rendered services to appellant which the judgment was assigned to secure, but it was also intended to secure payment for services and expenses to be rendered in the future, and he continued to render services and incur expenses after he and appellant were brought into this suit and had full notice of appellee's equities. For these services and expenses subsequent to such notice, and in defending appellant's claim and his own to priority over appellee in this suit, he charged and claimed the right to payment out of the judgment. By this means there has been a very large increase in his claim after actual notice of appellee's equities. The only valuable consideration actually passing between him and appellant prior to notice were the services performed and the expenses incurred up to that time. A valuable consideration is an essential requisite to secure an equitable right to precedence in such a case as this, and if notice is received before the consideration is actually parted with, it must be held a valid and binding notice, which will preclude an assignee from acquiring any right upon a subsequent consideration as against the prior equity. After such notice Gross was not bound to perform the services or incur the expenses upon the faith of the security, and would have had ample relief against his agreement on account of the failure of the security. To permit him, after notice, to go on and consume the whole or a large part of the value of the property in litigation, to the further impairment or destruction of the prior equitable right, would be most inequitable and unjust. He testified to his subsequent services and disbursements, and his charges therefor, as well as the continuing charges in this litigation, and the judgment of the appellate [370] court directed the circuit court to ascertain the amount due him from appellant and allow the same as a first lien. We think that this was wrong.

The judgment of the appellate court and decree of the circuit court are reversed and the cause is remanded to the circuit court, with directions to ascertain the amount equitably due to William L. Gross from appellant for services and expenses to secure which the judgment was assigned to him, up to the service of process on him under the amended bill in this case, and to make his claim a first lien for such amount and appellee's mortgage a second lien, and to enter a decree of foreclosure accordingly.

JUDGMENT—ASSIGNMENT OF.—Judgments may be assigned like choses in action: Wright v. Yell, 13 Ark. 503; 58 Am. Dec. 336. At common law, the effect of the assignment of a judgment was merely to transfer an equitable title. It did not authorize the assignee to bring an action thereon in his own name. This rule has, however, been generally abolished in this country: Extended note to Dugas v. Mathews, 54 Am. Dec. 366, 367. An assignee of a judgment is not affected by the latent equities of third persons not parties to the judgment, of which he had no notice at the time of the assignment: Western Nat. Bank v. Maverick Nat. Bank, 90 Ga. 339; 35 Am. St. Rep. 210, and note.

JUDGMENT LIEN—NATURE OF.—A judgment lien is not a specific lien, but only a general lien on the defendant's lands: Pettit v. Shepherd, 5 Paige, 493; 28 Am. Dec. 437. It attaches to the actual not the apparent, interest of the defendant: Burke v. Johnson, 37 Kan. 337; 1 Am. St. Rep. 252; and is subject to all equities existing against such lands in favor of third persons at the time of the recovery of the judgment: Leonard v. Broughton, 120 Ind. 536; 16 Am. St. Rep. 347, and note.

JUDGMENTS—VACATION OF—WHO MAY COMPLAIN OF.—One cannot complain of an erroneous decree who has no legal or equitable interest affected thereby: Bank of Utica v. Mersereau, 3 Barb. Ch. 528; 49 Am. Dec. 189. Upon the general subject of the vacation of judgments, see monographic note to Furman v. Furman, 60 Am. St. Rep. 633-663.

Cox v. Stern.

[170 Illinois, 442.]

AN AFFIDAVIT IS a declaration on oath in writing, sworn to by a party before some person authorized to administer oaths.

AFFIDAVIT, VENUE OF.—IF THE PLACE where an affidavit was taken does not appear therefrom, but it does appear to have been made before a notary public, it will be presumed that he administered it in the county within which he was authorized to administer oaths.

NOTARIES PUBLIC, SEALS OF MAY AID AFFIDAVIT.—If, from the venue of an affidavit, it cannot be ascertained where the oath was administered nor for what county the notary who administered it was authorized to act, his seal may be looked at to ascertain of what county he was an officer.

JUDICIAL NOTICE—NOTARIES PUBLIC.—The courts of a county will take judicial notice of the notaries of such county.

RECORDING DEEDS—SEALS OF NOTARIES.—The recorder should copy the inscription of the seals of notaries public upon instruments filed for record.

AFFIDAVITS.—THE JURAT of an officer is not an affidavit, nor, strictly speaking, any part of it. The omission of such jurat is, therefore, not fatal to the affidavit, if it appears by extrinsic evidence that it was, in fact, sworn to by the parties named therein.

CHATTEL MORTGAGE, AFFIDAVIT, DEFECTS IN.—The fact that an affidavit to a chattel mortgage does not show in what county it was taken, and the jurat is, as to some of the parties, not signed by the notary, does not invalidate the mortgage nor the record thereof, if, from the seal of the notary, the county in which he was authorized to act appears, and there is extrinsic evidence showing that the affidavit was made in that county by all the apparent parties thereto.

J. A. Bellatti, for the appellant.

Edward P. Kirby and Williams, Linden, Dempsey & Gott, for the appellee.

443 CARTER, J. This was a suit in replevin, by appellee, for household furniture, carriage, horses, etc., taken by appellant, as sheriff of Morgan county, under four executions issued on judgments against Bessie and Henry Schoenfield. Appellee claims under a chattel mortgage executed by the Schoenfields to him, which mortgage was sought to be extended, under the statute, by filing an affidavit for record in the recorder's office of Morgan county. The circuit court gave judgment for appellee that he have the property, and for costs. Appellant appealed to the appellate court, where the judgment was affirmed, and he has further appealed to this court.

444 The only point discussed by appellant before the appellate court, and the only one made in this court, is, that the alleged affidavit was insufficient to extend the mortgage; that it really was no affidavit, and that it was error to admit the same in evidence, and error also to admit parol evidence to aid and supplement the said affidavit.

The venue and commencement of the affidavit are as follows:

"State of Illinois,   }
    County of Illinois. }   ss.

"We, Henry L. Williams, attorney for Ferdinand Stern, of Cook county, state of Illinois, and Henry Schoenfield and Bessie Schoenfield, of Morgan county, state of Illinois, being duly sworn, each for himself and herself, says that," etc.

The conclusion and certificates are as follows:

"And affiants make this affidavit for the purpose of extending the time of payment of said debt, and the lien of said chattel mortgage on the property therein mentioned, according to the statute in such case made and provided. Such chattel mortgage is hereby extended by agreement of Henry Schoenfield and Bessie Schoenfield, mortgagors, and Henry L. Williams, attorney for the said Ferdinand Stern, mortgagee, to the twenty-third day of March, A. D. 1897.

"HENRY L. WILLIAMS,

"Att'y for Ferdinand Stern, Mortgagee.

"BESSIE SCHOENFIELD.

"HENRY SCHOENFIELD.

"Subscribed and sworn to by the said Henry L. Williams before me this 25th day of March, A. D. 1895.

"CHARLES E. ANTHONY,

"[Notarial Seal.]   Notary Public.

"Subscribed and sworn to by said Henry Schoenfield and Bessie Schoenfield before me this —— day of March, 1895."

The notarial seal was inscribed: "Charles E. Anthony, Notary Public, Cook county, Illinois." On the back of the affidavit was a duly executed certificate of acknowledgment of the justice of the peace in Morgan county that the Schoenfields appeared before him and acknowledged that they signed said affidavit; but, of course, such an acknowledgment cannot take the place of the required oath.

445 Objections are made that the instrument in question is not an affidavit, but only a statement; that after admitting the parol evidence it is, at most, only a sworn statement; that it has no venue, and that there is no signature or date to the jurat referring to the Schoenfields; that the statute requires an affidavit in order to extend a chattel mortgage; that the affidavit must be

perfect and complete, and must so appear of record, to be valid against creditors, and that parol evidence is inadmissible to aid or sustain the same.

The statute allowing the lien of a chattel mortgage to be extended requires the filing for record of an affidavit setting forth particularly certain facts enumerated in the statute: See Rev. Stats., c. 95, sec. 4, as amended in 1891. It nowhere directs or specifies anything in regard to the formal parts or authentication of the affidavit. Bouvier's Law Dictionary defines an affidavit to be "a statement or declaration reduced to writing, and sworn or affirmed to before some officer who has authority to administer an oath." And in 1 Encyclopedia of Pleading and Practice, 309, it is said: "An affidavit is a voluntary ex parte statement, formally reduced to writing and sworn to or affirmed before some officer authorized by law to take it." This court said in Harris v. Lester, 80 Ill. 307: "An affidavit is simply a declaration on oath, in writing, sworn to by a party before some person who has authority under the law to administer oaths."

As to the venue, we held in Hertig v. People, 159 Ill. 237, 50 Am. St. Rep. 162, that a notary public "being a public officer, it will be presumed he administered the oath in the county within which he was authorized to administer oaths, for the presumption is that he has done his duty." The venue of this instrument is: "State of Illinois, County of Illinois,—ss." As there is no such county in this state, we must look at the seal of the notary to ascertain for which county he was authorized to administer oaths. The seal bears the following inscription: "Charles E. Anthony, Notary Public, 446 Cook County, Illinois." The statute, chapter 99, section 7, provides that "each notary public shall . . . . provide himself with a proper official seal, ... upon which shall be engraved words descriptive of his office, and the name of the place or county in which he resides." It will be presumed that the notary has complied with the statute, and that the inscription on his seal speaks the truth. We think the venue sufficiently appears. Indeed, if the instrument had been filed in Cook county, it would have been good without a seal, as the courts will take judicial notice of the notaries in their county: Schaefer v. Kienzel, 123 Ill. 430.

Appellant insists that the inscriptions on notaries' seals never appear of record, but that the recorder simply makes a scrawl. and writes in it the word "Seal." There is no merit in this contention. The recorder should copy such inscriptions on the seals.

It is next contended that the instrument is inoperative as an affidavit because the jurat as to the oaths of the Schoenfields is not signed or authenticated in any way. But the jurat of the officer is not the affidavit, nor, strictly speaking, any part of it. It is simply evidence of the fact that the affidavit was properly sworn to by the affiant: Williams v. Stevenson, 103 Ind. 243; 1 Ency. of Pl. & Pr. 316, and notes. It has been frequently held, both in this state and elsewhere, that affidavits for attachment are not void because the clerk or officer failed to affix his signature to the jurat: Kruse v. Wilson, 79 Ill. 233.

But it is contended that there is a difference between attachment cases and the case at bar, because in attachment cases the affidavit is merely the initial proceeding of the cause and may be amended at the trial, while in this case the statute requires that the record should disclose all the facts, and no parol evidence can add to that record, for creditors are not bound to look beyond the record. We are referred to Colman v. Goodnow, 36 Minn. 9, 1 Am. St. Rep. 632, Stetson etc. Mill Co. v. McDonald, 5 Wash. 496, and Hill v. ⁴⁴⁷ Alliance Bldg. Co., 6 S. Dak. 160, 55 Am. St. Rep. 819, as supporting appellant's contention. In the first two cases the court held the affidavit defective for want of a seal to the jurat, and the third case was based on the other two, in that case one jurat having the seal of the notary but no signature, and the other being by a foreign notary, with no seal or certificate of authority attached. We have held that a seal is not required by the statute to be affixed to a jurat to be used within the county of the officer. The statute provides nothing as to the jurat or mode of authenticating the affidavit: Schaefer v. Kienzel, 123 Ill. 430. The decisions referred to, therefore, can hardly be regarded as authority on this point.

We are also referred to McDermaid v. Russell, 41 Ill. 489, where the court said: "The affidavit of nonresidence does not appear to have been sworn to before any officer. For that omission it was no affidavit, and gave no authority to the court to enter an order for publication." No copy of the affidavit is given, and nothing appears to show how it appeared that no oath was administered: See, also, Bickerdike v. Allen, 157 Ill. 95.

The affidavit in this case begins with the names of the parties, and then follows, "being duly sworn, each for himself and herself, says." They are referred to as "affiants" in the body of the instrument a number of times, and the same concludes, "and affiants make this affidavit," and their names are signed. The oath of the attorney, Williams, is properly authenticated, but not so the oaths of the Schoenfields. The record in the recorder's of-

fice then disclosed, or at least contained the statement, that all
the parties were sworn, but failed to show the evidence of the
officer who administered the oaths to two of them.   Is this such
an affidavit as the statute contemplates, or is it void as to creditors because the evidence that the oath was actually and duly administered was not preserved by a proper certificate of the officer
attached? We have carefully examined all the cases in this [448]
court on the subject of defective affidavits to which we have been
referred, and find that, as a general rule, they were held insufficient on account of defects in matters of substance, which could
not be aided by parol.   In McDermaid v. Russell, 41 Ill. 489, it
does not appear that there was any evidence that the affidavit was
sworn to.   But the case is different here.   We think enough appears in the record, no objection being made to the substance of
the affidavit, to show a substantial compliance with the statute,
upon proof being made of the truth of the statement in the affidavit that the affiants were duly sworn—that is, that the statements contained in the instrument were made on their respective
oaths.

We are of the opinion that the jurat or certificate of the officer
administering the oath is not a necessary part of the affidavit,
but that it may be shown aliunde that the statements contained
in the instrument were in truth and in fact made as they purported to be—on oath duly administered by an officer duly authorized.   The statute prescribes no form for the affidavit, and
makes no provision as to the form in which the evidence of the
oath shall be preserved or made to appear, but only requires that
an affidavit shall be filed, etc.   Of course, common prudence
would dictate that a properly executed jurat, or certificate of the
officer showing the oath, should be attached; but when attached
it is not conclusive, but may be shown to be false, and if shown
to be false, and that no oath was in fact administered, the instrument would not be an affidavit.

We are of the opinion that the record was sufficient to give
notice to third persons that the alleged affidavit was made on
oath, and that parol evidence was admissible on the trial to prove
that the oath was actually taken.   The judgment of the appellate
court will therefore be affirmed.

Wilkin and Cartwright, JJ., dissenting.

AFFIDAVIT—WHAT IS.—An affidavit is simply a declaration on
oath, in writing, sworn to by a party before some person having
authority under the law to administer oaths, and need not be entitled in any particular cause, or in any particular way, or be pre-

ceded by any caption: Hertig v. People, 159 Ill. 237; 50 Am. St.
Rep. 162, and note. See Beebe v. Morrill, 76 Mich. 114; 15 Am.
St. Rep. 288.

AFFIDAVITS.—AN AFFIDAVIT HAVING NO VENUE, but subscribed by a notary public of the county, is good, for the court will
take judicial notice that he is a notary of the county, and will presume that he administered the oath only in the county in which
he was authorized to act: Hertig v. People, 159 Ill. 237; 50 Am. St.
Rep. 162.

NOTARIES PUBLIC.—COURTS WILL TAKE JUDICIAL NO-
TICE of the notaries public in the counties in which they are held:
Hertig v. People, 159 Ill. 237; 50 Am. St. Rep. 162, and note.

AFFIDAVITS—JURAT.—The jurat of an affidavit offered in evidence may be amended by adding thereto a reference to the seal of
the notary before whom the affidavit was made, which reference
was omitted in the original jurat: Hallett v. Chicago etc. Ry. Co., 22
Iowa, 259; 92 Am. Dec. 893.

Postal Telegraph Cable Company *v*. Eaton.

[170 Illinois, 513.]

HIGHWAYS, RIGHTS OF LANDOWNER IN LANDS BE-
NEATH.—Where a highway is laid out over lands outside of an incorporated city, town, or village, the public acquires only an easement of passage, with the rights and incidents thereto, while the
owner of the land over which the road is laid out retains the fee and
ownership of everything connected with the soil, for all purposes not
incompatible with the right of the public to the free use of the road
as a public highway.

HIGHWAYS.—EJECTMENT MAY BE MAINTAINED BY
THE OWNER OF LAND over which there is a public highway against a telegraph corporation which has constructed and is
maintaining its line upon such highway without his consent and
without compensating him therefor.

HIGHWAYS, ADDITIONAL SERVITUDE.—A telegraph line
constructed and maintained upon the public highway constitutes an
additional servitude, and the owner of the land is entitled to compensation therefor. If not compensated, he may maintain an action
to dispossess the telegraph corporation.

HIGHWAYS, TELEGRAPH CORPORATIONS.—The consent
of the proper officers of a county that a telegraph line be constructed
and maintained upon a public highway is not binding on a landowner,
who, if he be not properly compensated, may maintain an action
against the corporation maintaining such line. The landowner is
protected by the declaration of the constitution that private property
shall not be taken or damaged without just compensation.

HIGHWAYS.— ONE WHO PURCHASES LAND, PART OF
WHICH IS A PUBLIC HIGHWAY, upon which a line of telegraph
has been constructed without the consent of the owner and without
compensation to him, acquires the right which his grantor had to
maintain ejectment against the telegraph corporation, unless duly
compensated for the additional servitude which it imposes on the
highway.

William P. Bradshaw, Loesch Bros. & Howell, and Frank J. Loesch, for the appellant.

Travous & Warnock, for the appellee.

[514] CRAIG, J. This was an action of ejectment brought by Henry A. Eaton, appellee, against the Postal Telegraph-Cable Company, for the purpose of compelling the removal of the defendant's line of telegraph poles from a public highway known as the Edwardsville and Hillsboro road, which was located over and upon appellee's land.

It appears from the record that the Board of Trade Telegraph Company in 1882 constructed its telegraph line over a public highway known as the Edwardsville and Hillsboro road by the consent of the board of supervisors of Madison county, under a resolution of the board adopted at a regular meeting upon the request of the telegraph company. The resolution granting the right contained the following conditions: "Said line shall start at or near New Douglas and run in a southwest direction, and terminate at or near Venice, in said county, the poles to be set not over two and one-half feet from the margin of the road, not to interfere with ditches and water drains; poles to be eighteen feet high and well set and braced, and the wire to be kept tight, and they are to establish but one line, and by them securing the right of way in the several townships." The telegraph company went on and constructed its line under this resolution [515] of the board of supervisors, without, however, obtaining consent or right of way from the landowners along the highway. The board of Trade Telegraph Company operated its line until 1886, when the line was leased to appellant, the Postal Telegraph-Cable Company, and that company has continued to operate the line since that time under its lease.

It is not denied that a telegraph company organized under the laws of this state may, under our eminent domain act, acquire property upon which it may erect its telegraph line. Indeed, section 2 of the act relating to telegraph companies (Rev. Stats. 1874, p 1052) makes provision for such companies to acquire property, as follows: "Every such company may enter upon any lands for the purpose of making surveys and examinations with a view to the erection of any telegraph line, and take and damage private property for the erection and maintenance of such lines, and may, subject to the provisions contained in this act, construct lines of telegraph along and upon any railroad, road, highway, street or alley, along or across any of the waters or lands

within this state, and may erect poles, posts, piers, or abutments
for supporting the insulators, wires, and other necessary fixtures
of their lines, in such manner and at such points as not to in-
commode the public use of the railroad, highway, street, or alley,
or interrupt the navigation of such waters." Section 4 of the
same act provides: "No such company shall have the right to
erect any poles, posts, piers, abutments, wires, or other fixtures
of their lines along or upon any road, highway, or public ground
outside the corporate limits of a city, town, or village without
the consent of the county board of the county in which such
road, highway, or public ground is situated, nor upon any street,
alley, or other highway or public ground within any incorporated
city, town, or village without the consent of the corporate authorities of such city, town, or village."

516 It is contended in the argument that the county board
having given consent to occupy the highway, and the consent
having been acted upon, the owner of the fee of the highway
cannot maintain an action of ejectment. Where a highway is
laid out over lands outside of an incorporated city, town, or
village, the public acquires only an easement of passage over the
lands, with the rights and incidents thereto, while the owner of
the land over which the road is laid out retains the fee and ownership of everything connected with the soil, for all purposes not
incompatible with the right of the public to a free and unob-
structed use of the road as a public highway: Palatine v. Kreuger,
121 Ill. 72. Elliott, in his work on Roads and Streets, page 519,
in the discussion of the question says: "The abutter has the exclusive right to the soil, subject only to the easement of the right
of passage in the public and the incidental right of properly
fitting the way for use. Subject only to the public easement,
he has all the usual rights and remedies of the owner of the
freehold. He may sink a drain under the road, ... he may
mine under it. The herbage and trees growing thereon belong
to him." At pages 535 and 536 the author says: "He may maintain trespass against one who unlawfully cuts and carries away
the grass, trees, or herbage, and even against one who stands
upon the sidewalk in front of his premises and uses abusive
language against him, refusing to depart. He may also maintain
ejectment against a railroad company which has placed its track
upon his side of the street without paying or tendering damages
therefor, or against an individual who has wrongfully and unlawfully encroached thereon." In Cole v. Drew, 44 Vt. 49, 8 Am.
Rep. 363, in considering the question the court said: "The owner

of the soil over which a highway is located is entitled . . . . to
the entire use of the land, except the right which the public
have to use the land and materials thereon for the purposes of
building and maintaining a highway suitable for [517] the safe
passage of travelers. This doctrine has been long established."

Other cases holding the same doctrine might be cited, but the
rule that the owner of the land upon which a public highway
is laid out has the exclusive right to the soil, subject to the easement of the right of travel in the public, and the incidental right
of keeping the highway in proper repair for the use of the public is so well established that the citation of other authorities is
not deemed necessary.

If, then, appellee was the owner of the fee subject to the easement, as we have seen he was, has he the right to maintain ejectment? In Smith v. Chicago etc. R. R. Co., 67 Ill. 191, it was
held that ejectment would lie against a railroad corporation by
the owner of the fee, for land taken and used by it for the purposes of its road, where the land had not been condemned under
proceedings instituted for that purpose in the mode prescribed
by law. If an action of ejectment may be maintained against
a railroad company by the owner of the fee where land has been
taken by the railroad company without instituting proceedings
to condemn, upon the same ground no reason occurs to us which
would prevent the owner of the fee from maintaining an action
of ejectment where possession has been taken by a telegraph company. Indeed, the two cases stand upon the same ground, and
if a recovery may be had in the one case a recovery may also be
had in the other.

The question whether the owner of the fee of a highway may
bring ejectment has arisen in other states, and it has been expressly held that the action will lie. In Terre Haute etc. Ry.
Co. v. Rodel, 89 Ind. 128, 46 Am. Rep. 166, in the discussion
of the question the court said: "The doctrine that the owner of
the fee may maintain ejectment for the land covered by a public highway is as old, at least, as Goodtitle v. Alker, 1 Burr. 133.
Lord Mansfield there said: 'I see no ground why the owner of
the soil may not bring [518] ejectment as well as trespass. . . . .
'Tis true, he must recover the land subject to the way; but
surely he ought to have a specific remedy to recover the land itself, notwithstanding its being subject to an easement upon it.' "
The court again says, on page 167: "We have no doubt at all
as to the right of the owner of the fee to maintain ejectment
against a wrongdoer, although the fee is burdened by a public

easement. Our own cases, as we have shown, so declare, and so do all the well-considered cases": See, also, Carpenter v. Oswego etc. R. R. Co., 24 N. Y. 655, and Robert v. Sadler, 104 N. Y. 229; 58 Am. Rep. 498.

In Indianapolis etc. Ry. Co. v. Hartley, 67 Ill. 439, 16 Am. Rep. 624, it was held that where the public have acquired an easement over a person's land for an ordinary street or highway, the location of the track of a railroad on the same is an additional burden and servitude upon the land, which will entitle the owner to additional compensation; that such an act is an exclusive appropriation by the railroad company of the soil to its own use which the owner had the right himself to use for any purpose not inconsistent with the public easement, and that hence it is taking private property for public use, which cannot be done without making just compensation.

In Board of Trade Tel. Co. v. Barnett, 107 Ill. 507, 47 Am. Rep. 453, an action of trespass was brought by an owner of land abutting on a highway to recover damages alleged to have been sustained by the erection of a telegraph line on the highway, and the court held that the construction and maintenance of a telegraph line upon the highway was a new and additional burden on the fee, to which it was not contemplated it should be subjected when the road was laid out, and that the owner of the fee was entitled to recover additional compensation for such use; that if the construction of the telegraph line was an additional burden on the fee, as the fee belonged to the appellee that burden could not be imposed upon the land unless compensation was made as provided by law.

[519] The appellee here was the owner of the fee, subject to the easement of the public to use the land for a public highway. He had been compensated for this public use, and could make no objection to the right of the public to use the land for a public highway, but no additional burden could be imposed upon the fee without compensation. When appellant, therefore, entered upon and took possession of the land and erected its line without instituting proceedings to condemn, as required by law, it was a trespasser, and no reason appears why appellee might not sue in trespass and recover such damages as he had sustained, or bring ejectment and regain his property in the condition it was in when appellant entered upon it.

But it is said the telegraph company obtained the right to construct its line from the county board of Madison county, and the authority of the county officers to grant a license of this character cannot be questioned in a proceeding of this kind. The consent of the county board of Madison county that the line might be erected on the public highway would no doubt be binding on the county and the road authorities in the several towns through which the highway runs upon which the line was authorized to be constructed, but the county board could give no consent which would be binding on any owner of the fee in the highway where the line was constructed. The right of the owner of the fee was beyond the control of the county board. His right is predicated on that provision of the constitution which declares that "private property shall not be taken or damaged without just compensation." The legislature had no authority to confer power on the county board to authorize the appellant company to take appellee's land without compensation, and hence the county board was powerless to give such authority. But it will not be necessary to consider this question further, as it was settled against appellant in Board of Trade Tel. Co. v. Barnett, 107 Ill. 507, 47 Am. Rep. 453, as will be found upon an examination of that case.

520 It is, however, said that appellee purchased the land after the telegraph line was constructed, with full notice that the line had been constructed, and hence he took the land with the burden upon it. It is no doubt true that appellee purchased the land subject to all rights appellant possessed in it; but the trouble with appellant is, by taking possession without making compensation to the owner of the fee it acquired no rights as against such owner, and when appellee purchased he acquired all the rights in the land possessed by his grantor, and if his grantor was entitled to bring ejectment this right passed to appellee. Whether appellee could maintain trespass, or whether he would be barred by the statute of limitations had such an action been brought, is a question not presented by this record. The sole question here is the right of appellee to maintain ejectment. The circuit court held that he had that right, and we think the judgment correct, and it will be affirmed.

HIGHWAYS—TITLE OF ABUTTING OWNER.—The property in the soil of a highway is not in the public, but in the owner of the land over which it passes: Note to Chicago etc. Ry. Co. v. Milwaukee etc. Ry. Co., 60 Am. St. Rep. 142. The owner of the land over which the highway passes retains the fee thereof and all rights of property therein not incompatible with the public easement therein: Note to Cater v. Northwestern Teleph. etc. Co., 51 Am. St. Rep. 549. The legislature cannot take away these rights, except to appropriate the land to a public use upon payment of compensation: Kincaid v. Indianapolis Nat. Gas. Co., 121 Ind. 577; 19 Am. St. Rep. 113, and note.

The lotowner's interest in the street is just as indefeasible and secure from legislative impairment as is his title to his lot: Moose v.
Carson, 104 N. C. 431; 17 Am. St. Rep. 681.

HIGHWAYS — RIGHTS OF ABUTTING OWNERS — ADDI-
TIONAL SERVITUDES—TELEGRAPH COMPANIES.—Although
there is still a conflict of authority upon the subject, it seems that
the weight of authority with which the principal case is in accord,
sustains the doctrine without qualification that a telegraph or
telephone line along a public street or highway is no part of
the equipment of the street, but is foreign to its use, and the
imposition of an additional burden for which the abutting owner
must be compensated; and also that the legislature has no power to
authorize the imposition of such servitude, except on condition that
due compensation shall be made therefor to such abutting owner:
Monographic note to Chesapeake etc. Tel. Co. v. Mackenzie, 28 Am.
St. Rep. 229-236; Western Union Tel. Co. v. Williams, 86 Va. 696; 19
Am. St. Rep. 908.

HIGHWAYS—RIGHTS OF ABUTTING OWNERS — EJECT-
MENT.—After some dicta and extrajudicial opinions to the contrary,
it is now settled that the owner of land over which a highway
passes may maintain ejectment therefor against any person who
encroaches thereon: Monographic note to Mayhew v. Norton, 28 Am.
Dec. 804.

CHICAGO & ALTON RAILROAD CO. v. MARONEY.

[170 ILLINOIS, 520.]

MASTER AND SERVANT, SAFE PLACE IN WHICH TO
WORK—DEFECTIVE SCAFFOLDING.—If a workman is employed
to assist in the erection of a house, and scaffolding for his use is constructed by his employer, and as so constructed, is defective and unsafe, and hence gives way and injures such employé, his employer is
answerable therefor, whether he knew that the scaffolding was unsafe or not, or the employé had equal opportunity with his employer
to know that the scaffolding was unsafe and insufficient. The ruling
would be different if the scaffolding had originally been properly
constructed and had become unsafe by a defect subsequently arising.

MASTER AND SERVANT—SAFE PLACE IN WHICH TO
WORK.—A servant or other employé has the right to assume that
his master or employer has discharged the duty of furnishing a safe
place in which his employé is to work and to act upon such assumption in the absence of actual knowledge to the contrary.

MASTER AND SERVANT—FELLOW-SERVANTS.—If a ser-
vant is injured by the failure of the master to furnish him a safe
place in which to work, the latter cannot escape liability on the
ground that the injury was the result of the negligence of a fellow-
servant in constructing an unsafe appliance, for the master owes a
positive obligation to his servant which he cannot avoid by deputing
its performance to another servant.

James H. Teller, for the appellant.

Willard Gentleman and Edward W. Sims, for the appellee.

[523] BOGGS, J.   The errors assigned in this court are, that the trial court erred: 1. In denying the motion of the appellant company, entered at the close of all the testimony, to peremptorily direct a verdict in its favor; and 2. The court erred in its rulings in giving instructions for the appellee and in refusing certain instructions asked by the appellant company.

Counsel for appellant insists the appellee, in order to recover, was required to establish three propositions, i. e., (a) That the scaffold was defective; (b) The appellant company had notice thereof or was chargeable with notice; and (c) The appellee did not know of the alleged defect and had not equal means with the master of knowing. It [523] is urged there was no evidence tending to establish either the second or third proposition, and hence it is argued the court erred in refusing to direct a verdict in favor of the appellant company.

It will be observed the position taken by counsel for appellant ignores the charge of the third count of the declaration. We find that charge was not referred to in any instruction asked by either of the parties, and it is therefore apparent the only issues which the evidence, in the opinion of the parties, justified them in presenting to the jury were those arising under the first and second counts of the declaration. We may, therefore, assume the appellant is warranted in ignoring in this court the charge of negligence preferred in the third count. We may, then, confine our attention, upon this branch of the case, to the pertinency of the three propositions advanced by counsel for appellant.

The evidence abundantly tended to establish the first of these —that the scaffold was defective. Two witnesses, at least, testified that certain foot-locks and braces intended to be used in the construction of the scaffold, and necessary to properly strengthen it, were not used, but were thrown up on the floor of the scaffold. The section of scaffolding which fell was put up on Saturday afternoon, and the evidence tended to show it was not used on that day. It gave way within a few minutes after the appellee and other workmen went upon it on the following Monday morning.

We do not assent that it was requisite to a recovery it should have been proven that appellant had notice, or was chargeable with notice, the scaffold was unsafe or defective, as urged in the second proposition, or that appellee did not know, or had not equal opportunity with appellant of knowing, the scaffold was unsafe or insufficient, as urged in the third proposition. It was the duty of appellant to provide appellee a suitable and safe place and appliances in and with which to work: Chicago [524] etc. Co. v. Van Dam, 149 Ill. 337; Mobile etc. R. R. Co. v. Godfrey, 155 Ill. 78; Hess v. Rosenthal, 160 Ill. 621; Cooley on Torts, 561. In this instance the scaffold was such place or appliance which the appellant company was required to provide. It undertook to construct it, and the defect was in its construction. The fault was not latent in character, but, as the evidence tended to show, was the result of the negligent failure of employés of the appellant company to place in position certain foot-locks or braces necessary to support and strengthen the scaffold, which foot-locks and braces had been supplied to be used for that purpose. If the scaffold had been properly constructed and had become unsafe by reason of a defect subsequently arising, the doctrine that the liability of the appellant company depended upon notice of such subsequent defect might have had application, but not so when the defect occurs by reason of the failure of the appellant company to discharge the duty cast upon it by law of providing a safe place for the appellee to work. If it omitted its duty in this regard, no rule of law required it should be notified of its own failure before it should be deemed answerable for injuries resulting from such failure.

Nor is the third proposition, that it should affirmatively appear the appellee did not know of the defect, or had not equal means of knowing, etc., applicable in such state of case. The appellee had a right to assume the appellant company had discharged its duty (Monmouth Min. etc. Co. v. Erling, 148 Ill. 521, 39 Am. St. Rep. 187), and to act upon such assumption, in the absence of actual knowledge to the contrary: United States Rolling Stock Co. v. Wilder, 116 Ill. 100; Chicago etc. R. R. Co. v. Hines, 132 Ill. 161; 22 Am. St. Rep. 515; Pullman Palace Car Co. v. Laack, 143 Ill. 242; Pennsylvania Coal Co. v. Kelly, 156 Ill. 9; Wharton on Negligence, 211; Bishop on Noncontract Law, secs. 647, 648.

It is, however, insisted, the workmen employed by the appellant company to construct the scaffolding, and the [525] appellee, were fellow-servants, and that appellee cannot recover if he was injured by the negligence of a fellow-servant. The relation of fellow-servant, if it existed, cannot avail to relieve the appellant company of liability. The duty of the master to furnish safe means, places, and instrumentalities for the servant's use is, we declared in Hess v. Rosenthal, 160 Ill. 628, "a positive obligation toward the servant, and the master is responsible for any failure to discharge that duty, whether he undertakes its perform-

ance personally or through another servant.   The master cannot
divest himself of such duty, and he is responsible, as for his
own personal negligence, for a want of proper caution on the
part of his agent."   And in Chicago etc. R. R. Co. v. Avery,
109 Ill. 314, we said: "The master's own duty to the servant is
always to be performed.   The neglect of that duty is not a peril
which the servant assumes, and, where the performance of that
duty is devolved upon a fellow-servant, the master's liability in
respect thereof still remains.   Care in the supplying of safe instrumentalities in the doing of the work undertaken is the duty
of the master to the servant, hence the rule of nonliability on
the part of an employer for the negligence of a fellow-servant
has no application in this case, where the negligence in question
is the master's neglect of duty in the providing of safe appliances."

We find no error in the ruling of the court upon instructions.
The complaint as to instruction No. 1, given on behalf of appellee, is, it ignores the ground set up in the third count of the
declaration.   The instruction has reference only to liability by
reason of the alleged negligence charged in the first and second
counts of the declaration, and we know of no rule or reason
requiring a litigant to embrace in each instruction every ground
of liability averred in the different counts of the declaration.   On
the contrary, he may frame an instruction touching upon each
separate charge of negligence as set forth in any count.

[526] What we have hereinbefore said in response to the insistence of the appellant company that the liability of the master
and the right of the appellee to recover depended upon notice
or knowledge possessed by the parties, respectively, or which they
should have possessed, of the defective condition of the scaffolding, disposes of the objections to the other instructions given
on behalf of the appellee, and also the complaints as to the refusal of instructions asked by the appellant, except as to refused
instruction No. 3.   Instruction No. 3, asked by appellant, but
refused, was no doubt intended to advise the jury that if the
scaffold was properly constructed, and was "interfered with and
weakened afterward" by some unauthorized person, the appellant
company was not liable, unless it appeared it had notice of such
subsequent defect or the circumstances were such that it should
be charged with notice.   But the instruction as framed asked the
court to charge the jury that if the scaffolding was properly constructed and finished on Saturday and gave way on the following
Monday, as a matter of law the appellant company was not to

be deemed chargeable with notice. If involved in the case at all, it was a question of fact whether, under all the circumstances, the time intervening between the alleged completion of the scaffold and its fall was so short that it should be presumed the appellant could not reasonably have discovered the scaffold had been "interfered with and weakened." The law has no rule about it, consequently the court rightly declined to invade the province of the jury by assuming to decide a question of fact for them.

We think the record is free from error, and the judgment of the appellate court is affirmed.

MASTER AND SERVANT—DUTY TO FURNISH SAFE APPLIANCES.—A servant has a right to assume, without inquiry or examination, that the appliances furnished him are safe and suitable: Carter v. Oliver Oil Co., 34 S. C. 211; 27 Am. St. Rep. 815, and note; and he is not chargeable with contributory negligence for so assuming: Nord-Deutscher etc. Co. v. Ingebregsten, 57 N. J. L. 400; 51 Am. St. Rep. 604; extended note to Shortel v. St. Joseph, 24 Am. St. Rep. 321.

MASTER AND SERVANT—DUTY TO FURNISH SAFE APPLIANCES AND PLACE TO WORK.—A master must use due care in supplying his servants with safe appliances, and a safe place in which to work. He cannot escape liability by delegating these personal duties to another: Ell v. Northern Pac. R. R. Co., 1 N. Dak. 336; 26 Am. St. Rep. 621, and note; note to Nord-Deutscher etc. Co. v. Ingebregsten, 51 Am. St. Rep. 608; McElligott v. Randolph, 61 Conn. 157; 29 Am. St. Rep. 181, and note. Compare with the principal case, Kimmer v. Weber, 151 N. Y. 417; 56 Am. St. Rep. 630.

East St. Louis Connecting Railway Co. v. Eggmann.

[170 Illinois, 538.]

RAILWAYS, ORDINANCE RESPECTING, WHEN MAY BE URGED BY EMPLOYES.—An ordinance limiting the speed of railway trains while running within a municipality and requiring the ringing of a bell is designed for the protection of employés, as well as of the general public. Hence one employed by a corporation and working upon or under its track may recover if injured through the negligence of its agent in not ringing the bell and in running more rapidly than permitted by such ordinance.

JURY TRIAL.—AN INSTRUCTION SUMMING UP THE FACTS ASSUMED TO BE NECESSARY TO SUPPORT THE ACTION, and stating that if the jury find those facts to exist, their verdict should be for the plaintiff, is not the proper mode of instructing the jury, but if it omits no material fact essential to the right of recovery, a reversal will not be directed because of its having been given.

JURY TRIAL—INSTRUCTION AS TO THE EFFECT OF AN ACT.—The defendant in an action to recover for injuries to the per-.

son of the plaintiff's intestate is not entitled to an instruction that if the jury believe that if the decedent had not changed his position. he would not have been hurt, then the verdict should be for the defendant, if the court instructs the jury to consider the facts referred to in connection with all the evidence in the case for the purpose of determining whether the decedent was guilty of contributory negligence leading to his injury.

Charles W. Thomas, for the appellant.

J. M. Freels and A. R. Taylor, for the appellee.

539 WILKIN, J.   This is an action on the case by appellee, as administrator of Joseph F. Newland, deceased, against appellant, for negligently causing the death of his intestate, under the provisions of sections 1 and 2 of chapter 70 of the Revised Statutes.   Upon a trial in the city court of East St. Louis the plaintiff recovered a judgment for three thousand five hundred dollars and costs of suit.   On appeal to the appellate court for the fourth district, that judgment was affirmed, and the defendant below now prosecutes this further appeal.

The declaration charges that while the deceased was in defendant's employ as a carpenter, constructing a drain near or under defendant's track, on the bank of the Mississippi river, in East St. Louis, the defendant's employés in charge of one of its engines attached to freight-cars negligently and carelessly ran the same upon him, thereby so injuring him that he died.   It is charged that he was not a fellow-servant with those in charge of the engine **540** and that he was in the exercise of due care for his own safety.   The negligent acts charged against the servants controlling the engine are, that it was being run at a rate of speed exceeding six miles per hour, contrary to an ordinance of the city of East St. Louis, and that in violation of a like ordinance it was being run without ringing a bell upon the same, these acts of negligence being within the city limits of the city of East St. Louis, and causing the alleged injury.   It is then further alleged that said Newland left surviving him a widow, Mary S. Newland, his next of kin, and left no children, and that said widow, by his death, was deprived of her means of support, etc.

The substantial grounds of reversal insisted upon here were all considered, and, we think, correctly decided, by the appellate court, as stated in its opinion.   We concur in the views expressed in that opinion, and shall only notice a few of the points urged here for a reversal.

The first of these, in natural order, is that the declaration states no cause of action, and therefore the trial court erred in overruling the defendant's motion in arrest of judgment.   The ground of this position is, that the ordinance which the defendant is charged in the declaration with having violated was only intended to protect the public against the danger of moving trains and locomotives at public places, and could have no legal application, as between the railroad company and its employés, to locomotives being run in the company's private grounds. This same question was presented for decision in Illinois Cent. R. R. Co. v. Gilbert, 157 Ill. 354, and decided adversely to the contention here urged. That case was cited and followed in St. Louis etc. R. R. Co. v. Eggmann, 161 Ill. 155. We have given due consideration to the argument urging the overruling of these decisions, but find no sufficient reason for so doing. The power of the municipality to pass the ordinance, as reasonably tending to protect persons against injury, is not seriously questioned, and we can see no good reason for [541] holding that a person should be deprived of that protection merely because he is at the time an employé of the company, working in its yards or other private grounds. The declaration stated facts which, if proved, entitled plaintiff to recover.

Objections were made to the introduction of the ordinance, the principal objection being the same as that made to the sufficiency of the declaration, and it follows, from what has already been said, they were properly overruled. The ordinance being the basis of plaintiff's cause of action, proof of its existence was a necessary part of his case.

It is insisted that the giving of plaintiff's first instruction was reversible error, the objection stated being that it assumes the existence of certain material facts necessary to plaintiff's right of recovery. We agree with the appellate court that this is a misapprehension as to the purport of the instruction. It is a summing up of the facts assumed to be necessary to support the action, with the conclusion that if the jury find these facts to be established by the evidence their finding should be for the plaintiff. We have time and again condemned the practice of giving such instructions, and do not wish now to be understood as retracting or modifying anything which we have previously said in that regard. Such a method of presenting a cause of action or defense, under the guise of instructing the jury as to the law of the case, is not to be approved. It has, however, been the uniform rule of decision in such cases, that where an instruction of that character omits no material fact necessary to the right of recovery a reversal will not be ordered because of its having been given. We are inclined to concur with the appellate court in holding that the giving of plaintiff's first instruction in this case was not reversible error.

Appellant has no just ground of complaint of the modification of its third instruction. We do not regard the modification as prejudicial error. As asked, the instruction [542] should have been refused altogether. It was argumentative, and ignored the real issue in the case, namely, whether the defendant was guilty of the negligence charged in the declaration, thereby causing the alleged injury to the deceased while he was in the exercise of due care. It did not, as contended, instruct the jury that if the injury was the result of accident plaintiff could not recover, but in effect told them that if they believed that if the deceased had not changed his position as the engine approached him he would not have been struck, then, as a matter of law, his administrator could not recover, no matter what care or diligence deceased was then using to avoid such change in his position. The modification of the instruction gave the defendant the benefit of all the facts upon which it based the conclusion that the plaintiff could not recover, and told the jury that the facts so stated should only be considered in connection with all the other evidence in the case in determining whether deceased was guilty of negligence which directly contributed to his injury, and if they believed from the evidence, he was so guilty, plaintiff could not recover. We are unable to see how this modification in any way prejudiced the defense.

In our view of the case, it is not important to consider whether the defendant asked such an instruction, at the proper time, to find for the defendant as brings before this court a consideration of the question as to whether the evidence tends to support the verdict and judgment below as a matter of law. If, as we have said, the declaration presented a good cause of action, the questions for the jury were very simple: Did the evidence tend to prove that the locomotive and train were being run at a higher rate of speed than that permitted by the ordinance, or without ringing a bell, as therein required? Did that negligence directly contribute to the injury? and, Was the deceased at the time in the exercise of proper care for his own safety? It cannot be seriously contended that there [543] was no evidence produced upon the trial tending to establish the affirmative of each of these facts, and hence the verdict and judgment in the circuit court, affirmed in the appellate court, conclusively settle them.

We do not regard other grounds of reversal urged of sufficient importance to be further noticed than has been done in the reasoning and conclusion of the appellate court, as shown in its opinion. The judgment of that court will accordingly be affirmed.

INSTRUCTIONS — CORRECT AND INCORRECT — GROUND FOR REVERSAL.—Instructions should avoid any statement of the evidence which may indicate the conclusions of the judge respecting the facts directly disputed on the trial: McShane v. Kenkle, 18 Mont. 208; 56 Am. St. Rep. 579. An instruction may properly be refused if based upon an assumption of fact, and applicable only upon the jury finding the fact in the manner assumed: Arneson v. Spawn, 2 S. Dak. 269; 39 Am. St. Rep. 783; Lake Shore etc. Ry. Co. v. Bodemer, 130 Ill. 596; 32 Am. St. Rep. 218. Compare Baddeley v. Shea, 114 Cal. 1; 55 Am. St. Rep. 56. Though the instructions given to the jury were erroneous, the judgment will not be reversed if the conclusion reached by the verdict was sustained by the decided or plain preponderance of the testimony: Cunningham v. Bucky, 42 W. Va. 671; 57 Am. St. Rep. 878, and note.

RAILROAD COMPANIES--LIABILITY FOR INJURY TO SERVANTS—VIOLATION OF ORDINANCE.—Railroad employés are entitled to the same protection as other persons in crossing railroad tracks within a city in performance of their duties, under a city ordinance requiring a bell to be rung continuously: Illinois Cent. R. R. Co. v. Gilbert, 157 Ill. 354. An ordinance regulating the speed of railway trains in a city should not by construction be limited in its application to those portions of the city used by the public. Such ordinances apply to switchyards as well. A railroad employé may recover for personal injury resulting from a violation of such ordinance by his employer: Crowley v. Burlington etc. Ry. Co., 65 Iowa, 658. See St. Louis etc. R. R. Co. v. Eggmann, 161 Ill. 155.

PEOPLE *v*. CHICAGO LIVE STOCK EXCHANGE.

[170 ILLINOIS, 556.]

TRADE, REGULATIONS IN RESTRAINT OF.—A by-law of a stock exchange board limiting the number of solicitors which may be employed by any member within certain designated states, prohibiting the employment of any solicitors except upon a salary, and allowing a member to solicit only when counted as solicitors and while complying with the regulations of the by-laws, is in restraint of lawful trade, and therefore void.

CORPORATIONS.—THE BY-LAWS OF A CORPORATION MUST BE reasonable and for a corporate purpose, and always within the charter limits. They must be in subordination to the constitution and laws of the state, and not interfere with its policy, nor be hostile to the general welfare.

CORPORATIONS, FORFEITURE OF CHARTER BY ACTS IN RESTRAINT OF TRADE.—Attempts to place restriction on trade and commerce and to fetter individual liberty of action by preventing competition are hostile to the public welfare and affect the interests of the people. Such attempts of a corporation are abuses of its franchise and warrant the filing of an information in the nature of a quo warranto against it for the forfeiture of its charter.

Application by the state's attorney for Cook county, Illinois,

tion in the nature of a quo warranto against the Chicago Live
Stock Exchange.   This exchange was incorporated under the laws
of the state of Illinois.   Its objects, as stated in its charter, were
to establish and maintain a commercial exchange, to promote
uniformity in the customs and usages of merchants, to provide
for the speedy adjustment of all business disputes among its
members, to facilitate the receiving and distributing of livestock,
as well as to provide for, and maintain, a rigid inspection thereof, thereby to guard against the sale or use of unsound or unhealthy meats, and, generally, to secure to its members the benefits of co-operation in the furtherance of their legitimate pursuits.
The corporation enacted a by-law declaring that no solicitors
should be employed except upon a stipulated salary, not contingent on the commission earned; that members should file with
the secretary of the exchange the name and postoffice address of
their traveling solicitors, and should not employ exceeding three
solicitors for each firm in the states of Indiana, Michigan, Wisconsin, Illinois, Missouri, Iowa, and Minnesota.   Members of the
firm were permitted to solicit in those states, provided they were
counted as among the solicitors allowed therein and complied
in all respects with the restrictions governing solicitors.   It was
declared to be a violation of the by-law for any solicitor representing a member of the firm located in another market to solicit
for any Chicago firm in the states named.   Nonresident members or stockholders of the firms were forbidden to solicit unless
duly registered and employed as a solicitor.   Another by-law
was enacted under which any member of the firm violating the
rules respecting the employment of solicitors was fined for the
first offense not less than two hundred dollars nor more than one
thousand dollars, and for the second offense not less than five
hundred dollars nor more than one thousand.   If such fines were
not paid within three days, the firm was declared suspended from
membership and a third offense required the expulsion of the
offending member or firm.   The relator in this proceeding was
William McIlhany, a member of the exchange.   He and other
members had employed solicitors and were threatened with the
enforcement of the by-laws, and alleged that their expulsion
would ruin their business.   The defendant filed an affidavit in
defense stating that it did no business of any kind itself, but
was an organization for the mutual benefit of its members; that
it had a membership of about seven hundred persons, each of
whom voluntarily sought such membership, and agreed to abide
by such by-laws and rules as the board might make.   The trial

court held that the by-law was valid, and refused leave to file the information. From its action this appeal was prosecuted.

Jacob J. Kern, state's attorney, and Moran, Kraus & Mayer, for the appellant.

Peck, Miller & Starr, for the appellee.

566 PHILLIPS, C. J. This corporation, organized as stated in its certificate or organization, was formed "to establish and maintain a commercial exchange; to promote uniformity in the customs and usages of merchants; to provide for the speedy adjustment of all business disputes between its members; to facilitate the receiving and distributing of livestock as well as to provide for and maintain a rigid inspection thereof, thereby guarding against the sale or use of unsound or unhealthy meats; and generally to secure to its members the benefits of co-operation in the furtherance of their legitimate pursuits." The purpose of this corporation, as expressed in this certificate of incorporation, is undoubtedly, if carried out to the fullest extent, in the interest of the people.

The common law refused to recognize restrictions upon trade and business among the citizens of a common country. Under this rule of the common law, the right of the laborer to dispose of his skill and industry, and to contract in reference to the same with whom he pleased and at such contract rates as might be agreed on, was recognized and not allowed to be trammeled with restrictions which interfered with individual action and liberty. Combinations and associations of men have no right to place restrictions upon the right of an individual to contract and engage in business, employing such means and agencies as are not prohibited by law. The natural flow of trade and commerce must be unrestricted, and men engaged therein may accelerate its current by all means not unlawful. To this end men engaged in trade and commerce may advertise, employ men to solicit business, and offer rewards and inducements to secure trade without violating the law of the land, and in so doing are exercising a right which is in the interest of the public, because competition cannot be hostile to public interests. Efforts to prevent competition and to restrict individual efforts and **567** freedom of action in trade and commerce are restrictions hostile to the public welfare, not consonant with the spirit of our institutions and in violation of law.

We said in Frorer v. People, 141 Ill. 171, 181: "The privilege of contracting is both a liberty and a property right, and if A is denied the right to contract and acquire property in a manner which he has hitherto enjoyed under the law, and which B, C, and D are still allowed by the law to enjoy, it is clear that he is deprived of both liberty and property to the extent that he is thus denied the right to contract. Our constitution guarantees that no person shall be deprived of life, liberty, or property without due process of law: Const., art. 2, sec. 2. And says Cooley: 'The man or the class forbidden the acquisition or enjoyment of property in the manner permitted the community at large would be deprived of liberty in particulars of primary importance to his or their pursuit of happiness.' "

In More v. Bennett, 140 Ill. 69, 33 Am. St. Rep. 216, we said: "Whatever may be the professed objects of the association, it clearly appears, both from its constitution and by-laws and from the averments of the declaration, that one of its objects, if not its leading object, is to control the prices to be charged by its members for stenographic work by restraining all competition between them. Power is given to the association to fix a schedule of prices which shall be binding upon all its members, and not only do the members, by assenting to the constitution and by-laws, agree to be bound by the schedule thus fixed, but their competition with each other, either by taking or offering to take a less price, is punishable by the imposition of fines, as well as by such other disciplinary measures as associations of this character may adopt for the enforcement of their rules. The rule of public policy here involved is closely analogous to that which declares illegal and void contracts in general restraint of trade, if it is not, indeed, a subordinate application of the same rule. As said by Mr. Tiedeman: 'Following the reason of the rule which prohibits [568] contracts in restraint of trade, we find that it is made to prohibit all contracts which in any way restrain the freedom of trade or diminish competition or regulate the prices of commodities or services.' "

In Braceville Coal Co. v. People, 147 Ill. 66, 37 Am. St. Rep. 206, it was said: "Property, in its broader sense, is not the physical thing which may be the subject of ownership, but it is the right of dominion, possession, and power of disposition which may be acquired over it; and the right of property preserved by the constitution is the right not only to possess and enjoy it, but also to acquire it in any lawful mode or by following any lawful industrial pursuit which the citizen, in the exercise of the liberty guaranteed, may choose to adopt.

Labor is the primary foundation of all wealth. The property which each one has in his own labor is the common heritage, and, as an incident to the right to acquire other property, the liberty to enter into contracts by which labor may be employed in such way as the laborer shall deem most beneficial and of others to employ such labor, is necessarily included in the constitutional guaranty."

In other jurisdictions the rule is the same. In Rex v. Wardens, 7 Term Rep. 540, it was held that a by-law limiting the number of apprentices which any member of the company might take was void. In the case of Tailors of Ipswich, 11 Coke, 53, a corporation known as the Tailors of Ipswich enacted a by-law to prohibit any tailor from exercising his trade until he had presented himself before the corporation and proved that he had served seven years as an apprentice. This by-law was held void, as being in restraint of trade: See, also, Gunmakers' Soc. v. Fell, Willes, 384. Sustaining the same propositions are Stanton v. Allen, 5 Denio, 434; 49 Am. Dec. 282; People v. Fisher, 14 Wend. 9; 28 Am. Dec. 501; Morris Run Coal Co. v. Barclay Coal Co., 68 Pa. St. 173; 8 Am. Rep. 159; People ex rel. v. Medical Soc. of Erie, 24 Barb. 570.

A case similar to that now under consideration was before the court of appeals of Kentucky in Huston v. Reutliger, **569** 91 Ky. 333; 34 Am. St. Rep. 225. There the Louisville Board of Underwriters passed a by-law which, among other things, prohibited local companies from employing more than one solicitor, and regulated the manner in which the salary of such solicitor was to be paid. For a violation of this by-law the offending member of the board would forfeit all rights as a member of the association. A local company which had employed more than one solicitor sought to enjoin the enforcement of the forfeiture on the ground that the association had no authority to control the members in the employment of solicitors, etc. A decree was entered in accordance with the prayer of the bill, which, on appeal, was affirmed, the court saying: "The majority of the members, under the guise of producing harmony in this business association, have taken from their individual members the right to determine how many men they shall employ in their private business, and then only such as the association may think fit for the position. Nor can they employ a solicitor for a less period than six months, or offer a solicitor employment within twelve months after the solicitor has severed his connection with any member; are compelled to discharge those in their employ if

they have more than one; and, if these by-laws are enforced, have
placed their business under the control of the majority vote of
the association—a power the exercise of which was not given by
the fundamental law of the order, and doubtless not contemplated when the association was formed. . . . . The common-law
rule, recognized and adopted when business relations were not
so multiplied and extensive as now and when less necessity existed for enforcing it, condemned all such restrictions upon trade
and business intercourse with men as is found to exist in this
case. The right of one to control his own property as he pleases,
and to employ those necessary to aid him in his business upon
such terms as may be agreed upon, when not in violation of the
law of the land, is the rule of the common law and the right of
the laborer to dispose [570] of his skill and industry to whom he
pleases and for the price agreed on is embraced within the same
rule. In all classes of business, the employer and employé should
be allowed to contract with each other unrestrained by others who
may demand that the one shall give more or the other receive
less, and, as a general rule, when restrictions are placed upon
their rights by combinations or associations of men, they will
be regarded as in violation of law, and void."

When a corporation is created there goes with it the power to
enact by-laws for its government and guidance, as well as for
the guidance and government of its members. This power is
necessary to enable a corporation to accomplish the purpose of
its creation. But by-laws must be reasonable and for a corporate
purpose, and always within charter limits. They must always be
strictly subordinate to the constitution and the general law of the
land. They must not infringe the policy of the state nor be hostile to public welfare. The by-law in this case is a restriction
on freedom of trade and business. It trammels competition and
prohibits an individual from contracting and engaging in business, and from using such agencies and means as he may desire
not hostile to general law. It is not required for corporate purposes, nor is it included within the purposes declared in the certificate of incorporation. It is therefore unlawful, as this corporation had no right to exercise this power of enacting it under
its franchise.

It is not every misconduct on the part of a corporation, or
act not consonant with the purpose of its creation, that will destroy its life. An act to thus result must be one which tends
to produce injury to the public by affecting the welfare of the
people. Where this results there is an abuse of corporate fran-

chise: People v. North River Sugar etc. Co., 121 N. Y. 582; 18 Am. St. Rep. 843. Attempts to place restrictions on trade and commerce and to fetter individual liberty of action by preventing competition are [571] hostile to public welfare and affect the interests of the people. Such attempts by a corporation are an abuse of its corporate franchise. Public policy requires that corporations, in the exercise of powers, must be confined strictly within their charter limits, and not be permitted to exercise powers beyond those expressly conferred. The state provides for the creation of corporations. The corporation is its creature, and must always conform to its policy. This duty on the part of corporations to do no acts hostile to the policy of the state grows out of the fact that the legislature is presumed to have had in view the public interest when a charter was granted to the corporation, and no departure from its charter purposes will be allowed which would be hurtful to the public. Where such act is done by a corporation the state may proceed to claim a forfeiture of its charter by an information in the nature of quo warranto.

The petition for leave to file an information in the nature of quo warranto should have been granted. The judgment of the circuit court was therefore erroneous and is reversed, and the cause is remanded with directions to grant leave to file the information.

CORPORATIONS—POWER TO ENACT BY-LAWS—THEIR EFFECT.—A by-law of a corporation is void if contrary to law, as where it imposes a forfeiture of goods, or is in restraint of trade, or is enforceable by extraordinary penalties: Matter of Long Island R. R. Co., 19 Wend. 37; 32 Am. Dec. 429. By-laws in restraint of trade are void: Monographic notes to Sayre v. Louisville Benev. Assn., 85 Am. Dec. 619, and People's etc. Bank v. Superior Court, 43 Am. St. Rep. 154. See, also, American etc. Co. v. Chicago Live Stock Exchange, 143 Ill. 210; 36 Am. St. Rep. 385, and note.

CORPORATIONS—FORFEITURE OF FRANCHISE—QUO WARRANTO.—If a corporation misuses, or abuses, powers granted by its charters in creating a monopoly or otherwise, it may be ousted from its franchises in quo warranto proceedings: Distilling etc. Co. v. People, 156 Ill. 448; 47 Am. St. Rep. 200. See People v. Milk Exchange, 145 N. Y. 267; 45 Am. St. Rep. 609. Also, monographic note to State v. Atchison etc. R. R. Co., 8 Am. St. Rep. 179-202, on the forfeiture of corporate franchises.

MARTIN v. MARTIN.

[170 ILLINOIS, 639.]

PARTITION, RIGHT TO.—As a general rule an adult tenant in common may demand partition as a matter of right.

PARTITION, WAIVER OF RIGHT TO BY ORAL AGREEMENT.—An oral agreement between tenants in common in view of what they believe to be the temporary depreciation in the market value of their real property that they will not seek to divide their lands, but will jointly rent them and divide the rentals, that each will endeavor to obtain purchasers satisfactory to all, and then all will join in a conveyance, followed by their joint leasing of the property for a term of years. estops any of them, during the continuance of such lease, from maintaining a suit for the partition of their property.

Suit in chancery by Joseph S. Martin against John W. Martin and others for the partition of certain property of which the plaintiff and the defendants had become seised as children of Catherine Martin. The defense pleaded was that the children, soon after becoming the owners of the property, in view of the depreciation of its market value, entered into a verbal agreement not to seek to divide it, but to allow it to remain as it was and jointly rent it and divide the rentals, and that they would endeavor to obtain purchasers and all would join in a conveyance if a satisfactory sale could be obtained, and that one of their number should take control of the lands. In pursuance of this agreement, the lands were rented for terms expiring March 1, 1898, and leases executed therefor. Exceptions were filed by the complainant to this defense and sustained by the court. Thereafter a decree was entered appointing commissioners to make a partition, and they, having reported that the land was not susceptible of division, an order was entered that it be sold and its proceeds divided among the owners thereof. Two of the defendants appealed.

H. C. Ward, for the appellants.

Walter Stager, for the appellee.

⁶⁴² BOGGS, J. A single question is presented by the record, and that is whether the court correctly ruled the exceptions to the answer were well taken. The general rule is, an adult tenant in common may demand partition as a matter of right: Hill v. Reno, 112 Ill. 154; 54 Am. Rep. 222; Trainor v. Greenough, 145 Ill. 543; Ames v. Ames, 148 Ill. 321. But there are certain well-recognized exceptions to the rule. In Hill v. Reno, 112 Ill. 154, 54 Am. Rep. 222, an instance of such exception

is stated in the following language: "If several tenants in common or joint tenants should covenant between themselves that
the estate should be held and enjoyed in common, only, equity
would not, in the absence of special equities, award a partition
at the suit of some of the parties, against the objections of the
others." And this court in the same case expressly declared
"that equity will not award a partition at the suit of one in the
violation of his own agreement. . . . . The objection to partition in such cases is in the nature of an estoppel." Mr. Freeman, in his work on Cotenancy, section 457, declares the absolute
right to partition is possessed by an adult tenant in common in
the absence of "special obligations existing independent of the
cotenancy." The conclusion reached by the author of that portion of the American and English Encyclopedia of Law devoted
to the subject of "Partition" (17 Am. & Eng. Ency. of Law, 693)
is, that the absolute right to a partition may be waived by agreement. The supreme court of Michigan, in Eberts v. Fisher, 51
Mich. 294, held that a tenant in common might become estopped,
by his agreement, to demand partition, and that an agreement
to lease the premises for a term of years, shown to have been
made in the case, was sufficient to warrant a decree dismissing
the bill for partition.

643 It seems clear, upon both principle and authority, a tenant
in common may become estopped to demand partition by his
covenant that the land shall be held in common.

But it is urged in behalf of complainant the agreement set
out in the answer in the case at bar was verbal, merely, and
therefore not enforceable, by reason of the familiar provision of
the statute of frauds and perjuries that no one shall be charged
upon a verbal contract concerning any interest in lands. The
complainant came, by his bill, into a court of equity, and the
equitable rule is that a verbal contract affecting or concerning
an interest in lands may be enforced, notwithstanding the statute of frauds and perjuries, if it has been so far performed as
that to permit the party to repudiate it would of itself be a
fraud: Morrison v. Herrick, 130 Ill. 631; Koch v. National etc.
Bldg. Assn., 137 Ill. 497. It appeared from the averments of
the answer that the complainant and respondents mutually agreed
with each other that "they would not seek to divide the land in
view of the fact the salable value of real estate had been greatly,
but, as the parties believed, only temporarily, depreciated in
value, and that the complainant and respondent, David L. Martin, should take charge and control of the lands," and that the

complainant and the respondents would endeavor to secure purchasers for the land at satisfactory prices, etc. The answer further alleged that the complainant and defendants joined in leasing the lands to different tenants for terms expiring on the first
day of March, 1898, and that such tenants were in possession of
the lands under said leases. It does not appear from any averment of the answer that the parties agreed upon a definite period
of time during which neither should take steps to have the
lands partitioned. It clearly appears that the agreement was
entered into upon the mutual understanding of the parties that
the real estate was so situate it could not be partitioned, and
that an effort to divide it by proceedings in court would result
in a sale of the land and 644 distribution of the proceeds of
the sale, and that the purpose of the agreement was to avoid a
sacrifice of the land at a forced sale while values were depreciated.
It was not practicable, therefore, for that reason, to fix a definite period for the expiration of the agreement, but it is manifest from the acts of the parties in jointly leasing the lands and
vesting the tenants with full right of possession and control
thereof until the first day of March, 1898, that it was their
intention the said agreement should remain in full force until
that time, and no reason is perceived why the agreement, if otherwise enforceable, should not be regarded as binding the parties to refrain from seeking to partition the lands until such
leases should expire. The execution of the leases would neces-
sitate a sale subject to the rights of the lessees, should such a
sale be made prior to the termination of their leases, and for
that reason would tend to further reduce the price likely to be
received for the property. The leases were in part performance of
the verbal agreement, and in character such as to evince they
would not have been executed but for the agreement. The execution of the leases and the investiture of possession in the
tenants so changed the situation and rights of the parties as
to make a repudiation of the agreement so unjust and unfair
that equity ought not permit it to be repudiated. It would be
inequitable to allow the complainant, while seeking the aid of
a court of conscience, to invoke the statute of frauds to enable him to avoid an agreement which he had so partly performed, and which agreement, if enforced, would operate to
estop him from asking the relief prayed for by his bill. The
mutual undertakings of the parties to the agreement supplied
the requisite consideration to uphold it.

We think the court erred in sustaining exceptions to the an-

swer. The decree awarding partition of the lands must be and
is reversed and the cause remanded to the circuit court, with
instructions to overrule the exceptions to the answer. The decree rendered in answer to the [645] prayer of the bill that the
error or mistake in·the description of the property in the deed
executed to Catherine Martin be corrected, is affirmed. The
costs in this court will be taxed to appellee, Joseph S. Martin.

PARTITION BETWEEN COTENANTS.—Every cotenant is entitled to demand partition though it may be inconvenient, injurious,
or even ruinous to one or more of the parties in interest: Donnor v.
Quartermas, 90 Ala. 164; 24 Am. St. Rep. 778; Charleston etc. R. R.
Co. v. Leech, 33 S. C. 175; 26 Am. St. Rep. 667, and note.

PARTITION—WHEN COTENANT MAY NOT DEMAND.—One
tenant in common cannot, without the consent of his cotenants, have
a partition of lands which they have devoted to a particular use,
which use enters into the consideration of the contract creating it:
Appeal of Latshaw, 122 Pa. St. 142; 9 Am. St. Rep. 76. See monographic note to Nichols v. Nichols, 67 Am. Dec. 703-712, as to who
may compel partition; Cannon **v.** Lomax, 29 S. C. 369; 13 Am. St.
Rep. 739, and note.

CASES

SUPREME COURT

OF

INDIANA.

STATE v. CLAPP.

[147 INDIANA, 244.]

MORTGAGES—FORECLOSURE BY SAME PERSON—SUR-PLUS—PRIORITY.—If two mortgages, of different dates, on the same land, against the same mortgagor, are foreclosed on the same day, but separate decrees are rendered, and the land is afterward sold under the junior mortgage, the junior mortgagee bidding it in for the amount of his decree, but there is subsequently another sale under the senior mortgage, at which the senior mortgagee bids in the land for a sum exceeding the amount of his decree, the surplus being paid to the clerk of the court, the junior mortgagee is entitled to such surplus to the amount of his mortgage. The mortgagor, as owner, is not entitled to such surplus until the junior mortgage debt has been satisfied.

MORTGAGES—FORECLOSURE—VALUE—SATISFACTION OF LIEN.—The value of land, for the purpose of satisfying a mortgage lien against it, is the amount for which it sold at a sheriff's sale, on a decree of foreclosure.

T. M. Eells and H. G. Zimmerman, for the appellant.

L. H. Wrigley and L. W. Welker, for the appellee.

244 HOWARD, J. The appellee held two mortgages executed by the relator upon an eighty-acre tract of land. Both mortgages were foreclosed at the same time; but there was a separate judgment rendered against the relator for the amount due the appellee in each case. For some unexplained reason, the appellee first **245** sued out an order of sale under his junior decree. At this sale he bid in the land for the amount of his junior judgment and costs, paying the costs to the sheriff and receipting for the amount of his debt. Thereupon the sheriff delivered to the appellee a certificate of sale. Afterward, the appellee sued out an order of sale under his senior decree. At this sale the attorneys for the relator bid two thousand five hundred and sixty dollars for the land, and appellee bid two thousand five hundred and sixty-one dollars. The land was accordingly sold to appellee for the amount of his bid. Thereupon the appellee paid all costs to the sheriff and receipted to him for the amount of his senior judgment, leaving a balance of twelve hundred and twenty-one dollars and thirty-two cents, which appellee paid over to the sheriff, and which was by the sheriff paid into the hands of the clerk of the court. The appellee also took from the sheriff a certificate of sale of the land under said senior decree.

The relator brought this action for payment to him of said surplus of twelve hundred and twenty-one dollars and thirty-two cents, claiming that as owner of the land he was entitled to it under the statute, section 1118 of Burns' Revised Statutes of 1894 (Rev. Stats. 1881, sec. 1104). To the action so brought the appellee appeared, and filed his answer and cross-complaint, setting up in the cross-complaint his junior mortgage and decree thereunder, and asking that such surplus be applied in part payment of the amount due thereon. To this cross-complaint the court sustained a demurrer; but the judgment was reversed: Clapp v. Hadley, 141 Ind. 28; 50 Am. St. Rep. 308.

On the return of the case to the trial court, the relator answered the cross-complaint, admitting the material facts as therein set out, but averring that the proceedings in the two sales disclosed the payment in full of the amount due on both decrees and the consequent release of both the senior and the junior lien, and also, that the fair cash value of the land was **246** largely in excess of principal, interest, and costs on both judgments.

The facts were found by the court, with conclusions of law in favor of appellee, and judgment was rendered accordingly.

The finding of the court shows, what is also clear from the record, that the debt due appellee on his junior mortgage has not been paid. The question to be decided, therefore, is whether the surplus in the hands of the clerk, paid in on the sale under the decree foreclosing the senior mortgage, should be applied in part payment of the amount due appellee on his junior mortgage, or whether it should be turned over to the relator as owner.

It is clear that the court has decided this question correctly. Indeed, the question is hardly debatable, under the holdings of this court on the first appeal. There we decided that the purchase under the junior decree was not effective to satisfy the debt secured by the junior mortgage, so as to bring the relator, as owner, within the statutory provisions as to the surplus left after the senior sale. This conclusion necessarily followed from the fact that the purchase under the senior decree extinguished any claim under the junior purchase which could ripen into title to the land. That, too, must be the decision at this time. The senior decree, while establishing the priority of the senior mortgage lien to the land, did not, of course, extinguish the junior decree. The relator remained indebted to the appellee on the junior decree just the same as he was before the senior lien upon the land had displaced the junior lien. And although the junior lien on the land was displaced by the senior lien, the junior lien was not thereby lost, provided there were any proceeds arising from the land upon which that junior lien could rest. There were, as we [247] have seen, such proceeds in the surplus left of the amount bid on the senior sale, and this to an extent sufficient to satisfy about one-half of the indebtedness evidenced by the junior decree. From the decision on the former appeal, sustained as it is by reason and by authorities, it is very clear, we think, that the relator, as owner, could receive no part of any surplus, but what might remain after satisfying the liens in the order of their priority.

It also follows that the court did not err in refusing to hear evidence as to the fair cash value of the land. For the purposes of the decrees and the satisfaction of the liens, the value of the land was that which was bid for it at the sheriff's sale: Bowen v. Van Gundy, 133 Ind. 670, 676. The only exception to this would be where it was shown that the true value of the property was so grossly out of proportion to the price for which it was sold that it might be inferred that there was fraud in the transaction. That is not the case here: Sowle v. Champion, 16 Ind. 165, and note; Kerr v. Haverstick, 94 Ind. 178; 22 Am. & Eng. Ency. of Law, 680, and cases cited in notes. Besides, in case land sells for less than its value at foreclosure sale, the statute provides a year for redemption, during which time any considerable difference between the value and the selling price may be protected by such redemption.

Other questions discussed by counsel are, as we think, sufficiently covered by what we have said.

The judgment is affirmed.

MORTGAGES — FORECLOSURE — DISTRIBUTION OF SUR-PLUS.—A mortgagee holding two mortgages on the same land against the same mortgagor, and a certificate of purchase under a foreclosure sale of the second mortgage, at which he bid the amount of the principal, interest, and costs, is entitled to a lien for the payment of the amount secured by such mortgage upon the surplus arising from a subsequent sale under the first mortgage, although the decrees foreclosing the mortgages were obtained at the same time, without provision made in either for the distribution of any surplus arising from a foreclosure sale: Clapp v. Hadley, 141 Ind. 28; 50 Am. St. Rep. 308.

CLEVELAND, CINCINNATI, CHICAGO AND ST. LOUIS RAILWAY COMPANY *v.* CITY OF CONNERSVILLE.

[147 INDIANA, 277.]

STATUTES—PASSING UPON CONSTITUTIONALITY OF.— Courts will not pass upon the constitutionality of an act of the legislature, if the merits of the case in hand may be fairly determined without doing so.

MUNICIPAL CORPORATIONS—POWER TO REQUIRE LIGHTS AT RAILWAY CROSSINGS—INVALID ORDINANCE.— A city having legislative power to require lights, for the "security and safety of citizens," at railway crossings therein, is not authorized to require lights unnecessary to that end. Hence, an ordinance requiring a railroad company to light, at the crossings, every night from dark to dawn, each of ten streets crossed by its railway, and to employ in such lighting arc lamps of nominal two thousand candle power, to be suspended at least twenty-five feet above the tracks, is invalid, where no trains are run over the road through the city after 8 o'clock on any night.

Byron K. Elliott, William F. Elliott, and G. C. Florea, for the appellant.

Reuben Conner and J. M. McIntosh, for the appellee.

278 HACKNEY, J. In attempting to exercise the power granted by the act approved March 4, 1893 (Acts 1893, p. 302), the appellee, the city of Connersville, adopted an ordinance, declared by the bill to be for the purpose of providing for the safety of persons from the running of railroad trains through said city, the first section of which ordinance was as follows:

"Section 1. Any railroad company or railway company running and operating its engines and cars upon what is known as the White Water Division of the Cleveland, Cincinnati, Chicago & St. Louis Railway Company, situated in said city, is hereby required to erect and maintain an arc electric lamp or light, and keep the same supplied with an ample supply of electricity, and lighted from dusk to dawn of each and every night, at the points where said railroad crosses the streets of said city, viz: One light or lamp where said railroad crosses Central avenue, near the south end of said city; one where said railroad crosses First street; one where said railroad crosses Second street, in said city; one where said railroad crosses Third [279] street; one where said railroad crosses Fourth street; one where said railroad crosses Fifth street; one where said railroad crosses Sixth street; one where said railroad crosses Seventh street; one where said railroad crosses Eighth street, and one where said railroad crosses Ninth street, in said city; each of said lights or lamps to be of two thousand nominal candle power, and may be the same kind of electric lamps or lights now used by said city in lighting the streets of said city, said lights or lamps to be suspended not less than twenty-five feet above said tracks."

Other sections related to other railway companies and prescribed penalties for violating the requirements of each of the sections.

The appellee prevailed in the lower courts, and the appellant, in this court, attacks the validity of said act, under various provisions of the state and federal constitution, and the validity of said ordinance under said act.

It is the generally recognized rule that the courts will not pass upon the constitutionality of acts of the general assembly if the merits of the case in hand may be fairly passed upon without. In the present case, in our opinion, the invalidity of the ordinance must be declared and therefore the validity of the act will not be questioned.

It will be observed that by the provisions of the ordinance the appellant was required to light, at the crossings, every night from dark to dawn, each of ten streets crossed by its railway, and to employ in such lighting arc lamps of nominal two thousand candle power to be suspended at least twenty-five feet above the tracks.

In the recent case of Shelbyville v. Cleveland etc. Ry. Co., 146 Ind. 66, it was said by this court: "Under the authority so given, the ordinance [280] provided for electric lights, which provision, we think, was authorized, inasmuch as electric lights were maintained by the city; but it was also provided in the ordinance that the lights should be of the 'arc pattern,' thus confining the company to a particular kind of electric lighting, and possibly to particular lamps in use in the city. Doubtless, under the statute, the ordinance could have required the light to be of a power sufficient to light the crossing, not to exceed that in use in the city; but there could be no authority further to interfere with the company's freedom of contract in providing such electric lights as it might prefer."

It was, in that case, further declared that, under the legislative intent, in enacting said statute, it should be kept in mind that only the safety and security of the citizen from the running of trains was to be enforced by cities and not simply the lighting of streets.

From the record in this case it appears that appellant ran no trains over its road through said city after 8 o'clock any night, and when we recall the provision of the ordinance requiring lights from dark until dawn, each night, there is more than a shadow of support to the proposition that the safety and security of the citizen was not the one object of the ordinance.

It is true that railway companies may run extra trains, those not scheduled, but possibly an ordinance might be so framed as to require the light for a specified reasonable time before the arrival and after the departure of each train during any night, and that security would be obtained thereby without unnecessary burden upon the companies, and thus avoid the ulterior object, lighting streets.

The existence of power to require lights for the "security and safety of citizens" at railway crossings does not imply that cities may, under the guise of that [281] power, require, arbitrarily and without control or restraint, lights, either in volume or at times, entirely unnecessary to that end. If they do so require, they exceed the limited power vested by the act in question. While it is perhaps true that a measure of discretion is lodged in the common council as to the streets requiring lights, and the volume of light necessary to the safety sought, the exercise of that discretion does not admit of requirements which at first blush are far beyond any reasonable necessities.

Upon the authority cited, and for the reasons we have suggested, the ordinance in question was and is void, and the judgment is reversed, with instructions to set aside the judgment and dismiss the cause.

————

STATUTES—CONSTITUTIONALITY.—A law will not be declared unconstitutional unless it is clearly and palpably in violation of the constitution: Hanna v. Young, 84 Md. 179; 57 Am. St. Rep. 396.

MUNICIPAL CORPORATIONS—LIGHTING STREETS.—A city has power to light its streets and its action is not subject to judicial control, except where the power or discretion of the city has been grossly abused to the oppression of the citizen: Note to Rockebrandt v. Madison, 53 Am. St. Rep. 350; Crawfordsville v. Braden, 130 Ind. 149; 30 Am. St. Rep. 214, and note.

EVANSVILLE STREET RAILROAD COMPANY v. GENTRY.

[147 INDIANA, 408.]

STREET RAILWAYS—CROSSINGS—DUTY OF FOOT PAS-
SENGERS.—A person about to cross a street railway track in a city
is not required to stop, look, and listen, before he crosses, unless
there is some circumstance which would make it ordinarily prudent
to do so.

STREET RAILWAYS—FOOT PASSENGERS—RELATIVE
RIGHTS AND DUTIES AT CROSSINGS.—A street-car has a right
to pass over a crossing, but foot passengers have special rights at
street crossings. They must, of course, use their sense of sight, hearing, and feeling to avoid injury; but it is also the duty of the motorman of an electric car to have it under full control as it passes over
such a crossing.

STREET RAILWAYS—NEGLIGENCE AT CROSSINGS.—It
is negligence for the motorman of an electric car, on a double-track
road, especially after receiving orders to slow up his car at street
crossings where a car is standing on the other track, taking on or letting off passengers, to run his car over such a crossing, at an unusual rate of speed, without slowing up; and, if death is thereby
caused, without fault of the person killed, the street company is answerable therefor in damages.

NEGLIGENCE, CONTRIBUTORY, MUST BE NEGATIVED.
One who seeks damages for an injury caused by another must, at
least, prove some fact or circumstance showing that he was not
himself guilty of negligence contributing to the injury.

STREET RAILWAYS—ACCIDENT AT CROSSING—PROOF
AS TO WANT OF CONTRIBUTORY NEGLIGENCE.—If a passen-
ger on a street car, running on a double-track road, attempts, after
alighting, to cross both tracks, but is struck and killed by a car
coming from the opposite direction, it will not be presumed, in an
action to recover for the death, that the decedent was free from
contributory negligence, although the approaching car was being
run in a reckless and negligent manner, if the evidence is silent as to
the acts of the decedent from the time he stepped off the car until he
was struck, and the interval was long enough to have permitted him
to cross the tracks in safety. There can be no recovery without, at
least, some slight proof of want of contributory negligence on the
part of the decedent.

Alexander Gilchrist, C. A. De Bruler, and L. C. Embree, for
the appellant.

J. E. Williamson, C. A. Buskirk, J. W. Brady, and Chamberlain & Turner, for the appellee.

[409] HOWARD, J.   The evidence in this case shows that appellant has a double-track street railroad on Second street, in
the city of Evansville; that appellee's decedent, Joseph Bradt,
was a passenger on car 70 of said line, going south, on the evening of the accident, December 20, 1892; that as said car approached the north crossing of Jefferson avenue, about 6 o'clock
that evening, it slowed up, preparatory to coming to a full stop

at the south crossing over said avenue; that when the car
reached the first, or north crossing, it was already moving quite
slowly, and the decedent [410] stepped off, his home being on the
north side of the avenue and east of Second street; that the
door by which he left the car was at the rear end, and the steps
descended to the west side of the car; that to reach his home he
would, therefore, have to cross both tracks of the street railroad;
that car 70 came to a full stop when it reached the south side
of Jefferson avenue; that after car 70 had come to a full stop,
car 72 was seen half a block south coming north on the other
track; that from one crossing to the other, on Jefferson avenue,
is about fifty feet; that one of the passengers who got off car
70 at the south crossing, passed around and to the east side
of the car, intending to cross the tracks just as car 72 rushed
by him to the north; that immediately thereafter a cry was
raised that a man was struck by car 72; that decedent was found
insensible and bleeding forty-five feet north of the north crossing, lying in the five-foot space between the two lines of track;
that car 72 went over the crossings at an unusual rate of speed,
the usual rate for the whole trip being from twelve to fourteen
miles an hour; that the motorman of car 72 had received orders
to slow up his car at crossings whenever a car was standing on
the other track taking on or letting off passengers, but did not
do so on this occasion, although car 70 was standing on the
south crossing, and it was well known that at this crossing many
persons were in the habit of getting off and on the street-cars.
It was already dark that evening. Car 72 had a headlight, and
was lit up by electricity. Joseph Bradt died without recovering
consciousness. He was a sober and industrious man, and his
usual way home was by this street-car line. He was foreman
in the Heilman Plow Company's works, situated over a mile
from the crossing. The president of the company testified that
Mr. Bradt was somewhat disturbed in [411] mind as be left the
factory, having just learned by telephone that his wife had run
the needle of her sewing-machine into her finger, and that he
had brought a pair of tweezers with him to extract the needle.
_ Appellee contends that this evidence shows negligence on the
part of the motorman of car 72, and also that Joseph Bradt was
killed by reason of such negligence, and without fault of his
own. Appellant contends that even if the motorman was negligent, yet that Joseph Bradt, having left car 70 at the north
crossing, was not, at the time of the accident, a passenger of
the company's, and, therefore, even if the motorman of car

72 was negligent in disobeying the order requiring him to slow up at the crossing, this negligence did not violate any duty owed to Mr. Bradt as a passenger; and, moreover, that the evidence does not show that the decedent was himself free from negligence, on his part, contributing to his death.

The rules that govern as to the crossing of steam railroads by travelers upon the highway are not fully applicable to street railroad crossings in cities. Foot passengers have special rights at street crossings, which crossings are, in effect, but extensions of the sidewalks over the streets. And, although a street-car or other vehicle moving along the street has a right, also, to pass over the crossing, yet, as has been well said, it behooves the motorman of the electric-car, or the driver of any other vehicle, to be vigilant in approaching a cross-walk, so as to avoid injury to a foot passenger, even though the latter may be careless in hurrying over. In a city, the people must hasten to their business, and cannot wait until all pass by who wish to use the roadway over which they must cross. The rule, therefore, to stop and look and listen cannot apply as it does to the crossing of a steam railroad track. It is, of course, true here, as elsewhere, that [412] everyone must use his senses of sight, hearing, and feeling, and so avoid injury to himself or to others; but it is also true that this rule applies to the controller of the vehicle on the street quite as much as to the foot passenger on the crossing. The street-car, therefore, ought to be under full control as it passes over the crossing; and, as said in Cincinnati Street Ry. Co. v. Whitcomb, 66 Fed. Rep. 915, it is not the law that persons crossing street railway tracks in a city are obliged to stop, as well as look and listen, before going over such tracks, unless there is some circumstance which would make it ordinarily prudent to do so. Other authorities showing that the rules which must be observed in crossing the tracks of the steam railroads do not strictly apply to the crossing of electric or cable car lines in cities are, Young v. Atlantic Avenue R. R. Co., 10 Misc. Rep. 541; 31 N. Y. Supp. 441; Kennedy v. Metropolitan Street Ry. Co., 11 Misc. Rep. 320; 32 N. Y. Supp. 153; Kennedy v. St. Paul City Ry. Co., 59 Minn. 45; Holmgren v. Twin City Rapid Transit Co., 61 Minn. 85; Citizens' Street R. R. Co. v. Spahr, 7 Ind. App. 23; Citizens' Street Ry. Co. v. Albright, 14 Ind. App. 433.

There can be little doubt that the running of car 72 at the unusual rate it ran over the crossing of Jefferson avenue on this occasion was negligence; so that if the death of Joseph Bradt was thereby caused, without fault on his part, the appellant would be liable. The usual rate of travel on this line was from twelve to fourteen miles an hour; and the more rapid rate at which car 72 rushed over this much frequented crossing was little less than wanton and reckless disregard of human life, to say nothing of the rights of foot passengers and of the rights of those who took passage on or left the street-cars at this point.

In Cincinnati Street Ry. Co. v. Snell, 54 Ohio St. [413] 197, the supreme court of Ohio held that when a street railway company operating a double-track road discharges a passenger at a street crossing, having reason to know that such passenger, in order to reach his destination, must cross its tracks, it is the duty of the company to regard the rights of the passenger while on the crossing, and to control the speed of cars on its tracks and give such warning of their approach as will reasonably protect the passenger from injury; that omission of such duty is negligence, and a person injured by reason thereof may maintain an action against the company for damages, unless prevented by his own negligence, contributing to the injury.

Had Joseph Bradt, therefore, got off car 70 at the south crossing of Jefferson avenue, and, relying on the rule of the company to slow up the other car at that point, turned around to cross the tracks of the street railroad on his way to his home, and then been struck by car 72, which at that time was coming north at the rate shown in the evidence, we should have no hesitation in holding that his administrator should recover for his death caused thereby. The decedent would have had a right to rely upon the custom of the company to allow the passengers alighting from its car, time to cross the street to their place of destination.

But the decedent did not alight at the south crossing, but at the north. Before his car reached the north crossing it had already begun to slow up for the usual place of stopping at the south, or further crossing. By the time it reached the first or north crossing, it was moving so slowly that he had no trouble in stepping off, as he did; that being the side of the street on which he lived. The car then proceeded still more slowly across Jefferson avenue, a distance of about fifty feet, where it came to a full stop. After it [414] stopped, car 72 was seen coming from the south on the other track, about half a block, or one hundred and fifty feet away. It is true that car 72 was coming at an unusual and very rapid rate, a negligent rate, so far as the crossing was concerned; yet, the car was still two hundred feet awa from the place where the decedent alighted from car

70; and, in addition, it does not seem reasonable that the decedent should have stood on the spot where he alighted for the whole time that his own car 70 had been slowly moving over from the north to the south crossing. Besides, it was a still evening, and already dark. Car 70 was standing still, and the noise of the coming car 72 must have been distinctly and easily heard; while its headlight shone directly north, and the inside was lit up with electricity. It seems impossible to conceive that the decedent could have stood during all this period from the time car 70 left him at the north crossing until car 72 reached the same crossing and struck him. He was in a hurry to reach home to relieve his wife of the painful injury to her hand. He had simply to cross two tracks, about fifteen feet, while his own car was slowly going fifty feet and the other car coming on two hundred feet more. The case is not at all the same as if he had alighted from car 70 at the south crossing and been caught by car 72 as he turned around to go over the tracks behind car 70. In the latter case he might not see or hear car 72, and would have good right, even if he knew it was coming, to believe that he should have time to cross the tracks before that car could reach the crossing. In the case before us, his time was greatly increased, as were his opportunities to see and hear the coming car.

Much is made by counsel for appellee of the fact that it was the custom at this crossing for cars to stop when meeting a car coming from the other direction, especially when the latter was standing to deliver or [415] receive passengers; that the motorman of car 72 had received explicit directions to slow up at this crossing, and that the decedent had a right, therefore, to act upon the belief that car 72 would stop at the south crossing. The trouble with this contention is, that there is not one particle of evidence to show that the decedent had any knowledge of such custom, or of the order to the motorman, or that he placed any reliance on either.

The evidence is absolutely silent as to the acts of the decedent from the time he stepped off car 70 until he was struck by car 72. It is not even clear that he was at the crossing when he was struck. He was found about forty-five feet north of the crossing, in the space between the two lines of track. Whether he had walked up on the west side of the tracks and was proceeding to cross to the east when he was struck, or whether he was struck at the crossing and carried north by the car and thrown where he was found, is altogether uncertain.

It is true that but little evidence may be needed to negative contributory negligence on the part of one injured by the act of another. The instincts of self-preservation and the desire to avoid injury or pain to one's self might be sufficient, in connection with some slight positive testimony, whether circumstantial or otherwise, to enable us to conclude that one who suffers an injury did not help to bring it upon himself. But there must be some evidence of due care. So many instances are known to us of lack of prudence, forgetfulness, absent-mindedness, or like want of ordinary care, on the part of otherwise prudent and thoughtful persons, that we cannot conclude, without some facts proved, some circumstances shown, that a person's injury was not brought upon him through his own inexcusable fault. Accordingly, the rule [416] has become firmly established that one who seeks damages for injury caused by another must show that he was not himself guilty of negligence contributing to the injury. Here, there is no such showing whatever. Without at least some slight proof of want of contributory negligence on the part of the decedent there can be no recovery: Toledo etc. Ry. Co. v. Brannagan, 75 Ind. 490; Indiana etc. Ry. Co. v. Greene, 106 Ind. 279; 55 Am. Rep. 736; Cincinnati etc. Ry. Co. v. Howard, 124 Ind. 280; 19 Am. St. Rep. 96; Pittsburgh etc. Ry. Co. v. Bennett, 9 Ind. App. 92; Weston v. Troy, 139 N. Y. 281; Cordell v. New York Cent. etc. R. R. Co., 75 N. Y. 330.

In the last case cited it was said: "When a person has been killed at a railroad crossing, and there are no witnesses of the accident, the circumstances must be such as to show that the deceased exercised proper care for his own safety. When the circumstances point just as much to the negligence of the deceased as to its absence, or point in neither direction, the plaintiff should be nonsuited The presumption that every person will take care of himself from regard to his own life and safety cannot take the place of proof. Because human experience shows that persons exposed to danger will frequently forego the ordinary precautions of safety."

While we are, therefore, of opinion that the evidence shows that the appellant was guilty of negligence in the reckless manner of running car 72 over the crossing, yet, we are equally clear that there is nothing to show that the decedent was not himself guilty of negligence contributing to his own injury and death.

The judgment is reversed, with directions to grant a new trial.

STREET RAILWAYS—FOOTMEN—RELATIVE RIGHTS AND
DUTIES AT CROSSINGS—NEGLIGENCE.—Travelers, as well as
street-car companies, must use reasonable care to avoid collisions,
accidents, and injuries at street crossings: Note to Hall **v.** Ogden
City etc. Ry. Co., 57 Am. St. Rep. 735. The duty to look and listen
required before crossing the track of a steam railway does not apply
with equal force to one in crossing the tracks of a street railway:
Consolidated Traction Co. **v.** Scott, 58 N. J. L. 682; 55 Am. St. Rep. 620.
An electric street railway is required to so regulate the movements of
its cars when receiving or discharging passengers from a standing car
as not to unnecessarily expose pedestrians to danger from collision
with a passing car on an adjacent track: Consolidated Traction Co.
v. Scott, 58 N. J. L. 682; 55 Am. St. Rep. 620. The failure of a motorman to keep his car under control when approaching a public crossing
is negligence on the part of the street railway company: Hall **v.** Ogden City etc. Ry. Co., 13 Utah, 243; 57 Am. St. Rep. 726. A high
rate of speed is, if not negligence per se, a circumstance from which
negligence may be inferred: Bittner **v.** Crosstown St. Ry. Co., 153 N.
Y. 76; 60 Am. St. Rep. 588.

CONTRIBUTORY NEGLIGENCE—PROOF OF WANT OF.—The
plaintiff must prove want of contributory negligence where the circumstances are not such as to raise any presumption of due care
on his part: Note to Flannegan v. Chesapeake etc. Ry. Co., 52 Am. St.
Rep. 902. If the issue is negligence, it must be alleged and made to
appear from the evidence that the plaintiff was not guilty of negligence contributing to the injury, and if from the whole evidence it
cannot be determined whether or not he was free from such negligence, he cannot recover, unless the defendant is chargeable with
willful wrong: Brannen v. Kokomo etc. Road Co., 115 Ind. 115; 7
Am. St. Rep. 411. That contributory negligence is purely a matter
of defense, which the plaintiff is not bound to negative in his complaint, see Rolseth v. Smith, 38 Minn. 14; 8 Am. St. Rep. 637.

BUCK *v.* FOSTER.

[147 INDIANA, 530.]

LICENSE TO USE ANOTHER'S LAND—REVOCABILITY
OF.—A mere naked license to use the land of another is revocable
at the pleasure of the licensor, but when the license has been acted
upon and expense incurred in reliance thereon, it cannot be revoked
without at least placing the licensee in statu quo.

VENDOR AND PURCHASER—CONVEYANCE FREE OF
IRREVOCABLE LICENSE—DRAINAGE THROUGH DITCH.—
One who purchases land without notice of an adjoining owner's right
of drainage through a ditch thereon, and without knowledge of such
facts as would put a man of ordinary prudence upon inquiry, takes
the land free of such right, although it is an irrevocable license,
and his deed thereto, even to one who does have notice or knowledge
of that right, conveys it free of the right.

B. W. Langdon and W. R. Coffroth, for the appellant.

John M. La Rue, for the appellee.

530 MONKS, J. Appellant brought this action to recover
damages for obstructing the flow of water and backing it upon
his land and for a mandatory injunction to compel the removal

of said obstruction. A demurrer to the fourth paragraph of complaint for want of facts was sustained. A trial of the cause upon the issues joined upon the other paragraphs of complaint resulted in a finding and judgment against appellant.

The only error assigned calls in question the action of the court in sustaining the demurrer to the fourth paragraph of complaint.

It appears from said fourth paragraph of complaint that appellant and one Randles, appellee's remote grantor, were owners of adjoining lands through which was a ditch to drain their lands, but which was inadequate for that purpose; that it was agreed between them that appellant should at his own cost and expense deepen, widen, and straighten said ditch running through the lands of both parties, in consideration of which appellant was to have the right thereafter to drain his land through said improved ditch, contemplated by said agreement, across the land of the adjoining owners; that said ditch was so deepened, straightened, and widened over the land of both parties at the expense of appellant in labor and money to a substantial amount under said agreement, and was sufficient to completely drain said lands of both parties, and that said drainage was of great benefit to said lands; that appellant owned a right of way over appellee's land for the flow of surplus water through said ditch; that Randles sold and conveyed said real estate over which said ditch was constructed to one Bryant in 1888, who afterward [532] sold and conveyed the same to appellee. That appellee had notice of said ditch and the purposes for which it was used when he purchased said land. That appellee, in March, 1894, built a dam across said ditch where it enters upon his land and filled up the same below the dam and thereby backed up the water on appellant's land to his damage, etc.

It is well settled that a mere naked license to use the land of another is revocable at the pleasure of the licensor, but when the license has been executed and acted upon and expense incurred in reliance upon such license, it cannot be revoked without at least placing the licensee in statu quo: Parish v. Kaspare, 109 Ind. 586, and cases cited; Nowlin v. Whipple, 120 Ind. 596, 599, and cases cited; Ferguson v. Spencer, 127 Ind. 66; Saucer v. Keller, 129 Ind. 475.

In Ferguson v. Spencer, 127 Ind 66, this court said: "Where a license has been executed by an expenditure of money, or has been given upon a consideration paid, it is either irrevocable altogether, or cannot be revoked without remuneration, the reason being that to permit a revocation without placing the other party in statu quo would be*fraudulent and unconscionable. . . . . Where a license is coupled with an interest, or the licensee has done acts in pursuance of the license which create an equity in his favor, it cannot be revoked: East Jersey Iron Co. v. Wright, 32 N. J. Eq. 248.''

It is alleged in the paragraph of complaint in controversy that appellant by an agreement obtained the privilege of draining the land through said ditch across the land of appellee's remote grantor; that said privilege was a valuable one; to obtain which, he expended money and performed labor in reliance upon said agreement made with appellee's remote grantor; [533] and that appellee had notice of said ditch and appellant's right to use the same to drain his said lands.

There is no allegation that Bryant, appellee's grantor, had notice or knowledge of appellant's alleged right of drainage, when he purchased said real estate, nor do the averments of said paragraphs show that he had notice of such facts as put him upon inquiry. If Bryant had no actual knowledge of appellant's rights as set forth in said paragraph, nor of such facts as would have put a man of ordinary prudence upon inquiry, before the time he purchased said real estate, then he took it free from any right of appellant to drainage over the same (Brown v. Budd, 2 Ind. 442; Catherwood v. Watson, 65 Ind. 576, 579; McCarty v. Pruett, 4 Ind. 226; Gaar v. Millikan, 68 Ind. 208, 211), and his deed to appellee conveyed said real estate free from said right, even though appellee had knowledge of appellant's rights as alleged in said fourth paragraph: Brown v. Budd, 2 Ind. 442; Hampson v. Fall, 64 Ind. 382, 387; Sharpe v. Davis, 76 Ind. 17, 22; Studabaker v. Langard, 79 Ind. 320, 323; Arnold v. Smith, 80 Ind. 417, 422; Trentman v. Eldridge, 98 Ind. 525, 538; Brown v. Cody, 115 Ind. 484, 488; 16 Am. & Eng. Ency. of Law, 841.

The court did not err, therefore, in sustaining appellee's demurrer to said paragraph of complaint.

Judgment affirmed.

———

LICENSE TO USE LAND—REVOCATION.—A mere license to use another's land is revocable at the pleasure of the licensor: See monographic note to Lawrence v. Springer, 31 Am. St. Rep. 712-719, discussing the nature and revocation of parol licenses; but such a license is not revocable at the pleasure of the licensor when it is given upon a valuable consideration, or money has been expended on the faith that it is to be perpetual or continuous. To permit a revocation, under such circumstances, without placing the other party in statu quo, would be fraudulent and unconscionable: Note to Lawrence v. Springer, 31 Am. St. Rep. 717. An oral license to maintain a ditch on another's land for permanent use is revocable by the licensor, although money has been expended thereon by the licensee: Hathaway v. Yakima etc. Power Co., 14 Wash. 469; 53 Am. St. Rep. 874. Contra, Flickenberger v. Shaw, 87 Cal. 126; 22 Am. St. Rep. 234; note to Lawrence v. Springer, 31 Am. St. Rep. 719.

LICENSE—CONVEYANCE OF LAND SUBJECT TO—BONA FIDE PURCHASER.—A bona fide purchaser is entitled to protection: Note to Anthony v. Wheeler, 17 Am. St. Rep. 288. A parol license is revoked by a conveyance of the property subject to it: Note to Lawrence v. Springer, 31 Am. St. Rep. 714. A purchaser with notice from a purchaser without notice takes a good title: Doyle v. Wade, 23 Fla. 90; 11 Am. St. Rep. 334.

STATE *v.* PARSONS.

[147 INDIANA, 579.]

GUARDIAN AND WARD—SUIT TO SET ASIDE FINAL SETTLEMENT.—A guardian's final settlement made by him with his ward, and approved by the court after the ward becomes twenty-one years of age, or if a female, after she marries a man of that age, cannot be set aside, modified, or corrected after the expiration of three years from the date of its approval; nor can it be set aside in an action brought within three years except for fraud or mistake.

GUARDIAN AND WARD—FINAL SETTLEMENT—WHAT IS NOT.—A final report made by a guardian who resigns and pays over a balance in his hands to his successor, is not a final settlement required by statute.

GUARDIAN AND WARD—PARTIAL SETTLEMENT—COLLATERAL ATTACK.—A partial settlement, approved by the court, made by a guardian who resigns, cannot be attacked collaterally. It is binding as to all matters properly embraced therein until set aside, corrected, or modified in some direct proceeding brought for that purpose.

GUARDIAN AND WARD—ACTION ON BOND—JOINDER. An action on a guardian or administrator's bond, or against such guardian or administrator personally, and to set aside a final or partial settlement, may be joined if brought in the court having control of such settlements.

GUARDIAN AND WARD—LIMITATION OF ACTION ON BOND.—An action for the breach of a guardian's bond, committed prior to the enactment of the Indiana civil procedure act of 1881, must be brought, under the present statute of that state, within twenty years after the cause of action has accrued.

MOTIONS—REMEDY FOR INDEFINITENESS IN PLEADING.—If, in an allegation concerning the concealment of a cause of action, circumstances of discovery, and time when made, are not sufficiently certain and definite, the remedy is by a motion to make more specific.

PLEADING—STATUTE OF LIMITATIONS—REPLY.—The plaintiff need not anticipate, and attempt to avoid, in his complaint, the defense of the statute of limitations. If it is pleaded as a defense, and the facts bring the case within any of the exceptions to the statute, the proper practice is to set them up in the reply.

GUARDIAN AND WARD—JOINT SUIT UPON TWO BONDS.—Under a statute providing that, if more than one bond is given for the performance of a duty, a joint suit may be brought, it is proper to sue upon two bonds of a guardian in the same action, although they were not signed by the same sureties.

FRAUDULENT CONVEYANCES—COMPLAINT—NO PROPERTY.—In a suit to set aside a conveyance of real estate as fraudulent, an allegation in the complaint that the grantor had no property subject to execution at the time of his death, and that his estate is wholly insolvent, is sufficient to show that there is no property of the estate with which to pay the claim except by setting aside the conveyance.

FRAUDULENT CONVEYANCES—COMPLAINT — GRANTEE'S KNOWLEDGE OF FRAUDULENT PURPOSE.—In a complaint to set aside a conveyance of real estate as fraudulent, an allegation that the grantee received the conveyance with knowledge of the fraudulent purpose of the grantor is sufficient, even if the complaint shows that a valuable consideration was paid. It is not necessary to aver that the grantor "had no property from the making of the conveyance until his death."

FRAUDULENT CONVEYANCES—COMPLAINT—EXEMPTION FROM EXECUTION.—A complaint to set aside a conveyance of real estate as fraudulent need not allege that the land conveyed was worth more than the amount allowed by law as exempt from execution. That is a matter of defense.

FRAUDULENT CONVEYANCES — SUIT BY WARD AGAINST GUARDIAN.—The solvency or insolvency of the sureties on a guardian's bond does not affect a ward's right to have his guardian's conveyance of real estate, made during the latter's lifetime, set aside as fraudulent, in order that it may be sold by the administrator for the payment of the debts of the decedent.

FRAUDULENT CONVEYANCES—COMPLAINT—ALLEGATION AS TO SUFFICIENCY OF ASSETS—DECEDENT'S ESTATE.—In a suit by a creditor of a guardian, against the latter's administrator, to set aside a conveyance of real estate, made by the guardian in his lifetime, as fraudulent, the primary object of the suit being to collect the amount due on the guardian's bond, the complaint must aver that assets of the estate in the hands of the administrator are not sufficient to pay decedent's debts, including the claim of the plaintiff.

Action brought by the relator, Little, against Parsons and others, appellees, for purposes specified in the opinion.

J. F. Neal and S. D. Stuart, for the appellant.

George Shirts, I. A. Kilbourne, T. J. Kane, and R. K. Kane, for the appellee.

[581] MONKS, J.   This action was brought by the relator on two bonds given by one Beeson to secure the faithful performance of his duties as guardian of the relatrix. One bond was executed in 1873 by said guardian, with the appellee, Harbaugh, as surety, and the other in 1874, with appellee, Burns, as surety. Said Beeson died in January, 1892, and appellee, Nagle, was duly appointed administrator of said estate. It is also sought to set aside a conveyance of real estate made by the guardian, Beeson, in his lifetime, to the appellee, Parsons, as fraudulent, and

subject the same to the payment of the debts of said decedent Beeson.

In 1877 Beeson filed his final report as such guardian, and resigned. After his resignation he paid over to his successor as such guardian the balance in his hands as shown in said report. It is alleged as one of the breaches of said bonds that Beeson received during said guardianship nine hundred and seventy-six dollars for which he did not account in said report, or in any other manner, but fraudulently converted the same to his own use. For all that appears from the paragraphs of complaint upon that bond, said final report was never approved, nor otherwise acted upon by the court.

The separate demurrer of each appellee was sustained to the complaint, and judgment was rendered in favor of appellees upon demurrer.

The only objection urged to the complaint by appellees, Harbaugh and Burns, who were the sureties on said bonds, is that the action on said bonds is barred by the statute of limitations. A guardian's final settlement made by him with the ward, and approved by the court after the ward becomes twenty-one years of [582] age, or if a female, after she marries a man of that age, cannot be set aside, modified, or corrected, after the expiration of three years from the date of its approval; nor can it be set aside in an action brought within said three years except for fraud or mistake: Candy v. Hanmore, 76 Ind. 125, 129, and cases cited; Horton v. Hastings, 128 Ind. 103, and cases cited. The approval of such final settlement and the discharge of the guardian would preclude the bringing of an action against the guardian on his bond, concerning any matter embraced in such settlement, so long as it remained in force: Horton v. Hastings, 128 Ind. 103; Candy v. Hanmore, 76 Ind. 125.

The final report made by said guardian, in 1877, when he resigned and paid over the balance in his hands to his successor, even if approved by the court, was only a partial settlement, and was not a final settlement within the contemplation of the statute: State v. Peckham, 136 Ind. 198, and cases cited. Such partial settlement, when approved by the court, cannot be attacked collaterally, but is binding as to all matters properly embraced therein and adjudicated until set aside, corrected, or modified in some direct proceeding brought for that purpose: State v. Peckham, 136 Ind. 198; Parsons v. Milford, 67 Ind. 489; Lang v. State, 67 Ind. 577; Wainwright v. Smith, 106 Ind. 239;

Naugle v. State, 101 Ind. 284; Taylor v. Calvert, 138 Ind. 67, and cases cited.

An action on a guardian or administrator's bond, or against such guardian or administrator personally, and to set aside a final or partial settlement may be joined if brought in the court having control over such settlements: State v. Peckham, 136 Ind. 198.

As the bonds in suit were given, and the breach thereof alleged occurred prior to the enactment of the act concerning civil procedure in 1881, the same are [583] governed by the fifth clause of section 211, page 76, of 2 Revised Statutes of 1852, section 211, page 124, of 2 Davis' Revised Statutes 1876, which provides that actions upon contracts in writing must be brought within twenty years after the cause of action has accrued.

The alleged breach of said bonds occurred in April, 1877, and the right of action thereon accrued at once, and the statute began to run: Peelle v. State, 118 Ind. 512, 514, and cases cited. This action was commenced March 5, 1894, which was within twenty years after the cause of action accrued. It is true that in Jones v. Jones, 91 Ind. 378, and in Lambert v. Billheimer, 125 Ind. 519, it was held that the right of a ward to maintain an action against his guardian for a failure to account for money due the ward is barred in six years from the time the ward becomes of age, but in those cases the action, as the records show, was not on the bond or other contract in writing, but on account for money had and received. It was correctly held, therefore, in said cases that they were governed by the six-year statute of limitations.

We are also of the opinion that even if sufficient time had run to bar the action, that the allegations concerning the concealment of the cause of action were sufficient to bring the case within the provision of section 301 of Burns' Revised Statutes of 1894 (Rev. Stats. 1881, p. 300). If the allegation concerning the concealment, circumstances of discovery, and time when made was not sufficiently certain and definite, the remedy was by a motion to make more specific.

However, the statute of limitations is a defense, and it was not necessary to anticipate and attempt to avoid such defense in the complaint. When any statute of limitations is pleaded as a defense, if the facts bring the case within any of the exceptions to the [584] statute they may be set up in the reply. This is the proper practice.

Section 254 of Burns' Revised Statutes of 1894 (Acts 1889, p. 264), provides: "That whenever any public officer or other person is required by the laws of this state to give bond for the performance of his duties, and more than one bond is given by the same officer or person for the performance of such duties, either during the same period of time or for successive periods of time, any person entitled to sue upon either of said bonds may bring a joint suit upon all or any number of said bonds, and in such action the liability of all the respective sureties thereon shall be determined by the court or jury."

Under this section, if any public officer, guardian, executor, administrator, commissioner, or other person required by the laws of this state to give bond for the performance of his duties, if he give more than one bond, may be sued upon all or any one or more of the bonds so given in the same action. It was proper, therefore, to sue upon both bonds in the same action, although they were not signed by the same sureties.

Appellee, Parsons, urges that the third paragraph was not sufficient to withstand his demurrer, for the reason that it is not averred therein that the "grantor, Beeson, had no property from the making of the conveyance until his death." Such an averment was not necessary: Bottorff v. Covert, 90 Ind. 508, 514; Cox v. Hunter, 79 Ind. 590; Bruker v. Kelsey, 72 Ind. 51; Galentine v. Wood, 137 Ind. 532; Henry's Probate Law, secs. 199, 200.

It was averred in said paragraph that he (Beeson) had no property subject to execution at the time of his death, and that his estate is wholly insolvent. This was sufficient to show that there was no property of [585] said estate with which to pay relator's claim except by setting aside said conveyance: Bottorff v. Covert, 90 Ind. 508; Taylor v. Johnson, 113 Ind. 164. Appellee, Parsons, also contends that said third paragraph is insufficient, because, although it averred that he paid no consideration for the conveyance of said real estate, it appears from the allegations of said paragraph that he paid full consideration therefor. It is sufficient in a complaint to set aside a fraudulent conveyance to allege either that the grantee received said conveyance with knowledge of the fraudulent purpose of the grantor, or that the grantee was a mere volunteer who paid no consideration: Rollet v. Heiman, 120 Ind. 511, 514; 16 Am. St. Rep. 340. Conceding, without deciding, that said paragraph shows that a valuable consideration was paid, yet the paragraph is sufficient for the reason that it was alleged that said appellee, Parsons, received said conveyance with full knowledge of the fraudulent intent of Beeson, the grantor. It was not necessary to allege that the land conveyed was worth more than the amount allowed by law as exempt from execution. If the same was exempt that was a matter of defense: Slagle v. Hoover, 137 Ind. 314, 316; Moss v. Jenkins, 146 Ind. 589.

The solvency or insolvency of the sureties on the guardian's bond cannot affect the right of the relatrix to have the conveyance of the real estate to the appellee, Parsons, by Beeson, the principal on said bonds set aside, if fraudulent, in order that the same may be sold by the administrator for the payment of the debts of the decedent, Beeson. There is no allegation in the fourth paragraph that the estate of said Beeson was insolvent, or that the assets of said estate in the hands of the administrator were not sufficient to pay all the debts of said decedent including the claim of the relatrix. Unless necessary to the payment of the claim [556] of the relatrix, she has no ground upon which to attack the conveyance to said Parsons: Brumbaugh v. Richcreek, 127 Ind. 240; 22 Am. St. Rep. 649. The fourth paragraph was, therefore, not sufficient to withstand the demurrer.

It was said by this court, in Bowen v. State, 121 Ind. 235: "The primary object of the suit is to collect the amount due on the bond, and the plaintiff may join in his complaint such other matters as are necessary for a complete remedy and speedy satisfaction of his judgment."

The judgment of the court is reversed, with instructions to overrule the demurrers to the first, second, and third paragraphs of the complaint, and permit appellant to file an amer'ed complaint if desired, and for further proceedings not inconsistent with this opinion.

GUARDIAN AND WARD—CONCLUSIVENESS OF SETTLEMENT.—The report of a guardian after its approval by the court must at least be taken as prima facie correct, and is conclusive until he who assails it overthrows it by proof: Note to Gillett v. Wiley, 9 Am. St. Rep. 597. In the absence of fraud, settlements of guardians are conclusive; but they may be set aside for fraud: Note to Lataillade v. Orena, 25 Am. St. Rep. 226.

PLEADING.—THE REMEDY FOR UNCERTAINTY in a pleading is by motion to have it made more specific: Meagher v. Morgan, 3 Kan. 372; 87 Am. Dec. 476.

STATUTE OF LIMITATIONS — DEFENSE — REPLY. — If the statute of limitations is pleaded as a defense, the matters upon which the plaintiff relies for relief against such defense may be deemed to have been pleaded in his reply thereto: Fox v. Tay, 89 Cal. 339; 23 Am. St. Rep. 474.

FRAUDULENT CONVEYANCES — COMPLAINT — GUILTY KNOWLEDGE.—An allegation that a transfer was made with intent

to defraud creditors of the grantor, and that the grantee well knew
the intention of the transfer, is a sufficient averment of fraud to
support an attack upon such transfer as fraudulent, although there
is no allegation that the grantor had no other property subject to
execution: Probert v. McDonald, 2 S. Dak. 495; 39 Am. St. Rep. 796.
A grantee with knowledge of fraud is not protected although he paid
a full and valuable consideration: See monographic note to State v.
Mason, 34 Am. St. Rep. 398, on knowledge of vendee as affecting
the validity of fraudulent conveyances; note to Cole v. Millerton Iron
Co., 28 Am. St. Rep. 618.

Buck *v.* Miller.

[147 Indiana, 586.]

TAXES—SITUS OF CHOSES IN ACTION FOR THE PUR-
POSE OF TAXATION.—In determining whether bonds, stocks,
notes, and mortgages executed by nonresidents of the state, may be
taxed, it is to be observed that it is the credit, and not the debt,
to which value attaches, and which is, therefore, taxable. It makes
no difference where the debtor lives, or where the debt was contracted, the chose in action, or credit, is taxable here, if the bond,
note, or other evidence of the amount due the creditor is itself within
the jurisdiction of this state.

TAXES—SITUS OF PERSONAL PROPERTY, GENER-
ALLY, FOR THE PURPOSE OF TAXATION.—Personal property,
in general, is taxable where its owner resides; but the situs of such
property, for the purpose of taxation, does not always or necessarily
follow the domicile of the owner.

TAXES—SITUS OF PERSONAL PROPERTY USED IN
BUSINESS FOR THE PURPOSE OF TAXATION.—Personal prop-
erty used in business in this state, either by the owner or his agent,
is taxable here, although the owner may reside elsewhere; and this
is true of credits and moneys, as well as of other forms of personal property. Hence, if money, notes, and mortgages are used in
this state in the business of buying and selling property, and in making loans and investments, the money so used being collected and
reloaned, such money, notes, and mortgages, if retained in this state,
are taxable here.

TAXES—COLLECTION — INJUNCTION.—The collection of
taxes cannot be enjoined, if any of the taxes against which the injunction is sought were legally assessed, where no payment of the
valid taxes, or tender thereof, is shown to have been made.

TAXES—SITUS—TEST.—In determining the proper place to
tax property, the test is to find its place of location and use, the
place where, if a security or obligation, it is a credit, not where it is
is a debit.

TAXES—ASSESSMENT OF OMITTED PROPERTY.—Under
a statute requiring a county auditor to give notice of his intention
to assess omitted property, he is not required to go outside of his
own county to give notice of his intention to assess such property.

TAXES—OMITTED PROPERTY—DECEDENT'S ESTATE
—LIEN.—Taxes assessed in pursuance of statutory provisions for the
assessment of omitted property are a lien on all property in the
county belonging to a decedent's estate. It is immaterial whether
the property is found in the custody of executors, administrators,
trustees, heirs, or devisees; and the lien can be released only by
payment of the taxes.

TAXES—ASSESSMENT OF OMITTED PROPERTY.—ALL PRESUMPTIONS are in favor of the correctness of the proceedings of the county auditor in assessing omitted property, and those who question such proceedings must point out error if it exists.

TAXES — COLLECTION — INJUNCTION — SUFFICIENCY OF ALLEGATIONS IN COMPLAINT.—In applying for an injunction to restrain the collection of taxes, an allegation in the complaint that the owner of the property was a nonresident of the state is not equivalent to an averment that his personal property and business were not in the state.

Action to enjoin the collection of taxes, brought by the appellants, Buck and others, against Miller, treasurer of Tippecanoe county.

Byron W. Langdon, W. R. Coffroth, and Addison C. Harris, for the appellants.

John M. La Rue and Will R. Wood, for the appellee.

[587] HOWARD, J. The appellants, as trustees under the last will of Job M. Nash, deceased, have brought this **[588]** action to enjoin the collection of taxes assessed against trust funds in their hands to the amount of two hundred and sixty-eight thousand dollars. It is alleged in the complaint that the county auditor, after notice given to the executors, placed upon the tax duplicate, as omitted property of the estate of said decedent, certain stocks, bonds, notes, and mortgages, of which the said trust funds form a part, and which had been held and owned by the said Nash during the years from 1881 to his death in 1893, and had been by him omitted and withheld from taxation during all that time.

It further appears that, from 1880 to 1886, all loans or investments made in this state by Job M. Nash were managed by him in person; and that, from 1887 until his death in 1893, he had in his service an agent in Tippecanoe county to take charge of his real and personal property in the state and to conduct his loan and investment business therein. It is also alleged "that said Job M. Nash was a citizen of and domiciled in another state than the state of Indiana during the whole of the year 1881, and continued to be such citizen and so domiciled until his death."

The theory of appellant's complaint seems to be that all those obligations due Job M. Nash or his estate which were executed by nonresidents of the state are not taxable here. It is explicitly alleged: "That the said bonds, stocks, notes, and mortgages so executed by nonresidents of the state of Indiana were not and are not subject or liable to taxation in the state of Indiana, as they believe." And again: "The plaintiffs further say that they have not, nor has either of them, made any return for taxation in Indiana of any bond, note, mortgage, or other chose in action, payable by or executed by any person or persons or corporation, who was or were not inhabitants or citizens of the state [589] last aforesaid, nor any mortgage not on lands in said state."

It is, however, the credit, and not the debt, to which value attaches, and which is, therefore, taxable. It can, consequently, make no difference where the debtor lives, or where the debt was contracted, provided only the bond, note, or other evidence of amount due the creditor is itself within the jurisdiction of the state. By section 3 of the tax law (Burns' Rev. Stats. 1894, sec. 8410) it is provided that: "All property within the jurisdiction of this state, not expressly exempted, shall be subject to taxation." By sections 51 and 53 of the same act credits are classed as personal property. Personal property, in general, is assessed where its owner resides. But the situs of such property, for the purpose of taxation, does not always or necessarily follow the domicile of the owner: Eversole v. Cook, 92 Ind. 222. Many such exceptions, too, are made in section 11 of the tax law, among them the following, in clause 4: "Personal property of nonresidents of the state shall be assessed to the owner or to the person having the control thereof in the township, town, or city where the same may be, except that where such property is in transit to some place within the state, it shall be assessed in such place": Burns' Rev. Stats. 1894, sec. 8421.

If, therefore, personal property is used in business in this state, it will be assessed here, even though the owner may reside elsewhere; and this must be true of credits and moneys as well as of other forms of personal property. A business may be done in buying and selling property and making loans and investments, collecting and reloaning the money so used, from year to year, and if the money, notes, and mortgages so used are retained in this state they will be subject to taxation here as well as any other kind of [590] personal property: See In re Whiting's Estate, 150 N. Y. 27; 55 Am. St. Rep. 640; In re Houdayer's Estate, 150 N. Y. 37; 55 Am. St. Rep. 642.

"It is the general rule of law," said this court in Herron v. Keeran, 59 Ind. 472, 26 Am. Rep. 87, "that the domicile of the owner is the place where, by a legal fiction, his personal property is regarded as having its situs, and where it is to be taxed: Commonwealth v. Chesapeake etc. R. R. Co., 27 Gratt. 344. But this rule is now departed from in most states, as to chattels having a permanent situs in a state other than that of the residence of the owner: Rieman v. Shepard, 27 Ind. 288; Burroughs on Taxation, 41. And the same departure has been taken in regard to notes and evidences of debt in the hands of an agent of the owner who resides in another state or country, which notes are taken for money loaned, and held for renewal or collection, with the view of reloaning the money by the agent in the same state, the business being permanent in the hands of the agent: Burroughs on Taxation, 44, et seq; People v. Board etc., 48 N. Y. 390." See, also, Forcsman v. Byrns, 68 Ind. 247; New Albany v. Meckin, 3 Ind. 481; 56 Am. Dec. 522.

If notes and other choses in action were in this state temporarily, however, or in the hands of an attorney for collection merely, it would, of course, be different: Herron v. Keeran, 59 Ind. 472; 26 Am. Rep. 87. Still more, where the credit is owned and held in another state by a nonresident of this state: See In re Bronson, 150 N. Y. 1; 55 Am. St. Rep. 632. In such a case, the note or bond so owned and held cannot be taxed here, even though secured by lien on property in this state: Senour v. Ruth, 140 Ind. 318. It is the note or bond so held, and not its mere security, that is regarded as the evidence of value, and hence taxable.

While injunction is the proper remedy against the [591] collection of taxes where the assessment is wholly void (Senour v. Ruth, 140 Ind. 318), yet the burden is upon the plaintiff to allege and prove facts necessary to show that the whole of the property in question was not subject to assessment for taxation: Saint v. Welsh, 141 Ind. 382. If any of the taxes against which the injunction is sought were legally assessed, then, in the absence of a showing of payment or tender, no relief can be granted: South Bend v. University of Notre Dame Du Lac, 69 Ind. 344; Shepardson v. Gillette, 133 Ind. 125.

In the case at bar, there is no claim made that the bonds, notes, and other obligations placed upon the duplicates as omitted property were not, in fact, in the state and subject to its jurisdiction at the several times when, by the decision of the auditor, they should have been returned for taxation. On the contrary, it is alleged in the complaint that during a part of this period the decedent was himself engaged in the business of making loans and investments in the state, while during the remainder of the time he was represented in this business by a local agent. If he lived here and did business in the state, having with him his moneys, stocks, bonds, notes, and mortgages, as the capital and means of doing such business, then it would be immaterial whether he might claim citizenship in some other state or not.

The law could not thus be evaded. His property so used in business and so held in this state would be subject to taxation under the statute cited. It would, of course, be the same if the property and business remained here in charge of an agent. The complaint nowhere states that the omitted property was not in the state at the times when the owner or holder failed to return it for taxation. Neither is it anywhere claimed that any taxes were in any place ever paid on such property. The [592] plaintiffs content themselves with simply alleging that the domicile of the decedent during the period in question was in some other state, not named, and that the obligations placed upon the duplicate as omitted property were executed by and due from nonresidents of the state. This is not enough, and the court did not err in sustaining the demurrer to the complaint.

Judgment affirmed.

ON PETITION FOR REHEARING.

HOWARD, J. It would not be difficult to take the several arguments in appellant's numerous briefs, filed in favor of the petition for a rehearing of this case, and arrange them, consecutively, in such a manner that they should mutually destroy one another. So we sometimes find a series of algebraic equations, each most formidable, when looked at by itself, but all of which, when added together, term by term, are mutually canceled, and there is nothing left but zero equals zero.

It is first contended that we erred in holding that Mr. Nash's "bonds, stocks, notes, and mortgages executed by nonresidents were liable to taxation in Indiana." If we understand that contention, it must mean that bonds, stocks, notes, and mortgages can be taxed only in the state where they are issued or executed, that is, in the state where the debtor resides, or where the company issuing the stock is located. But, in the case chiefly relied upon in appellant s main brief (Railroad Co. v. Pennsylvania (Case of State Tax on Foreign-held Bonds), 15 Wall. 300), it was held by the supreme court of the United States that the state of Pennsylvania could not tax bonds issued by a Pennsylvania railroad company, but owned and held in a foreign state. And, in Senour v. Ruth, 140 [593] Ind. 318, also relied upon in the same brief, it was held by this court that credits resulting from loans evidenced by promissory notes, but owned and held by nonresidents in another state, even though secured by mortgages on property in this state, are not taxable here. There can be no

doubt that the two cases cited are good law; but, if so, what becomes of appellants' contention, that "bonds, stocks, notes, and
mortgages executed by nonresidents" are not taxable in Indiana?

According to the two authorities cited, the bonds, stocks, notes,
and mortgages, although executed by nonresidents, are to be
taxed in the state where they are held and owned, it being immaterial where they were executed. In Railroad Co. v. Pennsylvania, 15 Wall. 300, and in Senour v. Ruth, 140 Ind. 318, the
effort was made to tax the obligations where they were executed;
but the courts held that they must be taxed where they are held
and owned. Taking appellant's contention, that Mr. Nash's
bonds, stocks, notes, and mortgages could not be taxed here, because they were executed by nonresidents, and taking the authorities cited by appellants, that they could not be taxed in the state
where they were issued or executed, because they were held and
owned elsewhere, and we have the beautiful result that they
could be taxed nowhere.

This would suggest a most excellent plan by which the holders
of this class of property might escape taxation altogether. For
example, let those in Ohio convert all their means into bonds,
stocks, notes, and mortgages, issued and executed by residents of
Ohio, and let those of Indiana invest likewise in bonds, stocks,
notes, and mortgages, issued and executed by residents of Indiana;
and then let the holders of the [594] Ohio securities move into Indiana, and the holders of the Indiana securities move into Ohio,
and it is done.

Those wealth movers must, however, be careful not to bring
their domicile along with them. They may, of course, indeed
they must, live and do business in the state into which they move;
but they should be cautious to have their residence and domicile
elsewhere. The complaint before us is drawn very circumspectly
in this regard. It is carefully alleged: "That said Job M. Nash
was a citizen of and domiciled in another state than the state of
Indiana." It was, indeed, a wise precaution that suggested this
manner of statement, and so avoided any indication as to the
particular state where Mr. Nash's domicile might be. Otherwise, the state of which he was actually a citizen, and the taxing
officers of such state. might have taken advantage of the information thus incautiously given, and have assessed his bonds, stocks,
notes, and mortgages. But, provided the allegation is always,
as in this case, that he was "a citizen of and domiciled in another
state," then his personal property subject to taxation, like the

youth's gold under the rainbow, will always be a little further off,
and so escape taxation altogether.

The property owner, to be sure, may have certain occasional
twinges of conscience—that he is sponging off the community,
that he is receiving the benefits of the laws for the protection of
his property, that the courts are open to him for the collection of
his bonds and notes and the foreclosure of his mortgages; in a
word, that all his personal property and business interests are as
carefully guarded as if he were "a citizen of and domiciled in"
the state; but that all these things are done for him at the expense of his neighbors, the citizens of the state, who pay their
taxes regularly from year to year. Those twinges of conscience
will, [595] however, grow more dulled from year to year, and
finally, perhaps, cease altogether; and, in time, if he perseveres,
he will come to regard it as his sacred right to bring all his bonds,
stocks, notes, and mortgages into the state, and so set himself up
in the real estate, loan, and mortgage business, without being at
all hampered by local or state taxes, at the same time that he en-
joys all the rights, privileges, and protection of citizenship.

Notwithstanding all this, we are still firmly of the opinion, as
heretofore expressed, that if personal property is used in business
in this state it ought to be assessed for taxes, even though the
owner may claim to be a citizen of and domiciled in another
state; and that this must be true of moneys and credits as well
as of other forms of personal property. We are still of opinion,
also, that a business may be done in buying and selling property,
including bonds, stocks, notes, and mortgages, and in making
loans and investments, collecting and reloaning from year to year,
and that if the moneys and securities so used are retained in this
state, they should be subject to taxation here, quite the same as
any other kind of property. For purposes of taxation, the term
"personal property" includes bonds, notes, choses in action, and
other evidences of credits: 1 Desty on Taxation, 328; Cooley on
Taxation, 270-272, notes; Boyd v. Selma, 96 Ala. 144. And the
situs of such property for taxation must be the place where it is
used in business: 1 Desty on Taxation, 323; Cooley on Taxation,
15; Burroughs on Taxation, 59; In re Jefferson, 35 Minn. 215;
People v. Davis, 112 Ill. 272; Redmond v. Board etc., 87 N. C.
122; Board etc. v. Leonard, 57 Kan 531; 57 Am. St. Rep. 347.

Counsel next contend that we erred in holding that Mr.
Nash's notes and mortgages, executed by residents [596] of Indi-
ana, were taxable here, except when he had an agent in the state.
The first contention was that obligations executed by residents

of another state could not be taxed here; now it is, that those executed in Indiana cannot be taxed here. One of these contentions must overthrow the other; they cannot both stand, even according to counsels' own argument. But the argument itself is fallacious. The test as to where the right to tax property exists is its place of location and use; the place where, if a security or obligation, it is a credit, not where it is a debit. It is quite immaterial whether the notes or other obligations were executed or were due by residents or nonresidents of the state. If they were owned, held, and used in Indiana, they were taxable here; and this, too, whether the business here in which they were used was conducted by Mr. Nash in person or by some one else for him.

The third contention of appellant, that we erred in holding that certain Indiana notes already taxed were again subject to taxation, shows that counsel have not well considered the opinion of the court. No such holding was made. If, as a matter of fact, the auditor thus retaxed any property which had been already taxed, appellants should have pointed it out to the auditor and asked to have the lists corrected in that particular. But even if such error were made, it would be no justification of appellants' request to enjoin the collection of all the taxes, including those which were justly due.

In the fourth place, counsel contend that we erred in holding that the auditor had jurisdiction to make the assessment of the omitted property. That is an idle claim. The statute expressly gives such power to the auditor, on his compliance with the conditions therein stated as to notice and other matters: [597] Tax Law, sec. 142; Burns' Rev. Stats. 1894, sec. 8560 (Acts 1891, p. 199); Rev. Stats. 1881, sec. 6416; Reynolds v. Bowen, 138 Ind. 434. Due notice was given. The statute requires the auditor, that "if the person claiming to own such property, or occupying it, or in possession thereof, resides in the county and is not present, he shall give such person notice, in writing, of his intention to add such property to the tax duplicate." The only persons in the county claiming to own such property or any part of it, or occupying or in possession of it, were one of the executors and a trustee under the will. To these he gave the statutory notice, and this would, doubtless, have been sufficient. But, through superabundance of caution, the auditor gave notice also to the remaining executor, a resident of Ohio. Besides, it is to be remembered, the assessment and taxation of property is not the bringing of an action in court. The power to prescribe how such assessment and taxation shall be made resides in the legislature, the supreme law-making power of the state. Taxes are not debts, in the ordinary sense of that term, but are rather contributions for the support of the body politic; and it is competent for the legislature to provide how such contributions shall be collected: Geren v. Gruber, 26 La. Ann. 694; Catlin v. Hull, 21 Vt. 152. Following the mode of procedure prescribed by the legislature, if there were no one in the county who claimed to own the property here in question, or who occupied or had possession of it, the state would not thereby be deprived of the means of taxing it. It is only such an owner, claimant, or occupant as "resides in the county and is not present" before the auditor that need be notified. The assessment officer is not required to go outside his own county to give notice to any one of his intention to assess omitted property. [598] In this case, the auditor did more than he was required to do.

The fifth contention is, that we did not hold that appellants were entitled to take evidence to show that Mr. Nash was a nonresident of the state. For the purpose of the complaint, however, it was sufficient to have made the allegation of nonresidence, and we are concerned only with the sufficiency of that pleading.

It is next said that we erred in holding that the trust estate was liable to pay taxes which Mr. Nash had neglected to pay. The state and the municipalities to which Mr. Nash owed taxes are not concerned specially with any trust he may have created for the management of a part of his estate. He died owing certain taxes which he had avoided paying for a great many years. Those taxes have now been assessed in pursuance of statutory provisions for the assessment of omitted property. The taxes are a lien on all property in the county belonging to his estate. This lien can be released only by payment of the taxes. He could not by giving away his property relieve it of the burden cast upon it by the law. It is immaterial to the state whether the property is found in the custody of executors, administrators, trustees, heirs, or devisees. The state seeks out the property itself, or any part of it that can be found, and demands of those claiming to own or use it that the taxes be paid. Nor is the seventh contention any more available. The property of the estate cannot be changed from one form into another, so as to avoid the taxes due and unpaid.

The complaint shows that the county auditor, in pursuance of the provisions of the statutes, placed upon the tax duplicate certain personal property omitted from his assessment lists by Job M. Nash, deceased, for the years from 1881 to the time of his

death, ⁵⁹⁰ in 1893. All the presumptions are in favor of the
correctness of the proceedings of the auditor; and if, in fact, any
of the chattels so placed upon the duplicate as omitted property
were placed there wrongfully, such fact must be shown by those
who call in question the regularity of the auditor's official acts.
A negative complaint, or one that is silent in any essential matter, will not do; the errors, if any, must be pointed out.

In a supplemental brief, counsel, not questioning the correctness of the statement in the principal opinion, that "the complaint nowhere states that the omitted property was not in the
state at the time when the owner or holder failed to return it for
taxation," yet contends, in effect, that the allegation that Mr.
Nash was not at such time a resident of the state is equivalent
to an allegation that his personal property and business were not
here. We think, however, that we have shown, both in the original opinion and in this, that the location of personal property,
particularly for the purpose of taxation, does not necessarily follow the domicile of the owner. The property is taxable where it
is owned, held, and used in business, and where it is protected by
the laws of the community in which it is so held and used; and
the circumstance that the owner, whether for honest or other motives, claims a residence elsewhere, is not controlling. It is, of
course, quite different, as already many times said, where the
property is temporarily in the state, as, for instance, where securities are sent into the state for collection, inspection, safekeeping, or the like. It would be a most immoral doctrine, however, to hold that securities could not be taxed at the residence
of the owner, because they were held at another place, and could
not be taxed where they were held, because the owner resided
elsewhere. It would be a still more grievous wrong to hold that
a man might retain his ⁶⁰⁰ residence in New York or Ohio, but
bring his property, whether money, or bonds, stocks, notes, and
mortgages, to Indiana, and here engage in a general real estate,
loan, and investment business, and so avoid paying taxes at the
place where he must call upon the law, its courts and officers, to
protect and aid him in the safe and profitable carrying on of his
business. A mere statement of such a claim is enough to show
its outrageous character.

Nor were appellants ignorant of the necessity of alleging that
the bonds, stocks, notes, and mortgages were not in the state of
Indiana at the time when the owner or holder failed to return
them for taxation. Speaking of certain of those mortgages, as to
one of the years in question, it was not found difficult to allege

in the complaint: "That said eleven mortgages last aforesaid
were not, nor were any of them, in the state of Indiana, nor were
they or any of them in the possession or under the power or control of said agent or of any one else in the state of Indiana on
the first day of April, 1893." This allegation itself might not
be sufficient to show that even the mortgages named might not
have been taxable for the year named; but we have set out the
allegation as showing appellants' ability to express in vigorous
and definite language the fact that the mortgages were not in the
state, and hence not subject to taxation. But if it be so emphatically alleged that the mortgages named were not in the state
when the auditor claimed they were taxable, we may well presume
that the remaining bonds, stocks, notes, and mortgages, for all
the other years, were in the state of Indiana at the several times
when they should have been returned for taxation. The maxim
quoted by counsel is here in point: Expressio unius, exclusio alterius. Mr. Anderson, in his Dictionary of Law, paraphrases
this maxim as follows: [601] "Express mention of one act, condition, stipulation, class, or number, person or place, implies the
exclusion of another or others not mentioned." It would have
been easy for the complaint to have alleged, if it were true, that
none of Mr. Nash's securities, as placed upon the duplicate, were
in the state of Indiana at the several times when the auditor held
that they were liable for taxation, but that, at such times, as was
the case in Senour v. Ruth, 140 Ind. 318, Railroad Co. v. Pennsylvania, 15 Wall. 300, and other cases cited by counsel, the securities were "held and owned by nonresidents in another state."

In Pullman Car Co. v. Pennsylvania, 141 U. S. 18, the supreme court of the United States, citing numerous authorities,
said: "For the purposes of taxation, as has been repeatedly affirmed by this court, personal property may be separated from its
owner; and he may be taxed, on its account, at the place where
it is, although not the place of his own domicile, and even if he
is not a citizen or a resident of the state which imposes the tax."

The following, from the recent vigorous opinion of Mr. Justice Brewer, speaking for the supreme court of the United States,
in Adams Express Co. v. Ohio State Auditor, 166 U. S. 185, may
fitly conclude this opinion, which has, perhaps, been unnecessarily extended:

"It is a cardinal rule which should never be forgotten that
whatever property is worth for the purposes of income and sale
it is also worth for purposes of taxation. . . . . Substance of
right demands that whatever be the real value of any property,

that value may be accepted by the state for purpose of taxation,
and this ought not to be evaded by any mere confusion of words.
Suppose an express company is incorporated to transact business
within the limits of [602] a state, and does business only within
such limits, and for the purpose of transacting that business purchases and holds a few thousands of dollars' worth of horses and
wagons, and yet it so meets the wants of the people dwelling in
that state, so uses the tangible property which it possesses, so
transacts business therein that its stock becomes in the markets
of the state of the actual cash value of hundreds of thousands of
dollars. To the owners thereof, for the purposes of income and
sale, the corporate property is worth hundreds of thousands of
dollars. Does substance of right require that it shall pay taxes
only upon the thousands of dollars of tangible property which
it possesses? Accumulated wealth will laugh at the crudity of
taxing laws which reach only the one and ignore the other, while
they who own tangible property, not organized into a single producing plant, will feel the injustice of a system which so misplaces
the burden of taxation. . . . .

"It is suggested that the company may have bonds, stocks, or
other investments which produce a part of the value of its capital
stock, and which have a special situs in other states or are exempt
from taxation. If it has, let it show the fact. Courts deal with
things as they are, and do not determine rights upon mere possi-
bilities. . . . . Where is the situs of this intangible property?
Is it simply where its home office is, where is found the central
directing thought which controls the workings of the great machine, or in the state which gave it its corporate franchise; or is
that intangible property distributed wherever its tangible property is located and its work is done? Clearly, as we think, the
latter. . . . . It may be true that the principal office of the corporation is in New York, and that for certain purposes the
maxim of the common law was, 'Mobilia personam sequuntur';
but that maxim [603] was never of universal application, and seldom interfered with the right of taxation. . . . . It would certainly seem a misapplication of the doctrine expressed in that
maxim to hold that by merely transferring its principal office
across the river to Jersey City the situs of twelve million dollars
of intangible property, for purposes of taxation, was changed
from the state of New York to that of New Jersey."

And the following from the same opinion: "In the complex
civilization of to-day a large portion of the wealth of a community consists in intangible property, and there is nothing in the

nature of things or in the limitations of the federal constitution which restrains a state from taxing at its real value such intangible property. Take the simplest illustration: B, a solvent man, purchases from A certain property, and gives to A his promise to pay, say, one hundred thousand dollars therefor. Such promise may or may not be evidenced by a note or other written instrument. The property conveyed to B may or may not be of the value of one hundred thousand dollars. If there be nothing in the way of fraud or misrepresentation to invalidate that transaction, there exists a legal promise on the part of B to pay A one hundred thousand dollars. That promise is a part of A's property. It is something of value, something on which he will receive cash, and which he can sell in the markets of the community for cash. It is as certainly property, and property of value, as if it were a building or a steamboat, and is as justly subject to taxation. It matters not in what this intangible property consists—whether privileges, corporate franchises, contracts, or obligations. It is enough that it is property which, though intangible, exists, which has value, produces income, and passes current in the markets of the world. To ignore this intangible property, or to hold that it is not subject to taxation at its accepted value, [604] is to eliminate from the reach of the taxing power a large portion of the wealth of the country."

Petition overruled.

Situs of Personal Property for the Purpose of Taxation.[*]

Taxation of Personal Property.—The place where personal property may be taxed is shown in the extended note to New Albany v. Meekin, 56 Am. Dec. 523-537. Many cases on the subject have, however, been decided since that note was written, and it is the purpose of this note to show what these decisions have been. It is a maxim of the law that movable things follow the person. Hence, for the purposes of taxation, one rule is, that the situs of personal property follows the domicile of the owner, where there is no statute fixing the situs of such property: Mills v. Thornton, 26 Ill. 300; 79 Am. Dec. 377; Sangamon etc. R. R. Co. v. County of Morgan, 14 Ill. 163; 56 Am. Dec. 497; Corn v. Cameron, 19 Mo. App. 573; Hall v. Fayetteville, 115 N. C. 281; Railey v. Board of

---

* REFERENCE TO MONOGRAPHIC NOTES.

Place where property may be taxed: 56 Am. Dec. 523-537.
Taxation of credits: 74 Am. Dec 93-96.
Power of states to tax shares, capital stock, real estate, or other property of national banks: 96 Am. Dec. 290-297.
Taxation of foreign corporations: 96 Am. Dec. 338-345.
Who is a manufacturer: 52 Am. Rep. 107-112.
Constitutionality of state regulations of interstate commerce: 27 Am. St. Rep. 547-568.
Taxation of patent rights and patented articles: 37 Am. St. Rep. 747-751.
Taxation of collateral inheritances: 41 Am. St. Rep. 580-585.

Assessors, 44 La. Ann. 765; People v. Caldwell, 142 Ill. 434. Intangible property, such as bonds, mortgages, and other evidences of debt, is, therefore, taxable, as a general rule, at the domicile of the owner, unless it has been otherwise provided by statute: Commonwealth v. American Dredging Co,. 122 Pa. St. 386; 9 Am. St. Rep. 116. But the common-law maxim, "Mobilia personam sequuntur," was never of universal application, and seldom interfered with the right of taxation: Adams Exp. Co. v. Ohio, 166 U. S. 185, 224, per Mr. Justice Brewer. As observed by Mr. Justice Story, "although movables are for many purposes to be deemed to have no situs, except that of the domicile of the owner, yet this being but a legal fiction, it yields whenever it is necessary for the purpose of justice that the actual situs of the thing should be examined": Story on Conflict of Laws, 8th ed., sec. 550. See, also, Prairie Cattle Co. v. Williamson, 5 Oklahoma, 488, 492; First Nat. Bank v. Smith, 65 Ill. 44, 53; Graham v. Board of Commrs., 31 Kan. 473; Hardesty v. Fleming, 57 Tex. 395; Pierce v. Eddy, 152 Mass. 594. "The old rule, expressed in the maxim, Mobilia sequuntur personam, by which personal property was regarded as subject to the law of the owner's domicile, grew up," says Mr. Justice Gray, who delivered the opinion of the court in Pullman's Palace Car Co. v. Pennsylvania, 141 U. S. 18, 22, "in the middle ages, when movable property consisted chiefly of gold and jewels, which could be easily carried by the owner from place to place, or secreted in spots known only to himself. In modern times, since the great increase in amount and variety of personal property, not immediately connected with the person of the owner, that rule has yielded more and more to the lex situs, the law of the place where the property is kept and used."

At the present day, the separation of the situs of personal property from the domicile of the owner for the purposes of taxation is a familiar doctrine, and, as a state has entire dominion over all personal property within its confines, it has a right, in the absence of any constitutional prohibition, to tax all personal property found within its jurisdiction, without regard to the place of the owner's domicile. The owner may be taxed, on account of the property, at the place where it is, although not the place of his own domicile, and even if he is not a citizen or a resident of the state which imposes the tax: Story on Conflict of Laws, 8th ed., sec. 550; Denver etc. Ry. Co. v. Church, 17 Colo. 1; 31 Am. St. Rep. 252; First Nat. Bank v. Smith, 65 Ill. 44, 53; Mills v. Thornton, 26 Ill. 300; 79 Am. Dec. 377; Pullman Palace Car Co. v. Pennsylvania, 141 U. S. 18, 22; Marye v. Baltimore etc. R. R. Co., 127 U. S. 117, 123; Coe v. Errol, 116 U. S. 517, 524; affirming Coe v. Errol, 62 N. H. 303; Brown v. Houston, 114 U. S. 622; State Railroad Tax cases, 92 U. S. 575, 607; Tappan v. Merchants' Nat. Bank, 86 U. S. 490, 499; State v. Falkinburge, 15 N. J. L. 320; People v. Niles, 35 Cal. 282; Barnes v. Woodbury, 17 Nev. 383, 385; In re Jefferson, 35 Minn. 215; People v. Caldwell, 142 Ill. 434; Eversole v. Cook, 92 Ind. 222; New Albany v. Meekin, 3 Ind. 481; 56 Am. Dec. 522.

The personal estate of a citizen of another state, when employed in this state, is as much the subject of taxation as property of the same kind belonging to our own citizens; and the fact that it is also elsewhere held subject to taxation is not a circumstance which interferes with the exercise of the power in the state where it is: Battle v. Mobile, 9 Ala. 234; 44 Am. Dec. 438. On the other hand, visible, tangible, personal property, permanently located in another state, is taxable within such jurisdiction, irrespective of the residence or domicile of the owner: Commonwealth v. American Dredging Co., 122 Pa. St. 386; 9 Am. St. Rep. 116. If the owner of personal property within a state resides in another state which taxes him for that property as part of his general estate attached to his person, this action of the latter state does not in the least affect the right of the state in which the propery is situated to tax it also: Coe v. Errol, 116 U. S. 517, 524; affirming Coe v. Errol, 62 N. H. 303; Battle v. Mobile, 9 Ala. 234; 44 Am. Dec. 438; Prairie Cattle Co. v. Williamsou, 5 Oklahoma, 488.

The imposition of a tax is the exercise of a legislative, not a judicial, function; and the legislature may, in the absence of any constitutional restriction, authorize personal property to be taxed either at the domicile of the owner or where the property is situated: Hall v. Fayetteville, 115 N. C. 281. It is clear that it may authorize tangible, movable property to be taxed where it is situated; in other words, it may separate the situs of such property from the domicile of the owner for the purposes of taxation: Liverpool etc. Ins. Co. v. Board of Assessors, 44 La. Ann. 760; Railey v. Board of Assessors, 44 La. Ann. 765; Coe v. Errol, 62 N. H. 303; affirmed in Coe v. Errol, 116 U. S. 517; Corn v. Cameron, 19 Mo. App. 573; and the present tendency is to exercise this power with respect to some kinds of intangible personal property: First Nat. Bank v. Smith, 65 Ill. 44, 54; Board of Supervisors v. Davenport, 40 Ill. 197. Thus, the statutes of Tennessee and of Illinois fix the situs of shares of stock, in domestic corporations, for the purpose of taxation, at the place where the corporation is located, even as against nonresident stockholders: Street R. R. Co. v. Morrow, 87 Tenn. 406; First Nat. Bank v. Smith, 65 Ill. 44, 53. And this has been said to be a very proper and even necessary exercise of legislative power. With respect to national bank shares, such a statute has been said to prescribe no unreasonable rule. "It places the situs of bank shares where, from the very nature of the property, it ought to be placed for the purposes of taxation. The act of Congress itself contemplates a severance of the situs of such shares from the person of their owner, by providing that they should not be taxed except in the state where the bank is established. But apart from this, it is really much more reasonable to fix the situs of shares at the place where the bank is located, and where it must continue to do its business or wind up its affairs, than to separate, by legislation, tangible personal property from the person of its owner. The latter may be in one county to-day, and in another to-morrow. Its actual situs is liable to constant change, and the title may be transferred by the owner wherever he may be. But not so with bank shares. The legislature, then, did no violence to the nature of this property when it fixed the situs of the shares at the locality of the bank":

First Nat. Bank v. Smith, 65 Ill. 44, 55. "Shares are not debts of the corporation, as are its bonds or other obligations. The fiction that personal property has no situs but that of the owner will always yield whenever the actual fact is opposed to the fiction, and when the purposes of justice likewise demand that the actual situs shall be examined. Shares are a species of intangible personal property. They have no actual situs such as tangible personals may have. The situs of such an anomalous kind of intangible property may very well be fixed, for the purposes of taxation, at the place where the corporation has its situs. Such a situs is more nearly in accord with the fact than any other, and the location is in accord with reason and the demands of justice": Street R. R. Co. v. Morrow, 87 Tenn. 406, 428. See, also, Tappan v. Merchants' Nat. Bank, 19 Wall. 490, 500; Grundy County v. Tennessee Coal Co., 94 Tenn. 295. So, as the term "personal property" includes, for the purpose of taxation, bonds, notes, choses in action, and other evidences of credits, such property, if used in business here, is taxable in this state, although the owner may reside elsewhere: See principal case and subdivision, infra, "Property Used in Business." This is another departure from the old rule that the domicile of the owner is the place where, by a legal fiction, his personal property is regarded as having its situs, and where it is to be taxed.

A personal property tax is to be assessed against the owner, at the place of his residence, or domicile, except so far as the rule may be changed by statute: People v. Caldwell, 142 Ill. 434; King v. McDrew, 31 Ill. 418; Hall v. Fayetteville, 115 N. C. 281; Street R. R. Co. v. Morrow, 87 Tenn. 406. If the situs of intangible personal property, such as choses in action, notes, accounts, etc., is not fixed by statute, its situs, for the purpose of taxation, is at the domicile of the owner: Grundy County v. Tennessee Coal Co., 94 Tenn. 295, 317. The statutes of Tennessee, it will be noticed, do not, in direct terms. fix the situs, for taxation, of intangible, incorporeal property, which enters into the value of the capital stock, or assets of a corporation, such as notes and other choses in action: Grundy County v. Tennessee Coal Co., 94 Tenn. 295, 322; though they do fix the situs of shares of stock, in domestic corporations, for the purpose of taxation, at the place where the corporation is located: Street R. R. Co. v. Morrow, 87 Tenn. 406. The legislature cannot, by statute, impose a tax upon tangible, personal property, unless such property has an actual situs within the state where the tax is assessed, and at the time when the property is subject to assessment: Coe v. Errol, 62 N. H. 303; affirmed in Coe v. Errol, 116 U. S. 517; Board of Commrs. v. Wilson, 15 Colo. 90; Corn v. Cameron, 19 Mo. App. 573; note to New Albany v. Meekin, 56 Am. Dec. 533, discussing the situs of personal property with respect to the day of assessment. Neither can it so impose a tax upon intangible, incorporeal personal property, without it is held or owned within the state: See principal case; for the power of taxation by any state is limited to persons, property, or business within its jurisdiction: State Tax on Foreign-held Bonds, 15 Wall. 300, 324; Tappan v. Merchants' Nat. Bank, 19 Wall. 490, 499. Compare note to New Albany v. Meekin, 56 Am. Dec. 524; Lockwood v. Weston, 61 Conn. 211.

Residence or Domicile of Owner.—This question is discussed at length in the note to New Albany v. Meekin, 56 Am. Dec. 531-533. A change of domicile, so far as it concerns the question of taxation, cannot be effected by intention alone, and without actual removal. A person is liable to taxation as a citizen of a certain county so long as he continues in fact to reside in such county: Stoddert v. Ward, 31 Md. 562; 100 Am. Dec. 83. The residence of an unmarried man, for the purposes of taxation, is not where certain of his trunks and clothing are kept, but in the county where he spends nearly all his time, where his interests are, and where he allows himself to be assessed for a small amount of his personal property without objection: King v. Parker, 73 Iowa, 757. A citizen has a right to reside in the country and to do business in a city, but it must be an actual residence. He will not be allowed to avoid taxation in the city by maintaining a nominal residence in the country while his actual residence is in the city: Detroit Transp. Co. v. Board of Assessors, 91 Mich. 382. A corporation must have a local habitation. It cannot fix a nominal domicile in the country while its actual domicile for business is in the city. It is a resident of the place in the state where its business is carried on, as well as of the state creating it: Detroit Transp. Co. v. Board of Assessors, 91 Mich. 382; Milwaukee Steamship Co. v. Milwaukee, 83 Wis. 590; for a corporation may be deemed to have two domiciles, when the just construction of a statute so requires: Ricker v. American etc. Trust Co., 140 Mass. 346, 350. Partnerships, like corporations, may have a residence, and, for the purposes of taxation, they dwell at the place where their meetings are held and their business is carried on: Ricker v. American etc. Trust Co., 140 Mass. 346, 350.

Taxation of Choses in Action, Generally.—It is a general rule, recognized not only in the state courts, but in the United States courts, that the situs of intangible personal property, such as choses in action, notes, accounts, etc., is, for the purpose of taxation and in the absence of any statute fixing a different situs, at the domicile of the owner; and, if the legislature fails to fix the location of such property for taxation, it is evident that it must be held to be the domicile of the owner, in cases of corporations as well as of individuals or executors: Grundy County v. Tennessee Coal Co., 94 Tenn. 295. 317, per Wilkes, J; monographic note to New Albany v. Meekin. 56 Am. Dec. 523-537; Matter of Bronson, 150 N. Y. 1; 55 Am. St. Rep. 632; State v. Earl, 1 Nev. 394; Kirtland v. Hotchkiss, 100 U. S. 491, 499; affirming Kirtland v. Hotchkiss, 42 Conn. 426; 19 Am. Rep. 546; Bonaparte v. Tax Court, 104 U. S. 592. The situs of particular choses in action for the purpose of taxation is discussed elsewhere in this note under appropriate heads.

Taxation of Bonds.—A bond for the payment of money is a mere chose in action, a right to recover a sum of money upon a given contingency. It is personal property, and subject to taxation, but it is intangible property, and belongs to the owner or holder, and not the debtor. It can, therefore, have no actual situs, unless one has been fixed by statute, and is taxable, as a rule, at the owner's domicile: See principal case; State Tax on Foreign-held Bonds, 15

Wall. 300; note to New Albany v. Meekin, 56 Am. Dec. 527; State
v. Board of Assessors, 47 La. Ann. 1544; Staunton v. Stout, 86 Va.
321; Street R. R. Co. v. Morrow, 87 Tenn. 406; State v. Ross, 23 N. J. L.
517. "It is undoubtedly true," said the court, in State Tax on Foreign-held Bonds, 15 Wall. 300, 323, concerning bonds issued to, and
held by, nonresidents of the state, "that the actual situs of personal
property which has a visible and tangible existence, and not the
domicile of its owner, will, in many cases, determine the state in
which it may be taxed. The same thing is true of public securities
consisting of state bonds and bonds of municipal bodies, and cir-
culating notes of banking institutions; the former, by general usage,
have acquired the character of, and are treated as, property in the
place where they are found, though removed from the domicile of
the owner; the latter are treated and pass as money wherever they
are. But other personal property, consisting of bonds, mortgages,
and debts generally, has no situs independent of the domicile of the
owner, and certainly can have none where the instruments, as in the
present case, constituting the evidences of debt, are not separated
from the possession of the owners." See, also, State v. Board of
Assessors, 47 La. Ann. 1544.

Railroad bonds issued by a corporation of another state, but held
in this state by the owner, have their situs here and are taxable
in this state, although they are secured by a mortgage on railroad
property situated in the state where they were issued: Mackay v.
San Francisco, 113 Cal. 392. Bonds and other choses in action follow
the person of their owner, and cannot be regarded as situated in the
state of which the debtor is a resident, when they and their holder
are both within another state: Matter of Bronson, 150 N. Y. 1; 55 Am.
St. Rep. 632. Bonds of corporations in this state, or of residents
thereof, held by an inhabitant of another state, are not taxable in
this state, as neither the bondholder nor the property is within the
jurisdiction of the state: State v. Ross, 23 N. J. L. 517; Street R. R.
Co. v. Morrow, 87 Tenn. 406. The commonwealth of Pennsylvania
cannot, consistently with the constitution of the United States, impose upon the New York, Lake Erie and Western Railroad Company, a New York corporation, the duty—when paying in the city
of New York the interest due upon scrip, bonds, or certificates of indebtedness held by residents of Pennsylvania—of deducting from the
interest so paid the amount assessed upon bonds and moneyed capital
in the hands of such residents of Pennsylvania: New York etc. R. R.
Co. v. Pennsylvania, 153 U. S. 628, 639; Delaware etc. Canal Co. v.
Pennsylvania, 156 U. S. 200. Compare Commonwealth v. New York
etc. R. R. Co., 129 Pa. St. 478. If a domestic corporation holds bonds
of foreign corporations issued to it in payment for patent rights
granted, the amount of capital invested in such bonds is taxable
here, as the bonds are presumably held at the office of the domestic
corporation in this state, and they, as well as all other choses in
action, unless kept, employed, or used outside of the state, have
their situs at the domicile of the owner: People v. Campbell, 138 N. Y.
543, 547. If an insurance company, doing business in another state
than that of its domicile, finds it necessary to purchase bonds of that

state and to deposit them in its treasury as an indemnity for the payment of risks in such state, the bonds are the avails and incidents of the insurance business, segregated from commerce, and are, therefore, taxable at the domicile of the company: State v. Board of Assessors, 47 La. Ann. 1544.

If the constitution requires the taxation of bonds, the legislature has no power to exempt them: Mackay v. San Francisco, 113 Cal. 392; and the bonds of a corporation have their situs, for the purpose of taxation, in the absence of any special provision affecting them, at the place of the bondholder's residence—not at the place where the corporation is situated; and this situs cannot be altered, by statute, as to pre-existing bonds, without violating the obligation of contract: Street R. R. Co. v. Morrow, 87 Tenn. 406. Resident bondholders of Tennessee are taxable, for county or city purposes, upon the bonds of domestic corporations held and owned by them, only at the place of the bondholder's residence, not at the place where the corporation is located, if that is different: Street R. R. Co. v. Morrow, 87 Tenn. 406. If a state statute provides that the bonds of a corporation secured by mortgage upon property wholly within the state shall be taxed in the same manner as bonds secured by mortgage upon property partly within and partly without the state, and there is no express provision for the taxation of the latter kind of bonds, but it is elsewhere provided that all bonds issued by any corporation, belonging to residents of the state, shall be liable to taxation, the bonds of a corporation secured by mortgage upon property partly within the state would be liable to taxation under such latter provision, and the bonds of a corporation secured by mortgage upon property wholly within the state are liable to taxation in the hands of residents, notwithstanding a statute exempting, for the purpose of valuation and assessment, mortgages upon property wholly within the state, as well as the mortgage debts secured thereby. "The exemption of the mortgage debt of an individual and the taxation of the mortgage bonds of a corporation in the hands of the respective creditors is not an arbitrary and unreasonable discrimination between the same classes of property": Simpson v. Hopkins, 82 Md. 478, 489. Bonds issued by a corporation, doing business within a state, and held by other corporations of the state in trust for persons "whose residence is unknown," are subject to a tax imposed by such state: Commonwealth v. Lehigh Valley R. R. Co., 120 Pa. St. 429. For other cases relative to the situs of bonds for the purposes of taxation, see subdivisions, infra, "Taxation of Collateral Inheritances"; "Property of Decedents"; and "Property Held in Trust."

Taxation of Collateral Inheritances.—The situs of property, for the purpose of taxation, under the inheritance tax act, or what is now known as the transfer tax act, which imposes a tax upon the right of succession, is discussed in the monographic notes to State v. Hamlin, 41 Am. St. Rep. 580-585, on the taxation of collateral inheritances, and New Albany v. Meekin, 56 Am. Dec. 536, on the place where property may be taxed. Bonds and certificates of stock, whether of foreign or domestic corporations, actually within the

state at the time of the death of a nonresident decedent, are subject
to the inheritance or transfer tax act, where such a law exists:
Matter of Whiting, 150 N. Y. 27; 55 Am. St. Rep. 640; though
habitually kept by him in a safe deposit vault in the state; Matter
of Morgan, 150 N. Y. 35. So with personal property in the state,
owned by a nonresident intestate at the time of his death, and which
was habitually kept or invested by him there: Matter of Romaine,
127 N. Y. 80. Moneys on deposit within the state in one of its
banks, though belonging to a nonresident, are, upon his death, subject to the inheritance or transfer tax act; and they are not any the
less subject to the tax because they are on deposit with a trust company, commingled with other moneys which the depositor held in
trust for a third person: Matter of Houdayer, 150 N. Y. 37; 55 Am.
St. Rep. 642.

Bonds issued by the United States are not subject to the inheritance or transfer tax act: Matter of Whiting, 150 N. Y. 27; 55 Am.
St. Rep. 640; and a statute imposing an inheritance tax upon a transfer by will or by the intestate laws of property within the state,
when the decedent was not a resident thereof at the time of his
death, does not apply to bonds and other indebtedness not within
the state at his death due to him from a corporation organized and
existing in another state, but does include stock in such corporation
held by him, whether the certificates of such stock are within the
state at that time or not: Matter of Bronson, 150 N. Y. 1; 55 Am. St.
Rep. 632. The interest which a shareholder in a corporation has is
property which may be deemed as existing within the state of which
the corporation is a resident, and, therefore, shares of stock held by a
nonresident stockholder of the corporation, though the certificates
thereof are at the place of his domicile at the time of his death,
are property within the state, and, as such, subject to the inheritance
tax imposed on all property within the state transferred by will or
the intestate laws, where the decedent was a nonresident at the
time of his death: Matter of Bronson, 150 N. Y. 1; 55 Am. St. Rep.
632. Compare subdivision, infra, "Taxation of Shares of Stock."
The legal situs of that species of property represented by certificates
of corporate stock is where the corporation exists, or where the
shareholder has his domicile. Hence, if a testator, domiciled in
Great Britain, dies in Africa, and leaves stocks and bonds in the
state of New York at the time of his death, such stocks and bonds
of corporations as are outside of that state are not property in that
state, within the meaning of the collateral inheritance tax act of
that state, and are not, therefore, properly taxable in New York:
Matter of James, 144 N. Y. 6. Compare Matter of Enston, 113 N. Y.
174.

Taxation of Debts and Credits.—"There is no doubt," says the
supreme court of Louisiana, "of the legislative power to modify the
rule of comity, mobilia personam sequuntur, in many respects. Movables having an actual situs in the state may be taxed there, though
the owner be domiciled elsewhere. Even debts' may assume such
concrete form in the evidences thereof that they may be similarly
subjected when such evidences are situated in the state, as in the

case of bank notes, public securities, and, possibly, of negotiable promissory notes, bills of exchange, or bonds. But as to mere ordinary debts, reduced to no such concrete forms, they are not capable of acquiring any situs distinct from the domicile of the creditor, and no legislative power exists to change that situs so far as nonresident creditors are concerned": Railey v. Board of Assessors, 44 La. Ann. 765, 770. A debt is not the property of the debtor, in any sense, but is his obligation, and has value only in the hands of the creditor. Hence, its situs is necessarily where it is owned and not where it is due: Railey v. Board of Assessors, 44 La. Ann. 765; Liverpool etc. Ins. Co. v. Board of Assessors, 44 La. Ann. 760, 764. As said by the supreme court of the United States: "To call debts property of the debtors is simply to misuse terms. All the property there can be in the nature of things, in debts, belongs to the creditors to whom they are payable, and follows their domicile wherever that may be. Their debts can have no locality separate from the parties to whom they are due": State Tax on Foreign-held Bonds, 15 Wall. 300, 320. A nonresident creditor of a state is not, by reason of the fact that a resident thereof owes him a debt, a holder of property within its limits. The credit is not within the state's jurisdiction, and is of no value to the debtor. It is not property within the state, but property of the creditor taxable at his place of residence: Liverpool etc. Ins. Co. v. Board of Assessors, 44 La. Ann. 760. Debts due to nonresidents cannot, therefore, be taxed within the state: Liverpool etc. Ins. Co. v. Board of Assessors, 44 La. Ann. 760, 764; Railey v. Board of Assessors, 44 La. Ann. 765; Jack v. Walker, 79 Fed. Rep. 138; note to New Albany v. Meekin, 56 Am. Dec. 529; Parker v. Strauss, 49 La. Ann. 1173. Compare, People v. Willis, 133 N. Y. 383. A debt has its situs at the residence of the creditor and may be taxed there: State v. Gaylord, 73 Wis. 316, 325.

Thus, a foreign insurance company domiciled out of the state and collecting premiums here is not liable for a tax levied on the premiums, as they are "credits" having a situs at the domicile of the company: Railey v. Board of Assessors, 44 La. Ann. 765. Debts owned by a nonresident of the state of Ohio, evidenced by notes and mortgages upon real estate, are not taxable there, although the notes and mortgages are in the hands of a resident agent, who made the loans, and who collects and remits the principal and interest as they become due: Jack v. Walker, 79 Fed. Rep. 138. Compare subdivision, infra, on "Property Used in Business." The domicile of the holder of evidence of a debt is the situs of the debt for the purpose of taxation: State Bank v. Richmond, 79 Va. 113.

"Credits" are taxable, although the property for which they were given is also taxable: See monographic note to People v. Worthington, 74 Am. Dec. 93, 95, on taxation of credits; Goldgart v. People, 106 Ill. 25. They have their situs at the domicile of the creditor, and are taxable at the place of his domicile. The fact that the debt is secured by mortgage of property situated in another state does not affect it for the purpose of taxation: See principal case; Mackay v. San Francisco, 113 Cal. 392; Grant v. Jones, 39 Ohio St. 506; Senour v. Ruth, 140 Ind. 318; Goldgart v. People, 106 Ill. 25. A credit in favor of a nonresident is, of course, a debit against a citizen of this state: Senour v. Ruth, 140 Ind. 318. If a nonresident creditor has debts due him from a resident of this state, such credits follow his person, leaving nothing here to which jurisdiction can attach, it being the credits, not the debts, which are taxable: Goldgart v. People, 106 Ill. 25. But if the owner of credits resides in this state, there is jurisdiction over his person and over his credits, as they accompany him, in the absence of anything showing that they have a situs elsewhere: Goldgart v. People, 106 Ill. 25. Solvent credits, evidenced by negotiable promissory notes owned by a resident of the state of Alabama, are taxable at the place of the owner's residence, though the notes are payable in another county of that state, where the makers thereof reside, and are secured by mortgages on land there, and notwithstanding the fact that the notes and mortgages themselves are kept, not by the owner at his place of residence, but by his agent in such other county, for collection and reinvestment: Boyd v. Selma, 96 Ala. 144. Compare subdivision, infra, "Property Used in Business." For the purpose of taxation, the domicile of an administrator is the legal situs of the credits belonging to the estate in his charge: Sommers v. Boyd, 48 Ohio St. 648.

A state legislature has power to tax persons residing in the state for money lent by them to persons residing out of the state and secured upon real property out of the state: Kirtland v. Hotchkiss, 42 Conn. 426; 19 Am. Rep. 546; affirmed in Kirtland v. Hotchkiss, 100 U. S. 491. It has been held in Louisiana that moneys standing to the credit of a nonresident firm on the books of a bank there are not taxable in that state, upon the theory that the relation between a bank and its customers is that of debtor and creditor, and that such a debt is not distinguishable from those due to the foreign firm from any other cause: Clason v. New Orleans, 46 La. Ann. 1; Parker v. Strauss, 49 La. Ann. 1173.

Taxation of Judgments.—Debts have their situs at the domicile of the creditor, and do not lose their situs because of being reduced to judgment at the domicile of the debtor. Hence, a debt, though evidenced by a judgment, being located at the domicile of the creditor, is not taxable elsewhere: Meyer v. Sheriff, 41 La. Ann. 645. Judgments rendered by the courts of Kansas in favor of nonresidents are not taxable in that state, as they have not been given a situs, by statute, for the purpose of taxation: Board of Commissioners v. Leonard, 57 Kan. 531; 57 Am. St. Rep. 347. A judgment for a debt, and foreclosing a mortgage given to secure it, is subject to taxation only in the county where the owner of the judgment resides, and only the money due on the judgment is taxable: People v. Eastman, 25 Cal. 600.

Taxation of Mortgages.—A mortgage, being a mere chose in action, follows the person of the owner, and is taxable only in the state in which he resides: Jack v. Walker, 79 Fed. Rep. 138; State Tax on Foreign-held Bonds, 15 Wall. 300, 324; Holland v. Board of Commissioners, 15 Mont. 460; note to New Albany v. Meekin, 56 Am. Dec. 529. The mortgage is not taxable as such. It is the debt secured by the mortgage that is taxable, and the debt, where the creditor resides in the state, has no situs for the purpose of taxation, apart from the residence of the owner: People v. Eastman, 25 Cal. 601. A mortgage owned by a resident of this state, given upon land situated in another state where a tax has been assessed upon the land and paid within the preceding year, is taxable here: Darcy v. Darcy, 51 N. J. L. 140. Mortgages of nonresidents may be taxed where recorded without regard to the time of the execution of the contract: Mumford v. Sewall, 11 Or. 67; 50 Am. Rep. 462.

Taxation of Negotiable Instruments.—The same rule that applies to the taxation of other choses in action prevails as to notes. They follow the domicile of the owner or creditor, and are taxable there: See monographic note to New Albany v. Meekin, 56 Am. Dec. 529. If they are not within the state, they cannot be taxed: Senour v. Ruth, 140 Ind. 318, 320. Neither can they be taxed if they are in this state merely for collection: Fisher v. Commissioners, 19 Kan. 414. Notes held by a bank located in a city are, however, taxable by the city, wherever the makers may reside, whether in or out of the city or in or out of the state: State Bank v. Richmond, 79 Va. 113. The taxation of negotiable instruments has been necessarily discussed elsewhere in this note. See, particularly, subdivision supra, "Taxation of Debts and Credits."

Taxation of Shares of Stock.—Shares of stock in a corporation, like other forms of intangible personal property, are taxable at the domicile of the owner, wherever that may be, unless it is otherwise provided by statute: Ogden v. St. Joseph, 90 Mo. 522, 529; Watson v. Fairmont, 38 W. Va. 183; collected cases in note to People v. Worthington, 74 Am. Dec. 95. And this rule applies to shares of stock in foreign corporations as well as to shares in domestic corporations. Shares of stock in a foreign corporation, owned by persons residing in this state, may be lawfully taxed to them here, although the capital of such corporation is taxed in the state where the corporation is located: Bradley v. Bauder, 36 Ohio St. 28; 38 Am. Rep. 547; Worth v. Commissioners, 82 N. C. 420; 33 Am. Rep. 692; Lockwood v. Weston, 61 Conn. 211; Seward v. Rising Sun, 79 Ind. 351; Worth v. Commissioners, 90 N. C. 409; McKeen v. County of Northampton, 49 Pa. St. 519; 88 Am. Dec. 515; Dwight v. Mayor, 12 Allen, 316; 90 Am. Dec. 149; collected cases in note to New Albany v. Meekin, 56 Am. Dec. 527; or a tax against the same shares has been there assessed and paid: Dyer v. Osborne, 11 R. I. 321; 23 Am. Rep. 460; Seward v. Rising Sun, 79 Ind. 351. Contra, State v. Smith, 55 N. J. L. 110. And it makes no difference whether the corporation is a public or private one: Lockwood v. Weston, 61 Conn. 211. Shares of stock of corporations in New Jersey held by the inhabitants of another state are not taxable in New Jersey: State v. Ross, 23 N. J. L. 517, 523. So, in New York, it is held that as to stock in corporations of other states, it is capital employed outside of the state, and is not taxable in New York, where the property represented by the shares of stock, is outside of that state: People v. Campbell, 138 N. Y. 543, 546; People v. Wemple, 148 N. Y. 690.

The capital stock of a corporation and the shares of the capital stock are distinct things, and both may be taxed without imposing double taxation: State Bank v. Richmond, 79 Va. 113; Farrington v. Tennessee, 95 U. S. 679, 686, 687; Commonwealth v. Charlottesville etc. Loan Co., 90 Va. 790; 44 Am. St. Rep. 950; Street R. R. Co. v. Morrow, 87 Tenn. 406. The state may, by statute, impose a tax upon the capital of a corporation, and also upon the shares of stock therein, held by resident and nonresident shareholders: Commonwealth v. Charlottesville etc. Loan Co., 90 Va. 790; 44 Am. St. Rep. 950; and shares of stock may be separated from the person of the owner, by statute, and be given a situs of their own: Tappan v. Merchants' Nat. Bank, 19 Wall. 490. The situs of·shares of stock may, for the purpose of taxation, be fixed, by statute, at the place where the cor-·poration is located, or at its principal place of business, even as against nonresident stockholders: Street R. R. Co. v. Morrow, 87 Tenn. 406; Wiley v. Commissioners, 111 N. C. 397. Under the Connecticut statute, stock owned by residents in nonresident corporations whether public or private, is taxable only in case such shares are not taxed in the state where the corporations are located: Lockwood v. Weston, 61 Conn. 211. Under the Massachusetts statute subjecting to taxation "shares or property in any incorporated company for a bridge or turnpike road," a resident of that state is liable to be taxed for stock held by him in a turnpike company of another state: Great Barrington v. County Commrs., 16 Pick. 572. The capital stock of a corporation issued for, or invested in, patents or patent rights, is not subject to taxation under state laws: Commonwealth v. Edison Electric Light Co., 157 Pa. St. 529; 37 Am. St. Rep. 747, and monographic note thereto on the taxation of patent rights and patented articles. As to the situs of shares of stock for the purpose of taxation, see, also, subdivisions, infra, "Property of Corporations," "Property of Railroad Companies," and "Property of National Banks."

Property within the State, Generally.—All personal property within the state, which has acquired a situs therein, owned either by residents or nonresidents, is subject to taxation by the state: Senour v. Ruth, 140 Ind. 318; Goldgart v. People, 106 Ill. 25; Parker v. Strauss, 49 La. Ann. 1173. Water pipes and fire plugs are taxable in the district where found whether considered as real or personal property: Riverton etc. Water Co. v. Haig, 58 N. J. L. 295. The actual situs of personal property, and not the domicile of the owner, is the material inquiry in determining the liability of tangible personal property to taxation. If it is brought into this state for the purpose of business, for an indefinite time, and not merely for·a transitory purpose, it becomes incorporated with the property in this state for revenue purposes, and is taxable here, although its owner's domicile is in another state: National Dredging Co. v. State, 99 Ala. 462. Compare subdivision, infra, "Property Used in Business." Moneys and notes secured by mortgages of land in another state, in the hands of an agent in that state to be loaned, collected, and reloaned, but belonging to a resident of this state, are "property in this state" and taxable here, on the principle that a debt has its situs at the residence of the creditor, and may be taxed there: State v. Gaylord, 73 Wis. 316, 325. This does not, however, prevent the taxation of the property by the state in which it is used in business: See subdivision, infra, "Property Used in Business." Where state statutes have been made applicable to village assessments, it being provided by such statutes that "all debts" due upon contracts are personal property and that every person residing in a town shall be assessed therein for all personal estate owned by him, or in his possession, or under his control as agent, trustee, etc., debts due to nonresidents, upon contracts for the sale of real estate situated within the state, but not within the village limits, which contracts are in the hands of an agent residing in such village, are taxable against such agent: People v. Willis, 133 N. Y. 383. Chattels purchased in one state by a citizen of another, and remaining in the former to receive a finishing process of manufacture, are taxable in the state where purchased: Standard Oil Co. v. Combs, 96 Ind. 179; 49 Am. Rep. 156.

Property stored for sale in a warehouse within the state is taxable therein the same as other personal property: State v. Deering, 56 Minn. 24; Hood v. Judkins, 61 Mich. 575; but attached goods in the hands of a sheriff, and stored away, are assessable to the owner, and not to attaching creditors who are nonresidents of the township where the goods are stored, and who are not engaged in any business therein: Kalkaska v. Fletcher, 81 Mich. 446. Lumber at a railway station for transit merely, and kept there in piles for convenience of shipment, upon grounds not owned or hired for the purpose, is not taxable at that place as property in "storage": Monroe v. Greenhoe, 54 Mich. 9. The placing of lumber at a railway station, merely for convenience in loading and shipping, and for a temporary purpose, is not "stored": Hood v. Judkins, 61 Mich. 575. So, lumber upon the premises of a manufacturer, under a contract of sale to dealers whose place of business is elsewhere, is not taxable where it is, as if in a place of "storage," where something yet remains to be done to complete the transfer to the purchasers: Osterhout v. Jones, 54 Mich. 228.

Logs and lumber are liable to taxation like other personal property. In Michigan, logs in camp are taxable at the place where the camp is located, if there is an office there receiving funds and making returns to headquarters: Ryerson v. Muskegon, 57 Mich. 383. Logs are not taxable in the township where they are temporarily left afloat for sawing if the firm to which they belong has its place of business in another township and the partners live elsewhere: Torrent v. Yager, 52 Mich. 506. Logs left by an Iowa company in a bayou on the Illinois side of the Mississippi river for safekeeping are taxable in Illinois: Burlington Lumber Co. v. Willetts, 118 Ill. 559. Under the Wisconsin statute, all sawlogs cut within six months prior to April 1st are to be assessed in the assessment district in which they are banked or piled, except those to be sawed or manufactured in a mill in that state, owned by the owner of such logs: State v. Bellew, 86 Wis. 189; but logs which have been cut in one town within six months previous to April 1st, and piled there for shipment, and which have been actually shipped into another town prior to that date, cannot be said, under that statute, to have acquired a situs for assessment and taxation in the town where they were piled for shipment. They are, therefore, subject to assessment and taxation in the town into which they have been shipped: Day v. Pelican, 94 Wis. 503. The principle of assessing cumbrous articles like logs, lumber, and manufacturers' stock at the place where they are kept, and where they have a legal situs, applies, of course, to other articles of a similar character.

Property in Cities, Counties, Towns, and Townships.—A city has no power to collect taxes on property situated outside of its corporate limits: Coln v. Cameron, 19 Mo. App. 573. So if, at the time of a testator's death, his domicile was beyond the corporate limits of a city, bonds belonging to his estate are not assessable and taxable by the city, though, at the time of the assessment and levy was made, his executors resided within the city: Staunton v. Stout, 86 Va. 321. Stock of the city of Baltimore, held by a nonresident of the state of Maryland, is not subject to taxation in that state: Mayor v. Hussey, 67 Md. 112.

In Illinois, personal property is taxable in the county, town, or district where the owner resides, although it may be in another county and be in use there: King v. McDrew, 31 Ill. 418. So, if a party in that state has a farm situated partly in one county and partly in another, he is taxable on his personal property in the county where he has his actual residence, whatever may be his motive for choosing one county in preference to the other: People v. Caldwell, 142 Ill. 434. In California, personal property is taxable in the county wherein it is situated, except money and gold dust, which may, at the option of the owner, be taxed in the county of his residence: People v. Niles, 35 Cal. 282, 286. The situs of money belonging to the estate of a decedent is in the county where he resided at the time of his death, and the situs is not changed by placing the money on general deposit in a bank of another county: San Francisco v. Lux, 64 Cal. 481. But, even in California, to authorize the taxing of personal property in any other county than that in which the owner resides, it must have a situs of its own, independent of the domicile of its owner. That is, it must appear that the property is being, to some extent, kept or maintained in such county, and not there casually, or in transitu, or temporarily in the ordinary course of business or commerce: People v. Niles, 35 Cal. 282, 287. It is recognized that personal property may acquire such a local situs in the county in which it is kept and used as to become liable to taxation there, although its owner resides in another county, and has there returned the property for taxation. A portable sawmill, and a yoke of oxen used in connection with it are illustrations of such property: Trammell v. Connor, 91 Ala. 398. An assessment to the owner, however, at his place of residence, is not void for want of jurisdiction, although the property is by law properly assessable in another county where it is kept and used: Clarke v. County of Stearns, 47 Minn. 552. Under the Iowa code, which provides that, if a person is doing business in more than one county, the property kept in one of the counties shall be taxed in that county, the capital invested by a manufacturer residing in one county, but doing business in another, is taxable in the latter county, although there may have been a tem-

porary suspension of business during the year, and a removal of the
property used in carrying on the business, but not of the property
assessed, to the county of the manufacturer's residence: Dean v.
Solon, 97 Iowa, 303, 308. Railroad ties, telegraph poles, and posts
kept for sale are "merchants' goods, wares, and commodities," within
the meaning of the Wisconsin statute, and are taxable where they
are kept for sale, though the owner resides in another county of that
state: Torrey v. Shawano County, 79 Wis. 152. If such property is
purchased in one county, by merchants residing and doing business
in another county, and is left and kept in piles upon a railroad company's right of way, where the purchase is made, until resold by the
owners at their place of business, the property is taxable in the
county where it has been so left and kept: Torrey v. Shawano Co.,
79 Wis. 152. If a manufacturing corporation, organized under the
laws of New York, carries on its operations in two counties of that
state, and its principal financial office is located in one of such
counties, its personal estate is to be taxed in that county: Peter
Cooper's Glue Factory v. McMahon, 15 Abb. N. C. 314. Personal
property in Texas, belonging either to a corporation or a natural
person, is taxable in the county where it is situated, unless such
county has not been organized, in which event it is taxable in the
county to which such county has been attached for judicial purposes: Llang Cattle Co. v. Faught, 69 Tex. 402; or in the nearest
organized county: Dupree v. Stanley Co., 8 S. Dak. 30.

If a person resides in a town in Indiana, and his personal property belongs elsewhere, such property is not taxable by the town:
Eversole v. Cook, 92 Ind. 222. A permanent resident of one town,
having been assessed therein on his personal property, including his
credits, cannot be assessed on such credits in another town of the
same county: Sivwright v. Pierce, 108 Ill. 133. In North Carolina,
the legislature has provided that shares of stock in a corporation
doing business outside the corporate limits of a town, and owned by
persons residing therein shall be taxed at the principal place of
business of the corporation. They are not, therefore, taxable by
the town: Wiley v. Commissioners, 111 N. C. 397, 402. A town, having authority under its charter to tax the property of nonresidents
"doing business within the limits" of the town, upon their respective
avocations and business, stock in trade, and "solvent credits" growing "out of their business located as above, just as though they
were actual residents," is not empowered to tax money held by a
nonresident administrator of a decedent who died in the town, although the administrator has an office in the town: Hall v. Fayetteville, 115 N. C. 281. Under a statute providing that "horses kept
throughout the year in places other than those where the owners
reside shall be assessed to the owners in the places where they are
kept," a person who owns a farm situated in two towns, with a
house in one and a barn in the other, is taxable in the latter for his
horses, which are habitually kept, fed, and watered in the barn,
although used on the entire farm: Pierce v. Eddy, 152 Mass. 594.

In New Jersey, "visible personal estate" must be assessed for taxes
in the township, ward, or taxing district where it is found: State

v. Dalrymple, 56 N. J. L. 449; and personal chattels of nonresidents
are there to be taxed in the township where they are found: State
v. Ross, 23 N. J. L. 517. Lumber is assessable to the owners in the
township where it is piled: Hood v. Judkins, 61 Mich. 575; but if a
lumber company has its office in a city, and has no yard, and pays
no taxes there, its lumber may be taxed in a remote township where,
by contract with a company that has its mill and storageroom there,
it is manufactured and piled on the latter's docks, from which,
after remaining until it is seasoned, it is taken by purchasers: Manis-
tique Lumbering Co. v. Witter, 58 Mich. 625.

Property in Trade—Business by Agents.—Personal property employed
in trade is taxable in the town where it is so employed: Gower
v. Jonesboro, 83 Me. 142. Railway cars used by a manufacturer in
the transportation of his manufactures are properly taxable with
the stock in trade as appurtenant to the business: Comstock v.
Grand Rapids, 54 Mich. 641. Under a statute providing that personal
property pertaining to the business of a merchant shall be taxable
in the town or district where his business is carried on, the property
is taxable where it is kept for sale. The mere buying of property
in some town or district other than that of his residence does not
render it assessable at the place of purchase: Minneapolis etc. Elevator Co. v. Board of Commrs., 60 Minn. 522. So, under a statute
providing that personal property pertaining to the business of a
manufacturer shall be taxable in the town or district where the business is carried on, if a person hires the owners of a manufacturing
plant to have his materials manufactured for him he becomes himself a manufacturer, and may be taxed at the place of such plant
on materials in transit to that place, to be there so manufactured for
him, although he resides elsewhere in the state, and owns and
operates a similar manufacturing plant at the place of his residence: State v. Clarke, 64 Minn. 556. "Merchants' goods, wares,
and commodities" are taxable where they are kept for sale: Torrey
v. Shawano County, 79 Wis. 152. Lumber is "merchants' goods,"
and taxable where it is located, irrespective of the residence of the
owner or his agent, although no sales are made at such place, if
actual sales are made while it is there, and it is delivered from that
place to the purchasers: Washburn v. Oshkosh, 60 Wis. 453; Sanford
v. Spencer, 62 Wis. 230. But debts due are not included within the
term "all goods, wares, merchandise, and other stock in trade"
made taxable by statute: New York Biscuit Co. v. Cambridge, 161
Mass. 326. If an executor keeps his testator's former shop open and
sells the goods therein, replenishing the stock, occasionally, with
small purchases, although for the sole purpose of settling the estate and closing the business, the stock of goods is taxable, under the
Massachusetts statute, in the city where the shop is hired and the
business carried on, although the testator last dwelt in another city:
Cotton v. Boston, 161 Mass. 8. Under the Massachusetts statute,
"all machinery employed in any branch of manufactures shall be assessed where such machinery is situated or employed; but an assessment thereunder is not necessarily limited to machinery which has
been affixed to land in such a manner as to become a part of the

real estate: Troy Cotton etc. Mfy. v. Fall River, 167 Mass. 517, 522. But quarrying stone and crushing it for use on roads and other similar purposes is not a manufacturing business within such statute: Wellington v. Belmont, 164 Mass. 142. Neither is the cutting of ice on the surface of a pond, and storing the pieces so cut in a building, a "manufacture," so as to render the machinery employed therein taxable to the owner: Hittinger v. Westford, 135 Mass. 258. As to what makes a "place of business," and what does and does not constitute "stock in trade" within the meaning of the Massachusetts statutes, relative to taxation, see Cloutman v. Concord, 163 Mass. 444; Barker v. Watertown, 137 Mass. 227; Farwell v. Hathaway, 151 Mass. 242; Singer Mfg. Co. v. County Commrs., 139 Mass. 266.

If a nonresident of the state surrenders the possession of his property, such as money and choses in action, to the control of agents in another state who have power to manage, loan, or invest the same there, he thereby subjects such property to the jurisdiction of that state for the purposes of taxation. The legal fiction that the situs of such property is at the domicile of the owner yields to the requirements of justice, and the actual situs is the place where the property is actually situated and employed in business, and where such agent resides: Billinghurst v. Spink County, 5 S. Dak. 84; note to New Albany v. Meekin, 56 Am. Dec. 530; Bowman v. Boyd, 21 Nev. 281; Bluefields Banana Co. v. Board of Assessors, 49 La. Ann. 43; State v. Board of Assessors, 47 La. Ann. 1544. There is no distinction between money and other special or personal property, in the application of this principle: Billinghurst v. Spink County, 5 S. Dak. 84, 98; Hutchinson v. Board of Equalization, 66 Iowa, 35; Board of Supervisors v. Davenport, 40 Ill. 197; Bluefields Banana Co. v. Board of Assessors, 49 La. Ann. 43; and the rule applies to "credits" invested or used in business, in one state by a resident of another: Grant v. Jones, 39 Ohio St. 506; Board of Supervisors v. Davenport, 40 Ill. 197; In re Jefferson, 35 Minn. 215. Contra, Jack v. Walker, 79 Fed. Rep. 138. As said in a Minnesota case: "For many purposes the domicile of the owner is deemed the situs of his personal property. This however, is only a fiction from motives of convenience, and is not of universal application, but yields to the actual situs of the property when justice requires that it should. It is not allowed to be controlling in matters of taxation. Thus, corporeal personal property is conceded to be taxable at the place where it is actually situated. A credit, which cannot be regarded as situated in a place merely because the debtor resides there, must usually be considered as having its situs where it is owned—at the domicile of the creditor. The creditor, however, may give it a business situs elsewhere, as where he places it in the hands of an agent for collection or renewal, with a view to reloaning the money and keeping it invested as a permanent business": See In re Jefferson, 35 Minn. 215, 220, and numerous cases there cited; Goldgart v. People, 106 Ill. 25. In order, however, to render such property liable to taxation elsewhere than at the domicile of its owner, its situs must be "permanent" in its nature, though not so permanent as real estate. Otherwise it is taxable at the owner's residence: Boyd v. Selma,

96 Ala. 144, 155. Compare State v. Gaylord, 73 Wis. 316. If, however, money is loaned to a person in this state by a nonresident having no agent here, the loan is not taxable in this state, though secured by a mortgage on property here, where the loan was accomplished outside of this state, though the negotiations for it were made in this state: State v. Smith, 68 Miss. 79. A statute providing for the assessment and taxation of money loaned or employed in this state applies only where the person owning the same, and upon whom a tax is to be imposed, resides, or has a place of business, or a location, or agent, within the state: State v. Smith, 68 Miss. 79. Such a statute is constitutional: Hutchinson v. Board of Equalization, 66 Iowa, 35.

Property Consisting of Livestock.—It is not necessary that the owner should reside within the state to render personal property, such as livestock, situated within the state, liable to taxation: Hardesty v. Fleming, 57 Tex. 395. If cattle owned in another state or terrritory actually range or graze in a certain county of this state during the entire year, they are taxable in that county of this state: Prairie Cattle Co. v. Williamson, 5 Oklahoma, 488. But livestock purchased abroad after May 1st are not taxable for that year in Colorado: Board of Commrs. v. Wilson, 15 Colo. 90. Compare Graham v. Board of Commrs,. 31 Kan. 473, showing that it is unconstitutional to tax migratory cattle.

Cattle in pastures which lie in two or more counties of the same state are taxable, under the Texas statute, in the several counties, in the proportion which the pasture land in each county bears to the whole pasture: Nolan v. San Antonio Ranch Co., 81 Tex. 315, 316. If the owner of cattle or horses resides in one county but his stock graze in another county, or are kept there, they are taxable in the latter county: Note to New Albany v. Meekin, 56 Am. Dec. 527; State v. Falkinburge, 15 N. J. L. 320; Graham v. Board of Commrs., 31 Kan. 473; Smith v. Mason, 48 Kan. 586; notwithstanding they are managed and controlled from the "home ranch" of the county in which the owner resides: State v. Shaw, 21 Nev. 222. If, however, the animals are kept at the "home ranch" a portion of the year, though they may roam and graze in other counties a part of the time, their situs, for the purpose of taxation, is at the "home ranch," where they belong: Barnes v. Woodbury, 17 Nev. 383; Ford v. McGregor, 20 Nev. 446; Whitmore v. McGregor, 20 Nev. 451; Holcomb v. Keliher, 5 S. Dak. 438; People v. Caldwell, 142 Ill. 434. So, where they are fed only a portion of the time in another county and are then moved to the home farm: People v. Caldwell, 142 Ill. 434. A statute requiring livestock connected with a farm upon which the owner does not reside to be assessed in the district where such farm is situated, does not apply where the farm on which the animals are kept lies in several districts or two different counties, and the animals pass from one part of the farm to another: People v. Caldwell, 142 Ill. 434.

Property of Partnership.—Personal property belonging to a partnership is assessable in the locality where it is situated, if the firm has its place of business there: Williams v. Saginaw, 51 Mich. 120; Hopkins v. Baker, 78 Md. 363; Tide Water Pipe Co. v. State Board

of Assessors, 57 N. J. L. 516; but logs cannot be taxed in the township where they have been temporarily left afloat for sawing, if the
firm owning the property has its place of business in another township and the partners live elsewhere: Torrent v. Yager, 52 Mich. 506.

Property of Decedents.—If there is no statute to the contrary, the
situs of the personal property of a decedent is at the last domicile
of the testator. It is, therefore, taxable there and not elsewhere:
Staunton v. Stout, 86 Va. 321; note to New Albany v. Meekin, 56
Am. Dec. 536; San Francisco v. Lux, 64 Cal. 481. Some cases, however, hold that the personalty of a decedent may be taxed at the
executor's residence: Note to New Albany v. Meekin, 56 Am. Dec.
536. Compare Hayden v. Roe, 66 Wis. 288. If a portion of the
mortgages and moneys of a decedent's estate is in the possession of
each of two executors residing in different townships of one county,
the part held by each should, under the Iowa statute, be assessed
where the executor having it lives, though the decedent lived in the
township of the other executor. But if personal property in the
possession of an executor, residing in one township, has a fixed
location in another, the property is not necessarily taxable in the
township of the executor's residence; neither does it follow, from
the mere fact that personal property is in a given taxation district
at the time when an assessment is required to be made, that it
must be assessed in that district. Yet personal property, in the
possession of an executor, in the township of his residence, is taxable there: Burns v. McNally, 90 Iowa, 432, 440. For the purposes of the application of the transfer tax act of New York, it is
not important whether the transferees reside in that state, or elsewhere, at the time of the imposition of the tax: Matter of Green,
153 N. Y. 223.

Property of Infants.—The personal property of a ward, in Iowa,
is assessable only in the county where the guardian lives: Hinkhouse
v. Wilton, 94 Iowa, 254; but under the Maryland statute it is taxable
in the county where the guardian was appointed, although both
guardian and ward reside in another county: Baldwin v. Commissioners, 85 Md. 145. Compare note to New Albany v. Meekin, 56 Am.
Dec. 535.

Property Held in Trust.—Except as controlled by statute, personal
property subject to a trust must be assessed at the trustee's domicile, that being the domicile of the legal owner: Note to New Albany v. Meekin, 56 Am. Dec. 535, discussing the subject; Guthrie v.
Pittsburgh etc. Ry., 158 Pa. St. 433, 438; Price v. Hunter, 34 Fed.
Rep. 355; Clark v. Powell, 62 Vt. 442; Walla Walla v. Moore, 16
Wash. 339; 58 Am. St. Rep. 31. "There seems," says Stiness, J., in
Allman, Petitioner, 17 R. I. 362, "to have been substantial uniformity in holding a trustee liable to taxation for property held by him
within the state in which the tax is assessed." Thus, mortgages held
by a trustee in Rhode Island, are taxable in that state, although he
was appointed by a South Carolina court under the will of a deceased
resident of that state, and the cestui que trust, who has the permanency of the income of the trust estate resides in New York: Allman, Petitioner, 17 R. I. 362. A state has the power to tax property

within its borders held by a resident trustee for a nonresident cestui que trust: Price v. Hunter, 34 Fed. Rep. 355. A statute providing that personal estate "held in trust" shall be taxable applies to any such estate which is, in fact, a trust fund: Clark v. Powell, 62 Vt. 442.

The Massachusetts statute in respect to personal property held in trust provides that if the "trustee is not an inhabitant of the commonwealth, it shall be assessed to the person to whom the income is payable in the place where he resides." This statute has been held to be constitutional, and to apply to a case where the trust was created by the will of a testator who lived and died in another state, and whose will was proved and allowed in such state, but never proved in Massachusetts: Hunt v. Perry, 165 Mass. 287.

Upon the death of the owner of personal property, leaving a will and appointing executors, who by the duties imposed upon them are really made trustees of his estate, the situs of such personal property, for the purposes of taxation, is at the domicile of such executors, and not in that of the decedent at the time of his death: Walla Walla v. Moore, 16 Wash. 339; 58 Am. St. Rep. 31; State v. Jones, 39 N. J. L. 650. A tax upon personal property in possession, or under control, of an executor should be against the person holding the office in his representative character, and such tax can be assessed only in the township where the executor resides, for all such property wherever situated: State v. Collector, 39 N. J. L. 79. If of three executors of the same estate, two of them reside within the corporate limits of a village, the other without such limits, and the three have possession, in law, of the taxable moneys, credits, bonds, and stocks of the estate, each executor is taxable, at his place of residence, with one-third thereof: State v. Matthews, 10 Ohio St. 432. An administrator with the will annexed stands like an executor in reference to a trust fund, and, in Vermont, if none of the beneficiaries entitled to the income reside in that state, the fund is taxable where the administrator resides: Clark v. Powell, 62 Vt. 442.

A trustee residing in another state, but holding no property in this state, is not taxable here at the place where his cestui que trust resides: Anthony v. Caswell, 15 R. I. 159; People v. Coleman, 119 N. Y. 137, 140. A trustee residing here, and having possession of securities, may be assessed for them as a trustee in possession, even if there are other trustees nonresidents, but a resident trustee cannot be assessed for securities not held by him and not within the state, but which are in the possession of one of the nonresident trustees. So, if two of three cotrustees reside in this state, and the other resides in another state, and the beneficiaries are also nonresidents, an assessment of securities in the hands of the nonresident trustee is void: People v. Coleman, 119 N. Y. 137. The New York statute provides that "all debts and obligations for the payment of money due or owing to persons residing within this state, however secured, or wherever such securities shall be held, shall be deemed, for the purposes of taxation, personal estate within the state, and shall be assessed as such, to the owner or owners thereof, in the town, village, or ward in which such

owner or owners shall reside at the time such assessment shall be
made, etc."; but this statute is held not to apply to trust property in
the form of securities on property out of the state, where the cestui
que trust and remaindermen all live without the state. Such property is not taxable in New York: People v. Commissioners, 21 Abb.
N. C. 168. If trustees as tenants in common own choses in action
which are taxable as private property, and some of the trustees
reside within, and some without, the limits of a city, it may tax the
shares of those trustees residing within pro rata, but it cannot tax
the shares of those residing without the city limits; and this is true
irrespective of the question as to whether a majority or minority of
the trustees reside in the city: Trustees v. City Council, 90 Ga. 634.

Property of Corporations.—A state may tax corporate property
found within its limits: Pullman Palace Car Co. v. Pennsylvania,
141 U. S. 18, 25. A corporation is legally taxable at its place of
business: Portland v. Union Mut. Life Ins. Co., 79 Me. 231, 232. For
the purposes of taxation the domicile of a domestic corporation is,
in the absence of other controlling charter or statutory provisions,
at the place fixed for the regular meetings of the stockholders,
although its directors may meet, its officers reside, and much of its
business be transacted, at other places in and out of the state,
where it also has offices; Grundy County v. Tennessee Coal Co.,
94 Tenn. 295. But the holding of a charter from one state, when
the corporate property is located or corporate business transacted
in another state does not relieve the corporation in both or either
state from taxation, in any form which the legislative power may,
under its constitution, adopt: Standard etc. Cable Co. v. Attorney
General, 46 N. J. Eq. 270; 19 Am. St. Rep. 394.

The capital stock of a corporation, as well as its shares of stock,
may be taxed, for they are distinct things, and it is not double taxation: State Bank v. Richmond, 79 Va. 113. All of the capital stock
of a corporation formed by consolidating corporations of different
states is properly taxable in one of such states, as the corporate
existence springs from the legislation of the state seeking to impose
such tax, and the corporation is to be regarded and treated by
the authorities of such state as domiciled there, and liable to taxation upon all its property which is of such a nature as to be taxable
at the residence of the owner. "The kind of property denominated
as 'capital stock' does not mean shares of stock, either separately
or in the aggregate, but designates the property of the corporation
subject to taxation as an homogeneous unit, partaking of the nature
of personalty, and subject to the burdens imposed upon it at the
domicile of the owner": Keokuk etc. Bridge Co. v. People, 161 Ill.
132, 142. The power of taxation, however, being limited to subjects
within the jurisdiction of the state, the whole of the capital stock of
foreign corporations cannot be taxed irrespective of its place of investment; but its capital stock may be taxed to the extent that it
brings such property, that is, the capital stock, within the state
in the transaction of its business. Thus, in Commonwealth v.
Standard Oil Co., 101 Pa. St. 119, it was held that the Standard Oil
Company, an Ohio corporation, had not, by any of its transactions,

brought all of its capital stock into Pennsylvania actually or constructively; that it was not taxable in Pennsylvania upon such portion of its capital stock as represented shares of stock owned by it in Pennsylvania corporations, or its interest in limited partnerships of that state; and that it was not taxable upon that portion of its capital stock which represented the capital used in the purchases of petroleum in Pennsylvania, bought through brokers and others in that state, without making a permanent investment there, and which petroleum was shipped to and refined at the refineries of the company beyond the limits of the state. The capital stock of a bank is to be taxed in the county where such bank is located: Bank of Bramwell v. County Court, 36 W. Va. 341. If a corporation created by the laws of a sister state employs the whole or any part of its capital here, and thus has the benefit and protection of the government and laws of the state to the extent of the capital so employed, there is no reason why it should not be subject, to the extent of such capital, to the same burdens and obligations as a domestic corporation: People v. Wemple, 131 N. Y. 64; 27 Am. St. Rep. 542. For a further discussion as to the place where the property of corporations is to be taxed, see the extended note to New Albany v. Meekin, 56 Am Dec. 531. See, also, subdivisions, supra, "Taxation of Bonds,' and "Taxation of Shares of Stock."

Property of National Banks—Stock.—It seems that shares in national banks are in the nature of choses in action: First Nat. Bank v. Smith, 65 Ill. 44. They are personal property, and, although they are, in one sense, a species of intangible and incorporeal personal property, the law creating them had power to separate them from the person of their owner for the purpose of taxation, and give them a situs of their own: Tappan v. Merchants' Nat. Bank, 19 Wall. 490. Hence, shares in such banks may be taxed by the state, at the place where the banks are located, without regard to the domicile or place of residence of the shareholders: First Nat. Bank v. Smith, 65 Ill. 44; Tappan v. Merchants' Nat. Bank, 19 Wall. 490. In the absence of any special provision made for the taxation of such shares, the owner thereof should be taxed therefor in the city or town where he resides, and not in the city or town where the bank is located: Clapp v. Burlington, 42 Vt. 579; 1 Am. Rep. 355. Stock of a national bank cannot be taxed by any state except that within which the bank is located, it having been withdrawn from taxation under the authority of other states: De Baun v. Smith, 55 N. J. L. 110: Tappan v. Merchants' Nat. Bank, 19 Wall. 490. Thus, shares of capital stock in a national bank located in New York City, and owned by a resident of Boston, Massachusetts, cannot be assessed to the latter in Massachusetts: Flint v. Board of Aldermen, 99 Mass. 141; 96 Am. Dec. 713. The Massachusetts statute providing for taxing national bank shares owned by nonresidents has been held not to be unconstitutional: Providence Inst. v. Boston, 101 Mass. 575. The power of states to tax shares, capital stock, real estate, or other property of national banks, is discussed in the extended note to Commonwealth v. First Nat. Bank, 96 Am. Dec. 290-297. See, also, subdivision, supra, "Taxation of Shares of Stock," and note to New

Albany v. Meekin, 56 Am. Dec. 530, showing where national bank
stock is to be taxed.

Property of Railroad Companies—Rolling Stock, etc.—Two modes
of assessment for taxation are prescribed in some of the states; one
by a state board of equalization; the other, by county boards and
local assessors: See Cal. Const., art. 13; Quincy etc. Ry. Co. v. People, 156 Ill. 437; California v. Central Pac. R. R. Co., 127 U. S. 1.
But it is within the power of the legislature of the state, unless restrained by some constitutional provision, to provide in any proper
manner for the valuation of railroad property and to fix its situs
for the purpose of taxation: Dubuque v. Chicago etc. R. R. Co., 47
Iowa, 196, 202. In Georgia, railroad companies are subject to
municipal taxation. Thus, if a railroad runs through several counties, the unlocated personalty of the corporation may be taxed in the
several counties, in the proper proportions, as the corporation is to
be considered as "residing sub modo in all the counties along its line
of road; and therefore in one as much as in the other": Sparks v.
Mayor, 98 Ga. 301. So, in Nebraska, the personal property of a railroad company outside of its right of way is taxable by the counties
in which it is situated, without regard to the use for which it is
designed: Chicago etc. R. R. Co. v. Hitchock County, 40 Neb. 781,
See Sangamon etc. R. R. Co. v. County of Morgan, 14 Ill. 163; 56 Am.
Dec. 497.

If a railroad runs into or through two or more states, its value, for
the purpose of taxation, in each state, is fairly estimated by taking
that part of the value of the entire road which is measured by the
proportion of the length of the particular part in that state to that
of the whole road: Pittsburgh etc. Ry. Co. v. Backus, 154 U. S. 421;
New York etc. R. R. Co. v. Pennsylvania, 158 U. S. 431; and the
stocks and bonds of an interstate railway are liable to taxation by
any state in which it is situate in proportion to the length of the
road in such state: Pittsburg etc. Ry. Co. v. Commonwealth, 66 Pa.
St. 73; 5 Am. Rep. 344.

The rolling stock of a railroad company is personal property:
Randall v. Elwell, 52 N. Y. 521; 11 Am. Rep. 747; Baltimore etc. R. R.
Co. v. Allen, 22 Fed. Rep. 376; though it has been held to be within
the power of the legislature to treat it as real property, for the purposes of taxation: Louisville etc. R. R. Co. v. State, 25 Ind. 177; 87
Am. Dec. 358. A state has a right to tax all personal property found
within its jurisdiction, without regard to the place of the owner's
domicile. It has the right, therefore, to tax railway cars found within its boundaries, although they are engaged in interstate commerce,
and, though used, are not owned by the company to which they are
assessed: Denver etc. Ry. Co. v. Church, 17 Colo. 1; 31 Am. St. Rep.
252; Pullman Palace Car Co. v. Pennsylvania, 141 U. S. 18;
Pullman Palace Car Co. v. Hayward, 141 U. S. 36; Pullman Palace Car Co. v. Twombly, 29 Fed. Rep. 658. It has been held, on
the contrary, that the rolling stock of a foreign railroad company
passing across the state for the purpose of interstate commerce is
not subject to taxation in that state: Bain v. Richmond etc. R. R.
Co., 105 N. C. 363; 18 Am. St. Rep. 912. Vehicles of transportation,

such as sleeping, drawingroom, and parlor cars, used constantly and continuously upon a single run, acquire a situs, however, according to the better opinion, for the purpose of taxation, independent and irrespective of the domicile of the owner; and such situs is not destroyed by the fact that the owner, having many vehicles of like character, and lines in various parts of the United States, transfers them now and then from one line to another, provided a constant and continuous use of such vehicles is preserved upon the single run. If such vehicles are used upon a run extending through two states, there is a situs for taxation in each state according to a fair proportion of the value of the property so used: Pullman Palace Car Co. v. Twombly, 29 Fed. Rep. 658.

All rolling stock owned, used, or operated by a domestic railway company is, by the Colorado statues, placed upon the same footing with reference to state taxation, regardless of the interest, as lessee or owner, of the company so operating it. It is not exempt from taxation merely because, in performing its regular journeys, it sometimes passes out of the state and becomes temporarily useful in operating other railroads: Denver etc. Ry. Co. v. Church, 17 Colo. 1; 31 Am. St. Rep. 252. Pullman sleeping-cars controlled and operated by a domestic railway company, though owned by a foreign corporation, may be assessed to the domestic corporation for state taxes when found within the borders of the state: Denver etc. Ry. Co. v. Church, 17 Colo. 1; 31 Am. St. Rep. 252; Pullman Palace Car Co. v. Pennsylvania, 141 U. S. 18, 25; Carlisle v. Pullman Palace Car Co., 8 Colo. 320; 54 Am. Rep. 553; although they are employed one-third of the time outside the state in the transaction of business: Denver etc. Ry. Co. v. Church, 17 Colo. 1; 31 Am. St. Rep. 252. Compare Kennedy v. St. Louis etc. R. R. Co., 62 Ill. 395. On the other hand, it is held that rolling stock owned by a railroad incorporated under the laws of one state, and employed in operating railroads leased by it in another state, is personal property taxable to the road in the state of its domicile and not in the state where it is so used; and that the rolling stock of the Baltimore and Ohio Railroad Company, a foreign corporation, used in operating leased roads in the state of Virginia, is not liable to taxation under the laws of that state: Baltimore etc. R. R. Co. v. Allen, 22 Fed. Rep. 376; Marye v. Baltimore etc. R. R. Co., 127 U. S. 117. So, a railroad company in Missouri cannot be taxed, under the laws of that state, for cars of the Pullman Palace Car Company, leased and operated by it: State v. St. Louis Co., 84 Mo. 234. For other cases showing where the rolling stock of railroads is to be taxed, see note to New Albany v. Meekin, 56 Am. Dec. 535.

Property Consisting of Vessels.—Unless vessels registered under the laws of the United States have an actual situs elsewhere, they are taxable at their home port, the domicile of their owners: Hayes v. Pacific Mail S. S. Co., 17 How. 596; Morgan v. Parham, 16 Wall. 471; St. Louis v. Ferry Co., 11 Wall. 423; Wiggins Ferry Co. v. East St. Louis, 107 U. S. 365; Johnson v. De Bary-Baya Merchants' Line, 37 Fla. 499. As said by the supreme court of the United States: "Ships or vessels, indeed, engaged in interstate or foreign commerce upon the high seas or other waters which are a common highway, and having their home port, at which they are registered under the laws of. the United States, at the domicile of their owners in one state, are not subject to taxation in another state at whose ports they incidentally and temporarily touch for the purpose of delivering or receiving passengers or freight. But that is because they are not, in any proper sense, abiding within its limits, and have no continuous or actual situs within its jurisdiction, and therefore, can be taxed only. at their legal situs, their home port and the domicile of their owners"; Pullman Palace Car Co. v. Pennsylvania, 141 U. S. 18. The "home port" of a regularly registered vessel is the port nearest to which her owner, husband, or acting and managing owner usually resides: Morgan v. Parham, 16 Wall. 471; Johnson v. De Bary Baya Merchants' Line, 37 Fla. 499. But if a tugboat, steamboat, or other vessel is regularly employed in business in one state, though the vessel is registered at the port of the owner's domicile in another state, it is taxable in the former state, especially where its business is wholly within the former state, and the vessel is to remain there for an indefinite time. It may then be said to "abide" there, and becomes incorporated with the property of the state. Where situs is shown, "neither foreign registry nor foreign ownership is of any consequence"; National Dredging Co. v. State, 99 Ala. 462; Lott v. Mobile Trade Co., 43 Ala. 578, 581; Lott v. Morgan, 41 Ala. 246; Pomeroy Salt Co. v. Davis, 21 Ohio St. 555; Irvin v. New Orleans etc. R. R. Co., 94 Ill. 105; 34 Am. Rep. 208; Battle v. Mobile, 9 Ala. 234; 44 Am. Dec. 438; St. Louis v. Consolidated Coal Co., 113 Mo. 84. In Michigan, however, it is held that a vessel enrolled and licensed or registered under the navigation laws of the United States, and owned by a nonresident, does not become subject to the taxing power of that state by engaging in business therein: Roberts v. Charlevoix, 60 Mich. 197.

As vessels having no actual situs elsewhere are taxable at the owner's residence, a vessel sailing from the port in which the owner resides is not taxable in another county from the fact that it is temporarily in such county for the purpose of being freighted: People v. Niles, 35 Cal. 282. A share of the part owner of a steamboat occasionally touching at a city in which he resides, but not enrolled or usually lying there, is not taxable there under a charter providing for the taxation of property within that city: New Albany v. Meekin, 3 Ind. 481; 56 Am. Dec. 522. Under the Indiana statute, all watercraft is taxable at the place of the owner's residence, without regard to its actual situation: Cook v. Port Fulton, 106 Ind. 170. Steamboats may be taxed where the owner resides, though they are navigated beyond the boundary of the state; and a statute requiring them to be so taxed is constitutional: Perry v. Torrence, 8 Ohio, 521; 32 Am. Dec. 725.

In Pennsylvania, it is held that unregistered vessels, not permanently located anywhere, have their situs for taxation at the domicile of their owner, although, if registered, they are taxable at their home port of registry. Hence, unregistered vessels belonging to a Pennsylvania corporation, and not permanently located, but carried

from state to state, are held to be taxable in that state, although
they were built out of the state, and some of them were never within
it: Commonwealth v. American Dredging Co., 122 Pa. St. 386; 9
Am. St. Rep. 116. Compare note to New Albany v. Meekin, 56 Am.
Dec. 526, showing that vessels are taxable at their home port.

Property of Nonresidents.—The question as to where the property
of a nonresident is taxable is discussed in the extended note to New
Albany v. Meekin, 56 Am. Dec. 533, 534, as well as elsewhere in this
note. It has been shown in this note that nonresidence is of no
consequence where personal property has an actual situs apart from
the owner's domicile: See National Dredging Co. v. State, 99 Ala.
462, 468. But, where no actual situs is proved, a chose in action
follows the owner; and, if he resides out of the state, the state has
no jurisdiction either of the person or of the thing proposed to
be taxed, and can tax neither: State v. Earl, 1 Nev. 394; Corn v.
Cameron, 19 Mo. App. 573. While personal property may be so
kept and used, within a certain locality, as to be taxable there,
notwithstanding the domicile of the owner, and that he may be
elsewhere, yet this is the exception to the general rule and it devolves upon the authorities seeking to impose the tax to prove that
the property is within their jurisdiction under such circumstances
as to show that it has an actual situs there: Corn v. Cameron, 19
Mo. App. 573. It is, of course, not always necessary that the owner
of personal property should reside within the state to render such
property, situated within the state, liable to taxation: Hardesty v.
Fleming, 57 Tex. 395; but the property, to be taxable here, must have
a situs here. It must be used or employed here, not temporarily,
but permanently. Thus, notes and mortgages belonging to a nonresident, but placed in the hands of an agent in this state for collection
and reloaning in this state are taxable here: Finch v. County of
York, 19 Neb. 50; 56 Am. Rep. 741; but choses in action, such as
mortgages, bonds, notes, accounts, and stocks owned by a nonresident, and left in this state temporarily for safekeeping or merely
for collection, are not taxable here: Herron v. Keeran, 59 Ind. 472;
26 Am. Rep. 87. Cases of this kind are clearly distinguishable from
each other.

Property Imported or Exported.—Imported goods from foreign countries are not subject to taxation under state laws until the packages
are broken, or they have been sold by the importer: Brown v. Maryland, 12 Wheat. 419, 449; Low v. Austin, 13 Wall. 29, 34; Murray v.
Charleston, 96 U. S. 432, 446; State v. Board of Assessors, 46 La.
Ann. 145; 49 Am. St. Rep. 318. Goods imported do not lose their
character as imports, and become incorporated into the mass of
property of the state, until they have passed from the control of
the importer or been broken up by him from their original cases:
Low v. Austin, 13 Wall. 29, 34; but if "the importer has so acted
upon the thing imported that it has become incorporated and mixed
up with the mass of property in the country, it has, perhaps, lost its
distinctive character as an import, and has become subject to the
taxing power of the state": Brown v. Maryland, 12 Wheat. 419;
Murray v. Charleston, 96 U. S. 432, 441. The terms "imports" and

"exports," as used in that clause of the federal constitution which
says that "no state shall levy any imposts or duties on imports or
exports," do not refer to articles transported from one state to
another, but only to articles imported from or carried to foreign
countries: Woodruff v. Parham, 8 Wall. 123; Brown v. Houston, 114
U. S. 622. Property in a state intended for exportation is taxable
in that state so long as it remains a part of the general mass of
property in the state. The owner has a perfect right to change
his mind, and, until the property is actually put in motion, for
some place out of the state, or committed to the custody of a carrier
for transportation to such place, it is taxable there: Coe v. Errol, 116
U. S. 517, 526; Turpin v. Burgess, 117 U. S. 504.

Property Used in Interstate Commerce.—A state has power to tax
all property having a situs within its limits, and property employed
in interstate commerce is not on that account withdrawn from the
power to tax. There must not, however, be any discrimination
against such property because it is so used, nor against property
brought from other states or countries because of that fact. There
is nothing in the constitution or laws of the United States which
prevents a state from taxing personal property, employed in interstate or foreign commerce, like other personal property within its
jurisdiction: Pittsburg etc. Coal Co. v. Bates, 156 U. S. 577; Fick-
len v. Shelby County Taxing Dist., 145 U. S. 1, 16; Pullman Palace
Car Co. v. Pennsylvania, 141 U. S. 18, 23; Pullman Palace Car
Co. v. Hayward, 141 U. S. 36; Coe v. Errol, 116 U. S. 517; affirming
Coe v. Errol, 62 N. H. 303; Brown v. Houston, 114 U. S. 622; Denver etc. Ry. Co. v. Church, 17 Colo. 1; 31 Am. St. Rep. 252; monographic note to People v. Wemple, 27 Am. St. Rep. 560; Pullman
Palace Car Co. v. Twombly, 29 Fed. Rep. 658. Contra, Bain v.
Richmond etc. R. R. Co., 105 N. C. 363; 18 Am. St. Rep. 912. Thus
coal mined in Pennsylvania and sent by water to Louisiana to be sold
in an open market in the city of New Orleans on account of the
Pennsylvania owners becomes mingled, on its arrival there, with the
general property of that state and is taxable under its general laws,
although it may, after its arrival, be sold from the vessel on which
the transportation was had, without being landed, to be taken out
of the country on a vessel bound to a foreign port: Brown v. Houston, 114 U. S. 622, 632. "The coal," said the court, "had come to
its place of rest, for final disposal or use, and was a commodity in
the market of New Orleans. It might continue in that condition
for a year or two years, or only for a day. It had become a part
of the general mass of property in the state, and as such was taxed
for the current year (1880), as all other property in the city of New
Orleans was taxed": Brown v. Houston, 114 U. S. 622, 632. So, coal
shipped by the owners at Pittsburg, Pennsylvania, in their own
barges to Baton Rouge, Louisiana, to supply orders or to be sold
there, is subject to local taxation in the latter state as "stock in
trade," though the coal is moored at Baton Rouge in the original
barges in which it was shipped at Pittsburg: Pittsburg etc. Coal Co.
v. Bates, 156 U. S. 577. Goods brought from one state to another
become lawful objects in the latter state the moment they reach their

destination, and are there kept, ready and offered for sale, at any
point within the place of destination; and it is immaterial that
they remain unloaded on the vessel that brought them, without
being consigned to any particular point or to any specially authorized agent: Pittsburg etc. Coal Co. v. Bates, 40 La. Ann. 226; 8 Am.
St. Rep. 519. The intangible property of express companies is
taxable in the state where such property exists: Adams Exp. Co. v.
Ohio, 165 U. S. 194; American Exp. Co. v. Indiana, 165 U. S. 255,
Adams Exp. Co. v. Ohio, 166 U. S. 185. "No fine-spun theories about
situs," says Mr. Justice Brewer, of the United States supreme court,
"should interfere to enable these large corporations, whose business
is carried on through many states, to escape from bearing in each
state such burden of taxation as a fair distribution of the actual
value of their property among those states require": Adams Exp. Co.
v. Ohio, 166 U. S. 185, 225. It is held in Michigan that lumber
brought into that state after May 1st is not taxable in that state for
the year beginning on that date: Johnson v. Lyon, 106 Ill. 64.
Property intended for exportation from one state to another is taxable in the former state, as a part of the general mass of the property in that state, until actually started in course of transportation
to the state of its destination, or delivered to a common carrier for
that purpose: Coe v. Errol, 116 U. S. 517; affirming Coe v. Errol, 62
N. H. 303; Carrier v. Gordon, 21 Ohio St. 605. Thus, logs cut in New
Hampshire to be transported upon a river to Maine, but waiting at a
place in New Hampshire for a convenient opportunity for such
transportation, are still a part of the general mass of property in
New Hampshire, and liable to taxation in that state, if taxed in
the usual way in which such property is taxed in the state: Coe v.
Errol, 116 U. S. 517. The carrying of property to, and depositing it
at, a depot for the purpose of transportation from one state to
another is no part of that transportation: Coe v. Errol, 116 U. S. 517;
affirming Coe v. Errol, 62 N. H. 303. Property brought into the state
for the purpose of early exportation therefrom is, while in the
hands of the owner and not in the course of transit, property permanently within the state, and as such is subject to state taxation
thereby: Myers v. County Commrs., 83 Md. 385; 55 Am. St. Rep. 349.

Property in Transitu—Property Temporarily Here.—Property in
transitu is not taxable in jurisdictions through which it passes:
See monographic note to New Albany v. Mecklin, 56 Am. Dec. 534;
Brooks v. Arenac, 71 Mich. 231; Pardee v. Freesoil, 74 Mich. 81; Corning v. Masonville, 74 Mich. 175.

Thus cattle in transitu, stopping in a township, for the temporary
rest and refreshment of the drove on a journey, are not taxable therein: State v. Falkinburge, 15 N. J. L. 320, 327. But logs and lumber
piled along a railroad track, awaiting the convenience of the owner,
or facilities for shipment, are not in transit: Maurer v. Cliff, 94
Mich. 194; Plainfield v. Sage, 107 Mich. 19. And logs piled on ice
in a river of one state, awaiting the opening of the river, to be
floated down into another state, to be there manufactured into lumber, are not in transit from one state to another and are taxable

where piled: C. N. Nelson Lumber Co. v. Loraine, 22 Fed. Rep. 54. But it seems that logs banked into a stream, and only awaiting the time of high water to be floated to their place of destination, or assorting ground, are in transit: Corning v. Masonville, 74 Mich. 177.

Personal property is not taxable in a state through which it is merely passing in the usual course of transportation: Coe v. Errol, 62 N. H. 303, affirmed in Coe v. Errol, 116 U. S. 517; Burlington Lumber Co. v. Willetts, 118 Ill. 559; Case of State Freight Tax, 15 Wall. 232; Erie Ry. Co. v. Pennsylvania, 15 Wall. 282. The personal property of a nonresident of Indiana at a railroad station, and awaiting shipment to the residence of the owner, is held to have no permanent situs there, and not to be taxable in that state: Standard Oil Co. v. Bachelor, 89 Ind. 1. Although property in transitu is temporarily detained from any cause, while passing through or across a state, it is not subject to taxation at the place where such detention occurs: State v. Engle, 34 N. J. L. 425; Burlingtou Lumber Co. v. Willetts, 118 Ill. 559; State v. Carrigan, 39 N. J. L. 35; Pardee v. Freesoil, 74 Mich. 81; Coe v. Errol, 116 U. S. 517; affirming Coe v. Errol, 62 N. H. 303. As where it is delayed merely for separation and assortment for shipment: State v. Engle, 34 N. J. L. 425; or where it is delayed within the state awaiting shipment to other states: State v. Carrigan, 39 N. J. L. 35. In such cases, the property has no situs at the point of delay or detention for the purpose of taxation.

Property which is in a state merely for temporary purposes is not taxable there, although the statute provides that "all personal property within the state" shall be taxed: Senour v. Ruth, 140 Ind. 318, 320. Otherwise, bills, notes, and bonds in the possession of a temporary visitor in the state; in fact, those in possession of a traveler passing through it might be taxable in it, as they would be within the state, and come within the letter of the statute: Senour v. Ruth, 140 Ind. 318, 320; Herron v. Keeran, 59 Ind. 472, 26 Am. Rep. 87. A traveling circus and menagerie, owned by a nonresident, and brought into this state, to be exhibited at various places, and then taken into and through other states, for a like purpose, is not taxable here: Robinson v. Longley, 18 Nev. 71. A portable steam sawmill temporarily located in a town is not taxable there as "machinery employed in any branch of manufactures" and "situated or employed" there: Ingram v. Cowles, 150 Mass. 155. But property cannot escape taxation in a given locality on the ground of being temporarily present, or as being in transitu, unless there is at least an intention and fixed purpose to remove it within a reasonable time. An intention to remove it at some future time, depending upon certain contingencies which may or may not happen, is wholly insufficient: State Trust Co. v. Chehalis County, 79 Fed. Rep. 282. "To say," says the court in Carrier v. Gordon, 21 Ohio St. 605, 609, "that the simple purchase of property, with an intention to remove it, would relieve it from liability to taxation, would be to make its liability depend upon the mere intention of the owner, and subject to change as often as the owner changed his intention. There would be no safety or certainty in such a rule. The safer and better rule is the one indicated to consider property actually in transit as belonging to the place of its destination, and property not in transit as property in the place of its situs, without regard to the intention of the owner, or his residence in or out of the state."

TOWNSEND *v.* STATE.

[147 INDIANA, 624.]

CONSTITUTIONAL LAW—WASTE OF PROPERTY.—No one has an inalienable right to waste his property, such as natural gas, to the injury of the public.

CONSTITUTIONAL LAW—WASTE OF NATURAL GAS.—A statute which declares that it is a waste of natural gas to burn it in flambeau lights, and which forbids such use, under penalty of a fine, does not violate those provisions of the federal constitution providing that no person shall be deprived of his property without due process of law.

CONSTITUTIONAL LAW—WASTE OF NATURAL GAS.—A statute which prohibits the burning of natural gas in flambeau lights, for illuminating purposes, does not contravene that clause of the bill of rights which guarantees to every person life, liberty, and the pursuit of happiness.

CONSTITUTIONAL LAW—WASTE OF NATURAL GAS.—A statute which prohibits the waste of natural gas is an exercise of the police power of the state, and the legislative determination that the burning of natural gas, in flambeau lights, is a wasteful use of it, is conclusive on the courts.

CONSTITUTIONAL LAW—WRONG AND UNJUST STATUTES.—Whether a statute encroaches upon the natural rights of the citizen is a legislative, and not a judicial, question, and courts cannot overthrow it upon that ground. They do not deal with the mere justice, propriety, or policy of a statute.

CONSTITUTIONAL LAW—LIMITATIONS UPON LEGISLATIVE POWER.—The only limitations upon the power of the legislature are those imposed by the state constitution, the federal constitution, and valid treaties and acts of Congress.

CONSTITUTIONAL LAW—JUDICIAL ACTION BY LEGISLATURE.—The legislature does not exercise judicial functions by declaring that the use of natural gas in flambeau lights is a wasteful and extravagant use thereof. Such a declaration in a preamble would not invalidate an act, even if it were judicial action, as the preamble is not an essential part of the statute.

CRIMINAL LAW—WASTE OF NATURAL GAS.—The offense created by a statute which prohibits the burning of natural gas in flambeau lights, thereby wasting it, is a continuous one, and a conviction therefor bars another prosecution for all violations of the statute by the defendant prior to the prosecution pending. Hence, evidence that he burnt natural gas, in a flambeau light, prior to the time charged is admissible.

APPEAL.—ERROR NOT PRESENTED BY THE RECORD cannot be considered on appeal.

John Cantwell, S. W. Cantwell, and L. B. Simmons, for the appellant.

W. A. Ketcham, attorney general, Merrill Moores, Jay A. Hindman, A. M. Waltz, J. C. Blacklidge, and C. C. Shirley, for the appellee.

⁶²⁵ McCABE, J. The appellant was prosecuted before a justice of the peace by affidavit charging that on the ninth day of October, 1895, and at divers other times at said county of Blackford and state of Indiana, before that, he did then and there knowingly and unlawfully use, light, and burn natural gas for illuminating purposes in what is known as flambeau light. The justice overruled a motion to quash the affidavit ⁶²⁶ and upon a trial found the defendant guilty, assessing his fine at one dollar and rendered judgment upon the finding and for costs, fr m which he appealed to the Blackford circuit court. He there renewed his motion to quash, which that court overruled, and, upon his plea of not guilty, a jury, upon a trial, found him guilty, fixing his punishment at a fine of one dollar, upon which the court rendered judgment over appellant's motion for a new trial. The assignment of errors calls in question the rulings above named, which rulings are the only questions presented by this appeal.

The statute, with a violation of which appellant was charged in the affidavit, provides that: "The use of natural gas for illuminating purposes, in what are known as flambeau lights, is a wasteful and extravagant use thereof, and is dangerous to the public good, and it shall therefore be unlawful for any company, corporation, or person, for hire, pay, or otherwise, to use natural gas for illuminating purposes in what are known as flambeau lights in cities, towns, highways, or elsewhere; provided, that nothing herein contained shall be construed as to prohibit any such company, corporation, or person from the necessary use of such gas in what are known as 'jumbo' burners inclosed in glass globes, or lamps, or by the use of other burners of similar character so inclosed, as will consume no more gas than said 'jumbo' burners": Burns' Rev. Stats. 1894, sec. 2316 (Acts 1891, sec. 1, p. 55).

Section 3 of the act provides that on conviction the person so convicted shall be deemed guilty of a misdemeanor and fined in any sum not exceeding twenty-five dollars, and for a second offense in any sum not exceeding two hundred dollars: Burns' Rev. Stats. 1894, sec. 2318 (Acts 1891, sec. 3, p. 55).

It is contended that the circuit court ought to have sustained the motion to quash the affidavit because [627] the act violates the provision in the fourteenth amendment to the federal constitution that no state shall "deprive any person of life, liberty, or property without due process of law," in that it deprives the owner of a gaswell of his property in the gas; and also that it violates the fifth amendment of the federal constitution providing that "no person shall be deprived of life, liberty, or property without due process of law." Also that it violates section 1 of the bill of rights of the state constitution, declaring "that all men are created equal; that they are endowed by their Creator with certain inalienable rights; that among these are life, liberty, and the pursuit of happiness"; also the twenty-first section providing that : "No man's property shall be taken by law without just compensation," and also section 23 providing that: "The general assembly shall not grant to any citizen, or class of citizens, privileges or immunities which upon the same terms shall not equally belong to all citizens." Counsel have not pointed out or explained how the act violates this last provision in the bill of rights, nor do we see or know how it can do so, and hence we conclude that it does not.

Nor have they pointed out or explained how it violates the provision securing the inalienable right to life, liberty, and the pursuit of happiness to each individual, and we are unable to perceive how it does so. While our republican government guarantees the right to pursue one's own happiness, yet that government is charged with the duty of protecting others than appellant in the pursuit of their happiness, and hence the inalienable right to pursue one's own happiness must necessarily be subject to the same right in all others. Hence, when that right is asserted in such a manner as to conflict with the equal right to the same thing in others, it is not an inalienable right, nor [623] a right at all, but is a wrong. This demonstrates the wisdom of the maxim that true liberty must be regulated and restrained by law. If, therefore, it makes appellant happy to waste natural gas for the want of which others are made to suffer and be unhappy, as the direct result of such waste, then the pursuit of such happiness is not an inalienable right but a positive wrong. That leaves no objection to consider except that it deprives the individual of property without due process of law, or without compensation in violation of the provisions quoted from the federal and state constitutions.

It is agreed on both sides that the act is an exercise of, and that it calls into exercise, the police power of the state.

It is true that natural gas when brought to the surface and secured in pipes is property belonging to the person in whose pipes it is secured: State v. Indiana etc. Min. Co., 120 Ind. 575; Jamieson v. Indiana etc. Oil Co., 128 Ind. 555.

But the act in no way deprives the owner of the full and free use of his property. It restrains him from wasting the gas to the injury of others, to the injury of the public.

It might present a very different and serious question whether the legislature has the power to prevent him from wasting his own property, if by so doing he in no way injured others as appellant's learned counsel erroneously assume.

In People's Gas Co. v. Tyner, 131 Ind. 281, 282, 31 Am. St. Rep. 433, this court, appropriating the language of the supreme court of Pennsylvania in Westmoreland etc. Gas Co. v. De Witt, 130 Pa. St. 235, said: "Water and oil, and still more strongly gas, may be classed by themselves, if the analogy be not too fanciful, as minerals ferae naturae. In common with animals, and unlike [620] other minerals, they have the power and tendency to escape without the volition of the owner. Their 'fugitive and wandering existence within the limits of a particular tract is uncertain.' . . . . They belong to the owner of the land, and are a part of it, so long as they are on or in it, and are subject to his control; but when they escape, and go into other land, or come under another's control, the title of the other owner is gone. Possession of the land, therefore, is not necessarily possession of the gas. If an adjoining, or even a distant, owner, drills his own land, and taps your gas, so that it comes into his well and under his control it is no longer yours but his." It is not to prevent an adjoining or a distant owner from doing this that the act in question was passed. But it was to prevent him from needlessly wasting the gas which he is drawing from the general reservoir which nature has furnished, and which experience and prudence teach is liable to be exhausted. It was further said in the Tyner case, from which we have just quoted: "The rule that the owner has the right to do as he pleases with or upon his own property is subject to many limitations and restrictions, one of which is that he must have due regard for the rights of others. It is settled that the owners of a lot may not erect and maintain a nuisance thereon whereby his neighbors are injured."

By People's Gas Co. v. Tyner, 131 Ind. 281, 282, 31 Am. St.

Rep. 433, this court has likened natural gas and laws regulating
the same to wild animals and laws regulating the taking of such
animals. The supreme court of Minnesota in State v. Rodman,
58 Minn. 393, having under consideration the constitutionality
of a certain game law of that state, said: "We take it to be the
correct doctrine in this country that the ownership of wild animals, so far as they are capable of ownership, is in the state,
⁶³⁰ not as proprietor, but in its sovereign capacity, as the representative, and for the benefit, of all its people in common. The
preservation of such animals as are adapted to consumption as
food, or to any other useful purpose, is a matter of public interest; and it is within the police power of the state, as the representative of the people in their united sovereignty, to enact
such laws as will best preserve such game, and secure its beneficial use in the future to the citizens, and to that end it may
adopt any reasonable regulations, not only as to time and manner in which such game may be taken and killed, but also by
imposing limitations upon the right of property in such game
after it has been reduced to possession." Fish laws are of the
same general nature. And their constitutionality has been upheld.

In Gentile v. State, 29 Ind. 415, 417, it was said: "The proposition is that the legislature 'has no power to pass a law denying or abridging the right of the people of the state to fish in
their own waters, and upon their own soil, at pleasure'; that
landowners derive titles from the United States, and their grants
include all unnavigable streams of water passing over their
lands, with the exclusive right to fish therein, within their own
boundaries; and that where the land bounds on such a stream
the stream is the common property of the adjoining proprietors,
who have the exclusive right of fishing. And it is claimed that
this right to fish may be exercised at all times, at the will of the
landowner, and is not subject to be controlled, restrained, or
abridged by the legislature. . . . . The proposition of appellant's counsel is erroneous, in confounding the exclusive right
of the owner of the stream to fish therein with the right of the
property in the fish before they are taken. But fish are ferae
naturae, and as far as any right of property ⁶³¹ in them can exist, it is in the public or is common to all. No individual property in them exists until they are taken and reduced to actual
possession: 2 Blackstone's Commentaries, 392. They are na-
tives of the water; it is there they generate and live and grow,
and no individual property in them can attach whilst they re-

main there free. . But, as they are valuable for food, the public
has an interest in their protection and growth. . . . . The same
principle precisely is involved in the numerous game laws of
this and other states, the constitutionality of which, we believe,
has never been seriously controverted. Whether the fish inhabit-
ing most of the watercourses of this state are sufficiently numerous or valuable to require or justify the enactment of this statute,
is a question for the legislature alone, and with which the courts
have nothing to do. The question presented here is, Had the
legislature the power, under the constitution, to enact the law?
And if so, then if it be found impolitic, the remedy is by an application to the legislature for its repeal. . . . . We find nothing
in the constitution restricting the power of the legislature over
the subject, and therefore hold the statute constitutional." To
the same effect and following that case are State v. Hockett, 29
Ind. 302; State v. Boone, 30 Ind. 225; Stuttsman v. State, 57
Ind. 119. The principle governing in these cases is very much
in point in the question now before us.

It was for the preservation of the fish for the benefit of all
the people of the state that that statute was enacted prohibiting
the taking of any fish in any way for a period of two years from
and after the taking effect of the act, even by an owner of the
lake, stream, or river, and even though the fish were to be used
in the laudable supply of needed food. That was the assertion
of a far greater and more sweeping power than 632 is involved
in the act now before us. It only attempts to restrain all persons from drawing from the general reservoir of nature a needless amount of natural gas only to be wasted. All persons in
the state are far more interested in preventing such needless
waste of gas than they were in preventing the owners of lakes
and streams from taking any fish at all therefrom for a period of
two years, though for necessary food. To the same effect are
Commonwealth v. Gilbert, 160 Mass. 157; Commonwealth v.
Look, 108 Mass. 452; Commonwealth v. Alger, 7 Cush. 53; Commonwealth v. Tewksbury, 11 Met. 55; Cole v. Eastham, 133
Mass. 65; Rideout v. Knox, 148 Mass. 368; 12 Am. St. Rep. 560;
Blair v. Forehand, 100 Mass. 136; 97 Am. Dec. 82; 1 Am. Rep.
94; Phelps v. Racey, 60 N. Y. 10; 10 Am. Rep. 140; Davis v.
State, 68 Ala. 58; 44 Am. Rep. 128; Lawton v. Steele, 152 U. S.
133.

The case of Commonwealth v. Tewksbury, 11 Met. 55, was a
case in which Tewksbury was indicted for the violation of a
statute of Massachusetts providing that: "Any person who shall
take, carry away, or remove, by land or by water, any stones,

gravel, or sand, from any of the beaches in the town of Chelsea,
. . . . shall, for each offense, forfeit a sum not exceeding twenty
dollars," etc. He defended on the grounds that he was the
owner of the land in fee and the statute did not intend to prohibit the owner from taking gravel from it; and, if the statute
did so intend, it was unconstitutional under article 10 of the
declaration of rights, which like our own constitution, provided
that "no part of the property of any individual can be taken
from him or applied to public uses without making him reasonable compensation therefor." The great jurist, Chief Justice
Shaw, delivering the judgment of the court said: "The court
are of the opinion that such a law is not a taking of property for
public use, within the meaning of the constitution, but is a just
and legitimate exercise [633] of the power of the legislature to regulate and restrain such particular use of property as would be inconsistent with, or injurious to, the rights of the public. All
property is acquired and held under the tacit condition that it
shall not be so used as to injure the equal righs of others, or to
destroy or greatly impair the public rights and interests of the
community. . . . . Without hazarding an opinion upon any
other question, we think that a law prohibiting an owner from
removing the soil composing a natural embankment to a valuable,
navigable stream, port, or harbor, is not such a taking, such an
interference with the right and title of the owner, as to give
him a constitutional right to compensation, and to render an
act unconstitutional which makes no such provision, but is a just
restraint of an injurious use of the property, which the legislature have the authority to make."

In Lawton v. Steele, 152 U. S. 133, Mr. Justice Brown, of
the supreme court of the United States, delivering the opinion
of that court, said: "The extent and limits of what is known as
the police power have been a fruitful subject of discussion in the
appellate courts of nearly every state in the Union. It is universally conceded to include every essential to the public safety,
health, and morals, and to justify the destruction or abatement,
by summary proceedings, of whatever may be regarded as a public nuisance. . . . . Beyond this, however, the state may interfere wherever the public interests demand it, and in this particular a large discretion is necessarily vested in the legislature to
determine not only what the interests of the public require, but
what measures are necessary for the protection of such interests."

If this be a correct enunciation of the law on the subject in
hand, and we think it is, it disposes of much of the argument of

the learned counsel as to the [634] question of fact involved in the act in question as to whether, in fact, burning natural gas by flambeau lights is a waste of natural gas. When the legislature inquired into that fact their determination was conclusive on the courts: Gentile v. State, 29 Ind. 415; Jamieson v. Indiana etc. Oil Co., 128 Ind. 555; Mode v. Beasley, 143 Ind. 306, and cases cited on page 315; Woods v. McCay, 144 Ind. 316, and cases cited on pages 322, 323; Board etc. v. State, 147 Ind. 476.

The contention of appellant that the act is void because, as he asserts, it violates the spirit of our institutions, or impairs those rights which it is the object of free government to protect, cannot be maintained, nor can it be declared unconstitutional simply because it may be wrong and unjust: Welling v. Merrill, 52 Ind. 350; Logansport v. Seybold, 59 Ind. 225; State v. Gerhardt, 145 Ind. 439.

Whether a statute encroaches upon the natural rights of the citizen is a legislative, and not a judicial question, and courts cannot overthrow it upon that ground: Hedderich v. State, 101 Ind. 564; 51 Am. Rep. 768; Eastman v. State, 109 Ind. 278; 58 Am. Rep. 400; Phenix Ins. Co. v. Burdett, 112 Ind. 204; Maxwell v. Board etc., 119 Ind. 20; Johnston v. State, 128 Ind. 16; 25 Am. St. Rep. 412; Jamieson v. Indiana etc. Oil Co., 128 Ind. 555.

With the justice, the propriety, or the policy of a statute the courts have nothing whatever to do, so long as the act does not infringe some provision of the constitution, state or federal, or some valid treaty or law of Congress. The State legislature possesses all legislative power, except such as has been delegated to Congress and prohibited by the constitution of the United States, to be exercised by the United States, and such as are expressly or impliedly withheld by the state constitution from the state legislature. The only limitations, therefore, upon the power of the legislature [635] are those imposed by the state constitution, the federal constitution, and the treaties and acts of Congress adopted and enacted under it: State v. McClelland, 138 Ind. 395, and authorities there cited; Hedderich v. State, 101 Ind. 564; 51 Am. Rep. 768.

Therefore, the doctrine invoked by the appellant, that a statute may be overthrown by the courts on the ground that it is unreasonable, is contrary to our decisions and has no place in our jurisprudence.

We have seen that the only constitutional barriers claimed by appellant as having been violated by the act are not so violated thereby.

It is further contended that the act violates section 1 of article 7 of the state constitution, providing that: "The judicial power of the state shall be vested in a supreme court, in circuit courts, and in such other courts as the general assembly may establish" in that it declares the use of natural gas in flambeau lights a wasteful and extravagant use thereof. This, it is claimed, is a judicial determination of what constitutes a wasting of gas. It is nothing more than a recital of the fact that the legislature ascertained by investigation, and the ascertainment of which gave rise to the enactment.

We have seen that there are facts that the legislature may inquire into and ascertain in order to apply the proper remedy by legislation: Gentile v. State, 29 Ind. 415; Jamieson v. India a etc. Oil Co., 128 Ind. 555; Mode v. Beasley, 143 Ind. 306, and cases there cited; Wood v. McCay, 144 Ind. 316, and cases c.ted; Board etc. v. State, 147 Ind. 476.

Very many statutes, if not all of them, are enacted through the influence of the investigation into the facts by the legislature, and the ascertainment thereof by the legislature, and many of them contain a recital of such facts set forth in what is called the preamble, [636] which is defined as a clause introductory to and explanatory of the reasons for passing the act.

Such preamble is in no sense judicial action. And if it were, it would not invalidate the act because it is not an essential part of the statute: Copeland v. Memphis etc. R. R. Co., 3 Woods, 660; Beard v. Rowan, 9 Pet. 317; Commonwealth v. Smith, 76 Va. 484; Potter's Dwarris on Statutes, 265; Endlich on Statutes, sec. 63; Sutherland on Statutory Construction, sec. 212. We therefore hold that none of the objections to the validity of the act are well taken.

Under the motion for a new trial, the action of the circuit court in giving certain instructions is called in question. The instructions, in effect, told the jury that if the facts stated in the affidavit were proven beyond a reasonable doubt, the jury should find the defendant guilty. The only objection urged to such instructions is the invalidity of the statute, as already indicated. It follows from what we have already decided above that there was no error in giving the instructions.

Complaint is made that the court permitted the state to propound to a juror the following question: "Mr. Jonagon, do you

feel that you could return a verdict according to the law as
given you by the court and the evidence as may be given you
by the witness?"

Appellant's counsel refer us to the motion for a new trial for
this question and their objection thereto, wherein such question
and objection are recited. But it has been so often decided by
this court that such matters cannot be brought into the record
by copying them into the motion for a new trial that we deem
it unnecessary to cite a full list of the cases: Deal v. State, 140
Ind. 354, and cases there cited. We turn to the bill of exceptions and find the question and the court's ruling, overruling
appellant's objection thereto, [637] and the juror's answer to the
question in the affirmative; but what the appellant's objection to
the question was is not stated. There is an objection stated in
the motion for a new trial, with the grounds thereof. But it not
being a part of the record we have no legal means of knowing
that appellant ever stated to the court any grounds or reasons
for his objection. Therefore, if the overruling of such objection
was even error, the record fails to make it appear.

Permitting the state to ask the following questions of the
juror De Witt is complained of: "Have you formed or expressed
any opinion as to the constitutionality of the law enacted for the
purpose of preventing the use of gas for illuminating purposes
in what are known as flambeau lights?" The juror answered
in the affirmative, but the question, objection thereto, and ruling of the court thereon is in the same condition as the preceding
one, hence no question as to the correctness of the ruling is
presented by the record.

Complaint is made that the court in the hearing of the jury,
while the juror De Witt was being examined on his voir dire,
remarked: "This jury is not here to try the constitutionality of
this law." There was no request made to discharge the jury.
There was no available error in the remark, especially as appellant made no motion to discharge the jury (Coleman v. State,
111 Ind. 563; Kurtz v. State, 145 Ind. 119), and as there is no
question that the appellant was guilty of violating the statute.
Besides, after making the remark, the court, at the proper time,
among other things, instructed the jury that, under the constitution of the state, they had the right to determine the law
for themselves.

Similar questions to those above mentioned were put and permitted to be answered by the jurors Campbell and Millikan,
but they are in the same condition [638] as the other questions, ob-

jections, and answers, and, like them, the record fails to show what the objections were, and hence fails to make any error in that respect affirmatively appear.

The state having proved by a certain witness that the defendant burned natural gas in flambeau light on the eighth or ninth day of October, 1895, then proved, over objection of defendant, that he did so at other times prior thereto. There is no merit in the objection, as the offense created by the act is a continuous one, a conviction of which bars another prosecution for all violations of the statute by the defendant prior to the pending prosecutions: Freeman v. State, 119 Ind. 501; State v. Lindley, 14 Ind. 430.

We therefore conclude that the circuit court did not err in overruling the motion to quash, or for a new trial.

Judgment affirmed.

CONSTITUTIONAL LAW—UNJUST STATUTES—LEGISLATIVE POWER.—The remedy for unjust or unwise legislation lies with the people, not the courts: People v. Mayor, 4 N. Y. 419; 55 Am. Dec. 266. Courts do not declare an act invalid because it may be unwise or detrimental to the best interests of the state: People v. Kirk, 162 Ill. 138; 53 Am. St. Rep. 277. They do not deal with the policy of a law. That is a question for the legislature: Lommen v. Minneapolis Gaslight Co., 65 Minn. 196; 60 Am. St. Rep. 450. The legislature is clothed with all powers of legislation that do not conflict with the constitution of the state, or of the United States: People v. Kirk, 162 Ill. 138; 53 Am. St. Rep. 277.

CONSTITUTIONAL LAW—REGULATING USE OF PROPERTY. The legislature may so regulate the use which an owner makes of his property as to protect the rights of the public: State v. Yopp, 97 N. C. 477; 2 Am. St. Rep. 305, and note.

APPEAL.—ERROR IS NOT AVAILABLE, on appeal, unless it affirmatively appears from the record: Beard v. Murphy, 37 Vt. 99; 86 Am. Dec. 693; Backus v. Clark, 1 Kan. 303; 83 Am. Dec. 437; Barber v. Hall, 26 Vt. 112; 60 Am. Dec. 301; Tarver v. Torrance, 81 Ga. 261; 12 Am. St. Rep. 311.

GOUGAR *v.* TIMBERLAKE.

[148 INDIANA, 38.]

ELECTIONS—SUFFRAGE—NATURE OF RIGHT—WHO ENTITLED TO.—Suffrage is not a natural right, but a political privilege, and is held only by those to whom it is granted, either by the constitution or written laws of the state.

ELECTIONS—SUFFRAGE IS A STATE RIGHT.—Suffrage is not given by the federal constitution, but is a right of the states.

ELECTIONS — SUFFRAGE — QUALIFICATIONS UPON RIGHT OF—SEX.—Qualifications may be lawfully imposed upon the privilege of suffrage, and sex is made such a qualification by a con-

stitution which gives to male citizens, in express terms, the right
to vote, without mentioning female citizens.

ELECTIONS—CONSTRUCTION OF CONSTITUTION AND
STATUTE.—The general rule of construction, that that which is
expressed makes that which is silent cease, applies to a constitution
and statute which give to male citizens, in express terms, the right
to vote, but do not expressly negative the privilege to female
citizens.

ELECTIONS—WOMEN SUFFRAGE.—The right to vote can-
not be extended to women under a constitutional provision which expressly grants to male citizens, of the age of twenty-one years, the
right of suffrage, but which is silent as to female citizens.

H. B. Sayler, S. M. Sayler, J. M. Sayler, Helen M. Gougar,
and John D. Gougar, for the appellant.

A. A. Rice and W. S. Potter, for the appellees.

39 HACKNEY, J. The question in this case is, Have women,
under existing laws in this state, the privilege of suffrage, or is
sex a qualification upon the right to vote for public officers?

The constitution of this state, article 2, section 2, provides
that: "In all elections not otherwise provided for by this constitution, every male citizen of the United States, of the age of
twenty-one years and upward," etc., "shall be entitled to vote,"
etc. The statute as to the qualification of electors (Burns' Rev.
Stats. 1894, sec. 6192), is substantially in the language of the
constitution cited. It will be observed that the language employed grants to males the right to vote, and that it does not
expressly negative the privilege to female citizens.

In this respect, our constitution is like that of every state in
the Union, and proceeds upon the assumption that the privilege
of voting is not an inherent or natural right, existing in the
absence of constitutional and legislative grant and to be limited
or restricted only by constitutional or legislative provision. If
this assumption is correct, and there is no right of suffrage except as it is given by the constitution and written laws, we have
reached the solution of the question at issue. Back of the constitution, and resting with those having the power to make and
unmake constitutions, is the fountain and source of all power.
From that source we receive such political rights as we posses,
and our concurrence in the constitution is our consent to such
an abridgment of our natural rights as that sacred instrument
may contain. If suffrage is a natural right, it is not abridged
as to any citizen on account of sex, but if it is a political privilege, it is held only by those to whom it is granted. **40** That
it is a political privilege and not a natural right has been af-

firmed, not only in this assumption of the framers of every constitution in the land, but it has been declared by all authority and precedent without exception.

Judge Cooley, in his Principles of Constitutional Law, page 248, declares that "participation in the suffrage is not of right, but it is granted by the state on a consideration of what is most for the interest of the state. Nevertheless, the grant makes it a legal right until it is recalled, and it is protected by the law as property is." Again he says, page 259: "During the last quarter of a century, while the agitation for an enlargement of civil rights has been violent, sentiment has had a great and extraordinary influence on public affairs in America. It has much affected the discussion of political privileges, and considerable numbers have insisted that suffrage was a natural right, corresponding to the right to life and liberty, and equally unlimited. Unless such a doctrine is susceptible of being given practical effect, it must be utterly without substance; and so the courts have pronounced it." One of the reasons for this conclusion, said by the distinguished jurist to be insurmountable, is, that "suffrage cannot be the natural right of the individual, because it does not exist for the benefit of the individual, but for the benefit of the state itself. Suffrage is participation in the government; in a representative country it is taking part in the choice of officers, or in the decision of public questions. . . . . The purpose is therefore public and general, not private and individual. . . . . Suffrage must come to the individual, not as a right, but as a regulation which the state establishes as a means of perpetuating its own existence, and of insuring the people the blessings it was intended to secure": Cooley's Constitutional Law, 260. See, to the [41] same effect, Cooley's Constitutional Limitations, 6th cd., 752; Story on the Constitution, 5th cd., c. 9, secs. 577-584; Black's Constitutional Law, 466; 2 Burgess on Political Science, 110; Minor v. Happersett, 21 Wall. 162; Anderson v. Baker, 23 Md. 531; 2 Lieber's Miscellaneous Writings, 204, 205; Bloomer v. Todd, 3 Wash. Ter. 599; Morris v. Powell, 125 Ind. 281; 2 Bryce's American Commonwealth, 437.

Black's Constitutional Law, says: "It has sometimes been contended that the right to take part in the administration of government or in the choice of those who are to make and execute the laws, by means of the ballot, is a natural right, standing in the same category with the rights of life, liberty, and property. . . . . But it remains not less true that the right of suffrage is not a natural right, but a political right; not a personal right, but a civil right. It does not owe its existence to the mere fact of the personality of the individual, but to the constitution of civil government. Nor is it even a necessary attribute of citizenship. These principles are established by the following considerations: 1. The exercise of an absolutely universal suffrage would imperil the very continuance of the government; 2. The right of suffrage does not exist for the benefit of the individual, but for the benefit of the state itself; 3. There have been restrictions upon the suffrage in all democratic or republican governments known to history, even the most free."

After presenting some of the reasons for and against a more universal suffrage, Mr. Justice Story (Story on the Constitution, 5th ed., 581), says: "Without laying any stress upon this theoretical reasoning, which is brought before the reader, not so much because it solves all doubts and objections, as because it presents a view of the serious difficulties attendant upon the assumption of an original and unalienable right of suffrage, as originating [42] in natural law, and independent of civil law, it may be proper to state that every civilized society has uniformly fixed, modified, and regulated the right of suffrage for itself, according to its own free will and pleasure." Again he says, in concluding section 582: "So that we have the most abundant proofs that among a free and enlightened people, convened for the purpose of establishing their own forms of government and the rights of their own voters, the question as to the due regulation of the qualifications has been deemed a matter of mere state policy, and varied to meet the wants, to suit the prejudices, and to foster the interest of the majority. An absolute, indefeasible right to elect or be elected seems never to have been asserted on one side or denied on the other; but the subject has been freely canvassed as one of mere civil policy, to be arranged upon such a basis as the majority may deem expedient with reference to the moral, physical, and intellectual condition of the particular state."

Dr. Lieber says (2 Lieber's Miscellaneous Writings, 204, 205): "The adoption of universal suffrage has led many persons to the belief and broad assertion that the right of voting is a natural right, and, if it is a natural right, it ought, as a matter of course, to be extended to women; while, on the other hand, many persons seem to profess that no qualification whatever . . . . should be demanded as a requisite for the right of voting. All these are erroneous conceptions. . . . . But how can so special a right as that of voting for a representative be a natural

right, when the representative government itself is something that does not spring directly from the nature of man,
however natural it may be in another sense of the word—that is
to say, consistent with the progress of civilization? It is the
latest and highest of all civilized governments; but where was [43]
the natural right of suffrage under the patriarchal government
—in the Mosaic commonwealth, founded on a hereditary and
priestly nobility; where in the Asiatic despotism—types of government necessary in their season—when nothing and nobody
was voted for? . . . . The representative system is the only
means of protecting individual liberty, and preventing democratic despotism. The right of suffrage, therefore, is a noble
right, or ought to be so; but it is not a natural right. It is a
political right, to which Providence has led man in the progres-
sive course of history."

In Morris v. Powell, 125 Ind. 281, 315, this court said: "It
is because this right of suffrage is a political right abiding in the
fountain of power, that the legislature cannot lay so much as
a finger upon it, except when expressly authorized by the organic
law, and for this reason it is that the legislature cannot make
a classification of its own, no matter whether there is or is not
equality. It is because the right of suffrage is a political right.
as has been decided by the supreme court of the United States,
and by other courts, that the provisions of the constitution
respecting the bestowal of special privileges and immunities have
no application to legislation upon the subject."

Our constitution sought to establish a representative government, a government wherein only limited numbers express the
will of all the people; and it was declared that those to represent
the whole number should be males, possessing the qualifications
enumerated. The government thus established is but the age t
or trustee of the state, the people; and it has derived its auth r-
ity through the constitution. In forming this government the
people declared that their authority should be exercised by and
at the command of males of a designated class. That the exercise of [44] such authority may be intrusted to enlarged classes
with fewer restrictions, there is and can be no doubt; but to do
so is with those who gave the authority, the people; and it is
no more within the power of the judicial or the legislative branch
of the government to modify the will of the people as expressed
in the constitution, than it is for the agent, in any case, to stand
above the principal in authority.

As said in Morris v. Powell, 125 Ind. 281: "The right of

suffrage is one for the consideration of the people in their capacity as creators of constitutions, and is never one for the
consideration of the legislature," and we may add, of the courts,
"except in so far as the constitution authorizes a regulation of
its mode of exercise. The people create, define, and limit their
own right to vote."

Those of us who have come into the state since the adoption
of the constitution, and those who did not vote for its adoption,
as well as those who may have voted against its adoption, are
alike bound by its provisions, and we can exercise no political or
governmental right or privilege which is not given by it. Such
privilege as that of suffrage was not given to women; and if it
only exists by grant, as we have shown, it must be admitted that
those to whom it was given may exercise it as the agents of the
state, the whole people, males and females, not possessing it. If
an agency exists which is contrary to our ideas of advancing
civilization and the highest sense of liberty, our privilege is to
change it, but only through the authority of the principal, the
state.

That the privilege of voting does not exist in the absence of
grants from the people or their authorized representatives is consistent with the decisions which declare that legislatures may not
abridge the privilege as declared in the constitutions by adding
restrictions [45] or limitations not therein defined: Green v. Shum-
way, 39 N. Y. 418; McCafferty v. Guyer, 59 Pa. St. 109; People
v. Canady, 73 N. C. 198; 21 Am. Rep. 465; Monroe v. Collins,
17 Ohio St. 665; Rison v. Farr, 24 Ark. 161; 87 Am. Dec. 52;
Randolph v. Good, 3 W. Va. 551; Brown v. Grover, 6 Bush, 1;
State v. Williams, 5 Wis. 308; 68 Am. Dec. 65; State v. Baker,
38 Wis. 71; Davies v. McKeeby, 5 Nev. 369; Clayton v. Harris, 7
Nev. 64; Cooley's Constitutional Limitations, 6th ed., 753; Black
on Constitutional Law, 471; Morris v. Powell, 125 Ind. 281;
Quinn v. State, 35 Ind. 485; 9 Am. Rep. 754. See, also, Feible-
man v. State, 98 Ind. 516, where the same principle is adhered to.

Giving full force to the decisions of this court just cited, there
is no escape from the conclusion that sex is one of the qualifications, under our constitution, upon the privilege of suffrage. It
was held in Morris v. Powell, 125 Ind. 281, and Quinn v. State,
35 Ind. 485, 9 Am. Rep. 754, that the qualifications specified in
the constitution could not be enlarged or diminished, and in the
former it was particularly pointed out that sex was a qualification. Not only do authority and the assumption by all of the
states, in the form of their grants of suffrage, establish the theory

that the privilege exists only with those to whom it is expressly given, but it is supported by the fact that if it should be held that females were not denied the privilege, there would be an entire absence of restriction upon the privilege as to them. Age, residence, and naturalization would be required of males; but as to females, the youngest and the oldest, nonresid.nt:, aliens, and all, there would be no restriction. If intention should be considered as a rule of construction, and it is always of first importance, there could be little doubt that the framers of the constitution did not intend any such consequences.

The direct question before us has frequently been [46] decided by courts of the highest authority: Spencer v. Board etc., 1 Mc-Ar. 169; 29 Am. Rep. 582; Van Valkenburg v. Brown, 43 Cal. 43; 13 Am. Rep. 136; Minor v. Happersett, 21 Wall. 162; Bloomer v. Todd, 3 Wash. Ter. 599; United States v. Anthony, 11 Blatchf. 200.

It is insisted further that the fourteenth amendment to the constitution of the United States secures to the appellant the elective franchise. The provision referred to is that: "All persons born or naturalized in the United States, and subject to the jurisdiction thereof, are citizens of the United States and of the state wherein they reside. No state shall make or enforce any law which shall abridge the privileges or immunities of citizens of the United States; nor shall any state deprive any person of life, liberty, or property without due process of law, nor to deny any person within its jurisdiction the equal protection of the laws."

If this amendment had created universal suffrage, there would have been no need for the Fifteenth Amendment, which provides that "the right of the citizens of the United States to vote shall not be denied or abridged by the United States, or by any state, on account of race, color, or previous condition of servitude": Judge Cooley says: "The constitution of the United States confers the right to vote upon no one. That right comes to the citizens of the United States, when they possess it at all, under state laws, and as a grant of state sovereignty. But the Fifteenth Amendment confers upon citizens of the United States a new exemption, namely, an exemption from discrimination in elections on account of race, color, or previous condition of servitude": Cooley on Constitutional Law, 277. In the same work, page 274, he says: "The second clause of the fourteenth article was intended to influence the states to bring about by their voluntary action the same result that is now accomplished [47] by this

amendment. It provided that when the right to vote was denied
to any of the male inhabitants of a state, being twenty-one years
of age and citizens of the United States, or in any way abridged
except for participation in crime, the basis of representation in
Congress should be reduced in the proportion which the number
of such male citizens should bear to the whole number of male
citizens twenty-one years of age in such state. By this, the purpose was to induce the states to admit colored freemen to the
privilege of suffrage by reducing the representation and influence
of the states in the federal government, in case they refused."
That suffrage is not given by the federal constitution, but is the
right of the states: See, also, Story on the Constitution, sec.
1932; Black's Constitutional Law, 467; Minor v. Happersett, 21
Wall. 162; Bloomer v. Todd, 3 Wash. Ter. 599; United States v.
Reese, 92 U. S. 214; United States v. Cruikshank, 92 U. S. 542;
United States v. Crosby, 1 Hughes, 448; Kinneen v. Wells, 144
Mass. 497; 59 Am. Rep. 105; Desty's Federal Constitution, 237;
Huber v. Reiley, 53 Pa. St. 112; United States v. Anthony, 11
Blatchf. 200; Spencer v. Board etc., 1 McAr. 169; 29 Am. Rep.
582; Spragins v. Houghton, 3 Ill. 377; Anthony v. Halderman,
7 Kan. 50; Van Valkenburgh v. Brown, 43 Cal. 43; 13 Am. R p.
136.

It is upon this theory alone that the great variety of provisions with reference to suffrage and the qualifications upon the
privilege is found in the several constitutions of the states, and,
although not always in accord, they are not in conflict with the
constitution of the United States. Appellant is in error in assuming that citizenship and suffrage are by the federal constitution made inseparable. Many are citizens, and not voters, unless
we may hold that the state constitution does not discriminate
against persons on account of age, residence, etc., and that dis-
franchisement for [48] crime, etc., may not be made by law. Nor
do negroes get their right of suffrage, under the fourteenth
and fifteenth amendments to the constitution, simply by reason
of citizenship, as appellant earnestly insists. The fifteenth
amendment, as we have shown, takes from the state the right, in
extending the privilege of suffrage, to discriminate against citizens "on account of race, color, or previous condition of servitude." It cannot be said, therefore, that the constitution of Indiana is in conflict with the fifteenth amendment in discriminating against the appellant on account of sex.

By the language of all of the constitutions, which but affirms
the right of voting to those intended to possess it; by the hold-

ings of the courts passing upon the question of the origin, exit-
ence, and grant of political privileges, including the decisions
cited from this court, and upon the reasoning of those eminent
authors who have written upon constitutional law, it must be held
that the general rule of construction, that that which is expressed
makes that which is silent cease, applies in the case before us.

It is insisted, however, against this conclusion, that the decision of this court in In re Leach, 134 Ind. 665, denies the application of the rule or maxim, Expressio unius, exclusio alterius.

That case involved the right of women, possessing the qualifications required by the rules of the court in which they sought
to practice law, to be admitted to practice in the profession of
the law in such court. The constitution, as to the practice of
law, extended the right to voters, and as to others was silent.
The maxim quoted was there denied application, because, as it
was believed, the right to practice law was not a political question, was governmental in no respect, but that it belonged to that
class of rights inherent in [49] every citizen, and pertained to the
fundamental duty of every inhabitant to gain a livelihood; that
this duty involved the privilege of choosing any honorable vocation or profession not forbidden by law, and recognizing the existing right of the people, in the constitution or by legislation,
to regulate the manner of pursuing that vocation or profession.
Constitutions had not recognized the practice of an honorable
profession as a governmental question. Throughout the ages it
had been deemed proper, in the interest of the public, that legislative regulation of the legal profession might be enacted and
enforced. It was, therefore, believed that the constitutional gra t
of the privilege of practicing law to a class was not intended
as a denial of the right to others. It was not thought that the
grant was more than a measure of regulation as to the class especially mentioned, nor that it was in effect an inhibition as to others. Judge Cooley says (Cooley's Constitutional Limitations,
484): "To forbid to an individual or a class the right to the acquisition or enjoyment of property in such manner as should be
permitted to the community at large would be to deprive them of
liberty in particulars of primary importance to their 'pursuit of
happiness'; and those who should claim a right to do so ought to
be able to show a specific authority therefor, instead of calling
upon others to show how and where the authority is negatived.'

In Story on the Constitution, section 1934, it is said that the
right "to acquire, possess, and enjoy property," and "to choose
from those which are lawful the profession or occupation of life,"

are among the privileges which the states are forbidden, by the constitution of the United States to abridge. In re Leach, 131 Ind. 665, we do not regard as an authority upon the question before us.

[50] We are not prepared to say, under the existing social conditions, considering the marked intellectual advancement of women since the adoption of the present constitution, that the elective franchise should not be given them. There are many questions to be settled by the ballot which would enlarge the sphere of freedom, would advance the morals and lighten the burdens of humanity, would redeem homes from the wreckful influences of intemperance, and would stay the mad pace of partisan bias and corruption. But to what extent the ballot in the hands of women would tend to increase or to destroy their present great influence in the affairs of man, the home, and the state cannot be known in advance of the experiment.

Whatever the personal views of the judges upon the advisability of extending the franchise to women, all are agreed that under the present constitution it cannot be extended to them.

The judgment of the lower court, in sustaining the demurrer of the appellees to the appellant's complaint for damages in denying her the right to vote, is affirmed.

ELECTIONS—SUFFRAGE—RIGHT OF WOMEN TO VOTE.— The elective franchise is not a natural right, but rests upon the authority of laws defining the qualifications of those who may exercise it: Spencer v. Board of Registration, 1 McAr. 169; 29 Am. Rep. 582. All citizens are not necessarily voters. A woman is a citizen, but as a citizen has no right to vote: Note to Schuchardt v. People, 39 Am. Rep. 38; Van Valkenburgh v. Brown, 43 Cal. 43; 13 Am. Rep. 136. The only restriction upon the power of the states to fix the qualifications of voters is that imposed by the fifteenth amendment to the constitution of the United States, which forbids any discrimination "on account of race, color, or previous condition of servitude": See monographic note to Blair v. Ridgely, 97 Am. Dec. 263, on the power of a state to impose qualifications for voters and holders of offices. A state constitutional provision ordaining that "every male citizen of the United States shall be entitled to vote" confines the right of suffrage to men, and excludes women. Such provision does not violate the federal constitution: Minor v. Happersett, 21 Wall. 162; note to Spencer v. Board of Registration, 29 Am. Rep. 588.

ADAMS *v.* VANDERBECK.

[148 INDIANA, 92.]

INSTRUCTIONS—APPEAL—STATUTE—PRESUMPTION.—
A statute dispensing with the necessity of bringing up the evidence,
on appeal, as to the question of the correctness of instructions, makes
no change in the practice as to instructions given, for it must be
presumed, in the absence of the evidence, that they were applicable
to it.

VENDOR AND PURCHASER — MORTGAGE — PRECE-
DENT DEBT—BONA FIDE PURCHASER.—It is proper to instruct
the jury, in an action to quiet title to real estate, that the holder
of a conveyance which is, in effect, a mortgage given to secure a
precedent debt, is not a bona fide purchaser.

VENDOR AND PURCHASER—CONVEYANCE IN PAY-
MENT OF PRECEDENT DEBT—BONA FIDE PURCHASER.—An
absolute conveyance of land by a debtor, in payment and satisfaction
of a pre-existing debt owing by the grantor to the grantee, makes
the grantee a bona fide purchaser, as against a prior equity in the
land of which he had no notice.

VENDOR AND PURCHASER—CONVEYANCE IN PAY-
MENT OF PRECEDENT DEBT—BONA FIDE PURCHASER—EN-
FORCEMENT OF EQUITY.—If land is conveyed by the owner to
another in payment and satisfaction of a debt due from the owner
to that other who is ignorant of an equity in the land in favor of a
third person, the enforcement of that equity against the land does
not revive the indebtedness for the payment and satisfaction of
which the land was conveyed. The grantee, in such a case, is as
much a bona fide purchaser for value as if he had paid cash.

INSTRUCTIONS—PRESUMPTION ON APPEAL.—It will be
presumed on appeal that the instructions given were applicable to
the evidence, if it is expressly so stated in a bill of exceptions,
although certain testimony set out therein tends to contradict such
statement.

Clay C. Hunt and M. E. Forkner, for the appellants.

Brown & Brown and D. W. Chambers, for the appellees.

98 McCABE, J. The appellees sued the appellants to quiet
title in and to certain real estate, particularly described, situate
in Henry county, which appellees claim to own. The issues
made by the defendants' answer of a general denial as to a part of
the land, and a disclaimer as to the rest, were tried by jury, resulting in a verdict and judgment in favor of the plaintiffs, the
appellees, over defendants' motion for a new trial and venire de
novo.

The action of the circuit court in overruling the motion for a
new trial, and for a venire de novo, is called in question by the
assignment of errors.

Among the reasons assigned therefor in the motion for a new
trial, and now urged as cause for reversal, are that the court erred
in the giving to the jury certain instructions, and refusing and

modifying an instruction. There is in the transcript what purports to be a bill of exceptions purporting to incorporate the evidence into the same, but it is conceded, even by the appellants, that it was not filed in time, and forms no part of the record.

[94] There is another bill of exceptions, numbered 1, embracing the instructions about which complaint is made. In this bill it is recited that the instructions were applicable to the evidence in accordance with the statute dispensing with the necessity of bringing up the evidence on appeal prosecuted upon the question of the correctness of instructions: Burns' Rev. Stats. 1894, sec. 662 (Rev. Stats. 1881, sec. 650). This statute makes no change in the practice as to instructions given, but does as to those refused, because as to those given, this court, without the aid of the statute, presumes that instructions were applicable in the absence of the evidence: Drinkout v. Eagle Machine Works, 90 Ind. 423; Rozell v. Anderson, 91 Ind. 591; Shugart v. Miles, 125 Ind. 445; Kinney v. Dodge, 101 Ind. 573. Therefore we must presume that the instructions given were applicable to the evidence.

So much of the instructions as are complained of read as follows: "But if Reed took a conveyance of the land in controversy before Hume's deed was made in discharge of or as security for a precedent debt, Reed would not be an innocent purchaser and could acquire no title as against Hume, although his deed would precede the deed to Hume"; and again, "but if Reed acquired his title in payment of a precedent debt he would not be a purchaser in good faith, and could not hold as against Hume's title; and if there was a misdescription of the land in the mortgage, and if said misdescription was perpetuated in the deed to Hume from Reeder, and in the deed from Hume to Vanderbecks, the plaintiffs, and if at a subsequent period Hume and Reeder and Reeder's wife joined in a deed made by them to Vanderbecks for the purpose of correcting said misdescription, said misdescription would not affect the plaintiffs' title, unless in the mean time an innocent purchaser had acquired a title to said [95] land, pending said misdescription, and a deed made to Reed or any third party in payment of, or as security for a precedent debt, would not give them a standing as an innocent purchaser. In such case, if you believe from the evidence that the deed from Thomas B. Reeder to Reed was in payment of or as security for the payment of a precedent debt, you should find for the plaintiff."

So far as these instructions relate to the mortgage, or security taken to secure a precedent debt, not being sufficient to constitute the taker thereof a bona fide purchaser, they are undoubt-

edly correct, which appellants' counsel do not question: Busen-
barke v. Ramey, 53 Ind. 499; Gilchrist v. Gough, 63 Ind. 576;
30 Am. Rep. 250; Davis v. Newcomb, 72 Ind. 413; Hewitt v.
Powers, 84 Ind. 295; Louthain v. Miller, 85 Ind. 161; Wert v.
Naylor, 93 Ind. 431.

But, as applicable to a conveyance in payment of a precedent
debt, they present a different question. We are bound to presume that there was evidence to which each one of the features
of the instructions mentioned was applicable.

The question presented in Wert v. Naylor, 93 Ind. 431, is there
thus stated: "Will a conveyance of land by a debtor to a credi.or,
in payment and satisfaction of a precedent debt, make the credi-
itor a bona fide purchaser of the land, as against prior equities of
which he had no notice? . . . . In the case at bar, the conveyance was not a mere security. It was an absolute conveyance,
and it is alleged in the third paragraph of the answer, and in the
finding of the court, that such conveyance was taken in full payment and satisfaction of one thousand dollars of the precedent
debt, and without notice of the plaintiff's claim. . . . . A man
who merely takes security for a debt gives up nothing, but if he
satisfies the debt itself, he does give up something, and he gives
more than he who merely extends the time for payment of the
precedent debt, which has often been held sufficient. . . . . Pomeroy in his Equity Jurisprudence, volume 2, page 208, says that
the weight of authority is in favor of the doctrine that the extinguishment or surrender of a precedent debt, in consideration
of the conveyance of land, makes the grantee a bona fide purchaser even against prior equities."

To the same effect are numerous cases cited in the opin'on
from which we have quoted. Petry v. Ambrosher, 100 Ind. 510,
Tarkington v. Purvis, 128 Ind. 182, and Orb v. Coapstick, 136
Ind. 313, are not in point and not in conflict with the case above
cited.

We may presume that there was evidence of a conveyance of
land in payment and satisfaction of a pre-existing debt owing by
the grantor to the grantee, and by agreement of the parties the
debt was satisfied and extinguished by the conveyance, and that
the grantee had no notice of any prior equity in the land.

The instructions tell the jury that such a purchaser would not
be a bona fide purchaser.

It is true, according to the authorities cited, the grantee in such
case must have taken the conveyance without any notice of the
prior equity. But the instructions tell the jury that, if the conveyance was made in satisfaction and payment of a precedent

debt, the grantee would not be a bona fide purchaser. Under such instruction, the jury would be bound to find that the grantee was not a bona fide purchaser, even though the evidence showed that he had no notice of the prior equity. That is not the law.

It is true, if this feature of the instructions would be correct under any supposable state of the evidence, then we are by the established law of this state required to presume that such state of evidence existed in the absence of the evidence in the record. But we [97] are also required, as before remarked, to presume that there was evidence from which the jury might have found that the conveyance mentioned in said instructions was made in payment and satisfaction of a pre-existing debt due from the grantor to the grantee, because, if there was no such evidence that feature of the instructions was not applicable to the evidence. Hence, we must hold that feature of the instructions erroneous, and that the circuit court erred in overruling the motion for a new trial.

The judgment is reversed, with instructions to grant defendant's motion for a new trial.

ON PETITION FOR REHEARING.

McCABE, J. The first point made for a rehearing is that we erred in the original opinion in following and adhering to the doctrine laid down in Wert v. Naylor, 93 Ind. 431.

That case concedes that he who takes a mortgage or conveyance as a security for the payment of a precedent debt is not a bona fide purchaser for value, as against the holder of a secret equity in the land, because he parts with nothing. But it holds that where he takes a conveyance of such land in payment and satisfaction of a precedent debt, that he is a bona fide purchaser for value, and entitled to hold such land, as against the holder of the equity of which such purchaser has no notice or knowledge.

While counsel for appellees do not deny that the rule thus laid down in that case is in harmony with the weight of authority elsewhere, yet they contend that such rule is in conflict with other decisions by this court, and is unsound and unjust, and opens the door to great fraud, and impliedly insist that it ought to be [98] overruled. We have already seen in the original opinion that the case is not in conflict with our other cases.

The fraud to which they claim that the doctrine there laid down opens the door is, that the holder of an equity in the land may be deprived of the entire value or purchase price paid for the land, where he has not taken a deed, by one who is ignorant of such equity, and who takes the land in payment and satisfaction of an antecedent debt; that is to say, the one who has thus changed his position, because he has parted with no value, as they contend, and hence not a bona fide purchaser. And it is insisted, in effect, that if the holder of the equity is allowed to enforce his equity and hold the land, the purchaser in consideration of the antecedent debt has lost nothing, because he may then enforce his debt, though he may have surrendered and canceled the evidences thereof, for the reason that the consideration which he was to receive therefor has failed. But that is a mistake. He may have taken a quitclaim deed, and in any event he receives a conveyance of the legal title to the land. This cannot be said to be of no value whatever. If by warranty deed, he has the warranty of title of his grantor.

It is said in Hardesty v. Smith, 3 Ind. 39, that: "When a party gets all the consideration he honestly contracted for, he cannot say he gets no consideration, or that it has failed. If this doctrine be not correct, then it is not true that parties are at liberty to make their own contracts." This language was quoted by Elliott, J., speaking for this court in Wolford v. Powers, 85 Ind. 296, 44 Am. Rep. 16, where it is further said that: "The same principle is declared and enforced in many of our own cases: Kernodle v. Hunt, 4 Blackf. 57; Harvey v. Dakin, 12 Ind. 481; Baker v. Roberts, 14 Ind. 552; Taylor v. Huff, 7 Ind. 680; Louden v. Birt, 4 Ind. 566; Smock v. Pierson, 68 Ind. 405; 34 Am. Rep. 269; Neidefer v. Chastain, 71 Ind. 363; 36 Am. Rep. 198; Williamson v. Hitner, 79 Ind. 233." And we add Laboyteaux v. Swigart, 103 Ind. 596; Price v. Jones, 105 Ind. 543; 55 Am. Rep. 230; Keller v. Orr, 106 Ind. 406.

When, therefore, land is conveyed by the owner to another in payment and satisfaction of a debt due from the owner to that other who is ignorant of an equity in the land in favor of a third person, the enforcement of that equity against the land does not revive the indebtedness for the payment and satisfaction of which the land was conveyed. Therefore, a purchaser of land in consideration of the payment and satisfaction of a debt due the grantee is as much a bona fide purchaser for value as if he had paid cash. And if he is not to be protected as such, the rule which appellees' learned counsel invokes and asks us to adopt opens a wider door for wrong and fraud than the rule laid down by this court in Wert v. Naylor, 93 Ind. 431, which he asks us to overrule. We think we ought to adhere to the rule laid down in that case.

The only other point made for a rehearing is, that we erred in

holding that "we are bound to presume that there was evidence
to which each one of the features of the instructions mentioned
was applicable." Counsel for appellees contend that the bill of
exceptions affirmatively shows .that there was no evidence to
which the erroneous instructions were applicable, and hence that
it was harmless. It, however, rarely happens that instructions
that are wholly inapplicable to the case made by the evidence are
harmless. In Blough v. Parry, 144 Ind. 163, and the numerous
cases there cited, such instructions were held harmful.

This appeal being prosecuted on the correctness of [100] the instructions given and refused, under section 662 of Burns' Revised Statutes of 1894 (Rev. Stats. 1881, sec. 650), the trial court
certified that the instructions given and refused were applicable
to the evidence without setting out all the evidence in the record.

The instructions on which we reversed were instructions given,
and not those refused. We there held, as had been previously
held, that the section of the statute cited made no change in the
practice as to instructions given, as the presumption always must
be, in the absence of the evidence, that instructions given were
applicable to the evidence. But, in addition to that presumption, the trial court has certified in the bill of exceptions incorpo-
rating the instructions, "that the instructions given by the court,
as above stated, ... were each and all applicable to the evidence in said cause."

Appellees' counsel, however, insist that the presumption and
certificate of the trial judge that the instructions were applicable
to the evidence are overcome by the following evidence and recital contained in the same bill of exceptions not purporting to
contain all the evidence, to wit: "Mr. Reeder testified . . . . as
follows: '. . . . you may state what the fact is as to whether Jesse
M. Reed purchased those lands of you, or whether it was by reason of liabilities that he had assumed for you? A. It was on
account of Mr. Reed having indorsed for me and I wanted to
make him safe. He was related to my wife. He was a cousin to
my wife, and I deeded him the land with the understanding that
at some time, if ever I got able to, that I should pay him for all
that he had paid for me, and redeem the land.' And this was all
the evidence on the subject of the consideration for the land
deeded from Reeder to Reed." This is not sufficient to overcome the direct statement in the bill of exceptions that [101] the
instructions were applicable to the evidence; at all events, one
statement is as strong as the other. That is as favorable to the
appellees as they have a right to ask. Even if we construe the

last statement quoted as directly conflicting with the first, which is as favorable to appellees, if not more so, than they have a right to ask, then we have both statements completely nullified. That being so, the presumption that the instructions given were applicable to the evidence must prevail. But, as before observed, it does not relieve the appellees from the consequences of the erroneous instructions by showing, even if we concede that to be the case, that they were not applicable to the evidence.

We see no way of escaping the consequences of giving the erroneous instructions.

Petition overruled.

VENDOR AND PURCHASER—MORTGAGE—CONVEYANCE—PRECEDENT DEBT—BONA FIDE PURCHASER.—The holder of a mortgage given for a precedent debt is a purchaser for value: Hanold v. Kays, 64 Mich. 439; 8 Am. St. Rep. 835; Gilchrist v. Gough, 63 Ind. 576; 30 Am. Rep. 250; and a precedent debt constitutes a valuable consideration for a conveyance: McMahan v. Morrison, 16 Ind. 172; 79 Am. Dec. 418. Other cases, however, hold that one who purchases property or takes a security for an antecedent debt is not entitled to the protection of a statute purporting to protect purchasers and encumbrancers in good faith for value: Union Nat. Bank v. Oium, 3 N. Dak. 193; 44 Am. St. Rep. 533. That one who takes an estate in payment of, or as security for, a previous debt is not a bona fide purchaser, see Dickerson v. Tillinghast, 4 Paige, 215; 25 Am. Dec. 528. If the consideration of a deed is a pre-existing debt, or if a mortgage is taken on the land to secure such indebtedness, it will not, in Texas, support the claim of bona fide purchaser: Note to Hanold v. Kays, 8 Am. St. Rep. 841. Compare discussion of the Indiana cases, on this subject, especially as to prior equities, in the note to McMahan v. Morrison, 79 Am. Dec. 421.

INSTRUCTIONS—PRESUMPTION ON APPEAL.—If none of the testimony is incorporated in the "case," the supreme court is bound to assume that the instructions given to the jury were applicable to the case made: State v. Levelle, 34 S. C. 120; 27 Am. St. Rep. 799.

Pittsburgh, Cincinnati, Chicago and St. Louis Railway Company v. Mahoney.

[148 Indiana, 196.]

CARRIERS—RAILWAY COMPANIES AS PRIVATE CARRIERS—EXEMPTION FROM NEGLIGENCE—EXPRESS MATTER.—A railway company, although it is a public or common carrier, may contract as a private carrier to transport express matter for express companies as such matter is usually carried, and in that capacity may properly require exemption from liability for negligence as a condition to the obligation to carry.

MASTER AND SERVANT—EXEMPTION FROM LIABILITY FOR NEGLIGENCE—EXPRESS AND RAILROAD COMPANIES—NOTICE TO SERVANT.—If there is a contract between an express company and a railroad company to the effect that the former will hold the latter harmless against claims by employés of the express company for the negligence of the railroad company, an employé of the express company, performing duties for it in its relations to the railroad company, is chargeable with notice of such private contract, and is subject to it, especially where he has assumed all risks of the employment, including the assumption by the express company in favor of the railroad company.

MASTER AND SERVANT—EXEMPTION FROM NEGLIGENCE IN CONTRACT BETWEEN EXPRESS COMPANY AND RAILROAD COMPANY—SERVANT'S RELEASE OF EXPRESS COMPANY.—If an employé of an express company, performing duties for it in its relations to a railroad company, releases the express company from all liability for injury sustained by the negligence of the express company "or otherwise," and there exists, at the time, a contract between the express company and the railroad company to the effect that the former will hold the latter harmless against claims by employés of the express company for the negligence of the railroad company, the administrator of such employé cannot maintain an action against the railroad company for negligently causing his death by suddenly closing the opening between parts of a train while he was passing through it in the discharge of his duty, as the word "otherwise" in the employé's contract with the express company covers all the risks involved, including liability for negligence on the part of the railway company. The employé did not stand independent of the contract between the two companies.

AFFIDAVIT—OATH WITHOUT AFFIANT'S SIGNATURE. It seems that a statement made under oath may be an affidavit without the signature of the affiant.

MOTIONS AND ORDERS—MODIFYING MANDATE.—A motion to modify a mandate of the supreme court is in the nature of a petition for a rehearing, and may be filed, during the time allowed for a rehearing, on behalf of a party who has not waived it, although the opinion has been certified to the court below.

MOTIONS AND ORDERS—PLEADINGS—STRIKING OUT. If averments in a pleading are in any way material, they ought not to be struck out on motion, and the test of materiality is whether they tend to constitute a cause of action or defense; if they do, they are not irrelevant and ought not to be suppressed.

MOTIONS AND ORDERS—MODIFYING MANDATE—JUDGMENT—NEW TRIAL.—If a judgment is reversed because of the trial court's error in striking from answers certain contracts filed as exhibits thereto, which contracts were thereby taken out of the issues, a motion to modify the mandate of the supreme court so as to give the defendant a judgment instead of a new trial will not be sustained.

Action for damages, brought by Mahoney, administrator, against the railroad company for negligently causing the death of Oscar P. J. Romick.

N. O. Ross, G. E. Ross, and Bell & Purdum, for the appellant.

F. Winter, M. Winfield, Kistler & Kistler, Fausler & Mahoney, and Blacklidge & Shirley, for the appellee.

[197] HACKNEY, J.   In December, 1894, Oscar P. J. Romick was an employé of the Adams Express Company, at the city of

Logansport, caring for express matter entering and going from said city on the line of the appellant's railway.   Between 2 and 3 o'clock on the morning of the 13th of said month, while passing from the south side of appellant's two parallel tracks, near the passenger depot, and from the express company's storeroom to the north side of said tracks, said Romick entered between two cars of a passenger train, separated by a space of from six to ten feet, just as additional cars were driven against those of one division of said train, and he was caught and crushed between said two cars.   From his injuries he died, and the appellee, charging the appellant with negligence in driving said additional cars without warning and without watchman at the point of the cut in the train, sued the appellant for damages.

The appellant's third answer to the complaint alleged a special contract between the appellant and said express company, whereby the former agreed to carry upon its passenger trains the express matter and messengers of the latter, said express company supplying its own servants, and handling the express matter by its own agents; that as a part of said special contract the express company agreed "to assume all risks of loss or damage that may arise out of, or result from, its operations under this agreement, and to save and hold harmless" the railway company "against the same, and especially to protect" it "against claims that may be made upon it for loss or [198] damage, either to the employés of the" express company "or the property in its charge, whether the loss may occur through the gross negligence of the" railway company "or its employés or otherwise."   It was alleged, also, that between Romick and the express company existed the following contract: "Whereas, O. P. J. Romick, the undersigned, has made application to be employed by the Adams Express Company as a servant of said company at a stipulated rate of compensation for his services, which rate said company is willing to pay only if the undersigned will assume all risks of said employment and release said company therefrom, as hereinafter set forth.   Now, therefore, in consideration of such employment, to be given by said company and the compensation to be paid therefor, and in consideration of one dollar, lawful money of the United States, paid by the Adams Express Company to the undersigned, the receipt whereof is hereby acknowledged, the undersigned, for himself, his heirs, executors, administrators, and assigns, hereby covenants and agrees that in no case shall said company be liable by reason of any act or negligence of its agents, servants, or employés, or any of them, or otherwise, causing any

injury to his person or property, or causing his death, while he
shall remain in its employ, and he accepts said employment with
full knowledge and notice of all the risks involved therein, which
he assumes. And the undersigned hereby releases said company
from any and all liability for and in respect of any such damage,
injury, or death, by reason of negligence or otherwise." Said
contract was signed by said Romick, was duly attested, and had
appended thereto the following statement, made and sworn to by
said Romick concurrently with said contracts:

"O. P. J. Romick, being duly sworn, says that he is [199] the
individual who executed the foregoing release and contract:
That he has read or heard read the same before execution, and
understands that by signing such contract he has released the
Adams Express Company, and all other carriers employed by it,
from all liability to him for his death or personal injury, from
any cause, whether negligence of either of said companies or
their servants or agents or otherwise." Upon motion of the appellee, the trial court struck out said contracts as exhibits to said
answer, and the allegations of the answer pertinent to said contracts; and thereafter sustained a demurrer to said answer, which
answer, denuded of said allegations, was not more than an admission of the injuries, and a denial of negligence. These rulings
are urged as error, and appellee's learned counsel concede in oral
argument that if the language of the contracts is sufficiently direct and comprehensive to include a release, on his part, of a
right of action for injuries from the appellant's negligence, said
rulings were erroneous and the judgment should be reversed. It
had been urged in the briefs for appellee that a contract of release from the results of negligence was void as against public
policy, and the following authorities were cited in support of that
proposition: Roesner v. Hermann, 8 Fed. Rep. 782; Railway Co.
v. Spangler, 44 Ohio St. 471; 58 Am. Rep. 833; Western etc.
R. R. Co. v. Bishop, 50 Ga. 465; Kansas Pac. Ry. Co. v. Peavey,
29 Kan. 169; 44 Am. Rep. 630; Johnson v. Richmond etc. R. R.
Co., 86 Va. 975; Louisville etc. R. R. Co. v. Orr, 91 Ala. 548;
Hissong v. Richmond etc. R. R. Co., 91 Ala. 514; 2 Thompson
on Negligence, 1025; 1 Cent. L. J. 465; Arnold v. Illinois Cent.
R. R. Co., 83 Ill. 273; 25 Am. Rep. 383; Jacksonville etc. Ry.
Co. v. Southworth, 135 Ill. 250; Purdy v. Rome etc. R. R. Co.,
125 N. Y. 209; 21 Am. St. Rep. 736; [200] Maney v. Chicago etc.
R. R. Co., 49 Ill. App. 105; Newport etc. R. R. Co. v. Eifort, 15
Ky. Law Rep. 600; Runt v. Herring, 2 Misc. Rep. 105; 21 N. Y.
Supp. 244.

These authorities probably sustain the proposition stated when applied to exemption against negligence in the discharge of a public or quasi public duty, such as that owing by a common carrier to an ordinary shipper, passenger, or servant. In a recent decision of this court, however, that of Louisville etc. Ry. Co. v. Keefer, 146 Ind. 21, 58 Am. St. Rep. 348, we recognized the well-established rule that railway companies, although public or common carriers, may contract as private carriers, such as that of transporting express matter for express companies as such matter is usually carried, and in that capacity may properly require exemption from liability for negligence as a condition to the obligation to carry: See, also, Express Cases, 117 U. S. 1; Hosmer v. Old Colony R. R. Co., 156 Mass. 506; Bates v. Old Colony R. R. Co., 147 Mass. 255; Chicago etc. Ry. Co. v. Wallace, 66 Fed. Rep. 506; Coup v. Wabash etc. Ry. Co., 56 Mich. 111; 56 Am. Rep. 374; Forepaugh v. Delaware etc. Ry. Co., 128 Pa. St. 217; 15 Am. St. Rep. 672; Hartford Fire Ins. Co. v. Chicago etc. Ry. Co., 70 Fed. Rep. 201; Quimby v. Boston etc. R. R. Co., 150 Mass. 365; Muldoon v. Seattle etc. Ry. Co., 10 Wash. 311; 45 Am. St. Rep. 787; Griswold v. New York etc. R. R. Co., 53 Conn. 371; 55 Am. Rep. 115.

Contracts of exemption from such liability have been upheld for many years in the courts of New York without regard to the distinction between exemptions from those duties arising from the obligations of common carriers and those which the carriers are not required [201] to perform, but may perform upon terms prescribed by them. In that state, however, impressed, perhaps, by the question of public policy, which in other states defeats contracts of exemption from the consequences of neglecting quasi public duties, it has been held that contracts of exemption must be strictly construed and with all presumptions indulged against an intention to exempt liabilities for negligence. Some of these cases are Kenney v. New York etc. R. R. Co., 125 N. Y. 422; Brewer v. New York etc. R. R. Co., 124 N. Y. 59; 21 Am. St. Rep. 647; Mynard v. Syracuse etc. R. R. Co., 71 N. Y. 180; 27 Am. Rep. 28.

In the early case of Wells v. Steam Nav. Co., 2 N. Y. 204, it was held, however, that the right to contract for a restricted liability existed with reference to private carriers.

Learned counsel for the appellee insist that the rule of strict construction should be applied to the contracts before us, and that under the rule the contract between the Adams Express Company and the appellant is one of indemnity only; that the contract between Romick and the express company exempted only the express company, and extended but to the ordinary risks of the employment with that company, not including the negligence of that company or of the appellant, and that, in construing the contract between Romick and the express company, the sworn statement of Romick should be cast out, because it does not contain his signature, and because it was not embodied in the contract. The only reason assigned in the motion for striking out the exhibits was that they were void as against public policy. This reason, upon the authorities we have cited, was not sufficient and should not have prevailed, but if the exhibits, for any other reason, should have been stricken out, the ruling [202] was probably harmless. There was no separate specification in the motion directed to the verified statement of Romick, and it went out under the general motion. There is no contention that the exhibits should have been stricken out because not the basis of the answer, and, therefore, not properly capable of becoming a part of the answer by exhibit; nor is it claimed that they were immaterial to the answer upon the theory thereof. The latter claim could not be sustained under the rule recently announced in Atkinson v. Wabash R. R. Co., 143 Ind. 501, where it was said that: "It is settled that where averments or matter in a pleading are in any way material, they ought not to be struck out on motion, and the recognized test of their materiality is to inquire whether they tend to constitute a cause of action or defense; if they do they are not irrelevant and ought not to be suppressed": Citing authorities.

That the exhibits tended to constitute and to support a cause of defense is without serious doubt; and, when we observe the character of attack made upon them in this court, their sufficiency to constitute a defense is the question, and not whether they tend to do so. In other words, the argument here is that which would apply to a demurrer, and has no place upon the motion. While regarding the ruling upon the motion as an error for which the judgment should be reversed, the force and effect of the contracts will necessarily arise upon another trial, and seems now to arise upon the appellant's motion for judgment on the special verdict, it having been found that Romick's only rights upon and about the tracks and right of way, on the occasion of his injury, were by the terms of said two contracts, not including the verified statement. In an interpretation of the language employed in the contracts, we are to be controlled by the usual [203] rules for the ascertainment of the intention of the parties, looking to the words in their ordinary meaning, and not by the rule of strict construction here insisted upon, and that adopted in New York, with reference to contracts restricting liability of common carriers.

As said in Hartford Fire Ins. Co. v. Chicago etc. Ry. Co., 70 Fed. Rep. 201: "The burden is on the party who seeks to put a restraint upon the freedom of contracts to make it plainly and obviously clear that the contract is against public policy." We have held the contracts before us not against public policy, and we must, therefore, subject them to the same tests of interpretation that other lawful contracts should receive. As between the express company and the appellant, their contract saving the latter from liability for injuries to the former's servants could not, in its very nature, be more than an assumption or indemnity, as there could be no waiver of a right belonging to another standing independent of them. But it yet remains to determine whether Romick stood independent of the contract and the parties thereto. That contract, whether an assumption, indemnity, or waiver, included the demand sued upon in this case, for it covered a claim for damage to an employé of the express company, alleged to have occurred through the negligence of the railroad company, taking the very words of the clause, quoted above, from that contract. By the provisions of that contract the rights of the express company were fully measured. Its only right to be upon the tracks and right of way, through and by its servants, was by the provisions of that contract. Its license came only from the contract, and the appellee introduced the contract in evidence to show the right of his decedent to be upon the tracks. The express company, operating by its servants, was present, on the occasion [204] in question, by Romick, its agent. His rights were those of the express company, and could not be greater. He was there by the license given the express company, and he could not accept the license and reject the conditions upon which it was granted. It is said, however, that it does not appear from allegation or proof that he knew of the conditions upon which the license was given, and we are aware that it was decided in Brewer v. New York etc. Ry. Co., 124 N. Y. 59, 21 Am. St. Rep. 647, that the express agent must have notice of the contract of exemption to be bound thereby. But with what reason can it be said that the railroad company should have given notice to the employés of the express company of the particular provisions of the contract under which they were admitted upon and permitted to use the property of the rail-

road company? Since the contract is the basis of rights which
he assumes and exercises, it should rather be said that he must
inform himself of its provisions. Unlike the theory of the holdings in New York, our court holds such contracts as standing,
not upon the relationship of a common carrier, but as existing
only in the private agreements of the parties. Therefore, when
Romick took employment with the express company, he was
obliged to know that his rights and privileges did not depend
upon the law as to common carriers, nor upon public or quasi
public duty of the railroad company, but that they rested upon
private contract, to which he became subject in the performance
of his duties for the express company in its relations to the appellant. He did not, therefore, occupy a position with relation
to the railroad company independent of the contract between
said two companies, but was chargeable with knowledge of the
limitation upon the appellant's liability.

If we accept the construction of the contract between [205] the
companies that it was an assumption or an indemnity which
supplied a liability to the appellant for any claim it might be
required to pay on account of an injury inflicted, and we then
look to the contract between Romick and the express company,
we find that he there assumed all the risks of the employment,
released the express company from any and all liability on account of his injury or death from negligence or otherwise, and
agreed that in no case should the express company be liable for
his death or injury from any act or negligence of any agent, servant or employé of such company, or otherwise. While it is
not clear that the words "agents, servants, or employés," used
in this contract, related directly to the appellant, since it was but
in a limited sense an "agent, servant, or employé" of the express
company, yet, when we have charged the decedent with notice
of the contract between the two companies, creating an obligation on the part of the express company to pay for the injury
or death of its employés, the last clause in his contract is more
than a general restatement of what is particularly stated before.
He "released said company from any and all liability for and in
respect of any such damage, injury, or death, by reason of negligence or otherwise." The words "such damage, injury, or
death" refer to the stated damage to property, injury to person,
or to his death, but they are not confined to the special negligence previously stated, but to negligence generally or otherwise. The word "otherwise" includes such liability as might

arise from any other cause or in any different manner. A contract assuming or releasing the employer from the ordinary risks
of a service would be a useless ceremony, for it could but do
that which the law does without it. Giving the parties credit
for a purpose to create an effective and rational [200] contract, we
would naturally look for a purpose not already accomplished,
and, when we consider the two contracts before us in the light
of such an object or purpose, we gather strength in the conclusion that the parties were contracting against unusual risks and
liabilities. The word "otherwise," as it is twice employed in
Romick's contract, must be deemed to include some liability not
expressly mentioned or such as might arise out of the relations
of the parties and within the general scope of his service and
connection with them. Giving the word such force, it would
reach liabilities beyond those expressly mentioned, and beyond
those claims for damages, injuries, or death arising from the ordinary hazards of the service, for such claims present no liability.
It would include "all the risks involved," ordinary as well as
extraordinary; and it would include the assumption by the express company in favor of the appellant. So that to treat the
contract with the railroad company as a release, accepted by the
decedent, and acted upon, or as an assumption or indemnity, the
decedent, by his contract, took the place of the express company,
assumed its liability, and released it from the same. Appellee's
decedent could not collect for the death a sum which the decedent, by the terms of his contract, agreed to release and assume.

   We do not understand that a statement under oath may not
be an affidavit without the signature of the affiant: Turpin v.
Eagle Creek etc. Gravel Road Co., 48 Ind. 45; Bonnell v. Ray,
71 Ind. 141; 1 Ency. of Pl. & Pr. 354, and authorities there cited.

   We offer no suggestion as to the effect of the statement, with
proper allegations as to the construction of the contract in case
of ambiguity, but its relevancy to the defense pleaded was such
that it should not have been stricken out, but should have received construction [201] upon demurrer. In view of the fact that
the special verdict contains findings relative to the contracts
which were not within the issues, we do not make any direction
as to the motion for a venire de novo, and for judgment in
favor of the appellant.

   The judgment of the lower court is reversed, with instructions
to overrule the appellee's motion to strike out parts of the answer.

ON MOTION TO MODIFY MANDATE.

HACKNEY, J. On the twenty-fourth day of May, 1896, the appellee filed with the clerk of this court his waiver of the right to petition for a rehearing, and, on the same day, the clerk certified to the clerk of the lower court the opinion heretofore rendered in this cause. On the twenty-eighth day of the same month, the appellant filed its motion herein so to modify the mandate heretofore entered in this cause as to direct a judgment in its favor. To the latter motion the appellee enters a special appearance, and moves to dismiss the same, because: 1. The opinion has been so certified down; and 2. Because of the absence of merit in the motion.

Under section 674 of Burns' Revised Statutes of 1894, and rule 37 of this court, jurisdiction is retained in this court for sixty days from the adjudication of a cause to entertain the petition for a rehearing by either party, and this right to be further heard cannot be defeated as to one of the parties by a waiver filed by or on behalf of another. The motion to modify a mandate entered by this court in a cause is in the nature of a petition for a rehearing, and may, at least during the time allowed for a rehearing, be filed on behalf of a party who has not waived it. The appellee's motion to dismiss will, therefore, be overruled.

208 The appellant's motion should not be sustained, for the reason that the error upon which the reversal was made primarily was that the court below had stricken from the answer certain contracts, which were thereby taken out of the issues. But for that ruling a reply and additional evidence might have presented the case in a different form. That ruling was the evidence that the trial court, from the time the ruling was made, proceeded upon an erroneous theory.

While we have construed the contracts in the light in which they were presented by the record, we feel that with an error committed so early in the case, and that error followed throughout, it would be prejudicial to the rights of the appellee to deny him an opportunity to plead to either of such contracts when answered by the appellant.

The motion to modify is overruled.

Relations of Express Companies, and Their Employés, to Other Common Carriers.*

Scope of Note—Reasonable Express Accommodations.—In the monographic note to Ballard v. American Exp. Co., 61 Am. St. Rep. 358, will be found a discussion of the duties and liabilities of express companies as common carriers. These carriers usually employ another common carrier, such as a railroad, steamboat, or stage company to assist them in performing the service required. This is generally done by special contract, and it is our purpose here to discuss particularly the new relations created between the carriers by such express contracts. A common carrier, such as a railroad company, does not often hold itself out as a common carrier of common carriers, notwithstanding it may be bound to furnish the public all reasonable express accommodations. A railroad company generally arranges, at the earliest practicable moment, to take one express company on some or all of its passenger trains, or to provide some other way of doing an express business on its lines, so as to discharge its duty to the public of furnishing reasonable express accommodations; but it is not the practice to grant such a privilege to more than one company at the same time, unless a statute or some special circumstances make it necessary or desirable. And where only one express company at a time is admitted to the privileges offered by a railroad company, the nature of the express business is such as to require an express contract.

"The reason," says Mr. Chief Justice Waite, in rendering the opinion of the court in Express cases, 117 U. S. 1, 23, "is obvious why special contracts in reference to this business are necessary. The transportation required is of a kind which must, if possible, be had for the most part on passenger trains. It requires not only speed, but reasonable certainty as to the quantity that will be carried at any one time. As the things carried are to be kept in the personal custody of the messenger or other employé of the express company, it is important that a certain amount of car space should be specially set apart for the business, and that this should, as far as practicable, be put in the exclusive possession of the expressman in charge. As the business to be done is 'express,' it implies access to the train for loading at the latest, and for unloading at the earliest, convenient moment. All this is entirely inconsistent with the idea of an express business on passenger trains free to all express carriers. Railroad companies are by law carriers of both persons and property. Passenger trains have from the beginning been provided for the transportation primarily of passengers and their baggage. This must be done with reasonable promptness and with reasonable comfort to the passenger. The express business on passenger trains is in a degree subordinate to the passenger business, and it is consequently the duty of a railroad company in arranging for the express to see that there is as little interference as possible with the wants of passengers. This implies a special understanding and agreement

---

* Reference to Monographic Note.

Right of carrier to exact special contract of shipper; 46 Am. St. Rep. 777-780. Passengers who are, and when they become such; 61 Am. St. Rep. 75-104. Duties of express companies as common carriers; 61 Am. St. Rep. 358-385.

as to the amount of car space that will be afforded, and the conditions on which it is to be occupied, the particular trains that can be
used, the places at which they shall stop, the price to be paid, and
all the varying details of a business which is to be adjusted between
two public servants, so that each can perform, in the best manner,
its own particular duties. All this must necessarily be a matter of
bargain, and it by no means follows that, because a railroad company can serve one express company in one way, it can as well serve
another company in the same way, and still perform its other obligations to the public in a satisfactory manner. The car space that
can be given to the express business on a passenger train is, to a
certain extent, limited, and, as has been seen, that which is allotted
to a particular carrier must be, in a measure, under his exclusive
control. No express company can do a successful business unless it
is at all times reasonably sure of the means it requires for transportation. On important lines one company will at times fill all the
space the railroad company can well allow for the business. If this
space had to be divided among several companies, there might be
occasions when the public would be put to inconvenience by delays
which could otherwise be avoided. So long as the public are served
to their reasonable satisfaction, it is a matter of no importance who
serves them. The railroad company performs its whole duty to the
public at large and to each individual when it affords the public all
reasonable express accommodations. If this is done, the railroad
company owes no duty to the public as to the particular agencies
it shall select for that purpose. The public require the carriage,
but the company may choose its own appropriate means of carriage,
always provided they are such as to insure reasonable promptness
and security."

Equal Express Facilities—Statutes.—In Express cases, 117 U. S. 1,
certain railroad companies had undertaken to perform for the public the express business which had been done before that time, over
the same lines, by express companies. The express companies applied for space in the express cars for their goods and messengers,
and the railroad companies refused to furnish the space or to carry
their messengers. Suits were therefore brought to compel the railroads to furnish the desired express facilities, the exact question
being whether the express companies could demand as a right what
they had theretofore only as by permission. The court, in deciding
the cases, conceded, as we understand the opinion, that a railroad
company, as a common carrier, must afford the public all reasonable express accommodations; but held that it is not obliged, either
by the common law, or by usage, to do more than this, as an express
carrier; that it is not required to transport the traffic of independent
express companies over its lines in the manner in which such traffic
is usually carried and handled; and that it need not, in the absence
of a statute, furnish to all independent express companies equal
facilities for doing an express business upon its passenger trains.
The court pointed out the fact that railroad companies have always
encouraged the express business; that they have not refused to transport express matter for the public, upon the application of some

express company; that the public has a right to demand the transportation, by railway facilities, of that class of matter which is known as express matter; but that, in this particular case, the express companies had never been allowed to do business on any road except under a special contract, and that, as a rule, only one express company had been admitted on a road at the same time: Express cases, 117 U. S. 1, 20, 26. "If the general public were complaining," said the court, "because the railroad companies refused to carry express matter themselves on their passenger trains, or to allow it to be carried by others, different questions would be presented. As it is, we have only to decide whether these particular express companies must be carried, notwithstanding the termination of their special contract rights. The question is, not whether these railroad companies must furnish the general public with reasonable express facilities, but whether they must carry these particular express carriers for the purpose of enabling them to do an express business over the lines": Express cases, 117 U. S. 1, 27, 28. We understand from the opinion in this case that a railroad company as a common carrier, performs its whole duty to the public at large and to each individual, so far as the carriage of express matter is concerned, though it admits, on its road, only one express company at a time, where that affords the public all reasonable express accommodations: Express cases, 117 U. S. 1, 24, 26.

Prior to the decision of the Express cases, 117 U. S. 1, some of the federal circuit courts had been holding that express companies had a right to do business upon railroads: Southern Exp. Co. v. St. Louis etc. Ry. Co., 10 Fed. Rep. 210; Wells v. Oregon Ry. & Nav. Co., 15 Fed. Rep. 561; Wells, Fargo & Co. v. Oregon Ry. & Nav. Co., 18 Fed. Rep. 517; Wells, Fargo & Co. v. Northern Pac. Ry. Co., 23 Fed. Rep. 469; that a railroad company was bound to furnish facilities for the transaction of an express company's business, at a reasonable rate of compensation: Southern Exp. Co. v. St. Louis etc. Ry. Co., 10 Fed. Rep. 210; Wells v. Oregon Ry. & Nav. Co., 15 Fed. Rep. 561; Wells, Fargo & Co. v. Oregon Ry. & Nav. Co., 18 Fed. Rep. 517; Wells, Fargo & Co. v. Oregon Ry. & Nav. Co., 19 Fed. Rep. 20; Fargo v. Redfield, 22 Fed. Rep. 373; Wells, Fargo & Co. v. Northern Pac. Ry. Co., 23 Fed. Rep. 469; that railroads, as common carriers, were not authorized to do an express business, or to insist on doing exclusively such business on their roads, or to give the exclusive right to any express company to do business on their railroads, but that all express companies had to be received on the same terms: Dinsmore v. Louisville etc. Ry. Co., 2 Fed. Rep. 465; Southern Exp. Co. v. Louisville etc. R. R. Co., 4 Fed Rep. 481; Texas Exp. Co. v. Texas etc. Ry. Co., 6 Fed. Rep. 426; Southern Exp. Co. v. Memphis etc. R. R. Co., 8 Fed. Rep. 799; Southern Exp. Co. v. St. Louis etc. Ry. Co., 10 Fed. Rep. 210; Wells v. Oregon etc. Ry. Co., 18 Fed. Rep. 667; Wells, Fargo & Co. v. Oregon Ry. & Nav. Co., 19 Fed. Rep. 20; and that a railroad company could not fix an absolute demand against an express company for carriage: Southern Exp. Co. v. St. Louis etc. Ry. Co., 10 Fed. Rep. 210. As announcing the rule in the federal courts these cases are of little or no value since the decision of the Express cases,

117 U. S. 1, holding that independent express companies have no absolute rights upon railroads.

In the state courts there has also been a contrariety of opinion upon the question. Thus, in Sandford v. Catawissa etc. R. R. Co., 24 Pa. St. 378, 64 Am. Dec. 667, it was held that an express company engaged in transporting small packages has a right to the benefits of a railroad as much as the owners of the packages possess in person; and that exclusive privileges could not be granted by a railroad company to one express company over another. In this case the railroad company sought, by contract, to give an express company the exclusive privilege of transportation on its passenger trains, and the court remarked: "The railroad corporation has no right to do this. The power to regulate the transportation on the road does not carry with it the right to exclude any particular individuals, or to grant exclusive privileges to others. Competition is the best protection to the public, and it is against the policy of the law to destroy it by creating a monopoly of any branch of business. It cannot be done except by the clearly expressed will of the legislative power. If it possessed this power, it might build up one set of men and destroy others; advance one kind of business and break down another; and might make even religion and politics the tests in the distribution of its favors. Such a power in a railroad corporation might produce evils of the most alarming character. The rights of the people are not subject to any such corporate control. Like the customers of a gristmill, they have a right to be served, all other things equal, in the order of their applications. A regulation, to be valid, must operate on all alike. If it deprives any persons of the benefits of the road, or grants exclusive privileges to others, it is against law and void": Sandford v. Catawissa etc. R. R. Co., 24 Pa. St. 378; 64 Am. Dec. 667. Mr. Justice Field, dissenting in Express cases, 117 U. S. 1, 34, said: "I am clear that railroad companies are bound, as common carriers, to accommodate the public in the transportation of goods according to its necessities, and through the instrumentalities or in the mode best adapted to promote its convenience. Among these instrumentalities express companies, by the mode in which their business is conducted, are the most important and useful."

Under statutes requiring railroad companies to furnish all persons and expressmen equal facilities for the transportation of agents and servants, as well as merchandise and other property, a railroad company is answerable in damages for not furnishing to the plaintiff terms, facilities, and accommodations for his express business on the defendant's road, reasonably equal to those furnished by the defendant to another express company: McDuffee v. Portland etc. R. R., 52 N. H. 430; 13 Am. Rep. 72; New England Exp. Co. v. Maine Cent. R. R. Co., 57 Me. 188; 2 Am. Rep. 31; Sandford v. Catawissa etc. R. R. Co., 24 Pa. St. 378; 64 Am. Dec. 667. In Sargent v. Boston etc. R. R. Corp., 115 Mass. 416, the plaintiff sought to recover damages of the defendants for breaking up its business as an expressman over the railroads of the defendants. The statute of the commonwealth obliged each railroad therein to give to all persons or companies reasonable and "equal terms, facilities, and accommodations" for the transportation of merchandise. The plaintiff had been furnished with express facilities for many years, and had acquired a valuable business, but the railroad companies finally made arrangements to lease express privileges to the highest bidder, and did so, notifying the plaintiff to vacate. The court held that the companies were not bound to furnish the plaintiff with facilities and accommodations different in kind from those furnished to the general public; and that the statute did not make it unlawful for a railroad company to carry on the express business itself. "The gravamen of the complaint," said the court "is not that the defendants have refused to give the plaintiff 'equal terms, facilities, and accommodations' with other persons and companies, but simply that they have refused to give him such facilities as he requires, for his special business as carrier, over their roads. His claim must stand upon the right to demand such facilities independently of any enjoyment of like facilities by others. As an absolute right this cannot be maintained." The court furthermore said that "railroads cannot be required to convert their passenger trains to the purpose of freight at the discretion of parties not responsible for the management of the trains; nor can they be compelled to admit others than their own agents and servants upon their trains or to their stations for the custody, care, receipt, and delivery of freight or parcels": Sargent v. Boston etc. R. R. Corp., 115 Mass. 416, 421. But, while one cannot, under such a statute, claim express facilities and accommodations not furnished to the general public, he does have a right to insist upon "equal terms, facilities, and accommodations." Thus, a person engaged in a local express business, between points in the state of Massachusetts, on the freight trains of a railroad company, is entitled under such a statute, to have the privilege of doing his express business on the passenger trains of the company upon terms, and with facilities and accommodations, which shall be reasonable, and equal to those furnished to others doing the same kind of business on the road, having regard to the amount and character of the service, and also to such reasonable regulations of the business as may be required for the public interest and the efficient operation of the road; Kidder v. Fitchburg R. R. Co., 165 Mass. 398.

"A railroad corporation," says the court, in McDuffee v. Portland etc. R. R., 52 N. H. 430, 13 Am. Rep. 72, "carrying one expressman, and enabling him to do all the express business on the line of their road, do hold themselves out as common carriers of expresses; and when they unreasonably refuse, directly or indirectly, to carry any more public servants of that class, they perform this duty with illegal partiality. The statute under which this case was decided required the railway company to furnish "all persons and expressmen equal facilities": McDuffee v. Portland etc. R. R. Co., 52 N. H. 430; 13 Am. Rep. 72. In New England Exp. Co. v. Maine Cent. R. R. Co., 57 Me. 188, 2 Am. Rep. 31, the railroad company, by agreement, gave to the Eastern Express Company the exclusive right, for four years, to use a certain apartment in a car attached to each of its passenger trains for the purpose of carrying an express messenger and merchandise, and agreed

that it would not let any space in its passenger trains during
the continuance of such contract to any other express carrier. Before the expiration of the contract, the railroad company refused,
upon any terms, to receive the express matter of another express
company, when and where they received that of the contracting
express company. The court determined that it was not within the
power of the railroad company to grant any such exclusive privilege,
and that it was liable in damages for so doing. Appleton, C. J., in
delivering the opinion of the court, said: "The very definition of
a common carrier excludes the idea of the right to grant monopolies, or to give special and unequal preferences. It implies indifference as to whom they may serve, and an equal readiness to
serve all who may apply, and in the order of their application.
The defendants derive their chartered rights from the state.
They owe an equal duty to each citizen. They are allowed to impose a toll, but it is not to be so imposed as specially to
benefit one and injure another. They cannot, having the means of
transporting all, select from those who may apply some whom they
will, and reject others whom they can, but will not, carry. They
cannot rightfully confer a monopoly upon individuals or corporations. They were created for no such purpose. They may regulate transportation, but the right to regulate gives no authority
to refuse, without cause, to transport certain individuals and their
baggage or goods, and to grant exclusive privileges of transportation to others. The state gave them a charter for no such purpose.
Such is the common law on the subject. The legislation of the state
has been in accordance with and in confirmation of these views."
The statute under which that case was decided provided that all
engaged in the business of carrying express matter "should have
reasonable and equal terms, facilities, and accommodations for the
transportation of themselves, their agents and servants, and of any
merchandise and other property, upon any railroad owned and operated within the state, and of the use of the depot and other buildings and grounds of such corporation, and at any point of intersection
of two railroads reasonable and equal terms and facilities of inter-
change"; and the court said: "The defendants (the railroad company) cannot object to this statute, unless they had, before its passage, an unlimited right to impose unreasonable and unequal terms,
to give special privileges, to confer monopolies, selecting from the
great public, from whom they acquired their powers and franchise,
who shall be the special and selected objects of their bounty, and
who shall not. The wildest and most extravagant supporter of
vested rights will hardly claim this. It would imply madness or
crime on the part of the legislature granting such rights. If, then,
the defendants have no such right, the grant of a monopoly to one
corporation at the expense of the general public is alike a violation
of the common as of the statute law, and cannot be upheld." Statutes requiring railroad companies, either in express terms or by
judicial interpretation, to furnish equal facilities to all express companies, are of comparatively recent origin, and thus far seem not to
have been generally adopted.

On the contrary, it has been held that a railroad company cannot be compelled to furnish express facilities to a special express company to conduct an express business over its road the same as it provides for itself or affords to some special express company, when it affords express facilities for all matter offered, has not held itself out as a common carrier of express companies, and is not compelled by special statute. In such a case, its refusal to carry a special express company over its road is not a violation of a railroad commission's rule that "no railroad company shall, by reason of any contract with any express or other company, decline or refuse to act as a common carrier to transport any articles proper to be transported by the train for which it is offered": Atlantic Exp. Co. v. Wilmington etc. R. R. Co., 111 N. C. 463; 32 Am. St. Rep. 805; following Express cases, 117 U. S. 1, which hold that, in the absence of some special statute, there is no law requiring railroads to furnish express facilities to all express companies which may demand them. See, also, Louisville etc. Ry. Co. v. Keefer, 146 Ind. 21; 58 Am. St. Rep. 348.

Contract to Transport Express Matter—Injuries Occasioned by Negligence of Railroad Company.—The authorities above cited and quoted from show, we think, that the prevailing opinion is, that, in the absence of some controlling statute, a common carrier is not bound to furnish equal facilities to all express companies that may wish to be carried, but this question must not be confused with that growing out of the relations of the parties under a contract of carriage which has been entered into by them. In other words, the carrier's right to exclude express companies from its line has nothing to do with its express contract relations. In speaking of the Express cases, 117 U. S. 1, Taft, C. J., says, in Voight v. Baltimore etc. Ry. Co., 79 Fed. Rep. 561, 564, holding that a railroad company is under no obligation to carry an express messenger, as such, that: "The plain intimation of the opinion of the court was that the express business had become such a necessity that it was the duty of a railroad company to furnish express facilities to the public; but the point in judgment was that a railroad company was not obliged to furnish to an independent express company means for carrying on the express business upon its road. The court held that the railroad company was not a common carrier of common carriers, and that it sufficiently complied with any obligation which it was under to the public to furnish to them express facilities, if it made a contract with one company to do all the express business upon its road. It follows from that case that, if a railroad company chooses to do its own express business, it may exclude all express companies from its line. The case does not decide that the railroad company, when it contracts to transport the express matter of an express company, is not discharging its duty as a common carrier in offering the public express facilities. It is true that it is under no obligation to carry an express messenger as such. It may stipulate with the express company that it will provide one of its own servants to take charge of the express matter while upon its trains. But when it does carry an express messenger, it is discharging its function as a

common carrier of persons. An express messenger is not a different
kind of freight from an ordinary passenger upon its passenger trains,
except that he travels in a special car provided by the railroad company. He would have the right to demand of the railroad company
that he should be carried in the passenger train, if he tendered his
fare. If the company, in order to discharge its duty to the public,
to afford express facilities upon its line, agrees to carry him in a
special car in a passenger train, he does not thereby lose his rights
and character as a passenger. This may be seen from the ruling of
the supreme court in an analogous case. A railroad company is a
common carrier of cattle. It is under no obligation to carry drovers
to attend the cattle. It may assume this duty itself, and provide servants of its own to water and care for the live freight. When it
does, however, make a contract allowing a drover to ride upon its
cattle train, furnishing, as one of the terms of the contract of
affreightment, free transportation for the purpose, he is carried as a
passenger for hire by the railroad company as a common carrier.
The reason is, that the railroad company is bound to carry the drover
if he presents himself and pays his fare upon its passenger trains,
and if, for any purpose of its own, the railroad company sees fit
to allow the drover to ride upon its freight trains, though it is not
under any obligation to carry him upon such trains, in doing so it
does not lose the character of a common carrier carrying a passenger
for hire: Railroad Co. v. Lockwood, 17 Wall. 357."

While a railroad company is under no obligation to carry an express messenger as such, if he is carried under a contract with the
railroad company made by the express company for the transportation of express matter in his charge, he is, by the weight of authority,
considered a passenger for hire, though he is carried in a special
car, and entitled to the rights of such a passenger, because the railroad company is then discharging its function as a common carrier
of persons: Voight v. Baltimore etc. Ry. Co., 79 Fed. Rep. 561; Brewer
v. New York etc. R. R. Co., 124 N. Y. 59; 21 Am. St. Rep. 647; Pennsylvania Co. v. Woodworth, 26 Ohio St. 585; Yeomans v. Contra Costa
etc. Co., 44 Cal. 71; Jennings v. Grand Trunk Ry. Co., 15 Ont. App.
477. Same principle as to mail agents, see Gulf etc. Ry. Co. v. Wilson, 79 Tex. 371, 23 Am. St. Rep. 345. Even where there is no
special contract between the express company and the railroad company, the latter company owes to the express messenger the same
duty that it owes to an ordinary passenger: Fordyce v. Jackson, 56
Ark. 594; and, in the absence of an express stipulation to the contrary, is answerable to him for an injury caused by its negligence,
though the messenger has paid no fare: Blair v. Erie Ry. Co., 66
N. Y. 313; 23 Am. Rep. 55. The general rule is, that a contract
whereby a passenger on a railroad train agrees not to hold the
railroad company answerable for an injury to him caused by the
negligence of the company or its servants is void as against public
policy, and this rule applies to an express messenger carried by a
railroad company in a special car, under a contract with the express
company: Voight v. Baltimore etc. Ry. Co., 79 Fed. Rep. 561; Brewer

v. New York etc. R. R. Co., 124 N. Y. 59; 21 Am. St. Rep. 647; Kenney
v. New York etc. R. R. Co., 125 N. Y. 422.

It appears to be perfectly reasonable that a person entering into
a contract of service with one employer may not, without his knowledge or assent, be made to assume the hazards of a service conducted
by another, and in which he is not engaged, and thus be personally
subjected to the consequences of the negligence of the latter, without remedy against him. A railway company is, therefore, answerable for its negligence resulting in the death of an express messenger
carried on its road free, under a contract between it and the express
company, in which it is stipulated that in no event, whether of
negligence or otherwise, shall the railway company be responsible for
property carried by it free of charge, where there is no evidence that
such messenger had any knowledge of the provisions of the contract.
When he entered the service of the express company he assumed
the ordinary hazards incident to that business in his relation to that
company, but there was no presumption or implied understanding
that he took upon himself the risks of injury he might suffer from
the negligence or fault of the railway company: Brewer v. New
York etc. R. R. Co., 124 N. Y. 59; 21 Am. St. Rep. 647.

Under the law of New York, general words in the contract of a
common carrier limiting its liability are not construed as exempting
it from liability for negligence, if they are susceptible of another
construction. In that state a contract between an express company
and a railroad company, in relation to the carriage of express matter
over the road, provided that the railroad company should be "expressly released from and guaranteed against any liability for any
damage done to the agents" of the express company, "whether in
their employ as messengers or otherwise." A messenger in the
employ of the express company was killed through the negligence of
the railroad company, and in an action by his administratrix to recover damages for the death it was held that the contract might
be read, not necessarily as releasing or preventing an action by
employés of the express company against the railroad company for
damages for injuries received while on the road, but as an agreement to indemnify the railroad company in the event of such an
action, and that the plaintiff was entitled to recover: Kenney v. New
York etc. R. R. Co., 125 N. Y. 422. The decision, however, was placed
upon the ground that the contract did not in unmistakable language
provide for an exemption from liability for the negligence of the
defendant's employés. "The rule," said the court, "is firmly established in this state that a common carrier may contract for immunity
from its negligence, or that of its agents; but that, to accomplish
that object, the contract must be so expressed, and it must not be
left to a presumption from the language. Considerations based upon
public policy and the nature of the carrier's undertaking influence the
application of the rule, and forbid its operation, except where the
carrier's immunity from the consequences of negligence is read in the
agreement ipsissimis verbis": Kenney v. New York etc. R. R. Co.,
125 N. Y. 422, 425. On the other hand, in Texas, an express com-

pany entered into a contract with a railroad company whereby the former assumed "all risk of loss or damage arising out of or resulting from its operations under this agreement," and agreed to "hold harmless the said railway company against the same," and the court said: "We do not think it was intended by that clause to bind the express company to indemnify the railway against injuries to a messenger resulting from the negligence of the railway company." The railway company, it was said, could not, by contract, make a third party responsible for its negligence and wrong, so as to bind the latter, even with his consent: San Antonio etc. Ry. Co. v. Adams. 6 Tex. Civ. App. 102. Another view of the relations existing between an express company and other common carriers is, that a common carrier may, under some circumstances, become a private carrier. This will now be noticed in the following separate subdivision of this note.

Common Carrier Becoming a Private Carrier.—A common carrier may become a private carrier or bailee for hire where, as a matter of accommodation, or special engagement, he undertakes to carry something which it is not his business to carry: Railroad Co. v. Lockwood, 17 Wall. 357, 377; Robertson v. Old Colony R. R. Co., 156 Mass. 525; 32 Am. St. Rep. 482; Coup v. Wabash etc. Ry. Co., 56 Mich. 111; 56 Am. Rep. 374; Chicago etc. R. R. Co. v. Wallace, 66 Fed. Rep. 506; New Jersey Steam Nav. Co. v. Merchants' Bank, 6 How. 344, 382. This is well illustrated by the "Circus cases." In these cases the railroad company agreed to haul over its road the train of cars belonging to the circus proprietor, and containing the animals and the company of persons engaged in the circus. It was held that the railway company was not liable as a common carrier, but acted as a private carrier, and might exempt itself, by contract, from liability for the negligence of itself and its servants in the hauling of the circus train, as it might refuse absolutely to receive the cars of the circus company and to haul them: Coup v. Wabash etc. Ry. Co., 56 Mich. 111; 56 Am. Rep. 374; Chicago etc. R. R. Co. v. Wallace, 66 Fed. Rep. 506; Robertson v. Old Colony R. R. Co., 156 Mass. 525; 32 Am. St. Rep. 482. So the rights of a shipper of specie may be controlled by a valid contract between an express company and a steamboat company: New Jersey Steam Nav. Co. v. Merchants' Bank, 6 How. 344. And this principle has been applied, in Indiana, to a contract exempting a railroad company from liability in the carriage of express matter and express messengers: See principal case. In that state a railway company, while carrying goods for an express company under a special contract, is held to be a private and not a common carrier, and may, by contract between the express company, its messengers, and itself, exempt itself from liability for injury to such messengers, however caused, while they are in charge of express matter on its trains: Louisville etc. Ry. Co. v. Keefer, 146 Ind. 21; 58 Am. St. Rep. 348. This holding is, of course, upon the theory that a railroad company, in transporting an express company's matter, and its agents, in performing a service foreign to its duties as a common carrier, and which it cannot be compelled to perform. It has also been held in Massachusetts that if an express messenger, holding a season ticket from a railroad company, and desiring to ride for the conduct of his business in a baggage-car, in contravention of its rules, agrees to assume all risk of injury therefrom, and to hold the company harmless therefor, it is a valid contract, exempting the railroad company from an injury received by the messenger through the negligence of the company, although the contract does not expressly exempt the railroad company from accidents occurring through its own negligence: Bates v. Old Colony R. R. Co., 147 Mass. 255; Hosmer v. Old Colony R. R. Co., 156 Mass. 500. The conclusion of the court in these cases was based on the fact that the place where the plaintiff was riding was one in which the defendant was not under obligation to carry him. The contract gave him the privilege which he sought for his own convenience, and while it did not expressly exempt the railroad company from accidents occurring through its own negligence, it was given that effect. The Indiana and Massachusetts cases above cited are not, however, in accord with the weight of authority, that a change of employment does not necessarily follow a change of liability. It is true that a common carrier cannot be compelled to carry outside of its business, as in the case of dogs and menageries, but it must carry express matter to the extent needed by the public, though it is not required to furnish facilities to all express companies, and an express messenger is one of the public whom a railroad company is bound to carry in some kind of a car, though it is not bound to carry him as an express messenger. Such carriage may be refused to the extent above indicated in this note, but when it is undertaken, the railroad company is, according to at least a preponderance of authority, discharging its function as a common carrier of persons and property: Voight v. Baltimore etc. Ry. Co., 79 Fed. Rep. 561; Railroad Co. v. Lockwood, 17 Wall. 357, 377; Brewer v. New York etc. R. R. Co., 124 N. Y. 59; 21 Am. St. Rep. 647; Pennsylvania Co. v. Woodworth. 26 Ohio St. 585; Yeomans v. Contra Costa etc. Co., 44 Cal. 71; Jennings v. Grand Trunk Ry. Co., 15 Ont. App. 477; Gulf etc. Ry. Co. v. Wilson, 79 Tex. 371; 23 Am. St. Rep. 345; and not as a private carrier, or bailee for hire.

Mr. Justice Bradley, in delivering the opinion of the supreme court of the United States, in Railroad Co. v. Lockwood, 17 Wall. 357, 376, used this language: "It is argued that a common carrier, by entering into a special contract with a party for carrying his goods or person on modified terms, drops his character and becomes an ordinary bailee for hire, and, therefore, may make any contract he pleases. That is, he may make any contract whatever, because he is an ordinary bailee; and he is an ordinary bailee because he has made the contract. We are unable to see the soundness of this reasoning. It seems to us more accurate to say that common carriers are such by virtue of their occupation, not by virtue of the responsibilities under which they rest. Those responsibilities may vary in different countries, and at different times, without changing the character of the employment. The common law subjects the common carrier to insurance of the goods carried, except as against the act of God or public enemies. The civil law excepts, also, losses by

means of any superior force, and inevitable accident. Yet the employment is the same in both cases. And if, by special agreement,
the carrier is exempted from still other responsibilities, it does not
follow that his employment is changed, but only that his responsibilities are changed. The theory occasionally announced, that a
special contract as to the terms and responsibilities of carriage
changes the nature of the employment, is calculated to mislead. The
responsibilities of a common carrier may be reduced to those of
an ordinary bailee for hire, whilst the nature of his business renders
him a common carrier still. Is there any good sense in holding that
a railroad company, whose only business is to carry passengers and
goods, and which was created and established for that purpose alone,
is changed to a private carrier for hire by a mere contract with a
customer, whereby the latter assumes the risk of inevitable accidents
in the carriage of his goods. Suppose the contract relates to a single
crate of glass or crockery, whilst at the same time the carrier
receives from the same person twenty other parcels, respecting
which no such contract is made. Is the company a public carrier as
to the twenty parcels and a private carrier as to the one? A common carrier may, undoubtedly, become a private carrier, or a bailee
for hire, when, as a matter of accommodation or special engagement, be undertakes to carry something which it is not his business
to carry. For example, if a carrier of produce, running a truck boat
between New York City and Norfolk, should be requested to carry
a keg of specie, or a load of expensive furniture, which he could
justly refuse to take, such agreement might be made in reference
to his taking and carrying the same as the parties chose to make,
not involving any stipulation contrary to law or public policy. But
when a carrier has a regularly established business for carrying all
or certain articles, and especially if that carrier be a corporation
created for the purpose of the carrying trade, and the carriage
of the articles is embraced within the scope of its chartered powers,
it is a common carrier, and a special contract about its responsibility
does not divest it of the character."

A common carrier cannot, by any special contract, exempt himself
from liability for loss occasioned by its negligence, or that of its
servants or agents: Notes to Meuer v. Chicago etc. Ry. Co., 49 Am. St.
Rep. 908; Duntley v. Boston etc. R. R., 49 Am. St. Rep. 613; Jones
v. St. Louis etc. Ry. Co., 125 Mo. 666; 46 Am. St. Rep. 514; Willock
v. Pennsylvania R. R. Co., 166 Pa. St. 184; 45 Am. St. Rep. 674; Johnson v. Alabama etc. Ry. Co., 69 Miss. 191; 30 Am. St. Rep. 534; note
to Pacific Exp. Co. v. Foley, 26 Am. St. Rep. 120; Johnson v. Richmond etc. R. R. Co., 86 Va. 975. Contra, Kenney v. New York etc. R. R.
Co., 125 N. Y. 422, 425; Brewer v. New York etc. R. R. Co., 124 N. Y.
59, 21 Am. St. Rep. 647; Mynard v. Syracuse etc. R. R. Co., 71 N. Y.
180; 27 Am. Rep. 28; Bissell v. New York etc. R. R. Co., 25 N. Y. 442;
82 Am. Dec. 369. This rule applies to express companies as well as to
railroad companies and other common carriers: See monographic
note to Bullard v. American Exp. Co., 61 Am. St. Rep. 358, discussing
the duties and liabilities of express companies as common carriers;
and it will be noticed that even in Indiana, a railroad company, while

performing its duty as a common carrier, cannot protect itself by contract from liability for negligence to a passenger; though it is there held that a railroad company is not obliged to carry an express messenger as such, and that, when he is carried under a special contract, he is not a passenger: Louisville etc. Ry. Co. v. Keefer, 146 Ind. 21; 58 Am. St. Rep. 348.

Other Matters.—An express company employing a railroad company to carry goods contracted to be transported by it, becomes primarily liable, in case of loss, to the consignor for the negligent acts of the railroad company, as the railroad company is then the agent of the express company, and the express company is answerable for loss occasioned by its own agents: Muser v. American Exp. Co., 1 Fed. Rep. 382; Hooper v. Wells, Fargo & Co., 27 Cal. 11; 85 Am. Dec. 211; Bank of Kentucky v. Adams Exp. Co., 93 U. S. 174; Boscowitz v. Adams Exp. Co., 93 Ill. 523; 34 Am. Rep. 191. The carrier is also liable to the owner for all the goods shipped on a public conveyance by an express company, without regard to any contract to the contrary between the carrier and the express company. Although the carrier may have no custody or control of the goods, he is liable to the owner in case of loss, if he allows them to be brought on board: New Jersey Steam Nav. Co. v. Merchants' Bank, 6 How. 344, 385; The D. R. Martin, 11 Blatchf. 233, 235. If a railroad company does its own express business, one who accepts service with the company as an express messenger is, ordinarily, to be considered as a fellow-servant of the engineer and other subordinate employés engaged in operating the trains of the company on which he is carried while performing this duty as express messenger: Baltimore etc. R. R. Co. v. McKenzie, 81 Va. 71, 83. If a messenger of an express company, who is entitled to be carried on the freight-cars of a railroad, is employed by the superintendent of the road to act as brakeman for one trip, and, while so employed, he is, by the negligent conduct of the engineer, thrown from the cars and injured, he may maintain an action against the railroad company, whether considered as a passenger or employé on that train: Chamberlain v. Milwaukee etc. R. R. Co., 11 Wis. 238. An express messenger on a railway train is not the servant of the railroad company, and the company is not, therefore, answerable for his wrongful acts: Louisville etc. Ry. Co. v. Douglass, 69 Miss. 723; 30 Am. St. Rep. 582. A railroad company is not bound, under a contract to run special express trains, to expedite the service of trains, except upon payment, by the express company, of the increased cost: Park v. New York etc. R. R. Co., 72 Fed. Rep. 594. Express companies, independently organized as corporations to transact the express business on their own account, are not subject to the provisions of the interstate commerce act: United States v. Morsman, 42 Fed. Rep. 448.

DENNIS *v.* HOLSAPPLE.

[143 INDIANA, 297.]

WILLS—VALIDITY OF, WHERE BENEFICIARY IS NOT NAMED.—It is not essentially necessary that a testator, in his will, name the legatee or devisee, in order to give effect to the bequest. It is sufficient if he is so described therein as to be ascertained and identified. Hence, if a testatrix devises all of her property to whoever shall take care of her, at her request, providing that the person so selected shall have a written statement to that effect, the will is not invalid for the reason that no devisee is named.

EVIDENCE, EXTRINSIC, TO EXPLAIN WILL.—A will may be explained by extrinsic evidence as to the person intended, the thing intended, or the intention of the testator, as to each, when the employment of such evidence does not result in making more or less of the will than its terms import.

EVIDENCE, EXTRINSIC, TO IDENTIFY DEVISEE.—If a testatrix devises all of her property to whoever shall take care of her, at her request, providing that the person so selected shall have a written statement to that effect signed by her, a letter written by her to her granddaughter after the execution of the will, informing the latter that the testatrix is sick and requesting her to come and take care of her, that she has made her will, and that she desires the granddaughter to have all of her estate, is admissible in evidence, in a controversy over the will, for the purpose of identifying the devisee.

Harvey Morris and Alspaugh & Lawler, for the appellant.

John A. Zaring and M. B. Hottel, for the appellee.

298 JORDAN, J. This was a proceeding in the lower court by the appellee, Ella Holsapple, to secure a construction of the last will of Emily J. Schull, deceased, and to obtain an order directing the appellant, the administrator, to turn over to the former certain property to which she claimed to be entitled as a devisee under the will in question. She prevailed in the action and obtained the relief demanded. Prior to the institution of this proceeding the will had been duly probated, and appellant appointed as administrator of the estate with the will annexed. The errors assigned are based upon the sufficiency of the complaint upon demurrer, and overruling appellant's motion for a new trial. The will over which the controversy arose was duly executed by Emily J. Schull on April 9, 1889, and was probated in the circuit court of Washington county, Indiana, January 7, 1896, in which county the testatrix resided and died. The will, omitting the attesting clause, is as follows:

"The following is the last will and testament of Emily J. Schull, of Salem, Indiana, to wit: So far as my property which I leave at my death is concerned, I declare the following to be

my desire and will: 1. Any valid debts due.from me at my
death shall be paid; 2. I command that my funeral at my death
shall be decent and rendered in a proper manner; 3. Also I direct
my executor to erect at my grave a proper monument not to
cost less than seventy-five dollars ($75.00); 4. Whoever shall
take good care of me and maintain, nurse, clothe, and furnish
me with proper medical treatment at my request, during the
time of my life yet, when I shall need the same, shall have all
of my property of every name, kind, and description left at
my death; 5. The person, or persons, whom shall be selected
by me to earn my estate, as provided in 4th clause, shall have
a written statement signed by me [299] to that effect to entitle
her, him, or them to my estate; 6. Samuel B. Voyles of Salem
is nominated for my executor of this will."

On January 6, 1895, the testatrix wrote and sent the following letter to the appellee: "Well, Ella, I am sick; I want you
to come and stay with me. I don't think I can live many weeks;
if you don't come I will try and get some of Lina Clark's to
stay. If you don't come you will rue it. I have made my will,
and whoever stays with me at my last hours gets everything I
leave, except funeral expenses paid. I don't want your father
or the Schulls to have a cent of my earnings, and want you to
have everything I have after my death and funeral expenses are
paid. Don't fail to come."

This letter, together with the will, upon the trial, over appellant's objections was admitted in evidence. There is no controversy over the facts. Among other things, it was admitted by
the parties upon the trial that appellee was the granddaughter
of the testatrix and the person to whom the letter above set out
was addressed. That she received the same, and, in response
to the request therein, she came and remained with Mrs. Schull,
waited upon, and took care of her until she died. The contention, substantially of appellant's learned counsel is: 1. That the
will is invalid for the reason that it does not name any devisee;
2. That the testatrix undertook by her pretended will to reserve
to herself the right or power to name the beneficiary by the written statement mentioned in the will, and which was written after
the execution thereof. They further insist that the person to
whom Mrs. Schull attempted to bequeath her estate is not made
certain by the will, and that the latter does not furnish the means
by which a devisee can be identified.

For any and all of these reasons they insist that, [300] under the
law, the will is void and the court erred in admitting it and the

letter in question in evidence, and in hearing evidence to identify appellee as the beneficiary under the will.

We concur with the contention of counsel for appellant, that
a testator, under the law, is not authorized or invested with the
power of reserving in his will the right to name or appoint a
legatee or devisee by means of a written statement, or instrument of the character or kind as is the letter heretofore referred
to and set out in this opinion. Neither are courts permitted to
receive extrinsic evidence in order to add to, vary, or change the
literal meaning of the terms of a will, or to give effect to what
may be supposed or presumed to have been the unexpressed intention of the testator. However, it is a well-affirmed legal principle, that a will may be explained by such evidence: 1. As to
the person intended; 2. The thing intended; 3. The intention of
the testator, as to each, when the employment of such evidence
does not result in making more or less of the will than its terms
import. Or, in other words, the law never opens the door to
parol evidence in order to add to or take from such instruments,
but for the legitimate purpose only of applying their terms or
provisions to the objects or subjects therein referred to, and in
order to reach a correct interpretation of such language or terms
as are therein expressed: Grimes v. Harmon, 35 Ind. 198; 9 Am.
Rep. 690; Daugherty v. Rogers, 119 Ind. 254; Sturgis v. Work,
122 Ind. 134; 17 Am. St. Rep. 349; Hartwig v. Schiefer, 147
Ind. 64.

Courts, however, in the main, entertain great respect for the
will of those who are dead, and it is always their earnest desire
to carry into effect the terms and provisions thereof, and it is
only when the instrument violates, or is not in accord with the
well-settled [301] rules of law, or is utterly uncertain, that the
carrying out of the disposition of the estate thereunder is denied.
The authorities fully affirm the rule that it is not essentially
necessary that the testator, in his will, name the legatee or devisee, in order to give effect to the bequest. It is sufficient, if
he is so described therein as to be ascertained and identified:
1 Redfield on Wills, 274; see Schouler on Wills, secs. 573, 584-
586, 592, 593; Beach on Wills, sec. 83, p. 148; Cheney v. Sel-
man, 71 Ga. 384; Hart v. Marks, 4 Bradf. 161; Stubbs v. Sargon,
2 Keen, 255; 14 Eng. Ch. 507. Extrinsic evidence, however,
in such cases does not create the devisee or legatee, but only serves
to point out the person intended as such by the testator in his
will.

In Hart v. Marks, 4 Bradf. 161, in course of the opinion, it is said: "Parol proof may always be used to apply the will—that is, to ascertain the person intended by the testator, by a description. . . . . It is entirely competent to point out by proof the person who answers the description of a legatee, as contained in the will." The will involved in the case of Stubbs v. Sargon, 2 Keen, 255, devised certain freehold estates to trustees, the annual income of which was to be paid to the sister of the devisor, during the life of the former, and after her death to dispose of the estate to the partners of the testatrix who should be in partnership with her at the time of her death, or to whom she might have disposed of her business. The court held in that appeal that this was a good devise to the persons to whom it was ascertained, that the testatrix had disposed of her business, in her lifetime.

In 1 Redfield on Wills, 275, the learned author, in his comments upon this decision, says: "This was regarded as nothing more than a description of the legatee, [302] instead of naming him, and we suppose the right to do that was never questioned. And whether the legatee were to be ascertained, at the date of the will, or at the death of the testator, or upon the determination of an intervening estate, which should only begin at the decease of the testator, has never been considered material. One may give real or personal estate to his wife, to the children of his brother, or to the next of kin of the testator, after the decease of all his lineal descendants, and in all of these cases, and in many others, the devise may be so expressed as to raise a serious question, not only in regard to the identity of the persons, which may be ascertained by resort to extraneous evidence, but also as to the period at which the description of persons, or classes is to be applied, and this must be removed by legal construction. But we have never supposed any doubt could exist in regard to the complete disposition of the property under such a devise."

In the light of the principles declared and supported by the authorities to which we have referred, and others of a like import, we may proceed to consider and determine the question involved under the will in controversy. An examination of its terms and provisions discloses that the evident intent and purpose of the testatrix thereunder was to make, at her death, the object of her bounty the person who, at her request, should take good care of her, and provide for and administer to her wants and necessities as therein provided. The manifest purpose of the provision embraced in clause 5, when construed in connection with clause 4, was to fix or declare what should be the requisite proof of the fact that the person who performed the required services and complied with the conditions imposed by clause 4 had been selected and requested to do so by the testatrix. The written statement, [303] as mentioned, was to be the evidence of such fact. The provision of clause 5 cannot be considered as a reservation to appoint, in the future, under the written statement referred to, the person who was to take the property bequeathed. The statement or request signed and sent to appellee by Mrs. Schull, in pursuance of this provision in her will, was not testamentary. No one was appointed thereby to take the estate devised. It simply advised appellee of the provisions made by the will, and requested her to come and stay with the testatrix, and could be employed only as it was upon the trial to aid in the identification of the person described, and declared in the will to be entitled to the bequest. The will, although not skillfully drawn, nevertheless, we think, made a complete disposition of all of Mrs. Schull's estate. It is true, as insisted, that it did not name any particular person as devisee, nor was there anyone at the time of its execution who occupied the status, or answered to the beneficiary therein described; still, however, it so designated the person whom the testatrix contemplated and intended should have the estate bequeathed, that he or she, by the means thereof, at her death could be clearly identified and ascertained by the aid of extraneous facts. It was at least in this respect sufficiently certain as to fall within the principle of the ancient maxim of the law, Id certum est quod certum reddi potest.

The testatrix substantially declared therein that whoever, at her request, performed the services exacted thereunder, and complied with the conditions imposed, should have all of her property of "every name, kind, and description," and further provided that the person selected by her to serve as mentioned should have the statement referred to in clause 5. These facts were the standard or test by which the beneficiary was to be determined. In the search to [304] ascertain the person entitled to the property according to the terms of the instrument, it was legitimate to prove all facts referred to in the will, going to identify such person: 7 Am. & Eng. Ency. of Law, 93. The will is not in the condition it would be had the name of the devisee been entirely blank with no sufficient terms or provisions therein descriptive of the beneficiary intended. Under such circumstances, parol evidence could not be invoked, and the will would be void in this respect for uncertainty.

Appellee is the only one who claims, under the will, the property devised. The evidence, together with the agreement of the parties, conclusively shows that she, at the time of the death of the testatrix, occupied the status, and in all respects responded to the person described, to whom Mrs. Schull intended her estate to go; while the insistence of appellant's counsel may be conceded, that, in making her will, Mrs. Schull left the person whom she thereby intended to become the object of her bequest to depend, in a sense, upon the happening of future events. This person, it is true, depended upon the future volition of the testatrix in being chosen to perform the exacted services, and upon the consent of the latter in accepting the request, and in discharging the obligation imposed by the will; but the subsequent volition exercised by Mrs. Schull in this respect cannot be deemed or considered in a legal sense as testamentary in its nature or character. It is no more so than had she been a feme sole at the time she executed her will, and thereby devised her estate to her surviving husband. To illustrate: An unmarried man may make a valid bequest to his wife and children, although he has neither at the execution of the will. If, however, he leaves surviving him either a widow, or children, at his decease, she or they, as the case may be, would take under the will, though not [305] sustaining that relation to him at the date of its execution. That this would be the result, under such a will, it is said in a footnote in 1 Redfield on Wills, page 276, has never been questioned, although the person who became the wife of the testator depended, in a sense, upon the future will of the testator in making the selection, and also upon the consent of the person who became his wife. Without further extending this opinion we sustain the validity of the will in dispute, and, under the circumstances of the case, the court did not err in admitting in evidence the letter or statement in question, nor in admitting the other facts to prove that appellee was the person who at the request of the testatrix discharged the obligations imposed by the will. The complaint was sufficient for the relief demanded, and the demurrer thereto was properly overruled, and also the motion for a new trial.

Judgment affirmed.

WILLS—EXTRINSIC EVIDENCE TO IDENTIFY DEVISEE OR LEGATEE.—For the purpose of determining the object of a testator's bounty in a will, extrinsic evidence is admissible to identify the devisee or legatee: Chappell v. Missionary Soc., 3 Ind. App. 356; 50 Am. St. Rep. 276, and monographic note thereto on extrinsic evidence to explain wills.

WINDFALL MANUFACTURING COMPANY *v.* PATTERSON.
[148 INDIANA, 414.]

INJUNCTION AGAINST NUISANCE—BUSINESS.—A business which is a nuisance per se, as well as one that is so conducted as to become an actual nuisance, will be enjoined; but a business which merely threatens to become a nuisance will be enjoined only where the court is satisfied that the threatened nuisance is inevitable.

INJUNCTION AGAINST NUISANCE—GASWELL.—The sinking of a gaswell to supply fuel for a manufacturing plant is not a nuisance per se, and cannot be enjoined as such.

INJUNCTION AGAINST NUISANCE—GASWELL NEAR DWELLING.—The mere drilling of a gaswell within about fifty yards of a dwelling will not be enjoined on the ground that if it is completed there will be a loud noise, pollution of the air, danger from fire or explosion, on account of the natural gas, or danger by reason of the well overflowing with oil or water, thus causing great damage to, and depreciation of, property, if it is not shown that gas, water, or oil will be found, and that the well cannot be so operated as to avoid the apprehended injuries if such gas or liquids are found.

J. C. Blacklidge, C. C. Shirley, R. B. Beauchamp, W. W. Mount, and W. O. Dean, for the appellant.

M. Bell, W. C. Purdum, Gifford & Nash, and Gifford & Coleman, for the appellees.

414 HOWARD, J. The appellees alleged in their complaint that the appellant was "threatening to and proceeding to drill a gaswell" within one hundred and fifty-two feet of appellees' dwelling, and asked that the appellant be restrained from digging said well, and from digging any well, or laying pipes therefrom "at any other point within three hundred feet" of appellees' property.

The complaint was in two paragraphs, to the first of which, named second in the record, there was a **415** special paragraph of answer; and to this answer a demurrer was sustained. The cause was submitted to the court for trial, and judgment rendered enjoining the company from drilling the well. The rulings on the pleadings, and the overruling of the motion for a new trial are assigned as errors.

It is doubtful whether the evidence is in the record. There is a certificate by a reporter that the evidence was taken down by him in shorthand and then transcribed into the longhand writing to which he certifies. The clerk also certifies "that the evidence set out in the bill of exceptions is the same that was taken by John Ingels, who is the official court reporter of the Howard circuit court." We might, perhaps, presume that the

reporter was sworn; but there is nothing to show that his transcript of the evidence was filed with the clerk before it was incorporated in the bill of exceptions, or, indeed, that it was ever
so filed and incorporated. The questions, however, which might
be considered in passing upon the motion for a new trial are,
in a great measure, those raised upon the pleadings. The main
facts do not seem to be in dispute.

It appears that the appellant company was organized in 1891,
for the purpose of buying land and machinery to engage in the
manufacture of brick and drain tile. In pursuance of this object,
the company, during the same year, purchased twenty-two acres
of land near the town of Windfall. The land was believed to
contain an unlimited supply of natural gas, such as was needed
to operate the business in which appellant was to engage. During
the same year, at a cost of twenty-five thousand dollars, the company erected its plant and machinery, locating the same near the
highway on the west line of said tract, and within two hundred
feet of the land afterward purchased by appellees. In that year,
[410] also, the company drilled a gaswell near the southeast corner
of its land, and obtained a sufficient flow of gas to run its factory until the year 1895, when the gas failed in that well.

It is averred in the answer that the twenty-two acre tract of
land is not large enough to afford more than two sites for the
location of a gaswell, such as would probably furnish gas in sufficient quantity to operate the factory; that on the failure of the
east well, it was necessary to suspend the operations of the
factory until another well should be located and drilled; that
three years after the location of the plant, the appellees, with
full knowledge of all the facts, purchased the land on which they
erected the dwelling-house in question; that in 1895, on the failure of appellant's first well, and while appellant was prospecting
for the location of a second well, the appellee, William E. Patterson, gave his consent that a well might be sunk on the west
side of appellant's land, not to be nearer than one hundred and
fifty feet to appellees' said dwelling; and that appellant, relying
upon this agreement, proceeded to drill the well here in question, and to lay the gas mains therefrom; that after the company
had been engaged for four days in sinking the well, and when
they were about to begin drilling the rock, the restraining order
was issued; and that the point selected for drilling the second
well was the farthest possible from the first well, and the best
that could be selected.

The reasons given in the complaint to show why the injunction should be issued were: That if the proposed well should be completed, there would be a continuous loud noise, depriving appellees of the enjoyment of their property and greatly depreciating its value; that natural gas is a very explosive and inflammable substance, and when confined under the surface of the earth, permeates the soil for hundreds of feet; [417] and, as soon as freed in the air, produces a stench, tarnishes paint, furniture and silverware, and renders the atmosphere unfit to breathe for many feet around the place of such escape; that the pipe line, if constructed to carry gas at rock pressure, as intended, would endanger the lives and property of appellees and their families; that gaswells attract the electric fluid and are exceedingly liable to be struck by lightning; that in the digging of said well there is danger of bringing from the earth other substances, such as water and oil; and that, if the well should overflow with either oil or water, great damage would result, rendering appellees' property unfit for the purposes for which they hold the same.

The dangers thus apprehended by appellees were such as might arise in case the well should be sunk, and gas, oil, or water be found. It is not said that any evil result could come merely from the drilling of the well. But the well might be sunk into the trenton rock, and yet no gas, oil, or water be brought to the surface. It is not clear, therefore, that the danger apprehended is so imminent as to warrant the issue of a restraining order. In addition, it may be questioned whether an injunction should in any event issue, unless it be true that a gas, oil, or water well is a nuisance per se, or unless it should be made to appear that the well and pipes of appellant were to be improperly put down and afterward carelessly attended to.

In Dalton v. Cleveland etc. Ry. Co., 144 Ind. 121, the appellant sought to enjoin the erection on appellee's right of way of a coal chute, to be used for supplying its engines with coal, and to be situated very near to a building owned and used by appellant as a dwelling and business house. It was alleged that from the height and character of the structure it would [418] greatly interfere with appellant's access, view, light, and air, would cause unusual, loud, and offensive noises, disturb sleep, cause coal dust, fumes of sulphur, and other noisome gases to be blown into appellant's building, injuring furniture, stock in trade, and in other ways greatly impairing the value of appellant's property, and causing annoyance, discomfort, and danger to appellant and to the occupants of his building. The court, in that case, while not denying that unlawful uses of the structure might be restrained, yet held that, as the erection of the building would of itself not constitute a nuisance, a writ could not issue, for the reason that the threatened evils might never result. The case of Keiser v. Lovett, 85 Ind. 240, 44 Am. Rep. 13, and other authorities were there cited, and the court concluded that: "Each of these cases recognizes the rule that equity will not restrain that which is not a nuisance upon the claim that it may be so used as to constitute a nuisance."

A business which is a nuisance per se, as also one that is so conducted as to have become an actual nuisance, will be enjoined. But a business which merely threatens to become a nuisance will be enjoined only where the court is satisfied that the threatened nuisance is inevitable; and, since the remedy is so severe, resulting often in wholly depriving an owner of the use of his property, the court will proceed with the utmost caution in restraining such threatened and possible injuries.

It was said in Duncan v. Hayes, 22 N. J. Eq. 25, that "A court of equity will not restrain, by injunction, any lawful business, or the erection of any building or works for such business, because it is supposed or alleged that such business will be a nuisance to a dwelling-house near it; it must be clear that the business will be a nuisance, and that it cannot be carried on so as not to be such."

[419] And, in McCutchen v. Blanton, 59 Miss. 116, the court said: "Every doubt should be solved against the restraint of a proprietor in the use of his own property for a purpose seemingly lawful, and conducive both to individual gain and the general welfare. Relief by injunction is so severe in its consequences that it is not to be granted in such a case, except when the right to it is clearly and conclusively made out. To interfere with one's right to use his own land for the production of what he pleases, in a case of doubt, would be a flagrant abuse of power. It is not enough to show a probable and contingent injury, but it must be shown to be inevitable and undoubted": See, also, Cleveland v. Citizens' Gas Light Co., 20 N. J. Eq. 201; Ryan v. Copes, 11 Rich. 217; 73 Am. Dec. 106, and note; Doellner v. Tynan, 38 How. Pr. 176; Rhodes v. Dunbar, 57 Pa. St. 274; 98 Am. Dec. 221; Huckenstine's Appeal, 70 Pa. St. 102; 10 Am. Rep. 669; Gilbert v. Showerman, 23 Mich. 448; Owen v. Phillips, 73 Ind. 284; Barnard v. Sherley, 135 Ind. 547; 41 Am. St. Rep. 454.

In Doellner v. Tynan, 38 How. Pr. 176, it was held that where a street in a city ceases to be used as a place of residence, and is changed to a place of business, no one or two persons, who may, for any reason, desire to continue their residence therein, should be allowed to prevent the carrying on of a lawful and useful trade, merely because they are or may be subjected to annoyance, or even loss thereby. And, in Gilbert v. Showerman, 23 Mich. 448, the court refused to restrain the carrying on, in a proper manner, of a steam flouring mill in the business part of a city, notwithstanding the use of such building for that purpose caused annoyance to the complainant and his family and rendered the occupation of his building, as a residence, less desirable than it otherwise would be. In that case, Judge [420] Cooley said: "The most offensive trades are lawful, as well as the most wholesome and agreeable; and all that can be required of the men who shall engage in them is, that due regard shall be had to fitness of locality. They shall not carry them on in a part of the town occupied mainly for dwellings, nor, on the other hand, shall the occupant of a dwelling in a part of the town already appropriated to such trades, have a right to enjoin another coming in because of its offensive nature. Reason, and a just regard to the rights and interests of the public, require that in such case the enjoyments of pure air and agreeable surroundings for a home shall be sought in some other quarter; and a party cannot justly call upon the law to make that place suitable for his residence which was not so when he selected it."

In the case at bar, the appellant, in locating its brick and tile works, for which natural gas was to be used as fuel, selected a place retired from all residences, and there erected its plant and machinery at great expense. The business so commenced was continued for three years before the appellees came and erected their dwelling upon land across the highway from appellant's land and within two hundred feet of its brick and tile works. Certainly, therefore, unless the works should constitute a nuisance per se, or unless they were so conducted as to become a nuisance in fact, the appellees are not in a position to demand that equity restrain the appellant in the use of its property.

A nuisance per se, as the term implies, is that which is a nuisance in itself, and which, therefore, cannot be so conducted or maintained as to be lawfully carried on or permitted to exist. Such a nuisance is a disorderly house, or an obstruction to a highway or to a navigable stream. But a business lawful in itself cannot be a nuisance per se, although, because of surrounding [421] places or circumstances, or because of the manner in which it is conducted, it may become a nuisance. Certain kinds of business or structures, as powderhouses or nitroglycerine works, are so dangerous to human life that they may be maintained only in the most remote and secluded localities. Others, as slaughter-houses and certain foul-smelling factories, are so offensive to the senses that they must be removed from the limits of cities and towns, and even from the near neighborhood of family residences. Yet there must be some proper place where every lawful business may be carried on, without danger of interference on the part of those who, in some slight degree, may be annoyed or endangered by the nearness of the objectionable occupation.

Of course, all persons have the right to insist that a business in any degree offensive or dangerous to them shall be carried on with such improved means and appliances as experience and science may suggest or supply, and with such reasonable care as may prevent unnecessary inconvenience to them. By such care and improved methods and appliances, many occupations formerly regarded as nuisances may now be carried on, even in populous neighborhoods, without annoyance to anyone. So, an establishment in some degree offensive, as a livery stable, may be kept so cleanly, so free from anything to offend the sense of sight or of smell, that the proprietor may invite his most fastidious visitors to any part of it; although the same establishment might also be so kept as to be an abomination even to the passer-by upon the highway.

It cannot be said that a plant for the manufacture of brick and drain tile, or even a gaswell sunk to supply fuel for such a plant, is a nuisance per se. The business is lawful, and, if located in a proper place, and conducted and maintained in a proper manner, [422] neither the plant nor the well can be treated as a nuisance.

Appellees voluntarily selected the neighborhood of appellant's plant for their residence, three years after the appellant began business there; and while this circumstance is not controlling, yet it is one that must be taken into consideration. Nor will it be sufficient answer that appellant's gaswell was on the east side of the brickyard at the time the appellees selected their home on a lot within two hundred feet of the factory. Experience has shown that gaswells are of short life, and that, after the failure of one well, another, in order to be successful, must be located at a considerable distance from the first. It is averred that there was room for but two wells on this twenty-two acre tract, and that the location of the proposed well is the farthest possible from the first well and the best that could be selected. It is, besides, admitted by the demurrer to the answer that the appellee,

Willard E. Patterson, agreed that the second well should be located within one hundred and fifty feet of his house; and, while it is possible that such agreement might not bind his co-appellee, yet the circumstance shows that the appellant, in locating its well at the distance of one hundred and fifty-two feet from appellee's dwelling, was proceeding carefully and with due regard to appellees' rights.

Unless, therefore, it should be made to appear that the gaswell could not be so managed and maintained as not to be of more than slight or barely possible danger or annoyance to appellees, it does not seem that they could have any sufficient cause to ask that the sinking of the well be restrained. The record does not show, nor have we any means of knowing, that a well at a distance of one hundred and fifty-two feet, or over nine rods, from a dwelling-house, cannot be so maintained and cared for as not to cause the injury and annoyance claimed to be threatened to appellees in this case.

[423] It is to be remembered that before a court of equity will restrain a lawful work, from which merely threatened evils are apprehended, the court must be satisfied that the evils anticipated are imminent and certain to occur. An injunction will not issue to prevent supposed or barely possible injuries. In the case before us, it is not shown that even if the gaswell were in operation it could not be so managed and cared for as to avoid all the injuries apprehended. But, more than this, there might never be any gas found in the well. This, the appellees practically concede, when they recite that, although gas might not be found, yet that oil, or even water, coming from the well would be dangerous to their residence. This is altogether too speculative. If the appellant company is willing to invest its money in a well from which may be brought to the surface of the earth an uncontrollable element productive of the evils feared by appellees, it must be allowed to do so at the hazard to itself of all the consequences for which it would thus become liable. But if the well may be sunk, and the gas, oil, or water therefrom, if any, can be so controlled and managed as to cause no appreciable injuries to appellees or to anyone else, then such reasonable and lawful use of property ought not to be prevented by the courts. To do so would be sheer usurpation of arbitrary power.

We do not think the statute alluded to, section 5108 of Burns' Revised Statutes of 1894 (Acts 1889, p. 22), in relation to condemnation proceedings for gaspipe lines, and providing that lands for such purposes shall not be condemned within seventy-

five yards of any dwelling or barn, has any application here.
Appellant had not instituted any condemnation proceedings, but
was at work on its own land. Besides, the statute permits pipes
to be laid along a public highway, notwithstanding the nearness
of the buildings named; and, in the [424] case at bar, not only
was appellant engaged in sinking a well and laying pipes on
its own lands, but there was a public highway between its lands
and those of the appellees.

We are, therefore, not satisfied, that the record presents a case
warranting the issuing of the writ of injunction. The judgment
is reversed, with instructions to sustain the demurrer to each
paragraph of the complaint, and to overrule the separate demurrers to the second paragraph of the answer, and for further proceedings not inconsistent with this opinion.

INJUNCTION AGAINST NUISANCES—LAWFUL BUSINESS.—
A business will not be enjoined as a nuisance unless it inflicts on
the complainant a real and substantial injury: Note to State v. Taft,
54 Am. St. Rep. 771. A lawful business may be so carried on as to
become a nuisance: Note to Wylie v. Elwood, 23 Am. St. Rep. 683;
but to justify a remedy by injunction, both injury and damage must
exist. Equity will not enjoin it if the injury is doubtful, eventual.
or contingent: Rhodes v. Dunbar, 57 Pa. St. 274; 98 Am. Dec. 221;
McGregor v. Silver King Min. Co., 14 Utah, 47; 60 Am. St. Rep. 883.

DAVIS v. CLEMENTS.

[148 INDIANA, 605.]

INJUNCTION AGAINST ENFORCEMENT OF JUDGMENT
—COLLATERAL ATTACK.—A proceeding to enjoin the enforcement of a judgment or decree by execution or decretal order is a collateral attack upon the judgment, and cannot be maintained for
mere errors or irregularities, but only by showing that the judgment
or decree, or the part thereof, the enforcement of which is sought
to be enjoined, is void.

INJUNCTION AGAINST ENFORCEMENT OF JUDGMENT
—COMPLAINT FOR—DEMURRER.—A judgment of a court of general jurisdiction will be presumed, on appeal, to be valid. Hence,
unless the facts stated, in a complaint in an action to enjoin the enforcement of such judgment, are sufficient to overcome or exclude
this presumption, a demurrer to the complaint should be sustained.

INJUNCTION AGAINST ENFORCEMENT OF JUDGMENT
—COMPLAINT FOR, WHEN INSUFFICIENT.—A complaint in an
action to enjoin the enforcement of a judgment ordering the foreclosure and sale of real estate is insufficient where it does not allege
what the record of the case, in which the decree was rendered, shows
on the subject.

PLEADING.—FACTS, NOT CONCLUSIONS should be stated
in pleadings.

H. H. Ristine, for the appellant.

M. M. Bachelder and George Harvey, for the appellee.

[606] MONKS, J. This action was brought by appellee against appellant, as sheriff of Montgomery county, to enjoin him from paying out money as ordered by a judgment and decree of fore-closure, as shown by a copy of the decree in his hands for exe-cution.

It is alleged in the complaint that "the Ladoga Building, Loan, etc. Association, on December 14, 1895, obtained in the Mont-gomery circuit court against appellee and her husband, a judg-ment for five hundred and forty-one dollars and eleven cents and costs and a decree of foreclosure for the sale of certain real estate (describing it); that in said decree the appellant as sheriff was ordered to sell said real estate and apply the proceeds of sale as follows: 1. To the payment of costs; 2. On judgment of the Ladoga Building etc. Association; 3. On judgment of record, held by Daniel J. Davis and Thomas Rankin against Robert Clements; 4. On judgment of John Maloney against Robert Clements; that Robert Clements is and was at the time of exe-cuting mortgage to the Ladoga Building etc. Association the owner in fee simple of said real estate, and that the appellee was at the time of execution of said mortgage, and ever since has been the wife of said Clements; that she signed said mortgage and is entitled to a one-third interest in said real estate, and is entitled to have said cost and judgment on mortgage paid out of said Clements' two-thirds interest in said real estate, before coming into her one-third interest, and that she is entitled to have one-third of the proceeds of the sale of said land paid to her before any shall be applied on the other judgments against said Clements; that the decree ordering an appli-cation of any of the proceeds from said sale upon other judgments [607] than the Ladoga Building etc. Associa-tion is not binding upon her one-third interest; that she was not made a party to a cross-complaint by any codefend-ant in said foreclosure proceedings; that the appellant has ad-vertised said real estate to be sold on the twenty-fifth day of July, 1896, and he will sell the same on that day, and will, unless otherwise ordered by the court, apply the proceeds in the order named in said decree, which would greatly injure her and defraud her of her one-third interest in said real estate; that said real estate is worth twelve hundred dollars, and she will thereby be defrauded out of four hundred dollars," etc. Appellant's demurrer to the complaint for want of facts was overruled.

After issues were formed, the cause was tried by the court, and a special finding made and conclusions of law stated thereon in favor of appellee, to each of which conclusions of law appellant excepted.

Before the trial of said cause, appellant sold said real estate on said decree for twelve hundred dollars, and the court rendered judgment on the special finding, that appellant pay to the clerk of the court, for the benefit of appellee, all the proceeds of said sale remaining after the payment of the cost of said sale and the amount of the judgment and decree in favor of the Ladoga Building etc. Association, not exceeding, however, four hundred dollars.

It is settled law that a proceeding to enjoin the enforcement of a judgment or decree by execution or decretal order is a collateral attack upon the judgment, and cannot be maintained for mere errors or irregularities, but only by showing that the judgment or decree, or the part thereof, the enforcement of which is sought to be enjoined, is void: Shrack v. Covault, 144 Ind. 260; Krug v. Davis, 85 Ind. 309, and cases cited; Earl v. Matheney, 60 Ind. 202; Gum-Elastic Roofing Co. v. Mexico Pub. Co., 140 Ind. 158, and cases cited; Fitch v. Byall (Ind. App., May 20, 1897), 47 N. E. Rep. 180.

608 The presumption is, that the part of the decree sought to be impeached by appellee, a party thereto, being rendered by a court of general jurisdiction, is valid, and unless the facts stated in the complaint are sufficient to overcome or exclude this presumption, the demurrer thereto should have been sustained: Exchange Bank v. Ault, 102 Ind. 322, 327; Bailey v. Rinker, 146 Ind. 129, and cases cited; Cassady v. Miller, 106 Ind. 69, 71, 72, and cases cited; Indiana Oolitic Limestone Co. v. Louisville etc. Ry. Co., 107 Ind. 301, 305, and cases cited; Sims v. Gay, 109 Ind. 501, 503, and cases cited; Phillips v. Lewis, 109 Ind. 62, 68; Nichols v. State, 127 Ind. 406, 413.

Appellee contends that codefendants can have no relief as between themselves, except upon a cross-complaint to which the defendants between whom the relief is sought are made parties, and that, under this rule, the complaint was sufficient to withstand the demurrer for want of facts. While there are authorities which sustain the rule as stated by appellee, there are cases which hold that adverse interests between codefendants may be passed upon and a decree made between them, grounded upon the pleadings and proof between the complainant and defendants, and founded upon and connected with the subject matter in litigation between the complainant and one or more of the defendants: See 5 Ency. of Pl. & Pr. 637, 638, where the cases are collected. See also, Elliott v. Pell, 1 Paige, 263; 2 Daniell's Chancery Practice, sec. 1370, note 6; Story's Equity Pleading, sec. 392, note 3; Van Fleet on Collateral Attack, secs. 749, 750; 1 Van Fleet on Former Adjudication, 573. But if the rule, as stated by appellee, be correct, which we need not and do not decide, the complaint was not sufficient. The part of the complaint which it is claimed brings the case within the rule stated, and shows that appellee [609] is not bound by the order to pay the judgment in favor of Davis and Rankin, and the judgment in favor of Maloney is, "that she was not made a party to a cross-complaint by any codefendant in said foreclosure proceedings." It is not alleged in the complaint that the Ladoga Building etc. Association commenced the action in which the decree was rendered; so far as the facts alleged show, the other parties to said decree, Davis and Rankin, or Maloney, may have commenced the same by complaint against the Ladoga Building etc. Association, appellee, and others as defendants, and such association may have obtained its judgment and decree on a cross-complaint. It is not shown by the complaint that the part of the decree assailed was rendered upon a cross-complaint. For all that appears from the complaint, it may have been rendered upon the complaint to which appellee was a party. Even if it were alleged that the Ladoga Building etc. Association commenced the action, making appellees, Rankin and Davis and Maloney, defendants thereto, it would not be sufficient, upon appellee's theory of the case, even if correct, to aver that she was not made a party to any cross-complaint. To properly present the question the complaint must allege what the record of the case in which the decree was rendered shows on the subject: Phillips v. Lewis, 109 Ind. 62; Krug v. Davis, 85 Ind. 309; Cassady v. Miller, 106 Ind. 69; Bailey v. Rinker, 146 Ind. 129.

The allegation "that she is entitled to have one-third of the proceeds of the sale of said land paid to her before any shall be applied on other judgments against Robert Clements," states only a legal conclusion. The facts concerning said judgments, and date when rendered, and whether specific or only general liens, should be stated. Facts, not conclusions, should [610] be stated in pleadings: Caskey v. Greensburg, 78 Ind. 233, 237, and cases cited; Krug v. Davis, 85 Ind. 309, and cases cited; State v. Casteel, 110 Ind. 174, 187; Lawrence v. Beecher, 116 Ind. 312, 316; Western Union Tel. Co. v. Taggart, 141 Ind. 281, 283.

The conclusions of law stated by the court in favor of appellee are erroneous for the same reasons which render the complaint insufficient.

Judgment reversed, with instructions to sustain the demurrer to the complaint, and for further proceedings not inconsistent with this opinion.

INJUNCTION AGAINST JUDGMENTS.—Merely erroneous and irregular judgments, wuether against infants or adults, cannot be enjoined. Void judgments can be enjoined: Note to St. Louis etc. Ry. Co. v. Lowder, 60 Am. St. Rep. 569. But see Scott v. Runner, 146 Ind. 12; 58 Am. St. Rep. 345; Wilson v. Shipman, 34 Neb. 573; 33 Am. St. Rep. 660. When relief is granted in chancery from a judgment at law, the interference is in all cases indirect: See monographic note to Little Rock etc. Ry. Co. v. Wells, 54 Am. St. Rep. 260, on relief in equity, other than by appellate proceedings, against judgments, decrees, and other judicial determinations.

PRESUMPTION ON APPEAL IN FAVOR OF JUDGMENT.— The judgment of a court of general jurisdiction is presumed, on appeal, to be regular and valid: Searls v. Knapp, 5 S. Dak. 325; 49 Am. St. Rep. 873.

CASES

IN THE

SUPREME COURT

OF

IOWA.

LARSON *v.* WILLIAMS.

[100 IOWA, 110]

JUDGMENT—VACATING, IN EQUITY, AFTER TIME FIXED BY STATUTE.—Although a time is prescribed by statute, within which a judgment may be vacated for irregularity or fraud in obtaining it, yet a court of equity has power to vacate it, for such cause, after the time so fixed by statute, if proper reasons are shown for not making such application within the time, as where the person against whom it was pronounced did not learn of its rendition until after the expiration of the statutory time for setting it aside.

JUDGMENT, PERSONAL, AGAINST WIFE, BY DEFAULT IS UNAUTHORIZED, WHEN.—If an unmarried man contracts to have a house built for himself, but he afterward marries, and proceedings are instituted against both husband and wife to foreclose a mechanic's lien on the building, a personal judgment by default against her is unauthorized, where there is no averment in the petition which warrants it, although notice was served on both husband and wife that a personal judgment would be taken as to both.

JUDGMENT—PROCUREMENT OF, BY FRAUD—VACATING IN EQUITY.—In an action against a husband and wife to foreclose a mechanic's lien, it is an irregular and fraudulent practice for the successful party to procure a judgment by default against the wife, which judgment is not authorized by the petition, and which the plaintiff knows is not authorized by it. Hence, she may have it vacated, in equity, for "irregularity" and "fraud practiced in obtaining it," after the time fixed by statute for setting it aside on those grounds, where she did not know of its rendition until after the expiration of such time.

Action in equity to cancel a judgment, and to restrain the enforcement thereof. The judgment was rendered in an action in which Williams & Betenbender, the present defendants, were the plaintiffs, and Peter Larson and Celia Larson, his wife, were the defendants. In January, 1889, Williams & Betenbender orally contracted to build a house for Peter Larson. He was, at that time, unmarried, but he did marry afterward. In April, 1889, Williams & Betenbender filed a statement for a mechanic's lien, which statement showed the oral contract "with Peter Larson," that he was the owner of the land, and that the house was built for him. The statement of accounts was with Peter Larson. A foreclosure suit was instituted. Both husband and wife were made parties, and notice was served on both that, unless they should appear and defend, judgment would be taken against them, but no fact was stated in the petition authorizing a personal judgment against the wife. Both parties defendant having made default, a judgment was rendered against them. Counsel for Williams & Betenbender, knowing that the petition did not warrant it, drew, and had signed, a decree giving personal judgment against the wife. She did not discover this until it was too late to set the judgment aside, under the statute. She then brought the present suit against Williams & Betenbender to cancel the judgment, alleging a want of jurisdiction to enter a personal judgment against her, there being no allegation in the petition showing any personal liability on her part. She further alleged that the judgment was obtained against her by fraud practiced by the successful parties and their attorney, as shown above and in the opinion. The personal judgment against her was set aside and Williams & Betenbender appealed. Upon the original hearing of the cause in the supreme court, Given, C. J., rendered an opinion, affirming the judgment of the trial court, but as the case is sufficiently presented by the opinion on rehearing that opinion alone is reported.

M. R. and J. B. McCrary, for the appellants.

M. W. Beach, for the appellee.

[116] KINNE, J.   1. This cause was heard in this court, and an opinion filed affirming the judgment of the lower court. A rehearing has been granted, and the cause is again before us for determination. Without entering into a lengthy discussion of the facts, it may be said that there was nothing in the petition in the case of Williams & Betenbender v. Peter and Celia Larson, or in the issues involved in that case, to warrant a personal judgment as against Celia Larson. She was not a party to the contract out of which the lien arose. She was not the wife of Peter Larson when the contract was made, or when the labor was done

for which a lien was thereafter established. The only reason for making her a party was, that at the time the foreclosure suit was instituted, she was the wife of Peter Larson. No one, on reading the petition, would understand that any facts were pleaded which tended to show a personal liability on the part of Celia Larson.

2. The claim is, that the original notice claimed a personal judgment against the plaintiff, and, as she made default in the action, she is now concluded by the judgment, whether it was procured by fraud practiced by the plaintiffs and their attorney, or not. It is said that this action is not brought within the time limited by the statute. We have often held that, independently of the statute, a court [117] of equity will grant new trials, in actions at law, after the time for applying for relief under section 3157 of the code, has elapsed, if proper reasons are shown for not making such application within the time: Bowen v. Troy Portable Mill Co., 31 Iowa, 460; Partridge v. Harrow, 27 Iowa, 97; 99 Am. Dec. 643; Hoskins v. Hattenback, 14 Iowa, 314; Young v. Tucker, 39 Iowa, 596; District Tp. v. White, 42 Iowa, 613; McConkey v. Lamb, 71 Iowa, 638; Lumpkin v. Snook, 63 Iowa, 515. This action is not predicated upon the statute. It is an attempt to invoke the equitable powers of the court as to vacating judgments, on a proper showing, after the time fixed in the statute for so doing has expired. In the two cases last cited, it is held that the jurisdiction of a court of equity in such cases is limited to the granting of relief on the grounds enumerated in section 3154 of the code. Do the facts alleged and proven on the trial bring this case within the provisions of that section? Among the grounds enumerated in said section are the following: "For mistake, neglect, or omission of the clerk, or irregularity in obtaining a judgment or order; . . . . for fraud practiced by the successful party in obtaining the judgment or order." We think the facts alleged and established make these grounds applicable in this case. Here was a petition which contained no allegations authorizing a personal judgment against Celia Larson. Counsel taking the decree of the court knew such to be the fact. As a lawyer, he knew that Celia Larson might confidently rely upon the fact that nothing was sought, as against her, save the extinguishment of her dower right in the premises. Having no defense to make to that claim, she was not called upon to appear and to answer to the petition. It matters not that the notice said that a personal judgment would be asked against her, as [118] she had a right to rely upon the fact that the petition contained no averment warranting such relief. It is claimed that, as the court by the notice

had jurisdiction of the person of Celia Larson, and by law had
jurisdiction in a proper case to render a personal judgment as to
the subject matter, therefore jurisdiction was in all respects complete, and, having failed to appear, she is concluded from now
being heard. Such claim is not well founded. It is said in
Bosch v. Kassing, 64 Iowa, 314: "It is true a defendant may be
concluded by a default where the facts stated in the petition do
not constitute a good cause of action in law, or where the petition
is so defective as to be vulnerable to a demurrer; but where the
petition omits the necessary averment to show liability against
the defendant, the court may, and should, even upon default, refuse to enter judgment." Clearly, then, procuring the court to
enter such a judgment, under the circumstances, was an "irregularity in obtaining a judgment," under the statute we are considering. So, also, procuring such a judgment upon a petition not
containing any averment authorizing it, and with a full knowledge of the facts, was practicing a fraud within the meaning of
the statute. In Lumpkin v. Snook, 63 Iowa, 518, in construing
this provision of the statute, this court said: "The term 'fraud'
is used in this section in its ordinary sense, 'and it would involve
any act or omission, or concealment which involves a breach of
legal or equitable duty, trust, or confidence, and is injurious to
another, and by which an undue or unconscientious advantage is
taken of another': Story's Equity Jurisprudence, sec. 187." Here
was an act done, in taking the judgment against Celia Larson,
which was a violation of a plain legal duty—an act done by counsel in violation of the duty he owed the court; and it cannot be
doubted, if counsel had advised the court of the [119] condition of
his petition, such judgment would not have been rendered. Taking advantage of his position as an attorney, and of the confidence
which the court no doubt reposed in him, he proceeded to procure a judgment which was wholly unwarranted. He thereby
perpetrated a fraud upon the court and this plaintiff, to the injury of the plaintiff.

Counsel for the defendant herein was a witness in this case,
and the following is a portion of his cross-examination: "Mrs.
Larson was made a party because I didn't know but the land was
in her name, and I wanted judgment against both of them. Q.
Then why was a personal judgment taken against her in the decree? A. Because I wanted a judgment against her. Q. It was
not based on any fact, or any contract, or any liability on her
part? A. I can't tell you whether it was or not. I don't know
about any contract now. I don't mean to say I didn't pay any

attention to that.   I drew the decree in which judgment was rendered against her.   Q. Now, in drawing that decree, upon what
fact did you base it that you had a right to a decree against her?
A. I based it on the fact that she had personal notice that we
would ask for a personal judgment.   Q. Did the notice state to
her that you would ask for a personal judgment?   A. The notice stated to her—it's the best evidence—that I would ask for a
judgment against her.   Q. As a matter of fact, there was nothing on the face of the petition to show that there was any liability
on her part?   A. Petition is the best evidence.   Q. I would like
to have you answer the question.   Is there any fact stated in the
petition that says that she would be liable to have a judgment
taken against her?   A. Not any more than is stated in the petition.   Q. What is that that is stated in the petition that gave you
any right to any personal judgment against her?   What fact is
there stated in the petition that shows that she [120] would be liable
to any judgment?   A. The petition is the best evidence.   Let
me have the petition, and I will read it.   (Witness is handed petition.)   Q. Go on.   I want you to state what there is in the petition that shows any liability on her part.   A. Nothing more than
the statements there made.   Q. Then you didn't understand, at
the time you drew the petition, that she had made a contract, or
in any way made herself personally liable?   A. I didn't investigate the matter.   If the land was in her name I wanted a personal
judgment against her.   Q. If the land wasn't in her name, then
what?   A. I wanted it anyhow.   Q. Whether she was liable, or
not?   A. I had served her with a notice that I was going to ask
for it, and that is why I wanted it."   From this examination, it
will be seen that the decree embracing the provisions for a personal judgment was prepared by counsel; that he knew that the
petition contained no allegation authorizing a personal judgment
against Celia Larson, yet he persisted in obtaining such a judgment.   Not having reason to believe, from the allegations of the
petition, that any personal judgment could be entered against
her, she was not negligent in not defending against relief which
could not be legally given under the statements of the petition.
She did not learn of the rendition of this judgment until long
after the time to avail herself of the remedy provided by statute
had passed.   She then instituted this action to cancel the judgment.

We have not considered the question as to whether or not defendants herein or their counsel made statements to the plaintiff
herein which were calculated to prevent her from making defense

to the mechanic's lien suit.   It is due counsel to say that, after a
re-examination of the record, in the light of further arguments, we
reach the conclusion that the [121] statements and representations
made by defendants herein, or their counsel, to Celia Larson, if
any, related to another case, which was tried months after the
mechanic's lien suit.   It seems to us, however, that the act of
counsel in procuring this personal judgment against Celia Larson,
when there was no foundation therefor in the petition, was such a
fraud in law as should warrant the relief asked in this action, and
that the decree of the district court was right.

Affirmed.

JUDGMENT—VACATING FOR FRAUD AFTER TIME FIXED
BY STATUTE.—The court has power to set aside a judgment for
fraud and deceit practiced by a party thereto, and may do so after
the lapse of the period designated by statute for setting judgments
aside: Furman v. Furman, 153 N. Y. 309; 60 Am. St. Rep. 629. See,
also, note to Cadwallader v. McClay, 40 Am. St. Rep. 498. If the
defendant had no knowledge of the pendency of the action, could
not have protected his rights therein, and his failure to defend was
not a negligent omission on his part, he is entitled to equitable relief: Dunlap v. Steere, 92 Cal. 344; 27 Am. St. Rep. 143.

JUDGMENT—COMPLAINT NECESSARY TO SUPPORT.—A
complaint, even in a court of general jurisdiction, must set forth a
cause of action by alleging facts sufficient to authorize the court
to render a judgment, as a judgment cannot be based upon facts
not pleaded. Hence, a judgment of a court of record, not based upon
a complaint or written statement of the cause of action, is void:
Beckett v. Cuenin, 15 Colo. 281; 22 Am. St. Rep. 399.

ROBINSON *v.* BERKEY.

[100 IOWA, 136.]

SALES—SETTLEMENT UPON DELIVERY—WARRANTY
WITH CONDITION—WAIVER.—If machinery is sold under a warranty which is not to take effect if the machinery is not settled for
at the time and place of delivery, the failure to settle is a condition of
the warranty, and, unless settlement is waived, the failure to settle
is a waiver of the warranty, and, in the absence of any excuse,
pleaded and established, for such failure, is a good answer to an
alleged breach of warranty.

CORPORATIONS—POWER OF AGENT TO CHANGE
CONTRACT.—An agent of an incorporated company may, if he has
authority to do so, waive compliance with the conditions of a contract made between the company and a third person, although it
contains a provision that no agent shall have power to bind the
company by any change in the contract.

TRIAL—WAIVER OF SUBMISSION OF FACT—IN-
STRUCTIONS.—Although a party's instructions, as asked, are based
on a claim, under the record of a right to a verdict as a matter of

law, that is no waiver of his right to have a question of fact submitted to the jury if his instructions are refused.

INSTRUCTIONS—PRESENTMENT OF ISSUES—APPROPRIATE LANGUAGE.—If the pleadings contain a plain statement of the matter in controversy, the court may use the language of the pleadings in presenting the issues to the jury, but if the language of the pleadings is technical, the issues should be presented in the language of the court.

TRIAL—FINDING ON EACH OF SEPARATE COUNTS—GENERAL VERDICT.—If a cause of action is presented in two counts, each setting forth a cause of action, it is not error for the court, although the plaintiff is entitled to a general verdict, to submit the cause to the jury to find independently on each count, as separate findings on separate causes of action are general, not special, verdicts.

PLEADING—ULTIMATE FACTS—LEGAL CONCLUSIONS. A pleading should state the ultimate facts, and not the evidence of such facts. Legal conclusions are not to be pleaded.

Action to recover the price of machinery sold. On May 5, 1893, Berkey & Martin ordered of the plaintiff company a thresher, self-feeder, band cutter, and a Perfection weigher, at the agreed price of eight hundred and twenty-five dollars, for which Robinson & Co. were to receive in exchange another thresher, stacker, weigher, and sieve, of the value of three hundred and seventy-five dollars, and two notes, each for two hundred and twenty-five dollars, one due on January 1, 1894, and the other on January 1, 1895. There was a warranty that the thresher was well made, of good materials, and that with proper management it would do as much and as good work as any other of similar size made for the same purpose. Robinson & Co. also agreed, in the contract of warranty, to make the machinery fill the warranty, the purchaser being required to render all necessary and friendly assistance and co-operation in making the machinery a practical success. On the same day, the defendant firm ordered of the plaintiff company a Farmer's Friend straw stacker, to be attached to the thresher, for the agreed price of two hundred and fifty dollars, for which two notes, of equal amount, were to be given, due at the same time as the others. There was also a warranty as to this machinery. The machinery under both orders was delivered, and the notes, as agreed upon in both orders, were made and placed in the hands of R. L. Dunlap, who was the agent of Robinson & Co., at Iowa City. The property to have been received by Robinson & Co. in exchange was never given to that firm, and Berkey & Martin, by injunction proceedings, prevented the delivery of the notes by Dunlap to Robinson & Co., which firm then brought this action to recover of Berkey & Martin the sum of one thousand and seventy-five dollars, the agreed price of the machinery under the two orders. The defendant firm, as such and as individuals, admitted the above facts, but pleaded, by way of defense, a breach of the warranties; that, upon the failure of the plaintiff company to make the machinery do work as warranted, they rescinded the contract of sale, and offered to return the machinery, which was refused; and that they then enjoined the delivery of the notes to the plaintiff company, to avoid their passing into the hands of innocent purchasers, and to enforce their right of rescission. There was a judgment for the defendants and the plaintiff company appealed.

Remley & Ney, for the appellant.

Baker & Ball and Joe A. Edwards, for the appellees.

[139] GRANGER, J. 1. The following is a part of the contract of warranty in the first order: "Failure to settle for the machinery at the time and place of delivery . . . . shall be a waiver of the warranty, and release the warrantor, without in any way affecting the liability of the purchaser for the price of the machinery or the notes given therefor." Appellant claims that the neglect of the defendants to deliver the old machinery, and their action in stopping the delivery of the notes to plaintiff, is a waiver of the warranty, and hence, that no advantage can be taken of it to defeat a recovery. It relies on Davis v. Robinson, 67 Iowa, 355, which case was again appealed and reported in 71 Iowa, 618. It is not to be doubted, on the authority of that case, that, if there was a failure to settle by the delivery of the old machinery and the giving of the notes, it waives the warranty, the breach of which is defendant's only defense, and plaintiff should recover, unless defendant pleads and establishes a legal excuse for not so doing. In the answer defendants admit the failure to deliver the machine, and that, as we view it, is the practical effect of their plea as to the notes. So that, unless they plead and establish an excuse for the [140] failure, the warranty is waived. It is contended in argument, that this is done, and the following appears in the answer: "They admit that they executed their promissory notes and left them with one R. L. Dunlap, and that they afterward procured a temporary injunction restraining Dunlap from delivering the same to the plaintiff. . . . . Further answering the said first count, they admit that they refused to deliver to plaintiff the said 33-inch cylinder, Roberts, Thorp & Company thresher, the Reeves stacker, the Perfection weigher,

the oats and timothy sieves; but they deny that they have continued to use the same, and aver that they have only refused to deliver, as they refused to deliver the said notes—that is, until the
said new outfit by them purchased should be made to comply with
the warranties given by the plaintiff in making the sale thereof;
and they say plaintiff agreed thereto." We assume that it would
not be contended that the plea, failure, or refusal is of any avail,
except as it is supported by the alleged agreement of plaintiff.
Of course, if the failure to deliver was by agreement with plaintiff, it would be good. In argument it is urged that the agreement is shown to have been made with the agent, Dunlap, and it
is insisted that he had authority to do so; but we are not called
upon to consider that question, because, on the trial, the issue we
are considering seems to have been excluded. By operation of
law, the averment as to the additional agreement was denied, and
the case presented an issue on which appellees now insist there
was testimony. It is insisted that the testimony is uncontradicted. If by that it is meant that it is so uncontradicted that
the fact is to be taken as established, it is a misapprehension.
The fact remains to be found. The fact of the authority of the
agent with whom the agreement is said to have been made is at
least doubtful in view of [141] correspondence had. The court, in
its instructions, specified the issues to be considered, and in express terms limited them to two, being the two breaches of warranty alleged. In the first instruction, after stating the issues,
the court said: "In connection with this warranty there are certain conditions to be performed by the purchaser; but under the
evidence in the case there is no issue for your determination upon
the performance of those conditions, except as to whether assistance was rendered to the plaintiff in attempting to make said
machine work as hereinafter explained." Certainly, the failure
of settlement was a condition of the warranty. It was pleaded,
and admitted, and a plea in excuse or avoidance made, which was
at issue. The above language excludes it from the consideration
of the jury, and nowhere in the instructions is there language to
overcome its effect. The result is, that the court determined
this issue for defendants, with the burden on them, for it permitted them to recover alone on the issues as to the warranties. Appellant asked several instructions on the question as to the failure
to settle for the machinery, which were refused, so that it is apparent that the point was in no way waived. It is true that appellant's instructions, as asked, are based on a claim, under the
record, of a right to a verdict as a matter of law; but that is no

waiver of a right to have the question of fact submitted, if his instructions were refused, for, without a finding of the fact of an agreement as alleged, it was entitled to an instruction, asked, that a jury return the verdict for plaintiff.

2. Appellant makes a claim that, on this branch of the case, we should direct a judgment for the plaintiff; but we think not. If the facts as to the settlement are as alleged, we do not see why defendants should not be permitted to prove them. It is [142] thought that, because of a provision in the contract, that no agent or salesman has power to bind the company by either verbal or written contracts or promises outside of the contract as written, no such change could be made. Such a condition, if valid, would prohibit absolutely a change by the parties, because the plaintiff is a corporation, and could only make a change by its agents. In Osborne v. Backer, 81 Iowa, 375, and again in Peterson v. Wood etc. Machine Co., 97 Iowa, 148, 59 Am. St. Rep. 399, we considered the legal effects of such a condition in a contract, and held that it did not prevent an agent from changing a contract. All has been said in support of the holding that need be. Under the issues as found, we think it competent for the defendants to show the agreement alleged, by showing authority in the agent, and the agreement.

3. In view of a new trial, it may be well to notice some other questions that may now properly be settled. It appears from the abstract that the court, in presenting the issues, attached carbon copies of the pleadings, amendments, and exhibits, entire. The court then said to the jury: "Upon said petition and answer as amended, the issues in the case arise, and the evidence in the case has to be considered by you in relation to said issues, as explained in these instructions." It is not to be said that the instructions are such as to aid the jury to know the issues. The petition is quite brief, with the contracts and warranties attached. The answer is quite lengthy, and the pleadings are, throughout, couched in language peculiar and adapted to pleading. It is not apt language for the ordinary juror, while to the legal student it is forcible and intelligible. We doubt if any juror could take the pleadings in this case and understand the issues. This court has disapproved the practice in several cases, and it has also said that, when [143] the pleadings contain a plain statement of the matter in controversy, it may use the language of the pleadings: See Lindsey v. Des Moines, 68 Iowa, 368, and several other cases; and see, also, Crawford v. Nolan, 72 Iowa, 673. We think the issues should be presented in the language of the court.

4. The petition is in two counts, each presenting a cause of action, and the court submitted the case to the jury so that it should find independently on each cause; and of this appellant complains, on the ground that it was entitled to a general verdict. The separate findings, on the separate causes of action, are general verdicts. They were not special verdicts. "A general verdict is one in which the jury pronounces generally for the plaintiff or defendant upon all or upon any of the issues": Code, sec. 2806. "A special verdict is one in which the jury finds facts only": Code, sec. 2807.

5. There was a motion of some eleven divisions, each asking to strike some part of the answer. The ground of most of them is, that the averments state conclusions, and not proper facts. One of them is as follows, and includes the argument: "3· The plaintiff moved to strike out the following words from the fourth page of defendant's answer: 'And these defendants say that, with proper management, the said machine would not, and could not, and did not, do as much work, or as good work, as other machines of similar size, for the same purpose.' Such a statement is absolutely a conclusion, and no evidence can be introduced thereunder to establish it as a statement of a fact. If a witness were put upon the stand, and these questions were asked him, the court should certainly overrule them." We think the pleadings in accord with the rule. It is a statement of facts to be established by evidence. It is preceded [144] by a minute statement of the particular facts on which the conclusion is based. The argument indicates that the facts should be pleaded so as not to be objectionable as questions to a witness. That would be pleading the evidence, which is not required. The pleading should state ultimate facts, and not the evidence of such facts: Davenport Gas Light etc. Co. v. Davenport, 15 Iowa, 6; Lumbert v. Palmer, 29 Iowa, 104. Legal conclusions are not to be pleaded, and, likely, conclusions of facts may be so stated as not to be sufficiently plain. In this case that is not the fact. The facts are pleaded minutely, and the language objected to is but an averment of conclusions from such facts, and to fix their relations to the terms of the warranty.

It is not necessary that other questions should be considered; the judgment will stand reversed.

SALES—RESCISSION—BREACH OF WARRANTY.—If a farming implement. sold under a warranty, is materially different from what it is warranted to be, and will not serve the purpose for which it is warranted, the vendee may return and rescind the sale, although

the note he gave to secure the payment of the purchase price contains a provision that "no promise or contract outside of this note
will be recognized": Gale etc. Mfg. Co. v. Stark, 45 Kan. 606; 23 Am.
St. Rep. 739.

TRIAL—CAUSE OF ACTION—DIFFERENT COUNTS.—There
need be but one finding or verdict where the same cause of action is
stated in general counts; and the judgment cannot be arrested, where
there is a nominal verdict for the plaintiff on one, and a substantial
verdict on the other, upon the ground that there are two verdicts for
the same cause of action: Lancaster v. Connecticut etc. Life Ins.
Co., 92 Mo. 460; 1 Am. St. Rep. 739.

PLEADING—FACTS—LEGAL CONCLUSIONS.—Facts only must
be stated in pleadings. Evidence of facts should not be pleaded:
Green v. Palmer, 15 Cal. 411; 76 Am. Dec. 492; Gray v. Osborne,
24 Tex. 157; 76 Am. Dec. 99; McCaughey v. Schuette, 117 Cal. 223;
59 Am. St. Rep. 176. Legal conclusions should not be pleaded: Morrison v. Insurance Co., 69 Tex. 353; 5 Am. St. Rep. 63.

O'LEARY & BROTHER AND STAVER & ABBOTT MANU-
FACTURING COMPANY v. MERCHANTS AND BAN-
KERS' MUTUAL INSURANCE COMPANY.

[100 IOWA, 173.]

INSURANCE, ADDITIONAL—WHEN VOID.—If a policy of
insurance, assented to by the insured, provides that it shall become
void if the insured contracts other insurance on the property without
the written consent of the company, indorsed on the policy, additional insurance, obtained without the required indorsement,
renders the policy void, although the secretary of the company consents, by letter, to the additional insurance.

INSURANCE, ADDITIONAL—WRITTEN CONSENT.—If a
policy of insurance, assented to by the insured, provides that additional insurance shall be void, without the written consent of the
company is indorsed on the policy, and that no agent shall have
power to waive any provision of the policy, the written consent of
the secretary and general agent of the company to additional insurance is not the consent of the company, and such additional insurance, so consented to by the secretary, is void, where there is
no proof of his authority to give such consent, or to waive the indorsement.

Action upon a fire insurance policy, issued to O'Leary & Plank.
The interest of Plank therein was afterward assigned to O'Leary
& Brother. The property was destroyed by fire. Subsequently,
O'Leary & Brother assigned their claim against the defendant
company to the Staver & Abbott Manufacturing Company, a
creditor of the insured. The additional insurance procured made
the whole insurance, at the time of the fire, about equal to the
value of the property. The plaintiffs claimed that they procured
the additional insurance by writing a letter to the company, and
that they received a letter in reply, from the secretary, consent-

ing to the additional insurance. Neither letter, nor a copy
thereof, was produced on the trial, but O'Leary and his brother
both testified, as witnesses, to the contents of the alleged letters.
The secretary of the company testified that he neither received
nor answered such a letter, and no reason was shown in the
whole record why the consent of the company was not obtained in the manner provided for in the contract. The insurance company contended that, while the evidence was conflicting as to whether a letter was written and answered, the evidence did not show that the plaintiffs had complied with their
contract. There was a verdict and judgment for the plaintiffs,
and the defendant appealed. On the original hearing in the
supreme court, Rothrock, C. J., rendered an opinion in which
it was considered that the main question in the case was whether
the contract of insurance had been complied with on the part
of the plaintiffs. As this controlling question is discussed in
the opinion on rehearing, and, as the case may be clearly understood therefrom, that opinion alone is reported.

James A. Howe and Read & Read, for the appellant.

Thomas Stapleton and T. S. Kitchen, for the appellees.

[177] KINNE, J. This cause was heard at the January term,
1896, and an opinion filed on February 7, 1896, reversing the
judgment of the lower court. A rehearing having been granted,
and the case again argued, it is now before us for determination.
In the former opinion but one question was considered, as we
then deemed it the controlling question in the case. On re-examination of the case, we are still of the opinion that no other question argued requires special consideration. The policy provided
that: "This contract shall be void and of no effect unless consent
in writing is indorsed hereon by the company in each of the following instances, viz: If the assured shall now have, or hereafter
make or procure, any other contract of insurance, whether valid
or not, on property conveyed in whole or in part by this contract.
. . . . No agent of this company has any authority to waive,
modify, erase, or strike out any of the printed conditions of this
contract. And it is mutually understood and agreed by and between this company and the assured that this contract is made
and accepted upon and with reference to the foregoing terms,
conditions, stipulations, and restrictions, all of which are a part
of this contract." [178] After the policy had been issued, O'Leary
& Brother procured additional insurance thereon in other compa-

nies in the sum of fifteen hundred dollars. No written consent for the same was ever given by the company, unless that hereafter mentioned can be so construed; and no consent was ever indorsed upon the policy by the company. The plaintiffs allege that O'Leary & Brother, in writing, informed the defendant's secretary of their desire to take additional insurance, and that the defendant consented thereto in a letter written and signed by the defendant's secretary. Defendant takes issue on these averments, and also pleads the conditions of the policy above set out; avers that additional insurance was procured upon the property by O'Leary & Brother, without the knowledge or consent of the company, and in violation of the terms and conditions of the policy. Evidence was introduced tending to sustain the respective allegations. Appellant contends that, even if it be found that O'Leary & Brother wrote to the defendant for permission to take the additional insurance, and if the secretary replied in writing consenting thereto, still it is not shown that plaintiffs have complied with the terms and conditions of the policy with respect thereto. Their claim is, that the consent to additional insurance must be in writing by the company, and must be by it indorsed upon the policy. Appellees claim that, if consent in writing was given by defendant's secretary, it is a compliance with the terms of the policy, though it was never indorsed thereon. The secretary of the company, who in this instance gave the consent to the additional insurance if it was given, was not the company, and could not consent for it, unless authorized so to do. Here is a positive provision of a contract, expressly assented to by the assured, whereby all agents of the company are prohibited from doing the [179] act claimed to have been done in this case. The secretary, though an officer, and, as the evidence shows, a general agent, is nevertheless an agent within the provision of the contract prohibiting agents from consenting to additional insurance. True it is, this defendant is a corporation, and must, of necessity, act through its agents; and it may be that, as a general agent of the defendant, he was, by the laws of the corporation, clothed with power to act for it in the matter of consenting to the taking of additional insurance. There is, however, no evidence in this record as to the character and extent of his powers further than that he countersigned policies, did consent to an assignment of this policy, and approved the risks taken by the company. It is urged that because he was a general agent we may presume that he had power to waive an express provision of the policy prohibiting him from doing the act which it is claimed he did do. If

the act in controversy was one not prohibited by the express terms
of the contract, or if the contract was silent respecting it, it may
be that we should be warranted in presuming that such power was
possessed by the secretary and general agent, as it is manifest that
the power to do the act must, of necessity, rest somewhere. In
this case the company itself has taken from its secretary, by the
terms of the contract, whatever power he might otherwise have
had to consent to additional insurance, except as is provided in
the policy. In the absence of evidence that power had been reposed in the secretary and general agent by the by-laws of the
company, or in some other way, to abrogate and set aside the express provisions of the policy, which are a clear limitation upon
his powers, the latter are binding upon him as well as upon the
assured, who assented thereto. As said in Mechem on Agency,
section 287: "The general agent, therefore, binds his principal
when and [180] only when, his act is justified by the authority conferred upon him." Nor can we presume that Kirkman had
authority to act contrary to, and in violation of, the terms of the
contract: Hollis v. State Ins. Co., 65 Iowa, 458. If authority to
do the act in question rested in the secretary and general agent,
notwithstanding the provisions of the policy, it should have been
shown by the plaintiffs. Our conclusion, then, is that the secretary and general agent, in view of the provisions of the policy,
and in the absence of evidence showing authority, did not have
authority to consent, as it is claimed he did, to the taking of the
additional insurance. No case has been before this court in
which the provisions of the policy were exactly like those in the
case at bar. In Kirkman v. Farmers' Ins. Co., 90 Iowa, 457, 48
Am. St. Rep. 454, a policy was considered which contained provisions very similar to those contained in the policy before us.
It was said in that case: "There is no question as to the rights of
the parties under such a contract as this. There is no statute of
this state by which insurance companies are bound by all the acts
of the agents which they send out to deal with the public, and the
courts cannot say that a contract limiting the power and authority
of agents is void. The plaintiff in this case must be held to have
assented to this stipulation in the policy, and for aught that appears, she is bound thereby." This case was followed in Ruthven
v. American etc. Ins. Co., 92 Iowa, 316. In Taylor v. State Ins.
Co., 98 Iowa, 521, 60 Am. St. Rep. 210, in referring to similar
conditions in a policy, we said: "The conditions of a policy upon
which the defendant relies are, in the absence of statutory regulations, valid, and binding upon the plaintiff": See, also, Zimmer-

man v. Home Ins. Co., 77 Iowa, 685. Without now determining whether, in case the secretary and general agent had [181] power to consent to the additional insurance, such consent would be binding upon the company, it not having been indorsed upon the policy, it may be proper to add that the cases relied upon by plaintiffs as holding that a waiver, if in writing, need not be indorsed upon the policy, even when so required by the contract of insurance, do not contain provisions like those in the case at bar. The provisions in the policy before us are not only materially different, but this policy contains additional provisions, which may have an important bearing upon the question presented. In the view we have taken, it was error to admit the evidence regarding the consent to the additional insurance. The jury should have been instructed that, as plaintiffs had not complied with the provisions of the policy with reference to additional insurance, they could not recover.

For the reasons given the judgment below is reversed.

INSURANCE—WRITTEN WAIVER—INDORSEMENT ON POLICY—ORAL WAIVER.—While the policy of insurance, in the principal case, provided that the contract of insurance should become void if the insured contracted other insurance on the property, without consent in writing indorsed on the policy by the company, there was also a provision in it which prohibited any agent of the company from consenting to such additional insurance. It was therefore held that the secretary and general agent of the company, in view of these provisions of the policy, and in the absence of evidence showing authority, did not have authority to consent, as it was claimed he had, to the taking of additional insurance. The question as to what constituted the "consent" of the company was involved, and no officer or agent of the company was authorized to waive conditions of the policy. But these questions did not involve a waiver of proofs of loss, and the court did not hold that the company could not itself, or by agent authorized to do so, waive the provisions of a policy as to proofs of loss, and that waivers must be in writing on the policy, though it did hold that the written consent of the company to additional insurance must be by it indorsed upon the policy. Such a case is distinguishable from one like that of O'Leary v. German-American Ins. Co., 100 Iowa, 390, in which the only limitation in the policy is that there shall be no waiver unless it is indorsed on the policy in writing. The requirement as to writing may be waived by the company itself, or by any agent of the company having authority so to do. Hence, although a policy of insurance provides that no officer, agent, or representative of the insurance company shall be held to have waived any of the conditions of the policy unless the waiver is in writing and is indorsed on the policy, yet an agent of the company may be authorized by it to waive proofs of loss, under such a policy, and there is no error in submitting to a jury the question whether the agent had authority to, and did, waive proofs of loss, nor in instructing them that such waiver may be by parol. A limitation in a policy of insurance that there shall be no waiver unless it is indorsed on the policy in writing is quite different from a limitation which prohibits all agents of the company from waiving conditions of the policy: O'Leary v. German-American Ins. Co., 100 Iowa, 390.

INSURANCE—CONSTRUCTION OF STIPULATIONS—ADDITIONAL INSURANCE—WAIVER.—The procuring of additional valid insurance in violation of an express condition of the first policy, without the written consent of the insurer, evidenced in the mode prescribed, avoids the policy, unless the company has waived the right to insist upon such forfeiture: Note to Wheaton v. North British etc. Ins. Co., 9 Am. St. Rep. 234; Queen Ins. Co. v. Young, 86 Ala. 424; 11 Am. St. Rep. 51; Snyder v. Dwelling-House Ins. Co., 59 N. J. L. 544; 59 Am. St. Rep. 625; Taylor v. State Ins. Co., 98 Iowa, 521; 60 Am. St. Rep. 210. Additional insurance taken upon the authority of a waiver by one unauthorized to waive any provision or condition of the policy avoids the policy: Bard v. Penn etc. Ins. Co., 153 Pa. St. 257; 34 Am. St. Rep. 704; Taylor v. State Ins. Co., 98 Iowa, 521; 60 Am. St. Rep. 210. But a stipulation, in a policy of fire insurance, that no agent of the company shall have power to waive "any provision or condition" thereof, applies only to those conditions and provisions in the policy which relate to the formation and continuance of the contract of insurance, and are essential to the binding force of the contract while it is running, and does not apply to those conditions which are to be performed after the loss has occurred, in order to enable the assured to sue upon his contract. Hence, after a loss has happened, conditions in the policy with respect to notice of loss and preliminary proofs may be waived by parol, although the policy contains such a stipulation: Snyder v. Dwelling-House Ins. Co., 59 N. J. L. 544; 59 Am. St. Rep. 625. Compare note to Hutchinson v. Western Ins. Co., 64 Am. Dec. 221. In the note to Thomas v. Builders' etc. Ins. Co., 20 Am. Rep. 322, are a number of cases cited to the point that an agent of the company can waive a condition as to other insurance.

STATE *v.* BRADY.

[100 IOWA, 191.]

TRIAL—CHALLENGE FOR CAUSE—WHEN NOT GOOD.—A challenge of a juror, in a criminal case, should be overruled, where he testifies that he can render a true and impartial verdict upon the evidence and instructions of the court, and upon that alone, without regard to what he may have heard and read about the case.

EVIDENCE—OTHER DISTINCT OFFENSES.—In a criminal case, other distinct offenses cannot be proved for the purpose of raising an inference that the defendant committed the crime in question, or to show that he had a tendency to commit that crime; but evidence of such distinct offenses is admissible for the purpose of showing the knowledge, intention, and bad faith of the defendant.

EVIDENCE—OTHER DISTINCT OFFENSES.—Upon an indictment of an overseer of the poor, charged with defrauding a county by filing a fraudulent claim with the county auditor for the transportation of an indigent poor person, evidence of all claims of a like character, for the transportation of other indigent poor persons, filed by him with that officer, together with the records of the transportation companies, is, in connection with evidence tending to show their fraudulent character, admissible for the purpose of establishing the defendant's knowledge of the falsity of the claim in question. It is also admissible to show the existence of a systematic scheme or plan to defraud the county, and thus to negative the idea that the filing of the claim in question was accidental, or made through oversight or mistake.

EVIDENCE—EXPLAINING MARKS UPON PAPER OFFERED.—It is the duty of the state, in a criminal case, such as a prosecution for defrauding a county by filing fraudulent claims against it for the transportation of indigent poor persons, to explain marks upon a paper offered in evidence, and which were not upon it originally, in order to make it admissible, and such explanatory evidence, made by a county officer, as a witness, is not prejudicial, though the witness, in making the explanation, is compelled to impress the jury with the fact that the marks were made to check up fraudulent claims charged to have been made by the defendant.

EVIDENCE—COMPETENCY OF TABULATED STATEMENTS.—Tabulated statements, taken from voluminous and numerous claims and records already in evidence, and made by competent persons for the purpose of assisting the jury in arriving at their verdict, are competent evidence.

APPEAL—ADMISSION OF EXHIBITS IN EVIDENCE—OBJECTIONS.—A specific objection to the admission of an exhibit is not available on appeal, where the only objection made in the court below was a general one.

WITNESSES—COMPLICATED AND VOLUMINOUS RECORDS AND CLAIMS—CLASSIFICATION AND TABULATION—TESTIFYING FROM PAPERS OFFERED IN EVIDENCE.—Upon the trial of an indictment of an overseer of the poor, charged with defrauding a county by filing a fraudulent claim against it for the transportation of an indigent poor person, where evidence of fraud as to other like claims, together with the records of transportation companies, is introduced in evidence, and the records are complicated, and the claims are numerous, it is not an abuse of discretion for the trial court to permit a witness to make a tabulated statement from the records, to classify the claims, and to testify from his examination of the various papers in evidence, especially where no prejudice is shown, and the purpose is to facilitate the trial and aid the jury in arriving at just results.

EVIDENCE — MEMORANDA — ADMISSIBILITY OF.—The record of a railroad ticket office, or memoranda showing the daily sales of tickets, is admissible in evidence, if the witness, who identifies the record, knows that it was correct when made, although he has no independent recollection, either before or after examining it, of the sales to which it refers.

FALSE PRETENSES—INSTRUCTIONS—"FALSELY."—In a prosecution for cheating by false pretenses, an instruction using the word "falsely," in connection with "representations" made, is not erroneous, if it manifestly means something more than "mistakenly," or "untruly," and must have been, in the light of other instructions, so understood by the jury.

Indictment for the crime of cheating by false pretenses. The defendant was convicted and appealed.

Steck & Smith, for the appellant.

Milton Remley, attorney general, Sumner Siberell, county attorney, J. C. Mitchell, and W. A. Work, for the state.

[193] DEEMER, J. During the year 1893, the defendant was the duly appointed and acting overseer of the poor in and for the city of Ottumwa. He was authorized by the board of supervisors to furnish transportation to indigent poor persons found within his jurisdiction, in order that they might be carried to the places of their respective legal settlements, in order that they might not become a charge upon the county of Wapello. For the amounts paid in procuring this transportation he would file an account against the county, and the county auditor was authorized by the board to issue warrants from time to time for the amount of the claims so filed. During the year for which he was appointed, the defendant filed more than [194] five hundred and eighty claims for transportation, alleged to have been furnished to paupers, aggregating more than fourteen hundred dollars. The indictment alleges that on or about the eleventh day of July, 1893, the defendant filed with the auditor of the county a claim for three dollars for transportation furnished a woman and three little children to Chillicothe, Missouri; that this woman gave her name as Eliza Young, and said she wanted to get to Leavenworth, Kansas; that the defendant, when he filed the claim, knew that he had not furnished any transportation to Chillicothe, Missouri, to any woman claiming her name as Eliza Young, and three little children, and that he knew that no woman claiming her name was Eliza Young, had applied to him for transportation to Leavenworth, Kansas, or to Chillicothe, Missouri, and that he well knew that every recital or statement in his said claim was false; and that he filed the claim designedly, willfully, and falsely, with intent to defraud, and by such false pretense did obtain from the auditor a warrant for the amount of the claim. There was evidence tending to support each allegation of the indictment, and upon such evidence the defendant was convicted, and sentenced to the penitentiary for the term of two years.

1. The first error assigned relates to the overruling of a challenge interposed by defendant to a trial juror. This juror testified that he had read an account of the crime charged against the defendant in all the papers which made mention of it; that he had heard the matter talked about, and that he had formed some opinion with reference to the guilt or innocence of the defendant, which he still retained; that it would require some showing on the part of the defendant to remove this opinion. The juror further said: "I say I have heard and read of this case. I think I could put aside what I have [195] heard and read, and go into the trial of this case, and render a true and impartial verdict upon the evi-

dence and instructions of the court, and upon that alone, without
regard to what I may have heard and read. I think I could do
that, the same as if I had never heard of it, but I had rather not sit
on the jury. The opinion I formed, I suppose, is an unqualified
opinion. I would try to hear the evidence in this case, and the
instruction by the court, and render a true verdict, without reference to the opinion, and without reference to what I have read
and heard, and I believe I could." The statements elicited from
this juror were very similar to those appearing in the case of
State v. Munchrath, 78 Iowa, 268, and, following that case, we
hold that there was no error in overruling the challenge.

2. The court permitted the state to introduce in evidence all
the claims filed with the auditor by the defendant, for transportation claimed to have been furnished by him to poor persons during the year 1893, and down to the twelfth day of January, 1894.
It also permitted the state to introduce the records of the Chicago, Milwaukee & St. Paul Railroad, the Wabash Railroad, the
Chicago, Burlington & Quincy Railroad, and the Chicago, Rock
Island & Pacific Railroad, showing, or purporting to show, the
ticket sales in their respective offices at the city of Ottumwa during the year 1893.   The admission of this evidence is complained
of. It is said in argument that it is not competent for the state
to give in evidence facts tending to prove other distinct offenses,
for the purpose of raising an inference that the defendant has
committed the crime in question; nor is it competent to show that
he has a tendency to commit the offense with which he is charged.
That such is the general rule must be conceded. But to this
rule there are at least two well-defined exceptions, which are well
stated [196] by Justice Stephen, in his work on Evidence, articles
10-12, as follows: "A fact which renders the existence or nonexistence of any fact in issue probable by reason of its general re-
semblance thereto, and not by reason of its being connected
therewith in any of the ways specified in articles 3-10, both inclusive, is deemed not to be relevant to such fact, except in the cases
specially excepted in this chapter.   11. Acts Showing Intention,
Good Faith, etc.—When there is a question whether a person
said or did something, the fact that he said or did something of
the same sort on a different occasion may be proved, if it shows
the existence, on the occasion in question, of any intention,
knowledge, good or bad faith, malice, or other state of mind, or
of any state of body or bodily feeling, the existence of which is in
issue, or is deemed to be relevant to the issue; but such acts or
words may not be proved merely in order to show that the person

so acting or speaking was likely, on the occasion in question, to
act in a similar manner. 12. Facts Showing System.--When
there is a question whether an act was accidental or intentional,
the fact that such act formed part of a series of similar occur-
rences, in each of which the person doing the act was concerned,
is deemed to be relevant." The first of these exceptions we have
frequently recognized and applied to cases of this character: See
State v. Jamison, 74 Iowa, 613; State v. Walters, 45 Iowa, 389;
State v. Saunders, 68 Iowa, 370; State v. Stice, 88 Iowa, 27; State
v. Lewis, 96 Iowa, 286; State v. Kline, 54 Iowa, 183. The evidence we have referred to is clearly admissible under the first of
these exceptions stated above, for the purpose of showing the
knowledge, intention, and bad faith of the defendant. It seems
to us that the evidence was also admissible for the purpose of
proving a systematic [197] scheme or plan on the part of the defendant to cheat and defraud the county, thus negativing the idea
that the presentation of the claim in question, was accidental, or
through oversight, or mistake: 1 Greenleaf on Evidence, 15th
cd., sec. 53, note, and cases cited, Commonwealth v. Robinson,
146 Mass. 571. The jury may well have found, from the evidence complained of, that the filing of the claim, and the receipt
of the warrant charged in the indictment, was a part of a plan, or
scheme, adopted by the defendant to cheat and rob the county.
For this purpose, as well as for the purpose of establishing the
defendant's knowledge of the falsity of the claim, the evidence
was admissible.

3. The claims filed by defendant, and which were introduced
in evidence, had blue lead pencil checks and figures upon them,
which it is admitted were not there when defendant presented
them to the auditor. The state introduced a witness to account
for these figures, in the person of the deputy county auditor. He
testified that he placed the marks and characters upon the claims,
and that he did it for the purpose of showing that where he made
checks he found no tickets sold, on the date of the claim, to the
station to which transportation was claimed to have been furnished; and that, where he had made figures, they were put on to
show that the actual railway fare was either more or less than
the amount claimed by the defendant. Error is assigned upon
the admission of these claims in evidence, because of the presence
of these marks. We do not think the objection was well founded.
It was necessary for the state to satisfactorily account for these
marks upon the papers, before they could be received in evidence.
This it did by the evidence in question, and, while it was permit-

ted to unduly impress upon the minds of the jury the object and purpose of the witness [198] in putting the marks and characters upon these papers, yet we think such evidence was not prejudicial, for reasons hereafter to be stated.

4. Complaint is made of the ruling of the court in admitting what is known as Exhibits 7 and 13 to the jury. Exhibit 7 is a tabulated statement made by one Patten, the agent of the Chicago, Milwaukee & St. Paul and the Wabash and Iowa Central Railroads, from the records of said companies, showing sales of tickets at Ottumwa during the year 1893, which were introduced in evidence after having been properly identified. Exhibit 13 was a written statement prepared by the auditor, and his deputy, and purports to be a list of all the names of all paupers for which defendant filed claims for transportation, and received county warrants thereon, during the year 1893, and up to January 12, 1894, also the dates upon which the transportation was furnished, and places to which paupers were claimed to have been sent, and the amount paid for transportation. This statement was made up from the claims introduced in evidence, which aggregated more than five hundred. The records from the ticket offices were necessarily long, and somewhat complicated, as they covered the ticket sales of the different offices for the period of nearly one year. It is said that these exhibits were not the best evidence— that they were secondary, hearsay, and incompetent. It is no doubt true that they were not substantive evidence tending to establish either the number or amount of claims filed by the defendant, nor of the number of tickets sold by the different railway companies. They were simply tabulated statements, made by competent persons, taken from voluminous and numerous claims and records which were already in evidence, made for the purpose of assisting the jury in arriving at their verdict. As such, they were competent: State v. [199] Cadwell, 79 Iowa, 432; 1 Rice on Evidence, 237; Von Sachs v. Kretz, 72 N. Y. 548; Bradner on Evidence, 308-310; Casey v. Ballou Banking Co., 98 Iowa, 107; 2 Rice on Evidence, 745, 746, and cases cited.

5. As to the first thirty-one entries on Exhibit 13, there is no evidence showing, or tending to show, that no tickets were sold to the persons indicated on this exhibit; for Mr. Van Patten did not take charge of the railway offices until March 24, 1894, and all that portion of Exhibit 7, antedating March 24th, was withdrawn from the evidence. The objection defendant made to the exhibit when it was offered by the state did not point out the claim now relied upon by the defendant. His objection was, that it was

incompetent, immaterial, secondary, and not the best evidence; not evidence of anything. Had the defendant made a specific objection to that part of the exhibit referred to, there is no doubt the court would have found some way to protect him without excluding evidence to which the state was entitled. Not having done so, he cannot now complaint: State v. Day, 60 Iowa, 100; Rindskoff v. Malone, 9 Iowa, 540; 74 Am. Dec. 367. But: aside from all this, we think it clearly appears that the defendant suffered no prejudice from the ruling. This exhibit were merely a tabulated statement of the claims filed with the county by the defendant, and if there was nothing to indicate that these first thirty-one claims were fraudulent, it is difficult to see how the defendant could have been prejudiced. The presumption would be that the claims were bona fide. Just how defendant would be prejudiced by proof of bona fide claims filed by him, we are unable to see.

6. Another witness was permitted to classify the claims filed by the defendant, to state the aggregate amount thereof, the total number of fares claimed to Chillicothe, Missouri, and the amount of the 200 fare claimed in each instance. He was also allowed to state what the actual fare was to the various points where defendant claimed to have sent paupers, and, finally, to give the difference between the amount of fare claimed by defendant, and the actual charge made by the railway companies. Most, if not all, of the testimony of this witness was based upon his examination of the various papers in evidence; and we do not think the trial court abused its discretion in allowing such evidence to be introduced for the purpose of facilitating the trial, and aiding the jury in their efforts to arrive at just results. This practice seems to be justified by the authorities before cited, and we can see no good reason for disturbing the verdict on account of this procedure. The same reasoning will apply to the evidence of the deputy auditor, who made the pencil marks upon the claims filed by the defendant, to which we have before referred. It must be borne in mind that the records, statements, and claims from which these witnesses made their statements, and upon which they founded their conclusions, were all properly in evidence, and open to the inspection at all times of defendant and his counsel. This original evidence went into the juryroom, with the exhibits before referred to; and, if there were any discrepancies, it was the duty of counsel to have called attention thereto, in order that the original records and claims might be examined, in order to determine upon the accuracy of these exhibits. While the course

pursued was somewhat unusual, yet the procedure seems to be
sustained by authority, and we do not think that we ought to interfere with the discretion of the trial judge in such matters,
especially where, as in this case, no prejudice is shown.

7. It is contended that the lower court erred in admitting the
records from the ticket offices, showing [201] daily sales at the city
of Ottumwa during the year 1893. This claim presents the question of most doubt in the case. It must be conceded that these
records are not books of account such as the statute contemplates.
They are, in a sense, ex parte statements made and caused to be
made by the witnesses who identified them, and are what might
properly be termed "memoranda," made by the witnesses at the
time of the transaction. Are these memoranda admissible in evidence, or can they be used by the witnesses who produced them,
simply, as an aid to their recollection? This question has been
given widely different answers by the courts of this country and
of England. The old common-law rule seemed to be that such
memoranda were not admissible; that they could be read by the
witness after proper foundation had been laid, even though the
witness had no recollection of the matters, even after having read
them. The modern doctrine, at least in this country, seems to
be that such documents are admissible in evidence, and that the
court will not go through the useless ceremony of having the
witness read a document relating to a fact of which he had no
present recollection, except that he knew it was correct when
made. The previous holdings of this court on the question do
not seem to be in entire accord upon the question: See Taylor v.
Chicago etc. Ry. Co., 80 Iowa, 431; Iowa State Bank v. Novak, 97
Iowa, 270; Adae v. Zangs, 41 Iowa, 536. Without attempting to
reconcile these cases, we think it sufficient to say that we are constrained to apply the modern—so-called American—rule to this
case, and hold that the records were admissible. The evidence
showed that the agent of the Chicago, Milwaukee & St. Paul, and
the Wabash and Iowa Central railroads kept a daily record of the
tickets sold at his office, over the respective lines which he represented; that he was required to do so by a [202] rule or regulation
of the several companies; that he kept the record introduced in
evidence as "Exhibit 8," from March 24, 1893, to January 10, 1894.
This record stated to what stations the tickets were sold, and the
day of the sale. The agent of the Chicago, Burlington & Quincy
Railroad testified that he used a machine in selling tickets over
his line, in which there were two pieces of paper. This machine
printed a ticket when called for, upon a piece of paper, and at

the same time printed a stub, which was, in effect, a duplicate of
the ticket sold.   This stub was sent in to the main office of the
railway company, as a record of sales.   He also testified that this
machine printed a register at the same time.   The witness presented this record made by the machine for the year 1893, printed
upon the stubs before referred to, and it was introduced in evidence.   This same witness was also agent for the Rock Island
Railroad Company, and he testified that he personally kept a
record of the tickets sold over this road during the year 1893, and
that the record was correctly kept.   This record was also introduced in evidence.   Now, it is clear from this statement of the
case that none of these witnesses could remember the number
of tickets sold by them during the whole year, and it would be
absolutely impossible for them to remember with certainty the
places to which they sold tickets on any particular day.   They
would have to rely upon these records, which they identified.   It
is conceded that they might rely upon them, and might have
read from them to the jury, although they may not have been
able to remember a single sale.   To use the language of Hamers-
ley, J., in the case of Curtis v. Bradley, 65 Conn. 99, 48 Am. St.
Rep. 177: "It seems to us to be pressing the use of a legal fiction
too far for a court to permit the statement made by such paper
[203] to be read in evidence, while holding that the law forbids the
admission as evidence of the paper which is the original and only
proof of the statement admitted.   In other words, it would seem
as if, in admitting the paper to be read, the court, of necessity,
admitted the paper as evidence, and therefore, by the concurrent
authority of all courts, the paper is itself admissible."   The
learned judge further said: "All courts rightly hold that the
thing used to refresh the memory is not, by reason of such use,
itself admissible in evidence.   When, in the application of the
rule, a document like the one in question was presented to a witness, and absolutely failed to refresh his memory, its exclusion as
a means of refreshing his memory became imperative, but the evidence of the document was so clearly essential to a fair and just
trial that its use in some form seemed absolutely imperative.
Instead of treating the paper as itself competent documentary
evidence, resort was had to a palpable fiction.   The paper is read
by the witness, and the knowledge the witness once had of the
facts stated by the paper is imputed to him as still existing, and
the statement of the paper is received as the testimony of the
witness, and the paper itself—the only witness capable of making
the statement—is excluded   The use of such a fiction in the ad-

ministration of justice can rarely, if ever, be justified. It is certainly uncalled for in this instance. The principles of law involved to justify the fiction are amply sufficient to support—indeed, to demand—the admission of the document as evidence. There is no occasion to sacrifice truth in order to secure justice, as regards its admissibility as evidence. There is no substantial difference between this paper and any other tangible object, capable of making a truthful and relevant statement." This reasoning is so cogent and logical that we adopt it as peculiarly applicable in [204] the case at bar, and need do nothing further than cite the following additional authorities in support of the rule: Guy v. Mead, 22 N. Y. 462; Haven v. Wendell, 11 N. H. 112; Owens v. State, 67 Md. 307; Donavan v. Boston etc. R. R. Co., 158 Mass. 450; People v. Dow, 64 Mich. 717; 8 Am. St. Rep. 873; 2 Rice on Evidence, 748-751. There was no error in the admission of this evidence.

8. The court, after specifically instructing the jury that the defendant was on trial for the one offense charged in the indictment, and no other, and that, if found guilty, it must be on this specific charge, concluded this paragraph of the charge as follows: "You may and should, therefore, consider all evidence, if any there is, which tends to show that defendant had obtained other warrants from Wapello county by falsely representing that he had transported other paupers, to aid you in determining whether or not he falsely represented in this case that he had transported a woman calling herself Eliza Young, and her children, to Chillicothe, Missouri, and whether or not such representations, if made by him, were fraudulently and falsely made, with the intent to obtain a warrant in this case." Complaint is made of this last sentence in the instruction. We have already sufficiently indicated our views with reference to this matter, and need only say that the word "falsely," as used in the instruction, manifestly meant something more than "mistakenly," or "untruly." The jury, in reading this instruction in connection with the others, could not fail to have construed the word to mean something designedly untrue or deceitful, and as involving an intention to perpetrate some fraud. This construction of the instruction was proper. The fourth instruction asked by the defendant, relating to the same matter, was properly refused because it practically withdrew all evidence as to [205] similar offenses, from the consideration of the jury. As sustaining the instruction, see authorities before cited, as well as the following case: Commonwealth v. Blood, 141 Mass. 571.

The alleged misconduct of counsel for the state in his address to the jury is not considered, because not properly made of record. Other questions discussed by counsel are disposed of by what had already been said, and we conclude by saying that we discover no prejudicial error, and the judgment is therefore affirmed.

TRIAL—CHALLENGE FOR CAUSE—OVERRULING.—If a juror testifies, on his voir dire, that he can fairly try the case, according to the law and the evidence, and a true verdict render, notwithstanding what he may have heard and read, he is a competent juror, and it is not error to overrule a challenge for cause in such a case: State v. Kelly, 28 Or. 225; 52 Am. St. Rep. 777, and note; Wade v. State, 35 Tex. Crim. Rep. 170; 60 Am. St. Rep. 31, and note.

EVIDENCE—OTHER DISTINCT OFFENSES.—Evidence of a crime different from the one charged is never admissible except for the purpose of showing motive, interest, or guilty knowledge: People v. Greenwall, 108 N. Y. 296; 2 Am. St. Rep. 415; State v. Reed, 53 Kan. 767; 42 Am. St. Rep. 322; Ingram v. State, 39 Ala. 247; 84 Am. Dec. 782. Evidence tending to prove other offenses is not necessarily incompetent, if it is pertinent to the point in issue, and tends to prove the crime charged: Farris v. People, 129 Ill. 521; 16 Am. St. Rep. 283. Acts which are part of one general scheme or plan of fraud, designed or put in execution by the same person, are admissible to prove that an act which has been done by some one was, in fact, done by the person who designed and pursued the plan, if the act in question was a necessary part of the plan: Note to Johnson v. Gulick, 50 Am. St. Rep. 632. As to when evidence of other crimes is admissible against the defendant in a criminal prosecution, see the extended note to Strong v. State, 44 Am. Rep. 299-308.

APPEAL—REVIEW OF EVIDENCE—SPECIFICATION OF ERROR.—Evidence will not be considered on appeal unless the particulars wherein it is insufficient are specified: Note to Bohannon v. Combs, 10 Am. St. Rep. 330; Gunter v. State, 111 Ala. 23; 56 Am. St. Rep. 17; and an objection to evidence not made at the time it is offered is waived: State v. Crosswhite, 130 Mo. 359; 51 Am. St. Rep. 571.

EVIDENCE—COMPETENCY OF MEMORANDA.—Entries upon the books of third persons, of their daily transactions, made by persons whose duty it was to make them, and who testify to their correctness when made, but who have no present recollection of the transactions, are competent to be read in evidence: State v. Shinborn, 46 N. H. 497; 88 Am. Dec. 224. If a witness can testify that, at or about the time a memorandum was made, he knew its contents, and that he knew them to be true, his testimony and the memorandum are both competent evidence, although the witness cannot testify to the facts as a matter of independent recollection, after refreshing his memory by an examination of the memorandum: Note to Curtis v. Bradley, 48 Am. St. Rep. 191.

Citizens' National Bank v. Loomis.

[100 Iowa, 266.]

THE ASSIGNMENT OF A JUDGMENT necessarily carries with it the cause of action on which it is based, together with all the beneficial interest of the assignor in the judgment and all its incidents.

· THE ASSIGNMENT OF A JUDGMENT in an action in which an attachment has been allowed and property seized thereunder, passes to the assignee the judgment creditor's right to recover damages of the sheriff for negligence in the care of the property seized by allowing a disposition to be made of it.

SHERIFFS—ATTACHMENT—RETURN—WHAT IS SUFFICIENT.—A sheriff's return of a levy upon property states all that the law requires when it shows that he has levied upon property, contains a description thereof, and shows what disposition had been made of it.

SHERIFFS—ATTACHMENT—RETURN—DISPOSITION OF PROPERTY.—Under a statute requiring a sheriff to show, by his return, what disposition he has made of attached property, it might be proper to show that he has turned it over to a receiptor, if such is the fact, but he is not required to show that such action was taken in pursuance of the plaintiff's directions.

SHERIFFS — ATTACHMENT — RETURN — NOT CONCLUSIVE WHEN.—The return of a sheriff on a writ of attachment is not conclusive against him as to matters which he is not required to state. Hence, in an action against him for a negligent loss of the property, he may introduce parol evidence of such matters for this does not tend to contradict the return.

SHERIFFS — ATTACHMENT — RETURN — WHAT DOES NOT CONTRADICT.—The return of a sheriff is not contradicted by evidence of a fact that he is not required to state therein. Hence, if his return on a writ of attachment shows that he holds the property "subject to the order of the court," evidence, in an action against him for a negligent loss of the property, that it was delivered to a third person, as receiptor, by direction of the attorney for the plaintiff in the attachment. is admissible, because evidence that the property is held by a receiptor, under the direction of the judgment creditor, is not a contradiction of the return.

SHERIFFS—ATTACHMENT—LIABILITY FOR RECEIPTOR'S NEGLIGENCE.—A sheriff who levies a writ of attachment and delivers the property to a third person as receiptor, by direction of the plaintiff in the attachment, or his attorney, is not answerable for the receiptor's negligence whereby the property is lost.

DEFINITIONS—"AGREEMENT" BETWEEN ATTORNEY AND CLIENT.—An order or direction given by an attorney, to a sheriff, to turn over attached property to a third person, for safekeeping. is not an "agreement" within the meaning of a statute prescribing how an agreement between attorney and client shall be proved.

Action brought by the Citizens' National Bank against a sheriff, C. C. Loomis, for the negligent loss of property attached by that officer. In 1889, one Smith had commenced an action against one Hess to recover rent. A landlord's attachment was issued, and was served by the sheriff, who made a return, certifying that he had, on a certain day, levied on certain personal property describing it, and stating that he held the property "subject to the order of the court." On the back of the writ was a receipt for the property given by J. M. Griffith, and showing that the property had been put in his charge for safekeeping. Smith obtained a judgment, which, on appeal to the supreme court, was affirmed in Smith v. Hess, 83 Iowa, 238. A special execution was subsequently issued for the sale of the attached property. This was returned unsatisfied, no property being found. The judgment was afterward assigned to the plaintiff bank, which, in March, 1892, instituted this action against the sheriff to recover the amount of such judgment and costs. There was a verdict and judgment for the defendant. It appeared on the trial that the property levied on was sufficient to have satisfied the judgment, interest, and costs, and that at the time the judgment was affirmed by the supreme court against Hess he was, and ever since had been, insolvent. The bank appealed.

Gatch, Connor & Weaver, and J. A. McCall, for the appellant.

Read & Read and D. F. Callender, for the appellee.

[268] KINNE, J. 1. Appellee insists that, even if there was error in the ruling of the court in the respects hereafter spoken of, the same was without prejudice, for the reason that plaintiff has no right to prosecute this suit. The claim is, that the assignment of the judgment alone did not carry with it to plaintiff the right to sue the sheriff for damages arising by reason of his alleged negligence in permitting the property levied upon to be disposed of. Just what rights will pass by the assignment of a judgment to an assignee, other than the right to enforce the judgment in the usual way, has never been determined by this court. In this case, the assignment, in terms, related to the judgment only. If, therefore, plaintiff has a right to sue the sheriff for [269] negligence, it is because such right passed by the assignment of the judgment, as an incident to it. If appellee's claim is sound, then no right of action, as against the sheriff, for damages, passed to the plaintiff bank by the assignment. Now, the right, if any, to recover damages, existed and was vested in Smith, the possessor of the judgment, prior to the time the assignment was made. If it did not pass by the assignment of the judgment, it must still remain in Smith. It can hardly be successfully contended that Smith might part with all his inter-

est in the judgment, and still reserve to himself the right to sue the sheriff for damages arising out of failure to do his duty in relation to the disposition of the property which had been taken on a writ issued by virtue of the very claim upon which the judgment itself was based. Nor can it be said that the assignment of the judgment had the effect of absolving the sheriff from liability for negligence in caring for the attached property. Hence, we think, if a cause of action existed against the sheriff for damages for such negligence, prior to the assignment of the judgment, it must be held to still exist in favor of some one, inasmuch as there is no claim that it has been satisfied, or been barred by the statute of limitations. As we have indicated, Smith, having parted with his interest in the judgment, could not maintain an action against the sheriff, because it was the interest in the judgment, alone, which entitled him to claim damages for the negligent loss of the property upon which he relied for the satisfaction of the same. Now, the original case was by the defendant appealed to this court, where the judgment was affirmed. A special execution properly issued for the sale of the attached property. That the right to this execution passed by the assignment of the judgment cannot be doubted. So, also, the assignee would have the right to have the property [270] sold, and the proceeds applied in payment of the judgment. Now, if the sheriff has, by negligence, permitted the property to be lost, destroyed, or disposed of, so that it cannot be reached by this special execution, he has thereby deprived the present holder of the judgment of a substantial right, for which, in a proper case, he should be held liable to make restitution. It is the general rule that the "assignment of a judgment necessarily carries with it the cause of action on which it is based, together with all the beneficial interest of the assignor in the judgment and all its incidents": 2 Freeman on Judgments, sec. 431; Ullmann v. Kline, 87 Ill. 268; Ryall v. Rowles, 1 Atk. 165; 2 White and Tudor's Leading Cases in Equity, 1667; Schlieman v. Bowlin, 36 Minn. 198. In the Minnesota case above cited, which was an action upon a replevin bond by the assignee of the judgment, the court said: "It is a familiar rule in equity, of universal application, that the assignment of a demand entitled the assignee to every assignable remedy, lien, or security available by the assignor as a means of indemnity or payment, unless expressly excepted or reserved in the transfer of the demand. The assignment of the demand, which is the principal thing, operates as an assignment of all securities for its recovery or collection, and upon such securities the assignee, as the real party in interest, may maintain an action in his own name": 2 Jones on Mortgages, secs. 829, 1316, 1377. In the Illinois case it was held that an appeal bond was but an incident of the debt, and a right to sue thereon was vested in the assignee of the judgment. As supporting the general rule above stated, see 1 Am. & Eng. Ency. of Law, 884; 2 Black on Judgments, secs. 948, 952. So it has been held that the assignee of a judgment takes the assignor's right to enforce the judgment by supplemental proceedings: Burns v. Bangert, 16 Mo. App. 22. We are aware of the fact that there are some authorities which [271] do not go to the extent of those above cited. Thus, in Michigan it has been held that where an attachment was issued and levied upon property, and a statutory bond given to the sheriff by the defendant, who retained possession of the property, and the judgment was afterward assigned by an instrument that did not mention the bond, such assignment did not authorize the assignee to sue upon the bond in his own name: Forrest v. O'Donnell, 42 Mich. 556. And see Timberlake v. Powell, 99 N. C. 233. We think that the assignment of the judgment in the case at bar carried with it the right to the assignee to avail himself of any remedy or means of indemnity, security, or payment possessed by, or which could have been made available to, the assignor, as against the sheriff.

2. On the trial, the defendant introduced evidence tending to show that, at the time the property was levied upon, the attorney for the plaintiff in that action directed the deputy sheriff, who made the levy, to place the goods in the custody of one Griffith, as receiptor, and that it was done. The receipt of Griffith for the goods appears on the writ, but not in the return. This evidence, and more of a similar character, was objected to, on the ground that it tended to contradict the return of the officer. The court held that the return could not be contradicted by parol, but said: "The fact that, by direction of plaintiff, it [the property] was turned over to the receiptor, if it was, does not contradict the levy." It may be conceded to be the general rule that a sheriff's return cannot be contradicted by parol evidence; that in a suit by the creditor against the sheriff, his return is prima facie, if not conclusive, evidence against the officer: Tillman v. Davis, 28 Ga. 494; 73 Am. Dec. 786; Crocker on Sheriffs, sec. 46; Murfree on Sheriffs, sec. 866; Macomber v. Wright, 108 Mich. 109; [272] Drake on Attachments, secs. 204, 206; 1 Shinn on Attachments, secs. 226, 227; 22 Am. & Eng.

Ency. of Law, 683, 684. By an examination of the foregoing authorities, and the cases therein referred to, it will be seen that there are many exceptions to this rule. Our statute provides: "The sheriff shall return upon every attachment what he has done under it. The return must show the property attached, the time it was attached, and the disposition made of it": Code, sec. 3010. It is also well settled that return upon a writ of attachment is evidence only of what can properly be embraced in the return. In Aultman v. McGrady, 58 Iowa, 118, it is said: "There is no provision for a return showing the acts of anyone but the officer. A statement in the return purporting to show the acts of some one other than the officer is without authority of law, and surplusage." The provisions as to returns on executions are substantially the same as those relating to a return on a writ of attachment. Therefore, a return embracing matters not required by statute, or which relate to acts done outside of the officer's duty, would not be receivable as evidence of such facts, nor would it in any way conclude the parties: 1 Shinn on Attachment, sec. 227; Freeman on Executions, secs. 364, 366; Charles City Plow etc. Co. v. Jones, 71 Iowa, 238; Murfree on Sheriffs, sec. 867. Under the authority of Aultman v. McGrady, 58 Iowa, 118, the sheriff was not required to set out in his return the fact, if such it was, that he had delivered the attached property to Griffith, the receiptor, in pursuance of the directions of the plaintiff. That would have been the recital of the acts of persons other than the officer, which the statute does not require to appear in the return. Now, it might be proper to show in the return the fact that the officer had turned the goods over to a party named as a receiptor, but to set out [273] that such action was taken at the request or direction of some one is not within the requirements of the statute. While the fact of the placing of the property in the hands of Griffith as a receiptor did not appear in the return, it did appear from Griffith's receipt on the back of the writ. Surely, no prejudice could arise because the naked fact that the property had been placed in the hands of some one as receiptor did not appear in the return. So far as the plaintiff was concerned, that fact, if stated in the return, would not have advised it that the property was placed in the receiptor's hands by the direction of its assignor.

Counsel for appellant says: "We grant that it was not necessary to state in the return the simple and unqualified fact that the officer had left the property with the receiptor, but insist that, to save himself from being liable on his return for its negligent loss, it was necessary to state the fact, if a fact, that he did so by direction of the judgment creditor." The contention appears to us, in view of the requirements of the statute, to be unsound. The return stated all that the law required. To have set forth the fact that, by direction of the judgment creditor, the property had been placed in Griffith's hands, would have been the recital of the fact or direction of one other than the officer, and, as we have seen, was not proper. The evidence introduced over plaintiff's objection was as to a fact not required to be stated in the return, and therefore properly no part of it, and hence it did not tend to contradict the return.

It is said that, because the sheriff's return shows that he holds the property subject to the order of the court, therefore evidence that it is held by a receiptor, under the direction of the judgment creditor, is a contradiction of the return. We do not think this is so. In a sense, at least, the property, having been levied upon by the officer, is in his [274] possession, even though in the hands of a receiptor nominated by a judgment creditor. "When the property attached is by the officer delivered into the hands of a keeper or receiptor, such person is the agent of the officer making the attachment, and for his torts or negligence in respect to the property the officer is liable. When, however, the property is delivered to a bailor named by the plaintiff, the officer is relieved thereafter from responsibility to the plaintiff for the safekeeping of it": 1 Shinn on Attachment, sec. 392. Ordinarily, and in the absence of evidence to the contrary, it would be presumed that the possession of the receiptor was the possession of the sheriff. Nor does it cease to be such because, by reason of his own acts, the judgment creditor is not in a position so that he may hold the officer personally liable for damages which arise by reason of the receiptor's negligence. The property attached, though left with a receiptor by direction of the judgment creditor, is still in the custody of the sheriff. If it were not so, the levy would, in law, be abandoned: Drake on Attachment, 7th ed., sec. 350. We are of the opinion that the evidence objected to was properly admitted, and that it did not contradict the return of the officer.

3. There can be no doubt that the officer levying the attachment had the right to deliver the property to Griffith, the receiptor, by direction of the judgment creditor, the plaintiff in that action; and, if he did so by the direction of said plaintiff, or his attorney, he would be relieved from personal liability: Davis v. Maloney, 79 Me. 110; Shepherd v. Hall, 77 Me. 569;

Drake on Attachment, 7th ed., sec. 361; Jenney v. Delesdernier, 20 Me. 183; Willard v. Goodrich, 31 Vt. 597; Strong v. Bradley, 14 Vt. 55; Donham v. Wild, 19 Pick. 520; 31 Am. Dec. 161; 1 Shinn on Attachment, sec. 392. It [275] is said in Freeman on Executions, second edition, section 108: "One inquiry will be answered here. Who is entitled to control the writ? The officer should always bear in mind that the writ is intended for the benefit of the plaintiff, who alone is interested in its enforcement. The interests and wishes of the plaintiff should at all times be respected. . . . . But all directions of the plaintiff not savoring fraud or undue rigor and oppression must be obeyed, or the officer will be held liable for injuries flowing from his disobedience."

4. It is said that the testimony admitted showed an agreement, and that parol evidence should not have been admitted to establish it. Our code, section 213, provides that an attorney and counselor has power "to bind his client to any agreement, in respect to any proceeding within the scope of his proper duties and powers; but no evidence of any such agreement is receivable, except the statement of the attorney himself, his written agreement signed and filed with the clerk, or an entry thereof upon the records of the court." It is claimed in this case that the direction to turn the property over to Griffith, the receiptor, was given by the attorney for the judgment creditor. He denies so doing; hence it is said the evidence of the deputy sheriffs was not admissible. If this direction of the attorney to place the property in Griffith's hands as a receiptor was given, and if it can be said to constitute an agreement, within the meaning of the statute, then the testimony should not have been admitted. That it was not an agreement in a statutory sense seems too clear to admit of a doubt. It was simply an order or direction given to the sheriff, which, it is claimed, he complied with.

[276] We have considered every question raised which is deemed of importance, and reach the conclusion that there was no error in the respects complained of.

Affirmed.

___

ASSIGNMENT OF JUDGMENT.—A judgment may be assigned: Wright v. Yell, 13 Ark. 503; 58 Am. Dec. 336; Mitchell v. Hockett, 25 Cal. 538; 85 Am. Dec. 151; Isett v. Lucas, 17 Iowa, 503; 85 Am. Dec. 572; Gardner v. Mobile etc. R. R. Co., 102 Ala. 635; 48 Am. St. Rep. 84; and the assignee takes it with all the equities and defenses which might have been asserted against it in the hands of the assignor; Note to Western Nat. Bank v. Maverick Nat. Bank, 35 Am. St. Rep. 215. Compare monographic note to Dugas v. Mathews, 54 Am. Dec. 366-369, on assignment of judgments at common law.

SHERIFF'S—ATTACHMENT—RETURN.—A sheriff's return on attachment must show that the statute has been complied with: Note to Hall v. Stevenson, 20 Am. St. Rep. 808. A sheriff's return, even in a proceeding against him, cannot be contradicted: Note to Boone County v. Lowry, 9 Mo. 23; 43 Am. Dec. 532; but it is prima facie evidence, even in his own favor: State v. Devitt, 107 Mo. 573; 28 Am. St. Rep. 440.

HARRIS v. BRINK.

[100 IOWA, 366.]

FRAUDULENT CONVEYANCES—FUTURE SUPPORT—VALIDITY OF DEED.—If the consideration for a conveyance is an agreement for the future support of the grantor, the transaction is fraudulent in law as to his creditors, to the extent which the value of the property is in excess of the support furnished.

FRAUDULENT CONVEYANCES—FUTURE SUPPORT—REMEDY OF EXISTING CREDITORS.—Existing creditors may avail themselves of property, conveyed for future support, for the payment of their claims, when the debtor has no other property out of which payment can be enforced.

FRAUDULENT CONVEYANCES—FUTURE SUPPORT—SUIT TO SET ASIDE.—If property is conveyed by a debtor for his future support, and the parties have acted in good faith, the conveyance may be sustained, so far as the consideration paid by the grantee, without notice, is involved, but will be set aside as to any value in the property in excess of the amount paid; and, in such a case, the grantee is chargeable with the value of the use of the property.

FRAUDULENT CONVEYANCES—FUTURE SUPPORT—LIEN OF CREDITORS.—If a debtor conveys his property, in consideration of his future support, an existing creditor, having no other means of enforcing his claim, is entitled, in equity, even after the grantor's death, to have his claim established as a lien against the property to the extent that the value of the property and of its use, exceeds the amount of the support actually furnished, in good faith, by the grantee.

Suit in equity, brought by Henry Harris, to set aside a conveyance of real estate, made by John Harris, to the defendant, Harriett Brink, to subject the property to the payment of a debt due to the plaintiff from John Harris, and to obtain other relief. There was a decree for the defendant, and the plaintiff appealed.

Stilwell & Stewart, for the appellant.

M. B. Hendrick, for the appellee.

366 ROTHROCK, C. J. John Harris died on the sixth day of September, 1891. The plaintiff claims that when Harris died he was indebted to the plaintiff in the sum of two hundred and fourteen dollars and fifty cents and interest. The deceased

had no money and no property of any kind when he died. He
had been the owner of a farm of forty acres, and some cattle,
and some other personal property. On the twenty-sixth day of
May, 1890, he executed and delivered to the defendant a quitclaim deed for the farm. The following is a copy of said conveyance: "I, John Harris, widower, in consideration of eight
hundred dollars [367] in hand paid, do hereby sell and quitclaim
unto Mrs. Hattie Brink the following described premises, the
NE NW of 22-98-6. And it is expressly agreed that a part of
the consideration herein is the future support of the said John
Harris by the said Hattie Brink, and a failure of the said Hattie
Brink to furnish the said John Harris proper support and all
necessary clothing and forty dollars cash each year, and care in
sickness and in health, and furnish and pay all doctor bills of
John Harris during all his life, shall be a failure of the consideration hereof, and shall work a forfeiture of this deed, and the
said Hattie Brink, on condition that she shall give my body a
suitable burial, shall have all property, personal and real, left
by me at my death, and the said John Harris hereby relinquishes
his right of dower and homestead in and to the same." There
was no encumbrance, or lien, upon the land, and there is no
question that Harris was the owner in fee simple, and had the
right to sell and dispose of it. He had no wife living and no
children. He had owned the farm for many years, and he and
a daughter occupied it as a home. He conveyed the land to his
daughter, and at her death, which occurred May 13, 1890, he inherited the property from her. The plaintiff is a brother of
John Harris. He alleges in the petition that the conveyance to
Mrs. Brink was fraudulent as to the creditors of Harris, and that
it was absolutely void as to the heirs of Harris, for the reason
that he was incapable mentally of making a disposition of his
property by deed. It is also averred that the plaintiff is the
only heir at law of the deceased, and the relief demanded is that
his claim as a creditor be established as a lien upon the farm,
and that he be declared to be the owner of the fee in the land
by inheritance. All of the averments of the petition were denied in the answer. Numerous witnesses [368] were examined by
the respective parties. We will not set out and review the testimony. It will be sufficient to state facts which we believe to
be established by a preponderance of the evidence: 1. At the
time of the death of John Harris he was indebted to the plaintiff in the sum of two hundred dollars. All of his claim, except
thirty-five dollars for money loaned, consisted of items of account

for the use of horses, and for hogs sold to the deceased, and for hay and grain furnished to him to feed his stock. The amount claimed in the petition was two hundred and fourteen dollars and fifty cents. We deduct all in excess of two hundred dollars, for the reason that we think one charge for a coat ought not to have been made, and other items appear to be overestimated. This account ought to draw interest at six per cent from November 15, 1890. 2. John Harris was about seventy-six years old when he died. For a number of years before his death he was greatly afflicted with rheumatism, so that he was very feeble, and walked with difficulty, and in a stooping position. But there is no satisfactory evidence that he was mentally incapable of making a contract or a will. He knew just what he was doing when he executed the deed to Mrs. Brink. 3. A few days after the conveyance was made, Harris, by a bill of sale, transferred some cattle to the defendant, of the value of seventy dollars. At the time of both transactions, defendant knew that Henry Harris claimed that John Harris was indebted to him. She also knew that W. C. Earle had a claim against him. It is true that she did not know that the claims were valid obligations. John Harris denied to her that he was in debt to the plaintiff. 4. At the time of the conveyance the farm was worth twelve hundred dollars, and the cattle were of the value of seventy dollars. At the date of the trial in the district court, the defendant had been in possession of [369] the farm for about five years, and the use and occupation was worth five hundred dollars. The defendant paid debts and funeral expenses of Harris and his daughter, and nursed and cared for him until he died, and the total value of the services and money paid was six hundred and thirty-five dollars. It therefore appears to us that, including the use of the farm, the defendant had received property of the value of seventeen hundred and seventy dollars, for which she has given as a consideration about six hundred and thirty-five dollars. The principal part of this sum consists of the value of the services rendered in caring and providing for Harris from the time of the death of his daughter until he died.

It appears to be well settled that, where the consideration for a conveyance is an agreement for the future support of the grantor, the transaction is fraudulent in law as to the creditors, to the extent which the value of the property is in excess of the support furnished. The authorities proceed upon the theory that it is the legal duty of a debtor to pay his debts, rather than to provide for his future support, and that existing creditors may

avail themselves of property conveyed for future support for the
payment of their claims, when the debtor has no other property
out of which payment can be enforced: Walker v. Cady, 106
Mich. 21; Kelscy v. Kelley, 63 Vt. 41; Farlin v. Sook, 30 Kan.
401; 46 Am. Rep. 100; Henry v. Hinman, 25 Minn. 199; Faber
v. Matz, 86 Wis. 370. And where the parties have acted in good
faith, the conveyance may be sustained, so far as the consideration paid by the grantee, without notice, is involved, but will be
set aside as to any value in the property in excess of the amount
paid; and in such case the grantee is chargeable with the value
of the use of the property: Loos v. Wilkinson, 110 N. Y. 195;
Gould [370] v. Hurto, 61 Iowa, 45; Redhead v. Pratt. 72 Iowa, 99;
Gaar v. Hart, 77 Iowa, 597. Applying these well-settled principles to the facts as we have found them to be, we think the
plaintiff is in equity entitled to have his claim to the amount of
two hundred dollars, with interest, as above stated, established
as a lien against the farm. We do not believe that the defendant acted in bad faith. She did faithful service for John Harris
and his daughter, for which she should be well recompensed.
While she knew that the plaintiff had some demands which he
asserted against Harris, yet her information from him was, that
he was in no way indebted to his brother. The decree of the
district court is reversed, and the cause is remanded to the district court for judgment and decree, in harmony with this
opinion.

———

FRAUDULENT CONVEYANCES—FUTURE SUPPORT.—While
an agreement for future support is a valuable consideration, it is not
sufficient to sustain a conveyance, when to do so will operate to the
prejudice of the grantor's existing creditors, though no actual fraud
was intended by any one of the parties to the transaction: Harting
v. Jockers, 136 Ill. 627; 29 Am. St. Rep. 341. One cannot transfer
all his property in consideration of support for life without first
satisfying his existing debts; and, without this, a fraudulent intent
to hinder and delay creditors follows necessarily as a conclusion
of law, regardless of what the parties to the transaction in fact intended: Davidson v. Burke, 143 Ill. 139; 36 Am. St. Rep. 367. If a
portion of the consideration for a conveyance is an agreement that
the grantee will support the grantor, such agreement will be treated
as a fraud upon the creditors of the grantor, though the remaining
portion of the consideration involved the expenditure of money on
the part of the grantee: Harting v. Jockers, 136 Ill. 627; 29 Am. St.
Rep. 341.

NEWBURY *v.* GETCHEL & MARTIN LUMBER AND MAN-
UFACTURING COMPANY.

[100 IOWA, 441.]

MASTER AND SERVANT—EMPLOYÉ AS VICE-PRIN-
CIPAL.—The mere fact that one employé has authority over others
does not make him a vice-principal, or superior, so as to charge the
master with his negligence; but this rule relates to the negligence
of the foreman, as such, and not to his want of care in doing those
things which the master is obliged to perform by virtue of the relation existing between him and his servant.

MASTER AND SERVANT—LIABILITY OF MASTER—
TEST.—The liability of a master for injury to his servant depends
upon the character of the act, in the performance of which the injury occurs, and not upon the rank of the employé who performs it.
If it is one pertaining to a duty which the master owes to his servants, he is answerable to them for the manner of its performance;
but if the act is one which pertains only to the duty of an operative,
the employé performing it is a mere servant and the master is not
answerable to a fellow-servant for its improper performance.

MASTER AND SERVANT—MINOR EMPLOYÉ—MASTER'S
DUTY—WARNING.—It is the duty of a master who knowingly employs a youthful, or inexperienced servant, and subjects him to the
control of others, to see that he is not employed in a more hazardous position than that for which he was employed, and to give
him such warning of his danger as his youth and inexperience demand; and the master cannot relieve himself of this duty by showing that he delegated its performance to another servant who was
at fault in performing it.

MASTER AND SERVANT—EMPLOYÉ AS VICE-PRIN-
CIPAL.—A servant, agent, or employé, while performing a duty required of the master, stands in the place of the master, and becomes a vice-principal. The master is, therefore, answerable for his
negligence.

MASTER AND SERVANT—INJURY BY FELLOW-SER-
VANT—MASTER'S LIABILITY.—A master is not answerable for an
injury to his servant occasioned by the negligence of a fellow-servant.

MASTER AND SERVANT—INJURY BY FELLOW-SER-
VANT—MASTER'S LIABILITY.—If a minor is employed to cut wood
into kindling by means of a "cut-off" saw, but a fellow-servant sets
him at such work with a rip-saw, thus putting him in a place of
increased danger, and he is injured, he may, where he shows himself
free from contributory negligence, recover of the master, if it is
found that the fellow-servant had authority to direct him where and
how he should work, especially if the fellow-servant ordered him
into the more hazardous employment without giving him warning
of the dangers incident to the use of the rip-saw, in such work,
and that it was more dangerous to use than the "cut-off" saw. It is
otherwise, however, where the fellow servant is not shown to have
had any such authority.

MASTER AND SERVANT—WARNING TO SERVANTS
—MASTER'S DUTY.—A master's duty to warn his servant of the
dangers incident to his work, extends only to those dangers which
the master knows, or has reason to believe, the servant is ignorant
of. He is not required to give warning of dangers known to the
servant, or that are so open and obvious that, by the exercise of
care, he would know of them, and the jury should be so instructed.

INSTRUCTIONS—THEORY SUPPORTED BY SOME EVIDENCE.—It is proper to give an instruction on a theory which is supported by some evidence, although it may be opposed by a preponderance of evidence.

MASTER AND SERVANT—ORDERS—PURPOSES.—An order to a servant designed for one purpose, and misunderstood by him for another, is not an order for the latter purpose.

MASTER AND SERVANT—MINOR EMPLOYE—FELLOW SERVANT—VICE-PRINCIPAL.—The fact that a servant, injured by the negligence of a fellow-servant, was a minor, does not make the fellow servant a vice-principal.

MASTER AND SERVANT—MINOR EMPLOYE—CONTRIBUTORY NEGLIGENCE—CONSIDERATION OF MINORITY.—If a minor is employed to cut wood into kindling by means of a "cut-off" saw, and a fellow-servant sets him at such work with a rip-saw, thus making the employment more hazardous, and he is injured, it is proper, in an action by him against the master, to instruct the jury, upon the subject of contributory negligence, that they should consider the plaintiff's minority solely upon the question as to whether or not one of his years and experience and intelligence could, and did, know or appreciate the danger, if any, there was in operating the rip-saw.

MASTER AND SERVANT—MINOR EMPLOYE—RIGHTS OF.—A master having furnished to his servant a proper machine with which to work, is not answerable if it is used for an improper purpose; but this rule is not applicable to the case of a minor who obeys the orders of his superiors and uses machines for the purpose of his employment as directed by them, he having no knowledge as to what machines he should use, except as he is informed by his superiors. He has a right to assume that they will subject him to no greater risks than his contract of employment contemplated, and that, on account of his age and inexperience, they will furnish him proper machines, and give him the needed information as to how to operate them.

APPEAL—REDUCING VERDICT—HARMLESS ERRORS.— Error in allowing a petition to be amended, after verdict, by stating an increased amount of damages, and error in instructing the jury as to the amount recoverable, are cured by the court's action in reducing the verdict to a less sum, and are, therefore, harmless.

DAMAGES—DISFIGUREMENT AS ELEMENT OF—NEGLIGENCE.—In personal injury cases, the plaintiff's disfigurement of person may be considered as an element of damages.

DAMAGES—MEDICAL EXPENSES AS ELEMENT OF— MINORS—NEGLIGENCE.—In an action for personal injuries brought by a minor, he cannot, as an element of damages, recover the cost of medical services rendered, at least, until he has paid the bill, for his parents are primarily liable for it.

APPEAL—REMITTING PART OF VERDICT—DISCRETION.—A ruling of the trial court, in an action for personal injuries, requiring the plaintiff to remit a part of the verdict, will not be disturbed where no abuse of discretion is shown.

Action at law, brought by Harry A. Newbury, by his next friend, Maggie Newbury, to recover damages for personal injuries sustained by the plaintiff while employed by the defendant company in its mill. There was a judgment for the plaintiff and the defendant appealed.

Guernsey & Bailey and Barcroft & McCaughan, for the appellant.

McVey & Cheshire, for the appellee.

443 DEEMER, J. The defendant is a corporation engaged in the manufacture of sash, doors, blinds, and other woodwork. In the month of September, 1891, the plaintiff, Harry A. Newbury, a boy seventeen years of age, entered into the employ of the defendant, to work in and about its factory. He was put to work in a room known as the "Sash and Blind Department," over which one Page was foreman. He was engaged as a sort of a "roustabout," and one of his duties was to clean up the refuse pieces of wood that accumulated from time to time in the room where he worked, and to saw them into proper lengths for kindling. Plaintiff had done this cleaning and sawing on an average of about once every other day from September, 1891, to some time in the month of May, 1892, at which time the accident happened which will be hereafter referred to. In the department where the plaintiff worked, there were two circular saws —one known as a cut-off and the other as a rip-saw. The cut-off saw was mounted on a table which was about three and one-half feet wide, six feet long, and two feet five inches high. The saw was about twenty inches from the end of the table at which the operator stood. It projected a few inches above the table, and the lumber which the operator desired to saw was placed upon a sliding carriage, which carriage was then pushed, with the lumber thereon, against the saw, by the operator, who would place his hands either behind the sliding carriage, or upon the lumber, and at safe distance to the left of the saw. Plaintiff was instructed in the use of the saw, and was directed to place both hands to the left of the saw while using it, in order to avoid **444** danger. The rip-saw was mounted upon a similar table but it had no carriage. To the right of this saw was a movable gauge, which could be adjusted so as to rip the lumber accurately and smoothly to the required width. Designed as they were for special purposes, the saws were differently constructed. The teeth of the cut-off saw were smaller than the rip-saw, and so set that they made a wider path through the wood than did the rip-saw. There was the same difference between them that there is in the ordinary cross-cut and rip-saws; the difference being due, of course, to the fact that one is made to cut across the grain of the wood, and the other with it. Prior to the time of the accident, the plaintiff had used the cut-off saw in cutting the refuse matter, but he had not always followed the directions of his employer with reference to the proper place of putting his hands while using this machine. On the —— day of May, 1892, plaintiff was directed by the foreman of the room to clean up the shop and saw up the refuse matter for kindling. This he proceeded to do, and while so engaged, the foreman left the room. While engaged in his work, and during the absence of the foreman, one Garrity, who was employed about the mill, came to the plaintiff, and said he desired to use the cut-off saw, and plaintiff claims that Garrity ordered him to use the rip-saw for cutting up the kindling. Newbury claims that, as he had never used the rip-saw for this purpose, he asked Garrity how to use it, and that Garrity, in response to this request, went to the saw, pushed back the gauge so it would not interfere with the lumber, started it, placed a handful of strips upon the table, and, with one hand to the left and the other to the right of the saw, pushed them against it, and thus sawed the lumber into the required lengths for kindling. Plaintiff also claims that Garrity repeated this operation two or **445** three times and said to him (plaintiff) that that was the way to do it. Newbury says that he proceeded with his work as directed, and that (to quote plaintiff's own language): "I was standing at the north end of the table, looking south. The north end of the table is about three feet north of the saw. I was working on the rip-saw, cross-cutting, the same as Dick Garrity had told me to, and while doing that I picked up another handful of the strips, and went to push them into the saw, and pushed one handful through all right, and the next time I tried it they wedged on the saw. The rip-saw did not take out enough of the wood, but what it left there wedged on the sides of the saw, and it kind of made the saw jerk; and when the saw jerked it stopped it a little bit, and it caught a bigger stick, I suppose. I do not know exactly how it happened, but it was in that way. At the time the saw jerked there, my right hand was gripping the end of the lumber. The rip-saw was going up in the center of the table, and I had both hands on the wood, and ran it along like that, and my right hand was on the right hand end of the stick. In pushing it down that way, I was holding both ends, and they went down there and wedged, and it commenced to jerk; and I tried to push it on through, and it gave a heavy jerk, and threw my hand over on to the center of the saw, like that, and my hand was sawed off."

The negligence charged against the defendant is the order of Garrity to do the work with the rip-saw, without informing him (plaintiff), who, by reason of his years, was without knowledge or experience sufficient to comprehend the character of the work, of the dangers incident thereto, and in ordering plaintiff to do the work he did so, without informing him that it was more dangerous than when done with the cut-off saw. It will be noticed that [446] plaintiff does not claim that he was not furnished with proper tools with which to do his work. The cut-off saw is conceded to be the proper machine for the purpose, and it was the duty of the plaintiff to use it, in the absence of proper directions to use another. The negligence charged is that of Garrity, in ordering him to do the work with the rip-saw without informing the plaintiff of the dangers incident to its use. But defendant cannot be held responsible for this, unless it is to be charged with the negligence of Garrity. Whether it should be so charged or not is the principal question in the case to determine. We must look to the evidence relating to Garrity's authority. It appears that Samuel Martin was, and is, the vice-president and general manager of the defendant corporation. Adolph Vieser was mill manager at the time of the accident, and O. A. Page was foreman of the department where plaintiff was employed. Page had charge of all the men in the room where plaintiff worked, and had authority to direct them as to their work. He had no authority to employ workmen, nor did he directly discharge them. It appears, however, that his requests for discharge were generally, if not universally, respected and acted upon. Martin employed the plaintiff, and directed him to go to Page's department, where he would be informed by Page as to his duties, and that he must obey Page. Garrity was a workman in the same room with plaintiff. He did machine work, principally, although he occasionally worked at the bench, on blinds. There is also testimony tending to show that early in the spring of 1892, while Page was absent from the factory, Garrity directed the men in the department in which plaintiff was engaged, and that at other times, when Page was out of the room, Garrity called plaintiff to his assistance, and directed him in his work, and that, when Page was not present, Garrity was in charge, [447] and gave directions to the men. It also appears that, for two or three days prior to the accident, Newbury was assisting Garrity, and working under his directions. In order to charge defendant with knowledge of the fact that plaintiff was working under the direction of Garrity, the following testimony was delivered by plaintiff: "Dick Garrity wanted me to do something there one day—me and Law Martin, I think it was, that

was working there at the same time—and we were not going to
do it; we were going to do something else; and Dick went and
saw Page about it, and Page told us to go ahead; that Dick was
an old hand there and we should mind him; he would tell us
what to do. From that time to the time of the injury, I was
in the habit of obeying Richard Garrity, when he ordered me
to do it." It also appears from the evidence that Martin was
frequently present at the room where plaintiff worked; that he
often noticed Garrity call Newbury to his assistance; and that
he noticed Newbury was assisting, helping, and obeying Garrity;
and that Garrity was the most experienced man in the department, except Page.

From this statement of the evidence, it will be seen that the
controlling point in the case is the determination of the question as to whether the negligence of Garrity is to be attributed
to the defendant. If Garrity was a mere fellow-servant with
plaintiff, then defendant is not responsible for his negligence.
If, on the other hand, he is and was a vice-principal, then defendant would be chargeable with his negligence. It is conceded
by all parties that Martin and Vieser were vice-principals.
Whether Page is to be so classed or not is a more difficult question, but one not necessarily determinative of the case, for the
real question is as to the authority of Garrity. Let it be conceded, for the purposes of the case, that Page was a vice-principal, and yet there is no liability, [448] for it is the negligence of
Garrity, and not of Page, that is relied upon. What, then, was
Garrity's authority? He had no power to employ or discharge
men. The evidence tended to show that he had the right to
call other employés to his assistance at all times, and that when
Page was absent he was foreman of the shop, or of the department in which he worked. But as such foreman he had no more
authority than usually devolves upon such a person. We have
frequently held that the mere fact that one employé has authority over others does not make him a vice-principal or superior, so as to charge the master with his negligence: Peterson
v. Whitebreast etc. Min. Co., 50 Iowa, 673; 32 Am. Rep. 143;
Foley v. Chicago etc. Ry. Co., 64 Iowa, 650; Benn v. Null,
65 Iowa, 407; Baldwin v. St. Louis etc. Ry. Co., 68 Iowa, 37;
Hathaway v. Illinois Cent. Ry. Co., 92 Iowa, 337. This rule,
of course, relates to the negligence of the foreman, as such, and
not to his want of care in doing those things which the master
is obliged to perform by virtue of the relation existing between
him and his servant. The rule is well settled, although not

always correctly applied, that the liability of the master is made
to depend upon the character of the act, in the performance of
which the injury occurs, and not upon the rank of the
employé who performs it. If it is one pertaining to a duty
the master owes to his servants, he is responsible to them
for the manner of its performance. But, if the act is one
which pertains only to the duty of an operative, the employé
performing it is a mere servant, and the master is not liable to
a fellow-servant for its improper performance. For instance, it
is the duty of the master to make reasonable efforts to supply
his employés with safe and suitable machinery, tools, and appliances, and thereafter to make like efforts to keep the same in repair, and in a safe and serviceable condition. [449] He is also
required to exercise reasonable care in selecting and retaining
a sufficient number of competent servants to properly carry on
the business in which the servant is employed. It is another
duty to make and publish such rules and regulations as are
reasonably necessary to protect his employés against injury incident to the performance of their duties. And it is further
the duty of the master who knowingly employs youthful, or inexperienced servants, and subjects them to the control of others,
to see that they are not employed in a more hazardous position
than that for which they were employed, and to give them such
warning of their danger as their youth and inexperience demand.
These are duties of which the master cannot relieve himself
by showing that he delegated their performance to another servant, who was at fault in performing them. In the performance
of his duties the servant, agent, or employé stands in the place
of the master, and becomes a vice-principal, and the master is
responsible for his negligence: Fink v. Des Moines Ice Co., 84
Iowa, 321; Haworth v. Seevers Mfg. Co., 87 Iowa, 765. There is
no pretense that this case falls within either of the first three
exceptions to the general rule of nonliability for the negligence
of fellow-servants above stated. But it is claimed that it does
come squarely within both exceptions stated in the last; that is
to say, that the defendant, through its servant and agent, Garrity, ordered plaintiff, into a more hazardous place to work than
that for which he was employed, and that Garrity gave him improper and negligent instructions as to how to use the saw, and
failed to warn him of the dangers pertaining to its use. Now,
if it be found that Garrity had authority to direct the plaintiff
as to where and how he should work, and it is further shown that
he ordered him into an employment [450] more hazardous than

that for which he was engaged, or that Garrity failed to give
him such warning of his danger as his youth and inexperience
demanded, then the defendant would be responsible for Garrity's
negligence, and plaintiff would be entitled to recover, provided
he showed himself free from contributory negligence. Upon
these propositions the court below gave the following instructions: "If you find, under the directions given you in the last
preceding instruction, that the order or direction made by Garrity to the plaintiff, to use the rip-saw for the purpose it was
being used at the time of the injury, was the order of the defendant, then you are further instructed that it is the duty of the
master who knowingly employs a youthful servant, and subjects
him to the control of another servant, to see that he is not
employed in a more hazardous position than that for which he
was employed, and to give him such warning of his danger as
his youth or inexperience demands. And if you find that the
use of the rip-saw, for the purpose and in the manner it was
being used by the plaintiff at the time of the injury, was more
hazardous than the use of a cross-cut saw, when used for the
same purpose, or that the use of the rip-saw, in the manner and
for the purpose it was being used at the time of the injury, was
more hazardous and dangerous than when used for ripping lumber, then it was the duty of the defendant to explain, or have
some competent person explain, to the plaintiff, the extra hazard
or danger, if any, connected with the operation of said rip-saw
when used in the manner and for the purpose it was being used
by the plaintiff at the time of the injury. And if the defendant failed so to explain, or cause to be explained, to the plaintiff, such increased hazard or danger, if any, then the defendant
in so failing to do will be deemed negligent and liable to the
plaintiff if such order to use the rip-saw was the direct and
451 immediate cause of his injury unless you find from the
evidence that the plaintiff at the time of the injury, had acquired knowledge from other sources, or by experience, of such
extra hazard or danger in using said rip-saw in the manner and
for the purpose it was used at the time of the injury." This
instruction is criticised because, it is argued, it states the duty
of the master too broadly. It is contended on the part of defendant that the duty of the master is to warn as to such dangers,
and such only, as he has reason to believe, as an ordinarily prudent man, are not known to the servant. The instruction quoted
relates to the duty of the master who orders his servant into
a more hazardous position than that for which he was employed,

and fails to explain to him the dangers incident to his work. And, in so far as it makes this duty absolute, it seems to us that the instruction is wrong. The correct rule is as stated in the case of Yeager v. Burlington etc. Ry. Co., 93 Iowa, 1, as follows: "The duty of the master to instruct and warn the servant only arises as to dangers which the master knows, or has reason to believe, the servant is ignorant of. It does not arise as to dangers known to the servant, or that are so open and obvious as that, by the exercise of care, he would know of them": Citing Reynolds v. Boston etc. R. R. Co., 64 Vt. 66; 33 Am. St. Rep. 908; St. Louis etc. Ry. Co. v. Davis, 55 Ark. 462; Dysinger v. Cincinnati etc. Ry. Co., 93 Mich. 646; Levey v. Bigelow, 6 Ind. App. 677; Evansville etc. R. R. Co. v. Henderson, 134 Ind. 636; Merryman v. Chicago etc. Ry. Co., 85 Iowa, 634; Downey v. Sawyer, 157 Mass. 418. In view of the evidence, it was highly important that the jury be correctly informed as to when, and under what circumstances, it was the duty of the master to warn his servant of the dangers incident to his work.

452 2. The eighth instruction is complained of. It is as follows: "Further, regarding the relation of fellow-servants, you are instructed that the master may so act, and instruct his servants to obey one of their number in the performance of their work for the master, that in the performance of such duties so required by the master, the servant so authorized to transact the business of the master in the performance of such duties for the time, as to such servants who have received of the master a direction to obey, becomes the agent or representative of the master, in such sense that the master is liable for the negligence of the servant so invested with authority, while in the performance of the duties directed in the manner aforesaid by the master. And if you find from the evidence that Samuel Martin, the vice-president and general manager of the defendant corporation, told the plaintiff to obey Foreman Page, and that Page would tell him what to do, and that thereafter Page told the plaintiff, prior to the time of the injury, to obey the orders or commands of Richard Garrity, and that Martin knew that plaintiff was under the direction of Richard Garrity, and required to obey the orders and instructions of Garrity, and acquiesce therein, then the said Garrity, when he told the plaintiff to use the rip-saw in the manner and for the purpose it was being used at the time of the injury, was the agent or representative of the defendant corporation, in such sense that the order of Richard Garrity to use the rip-saw in the manner and for the purpose it was being used at the time of the injury would be the order of the defendant to use the said rip-saw." The objections to it are that there is no evidence that Page told plaintiff that he should obey the orders and commands of Garrity, or that Martin knew that plaintiff was under the direction of Garrity, and was required to obey his orders.

453 These objections are without foundation, for we think there is evidence to establish both propositions. It may be that the preponderance of it is to the contrary, but we are not dealing with a question as to the weight of the evidence. It is also contended that the instruction is wrong for the reason that it holds the defendant to liability simply because Garrity was in control of the work as foreman or temporary overseer of the work. If we were to consider the instruction apart from the evidence in the case, it is likely that it would be condemned. But, as applied to the evidence, it was a correct statement of the law as we have announced it in the first paragraph of this opinion.

3. The ninth instruction was as follows: "As before stated, it is conceded that there was not any actual direction given by Page to the plaintiff, at the time of the injury, to obey Garrity in reference to the work at which he was engaged when injured, but it is claimed by the plaintiff that he was acting in obedience to prior directions from Martin to obey Page, and from Page to obey Garrity; and in determining whether or not plaintiff is justified in claiming that he was thus acting under the direction of the defendant in obeying Garrity, you are to consider all the evidence in relation to that matter; what, if anything, was said by Martin to plaintiff in relation to Garrity commanding or directing the plaintiff; what, if anything, he said and did in relation thereto; what, if anything, was said by Page to the plaintiff in relation to obeying Garrity; whether such commands, if any, were for the plaintiff to obey in particular instance or instances, or in every instance; and all facts and circumstances in evidence bearing upon said matter. And if, from the consideration of all the evidence and the circumstances, you believe that **454** Martin commanded the plaintiff to obey Page in all instances, and that Page commanded plaintiff to obey Garrity in all instances, or that Martin and Page gave plaintiff such commands to obey as a reasonably prudent boy of the age and experience of the plaintiff at that time would understand and believe to be an order to obey Page and Garrity in every instance, and plaintiff did so, in good faith, believe, then you would be warranted in finding that he was acting under the direction of defendant, in

obeying Garrity, but not otherwise." This instruction is criticised because it is said there is no evidence to support it. In this we cannot agree with counsel. Properly construed, it had evidence in its support, and it is not subject to the criticism made. The latter part of the instruction is also challenged because, it is said, it makes the defendant liable for the plaintiff's mere belief as to the orders given him. We think this objection is well taken. An order designed for one purpose and misunderstood for another would not be an order for the latter purpose: McCarthy v. Chicago etc. Ry. Co., 83 Iowa, 485.

4. Appellant's counsel make the following subheading to one division of their argument: "The fact that the plaintiff was a minor does not make Garrity a vice-principal."

This is a proper statement of the law, but we fail to find where the court below held anything to the contrary. The instructions tell the jury that they may consider the plaintiff's minority, in determining the question as to whether he had intelligence enough to appreciate the dangers that were involved in the employment, and that they might also consider the plaintiff's age, in determining whether or not he was guilty of contributory negligence. These instructions do not tend to hold the defendant [455] to liability because the minority of the plaintiff made Garrity a vice-principal.

In this connection, we may consider the objection lodged against the eleventh instruction. This part of the charge related to the subject of contributory negligence, and told the jury, in effect, that they should consider the plaintiff's minority solely upon the question as to whether or not one of his years and experience and intelligence could and did know or appreciate the danger, if any there was, in operating the rip-saw. This instruction was in accord with the voice of authority, and was properly given: Merryman v. Chicago etc. Ry. Co., 85 Iowa, 634; McMillan v. B. & M. Ry. Co., 46 Iowa, 231; Beach on Contributory Negligence, sec. 136.

5. Appellants' counsel say, in argument, that the defendant, having furnished the proper machine, is not liable, where the servant makes use of it for an improper purpose. This statement announces a correct rule of law. But does it apply to the case at bar? Here there was evidence tending to show that the plaintiff was not informed by any one that the cut-off saw was the one, or the only one, to be used in cutting the kindling; and that he was ordered to obey the directions of Page, and, in Page's absence, to obey Garrity. It was plaintiff's duty to obey all orders

given him by his superiors, unless their performance involved a hazard which no ordinarily prudent person would have subjected himself to.   In obeying his superiors, he had a right to assume that they would subject him to no greater risks than his contract of employment contemplated, and that, on account of his age and inexperience, they would furnish him proper machines, and give him the needed information as to how to operate them.   He had no knowledge as to what machines he should use, except as he was informed by his superiors.   And, in [456] using the machines which they directed him to operate, he was but doing a duty to his employers.   The rule of law relied upon by appellant's counsel is not applicable to the case.   Our conclusions on this branch of the case find some support in the case of Sprague v. Atlee, 81 Iowa, 1.

6. It is said that the evidence conclusively shows that plaintiff was guilty of contributory negligence, and that the verdict is contrary to the sixth instruction, which related to this subject.   In view of a new trial, it is better that we express no opinion upon these matters.

7. The court instructed the jury that, if they found for plaintiff, they could allow him as damages any sum not exceeding ten thousand dollars.

It appears from the record that the original petition asked for but five thousand dollars damages.   Afterward by leave of court, this petition was amended so that the prayer was for ten thousand dollars, but the clause in the petition stating plaintiff's damages was not amended.   This stood, as in the original petition, at five thousand dollars.   The verdict was for eight thousand dollars.   The court, however, reduced it to five thousand dollars; and after the verdict was returned the plaintiff, by leave of the court filed an amendment to his petition stating that he was damaged to the amount of ten thousand dollars.   The defendant complains of the instruction given by the court, and of the permission given the plaintiff to amend.   It is, no doubt, true that plaintiff could not cover the defect by amendment after verdict: See Cox v. Burlington etc. Ry. Co., 77 Iowa, 478.   But it clearly appears that no prejudice resulted to defendant by reason of the ruling.   The court reduced the verdict to the sum of five thousand dollars, and, in so doing, not only covered [457] the error with reference to the amended pleading, but also the error in the instruction.

8. The instruction with reference to the measure of damages

tells the jury that they may consider plaintiff's disfigurement of person as an element.

This is said to be error. We do not think so. We have uniformly held that this may be considered in personal injury cases. And such seems to be the general rule: 1 Sutherland on Damages, sec. 158, and authorities cited; Thomas on Negligence, 461 c.

9. Another element of damages, which the court permitted the jury to consider in the event they found for plaintiff, was for medical services rendered.

It appears that the doctor who attended the plaintiff charged eighty-one dollars for his work. Whether this charge was made against plaintiff, or his father, does not appear. But as the father, or, in the event of his death, the mother was primarily liable for the bill, we must assume it was charged to him or her. And, if so charged, then the plaintiff cannot recover this item. But, if not so charged, we do not think plaintiff was entitled to recover this item, under the showing made. The liability was primarily that of the father. He was liable for the support and maintenance of his minor son, and it must be presumed that he will meet his obligation. Plaintiff as a minor, cannot recover for these services; not, at least, until he has paid the bill: Tompkins v. West, 56 Conn. 478.

10. Misconduct on the part of the plaintiff's attorney was one of the grounds for a new trial. We have examined the record with reference to this matter, and find there is no reason for interfering with the discretion of the trial court in overruling the motion on this ground.

458 11. Some other questions are discussed by counsel. But as they are not likely to arise on another trial, we do not consider them.

12. Plaintiff appeals from the ruling of the court, requiring him to remit three thousand dollars of the verdict. We do not think he is in a position to complain: 1. On account of the condition of the pleadings, to which we have referred; 2. Because this matter rests peculiarly within the discretion of the trial court, and we see nothing to indicate that he abused this discretion.

For reasons pointed out, the judgment of the district court is reversed.

MASTER AND SERVANT—MASTER'S DUTY AND LIABILITY —MINOR EMPLOYES—FELLOW-SERVANTS.—One who is engaged with another in the same employment is not divested of the character of a fellow-servant by the mere fact that he has authority to direct the other in his work: Hayes v. Colchester Mills, 69 Vt. 1; 60 Am. St. Rep. 915. But see Foley v. California Horseshoe Co., 115 Cal. 184; 56 Am. St. Rep. 87. A master is not answerable to a servant for injuries inflicted on him by the negligence of another servant in the same common employment and not traceable to the personal negligence of the master: Note to Kimmer v. Weber, 56 Am. St. Rep. 634. A servant engaging in a dangerous employment assumes all the risks ordinarily incident thereto, including those which arise from the negligence of a fellow-servant. A minor, though a child of tender years, is within the application of this rule, but, in his case, it is modified by the duty of the master to warn him of the perils of the work and to instruct him how to avoid them: Hayes v. Colchester Mills, 69 Vt. 1; 60 Am. St. Rep. 915. When injury happens to a servant in the course of his employment, the master is answerable if it was occasioned by his negligence: Note to Sawyer v. Rumford Falls etc. Co., 60 Am. St. Rep. 265. If a servant, acting within the scope of his employment, requires his minor fellow-servant to perform a service requiring warning and instruction, the negligence of such servant in failing to give such instruction and warning is the negligence of the master, who is liable therefor. If an employé, although a fellow-servant of an injured employé, is charged with the master's duty to such employé, his failure in that duty is the negligence of the master, and the doctrine of fellow servants does not apply: Hayes v. Colchester Mills, 69 Vt. 1; 60 Am. St. Rep. 915. It is only in an extreme case that a minor should be held guilty of contributory negligence in obeying the orders of one representing his master: Foley v. California Horseshoe Co., 115 Cal. 184; 56 Am. St. Rep. 87. Infant employés are entitled to be instructed as to the dangers of their employment and how to avoid them. They do not, therefore, assume all the usual dangers incident to the employment: Note to Foley v. California Horseshoe Co., 56 Am. St. Rep. 95.

DAMAGES.—MEDICAL EXPENSES may be allowed as an element of damages in personal injury cases: Note to Standard Oil Co. v. Tierney, 36 Am. St. Rep. 603.

CASES

SUPREME COURT

KANSAS.

KELLOGG *v.* DOUGLAS COUNTY BANK.

[58 KANSAS, 43.]

APPELLATE PROCEDURE—PRESUMPTION IN FAVOR OF THE JUDGMENT.—If it appears by the record that the plaintiff took leave to amend his complaint in a respect indicated, it will be inferred that such amendment was made in the absence of any statement to the contrary and where the findings and evidence respond to the issues suggested by the proposed amendment.

BANK, FAILURE OF TO COMPLY WITH THE LAW.—In a suit upon a promissory note made to, and negotiated by a bank, the maker cannot defend on the ground that such bank had not complied with the law in procuring the certificate authorizing it to transact business, nor in making a statement required to be made by the banking law of the state.

NEGOTIABLE INSTRUMENTS — INDORSEMENT AND GUARANTY.—The writing on the back of a note, "For value received we hereby guarantee payment of within note at maturity, waiving demand, protest, and notice of protest," signed by the payee of the note, is both an indorsement and a guaranty, and hence passes the title thereto.

COLLATERAL SECURITY.—An indorsement as collateral security for a debt contracted at the time of the indorsement protects the indorsee to the extent of the debt the same as if the purchase were absolute.

FRAUDULENT TRANSFER.—IF A DEBTOR ORGANIZES A CORPORATION and transfers his property to it for the purpose of shielding himself from his creditors, the property so transferred being the chief part of his assets, and the corporators being members of his family, the transfer is fraudulent, and may be avoided by his creditors.

FRAUDULENT TRANSFER—WHO MAY ATTACK.—One holding a note made after a transfer may attack it as a fraud upon him if his note was a renewal of an obligation antedating such transfer.

(596)

Three actions were brought against Q. A. Kellogg, in which attachments were issued and levied upon property claimed by the Kellogg Mercantile Company, a corporation. In each case the action was upon a negotiable promissory note executed by the defendant to M. D. Ewing for the accommodation of the latter, and by him transferred to the plaintiff. In one of the cases the indorsement was in the form shown in the third subdivision of the syllabus. The corporation claimed the property attached by filing an interplea in each case. By consent all the cases were tried together. The defendant, finding himself in embarrassed circumstances because of the notes sued upon and other indebtedness greatly exceeding his assets, organized a corporation with a capital stock of fifteen thousand dollars, divided into one hundred and fifty shares, and transferred to it his stock of merchandise and the house in which he conducted his business. One hundred shares of stock were issued to the defendant and the remainder to his wife and nephew, who gave promissory notes therefor. That of the nephew having been surrendered soon after its execution, all his stock, except one share, was transferred to the defendant. Judgment was given in favor of the plaintiff for the amount sued for and sustaining the attachment. The defendant presented three petitions in error, all attached to one record.

J. W. Deford and J. M. Dunsmore, for the plaintiff in error.

Lapham & Brewster, for the Douglas County Bank et al., Lapham, Alexander & Co. et al.

J. D. McCleverty, for the Chemical National Bank et al.

[47] ALLEN, J. The sufficiency of the record to present the errors complained of is challenged. If there are really three separate cases, it is difficult to see how all may be prosecuted on one record: Parkhurst v. National Bank,•55 Kan. 100. As all of the cases were tried together in the district court, and all the parties laid claim to the attached property, and as all of the parties necessary to a consideration of the questions involved are made defendants in error in one or another of the petitions in error which are attached to the single case-made, we are inclined to treat the case here as a single one, and the three petitions in error as really one in substance. This practice, however irregular it may be, does not appear to prejudice the rights of any of the parties.

1. A copy of the note attached to the petition of the Douglas

County Bank fails to show any indorsement by Ewing to the plaintiff. It is urged that the note [48] was entirely without consideration as between Kellogg and Ewing, and that there was neither allegation nor proof of such a negotiation as would cut off Kellogg's defense of want of consideration. In answer to this, it is said that leave was taken by the plaintiff to amend the petition, and that, in support of the finding and judgment of the court, it must be inferred that an amendment was made showing that the note was properly indorsed. In the second paragraph of the facts as found by the trial court, we find the following: "Said note was duly indorsed to the plaintiff herein, and said plaintiff became the owner and holder of said note before the maturity thereof, in good faith, for value, and in the regular course of trade and business, without notice of any defense that Kellogg might have to said note as against C. T. Ewing." On the trial, Mr. Sparr, the president of the bank, testified, without objection, that the indebtedness to his bank on the note sued on was four thousand one hundred dollars and accrued interest; that the bank purchased it from Ewing's bank as a rediscount, and was the owner and holder thereof. The cross-examination was solely as to whether there should be a credit on the note. We find no statement in the case-made to the effect that it contains all the pleadings, nor is there anything from which we are required to infer that the petition was not amended so as to show a proper indorsement of the note. There is nothing indicating that the attention of the court was ever called to the want of a proper indorsement, and it seems altogether improbable that the question now presented was ever really before the trial court. All presumptions are in favor of the judgment.

2. It was not necessary for the plaintiff to show that [49] Ewing's Bank had received a certificate from the bank commissioner, authorizing it to transact business, nor that the bank had transmitted the statement required by the banking law. It would be a strange construction of the act to hold that securities negotiated by a bank would be rendered void by the failure of the banker to comply with the law. It would be absurd to visit on innocent purchasers of its paper penalties for a failure of the officers or proprietors of a bank to perform their duty. The law was intended to protect the public. The construction we are asked to place on it would aid in defrauding those who might deal with an unlawfully conducted bank.

3. The indorsement to the Chemical National Bank was sufficient. It was placed on the back of the note, and while it was

a guaranty of payment, it was also an indorsement of the note. The guaranty itself would be senseless and wholly inoperative unless the note was transferred by the payee to a third party. Such indorsements are not at all uncommon. The cases of Briggs v. Latham, 36 Kan. 205, and Hatch v. Barrett, 34 Kan. 223, are not in point. One was a transfer of a mortgage, the other a mere assignment of a note without recourse. This was both a guaranty, and an indorsement which passed a full title to the note: 2 Daniel on Negotiable Instruments, 4th ed., 1781; Robinson v. Lair, 31 Iowa, 9; Heard v. Dubuque County Bank, 8 Neb. 10; 30 Am. Rep. 811. And an indorsement as collateral security for a debt contracted at the time of the indorsement protects the indorsee to the extent of the debt, the same as if the purchase were absolute: State Sav. Assn. v. Hunt, 17 Kan. 532.

4. It is insisted that, in order to avoid the transfer of the property from Kellogg to the Kellogg Mercantile [50] Company, actual fraud must be shown; that constructive fraud is insufficient, and that there is no showing in this case of actual fraud. It is contended that the organization of the Mercantile Company was suggested by the attorney for the National Bank of Kansas City, as a means of securing Kellogg's indebtedness to it. It appears that Kellogg was asked by the attorney for the bank to secure his note by chattel mortgage on his stock; that he refused to do so, and that the representatives of the bank afterward suggested the organization of a corporation, and the transfer of a part of the stock as security for Kellogg's note to the Bank. After the corporation was organized, he did assign to the bank ten thousand dollars of the stock in the Mercantile Company to secure a new note for six thousand five hundred dollars, due in one year after date, with seven per cent interest. The fact that the organization of the corporation was suggested by the representatives of the Kansas City Bank does not conclusively prove good faith on the part of Kellogg in acting on the suggestion. He refused to give a chattel mortgage, on the ground that it would result in closing his business. He adopted the other course, and organized a corporation in order to shield himself from the attacks of his creditors, and enable him to carry on his business and enjoy the income therefrom. The incorporation seems to have been little but a paper scheme devised in his own interest. His wife and clerks were mere instruments in his hands, contributing no real capital and obtaining no substantial interest in the property. Clearly, a fraud may be committed in the transfer of a debtor's property to such a corporation, as

well as by a transfer to another individual for the purpose of placing it beyond the reach of creditors. In such case, the court was clearly warranted in [51] closely scrutinizing the transaction and declaring its real purpose, notwithstanding the elaborate fabrications of charters, by-laws, and paper transfers. There is no force in the contention that it was not a fraud as to the Chemical Bank because the note sued on was not given until after the creation of the corporation. The note was merely a renewal of a prior obligation, and the debt existed before the fraudulent transfer was made. No error appearing in the record the judgments are affirmed.

NEGOTIABLE INSTRUMENTS—RIGHTS OF HOLDERS AS COLLATERAL SECURITY.—An indorsee of negotiable paper taken before maturity as collateral security for an antecedent indebtedness, in good faith, and without notice of defenses, such as fraud, which might have been available as between the original parties, holds the paper free from such defenses: Rosemond v. Graham, 54 Minn. 323; 40 Am. St. Rep. 336, and note. Contra, Vann v. Marbury, 100 Ala. 438, 46 Am. St. Rep. 70; Smith v. Bibber, 82 Me. 34; 17 Am. St. Rep. 464, and note.

FRAUDULENT CONVEYANCES—WHO MAY ATTACK.—It is only those persons whose rights are interfered with, those who are injured by conveyances alleged to be fraudulent, that have the right to interfere to set them aside; Yeend v. Weeks, 104 Ala. 331; 53 Am. St. Rep. 50, and note. As to what creditors have the right to attack such conveyances, see monographic notes to Jenkins v. Clement, 14 Am. Dec. 703-709, and Hagerman v. Buchanan, 14 Am. St. Rep. 739-754.

NEGOTIABLE INSTRUMENTS—INDORSEMENT AND GUARANTY.—Indorsement thereon by the payee of a promissory note "For value received I hereby guarantee the payment of the within note and waive presentation, protest, and notice"; amounts to an indorsement with an enlarged liability: Heard v. Dubuque Co. Bank, 8 Neb. 10; 30 Am. Rep. 811. The words, "I hereby guarantee the payment of the within note, R. D. H." written on the back of a note, R. D. H. being the payee, constitute a valid indorsement: Myrick v. Hasey, 27 Me. 9; 46 Am. Dec. 583. The legal title to a negotiable note may be transferred by guaranty as well as indorsement: Crosby v. Roub, 16 Wis. 616; 84 Am. Dec. 720; Herring v. Woodhull, 29 Ill. 92; 81 Am. Dec. 296.

GERMAN INSURANCE CO. *v.* FIRST NATIONAL BANK,

[58 KANSAS, 86.]

FOREIGN INSURANCE CORPORATIONS—JURISDICTION OVER IN CAUSES OF ACTION ARISING WITHOUT THE STATE.—Under a statute providing that if the defendant be a foreign insurance corporation, an action may be brought against it in any county where the cause of action or some part thereof arose, and that if the defendant is an incorporated insurance corporation, and the action is brought in a county in which there is an agency, the service may be made on the chief officer of such agency, such corporation may be sued and process served upon its agent, though the cause of action is not based on a contract of insurance and did not arise within the state.

Jetmore & Jetmore, for the plaintiff in error.

Rossington, Smith & Dallas, and Clifford Histed, for the defendant in error.

[87] ALLEN, J. The First National Bank of Boonville, New York, obtained in the circuit court of Shawnee county a judgment for two thousand three hundred dollars against the Western Investment Loan and Trust Company, a Kansas corporation. Execution having been issued on the judgment and returned unsatisfied, this action was brought against the German Insurance Company of Freeport, Illinois, to charge it as a stockholder of the loan and trust company. It was alleged in the petition that the insurance company had duly subscribed for fifty shares of stock, of the par value of fifty dollars each, on which it had paid two thousand dollars; that there remained unpaid five hundred dollars on the subscription, and that the defendant was liable in the further sum of two thousand five hundred dollars under its statutory liability. A summons was issued and served on Joseph Groll and J. S. McKittrick, partners as Groll & McKittrick, managing agents of the defendant and chief officers of its agency at Topeka. The defendant appeared specially, and, on various grounds, moved to set aside the summons and the service thereof. The motion was overruled. The defendant made no further appearance in the case, and judgment was thereupon rendered in favor of the plaintiff for two thousand five hundred dollars and costs.

It is contended that the court had no jurisdiction over the defendant, and that the service on Groll & McKittrick was void. Section 69 of the Code of Civil Procedure reads: "Where the defendant is an incorporated insurance company, and the action is brought in a county in [88] which there is an agency thereof,

the service may be upon the chief officer of such agency." It
is contended that Groll & McKittrick were not chief officers
of an agency, within the meaning of the statute, but that they
were mere soliciting agents. Section 53 of the code provides:
"If said defendant be a foreign insurance company, the action
may be brought in any county where the cause, or some part
thereof, arose." It is urged that, under these provisions of the
statute, suits against a foreign insurance company can only be
maintained on insurance contracts; that both the parties to this
action are foreign corporations; that the plaintiff's cause of action is not based on any contract of insurance entered into in
this state, and that our courts can acquire no jurisdiction over
the defendant without service of process on one of its principal
officers. The old theory that a corporation resides only in the
state of its creation no longer obtains. It is now held that, for
the purpose of conferring jurisdiction on the courts, a corporation is present in any place where it transacts its business; and
that service of process may be made on its agents through whom,
as its instruments, its business is transacted. The intangible
corporation is held to be present wherever its business is carried
on, whether that be in the state where its charter was obtained,
or in any other sovereignty: St. Claire v. Cox, 106 U. S. 350.
Groll & McKittrick represented the insurance company, as its
agents, at Topeka, with authority "to receive applications for
insurance and moneys for premiums, and to countersign, issue,
and renew policies of insurance signed by the president and attested by the secretary." They were furnished blank policies,
signed by the president and the secretary, which they were authorized to fill out; and, when [89] countersigned and delivered
the policies became valid and binding on the company. Under
the prior decisions of this court, such an agency is a general
agency: American Cent. Ins. Co. v. McLanathan, 11 Kan. 533;
Western Home Ins. Co. v. Hogue, 41 Kan. 524; Phoenix Ins. Co.
v. Munger, 49 Kan. 178; 33 Am. St. Rep. 360. Unquestionably,
the insurance company was transacting business in Kansas, and
the persons served were in charge of its office and were the
chief officers of the agency.

It is sought to draw a distinction between actions on policies
of insurance and actions on other contracts; and, as a basis for
the distinction, section 53 of the Code of Civil Procedure, which
authorizes an action to be brought in any county where the
cause of action arose, and section 41 of chapter 50a of the
General Statutes of 1889, which provides for service of process

on the superintendent of insurance, are cited. In the case of Burlington Ins. Co. v. Mortimer, 52 Kan. 784, it was held that the different methods of service on insurance companies are cumulative; and that, in an action on a policy of insurance, service may be made on the chief officer of the agency.

The contention that the courts of this state are limited in jurisdiction to actions on policies of insurance is not sound. Issuing such policies and paying losses thereon, is by no means the only business an insurance company may lawfully transact. It may lawfully invest its money, employ agents, and contract debts and obligations of various kinds. There is certainly no valid reason why our courts have less power to enforce the payment of one obligation than of another. Nor is it essential that the contract sought to be enforced should have been entered into in this state. For the purpose of transacting the business for which it was created, the company resided here as well as in the state of Illinois, and is as much subject to our laws and the jurisdiction of our courts as any other corporation carrying on business here.

The judgment is affirmed.

———

INSURANCE—FOREIGN COMPANIES.—A corporation, in addition to its corporate home in the state of its creation, has a legal location, place of business, and corporate home in any jurisdiction in which it has property exposed to execution sufficient to satisfy any judgment which may be rendered against it, and in which, either by force of statutory law there binding upon it, or by its own act or agreement, or by the combined force of both, it so far becomes, in the person of its agent duly authorized for that purpose, a resident therein, as that a general personal judgment can be obtained, which will be binding upon it, and any property which it may have in any jurisdiction, as completely as if it had been sued and personally served in the state of its creation where it has its principal legal location and place of business: Crouse v. Phoenix Ins. Co., 56 Conn. 176; 7 Am. St. Rep. 298, and note. See Continental Ins. Co. v. Ruckman, 127 Ill. 364; 11 Am. St. Rep. 121.

ATCHISON, TOPEKA & SANTA FE RAILROAD COMPANY
v. SCHWARZSCHILD.

[58 KANSAS, 90.]

ATTACHMENT—LEVY OF JUNIOR BEFORE SENIOR.—
If several writs of attachment are placed in the hands of a sheriff,
they are entitled to priority in the order in which they are received,
and that officer cannot by levying the junior writ first give it precedence over the senior, nor can he by levying the senior writ first on
certain property and subsequently levying the junior writ on other
property restrict the right of the holder of the senior writ to the
property actually levied upon under it.

A. A. Hurd and Mills, Smith & Hobbs, for the plaintiff in
error.

Miller & Morris, for the defendant in error.

[90] JOHNSTON, J. Involved in this case is the question:
Which one of two attaching creditors shall have the preference in
the distribution of a fund derived from the sale of attached
property?

On April 21, 1893, the Schwarzschild & Sulzberger Company
brought an action against Frank E. Tyler [91] and obtained an
order of attachment. At 6 o'clock P. M. of that day, the
order was placed in the hands of the sheriff, who, forty minutes
later, levied upon the personal property of Tyler, appraised at
forty-nine thousand five hundred and thirty eight dollars and
thirty cents. It was soon found that the property levied upon
was mortgaged to secure a debt of fifty thousand dollars. On the
next morning, at 5:40 o'clock, a levy was made, under that order,
on real estate of the appraised value of forty-two thousand dollars, but which was afterward found to be covered by a mortgage
of fifty thousand dollars. Three orders of attachment were
issued in other cases and placed in the hands of the sheriff; after
which, and on April 22, 1893, the Atchison, Topeka & Santa
Fe Railroad Company instituted an action against Tyler, and
caused an attachment to issue which was placed in the hands of
the sheriff. At that time, the sheriff had in his possession four
orders of attachment previously issued against the property of
Tyler. On the evening of April 22d, at the request of the railroad company, the attachment issued at its instance was levied
upon the contents of four cars, which were in the yards of the
company and which it pointed out to the sheriff; and, in his
return the sheriff declared that, by virtue of that order, he levied
upon the property. An inventory of the property was made,
and it was appraised at four thousand six hundred and seven dol-

lars and thirty-two cents. On the morning of April 24th, at the request of the Schwarzschild & Sulzberger Company, the sheriff declared a levy in its favor upon the same property. The property, being of a perishable character, was ordered by the court to be sold, and it was sold for two thousand two hundred and ninety-two dollars. The controversy arises on the distribution of this fund.

Upon the evidence, the court found that the Schwarzschild & Sulzberger Company was entitled to a preference; of which ruling the railroad company [92] complains. Under our code, orders of attachment are entitled to priority of service in the order in which they are received: Civ. Code, sec. 196. It is also provided that "different attachments of the same property may be made by the same officer, and one inventory and appraisement shall be sufficient, and it shall not be necessary to return the same with more than one order": Civ. Code, sec. 203. It therefore appears that, when several orders against the same defendant are placed in the hands of an officer for service, the statute, rather than the discretion of the officer, fixes the priorities and determines the rights of the claimants. The officer cannot, in such a case, by a mere declaration, or by the writing of a return upon a junior order and a return of an inventory and appraisement therewith, give the junior order priority over an earlier order which he then holds in his possession. The case of Larabee v. Parks, 43 Kan. 436, practically determines the questions in this case. It was there held that, where several orders are issued against the same defendant and executed, the priority of levy is determined by the time of reception, and not by the order of execution. It was held that the statute prescribing the order of execution is mandatory upon the officer; and that if the sheriff disobeys the law, and attempts by the levy of a later order to give it priority over a former one, the injured party is not compelled to look to the sheriff for a remedy, by amercement or other proceeding, but may apply to the court and obtain the preference which the law gives him.

As the officer has no discretion as to the execution, the levy of one of several orders in his possession on the debtor's property will be deemed to inure to the benefit of the attaching creditors in the order of their priority. An attachment does not become a lien when it is issued; but when several are issued against the defendant [93] and placed in the hands of the sheriff, as in the present case, and an actual levy is made, a lien then attaches as the law provides. The officer cannot, by a declaration of levy under a junior attachment, change the rule of the law or give priority over a senior order; and the court may require the officer's return to be corrected, and may give the benefit to the creditor whose order of attachment was first delivered to the sheriff. The fact that the order obtained by the Schwarzschild & Sulzberger Company was first levied upon other property of considerable value will not affect the determination. That which was levied upon appears to have been mortgaged to secure indebtedness which exceeded the appraised value of the property; and from the return it appears that, when the levies were made, the officer had no actual notice or knowledge of the existence of the mortgages. If there was nothing left for seizure, or if the property levied upon was insufficient to satisfy their claims, the senior creditors will be deemed to have been in the same position as if no levy had been made, and, to the extent of the deficiency, to have had a right to demand of the junior attaching creditors the preference which the statute awards them. We think the court ruled correctly in fixing the priorities and in distributing the proceeds: Larabee v. Parks, 43 Kan. 436; Gillig v. Treadwell Co., 148 N. Y. 177; Pach v. Gilbert, 124 N. Y. 612; Callahan v. Hallowell, 2 Bay, 8.

The judgment of the district court will be affirmed.

ATTACHMENTS—PRIORITY BETWEEN—DUTY OF OFFICER. Successive attachments should be satisfied in the order of their priority, and not pro rata: Hepp v. Glover, 15 La. 461; 35 Am. Dec. 206, and note. Where a subsequent attachment has been first levied by the sheriff or his deputies, and the fund attached is under the control of the court, and the parties are all before the court, the chancellor should distribute the fund amongst the attaching creditors in the order in which attachments came into the sheriff's office. Kennon v. Ficklin, 6 B. Mon. 414; 44 Am. Dec. 776, and note. See McComb v. Reed, 28 Cal. 281; 87 Am. Dec. 115; note to Gillespie v. Keating, 57 Am. St. Rep. 625, 626.

BLAIR *v.* ANDERSON.

[58 KANSAS, 97.]

RES JUDICATA.—THE DECISION OF A MOTION which must be tried and determined by the court, and from which decision no appeal can be taken, is not conclusive upon the parties in a subsequent action presenting the same issues, but in which they are entitled to a trial by jury. Hence, if an assignee for the benefit of creditors moves to discharge an attachment, and the court makes special findings declaring the assignment fraudulent and void, and for that reason refuses to discharge the attachment, and the assignee thereafter brings an action in replevin to recover the same property, the former findings and decision on the motion do not constitute such a trial of the questions involved as precludes the assignee or his successor in interest from trying the title to the property in the regular and formal action of replevin.

Bond & Osborn and T. F. Garver, for the plaintiff in error.

Mohler & Hiller, for the defendant in error.

[97]ALLEN, J. Swain Pearson was a manufacturer of carriages, wagons, and other articles at Salina. On the 6th of April, 1893, he executed a deed of assignment for the benefit of his creditors to E. E. Swanson, [98] who took immediate possession of the assigned property. On the next day, the Paddock & Hawley Iron Company commenced an action in the district court against Pearson, and caused an attachment to be issued and levied on a portion of the property in the possession of the assignee. Subsequently, Swanson and Pearson filed separate motions to discharge the attachment; Swanson claiming the goods by virtue of the deed of assignment. These motions were heard by the court on oral evidence. Special findings of fact were made, and the court, as a conclusion of law, held the assignment fraudulent and void, and overruled the motions to discharge the attachment. Afterward, Swanson, as assignee, brought this suit, which is, in form, an action of replevin to recover the property levied on by the sheriff under the attachment in the case first mentioned. E. W. Blair, who was elected permanent assignee by the creditors, was afterward substituted as plaintiff. The defendant pleaded the decision of the court on the motions to discharge the attached property as an adjudication of the invalidity of the assignment. On demurrer to the answer, as well as on the trial of the case, the court sustained the defendant's position, and held the decision on the motions conclusive between the parties in this case. The sole question for our determination is the correctness of this ruling.

The question when a decision of a court on a motion becomes a final adjudication between the parties of the matters necessarily involved in the consideration of the motion is often one of much difficulty. Most of the cases in this court have arisen on orders confirming or setting aside sheriff's sales; and, in those cases, it is held that the order of the court is conclusive on all matters involved in the proceedings of the officer in executing the writ: Phillips v. Love, [99] 57 Kan. 828. It is, perhaps, unnecessary at this time to discuss the reasons for the rule in such cases, but it may be remarked that the order confirming a sale is made after judgment in the action, in pursuance of a provision of the statute requiring the court to examine the proceedings of the officer, and, if regular, to approve them, and direct a conveyance of the property sold. The determination of such a motion becomes a final order after judgment, and as such is reviewable on proceedings in error in this court. The order set up in this case as an adjudication of the rights of the parties was one refusing to vacate an attachment, and is not, under section 542 of the code, reviewable by proceedings in error. This action is brought by the assignee to recover the possession of specific personal property. In such a case, the parties have a right to a trial by jury. Motions to discharge attachments are tried by the court; and may be heard on affidavits and written evidence alone, without any opportunity for the cross-examination of witnesses. They may even be heard out of court, by the judge at chambers: Gen. Stats. 1889, par. 1962; Shedd v. McConnell, 18 Kan. 594; Wells, Fargo & Co. v. Danford, 28 Kan. 487. From these considerations, it is plainly apparent that an order overruling a motion to vacate an attachment lacks much of a formal adjudication of the title to the attached property. We think this case falls fairly within the rule followed in Stapleton v. Orr, 43 Kan. 170, Kendall etc. Co. v. August, 51 Kan. 53, and Miami County Nat. Bank v. Barkalow, 53 Kan. 68.

Though the questions considered on the hearing of the motions to discharge the attachment were the validity of the deed of assignment and the alleged fraud of the parties to it, the hearing on the motions was not such a trial of the questions as precludes the assignee, or his successor in interest, from bringing this [100] action and trying the title to the property in a regular and formal action. The fact that the suit of the Paddock-Hawley Iron Company was brought on a claim not due does not change the rule, though valid grounds for an attachment are prerequisites to the prosecution of an action on a claim not due. The hearing on a motion to vacate the attachment is in all respects the same as that in an action on a claim past due. The determination of the court as to the title of a third person to the attached property is no more conclusive in the one case than in the other. Though, between the parties to the record, the judgment finally rendered in the attachment suit may be conclusive of the right to the attachment, it is not, as to the assignee claiming as the representative of the creditors, conclusive of the right to the attached property.

The judgment is reversed, and the cause remanded for further proceedings.

RES JUDICATA—LIMITS TO RULE OF.--If a question has once been tried on its merits without fraud or collusion, by a court having jurisdiction of the parties and subject matter, it cannot be again litigated between the same parties in the same or any other judicial tribunal so long as the adjudication remains unreversed and in full effect: Martin v. Evans, 85 Md. 8; 60 Am. St. Rep. 292, and note. But the question must have been determined by final judgment, have been in issue under the pleadings, and actually litigated and determined: Fuller v. Metropolitan Life Ins. Co., 68 Conn. 55; 57 Am. St. Rep. 84, and note. A decision that sweeps away the rights of a party without giving him a chance to be heard is not res judicata: Nichells v. Nichells, 5 N. Dak. 125; 57 Am. St. Rep. 540. A judgment is no evidence of a matter coming collaterally in question merely: Wood v. Jackson, 8 Wend. 9; 22 Am. Dec. 603, and note. See, also, notes to Hawk v. Evans, 14 Am. St. Rep. 252, and King v. Chase, 41 Am. Dec. 682.

GILLE v. EMMONS.

[58 KANSAS, 118.]

A JUDGMENT OUTSIDE THE ISSUES IS VOID.—Hence, if in an action to foreclose a mortgage made by a husband and wife to secure notes executed by him only, a personal judgment is entered against her, there being no allegation in the complaint respecting her personal liability, such judgment is void as against her.

JUDGMENT, VACATING.—IF A JUDGMENT IS VOID as against a defendant, because outside of the issues, as where personal judgment is entered against a defendant in a foreclosure suit, when the complaint does not show any personal liability, such judgment may be vacated on motion at any time.

JUDGMENT.—THE AFFIRMANCE OF A VOID JUDGMENT does not give it any validity, nor deprive the defendant against whom it is void of the right to have it vacated on motion at any time.

Witten & Hughes, for the plaintiff in error.

Mills, Smith & Hobbs, for the defendant in error.

[119] JOHNSTON, J. This was an application by Carrie L. Emmons to vacate and set aside a judgment rendered against her without right or authority by the district court of Johnson county. It appears that, on February 4, 1887, D. R. Emmons executed two promissory notes for four thousand three hundred dollars each, payable one year after date with interest at the rate of eight per cent per annum, and to secure the payment of the same executed a mortgage upon a tract of land in Wyandotte county. Being a married man, his wife, Carrie L. Emmons, joined in the execution of the mortgage. Default was made in the payment of the notes, and, on March 12, 1888, an action was brought by James M. Gille, the owner of the notes and

mortgage, to recover a personal judgment against D. R. Emmons
and to foreclose the mortgage. Carrie L. Emmons was joined
as a defendant, and, as to her, the prayer of the petition was
that her equity of redemption in the mortgaged premises should
be foreclosed. In her answer she alleged that she was not interested in the controversy, which related to a failure of title
to part of the mortgaged land which was the consideration of the
notes and mortgage in question, except as the wife of D. R. Emmons. On January 26, 1889, the trial resulted in a judgment
in favor of Gille upon the notes and for a foreclosure of the
mortgaged premises. A journal entry was prepared by one of the
counsel for Gille, which was entered by the clerk, and, although
not asked for nor authorized by the pleadings, it was made to
appear that a personal judgment had been rendered against Carrie
L. Emmons for ten thousand one hundred and eighty-eight dollars. It seems that counsel for Gille did not intend to include
[120] her in the entry of personal judgment, and that her attorney
was not aware that such an entry had been prepared or made.
She had no knowledge that a judgment had been entered against
her until August, 1893, when an execution was taken out and
levied upon her property. She never was liable for the debt sued
on, and never, by any promise, pleading, or action, authorized
the creation of the debt which the mortgage was given to secure.
Shortly after the levy was made upon her property, she filed, in
the original cause, a motion asking that the judgment be vacated and set aside. A hearing was had at which the foregoing
facts were developed; and the court held the judgment to be
void and sustained the motion. This decision is assigned as error.

We entertain no doubt that the court reached a correct conclusion. The indebtedness of Carrie L. Emmons was not an issue
in the case, and was never submitted to the court for its determination. The mere fact that jurisdiction of the person was obtained by the court did not give it unlimited power to adjudge
any and every matter in which the parties to the action might be
concerned. A court cannot determine matters not brought to
its attention by some method known to the law, nor give effective
judgment upon a cause or subject matter not brought within
the scope of its judicial power. Although it may have jurisdiction in the class of cases to which a cause belongs, it cannot exercise its power until it is invoked by the parties; and if it goes
outside of the issues and adjudicates a question not submitted for
its decision the judgment is without force. The question was
recently examined by the supreme court of the United States in

Reynolds v. Stockton, 140 U. S. 254, where it was held that in
order to give a judgment rendered by even a [121] court of general
jurisdiction the merit and finality of an adjudication between the
parties, it must be responsive to the issues tendered by the pleadings; and that a judgment rendered upon another and different
cause of action than that stated in the complaint or submitted
to the court for its decision is without binding force. In that
case, Mr. Justice Brewer used the following language:

"We are not concerned in this case as to the power of amendment of pleadings lodged in the trial court, or the effect of any
amendment made under such power, for no amendment was made
or asked. And without amendment of the pleadings, a judgment
for the recovery of the possession of real estate, rendered in an
action whose pleadings disclose only a claim for the possession
of personal property, cannot be sustained, although personal service was made upon the defendant. The invalidity of the judgment depends upon the fact that it is in no manner responsive
to the issues tendered by the pleadings. This idea underlies all
litigation. Its emphatic language is, that a judgment, to be conclusive upon the parties to the litigation, must be responsive
to the matters controverted. Nor are we concerned with the
question as to the rule which obtains in a case in which, while
the matter determined was not, in fact, put in issue in the pleadings, it is apparent from the record that the defeated party was
present at the trial and actually litigated that matter. In such
a case the proposition so often affirmed, that that is to be considered as done which ought to have been done, may have weight,
and the amendment which ought to have been made to conform
the pleadings to the evidence may be treated as having been
made. Here there was no appearance after the filing of the answer, and no participation in the trial or other proceedings.
Whatever may be the rule where substantial amendments to the
complaint are permitted and made, and the defendant responds
thereto, or where it appears that he takes actual part in the litigation of the matters determined, the rule is universal that, where
he appears and responds only to [122] the complaint as filed, and
no amendment is made thereto, the judgment is conclusive only so
far as it determines matters which by the pleadings are put in
issue."

The same question was before the court of errors and appeals
of New Jersey, and it was there held that a judgment entirely
outside the issues in the record is invalid, and will be treated
as a nullity even in a collateral proceeding. It was said: "Juris-

diction may be defined to be the right to adjudicate concerning
the subject matter in the given case. To constitute this there
are three essentials: 1. The court must have cognizance of the
class of cases to which the one to be adjudged belongs; 2. The
proper parties must be present; and 3. The point decided must
be, in substance and effect, within the issue. That a court cannot
go out of its appointed sphere, and that its action is void with
respect to persons who are strangers to the proceedings, are propositions established by a multitude of authorities. A defect in a
judgment arising from the fact that the matter decided was not
embraced within the issue has not, it would seem, received much
judicial consideration. And yet I cannot doubt that, upon general principles, such a defect must avoid a judgment. It is impossible to concede that because A and B are parties to a suit, a
court can decide any matter in which they are interested, whether
such matter be involved in the pending litigation or not. Persons
by becoming suitors do not place themselves for all purposes
under the control of the court, and it is only over these particular
interests, which they choose to draw in question, that a power
of judicial decision arises": Munday v. Vail, 34 N. J. L. 422.
And again: "A judgment upon a matter outside of the issue
must, of necessity, be altogether arbitrary and unjust, as it concludes a point upon which the parties have not been heard":
Munday v. Vail, 34 N. J. L. 423.

[123] The supreme court of Ohio has held: "The judgment of
a court upon a subject of litigation within its jurisdiction, but
not brought before it by any statement or claim of the parties,
is null and void, and may be collaterally impeached": Spoors v.
Coen, 44 Ohio St. 497.

In treating upon this subject, Freeman, in his work on Judgments, states: "It is essential that the jurisdiction of the court
over the subject matter be called into action by some party and in
some mode recognized by law. A court does not have the power
to render judgment in favor of one as plaintiff if he has never
commenced any action or proceeding calling for its action; nor
has it as a general rule power to give judgment respecting a
matter not submitted to it for decision, though such judgment
is pronounced in an action involving other matters which have
been submitted to it for decision and over which it has jurisdiction": 1 Freeman on Judgments, 4th ed., secs. 120, 120 c. See,
also, Little v. Evans, 41 Kan. 578; Fithian v. Monks, 43 Mo.
502; Steele v. Palmer, 41 Miss. 88; Armstrong v. Barton, 42
Miss. 506; Lewis v. Smith, 9 N. Y. 502; 61 Am. Dec. 706; Un-

fried v. Heberer, 63 Ind. 67; Dunlap v. Southerlin, 63 Tex. 38;
1 Black on Judgments, sec. 242.

If there had been an attempt to set up a liability against Mrs.
Emmons, and the cause of action had been imperfectly or defectively stated, a judgment rendered thereon, although erroneous,
would be deemed to be valid until reversed on error or set aside by
some direct proceeding for that purpose. Here, however, there
was no attempt to state a liability against her, and the pleadings
plainly disclosed that she was not liable for the debt. There was
no amendment of the pleadings, and no purpose by any of the
parties that a liability should be asserted or a judgment taken
against her. Her liability was not within the judicial control of
the court nor subject to its determination. [124] The court had
no more power to award a judgment against her therein than it
would have had to adjudge that the title to her personal property
was in the plaintiff, or that the home in which she lived in another county was not a homestead. The judgment rendered
against her was a nullity, and subject to either direct or collateral attack. The validity of the judgment was challenged in
the same court and in the same case in which it was rendered.
It is true that the application to vacate was not made until more
than four years after the judgment was rendered, but, as the
judgment was void, the court was not hampered by a limitation
of time. The statute relating to proceedings for the vacation
and modification of judgments provides that "a void judgment
may be vacated at any time on motion of a party or any person
affected thereby": Civ. Code, sec. 575; Beach v. Shoenmaker, 18
Kan. 147; Hanson v. Wolcott, 19 Kan. 207.

The judgment was brought to this court for a review of the
questions which were in issue in the district court, and the
name of Carrie L. Emmons was added as a plaintiff in error. The
questions in controversy between D. R. Emmons and Gille were
determined in favor of the latter, and the judgment was affirmed.
The fact that Carrie L. Emmons was named as a plaintiff in
error, and that the judgment was affirmed in that proceeding,
did not operate to infuse life into the void judgment, nor prevent the trial court from setting it aside upon motion at any
time thereafter. If she had had knowledge of the existence of
the judgment against her, the proceedings could be regarded
as nothing more than an attempt to set aside a void judgment.
Being a nullity, it could be collaterally attacked; but, although
a nullity, it is sufficient to lay the foundation for a proceeding
in error: Earls v. [125] Earls, 27 Kan. 538. It may also, as we

have seen, be vacated and set aside at any time on motion of the defendant.

The order setting aside the judgment is affirmed.

JUDGMENT OUTSIDE OF ISSUES.—A judgment or decree outside of the issues, is, to that extent, without jurisdiction and void: Metcalf v. Hart, 3 Wyo. 513; 31 Am. St. Rep. 122. See extended note to Falls v. Wright, 29 Am. St. Rep. 78-84.

JUDGMENTS—VOID—CONFIRMATION OF.—Void judgments cannot be validated by citing the parties against whom they are rendered to show cause why they should not be declared valid: Jewett v. Iowa Land Co., 64 Minn. 531; 58 Am. St. Rep. 555, and note.

JUDGMENTS—VACATING BECAUSE VOID.—If a judgment is void for want of jurisdiction over the parties or the subject matter, there is no doubt that it may be vacated upon motion. A judgment may be void though the court had jurisdiction over the subject matter and the parties, if it proceeds to dispose of matters over which it was not authorized to act in the controversy before it, or to grant relief of a character which it has no power to grant. Such a judgment may be vacated on motion: Monographic note to Furman v. Furman, 60 Am. St. Rep. 642-644.

IN RE HURON.

[58 KANSAS, 152.]

NOTARIES PUBLIC, EXERCISE OF JUDICIAL POWER BY.—Under a constitution declaring that the judicial power of the state is vested in certain courts therein named and such other courts as may be prescribed by law, judicial power cannot be vested in a notary public.

CONTEMPT, JURISDICTION TO PUNISH.—To try the question of contempt and adjudge punishment is an exercise of judicial power.

CONTEMPT, PUNISHMENT OF BY NOTARIES.—A statute authorizing notaries public to take depositions and issue subpoenas to compel the attendance of witnesses before them, and declaring that the disobedience of a subpoena, or the refusal to be sworn, or to answer as a witness, or to subscribe the deposition when legally ordered, may be punished as a contempt of the court or officer by whom the attendance or testimony is required, is unconstitutional in so far as it undertakes to authorize notaries public to punish witnesses for contempt, because the power to so punish is judicial and cannot be vested in a notary.

David Overmyer and S. B. Bradford, for the petitioner.

Troutman & Stone and Thomas Berry, for the respondent.

¹⁵² JOHNSTON, J. A subpoena was issued by a notary public of Shawnee county and served upon George A. Huron, the petitioner, requiring him to appear before the notary and give testimony in a cause then pending in Franklin county. He

appeared in obedience to the subpoena, but refused to be sworn:
1. Because he was a defendant in the action and an attorney of
record, and expected to be present at the trial; and 2. Because
the attempt to take his deposition was not made in good faith,
or with any intention of using the deposition when taken, but
was for the mere purpose of ascertaining in advance the line of
defense and testimony of the defendants. An affidavit in behalf of the plaintiff was then filed, alleging good faith, and that
the depositions were intended to be used upon the trial of the
action and in an application for a receiver; and, further, that
the witness was a nonresident of the county where the action
was pending. The petitioner still persisting in his refusal to
testify, the notary held him guilty of contempt, and ordered
that he be committed until he should be willing to be [153] sworn
and to give his deposition. He petitions for release, insisting
that the case was not one in which his deposition could be taken,
and, further, that the notary public had no authority to compel
him to testify.

As the petitioner does not reside in the county where the action is pending, the plaintiff was clearly entitled to take his
deposition; Civ. Code, sec. 346; and the fact that he has been
named as a defendant, or that he is an attorney of record in
the case, will not prevent the taking of his deposition. No such
exceptions are expressed or implied in the statute. But, while
these objections are not tenable, there remains the more important question whether a notary public may punish a witness
for contempt in refusing to be sworn or to give his deposition.
"By section 348 of the Civil Code, the general power, without
any exception or limitation, is given to notaries public to take
depositions": Swearingen v. Howser, 37 Kan. 128. Other provisions of the code are, that the officer authorized to take depositions may issue subpoenas requiring witnesses to attend before
him and give their depositions, and that the disobedience of a
subpoena, or the refusal to be sworn and to answer as a witness,
or to subscribe a deposition, when lawfully ordered, may be
punished as a contempt of the court or officer by whom his attendance or testimony is required. If the witness fails to attend, provision is made for the issuance of an attachment commanding the arrest of the witness, and that he be brought before
the court or officer. The punishment for the contempt, where
the witness fails to attend in obedience to a subpoena, is a fine
not exceeding fifty dollars. In other cases, the court or officer
may imprison him in the county jail, there to remain until he

shall submit to be sworn, testify, or give his deposition: Civ. Code, secs. 326-332. Can the [154] notary exercise the power which the statute purports to confer?

It must be conceded that to try a question of contempt and adjudge punishment is an exercise of judicial power. Has that high judicial function been vested in notaries public? A majority of the court are of opinion that notaries public are not judicial officers, and that they cannot arrest and punish for contempt. The view of the court is, that the whole judicial power of the state is vested by the constitution, and can only be vested in such tribunals as are therein prescribed. It provides that "the judicial power of this state shall be vested in a supreme court, district courts, probate courts, justices of the peace, and such other courts, inferior to the supreme court, as may be prescribed by law": Const., art. 3, sec. 1. It will be observed that the judicial power is placed in the courts expressly mentioned and any inferior courts that may be created by the legislature; but is lodged in courts alone. Until a tribunal is created which rises to the dignity of a court, it cannot be vested with judicial power. A notary public is not a court in the sense in which the term is used in the constitution. He is simply an executive officer, who is chosen with reference to the duties to be performed by officers of that class. No limit is placed upon the number of notaries the governor may appoint in a county. The general authority conferred is to take proof and acknowledgment of deeds and instruments in writing, to administer oaths, to demand acceptance and payment of commercial paper and protest the same for nonacceptance or nonpayment, and to exercise such other powers and duties as by the law of nations and commercial usage may be performed by notaries public: Gen. Stats. 1889, par. 3927. The duties, including the mere taking [155] of testimony by deposition, are not judicial in their character; and in the commercial world a notary has not been regarded as a judicial officer. While the taking of testimony is incidental to a judicial proceeding, the notary, in taking the deposition, is not required to determine the relevancy and competency of testimony, but simply writes and authenticates the testimony given, with such objections as the parties desire to make. He is not designated as a court, nor clothed with the usual paraphernalia of such a tribunal. A court is said to be a tribunal organized for the public administration of justice at a time and place prescribed by law. No provision is made for pleadings, nor for the issuance of process by a notary, except to subpoena a witness to give his

testimony. If the witness refuses to be sworn or to testify and
is deemed subject to a charge of contempt, no rules are prescribed for a trial before the notary, nor is specific provision
made for obtaining evidence in order to determine whether such
witness is actually guilty of contempt. Up to the time of the
refusal of the witness, at least, the notary is only an executive
officer, and is exercising executive power. There is no such
thing as a punishable contempt of executive authority. While
an executive officer might be constituted a court, judicial power
cannot be conferred on him as merely ancillary to the exercise
of purely executive power. It is true that in In re Abeles, 12
Kan. 451, it was stated that a notary might commit a recusant
witness for contempt, but it does not appear that the constitutional phase of the question received much consideration, and
the decision is not deemed to be controlling. It has since been
accepted without serious dispute, and has been followed in other
cases without much discussion. It is, therefore, the view of the
court that the question has not before been authoritatively [156]
settled. Not every one who hears testimony and exercises discretion and judgment in a matter submitted to him is necessarily
a judicial officer; and whether notaries public have the attributes
and powers of courts is to be determined from the constitution.
Anciently, such officers were not clothed with judicial power;
and when the constitution was adopted they were not regarded
as having power to punish for contempt, nor as being in any
sense judicial officers. In Whitcomb's case, 120 Mass. 118, 21
Am. Rep. 502, it was contended that a city council had such power. The statute undertook to confer it, but it was held to be ineffectual. It was said that under the common law a city council had
no such power, and that, when the constitution of the commonwealth of Massachusetts was adopted, it was not part of the law of
the land that municipal boards or officers had power to commit or
punish for contempt. It was, therefore, held that they were not to
be regarded as a part of the judiciary, and that a statute which undertook to confer such authority upon them was unconstitutional
and void. It is asserted that, when our constitution was adopted,
notaries were not understood to have judicial power, and therefore, were not within the contemplation of the people in
providing for the creation of courts. In Ex parte Doll, 7 Phila.
595, it was held that a United States commissioner had not been
given authority to arrest and punish recusant witnesses for contempt; and the judge, in disposing of the case, remarked that
he very much doubted the power of Congress to invest a com-

missioner with such power: See, also, In re Mason, 43 Fed. Rep.
510; In re Kerrigan, 33 N. J. L. 344; Rhinehart v. Lance, 43
N. J. L. 311; 39 Am. Rep. 592. The attempt of the legislature
to confer judicial power on a mere executive officer of the government must be [157] deemed to be invalid. As was said in
Langenberg v. Decker, 131 Ind. 486: "The authority to imprison
resides where the constitution places it, and the legislature cannot give it residence elsewhere. The authority is essentially a
judicial one, abiding in the courts of the land. As it is a judicial
power, it is not created by the legislature . nor vested by that
body. . . . . Judicial power, like all sovereign powers, comes
from the people and vests where the people's constitution directs
that it shall vest. The legislature may name tribunals that shall
exercise judicial powers, unless the constitution otherwise provides, but the power itself comes from the constitution, and not
from the statute": See, also, Eastman v. State, 109 Ind. 278;
58 Am. Rep. 400; Lezinsky v. Superior Court, 72 Cal. 510. For
these reasons, it must be held that a notary public is not a judicial
officer, and that he has not been vested with power to commit and
punish for contempt.

The writer is unable to concur in the views expressed or in the
conclusion reached. Unlike some of the cases referred to, the
power to arrest and punish for contempt does not rest on inferences and implications. The legislature of our state has expressly provided that if a witness, who has been duly subpoenaed
to appear and to give his deposition before a notary public, refuses to appear or to testify, he may be punished for contempt.
It is competent for the legislature to create as many judicial
officers or tribunals as necessity or convenience suggests. The
only limitation upon that power is that those created shall be
inferior to the supreme court: Const., art. 3, sec. 1. Within that
limitation, they may be given as much or as little power as the
legislature in its wisdom and discretion may provide. The fact
that a very limited extent of judicial power is conferred [158] will
not thwart the legislative purpose. It is not necessary that the
person so clothed with judicial power shall be designated as a
court in order to be a court within the meaning of the constitution: Malone v. Murphy, 2 Kan. 250; State v. Young, 3 Kan.
445. The objection that notaries public are not carefully chosen,
and are not invested with the paraphernalia of courts, can have
little weight. They are certainly selected with as much care as
some of those expressly named in the constitution. They are
appointed by the chief executive officer of the state, are required

to take an oath of office and give a bond, and are provided with a
seal. To constitute them judicial officers, it is not necessary
that a clerk and a bailiff should be provided. It is enough that
they are vested with judicial authority and are authorized to act in
a judicial capacity when deciding the matters submitted to them.
It is immaterial that many of the duties of notaries public are
ministerial, so long as they are not inconsistent with the judicial
power vested in them. There is nothing incompatible between
the ordinary duties of a notary and the exercise of authority
in compelling witnesses to testify. The taking of testimony is
an incident of a judicial proceeding; and what could be more
appropriate than that the notary, who is authorized to administer
oaths and to take testimony, should be vested with the judicial
function to enforce the authority conferred? The legislature has
undertaken to confer this power; and, as the constitution authorizes the legislature to create inferior courts, and there is
nothing in their general duties inconsistent with the judicial
power, why may it not be conferred on notaries? In pursuance
of the constitutional authority, judicial functions have been
conferred on many officers and bodies; police, municipal, criminal, and special courts have [159] been created, and some of them
with quite limited jurisdiction. Judicial power has been conferred on the mayors of cities, coroners, clerks of the district
courts, boards of county commissioners, election and other boards
and officers, and an appeal is authorized to be taken directly from
most of them to the district court. In Mathews v. Commissioners of Shawnee Co., 34 Kan. 606, after naming several officers
on whom judicial power has been thus conferred, it is stated:
"Indeed, courts may be created by statute in a great variety of
ways; and courts so created are not courts provided for by the
constitution, but are simply 'such other courts, inferior to the
supreme court, as may be provided by law.'" That notaries public possess the power to compel a witness to appear and testify
has been the understanding of the profession since the code was
enacted; and for nearly a quarter of a century the doctrine has
received the sanction of this court. In In re Abeles, 12 Kan.
451, it was expressly held that the power had been conferred;
and it was reaffirmed in In re Merkle, 40 Kan. 27. The same
doctrine was recognized in In re Davis, 38 Kan. 408, and also
in In re Cubberly, 39 Kan. 291. The power of the legislature
to invest an officer with the mere power to try and commit for
contempt was the subject of special consideration in In re Sims,
54 Kan. 1; 45 Am. St. Rep. 261; and it was there held that

such power might be conferred on an executive officer, providing the judicial duties were not inconsistent with those which the officer was required to perform. Chief Justice Horton, in his concurring opinion, said: "The legislature has full authority to confer the power to imprison the witness for contempt, prescribed in paragraph 2543 of the General Statutes of 1889 upon justices of the peace, probate judges, notaries public, clerks of courts, or any individual, not the prosecuting attorney, or interested in the proceeding." [160] The views expressed in the opinions in that case clearly sustain the validity of the law and the exercise of the power by notaries public. The cases relied on by the petitioner are based upon an absence of statutory authority; and all concede that without such authority a notary public or other inferior judicial officer cannot commit or punish for contempt. Of course, as United States commissioners belong to that class, and there being no act of Congress conferring the right to try and punish for contempt, the courts of necessity held that no such power existed. In Works on Courts and their Jurisdiction, 501, it is stated that notaries public, and like officers authorized to take depositions, do not possess the power to punish a witness for contempt, unless there is a statute conferring it. After stating that a question exists whether such power can be conferred by statute, it is remarked: "It is believed, however, that it may properly be conferred, at least so far as it authorizes such officer to enforce obedience to a subpoena to procure a deposition that he is authorized to take. It is apparent from the later decisions on the subject that the power to punish has been greatly extended as respects courts and tribunals which may exercise the power, and has, as a rule, been recognized in all courts and tribunals exercising judicial functions, no matter what their grade or the limitations placed upon their jurisdiction." The ruling of the court in the present case leads to the result that, under the law as it now exists, no witness can be compelled to attend and give his deposition. A notary has the same authority under the statute as a judge of a court of record, a justice of the peace, or other officer authorized by the statute to take depositions. In such cases, judges and justices of the peace act independently of the courts with which they are connected, and their [161] powers in respect to contempt proceedings are based alone upon the statute in question.

The following cases sustain the view of the writer, that a notary public is authorized to try and punish for contempt: Ex parte McKee, 18 Mo. 599; Ex parte Mallinkrodt, 20 Mo. 493;

Ex parte Priest, 76 Mo. 229; In re Jenckes, 6 R. I. 18; Dogge v. State, 21 Neb. 272; Ex parte Krieger, 7 Mo. App. 367. See, also, Norton v. Graham, 7 Kan. 166; Prell v. McDonald, 7 Kan. 450; 12 Am. Rep. 423; Morris v. Vanlaningham, 11 Kan. 269; In re Johnson, 12 Kan. 102.

The majority of the court, however, entertaining a different view, and having reached a different conclusion, it follows that the petitioner must be discharged.

Doster, C. J., and Allen, J., concurring.

Johnston, J., dissenting.

NOTARIES PUBLIC—POWER CONFERRED BY STATUTE TO PUNISH CONTEMPT.—A notary public may be authorized to punish a witness for contempt in refusing to answer a material question on the taking of a deposition. The statute purporting to confer such authority is not in conflict with a constitution vesting all the judicial power of the state in certain courts: De Camp v. Archibald, 50 Ohio St. 618; 40 Am. St. Rep. 692, and note.

CONTEMPT—POWER TO PUNISH FOR.—The power to punish for contempt is never exercised except by legislative bodies or judicial officers, and cannot be conferred upon an executive officer while acting in his executive capacity: In re Sims, 54 Kan. 1; 45 Am. St. Rep. 261, and note; see De Camp v. Archibald, 50 Ohio St. 618; 40 Am. St. Rep. 692, and note; also, monographic note to Clark v. People, 12 Am. Dec. 178-186.

LANCASHIRE INSURANCE COMPANY *v.* BOARDMAN.

[58 KANSAS, 339.]

INSURANCE, MORTGAGE CLAUSE—CONDITIONS AVOIDING POLICY ON COMMENCEMENT OF SUIT TO FORECLOSE. Where a mortgage clause is attached to a policy making the loss payable to the mortgagee, as his interest may appear, and providing that, as to his interest, the policy shall not be invalidated by any act or neglect of the mortgagor, and the policy also contains a condition that, upon commencement of proceedings to foreclose or upon a sale under a deed of trust, or if any change takes place in the title or possession, whether by legal process, judicial decree, or voluntary transfer, "the policy shall be void, such condition is to be construed as operating against the mortgagor only, and not as avoiding the policy as against the mortgagee on the commencement of a suit by him to foreclose his mortgage, nor by the appointment of a receiver in such suit to take possession of the mortgaged premises.

Thomas C. Wilson and Myron H. Beach, for the plaintiff in error.

Holmes & Haymaker, for the defendant in error.

340 ALLEN, J. Boardman brought suit on a policy of insurance for two thousand five hundred dollars, issued by the plaintiff in error to Flora Cowley on the fifth day of December, 1889, alleging in his petition the execution of the policy, payment of the premium, and the destruction by fire of the property insured. It was also alleged that the Sedgwick Loan and Investment Company loaned Flora Cowley the sum of two thousand five hundred dollars, for which she executed her bond secured by mortgage covering the property insured; that, as additional security for the loan, the said Flora Cowley, with the consent of the duly authorized agent of the defendant, assigned the policy of insurance to the Sedgwick Loan and Investment Company; that said investment company duly assigned to the plaintiff the mortgage and the debt secured thereby, and that the defendant's agent attached to the policy what is denominated as a mortgage clause, which bears date the day on which the policy was issued and the essential parts of which read as follows:

"Policy No. 1,510,005, in name of Flora Cowley. Agency at Wichita, Kan. Loss, if any, payable to the Sedgwick Loan and Investment Company, mortgagee or trustee, or its assigns, as its interest may appear, as herein provided. It being hereby understood and agreed that this insurance, as to the interest of the mortgagee or trustee, only, therein, shall not be invalidated by any act or neglect of the mortgagor or owner of the property insured, nor by the occupation of the premises for purposes more hazardous than are permitted by the terms of this policy. Provided, that the mortgagee or trustee or assigns shall notify this company of any change of ownership or increase of hazard which shall come to his or their knowledge, and shall have permission for such change of ownership or increase of hazard duly indorsed on this policy. And provided further, that every increase of hazard not [341] permitted by the policy to the mortgagor or owner shall be paid for by the mortgagee or trustee or assigns, on reasonable demand and after demand made by this company upon, and refusal by the mortgagor or owner to pay, according to the established schedule of rates.

"It is also agreed that whenever this company shall pay the mortgagee or trustee or assigns any sum for loss under this policy, and shall claim that as to the mortgagor or owner no liability therefor exists, it shall at once and to the extent of such payment be legally subrogated to all the rights of the party to whom such payments shall be made, under any and all securities held by such party for the payment of such debt; but such subrogation shall be in subordination to the claim of said party for the balance of the debt so secured; or said company may, at its op-

tion, pay the mortgagee, or trustee or assigns, the whole debt
so secured, with all the interest which may have accrued thereon to the date of such payment, and shall thereupon receive
from the party to whom such payment shall be made, an assignment and transfer of said debt, with all securities held by said
parties for the payment thereof.

"The foregoing provisions and agreements shall take precedence over any provision or condition conflicting therewith contained in said policy. This clause is attached to, and is made
a part of, the said policy from the fifth day of December, 1889."

For a seventh defense, the defendant set up in its answer:
"That the said policy of insurance issued by it, bearing date
December 5, 1889, and numbered 1,510,005, contains the following provision, condition, and agreement, constituting a part
thereof and one of the considerations therefor, to wit: '1. . . . .
Upon the commencement of proceedings of foreclosure, or upon
a sale under a deed of trust, ... or if any change take place
in the title or possession, except in case of succession by reason
of the death of the assured, whether by legal process or judicial
decree or voluntary transfer or conveyance, ... then, and in
every such case, this policy is void.' [342] That the said W. F.
Boardman, plaintiff herein, heretofore, to wit, on or about the
first day of January, 1891, brought suit against the said Flora
Cowley and others in this court, to foreclose the mortgage referred to in the petition in this action."

It was then averred that on the application of the plaintiff a
receiver had been appointed who took possession of the mortgaged property; and that by reason thereof the policy was rendered void and the defendant discharged from all liability thereunder. To this part of the answer the plaintiff demurred, and
the demurrer was sustained by the court. The only question
presented is as to the correctness of this ruling.

An extended argument has been made and elaborate briefs filed
on behalf of the plaintiff in error, citing many authorities supposed to have application to the case. The contention is, that,
while the mortgage clause provides that no act or neglect of the
mortgagor shall invalidate the policy, the act of the mortgagee
in commencing foreclosure and obtaining the appointment of
a receiver avoids it. The language in the answer, copied from
the policy of insurance, is picked out from a long provision
stating many grounds of forfeiture. The concluding sentence
of the mortgage clause is: "The foregoing provisions and agreements shall take precedence over any provision or condition con-

flicting therewith, contained in said policy." The policy and
mortgage clause appear to have been issued contemporaneously.
The policy of insurance proper is written on a blank form
adapted to the insurance of the owner against loss. The provisions contained in the clause from which the excerpt copied
in the defendant's answer is taken are applicable to a policy issued to the owner, but many of them are wholly inapplicable
to a policy issued to a mortgagee.

343 The mortgage clause attached changes the insurance contract in the very essential particular of making the mortgagee
the beneficiary of the policy so long as the mortgage debt remains unpaid; and he alone is entitled to recover in case of a
loss: Westchester Fire Ins. Co. v. Coverdale, 48 Kan. 446.

The purpose of the clause in the original policy, so far as it
is lawful and enforceable, is to protect the insurance company
against any material change of the situation calculated to increase the hazard of the insurer. It provides against transfers
of the property, foreclosure, or change in title or possession; and
it is readily apparent that the insurer might be unwilling to continue a risk when the title of the insured was becoming impaired
either by a transfer of his interest, by its encumbrance, or by the
institution of legal proceedings, for the purpose of effecting a
transfer of the legal title, based on his own default in a mortgage contract. But these provisions appear in an entirely different light when construing the policy with the mortgage clause
attached, in an action brought by the mortgagee. The commencement by the mortgagee of proceedings to foreclose a mortgage is not prohibited by the express terms of the mortgage
clause, nor by any fair implication therein contained. If prohibited at all, it must be by reason of the provisions of the policy
quoted. Construing both the original policy and the mortgage
clause together, in the light of the plain purpose to insure the
interest of the mortgagee, the commencement of foreclosure proceedings cannot be held to be a violation of any stipulation forbidding the mortgagee. The insurer must have known, when
attaching the mortgage clause, that it might become necessary
for the mortgagee, in order to protect his interest under the
mortgage, to commence foreclosure proceedings; that this would
not 344 have a tendency to diminish the interest of the mortgagee in the property, but rather to increase it. It is settled that
an increase of the interest of the insured is no ground for a
forfeiture of the policy: Continental Ins. Co. v. Ward, 50 Kan.
346. Nor does the appointment of a receiver to take charge of

the property amount to such a change of possession as would vitiate the insurance. The receiver takes possession, as an officer of the court, for the benefit of the parties interested in the litigation: Thompson v. Phenix Ins. Co., 136 U. S. 287.

We have examined the authorities cited by counsel for plaintiff in error, and, while there is some language used in some of the cases tending to support his contention, no case is brought to our attention that seems controlling in this. The case of Dodge v. Insurance Co., 4 Kan. App. 415, was on a policy with a similar mortgage clause attached; and the questions involved in this case were there resolved adversely to the contention of the plaintiff in error.

We find no error in the ruling of the court sustaining the demurrer, and it is affirmed.

INSURANCE—MORTGAGE CLAUSE—CONSTRUCTION OF.—The cases in which a condition of forfeiture in a policy of insurance applies against a mortgagee to whom the loss has been made payable are collected, and the subject discussed in the monographic note to Oakland etc. Co. v. Bank of Commerce, 58 Am. St. Rep. 667-673. See, also, monographic note to King v. State etc. Ins. Co., 54 Am. Dec. 698-700. A mortgage is not foreclosed until the mortgagor's right of redemption is cut off, and a mortgagee is still protected by a policy of insurance made payable to him though he has foreclosed the mortgage and purchased the property at the sale, if the mortgagor retains the right to redeem from the sale: National Bank v. Union Ins. Co., 88 Cal. 497; 22 Am. St. Rep. 824.

PRICE *v.* ATCHISON WATER COMPANY.

[58 KANSAS, 551.]

DANGEROUS PREMISES ALLURING TO CHILDREN.—A landlord maintaining on his premises a reservoir filled with water to which children are attracted for the purpose of fishing and other sports, and who knows they frequent it for such purpose, and who takes no adequate means to exclude or warn them therefrom, is guilty of negligence, and hence answerable to the parents of a child who, being attracted there, falls in and is drowned.

NEGLIGENCE.—CHILDREN OF TENDER YEARS are not held to the same degree of care as persons of mature age. Hence a child of eleven years of age, who is attracted to a dangerous reservoir maintained on the defendant's premises, and who falls in and is drowned, is not necessarily chargeable with contributory negligence precluding his father from recovering for his death.

NEGLIGENCE, PLEADING, MOTION TO MAKE ANSWER MORE DEFINITE AND CERTAIN.—A complaint containing a general allegation of negligence is subject to a motion requiring it to be made more definite and certain. Therefore, if in an action to recover for the death of the plaintiff's child through falling into a dangerous reservoir on the defendant's premises, the latter pleads that if the plaintiff has suffered any damage, it is from his own negligence and that of such child; a motion on the part of the plaintiff to make the answer more definite and certain should be granted.

H. C. Solomon and Waggener, Horton & Orr, for the plaintiffs in error.

B. F. Hudson, for the defendants in error.

[552] DOSTER, C. J. Melrose H. Price, the son of plaintiffs in error, a bright, intelligent boy of about eleven years of age, was drowned in one of the reservoirs of the defendant in error. These reservoirs were two in number, and were situated in or near the corporate limits of the city of Atchison, in immediate proximity to a section of the residence portion of the city. They were of unequal size; one having a capacity of about one million one hundred thousand gallons, the other about three million gallons. The smaller one was used as a "settling basin," into which the water was pumped, and from whence it was discharged into the larger one through a pipe. The opening of this pipe into the larger basin was covered with an "apron," made of lumber, and designed to break the force of the water discharge and prevent injury to the walls of the reservoir. It was partially buoyed by the water, and rose and fell as the water supply increased or lessened. For four feet from the top the walls of the smaller reservoir were perpendicular, and thence slanted to the bottom; and its basin was about ten feet in depth in the deepest part. The walls of the larger reservoir slanted at an angle of about forty-five degrees, and its basin had a depth in its lowest part of about fifteen feet. It would be difficult, if not impossible, for a person falling into the larger basin to get out unaided, on account of the steepness of the walls. These reservoirs and appurtenant grounds occupied about three acres, and were attractive places for children, many of whom frequented there for fishing and for other sports. They were inclosed with a barb-wire fence ten to [553] twelve wires high. There were two gates through the fence, which, however, were always kept closed, and two rudely constructed contrivances designed for stiles, but being as described by some of the witnesses, "sheds," or large boxes, nailed to adjacent trees and inclosing most of the wires, but upon and over which it was not difficult for boys to climb from the outside. A watchman and custodian of these grounds was employed by the defendant. He was aware of the habit of the boys of the town to climb over the stiles, and permitted them to do so without objection. The boy, Melrose, without the consent

or knowledge of his parents, went with some companions to the reservoirs in question to fish and play, and, venturing upon the apron before described, for the purpose of crossing from one part of the reservoir wall to another, the end which projected out upon the water sank, precipitating him into the basin, where he drowned. Immediately upon starting to go upon the apron, one of his companions called to him and warned him of the danger of so going, saying to him he might fall in. To this he replied "Oh, no!" His parents had frequently warned him of the danger of going to the reservoir, and he had trespassed there but once before, and then without their knowledge.

The plaintiffs in error sued to recover damages for the loss of their son, occasioned by the negligent maintenance of the reservoir and the negligence of the defendant in permitting him access to the dangerous situation described. The above statement summarizes the evidence for the plaintiff. To this evidence a demurrer for insufficiency to prove a cause of action was sustained. This action of the court is alleged as error, and is brought here for review.

The contention arising upon the above state of facts divides itself into two principal questions: 1. [554] Was the defendant in error negligent, as to the deceased boy, in maintaining the dangerous reservoir? and 2. Was the deceased guilty of contributory negligence in venturing upon the slanting wall and projecting apron? These are questions of fact, and they should have been left to the jury for determination. They are not questions of law for decision by the court.

It is, however, contended by the defendant in error that, inasmuch as the deceased was a trespasser upon its grounds, it owed to him no duty to guard against the accident which occurred. Without doubt, the common law exempts the owner of private grounds from obligation to keep them in a safe condition for the benefit of trespassers, idlers, bare licensees, or others who go upon them, not by invitation, express or implied, but for pleasure or through curiosity: Cooley on Torts, 2d ed., 718; 1 Thompson on Negligence, 303; Dobbins v. Missouri etc. Ry. Co. (Tex., May 24, 1897), 41 S. W. Rep. 62. The common law, however, does not permit the owner of private grounds to keep thereon allurements to the natural instincts of human or animal kind, without taking reasonable precautions to insure the safety of such as may be thereby attracted to his premises. To maintain upon one's property enticements to the ignorant or unwary is tantamount to an invitation to visit, and to inspect and enjoy; and in such cases the obligation to endeavor to protect from the dangers of the seductive instrument or place follows as justly as though the invitation had been express. The rule collected out of the authorities is vigorously, but not too strongly, stated in 1 Thompson on Negligence, 304, 305: "There is also a class of cases which hold proprietors liable for injuries resulting to children although trespassing at the time, where, from the peculiar nature [555] and open and exposed position of the dangerous defect or agent, the owner should reasonably anticipate such an injury to flow therefrom as actually happened. In such case, the question of negligence is for the jury. It would be a barbarous rule of law that would make the owner of land liable for setting a trap thereon, baited with meat, so that his neighbor's dog, attracted by his natural instincts, might run into it and be killed; and which would exempt him from liability for the consequences of leaving exposed and unguarded on his land a dangerous machine, so that his neighbor's child, attracted to it and tempted to intermeddle with it by instincts equally strong, might thereby be killed or maimed for life. Such is not the law."

The principle involved is the same as that upon which those actions known as the "turntable cases" have been resolved, and in which it has been held, with few exceptions, that the maintenance, in an unguarded manner, of a dangerous apparatus for the shifting of locomotives, attractive to children residing or accustomed to playing near by, constitutes negligence upon the part of the companies. In one of these cases, it was quite well remarked by Mr. Justice Valentine: "Everybody knowing the nature and instincts common to all boys must act accordingly. No person has a right to leave, even on his own land, dangerous machinery calculated to attract and entice boys to it, there to be injured, unless he first take proper steps to guard against all danger; and any person who does thus leave dangerous machinery exposed, without first providing against all danger, is guilty of negligence. It is a violation of the beneficent maxim, Sic utere tuo ut alienum non laedas. It is true that the boys in such cases are technically trespassers. But even trespassers have rights which cannot be ignored, as numerous cases which we might cite would show": Kansas Cent. Ry. Co. v. Fitzsimmons, 22 Kan. 691; 31 Am. Rep. 203.

[555] The reasons upon which these cases proceed, and the authorities supporting the rule, are strongly set forth in Keffe v. Milwaukee etc. Ry. Co., 21 Minn. 207; 18 Am. Rep. 393. They

are, in brief, that where a person maintains upon his premises anything dangerous to life or limb and of a nature to invite the intrusion of children, he owes them a duty of precaution against harm, and is liable to them for injury from that thing, even though their own act, if not negligent, puts in operation its hurtful agency. One may not bait his premises with some dangerous instrument or quality, alluring to the incautious or vagrant, and then deny responsibility for the consequences of following the natural instincts of curiosity or amusement aroused thereby, without taking reasonable precautions to guard against the accidents liable to ensue. Rights can only be enjoyed subject to those limitations which regard for the weaknesses and deficiencies of others dictate to be humane and just. This rule has been applied, not only in the "turntable cases," but to others in which dangerous situations have been negligently maintained, and especially to cases of death or injury by falling into unguarded pools or vats of water: Brinkley Car Co. v. Cooper, 60 Ark. 545; 46 Am. St. Rep. 216; Pekin v. McMahon, 154 Ill. 141; 45 Am. St. Rep. 114.

Counsel for defendant in error endeavors to distinguish the "turntable" and other like cases from the one under discussion, upon the ground that, in such first-mentioned cases, the dangerous instruments or places were not inclosed, so as to exclude or warn trespassers, while, in the present case, the reservoirs had been so fenced as to render access to them difficult, to say the least, and in any event to operate as notice to stay on the outside because of the dangerous situation within. Whatever merit such precautionary measures might have under other circumstances, it is [557] sufficient to say that, in this case, they were not reasonably effective; because it was the daily habit of trespassing boys to mount the fence and frequent the reservoirs on the inside, and this habit was known to the company's responsible agent, and was not only tolerated but went unrebuked by him. Knowing the fence to be ineffective either as barrier or warning, it was the duty of the company to expel the intruders, or adopt other measures to avoid accident. Whatever advantage the defendant in error might have gained from the erection of a reasonably effective barrier or warning is neutralized by the facts of its knowledge that the boys did trespass, and its permission to them to do so. It is as though no fence at all had been erected.

The second question, viz., the contributory negligence of the deceased, can be shortly disposed of. What might be negligence in an adult will not of necessity be negligence in a child. Persons of tender years are not held to the same degree of care that a mature and experienced person is required to exercise. As remarked in Kansas Cent. Ry. Co. v. Fitzsimmons, 22 Kan. 691, 31 Am. Rep. 203: "Boys can seldom be said to be negligent when they merely follow the irresistible impulses of their own natures—instincts common to all boys. In many cases where men, or boys approaching manhood, would be held to be negligent, younger boys, and boys with less intelligence, would not be. And the question of negligence is in nearly all cases one of fact for the jury, whether the person charged with negligence is of full age or not."

This view of the law we believe to be taken by all the courts. It has been recently entertained by us in other cases: Kinchlow v. Midland Elevator Co., 57 Kan. 374; Consolidated etc. Ry. Co. v. Carlson, 58 Kan. 62.

[558] The defendant in error made its plea of contributory negligence in the following language: "Further answering, defendant alleges that, if the plaintiffs have suffered any damage whatever, it is through and by reason of their own negligence in the premises, and that of said Melrose H. Price." The case did not progress far enough to require evidence under this plea. Had it done so, the plaintiffs would have been uninformed as to the facts constituting the claim of negligence upon the part either of themselves or of the deceased boy. A motion by plaintiffs in error to require this answer to be made more definite and certain was made and overruled. It should have been sustained. The rule is the same in the case of an answer as it is in the case of a petition charging negligence. As to the latter it has been held: "If a petition contains but a general allegation of negligence, it is subject to a motion requiring it to be made more definite and certain, and it is error for the court to overrule a proper motion presented for that purpose": Atchison etc. R. R. Co. v. O'Neill, 49 Kan. 367.

The case is reversed, with instructions to award a new trial and to sustain the motion to make the answer more definite and certain.

———

NEGLIGENCE—CARE REQUIRED OF CHILDREN.—A child is held answerable only to the exercise of such care as is reasonably to be expected from children of his age and capacity: Railroad Co. v. Mackey, 53 Ohio St. 370; 53 Am. St. Rep. 641, and note; Spillane v Missouri Pac. Ry. Co., 135 Mo. 414; 58 Am. St. Rep. 580, and note.

NEGLIGENCE — DANGEROUS PREMISES — INJURIES TO CHILDREN.—Persons are required to use greater care in dealing

with children of tender years than with older persons who have
reached the age of discretion; and greater care is required to avoid
injury to such children, even though they are trespassers. Unguarded
premises supplied with dangerous attractions are regarded as holding out an implied invitation to children, which will make the
owner of the premises liable for injuries to them, even though they
be technical trespassers: Monographic note to Barnes v. Shreveport
City It. R. Co., 49 Am. St. Rep. 417. See, however, Moran v. Pullman Palace Car Co., 134 Mo. 641; 56 Am. St. Rep. 543, and note.

LAWRENCE *v.* LEIDIGH.

[58 KANSAS, 594.]

ELECTIONS—INMATES OF SOLDIERS' HOME, RIGHT
OF TO VOTE.—Under a constitutional provision declaring that no
person shall be deemed to have gained or lost a residence while kept
in any almshouse or other asylum at the public expense, inmates of
soldiers' homes by going to and residing in such home neither lose
their old, nor gain a new, residence, though they intend to reside
in the home permanently. Hence they are not entitled to vote except
at their place of residence before becoming such inmates. Such
home is an asylum within the meaning of the constitutional provision.

B. F. Milton and Overmyer & Mulvane, for the plaintiff.

Ed. H. Madison, for the defendants.

594 DOSTER, C. J. This is an original proceeding in quo
warranto, to determine the right of the defendant, as against
the plaintiff, to hold the office of county clerk of Ford county.
The parties were opposing candidates for the office named at
the general election in 1895. The defendant received a majority
of the votes cast, and thereafter qualified and entered upon the
duties of the position. The facts have been agreed upon, and
from them it appears that, outside of the ballots cast by certain
inmates of the State Soldiers' Home located in the county, the
plaintiff received a majority of the votes. The right of the
inmates of the Home to participate in the election is the sole
question for decision.

The legislation respecting the establishment and maintenance
of this Home and the government of its inmates began in 1889.
In that year, the legislature, by concurrent resolution, requested
our senators and representatives in Congress to endeavor to secure the donation to the state of the Fort Dodge Military Reservation, **595** in order "to provide for its indigent soldiers and
sailors proper and suitable homes for their declining years":

House Concurrent Resolution, No. 49. At the same session, in anticipation of the making of the donation asked, an act was passed establishing the Home, providing for its management, and making a conditional appropriation for its support. Since then, it has been, like all other state institutions, supported by biennial appropriations. The act in question provided: "All honorably discharged soldiers, sailors, and marines who served in the army and navy of the United States during the war of the Rebellion, and who may be disabled by disease, wounds, or old age, or otherwise disabled, and who have no adequate means of support, and who by reason of such wounds, old age, or disability are incapacitated from earning their living and who would otherwise be dependent upon public or private charity, together with such members of their families as may be dependent upon them for support, shall be entitled to admission to such institution, subject to the rules and regulations that may be established by the board of managers for the government thereof": Laws 1889, c. 235; Gen. Stats. 1889, par. 6235.

March 2, 1889, Congress authorized the desired conveyance to be made, upon the condition: "That said state . . . . shall within three years establish and provide for the maintenance thereon a home in which provision shall be made for the care and maintenance of officers, soldiers, sailors, and marines, who have served in the army, navy, or marine corps of the United States, their dependent parents, widows, or orphans, and under such rules and regulations as said state may provide": 25 U. S. Stats. at Large, c. 420, p. 1012.

In 1893, an act was passed specifying some additional details of management of the Home, and providing, among other things, that applicants for [596] admission should furnish a certificate by the board of county commissioners of the county of their residence, stating their inability to properly support themselves and families without aid from such county; and also providing that, save in certain specified exceptional cases, wives of inmates should not be admitted with them to the Home unless they had attained the age of forty years, nor girls over the age of fourteen, nor boys over the age of twelve years: Laws 1893, c. 148.

The state legislation thus noted, and the rules of the board of management authorized thereby, provide for the residence in separate cottages of such of the inmates and their families as can be accommodated in that way, and also provide for the cultivation by the inmates of the lands forming part of the Home, for the maintenance of the institution in that way, so far as it can be. Family and not communal life, in the case of such of the veterans as have families, is the rule of the institution, so far as the accommodations will allow; while as to unmarried men, barracks and mess privileges, somewhat after the manner of army life, are provided. A large majority of the inmates who voted were married men residing with their families upon the Home lands; and it is agreed in the statement of facts: "That all said persons, both married and single, at the time they moved from various counties in Kansas, where they resided previous to moving to the Home, abandoned their old homes with the intention of making their permanent abiding place and their homes in the State Soldier's Home at Fort Dodge, Kansas; that they actually took up their residence in the houses and quarters assigned them in said Home with the intention upon their part of making the same their home; and during the time they resided therein they intended and claimed said houses and quarters in said State Soldiers' Home to be their homes; and while they resided in said houses they had no other homes [597] and that they were their fixed habitations, to which, when they were absent, they intended to and did return."

The act of 1889 authorized the board of management to prepare and promulgate a system of government for the Home, embracing such regulations as might be necessary for the preservation of order, the enforcement of discipline, and the security of the health of the inmates. Conformity to these rules is, of course, required, and, as we assume, under the compulsion of discharge, although such is not so declared in the statute, nor does the agreed statement of facts so recite; but, it may be taken for granted that, under the rules of the institution, permanency of stay is conditioned upon obedience to the reasonable regulations prescribed.

The constitutional provisions bearing upon the question for decision are as follows: "Every white male person of twenty-one years and upward . . . . who shall have resided in Kansas six months next preceding any election, and in the township or ward in which he offers to vote, at least thirty days next preceding such election, shall be deemed a qualified voter": Const., art. 5, sec. 1. For the purpose of voting, no person shall be deemed to have gained or lost a residence by reason of his presence or absence while employed in the service of the United States, nor while engaged in the navigation of the waters of this state, or the United States, or of the high seas, nor while a student of any seminary of learning, nor while kept at any almshouse or other asylum at public expense, nor while confined in any public prison": Const., art. 5, sec. 3.

Upon the part of the plaintiff, it is insisted that the section last quoted precludes an inmate of the Soldiers' Home from acquiring at such Home the residence required by the section first quoted. Upon the part of the defendant, it is insisted that the section [598] last quoted does nothing more than declare a disputable presumption—does nothing more than declare that the fact of occupancy of a public asylum raises a presumption of disqualification, repellable, however, by evidence of removal of residence and fixity of intent to remain. If the contention of the defendant as thus stated be sound, there is no question but he has overcome in behalf of the inmates of the Home the presumption of disqualification to vote. The agreed statement of facts above quoted shows that these inmates abandoned their former places of abode with no intention of returning thereto, and took up their residence at the Soldiers' Home with the intention of permanently remaining there; such of them as had families removing them and their household goods and other personal belongings. We apprehend that the fact that their right to remain is conditioned upon their observance of the rules of the institution, and their ability to remain likewise conditioned upon the continuance of the bounty thus far provided, cannot be taken to qualify their intention to remain. Permanency of residence is always conditioned upon such contingencies as may thereafter occur, and an intent of the most fixed character to remain at a given place is always held subject to both the fortuitous and designed circumstances of the future. Nor can there be any question that, under the legislation of the United States and of this state and the rules of the board of management, the places provided for the veterans in question were provided for them as homes. The institution as an "asylum," place of retreat, or shelter, has grafted upon it the feature of home life, not only as respects its management, but its purpose as well.

The first matter of importance to determine is the character of the place in question. Is it an "asylum," [599] within the meaning of the constitutional provision quoted? Our judgment is that such is the case. The supreme court of Michigan had under consideration the precise question, and expressed its opinion thereon in the following language: "The Soldiers' Home is purely eleemosynary in character. To hold otherwise would be contrary to sound legal principle and good sense. The title to the act shows it. It is not the character of the beneficiaries, nor the cause of their inability to earn a living, nor the reason for grant-ing the bounty, which determines whether such an institution is charitable in its character. An institution established and maintained for the support of indigent persons who become blin1 or deaf in the service of their country or state is as much elee-mosynary as one established for the support of those who were born blind or deaf, or who have become so from other causes. All institutions in this state, established and maintained at the public expense, for the care, education, and support of the un-fortunate, belong to this class of institutions, and are included in the term 'asylum,' used in the above clause of the constitu-tion. It is immaterial whether they are called schools, retreats, homes, or asylums. It is equally immaterial what the feeling is which prompts their erection and maintenance. An 'asylum' is defined by Webster to be 'an institution for the protection or relief of the unfortunate.' Such is its meaning as used in the constitution. It follows that one's entry and residence in such an institution partake of the same character as the institution itself, and are likewise eleemosynary in character": Wolcott v. Holcomb, 97 Mich. 361-364.

The proposition next to be considered herein was also involved in the case in Michigan. Upon it the members of the court were divided in opinion, but no dissent was expressed from the view taken of the character of the institution as an asylum within the meaning of the constitution. In this view of the character of such institutions we also concur. We 600 cannot think that the plan of life at the Home, as family instead of communal, nor any other departure made by it from the ordinary method of conducting such institutions, changes its nature. Its eleemosy-nary character is fixed in its benevolent design, not in the meas-ure of control exercised over its inmates nor in the method of ad-ministering its charity. We have, therefore, no doubt that a home for the indigent veterans of the wars, such as the one estab-lished in this state, is an "asylum," as that word is used in the constitution. That its inmates are kept at public expense need not be argued; it is admitted.

The inquiry, then, occurs: Can such inmates acquire at this asylum a residence for voting purposes? This inquiry was also made in the case of Wolcott v. Holcomb, 97 Mich. 361, and was answered in the negative by a majority of the supreme court of Michigan, under constitutional provisions identical in language with ours. These provisions have already been quoted. For the purpose of their application to the precise case in hand, such of their terms as relate to collateral but not necessarily connected matter may be eliminated, so they may be read as follows: "Every male person of twenty-one years and upward who shall have resided in Kansas six months, and in the township or ward in which he offers to vote thirty days, next preceding any election, shall be deemed a qualified voter; but, for the purpose of voting, no person shall be deemed to have gained or lost a residence while kept at any almshouse or other asylum at public expense."

Thus read, there appears to us slight ground upon which to base a claim of competency to vote in the inmates of the Soldiers' Home. It will be observed that the provision quoted does not disfranchise these inmates. No more shall they be deemed to have lost their former residence than they shall be deemed to have gained a new one while kept at the asylum. No matter how settled their determination to abandon their former places of residence, nor how protracted their stay in their new home, the constitution preserves to them their electoral privileges in the event of their return. Whether that return be for the purpose of resuming the old habitation or for the purpose merely of casting a ballot, the right to vote, throughout all the time of absence, is fully retained.

It is no sufficient answer, upon the mere question of interpretation, to say that many to whom the right of voting is thus saved live at distances too remote and suffer other disadvantages too great to make its enjoyment practicable. The burden is no greater upon an inmate of the Home than upon many others whose lives are largely spent at distances far from the place which the law assigns for the exercise of the voting privilege, and upon whom travel thereto entails expense which can be illy borne.

The language of the constitution is: "For the purpose of voting, no person shall be deemed to have gained . . . . a residence while kept at any . . . . asylum at public expense." The Standard Dictionary gives the word "deem" the following definitions: "To hold in belief, estimation, or opinion." "To judge; adjudge; decide; sentence; condemn." "To have or be of an opinion." Its synonyms are "esteem" and "suppose." The defendant is constrained by the logic of his contention to rest his case upon the theory that the constitution simply declares a rule of evidence—simply raises a presumption of disqualification; but none of the shades or variations of meaning possessed by the word "deemed" admit the raising of such presumption upon the lan-

guage of the constitution.   For voting purposes, no person while
kept at an asylum at public expense shall be [602] adjudged or declared to have gained a residence; nor of him shall the gaining
of a residence be held in belief or estimation; nor as to him shall
anyone have or be of an opinion that he has gained such residence.   This is the meaning which the law, as well as common
usage, has affixed to the word "deemed": Commonwealth v.
Pratt, 132 Mass. 246; Blaufus v. People, 69 N. Y. 101-111; 25
Am. Rep. 148; Leonard v. Grant, 5 Fed. Rep. 11-16.   Such residence shall not be gained "while" kept at any asylum.   The definition of "while," as a conjunction and also as an adverbial modi-
fier, is, "during the time that; as long as."   Therefore, no residence shall be gained during the time that, or as long as, the
person is kept at an asylum.

The decisions upon the precise question are few in number.
But three have been called to our attention.   Those of Wolcott v.
Holcomb, 97 Mich. 361, and Silvey v. Lindsay, 107 N. Y. 55, are
to the same effect as the one we make.   That of Stewart v. Kyser,
105 Cal. 459, is in opposition.   It also appears, by records of the
United States district court for this district which have been called to our attention, that, in an unreported case, entitled United
States v. Rowdebush, being an indictment for illegally voting at
an election for representatives in Congress, a decision similar to
that of the supreme court of California was made upon an agreed
statement of facts; but we are constrained by what we regard as
the true interpretation of the constitution, derived out of the
settled and authoritative meaning of the words used, to follow
the New York and Michigan decisions, and to hold that, notwithstanding the abandonment by the veterans in question of their
former places of abode and their settlement at the Soldiers' Home
with the fixed intention of remaining there, they cannot acquire
a residence at such Home for voting purposes.

[603] It may also be remarked that such, too, is the plain statutory provision.   The law of 1893, chapter 148, section 5, declares:
"Inmates of this Home shall not lose their legal residence in the
county from which they came, nor acquire any legal residence in
Ford county, Kansas, while they remain as inmates of said
Home."   This statute is vigorously assailed as conflicting with
section 1, article 5, of the constitution, which fixes, as to residence, the general rule upon the subject of electoral qualifications.   Whether it does so conflict is involved in the question
just decided.   It does not conflict with the rule of exception contained in section 3 of the same article, but is in harmony with it;

and, therefore, if the case were to rest upon it and not upon the constitution itself, it could be upheld. Judgment for plaintiff is therefore ordered.

———

ELECTIONS—RESIDENCE OF VOTER—INMATES OF SOLDIER'S HOMES.—The residence of a voter is the place in which his habitation is fixed, without any present intention of removing therefrom: Berry v. Wilcox, 44 Neb. 82; 48 Am. St. Rep. 706. A permanent member of a soldier's home, who is not permitted to leave it without a license or furlough, has a residence at such home for the purpose of voting: Lankford v. Gebhart, 130 Mo. 621; 51 Am. St. Rep. 585. But if at the time he is admitted to such home, he has a legal residence elsewhere, which he has no intention to abandon, his residence remains unchanged: Monographic note to Berry v. Wilcox, 48 Am. St. Rep. 717. See Sinks v. Reese, 19 Ohio St. 306; 2 Am. Rep. 397.

———

BALL v. REESE.

[58 KANSAS, 614.]

CORPORATIONS, JUDGMENT AGAINST, EFFECT UPON STOCKHOLDERS.—If a judgment is rendered against a corporation, and proceedings are subsequently taken against its stockholders to enforce their liability, such judgment is conclusive against them of the liability of the corporation, and they cannot compel the creditor to go behind it and relitigate the questions determined between the corporation and himself.

Peters & Nicholson, for the plaintiff in error.

Bowman & Bucher, Branine & Branine, and A. L. Greene, for the defendants in error.

[615] JOHNSTON, J. This was a proceeding brought by W. E. Ball to enforce the individual liability of the defendants as stockholders in the Kansas Savings Bank, a corporation incorporated under the laws of Kansas, against which, on June 18, 1891, Ball obtained a judgment for ten thousand two hundred and twenty dollars on a certificate of deposit previously issued by the bank. In these proceedings the defendants undertook to show that the certificate of deposit was not a valid indebtedness of the corporation, because, as alleged, it was issued by its officers without authority. The trial court ruled that the stockholders could make any defense which the bank itself might have made, admitted testimony as to lack of authority by the officers to bind the bank, and upon such testimony held that there was in fact no indebtedness, that the judgment was not effectual, and that Ball was not entitled to an execution thereon against the stockholders.

The ruling cannot be sustained. The judgment was rendered by a court of competent jurisdiction, an execution thereon has been returned unsatisfied, and the remedies against the corporation have been exhausted. The judgment creditor is entitled to proceed against the stockholders, as the constitution and the statutes make them individually liable for the debts of the corporation; Const., art. 12, sec. 2; Gen. Stats. 1889, pars. 1192, 1206.

The question presented for decision is: What effect is to be given to the judgment against the corporation in a proceeding to enforce the statutory liability? Is it to be deemed conclusive upon the stockholders? Or can they go behind it and compel the creditor to relitigate the questions determined between the corporation and himself? The rule appears to be well settled, and the courts seem to be well nigh unanimous in [616] holding that the judgment is conclusive upon the stockholders as to the liability of the corporation, except for collusion or fraud, and, of course, a judgment is of no force against anyone where there is a lack of jurisdiction. The ruling proceeds upon the theory that the corporation represents its stockholders within the limits of its corporate power. Through its officers and agents it can make contracts binding upon its members, and as it has to bring and defend suits in regard to any interest of the corporation, its action in that respect, if there is good faith, necessarily binds the stockholders as to any matter in litigation. In this connection it has been said: "It must be borne in mind that a corporation is composed of its shareholders, and that a judgment obtained against the corporation is, in reality, a judgment obtained against the shareholders in their corporate capacity. There is no reason why the members of a corporation should be allowed to contest a creditor's claim twice—once in the suit against the corporation through the corporate agents and again in the suit brought to charge them individually. If the judgment against the corporation was obtained by fraud or through collusion with the company's agents, the shareholder may obtain relief through equitable proceedings": Morawetz on Private Corporations, 2d ed., sec. 886.

In his treatise on Corporations, Judge Thompson states that, although stockholders cannot appear and contest the merits of the action against the corporation, "yet when a judgment is rendered against the corporation it establishes, as conclusively as any judgment can establish the matter in litigation, the liability of the corporation to pay the debt. Like any judgment, it may be impeached for fraud or for want of jurisdiction by a party entitled to question it; but it cannot be assailed collaterally by a stockholder for any other cause when sought to be charged in respect [617] of it. It is valid until reversed in a direct proceeding, and concludes the stockholder who is in privity with the corporation": 3 Thompson on Corporations, sec. 3392. See, also, the numerous cases there cited.

The defendants appear to have relied upon some remarks in Howell v. Manglesdorf, 33 Kan. 194, where the judgment is spoken of as prima facie evidence against the stockholder, and his liability to the creditors of the corporation as in the nature of a guaranty. The character of the liability was not involved in the case, and no attempt was made to define it. Prima facie, the judgment is valid, even if obtained by collusion and fraud; and it is also true that the liability has some of the features of suretyship, because it is an additional security of the creditor for the liability of the corporation. While the liability is secondary and collateral, it is certainly not one of suretyship, as the term is ordinarily understood. In the case mentioned, the court was considering the question whether, in a proceeding like this, a notice might be served on the stockholder outside of the state, and did not have before it the conclusive effect of the judgment. In referring to the defense that might be made by the stockholder, it was said he might show that he was not a stockholder; or, if he had subscribed to the capital stock, that it had been forfeited or released, or had been sold and transferred, and the liability thereon assumed and succeeded to by another; or he might show that the judgment against the corporation was void, or that he had already paid the amount of his individual liability. There was no intimation, however, that he might relitigate the amount or validity of the indebtedness against the corporation. The general holding in this court has been that a judgment is final and conclusive between [618] the parties and their privies; and we think it must be held that every stockholder in a corporation is so far privy in interest in an action against the corporation that he is bound by the judgment against it. In the absence of fraud and collusion, the judgment must be held to be final and conclusive against the stockholder if the court rendering it has jurisdiction. As the judgment was valid, the court committed error in allowing the defendants to go behind it and contest matters which were conclusively settled by the judgment against the corporation.

Defendants have attempted to question the finding of the trial court that there was due service of summons in the action against

the corporation, but they are hardly in a position to challenge
that finding.   They are endeavoring to sustain the findings, and
are asking that the judgment of the court be affirmed.   No error
is alleged by them, and hence they are not entitled to a review of
that ruling.

The judgment will be reversed, and the cause remanded for further proceedings.

———

CORPORATIONS—JUDGMENT AGAINST—CONCLUSIVENESS
UPON STOCKHOLDERS.—A judgment against a corporation is conclusive against the stockholders in any action or proceeding to enforce their individual liability, and there is no legitimate distinction
between cases in which actions are brought against stockholders on
account of unpaid subscriptions and those wherein the object is to enforce the statutory or constitutional liability: Holland v. Duluth Iron
Min. etc. Co., 65 Minn. 324; 60 Am. St. Rep. 480, and note. See,
also, Tatum v. Rosenthal, 95 Cal. 129; 29 Am. St. Rep. 97, and
note.

CASES

SUPREME COURT

OF

LOUISIANA.

SUCCESSION OF VANHILLE.

[49 LOUISIANA ANNUAL, 107.]

WILLS, OLOGRAPHIC.—FIGURES may be used in an olographic will for the purpose of expressing the amount of a legacy.

Kenneth Baillio, for the appellee.

Gilbert L. Dupré, for the appellants.

107 WATKINS, J. The sole question in this case is whether a legacy in an olographic will expressed in figures is valid, and it is presented by an opposition on behalf of certain heirs by representation of the testator.

We make the subjoined extract from the brief of opponent's counsel, viz: "The deceased made an olographic will containing sundry legacies, among others, the following one, viz: 'Je donne mon argenterie et $300 de plus que cc quil doit heriter de ma succession a mon dernier fils Lucius G. Dupre.' The opponents contend that this donation is not made in conformity with law, and is, therefore, null and void."

Our code prescribes the following form for an olographic testament, viz: "The olographic testament is that which is written by the testator himself. In order to be valid, it must be entirely written, dated, and signed by the hand of the testator. It is subject to no other form," etc: Rev. Civ. Code, 1588.

The language of the French code is almost identical with that of our code. **108** "An olographic will shall not be valid unless it is written throughout, dated and signed by the testator," etc: Code Napoleon, art. 970.

To be valid, this kind of a testament must be "written throughout," or "entirely written by the hand of the testator." But this article is closely coupled with another found in the section which treats "of the opening and proof of testaments," which declares that "the olographic testament . . . . must be acknowledged and proved by the declaration of two credible persons, who must attest that they recognize the testament as being entirely written, dated, and signed in the testator's handwriting, as having often seen him write and sign during his lifetime": Rev. Civ. Code, 1655.

The latter article explains that the words of the former, "entirely written by the hand of the testator," mean "entirely written in the testator's handwriting."

The transcript shows that this provision of the law was complied with, and the fact established that the testament was entirely written in the handwriting of the testator.

This last article has been so amended as to require the judge a quo "to interrogate witnesses under oath touching their knowledge of the testator's handwriting and signature, and [to] satisfy himself that they are familiar therewith," etc: Act 119 of 1896.

And these essentials having been complied with, the will should have been admitted to probate. The judge a quo did admit it to probate in so far as its probate was not opposed; and subsequently overruled the opposition and probated it in its entirety, and opponents have appealed.

These articles were dealt with and interpreted in Fuentes v. Gaines, 25 La. Ann. 85, and Succession of Roth, 31 La. Ann. 315.

We are not aware of any decision of this court in which this precise question has been decided; but the French authorities have put the question at rest.

"At the moment," one author says, "that the testament is written in its entirety in the testator's hand, it avails for the purpose, whatever the manner it is written, and whatever the substance on which it is written. Therefore, that it is found on paper, parchment, cartoon paper, or of linen; whether written with ink, blood, or any other liquid, or written with a pencil; whether the will be expressed in abbreviations or quantities—i. e., amounts fully expressed, or in figures, etc. is of no importance, if, irrespective of this, the will can be read—all that is requisite": [109] 4 Marcade Explanation du Code Napoleon, 6; Code Napoleon, art. 970; 3 Troplong's Commentaries.

And in the annotations of another author on the Code Napoleon a number of commentators are quoted to the same ef-

fect as the foregoing extract from Marcade, viz: Pothier on Do-
nations and Testaments, c. 1, art. 2, sec. 2; Merlin on Testam.,
sec. 2, par. 4, art. 3 N. J.; 1 Duranton, tr. 9, n. 51; Coin Delisle,
n. 16; see Gilbert Codes Annotes, 427, No. 43, interpreting
Code Napoleon, art. 970.

We are of opinion that the legacy is valid.

Judgment affirmed.

WILLS - OLOGRAPHIC—ESSENTIALS OF.—An instrument entirely written, dated, and signed by the testator is clothed with all
the formalities of law required to constitute a valid olographic will:
Ehrenberg's Succession, 21 La. Ann. 280; 99 Am. Dec. 729. Formalities prescribed by law for the execution of olographic wills must be
strictly observed or the will will be void: Succession of Armant, 43
La. Ann. 510; 26 Am. St. Rep. 183. See Mitchell v. Donohue, 100
Cal. 202; 38 Am. St. Rep. 279, and monographic note to Lagrave v.
Merle, 52 Am. Dec. 591-593.

STATE *v.* SULLIVAN.

[4 , LOUISIANA ANNUAL, 197.]

CRIMINAL LAW—PLACE OF CRIME OF EMBEZZLE-
MENT.—If one is intrusted with property in one parish or county,
and there forms the intention of fraudulently appropriating it to
his own use, and, pursuant to such intention, goes with it to another
parish or county, where he accomplishes his object by pawning it,
his crime may be deemed committed in the place where he received
the property and formed the criminal intent, and hence he may be
convicted under an indictment charging him with committing the
crime in the latter place.

M. J. Cunningham, attorney general, and G. A. Gondran, district attorney, for the appellee.

R. McCulloh, for the appellant.

[197] NICHOLLS, C. J. The indictment in this case charges
that the defendant, "on the fifteenth day of September, [198] 1896,
with force and arms, in the parish of Ascension, and within the
jurisdiction of the twentieth judicial district court of the state
of Louisiana, being then and there a trustee of Henry O. Maher,
Jr., did then in his fiduciary capacity, fraudulently, wrongfully,
and feloniously use, conceal, and otherwise embezzle a gold
watch of the value of one hundred dollars, a gold chain of the
value of forty dollars, a gold locket of the value of ten dollars,
the whole valued at one hundred and fifty dollars, the lawful
property of said H. O. Maher, Jr., which had been there intrusted to his care, keeping, and possession by the said H. O.

Maher, Jr., with the felonious intent to convert the same to his own use and benefit and to deprive the said H. O. Maher, Jr., of his lawful property." The only matter called to our attention by counsel of defendant is contained in a bill of exceptions in which it is recited "that on the trial of the cause the state attempted to show that the watch which accused is charged in the information with having embezzled was pledged in the city of New Orleans by accused to a pawnbroker; and that to any and all evidence of any use made in the city of New Orleans of said watch, by said accused, defendant objected on the ground that the same was inadmissible under the information which charges the accused with having wrongfully converted said watch to his own use in the parish of Ascension—that the court overruled said objection, on the ground that should the state produce evidence to show that accused had formed the intention of converting the watch to his own use in the parish of Ascension and pursuant to said intention so formed in said parish had gone to the city of New Orleans and there pawned said watch, accused could be, under the law, prosecuted either in said city or in said parish; that said evidence was, therefore, admissible; that he would charge the jury that unless they found from the evidence that accused had formed the intent to convert said watch in the said parish they must discharge the said Sullivan"; that to this ruling defendant excepted and reserved a bill of exceptions.

Appended to the bill is the following statement of the judge: "As stated in the foregoing bill of exceptions, I allowed the state to show the fact that the property alleged to have been embezzled by defendant was pawned by him in the city of New Orleans, but I stated at the time that I would charge the jury that unless the accused had wrongfully appropriated the property in Ascension [199] parish, and had conceived the idea of converting it to his own use in said parish, they could not convict him, and I did so charge the jury, and expressly stated to them that if accused had only conceived the idea of appropriating the property in the city of New Orleans, he could not be convicted in Ascension parish." The accused was found guilty by the jury and sentenced to one year's imprisonment at hard labor in the penitentiary. He appealed.

No objection appears to have been made to the indictment, nor to the charge given by the court. No plea to the jurisdiction of the court was entered. Defendant went to trial without objection. The case comes to us on an objection by defendant to the reception of evidence under the recitals of the informa-

tion. Defendant's complaint is, that under the allegations of the
information it was not competent for the court to allow testimony
to show that the watch charged to have been embezzled was
pawned in the city of New Orleans. He made no motion to
strike out the evidence: See 3 Rice on Criminal Evidence, secs.
256 et seq. He made no attempt to make use of the fact complained of for a new trial.

In the brief filed in behalf of the defendant we understand
his counsel to maintain that as the "possession" of the jewelry
had been given to defendant by the owner, and his original possession was lawful, he continued to hold the same lawfully until
actual conversion. That even if he conceived in the parish of
Ascension the idea of disposing of the goods in the city of New
Orleans, and left that parish, taking the goods with him for the
purpose of there accomplishing his design, he was guilty of no
crime when he crossed the parish line. That he still held them
lawfully in possession, and the mere "intent to commit" did
not change the character of the possession; and that when the
intent to convert became coupled with the fact of conversion,
then, for the first time, was there a crime committed, and that
conversion took place in New Orleans.

The case comes before us with a judgment of the district
court for the parish of Ascension based upon the verdict of a
jury convicting defendant of embezzlement charged to have been
committed in the parish of Ascension. Upon what particular
evidence, or on what precise theory of the law the jury acted in
finding the verdict, we cannot say with any certainty. If the act
of appropriation or disposal, by defendant, of the property took
place in the city of New Orleans, as defendant intimates that
it did, we only come to a [200] knowledge of that fact inferentially
through reference made by counsel and the court to the admission
of the testimony against the reception of which he argued and
still complains. We understand him to say that but for that
evidence there would have been nothing before the jury to show
unlawful appropriation or conversion, and that the jury would,
but for this, have been forced to acquit him. Of the correctness of that proposition, we are not advised. We know nothing
of what occurred between defendant and Maher in the parish of
Ascension before defendant pawned the watch in New Orleans,
nor do we know anything of what occurred in that parish afterward: State v. Foster, 8 La. Ann. 292; 58 Am. Rep. 678. We
would infer from the judge's charge, followed as it was by the
verdict, that matters had occurred in Ascension parish of a char-

acter such as to warrant the verdict independently of the act of pawning in New Orleans. That act may have been only offered as "evidence" and cumulative evidence of a prior embezzlement, and may have been very properly admitted to show intent.

Defendant was indicted under section 905 of the Revised Statutes, which declares that "any servant, clerk, broker, agent, consignee, trustee, attorney, mandatary, depositary, common carrier, bailee, curator, testamentary executor, administrator, tutor, or any person holding any office or trust under the executive or judicial authority of this state or in the service of any public or private corporation or company, who shall wrongfully use, dispose of, conceal, or otherwise embezzle any money, bill, etc., ... shall suffer imprisonment," etc.

The term "embezzle," used in the statute, is one which has a well-recognized and accepted common meaning, as much so as the word to "burn" or to "carry away": See Bishop's Criminal Procedure, sec. 322.

Webster defines it as "to appropriate fraudulently to one's own use, as that intrusted to one's care; to apply to one's private use by a breach of trust, as to embezzle public money." It has received frequent judicial construction. It is a broader term than larceny under our law, but is not exclusive of it, as counsel contends: See State v. Wolff, 34 La. Ann. 1154.

It is not of the essence of the "commission" of the crime of embezzlement (if committed within the state), that all of the elements of the crime should be consummated in the same parish [201] though the question as to where the crime was committed affects the jurisdiction of the court in which the accused may be brought to trial.

Defendant's contention that the place of an ultimate unlawful sale or pawning of property by a person holding the same through fiduciary relations with the owner is the only test and criterion of the place where embezzlement of that property was effected, and that antecedent acts by him, in other localities, are to be taken and considered as merely acts leading up to an embezzlement there, is not, in our opinion, sound.

Though defendant does not present this case specifically as one involving the jurisdiction of the district court of the parish of Ascension over the trial of this cause, we think it may be well to say that if that question arose it sprung entirely from the evidence on the trial of the case, and not from the averments of the indictment or from defendant's pleadings.

We are of the opinion that if the jewelry received by the defendant and intrusted to him by H. O. Maher was received in the parish of Ascension, to be there returned, but that instead of doing so defendant conceived, in that parish, the intention of fraudulently appropriating the same to his own use, and in furtherance of that intention he took the same to the city of New Orleans for the purpose of there unlawfully and fraudulently selling or disposing of the same, and that he did there fraudulently sell and dispose of the same and appropriate the same to his own use, he was legally subject to indictment in the parish of Ascension for embezzlement: See 6 Am. & Eng. Ency. of Law, tit. Embezzlement; Campbell v. State, 35 Ohio St. 70.

For the reasons herein assigned the judgment appealed from is affirmed.

———

EMBEZZLEMENT—PLACE OF CRIME.—Embezzlement is committed, and a prosecution therefor may be maintained, in the county in which the accused took or received the property embezzled, or through or into which he may have undertaken to transport it: Monographic note to Simpson v. State, 44 Am. St. Rep. 83. Where the defendant received the property in one county, but performed the act of conversion in another, he cannot be tried in the county where he received the property, unless he conceived the intent of committing the crime when he received it: Monographic note to Calkins v. State, 98 Am. Dec. 161, on embezzlement.

———

STATE v. ITZCOVITCH.

[49 LOUISIANA ANNUAL, 366.]

MUNICIPAL CORPORATIONS, POWER TO ENACT ORDINANCES REGULATING SECONDHAND STORES. — Unless granted authority to do so by the legislature, a municipal corporation cannot by ordinance make it the duty of persons keeping a place where secondhand goods are sold, bought, or exchanged to furnish to the superintendent of police every day a descriptive list of the articles bought, sold, or exchanged, with a complete description thereof with the name, sex, color, apparent age, and general description and place of residence of the persons buying, selling, or exchanging the same. The authority to enact such an ordinance is not included within a general grant to the municipality of the right to exercise the police power.

MUNICIPAL CORPORATIONS, POWER OF TO DECLARE AN ACT CRIMINAL.—A municipality cannot, unless expressly authorized by statute, make that criminal which the legislature has not seen fit to make so.

James L. McLoughlin, assistant city attorney, and Samuel L. Gilmore, city attorney, for the city of New Orleans, appellee.

Albert D. Henriques, for the appellant.

366 McENERY, J. The city council of New Orleans enacted the following ordinance:

"Mayoralty of New Orleans,
"City Hall, September 3, 1896.
(No. 12619, Council Series.)

"An ordinance amending Ordinance No. 12512, Council Series.

"Be it ordained by the common council of the city of New Orleans, that Ordinance No. 12512, Council Series, be and the same is hereby amended so as to read as follows:

"Section 1. Be it ordained, that from and after the passage of this ordinance, it shall be the duty of every person keeping a shop or other place, whether as owner or agent, where second-hand goods are bought, sold, or exchanged, to furnish to the superintendent of police, at his office, between the hours of 3 o'clock P. M. every day in the year, a complete descriptive list of all articles bought, sold, or exchanged, at such shop or place, during the twenty-four hours last preceding, and since the furnishing of the last report, together with the name, sex, color, apparent age, and general description and **367** place of residence of the person or persons buying, selling or exchanging each of said articles; provided, that all dealers in goods of any kind or description, which shall have been used, or which shall have been transferred from the manufacturers to the dealer, and then received in the possession of third persons, whether the same consists of clothes, bicycles, or other vehicles, carpets, clothing, firearms, weapons, household utensils, or of articles of personal use, or of male or female wearing apparel, or of jewelry, gold or silver, shall be and are hereby declared to be secondhand dealers; provided, further, that secondhand furniture dealers, paying licenses as such, and who buy and sell furniture exclusively, either at auction or private residences, shall not be considered secondhand dealers within the meaning of this ordinance.

"Sec. 2. Be it further ordained, that whoever loans money on deposit or pledges of personal property, or who purchases personal property, or choses in action, on condition of selling the same back again at a stipulated price, is hereby defined and declared to be a pawnbroker."

"Sec. 3. Be it further ordained, that all keepers, whether as owners or agents, of shops or places commonly known as loan offices or pawnbroker shops, and all persons who habitually lend money on pawn or pledge of diamonds, jewelry, plate, valuables, clothing, firearms, or other movables or personal property, shall at the time of receiving any article of property whatsoever in pawn or pledge, enter in a book to be kept by them, respectively, a full and complete description of the articles of property so pawned or pledged, with the date and hour of receiving the same, and the name, description, and place of residence of the depositor or pledgor, and shall, on demand of the superintendent of police, or of any officer or person acting under his authority, exhibit to him, with the articles of property therein mentioned, the books of the description so required. It shall also be the duty of such keeper to make daily reports in the same manner required in the preceding section, save that the name and place of residence of the pledgor may be omitted therefrom. The reports herein provided for in this section shall be considered as confidential, and shall be for the private use of the police solely.

"Sec. 4. Be it further ordained, that the shops and places mentioned in sections 1 and 2 hereof shall be kept closed from the hour [368] of 10 o'clock P. M. to 6 o'clock A. M., except on Saturdays, when the hours of closing may be extended to 11:30 P. M.

"Sec. 5. Be it further ordained, that in the event that any day shall be a legal holiday, then the said report required by sections 1 and 2 shall be made on the day following and between the hours aforementioned.

"Sec. 6. Be it further ordained, that the proper blanks for the reports aforementioned shall be furnished at the office of the superintendent of police on application.

"Sec. 7. Be it further ordained, that it shall be unlawful for the owner or keeper of a shop described in section 1 to sell, exchange, barter, or remove from their place of business, or permit to be redeemed, any of the goods bought, exchanged, pledged, pawned, or deposited by, to, or with them for the period of seven days after the making of the report thereof provided for in this ordinance.

"Sec. 8. Be it further ordained, that it shall be unlawful for any owner or owners, keeper or keepers, agent or agents, or parties representing said owner or owners or proprietors of any secondhand store, pawnshop, or loan office to buy, pawn, pledge, or exchange any article or articles from any minor under the age of sixteen years, from a person appearing to be intoxicated, from a person known to be a notorious thief, or from a person known to have been convicted of larceny or burglary.

"Sec. 9. Be it further ordained, that in the event any person or persons shall tender for sale, pawn, or exchange any article or articles to the owner or owners, keeper or keepers, agent or agents, or parties representing said owner or owners or proprietors or keepers of any secondhand store, pawnshop, or loan office, and they having good reasons to believe that such article or articles were stolen it shall be their duty to have the person or persons so tendering the same immediately arrested.

"Sec. 10. Be it further ordained, that any violation of this ordinance shall be deemed a misdemeanor, and any person or persons violating any of the provisions of this ordinance shall be liable to a fine not exceeding twenty-five dollars, or imprisonment in the parish prison not exceeding thirty days, at the discretion of the recorder of the district in which the offense shall have been committed."

(Other sections omitted.)

360 The defendant who keeps a secondhand store in the city of New Orleans, was arrested and convicted for violating provisions of the above ordinance. He contested its legality and constitutionality in the recorder's court. He specifically avers that the city council was without authority or power to enact said ordinance.

The regulation of such establishments as are named in the ordinance is, undoubtedly, an exercise of police power, but they are of that character that the city council of New Orleans is without power to police them in the manner adopted in the ordinance without special legislative permission.

We presume there was a necessity for the attempt to regulate the establishments mentioned and provided in for the ordinance, but however great the necessity, without the sanction of legislative authority the city council was without power to enact such an ordinance. Under the grant of police power to the city no such power is vested in the city council. Hence its exercise was unlawful: 1 Dillon on Municipal Corporations, par. 317; City Charter, secs. 14, 15.

In the case of State v. Robertson, 45 La. Ann. 945, 40 Am. St. Rep. 272, this court held that an ordinance of the city council of New Orleans providing for the office of inspector and examiner with the power to examine engineers, and to grant certificates of competency and to inspect boilers, etc., was illegal, as the power to enact such an ordinance was not granted to the city and could not be inferred from the powers granted.

In State v. Von Sachs, 45 La. Ann. 1416, it was held the city council of New Orleans had no power to enact an ordinance requiring labor agents to give bond for a faithful discharge of duties as labor agents.

The language employed in that case is applicable here. "The

city council can exercise only such power as legislative authority
confers upon it. It can prohibit no business authorized by the
legislature, and, when it assumes that the legislature authorizes
the taxation of the occupation, ... it cannot, in authorizing
the business or occupation to be carried on, impose obligations
not authorized by the legislature."

The occupations attempted to be regulated are legitimate occupations licensed by the state, and the city can impose no burden upon the carrying on of these occupations not authorized
by the legislature.

In Clinton v. Phillips, 58 Ill. 102, 11 Am. Rep. 52, there was
[370] an effort made by the plaintiff city to regulate the sale of
intoxicating liquors for medicinal, mechanical, and chemical purposes, requiring a report quarterly of the kind and quantity sold
for such purposes, when and to whom sold, and on whose prescription. The ordinance was held to be illegal because there was
no power to enact it.

In Long v. Taxing Dist., 7 Lea, 134, 40 Am. Rep. 55, it was
held "a municipal corporation cannot, without special legislative
authority, pass an ordinance requiring merchants, parts of whose
business is the buying and repacking of loose cotton, in addition
to the other conditions prescribed by law and ordinance for taking
out merchant's license, to give bond to keep in a book specially
provided for the purpose a daily record of the name of each seller
of loose cotton and the quantity of each purchase, and that he
will keep such book at all times open to the inspection of the
police."

The ordinance was enacted to break up the stealing of loose
cotton. The court said: "The ordinance does not regulate the
administration of the local government, the convenient transaction of business or the conduct of the citizens with a view to
health and comfort, nor is it such as can be said to fall within
the general duties of municipal bodies. It is rather intended
to facilitate the enforcement of the criminal law against theft of
loose cotton."

And the ordinance under review was evidently intended to
facilitate the enforcement of criminal law in the detection of
thefts of personal property. The ordinance, no doubt, has accomplished good results, but there was no authority to enact
it. Legislative grant of power to enact such an ordinance must
be obtained before it can have any effectual force.

That part of the ordinance which makes the violation of any
of its provisions a misdemeanor is illegal, in that it makes or

creates an act a crime which the legislature has not seen fit to
do: State v. McNally, 48 La. Ann. 1450.

The ordinance above recited, No. 12619, council series, is declared to be null and void, and the judgment appealed from is
annulled and reversed, and it is ordered that the defendant be
discharged.

MUNICIPAL CORPORATIONS—POWER TO ENACT ORDI-
NANCES.—When an act is permitted by state law it cannot be prohibited by ordinance. The municipality cannot prohibit that which
the state has licensed: Monographic note to Robinson v. Mayor, 34
Am. Dec. 643.

MUNICIPAL CORPORATIONS—ORDINANCES REGULATING
PAWNBROKERS AND SECONDHAND CLOTHING DEALERS.
The business of pawnbroker, junk dealer, or dealer in secondhand
goods and merchandise is expressly within the control of the police
power of the state, and is properly subject to reasonable rules and
regulations, and a very clear abuse of this power must be shown in
order to justify the court in declaring the regulations unreasonable
and void: Grand Rapids v. Braudy, 105 Mich. 670; 55 Am. St. Rep.
472, and note. A city ordinance requiring every licensed pawnbroker to make out and deliver to the superintendent of police, every
day before noon, a legible and correct copy from a book to be kept
by him, of all things received on deposit or purchased during the
preceding day, together with the hour when received or purchased,
and a description of the pledgor or seller is not unreasonable:
Laurde v. Chicago, 111 Ill. 291; 53 Am. Rep. 625. See St. Joseph
v. Levin, 128 Mo. 588; 49 Am. St. Rep. 577. From these citations it
is apparent that the conclusion announced in the principal case does
not accord with that reached in other states.

STATE v. VOSS.

[49 LOUISIANA ANNUAL, 444.]

MUNICIPAL ORDINANCE MAKING CERTAIN ACTS
EVIDENCE OF CRIME.—An ordinance providing that it shall not
be necessary to prove the actual sale of lottery tickets in any place,
house, office, or premises, but any sign, ticket, sheet, bulletin, or
other device used to indicate that tickets are kept for sale or to
give information as to the result of any drawing shall be taken and
accepted as sufficient evidence of keeping a lottery house or shop,
is valid. Such an ordinance does not justify a conviction unless
there was guilty knowledge or intent.

MUNICIPAL ORDINANCE, CONSTRUCTION OF AS TO
EXTENT OF PUNISHMENT.—An ordinance providing that, upon
conviction, a person convicted shall be condemned to pay a fine not
exceeding twenty-five dollars or imprisonment not exceeding twenty-
five days, or both, on default of the payment of the fine, providing
that the fine shall not exceed twenty-five dollars nor the imprisonment more than thirty days, does not authorize a fine of the amount
named and an imprisonment of thirty days and a further imprisonment if the fine is not paid. In no event can the imprisonment exceed thirty days.

James J. McLoughlin, assistant city attorney, and Samuel L.
Gilmore, city attorney, for the appellee.

Chandler C. Luzenberg, for the appellant.

445 BREAUX, J. An affidavit charged defendant with having
violated an ordinance of the city council relative to lotteries. He
was tried, found guilty, and sentenced to pay a fine of twenty-
five dollars and to ten days' imprisonment, and, in default of
payment of the fine, to an additional imprisonment of twenty
days in the parish prison. Upon his trial he alleged that the
ordinance was illegal and unconstitutional. From the sentence
he has appealed.

In this appeal, the defendant, in the first place, urged that
section 2 of the crdinance, which reads as follows: "That it shall
not be necessary to prove the actual sale of lottery tickets in any
space, house, office, or premises, but any sign, tickets, sheets, bulletins or other device used to indicate that tickets are kept for
sale or to give information as to the result of any drawing or pretended drawing shall be taken and accepted as a sufficient proof
of the keeping of a lottery office or shop," was illegal and unconstitutional.

The complaint of the defendant was, that any ordinance which
makes the finding of a lottery ticket or device on the premises
or on the person of a defendant sufficient proof of his keeping
a lottery shop is depriving him of his liberty without due process
of law.

The section of the ordinance against which this complaint is
directed reads: "That it shall not be necessary to prove the actual
sale of lottery tickets in any space, house, office, or premises,
but any sign, tickets, sheets, bulletins or other device used to
indicate that tickets are kept for sale or to give information as to
the result of any drawing or pretended drawing, shall be taken
and accepted as a sufficient proof of the keeping of a lottery
office or shop."

The following is quoted by counsel for the appellant, and made
the basis of his clearly presented points in argument: "The law
delights in the life, liberty, and happiness of the subject; consequently, it deems statutes which deprive him of these, however necessary they may be, in a sense odious. For which, as for
kindred **446** reasons, as well as because every man should be able
to know certainly when he is guilty of crime, statutes which subject one to a punishment or penalty, or to a forfeiture or a summary process calculated to take away his opportunity of making

a full defense, or in any way deprive him of his liberty, are to be construed strictly": Bishop on Statutory Crimes, sec. 193.

Upon this point we agree with Mr. Bishop and with counsel, in such cases as those alluded to in the quotation; in our view, also, the construction should be strict, but from this agreement in opinion it docs not follow that the ordinance assailed should be declared a nullity upon the ground urged. In our judgment, as we read the ordinance, it does not say that the holder of a ticket is, by the mere fact that he is a holder, guilty as charged.

If one, without guilty knowledge or intent, is in possession of a lottery ticket, it cannot be taken of itself as being sufficient proof of guilt. One of the indispensable elements of crime is wanting. To constitute crime there must be joint operation of act and criminal intent. Under the language of the statute, to our thinking the fact that one is engaged in the business of selling tickets or in giving information as to the result of any drawing, or pretended drawing, constitutes the offense denounced. One accused is certainly not guilty unless it is satisfactorily shown that he knowingly had the tickets in his possession, or knowingly gave information as to the result of any drawing or pretended drawing. Either act is the offense denounced, and it may be made evident from either that the one thus committing the act is engaged in conducting a lottery shop, without thereby defeating the purpose of the ordinance.

The section requires, to convict an accused, "any sign, tickets, sheets, bulletins or other device used to indicate that tickets are for sale, or to give information as to the result of any drawing or pretended drawing," a well-known business, giving rise to the conclusion stated in the ordinance that he is conducting a lottery office.

In the second place, the appellant urges that any section of an ordinance which permits a recorder to sentence an accused to an imprisonment of more than thirty days is ultra vires and illegal.

It must be confessed that the language of the ordinance is not as clear as it might have been, but we think it sufficiently fixes the limit.

[447] Section 3 of the ordinance is as follows: "That whoever shall violate the provisions of this ordinance shall, upon conviction before the recorder within whose jurisdiction the offense is committed, be condemned by said recorder to pay a fine not to exceed twenty-five dollars, or imprisonment in the parish prison for a term not to exceed thirty days, or both, in default

of the payment of said fine; provided, that the fine shall not exceed twenty-five dollars, nor the imprisonment more than thirty days.

By Act 41 of 1890 the council may enforce obedience to and punish the violation of ordinances "by fine or imprisonment or both, or by imprisonment in default of the payment of the fine; provided, that the fine shall not exceed twenty dollars for each offense, nor the imprisonment more than thirty days."

The ordinance interpreted as a whole does not, in our judgment, exceed that limit. Without the proviso the recorder would be authorized to impose a fine of twenty-five dollars, with imprisonment of thirty days for the violation of the ordinance and an additional thirty days' imprisonment for the nonpayment of the fine; that is, if the fine were not paid the imprisonment might be as much as sixty days, but it is saved by the proviso limiting the fine to twenty-five dollars and all imprisonment to thirty days. The penalty is thereby kept within statutory limitation.

The sentence and fine imposed upon the accused were within the limit of the proviso.

The sentence and judgment appealed from are affirmed.

———

LOTTERIES — STATUTE PROHIBITING POSSESSION OF LOTTERY TICKETS.—A statute making it criminal for a person to have in his possession any ticket, slip, list, or record of prizes drawn in a lottery, or any record of any lottery ticket, or anything in the nature thereof, unless for the purpose of procuring and furnishing evidence of violations of the law, is constitutional, and the accused cannot escape conviction by proving that he did not know the nature and use of the prohibited articles found in his possession, and that they were given to him by another man to be delivered to a third, and that he to whom they were so given had no knowledge that they were in any way connected with the lottery business. The absence of guilty knowledge is, under this statute, but a matter for the court in imposing sentence for its violation: Ford v. State, 85 Md. 465; 60 Am. St. Rep. 337, and note. See In re Wong Hane, 108 Cal. 680; 49 Am. St. Rep. 138.

CRIMINAL LAW — PUNISHMENT — IMPRISONMENT UNTIL FINE IS PAID.—In California, though a statute authorizes one convicted of assault with a deadly weapon to be punished by "imprisonment in the state prison or in a county jail not exceeding two years, or by fine not exceeding five thousand dollars or by both," a court sentencing a prisoner to a state prison and to the payment of a fine cannot require him to be imprisoned in such prison until the fine is paid: Extended note to Ex parte Bryant, 12 Am. St. Rep. 204, on the right to imprison until a fine is paid.

STATE v. NAMIAS.

[49 LOUISIANA ANNUAL, 618.]

CONSTITUTIONAL LAW. — WHETHER THE POLICE POWER has been exercised within the proper limitations is a judicial question.

MUNICIPAL ORDINANCE REGULATING MARKETS.—An ordinance prohibiting all sales in the public markets after 12 o'clock noon, except fruits and vegetables in limited quantities, and forbidding the sale of fruits, vegetables, or other articles of food within six squares of the public markets by peddlers, is a valid exercise of the police power by a city.

James J. McLoughlin, assistant city attorney, and Samuel L. Gilmore, city attorney, for the city of New Orleans, for appellee.

Sholars & Schreiber, for the appellant.

[618] MILLER, J. The defendant, prosecuted and fined for selling fruits [619] and vegetables within six squares of a public market prohibited by an ordinance of the city council, takes this appeal, and claims the reversal of the sentence on the ground of the unconstitutionality of the ordinance.

The ordinance prohibits all sales in the public markets, after 12 o'clock M., except fruits and meats in limited quantities, and prohibits the sale of fruits, vegetables, and other articles of food within six squares of the public markets by peddlers. The defendant is a peddler of fruits and vegetables, and assails that portion of the ordinance which excludes him from selling within the area of six squares of the public markets.

The defendant's contention is, that the sale of fruits and vegetables within the prohibited area cannot be deemed injurious to the public health or cleanliness of the city, and hence the ordinance in this respect is not the exercise of the police power; he further contends the ordinance prohibiting the peddler, but allowing sales of vegetables and fruits within the six squares by grocers, is unequal, oppressive, and unjust, and in all aspects the prohibition placed by the ordinance is assailed as unconstitutional.

It is pressed on us with great earnestness of argument that the courts have the full power to scrutinize ordinances of the council professing to exert the police power, and to protect the citizens from the abuse of the power. Hence, it is argued that the ordinance, prohibitive of sales of fruit and vegetables, not decayed, but sound and fresh, having no relation to public health, should be held by us as not sanctioned by the police power. We have given full attention to the line of authority cited in this connection. It may be conceded, as it is put in one of the cases cited by defendant, it is for the legislative department to determine when the occasion arises for the exercise of the police power, but the subjects on which the power is exerted is for judicial decision. The police power has its limitations, and whether exerted within those limitations is necessarily a judicial question: Cooley's Constitutional Limitations, 568; Horr and Bemis on Municipal Police Ordinances, par. 217; Toledo etc. Ry. Co. v. Jacksonville, 67 Ill. 37; 16 Am. Rep. 611. If, therefore, this ordinance transcended the police power, our duty to declare it could not be questioned.

The market ordinances in their general scope have been frequently called in question before our courts: Morano v. Mayor etc., 2 La. 620 217; First Municipality v. Cutting, 4 La. Ann. 335; New Orleans v. Stafford, 27 La. Ann. 417; 21 Am. Rep. 563. It is true in the previous decisions the precise phase of this controversy was not presented. But the power of the council to fix the time, place, and mode of selling food was discussed. The conclusion was, such legislation was essential to the good government of the city, and that the power to prohibit sales of food for the daily consumption of the city was implied by the power to fix the location of the public markets. The locations of the public markets and the prohibition to sell elsewhere are linked. Public markets of absolute necessity, cannot be maintained without judicious restrictions to prevent sales in other places of food commodities. That restriction under this ordinance and the law is the restraint of such sales within six squares of the public market: Act No. 100 of 1878, p. 152. As Judge Dillon puts it: Under the delegation of the police power, the municipal corporation may establish markets and prohibit sales and purchases of marketable articles, except at designated market places: 1 Dillon on Municipal Ordinances, last ed., secs. 313, 1380. It is not, then, sufficient, in support of the objection to the ordinance, to say that the sale of fresh vegetables or fruit within six squares of a public market has no tendency to menace the public health. Public markets cannot be fixed at designated places if marketable commodities can be sold anywhere by peddlers. Hence the ordinance in our opinion, is to be supported, because part of the usual municipal function to establish markets.

It is urged on us that the ordinance is oppressive inasmuch as grocers are permitted, or at least left under no prohibition as to sales of fruits and vegetables. We do not think this would authorize us to hold the ordinance void. The distinction, whatever its effect, is the mere incident of a valid ordinance. Nor do we appreciate that the nonenforcement of this ordinance in the markets can support an objection to the ordinance itself.

It is therefore ordered, adjudged, and decreed that the judgment of the lower court be affirmed with costs.

POLICE POWER—LIMITS OF, A JUDICIAL QUESTION.— A determination by the legislature as to what is a proper exercise of the police power is not final and conclusive, but is subject to the supervision of the courts: Colon v. Lisk, 153 N. Y. 188; 60 Am. St. Rep 609· Chicago etc. R. R. Co. v. State, 47 Neb. 549; 53 Am. St. Rep. 557, and note. That the limits of the police power are fixed solely by legislative discretion, inside of constitutional boundaries: Walker v. Jameson, 140 Ind. 591; 49 Am. St. Rep. 222.

MUNICIPAL CORPORATIONS—ORDINANCES—REGULATIVE OF MARKETS.—Power given in a city charter "to regulate and manage markets" authorizes the city to adopt ordinances prohibiting the sale of commodities at stores, stalls, and places in the city outside of the market-houses. While the power "to regulate" does not authorize prohibition in a general sense, yet it confers authority to confine the business referred to to certain hours of the day, to certain localities or buildings in a city, and to prescribe rules for its prosecution within those hours, localities, and buildings: Ex parte Byrd, 84 Ala. 17; 5 Am. St. Rep. 328, and note; Jacksonville v. Ledwith,. 26 Fla. 163; 23 Am. St. Rep. 558, and monographic note thereto discussing the power of municipalities to establish and regulate markets. See St. Paul v. Laidler, 2 Minn. 190; 72 Am. Dec. 89; Ash v. People, 11 Mich. 347; 83 Am. Dec. 740; also monographic note to Caldwell v. Alton, 85 Am. Dec. 286-288.

SUCCESSION OF PETIT.
[49 LOUISIANA ANNUAL, 625.]

CONFLICT OF LAWS.—THE DOMICILE OF THE OWNER governs his contracts as to personal property and the distribution of that property when he dies. This rule is subject to the exception that the law of the domicile of the owner of personal property will not be enforced in another country to the prejudice of its citizens or when utterly opposed to the spirit and policy of its legislature.

CONSTITUTIONAL LAW—NATURAL CHILD, RIGHT OF TO INHERIT.—If the father of a natural child is domiciled in France, where he dies, and by whose laws such child, being acknowledged by the father, has the right to inherit one-half of his estate, this right will not be enforced in Louisiana, even as to the personal estate of the decedent, if he left relatives residing in that state who, by its laws, are entitled to such property, or some portion thereof, as heirs of the decedent. The right of a natural child to inherit any portion of the estate of its father, when he leaves surviving any heirs at law, is repugnant to the policy of the state as expressed in its statutes.

Henry Chiapella, for the appellant.

Denegre, Blair & Denegre, for the appellee.

626 MILLER, J. This is an appeal from the judgment dismissing the opposition to the account of the administratrix of the succession, asserting the right of the minor, Jean L. O. Petit, as the duly acknowledged natural child of the deceased to one-half of the proceeds of the succession property.

The deceased, George A. Petit, died in France, his domicile for years. By his last will he constituted the mother of the minor Jean L. O. Petit his universal legatee, but the will was annulled by the competent court in France. His legal heirs are his sisters and a brother, two residing here, one in Mississippi, and one in France. The minor on whose behalf the opposition is filed was duly acknowledged by the deceased in France as his natural child. The administratrix, in due course of administration, has sold and realized the proceeds of part of the succession property, has exhibited in her account the fund for distribution to the heirs, excluding from any participation in the distribution the natural child of the deceased.

Under the code, if the deceased, dying intestate, leaves no descendants or ascendants, his legal heirs are his brothers and his sisters, or their descendants. The natural child duly acknowledged is called to the succession of his father only when he leaves **627** no descendants, ascendants, collaterals, or surviving wife: Civ. Code, arts. 911, et seq., 917, 918. The account proposes that distribution the code prescribes, when the deceased, as in this case, making no will, that made in France having been annulled, leaves brothers and sisters and no ascendants or descendants.

It is claimed on behalf of the minor that his right to one-half of the property of the succession is fixed by the judgment of the court in France, and it is insisted that judgment is res judicata. We find no occasion to deal with the effect of a judgment rendered by the competent tribunal of one country contradictorily with the parties by or against whom the judgment is pleaded in the courts of another country. The suit in France was brought by the heirs at law to set aside the will, on the ground that the universal legatee, the mother of the minor, was interposed for his benefit, to evade the provisions of the Napoleon Code, forbidding testamentary dispositions in favor of natural children, when such dispositions trenched on the portions reserved by that code for brothers and sisters of the deceased. The under-tutor of the

minor joined in that suit, asserting his right and making his
mother a party.   We understand the French judgment as annulling the will and as withholding any decision in reference to the
distribution of the Louisiana property.   The material part of
the decree is: "Declare nul le legs fait à la dame Bayly, en ce
sens que le mineur Petit n'a droit qu'a a la moitié de l'actif de la
Succession; débouté la dame Bayly de sa demande en délivrance
du dit legs."   And the court adds: "Attendu que de la succession comprend des biens sis en France et des biens sis à a Lou-
isiane; que les legislations qui régissent les dits biens peuvent
être différentes; que le Notaire commis pour le partage prendra
tous renseignements et en cas de difficultés donnera son avis avec
l'estimation des immeubles et fera soumettre au Tribunal les
questions douteuses et litigieuses."   Wholly independent of this
decree the status of the minor child had been fixed by the
acknowledgment in due form by the father.   That status was not
in controversy, but conceded when the heirs at law brought the
suit to annul the will.   In our appreciation the decree is not the
basis of the demand of the minor asserted here, and hence the
decree is not res judicata in support of his demand in our courts
to take one-half of the property of the deceased.   He stands before us simply as the natural child of the deceased claiming a distribution accorded to him in France, but which our code denies
to natural children.

628 The general principle, not of statutory recognition, but enforced by the comity of nations, is that the law of the domicile
of the owner should govern his contracts as to personal property
and the distribution of that property when he dies.   Hence, it
is argued that as the law of France, the domicile of the testator,
gives the natural child one-half the property of his father who
leaves collateral heirs, that law and not our code must control
the distribution of the movables of the succession in Louisiana,
the argument conceding that our law governs the right of inheritance to all immovable property here.   The principle that gives
the foreign law operation in any other country, based entirely on
international comity, is subject to exceptions.   The personal capacities and disabilities fixed by the law of the domicile of the
party, as a general rule, will operate on him in other countries,
yet even these personal laws are not enforced by the courts of
other countries when that enforcement would prejudice the rights
or interests of their citizens.   Again, the foreign law will not be
enforced by the courts of another country in aid of a contract
made abroad, when the rights of the citizens of the country in

which the enforcement is sought would suffer, although the property within that country, the subject of the contract, is movable: Story on Conflict of Laws, secs. 23, 25, 302, 386, 550; Olivier v. Townes, 2 Mart., N. S., 93; Saul v. His Creditors, 5 Mart., N. S., 597; 16 Am. Dec. 212; Lee v. Creditors, 2 La. Ann. 603.

If these exceptions exist to the operation of the foreign law, on property in another country, it is not easy to appreciate why the foreign law, utterly opposed to the spirit and policy of our legislation, should be admitted by our courts to control the distribution to the heirs of the deceased of movable property here, merely because the deceased was domiciled in the country, the laws of which it is proposed to substitute for our own. In the argument for the natural child, it is urged that our code recognizes his heirship, and hence the inference is sought to be supported of no difference in the policy of France and Louisiana on that subject. The difference, in our view, is radical. Under the Napoleon Code the natural child is placed on a footing of equality as respects the right of inheritance with the brothers and sisters of the deceased. Our code, on the contrary, excludes the natural child from any inheritable right to the succession of the father, unless his succession would otherwise go to the state, and the code, thus viewing [629] the natural child, places him under the rubric of the code of irregular heirs: Civ. Code, arts. 757, 912 et seq. If in this case, then, we are to give effect to the French law, we disregard the spirit and text of the code as well as the public policy, the basis of our law on this subject; in thus deviating from our policy and legislation we deny the right of inheritance our code confers on two of our citizens included among the collateral heirs of the deceased; we enforce to their prejudice a title utterly repugnant to our system and derived solely from the foreign law and the force given to it, as is claimed by the comity due from one to another state. We are not aware of any case in which international comity has been thus applied.

The types of decisions of the class cited in the briefs in support of the claim of the natural child are numerous. The courts of one country charged with the administration of an estate, the principal administration being conducted in the courts of another country, the domicile of the deceased, will in a spirit of comity direct the transmission of the succession funds to the foreign country for administration there, but not until the claims of our own citizens are satisfied. Debts for many purposes will be deemed to follow the owner and be controlled by the law of his domicile: Succession of Packwood, 9 Rob. 443; 41 Am. Dec. 341.

In a contest between heirs all foreign our courts will ascertain
their rights in respect to movable property here by the standard
of the law of their foreign domicile, as was well illustrated in the
leading case of the heirs of Kosciusko: Ennis v. Smith, 14 How.
400. The right of a foreign administrator to control personal
property will be recognized when no prejudice to our citizens is
operated. In these classes of cases and others in which there
is no right asserted affecting our own citizens or repugnant to
our law and public policy, our courts will give effect to the foreign
law in subjecting to its operation movable property here. To all
the cases cited on behalf of the natural child we have given attention, and we have endeavored to indicate the difference in
principle between that applied in those cases and that involved
in this case.

We are not at liberty to enforce in this case the foreign law,
because, in our view, the comity of states does not exact the recognition by the courts of one country of the title of an heir based
on the foreign law opposed to our own law and detrimental to our
own citizens, if enforced. We think that in the discussion of the
subject by the jurists the limit of comity we have indicated finds
recognition. [630] In our own jurisprudence, with no direct adjudication on the particular phase presented in this case, we have
expressions carrying great significance against admitting the foreign law to interfere with the distribution to heirs our code establishes, although the property is movable and the owner had his
domicile in the foreign country. Thus the husband, who under
the common law becomes entitled to the personal property of his
wife, or to a part of it, in one case to be found in our reports, endeavored to assert against the heirs under our law his right here,
based on the foreign law to movable property of the deceased wife,
under administration here. The claim was denied, but the
authority of the case is weakened by the view expressed that the
title of the husband was not complete under the foreign law:
Marcenado v. Bertoli, 2 La. Ann. 980; Marcenaro v. Mordella, 10
La. Ann. 772. The tendency of the decision is, however, against
the title claimed under the foreign law opposed in that case to
the order of heirship our law establishes, but not exhibiting that
different and more impressive phase of repugnance to our code
manifest by the foreign law we are called on in this case to enforce. There is the greater reason to deny the operation here of
the foreign law.

There is another view. Our code gives effect to wills made out
of the state on movable property within the state. There is no

will in this case; that made in France having been annulled. When our courts carry into effect the testament made abroad, we execute the will of the deceased, not the foreign law. When there is no will, subject to such modifications as international comity demand, our courts enforce our law in distributing property within our jurisdiction to the heirs of the deceased owner. It is the law, therefore, of Louisiana that must be applied in this case, and that application is made by the judgment before us on this appeal: Civ. Code, art. 10491.

It is therefore ordered, adjudged, and decreed that the judgment of the lower court be affirmed with costs.

DISTRIBUTION—CONFLICT OF LAWS.—The disposition, succession to, and distribution of personal property, wherever situated, is governed by the law of the country of the owner's or intestate's domicile at the time of his death, and not by the conflicting laws of the various places where the property is situated: Smith v. Howard, 86 Me. 203; 41 Am. St. Rep. 537, and note; Cross v. United States Trust Co., 131 N. Y. 330; 27 Am. St. Rep. 597, and note; monographic note to In re Ingram, 12 Am. Dec. 96; extended note to Montgomery v. Milliken, 43 Am. Dec. 518-520.

DESCENT—RIGHTS OF BASTARDS—CONFLICT OF LAWS.—Legitimation in a foreign country does not make lawful heirs in other countries of those born out of lawful marriage, if the common law or statute of Merton prevails in the latter countries: Williams v. Kimball, 35 Fla. 49; 48 Am. St. Rep. 238; Smith v. Derr, 34 Pa. St. 126; 75 Am. Dec. 641. The right of a child to inherit in a country is not concluded by the fact that such child has been legitimated in the country of its domicile: Monographic note to Simmons v. Bull, 56 Am. Dec. 261. The authorities, however, are in conflict upon this question: Monographic note to In re Ingram, 12 Am. St. Rep. 103.

STATE v. KRAEMER.

[49 LOUISIANA ANNUAL, 766.]

CRIMINAL LAW, DRUNKENNESS AS AN EXCUSE FOR CRIME.—Voluntary drunkenness ordinarily constitutes no excuse for a crime committed under its influence, even though the intoxication is so extreme as to make the person unconscious of what he is doing or as to create a temporary insanity. If, however, the habit of drunkenness has created a fixed frenzy or insanity, whether permanent or temporary, as, for instance, delirium tremens, such frenzy or insanity is not deemed voluntary, and he who acts under its influence is to be judged as if his condition had not been brought about by his bad habits.

CRIMINAL LAW—DRUNKENNESS, WHEN A CRIMINAL INTENT IS ESSENTIAL TO A CRIME OR TO SOME GRADE THEREOF.—If the law requires a special intent to exist as an element of a crime, one who, when he does the act, is so drunk that he has not this intent, cannot be held guilty of a crime. Hence, if a man while drunk kills another, and the statute divides murder into two degrees, and to constitute the first a specific intent to take life is required, the slayer should not be found guilty of this higher degree of offense, if, at the time of his criminal act, his intoxication was such that he could not have this intent, unless it further appeared that he first resolved to kill the decedent and afterward drank to extreme intoxication and then carried out his former intention.

CRIMINAL LAWS — DRUNKENNESS—DELIRIUM TREMENS AS AN EXCUSE FOR CRIME.—One who was laboring under delirium tremens at the time of his commission of a criminal act, so that he did not know or realize what he was doing, is not excused, unless such delirium tremens antedated the fit of drunkenness during which such act was committed.

M. J. Cunningham, attorney general, and R. H. Marr, district attorney, for the appellee.

Paul W. Mount and James Wilkinson, for the appellant.

⁷⁶⁸ NICHOLLS, C. J. Defendant having been indicted for the murder of Mary Cooney, and the jury which tried him having returned a verdict of guilty without capital punishment, he was sentenced by the court to hard labor for life in the state penitentiary. From that sentence he has appealed.

He relies upon the following bill of exception:

"Be it remembered that on the trial of this cause a number of witnesses having testified before the jury that the accused, Nicholas Kraemer, had from his boyhood to the present time been considered by his associates as lightminded and had been known by the soubriquet of 'Crazy Nick'; that the drinking of liquor seemed to put him in a frenzy; that he had, previous to the time of the homicide, been a steady drinker and on the morning of the homicide he had come home after a night's absence at 8:30 A. M., terribly intoxicated; that he had called for his Sunday clothes and taking them into the yard chopped them up with a hatchet into little pieces, muttering, and when deceased tried to get him to desist, threatened her life with a hatchet; that it was further shown that three hours later he was seen in the back yard of a grocery near by shrieking; that at about the time of the homicide, 12:30 P. M., he returned to the house, walking straight, and went in to sit down to dinner with the deceased alone, from which place he came out, and was seen, bareheaded, walking rapidly and straight away from place where deceased had been left with her throat cut, and that when arrested was walking erectly with a staring look in his eyes; that he had taken a ten year old boy's hat and put it on his head, and when questioned, refused to answer, and it having been urged on his behalf by his counsel on the trial that, if the killing of the deceased had been done by accused, it was done: 1. Because he was insane and was not responsible for his acts; 2. Because such insanity, though possibly slight, was enhanced and made dangerous and homicidal by the use of liquor, which acted as a [769] poison to the mental disease of said accused, and that there was no motive for said act; 3. Because all the symptoms described in said testimony as to accused showed that such insanity or low order of intelligence was aggravated into homicidal mania by delirium tremens, from which he was suffering at the time it is claimed he killed Mrs. Cooney, the deceased.

"And on the part of the defense, counsel having requested the court to charge the jury as per the written request set forward and numbered and made a part of this bill of exceptions, and the court having failed to charge Nos. —— in said charge requested, and the said court moreover having failed to charge as to request Nos. ——, and the said court having moreover charged that any temporary insanity the result of drunkenness will not excuse crime, and that only permanent insanity the result of drunkenness will excuse crime, or in words of similar import or effect, and the said counsel for accused having thereupon, before the jury retired, taken the within bill of exceptions: 1. To the failure of the court to charge as requested; 2. To the refusal of the court to charge as requested; 3. To the charge of the court to the jury as herein stated.

"Counsel for the accused now having submitted this bill of exceptions to the district attorney, now tenders the same to this honorable court for its approval and signature.

"By the Court.—The jury were charged fully as to the law of insanity, whether brought about by intoxication or other causes. The jury were instructed that temporary insanity produced by undue indulgence in spirituous liquors furnished no excuse for homicide or other crime, but that fixed insanity did. As to special request No. 6, they were further instructed that delirium tremens, or fixed insanity, formed an excuse for the act, provided the party was not intoxicated at the time. My idea of the law is, that if the mental condition of the accused is the remote consequence of antecedent drunkenness, then he is not responsible, but that if his act takes place in a fit of intoxication, and is the immediate result of it, then he is. In my charge I endeavored to give the jury all the law applicable to the case."

The sixth special charge referred to in the bill of exception reads as follows: [770] "Delirium tremens, although the result or consequence of continual drunkenness, is insanity or a diseased state of mind, and affects responsibility for crime in the same way as insanity produced by any other cause.   Delirium tremens, like insanity, if it deprives a man of capacity of knowing right from wrong, saves him from any criminal responsibility for his acts."

The charge given by the court is not in the record, so that we cannot test the propriety of a particular portion of it by reference to it.   The only way in which we come to a knowledge of any part of it is through the statement made by the court itself at the foot of the bill of exceptions.

The recitals of the bill as to what the testimony in the case showed afford us no aid in passing upon the question before us, as the testimony was directed to the establishment of issues of fact, the conclusions as to which were to be disposed of, and were disposed of, by the jury.   What those conclusions were, upon the different issues raised, we do not know.   We know only the result reached in their verdict.   Whether the accused, as a fact, was at the time of the homicide insane or not we do not know, nor do we know, if insane, whether he was at that time suffering from delirium tremens.   The instructions asked seemed to have assumed that the nature, causes, and consequences of delirium tremens were fixed facts, known to and to be announced by the court to the jury, and to have further assumed as a fact that accused at the time of the homicide was under its influence and effects.   Those matters were matters, under expert and other evidence in the case, to be determined by the jury.

The doctrine with reference to drunkenness, in relation to crime, is thus stated by Bishop: "If a man, intending one wrong, accomplishes another, he is punishable for what is done, though not intended, except where a specific intent in distinction from mere general malevolence or carelessness is an essential element in the particular crime.   The law deems it wrong for a man to cloud his mind or excite it to evil action by the use of intoxicating drinks; and one who does this, then moved by the liquor while too drunk to know what he is about, performs what is ordinarily criminal, subjects himself to punishment; for the wrongful intent to drink coalesces with the wrongful act done while drunk and makes the act complete": Bishop's Criminal Law, 6th ed., c. 27, par. 397.

[771] The common law has always regarded drunkenness as being in a certain sense criminal.   Since, therefore, a man who intends one wrong and does another of the indictable sort is punishable, even when the wrong intended would not be so if actually done, voluntary drunkenness supplies in ordinary cases the criminal intent.   Thus, when a man voluntarily becomes drunk, that is

the wrongful intent, and if, while too far gone to have any further intent, he does a wrongful act, the intent to drink coalesces with the act done while drunk, and for this combination of act and intent he is liable criminally. It is, therefore, a legal doctrine, applicable in ordinary cases, that voluntary drunkenness furnishes no excuse for crime committed under its influence. It is so even when the intoxication is so extreme as to make the person unconscious of what he is doing, or to create a temporary insanity: Bishop's Criminal Law, pars. 399, 400. The author, referring to limitations of the doctrine, says: "The law holds men responsible for the immediate consequences of their acts, but not ordinarily so for those more remote. If, therefore, one drinks so deeply or is so affected by the liquor that for the occasion he is oblivious or insane, he is still punishable for what of evil he does under the influence of the voluntary drunkenness. But if the habit of drinking has created a fixed frenzy or insanity, whether permanent or intermittent, as for instance delirium tremens, it is the same as if produced by any other cause excusing the act. For whenever a man loses his understanding as a settled condition he is entitled to legal protection equally, whether the loss be occasioned by his own misconduct or by the dispensation of Providence": Bishop's Criminal Law, par. 406.

Referring to cases requiring specific intent the author says: "It is plain that when the law requires, as it does in some offenses, a specific intent, in distinction from mere general malevolence, to render a person guilty, the intent to drink and drunkenness following cannot supply this specific intent. Thus drunkenness as we have seen, does not incapacitate one to commit either murder or manslaughter at the common law; because to constitute either the specific intent to take life need not exist, but general malevolence is sufficient. But where murder is divided by statute into two degrees, and to constitute it in the first degree there must be the specific intent to take life, this specific intent does not, in fact, exist, and the murder is not in this degree, where one not meaning [772] to commit a homicide becomes so drunk as to become incapable of intending to do it; and then in this condition kills a man. In such a case the courts hold that the offense of murder is only in the second degree. This doctrine does not render it impossible for one to commit murder in the first degree while drunk. If he resolves to kill another, then drinks to intoxication and then kills him, the murder is of the first degree, because in this case he did specifically intend to take life. And a man, though drunk, may not be so drunk as to exclude the par-

ticular intent. Drunkenness short of the extreme point, therefore, will not reduce the murder to the second degree"; Bishop's
Criminal Law, pars. 401, 410.

"There are cases not requiring a specific intent where the precise state of the prisoner's mind is under special circumstances
important. Not conflicting with what has been previously laid
down, it is pretty well settled that there are circumstances on
which evidence of intoxication may be properly received to reduce
a homicide to manslaughter. Some judges seem not willingly
to yield this point, but the better opinion is, that if, for instance,
the question is whether the killing arose from a provocation which
was given at the time, or from previous malice, evidence of the
prisoner's having been too drunk to carry malice in his heart may
be admitted. And the consideration is not to be withheld from
the jury that his drunkenness may render more weighty the presumption of his having yielded to the provocation rather than
to the previous malice, because of the fact that the passions of a
drunken man are more easily aroused than those of a sober one.
This doctrine differs from the untenable one that drunkenness
excuses or palliates passion or malice. So intoxication is relevant to the question whether expressions used by a prisoner
sprang from a deliberate evil purpose, or were the mere idle words
of a drunken man. This evidence, moreover, assists in determining whether a defendant acted under the belief that his property
or person was about to be attacked."

In Haile v. State, 11 Humph. 154, it was said that when the
question was what was the actual mental state of the perpetrator
at the time the act was done, whether it was one of deliberation
and premeditation, then it was competent to show any degree of
intoxication that might exist, in order that the jury might judge,
in view of such intoxication, in connection with all the other facts
and circumstances, whether the act was premeditatedly and deliberately done. [773] The court, however, said that when the
question was whether drunkenness could be taken into consideration in determining whether a party be guilty of murder in the
second degree, the answer must be that it cannot. It was further
said that the law implied malice from the manner in which the
killing was done or the weapon with which the blow was stricken.
In such cases it is murder, though the perpetrator was drunk.
And no degree of drunkenness will excuse in such case, unless
by means of drunkenness an habitual or fixed madness is caused.

"The law in such cases does not seek to ascertain the actual
state of the perpetrator's mind, for the fact from which malice is

implied having been proved, the law presumes its existence, and proof in opposition to this presumption is irrelevant and inadmissible. Hence, a party cannot show that he was so drunk as not to be capable of entertaining a malicious feeling. The conclusion of law is against him."

In a note to Bishop's Criminal Law, paragraph 400, Lord Coke is quoted as saying that although he who is drunk is for the time non compos mentis, yet this drunkenness did not extenuate his act or offense, nor turn to his avail, but it is a great offense in itself, and therefore aggravates his offense. The author adds that it is not, however, strictly true that drunkenness aggravates a crime; it simply furnishes no excuse: Quoting McIntyre v. People, 38 Ill. 514.

Drunkenness in its relation to crimes has been considered a number of times by this court. Among the cases bearing upon the subject, we note State v. Mullen, 14 La. Ann. 577; State v. Coleman, 27 La. Ann. 692; State v. Watson, 31 La. Ann. 379; State v. Willis, 43 La. Ann. 407; State v. Ashley, 45 La. Ann. 1036; State v. Hill, 46 La. Ann. 27; 49 Am. St. Rep. 316.

We have given careful consideration to the argument in behalf of defendant by his counsel, and have reached the conclusion that, tested by the principles laid down in the commentators, the decisions of courts other than those of Louisiana and by our jurisprudence defendant has shown no proper case for relief.

We think that the jury was substantially instructed that when a prisoner urges that he should be held "excused" from criminality for a homicide which he had committed (we use that term in contradistinction to a plea for reduction of the grade of criminality charged) by reason of his having been laboring under "delirium tremens" at the time of the commission of the act, and that he was [774] therefore unable to know, realize, or appreciate what he was doing, the delirium tremens must be shown to have antedated the fit of drunkenness, during the existence of which the act was committed.

In other words, that if a person, being in possession of his mental faculties, voluntarily gets into a fit of drunkenness, and during such drunkenness commits a homicide under a diseased mental condition occasioned by the same, he cannot set up such diseased mental condition as an excuse for his act; that in order that a man should stand excused for a homicide committed during drunkenness and while in a diseased mental condition, the diseased mental condition which excuses the homicide should be able to be successfully urged as an excuse for the act of getting drunk.

It is a well-known fact that men who, at the time of voluntarily getting drunk are in full possession of their mental faculties, and who are in the same condition when the fit of intoxication passes away, frequently commit acts during the drunkenness of which they have absolutely no recollection on regaining a condition of sobriety—acts committed under a substantial condition of temporary insanity. All writers agree that a homicide committed under such conditions does not stand excused. The effect of drunkenness upon the mind and upon men's actions when under the full influence of liquor are facts known to everyone, and it is as much the duty of men to abstain from placing themselves in a condition from which no such danger to others is to be apprehended as it is for men to abstain from firing into a crowd or doing any other act likely to be attended with dangerous or fatal consequences. It would open the door wide to the commission of crime were we to justify the commission of a homicide committed under a condition of mind designated as delirium tremens, when it was, in all probability, nothing more nor less than the condition of mind usually resulting from a condition of thorough drunkenness.

It would be utterly impossible to distinguish between the two conditions of mind, if, in reality, there be a difference between the two.

It is, of course, as possible for an insane man to get drunk as a sane one. The addition of drunkenness to insanity does not withdraw from such person the protection due to insanity, but when such a person commits a homicide during drunkenness reliance must be placed upon the original insanity itself, not upon the subsequent drunkenness. We are of opinion the judgment should be affirmed. [775] We have no different degrees of murder in this state, but parties accused get all the benefit which would arise from grading the crime in the flexibility given to the punishment which is to be meted out in any given case, by allowing the jury, under a charge of murder, to bring in a verdict of guilty without capital punishment. The jury are enabled to give to the accused the benefit of any extenuating or mitigating circumstances which would save them from suffering the extreme penalty of the law. We gather from the record that the deceased in this case came to her death by having her throat cut by the defendant. The jury evidently gave some effect to the condition of drunkenness which, we infer, must have been established on the trial.

The judgment is affirmed.

CRIMINAL LAW—DRUNKENNESS AS A DEFENSE—DELIRIUM TREMENS.—Drunkenness is no excuse for committing a crime; State v. Shores, 31 W. Va. 491; 13 Am. St. Rep. 875. To excuse crime, intoxication must be of such a degree as to render the offender incapable of entertaining an intent to commit such crime. If it falls short of this it is worthless as a defense: Warner v. State, 56 N. J. L. 686; 44 Am. St. Rep. 415, and note. Temporary insanity produced by recent intoxication is not a defense to any crime, but is permitted to be shown in murder cases to determine the degree, and in all criminal prosecutions to mitigate or lessen the penalty: Ivers v. State, 31 Tex. Crim. Rep. 318; 37 Am. St. Rep. 811, and note; Garner v. State, 28 Fla. 113; 29 Am. St. Rep. 232, and note. It has been held that delirum tremens rendering one irresponsibly insane is an excuse for crime; Carter v. State, 12 Tex. 500; 62 Am. Dec. 539.

SUCCESSION OF ROBERTSON.

[49 LOUISIANA ANNUAL, 868.]

WILLS—OLOGRAPHIC, PRINTED HEADING OR DATING.—If will is written on a printed heading, so that in dating it the writer uses the figures printed on the paper as a part of his dating, it is not wholly written, dated, and signed by his hand, and therefore is not a valid olographic will.

WILLS, OLOGRAPHIC.—THE COURT MAY DETERMINE FROM AN INSPECTION that part of a will was printed. Where the original will is before the court, it will look at it and take notice that a date thereon is partly printed and not wholly written by the testator, though the witness, whose attention was not directed to the printed heading, testified in general terms that the will was wholly in the handwriting of the testator.

W. S. Benedict, for the appellant.

Buck, Walsh & Buck, for the appellee.

⁸⁶⁸ BREAUX, J. This appeal is prosecuted from a judgment of the district court in which it is decreed that the will of R. L. Robertson, Jr., probated on the sixth day of August, 1895, is a nullity.

The following is a copy of the olographic will annulled.

"New Orleans, December 12, 1892.

"I, Richard Lamb Robertson, being of sound mind and body, and in full possession of all my faculties, do make this my will and testament:

"To my dearly beloved wife, Cora Celeste Davidson, I owe all my present prosperity, and I give to her all my personal property, and leave to her the usufruct of all my estate during her life.

869 "I also appoint her my sole executrix, without bond and with full seizin.

"(Signed)   RICHARD LAMB ROBERTSON.

"Witness: Joseph B. Wolfe, Jr."

We have had occasion to refer to this testament in a case heretofore decided, having the same title: Succession of Robertson, 49 La. Ann. 80.

The will, the validity of which was assailed, was written on one of the letterheads of the testator, having the words "New Orleans" and the figures "189" of the year in print. The following is the only written date of the will: December 12-2. The appellant, widow of the deceased, R. L. Robertson, Jr., urges that the will in contest fulfills all the requirements of the law.

The requisites under the article of the Civil Code to the validity of the olographic will "that it be dated," does not import the necessity of mentioning the place at which it was dated.

The printed words, "New Orleans," give rise to no issue in the case. It is different in regard to the date of the will, which in order to be valid must be "entirely written, dated, and signed by the hand of the testator." Under the precise language of the article, the date is one of the essential formalities of an olographic testament. The nullity is formally pronounced by the law itself. It has been decided that absence or uncertainty of the month or the day of the testament is cause to decree it null; for better reason, the ruling should be the same where the year is not stated or is left to mere conjecture. The "year" printed or written by another is not a date in the hand of the testator, made the essential of a valid will. The law enjoins the date on two grounds: the first, the most essential, is in order that the precise date the testator made a disposition of his property may be known, rendering it possible to determine whether the testator had the capacity of giving at the time the testament was made. The second ground is secondary; if there are two testaments, it should be manifest which is the last, in case of opposing or incompatible disposition. In either case, the date written by the testator is an essential. We have cited these "motives" or grounds in support of the raison d'etre of the law, but without these "motives" or grounds, it is enough to 870 justify the decree declaring the will null that a substantial condition to its validity is lacking.

In Lewis v. Executor, 5 La. 396, this court said: "The law in its anxiety to guard against the testator being circumvented or practiced on, will not permit a testament to have any effect, no matter how strong the moral evidence may be that it contains truly his last disposition of his property. The formality (our code says) must be observed, otherwise the testaments are null and void. . . . . Courts of justice, therefore, can do nothing else but inquire, when a case of this kind arises, whether the formalities have been pursued."

The appellant insists that there is no proof before the court that the date was printed as stated, and urges that in these days of skilled penmen and draughtsmen, the eye to which print or engraving is manifest cannot always be trusted in opposition to the oath of three reputable witnesses.

The testament as written by the testator is before us. It is manifest that the date is printed. The testimony of witnesses, whose attention was not directed to the printed heading of the paper on which the testimony was written, cannot make that to be written which is not written. It is too plain to admit of question that the words and figures are printed.

Lastly, the appellant cites authorities in support of the proposition that writing, in its legal sense, includes what is printed as well; that while it is decided, for instance, to be essential to a deed that it should be in writing, yet printed forms have been in use from time immemorial. The appellant also quotes the definitions from a number of dictionaries as evidence that writing not only means words traced with the pen or stamped, but printed or engraved words. The argument would lead to the conclusion that it would be possible for a printer or engraver to print or engrave a portion of his testament.

Writing must be taken in its ordinary sense—to set down legible characters with pen and ink. The writing essential to a deed may include printed words without violating a prohibitory law. But in the matter of an olographic testament, it must be written; the pain of nullity is inevitable.

The judgment is therefore affirmed.

WILLS, OLOGRAPHIC—WHAT CONSTITUTES.—A will consisting in a printed form with the blanks filled in the testator's handwriting is not an olographic will and no part of it can stand: Estate of Rand, 61 Cal. 468; 44 Am. Rep. 555. Formalities prescribed by law for the execution of olographic wills must be strictly observed or the will is void: Succession of Armant, 43 La. Ann. 310; 26 Am. St. Rep. 183. See extended note to Lagrave v. Merle, 52 Am. Dec. 591-593. Substantially the same question involved in the principal case was decided in the same manner in Estate of Billings, 64 Cal. 427.

BAYSSET v. HIRE.

[49 LOUISIANA ANNUAL, 904.]

LIBEL, PRIVILEGED COMMUNICATION.—A FATHER who honestly believes disparaging reports about a suitor of his daughter, and who repeats such reports to friends of the suitor in confidence, without intending to injure him, but to convey to him that his attentions to his daughter must cease, is not guilty of slander. His legal and moral duty as a father makes his communication privileged, if not prompted by malice, and before a recovery can be had against him by the suitor, he must assume the burden of proving that the father was actuated by malice.

Clegg & Quintero, for the appellant.

B. B. Howard, for the appellee.

904 BREAUX, J. This suit was brought by the plaintiff to recover damages for slander committed, it is charged, by the defendant. The damages affected his reputation, caused loss in business, wounded his feelings, and brought about a severance of the betrothal between himself and defendant's daughter, he, in substance, avers.

The defendant, in his answer, admitted that he had made the statement as alleged by the plaintiff, but he especially denied that the **905** statement was made in any spirit of malice, revenge, or hatred, or that it had, in any manner, damaged the plaintiff. He also averred that he entertained kindly feeling for the plaintiff; that he was paying his address to his daughter, to which he objected; that the statements he made were to friends of the plaintiff in confidence, without intending to injure him, but to convey to him that his visits must cease. The case was tried before a jury. The verdict was for the defendant.

The vexatious and painful reports against the plaintiff, of which he complains, were of a date long anterior to the date that the defendant made the statements he is charged with having made. Such reports, if unfounded, are always to be regretted, and those who maliciously and wantonly circulate them are as blamable and censurable as those by whom they were originated.

It remains that the case before us is exceptional. It is the case of a father who sought to prevent his daughter from receiving the address of the plaintiff—in other words, the plaintiff sought defendant's daughter in marriage. The father, on account of injurious reports against the young man, deemed it proper to interfere.

It is true that rumor with her thousand tongues exaggerates everything. She rejoices in her task of telling alike of facts and fictions; of things done and things not done. Such reports as those circulated in this instance are nearly always disproved with great difficulty. The father owed no duty to the plaintiff which could possibly prevent him from carrying out a determination prompted by affection and tenderness for his daughter. Reports, such as those evident by the record, circulated about a Caucasian of the purest type, would be enough to influence the conduct and utterances of a prudent parent when considering with the members of his family, or in conversation with close friends, the advisability of his daughter's marriage.

In justice to the plaintiff, we deem it proper to state that witnesses of the highest respectability have testified that members of the family against whom the grievous charges were directed were at the time treated and considered as white, and that as such they were admitted in religious and other circles where none but white persons were admitted. It was plaintiff's misfortune that there were adverse reports about him. In view of the occasion and exigency, the question [900] was whether the father, who is now the defendant, honestly believed the report to be true. In our judgment, whether the rumor was true, or even whether the defendant had reasonable grounds to believe these reports, are not essentials to free him from the reproach of being a defamer, if he believed the report to be true.

In our view, the occasion was one of qualified privilege, and the purpose of the defendant was to prevent a threatening injury, and not for the purpose of slandering. The disclosure made by him to the plaintiff was made bona fide, and the utterances while conversing with intimate friends do not disclose the least malice. We have before stated the occasion was one of qualified privilege. In that case, to sustain his action, the plaintiff must show actual malice. The onus is with him. We think the plaintiff has failed in his attempt to prove malice. Without this proof, if the defendant honestly believed the report true, he cannot be held in damages.

We believe, as substantially urged by counsel for the plaintiff, that the pleadings on the part of the defendant were stronger than the occasion required. But the answer and the evidence were considered as a whole by us, and we reach the conclusion that the defendant in his defense had not alleged more than had been reported to him.

Mr. Cooley, in his book on Torts, page 214, said: "To require him at his peril to keep strictly within the limits of what he could prove to be true would be to make no allowance for the confidence properly belonging to the relation, or for the agitation and alarm which paternal feelings would naturally experience when an alliance believed to be improper was proposed. The case suggested is one of a large class of cases in which the like privilege is allowed, and in which it is necessary to show, not only that the communication was false, but also that it was made with evil intent."

Much must be allowed to the thoughtful father who seeks to guide his children in the right direction. Unless he is reckless and inconsiderate in his statement his utterances are not actionable.

"If fairly warranted by any reasonable occasion or exigency, and honestly made, such communications are protected for the common convenience and welfare of society, and the law has not restricted the right to make them, within any narrow limits": Baron Parke in Toogood v. Spying, 4 Tyrw. 582.

"The privilege is not defeated by the mere fact that the communication [907] is made in terms that were intemperate or excessive from over-excitement": Atwill v. Mackintosh, 120 Mass. 177, 183; citing Brow v. Hathaway, 13 Allen, 239; Harrison v. Bush, 5 El. & B. 344; Joannes v. Bennett, 5 Allen, 169; 81 Am. Dec. 738.

It follows from the foregoing that communications within the qualified privilege are not actionable merely because they are false or defamatory, but express malice must be made evident.

It is ordered, adjudged, and decreed that the judgment appealed from is affirmed.

SLANDER—PRIVILEGED COMMUNICATIONS—WHAT ARE.— Words spoken in the discharge of a duty, and in good faith, or spoken to those who have an interest in the communication, are not actionable, unless actual malice be proved: Bradley v. Heath, 12 Pick. 163; 22 Am. Dec. 418, and note; Farls v. Starke, 9 Dana, 128; 33 Am. Dec. 536. See note to Vanderzee v. McGregor, 27 Am. Dec. 158. It has been held that a letter to a woman, containing libelous matter concerning her suitor, cannot be justified on the ground that the writer was her friend and former pastor, and the letter was written at the request and with the approval of her parents: Monographic note to Shurtleff v. Stevens, 31 Am. Rep. 714. See, also, Byam v. Collins, 111 N. Y. 143; 7 Am. St. Rep. 726.

STATE *v.* ARDOIN.

[49 LOUISIANA ANNUAL, 1145.]

CRIMINAL LAW—ALIBI, PROOF OF.—Where alibi is a defense, the proper charge is, that the evidence in support of it should be considered in connection with all the other evidence in the case, and if, on the whole, there is reasonable doubt of the defendant's guilt, he should be acquitted.

EVIDENCE—ALIBI, BURDEN OF PROVING.—It is error to instruct the jury that the burden of proof is upon the accused to establish an alibi by a preponderance of the evidence. The setting up of the alibi does not change the presumptions nor the burden of proof, and if, because of it or anything else, the jury is not satisfied beyond a reasonable doubt of the guilt of the accused, he should be acquitted.

JURY TRIAL — INSTRUCTIONS, CORRECT MINGLED WITH INCORRECT.—While an inaccurate or incomplete instruction may be cured by subsequently supplying the defect or accurately stating the law, an absolute misstatement of the law is not cured by a correct statement elsewhere in the charge.

M. J. Cunningham, attorney general, and R. E. Lee Garland, district attorney, for the appellee.

E. B. DuBuisson and John N. Ogden, for the appellant.

[1146] BLANCHARD, J. The judgment appealed from having been affirmed, a review of the case, on the application for rehearing, induced the court to grant the rehearing; and now, on a further consideration, we have become satisfied of the incorrectness of some of the views expressed in our former opinion relating to the law governing the defense of alibi.

We now hold that it was error for the judge a quo to charge that: "It is obviously essential to the satisfactory proof of an alibi that it should cover the whole of the transaction in question, so as to render it impossible that the prisoner could have committed the act; it is not enough that it renders his guilt improbable merely."

It was also error to charge that: "If, therefore, the proof of an alibi does not outweigh the proof that he (the defendant) was at the place where the crime was committed, it is not sufficient." And it was additional error to charge that: "When the defense is that of an alibi the law casts the burden upon the defendant to reasonably satisfy the jury that he was elsewhere at the time of the commission of the offense. The rule of law, as applicable to the defense of an alibi, does not require of the defendant to reasonably satisfy the jury of his exact whereabouts [1147] every moment of the time necessary to cover the period when the offense was committed, but he is required to prove such a state of facts or circumstances as to reasonably satisfy the jury that he was else-where than at the place where, and the moment when, the offense was committed."

Where alibi is a defense, the proper charge is, that the evidence in support of it should be considered in connection with all the other evidence in the case, and if, on the whole evidence, there is reasonable doubt of defendant's guilt, he should be acquitted.

It is error to instruct that the burden of proof is upon the accused to establish an alibi by a preponderance of the evidence: Beck v. State, 51 Neb. 106; Casey v. State, 49 Neb. 403; Gravely v. State, 38 Neb. 870.

In State v. Reed, 62 Iowa, 40, it was held that alibi is not a defense within any accurate meaning of that word, but a mere fact shown in rebuttal of the state's evidence.

The setting up of an alibi does not change the presumptions and burden of proof, and if because of it, or anything else, the jury are not satisfied beyond a reasonable doubt of the guilt of the accused, they must acquit: Bishop's New Criminal Procedure, sec. 1066.

Whatever the accused brings forward in denial of the allegations, or of the proofs which the prosecution has adduced, the burden still remains on the state, and it never shifts to him: Bishop's New Criminal Procedure, sec. 1049.

The charge to the jury in its different parts should not be conflicting; and while a merely inaccurate or incomplete instruction may be cured by subsequently applying the defect or accurately stating the law, an absolute misstatement of the law is not cured by a correct statement elsewhere in the charge: Beck v. State, 51 Neb. 106; Barr v. State, 45 Neb. 458.

The errors of the court a quo, pointed out above, being of the character last mentioned, could not be cured by what the judge subsequently charged as set forth in our original opinion.

It is therefore ordered that the judgment of this court hereinbefore rendered be set aside, and it is now ordered and decreed that the verdict and sentence appealed from be annulled, avoided, and reversed, and that the case be remanded to be proceeded with according to law.

Miller, J., concurred in the decree.

Nicholls, C. J., absent; ill.

CRIMINAL LAW—ALIBI—BURDEN OF PROOF—INSTRUC-TIONS.—The whole evidence, including that relating to an alibi, should be considered and weighed, and if, after such consideration, the jury have a reasonable doubt of the defendant's guilt arising out of any part of the evidence, they must acquit: Prince v. State, 100 Ala. 144; 46 Am. St. Rep, 28, and note. The preponderance of evidence must be in favor of an alibi, but it need not be sufficient to remove all reasonable doubt thereof: State v. Jackson, 36 S. C. 487; 31 Am. St. Rep. 890, and note. The burden of proof is on the accused: Carlton v. People, 150 Ill. 181; 41 Am. St. Rep. 346. It is error to charge the jury that the alibi must be proved beyond a reasonable doubt: Miles v. State, 93 Ga. 117; 44 Am. St. Rep. 140.

INSTRUCTIONS—INCORRECT IN PART BUT CORRECT AS A WHOLE.—Where a charge as a whole is correct, the judgment will not be reversed, although an extract from the charge, taken by itself, is erroneous: Cushman v. Somers, 62 Vt. 132; 22 Am. St. Rep. 92; State v. Turner, 29 S. C. 34; 13 Am. St. Rep. 706. There is no necessity for qualifying each instruction by an express reference to the others: Owens v. Kansas City etc. Ry. Co., 95 Mo. 169; 6 Am. St. Rep. 39, and note; see Gibson v. State, 89 Ala. 121; 18 Am. St. Rep. 96.

STATE *v.* SMITH.

[49 LOUISIANA ANNUAL, 1515.]

CRIMINAL LAW—REINDICTMENT NOT NECESSARY.—If an accused is tried under an indictment charging him with murder and found guilty of manslaughter, and, on moving for, obtains a new trial, he need not be reindicted before he can again be tried for the offense.

CRIMINAL LAW.—THE REFERENCE BY THE PROSECUTING ATTORNEY to the fact that the indictment charges the defendant with murder, but that on a former trial he was convicted of manslaughter only, and a new trial having been granted, that he is now on trial for the latter offense, is proper and not prejudicial to the accused.

CRIMINAL LAW—AUTREFOIS ACQUIT, PLEADING OF AS TO A HIGHER OFFENSE CHARGED.—If to an indictment of murder the defendant pleads autrefois acquit, and the plea is sustained as to the charge of murder, he may be tried for the lesser offense of manslaughter, included within the indictment, if it is clear that the action of the court sustaining the plea was not intended to go any further than to protect the defendant from further prosecution for murder.

M. J. Cunningham, attorney general, Alex. Hebert, district attorney, and P. A. Simmons, Jr., for the appellee.

Clarence S. Hebert, for the appellant.

1516 NICHOLLS, C. J. On January 13, 1897, the grand jury of the parish of Iberville indicted the defendant for murder. On this indictment he was tried by a petit jury on January 25th, and on the following day was found guilty of manslaughter. He immediately applied for a new trial on the ground: 1. That the verdict was contrary to law and the evidence; and 2. Because one of the jurors in the case was not a citizen of the parish. After evidence adduced the motion was sustained, but without assignment of the grounds upon which the ruling was made.

On July 12, 1897, at a subsequent term of the court, defendant filed the following plea in the case: "Now into the court by his undersigned counsel, comes the defendant, and, upon suggesting to the court that he has been acquitted of the charge of murder by a petit jury at the last jury term of this court in and for the parish of Iberville, pleads said acquittal in bar of any further proceedings against him for murder. Wherefore he prays that said charge of murder against him be dismissed, and further prays for costs and for general relief."

We find in this record the following entry as of the 13th of July:

"State v. Dennis Smith.—The plea of autrefois acquit filed in this cause was this day taken up, submitted, and sustained by the court in so far as the charge of murder was concerned."

The case was on the 15th of July fixed for trial for the 28th of the month. On that day leave was granted defendant's counsel to file a "protest," which, according to the record, was "taken up, submitted, and overruled by the court."

It read as follows: "Into this honorable court comes Dennis Smith, by his counsel, and, suggesting to the court that a plea of autrefois acquit urged by [1517] him, in so far as the charge of murder is concerned, has been sustained by the court, as appears from the minutes of the court hereto annexed as a part hereof, protests against going to trial in this case for the following reasons: 1. Because no indictment or information is filed in this case charging him with any crime, as required by law; 2. Because if any indictment or information has been filed herein, which is not admitted, but specially denied, no copy of same has been served on appearer, as required by law. Wherefore, the premises considered, appearer protests against going to the trial of this case until these requirements of the law have been complied with, and further prays for general, special, and equitable relief in the premises."

On the trial of this exception or protest it was admitted "that the indictment against the defendant for murder in suit No. 1355, State v. Dennis Smith, a true bill,, Charles E. Grace, foreman, indictment—murder—was served on the defendant as required by law, as stated in the return of the sheriff of said service."

The court, over defendant's objections, ruled him to trial, and he reserved a bill of exceptions to the ruling and action of the court. In this bill he stated and complained that, although the original indictment in the case was duly served on the accused previous to the first trial of the accused for murder, neither the same indictment with the verdict thereon nor any other indictment was served upon him.

The judge's addendum to the bill was as follows:

"The motion, so far as it affects the validity of the indictment, is not in the proper form as required by the rules of criminal practice, which should have an exception in bar or a motion in arrest of judgment. As the legal question presented under the second ground of the motion is also involved in the first, it may be considered of better consequence.

"The idea of defendant's counsel is that the defendant should have been reindicted. I regard this question as settled adversely to counsel's idea, and deem it only necessary to refer the court to the authority on the subject: State v. Bryd, 31 La. Ann. 419; State v. Hornsby, 8 Rob. 588; 41 Am. Dec. 314.

"The cases of State v. Chandler, 5 La. Ann. 489, 52 Am. Dec. 599, and State v. Desmond, 5 La. Ann. 398, were remanded to be tried evidently on the same indictment. The counsel for defendant was apprehensive that the [1518] jury might be misled by the charge of murder, and desired that i* might be eliminated in advance by a motion that he presented. This was sustained in so far as the charge of murder was concerned. I understood that the counsel acquiesced in this proposition. Having been legally arraigned, as the record shows, and from the admission of the defendant previous to the first trial, a second arraignment was unnecessary.

"Defendant reserved two other bills of exception. The first bill recites that when the jurors were called and examined on their voir dire the district attorney proceeded to state to them that the accused had been indicted for murder, but that a petit jury had found him guilty of manslaughter, which in law amounted to an acquittal for murder, and that, therefore, the accused was only on trial for manslaughter; that accused objected to these explanations and statements, for the reasons stated in the bill of exceptions reserved to the ruling of the court to trial over his protest and objections, and because that the statements were calculated to prejudice the case of the accused; that the court overruled the objections and permitted the district attorney to make these statements and explanations to the jurors who were in turn accepted and sworn to try the case."

The judge made the following statement in regard to this bill:

"The question as stated by counsel is more elaborate than that propounded by the district attorney, which was that defendant had been indicted for murder and was now being tried for manslaughter, but I imagine that this is immaterial. The jurors were on their voir dire, and the question was essential in order to inform them of the character of the case to be tried, and was according to the rule which is invariably pursued in criminal trials. The question was also based upon facts apparent upon the indictment, which would have been disclosed to the jury when the indictment was delivered to them for deliberation. It would be necessary, further, for the court to state the facts involved in the question, in order that the jury might not be misguided and for the protection of the defendant."

The second bill was substantially to the same effect, differing simply in the fact that it is recited that the district attorney made the statements and explanations to the jury after the jurors had been sworn and after reading to them the indictment.

[1510] The court's addendum to this bill was that the objections in the same were substantially embodied in the other bills and presented the same idea; that the jury could not have been prejudiced, as they were instructed in the charge that the indictment for murder and the verdict indorsed thereon should not be allowed to influence them, and the latter part of this instruction was given at the request of defendant's counsel. That, in fact, the instruction and statement of the counsel were proper and necessary in order that the jury might fairly and properly perform their duty.

In the brief filed on behalf of the defendant his counsel declares: "There is only one point to be determined by the court, which is, Was there a valid subsisting indictment against the accused? If there was, it is certain that an explanation to the jurors as to how the defendant came to be tried for manslaughter was necessary, and it is also certain that the indictment had to be read to them, and the statements and explanations made by the district attorney at the time of reading to them were again necessary . . . . the whole controversy has arisen from the judge of the lower court sustaining the plea of autrefois acquit without reserving to the state any right she might have to proceed against the defendant for manslaughter. In other words, defendant contends that the court dismissed entirely the indictment against him absolutely and without reservation, sustaining his plea of autrefois acquit as to the charge of murder, and that if the district attorney still desired to prosecute for manslaughter he was

bound to have him reindicted by the grand jury, or he should
have filed an information charging that offense. . . . . It is
perfectly clear that a party convicted of murder on an indictment
charging murder can, if he obtains a new trial, be tried for murder on the same indictment. The theory of the law is, that
while the conviction for the lesser offense dismisses from the indictment, not actually, but by legal contemplation, the charge
of the greater offense, it retains in the indictment the charge of
the less offense. Suppose, however, a man is convicted of manslaughter on an indictment charging murder and a new trial is
granted, if the district attorney enters a nolle prosequi as to the
charge of murder, can he try the defendant for manslaughter on
the same indictment if he has not reserved the right to do so?
Most assuredly not. When the nolle prosequi is entered as to
the charge of murder without reservation, all the words in the
indictment that charge murder go, therefore [1520] there is no
charge of manslaughter left in the indictment." Defendant relies upon State v. Hornsby, 8 Rob. 584; 41 Am. Dec. 314; State
v. Byrd, 31 La. Ann. 419; Brittain v. State, 7 Humph. 159; People v. Porter, 4 Park. C. C. 524. It will be seen that defendant
concedes that but for the fact that he filed as he did a plea of
autrefois acquit so far as the charge of murder was concerned,
and that the court sustained the same, he would have no ground
of complaint, and his contention even now is simply that he cannot be tried on the original indictment but under an information or a newly found indictment. Where, upon the trial of a
person under an indictment for murder, accused is convicted of
manslaughter, but on appeal the conviction is set aside on his
motion, it is unquestionable [conceding that he might not be
liable to be put upon his trial a second time for murder] that he
may be tried for manslaughter on the same indictment—that
neither law nor jurisprudence require that he could only and
legally be tried on a new indictment specially charging manslaughter: State v. Dunn, 41 La. Ann. 612; State v. West, 45
La. Ann. 933. It is also clear that upon the second trial on the
original indictment the district attorney and the court would
necessarily have to explain to the jury the modification in the
situation, resulting from the effect of the verdict upon the first
trial: McQueen v. State, 103 Ala. 12; State v. Evans, 40 La.
Ann. 218. We have, in view of these facts, simply to inquire
whether the filing by the defendant of the plea of autrefois acquit as to the charge of murder, and the ruling of the court
thereon, had the effect which the defendant contends for.

It is useless to enter into a general discussion as to what the situation would have been had the district attorney entered in the case a formal nolle prosequi as to the charge of murder for the reason that there was no nolle prosequi at all entered.

The whole claim is, that by reason of the fact that defendant had under the circumstances of this case filed a plea of autrefois acquit so far as the charge of murder was concerned, and had succeeded in obtaining from the district court a ruling sustaining that position, the whole indictment necessarily fell. If it be assumed as a conceded fact that the defendant, by having been on trial before a jury under an indictment for murder, and by having been found guilty of manslaughter by the jury, was protected, under the circumstances of this case, through that verdict, from a further prosecution for [1621] murder, though the sentence was set aside and a new trial accorded defendant on his prayer (which is what the district court decided), the consequences to flow from that assumed condition of affairs would be those which the law itself attached to it. Defendant, by interposing before a second trial a plea of autrefois acquit, as he did, so far as the charge of murder was concerned, and by obtaining a ruling of the district court sustaining that claim, acquired through that ruling no position other and different as to the after-results of the declared existing situation from what he would have otherwise held had the actual legal situation been such as the court decreed it to be. The ruling, standing unreversed, would protect defendant from a second prosecution for murder, but it would leave untouched all questions as to defendant's liability under charges for crimes other than murder, and all questions as to the time and method of the presentation of such charges. These matters would have to be tested as they arose, by the application to them of legal rules and the jurisprudence of the state.

So tested, defendant's contention that he is entitled under the circumstances of this case to be brought to trial only upon a new indictment or an information specifically charging him with manslaughter finds no support. The indictment did not fall as the result of the court's decree—the charge against appellant under the existing indictment was simply reduced to manslaughter: State v. Evans, 40 La. Ann. 218. The situation is precisely the same to-day as if the district attorney of his own accord, without any plea filed by the accused, had announced to the jury that defendant, though charged with murder, could no longer be legally tried for murder, that he would be tried by them under the original indictment, but simply upon a charge of manslaughter. Had matters taken that shape and form, the accused, under the jurisprudence of the state, could have found no legal ground for complaint.

The court has decreed in this case that defendant is protected by the verdict of the jury, though set aside by the court, from any further prosecution for murder. The state has acquiesced in that decree. It is not before us for review. We have to accept it as the law of the case. It is clear, besides, that neither defendant's plea nor the court's action on it were intended to go further than to protect defendant from further prosecution for murder. The qualified language both of the plea and of the ruling upon it show that the former [1522] was not aimed at and did not result in throwing the whole indictment out of court. It could not be claimed under that language that it was either urged before the court or admitted by it that by reason of jeopardy incurred through the first trial defendant was protected against a charge of manslaughter. Appellant, as we understand, advances no pretension of that character.

The judgment, in our opinion, is correct, and it is hereby affirmed.

FORMER ACQUITTAL—DEGREES OF CRIME.—If an accused has been on trial for a homicide or other offense which embraces different degrees, and has been acquitted of the higher degree, he cannot again be put on trial for that degree, and it is the duty of the court to so inform the jury: Conde v. State, 35 Tex. Crim. Rep. 98; 60 Am. St. Rep. 22, and note. Upon this question, however, there is a conflict of opinion arising from a difference in theory as to the effect of granting a new trial. By some cases it is held that the effect of granting a new trial is to set aside the whole verdict and leave the case to be retried upon the same issues as the first trial: State v. Kessler, Utah, 142; post 911. The weight of authority is opposed to this view: Extended note to Commonwealth v. Arnold, 4 Am. St. Rep. 117-120. See, also, monographic note to Roberts v. State, 58 Am. Dec. 536-548, as to what facts sustain a plea of former acquittal or conviction.

TANNER *v.* MERRILL.

[108 MICHIGAN, 58.]

PAYMENT OF PART OF A DEMAND, WHEN EXTIN-GUISHES THE WHOLE.—If there is a dispute between a debtor and creditor respecting the amount due, payment of the part admitted to be due and the taking of a receipt in full, accompanied with the refusal to pay more, discharges the whole debt, in the absence of mistake, fraud, or undue influence.

ACCORD AND SATISFACTION.—If there is a controversy between a debtor and creditor as to the amount due, and the debtor tenders the amount which he claims to be due on condition that the creditor accept it in discharge of the whole demand, and it is thereupon accepted, there is an accord and satisfaction, and the creditor cannot maintain a subsequent action to recover the difference between the amount received and that which he claimed to have been due.

D. P. Foote, for the appellants.

Rowland Connor, for the appellee.

58 HOOKER, J. The defendants appeal from a judgment recovered against them at circuit. They are lumbermen, and the plaintiff worked for them at Georgian Bay, his transportation from Saginaw to that place having been paid by them. When he quit work, a question arose as to who should pay this, under the contract of employment, and defendants' superintendent declined to pay any transportation. **59** The plaintiff needed the money due him to get home, and showed a telegram announcing the illness or death of his mother, and said that he must go home, to which the superintendent replied that "he did not pay any man's fare"; whereupon a receipt in full was signed, and the money due, after deducting transportation, was paid. ·The plaintiff testified that they had no dispute, only he claimed the fare and the superintendent refused to allow it.

The most important question arises over a request to charge upon the part of the defendants, which reads as follows: "The testimony of the plaintiff is, that at the time the receipt put in evidence in this case was signed by him, he claimed that his railroad fare should not be deducted from his wages; that this was denied by the agents and superintendent of defendants, and it was taken out of his wages; that he then signed the receipt with full knowledge of its contents, and of the fact that his railroad fare had been taken out of his wages. This being so, the receipt in this case, upon the plaintiff's own testimony, cannot be contradicted. While a receipt may be contradicted in certain cases, it must be in a case of mistake, ignorance of fact, fraud, or when some unconscionable advantage has been taken of one by the other party. Therefore, the receipt, in this case, shows a full settlement of all claims plaintiff had against the defendants."

The only theory upon which it can be contended that this request should have been given is, that the plaintiff accepted less than he claimed, but no more than defendants admitted, to be due, and gave a receipt in full when the defendants' superintendent refused to pay more. We do not discover any testimony tending to show an agreement to accept as payment, either in full or by way of compromise, except the receipt, and the question resolves itself into this, whether a receipt in full is conclusive of the question of defendant's liability, when it is given upon payment of a portion of a claim admittedly due, accompanied by a refusal to pay more, in the absence of mistake, fraud, duress, or undue influence.

⁶⁰ It is urged upon behalf of the plaintiff that receipts are always open to explanation, and that there is no consideration to support the acceptance of a portion of a valid claim as full payment. The cases which counsel cite do not support the broad contention of plaintiff's counsel, which would seriously derange business affairs if it should be sustained. The doctrine that the receipt of part payment must rest upon a valid consideration to be effective in discharge of the entire debt is carefully limited to cases where the debt is liquidated, by agreement of the parties or otherwise, which was not the case here. It was in dispute. In the case of St. Louis etc. R. R. Co. v. Davis, 35 Kan. 464, the opinion says that "it is a well-settled principle

of law that the payment of a part of an ascertained, overdue,
and undisputed debt, although accepted as full satisfaction, and
a receipt in full is given, does not estop the creditor from recovering the balance.   In such a case the agreement to accept a
smaller sum is regarded to be without consideration." The case
of Day v. Gardner, 42 N. J. Eq. 199, was one where the agreement was to forgive a debt, implying its existence. In Hasted
v. Dodge (Iowa, Dec. 13, 1887), 35 N. W. Rep. 462, the opinion
of Mr. Justice Rothrock shows the debt not to have been in dispute.   Moreover, the doctrine was not applicable to the case
for reasons shown: See, also, American Bridge Co. v. Murphy,
13 Kan. 35. In Bailey v. Day, 26 Me. 88, the claim was
liquidated by judgment. In Hayes v. Massachusetts Life Ins.
Co., 125 Ill. 639, the court apply the doctrine relied upon, but
expressly state that "this rule has no application where property other than money is taken in satisfaction, or where there is
an honest compromise of unliquidated or disputed demands":
See, also, Bishop on Contracts, sec. 50; 2 Parsons on Contracts,
618. In Marion v. Heimbach, 62 Minn. 215, the court say:
"But where the claim is unliquidated, it would seem to be true
that if the creditor is tendered a sum less than his claim, upon
the condition that, if it is accepted, it must be in full satisfaction of his whole claim, his acceptance is an accord and satisfaction": See, [61] also, Fuller v. Kemp, 138 N. Y. 231, where the
same doctrine is held; Fire Ins. Assn. v. Wickham, 141 U. S. 577.

The important fact to ascertain is, whether the plaintiff's
claim was a liquidated claim or not. If it was there was no consideration for the discharge. If not, the authorities are in substantial accord that part payment of the claim may discharge
the debt, if it is so received. Upon the undisputed facts, the
claim of the plaintiff, as made, was not liquidated. It was not
even admitted, but, on the contrary, was denied, because the defendants claimed that it had been partially paid by a valid offset.
While the controversy was over the offset, it is plain that the
amount due the plaintiff was in dispute. If so, it is difficult to
understand how it could be treated as a liquidated claim, unless
it is to be said that a claim may be liquidated piecemeal, and that,
so far as the items are agreed upon, it is liquidated, and to that
extent is not subject to adjustment on a basis of part payment.
Cases are not numerous in which just this phase of the question
appears. This would seem remarkable, unless we are to assume
that, in calling a claim unliquidated, the courts have alluded to
the whole claim, and have considered that, where the amount is

not agreed upon, the claim as a whole is unliquidated, and therefore subject to adjustment. If this is not true, no man can pay an amount that he admits to be due without being subject to action whenever and so often as his creditor may choose to claim that he was not fully paid, no matter how solemn may have been his acknowledgment of satisfaction, so long as it is not a release under seal.

The general rule is a technical one, and there are many exceptions. It has been said that it "often fosters bad faith," and that "the history of judicial decisions upon the subject has shown a constant effort to escape from its absurdity and injustice": Harper v. Graham, 20 Ohio, 105; Kellogg v. Richards, 14 Wend. 116; Brooks v. White, 2 Met. 283; 37 Am. Dec. 95. Again, [62] it is said to be "rigid and unreasonable," and "a rule that defeats the expressed intentions of the parties, and, therefore, should not be extended to embrace cases not within the letter of it": Wescott v. Waller, 47 Ala. 492; Johnston v. Brannan, 5 Johns. 268; Simmons v. Almy, 103 Mass. 35. See Milliken v. Brown, 1 Rawle, 391, where the rule is vigorously denounced. It has no application in cases of claims against the government. If one accepts the amount allowed it is a discharge of the whole claim: United States v. Adams, 7 Wall. 463; United States v. Child, 12 Wall. 232. See, also, Wapello Co. v. Sinnaman, 1 G. Greene, 413; Brick v. County of Plymouth, 63 Iowa, 462; Perry v. Cheboygan, 55 Mich. 250; Calkins v. State, 13 Wis. 389. Again, it has been repeatedly held that part payment is a bar to a claim for interest. Another exception is found in composition with creditors.

It is believed that we may safely treat this claim as one claim, not as two, and as unliquidated, inasmuch as it was not admitted. In McGlynn v. Billings, 16 Vt. 329, the defendant after an examination of accounts, claimed that he owed the plaintiff eighty-two dollars, and drew a check for that sum, and tendered it as payment in full. It was refused and it was delivered to a third person, with directions to deliver it whenever the plaintiff would receive it as payment in full. This was done, and it was held to discharge the debt. In Hills v. Sommer, 53 Hun, 392, the plaintiffs shipped lemons to dealers in St. Joseph, Missouri, and were notified that some were defective, with a claim of a specific rebate, which plaintiffs refused to allow. A draft was subsequently sent for the amount which the defendants had previously expressed their willingness to allow, with a letter stating that it was in payment of the invoice. The draft was cashed, and

action brought for the remainder of the claim. Verdict was
directed for the defendants. Pierce **v.** Pierce, 25 Barb. 243,
seems to be a similar case. In Potter v. Douglass, 44 Conn. 541,
plaintiff refused forty-five dollars, which was [68] tendered in
full payment of a claim. He took it, however, on account, as
he said, and wrote a receipt to that effect, which defendant refused, for the reason that it stated that the money was received
on account. The plaintiff, however, kept the money. It does
not appear that this amount of forty-five dollars was disputed.
Apparently, it was not. Yet the court called the claim an unliquidated demand, and held it to have been discharged. In Perkins v. Headley, 49 Mo. App. 562, it is said: "But if there is a
controversy between him [the creditor] and his debtor as to
the amount which is due, and if the debtor tenders the amount
which he claims to be due, but tenders it on the condition that
the creditor accept it in discharge of his whole demand, and
the creditor does accept it, that will be an accord and satisfaction
as a conclusion of law."

While no Michigan case decisive of this question is cited, and
we recall none, it was held in Houghton v. Ross, 54 Mich. 335,
that: "A receipt which states its purpose to be for a complete
settlement, and which covers the whole period of dealing, is
equivalent to an account stated; and though it is open to explanation as to errors or omissions, it cannot be treated as if it had
not been meant to cover everything."

And in Pratt v. Castle, 91 Mich. 484, it was said that: "1. Settlements are favored by the law, and will not be set aside, except
for fraud, mistake, or duress; 2. A settlement evidenced by the
execution of mutual receipts of 'one dollar, in full for all debts,
dues, and demands to this date,' except as to certain specified
items, is conclusive, in the absence of fraud or mistake, as to
all prior dealings between the parties not covered by the excepted
items": See, also, Dowling v. Eggemann, 47 Mich. 171.

It therefore appears that such settlements should have weight,
and it seems reasonable to hold that the rule contended for does
not apply, for the reason that this was an [64] unliquidated demand, although a certain portion of it was not questioned.
Clearly, the claim was disputed, and, so far as this record shows,
the defendant's superintendent was given to understand that the
money paid was accepted in full satisfaction, as plaintiff's own evidence shows that he gave the receipt without protest, and without stating to the defendants' superintendent what he said, aside,
to his fellow laborers, that it would make no difference if they

did give the receipts. To hold otherwise would be a recognition
of the "mental reservation" more effective than just. Upon the
plaintiff's own testimony, he accepted the money with the knowledge that the defendants claimed that the amount paid was all
that was his due, and gave a receipt in full. There is nothing in
the case to negative the inference, naturally to be drawn from
this testimony, that there was an accord and satisfaction of an
unliquidated demand.

The judgment must be reversed. No new trial should be
ordered.

Long and Grant, JJ., concurred with Hooker, J.

Montgomery, J., and McGrath, C. J., dissented.

_____

PAYMENT—ACCEPTANCE OF LESS THAN THE SUM
DUE.—Whether the payment of a less sum will operate as a discharge of the entire debt when the parties agree that it shall be in
full satisfaction, depends entirely upon whether there is any consideration existing to support such agreement. The slightest consideration will suffice to answer the requirements of this rule and
make the agreement binding: Monographic note to Jones v. Perkins,
64 Am. Dec. 139. The acceptance from the maker by the payee of
a note of a sum less than that actually due, with a distinct agreement
that such payment is made in full satisfaction of the debt, accompanied by a surrender of the note, extinguishes the entire debt;
Clayton v. Clark, 74 Miss. 499; 60 Am. St. Rep. 521, and note; note
to Nassoiy v. Tomlinson, 51 Am. St. Rep. 699. See, however, White
v. Kuntz, 107 N. Y. 518; 1 Am. St. Rep. 886, and note.

ACCORD AND SATISFACTION—WHAT AMOUNTS TO.—
Accord is a satisfaction agreed upon between the party injuring and
the party injured, which when performed is a bar to all actions upon
this account: Mitchell v. Hawley, 4 Denio, 414; 47 Am. Dec. 260. To
constitute accord and satisfaction, it must appear that the satisfaction made was advantageous to the plaintiff, and it must be averred
and proved that it was accepted: Diller v. Brubaker. 52 Pa. St. 498;
91 Am. Dec. 177. It is the general rule that the payment of a less
sum, though accepted in full, where there is a certain amount due,
cannot be taken as a good accord and satisfaction: Harrison v. Close,
2 Johns. 448; 3 Am. Dec. 444; Rose v. Hall, 26 Conn. 392; 68 Am. Dec.
402. See monographic note to Jones v. Perkins, 64 Am. Dec. 138,
139.

MUTUAL FIRE INSURANCE COMPANY *v.* PHOENIX FURNITURE COMPANY.

[108 MICHIGAN, 170.]

JUDGMENT OF SISTER STATE.—A judgment or decree of the courts of one state is conclusive in those of another, if the court pronouncing it had jurisdiction of the cause and the parties.

JUDGMENT AGAINST CORPORATIONS, WHETHER BINDING UPON STOCKHOLDERS.—A judgment against a corporation determining the amount of its indebtedness and of its assets, and directing an assessment upon its members or stockholders, for the purpose of paying its debts and expenses, is conclusive in a subsequent action brought in another state against one of such members, or stockholders, to collect his proportion of such assessment.

JUDGMENTS—CORPORATION AND STOCKHOLDERS, PRIVITY BETWEEN.—A stockholder is so far an integral part of the corporation that, in view of the law, he is privy to proceedings touching the body of which he is a member, and a judgment against it establishing the existence and amount of its liabilities is conclusive against him in proceedings to compel him to discharge his proportion thereof.

JUDGMENTS AND DECREES CANNOT BE ATTACKED COLLATERALLY because they include items which courts other than those by whom they were rendered may hold to be illegal.

Action by a receiver of a mutual insurance company upon a premium note dated Chicago, May 1, 1889, promising to pay, in installments, the sum designated therein at such time as the directors of the company might order and assess. In October, 1890, an action was brought in the circuit court of Cook county, Illinois, against the corporation, in which a receiver was appointed. After the appointment of such receiver, the court determined the amount of the assets and of the indebtedness of the corporation and the reasonable expenses of the suit and receivership, and authorized the receiver to assess upon each of the members of the corporation sixty-five per cent of the amount of his premium note. The receiver made the assessment as authorized, and this action was brought to recover the defendant's proportion thereof. The plaintiff obtained judgment and the defendant appealed.

Fletcher & Wanty, for the appellant.

D. J. Schuyler and Mark Norris, for the appellee.

171 GRANT, J. After a full argument upon the rehearing of this cause, we are satisfied that we were in error in reversing the judgment. The testimony was not returned, and the case is before us on findings of fact and law, to which no exceptions

were taken. The sole question, therefore, is, Do the facts found
support the judgment?

[172] We held in Detroit etc. Ins. Co. v. Merrill, 101 Mich. 393,
that the defendants, under such a note, were not liable to an
assessment for unearned or return premiums. That case would,
of course, control this, unless the decree of the Illinois court is
conclusive upon the courts of this state. The constitution of
the United States declares that "full faith and credit shall be
given in each state to the public acts, records, and judicial proceedings of every other state": U. S. Const., art. 4, sec. 1. In
the early case of Mills v. Duryee, 7 Cranch, 481, it was held that
the decrees and judgments of the courts of one state were conclusive in the courts of sister states. This case has since been
uniformly followed. Where a court has jurisdiction of the cause
and of the parties, its judgment is conclusive in other courts,
and the only remedy is by direct proceeding in the original cause:
Hanley v. Donoghue, 116 U. S. 4; Cole v. Cunningham, 133
U. S. 111; Bonesteel v. Todd, 9 Mich. 371; 80 Am. Dec. 90. It
is conceded that as against the corporation itself, and the directors and officers thereof, the rule applies. It is, however, contended that [173] it does not apply to a stockholder of such corporation who is not made a direct party to the original suit.
That is the question in this case.

We are not dealing with a case where a stockholder is interposing the defense of payment or any other defense which was
not passed upon in the original suit against the corporation. In
such a case there is no judgment or decree of the court of a sister state which other courts must recognize. But the very point
now urged as a defense was involved and determined by the Illinois' court. This was an Illinois contract. These notes were
choses in action, were first in possession of the company in Illinois, were turned over by it to the receiver, and were under the direct control of the Illinois court. That court entered a decree, upon evidence placed before it, determining the amount of assets
and debts, and the amount of the assessment necessary to liquid-
ate its liabilities. If every stockholder may now contest this decree, the difficulty thus thrown in the way of an orderly and practical settlement of the affairs of the insolvent corporation is [174]
apparent. Different courts might adopt different rulings upon
the amount of the assessment. We think the better doctrine is,
that each stockholder or member of the corporation is an integral
part thereof, and is represented in such suit through the corporation itself, and that such decree is binding and conclusive upon

him. Two courts have so held in regard to the case now under consideration: Rand v. Insurance Co., 58 Ill. App. 528; Parker v. Stoughton Mill Co., 91 Wis. 174; 51 Am. St. Rep. 881.

In the latter case two points were raised: 1. That the receiver in Illinois could not sue in the courts of Wisconsin; and 2. That the assessment was inequitable and unjust, and hence should not be enforced. The distinction between the rights of property situated in other states, and those of choses in action, is there very clearly pointed out. Upon the first point the court say: "There is no question here of a transfer of property in this state. No such transfer was attempted. The property in question—that is, the defendant's note and its liability to pay assessments—was in Illinois, at the office of [175] the company. They were choses in action, and their situs was at the residence of the company."

Upon the second point the court say: "If a judgment is conclusive in the state where rendered it is conclusive here. The decree by which the assessment in question was made was undoubtedly conclusive on the members or policy holders of the defunct company, unless attacked in a direct proceeding, notwithstanding they were not present when it was rendered. . . . . We can come to no other conclusion than that we are bound, under the constitutional requirement of 'full faith and credit,' to hold that the decree making the assessment in question, being conclusive in Illinois upon all members and policy holders, unless attacked by direct proceeding, is conclusive here, and not open to collateral attack."

The point appears to be expressly decided in Hawkins v. Glenn, 131 U. S. 319. The proceedings in that case were substantially the same as in this. The defense was that the stockholder was not a party to the suit, that the cause of action was barred by the statute of limitations, that he was not responsible on one hundred and fifty shares, and that interest should not have been allowed. The stockholder was sued in North Carolina. A decree had been rendered in a court of chancery in Virginia, which had ascertained the [176] extent of the liabilities and assets of the corporation, and decreed the assessment required to pay its liabilities. The court held the decree conclusive, and, in deciding it, speaking through Chief Justice Fuller, said: "A stockholder is so far an integral part of the corporation that, in view of the law, he is privy to the proceedings touching the body of which he is a member": Citing Sanger v. Upton, 91 U. S. 56. The same question was again before the court in Glenn v. Liggett,

135 U. S. 533, and the same conclusion reached, quoting from
Hawkins v. Glenn, 131 U. S. 319. The same was held in Lycoming Fire Ins. Co. v. Langley, 62 Md. 211.

The learned counsel for the defendant cite Chandler v. Brown,
77 Ill. 333, and Lamar Ins. Co. v. Gulick, 102 Ill. 41. These
cases are distinguished from a case like the present in Great
Western Tel. Co. v. Gray, 122 Ill. 630. The two former cases
were based upon a statute which provided that stockholders
should be made parties to the suit: Ill. Rev. Stats. 1891, c. 32,
secs. 1-49. The decree of the Illinois court in this case was
based upon an act in regard to the dissolution of insurance companies: Ill. Rev. Stats. 1891, c. 73, secs. 103-111. This does not
provide for any service upon or notice to the stockholders [177]
or members, but confers the entire jurisdiction in such cases
upon the courts. Upon the question of notice to stockholders,
see Wardle v. Cummings, 86 Mich. 400.

Mr. May, in his work on Insurance, volume 2, section 557,
says "the receiver of an insolvent company stands upon no better footing" than would the directors in making an assessment;
and cites Jackson v. Roberts, 31 N. Y. 304; Embree v. Shideler,
36 Ind. 423. If these decisions sustain the rule contended for,
we could not follow them, as we think they are opposed to the
clear weight of authority. The New York statute is clearly
different from that in the present case. It reads as follows: "In
case the corporation, in regard to which a receiver has been or
shall hereafter be appointed, is or shall be a mutual insurance
company, such receiver shall have full power, under the authority and sanction of the court appointing him, to make all such
assessments on the premium notes belonging to such corporation
as may be necessary to pay the debts of such corporation, as by
the charter thereof the directors of such corporation have authority to make; and the notice of such assessment may be given in
the same manner as is provided in the charter of said company
for the directors of said company to give; and the said receiver
shall have the like rights and remedies upon and in consequence
of the nonpayment of such assessments as are given to the corporation or the directors thereof by the charter of such corporation": Laws 1852, c. 71, sec. 2.

It thus appears that the power of the receiver was expressly
limited to the power of the board of directors, and to the modus
operandi of collecting the assessments.

In Embree v. Shideler, 36 Ind. 423, it appeared upon the face
of the complaint that neither the receiver, nor the court to which

he had reported his action, had examined and determined upon the validity of the claims against the company. This was expressly required by the charter of the company. It was therefore said that "the assessment is the act of the receiver, and in and with him is the authority to act in the premises."

[178] The decree in the present case was erroneous only in that it included some items which, under Detroit etc. Ins. Co. v. Merrill, 101 Mich. 393, this court would have excluded. Judgments and decrees cannot be attacked collaterally because they include items which courts, other than those by whom they were rendered, might hold to be illegal: See Morawetz on Private Corporations, sec. 822.

The judgment must be affirmed.

Montgomery and Hooker, JJ., concurred with Grant, J.

JUDGMENTS OF SISTER STATES — CONCLUSIVENESS OF.—A judgment of a court of one state having jurisdiction of the parties and of the subject matter is, in the absence of fraud, binding upon the courts of another state in a suit involving the same parties and subject matter, though the suit in the latter state was instituted first: Memphis etc. R. R. Co. v. Grayson, 88 Ala. 572; 16 Am. St. Rep. 69, and note. See note to Messier v. Amery, 1 Am. Dec. 324-326. A judgment rendered in one state has the same effect and is as conclusive in any other state where brought into controversy as in the state where rendered: Peet v. Hatcher, 112 Ala. 514; 57 Am. St. Rep. 45, and note; Parker v. Stoughton Mill Co., 91 Wis. 174; 51 Am. St. Rep. 881.

JUDGMENTS AGAINST CORPORATIONS—CONCLUSIVENESS UPON STOCKHOLDERS. — A judgment against a corporation is conclusive against the stockholders in any action or proceeding to enforce their individual liability, and there is no legitimate distinction between cases in which actions are brought against stockholders on account of unpaid subscriptions and those wherein the object is to enforce the statutory or constitutional liability: Holland v. Duluth Iron etc. Co., 65 Minn. 324; 60 Am. St. Rep. 480, and note; Nichols v. Stevens, 123 Mo. 96; 45 Am. St. Rep. 514, and note. See monographic note to Thompson v. Reno Sav. Bank, 3 Am. St. Rep. 815, 858; also, Tatum v. Rosenthal, 95 Cal. 129; 29 Am. St. Rep. 97, and note.

JUDGMENTS — COLLATERAL ATTACK — WHEN ALLOWABLE.—A judgment may be collaterally impeached by one not a party or privy where the court rendering it had no jurisdiction of the case; where it was obtained by fraud or collusion, or where it was erroneously or unlawfully entered up to the prejudice of rights of third parties. Beyond this the law does not authorize parties to proceed in the collateral impeachment of judgments: Sidensparker v. Sidensparker, 52 Me. 481; 83 Am. Dec. 527. For an exhaustive discussion of the subject, see the monographic note to Morrill v. Morrill, 23 Am. St. Rep. 104-119; also note to Brown v. Wilson, 52 Am. St. Rep. 239.

MARKEY v. COREY.

[108 MICHIGAN, 184.]

NEGOTIABLE INSTRUMENTS—ASSIGNOR'S LIABILITY.
ONE WHO WRITES AND SIGNS ON THE BACK of a negotiable
instrument an assignment thereof is liable as an indorser to the same
extent as if he had merely indorsed his name without any other
words.

NEGOTIABLE INSTRUMENTS.—THE NEGOTIABILITY
OF A PROMISSORY NOTE IS NOT DESTROYED by writing thereon a statement that it is given in accordance with the terms of a
contract of even date between the same parties, though such contract, on being examined, shows that the note was one of three
given at the same time, payable at different dates, and that in the
contract the maker agreed that if any of them should not be paid
within ninety days after becoming due, then the payee had the right
to declare all the other notes to have become due and payable.

Edgar Weeks and Moore & Moore, for the appellant.

Ervin Palmer, for the appellees.

185 LONG, J. Defendant Corey entered into a written contract with Waldo and Varney for the sale of certain personal
property at the sum of two thousand five hundred dollars, payable two hundred dollars the first year, five hundred dollars the
second, and six hundred dollars each year thereafter, until the
whole amount should be paid, according to five promissory notes
executed at the same time. The contract also provided that certain stock should be deposited by the purchasers as further security for the payments. It was then provided: "But in case
said payments shall not be made as above provided, and in case
either or any of said payments shall remain unpaid for the period
of ninety days, then the party of the first part shall, at his
option, have the right to declare the whole remaining amounts
represented by said notes to have become due and payable."

On the face of each of the promissory notes was written:
186 "This note is given in accordance with the terms of a certain contract under the same date, between the same parties."

Subsequently the plaintiffs received from defendant Corey
an assignment of all his right, title, and interest in and to the
contract, stock, and notes. On the back of the note in suit was
indorsed: "I hereby assign the within note to Matthew M. Markey and Catherine Sundars."

This five hundred dollar note was not paid, and was protested,
and the plaintiffs brought this suit upon it against Waldo and
Varney as makers, and Corey as indorser. The declaration was
upon the common counts in assumpsit, with a copy of the note

attached. On the trial, however, the court permitted the plaintiffs to amend the declaration by averring the assignment of the contract and note. The case proceeded to trial, and plaintiffs' counsel offered in evidence the note and indorsement of assignment on it, together with the certificate of protest. Defendant's counsel objected to their introduction as against defendant Corey, claiming: 1. That the note in question was not a promissory note, and that plaintiffs could not recover upon it against Corey as indorser, but that, if they took any title to it, it was under the assignment; 2. That the contract was evidenced by the note and the other writing—the contract of sale. Plaintiffs' counsel then put in evidence, under objection, the contract of sale. The court thereupon directed a verdict in favor of plaintiffs for the amount of the note and interest, from which judgment defendant Corey alone appeals.

It is insisted here, by counsel for defendant Corey: 1. That if the plaintiffs took title to the note, it was under the assignment, and that, therefore, they could not sue in their own names, but, if they had a right of action, it must be brought in the name of the original party to the contract; 2. That the two papers must be taken as constituting [187] the contract, and that the note was not, therefore, a promissory note; 3. That Corey, by making the assignment to the plaintiffs, was not the indorser of the note, and could not be held liable as such.

The usual mode of transfer of a promissory note is by simply writing the indorser's name upon the back, or by writing also over it the direction to pay the indorsee named, or order, or to him or bearer. An indorsement, however, may be made in more enlarged terms, and the indorser be held liable as such. In Sands v. Wood, 1 Iowa, 263, the indorsement was, "I assign the within note to Mrs. Sarah Coffin." In Sears v. Lantz, 47 Iowa, 658, the indorsement on the note was, "I hereby assign all my right and title to Louis Meckley." And in each case the party so assigning was held as indorser, the court in the latter case saying of Sands v. Wood, 1 Iowa, 263: "He used no words that, in and of themselves, indicated that he had bound or made himself liable in case the maker, after demand, failed to pay the note. But it was held the law, as a legal conclusion, attached to the words used the liability that follows the indorsement of a promissory note": See, also, Duffy v. O'Conner, 7 Baxt. 498; Shelby v. Judd, 24 Kan. 166; Brotherton v. Street, 124 Ind. 599.

The rule of the American cases is well stated in Daniel on Negotiable Instruments, section 688 c, as follows: "The question arising in such cases is a nice one, and depends upon rules of legal interpretation. The mere signature of the payee, indorsed on the paper, imports an executed contract of assignment, with its implications, and also an executory contract of conditional liability, with its implications. The assignment would be as complete by the mere signature as with the words of assignment written over it. The conditional liability which is executory is implied by the executed contract of assignment, and the signature under it, which carries the legal title; and the question is, Does the writing over a signature an express assignment, which the law imports from [188] the signature per se, exclude and negative the idea of conditional liability, which the law also imports if such assignment were not expressed in full? We think not. . . . . When the thing done creates the implication of another to be done, we cannot think that the mere expression of the former in full can be regarded as excluding its consequence, when that consequence would follow if the expression were omitted."

The language used in the assignment to the note in suit does not negative the implication of the legal liability of the assignor as indorser, and as the words are to be construed, as strongly as their sense will allow, against the assignor, he must be held as indorser. This rule is fully supported in Hatch v. Barrett, 34 Kan. 230. See, also, Adams v. Blethen, 66 Me. 19; 22 Am. Rep. 547.

In the case of Aniba v. Yeomans, 39 Mich. 171, the assignment read as follows: "I hereby transfer my right, title, and interest of the within note to S. A. Yeomans." Mr. Justice Marston said in that case: "The right or interest passing, therefore, under the usual and customary indorsement, is much greater than the mere right, title, and interest of the payee; and where the transfer, as made, only attempts to pass the title and interest of the payee of the note, no greater right or interest than he then held can pass."

In other words, the learned justice seemed to think that the words used limited the transfer to the right and title he then held. While this holding appears to be at variance with the cases elsewhere, we think it readily distinguishable from the present, as here the words are, "I hereby assign the within note to Matthew M. Markey and Catherine Sundars," and do not purport to limit the liability of Corey as an indorser.

In Stevens v. Hannan, 86 Mich. 307, 24 Am. St. Rep. 125, the note sued upon was negotiable in form, and made payable 'to Batchelder, and he assigned it before maturity, as follows: "For value received, I hereby assign all interest in and to this note to Ralph E. Watson." Defendant insisted in [189] that case that the plaintiff could not sue in his own name, but should have sued in the name of the payee. It was said by Mr. Justice McGrath: "I do not think the point is well taken. . . . . If Batchelder's indorsement did not affect its negotiability, then Watson's indorsement entitled the plaintiff, as holder of the note, to sue in his own name."

It must be held, therefore, that the memorandum on the note did not relieve Corey from his liability as indorser.

The court was not in error in admitting the contract in evidence, as its purpose was to show that the note was not in fact limited by its provisions, and those provisions of the contract cited did not destroy the negotiability of the note: Daniel on Negotiable Instruments, sec. 48.

The judgment must be affirmed.

The other justices concurred.

NEGOTIABLE INSTRUMENTS — ASSIGNMENT — LIABILITY OF ASSIGNOR.—The law implies on a simple assignment of a note a promise by the assignor to refund the consideration of the assignment if the note be not justly demandable, or if by the obligor's insolvency or removal from the jurisdiction within which he resided at the date of the assignment, the assignee by ordinary diligence cannot coerce payment: Graves v. Tilford, 2 Duvall, 108; 87 Am. Dec. 483. See Mason v. Wash. Breese, 39; 12 Am. Dec. 138, and note; also, notes to Brown v. Montgomery, 75 Am. Dec. 407, and Emmerson v. Claywell, 58 Am. Dec. 647.

NEGOTIABLE INSTRUMENTS—PROVISIONS NOT AFFECTING NEGOTIABILITY.—Neither a provision in a promissory note for a specified additional interest after maturity, nor a recital therein to the effect that it may become due at the holder's option and by reason of the maker's default, at a date earlier than that fixed, destroys the character of the note as a negotiable instrument: Merrill v. Hurley, 6 S. Dak. 592; 55 Am. St. Rep. 859, and note; Heard v. Dubuque County Bank, 8 Neb. 10; 30 Am. Rep. 811; Kirk v. Dodge County Mut. Ins. Co., 39 Wis. 138; 20 Am. Rep. 39. See, also, Riker v. Sprague etc. Co., 14 R. I. 402; 51 Am. Rep. 413, and note.

DOWLING *v.* LIVINGSTON.
[108 MICHIGAN, 321.]

LIBEL—CRITICISM OF A BOOK.—When an author places his book before the public, he invites criticism, and however hostile the criticism may be and however much damage it may cause him by preventing sales, the critic is not liable to an action for libel, if he has made no misstatement of any material fact contained in the book and does not attack the character of the author. The propositions contained in the book the critic is at liberty to attack or denounce with sarcasm and ridicule.

LIBEL, CRITICISM OF A BOOK—UNDESERVED RIDI-CULE.—An instruction in an action brought by an author for the hostile criticism of his book, that the defendants had the right to ridicule it, if, in the candid judgment of any fair mind, it or any part thereof, deserved ridicule, is not sufficiently favorable to the defendant, because he had the right to use ridicule if he believed in good faith that the book deserved it, whether he is mistaken in this belief or not, and whether any fair mind would have agreed with his opinion or not.

LIBEL, CHARGE OF PLAGIARISM, WHAT IS NOT.—To charge one author with quoting from another without giving him credit is not libelous. It does not amount to an accusation of plagiarism.

LIBEL.—TO CALL A REMEDY PROPOSED BY AN AU-THOR A QUACK REMEDY is not libelous.

LIBEL—INCORRECT STATEMENT.—A statement in a review of a book that certain measures advocated therein had not the merit of originality, as Horace Greeley had advocated the same thing for fifty years, is not libelous, though, as a matter of fact, it is not true that Horace Greeley advocated the same thing for fifty years, or at all.

Action for libel. The plaintiff was the author of a book, and the defendants were publishers of a newspaper. The plaintiff requested that his book be reviewed, and it was thereupon submitted by the defendants to a critic for that purpose. The review which this critic prepared, and which was subsequently published by the defendants and constituted the basis of the present action, was as follows:

"MR. DOWLING'S BOOK.
"The Wage-Worker's Remedy.

"Morgan E. Dowling's little book, the 'Wage-Worker's Remedy,' is a well-meant, but rather hysterical, attempt to solve the labor question. Although utterly lacking scientific value, it is interesting to most Journal readers, because the author is a Detroit man, and because it reveals how the average mind is groping and floundering in the midst of a forest of contradictions and in swamps of bad logic to the discovery of the truth. We do not claim to know beyond question the right path, but feel sure that Mr. Dowling has hopelessly lost his way.

"In the first place, Mr. Dowling's view is entirely confined to this country. His wage worker is the American wage worker. This is mainly why his effort has no value as a contribution to economic science. What would be thought of a writer who tried to explain the law of the correlation of forces wholly from the American or the French standpoint? The truths of political economy are, of course, world-wide, like all truth. Rent and interest and wages must rise and fall in the United States in obedience to the same eternal laws that govern them elsewhere. To think otherwise is to doubt the harmony and simplicity of God's rule.

"Bearing this in mind, one of the author's nine remedies for low wages and lack of employment is seen to be inadequate. For instance, he would suspend immigration to this country; yet Italy, Germany, and Poland, all having emigration instead of immigration, and enjoying to a small degree some of his other remedies, are suffering from low wages. Ireland still seems to be too crowded, although, from famine and emigration, her population has been reduced one-half in less than a century. Surely, France's low wages have not been caused in any way by immigration, and war and starvation and a low birth rate have kept her population within reasonable limits, almost at a standstill.

"Another of Mr. Dowling's remedies for low wages is government ownership of railroads, street railways, telegraph lines, and telephones. This is funny. He doesn't stop to think, but disposes of the whole subject almost with one flourish. If he had stopped for even a moment, it might have occurred to him that wages were low before the telegraph and locomotive were known. In his hasty opinion, governmental operation of street-cars would realize Mayor Pingree's dream of a three-cent fare, and that would lead to more travel, and hence to the employment of more men. There you are. The whole question of labor is solved! But electricity has displaced horses (outside Detroit); travel on street-cars has doubled; and yet wages have fallen. We, of course, are using the word 'wages' in its strict economic sense, whereas Mr. Dowling for the moment has in mind only the wages of one set of men. The reduction of street-car fares, he says, would be equivalent to raising the wages of those wage workers who used the cars. Has he never thought of the influence of street-car improvements on rent? May it not be possible that the landowner, not the wage earner, would absorb the benefits of such improvements? We are not arguing against the restriction of immigration, and governmental ownership and management of these natural monopolies. They may be desirable in themselves, but as a solution of the labor problem they are ridiculous.

"Mr. Dowling disclaims being a paternalist; yet he advocates the most astounding piece of socialistic policy. He inveighs against class legislation, and then proposes some legislation of that kind. He would have the government forbid a higher rate of interest than four per cent and a lower rate of wages than two dollars a day. Such childish suggestions were bad enough in the Middle Ages, when the laws of political economy were unknown. An old king commanded the tide to recede, and an English parliament undertook to fix a maximum wage. Both were excusable, for they were ignorant. We know better to-day. Like the tide, wages follow certain unchangeable laws. The old king might have erected a stone wall against the tide, but the tide would have gone on working just the same, until it overflowed the obstruction or undermined it or pushed it over. So the law of wages does not cease to operate when artificial obstructions are put in the way of its sweep. Something may fall and smash, but it will not be the fault of the economic law. The law itself is all right, being the will of the Creator, and any patchwork by the finite mind cannot but lead to bad results.

"Mr. Dowling simply does not understand what 'wages' are, in the meaning given to the word by political economy. He has constantly in mind the popular meaning of the word as applied to 'wage earners.' In political economy, however, the meaning of the word 'wages' is broader. It is the return for any service or for any productive labor. Thus, many are their own employers, and receive as wages what they themselves produce. How could the legislature compel an express-wagon driver or a small market gardener or a small shopkeeper to pay himself at least two dollars a day? The merchant is both a capitalist and a wage earner, as political economy regards him. His profits are made up of interest on his capital, and of wages of superintendence. He may have, let us say, fifty clerks employed, at an average rate of one dollar and fifty cents a day. The law suddenly compels him, according to Mr. Dowling's scheme, to pay them not less than two dollars a day, increasing his expenses twenty-five dollars a day. He is himself a laborer, a wage worker, as truly as are his clerks, and nine times out of ten a harder and more anxious worker, for upon him rests responsibility, and the shame should failure come. His own wages may already be cut down fearfully by high rent and competition; yet Mr. Dowling would arbitrarily make him pay higher wages to his clerks than the labor market required. Of course, like all quack remedies, it would intensify the trouble if it had any effect at all. Besides trickery and lying, it would cause business failures and the employment relatively of less clerks. The tide might be dammed up for a moment, but its strength would be felt.

"About one-third of Mr. Dowling's book is devoted to praising Henry George, and to refuting his ideas. In the opening chapter he quotes from George without giving him credit, and outdoes him in raising alarm over present social conditions, even saying that revolution is at hand unless something is quickly done to appease the wrathful and wronged masses. In the last chapter he has apparently cooled off, forgotten his alarm, and believes that material progress tends to benefit all. One wonders what he made a fuss for first, especially when it is found that he believes that some poverty is sure to exist anyway. He says Henry George's scheme is socialistic, and then he proposes an extension of governmental powers which would make Sam Goldwater happy. He denounces the single-tax scheme as robbery, and then advocates it, at least so far as it is applied in New Zealand. He would exempt improvements largely, and tax land values so high as to prevent speculation in land, which is all any single taxer dares to hope will be accomplished in a generation or two to come. After giving his programme of nine remedies, Mr. Dowling thinks of many more. He would prohibit the acquirement of more land by any man than is actually needed by him for business or homestead purposes. This is pretty strong for one who has just been defending the institution of private property in land as all right, and it hasn't the merit of originality, for Horace Greeley advocated the same thing fifty years ago.

"It is altogether an amusing book, as full of contradictions and absurdities as a schoolboy of tricks. Mr. Dowling gravely assures the reader that the remedy for poverty is 'steady work, shorter hours, and fair wages.' He might have added that food is an excellent remedy for hunger.

"'The Wage-Worker's Remedy' is on sale at Hunt & Eaton's, 189 Woodward Ave."

Cutcheon, Stellwagen & Fleming, for the appellants.

Morgan E. Dowling, in pro. per.

[326] GRANT, J. (after stating the facts). The propositions advocated by the plaintiff are thus stated in the third chapter of his book:

"1. The suspension of all immigration to this country; 2. The making of eight hours a legal day's work; 3. The prohibition of marriage under the age of twenty-one years; 4. The prohibition of the employment of children under fifteen years of age in workshops, factories, and mines; 5. The fixing of the minimum rate of wages at two dollars per day for all laborers, except domestic and farm laborers; 6. The reduction of the legal rate of interest to four per cent per annum; 7. The purchase of all street railways, and the placing of them under the control and management of the municipal authorities; 8. The purchase of all telegraph, telephone, and railroad lines in the United States, and the placing of them under the control and management of the national government; 9. The prohibition of the purchase of lands in this country by nonresident aliens, and the compelling of all nonresident aliens who now own lands to sell them within a specified time, or forfeit their titles."

The book is mainly devoted to a discussion and elucidation of these propositions. No malice was shown on the [327] part of the defendants, unless it is fairly deducible from the article itself. On the contrary, it appears to be conclusively established that the defendants did not entertain any malice toward him, and that the book was placed by them in the hands of their critic, who wrote the article, without any comment or instruction.

When an author places his book before the public, he invites criticism, and, however hostile that criticism may be, and however much damage it may cause him by preventing its sale, the critic is not liable in an action for libel, provided he makes no misstatement of any material facts contained in the writing, and does not attack the character of the author. The book and the criticism are both before the public. The language we used in Belknap v. Ball, 83 Mich. 589, 21 Am. St. Rep. 622, applies to this case: "When language is truthfully stated, the criticism thereon, if unjust, will fall harmless, for the former furnishes a ready antidote for the intended poison. Readers can then determine whether the writer has, by the publication, libeled himself or the candidate. When the language is falsely and maliciously stated, privilege ceases to constitute a defense." We think that case and the authorities there cited establish the principle governing this.

Townshend on Slander and Libel, section 258, states the rule as follows: "As criticism is opinion, it can never be primarily material to inquire into its justness. The right to criticise implies the right to judge for one's self of the justness of the criticism. It would seem to be but a delusion to say one has the right to criticise, provided the criticism be just. The justness or unjustness can never be more than matter of opinion. The test always is, Was the criticism bona fide? It is like the case of one writing concerning the sanity of another. The test of the justification is not, Was the statement such as a man of sound sense would have made? but, Was it the honest conviction of the publisher?"

328 The case of Bacon v. Michigan Cent. R. R. Co., 66 Mich. 166, has no application to this case. No question of criticism of an author's writing was there involved. The defendant had reported the plaintiff as having been discharged from its employ for stealing. The report was a direct attack upon his personal character. There is in both reason and authority a wide distinction between language uttered concerning a person and criticism of his writings: Townshend on Slander and Libel, sec. 255.

It was said in Campbell v. Spottiswoode, 3 Fost. & F. 428: "The article, no doubt, is pungent, bitter, and caustic. At the same time, public men, and, above all, public writers, must not complain if they are sometimes rather roughly treated. Public writers, who expose themselves to criticism, must not complain that such criticism is sometimes hostile. . . . . It was perfectly lawful for a public writer to say that it was an idle scheme, and that it was a delusion to suppose that, by forcing these papers [meaning the plaintiff's newspapers] into circulation by free distribution, the great cause of missions would be promoted, and, in short, to denounce the whole scheme as pernicious and delusive." In a note to the above case will be found cited several English cases sustaining the rule: See, also, Townshend on Slander and Libel, sec. 254.

It is not libelous to ridicule literary composition: Carr v. Hood, 1 Camp. 355, note. Lord Ellenborough in that case said: "One writer, in exposing the follies and errors of another, may make use of ridicule, however poignant. Ridicule is often the fittest weapon that can be employed for such a purpose. If the reputation or pecuniary interests of the person ridiculed suffer, it is damnum absque injuria. Where is the liberty of the press if an action can be maintained on such principles? . . . . Every man who publishes a book commits himself to the judgment of

the public, and any one may comment on his performance. If
the commentator does not step aside from [329] the work, or introduce fiction for the purpose of condemnation, he exercises a fair
and legitimate right."

It is unnecessary to cite or quote further from the authorities.
The rule of law in such cases is clear. In applying it to the present case, we find that the personal character and reputation of
the author are not attacked. His theories are. In no material
matter is there any misstatement of fact or of the propositions
set forth in the book. The critic was at liberty to attack or denounce them with sarcasm and ridicule.

The learned circuit judge instructed the jury that "the defendants had the right to ridicule this book if, in the candid judgment of any fair man, the book or any part of it deserved ridicule." This is not the law. As already shown, when the critic
correctly states the author, he (the critic) is the sole judge of
the language of his criticism. Many fair men might disagree
with him, and very likely would in this case. This is for the
public, and not for a jury, to determine. If the plaintiff's contention be the correct rule of law, then the protectionist might
maintain an action for libel against the free trader who attacks
his protection theories and arguments with sarcasm, ridicule, and
contempt.

Plaintiff insists that the defendants charged him with plagiarism because he did not give Henry George credit for a quotation
from his works. The quotation was inclosed in quotation marks,
but not credited to Mr. George, and the court very properly
charged the jury that this did not charge him with plagiarism.

The court also correctly instructed the jury that it was not libelous to call his remedy a "quack remedy."

It was not libelous to say that "Horace Greeley advocated the
prohibition of the acquirement of more land by a man than is
actually needed by him for his business or homestead purposes,"
even though it should appear that Mr. Greeley had not advocated such a doctrine.

Complaint is also made of the statement that "he [plaintiff]
denounces the single tax scheme as robbery." [330] In that part
of the book to which this statement has reference, plaintiff is
discussing the single tax theory of Mr. George, and is denounc-
ing his proposition to take the land from the present owners
without compensation, which he denounces as "a gigantic piece
of robbery." As stated in the book, this was a part of the single tax theory of Mr. George. The article complained of, how-

ever, correctly states the position of the plaintiff upon this subject.

The declaration contains no innuendoes, and although the criticism is undoubtedly severe and caustic, it does not exceed the bounds of legitimate criticism. The court should have directed a verdict for the defendants.

Judgment reversed, and a new trial ordered.

The other justices concurred.

LIBEL — CRITICISM OF BOOK — WHEN AMOUNTS TO.— Authors, artists, and all other persons voluntarily exposing the result of their labors to the public, seeking to gain favorable recognition of their work if found meritorious, become public characters, so far, at least as their works are concerned. Any periodical may publish an estimate of such works, whether favorable or unfavorable: and if unfavorable, it may use strong terms of condemnation, and expose the work to merciless ridicule. No action can be sustained for such adverse criticism, unless it is shown, or on its face it appears, to be actuated by malice in fact. But for any defamation of an author or artist not necessarily connected with his public works, the publisher of such defamation is answerable, though it may have been published as a part of a professed criticism of such work: Monographic note to McAllister v. Detroit Free Press Co., 15 ALL. St. Rep. 859.

STARLING v. SUPREME COUNCIL.
[108 MICHIGAN, 440.]

MUTUAL BENEFIT ASSOCIATIONS, CHANGE OF BY-LAWS OF.—If a mutual benefit society issues to a member a certificate of insurance, it cannot, by the subsequent adoption of a by-law, modify or change the contract without the consent of the member. Hence, if when a certificate is issued, it defines what shall be deemed a total disability, and declares the member to be entitled to a sum specified on the suffering by him of such disability, the society cannot, without his consent, afterward reduce the classes of total disability.

MUTUAL BENEFIT ASSOCIATIONS, LOSS OF MEMBERSHIP, WHEN DOES NOT BAR A RECOVERY.—If one was a member of a council of a mutual benefit association until that council broke up for want of members, and he then obtained a transfer card and deposited it within another council in the same city, which refused to accept him as a member, he cannot be compelled to apply for membership in a council in another city, and cannot be deprived of the benefit of the certificate issued to him on the ground that he had ceased to be a member, if he had paid to the supreme council all sums chargeable against him.

JURY TRIAL—MUTUAL BENEFIT ASSOCIATIONS—INSTRUCTION AS TO WHAT IS AN AVOCATION.—If the jury is instructed that to entitle plaintiff to recover he must be totally disabled from following any avocation, and that it is for the jury to draw from the evidence the inference of fact upon this subject, the defendant cannot be regarded as prejudiced by the further statement

on the part of the judge that the fact that a man may work for a
few moments or perhaps for a few months, is not necessarily conclusive evidence that he can follow some avocation.

J. H. Tatem, for the appellant.

Powell & Johnson, for the appellee.

441 MOORE, J. The defendant is a fraternal and mutual
benefit association, composed of social and beneficiary members,
with a membership of thirteen thousand. Its beneficiary fund is
derived from monthly assessments paid by its members. The
certificate of insurance issued to the plaintiff provides, among
other things, that the beneficiary, at the death of the insured,
shall be entitled to the sum of one dollar from each and every
active member in good standing, not to exceed two thousand
members, or if the insured shall become totally disabled for life,
so as to prevent his following his own or any other avocation, he
shall, upon satisfactory proof of such total disability, be entitled
to one-half of the above-mentioned amount, the remaining one-
half to be paid at the time of his decease, provided he shall comply with all the laws, rules, and regulations of the order. On
the back of the certificate was indorsed the following: "Total
disability shall consist of the following conditions: 1. An injury
which shall produce complete, total, and permanent disability
from following any avocation; 2. Paralysis so extensive as to
produce absolute disability to follow any avocation, and which is
conclusively permanent; 3. Rheumatic or gouty arthritis, followed by permanent anchylosis, so extensive as to produce total
disability; 4. Entire and hopeless loss of useful vision; 5. Hopeless and irremediable insanity."

In July, 1890, the plaintiff was stricken with paralysis, which,
he claims, totally disabled him for work, and entitled him to the.
sum of one thousand dollars, according to the terms of his certificate, and, inasmuch as his claim was not paid, he brought this
suit in 1893.

It is claimed, by way of defense, that in 1890, and before this
suit was brought, the causes of total disability were reduced to
three: 1. Entire and incurable loss of **442** vision; 2. Entire loss
of both arms, or both legs; 3. Hopeless and incurable insanity—
and that, inasmuch as the plaintiff had agreed to observe the rules
and regulations of the order, this change of causes of total disability would prevent his recovery for the total disability growing out of the paralysis. It has been held that, where a mutual
benefit society issued to a member a certificate of insurance, the

subsequent adoption of a by-law by the society could not modify or change the contract of insurance without the express consent of the member: Grand Lodge A. O. U. W. v. Sater, 44 Mo. App. 445; Insurance Co. v. Connor, 17 Pa. St. 136; Becker v. Berlin etc. Soc., 144 Pa. St. 232; 27 Am. St. Rep. 624; Morrison v. Wisconsin etc. Ins. Co., 59 Wis. 162. To the same effect is Becker v. Farmers' Mut. etc. Ins. Co., 48 Mich. 610.

It is also claimed that plaintiff is not entitled to recover, for the reason that, at the time of the commencement of this suit, he was not a member of the order. It seems to be established by the record that plaintiff, who was a resident of Detroit, was a member of Enterprise Council, of Detroit, until it broke up for want of members. He then obtained a transfer card from the supreme council at Buffalo, and deposited it with the North Star Council at Detroit. It was refused by that council. It is claimed by the defendant that, if the Detroit councils refused to receive him, he was under obligations to unite with a council in Grand Rapids or Buffalo. As this was a social as well as a beneficiary order, such a construction is unreasonable. The plaintiff sent payments of all assessments of which he had notice to the supreme council, at Buffalo, which received them for more than two years after he claims to have become totally disabled. The plaintiff had done all he could, and all he was bound to do, to retain his membership, and was not in fault.

Complaint is made of the charge of the trial judge. The record shows that the avocation of plaintiff was cutting leather in a shoe factory, which required a steady hand; that after 1890, his condition was such that he [443] could not longer follow it. There was some testimony that, for a short time in 1892, he had acted as an inspector of sidewalks. After the trial judge had charged the jury properly as to the law, this occurred:

"Mr. Powell: May it please the court, your honor has not defined what 'following an avocation' would be. I don't know whether you see fit to do that or not.

"The Court: I have not been requested to, in that respect. I will say, on that subject, that following an avocation, perhaps—

"Mr. Tatem: It is not a question of law, your honor.

"The Court: I think that is so, largely. But I will say this with reference to that: The fact that a man may carry a bucket of coal, or may carry a stick of wood, or perhaps may run a lawn mower over a lawn, will not, in itself, necessarily show that he is competent to follow some avocation. The fact that a man may work for a few moments, even though, perhaps, he may work for a few months, will not, necessarily—it is not conclusive evidence that he can follow some avocation. But, if you find that he can perform some kind of employment—if you find, as suggested by the counsel in this case, that he could keep a newspaper stand, or a peanut stand, or could do any work, or follow any line of employment—why, then, gentlemen of the jury, under those circumstances, he would not be entitled to recover. But you must remember it is not for me to say what inference shall be drawn from the evidence in this case. You have heard the evidence. It is for you to draw the inference of fact, and not for the court."

The court had fully charged the jury that, to entitle the plaintiff to recover, he must be totally disabled from following any avocation, and he again repeated that charge, and left it entirely for the jury to draw the inference of fact.

The judgment of the court below is affirmed, with costs.

The other justices concurred.

MUTUAL BENEFIT ASSOCIATIONS—CHANGE IN BY-LAWS OF.—While a mutual benefit society has the power to make, alter, abrogate, or amend its by-laws, it cannot so exercise this right that it will operate as a repudiation of its obligations or to work a forfeiture of rights previously vested in its members. A contract between a member and an association cannot be enlarged or changed except by the consent of both contracting parties: Monographic note to Lake v. Minnesota etc. Assn., 52 Am. St. Rep. 556, 557. See Daughtry v. Knights of Pythias, 48 La. Ann. 1203; 55 Am. St. Rep. 310.

MUTUAL BENEFIT ASSOCIATIONS — FORFEITURE OF MEMBERSHIP IN.—Forfeitures of insurance policies are not favored by the courts; and where a forfeiture is claimed, the courts will, if possible, preserve the equitable rights of the holders: Monographic notes to Lake v. Minnesota etc. Assn., 52 Am. St. Rep. 574, and Bankers' etc. Assn. v. Stapp, 19 Am. St. Rep. 783, discussing the numerous cases relating to the forfeiture of membership rights in mutual benefit societies.

MUTUAL BENEFIT ASSOCIATIONS—TOTAL DISABILITY —WHAT CONSTITUTES.—Under the by-laws of an association entitling a member to recover a stated sum, when, by reason of accident or disease, he becomes permanently disabled from following his usual or some other occupation, he is not precluded from recovery where he has been injured so as to be unable to pursue his ordinary occupation, though not incapacitated from pursuing another occupation in which his wages are much inferior, and which requires for its duties much less physical or mental ability: Niell v. Order of United Friends, 149 N. Y. 430; 52 Am. St. Rep. 738, and note; Pennington v. Pacific etc. Ins. Co., 85 Iowa, 468; 39 Am. St. Rep. 306. The words "totally disabled from the prosecution of his usual employment" mean inability to do substantially all kinds of his accustomed labor to some extent: Note to North American etc. Ins. Co. v. Burroughs, 8 Am. Rep. 218. See Baltimore etc. Assn. v. Post, 122 Pa. St. 579; 9 Am. St. Rep. 147.

MACOMBER v. DETROIT, LANSING & NORTHERN RAILROAD COMPANY.

[108 MICHIGAN, 491.]

LICENSE TO REMOVE STANDING TIMBER NOT EXERCISED IN THE TIME STIPULATED.—If a landowner sells the timber on his land, to be removed within a time specified, and the timber remains uncut after the expiration of that time, it reverts to the owner of the realty, but timber which is cut within that time becomes the personal property of the licensee and remains such, though it is not removed from the land within the time agreed upon.

McGarry & Nichols and George A. Farr, for the appellant.

Whittlesey & Kennedy and Vernon H. Smith, for the appellees.

491 MONTGOMERY, J. On the twenty-second day of July, 1892, the Cutler & Savage Lumber Company executed a writing to one John S. Wiedman, containing the following provisions: "The Cutler & Savage Lumber Company has this day sold to J. S. Wiedman, of Lake View, Michigan, all of the timber on the entire section 29, in town 13 north, of range 7 west. The said J. S. Wiedman is to remove the timber in two years from this date; and, in case the said Cutler & Savage Lumber Company **492** sell any of said land, the said J. S. Wiedman is to remove the timber from the land sold at once, on being notified of the said sale."

On the 4th of November, 1892, Wiedman sold the same timber to plaintiffs, and the lumber company afterward sold the land to one Fred Bissell. No notice of this sale or request for immediate removal was made. Plaintiffs, within the two years, cut the pine in question into logs, but had not removed the logs from the premises within the two years. Bissell removed them, and defendant represents his title. The question is, whether failure to remove the logs after they were cut, and within the two years named in the contract, forfeited the title.

Contracts containing similar provisions have been construed in the courts in a number of the states, and the weight of authority supports the defendant's contention that, as to timber remaining uncut at the expiration of the time limited under a contract such as this, the title reverts to the owner of the realty: See Pease v. Gibson, 6 Me. 84; Howard v. Lincoln, 13 Me. 123; Saltonstall v. Little, 90 Pa. St. 422; 35 Am. Rep. 683; Utley v. S. N. Wilcox Lumber Co., 59 Mich. 263; Haskell v. Ayres, 32 Mich. 93; 35 Mich. 89; Gamble v. Gates, 92 Mich. 510. None of the Michigan cases directly determine the status of timber cut and manufactured into logs during the time limited by such a contract as

that in question -but not removed until later. In Gamble v.
Gates, 92 Mich. 510, the contract covered all the timber standing,
lying, or being on the land. It was provided expressly that whatever of said timber should remain on said lands, after the limit
afforded, should' revert back, and become the property of the
first party. The case was determined by the terms of the contract. In Golden v. Glock, 57 Wis. 118, 46 Am. Rep. 32, a contract similar to that in question was held to convey title to only
such timber as was removed within the time limited, but considered all such timber as was manufactured into stave bolts as removed. In Hicks v. Smith, 77 Wis. 146, the same doctrine was
reaffirmed by [493] the same court. A contract not distinguishable from the one herein involved was considered, and it was held
that, as to trees cut into logs, the severance from the realty had
become complete. The property had become personalty, and its
character so essentially changed by such manufacture that it was,
in effect, removed from the premises, within the meaning of the
deed.

In Williams v. Flood, 63 Mich. 493, Mr. Justice Campbell,
speaking of such contract as the present, said: "It is not very important to discuss the exact nature of plaintiff's rights under the
written contract. Whatever they were, they included an absolute sale of all the timber described, subject only to such qualifications of the right of removal as the contract mentions. At
most, this condition would only operate by way of forfeiture.
The timber had all been paid for, and all belonged to the plaintiff, unless lost by forfeiture for nonremoval."

The same can be said of the present case, and, if we apply the
rule that forfeitures are not favored (Miller v. Havens, 51 Mich.
485), the rule of the Wisconsin court seems consistent with reason
and justice. It is no stretch to treat the severance of the timber
from the soil, and its manufacture into logs, as a removal, within
the terms of the provision for forfeiture. The case of Boisaubin
v. Reed, 1 Abb. Dec. 161, is opposed to the Wisconsin cases cited;
but we think the doctrine of the Wisconsin cases more just, and
are disposed to adopt it.

Judgment affirmed.

The other justices concurred.

**LICENSE TO CUT TIMBER—EFFECT OF—REVOCABILI-
TY.**—A license to enter on land and cut and carry away timber.
which the owner gives by virtue of a verbal contract for the sale of
standing timber to be cut and severed from the freehold by the purchaser, is revocable so far as it relates to timber not cut at the time:
Giles v. Simonds, 15 Gray, 441; 77 Am. Dec. 373, and note. For

although one having such a license has no title in the timber until it is severed, yet, upon such severance, even by a trespasser, the title of the licensee becomes perfect: Keystone Lumber Co. v. Kolman, 94 Wis. 465; 59 Am. St. Rep. 905, and note. To be available at all where no time is limited, such a license must be acted upon in a reasonable time, and must be considered as applying to the wood as substantially in the state of growth which it is then in: Gilmore v. Wilbur, 12 Pick. 120; 22 Am. Dec. 410; Heflin v. Bingham, 56 Ala. 566· 28 Am. Rep. 776. See note to Burton v. Scherff, 79 Am. Dec. 721.

PEOPLE v. SMITH.

[108 MICHIGAN. 527.]

EMPLOYERS AND EMPLOYÉS, SPECIAL LAWS FOR THE PROTECTION OF THE LATTER.—A statute requiring emery wheels which are in continuous use to be provided with blowers to carry away the dust arising from their operation is a valid exercise of the·police powers of the state.

CONSTITUTIONAL LAW—USE OF PUBLIC PROPERTY.—A statute may regulate the use of public property when the health, morals, or welfare of the public demand it.

CONSTITUTIONAL LAW—CLASS LEGISLATION, WHEN NOT FORBIDDEN.—A statute for the protection of all persons who are given continuous employment over dry emery wheels is not forbidden class legislation.

EMPLOYERS AND EMPLOYÉS—CONSTITUTIONAL LAW. A state has the right to require employers to provide and employés to use appliances intended for the protection of the latter, and the requirement may be applicable, though an employer and employé may have contracted that the appliance need not be furnished, if the law has relation to the public welfare or health, and it is clear that the regulation is reasonable.

CONSTITUTIONAL LAW—PRESUMPTION IN FAVOR OF LEGISLATIVE ACTION.—If the legislature has enacted a regulation for the benefit of the public or some general class thereof, and the regulation is assailed as an unnecessary and unreasonable interference with property rights, or with the right to contract, the presumption is in favor of the validity of the legislative action, and unless some plain provision of the constitution has been violated or it can be said that the regulation is not within the rule of necessity in view of facts of which judicial notice may be taken, the statute must be sustained.

Corliss, Andrus & Leete, and Arthur Webster, for the appellant.

Allan H. Frazer, prosecuting attorney, and Ormond F. Hunt, assistant prosecuting attorney, for the people.

⁵²⁸ HOOKER, J. The defendant was convicted of a violation of the statute requiring emery wheels to be provided with blowers to carry away the dust arising from their operation: Pub. Acts 1893, Act No. 111; 3 Howell's Stats., sec. 1690-1693. Counsel for

the defendant assert that they care to raise but one question, viz., the constitutionality of this law.

[529] It is not disputed that the state may regulate the use of private property, when the health, morals, or welfare of the public demands it. Such laws have their origin in necessity: Prentice on Police Powers, 4-8, 52, 54, 161, 433. Counsel say that this law is invalid because it does not apply to all, not even to all who use emery wheels, because some may use with water, and others may not work continuously. Again, it is contended that it is invalid because it prohibits a man from running his own machine continuously without protection. We need not concern ourselves with the last objection, because we have not the case before us, and for the reason that the law may be valid to the extent that others are protected, and invalid in the particular mentioned, if such a construction is unavoidable. For the purposes of this case, it may be said that all persons who are given continuous employment over dry emery wheels are within the provisions of this act. This singles out no class, as it applies to all persons who use emery wheels in that manner. Necessarily, the practical application is limited to those who engage in such business, but such is the case with many laws. All criminal laws apply only to those who choose to break them. This law applies to all who choose to use the emery wheel. The legislature has seen fit to permit certain uses of the dry wheel without a blower, while in other cases it is required. This is competent, and is not class legislation, as between operatives. It fixes the limits of use without a blower, and requires it after such limits are passed; but the rules apply to all.

The vital question in this case is the right of the state to require the employer to provide, and the employé to use, appliances intended for the protection of the latter. Laws of this class embrace provisions for the safety and welfare of those whom necessity may compel to submit to existing conditions involving hazards which they would otherwise be unwilling to assume. Among them [530] are provisions for fire escapes, the covering or otherwise rendering machinery safe, the condition of buildings, ventilations, etc. In the main, where the necessity is obvious, they commend themselves to those who have at heart the welfare of their fellows, and should be upheld if they do not contravene private rights.

The constitution secures to the citizen the rights of life, liberty, and private property, and, as the only value in the latter consists in its use, it follows that the right to use private prop-

erty is within the provision. There can, however, be no doubt
that the use of private property may be regulated by law. No
one would think of questioning the validity of laws regulating
the manufacture, use, and sale of dangerous drugs or explosives,
or laws designed to insure safety in railway travel. The inspection of boilers, fire escapes upon hotels, means of exit from
churches and other buildings which the public are wont to frequent, are familiar instances of the exercise of the police power.
These rules are defended upon the ground that they are necessary to the safety of the public; not the entire populace, but
such persons as shall lawfully place themselves in a position requiring such protection. Where the law is aimed at acts or conditions which threaten contagion—as where sewers, disinfection,
or quarantine is required—the necessity of and the power to
make such laws are obvious. But at first blush they may not be
so apparent where there is no direct danger to others than the
party whose business is sought to be regulated, and those with
whom he contracts. It is contended in this case that neither
the public welfare nor health is involved, inasmuch as the protection sought to be afforded is limited to the individual employé, who, by his contract of employment, signifies a willingness to use the machine in its dangerous condition, and therefore
cannot be heard to complain.

It is the law that a manufacturer may provide inferior, and
even dangerous, machinery, tools, and utensils; and [531] enterprises more or less hazardous are common and lawful. Men may
contract to use such machinery, or to perform dangerous service, and have no remedy if injured. But we are not aware that
the police power is limited by such contracts. As between the
parties themselves, the contract may cut off legal redress for injuries sustained; but we are not satisfied that the authority of
the state is limited to the protection of those who do not sustain
contract relations with each other. In the absence of a law requiring fire escapes, one who works in a high building and is
injured may be held to have assumed the risk incident to his
employment; but we know of no rule that precludes the state
from making a regulation requiring fire escapes to be placed upon
high buildings, though the only object be to facilitate the escape
of employés who are under contract to work there without such
appliances for escape. Fire escapes in hotels, and means of exit
in theaters and public halls, are required by law for the benefit of
patrons, who are there by virtue of contract relations with the
proprietor. So long as the rule is general, and the danger to the

public—i. e., that portion of the public who are subjected to the
danger—is clear, it is a proper subject for legislative intervention. In re Jacobs, 98 N. Y. 98, 50 Am. Rep. 636, is cited to
sustain the proposition contended for, but it cannot be said to
have decided the question, although allusion is made to voluntary submission to alleged dangerous conditions. The case does
not dispute the power to regulate the business of private persons
where the public welfare requires, but does deny the power of
regulation in the absence of such necessity, where the law has
no relation to the public welfare or health: See, also, Tiedeman's
Limitation of Police Power, sec. 122 c.

The case of People v. Warden of City Prison, 144 N. Y. 529,
is an interesting one upon this question, and although the decision there laid down is criticised (perhaps justly) by Mr. Justice
Peckham in a dissenting opinion, concurred in by two of his associates, the power [532] to regulate private affairs where the public necessity exists is asserted in an exhaustive opinion by the
same learned judge in the case of Health Department v. Rector
etc. of Trinity Church, 145 N. Y. 32, 43, 44, 45 Am. St. Rep.
578, in the course of which the power to regulate the appliances
for manufacturing is asserted. The opinion says: "Handrails
to stairs, hoisting shafts to be inclosed, automatic doors to elevators, automatic shifters for throwing off belts or pulleys, and
fire escapes on the outside of certain factories—all these were
required by the legislature from such owner, and without any
direct compensation to him for such expenditure. Has the legislature no right to enact laws such as this statute regarding factories, unless limited to factories to be thereafter built? Because
the factory was already built when the act was passed, was it
beyond the legislative power to provide such safeguards to life
and health, as against all owners of such property, unless upon
the condition that these expenditures to be incurred should ultimately come out of the public purse? I think to so hold would
be to run counter to the general course of decisions regarding
the validity of laws of this character, and to mistake the foundation upon which they are placed."

The trouble with these cases arises over the inability of the
courts to fix a rigid rule by which the validity of such laws may
be tested. Each law of the kind involves the questions: 1. Is
there a threatened danger? 2. Does the regulation invade a constitutional right? 3. Is the regulation reasonable? In the present case no controversy is raised over the first of these. Hence
we are not called upon to discuss it. As is implied by what has

been said, the constitutional right to use property without regulation is plain, unless the public welfare requires its regulation.
If the public welfare does require it, the right must yield to the
public exigency. And it is upon this question of necessity that
the third question depends. All, then, seems to be embraced
in the question of necessity. Unless the emery wheel is dangerous to health, there is no necessity, and consequently no power,
to regulate it. [533] Unless the blower is a reasonable and proper
regulation, it is not a necessary one. Who shall decide the question, and by what rule? Shall it be the legislature or the courts?
And, if the latter, is it to be determined by the evidence in the
case that happens to be first brought, or by some other rule?
Does it become a question of fact to be submitted to the jury or
decided by the court? Of all the devices known to human tribunals, the jury stands pre-eminent in its ability to determine
cases in direct violation of and contrary to law, without impairing the binding force of the law as a rule of future action. We
have known of instances where the question of the constitutionality of acts, as applied to the particular case on trial, has been
made to depend upon the finding of the jury upon the facts in
the case. But there is a manifest absurdity in allowing any tribunal, either court or jury, to determine from testimony in the
case the question of the constitutionality of the law. Whether
this law invades the rights of all the persons using emery wheels
in the state is a serious question. If it is a necessary regulation,
the law should be sustained, but, if an unjust law, it should be
annulled. The first case presented might show by the opinions
of many witnesses that the use of the dry emery wheel is almost
necessarily fatal to the operative, while the next might show exactly the opposite state of facts. Manifestly, then, the decision
could not settle the question for other parties, or the fate of the
law would depend upon the character of the case first presented
to the court of last resort, which would have no means of ascertaining whether it was a collusive case or not, or whether the
weight of evidence was in accord with the truth. It would seem,
then, that the questions of danger and reasonableness must be
determined in another way. The legislature, in determining
upon the passage of the law, may make investigations which the
courts cannot. As a rule, the members (collectively) may be expected to acquire more technical and experimental knowledge of
such [534] matters than any court can be supposed to possess, both
as to the dangers to be guarded against and the means of prevention of injury to be applied; and hence, while under our in-

stitutions the validity of laws must be finally passed upon by the courts, all presumptions should be in favor of the validity of legislative action. If the courts find the plain provisions of the constitution violated, or if it can be said that the act is not within the rule of necessity in view of facts of which judicial notice may be taken, then the act must fall; otherwise it should stand. Applying this test, we think the law constitutional, and the judgment is therefore affirmed.

The other justices concurred.

PER CURIAM. Our attention is called to the fact that under the opinion heretofore filed the act as originally passed might be held unconstitutional, inasmuch as it does not discriminate between dry and wet wheels, which last, it is said, cannot possibly produce dust, and therefore do not require the blower. This question was necessarily passed upon in the former opinion, as the amendment could not be sustained if the original act was invalid. In addition to what was said in the former opinion, we may say that two sufficient reasons may be given for not holding the first act void: 1. We are not able to say that a wheel may not be run with or without water at pleasure, in which case it would seem proper that the blower should be required as an efficient means of preventing its being run without water; 2. If this were not so, the act might be construed as applicable only to wheels capable of producing dust, as the language of the act clearly shows that it was intended to reach such, and an act should always be so construed as to bring it within the constitution, if it can be reasonably done: Coit v. Sutton, 102 Mich. 324.

———

STATUTES—CONSTITUTIONALITY OF—PRESUMPTION IN FAVOR OF.—All reasonable doubts must be solved in favor of legislative action. Every statute must, therefore, be sustained unless its conflict with the constitution is beyond reasonable doubt: State v. Camp Sing. 18 Mont. 128; 56 Am. St. Rep. 551, and note; State v. Roby, 142 Ind. 168; 51 Am. St. Rep. 174; Hanna v. Young, 84 Md. 179; 57 Am. St. Rep. 396, and note; monographic note to People v. Starne, 85 Am. Dec. 357.

POLICE POWER — DEFINITION OF — REGULATION OF OCCUPATIONS.—The police power of the state is the authority vested in the legislature by the constitution to enact all wholesome and reasonable laws that they may deem conducive to the public good: Note to People v. Wagner, 24 Am. St. Rep. 145. It extends to all regulations affecting the lives, limbs, health, comfort, good order, morals, peace, and safety of society: Extended note to Chicago etc. R. R. Co. v. State, 53 Am. St. Rep. 572; monographic note to State v. Goodwill, 25 Am. St. Rep. 889. The right of every person to pursue any lawful business, occupation, or profession, is subject to the paramount right, inherent in every government as a part of its police power, to impose such restrictions and regulations as the protection of the public may require: State v. Randolph, 23 Or. 74; 37 Am. St. Rep. 655, and note; monographic note to State v. Goodwill, 25 Am. St. Rep. 879. See State v. Fire Creek etc. Co., 33 W. Va. 188; 25 Am. St. Rep. 893. The legislature has no power to prevent persons who are sui juris from making their own contracts, nor can it interfere with the freedom to contract between workmen and employers: Ritchie v. People, 155 Ill. 98; 46 Am. St. Rep. 315.

STATUTES — DISCRIMINATION BETWEEN CLASSES AND PERSONS.—Laws public in their objects may be confined to a particular class of persons, if they are general in their application to the cases to which they apply, provided the distinction is not arbitrary but rests upon some reason of public policy: Note to Foster v. Police Commrs., 41 Am. St. Rep. 200. An act which applies to and embraces all of a class of persons who are or may come into like situations or circumstances is a general law: Monographic note to State v. Ellet, 21 Am. St. Rep. 781.

CASES

SUPREME COURT

MISSOURI.

HUDSON BROTHERS COMMISSION COMPANY *v.* GLENCOE SAND AND GRAVEL COMPANY.

[140 MISSOURI, 103.]

A TENDER MADE AFTER THE MATURITY OF NOTES SECURED by a deed of trust or mortgage does not discharge its lien. It has no greater effect on the security than on the debt. Hence, if the tender is not kept good, the trustee or mortgagee may proceed to sell the property, and the purchaser will acquire a good title.

RECORDING OF INSTRUMENTS.—If two instruments are executed on the same day and filed for record at substantially the same time, and the same person is the beneficiary in both, it is not material which was first recorded, or filed for record.

MERGER.—IF THE OWNER OF LANDS HAS EXECUTED A TRUST DEED THEREON AND A LEASE THEREOF to the same person, and the latter assigns the lease to a third person to whom the equity of redemption is also assigned by the landowner, the leasehold and the equity merge and become one estate, all of which is subject to the trust deed, and a sale thereunder passes title paramount to that of the person claiming under the assignment of the lease.

R. M. Nichols, for the appellant.

John W. Noble, George H. Shields, and John R. Warfield, for the respondents.

[108] MACFARLANE, J. This is an ejectment suit, instituted in the circuit court of St. Louis county, on the fourteenth day of November, 1893, by Hudson Brothers' Commission Company, a corporation, Benjamin F. and William A. Hudson and A. D. Scott, against Glencoe Sand & Gravel Company, a corporation, John E., Martha A., and Louis Beard, and afterward by

change of venue taken to the circuit court of the city of St.
Louis.

The petition, in the usual form, is to recover a tract of land
in St. Louis county. The answer of defendants, the Beards, was
a general denial, and an allegation that they were tenants of
defendant corporation. The answer of said corporation was a
general denial and two special defenses. The first of these
charges, in brief, that Mrs. Beard, by a trustee, was the original
owner of the land, and in 1885 made to plaintiffs a lease for a
term of twenty-five years, beginning [109] April 10, 1885, and
ending April 10, 1910, of the right of entering upon said land
and mining and carrying away gravel, sand, ballast, and fire
clay, and also to carry on all necessary quarrying and mining
operations thereon. The consideration for the lease was one-
fourth of the net profits of what was mined and taken from the
land. The lease was duly recorded April 17, 1885, at 10:28 in
the forenoon. That subsequently, on the said tenth day of
April, 1885, the said defendant Beard and her trustee conveyed
said property to one Henry L. Wilson in trust to secure to plaintiffs certain promissory notes of said date, maturing in one, two,
three, four, and five years, and bearing ten per cent interest,
aggregating the sum of eleven thousand two hundred and eighty
dollars, which deed of trust was recorded on the 17th of April,
1885, at 10:29 o'clock in the forenoon. That said defendants,
Beard, afterward paid large sums on said notes, aggregating two
thousand dollars, and were entitled to credits thereon for royalty
and rentals which had not been accounted for or credited. That
on August 11, 1890, defendant entered into a contract with
plaintiff for the purchase of said lease, together with the mortgage notes of Mrs. Beard, and the equity of redemption in the
land, for all of which defendant agreed to pay plaintiff the sum of
ten thousand dollars, of which sum three thousand seven hundred and fifty dollars was paid in cash and was to be credited
upon said notes, and the balance was to be paid in one year thereafter. That in pursuance of said contract plaintiff assigned to
defendant said lease and put it in possession of the land thereunder, and procured from said Beard and her trustee a deed
conveying to it her equity of redemption in the land. By this
defense it is alleged that defendant is in possession of the land
under said lease and the ownership thereof, and has always paid
the rents under its provisions, and is entitled to the possession
of the land thereunder.

[110] The second special defense charges that on the fourteenth

day of June, 1892, defendant tendered to plaintiff the sum of ten thousand four hundred and fifty-three dollars in payment of the notes secured by said deed of trust which plaintiff refused to accept, and refused to credit said notes by the cash payment of three thousand seven hundred and fifty dollars. That thereafter plaintiff, pretending that there was a default in the payment of said deed of trust, procured the said trustee to sell the land, under the powers contained in the deed of trust, purchased the same at the sale and received from the trustee a deed of conveyance therefor. Under this defense, defendant alleges that the tender had the effect of extinguishing and discharging the lien of the deed of trust and of making null and void the power of sale therein conferred, and the sale and deed thereunder was therefore void and of no effect.

The reply denies the new matter. Denies specially a sale or assignment of the lease. Admits the execution of the lease and deed of trust, but alleges that they were contemporaneous acts and intended as parts of the same transaction. Denies the tender, but admits the sale of the land under the deed of trust and the conveyance thereof by the trustee to plaintiffs.

The cause came to trial to a jury January 23, 1895. It was agreed that Mrs. Beard was the common source of title. Plaintiff read in evidence the deed of trust from Mrs. Beard, the trustee's deed to plaintiff, a certified copy of the lease mentioned, and evidence of rental value, and rested.

Defendant corporation offered to introduce evidence in support of its special defenses. Plaintiff objected to any evidence in support of these pleas on the ground that they constituted no defense to the action. The court held "that the facts thus pleaded in the answer were in the nature of an equitable defense, which, if sustained, should be so on terms that a court [111] of equity would deem just, and that if the defendants' counsel desired, the court would consider the question of whether or not there was a cause for equitable relief or defense made out by the answer; and if so, would hear the evidence pro and con, and pass judgment upon it." Counsel for plaintiff assented to that course, but the counsel for defendant declined to have his answer treated otherwise than as a plea at law to be passed on by the jury; whereupon the court instructed for the plaintiff, and the verdict and judgment were rendered accordingly. Defendant appealed.

1. By their special pleas defendants undertake to set up facts which they insist give them the legal right to continue in the

possession of the land. On the trial they disclaimed any equitable right to relief under them, and as defenses at law claimed
the right to prove the facts therein alleged. The court refused
to admit evidence for the purpose for which it was offered, and
these rulings are the only errors assigned. The questions for
consideration, therefore, on this appeal are whether, under the
facts stated in these defenses, assuming them to be true, defendants are entitled to remain in the possession of the premises in
question.

2. The second defense will be considered first. By that plea
defendants say that prior to the sale under the deed of trust they
tendered to plaintiff the amount due on the notes secured thereby, and that the tender thus made extinguished the mortgage
and power of sale thereunder, and the subsequent sale by the
trustee and his deed to plaintiff are therefore absolutely void.

The alleged tender was made by defendants long after the
maturity of the notes, and the question raised by the second defense is, whether the tender, if sufficient [112] in amount, discharged the lien of the deed of trust.

The question is one upon which there is much conflict in the
adjudications of the courts of this country. It is agreed, generally, that if a tender of the amount due on the secured debt is
made on the day of its maturity, the mortgage or deed of trust
given as security for it will be released and the lien thereof discharged. It has been expressly so decided by this court in the
case of Thornton v. National etc. Bank, 71 Mo. 221. Yet the
reasoning employed in the subsequent case of Landis v. Saxton,
89 Mo. 375, would appear to lead to a different result. But that
is a question we are not called upon to decide in this case, for
the tender was not made until after the maturity of the notes.

The question here in issue was recently considered by division
2 of this court in the case of McClung v. Missouri Trust Co., 137
Mo. 106. Burgess, J., who wrote the opinion in that case, after
a review of the authorities, reaches the conclusion that "the generally accepted doctrine is that the tender of the amount of the
indebtedness secured by the mortgage, made after default, will
not discharge the mortgage, but will stop the running of interest
from that time." To the numerous cases cited supporting that
doctrine may be added the following: Crain v. McGoon, 86 Ill.
431; 29 Am. Rep. 37; Matthews v. Lindsay, 20 Fla. 973; Parker
v. Beasley, 116 N. C. 1; Rowell v. Mitchell, 68 Me. 21. The
case, however, was finally decided upon the ground that no ten-

der had, in fact,.been made, and what was said, therefore, cannot fairly be regarded as a decision of the question here involved.

The question in issue in Olmstead v. Tarsney, 69 Mo. 399, was the effect of a tender of the amount due on a special tax bill, in respect to discharging the lien. The court treated the lien of a tax bill "as conferring [113] upon the owner thereof the same right which would have been conferred by a mortgage for that amount, and as being similarly subject to redemption." The two rules were stated and authorities sustaining each .cited, but, without reaching a conclusion, the case was decided upon another question.

In the case of Thornton v. National etc. Bank, 71 Mo. 232, the court expressly states that "A. B. Thornton, one of the debtors, at their maturity, tendered to the National Exchange Bank one-half of the notes that bank held against him and Bragg, and the bank refused to accept it, insisting upon payment of the whole amount." The court held that this tender extinguished the bank's lien on her property, she being only liable for that amount. The decision, therefore, was that a tender on the maturity of the notes extinguished the lien of the deed of trust.

The case of Landis v. Saxton, 89 Mo. 375, was a suit to enjoin the sale of land under a deed of trust. There was a dispute in respect to the allowance of a certain credit on the note. A tender, previous to commencing the suit, was made by the payee of the note of the amount he thought to be due, but the tender was not kept good by a deposit in court. On a trial, it was found that the payee was entitled to the credit claimed and that the full balance due on the note was tendered, still the court held: "While a tender was made by the plaintiff to the defendant, we do not understand that any deposit of the money tendered was ever made in court, and the only effect of the tender, if·sufficient in amount, was to stop the running of interest. The tender cannot have the effect to deprive the defendant of his security cre- ;ated by the deed of trust for so much as may be found due at the time the tender was made." This decision was predicated upon the statute which provides that, "where a tender and no deposit [114] shall be made, as provided in the next preceding section, the tender shall only have the effect, in law, to prevent the running of interest or accumulation of damages from and after the time the tender was made": Rev. Stats. 1879, sec. 1008; Rev. Stats. 1889, sec. 2938. The preceding section referred to relates to cases in which a tender is made before suit is brought.

It is evident that the court, or at any rate, the judge who wrote the opinion, held that the statute applied to mortgage debts as well as others, and that a tender only had the effect therein declared. The subsequent remarks of the judges indicate that without regard to the statute, and though a tender made after default may extinguish the lien, a court of equity will not relieve the mortgagor except in terms of full payment of the debt. The courts of appeals of this state, following Landis v. Saxton, 89 Mo. 375, hold that a tender after default of the amount due on a debt secured by chattel mortgage, does not extinguish the lien: McGuire v. Brockman, 58 Mo. App. 310; Woolner v. Levy, 48 Mo. App. 474; Berman v. Hoke, 61 Mo. App. 380.

We are of the opinion, therefore, that the question is not settled in this state, and may be considered as an original proposition, on reason and authority.

As has been seen, the greater number of courts of the states hold that a tender after default does not discharge the lien of a mortgage unless it be kept good. In addition to the authorities before cited some courts have held that the tender of the amount due on a mortgage debt has no greater effect than a common-law tender of the amount due on an unsecured debt. If kept good it only stops the running of interest. In Arkansas it is held that the tender of the mortgage debt stops interest on the debt, and as long as it is kept good destroys the power to sell the mortgaged premises for payment of the debt: Greer v. Turner, 36 [115] Ark. 17. A statute of Alabama allows the mortgagor to redeem after a sale under the mortgage by paying or tendering, within a specified time, to the purchaser or his vendee, the purchase money with interest and all lawful charges, and provides that "such payment or tender has the effect to reinvest him with the title." It was held by the supreme court of that state that the tender, in order to be effective, must be kept good: Alexander v. Caldwell, 61 Ala. 550. See, also, to the same effect, Brown v. Simons, 45 N. H. 211.

The common-law doctrine was that the estate of the mortgagor vested absolutely in the mortgagee, upon default in payment of the debt, at the time and place stipulated: 2 Coke on Littleton, 205 a. A breach of the condition worked an absolute forfeiture of the estate. On the other hand, if the mortgagor tendered the full amount due, at the time and place stipulated, and the mortgagee refused to accept payment, the mortgage was discharged for the reason that there had been no breach of the condition: Coke on Littleton, 207 a.

In order to prevent a forfeiture of the estate, courts of equity raised an equitable estate in the mortgagor, called the equity of redemption. While the legal estate, on breach of the condition, vested in the mortgagee, it was held in trust for the mortgagor, who had the right to redeem the estate or have it reinvested in him, by payment of the debt at any time before foreclosure. The right is purely equitable. A legal breach of the condition has already occurred, the legal title has vested in the mortgagee, and relief is afforded to the mortgagor alone on equitable principles. In dealing with the rights of mortgagors, after condition broken, this court has at all times been governed by equitable principles, and has refused to enforce forfeitures: Philips v. Bailey, 82 Mo. 639; [116] Whelan v. Reilly, 61 Mo. 567; Wolz v. Parker, 134 Mo. 465.

When the mortgagor is protected in rights on equitable considerations, why should not like considerations protect also the mortgagee? Why should a forfeiture be prevented in the one case and enforced in the other? A loss of the security would in many, indeed, in most, cases be a loss of the debt. It may be said also that a mortgagee will rarely, if ever, refuse payment of the amount he thinks due, and a refusal to accept a tender generally occurs only when there is a dispute as to the true amount. It would be most inequitable to require the acceptance of whatever is offered, or take the chance of forfeiting the whole. Nor could the mortgagor fairly complain that his tender did not effect a discharge of the mortgage, for he would still owe the debt and could stop the running of interest by keeping the tender good.

Take the case at bar as an illustration. Mrs. Beard is the debtor and mortgagor. Plaintiff is mortgagee and holder of the notes. Defendants hold the equity of redemption, and tender the amount due on the notes, which plaintiffs, not believing it sufficient, refuse to accept. The lien is discharged, and defendants have the absolute title to the land without paying for it; Mrs. Beard is deprived of the protection the deed of trust afforded her as maker of the notes, and plaintiff must look to Mrs. Beard for payment of the notes, or to defendant for breach of the agreement to purchase them. When a court of law undertakes to deal with the equity of redemption, it should, at the same time, regard the equities of the mortgagee and only declare a mortgage satisfied when the debt is paid.

It is held in the states of New York and Michigan (both of which hold that a tender after maturity discharges the mortgage) that a mortgagor coming into [117] a court of equity for affirmative relief must himself do equity, and pay the debt and interest at least up to the time of the tender. All that he can be equitably entitled to is relief from the interest and costs subsequent to the tender: Tuthill v. Morris, 81 N. Y. 94; Cowles v. Marble, 37 Mich. 158. In these cases the equities of the mortgagee is recognized in a court of equity, and they should in like manner be recognized by a rule of law that a mere tender does not discharge the mortgage.

The correct principle is so well expressed by the supreme courts of Illinois and New Jersey that we quote what is said by them in one case each. "We fail to appreciate," says Scholfield, C. J., of the former state, "why a court of equity, while interposing its authority to mitigate the rigor of the common-law rule against the mortgagor, should, at the same time, extend and make more rigorous the rule against the mortgagee. We do not perceive how this can be said to be in pursuance of the natural principles of justice. If a tender is made but not accepted, and is kept good, it is plainly right that the mortgagee should have only the tender. The mortgagor has been deprived of the use of his money, and the mortgagee has had ample time to reflect upon his rights, and has been at liberty to have them, whenever he would, by the acceptance of the tender. But when the tender is not kept good, the mortgagor has the use of the money, and the mortgagee, however ill-advised he may have been at the time of the tender, has no opportunity for revising and reconsidering his judgment, and thereafter accepting the money tendered": Crain v. McGoon, 86 Ill. 431; 29 Am. Rep. 37.

Depue, J., of the New Jersey supreme court, says: "When a court of law undertakes to deal with this equitable estate, it must do so upon principles of equity, [118] and keep in view the relief which would be afforded in equity, and protect the rights of the parties accordingly. The recognition of this equitable estate has been obtained in courts of law by the fiction of regarding the mortgagee, after his debt is satisfied, as a trustee of the legal estate for the mortgagor. Until the debt is paid, the legal seisin of the mortgagee is not a mere formal title, and no trust will be raised for the benefit of the mortgagor until the purpose for which the mortgage was made is answered": Shields v. Lozear, 34 N. J. L. 507; 3 Am. Rep. 256.

If, after condition broken, the mortgagor continues to hold the mortgage as security for his debt, a tender should have no greater effect upon the security than upon the debt itself. In such case, a tender does not discharge the debt at common law or under the statute heretofore quoted. The security is a mere accessory of the debt, and is only discharged when the debt is paid, except in cases in which principles of equity require a discharge.

Our opinion is, that a tender of the amount due on a mortgage debt, made after default, should not on principle discharge the mortgage, and should have no greater effect on the security than it has on the debt itself, and that the result will be the same whether the mortgagee holds the legal title in trust, or as a mere security. Defendants make no offer to redeem, but stand upon the strict legal rights they suppose their tender gives them. They state no legal defense to the action under this plea, and the court ruled correctly on it.

3. The facts charged in the first defense are that defendants, in August, 1890, purchased from plaintiff the lease, the deed of trust on the land, and the equity of redemption, for which they agreed to pay the amount then due on the mortgage notes, not to [119] exceed ten thousand dollars. Of this sum three thousand seven hundred and fifty dollars, was paid in cash and the balance they agreed to pay in one year thereafter. That plaintiffs thereupon assigned to defendants said lease, and secured from Mrs. Beard a deed conveying said land to defendants, subject to said deed of trust, and defendants were put in possession of said land under said lease. There is no allegation that any specific part of the purchase price was the consideration for the lease, or that the agreed price had been paid. Nor were any facts stated, such as making valuable improvements on the land, which would make it inequitable to take from them the possession.

The equity of redemption having been foreclosed, the defendants have no standing, unless they can maintain their right to the possession as assignee of the lease. This we think they cannot do.

The deed of trust and lease were executed by Mrs. Beard and were delivered to plaintiffs on the same day, and were filed for record by plaintiffs substantially at the same time. The certificate of the recorder shows that the lease was filed only one minute before the deed of trust, a difference which can be accounted for in the time taken to indorse the filing. But plaintiff was beneficiary in each, and there could have been no question of notice as affecting priorities, and the date of recording is a matter of no importance. The execution of the two instruments were evidently contemporaneous acts and constitute but one transaction.

It is also manifest that the purchase from plaintiffs by defendants of the equity of redemption, the lease and the mortgage notes, under which the latter sought to secure the entire title to the land, were intended to be, and were in fact, a single transaction. The consideration, ten thousand dollars, which defendant agreed to pay, was for all three rights purchased. It is evident that it was intended that the equity of redemption, the [120] mortgage, and the lease should go together, as it was intended the lease and the mortgage should when first executed. No equities are shown and none can be seen, which should prevent a merger of the lease into the greater title held by defendants, and to carry out the manifest intention of the parties we must hold that a merger took place. Great injustice would be done to plaintiff to hold otherwise. The agreement of plaintiff in effect was to vest the absolute title in defendants upon the payment of ten thousand dollars. Payment was not made, and the equity of redemption was foreclosed, and plaintiff thereby became the owner in fee of the premises. It cannot be thought for a moment that the parties intended that the lease should be kept separate and distinct from the title, and that defendants, without paying the agreed consideration, should enjoy the possession of the land until the termination of the lease in the year 1910.

In order to carry out the intention of the parties and to prevent gross injustice, we must hold that when defendants purchased the equity of redemption, lease, and mortgage, and was put into possession thereunder, the lease became merged in the greater estates, and the sale under the deed of trust passed the legal tender to plaintiffs free of the lease or any rights under it.

The judgment is affirmed.

Barclay, C. J., and Gantt, Sherwood, Brace, Burgess, and Robinson, JJ., concur.

———

TENDER—EFFECT OF UPON LIEN OF MORTGAGE.—
There is a conflict of judicial opinion as to the effect of a tender of a debt secured by a mortgage, made either upon the date of maturity or subsequent thereto. In some jurisdictions it is held to discharge the lien of the mortgage whether it is subsequently kept good or not, but this rule is not unquestioned. The various questions relative to tender are discussed in the monographic note to Moynahan v. Moore, 77 Am. Dec. 470-491, the question at issue in the principal case being noticed at page 489. See, also, Moore v. Norman, 43 Minn. 428; 19 Am. St. Rep. 247, and note; Renard v. Clink, 94 Mich. 1; 30 Am.

St. Rep. 458, and extended note; Maxwell **v.** Moore, 95 Ala. 166; 36 Am. St. Rep. 190, and note.

MERGER OF ESTATES — WHEN TAKES PLACE.—Whenever a greater and less estate meet and coincide in the same person, in the same right, without any intermediate estate, the less estate is immediately merged in the greater: Extended note to Speed v. Haun, 15 Am. Dec. 83. This rule at law is inflexible: Johnson v. Johnson, 7 Allen, 196; 83 Am. Dec. 676. See Boykin v. Ancrum, 23 S. C. 486; 13 Am. St. Rep. 698. As to when merger does not take place, see note to Boos v. Morgan, 30 Am. St. Rep. 245.

APPLEMAN *v.* APPLEMAN.

[140 MISSOURI, 309.]

DEED, DELIVERY OF, WHAT SUFFICIENT.—If a deed is simply sealed and acknowledged and left with the officer taking the acknowledgment, with instructions to hold it until called for by the proper person, and the grantee knew of, and assented to, the conveyance, and took and retained possession of the land described therein, but the deed, when called for by him, could not be found, it is, nevertheless, well delivered. ·

COSTS IN PARTITION, WHEN PROPERLY AWARDED AGAINST PLAINTIFFS.—If plaintiffs sue in partition and their title is denied as to a portion of the lands, and they alone contest this issue and are defeated thereon, it is proper to charge the costs of the trial against them.

W. H. Kennan and W. W. Fry, for the appellants.

George Robertson, for the respondents.

[311] BRACE, J. This is an action brought by a number of the heirs at law of Levi Appleman, deceased, against [312] the other heirs of said deceased, for partition of the real estate of which the said Appleman died seised, alleged to be three hundred and three acres as described in the petition. The only contested issues in the case arise upon the answer of the defendant Mary J. Appleman, a daughter of said deceased, who therein claimed that in the month of September, 1886, her father, the said Levi Appleman, in consideration of service theretofore rendered him, by his warranty deed duly signed, sealed, and acknowledged, conveyed to her, of the land described in the petition, "the northeast quarter of section 25, township 52, range 12, containing one hundred and sixty acres, and delivered the same to one G. W. Holloway for her; that afterward and while the deed remained in the hands of said Holloway, the same was lost or destroyed," and prayed that the title to said one hundred and sixty acre tract be vested in her. Issue upon this answer was joined by plaintiffs, in which, after a general denial of the alle-

gations of the answer, it was averred that if there was a deed
made as alleged in said answer, that the said Levi Appleman,
at the time of the making thereof, was of unsound mind and
incapable of making a valid conveyance, that the same was without consideration and was never accepted by said Mary J. Appleman. The issues were tried by the court and found for the defendant Mary J. Appleman, and the title to said one hundred
and sixty acres decreed to her, from which decree the plaintiffs
appeal.

After a careful consideration of all the evidence in the case,
we return the following answers to the questions raised by counsel for appellants in their brief.

1. It appears satisfactorily from the evidence that on the
eleventh day of September, 1886, the said Levi Appleman, by
his general warranty deed of that date, conveyed the said tract
of one hundred and sixty acres to his daughter Mary J. Appleman in consideration [313] of the love and affection which he
bore her, and of the obligation he felt he was under to her for
her long and faithful service to him after she had arrived at the
age of maturity. That said deed was duly signed, sealed, and
acknowledged before G. W. Holloway, a justice of the peace, and
with another like deed for other land executed in the same manner to his grandson Bell Jackson Appleman, was delivered to
the said Holloway with the direction "to take these deeds and
hold them until they are called for by the proper persons." That
the said Mary J. Appleman knew at the time or was thereafter
informed that said deed to her had been so executed and assented
thereto, and thereafter in the lifetime of her father took possession of the premises. That said deeds remained in the possession of Holloway some time, when the deed to the grandson
was called for and delivered to him. The deed of the daughter,
remaining in his possession a still longer time, could not, when
called for, be found, and remained lost at the time of the trial.
Under these circumstances, we think the deed was well delivered, the rule being in respect to a grantee not under disability
"that when such grantee is aware of the conveyance, and does
not dissent, and the conveyance is positively beneficial to him
or her, acceptance will be presumed": Hall v. Hall, 107 Mo.
101; Standiford v. Standiford, 97 Mo. 231. There can be no
question but that the "direction to deliver the deed to the proper
person" was a direction to deliver it to the grantee Mary J. Appleman, and as the deed took effect and the title passed to her

at the date of the delivery to Holloway, the subsequent loss of the deed could in no way affect her rights under the deed.

2. The weight of the evidence is, that the said Levi Appleman, at the time of the execution of the deed, was of sound mind and capable of disposing of [314] his property in a rational manner, and that he made the conveyance freely and voluntarily with full knowledge of his property, situation, surroundings, and circumstances and of all those who had any claims upon his bounty.

3. The court committed no error in taxing the costs of the trial of this issue against the plaintiffs; they alone contested the issue, and having lost it, should pay the costs. Finding no error, the judgment is affirmed.

Barclay, P. J., Macfarlane, and Robinson, JJ., concur.

DEEDS — DELIVERY OF — WHAT SUFFICIENT.—The delivery of a deed by the grantor to the officer who takes the acknowledgment, with unqualified instructions to deliver to the grantee whenever he calls for it, followed by an acceptance of the title conveyed, vests title to the land in the grantee, although the grantee permits the officer to retain the deed merely as a matter of convenience: Monographic note to Brown v. Westerfield, 53 Am. St. Rep. 545, as to what is a delivery of a deed. A deed being merely evidence of the grantee's title, its loss or destruction after delivery does not divest the title of the grantee: Brown v. Westerfield, 47 Neb. 399; 53 Am. St. Rep. 532.

COSTS—WHO ENTITLED TO.—In actions at law the prevailing party is entitled to costs, although he may recover only a part of his demand: Extended note to Saunders v. Frost, 16 Am. Dec. 405. In equity, costs are awarded, in the discretion of the court, to either party as justice may require; but the prima facie right thereto is in the prevailing party: Saunders v. Frost, 5 Pick. 259; 16 Am. Dec. 394, and note. See Turner v. Johnson, 95 Mo. 431; 6 Am. St. Rep. 62.

EMMONS *v.* GORDON.

[140 MISSOURI, 490.]

EXECUTORS, POWER OF TO ACT IN ANOTHER STATE. So far as concerns realty, a will beyond the jurisdiction where it is probated is inoperative and has no extraterritorial force, and the executor cannot, because of his appointment in accordance with the laws of one state, sell real property of his testator situated in another state, unless the will was there proved or the laws of that state, dispensing with probate anew, confer the requisite permission.

EXECUTOR, WHETHER MUST ACCOUNT FOR PROCEEDS OF LANDS SOLD IN ANOTHER STATE.—If an executor sells lands of his testator situate in another state without the will being there admitted to probate, such sales must be regarded as made without authority and as passing no title. Hence an action cannot be sustained against him or the sureties on his bond for the moneys received by him in consideration of such sales.

EXECUTORS.—THE SURETIES ON THE BOND OF AN EXECUTOR who, by the will is given power to sell realty, are answerable for proceeds received by him from the sale or rent of lands situated within the state.

W. W. Fry, for the appellants.

George Robertson, for the respondents.

[492] BURGESS, J. This proceeding was begun in the probate court of Audrain county, under section 48 of the Revised Statutes of 1889, to compel the defendant Gordon, as executor of the last will and testament of J. J. West, deceased, to account with the plaintiff as administrator de bonis non with the will annexed of said deceased, and for judgment against said Gordon and his securities and the heirs of William M. Sims, one of the sureties now deceased on his bond as such executor. The case went by appeal from the probate to the circuit court of Audrain county.

J. J. West, deceased, died testate. His will is as follows:

"Know all men by these presents, that I, Jeremiah J. West, of the county of Audrain and state of Missouri do make and publish this, my last will and testament.

"Item first. I desire, will, and direct that all my just debts shall be paid from the proceeds of my property, and to that end I will and direct my executor to sell at public or private sale, and on such terms as may seem best, all or so much of my property as may be necessary for the payment of my debts, and I hereby give him full power and authority to execute such deeds and conveyances to any and all of my [493] property as may be necessary to convey the title to the same. And I direct my executor to pay my debts as soon as may be after my decease.

"Item second. After the payment of my debts it is my will, and I hereby direct, that my executor pay over to my beloved wife, Zelophia West, the full net income and proceeds of all property remaining undisposed of and not necessary for the payment of debts. Said income and proceeds to be paid to my said wife, as it accrues for the support and maintenance of herself and her children during her natural life, and after the death of my beloved wife I will and direct that all my property remaining undisposed of be sold and the proceeds be divided equally between the following named of my children, that is to say: Jeremiah J. West, Jr., Enoch Bascum West, Mary Jane

Cox, Nancy Marvin Fowles, Martha Caples West, and Sarah Pierce West, until each one of the above-named children shall have received the sum of two thousand dollars, and after the above named of my children shall have received the sum of two thousand dollars each, then it is my will and I hereby direct that the rest and residue of my property be divided among all my children, share and share alike.

"Item third. I give and bequeath to my daughter Louisa Gardner the sum of five dollars, and also an interest or share in the residue of my estate if there shall be any after giving to my other children the sum of two thousand dollars each.

"Item fourth. It is my will, desire, and I so direct that my wife retain and keep all my household and kitchen furniture, beds and bedding, and two cows, and provisions for one year for herself and family.

"Item fifth. I hereby appoint John M. Gordon of Audrain county my executor, and direct him to execute and carry out this, my last will and testament.

494 "Item sixth. I commit my soul to God, who gave it, and direct that my body be decently buried. In witness whereof I have hereunto set my hand on this 11th day of April, 1879.

"J. J. WEST."

John M. Gordon qualified as executor and as such executed bond as follows:

"We, John M. Gordon as principal, and William M. Sims, Chas. W. Baker, C. T. Black, and Robert Luckie, Jr., as securities, are held and firmly bound unto the state of Missouri in the sum of ten thousand dollars, for the payment of which we do hereby bind ourselves, our heirs, executors, and administrators firmly by these presents.

"Sealed with our seals and dated at Mexico, in the state aforesaid, this 28th day of April, 1879.

"The condition of the above bond is that if the said John M. Gordon, executor of the last will and testament of J. J. West, deceased, late of Audrain county, Missouri, shall well and faithfully execute the said last will and testament and shall make true and faithful inventories, returns, and settlements of accounts of the estate of the said testator, according to law; and shall, moreover, do and perform all other matters and things touching the execution of said last will and testament, as are or shall be prescribed by law, or enjoined on him by the order, sentence, or decree of any court having competent jurisdiction, then this obligation to be void and of no effect; otherwise to remain in full force.

> "JOHN M. GORDON.   [Seal]
> "WILLIAM M. SIMS.   [Seal]
> "CHARLES W. BAKER.   [Seal]
> "C. T. BLACK.   [Seal]
> "ROBERT LUCKIE, Jr.   [Seal]

"Filed for record April 28th, 1879."

William M. Sims died some time prior to May 25, 1885, leaving a will which was duly probated on that [495] day in the probate court of Audrain county. Final settlement of his estate was made September 15, 1887. Mrs. Potts and Mrs. Clark were the only heirs of Sims, who with their husbands, J. A. Potts and C. F. Clark, are made defendants. The proceedings were dismissed as to C. T. Black, in the probate court on the twenty-third day of February, 1891. At the September term, 1895, of the Audrain circuit court the death of John M. Gordon was suggested of record, and the suit revived against the defendant Robert Luckie as his administrator, who entered his voluntary appearance.

At the time of West's decease he was the owner of a large personal estate and several tracts of land in the state of Missouri, and several large tracts of land in the state of Texas. Gordon sold the lands in Texas under the power conferred upon him by the will as executor, and as such received the purchase money and executed deeds therefor.

The trial court in passing upon the case and in rendering judgment, said: "The plaintiff has filed an itemized statement of the amounts he contends the defendant should be charged with in the final settlement. First and most prominent among them is a balance of the purchase price of land situate in Texas sold by Gordon as executor and only part of the consideration accounted for by him. That he failed to account for fifteen hundred and twenty-nine dollars and seventy-four cents of the purchase price, is proven beyond controversy. The defendants contend, and by their motion in the case so ask, that this court strike out of his settlement a charge made by him against himself of four thousand five hundred and fifty-five dollars and sixty-eight cents, proceeds of such sale, for the reason he had no authority as executor to sell the land or receive the purchase price and hence could not receive it as executor." The court then rendered the following judgment:

496 "Now on this February 10, 1896, this cause being called by the court, the said cause having been heard at the last September term and taken under advisement, the court doth find the following items in favor of the plaintiff and against the said John M. Gordon's estate as follows:

John M. Gordon, Executor..........................Dr.
To estate of J. J. West, deceased.

Amount received by him from Hy Barker, March 29, 1880..$	675	56
6 per cent interest thereon to Jan. 20, 1896.............	640	09
Amount received from Harrison, December 20, 1881........	269	50
6 per cent interest thereon to Jan. 20, 1896............	227	72
Amount received from Harrison, May 10, 1883.............	44	50
6 per cent interest thereon to Jan. 20, 1896............	33	88
Amount received from Harrison, balance on Eastern rent, March 1, 1885....................................	25	00
6 per cent interest thereon to Jan. 20, 1896............	16	22
Commission on interest improperly charged by executor in settlement May 12, 1885, on $377.15................	18	85
6 per cent interest thereon to Jan. 20, 1896...........	17	38
Excessive commission charged in settlement November 13, 1884, on $1,039.54.................................	51	97
6 per cent interest thereon to Jan. 20, 1896...........	35	00
Error in debit account of addition in settlement November 26, 1887......................................	6	00
6 per cent interest thereon to Jan. 20, 1896...........	2	91
Excessive commission charged in settlement, 1882, and again charged in settlement, November 13, 1884, on $573.74	20	68
6 per cent interest thereon to Jan. 20, 1896............	19	20
Commission on $4,555.68 debit item in second settlement stricken out	227	78
	$2,340	94

"And the court doth further strike from the said settlement of said John M. Gordon the item of $4,555.68 arising from the sale of Texas lands, thereby leaving a balance due the said John M. Gordon's estate of the sum of $2,214.74. Whereupon the court doth order and adjudge that said plaintiff revise his settlement as administrator in accordance herewith, and that costs hereof be adjudged against plaintiff and that execution is issued therefor.

497 "And it is further ordered that a certified copy of this judgment be certified back to the probate court of Audrain county."

From the judgment plaintiff appeals.

The question of chief importance involved in this appeal is as to whether or not Gordon and his sureties can be held liable upon his bond as executor of West for the moneys received by him for the Texas lands which were sold and deeded by him to the purchasers thereof, as such executor. There seems to be no question as to the sale of these lands by Gordon and the receipt of the purchase money by him. Indeed, the court found that he failed to account for $1,529.74 of the purchase price which was received by him, beside he had in a former settlement charged himself with the sum of $4,555.68 proceeds of such sale, but defendants contend that he ought not to be charged with the proceeds of such sale, for the reason that he had no authority as executor to sell the land or receive the purchase money, and therefore could not receive it as executor.

In Wilson v. Wilson, 54 Mo. 213, it is held that the difference between an administrator and an executor lies in the fact that the former derives his power from appointment by the probate court, and has no power until appointed, while an executor derives his power from the will, and the property vests in him from the time of the testator's death.

The expression made use of in that case to the effect that the real estate belonging to the testator at the time of his death vested in his executor at that time, is not to be understood as vesting the title absolutely and unconditionally in the executor, but rather the power of disposition, for under our laws real estate upon the death of the testator passes to his heirs, subject **498** to the power of disposal conferred upon his executor by the will, and where the will, as in the case in hand, directs that his lands shall be sold by his executor, it is clear that he is given but the naked power to sell, and that he has no interest in the land: Herbert v. Smith, 1 N. J. Eq. 141.

In Aubuchon v. Lory, 23 Mo. 99, it is said: "The real estate of a deceased person descends, upon his death, to his heirs, or passes to the devisees under his will. By the common law, the personal representative, whether executor or administrator, takes no interest in it, and our statute gives him nothing but the naked power to sell for the payment of debts, or to make short leases, under the directions of the county court."

An administrator's power as such does not extend beyond the boundaries of the state in which his letters of administration are granted, nor can he sue in the courts of any state, or take possession of property belonging to his intestate without becoming a trespasser, unless he first qualifies as administrator according to the laws of the state where suit is intended to be brought, or the property is situated. In other words, letters of administration have no extraterritorial force: Naylor v. Moffatt, 29 Mo. 126; Scudder v. Ames, 89 Mo. 522; In re Partnership Estate of Ames, 52 Mo. 290; State v. Osborn, 71 Mo. 86; McPike v. McPike, 111 Mo. 216. An administrator's actions are controlled by the probate court, under whose supervision they come, and while an executor derives his power to act as such with respect to the transfer of real estate, and can dispose of it as provided by the will by which he is appointed executor without first obtaining an order of court, he can only convey such property in conformity with the laws of the state where he attempts to operate under the will, and not from the will alone, and he and his sureties cannot, [499] therefore, be held liable upon his bond as executor for moneys received by him for lands sold in another state, not in compliance with the laws of that state. There are authorities, however, which announce a different rule, that is, which hold that where an executor qualifies as such in one state and sells lands in another state which belonged to his testator, under the power conferred upon him by the will, the executor and his securities will be required to account for the proceeds arising from the sale of such property by him: Hooper v. Hooper, 29 W. Va. 276; 2 Woerner on American Law of Administration, sec. 537; Judge of Probate v. Heydock, 8 N. H. 491. But the weight of authority unquestionably is in accord with the rule announced by this court, through Sherwood, J., in Cabanne v. Skinker, 56 Mo. 367, in which it is said: "So far as concerns the realty a will beyond the jurisdiction where it is probated is inoperative and has no extraterritorial force or validity; and the executor of such will cannot, because of his appointment in accordance with the laws of one state, thereby acquire authority to sue for, or in any manner intermeddle with, the property or effects of his testator, whether real or personal, in another state, unless the will be there proven, or the laws of such state dispensing with the probate anew confer the requisite permission: Kerr v. Moon, 9 Wheat. 565; Doe v. McFarland, 9 Cranch, 151; Story's Conflict of Law, sec. 474; McCormick v. Sullivant, 10 Wheat. 192; Lucas v. Tucker, 17 Ind. 41; Wills v. Cowper, 2 Ohio, 124. Under the circumstances, then, as detailed in the petition, Cabanne, the testator, must be regarded as having died intestate as to whatever lands in the territory of Colorado he was possessed of at the time of his decease; and those lands, of course, in consequence of his intestacy, descended in conformity to the laws of that territory [500] to his heirs at law. But as to who those heirs are, no information is afforded us. There is not the remotest information contained in the petition that the plaintiffs are those heirs, nor is it shown that the plaintiffs had any title, either legal or equitable, in the property in Colorado. If they had no interest in the land itself, they certainly could have none in the proceeds arising from the sale thereof. It being out of the power of the executor, as such, to have any control over, or right to interfere with, the property situate in Colorado, it must inevitably follow that neither he nor his sureties can, in consequence of any acts done in Colorado, be held liable on the bond given for the faithful performance of the duties pertaining to the executorship in this state."

In McCormick v. Sullivant, 10 Wheat. 192, it was held that title to lands by devise can be acquired only under a will duly proved and recorded, according to the law of the state in which the lands lie; and that the probate of a will in the state of Pennsylvania gave it no validity whatever in respect to lands situated in the state of Ohio, and as to which the court considered the deceased as having died intestate, and consequently that they descended to his heirs.

In Kerr v. Moon, 9 Wheat. 565, it was held that: "It is an unquestionable principle of general law that the title to, and the disposition of, real property must be exclusively subject to the laws of the country where it is situated." And it is also ruled in the same case that where lands were situated in Ohio which were claimed under a will made and proved in Kentucky, it was essential to the establishment of the title to prove that the will had been proven and recorded according to the laws of Ohio.

The same rule is announced in Story's Conflict of Laws, section 474, and in Lucas v. Tucker, 17 Ind. 41. [501] There was no evidence in this case that the will of West had ever been probated in the state of Texas, in the absence of which Gordon's sales of the lands in that state were without authority, passed no title, and he and his sureties upon his bond as executor are not responsible for the moneys received by him in consideration for such sales.

But for the proceeds of all lands received by him from the sale or rent of lands in this state he and his sureties are liable upon his bond: Dix v. Morris, 1 Mo. App. 93; Gamble v. Gibson, 59 Mo. 585.

Finding no reversible error in the record, the judgment is affirmed.

Barclay, C. J., Gantt, and Sherwood, JJ., concur; Brace and Robinson, JJ., dissent; Macfarlane, J., not sitting.

EXECUTORS AND ADMINISTRATORS — FOREIGN, POWERS OF.—A grant of administration cannot extend as a matter of right beyond the territory of the state in which it is granted: Vroom v. Van Horne, 10 Paige, 549; 42 Am. Dec. 94, and note; Schneller v. Vance, 8 La. 506; 28 Am. Dec. 140. An administrator or guardian cannot receive rents of lands outside the state in which he is appointed, nor can the probate court authorize him to receive them; and if he does receive them he does so in his own wrong, and is bound to pay the money to those entitled to it: Smith v. Wiley, 22 Ala. 396; 58 Am. Dec. 262, and note. See Governor v. Williams, 3 Ired. 152; 38 Am. Dec. 712. It has been held also that neither an administrator nor his bondsmen are liable for his intermeddling with his intestate's property in another state, but these comparatively early decisions must not be regarded as opposed to the weight of authority: Monographic note to Shinn's Estate, 45 Am. St. Rep. 670, 671.

EXECUTORS AND ADMINISTRATORS — LIABILITY OF SURETIES FOR SALE OF LANDS IN ANOTHER STATE.—Where land is sold in another state and the administrator receives the proceeds, his sureties are liable therefor: Monographic note to Commonwealth v. Stub, 51 Am. Dec. 520, 521. Contra, Fletcher v. Sanders, 7 Dana, 345; 32 Am. Dec. 96, and note. See, also, note to Shinn's Estate, 45 Am. St. Rep. 670, 671; Andrews v. Avory, 17 Gratt. 229; 73 Am. Dec. 355.

STATE *v.* EAST FIFTH STREET RAILWAY COMPANY.

[140 MISSOURI, 539.]

STREET RAILWAYS, PRIVILEGES OF, WHETHER ARE FRANCHISES OR LICENSES.—The privilege granted to a street railway corporation of laying its tracks on designated streets and running cars thereon, and to charge and receive fares from persons riding upon such cars, is not a mere license. It is a franchise without which the corporate charter would be of no value. This remains true, though the privilege or franchise is granted by a municipality under authority conferred by the state legislature. In making the grant the state must be regarded as acting through the municipality as its agent.

QUO WARRANTO, RIGHT TO MAINTAIN FOR THE FORFEITURE OF THE FRANCHISE OF A STREET RAILWAY.— Though the franchise of a street railway corporation was granted by the common council of a municipality, and the ordinance making the grant provided that on failure of the corporation to comply with the conditions thereof, it should forfeit its rights and powers, and that a suit to enforce such forfeiture might be maintained by the municipality, and in its name, the state may maintain quo warranto to enforce such forfeiture. Its power to proceed by quo warranto cannot be contracted away or enlarged by the city.

FRANCHISE, FORFEITURE OF.—A PROCEEDING IN EQUITY is not a proper remedy to enforce the forfeiture of a franchise.

STREET RAILWAYS, FORFEITURE OF FRANCHISE OF.
A street railway refusing or neglecting to run its cars for considerable periods of time when by its charter required to run them for sixteen hours each day, thereby forfeits its franchise, and such forfeiture may be enforced by quo warranto.

FRANCHISE, FORFEITURE OF.—THE INSOLVENCY of a street railway corporation constitutes no ground for forfeiting its franchise, if it continues to discharge its duties to the public.

AN ESTOPPEL IN PAIS MUST BE PLEADED.

QUO WARRANTO, ESTOPPEL TO MAINTAIN.—The fact that the municipality granting a street railway a franchise prevented it from laying its track at a designated place does not estop it as relator in a quo warranto proceeding from enforcing the forfeiture of the franchise for nonuser, if it appears that the acts of the municipality of which complaint is made by the corporation did not injure it.

QUO WARRANTO.—NONUSER OF A FRANCHISE cannot be justified in a proceeding to enforce a forfeiture because of such nonuser on the ground that the municipality granting the franchise had passed an ordinance repealing, or attempting to repeal, its grant.

QUO WARRANTO — FRANCHISE, FORFEITURE OF, WHETHER MAY BE WAIVED BY A CITY.—A municipality granting a franchise to a street railway corporation cannot waive the forfeiture thereof arising from nonuser. The streets of a municipality are for the use of the general public, and neither the city nor its officers can deprive the state of the right to proceed by quo warranto to enforce the forfeiture of the franchise.

Johnson & Lucas, for the appellants.

H. C. McDougal and C. O. Tichenor, for the respondent.

543 BURGESS J. This is a proceeding by the state at the relation of Kansas City, Missouri, by Marcy K. Brown, prosecuting attorney of Jackson county, Missouri, by quo warranto to oust defendants of their corporate franchises granted to them by said city by ordinances, to construct, maintain, and operate a street railway on certain streets in said city, upon the ground of their failure to comply with said ordinance, and the consequent forfeiture of their franchise rights under said ordinance.

The petition alleges that the relator was on the ninth day of May, 1889, and ever since has been, a municipal corporation under the laws of the state of Missouri, having full power and control over its streets. That defendants are corporations under the laws of this state, except defendant Thornton, who is trustee in a deed of trust executed by the East Fifth Street Railway Company on the first day of November, 1890, on the franchises hereinafter described. That by certain ordinances passed by said city, the right was given and accepted by said defendant railway company to construct, maintain, and operate a street railway on certain of its streets. That by reason of said **544** ordinances the defendant railway company claims the right to maintain and operate a street railway over certain streets named in said ordinance, and had in fact laid its tracks on said streets. But that said railway company had failed for eighteen months prior to November 12, 1892, to run cars over said streets, and had never complied with the provisions of said ordinances, although notice was given by relator to said company to run cars over said streets, but that it refused and still refuses so to do. That said railway company has failed and neglected for more than eighteen months prior to November 12, 1892, to keep in repair its tracks and roadbed, and permitted its tracks to become a nuisance, and has abandoned the rights granted in said ordinances.

The answer admits the acceptance of the ordinances by the railway company, and alleges that said ordinances constitute valid and subsisting contracts between said city and defendant railway company. The answer also admits that defendant railway company and defendant trust company are now and were during the dates mentioned in said information, corporations organized under the laws of the state of Missouri, and that the deed of trust mentioned in the information has not been released or satisfied, and that defendants, by reason of said ordinances, claim the right to run, maintain, and operate a street railway over the streets named in said ordinances. It then alleges that section 17 of ordinance number 42389 requires an action for forfeiture to be brought within six months after cause of forfeiture has arisen, and that causes are alleged in the information to have arisen eighteen months prior to the filing of the information. That defendant railway company was unlawfully prevented by the police of the city of Kansas from constructing its railway on Fifth street from Grand avenue [545] to Main street, and was harassed by litigation, whereby its credit was impaired and its financial operations so embarrassed that it was unable to procure funds necessary to complete its railway, and was compelled to mortgage the same in its uncompleted condition to pay the loss sustained by reason of the acts of the city of Kansas, and to cease, temporarily, the operation of its cars, but intends to resume such operation at the earliest moment the financial condition of the public and itself will permit.

It appears from the record that in December, 1881, by an ordinance of Kansas City, a franchise was granted to certain persons named in said ordinance to construct and operate a street railway on certain streets in that city.

The franchise was to continue for twenty years; the company

was to keep the tracks in repair, and the spaces between the tracks and for eighteen inches on the outside well paved; cars were to be regularly run for not less than sixteen hours per day, "during each and every day of the entire year." With the consent of the grantees of the franchise, a subsequent order was passed whereby the franchise was extended for thirty years from September 1, 1885, and the starting point fixed at Fifth street and Grand avenue, instead of Fifth and Main streets. In June, 1888, another ordinance was passed by said city which recites in its preamble, the following: "Whereas, the East Fifth Street Railway Company is the successor and owner of all franchises and ordinances above granted." This ordinance then, among other things, regulates the pavement of spaces between the tracks, and the keeping of them in good condition and repair. Section 12 of this ordinance provides for the equipment of the road and the running of the cars, and gave defendant [546] the right to collect a fare of five cents for each passenger. By a still later ordinance passed also in June, 1888, defendant was granted a franchise to extend its road to the eastern limits of the city. It had the right to operate its cars on this portion of its route by endless cable or noiseless steam power, with smokeless fuel. Section 17 of this ordinance reads as follows: "If the said railway company shall at any time fail, neglect, or refuse to obey and comply with any one of the provisions of this ordinance, then said company shall forfeit all rights, powers, and privileges by this ordinance granted and conferred, and this ordinance shall be null and void. Such forfeiture and such annulling of this ordinance may be had by proceedings instituted by the city of Kansas, in its own name and against said company, in a court of record in Jackson county, Missouri, and on proof of such failure, neglect, or refusal on the part of the said company; provided, that if any such proceedings be not commenced within six months after such failure, refusal, or neglect of said company to comply with any one of the provisions of this ordinance, then as to such failure, refusal, or neglect, the city shall be deemed to waive the effect thereof under this section of this ordinance."

From the date of the original ordinance, December 18, 1881, to the time of trial in the court below, the road was only operated for two or three months and then by electric-cars. The company then suspended operating the road from eighteen months to two years, after which it ran some steam-cars from one and a half to two years. For about three years before the time of the.

trial of this cause it ran no cars at all, and did nothing toward the operation of the road. Some time prior to the bringing of this proceeding, they sold their cars to some company in Texas, and paid the proceeds upon a mortgage upon the road, upon which was due about [547] one hundred and ten thousand dollars. The company is insolvent, but some of its officers testified that they expect to run it again. They seemed to have no idea when the company will operate the road again. The evidence on the part of defendant railway company showed that defendant was prevented by the Kansas City police force from laying its tracks on Fifth street between Grand avenue and Main street; that the company was harassed by litigation by the city and property owners, which greatly depreciated the value of its property. It also tended to show that said company had not abandoned its rights under said ordinances.

No notice was ever given by Kansas City to defendant railway company to run its cars. Nor was the information filed for more than six months after the alleged grounds for forfeiture arose.

At the conclusion of the evidence the court, at the request of the relator, gave the following declaration of law: "The court declares the law to be that if defendant has ceased to operate its road, that it has sold its rolling stock and has none with which to operate its road, and that it has no means with which to purchase more stock and is heavily in debt, then judgment must go for relator."

The court gave judgment of ouster against the defendants, from which they appeal.

1. Defendant's contention is, that quo warranto is not the proper remedy in this case; that the state has no interest in this controversy; that the "franchise" granted by it and the only one that it is interested in, is not the subject matter of this litigation; that the questions involved are of a personal nature, between the relator on the one hand, and the defendant railway company on the other, the relator alleging failure to comply with the terms and conditions of a contract [548] between it and defendant, and the defendant denying noncompliance and pleading estoppel, a question that can be fully settled by a court of chancery in an action brought by the relator against the defendant. Upon the other hand, it is claimed that there is a difference between the charter and a franchise independent of it, and that this proceeding is based upon that distinction.

In the case of Memphis R. R. Co. v. Commissioners, 112 U. S. 619, the court says: "The essential properties of corporate existence are quite distinct from the franchises of the corporation. The franchise of being a corporation belongs to the corporators, while the powers and privileges vested in and to be exercised by the corporate body as such are the franchises of the corporation. The latter has no power to dispose of the franchise of its members, which may survive in the mere fact of corporate existence, after the company has parted with all its property and all its franchises."

It may be said that corporate existence is as much a franchise as the franchises of the corporation. The former is not property in the ordinary acceptation of the term, cannot be transferred by ordinary conveyance, nor by sale under execution, unless the statutes of the state so provide, while corporate franchises are property, can be transferred by voluntary conveyance or by sale under execution against the corporation: New Orleans etc. R. R. Co. v. Delamore, 114 U. S. 501. In the case in hand, the privilege of laying its tracks on the designated streets, to run cars thereon, and to charge and receive fares from persons riding on its cars were franchises of the defendant railway company, without which the charter would be of no value. Such privileges were not mere licenses. A different view, however, seems to have been taken in the case of the People v. Mutual Gaslight Co., 38 Mich. 154, in which it was ruled that the right to lay pipes in the streets of a city is not a state ⁵⁴⁹ franchise but a local easement resting only on a contract or license, the violation of which does not concern the state, and is open to legal remedy. A similar view seems also to have been taken by the supreme court of Illinois in the case of Belleville v. Citizens' Horse Ry. Co., 152 Ill. 171. But those cases we think not in line with the great weight of authority. Thus Mr. Justice Field, in speaking of franchise in Morgan v. Louisiana, 93 U. S. 223, says: "But the term must always be considered in connection with the corporation or property to which it is alleged to appertain. The franchises of a railroad corporation are rights or privileges which are essential to the operations of the corporation, and without which its road and works would be of little value; such as the franchise to run cars, to take tolls, to appropriate earth and gravel for the bed of its road, or water for its engines, and the like. They are positive rights or privileges, without the possession of which the road of the company could not be successfully worked. Immunity from taxation is not one of them. The former may be conveyed to a purchaser of the road as part of the property of the company; the latter is personal, and incapable of transfer without express statutory direction." A franchise is of public concern which cannot be exercised by individuals at pleasure, but is of legislative origin, and from that source it must derive its power and authority to acquire rights and privileges for the public good. "It is an executed contract on the part of the state, the consideration for which is the benefit which the public will derive from its use and exercise": Ashland v. Wheeler, 88 Wis. 615; California v. Pacific R. R. Co., 127 U. S. 40; New Orleans Waterworks Co. v. Rivers, 115 U. S. 674; Wheat v. City Council of Alexandria, 88 Va. 742; Port of Mobile v. Louisville etc. R. R. Co., 84 Ala. 119; 5 Am. St. Rep. 342; Baltimore Trust etc. Co. v. Mayor etc., 64 Fed. Rep. 153.

550 This court has recognized the rights of street railways in the streets of a municipality as franchises and as vested rights which might be mortgaged by the company to whom the franchise belonged: Hovelman v. Kansas City etc. R. R. Co., 79 Mo. 643.

While the franchises involved in this controversy were derived directly from the city by the East Fifth Street Railway Company, under ordinances passed under the grant of power contained in the city charter, that power was conferred upon the city by the general assembly, so that the power came indirectly from the state, and in granting it the state acted through the city as its agent: Transportation Co. v. Chicago, 99 U. S. 641; Port of Mobile v. Louisville etc. R. R. Co., 84 Ala. 119; 5 Am. St. Rep. 342. The power of the city to grant the franchises in question is unquestionable.

We do not think, however, that the fact that the franchises in question are in a sense contractual in their nature, is a barrier to the prosecution of this suit if the facts alleged and proven be sufficient to oust defendant company of its franchises, notwithstanding section 17, supra, of the ordinance passed in June, 1888, provides that in case of failure, neglect, or refusal by the defendant railway company to obey and comply with any of the provisions of said ordinance, said company shall forfeit all rights, powers, and privileges conferred thereby, and that such forfeiture may be had by proceedings instituted by said city in its own name, against said company in a court of record in Jackson county, Missouri. The sovereign power of the state to proceed against defendant company by quo warranto for forfeiture of its franchises, even at the relation of the city, could not be contracted away or in any way abridged by the city. At most, such a provision in the ordinance only provided the city another remedy: Fath [551] v. Tower Grove etc. By. Co., 105 Mo. 545; President etc. **v.** State, 19 Md. 239.

Moreover, a proceeding in equity is not the proper remedy to enforce the forfeiture of a franchise. Pomeroy, in his work on Equity, second edition, section 459, says: "It is a well-settled and familiar doctrine that a court of equity will not interfere on behalf of the party entitled thereto, and enforce a forfeiture, but will leave him to his legal remedies, if any, even though the case might be one in which no equitable relief would be given to the defaulting party against the forfeiture." The same rule is announced in High on Extraordinary Remedies, second edition, section 660, in which it is said: "The dissolution of a corporation and the revocation of its franchises are generally considered matters of legal rather than of equitable cognizance, and unless a court of chancery is especially empowered to divest a corporation of its franchises, the more appropriate remedy for this purpose is by information in the nature of a quo warranto": Attorney General v. Tudor Ice Co., 104 Mass. 239; 6 Am. Rep. 227; National Bank v. Matthews, 98 U. S. 621. In Hovelman v. Kansas City etc. R. R. Co., 79 Mo. 643, this court said: "It is the settled rule that the acts of a corporation can be assailed for abuse or excess of its corporate powers only in a direct proceeding brought by the state for that purpose." The city granted the franchises in the interest of the public, and we see no reason why she should not be relator in this proceeding to have the franchises forfeited in the interest of the public also, if the facts and circumstances in proof justify such a result.

The question then arises, Was the nonuser of the franchises, by defendant company under the circumstances disclosed by the record, sufficient to justify the court in declaring their forfeiture? In considering this question, it may be said that the insolvency of the corporation [552] is of no importance except in so far as it may have a bearing upon the question of abandonment of its franchises by defendant, for if defendant continued to discharge its duties to the public, it makes no difference whether it was solvent or not. Were it otherwise, very many corporations might be ousted of their franchises at any time, to the great detriment of the members thereof as well also as the general public for whose benefit public corporations and franchises are presumed to be granted. The sale, however, by the defendant company of all of its rolling stock and its failure to operate its road for so long a time, and then not in accordance with the terms of the ordinances, tended very strongly to show an abandonment by defendant of its franchises. But whether there was an abandonment by defendant of its franchises or not, the evidence clearly shows that the ordinances granting the railroad company the franchises were never complied with. Electric-cars were run for about three months, and then steam-cars which it had no right to run, except upon the eastern extension of the road. It ran steam-cars for about eighteen months, and for three years next preceding the trial, it did not operate its road at all, while under the ordinances its cars were to be regularly run not less than sixteen hours per day, during every day in the year.

In the case of Roanoke Inv. Co. v. Kansas City etc. Ry. Co., 108 Mo. 50, it is said: "But while it is true that mere nonuser will not amount to an abandonment, it is well settled that an easement acquired by grant or its equivalent may be lost by abandonment. To constitute an abandonment of an easement acquired by grant, acts must be shown of such an unequivocal nature as to indicate a clear intention to abandon: Curran v. Louisville, 83 Ky. 628; Dyer v. Sanford, 9 Met. 395; 43 Am. Dec. 399; Hayford v. Spokesfield, 100 Mass. 491. It is said, however, [553] that abandonment will be more readily inferred when the easement was granted for public purposes than when it was created for private use." In Beach on Private Corporations, section 45, it is said: "It is conceded that a corporation may forfeit its charter or franchises for willful misuser or nonuser thereof. For it is a tacit condition annexed to the creation of every corporation that it shall be subject to dissolution by forfeiture of its franchise for willful misuser or nonuser in regard to matters which go to the essence of the contract between it and the state." On the same subject, Morawetz on Private Corporations, section 1018, says: "It has accordingly been held in various cases that if a corporation has assumed the performance of duties for the benefit of the public generally, it cannot neglect the performance of these duties without incurring a forfeiture of its franchises. Thus it is the duty of a corporation to build a turnpike road to maintain its road in repair as a thoroughfare for the public use. . . . . The same rule undoubtedly applies to other corporations of a similar character, such as ferry and bridge companies, canal companies, gas companies, etc."

The generally accepted doctrine is that the omission of an express duty imposed by the charter of a corporation is cause for its forfeiture, and in such circumstances the sovereign who granted the charter may insist on resuming the grant for breach of the duty imposed: Commonwealth v. Commercial Bank, 28 Pa. St. 383; Attorney General v. Petersburg etc. R. R. Co., 6 Ired. 456; Erie etc. R. R. Co. v. Casey, 26 Pa. St. 287. And where there has been a willful misuser or nonuser by a corporation it is subject to dissolution by forfeiture of its franchises: Mumma v. Potomac Co., 8 Pet. 281; Terrett v. Taylor, 9 Cranch, 51; Chicago Life Ins. Co. v. Needles, 113 U. S. 574; People v. Broadway R. R. Co., 126 N. Y. 29. "The rule in [554] regard to acts of misuser and nonuser is, that they must relate to matters of the essence of the contract between the sovereign and the corporation; and we see no reason why that rule should not be applied in the present case. Where duties are imposed upon a corporation from motives of public policy, a total neglect of the duty justifies a judgment of forfeiture": State v. Wood, 13 Mo. App. 142; Harris v. Mississippi Valley etc. R. R. Co., 51 Miss. 602. One of the duties imposed upon defendant by ordinance which it accepted and in which the public had an interest, was to run its cars sixteen hours every day in the year with which there was no compliance on its part, but a total neglect of its duty, hence nonuser. It was held in State v. Hannibal etc. Gravel Road Co., 37 Mo. App. 496, that quo warranto would lie where a corporation is charged with misuser or nonuser of its franchises.

2. But it is insisted by defendant that relator is estopped to maintain this action upon the ground: 1. That by its military force it prevented the company and still prevents it from completing its contract and entering on the enjoyment of its grant; 2. That the city by its common council passed an ordinance repealing, or attempting so to do, the grant made to defendant; 3. That relator compelled the defendant to tear up its turntable, and that by reason thereof necessitated and required the defendant to change its equipment and to dispose of the equipment purchased by it and then in use; 4. That relator, by litigation instituted before defendant ceased to operate the road, rendered impossible the operation of the road on the part of defendant, and is by reason thereof estopped from taking advantage of its own wrong.

With respect to the first proposition W. J. Smith, [555] president of defendant company, testified that even if the city had allowed the company to lay a track from Main to Walnut street that it would not have done the company any good until they got some right of way from the Metropolitan from Walnut to Grand

avenue, which it never succeeded in doing. It seems that Fifth
street between Walnut and Grand avenue, upon which there were
at the time two parallel tracks owned by the Metropolitan Street
Railway Company, is only thirty feet between the curbs, and
that there was no room for another track; hence, unless the defendant company could in some way have acquired the right to
use the Metropolitan tracks, that part of the route from Main
to Walnut, even had it been constructed, would have availed
nothing; therefore no justification or excuse for not operating
the road.

Nor do we see how the fact that the city may have passed an
ordinance repealing, or attempting to so do, the grant made to
defendant, could have afforded it any excuse for noncompliance
with the ordinances.

It is well settled that estoppel in pais must be pleaded, and as
the answer contains no allegation to the effect that the city compelled defendant to tear up its turntable, that question cannot
be considered by this court.

The records of the suits mentioned in the fourth proposition
are not copied into the bill of exceptions; so that it is impossible
to tell anything about the issues involved in them, or what possible effect they may have had upon defendant's failure to operate the road. The only litigation mentioned in the answer seems
to have been by the city, and the evidence shows that it resulted
in favor of defendant. But even the record in this suit is not in
the bill of exceptions.

5. A further contention is, that the record shows that the relator waived all the causes of forfeiture complained [556] of.
This contention is based upon section 17 of the ordinance, supra,
which in case of forfeiture by defendant of its franchises for
failure to comply with the provisions of said section, provides
that such forfeiture may be had by proceedings instituted by said
city in its own name in a court of record in Jackson county,
Missouri, and that if any such proceedings be not commenced
within six months after such forfeiture has accrued, the city shall
be deemed to waive the effect of such forfeiture. The streets
of Kansas City are for the use of the general public, and its officers had no right to contract with defendant by ordinance or
otherwise that nonuser of its tracks by the corporation for the
period of six months, or any other length of time, should not operate as a forfeiture of its franchises. To do so would be to recognize the authority of the city to grant the right of the use of
its streets for private purposes which it clearly has no right to

do. To lay railroad tracks in the streets of the city, and then
not use them, would not be a public use, and it is only in that
sense that a city has a right to grant the use of its streets to
any person or corporation, for the purpose of operating cars
thereon. To grant the use of its streets for a private use would
be a misappropriation of the street, and without authority upon
the part of the city. If the city had the right to provide by ordinance against the forfeiture of the franchises of defendant on
account of the nonuser of its tracks for a period of six months,
it had the same right to provide against its forfeiture for an indefinite period and thereby convert the use, which was and could
only be public, to a private use: State v. Murphy, 134 Mo. 548;
56 Am. St. Rep. 515. In the case of President etc. v. State, 19
Md. 278, it was said: "The consequence of the argument, that
an inability to keep the road in good order, owing to a [557] want
of means, relieves the company from the duties imposed upon
it by its charter, would be that the state would be obliged to
permit the existence of roads impassable and even dangerous.
Such, it may safely be asserted, is without support from authority. In fact, the conclusion would seem to be inevitable that if
(as is conceded) the state can authorize the construction of a
railroad anywhere within her jurisdiction, such authority is absolute, and can impose upon her no restriction, no loss of any other
of her sovereign rights and powers, and cannot operate to close
the doors of her own courts against her, when she wishes to inquire into the delinquencies of a corporation created by her
and responsible to her. [Citing cases.] . . . . The rule is, that
as against the state, no waiver can be presumed, unless a clear
intention to waive the forfeiture, with a full knowledge of the
facts, can be gathered from the legislation relied on to prove
such intention. . . . . Moreover, to maintain that such an act
is a waiver of any cause of forfeiture happening up to that time,
and then to argue that the charter cannot be vacated, because
the road is now (as the plea states) in as good order as it was
then, is to make the condition of the road at that time, and not
the charter, the standard of the obligations of the appellants for
all time. Such, of course, cannot be the true measure of their
liability. It is to the charter, and the charter alone, that we
must look for the character and extent of their rights and duties.
Nor would it by any means follow that because the state did not
choose, in 1839, to enforce a forfeiture, she designed to declare
that so long as the road was maintained as it then was, the com-

pany should be unmolested. The fourth plea insists that the conduct of the state, up to 1858, amounts to a waiver; that is, that the silence of the state, her failure to authorize proceedings against the company, [558] is to be held to be equivalent to a declaration that no cause of forfeiture had occurred. This, obviously, does not come up to the terms of the rule we have stated above. . . . . And to hold the silence of the state from 1839 to 1858 to be a conclusive argument against her present right to revoke franchises, when the conditions are forfeited on which those franchises were granted, would be to make the long-continued clemency and forbearance of the state the means of destroying her rights and restricting her powers."

Moreover, the city had no power or authority by ordinance or otherwise to take away from its sovereign the right to proceed by its public officer, the prosecuting attorney of the county, against the defendant by quo warranto for ouster of its franchises upon the ground of their forfeiture.

The judgment is affirmed.

Gantt, P. J., and Sherwood, J., concur.

ESTOPPEL — NECESSITY OF PLEADING.—Estoppels, to be available on the trial, must be specially pleaded, where there has been an opportunity for so pleading them: Monographic note to Tyler v. Hall, 27 Am. St. Rep. 344. Otherwise they are waived: Nickum v. Burckhardt, 30 Or. 464; 60 Am. St. Rep. 822, and note.

STREET RAILWAYS — FRANCHISES, NATURE OF.—A franchise by a city or right given by it to operate a street railway is something more than a mere easement to use the street for the time, in the manner, and under the conditions specified in the ordinance, and something more than a contract between the public acting through the city council on one hand, and the railway company on the other, where the ordinance has been accepted and acted upon by the grantee. It is also a grant from the state which when accepted by the grantee imposes upon it the duty of serving the public and it cannot lay this burden down at will, nor emancipate itself by merely ceasing to operate its cars: Wright v. Milwaukee Electric Ry. etc. Co., 95 Wis. 29; 60 Am. St. Rep. 74, and note.

STREET RAILWAYS — FORFEITURE OF FRANCHISE— PROPER ACTION AND PARTY PLAINTIFF.—The authority of a city to act for the state, and on its behalf, in granting franchises to build and operate street railways, where such authority has been delegated to it, does not include the power to institute and maintain actions to forfeit such franchises for misuse or abuse. They must be brought in the name of the state and cannot be maintained in the name of the city by a bill in equity: Milwaukee Electric Ry. etc. Co. v. Milwaukee, 95 Wis. 39; 60 Am. St. Rep. 81 and note. See monographic note to State v. Atchison etc. R. R. Co., 8 Am. St. Rep. 193 200.

FRANCHISES OF CORPORATIONS — FORFEITURE — GROUNDS FOR.—It is said to be a tacit condition annexed to every act of incorporation, that the franchises are subject to forfeiture and the corporation to dissolution for willful misuser or nonuser in regard to matters which go to the essence of the contract between the corporation and the state. Insolvency alone is not sufficient, but, undoubtedly, if a corporation is in such a financial condition that it cannot continue its operations with safety to the public, the state may dissolve it: Monographic note to State v. Atchison etc. R. R. Co., 8 Am. St. Rep. 180, 191; State v. Bailey, 16 Ind. 46; 79 Am. Doc. 406.

NELSON v. BROWN.

[140 MISSOURI, 580.]

STATUTE OF FRAUDS, AGREEMENT RESPECTING PURCHASE PRICE OF LAND, WHEN NEED NOT BE IN WRITING. If a purchaser of land agrees as part of the purchase price to pay certain indebtedness of the vendor secured by a mortgage thereon, and thereafter receives a conveyance of such land, this agreement is not within the statute of frauds and is enforceable though not in writing.

MORTGAGOR AND MORTGAGEE.—THE AGREEMENT OF THE PURCHASER TO PAY THE MORTGAGE DEBT as part of the purchase price does not, as between the mortgagor and mortgagee, convert the former into a surety, unless the latter had notice of the agreement. But if he has such notice, though he may treat both the purchaser and the mortgagor as debtors and enforce the liability against either, he is bound to recognize the condition of suretyship and to respect the rights of the sureties in all his subsequent dealings with them. If he releases the purchaser or makes a valid extension of the time of payment without the mortgagor's consent, he is thereby released. Should the mortgagor pay the debt, he is entitled to be subrogated to the rights and remedies of the mortgagee.

NEGOTIABLE INSTRUMENTS SECURED BY MORTGAGE, PURCHASER OF WITHOUT NOTICE.—One who becomes a bona fide purchaser of negotiable notes secured by mortgage before their maturity is not bound nor otherwise affected by an agreement between the mortgagor and a purchaser from him of the mortgaged premises whereby the latter assumes the payment of the mortgage debt.

PAYMENT, CONSIDERATION FOR EXTENSION OF TIME FOR.—The payment of interest in advance is a sufficient consideration for the extension of a note for a definite and fixed time.

MORTGAGE, RELEASE OF BY EXTENSION OF TIME FOR PAYMENT.—If a person intending to purchase real property calls on a mortgagee and notifies him of such intention and that he expects to assume the payment of the mortgage debt as part of the purchase price, and thereafter the mortgagee agrees to extend the time for payment in consideration of receiving certain interest in advance, this agreement is based upon a sufficient consideration, and, as the mortgagor is, under the circumstances, a mere surety, he is released by these extensions from all liability for the mortgage debt.

Beebe & Watson, for the appellants.

R. O. Rogers, for the respondent.

583 BURGESS, J. This is an action upon three negotiable promissory notes, of the same date, executed by defendant Brown to Charles R. Lockridge, due one, two, and three years after date, respectively, and to foreclose Brown's equity of redemption in certain city lots under a deed of trust in the nature of a mortgage made by Brown to one Victor B. Bell, trustee, to secure the payment of said notes, which were all indorsed **584** in writing, and for a valuable consideration sold and delivered to plaintiff by said Lockridge before maturity in the usual course of business. The petition is in the usual form in such cases. Bell made default.

For defense Brown alleges in his answer that after the execution of said notes he sold and conveyed said lots to one John W. Henry, who, in part consideration therefor, assumed and agreed to pay said notes; that Henry sold and conveyed said lots to one Frank Baird, who also assumed and agreed to pay said notes; that said Baird sold and conveyed said lots to one Joseph A. Mitchell, who also assumed and agreed to pay said notes; that on the —— day of March, 1891, said Joseph A. Mitchell sold and conveyed said lots to one George J. Mitchell, who also assumed and promised to pay said notes. That by virtue of said conveyances aforesaid and assumptions therein contained, this defendant became a mere surety for the payment of said notes. And that by reason of the several successive transfers and assumptions, said Henry, Baird, and Mitchell successively became principal debtors to the plaintiff on said notes, and that appellant by the same means became the surety of said several principal debtors, and that plaintiff, for valuable consideration, at the request of said Baird and Mitchell, extended the time of the payment of said notes without the knowledge or consent of appellant, by reason whereof he was discharged from liability on said notes.

Plaintiff filed reply to the answer, in which he denied all new matter set up therein. The case was tried by the court, a jury being waived. The court, at the instance of plaintiff, made a finding of facts, which is as follows: "On August 15, 1887, Charles R. Lockridge conveyed to Leon T. Brown, the defendant herein, lots 9 and 10, Mariner Place, an addition to Kansas City, Missouri, and on the same day the said **585** Brown to secure part of the purchase price of said lots, executed and delivered to said Lockridge a deed of trust covering the said property to secure three notes of eight hundred and eighty-eight dollars and eighty-nine cents each, due respectively in one, two, and three years after date, bearing interest at the rate of eight per cent per annum, said interest being payable semiannually, that is, on the fifteenth day of February and August of each year. Thereafter, on September 6, 1887, the said Brown, the defendant herein, conveyed said property by warranty deed to John W. Henry. The said deed recited that the conveyance was made subject to the aforesaid deed of trust given by Brown to Lockridge, but Henry, the grantee, did not agree to assume or pay the debt therein mentioned. Afterward, on January 6, 1888, the said John W. Henry conveyed said property by warranty deed to Frank Baird in which deed the said Baird assumed and agreed to pay the mortgage debt, heretofore mentioned in the deed of trust from Brown to Lockridge.

"Thereafter, on March 15, 1889, the said Frank Baird conveyed said property by warranty deed to Joseph A. Mitchell, and the said Mitchell also agreed to assume and pay said mortgage debt aforesaid. Shortly after the execution and delivery of the deed of trust from Brown to Lockridge, the said Lockridge sold and transferred the three notes therein mentioned to the plaintiff, George R. Nelson, for the consideration of the face value of said notes and interest thereon up to the day of sale thereof, which was before the first interest payment became due. The said Nelson became, and thereafter was the owner and holder of said notes, and received interest thereon on the fifteenth day of February, 1888, and the fifteenth day of August, 1888. On the fifteenth day of February, 1889, the said Joseph A. Mitchell entered into a contract with the said Baird for the purchase of the property aforesaid, [588] and upon ascertaining that neither of the three notes mentioned in said deed of trust had been paid, and that the first of said notes was due, and had been due for about six months, and that the interest thereon had not been paid on February 20, 1889, called in company with the agent who was negotiating the sale to him, namely, Mr. Hovey, upon Mr. Nelson, the plaintiff herein, and stated to him that he, Mitchell, was about to purchase the property above mentioned, but that he did not desire to make such purchase unless the notes held by Nelson could be extended for some time; and also said to Mr. Nelson at the time that he expected to purchase the property, and assume the payment of these notes as part of the consideration of such purchase. Nelson replied that he would extend the notes if he, Mitchell, would pay the interest up to February 15, 1889, and thereupon it was agreed between Mitchell and Nelson that Nelson would extend the said three notes until March 15, 1892, and Nelson indorsed on said notes, and each of them, that the same was extended to March 15, 1892. At the time of said agreement, and also at the time of the payment of the interest by Mitchell to Nelson, the interest on all of said notes up to February 15, 1889, was due and payable. At the time of the extension of said notes, the property aforesaid was of sufficient value to have paid off said notes if it had then been sold. It is proper to state that the evidence shows that the defendant Brown, and the agent Hovey, who conducted the negotiations for the sale between Baird and Mitchell, and who was present at the time the arrangement for the extension of the notes was made, were partners at that time, and had been ever since prior to August 15, 1887, and that the negotiations for the sale of the property from Baird to Mitchell was made through their office, but was personally attended to by Mr. Hovey. After [587] Mitchell became the owner of the property, the interest on all of said notes was paid as follows: On February 15, 1890; on August 15, 1890; on February 15, 1891, and on August 15, 1891, after which no interest was paid, and the interest, together with the face of the notes, now remains due and unpaid."

The court then declared the law to be as follows: "Assuming the position of the defendant to be true, namely, that he, the defendant, was entitled to be subrogated to the mortgage security on the premises conveyed when the sum became due, and to use the mortgage to reimburse himself to the extent of the value of the land mortgaged for the money he thus was liable for to Nelson, and that Nelson could not make a valid extension of the notes beyond the date of their maturity without releasing Brown from any liability thereon, yet it is clear to my mind that the agreement for the extension made in this case is not valid, for the reason that there was no consideration therefor. Had Brown, the defendant, paid the notes at their maturity to Nelson and proceeded against the land for the recovery of the amount thus paid, the agreement between Nelson and Mitchell as to the extension of such notes could not have been successfully pleaded in abatement of such action."

Judgment was then rendered in favor of plaintiff for the sum of three thousand four hundred and fifty-three dollars and ninety-nine cents, being the aggregate amount of the notes and interest, and for foreclosure of the deed of trust as prayed. Defendant appeals.

1. The first assignment of error is, that the court erred in excluding evidence offered by defendant to show that John W. Henry, as a part of the consideration for the conveyance of the

lots from Brown to him, agreed to assume the payment of the notes sued on.

The record shows that while defendant Brown was testifying as a witness in his own behalf in regard to [588] the purchase of the lots by him from Henry, he was asked by his counsel to state under what circumstances he made the purchase. An objection being made by plaintiff, the court inquired of defendant's counsel, if "he proposed to show that Nelson knew anything about the arrangement," and receiving the reply that "what the facts would show about that he did not know," the proffered testimony was excluded. This same witness was also asked the following question: "I will ask you to state whether or not Mr. Lockridge knew, at the time you made the purchase, and at the time you executed these notes, that you were making this purchase for Judge Henry?" Upon objection by plaintiff this testimony was also excluded.

If, at the time of the sale of the lots by Brown to Henry, it was agreed between them that, as a part of the consideration of the purchase price, Henry assumed and agreed to pay the notes in suit, the agreement was a valid and binding contract between them. The execution of the deed from Brown to Henry was sufficient to take the contract out of the statute of frauds. Where the contract of sale of real estate is fully executed by the vendor by executing and delivering a deed therefor, an agreement to pay an existing debt against the land, in part or in full payment of the purchase money for the land, is not within the statute of frauds, and is not required to be in writing, nor is it an agreement to pay the debt of another and therefore void if resting in parol, but is an original undertaking, and constitutes a part or all of the purchase money as the case may be: Ely v. McNight, 30 How. Pr. 97; Wright v. Briggs, 99 Ind. 563. But even if it was a part of the contract between Brown and Henry, and between all subsequent vendors and vendees by which such vendees respectively assumed and agreed to pay the notes in suit as part consideration for the [589] purchase price, in order to place Brown in the attitude of surety for the payment of the mortgage debt the holder of the mortgage must have had notice of the assumption of the debt by the vendee or purchaser of the lot; and without an offer upon the part of defendant to show such notice in addition to the fact of the assumption of the mortgage debt by Henry the evidence was properly excluded.

Moreover, the court made a finding of facts in which it is stated that "Henry did not agree to assume or pay the debt" to

Lockridge, and counsel for defendant in their brief admit that
"the findings of 'fact are supported by the evidence." "When
a grantee thus assumes payment of the mortgage debt as a part
of the purchase price, the land in his hands is not only made the
primary fund for the payment of the debt, but he himself becomes personally liable therefor to the mortgagee or other holder
of the mortgage. The assumption produces its most important
effect, by the operation of equitable principles, upon the relations
subsisting between the mortgagor, the grantee, and the mortgagee. As between the mortgagor and the grantee, the grantee
becomes the principal debtor primarily liable for the debt, and
the mortgagor becomes a surety, with all the consequences flowing from the relation of suretyship. As between these two and
the mortgagee, although he may treat them both as debtors and
may enforce the liability against either, still, after receiving notice of the assumption, he is bound to recognize the condition of
suretyship, and to respect the rights of the surety in all of his
subsequent dealings with them. Payment, therefore, by a grantee who has assumed the entire mortgage debt completely extinguishes the mortgage; he cannot be subrogated to the rights
of the mortgagee, and keep the mortgage alive for any purpose.
While the mortgagee [590] may release ·the mortgagor without
discharging the grantee, his release of the grantee, or his valid
extension of the time of payment to the grantee, without the
mortgagor's consent, would operate to discharge the mortgagor.
In short, the doctrines concerning suretyship must control the
dealings between these three parties. When land is thus conveyed, with an assumption of a mortgage by the grantee contained in the dèed, subsequent grantees holding under the conveyance are charged with notice, and the land continues to be
the primary fund for payment, as though the fact were recited
in their own deeds": 3 Pomeroy's Equity Jurisprudence, 2d ed.,
sec. 1206.

In such circumstances the vendee becomes personally liable
to the mortgagee for the mortgage debt, who may maintain a
personal action against him for the debt thus assumed: Heim v.
Vogel, 69 Mo. 529; Fitzgerald v. Barker, 70 Mo. 685.

The rule seems to be that if the owner of real estate encumbered by a mortgage sells it, and his vendee, as part payment of
the purchase price, assumes the payment of the mortgage debt,
the vendee becomes the principal, and the vendor is as to such
debt entitled to the same rights and remedies against the vendee,
whether legal or equitable, that a surety may have against his

principal: Orrick v. Durham, 79 Mo. 174; Fitzgerald v. Barker, 70 Mo. 685; Heim v. Vogel, 69 Mo. 529; 1 Brandt on Suretyship and Guaranty, sec. 37. Under such circumstances, the vendor, upon the payment of the debt, becomes entitled to be subrogated to the rights of the mortgagee, and in equity the property becomes, as it were, a primary fund for the payment of the debt. "And any valid agreement by the mortgagee with the grantee of the mortgagor to extend the time of payment, made without the consent of the mortgagor, discharges the latter. This statement of [591] the law is supported by the great weight of authority": Wayman v. Jones, 58 Mo. App. 313. In support of this position the following authorities are cited by the court: Home Nat. Bank v. Waterman, 134 Ill. 461; Union Mut. Life Ins. Co. v. Hanford, 27 Fed. Rep. 588; Spencer v. Spencer, 95 N. Y. 353; George v. Andrews, 60 Md. 26; 45 Am. Rep. 706; Calvo v. Davis, 73 N. Y. 211; 29 Am. Rep. 130; Fish v. Hayward, 28 Hun, 456; Murray v. Marshall, 94 N. Y. 611; Union Mut. Life Ins. Co. v. Hanford, 143 U. S. 187; Metz v. Todd, 36 Mich. 473; Remsen v. Beekman, 25 N. Y. 552; Hurd v. Callahan, 9 Abb. N. C. 374; Jester v. Sterling, 25 Hun, 344; Paine v. Jones, 14 Hun, 577; King v. Baldwin, 2 Johns. Ch. 559.

The notes were negotiable promissory notes of which plaintiff became the owner and holder for a valuable consideration before maturity, and his rights as such holder could not in any way be affected by reason of any contract or agreement with respect to the assumption of their payment made before he acquired them and of which he did not have notice at that time, so that, unless Nelson, for a valuable consideration, after he became the holder of the notes, extended the time of their payment by an agreement with Mitchell without the consent of Brown, he, Brown, was not discharged from liability thereon; otherwise he was. Upon this question the court found that on the fifteenth day of February, 1889, Joseph A. Mitchell, having entered into a contract with the said Baird for the purchase of said lots, and upon ascertaining that neither of the notes had been paid, and that the first one was due, and had been due for about six months, and that the interest thereon had not been paid, called, in company with the agent who was negotiating the sale to him, namely Hovey, upon the plaintiff, and stated to him that Mitchell was about to purchase said property, but that he did not desire to make the purchase [592] unless Nelson would extend the time of the payment of the notes; that he expected to purchase the property, and assume the payment of the notes as part consideration of the purchase price. Nelson replied that he would extend the notes if Mitchell would pay the interest on them up to February 15, 1889, and it was then agreed between Mitchell and Nelson that the notes would be extended until that time, and Nelson indorsed on each of said notes that the same was extended to March 15, 1892, up to which time Mitchell paid the interest. The court also further found that the defendant Brown, and the agent Hovey, who conducted the negotiations for the sale between Baird and Mitchell, and who was present when the arrangement for the extension of the notes was made, were partners at the time, and had been ever since prior to August 15, 1887, and that the negotiations for the sale of the property from Baird to Mitchell was made through their office but was personally attended to by Hovey. The notes were executed August 15, 1887, were due respectively, one, two, and three years from date, interest payable semiannually. On February 15, 1889, interest was due on said notes up to that time, and Joseph A. Mitchell having contracted for the lots, in consideration for the extension of said notes until March 15, 1889, and as a part of the purchase price for the lots paid to Nelson the interest then due on the notes, and in advance to March 15, 1892, whereupon Nelson indorsed on said notes and each of them that the same was extended to March 15, 1892. It has been held by this court that the payment of interest in advance is a sufficient consideration for the extension of a note to a definite and fixed time: Stillwell v. Aaron, 69 Mo. 539; 33 Am. Rep. 517; St. Joseph etc. Ins. Co. v. Hauck, 71 Mo. 465.

While it is true that Joseph A. Mitchell had not [503] consummated his purchase of the lots at the time of the contract with Nelson for the extension of the notes, he did so shortly thereafter, and testified that the amount of interest paid to Nelson was part of the contract price, and this is not disputed. It follows that the agreement for the extension was a valid agreement and as Brown was merely surety, that he, on paying the debt, would be entitled to be subrogated to the rights of the mortgagee or his assignee, but could not sell the lots under the mortgage until the expiration of the time to which the notes were extended. He would stand in the shoes of Nelson and would take the mortgage subject to Nelson's agreement with Mitchell.

In passing upon a similar question in Murray v. Marshall, 94 N. Y. 616, it was said: "When the creditor extended the time of payment by a valid agreement with the grantee, he at once, for the time being, took away the vendor's original right of subrogation. He suspended its operation beyond the terms of the mortgage. He put upon the mortgagor a new risk not contemplated and never consented to. The value of the land, and so the amount to go in exoneration of the bond, might prove to be very much less at the end of the extended period than at the original maturity of the debt, and the latter might be increased by an accumulation of interest. The creditor had no right thus to modify or destroy the original right of subrogation."

Our conclusion is, that defendant Brown by reason of the extension of the notes was released from any liability thereon.

From these considerations it follows that the judgment must be reversed and the cause remanded.

Gantt, P. J., and Sherwood, J., concur.

STATUTE OF FRAUDS—PAROL CONTRACT OF VENDEE TO SATISFY MORTGAGE OR LIEN UPON LAND PURCHASED.—An oral agreement by the purchaser of land to assume and pay a mortgage thereon is sufficient, and may be enforced in equity by the grantor or the holder of the mortgage: Monographic note to Klapworth v. Dressler, 78 Am. Dec. 84. See Jennings v. Crider, 2 Bush, 322; 92 Am. Dec. 487.

MORTGAGE — SURETYSHIP — AGREEMENT OF PURCHASER TO ASSUME MORTGAGE—RELEASE OF SURETY.— A grantee who covenants with the grantor to pay off a mortgage on the premises becomes in equity the principal debtor with respect to the mortgage debt, and the grantor becomes his surety: Klapworth v. Dressler, 13 N. J. Eq. 62; 78 Am. Dec. 69. And an extension by the mortgagee of the time of payment of the mortgage, without the mortgagor's consent, releases the grantor from personal liability: Calvo v. Davies. 73 N. Y. 211; 29 Am. Rep. 130; Cashman v. Henry, 75 N. Y. 103; 31 Am. Rep. 437. See monographic note to Klapworth v. Dressler, 78 Am. Dec. 73, 75. But if the extension of time be void, as for lack of consideration, no release of the surety is effected: Davis v. Stout, 126 Ind. 12; 22 Am. St. Rep. 535, and note.

NEGOTIABLE INSTRUMENTS SECURED BY MORTGAGE—TRANSFER OF RIGHTS OF PURCHASERS.—An innocent holder for value and before maturity of negotiable notes secured by a mortgage or vendor's lien, takes the notes, as well as the security, freed from equities arising between prior holders and the mortgagor and mortgagee or the vendor and vendee: Nashville Trust Co. v. Smythe, 94 Tenn. 513; 45 Am. St. Rep. 748, and note; Crosby v. Roub, 16 Wis. 616; 84 Am. Dec. 720, and note. See Duncan v. Louisville, 13 Bush, 378; 26 Am. Rep. 201; Williams v. Huntington, 68 Md. 590; 6 Am. St. Rep. 477.

NEGOTIABLE INSTRUMENTS—EXTENSION OF TIME—CONSIDERATION.—A renewal of a note previously given by the same parties is not a continuation of the prior obligation, but is a new, separate, and distinct contract: Galliott v. Planters' etc. Bank, 1 McMull. 209; 36 Am. Dec. 256; and must be based upon sufficient consideration: Davis v. Stout, 126 Ind. 1; 12 Am. St. Rep. 565, and note. See Peterson v. Russell, 62 Minn. 220; 54 Am. St. Rep. 634.

CASES

IN THE

SUPREME COURT

OF

NEVADA.

———

STATE *v.* LA GRAVE.

[23 NEVADA, 25.]

TO CONSTITUTE AN APPROPRIATION OF PUBLIC MONEY there must be money placed in a fund applicable to a designated purpose. The word "appropriate" means to allot, assign, set apart, or apply to a particular use or purpose, and an appropriation in the sense of the constitution must set apart a portion of the public moneys for a public use.

APPROPRIATION OF PUBLIC FUNDS, WHAT IS NOT.— A statute does not accomplish an appropriation of public moneys, though it declares it the duty of the county commissioners of every county in the state in which public arms, accouterments or military stores are now, or at any time hereafter shall be received, for the use of any volunteer organized militia company, to provide a suitable armory for organized militia companies within such county; that all claims for the expense of procuring and maintaining armories shall be audited and approved by the board of military auditors, and, upon approval, shall be presented to the state controller, who shall draw his warrant upon the state treasury for the amount so approved, and the state treasurer shall pay the same, on presentation, out of the general fund, such expenses not to exceed seventy-five dollars per month for any company, except that companies drilling with field pieces or machine guns may be allowed an additional sum of twelve dollars per month for each piece or gun.

A STATUTE IS NOT REPEALED BY IMPLICATION, unless the later statute contains negative words, or an intention to repeal is made manifest by some intelligible form of expression. The legislature, in passing a statute, is not presumed to intend to interfere with a former statute relating to the same subject matter, unless the repugnancy between the two is irreconcilable.

J. Poujade, for the relator.

Robert M. Beatty, attorney general, for the respondent.

²⁵ BELKNAP, J. A former application for mandamus was dismissed upon the ground of insufficiency of the petition: State

v. LaGrave, 22 Nev. 417. The application has been renewed upon a corrected statement.

[26] The question now is, whether an appropriation of the public funds has been made. It is claimed that it is made by section 11 of the act of 1895, as follows:

"Sec. 11. It shall be the duty of the board of county commissioners of any county in which public arms, accouterments, or military stores are now had, or shall hereafter be received, for the use of any volunteer organized militia company, to provide a suitable and safe armory for organized militia companies within said county. All claims for the expense of procuring and maintaining armories shall be audited and approved by the board of military auditors, and upon approval of such claims they shall be presented to the state controller, who shall draw his warrant upon the state treasury for the amount so approved, and upon presentation of said warrant the state treasurer shall pay the same out of the general fund. Such expenses shall not exceed seventy-five dollars ($75) per month for any company, except that each company regularly drilling with field pieces or machine guns, and using horses therewith, may be allowed an additional sum not to exceed twelve and 50-100 dollars ($12 50) per month for each piece or gun": Stats. 1895, p. 109.

It is said that fixing the maximum amount to be paid each company and directing the controller to draw his warrant for the amount and the treasurer to pay it constitutes an appropriation.

These matters alone do not accomplish that end. To constitute an appropriation there must be money placed in the fund applicable to the designated purpose. The word "appropriate" means to allot, assign, set apart, or apply to a particular use or purpose. An appropriation, in the sense of the constitution, means the setting apart a portion of the public funds for a public purpose. No particular form of words is necessary for the purpose, if the intention to appropriate is plainly manifested.

In Ristine v. State, 20 Ind. 339, the court said: "An appropriation of money to a specific object would be an authority to the proper officer to pay the money, because the auditor is authorized to draw his warrant upon an appropriation and the treasurer is authorized to pay such amount if he has appropriated money in the treasury. And such an [27] appropriation may be prospective, that is, it may be made in one year of the revenues to accrue in another or future years, the law being so framed as to address itself to such future revenues."

In McCauley v. Brooks, 16 Cal. 28, the court said: "To an ap-

propriation within the meaning of the constitution nothing more
is requisite than a designation of the amount and the fund out
of which it shall be paid."

The authorities to which we are referred do not support the
relator's contention. Except the case of Reynolds v. Taylor, 43
Ala. 420, all are cases in which an appropriation of money had
been expressly made in terms. In Reynolds v. Taylor, 43 Ala.
420, it was said that if the salary of a public officer is fixed and
the time of payment prescribed by law, no special annual appropriation is necessary.

Under existing facts, it is improbable that the provisions of the
statute were intended as an appropriation, because the number
of military companies that could have received its benefits was
indefinite and uncertain. These facts are: The law permits
one company in each of the fourteen counties of the state, and
excepts from this provision companies existing at the time of the
passage of the act: Stats. 1893, p. 96. We understand that at
present there are eight companies in the state, but that number
may be increased up to the maximum at any time.

If an appropriation had been intended, the act would conflict
with the provisions of the law of 1866 defining the duties of
state controller. Among these duties he is forbidden to draw
any warrant on the treasury except there be an unexhausted
specific appropriation to meet the same. And it is made his
duty, among other things, to keep an account of all warrants
drawn on the treasury, and a separate account under the head
of each specific appropriation in such form and manner as at all
times to show the unexpended balance of each appropriation:
Gen. Stats., secs. 1812-1831.

The foregoing requirements cannot be observed if the act of
1895 be construed as making an appropriation, because there is
no specific appropriation upon which a warrant could [28] be
drawn; and also the accounts cannot show the unexpended balance as required.

"By a specific appropriation we understand an act by which
a named sum of money has been set apart in the treasury and devoted to the payment of a particular claim or demand. . . . .
The fund upon which a warrant must be drawn must be one the
amount of which is designated by law, and therefore capable of
definitive exhaustion—a fund in which an ascertained sum of
money was originally placed, and a portion of that sum being
drawn an unexhausted balance remains, which balance cannot

thereafter be increased except by further legislative appropriation": Stratton v. Green, 45 Cal. 149.

The law of 1866 was intended to prescribe a uniform rule for
the controller. That of 1895 to provide a method by which
armory rent may be obtained when an appropriation shall have
been 'made. Thus construed there is no repugnancy between
the two acts and both may well subsist together.

"Repeals by implication are not favored," said Judge Field,
speaking for the court, in Crosby v. Patch, 18 Cal. 438. "Such
is the universal doctrine of the authorities. 'Whenever two
acts,' says the supreme court of Pennsylvania, 'can be made to
stand together, it is the duty of a judge to give both of them full
effect. Even when they are seemingly repugnant, they must,
if possible, have such a construction that one·may not be a repeal
of the other, unless the latter one contain negative words, or the
intention to repeal is made manifest by some intelligible form of
expression': Brown v. County Commrs., 21 Pa. St. 43. 'The invariable rule of construction,' says the supreme court of New
York, 'in respect to the repealing of statutes by implication is,
that the earliest act remains in force, unless the two are manifestly inconsistent with and repugnant to each other; or unless
in the latest act express notice is taken of the former, plainly indicating an intention to abrogate it. As laws are presumed to
be passed with deliberation, and with full knowledge of existing
ones on the same subject, it is but reasonable to conclude that
the legislature, in passing a statute, did not intend to interfere
with or abrogate any [20] former law relating to the same matter,
unless the repugnancy between the two is irreconcilable": Bowen
v. Lease, 5 Hill, 226.

"'It is a rule,' says Sedgwick, 'that a general statute without
negative words will not repeal the particular provisions of a
former one, unless the two acts are irreconcilably inconsistent.
The reason and philosophy of the rule, says the author, is, that
when the mind of the legislator has been turned to the details
of a subject, and he has acted upon it, a subsequent statute in
general terms, or treating the subject in a general manner, and
not expressly contradicting the original act, shall not be considered as intended to affect the more particular or positive previous provisions, unless it is absolutely necessary to give the latter act such a construction, in order that its words shall have any
meaning at all. So where an act of parliament had authorized
individuals to inclose and embank portions of the soil under the
river Thames, and had declared that such land should be free

from all taxes and assessments whatsoever.' The land tax act,
subsequently passed, by general words embraced all the land in
the kingdom; the question came before the king's bench, whether
the land mentioned in the former act had been legally taxed, and
it was held that the tax was illegal."

Mandamus denied.

APPROPRIATION OF PUBLIC MONEYS—WHEN CONSTI-
TUTED.—To an appropriation within the meaning of the constitution nothing more is requisite than a designation of the amount
and the fund out of which it shall be paid. It is not essential that
the funds to meet the same be at the time in the treasury, and, in
some instances, an act making an appropriation need not name the
fund out of which payment is to be made: Ingram v. Colgan, 106
Cal. 113; 46 Am. St. Rep. 221. See monographic note to Carr v.
State, 22 Am. St. Rep. 638-648, as to what are appropriations; and
State v. Moore, 50 Neb. 88; 61 Am. St. Rep. 538.

STATUTES—REPEAL BY IMPLICATION.—A repeal by implication does not exist unless there is a positive repugnancy between
the provisions of the new law and those of the old: State v. Walbridge, 119 Mo. 383; 41 Am. St. Rep. 663, and note. Repeals by implication are not favored, unless there is a strong and clear inconsistency between enactments: Note to Winona v. School Dist., 12
Am. St. Rep. 695. See, also, note to Towle v. Marrett, 14 Am. Dec.
209, 210.

STATE v. O'KEEFE.

[23 NEVADA, 127.]

ROBBERY, WHAT NECESSARY TO SHOW GUILTY PAR-
TICIPATION IN.—It is not necessary to sustain a conviction for
robbery to prove that the defendant took any money from the person of another with his own hands, or that he actually participated
in the assault. It is sufficient that he was present when the criminal
act was committed, that he came and went with the robbers, and
was present when they robbed and apparently acquiesced therein.
All who are present at any criminal act, rendering it countenance
and encouragement, and, especially, if ready to help, should necessity require, are liable as principal actors.

ATTEMPT TO COMMIT A CRIME.—Under a statute provid-
ing that the jury may find the accused guilty of any offense necessarily included in that with which he is charged, or an attempt to
commit the offense, one charged with robbery may be found guilty
of an attempt to rob.

CRIMINAL PROSECUTION.—A MISSTATEMENT OF THE
LAW BY THE PROSECUTING ATTORNEY should be corrected
by an instruction, and not by a motion to strike it out.

CRIMINAL PROSECUTION, WAIVER OF EXCEPTIONS.—
If an exception is taken to the admission of evidence, and subsequently the same evidence is introduced without objection, and no
attempt is made to disprove it, the exception is deemed waived.

F. M. Huffaker and George D. Pyne, for the appellant.

Robert M. Beatty, attorney general, and Langan & Knight,
for the respondent.

[130] BELKNAP, J. Appellant was tried separately upon an indictment charging him jointly with Charles Martin and Frank Conlan of the crime of robbery perpetrated upon the person of Jonathan Lees.

It was shown that Lees and McDonald during the daytime were in the front portion of a house occupied by McDonald, when a party of boys, among whom was the defendant, invaded the premises, separated the men by driving McDonald to the rear and detaining him there while the others robbed Lees of an inconsiderable sum of money. It was not definitely shown that defendant participated in the robbery other than he came with the robbers and left when they left, was present at the robbery and apparently acquiesced therein.

A verdict of "attempt to rob one Jonathan Lees" was returned. A motion for new trial was made and denied, and upon the judgment and order this appeal is taken.

The exceptions will be considered seriatim.

1. It is urged that the verdict is not responsive to the indictment. It must be admitted that the defendant could [131] not be convicted of the offense charged unless he actually or constructively committed it. If his liability arise from the act of another, it must appear that the act done was in furtherance of a common purpose. The common purpose of robbery is shown by the acts of the defendant. It was not necessary to have shown that the defendant took any money from the person of Lees by his own hands, or that he actually participated in the assault. If he was present, under the circumstances, the evidence would have justified the jury in finding him guilty of the robbery.

Bishop states the law as follows: "If persons combining in intent perform a criminal act jointly, the guilt of each is the same as if he had done it alone; and it is the same if, the act being divided into parts, each proceeds with his part unaided." Again: "All who are present at a riot, prize fight or any other crime, if lending it countenance and encouragement, and especially if ready to help, should necessity require, are liable as principal actors": Bishop's New Criminal Law, 630, 632.

"There can be no doubt of the general rule of law, that a person engaged in the commission of an unlawful act is legally responsible for all the consequences which may naturally or necessarily flow from it, and that, if he combines and confederates with others to accomplish an illegal purpose, he is liable criminaliter for the acts of each and all who participate with him in the execution of the unlawful design. As they all act in concert for a common object, each is the agent of all the others, and the acts done are, therefore, the acts of each and all": Commonwealth v. Campbell, 7 Allen, 541; 83 Am. Dec. 705.

The doctrine, as applied to cases of homicide is stated in 1 Hale's Pleas of the Crown, page 441, as follows: "If divers persons come in one company to do any unlawful thing, as to kill, rob, or beat a man, or to commit a riot, or do any other trespass, and one of them in doing thereof kill a man, this shall be adjudged murder in them all that are present of that party, abetting him, and consenting to the act, or ready to aid him, although they did but look on."

The court instructed the jury, in effect, that under the circumstances, if the defendant stood by, and by his presence aided or abetted those who committed the robbery, it was [132] sufficient. The matter was properly submitted to the jury. It was not necessary to have shown any other physical act. The statute (section 4292) provides that the jury may find the defendant guilty of any offense the commission of which is necessarily included in that with which he is charged, or an attempt to commit the offense. Upon the evidence, as we have seen, the jury could have found the defendant guilty of the robbery. As they have found him guilty of a lesser offense he cannot complain.

2. At the commencement of the trial, counsel for appellant announced in open court that they would introduce the codefendants as witnesses. They were not sworn, and the district attorney, in summing up, among other things, said: "From the fact that the defense did not place upon the witness stand the parties jointly indicted with this defendant, who were present at the commission of this robbery, and whom they had announced in court as their witnesses, and have had an opportunity to produce, the inference, I claim, is that this defendant either aided, abetted, assisted, or encouraged the commission of said robbery, and you are at liberty to infer his guilt from this circumstance, and the failure of the defense, by such witnesses, to explain the defendant's connection with the robbery."

Appellant moved to strike out the above statement, and, upon denial of the motion, excepted to the ruling. It will be observed that the inference drawn by the district attorney was one for which he alone, and not the court, was responsible. The most that can be said against it is, that it is a misstatement of the law. If so, the error could have been corrected by an instruction, and not, as in this case, by a motion to strike out. Such motion affords no adequate relief.

In Proctor v. De Camp, 83 Ind. 559, a similar question arose. The court said: "Errors in logic, or in law, occurring in the address to the jury, cannot be made a cause for overturning the verdict. If the error is of logic, if illogical conclusions are drawn or illicit inferences made, the courts cannot correct these by directing counsel to reason logically. If, however, counsel state the law incorrectly in their address to the jury, the adverse party can secure a correction. The [133] correction is not to be obtained by objecting to the statements of counsel during the argument, but by asking the court to give the law to the jury in its instructions."

Again, if error were committed, it was corrected by the instructions. In charging the jury the court, among other things, said: "In determining questions of fact presented in the case, you should be governed solely by the evidence introduced before you. . . . . You have entered upon your duties as jurors in this case by taking a solemn oath that you would render a true verdict according to the evidence. That duty and obligation are performed only when a verdict is rendered which is in accordance with the evidence. While you have a right to use your knowledge and experience as men in arriving at a decision as to weight and credibility of witnesses, yet your finding and decision must rest alone upon the evidence admitted in this trial. You cannot act upon the opinions and statements of counsel as to the truth of any evidence given, or as to the guilt or innocence of the defendant."

3. Exception was taken to the admission of evidence illustrating the manner in which Martin committed his part of the robbery. At the time the exception was taken the complicity between the defendants had not been as fully established as it afterward was, but the witness Lees, then under examination, had testified to the assault made upon him by several persons in whose company the defendant was. This was a sufficient foundation for the admission of the evidence.

4. Exception was taken to evidence given by the witness Lees touching a colloquy between himself and McDonald. After the exception had been taken, McDonald testified, fully corroborating Lees' statement, without objection, and no attempt was made to disprove the fact.

Under the circumstances the defendant was not prejudiced.

The judgment and order denying a new trial are affirmed.

ROBBERY—WHAT CONSTITUTES CRIME OF.—Robbery is the felonious and forcible taking from the person of another of goods or money of any value, by violence and putting him in fear: Commonwealth v. White, 133 Pa. St. 182; 19 Am. St. Rep. 628. But it is not necessary that the taking should be directly from the person of the owner. It is sufficient if it is done in his presence, against his will, by violence or putting him in fear: Crawford v. State, 90 Ga. 701; 35 Am. St. Rep. 242, and note. See monographic note to State v. McCune, 70 Am. Dec. 178-191.

ACCESSARIES AND ACCOMPLICES—WHO ARE PRINCIPALS—PARTICIPATION IN CRIME.—All persons who are present at the commission of a wrongful act, and participate therein by counsel and advice, are regarded as principals; and held liable as such; and the same rule prevails even in criminal cases: Willi v. Lucas, 110 Mo. 219; 33 Am. St. Rep. 436, and note. In misdemeanors, all who participate in the criminal act are deemed to be principals: Commonwealth v. Gannett, 1 Allen, 7; 79 Am. Dec. 693.

CRIMINAL LAW—ATTEMPT TO COMMIT CRIME.—As an attempt to commit a crime is an inferior degree of the crime and included in it, a conviction of the attempt under an indictment for the crime will be sustained: Extended note to People v. Moran, 20 Am. St. Rep. 745. The offense of assault and battery with intent to rob is not merged in the crime of robbery, but the prisoner may be prosecuted for either: Monographic note to State v. McCune, 70 Am. Dec. 191.

TRIAL—INSTRUCTIONS TO JURY.—In charging the jury all irrelevant matter found in the pleadings, evidence, or arguments of counsel should be stricken out: State v. Chandler, 5 La. Ann. 489; 52 Am. Dec. 599. See Angelo v. People, 96 Ill. 209; 36 Am. Rep. 132.

WATT *v.* NEVADA CENTRAL RAILROAD COMPANY.

[23 NEVADA, 154.]

IF INCOMPETENT EVIDENCE IS ADMITTED at a trial without objection, full weight must be given to it in considering whether the evidence is sufficient to sustain the findings.

RAILWAY, NEGLIGENCE, WANT OF PROPER APPLIANCES.—A finding that the defendant railway corporation omitted to use proper appliances to prevent the emission of sparks, burning coals, and fire from its locomotives will not be disregarded, when the evidence upon the subject is conflicting.

RAILWAYS—FIRES, DUTY TO USE APPLIANCES TO AVOID SPREADING OF.—It is the duty of a railway corporation to supply itself with such engines as will be least liable to set fire, and be reasonably safe from destroying the property of others along its line.

RAILWAY CORPORATIONS — NEGLIGENCE IN PERMITTING COMBUSTIBLE MATERIAL TO BE UPON THE RIGHT OF WAY.—A finding that a railway company negligently omitted to keep its right of way free and clear of dry and combustible material along and upon the plaintiff's land is sustained by testimony that dry grass grew along the track from eight inches to three feet in height, and more or less dry stubble grass had grown up in the center and on the edges of the track, and when the fire occurred, all this grass was as dry as could be.

RAILWAYS, COMBUSTIBLE MATERIALS UPON RIGHT OF WAY.—It is the duty of a railway corporation to keep its tracks and right of way free of such substances as are liable to be ignited by sparks or cinders from its engines.

RAILWAY CORPORATIONS—FIRE, LIABILITY FOR.—The finding that a fire was set by sparks which escaped from a railway locomotive is sustained by evidence that dry grass had been permitted to accumulate and remain upon the track and right of way, and that fire frequently sprang up among it after the passing of a locomotive, and that coals had been permitted to escape and remain on the track, and that many of the ties appeared to be burned.

NEW TRIAL—FINDING NOT SUSTAINED BY THE EVIDENCE.—If there is no substantial conflict in the evidence, and the verdict or decision is against such evidence, or the verdict or decision strikes the mind as manifestly and palpably contrary to the evidence, the supreme court will direct a new trial.

APPELLATE PROCEDURE, DUTY TO REVIEW THE EVIDENCE.—A statute declaring where the evidence taken altogether does not support the verdict, decision, or judgment, the appellate court should grant a new trial, imposes on that court the duty of reviewing the evidence, and determining whether an assailed finding is supported by it. If there is a substantial conflict in the testimony, the verdict of the jury or the findings of the trial court should not be disturbed; but, on the other hand, the appellate court should interpose when, upon all the evidence, it is clear that a wrong conclusion has been reached.

APPELLATE PROCEDURE, CONFLICT IN THE EVIDENCE, WHAT IS NOT.—Uncertain estimates and claims respecting the quantity of hay destroyed or produced cannot reach the rank of conflicting evidence as against testimony showing the total number of acres of hay as ascertained by a reliable survey on the ground and a fair average yield thereof, as admitted by the parties.

DAMAGES FOR PROPERTY DESTROYED.—THE COST OF REPLACING PROPERTY destroyed by other property of like character is not the criterion of damages, but it is the actual value of the property at the time and place of its destruction.

DAMAGES FOR DESTROYING PROPERTY ARE GOVERNED BY ITS MARKET VALUE, rather than by any special value it has to its owner.

DAMAGES FOR DESTROYING PROPERTY.—If one has hay for which he has no use, and will have no use until a severe winter shall come, its value for which allowance must be made, on its destruction by the negligence of another, is the same as if it belonged to one at the same place having no stock.

DAMAGES FOR DESTROYING PROPERTY HAVING NO MARKET VALUE AT THE PLACE OF DESTRUCTION.—If property situated at a place where it has no market value is destroyed by the negligence of another, its owner having no immediate use for it, the damages for which the wrongdoer is answerable are to be ascertained by finding the value of the hay at the nearest place where it has a market value and deducting therefrom the cost of putting it in a marketable shape and transporting it to that place. This rule remains applicable though the owner did not intend to sell the hay, but to keep it for his own use in the future, and at the time of its destruction could not have replaced it, except by purchasing at such market place and paying the cost of transporting it thence to the place where it was destroyed and where, in the event of his ever having use for it, it would be used.

EVIDENCE OF VALUE.—WHAT THE OWNER WOULD TAKE FOR HIS PROPERTY cannot be shown as proof of its value; neither can the use to which he intended to put it in the future. The measure of damages for its destruction is its market value.

DAMAGES—USE FOR WHICH PROPERTY WAS KEPT.— The fact that hay destroyed was put up and kept, because if ever there should come another winter like one which had occurred a few years before, the hay would be of very great value in preventing the starvation of stock, does not entitle its owner, on its destruction by the negligence of another, to recover a sum equivalent to the value of the stock which it might, at some future time, save from starvation, or any other than its market value at some place where it has such a value, less the expenses of transporting it there in a marketable condition.

O. A. Murdock, James F. Dennis, and Dickson, Ellis & Ellis, for the appellant.

Henry Mayenbaum, for the respondent.

[162] BONNIFIELD, J. This action was commenced by the plaintiff in the district court of the state of Nevada, in and for Lander county, to recover of the defendant damages for the destruction of a certain lot of hay, a hay press, and for injury to pasture land of the plaintiff, alleged to be caused by fire from the defendant's railroad engine. The case was tried by the court without a jury, and judgment given in favor of the plaintiff for $10,060 damages, the value of the property destroyed, as found by the court, with legal interest and $1,289.70 costs. The defendant appeals from the judgment and order of the court denying the motion for a new trial. One of the grounds on which said motion was based is: "Insufficiency [163] of the evidence to justify the decision of the court." The findings of fact on the issues made by the pleadings are very full and voluminous, and to each material finding the defendant excepted on the ground "that the same is wholly unsupported by the evidence and contrary thereto."

Appellant's counsel argues that the findings are not supported by competent evidence, and this court is asked to exclude all incompetent evidence from its consideration in reviewing the testimony to determine its sufficiency or insufficiency to support said findings. But evidence may tend to prove the issues in a case and yet be incompetent. If such evidence be admitted at the trial of a cause, full weight must be given it in considering the question whether or not the evidence is sufficient to sustain the findings: Vietti v. Nesbitt, 22 Nev. 390; Sherwood v. Sissa, 5 Nev. 349; McCloud v. O'Neall, 16 Cal. 397; Pierce v. Jackson, 21 Cal. 636; Hayne on New Trial and Appeal, sec. 98.

In the present case, all evidence offered was admitted without objection, by stipulation of the parties, except hearsay evidence.

The argument of counsel is more pertinent to the question as to the weight of the evidence than to the matter of its competency.

There is no contention as to the sufficiency of the findings of fact to support the judgment, and we do not deem it necessary to consider but a few of the many findings and review but portions of the evidence upon which they seem to be based. It is admitted by the defendant that its railroad track and right of way pass through the meadow land of the plaintiff where it is alleged the fire occurred and his property was destroyed. The court found "that on the eleventh day of October, 1893, the defendant, while running its train of cars on said track and right of way over and across said lands, carelessly and negligently used and operated a locomotive engine defectively constructed, and carelessly and negligently omitted to use proper appliances to prevent the emission of sparks, burning coals, and fire from said engine, and carelessly and negligently omitted to keep the said right of way free and clear of dry and combustible materials, but carelessly and negligently permitted the accumulation of large quantities of dry grass and weeds on said right of way [164] adjoining the said land of plaintiff, and negligently and carelessly permitted its said engine to emit and drop sparks, burning coals, and fire into said dry grass and weeds on said right of way adjoining plaintiff's said land, and thereby the defendant negligently and carelessly ignited and set on fire said grass and weeds, and negligently and carelessly permitted the said fire to spread in a continuous fire to said pasture lands, hay, and hay press, and carelessly and negligently permitted said pasture, hay, and hay press to be wholly destroyed by said fire without any fault of the plaintiff."

Proper Appliances: Is the finding that the defendant negligently omitted to use proper appliances to prevent the emission of sparks, burning coals, and fire from the engine supported by the evidence? It is admitted by the evidence on the part of the defendant that there was no wire or iron netting or screen in the ashpan of engine No. 1, the engine that hauled the train on the day the fire occurred. There is evidence on the part of the plaintiff that if there be no such netting in the back door of the ashpan, that when the back damper is open and the engine is moving forward, hot cinders and coals of fire are liable to and do drop out through the back door when the damper is up, and are liable to ignite the oil which leaks more or less from the train and set fire to combustible material on and by the side of the track; that there is naturally a certain amount of burning coals that drop into the ashpan, and, in the absence of such netting, the natural shaking of the engine in motion, when the damper is raised, will roll these coals out on the ground, and, if there be combustible matter on the ground, they will set it on fire; that when these coals drop out they may strike the end of the ties and roll three or four feet from the track; that it is necessary to have the back damper of the ashpan open to get draught; that both dampers are nearly always open except when crossing a bridge; that by some means said engine No. 1 set six fires in passing along on a ranch adjoining the plaintiff's ranch about a month before the fire in question. Walter Davis testified that he was engineer on this road about two and a half years; that he quit about the middle of February, 1893; that he generally ran with both [165] dampers open except when going over a bridge; that he fired about two years and a half for seven different men on this road before he became engineer; that these men always ran with both dampers open, and made him run that way. The testimony of Davis is pertinent as tending to show the habit on this road of running the engines with both dampers open: Grand Trunk R. R. v. Richardson, 91 U. S. 454. There is a great deal of other evidence tending to show the necessity of such netting in the ashpan to prevent fire escaping therefrom. On the contrary, there is evidence on the part of the defendant tending to prove that coals of fire or hot cinders will not escape through the door of the ashpan when the damper is up, even in the absence of said netting; that there is no necessity of having such netting; that the engineer who ran engine No. 1 on the day of the fire always kept the back damper of the ashpan closed, and that said engine was in good and safe condition, and had all the necessary appliances to prevent the escape of fire.

We cannot say that the evidence is not sufficient to support the finding as to the want of proper appliances. At least, there is a substantial conflict of evidence with reference thereto, and in such case the appellate court will not interfere: Vietti v. Nesbitt, 22 Nev. 390; State v. Yellow Jacket, 5 Nev. 415; Clark v. Nevada etc. Co., 6 Nev. 203.

"The rule that the supreme court will not consider the weight of conflicting evidence has been so often reiterated as to become somewhat monotonous": McCoy v. Bateman, 8 Nev. 126.

That it is the duty of a railroad company to supply its road with such engines as will be least liable to set fire and be reasonably safe from destroying property of others along its line, is well settled. "A railroad company is obliged to employ the best known appliances to prevent injury to others from fire, and the failure to do so is want of ordinary care and prudence": Longabaugh v. Virginia City etc. R. R. Co., 9 Nev. 271; Brighthope Ry. Co. v. Rogers, 76 Va. 443; Thompson on Negligence, 154, 155.

Rubbish on Right of Way: As to the finding "that the defendant negligently omitted to keep the said right of way free and clear of dry and combustible material along and [166] adjoining said land of plaintiff, and carelessly permitted the accumulation of large quantities of dry grass and weeds on said right of way adjoining said land," we are of opinion it is abundantly sustained by the evidence, which is without material conflict. The evidence is to the effect that the rye grass grows right along the side of the track from eight inches to three feet in height; that there was more or less dry stubble grass which had grown up in the center and on the edges of the track on the right of way through plaintiff's said land; that there was dry grass there all along the right of way; that it was not a foot from the end of the ties; that the tall grass extended along the track the length of the field; that at the place of the fire there was quite a bunch of rye grass more than at any other place along the line; that it was four or five feet high; that when the fire occurred this grass was very dry, as dry as it could be, and would easily take fire; that in the fall of the year it had not been cut off any farther than the end of the ties; that there was dry grass all along the right of way there, fifty feet on each side of the railroad, that was not cut, and that the dry grass they had cut between the rails was left there and would easily ignite.

We are of opinion that we are justified in saying that it is common knowledge, based on common observation in this railway age, that railroad engines of the most approved construction and with the best known appliances, and managed by the most skillful engineers and firemen, are liable to do and frequently, from necessity or by accident, emit sparks and fire capable of igniting dry rubbish or combustible matter along their pathway, and thus place the property of adjoining owners in imminent danger of destructive conflagrations and frequently cause the destruction of such property.

"A railroad company may be supplied with the best engines and most approved apparatus for preventing the emission of sparks, and operated by the most skillful engineers; it may do all that skill and science can suggest in the management of its locomotives; and still it may be guilty of gross negligence in allowing the accumulation of dangerous combustibles along the track, easily to be ignited by its furnaces and thence communicated to the property of adjoining [167] owners": Richmond etc. R. R. Co. v. Medley, 75 Va. 499; 40 Am. Rep. 734.

"The general rule is, that a railroad company must keep its track and right of way reasonably clear of all such substances as are liable to be ignited by sparks or cinders from its engines": Eddy v. Lafayette, 49 Fed. Rep. 807; 8 Am. & Eng. Ency. of Law, 14; Kellogg v. Chicago etc. R. R. Co., 26 Wis. 223; 7 Am. Rep. 69; Jones v. Michigan Cent. R. R., 59 Mich. 437; Black v. Aberdeen etc. R. R. Co., 115 N. C. 667. "A railroad company must be diligent in keeping its track clear of such combustible matter as is liable to be easily ignited": Longabaugh v. Virginia City etc. R. R. Co., 9 Nev. 271.

What Caused the Fire? We are of opinion that the evidence reasonably supports the finding that it was caused by fire from the defendant's engine. The testimony of the plaintiff is to the effect that, in passing up and down the railroad, he frequently saw trains pass and within an hour or so thereafter had seen the sagebrush and dry grass on fire, and he had seen fires started immediately after the train had passed; that he saw it thus in September, about a month before the fire in question; that he frequently saw ties burnt in the center along the track; that he saw coals scattered along the railroad, etc. Watt, Jr., testified to the same effect and that he was at the fire on the Watt ranch in about two hours after the train had passed; that he went to where the fire started and investigated it; that in his opinion the fire started right along the railroad track; that he could see coals on the edges of the rails in many places; that the wind was blowing from the railroad toward the stacks of hay; that the fire widened from the track across the meadow to the stacks; that in his opinion the engine set the fire; and nothing else.

Fred Steiner, whose ranch adjoins the plaintiff's ranch, testified, in effect, that he had seen many fires kindled by passing engines ever since the road was built; that he and his family always kept watch for fires when the trains passed his place, and had put out many fires set by the engines; that in the latter part of September, a short time before the Watt fire, the engine (No. 1) set six fires on his ranch in passing along a distance of a mile or a mile and a half.

O'Donald testified that in December, after the fire at [168] Watt's ranch, he put out two fires that had been set by the engine on his ranch, near the track and near the place where the fire occurred on the eleventh day of October, before.

Walter Davis testified, in substance, that he was engineer on this road for about two years and a half, and up to February, 1893; that he ran engines No. 1 and No. 5 from the start, then No. 1 and No. 2; that he frequently set fires by these engines along the road; that he had set as many as twelve to fifteen in a trip; that about two years ago he set fire to Watt's meadow, where the late fire occurred.

We are of opinion that the evidence affords reasonable presumption and inference that the defendant's engine was the agent that set the fire that destroyed the plaintiff's property, especially in the absence of evidence tending to point to any other agency or probable agency. In Gibbons v. Wisconsin Valley Ry. Co., 66 Wis. 161, the circumstances and evidence tending to show the origin of a fire are very much like these of the present case, and the court held that they were sufficient to justify the finding of the jury that the fire was set by the locomotive.

The Number of Tons of Hay: The court found that the number of tons of hay destroyed was 976. There were several modes adopted on the part of plaintiff at the trial in arriving at the estimated amount of hay.

1. The plaintiff testified, substantially, that he should think he stacked in 1890, 250 tons; that in 1891 he thought he stacked in the neighborhood of the same amount; that in 1892 he thought it was over 300 tons, or in that neighborhood; in 1893 he thought perhaps he stacked in the neighborhood of 200 tons; that he did not take any measurements only from observation; that he did not handle the business himself; that he might have been there, off and on, while the hay was being put up, but never stayed any length of time.

2. That he should judge that there were some 150 to 175 acres of hay land, somewhere along there; that he never measured it; that in a good year he thought "you could get two tons or over" of hay to the acre; that in 1891 and 1893 the crops were not so good as in 1890 and 1892; that two tons would be a fair average yield. Watt, Jr., who [169] harvested the hay each of the four years, estimated the number of acres of hay land at 150 to 165, and the yield per acre at 1¾ to 2 tons.

3. Estimates were made by Watt, Jr., from his recollection of the number of loads of hay hauled and stacked each year of the four years and from the estimated weight of each load as guessed at by him and the boys who helped in the harvesting.

4. Watt, Jr., testified to the measurements he made of the length and width of the burned ground where the several stacks had been standing, and to his estimate of the height of each stack; that he estimated that the stacks "would each square 16 feet high," and from these measurements and estimated heights he calculated 976 tons. Dennis Scully, a surveyor, measured the height of the two stacks of Fred Steiner on an adjoining ranch, and found one to be 10½ feet and the other 11 feet. Fred Steiner testified that he had taken notice of Watt's stacks a short time before they were burned; that a part of them probably was as high as his, but that he did not think they would average as high as his. Watt, Jr., testified that he was quite familiar with Steiner's stacks; that he thought some of Watt's were a little higher than Steiner's; but that they were "about the same, just about the same." And yet his calculation is based partly on 16 feet as the height of the Watt stacks, although the accuracy of Scully's measurements of the Steiner stacks was not questioned at the trial or in this court. If the Scully measurements of these stacks and the observations of Steiner and Watt, Jr., as to the relative height of the two sets of stacks can be relied on as being approximately correct, then the calculation of 976 tons, based on the measurement of the burnt ground where the stacks stood, and the estimated height of the stacks, 16 feet, gives a result too much by 5-16 of 976, or by 305 tons. There is nothing in the record by which it may be inferred that either the plaintiff or Watt, Jr., had any particular object in wishing to know the number of tons they put up each year, until after the hay was destroyed, or that they had, or retained in mind, very reliable data on which to base their several calculations, and it could not be expected that their conclusions under such circumstances [170] would be very accurate. Certain of their estimates, when tested by actual survey and measurements, are found to be very wild. Taking all the testimony given, and estimates made, on the part of the plaintiff, they would, doubtless, be sufficient to support the finding of 976 tons of hay as against other evidence of similar character and of no greater degree of certainty. But Dennis Scully made a survey of the meadow land for the defendant, and, when he was put on the witness stand, counsel for the plaintiff stated to the opposing counsel and to the court as follows: "Without going into an extensive examination, I will admit right here that Mr. Scully is a first rate surveyor and a faithful man." Mr. Scully produced a plat of his survey of "the hay land on Watt's Reese river ranch," and briefly testified in explanation

thereof and to its correctness. No suggestion was made that the survey as to the contents of the hay land was not correct, until it came to the argument of the case by briefs. Then counsel for plaintiff in the court below, and in argument in this court, claimed that Mr. Scully did not know the boundaries of the meadow except as they were pointed out to him by Mr. Cox and Mr. Murdock, and that there is no evidence that these lines were correctly pointed out to him. But in this contention we cannot agree with plaintiff's counsel. It is clear from the testimony of Mr. Scully that what were pointed out to him were the several designated places marked on the plat, to wit: "Fire first discovered," and "Boundary line of fire," and "End of hay stacks," which are no part of the survey of the contents of the meadow land. Besides, we are of opinion that a competent surveyor and reliable man could have no great difficulty in finding and tracing the boundaries of a tract of hay land that produces two tons of red-top hay to the acre. Mr. Scully found by his survey that the meadow or hay land contained 91.2 acres. The evidence of Mr. Watt and Watt, Jr., shows, and the court found, that of the hay land four acres were never cut. This leaves 87.2 acres from which the plaintiff's hay was harvested. Taking the 87.2 acres as a basis of connection with two tons of hay to the acre as the annual product, which the plaintiff testified would be a fair average yield, and which was corroborated by Watt, Jr., and [171] a nearer approach may be had and a more reliable result be obtained as to the actual number of tons destroyed than by any of the uncertain methods adopted by the plaintiff at the trial.

Notwithstanding the well-established rule which has been so often announced by this and other courts that, "where there is a substantial conflict in the evidence the appellate court will not disturb the decision of the court below," there is another rule as well established and of as binding force, both in actions at law and in equity, addressed to the conscience and judgment of the court of last resort, which cannot be ignored without doing violence to the plain principles of common justice in many cases, to wit: "If there be no substantial conflict in the evidence upon any material point and the verdict or decision be against such evidence upon such point, or where the verdict or decision strikes the mind, at first blush, as manifestly and palpably contrary to the evidence, the supreme court will direct a new trial": Hayne on New Trial and Appeal, sec. 288, and citations; Barnes v. Sabron, 10 Nev. 217.

The duty of the supreme court to look into the evidence and

grant a new trial "in cases where it appears that the evidence taken all together does not support the verdict or decision or judgment of the court," is made clear by the Statutes of 1893, page 88, as authoritatively construed in Beck v. Thompson, 22 Nev. 121. In that case the court, while recognizing the rule applicable in case of conflict of evidence as given above, said: "As already remarked, this statute (1893) has worked an important and quite radical change, and in a proper case, without regard to whether there are or are not findings, seems to impose upon this court the duty of reviewing the evidence, and determining whether the final result is supported by it. This statute was undoubtedly designed to cut through many technicalities that have so often prevented cases from being considered upon their merits, and should be construed in the same broad spirit in which it was enacted, but at the same time with such conservatism as will not result in the reversal of a case where substantial justice has been done. . . . . Where there is a substantial conflict in the testimony, the appellate court should undoubtedly [172] not substitute its judgment for that of the trial court, and should only interfere where, upon all the evidence, it is clear that a wrong conclusion has been reached."

We are of opinion that the uncertain estimates and calculations made on the part of the plaintiff to ascertain the quantity of hay destroyed, on which the finding of the court was based, cannot be considered as reaching the rank of conflicting evidence with the actual number of acres of hay land, as ascertained by a reliable survey of the ground, and the fair average yield of two tons per acre, as admitted by the plaintiff. A sense of justice impels us to hold that the evidence given at the trial is insufficient to support the finding of 976 tons, or of any greater number than 697.6 tons, and we are satisfied that the latter number is a very liberal allowance in favor of the plaintiff.

The Value of the Hay: The court found that the value of the hay destroyed was $10 per ton, and assessed the damages for its destruction at that sum. That the value of the hay at the time and place when and where it was destroyed is the criterion of damages in this case is not disputed by the parties, but there is a radical difference between them as to what that value was, and as to the rules to be adopted in arriving at the value. It is claimed by plaintiff's counsel that "the value of a thing is that which it takes to replace the thing at the time and place when and where it was to be delivered, or where and when it was taken or destroyed; that the value of the hay in question was the sum of money that it would have required to replace the same quantity and quality of hay in stack on the plaintiff's ranch"; and, therefore, that "the plaintiff is entitled to recover the value in the nearest market and the cost of transportation to his ranch with other necessary expenses to replace the hay." He cites several authorities to sustain his contention. The counsel for defendant denies the correctness of these propositions as applied to this case and also cites several authorities.

Doubtless, the rules adopted in the respective cases cited by plaintiff's counsel were applicable to the facts and circumstances of those cases, but we fail to see their applicability to the state of facts of the present case.

[173] Evidence of the cost of an article may be an element of proof to be considered in arriving at its value. In the case at bar, if the cost of producing the hay had been shown, it would have been proper for the court to have considered it as evidence tending to show value; and if there were no other facts incident to the condition of things involved calculated to affect the question of value, or which would outweigh such cost in arriving at a valuation, the court might have properly fixed the value at such cost. The cost of an article may be inconsiderable, and yet its value great; and its value may be trivial, and its cost great. Because the cost of substituting property is a certain sum, it does not necessarily follow that the value of the new property is the same sum, nor that the value of the original property is the cost of substituting other like property in its place.

How the cost of substitution of other property can add to or detract from the value of the property for which the substitution is made we are unable to perceive.

It is well settled that the cost of replacing other property for property destroyed is not the criterion of damages, but it is the actual value of the property at the time and place it was destroyed: Burke v. Louisville etc. R. R. Co., 7 Heisk. 451; 19 Am. Rep. 618; Wylie v. Smitherman, 8 Ired. 236; 1 Sutherland on Damages, 2d ed., 12, 105; Sedgwick on Damages, 40, 428.

But "where the value of the property destroyed is the criterion of the amount of damages to be awarded, and the property had no market value at the place of its destruction, then all such pertinent facts and circumstances as tend to establish its real and ordinary value at the time of destruction are admissible in evidence; such facts as will furnish the jury or court with such pertinent data as will enable them reasonably and

intelligently to arrive at a fair valuation, and are all elements
of proof to be considered by them": Jacksonville etc. Ry. Co.
v. Peninsular Land etc. Co., 27 Fla. 1.

"If the article in question has no market value, its value may
be shown by proof of such elements or facts affecting the question as exist. Recourse may be had to the items of cost, utility,
and use": Sutherland on Damages, 378, 654. If the property
[174] of which the owner is deprived is a marketable commodity, its market price is the value he is entitled to recover: Sedgwick on Damages, 433; Sullivan v. Lear, 23 Fla. 473; 11 Am.
St. Rep. 388; Sutherland on Damages, 1098. The market value
will govern rather than any special value to the owner: Sutherland on Damages, 1113; Brown v. Allen, 35 Iowa, 306.

In this case the value of the hay destroyed is the criterion of
damages, and there was no market at the ranch where it was
destroyed. The hay was produced on the plaintiff's land. The
plaintiff testified to the effect that he stored the hay in stack
each of the four preceding years in order to have it in case of
a recurrence of a severe winter, such as was experienced in
1889-90, in which he lost $100,000 worth of stock, of which he
could have saved $50,000 worth if he had had on hand the hay
in question; that he intended to continue to store hay for that
purpose for an indefinite number of years; that if a hard winter
did not come in ten years he would have ten years' accumulation of hay on hand; that if the hay had not been destroyed
he would have continued to keep it till a hard winter did come;
that he had no other use for it whatever; that if a hard winter did not come he might be compelled to use it, or some of
it, at some time in the indefinite future, on account of the increase of his stock; that this was a possibility, as his stock was
increasing rapidly; that he had not used any of the hay, and
had no need to use it since he commenced storing it in 1890,
which was four years before.

According to the plaintiff's own showing, it is manifest that
the hay had no value for present use as feed for his stock. What
facts or circumstances are there disclosed that would furnish
such pertinent data to a court or jury as would enable them
reasonably and intelligently to arrive at a fair valuation for
future use as feed for his stock? If there be any element of
proof of value for such future use, it is so hedged about with
simple conjecture, uncertainty, and speculation, and so environed
with matters problematic, as to be incapable of making an intel-

ligent impression upon the common judgment as to what that value would be.

"There must be proof of value or evidence of such facts as will warrant a deduction of the value with reasonable certainty. Neither courts nor juries are permitted to assess [175] values on conjecture. Value must be ascertained by a money standard and based on evidence, not on conjecture": Fraloff v. New York etc. R. R. Co., 10 Blatchf. 16; Sedgwick on Damages, 172. Compensation cannot be based on mere conjectural probability of future loss: Chicago City Ry. Co. v. Henry, 62 Ill. 142; Sedgwick on Damages, 244. Prospective damages are allowed only on proof that they are reasonably certain to occur: Clark v. Nevada etc. Co., 6 Nev. 203.

Where a plaintiff claims compensation for consequences of an injury which he has not yet experienced, he must prove with reasonable certainty that such consequences are to happen: De Costa v. Massachusetts etc. Co., 17 Cal. 613; Fry v. Dubuque etc. Ry. Co., 45 Iowa, 416; Lincoln v. Saratoga etc. R. R. Co., 23 Wend. 425; Clark v. Nevada etc. Co., 6 Nev. 203.

It is evident that the plaintiff in this case has sustained no damages, as yet, by reason of the destruction of his hay, beyond the value of the hay in the market. To allow him other damages would be giving him compensation for conjectural consequences, which is not allowable: Sedgwick on Damages, 888, 937. It would be compensation for conjectural consequences based on conjectural value. As the hay had no value for present use, and no ascertainable value for future use, as feed for plaintiff's stock, its value was no more and no less than if it had been the property of A, raised and stored at the same place, A having no stock.

That the market at Austin must be looked to for a solution of the question of the value of the hay, we understand, the counsel are agreed. At Austin, 37 miles distant by rail, there was a market for baled hay. The plaintiff's counsel, however, claims that the cost of transportation of the hay from Austin to the plaintiff's ranch, and other expenses such as unbaling and stacking it, should be added to the Austin market price in assessing the damages, while the defendant's counsel maintains that the cost of baling to put it into marketable shape, and the cost of transportation from the ranch to Austin, must be deducted from the market value at Austin. The contention of plaintiff's counsel is based on the theory that the plaintiff did not want to sell the hay, but wanted to keep it for his own use, but it appears that he did not want to purchase hay either to keep for his own use in [176] the place of the hay destroyed, for he made no effort to do so, evidently for the reason that the cost would have greatly exceeded the value of the hay. If the plaintiff can recover the cost of buying and replacing other hay on his ranch, it is evident that he would recover a sum greatly in excess of his loss, and that the fire would be the source of great profit, instead of being the cause of loss. It seems clear that the plaintiff has sustained no loss beyond the value of the hay in the market as a commodity for sale. And that value was the market price, less the cost of putting into market. A sense of common justice constrains us to hold that the evidence is insufficient to sustain the finding that the value of the hay destroyed was $10 per ton.

The plaintiff based his testimony of the value of the hay on the alleged facts, substantially, that he had stored it for future use in the event of a hard winter; that it would cost at least $20 per ton to replace it with other hay; that it was worth $20 per ton to him; that he would not have taken less for it; that it was not for sale, and that it was worth more than river hay such as was sold in the Austin market. But "it is quite immaterial what use he would have made of the hay in the future. The measure of damages is the market value": Berry v. Dwinel, 44 Me. 255; Washington Ice Co. v. Webster, 68 Me. 451; Stevens v. Springer, 23 Mo. App. 375; Smith v. Griffith, 3 Hill, 333; 38 Am. Dec. 639. "What the owner would take for his property cannot be shown as proof of its value": Sedgwick on Damages, 1294; Kiernan v. Chicago Ry. etc. Co., 123 Ill. 188.

"The price at which property would sell under special and extraordinary circumstances is not to be considered, but its fair cash market value if sold in the market under ordinary circumstances, and assuming that the owner is willing to sell and the purchaser is willing to buy": Brown v. Calumet Riv. R. R. Co., 125 Ill. 606. "In an action against a railroad company to recover damages for hay destroyed by fire set by defendant's locomotive, the measure of damages is the market value of the hay where burned. In case there is no local market, the value is properly fixed by the value at the nearest market, deducting the cost of transportation": Eddy v. Lafayette, 49 Fed. Rep. 807.

[177] As there is testimony tending to show that the hay destroyed was of better quality than the river hay sold in the Austin market, this evidence should be considered, in connection with the Austin market for river hay, in arriving at the

value of the plaintiff's hay. This hay was a marketable commodity, and therefore its market value at the time it was destroyed is the measure of damages. If there was no market for it where it stood, there was one at Austin, which was within reach and to which hay had sometimes been shipped from this section. In the absence of a showing that it had any greater market value where it was situated, its value in the Austin market, less the cost of transportation, must control.

The Hay Press: The value of the hay press was fixed by the finding at $200, the sum alleged in the complaint. We do not think this finding is supported by the evidence. We find no evidence in the record tending to show any greater value of the press than its cost at plaintiff's ranch.

The judgment and order appealed from are reversed and new trial granted.

ON PETITION FOR REHEARING.

BONNIFIELD, J. The plaintiff has petitioned for rehearing "on the ground that it is probable that the court in its decision has arrived at an erroneous conclusion and overlooked important questions which were necessary to be considered in order to arrive at a full and proper understanding of the case; and on the ground that petitioner verily believes that the court upon such rehearing will come to different conclusions from those announced in its former decision."

Counsel argues at great length that the court erred in its conclusions on all points wherein the decision was adverse to plaintiff's contention. The matter of the quantity of hay destroyed we will not further consider, but briefly notice counsel's contention as to measure of the value of the hay.

The case is reported in 44 Pac. Rep. 423, in which, after thorough and deliberate consideration, we held that: "In the absence of a showing that it had any greater market [178] value where it was situated, its value in the Austin market, less the cost of transportation, must control."

The plaintiff tried the case in the court below upon the theory, and his counsel contended there and on appeal, and now contends in his petition, that, as the plaintiff had harvested and stored the hay for use in the event of the occurrence of a hard winter like that of 1889-90, in which he lost $100,000 worth of stock, and could have saved $50,000 worth with the amount of hay defendant destroyed, the true measure of the value of the hay is such a sum of money as it would require to place on plaintiff's ranch the same quantity and quality of hay as that destroyed. He claimed on appeal from the evidence that no hay of the same quality as that destroyed could be procured at any place nearer than Carson valley. There is no evidence in the record of what the cost would have been to have bought and shipped hay from that place to replace the hay destroyed. He argued that, taking Austin as the supply point, there must be added to the Austin market price the cost of transportation from Austin to plaintiff's ranch, and the difference between the value of the plaintiff's red-top hay and the common river hay sold at Austin, and thus he figures the value of the hay destroyed at $32.50 per ton.

While we may admit that the sum of $32.50 per ton is a correct result of his theory, there is no ingenuity of argument, however learnedly and lengthily it may be presented, that can cover up from the ordinary mind the fallacy of the theory as applied to the facts and circumstances of this case. The fact that the plaintiff only claimed $15 per ton in his complaint or was allowed only $10, or now claims only the latter sum, does not relieve his theory of its fallaciousness as a guide in arriving at the value of $10, or any other sum, per ton.

If the value of the destroyed hay is to be based on what the value of like quantity and quality would be for use in the contingency of such a winter as plaintiff claims, then $50,000 would not be an unreasonable valuation for it.

He testified, and his counsel argues, that he could have saved $50,000 worth of stock in the hard winter named with the amount of hay the defendant destroyed. If that be so [179] it is as probable that such amount and quality of hay would be worth that sum in the event of such another winter as that such winter will again occur. But as neither history nor tradition furnishes any evidence of the occurrence in the past of such another winter as that of 1889-90 within the borders of this state outside of the Sierra Nevada mountains, we are of opinion that such contingent value is not the criterion by which it is to be determined what the plaintiff's hay was worth in 1893.

Counsel informs us "that for the purpose of providing against future deep snows the stock farmers commenced in 1889-90, and continued every year since, to store up all the hay they could for such purpose." But we are not so informed by the record, or otherwise, except as to the plaintiff. If the theory or contention be true that red-top hay is worth $32.50 per ton for the purpose of storing for use in the event of the coming of a winter

like that of 1889-90, and the farmers find it out, there ought
to be great revival in the hay business. That the value of
the hay destroyed was not $50,000 in the aggregate, or even
$32.50 per ton, we think counsel will not deny; if not, he must
admit that any theory of which either sum is the logical result
as to the value must be erroneous, and should be discarded in
this case.

Petitioner asks the court, in the event of its adhering to its
conclusions heretofore arrived at, to terminate this litigation by
ordering such judgment as it deems proper with the usual alternative that the plaintiff accept it or suffer a new trial. In view
of the necessary costs and expenses to which the parties would
be subjected by a new trial, we are inclined to grant the request.

Mr. Van Patton, defendant's witness and engaged in the livery
business at Austin, testified that the market value of hay in bale
in Austin was $12 per ton in the fall of 1893. Other witnesses
gave the value at $10 to $12. Exhibit 6 in evidence, being a
schedule of railroad freight rates, gives the rate of $3 per ton
for hay from "Canyon and Vaughn's and points between to Austin." Walter's or plaintiff's ranch, is between Canyon and
Vaughn's. There is no siding at Walter's, hence hay at plaintiff's ranch would have to be hauled by wagon to Canyon or
Vaughn's, where there are 180 sidings, for shipment by rail to
Austin. Canyon is the nearest station and distant three or four
miles from plaintiff's ranch, or Walter's station.

We find no evidence as to the cost of hauling hay from Walter's to either siding, but plaintiff's counsel in his brief put it
at $1 per ton from the siding to the ranch. So we will consider
$1 per ton reasonable cost for hauling from the ranch to the
siding where it could have been loaded on the cars. It is in
evidence that the rate for hauling general merchandise from
the Austin depot into town is $2.50 per ton, and that the cost
of baling hay was about $2 per ton. Taking the above items
of cost as approximately correct for putting hay into the
Austin market from plaintiff's ranch, the total cost would be
$8.50 per ton. As there is evidence tending to show that the
plaintiff's hay was worth more than the common river hay sold
in Austin, we are of opinion that it is reasonable to conclude
that his hay was worth the highest market price, $12 per ton.

We are of the opinion that the evidence would sustain a finding of a net market value of $3.50 per ton, and no more. The
evidence is that the hay press cost $80 in Caleco, Lake valley,
and the value of the labor in hauling it to his ranch the plaintiff

puts at $25 or $30. We are of opinion that the evidence would support a finding of $110 as the value of the press, and no more. The $100 damages assessed for injury to the meadow land we think the evidence justifies.

We are of opinion that the plaintiff is entitled, under the evidence and the law applicable to the case, to a judgment for the value of 697.6 tons of hay, at $3.50 a ton; for the value of the hay press, $110, and for damages to the meadow land, $100, amounting to $2,651.60, with legal interest from date of original judgment, besides the cost of suit, taxed at $1,289.70 in court below.

The judgment of this court herein is modified so as to read as follows:

It is therefore ordered that the plaintiff have twenty days from the filing hereof to file in this court a release of all damages claimed in this action, except the sum of $2,651.60, with legal interest thereon from April 10, 1895, till paid, and [181] that upon filing such release in due form within said twenty days, the judgment of the trial court be affirmed in said sum of $2,651.60, with interest as aforesaid, and costs of the court below in the sum of $1,289.70; but in default of filing such release that the judgment of the district court and the order denying a new trial be reversed and a new trial granted. And it is further ordered that appellant recover its costs on appeal.

Ordered, that the remittitur be stayed fifteen days to give appellant time to petition for rehearing if it desires to do so.

———

RAILROADS—NEGLIGENCE—FIRES CAUSED BY SPARKS —APPLIANCES TO PREVENT.—It is the duty of railroad companies to use the best devices available to prevent the escape of fire from their engines, irrespective of the use of other roads: Metzgar v. Chicago etc. Ry. Co., 76 Iowa, 387; 14 Am. St. Rep. 224, and note. If a railroad company negligently permits combustible material to accumulate on its track and right of way, and, setting fire thereto, negligently permits the fire to escape to adjoining lands and destroy the property of another, the company is liable in damages whether it started the fire negligently or not: Lake Erie etc. R. R. Co. v. Clark, 7 Ind. App. 145; 52 Am. St. Rep. 442. See Gulf etc. Ry. Co. v. Benson, 69 Tex. 407; 5 Am. St. Rep. 74, and note. But the mere fact of the existence of the fire will not charge the company with either negligence or want of skill: Henderson v. Philadelphia etc. Ry. Co., 144 Pa. St. 461; 27 Am. St. Rep. 652 and note; Bernard v. Richmond etc. R. R. Co., 85 Va. 792; 17 Am. St. Rep. 103, and note. See, further, Campbell v. Missouri Pac. Ry. Co., 121 Mo. 340; 42 Am. St. Rep. 530, and extended note.

APPEAL—SUFFICIENCY OF EVIDENCE.—If there is sufficient conflict in the evidence to put the determination of the issue within the province of the jury, the verdict cannot be disturbed on appeal on the ground of the insufficiency of the evidence to sustain it: Warner v. Southern Pac. Co., 113 Cal. 105; 54 Am. St. Rep. 327, and note. If there is not a clear preponderance of evidence against a finding it must be sustained on appeal: Singleton v. Hill, 91 Wis. 51; 51 Am. St. Rep. 868, and note.

NEW TRIAL—VERDICT AGAINST EVIDENCE.—That a verdict is palpably against the evidence is good ground for a new trial: Western Ry. Co. v. Mutch, 97 Ala. 194; 38 Am. St. Rep. 179, and note.

Of the Measure of Damages for the Destruction of Property Having No Market Value at the Time and Place of Destruction.

The principal case, in so far as it involved the question of what was the proper measure of damages, was an exceedingly embarrassing one, because it was not possible to adopt any measure insisted upon by either of the parties without leading to a questionable conclusion. The property destroyed had no market value at or near the place of its destruction, and the expenses of transporting it to the nearest market amounted to nearly as much as its value at the end of the transit. If the plaintiff was entitled to recover the market value of the property at the nearest market place and to add thereto the expense of shipping it there, his recovery must have been nearly twice the market value at the only available market place. If, on the other hand, the cost of transportation was to be deducted from the market value, his recovery must have been of nominal damages for property manifestly of substantial value, the destruction of which might prove an exceptional misfortune to him. The suggestion was made by both parties that the recovery of the plaintiff might properly be based upon the value of the property to him personally, he contending that its destruction might involve him in the loss of his livestock by starvation in the event of there being a harsh winter season approaching somewhere in the near future, and the defendant insisting that it was known that the plaintiff had not and would not have, any use for the property whatever, and hence that he had not proved that he would be damaged by its loss. The evidence tended to prove that the plaintiff's hay, had it been shipped to the nearest market, would have there been worth twelve dollars per ton, and that it would have cost about eight and a half dollars per ton to pay the expense of transportation. Assuming that the market price at the nearest available market was to be taken as a basis of valuation, the plaintiff's damages were twenty dollars and fifty cents per ton if it was the defendant's duty to bear the cost of transit, and three dollars and fifty cents per ton if it was plaintiff's duty to bear such cost. The trial court apparently did not adopt either theory, but allowed the plaintiff ten dollars per ton only, an allowance not justified by any theory either of the plaintiff or of the defendant, nor, so far as we can see, by any evidence before the court, but which, notwithstanding, was probably a nearer approach to substantial justice than would have been reached by the adoption of any of the theories of either of the parties.

Whenever a person has, by the negligent or other wrongful act of another, been deprived of property, and the former seeks to recover of the latter for the injury thus inflicted, we suppose the authorities agree that the plaintiff should be compensated for his loss. If the property had a market value at the place where it was situated when the owner was deprived of it, he would ordinarily be fully compensated if paid that value, because he can, if he chooses, replace the property with the sum so received. Hence it is that in actions to recover damages for the destruction of property its market value is usually resorted to to determine what these damages are, but evidence of the market value is merely an aid in determining the real value and is by no means conclusive: Sedgwick on Damages, 243. There is no doubt that where the property destroyed is marketable at the place of destruction, that its market value is usually the best test of its real value, and that the damages suffered will be restricted to such value, though for some additional reason the property may have been exceptionally useful to the plaintiff on account of which he was unwilling to part with it for such price as might have been obtained in the market: Jacksonville etc. Ry. Co. v. Peninsular etc. Co., 27 Fla. 1; Gripton v. Thompson, 32 Kan. 367; Burke v. Louisville etc. R. R., 7 Heisk. 451; 19 Am. Rep. 618; Stevens v. Springer, 23 Mo. App. 375.

The market value may properly be disregarded as a test of the damages suffered from the destruction of property: 1. Where, though the articles in question have some market value, such value is clearly not the true test of the injury suffered by the plaintiff; and 2. Where, from the situation of the property or its character or from some other cause, it cannot be said to have a market value. Hence it was held, where the assignee of a bankrupt sold fixtures on leased premises for thirty-six pounds, and such sum was the fair market price, yet if, as between an incoming and an outgoing tenant, they were worth eighty pounds, that the damages from such sale, if wrongful, were the larger sum: Thompson v. Pettitt, 10 Q. B. 101. This is but an application of the indisputable rule that one entitled to recover the value of property is entitled to have his recovery based upon the most useful or valuable purpose to which the property is adapted: Reed v. Ohio etc. Co., 126 Ill. 48; Chenango etc. Ry. Co. v. Braham, 79 Pa. St. 447. In other words, if property is shown to have a special value, the recovery of the plaintiff may be commensurate with that value, though in excess of the market price.

The market value is not a conclusive test of the value of property which is specially adapted to the use of its owner, and for that very reason cannot have a market value as do articles adapted to the common use. It has been said, "that the actual value to the owner is the just rule of damages in an action against one who converts it to his own use": Washington Ins. Co. v. Webster, 68 Me. 449. This language is liable to misconstruction in that, standing alone, it might tend to support the conclusion that in each case the question of what was the value of the property involved might be complicated with the further question of whether its value might be enhanced by the peculiar situation of the plaintiff, by his partiality for it, and by the fact that he happened to honestly place a higher value upon the property than that which would be placed thereon by other persons. It is true, however, that there are exceptional cases in which the value of the property to its owner must be

taken into consideration. Thus it was said in Suydam v. Jenkins,
3 Sandt. 621: "In most cases ,the market value of the property is
the best criterion of its value to the owner, but in some its value to
the owner may greatly exceed the sum that any purchaser would be
willing to pay. The value to the owner may be enhanced by personal or family considerations, as in the case of family pictures,
plate, etc., and we do not doubt that the 'pretium affectionis,' instead
of the market price, ought then to be considered by the jury or
court, in estimating the value. In these cases, however, it is evident that no fixed rule to govern the estimate of value can be laid
down, but it must, of necessity, be left to the sound discretion of a
jury in the exercise of a reasonable sympathy with the feelings of
the owner." It is true that, as a general rule, the amount of damages recovered by a person for being deprived of his property cannot
be enhanced by proving that it was more valuable to him than to
others, either owing to his partiality for it or to his having a special
need for it. From this rule must, however, be excepted those cases
in which the property, though having some market value, would not
sell in the market either for what it would require to replace it nor
for what it is reasonably worth to the owner or to any other person
similarly situated. Thus, to use a homely illustration, if my feet
happen to be exceedingly large and tender, and I therefore find it
necessary to supply myself with shoes of unusual size, the cost to
me will probably be greater than if they were of ordinary size, and
if I am deprived of them, the injury suffered by me will be cor-
respondingly great. They, however, would have little or no market
value, and to award me their market value, if they have any, will be
to deprive me of just compensation for their loss, if they are wrongfully taken from me. Hence, it is well settled that if one is entitled
to recover for articles of wearing apparel used by himself or his
family, or for household furniture which has been used by him or
them, that the amount of his recovery is not restricted to the price
which could be realized by their sale in the market. Thus, where
the question was, what should be the measure of damages for goods
which had been lost by a common carrier, the court said: "As to
certain other goods, such as wearing apparel in use, and certain
articles of household goods and furniture kept for personal use and
not for sale, while they have a real intrinsic value to the owner,
they have little or no market value whatever at the point of destination; they are not shipped as marketable goods. The market
value of many such articles depends on style and fashion, irrespective of actual value for use. In some cases the owner may not
be able to replace them in any market. In such cases the value
is to be properly fixed by considerations of cost and of actual worth
at the time of the loss, without reference to what they could be
sold for in a particular market or hawked off for by a secondhand
dealer where they happen to be unloaded": Denver etc. Ry. Co. v.
Frame, 6 Colo. 385. Where a similar question was involved, another
court said: "In fact, the lost articles seem to be of such character,
.viz., secondhand clothing, books, and table furniture, which had
been used by the plaintiff that they could not be said to have to him

a value at one place different from what they possessed at another. He could hardly supply himself in the market with goods in the same condition and so exactly suited to his purposes as were those of which he had been deprived. As compensation for actual loss is the fundamental principle upon which this measure of damages rests, it would seem that the value of such goods to the owner would furnish the proper rule upon which he should recover. Not any fanciful price which he might for special reasons place upon them, nor, on the other hand, the amount for which he could sell them to others, but the actual loss in money he would sustain by being deprived of articles so specially adapted to the use of himself and his family": International etc. Ry. v. Nicholson, 61 Tex. 553. In still another case against a railroad company to recover the value of property lost by it while in transit, the court said: "The court did not err in charging the jury that the plaintiff was entitled to recover the full value of clothing for use to him, in New York, and not merely what it could be sold for in money. The clothing was made to fit plaintiff, and had been partly worn. It would sell for but little, if put into the market to be sold for secondhand clothing, and it would be a wholly inadequate and unjust rule of compensation to give plaintiff, in such a case, the value of the clothing thus ascertained. The rule must be the value of the clothing for use by the plaintiff. No other rule would give him a compensation for his damages. This rule must be adopted, because such clothing cannot be said to have a market price, and it would not sell for what it was really worth": Fairfax v. New York etc. Ry. Co., 73 N. Y. 167; 29 Am. Rep. 119.

We have heretofore shown that the market value is only one of the tests of the real value. It hence follows that the absence of a market value is by no means conclusive against the right of the plaintiff to recover substantial damages: Atchison etc. R. R. Co. v. Stanford, 12 Kan. 379; 15 Am. Rep. 362. In that event, other tests must be applied and such evidence as may be available placed before the court or jury to aid it in determining the true value of the property in question. In an action against a railway corporation for destroying by fire buildings and other property of the plaintiff, the defendant asked that the jury be instructed that, in estimating damages for the property destroyed, they must be governed by its market value at the time and place of its destruction, and that it devolved upon the plaintiff to prove such value by a preponderance of the evidence. The trial court refused to instruct as requested, and, its refusal having been assigned as error, the appellate court, in determining the question, said: "Whenever there is a well-known or fixed market price for any property, the value of which is in controversy, it is proper, to establish the value, to prove such market price; but in order to say of a thing that it has a market value, it is necessary that there should be a market for such commodity; that is, a demand therefor, an ability, from such demand, to sell the same when a sale thereof is desired. Where, therefore, there is no demand for a thing— no ability to sell the same—then it cannot be said to have a market

value 'at a time when, or a place where,' there is no market for the
same. We think it would have been a very harsh rule, in a case
like this, to have confined the plaintiff to proof of the market value
of the property at the time and place of its destruction, in the absence of proof that at the time and place of such destruction there
was a market for such property. In cases where property is of a
well-known kind in general use having a recognized standard value,
it is not proper to circumscribe the proof of such value within the
limits of the market demand at the time when, and at the place
where, it was destroyed. Were the rule contended for to prevail,
then the compensation for personal property confessedly worth
thousands of dollars would be reduced to a pittance in cents if destroyed en route from market to market, in a thinly settled, barren
country where there was no demand, simply because of the demand
of 'time and place' of destruction. In actions of this kind, where the
value of the property destroyed is the criterion of the amount of
damages to be awarded, and the property destroyed has no market
value at the place of its destruction, then all such pertinent facts
and circumstances are admissible in evidence that tend to establish
its real and ordinary value at the time of its destruction, such facts
as will furnish the jury, who alone determine the amount, with
such pertinent data as will enable them reasonably and intelligently
to arrive at a fair valuation, and to this end the original market
value of the property, the manner in which it has been used, its
general condition and quality, the percentage of its depreciation
since its purchase or erection, through use, damage, age, decay, or
otherwise, are all elements of proof proper to be submitted to the
jury to aid them in ascertaining its value. And, to establish value
in such cases, the opinions of witnesses acquainted with the standard value of such properties are properly admitted": Jacksonville
etc. Ry. Co. v. Peninsular Land etc. Co., 27 Fla. 1, 120. "The market value, as signifying the price established by public sales, or
sales in the way of ordinary business, as of merchandise, is not
necessary to the assessment of damages, or an appraisal of property
as a subject of judicial valuation. Property is often the subject of
such legal valuation for which no proof of value in the market could
be given, because it is not bought in the course of trade and is not
known in the market, and therefore is incapable of any estimate
in that mode. In such case, the real value is to be ascertained from
such elements as are attainable"; Murray v. Stanton, 99 Mass. 345.
"The market price in the ordinary sense is generally, but not always, the test of value. For such a tort as the conversion of goods
the plaintiff may be entitled to recover large damages, though unable
to sell the goods at any price. He may be greatly injured by the
loss of goods which he could not sell, but which would be productive
of great benefit and therefore would be of great value without a
sale": Hovey v. Grant, 52 N. H. 569. What elements of value may
be taken into consideration and what tests of value applied when
there is no market value of the property in question, the courts in
their opinions have not undertaken to definitely prescribe. Probably all that can be done in such cases is to place before the jury

all the conditions and circumstances tending to show that the property has some value, leaving them to estimate therefrom, as best they can, what the true value is. If the property is useful for some valuable purpose, evidence of such use or of capacity for it, is properly receivable, and may constitute the basis for an award of damages. Thus where an action was for the recovery of damages sustained by the plaintiff by the burning of grass growing on land, the court said: "Evidence of the value of the grass as hay, as well as for pasturage purposes, should be admitted for the consideration of the jury, and from the showing of all the purposes for which the plaintiff's grass was useful and valuable, the jury should determine what its value was at the time at which, and place in which, it stood when burned. If the grass possessed a market value, that should be the criterion. But if, as is probable, there was no market value, conceding it as useful for pasturage, its value when thus used should be taken. Any evidence tending to show what the grass was worth put to any of the uses for which it was valuable should be admitted": Gulf etc. Ry. Co. v. Matthews, 3 Tex. Civ. App. 493; International etc. Co. v. Searight, 8 Tex. Civ. App. 593.

Expressions may be found in the opinions of courts indicating that neither the cost of the original construction or production of property, nor the amount of money which would enable the plaintiff to replace it after destruction, is admissible as a test of its value. We think, however, that in many cases both the cost of replacing and of original construction or production are properly admissible in evidence for the purpose of aiding the jury in determining the actual value of the property, but that it is not proper in any case to instruct them that their estimate should be based solely upon such cost. Thus in Burke v. Louisville etc. R. R. Co., 7 Heisk. 451; 19 Am. Rep. 618, which, like the principal case, was an action to recover damages for the destruction of property by fire ignited by sparks from a locomotive, the court instructed the jury that the "measure of damages would be just what it would cost in cash at the time and place of the burning to replace the house and each article consumed in it." The appellate court said: "We think that this part of the charge was inaccurate, and calculated to produce confusion in the estimate of damages. The better instruction would be the value · of the property destroyed at the time and place of the destruction." It will be observed in this criticism of the instruction the court does not intimate that the value of the property was necessarily restricted to its market value, nor that it was improper as a means of enabling the jury to estimate the true value to place before them evidence showing the cost of replacing it. A college issued a certificate of permanent scholarship, transferable at the pleasure of the holder, and which entitled him to the tuition of one pupil in perpetuo in such college. It afterward denied to a holder of such certificate the right thereby guaranteed to him, and he thereupon brought an action for damages, and, having established his right to recover, the question necessarily arose as to what was the measure of his damages. The court said: "It is not shown that the scholarship in question had any

marketable value. The right to appoint under it may never have
been exercised. In one sense it may have been worth more to one
person than to another. One owner may have used it every year,
and another may never have used it at all. In view of these intrinsic difficulties, we are rather inclined to adopt the view that
presumptively its true value is the contract price which the parties'
themselves have placed upon it in the contract of sale and purchase.
This price was five hundred dollars in lawful money—a sum for
which the defendant was accustomed to sell permanent scholar-
ships, and which purchasers commonly agreed to give. It is safe to
say that prima facie, at least, the value of the right was the price
agreed to be paid for it, in the absence of evidence showing to the
contrary": Howard College v. Turner, 71 Ala. 429; 46 Am. Rep. 326.
An action was brought against a railroad company to recover damages for the loss or destruction of family portraits painted by distinguished artists, but having no market value. The trial court charged
the jury that, in determining the value of family portraits, which had
no market value, they might look to the original cost of the same and
to the probable cost of replacing or repainting them. The appellate
court said: "In regard to a family portrait which might be repro-
duced, the artist and the subject being still accessible, it is not perceived why the owner would not be entitled to supply the lost portrait, and to recover of the carrier the cost. This is said to. be the
owner's right in case of lost articles generally. But when it is
impracticable to replace the painting, and where the original cost
was incurred at a time long past, and under circumstances differing
widely from those affecting the present value, the charge given
would be of doubtful applicability, and, at all events, should be
better qualified or explained so as to guard the jury against making
the first cost and the cost of replacing the exclusive measure of
value. We do not understand the plaintiff as claiming, or the charge
of the court as allowing, damages because of the peculiar value
attached by the owner to the portraits, the pretium affectionis, as it
is styled. The claim of the plaintiff seems to be that as works of
art, paintings by artists of established reputation, of subjects calculated to give those paintings value in the eyes of those who buy works
of art, the lost portraits had a value, aside from any peculiar value
for family reasons. As bearing on this claim, we cannot say that
the charge given was erroneous, although we think it would have
been better adapted to the case had it been qualified or explained":
Houston etc. R. R. Co. v. Burke, 55 Tex. 323; 40 Am. Rep. 808.
Where the evidence tended to show that the plaintiff's meadow was
destroyed by a fire set out by the defendant, the court instructed
the jury that the plaintiff was entitled to recover as damages the
cost of restoring the meadow to as good a condition as it was before
the fire; it was held that the instruction was correct, the court saying: "A meadow is in the nature of a permanent improvement and
not like annual crops. Its value is largely based upon the fact
that it possessed this character, and is not to be planted each year.
It is evident that plaintiff could not be fully compensated for his
loss unless allowed for the value of the meadow, and no more just

or reasonable way of determining that value can be suggested than by inquiring as to the cost of restoring it": Vermilya v. Chicago etc. Ry. Co., 66 Iowa, 606; 55 Am. Rep. 279. When, in an action to recover for the destruction of a hedge, the court instructed the jury that "the value of the destruction of the hedge would be the value of the labor in raising or planting or cultivating from seed to hedge," the appellate court denounced this instruction as erroneous on the ground that "any growing crop may be worth more or less than the cost of producing it": Williamson v. Miller, 55 Iowa, 86. This is doubtless true, and the vice of the instruction was in making the elements referred to a conclusive test of the value of the property in question; but in those cases in which the property destroyed does not consist of commodities commonly on sale in the market, and for which, therefore, no market value can be shown, we believe that the cost of production is always a proper element to be considered by the jury in estimating damages: Jacksonville etc. Ry. Co. v. Peninsular Land etc. Co., 27 Fla. 1.

In the principal case, there was no evidence of the cost of the production of the hay destroyed nor of the cost of replacing it, except by purchasing hay of like character at Austin and transporting it to the place where it had been destroyed. It is true that there was evidence of the use for which the plaintiff intended the hay, but as this use was not contemplated unless and until there should be a winter of unusual severity, and it could not be known when, if ever, such a winter would again occur in that neighborhood, it is evident that the use thus contemplated by the plaintiff could not afford any satisfactory basis upon which to estimate his damages, and that if any precise test should be attempted, it must have some connection with the market price of the property at the nearest market place. Plaintiff never intended to sell his hay there, and from his circumstances and all the evidence it was clear that, though it had never been destroyed, he, as a prudent man, would never have sent his hay to Austin to be sold, unless, indeed, from some unforeseen cause hay should become extremely valuable in that place, thus tempting him to change his plans. He therefore, in our judgment, very properly, insisted that he should be indemnified for the injury done him, and that such indemnity should, as near as possible, place him in the situation in which he was before the injury was inflicted, and hence that he should be awarded a sum which would enable him to replace the property destroyed by purchasing like property in the nearest and cheapest market, and carrying it to the place where it was intended for use and where the other property had been destroyed.

There is no doubt that when property had no market value at the place where it was destroyed, its value may often be established by ascertaining its market value at some other place to which it may be transported at an expense less than its market value at the end of the transit. The difficulty is in determining whether this cost of transportation is to be added to, or deducted from, the market value for the purpose of fixing the amount of the plaintiff's damages.

There are many cases in which it must be deducted. If the property is of a class which is intended to be marketable, and for that purpose its owner must have anticipated that he must send it to some market place or must sell it to some one who, in fixing the purchase price, must take into consideration the necessity of sending it to such place, then it is clear that the value of the property must be dependent upon the market place and the expense incident to taking it there, and that, in fixing its value, there must be deducted from its market price at the nearest market the expense of its transportation thither: Berry v. Dwinel, 44 Me. 255; Glaspy v. Cabot, 135 Mass. 435; Harris v. Panama R. R. Co., 58 N. Y. 660; Rice v. Manley, 66 N. Y. 82; 23 Am. Rep. 30; Brown v. Gilmore, 92 Pa. St. 40; McDonald v. Unaka etc. Co., 88 Tenn. 38; Eddy v. Lafayette, 49 Fed. Rep. 807. These were, however, cases in which the property in question was either intended for the market place by which its price was fixed after deducting the expense of transportation, or was so situated, or of such a character, that it was manifest that a prudent owner before making any use or disposition of it would transport it to that place or some other available market. The principle of these cases, therefore, is obviously not applicable to an inconsistent state of affairs or circumstances. The legitimate object of the acquisition of property may be to take it from, as well as to take it to, a market place, and its value to the owner may be increased in proportion to its distance from that place. A dealer in merchandise may purchase it in a large city or great market place for the purpose of taking it to the country or to a village with the object of there retailing it to his customers, and it may not have a market value in the latter place except for sale at retail. In transporting the property to his place of business the retailer necessarily incurs expense. If it is wrongfully destroyed or taken from him, is it not clear that his damages are to be measured by adding to the market value of the property at the place where it was bought the cost of transporting it to his place of business, rather than by deducting such cost from such market value? In truth, in all cases in which one has, or is entitled to have, property at a particular place where it has no market value, and is wrongfully deprived of such property and cannot supply himself with property of like character except by going to some other place where it has a market value and can be obtained, we think his damages should be measured by the cost necessary to be incurred by him in purchasing in that market and transporting the property purchased to the place where he had, or was entitled to have, the property which has been destroyed or of which he has been otherwise deprived. A contract was made for the sale of hay of a merchantable quality, and it was insisted that this contract had not been complied with, and that, on account of such noncompliance, it had been necessary for the purchaser to buy hay elsewhere, and under these circumstances the question was presented of what was the measure of damages for the failure to deliver the hay at the place stipulated for its delivery in the contract of sale. The court said: "Should it appear that goods of a kind like those sold could not be obtained at the time and place of delivery, and that no market price there existed, the party entitled to damages must, upon principle, be allowed to ascertain the market price at the nearest and most suitable place where the goods could have been purchased, and the difference between the market value there at the time and the price paid, adding the necessary cost of their transportation to the place of delivery, would be the measure of damages. The essence of the rule being to place the party injured in the same situation, by allowing him to supply himself as he would have been if the goods had been delivered": Furlong v. Polleys, 30 Me. 491; 50 Am. Dec. 635. This rule received confirmation from the only English decision falling within our observation pertinent to the subject here under consideration: O'Hanlon v. Great etc. Ry. Co., 6 Best & S. 484. That it is applicable where the circumstances are like those in the cases cited is unquestionable. To our mind it seems equally indisputable where the question presented, instead of being what is the measure of damages for failing to comply with a contract to sell property, is what is the measure of damages for its destruction by an act or neglect for which the defendant is answerable. Otherwise those who go to remote regions, taking or producing property there, must be subject to spoliation, because the property has not there a market value, and the cost of sending it to market may equal or exceed the prices which can there be realized for it.

STATE *v.* ZICHFELD.

[23 NEVADA, 304.]

MARRIAGE. COMMON LAW CONCERNING, WHEN NOT REPEALED BY STATUTES.—Statutory provisions requiring persons to take out a license for their marriage, and enacting how and by whom such persons may be joined in marriage, do not render a marriage contract without compliance therewith void. Hence the marriage of two persons effected by a written contract and without any other solemnization, but followed by the assumption of marital rights and obligations, is valid.

MARRIAGE, FORM OF CONTRACT OF.—No particular form is required to constitute a contract of marriage. It is sufficient that the parties in some form declare that they take each other as husband and wife. Statutory provisions concerning the solemnization of marriage are generally deemed directory merely.

BIGAMY—EVIDENCE THAT THE PARTIES TO A MARRIAGE AGREED TO DISREGARD OR DISCONTINUE IT.—In a prosecution for bigamy where the first marriage was by a contract between the parties, without any solemnization, a subsequent agreement between them settling their property rights and purporting to sever their marital relations is not admissible in evidence, though offered, solely as tending to prove the absence of criminal intent in contracting the second marriage.

CRIMINAL INTENT, ABSENCE OF.—One who does a thing forbidden by statute is liable to the punishment there imposed, though in so doing it he had no evil intent, unless the statute makes such intent an element of the crime. If a statute has made it criminal to do an act under peculiar circumstances, one who voluntarily does it under those circumstances is charged with the criminal intent of doing it.

BIGAMY, ABSENCE OF CRIMINAL INTENT.—One who, knowing his wife to be living, contracts a second marriage is guilty of bigamy, whether he intended to commit the crime or not. Hence a contract between him and his wife purporting to sever their marital relations is not admissible as evidence in his favor for the purpose of proving his want of criminal intent in contracting the second marriage.

Curler & Curler, for the appellant.

F. H. Norcross, district attorney, for the respondent.

807 BONNIFIELD, J. The appellant was convicted in the district court of the second judicial district, in and for Washoe county, of the crime of bigamy, and appeals from the judgment of the court and order denying his motion for a new trial. The following facts are not disputed: In the year 1893 in said county the appellant was married to Sophia Koser by written contract, without the services of any of the persons authorized by the statute to join persons in marriage, or to solemnize marriage. Subsequently, and in 1895, the parties separated by mutual consent, and the appellant, while he was so married to Sophia Koser, and knowing that said Sophia was still alive, was formally married to Lauretta **808** Bosford by J. J. Linn, a justice of the peace of Washoe county.

There is no contention as to the sufficiency of said first marriage to constitute a valid marriage at the common law; but counsel for appellant contend that our statute concerning marriages has superseded the common law, and that all marriages not entered into in conformity to the provisions of the statute are null and void. It is well settled that under the common law the marriage relation may be formed by words of present assent (per verba de praesenti), and without the interposition of any person lawfully authorized to solemnize marriages or to join persons in marriage.

The first act passed by our territorial legislature was an act entitled "An act adopting the common law." At the same session of the legislature it passed the act relating to marriages, of which the following is section 1: "That marriage, so far as its validity in law is concerned, is a civil contract to which the consent of the parties, capable in law of contracting, is essential." Although this act contains provisions requiring a license, directing how and by whom marriages may be celebrated, or by whom persons may be joined in marriage, and prescribing other regulations in reference thereto, the statute contains no express clause of nullity, making void marriages contracted by mutual consent

per verba de praesenti, except a prior license is obtained, or solemnization had in accordance with its provisions.

Authorities: The supreme court of the United States in Meis-
ter v. Moore, 96 U. S. 76 (opinion by Justice Strong), in construing the Michigan statute, which is substantially the same as
ours, said: "It [the instruction] certainly withdrew from the
consideration of the jury all evidence, if any there was, of informal marriage by contract, per verba de praesenti. That such
a contract constitutes a valid marriage at common law there can
be no doubt, in view of the adjudications made in this country
from the earliest settlement to the present day. Marriage is
everywhere regarded as a civil contract. Statutes in many states,
it is true, regulate the mode of entering into the contract, but
they do not confer the right. Hence they are not within the
principle that, where a statute creates a right and provides a
remedy for its enforcement, [309] the remedy is exclusive. No
doubt a statute may take away a common-law right, but there is
always a presumption that the legislature has no such intention,
unless it be plainly expressed.

"A statute may declare that no marriages shall be valid unless
they are solemnized in a prescribed manner, but such an enactment is a very different thing from a law requiring all marriages to be entered into in the presence of a magistrate or a
clergyman, or that it be preceded by license, or publication of
bans, or attested by witnesses. Such formal provisions may be
construed as merely directory instead of being treated as destructive of a common-law right to form the marriage by words
of present assent.

"And such, we think, has been the rule generally adopted in
construing statutes regulating marriage. Whatever directions
they may give respecting its formation or solemnization, courts
have usually held a marriage good at common law to be good
notwithstanding the statutes, unless they contain express words
of nullity. . . . . In many of the states, enactments exist very
similar to the Michigan statute, but their object has manifestly
been, not to declare what shall be requisite to the validity of a
marriage, but to provide a legitimate mode of solemnizing it.
They speak of the celebration of its right rather than of its validity, and they address themselves principally to the function-
aries they authorize to perform the ceremony. In most cases
the leading purpose is to secure a registration of marriage, and
evidence by which marriages may be proved; for example, by
certificate of a clergyman or magistrate or by exemplification of

the registry. In a small number of the states, it must be admitted, such statutes have been construed as denying validity to marriages not formed according to the statutory directions. . . . .

"As before stated, the statutes are held merely directory, because marriage is a thing of common-law right, because it is the policy of the state to encourage it, and because, as has sometimes been said, any other construction would compel holding illegitimate the offspring of many parents conscious of no violation of law.

"The Michigan statute differs in no essential particular [310] from those of other states, which have generally been so construed. It does not declare marriages void which have not been entered into in the presence of a minister or magistrate. It does not deny validity to marriages which are good at common law. The most that can be said of it is that it contains implications of an intention that all marriages, except some particularly mentioned, should be celebrated in the manner mentioned. . . . .

"The sixth section declares how they may be solemnized. The seventh describes what shall be required of justices of the peace and ministers of the gospel before they shall solemnize any marriage. The eighth section declares that in every case, that is, whenever any marriage shall be solemnized in the manner described in the act, there shall be at least two witnesses present besides the minister or magistrate. The ninth, tenth, eleventh, sixteenth, and seventeenth sections provide for certificates, registers, and exemplifications of records of marriage solemnized by magistrates and ministers. The twelfth and thirteenth impose penalties upon justices and ministers joining persons in marriage contrary to the provisions of the act, and upon persons joining others in marriage, knowing that they are not lawfully authorized so to do. The fourteenth and fifteenth sections are those upon which most reliance is placed in support of the charge of the circuit court. The former declares that no marriage solemnized before any person professing to be a justice of the peace or minister of the gospel shall be deemed or adjudged to be void on account of any want of jurisdiction or authority in such minister or justice, provided the marriage be consummated with full belief on the part of the persons so married, or either of them, that they have been lawfully joined in marriage. This, it is argued, raises an implication that marriages not in the presence of a minister or justice, or one professing to be such, were intended to be void. But the implication is not necessarily so broad. It is satisfied if it reach not beyond marriages in the mode allowed by the act of the legislature. The fifteenth section exempts people called 'Quakers' or 'Friends' from the operation of the act. . . . . As to them the act gives no directions. From this, also, an inference is attempted to be drawn that [311] lawful marriages of all other persons must be in the mode directed or allowed [by the statute]. We think the inference is not a necessary one. Both these sections, the fourteenth and the fifteenth, are to be found in the acts of other states, in which it has been decided that the statutes do not make invalid common-law marriages."

We think that in the above opinion by Justice Strong a clear and proper construction of the statute is given.

Bishop says: "It is well observed by Lord Stowell that in a state of nature no forms need be added to an agreement of present marriage to render it complete. , In the opinion of the Scotch people and of the people of a part of our states, marriage, emphatically a thing of nature, is properly regulated by the law of nature. But in England, in other of our states, and largely in Continental Europe, civilization has undertaken to refine and improve nature's law by denying marriage except under specified forms and ceremonies. The consequence of which is that shrewd rakes entrap simple girls into nature's marriage, then at their whim or exalted pleasure cast them off, and leave a family of children under the disabilities and disgrace of bastardy": 1 Bishop on Marriage, Divorce, and Separation, secs. 385, 386.

Bishop, after an extended review of the authorities on the subject which he cites, restates the doctrine recognized by the courts of nearly all the states having statutes similar to ours, as follows: "Any required formal solemnization of marriage is an impediment to entering into it; therefore, since marriage is favored in law, statutory provisions establishing forms are to be strictly interpreted, not being encouraged by the courts. In the absence of any statute or local usage controlling the question, only the consent treated of in our last two chapters is indispensable to the constitution of marriage; and legislation commanding formalities, even punishing those who celebrate marriage contrary to its provisions, or punishing the parties themselves, will not render a marriage had in disregard of it void, unless the statute expressly or by necessary implication declares this consequence. But it is otherwise of a statute which authorizes the intermarriage of persons before incompetent, for in this case there is no common law to fall back upon. And such parties must strictly [312] conform to the legislative direction to render their mar-

riage valid. In the ordinary case, wherein the common law may
be relied on except as excluded by the statute, only the particular
things which the statute declares to be nullifying if omitted need
be observed—all the rest being directory, and noncompliance
immaterial": Bishop on Marriage, Divorce, and Separation, sec.
449.

In an elaborate review of the authorities and an exhaustive
discussion of the question now under consideration, the supreme
court of Missouri, in Dyer v. Brannock, 66 Mo. 391, 27 Am. Rep.
359, held that a marriage by contract, without solemnization before a minister of the gospel or an officer of the law was valid,
the statute concerning marriages containing no positive declarations that a marriage not so solemnized shall be void. Numerous other authorities might be cited to the same effect as the
above, but we deem it unnecessary.

In Fitzpatrick v. Fitzpatrick, 6 Nev. 63, this court has construed section 2 of our statute, and the reasoning of the court is
applicable to the construction of all the sections relied on by
counsel for appellant, and by the authorities holding that the
statute nullifies common-law marriages. In that case the plaintiff brought suit to have her marriage declared annulled on the
ground that she was under age and the consent of her parent or
guardian had not first been obtained. Section 2 provides that
"male persons of the age of eighteen years and female persons
of the age of sixteen years . . . . may be joined in marriage;
provided always, that male persons under the age of twenty-one
years and female persons under the age of eighteen years shall
first obtain the consent of their fathers" or mothers or guardians,
respectively, "and provided further, that nothing in this act shall
be construed so as to make the issue of any marriage illegitimate,
if the person or persons shall not be of lawful age." The plaintiff's counsel contended that "the plaintiff, by reason of want of
age, was incapable of contracting a valid marriage, except with
the consent of her parent or guardian." He argued: "The statute provides that marriage by females under the age of eighteen
shall be contracted only with the consent of their parents or
guardian, and a penalty is imposed on the county clerk who shall
issue a license for the marriage of such minor without such consent. . . . . Besides, the statute of Nevada [313] is peculiar in
providing that nothing in it shall be construed to make the issue
of any marriage illegitimate, if the persons shall not be of lawful
age. Evidently, the legislature intended by this act that all marriages entered into except as provided in said act should be void.

If this was not their intention, then that portion of the act which provides against bastardizing the issue of such marriage is mere surplusage and without meaning, for the reason that it would be the merest folly to provide by statute that issue of a valid marriage shall not be illegitimate."

The court held, however, that: "That proviso did not indicate any such intent as claimed by counsel, as it only relates to issue of persons not of lawful age, that is, eighteen and sixteen years in males and females, respectively. . . . . That by the common law, and the statute law of this state, marriage is held to be a civil contract. To render the contract valid, the parties must be able and willing to contract. At common law, the age of capacity to make the contract of marriage was fixed at fourteen years for males, and twelve years for females. . . . . Marriage before such age is voidable at the election of either party, on arriving at the age of consent, if either of the parties be under age when the contract is made: 2 Kent's Commentaries, 44. The statute of this state does not alter the common law, save by substituting the ages therein named for the common-law ages, and it has generally, if not universally, been held, in construing similar statutes, that. in the absence of any provision declaring marriage made in violation of the statutory proviso void, it was a binding and valid contract, upon the theory that persons of the consenting or lawful age, voluntarily entering into a contract, should be held thereto, precisely as they would be held to any other lawful contract voluntarily assumed at the legal age or upon majority." It will be observed that the court held, in effect, that in the absence of any provision of the statute declaring the marriage of a minor, without the consent of parent or guardian, void, the marriage was valid, notwithstanding the explicit requirements of the statute that such consent shall first be obtained.

Our statute does not expressly, nor by necessary implication, [14] as we view it, render a marriage had in disregard of its prescribed formalities void. We are to presume that the legislature knew that marriages by contract are valid at common law; that they have thus been entered into from time immemorial, and are liable to continue to be so contracted, and if the legislature intended to prohibit such marriages and render them void, and thus entail upon the parties conscious of no wrongdoing, and their children, such evil consequences as must necessarily result therefrom, it would have expressed such intent in such terms as need no construction, and about which even laymen could have no doubt, and would thus have given due notice to all of the invalidity of informal marriages entered into simply by contract.

It seems to us clearly that the legislature, by the terms used in the first section of the marriage act, intended to specifically recognize the common law in respect to marriages. It therein declares "that marriage, so far as its validity in law is concerned, is a civil contract to which the consent of the parties capable in law of contracting is essential." If the legislature had intended that compliance with any of the provisions of the succeeding section should also be essential to its validity in law, we are of opinion it would have so expressed itself, and not left the definition of a valid marriage in law "a civil contract to which the consent of the parties capable in law of contracting is essential."

We are of opinion that the subsequent sections were enacted for the purposes named above in the opinion delivered by Justice Strong, and for the additional purpose of accommodating the views of those who do not believe in marriages by contract simply, and would not be satisfied with entering into the marriage relation except by some mode prescribed by the statute, and for the purpose of giving to the forms and ceremonies in practice among many classes statutory recognition.

While any form or ceremony the parties interested may choose is recognized by the statute, no particular form is required. The elements essential to a common-law marriage are required—a contract per verba praesenti. In the language of the statute, the parties "shall declare that they take each [315] other as husband and wife," not necessarily by word of mouth, but in some manner to declare such assent. From the great preponderating weight of authority and reason, we are of opinion that all other provisions of the statute are directory, so far as the validity of the marriage is concerned, and that a marriage by contract between parties competent to enter into that relation with each other is valid under our statute.

We, therefore, hold that the said marriage of the appellant to Sophia Koser is valid.

Errors Assigned: On the fourteenth day of September, 1895, about three weeks before the alleged second marriage of the defendant, he and his first wife, Sophia, entered into a written agreement between themselves in settlement of their property rights and agreed to then and there separate, and further agreed in terms as follows: "The parties hereto, each with the other, covenant and agree to sever their marital relations, and by these presents do sever their marital relations." Counsel for defendant offered to introduce this agreement in evidence, to which the district attorney objected on the ground that it was incompetent, irrelevant, and immaterial. The court sustained the objection. This ruling is assigned as error. Counsel argues, in substance, under the authority of State v. Gardner, 5 Nev. 377, that the agreement was proper evidence to go to the jury, as tending to show that there was no criminal intent on the part of the defendant in entering into the second marriage, he believing that the agreement had annulled the first marriage.

Criminal Intent: The rule adopted by the majority of the court in the said Gardner case, to the effect that where a statute forbids the doing of a certain thing, and is silent concerning the intent with which it is done, a person commits no offense, in law, though he does the forbidden thing, within all the words of the statute, if he had no evil or wrongful intent beyond that which is involved in the doing of the prohibited act, is disapproved, and the decision to that effect is hereby overruled. We recognize the well-settled rule that, where a specific intent is required by statute to constitute the crime, such specific intent enters into the nature of the act [316] itself, and must be alleged and proved beyond a reasonable doubt.

The statute under which the defendant was indicted, tried, and convicted provides: "Bigamy consists in the having of two wives or two husbands at one and the same time, knowing that the former husband or wife is still alive. If any person or persons within this state, being married, or who shall hereafter marry, do at any time marry any person or persons, the former husband or wife being alive, the person so offending shall be punished. . . . . Nothing herein contained shall extend to any person or persons whose husband or wife shall have been continually absent from such person or persons for the space of five years prior to the said second marriage, and he or she not knowing such husband or wife to be living within that time. Also, nothing herein contained shall extend to any person that is, or shall be, at the time of such marriage, divorced by lawful authority from the bonds of such former marriage, or to any person where the former marriage hath been by lawful authority declared void." There is no intent involved in this case except the doing of the thing forbidden to be done by the statute.

"Whatever one voluntarily does, he, of course, intends to do. If the statute has made it criminal to do any act under peculiar circumstances, the party voluntarily doing that act is chargeable with the criminal intent of doing it": Commonwealth v. Mash, 7 Met. 472.

"There was the intent to marry a second time, not knowing the husband to be dead, and who had been absent for about one year only, and this is the criminal intent which is of the essence of the offense": Jones v. State, 67 Ala. 84.

"Upon indictment for selling intoxicating liquor to a minor, without authority from his parents or guardian, it does not matter that the defendant did not know that such person was a minor. He is bound to know whether such person is a minor or not": Farmer v. People, 77 Ill. 322.

A statute of North Carolina authorized the sheriff to issue a license to sell liquor by retail, only on an order of the board of commissioners, upon application of the person seeking the license, and made it a criminal offense to retail liquor without a license. On the first day of January, 1883, [317] the board, upon application of Voight, ordered the license to issue, and on the same day revoked the order. Notwithstanding this revocation, the sheriff afterward, and on the last day of said January, issued the license, Voight knowing when he received the license that the order for its issuance had been revoked. Voight was prosecuted criminally for retailing liquor without a license. The trial court charged the jury "that if the jury were fully satisfied that the license was issued after the 1st of January, 1883, and defendant knew it was subsequent to the revoking order, and thereafter sold liquor as charged, ... they should convict, notwithstanding, at the time of the act, he had possession of the license." The supreme court approved the instruction, and said: "Nor is it a defense to a criminal accusation that the defendant did not intend to violate or evade the law, or supposed he had a right to sell, when he intended to do, and did do, the criminal and forbidden act. The criminal intent is inseparably involved in the intent to do the act which the law pronounces criminal": State v. Voight, 90 N. C. 741.

The provisions of a statute in Massachusetts are as follows: "Whoever falsely makes . . . . any certificate of nomination or nomination paper, or any part thereof, or files any certificate of nomination or nomination paper knowing the same, or any part thereof, to be falsely made . . . . shall be punished," etc. Connelly was convicted under this statute: 1. For falsely making nomination papers; 2. For filing the same. On appeal, the supreme judicial court held: "No fraudulent intent is necessary to constitute the offense. It is immaterial that the defendant did not intend to break the law. It is enough that he did the things made offenses by the statute": Commonwealth v. Connelly, 163 Mass. 539.

We cite the following additional authorities on the question of intent, which are in line with the ones given above: Walls v. State, 7 Blackf. 572; The Brig Ann, 1 Gall. 62; Regina v. Woodrow, 15 Mees. & W. 404; Myers v. State, 1 Conn. 502; State v. Goodenow, 65 Me. 30; State v. Whitcomb, 52 Iowa, 85; 35 Am. Rep. 258; State v. Peters, 56 Iowa, 263; Davis v. Commonwealth, 13 Bush, 318; Wharton's Criminal Evidence, 8th ed., sec. 725, and cases there cited.

[318] We, therefore, hold that the court did not err in excluding said agreement of the appellant and Sophia Zichfeld.

This opinion disposes of all the alleged errors; and, finding no error of the court in the record, the judgment and order appealed from are affirmed.

––––––

MARRIAGE AND DIVORCE — STATUTORY RESTRICTIONS REGARDING.—A statute providing for the procurement of a marriage license, and the other formalities to be observed in the solemnization of marriage, does not render void marriages entered into according to the common law, but not in conformity to such formalities unless the statute itself declares them so: State v. Bittick, 103 Mo. 183; 23 Am. St. Rep. 869, and note; Holmes v. Holmes, 6 La. 463; 26 Am. Dec. 482, and note; Cartwright v. McGown, 121 Ill. 388; 2 Am. St. Rep. 105.

MARRIAGE—CONTRACT OF—ESSENTIALS.—To complete a marriage nothing more is necessary than a full, free, and mutual consent between parties not incapable of entering into such state: Jackson v. Winne, 7 Wend 47; 22 Am. Dec. 563 and note: Voorhees v. Voorhees, 46 N. J. Eq. 411; 19 Am. St. Rep. 404, and note. A marriage without license by an unauthorized person is valid, if the parties consent thereto and afterward cohabit together: Farley v. Farley, 94 Ala. 501; 33 Am. St. Rep. 141, and note.

BIGAMY—CRIMINAL INTENT.—The fact that the defendant prosecuted for bigamy or polygamy had a bona fide and reasonable belief when contracting the second marriage that his first wife was dead does not entitle him to an acquittal: Commonwealth v. Hayden, 163 Mass. 453; 47 Am. St. Rep. 468. A mistaken belief on the part of a defendant charged with bigamy that his first marriage was void at the time of his second marriage, because his first wife had deserted him for more than three years prior thereto, is a mistake of law, and constitutes no defense: Medrano v. State, 32 Tex. Crim. Rep. 214; 40 Am. St. Rep. 775. See extended note to State v. Johnson, 93 Am. Dec. 253.

CRIMINAL LAW—CRIMINAL INTENT.—Whether or not a criminal intent or guilty knowledge is a necessary element of a statutory offense is a matter of construction to be determined from the language of the statute, in view of its manifest purpose and design: Commonwealth v. Weiss, 139 Pa. St. 247; 23 Am. St. Rep. 182, and note.

STATE *v.* MACK.

[23 NEVADA, 359.]

JURISDICTION OVER CRIMES COMMITTED ON LANDS PURCHASED BY THE UNITED STATES WITH THE ASSENT OF THE STATE.—If lands are purchased by the United States with the consent of the state, for the erection thereon of forts, arsenals, dockyards, or other needful buildings, the lands so purchased are within the exclusive jurisdiction of the United States. Among such needful buildings are courthouses and postoffices.

JURISDICTION OVER LANDS PURCHASED BY THE UNITED STATES—ATTEMPT OF THE STATE TO RESERVE JURISDICTION IN CRIMINAL CASES.—If a state consents to the purchase by the United States of lands to be used as a courthouse and postoffice, and assents to the exclusive jurisdiction of the United States "except the administration of the criminal laws of the state," this reservation includes only the right of the state to execute valid process upon the lands so purchased for the violation of state laws committed within the state, but not upon the lands so purchased.

James F. Dennis, William Woodburn, and R. M. Clarke, for the relator.

James R. Judge, attorney general, and A. J. McGowan, district attorney, for the respondent.

[361] MASSEY, J. This is an original application to the supreme court for a writ of certiorari. It appears from the petition and affidavit filed herein, and from the records and proceedings of the district court certified to this court, that the petitioner was indicted by the grand jury of Ormsby county on the eleventh day of December, 1896, for the crime of assault with a deadly instrument, with intent to inflict upon the person of another bodily injury; that the petitioner was duly arrested for the said offense and taken before said district court; that, when required to plead to said indictment, he interposed a special plea to the jurisdiction of the court, in which it was alleged that the offense charged in said indictment was committed upon certain lands in Carson City, Ormsby county, state of Nevada, purchased by the United States, by consent of the legislature of the state, for the erection of a courthouse, postoffice and other needful public buildings, and that upon which lands there had been erected, and the same were then used by the United States, the said needful public buildings. To this plea the district attorney demurred, alleging that the facts set up in the plea did not oust the jurisdiction of the state, and the district court sustained the demurrer, and required [362] the petitioner to plead to the merits of the indictment, and proceeded to set the action for trial for a certain day. It also appears from the record of

the district court that the district attorney admitted that the
alleged offense was committed upon lands purchased by the
United States with the consent of the legislature of the state of
Nevada, and that the United States had erected a postoffice and
courthouse thereon. Counsel for respondent concede that the
special plea to the jurisdiction of the district court, and the
proceedings thereon, are regular and proper, and that the proceedings in this court upon certiorari are proper and regular,
therefore no opinion is given on these questions.

From the facts above stated, the petitioner contends that the
said district court has no jurisdiction over the alleged offense
for the reason that the same was committed upon lands over
which, under the provision of article 1, section 8, of the federal
constitution, the United States has the right to exercise exclusive jurisdiction.

Article 1, section 8, of the federal constitution provides that
"Congress shall have power . . . . to exercise exclusive legislation, in all cases whatsoever, over such district, ... and to
exercise a like authority over all places purchased by consent of
the legislature of the state in which the same shall be, for the
erection of forts, magazines, arsenals, dockyards, and other needful buildings."

By act of Congress, approved January 13, 1885 (U. S. Stats.
1885, c. 19, p. 181), the secretary of the treasury was authorized
and directed "to purchase a site for, and cause to be erected
thereon, at the city of Carson City, in the state of Nevada, a suitable building, ... for the accommodation of the United
States courts, postoffice; . . . . provided, that no money to be
appropriated for said building shall be available . . . . until
the state of Nevada shall cede to the United States exclusive
jurisdiction over the same . . . . for all purposes except the administration of the criminal laws of said state and the service of
any civil process therein."

By an act of the legislature of the state of Nevada, approved
February 24, 1885 (Stats. 1885, p. 40), the jurisdiction of the
state was ceded to the United States, over all [303] lands selected
or acquired by the United States, "for the purpose of erecting
thereon a public building or public buildings for the accommodation of the United States courts, ... and the United
States shall have exclusive jurisdiction over the same . . . . for
all purposes except the administration of the criminal laws of
this state, and the service of any civil process therein or
thereon."

Section 5391 of the Revised Statutes of the United States makes the offense, charged in the indictment found by the state grand jury, punishable under the laws of the United States, when committed in any place "ceded to and under the jurisdiction of the United States."

The above are express provisions of state and federal law bearing directly upon the question to be determined in this action.

It has been held that when a purchase of land has been made by the United States with the consent of the legislature of the state, for any of the purposes enumerated in section 8, of article 1, of the federal constitution, the land so purchased, by the very terms of the constitution, ipso facto, falls within the exclusive jurisdiction of the United States: United States v. Cornell, 2 Mason, 60; Sharon v. Hill, 24 Fed. Rep. 726; Fort Leavenworth R. R. Co. v. Lowe, 114 U. S. 525; Story on the Constitution, secs. 1224-1227; Hare's Constitutional Law, 1142-1145; Ordronaux on Constitutional Legislation, 516, 517.

The supreme court of the United States in the case of Fort Leavenworth R. R. Co. v. Lowe, 114 U. S. 525, uses the following language: "When the title is acquired by purchase by the consent of the legislatures of the states, the federal jurisdiction is exclusive of all state authority. This follows from the declaration of the constitution that Congress shall have 'like authority' over such places as it has over the district which is the seat of government; that is, the power of 'exclusive legislation in all cases whatsoever.' Broader or clearer language could not be used to exclude all other authority than that of Congress; and that no other authority can be exercised over them has been the uniform opinion of federal and state tribunals, and of the attorneys general."

Counsel for respondent vigorously contend that the purchase of the land in Carson City by the United States for [364] the purposes designated in the act of Congress, approved January 13, 1885, above cited, does not come within the specific purposes named in section 8 of article 1 of the federal constitution; that the purchase of land for the erection of courthouses and post-offices by the United States, with the consent of the legislature of the state, does not, ipso facto, vest exclusive jurisdiction in the United States over such lands. This contention is not tenable.

The federal constitution provides for a judicial department; for the establishment of postoffices and post roads, and buildings are "needful" for the administration of justice, and for postof-

fices.   It is too narrow construction of section 8, article 1, of the
constitution to limit the exercise of exclusive jurisdiction by the
United States over lands purchased for the specific purposes
enumerated therein.   Under such construction the use of the
words "and other needful buildings" adds nothing to that
section.

Ordronaux, in his work on Constitutional Legislation, supra,
says: "The functions of the general government demanding the
establishment of forts, magazines, and dockyards, and the erection of postoffices, courthouses, mints, and other buildings in
various parts of the United States, the framers of the constitution made provisions accordingly for acquiring the necessary
sites.   It was contemplated that such places should be purchased
either from states or individuals, and as it was necessary for their
better government that Congress should have exclusive legislation over them, the clause requiring the legislature of the state
making the cession was introduced in order to avoid conflicts of
jurisdiction": See, also, Sinks v. Reese, 19 Ohio St. 306; 2 Am.
Rep. 397; Sharon v. Hill, 24 Fed. Rep. 726; Foley v. Shriver, 81
Va. 568; People v. Collins, 105 Cal. 504; Hare's Constitutional
Law, 1141-1143.

Counsel for respondent cite In re Kelly, 71 Fed. Rep. 545, as
strongly supporting their position.   That was a case wherein
the state of Wisconsin, by legislative enactment, ceded to the
United States jurisdiction over certain lands purchased by the
United States for the purpose of locating a "National Asylum
for Disabled Volunteer Soldiers."   The legal title to said lands
was not vested in the United States, but was [365] vested in a
corporation created by an act of Congress for the purpose.

The court (In re Kelly, 71 Fed. Rep. 545), in discussing the
right of the United States to exercise exclusive jurisdiction over
lands purchased by the United States with the consent of the
legislature for the purposes enumerated in section 8, article 1,
says: "The rule thus stated, whereby legislative consent operates
as a compete cession, is applicable only to objects which are specified in the above provision, and cannot be held to so operate,
ipso facto, for objects not expressly included therein.   Whether
it rests in the discretion of Congress to extend the provisions not
specifically enumerated, although for national purposes, upon
declaration as 'needful buildings,' and thereby secure exclusive
jurisdiction, is an inquiry not presented by this legislation."

The court then argues that the purchase of lands by the United States with the consent of the legislature of the state, irre-

spective of its use, does not vest in the United States exclusive
jurisdiction over the same; and that in determining the question
of jurisdiction, under purchases not made for the specific purposes enumerated in the federal constitution, the courts must
ascertain from the enactments whether it was intended that the
United States should exercise exclusive jurisdiction over such
lands because of any need or requirement of the exercise of the
same.　Applying this rule to the Kelly case, above cited, the
court therein properly held that the United States did not have
the right to exercise exclusive jurisdiction over the land purchased for the establishment of the "National Asylum for Disabled Volunteer Soldiers," for the reason there was a want of
affirmative showing of any congressional intention to secure exclusive jurisdiction, and the provisions of the law tended to show
that such jurisdiction was neither intended nor wanted, otherwise the legal title to the lands would have been taken in the
United States.

The case at bar is clearly distinguishable from the Kelly case,
supra.　The lands purchased under the act of January 13, 1885,
in Carson City, for the purposes specified therein, were so purchased for the erection of "needful buildings," within the
meaning of section 8 of article 1 of the federal constitution.
This is clearly manifest from the necessity of [366] the proper
exercise of the rights, powers, and duties, under the constitution,
of Congress to establish postoffices and post roads, and to create
and maintain federal courts.　The legislative intention that
such purchase was made under said section 8 is also clearly manifest from the condition of the act of January 13, 1885, prohibiting the expenditure of any portion of the money appropriated thereunder, until the state of Nevada had ceded to the
United States "exclusive jurisdiction" over such lands, and from
the act, and the title thereof, of the legislature of Nevada, approved February 24, 1885, above cited, ceding to the United
States "exclusive jurisdiction" over such lands.　Also, the legislature of Nevada, by an act thereof, approved January 18, 1883,
consenting to the purchase of lands within said state by the
United States, ceded "jurisdiction" (not exclusive) to the United
States over such lands, and attempted by an express proviso
therein to retain "concurrent jurisdiction": Stats. 1883, p. 13.
Considering this act with act of Congress of January 13, 1885,
and with the act of the legislature of Nevada of February 24,
1885, above cited, it is also clearly manifest that the attempt,
under the **act of 1883,** to retain concurrent jurisdiction in the

state was regarded by Congress as in contravention of the provisions of article 1, section 8, of the federal constitution, as no
purchase or appropriation for the purposes of the act was made
thereunder, and until after the act of February 24, 1885, became operative.

Counsel for respondent further contend that the proviso of
the act of February 24, 1885, ceding exclusive jurisdiction of the
state to the United States, "except the administration of the
criminal laws of the state," reserves to the state all criminal jurisdiction. This is also not tenable. If the purchase was made,
as has been held in this opinion, under the provisions of article
1, section 8, of the federal constitution, any attempt on the part
of the legislature to retain jurisdiction in the state over the lands
so purchased would be in contravention of said section, and
therefore void. Considering the legislative intention manifested
in the various acts, above cited, and that Congress and the legislature must have had in view the provisions of article 1, section
8, of the federal constitution in the passage of said acts, a
reasonable [307] and fair construction to be placed upon the provision reserving to the state the "administration of the criminal
laws" thereof, is simply the reservation to the state of the right
to execute criminal process upon the lands purchased for violation of the laws of the state, committed within the state, and
without the purchased lands. Giving the construction contended for would, in effect, destroy the purpose of the act.

It is a well-settled rule of construction that, when a statute is
of doubtful meaning, the first thing is to ascertain the intention
of the legislature that passed the act, and that intention must
be found, if possible, within the act itself; outside the statute,
courts will consider the mischief it was intended to suppress, or,
as the case may be, the objects or benefits thereby to be obtained:
Maynard v. Johnson, 2 Nev. 25.

From the act itself it is clear that the legislature intended to
consent to the purchase of lands within the state by the United
States for the purpose of erecting "needful public buildings,"
and to cede "exclusive jurisdiction" over the same to the federal
government, under the terms of article 1, section 8, of the federal constitution. Going outside of the statute, what object
was thereby to be attained? That the legislature intended to
consent to the purchase of lands within the state by the United
States for the purpose of erecting thereon "needful public buildings," and thereby vest in the United States exclusive jurisdiction over the same. No other object could be attained, for the

United States has the right to acquire lands within the state for needful buildings by other methods than the one provided in the constitution. The United States may purchase lands within the state, without the consent of the legislature thereof, but when so purchased, the possession is simply that of an ordinary proprietor, and the state retains jurisdiction over the same, within the limits of its authority: Fort Leavenworth R. R. Co. v. Lowe, 114 U. S. 525; United States v. Cornell, 2 Mason, 60.

Therefore the act of the legislature approved February 24, 1885, considered in the light of well-established rules of construction—from the language of the act itself and from the object to be obtained thereby—is simply the consent of the [368] state to the purchase of lands within its limits, by the United States for the purposes enumerated in said article 1, section 8, of the constitution, and such purchase vested exclusive jurisdiction over said lands in the United States.

The condition in the act of cession cannot be construed to mean that the state should reserve jurisdiction for the punishment of crime committed upon the purchased land. The apparent object of the condition was to prevent these lands from becoming the sanctuary for fugitives from justice for acts done within the jurisdiction of the state.

In Fort Leavenworth R. R. Co. v. Lowe, 114 U. S. 525, the supreme court of the United States, in commenting upon such provisions, uses the following language: "Now, there is nothing incompatible with the exclusive sovereignty or jurisdiction of one state that it should permit another state in such cases to execute its process within its limits. And a cession of exclusive jurisdiction may well be made with a reservation of this nature, which then operates only as a condition annexed to the cession, and as an agreement of the new sovereign to permit its free exercise as quoad hoc his own process."

For these reasons, the proceedings of the district court must be and are annulled.

No opinion is given upon the sufficiency of the indictment, as that question is not properly before this court.

JURISDICTION OF STATE COURTS OVER LANDS CEDED TO THE UNITED STATES.—Where a state court cedes to the United States lands for forts, etc., reserving concurrent jurisdiction to serve state process, civil and criminal, in the ceded place, such reservation merely operates as a condition of the grant, and does not defeat the exclusive jurisdiction of the United States over such place, and the state courts have no jurisdiction of crimes committed thereon: Lasher v. State, 30 Tex. App. 387; 28 Am. St. Rep. 922. See, also, Barrett v. Palmer, 135 N. Y. 336; 31 Am. St. Rep. 835; Exum v. State, 90 Tenn. 501; 25 Am. St. Rep. 700, and note thereto.

TAYLOR *v.* WANDS.

[55 NEW JERSEY EQUITY, 491.]

FRAUD, PROOF OF.—Evidence that merely excites suspicion that fraud may have existed is not sufficient. It must reasonably justify the inference of fraud.

FRAUD, ON HUSBAND'S CREDITORS.—A GIFT BY A WIFE to her sons in her last illness, in anticipation of death, though suggested by her insolvent husband, cannot be regarded as a fraud upon his creditors.

HUSBAND AND WIFE—SERVICES OF HUSBAND, RIGHTS OF HIS CREDITORS TO.—A married woman may employ her husband as her agent and make use of his business ability, experience, and energy in making her business successful. Earnings upon, or increase in, her capital in such business, though due in part to his services, belong to her, and are not liable to be seized by his creditors. Especially is this true when his services are rendered upon a compensation not shown to be an unusual compensation for such services. Instead of embarking in business in her own name, she may organize a corporation, supplying the capital, and the corporation may employ the husband in managing its business.

Garret D. W. Vroom, and Chauncey H. Beasley, for the appellants.

Peter Backes, for the respondent.

492 MAGIE, J. The decree appealed from was made upon a bill filed by Frederick J. Wands, assignee, the respondent, against John Taylor, Harry C. Taylor, William T. Taylor, the Taylor Provision Company, and others, the general purpose of which was to subject certain real and personal property, charged to be property of John Taylor, to a judgment entered by confession in the supreme court on April 7, 1893, in favor of respondent and against John Taylor and William C. Brandt.

The decree gave the relief prayed for by respondent in various particulars. Harry C. and William T. Taylor have appealed from the whole of the decree, but since they are only affected by it in two particulars, our attention may be confined to them. It adjudged that the surplus (by which was evidently meant the undivided earnings) of the Taylor Provision Company, so far as such surplus represented forty-eight shares of its capital stock standing in the name of appellants, was subject to the lien of respondent's judgment, and directed a reference to ascertain what surplus the company has. It further adjudged that the lands described in the bill, which formerly belonged to John Taylor, were also subject to respondent's judgment, and decreed that conveyances thereof made by John Taylor, under which, by divers mesne conveyances, the title to one of the tracts had come to Harry C. Taylor and the title to the remaining tracts had come to the Taylor Provision Company, should be annulled and set aside.

With respect to the part of the decree which dealt with the undivided earnings of the Taylor Provision Company, the issue **493** made by the pleadings, briefly stated, was this: The bill charged that John Taylor, Catharine M., his wife, and Harry C. and William T. Taylor, who are sons of John and Catharine M. Taylor, organized that company, but that all the stock was the property of John Taylor, and the shares held by Harry C. and William T. Taylor were held for John Taylor and to protect them from respondent's judgment. The prayer was, that appellants should be decreed to transfer all their stock in said company to a receiver to be appointed in the cause. Each appellant answered and denied the charge of the bill in this respect.

With respect to the part of the decree which dealt with the lands, the bill charged that John Taylor, with intent to defraud respondent and to protect said lands from respondent's judgment, had conveyed them to Edward H. Murphy, who afterward conveyed them to the Mechanics' National Bank of Trenton, which afterward conveyed them to Benjamin Van Cleve, who conveyed one tract to Harry C. Taylor and the remaining tracts to the Taylor Provision Company. The prayer on this subject was that the deeds should be set aside. Appellants' answer contained a specific denial of this charge.

The Taylor Provision Company did not at first file an answer, and a decree pro confesso was entered against it. But that de-

cree has since been opened and an answer has been filed by the
company, containing like specific denials.

It is scarcely necessary to observe that respondent's decree
upon these issues can only be supported by sufficient evidence
of the fraudulent character of the impeached transactions. Evidence which merely excites suspicion that fraud may have
existed will not be sufficient. It must reasonably justify an
inference of the actual existence of fraud.

As to the organization and stock of the Taylor Provision
Company, the only witnesses called by respondent were John
Taylor and the appellants. Upon their evidence the following
facts were established :

In 1860, upon the marriage of John Taylor with Catharine. M.
Taylor, a policy of insurance upon his life for $5,000 was, [494]
in some mode not disclosed by the evidence, made payable to
her. It does not appear who kept the policy alive by the payment of the premiums. It does not appear that John Taylor
paid any premium upon that policy after incurring the debt
whereon respondent's judgment was founded. In August, 1888,
the firm of John Taylor & Co., composed of John Taylor and
William C. Brandt, failed for a large amount. At that time
Mrs. Taylor had held the policy of insurance in question for
twenty-eight years, and there is nothing in the case to justify a
doubt as to her absolute right to it, free from any claim by
John Taylor's creditors. About the 1st of September, 1889,
she surrendered the policy to the company which had issued it
in consideration of a present payment to her of $2,400. On the
4th of September, 1889, the Taylor Provision Company became
incorporated by the filing of a proper certificate declaring that
its capital stock was to be $25,000, divided into two hundred
and fifty shares of $100 each, but that the company would com-
mence business upon payment of $5,000. It also appears that
fifty shares of the capital stock were subscribed, of which Mrs.
Taylor took forty-seven shares, each of the appellants took one
share and John Taylor took one share.

About the same time appellants obtained some money by the
surrender of a policy of life insurance upon the life of their
father, payable to them. There is no evidence that the money
thus acquired was not their own, free from any claim of their
father's creditors. If the fact were otherwise, it has not been
made to appear.

All the money procured by the surrender of the life insurance
policies was paid into the newly-formed company. Mrs. Taylor

paid in $2,400 and gave her duebill to the company for the difference between that sum and the par value of her forty-seven shares. John Taylor paid nothing for his share.

It is unnecessary to discuss whether this transaction was conducted in accord with the provisions of the corporation acts, for it could only be questioned in that respect by other stockholders or by creditors of the company.

Shortly after the formation of the company Mrs. Taylor [495] became sick and continued so until her death, in April, 1890. On January 31, 1890, when her death was expected by herself and her family, she transferred twenty-three of her shares of its stock to one of the appellants and twenty-three more to the other appellant, retaining one share in her own name. Her certificate was surrendered and new certificates issued to appellants. No consideration was paid for the stock; the transaction was a gift from the mother to her sons.

The vice-chancellor criticised this transaction as having been suggested by John Taylor. I am unable to perceive the justice of such criticism. John Taylor was hopelessly bankrupt. If his wife owned these shares of stock, or an interest in them, and died intestate, his creditors could require them to be applied to the satisfaction of their debts. But his duty to his creditors did not extend beyond such property as he had acquired. It did not require him to refrain from advising her as to the disposition of her property. There was, therefore, no legal or moral wrong in suggesting to her, or even entreating her, to bestow her property upon their sons, either by will or by gift inter vivos. Such a disposition by gift was made, and, in my judgment, appellants thereby acquired all the rights of their mother.

From this resumé of the evidence it is obvious that the decree prayed for, viz., the transfer of appellants' stock to a receiver for payment of respondent's judgment, was properly denied. There was no evidence to rebut the presumption that the $2,400 acquired by her by the surrender of the policy of life insurance was her own money. It follows that the shares of stock in the Taylor Provision Company, or such interest therein as she acquired with that money, became hers, and that she transferred her interest therein by the gift to appellants. The right of appellants to the shares originally taken and paid for by them is in no wise challenged.

The decree, however, subjects to respondent's judgment the accumulated earnings of the company which, upon division, would pertain to appellants' shares. In other words, it recog-

nizes the bona-fides of the transaction by which such shares
[496] were acquired, but decrees that the earnings upon the shares
belong not to appellants but to John Taylor and are subject to
his debts.

The evidence upon which the decree in this respect seems to
have been made may be thus stated: The Taylor Provision Company engaged in the same business as that which the firm of
John Taylor & Co. had previously carried on. John Taylor became the president and manager of the corporation. It does not
clearly appear but it may be inferred that the corporation owed
its success to his business ability and exertions. It appears, at
least, that while he was, as the vice-chancellor finds, the controlling spirit of the company, it established a good business and has
accumulated earnings of about $30,000.

From the opinion below, it seems that the conclusion respecting these earnings was based upon the lack of evidence to show
any agreement between the company and John Taylor as to accountings, or compensation or profits. But this put upon the
defendants below a burden which ought not to have been imposed on them. It was for respondent to establish fraud in the
transaction. As to accountings, it should be presumed, in the
absence of proof to the contrary, that such accountings as shareholders may require from officers of corporations were provided
for. The mere fact of large undivided accumulations of earnings justifies no inference of fraud, because the shareholders had
a right to leave their earnings undivided, and it may be inferred
that there was a necessity for more working capital than that
supplied by the original subscriptions. In respect to compensation of the president and manager, there is obvious error, for the
evidence shows that John Taylor is and has been receiving a salary of $3,000 a year as an officer of the company, for his services.

The decree, in so far as it subjects the accumulated earnings of
the Taylor Provision Company which represent appellants' forty-eight shares of stock to respondent's judgment, upon this evidence, is plainly erroneous.

In respect to such of the earnings as represent the two shares
originally subscribed and paid for by appellants, the decree has
[497] no foundation to rest upon. In respect to so much of the
earnings as represent the forty-six shares subscribed for by the
deceased Catharine M. Taylor, or such interest as she acquired
therein by the money she actually paid thereon, it is also without
support.

Under our married woman's act and the deliverances of our

courts on the subject, it is thoroughly settled that a married woman may embark her own money and capital in any separate business or trade; may make valid contracts respecting the same; may employ agents in carrying on such business or trade, and may avail herself of their skill and ability to make it successful. She may employ her husband as such an agent, and make use of his business ability, experience, and energy to the same purpose. Earnings upon or increase of her capital in such business or trade, though due in part to the services rendered by her husband, will still belong to her and will not be liable to be seized by the husband's creditors as his property. This was the doctrine declared in the court of chancery by Vice-Chancellor Van Fleet and approved by this court in Tresch v. Wirtz, 34 N. J. Eq. 124; 36 N. J. Eq. 356. It was applied in the court of chancery in Kutcher v. Williams, 40 N. J. Eq. 436, and more recently in this court in Coyne v. Sayre, 54 N. J. Eq. 702.

Had Mrs. Taylor established a business such as was carried on by the Taylor Provision Company and invested in it the money acquired by her upon the surrender of the life insurance policy and employed her husband to carry on that business in the same manner as he carried on the company's business, this doctrine would have been plainly applicable. For, while a court of equity will carefully scrutinize the employment of an insolvent husband by a wife in such a case, it could find nothing in the facts to indicate that the husband acquired any interest in the profits or earnings of the business. Had the husband's services been rendered to her gratuitously, such would probably be the conclusion, for the debtor is not obliged to work for the benefit of his creditor, but when, as in this case, the services were rendered upon compensation, not shown to be unusual compensation for such services, it is beyond doubt that the profits [498] and earnings of the business belonged to the wife, notwithstanding they were in part due to the husband's skillful services, precisely as they would do had she employed a stranger of like ability to carry on the business.

I am unable to distinguish between the case supposed and which the vice-chancellor concedes would require a different conclusion than that he reached, and the case actually presented by the evidence. Mrs. Taylor, instead of embarking her capital alone or in partnership with her sons in the business, organized a corporation to establish the business, and she and her sons took all the stock issued except one share and paid in all the working capital. Instead of employing her husband as her own agent or the agent of a firm composed of herself and her sons, the corporation, which they practically controlled, employed him as president and manager. The cases are identical and the profits and earnings represented by her stock were her own property and not liable to respondent's judgment.

There is nothing in the evidence to indicate it, but it may reasonably be inferred that a large part of the undivided earnings of the company were made after the stock of Mrs. Taylor had been transferred to appellants. With respect to the earnings after the transfer, the evidence is equally insufficient to justify the conclusion that they became the property of John Taylor. For these reasons the decree in the respect under consideration was erroneous.

It remains to consider that part of the decree appealed from which set aside certain conveyances and subjected the lands thereby conveyed to the Taylor Provision Company and to Harry C. Taylor to respondent's judgment.

To support the judgment in this respect respondent's evidence must show that John Taylor was the owner of said lands or of some interest in them liable to be taken in satisfaction of respondent's judgment.

The only witnesses called upon this subject were John Taylor and Benjamin Van Cleve. Neither Edward H. Murphy nor any officer of the Mechanics' National Bank of Trenton was examined as a witness.

[499] From the evidence of John Taylor the following facts appear: All the lands in question belonged to him at the time of the failure of the firm of John Taylor & Co., and the title was in him. The Mechanics' National Bank of Trenton was a large creditor of the insolvent firm. John Taylor conveyed the lands to Edward H. Murphy without any consideration, but with the intent that Murphy should convey them to said bank, which he afterward did. There was no agreement or understanding with the bank, except that it was to credit upon the debt of the firm whatever moneys it should obtain by a sale of said lands.

If the evidence of John Taylor is believed—and he is the only witness called respecting the transfer of his title to the bank—it is plain that his conveyances were absolute, and conveyed all his right, reserving no right of redemption. If the peculiar manner in which the title was conveyed to the bank is adapted to excite suspicion of the bona fides of the transaction, such suspicion is not sufficient to justify the rejection of the sworn statements of respondent's witness, to the effect that the design was

to prefer the bank to the other creditors of John Taylor. Such
a preference is not forbidden by law.

Since it thus appears that John Taylor parted with all his interest in the lands upon the transfer to the bank, it is obvious
that the decree can only be supported by evidence establishing
the fact that he subsequently acquired the title to said lands or
some interest therein.

The bank conveyed the lands to Van Cleve, who paid for
them partly in cash and partly by a note, which he afterward
paid. Both Van Cleve and Taylor testify that after Taylor had
heard that Van Cleve had agreed to buy the lands from the
bank, he expressed a desire to redeem the property at some future time, but both deny, in the most positive terms, that there
was any agreement or understanding by which Van Cleve was
bound to permit such redemption.

If this evidence is credited, it is plain that John Taylor acquired no interest in said lands from Van Cleve. But it is
argued in behalf of respondent that facts admitted by these witnesses are at variance with their evidence, and justify a [500] refusal to credit their denial that Van Cleve's purchase of the lands
from the bank was for the benefit of John Taylor. The facts
relied on are these: Van Cleve and John Taylor were old and
intimate friends. The sales of the greater and more valuable
parts of the lands made by Van Cleve to the Taylor Provision
Company were made for prices which reimbursed him for his
outlay in the purchase from the bank. The conveyance by Van
Cleve of one tract to Harry C. Taylor was without consideration.

A theory deduced from such admitted facts will not justify
discrediting the sworn evidence of unimpeached witnesses in respect to the intent and purpose of the respective conveyances,
unless it is absolutely inconsistent therewith. I do not think
such inconsistency appears.

With respect to the lands conveyed to the Taylor Provision
Company, there is no sufficient evidence to show that the prices
paid were below the fair market value at the time of the respective conveyances. The lands were conveyed to the company
in which John Taylor had but a nominal interest as holder of one
share of its stock.

With respect to the tract conveyed to Harry C. Taylor without consideration, it appears that it was heavily mortgaged.
There is no sufficient evidence of the market value of the equity
of redemption at the time the conveyance was made, but the fair
inference is that it was very small. If John Taylor's friend,

being protected from any loss upon his purchase from the bank, chose to convey to his friend's son this equity of redemption of trifling value, the inference that it was a gift is at least as reasonable as the inference sought to be deduced that the transfer was for the benefit of John Taylor. There is no evidence whatever that Harry C. Taylor accepted the conveyance with any agreement or understanding that he was to hold the tract for the benefit of his father.

Whatever suspicion the evidence on this subject may excite, it falls short, in my judgment, of establishing the claim of respondent. The decree, in the respect lastly considered, is therefore also erroneous.

[501] The result is that the decree appealed from, in the two respects which have been considered, and which are all in which appellants have an interest, must be reversed.

FRAUD—PROOF OF—CIRCUMSTANCES OF SUSPICION.— Fraud is never presumed but must be proved, and the burden of proving it is upon the party alleging it. Direct or positive evidence is not necessary, but it may be proved by circumstances which naturally, logically, and clearly indicate its existence. Circumstances of mere suspicion are not sufficient to prove it: Bank of Little Rock v. Frank, 63 Ark. 16; 58 Am. St. Rep. 65.

HUSBAND AND WIFE—SERVICES OF HUSBAND—RIGHT OF CREDITORS TO.—It has sometimes happened that a husband has devoted the major part of his time and all of his skill and ability either in the management of the separate property of his wife or in the conduct of business carried on in her name, and that her property has been augmented in value or her business caused to realize large profits, and the husband being indebted and having no other property, his creditors have claimed that they should in some manner be permitted to enforce their obligations against the fruits of the husband's labor and skill, though existing in the form of the wife's separate estate or business, and there are, doubtless, cases indicating that this claim of his creditors ought under some circumstances and by some mode of procedure to be sustained: Monographic note to Michigan Trust Co. v. Chapin, 58 Am. St. Rep. 497. See Brooks-Waterfield Co. v. Frisbie. 99 Ky. 125; 59 Am. St. Rep. 452, and note; Trefethen v. Lynam, 90 Me. 376; 60 Am. St. Rep. 271, and note. Contra, Boggess v. Richards, 39 W. Va. 567; 45 Am. St. Rep. 938. See, also, Trapnell v. Conklyn, 37 W. Va. 242; 88 Am. St. Rep. 30, and note.

HOLLOWAY *v.* APPELGET.

[55 NEW JERSEY EQUITY, 583.]

STATUTE OF LIMITATIONS, INJUNCTION AGAINST PLEADING.—A court of equity may, by the use of its injunctive power, disarm the defendant from using the statute of limitations fraudulently in an action at law, as where there has been a fraudulent concealment by the defendant of the cause of action against him, or, whether the act was fraudulent or not, when the defendant has employed means to mislead the plaintiff or to hide from him the fact that a cause of action has arisen. Hence if one employs an attorney to perform services in collecting certain municipal bonds, agreeing to pay him therefor ten per cent of any amount which may be realized on such bonds, and afterward settles with his creditor, or sells the bonds to another person acting for the creditor, without disclosing these facts to the attorney, equity will enjoin the pleading of the statute of limitations against an action by the attorney to recover his compensation brought upon discovering the facts entitling him to maintain it.

The vice-chancellor denied a decree in favor of the complainant. The decree was affirmed and the opinion of the vice-chancellor was approved by the court of appeals. It was as follows:

583 REED, V. C. This bill is filed to restrain the defendant from setting up the statute of limitations in an action at law brought by the complainant against the defendant and now pending in the Mercer **584** circuit. On March 5, 1884, the defendant was the owner of four bonds of the city of Rahway. On that date he consulted Mr. A. S. Appelget, an attorney at law, concerning the collection of the said bonds. The result of the consultation was that they entered into a contract in the following terms:

"In consideration of the services and expenditures to be rendered by A. S. Appelget, attorney at law, in collecting amounts due me on bonds of the city of Rahway, I hereby agree to allow him, as compensation therefor, ten per cent of the net amount he may be paid thereon, hereby requiring him not to settle for a less sum than the face value of said bonds and interest, without my consent, he to save me from all costs of suit.

"Dated March 5th, 1884.

(Signed) "JOHN K. HOLLOWAY,
"A. S. APPELGET."

One of the bonds was then due, and upon one of the other three there were coupons due. The four bonds were by Mr. Appelget, he having no safe, deposited in the Hightstown Bank. Afterward Mr. Holloway obtained an order from Mr. Appelget, by which he got the bonds from the bank. Mr. Appelget says

that Mr. Holloway promised to return them, for the purpose of
bringing suit, when the principal upon them became due. Mr.
Appelget brought suit on the bond that was due, and, in June,
1884, recovered judgment.

On June 18, 1884, Mr. Appelget wrote to Holloway the following letter:

"Dear Sir: I have entered up judgment for you against the
city of Rahway, for $2,832.34, and you will be entitled to interest
on this sum from June 16th, 1884, until it is paid. A law was
passed March 25th, 1884, and made to take effect immediately,
requiring all persons holding claims against Rahway to file with
the city clerk a dissent to receive the sum they offer by compromise within three months, and it must be on a form or blank
prepared by their city clerk. A most scoundrelly and outrageous
law, but you will have to look out for it and file the dissent before June 25th instant, or they may get the best of you on the
sly.   Respectfully yours,
                                     "A. S. APPELGET."

Upon the receipt of this letter, Mr. Holloway, instead of visiting Mr. Appelget, secured the services of another attorney [585]
to file the dissent. There appears to have been no other communication between the complainant and the defendant for several years, during which time the financial affairs of the city of
Rahway were in a bankrupt condition.

On December 31, 1885, Mr. Holloway sold the four bonds
to N. B. Conklin for the sum of fifteen hundred dollars. Mr.
Holloway says that he was induced to open communication
with Mr. Conklin through an advertisement which he saw in a
local newspaper, in which advertisement Conklin offered to purchase Rahway bonds. The bonds so purchased by Conklin were
turned into the city of Rahway and paid. Mr. Appelget first
discovered that the bonds had been paid, when, in 1894, the attorney of the city of Rahway requested him to have the judgment
which he had obtained against the city, for Mr. Holloway, satisfied upon the record. Afterward Appelget brought his action
against Holloway.

The question is, whether, in equity, Mr. Holloway is entitled
to invoke the statute of limitations in bar of Appelget's action
at law. In most of the cases, the bar has been set up in suits in
equity instituted for the purposes of obtaining relief in instances
of fraud. There, however, is no reason why a court of equity
should not, by the use of its injunctive power, disarm a defend-

ant from using the statute fraudulently in an action at law.   In
the case of Freeholders of Somerset v. Veghte, 44 N. J. L. 509,
where it was held that a fraudulent concealment of a cause of
action was no answer to the statute in an action at law, it was
admitted that relief could be successfully sought in equity.

It also appears that the equitable relief here invoked has been
granted mostly in cases where the act out of which the cause of
action arose was a fraudulent act, in its nature self-concealing,
such as embezzlements or thefts carried out by the falsification of
accounts or vouchers.   But it seems clear that a court of equity
will interfere, although the cause of action may not have arisen
out of a technically fraudulent act, if the defendant has employed any means to mislead the plaintiff, or to hide from him
the fact that a cause of action has arisen.

586 Now, the facts displayed in this case are such that I do not
see how the defendant could honestly have taken the course he
did.   He could not have forgotten, when he sold the bonds, that
he had entered into a written contract with Mr. Appelget to pay
him ten per cent of the amount collected.   He had been informed, by the letter already set out, that Mr. Appelget had entered up a judgment for a portion of the amount represented by
the four bonds.   Upon receipt of that letter, instead of going to
Mr. Appelget and consulting him, he employed another attorney
to file his dissent to the proposition of the city of Rahway.   He
never thereafter visited Appelget, but instead opened a correspondence with a broker, which resulted in a sale of the bonds
unknown to Appelget.   The whole affair has the unmistakable
appearance of an attempt to deprive Mr. Appelget of his percentage by dealing with a broker, on Holloway's own account,
surreptitiously.   It is within the range of possibility that Holloway may have believed that Mr. Appelget had abandoned all
hope of collecting the money, but in the face of Appelget's letter
informing him of the entry of the judgment, and the passage of
the statute affecting his claim, I do not see how he could have
formed such an opinion.

Nor do I see in what way Mr. Appelget was in laches in failing to discover that the bonds had been sold.   During all the
time intervening between the date of the contract between him
and the defendant and the date of the sale of the bonds, the des-
perate financial condition of Rahway was notorious.   There was
at the time no prospect of realizing any substantial part of the
debt, and it was natural that Appelget should wait, hoping for a
change in the condition of affairs.

Nor was the sale of the bonds discoverable except by accident. No inquiry about their custody was called for until a time should arrive when further litigation would be advisable. There was no act required by Mr. Appelget in the exercise of due diligence, which, if performed, would have led to a discovery of the sale, which he left unperformed.

I will advise a decree that the injunction be made perpetual.

⁵⁸⁷ PER CURIAM. Decree affirmed, for the reasons given in the court of chancery.

INJUNCTION AGAINST PLEADING STATUTE OF LIMITA-TIONS.—The power of a court of equity to restrain in a proper case, a defendant from pleading the statute of limitations, is recognized by all the authorities: Extended note to Wilkinson v. Flowers, 75 Am. Dec. 84. But it will not prohibit the use of this defense in a court of law except in plain cases of fraudulent abuse of the advantage of the lapse of time gained by the party seeking to use it: Bank of Tennessee v. Hill, 10 Humph. 176; 51 Am. Dec. 698, and note. See Thorndike v. Thorndike, 142 Ill. 450; 34 Am. St. Rep. 90, and note.

CASES

SUPREME COURT

OF

SOUTH CAROLINA.

RYAN v. SOUTHERN BUILDING AND LOAN ASSOCIATION

[50 SOUTH CAROLINA, 185.]

RES JUDICATA—USURY.—One against whom a judgment has been recovered foreclosing a mortgage and whose property is sold under such judgment and the proceeds paid to the plaintiff therein, cannot maintain an action against such plaintiff on the ground that the judgment included usurious interest. Since usury goes to defeat a recovery in whole or in part and is necessarily connected with the contract sued upon, the recovery of a judgment thereon, whether the defense of usury was pleaded or not, negatives its existence and estops the defendant from subsequently alleging usury in the judgment.

JUDGMENT, MERGER, EFFECT OF UPON USURIOUS CONTRACT.—If a contract claimed to be usurious becomes merged in a judgment, the original contract is extinguished. The judgment is a new debt not infected with the usurious nature of the cause of action.

Patterson & Holman, for the appellant.

R. C. Holman, B. T. Rice, and Bellinger, Townsend & O'Bannon, contra.

186 JONES, J. This is an action under section 1391 of Revised Statutes, for double the sum alleged to have been received of plaintiff by the defendant association in excess of lawful interest. The jury found a verdict in favor of plaintiff for two thousand eight hundred and sixty-four dollars and fifty cents, and from the judgment entered thereon the defendant, Tobin, as receiver of the defendant association, appeals on the ground that the circuit court erred in refusing his motion for nonsuit.

The defendant, Tobin, as receiver, in his answer, after a general denial, set up as a defense that "the action could not be maintained because the questions involved in said action were res judicata, for the reason that in an action in the court of common pleas for Barnwell county, the said Southern Mutual Building and Loan Association had brought an action and foreclosed a mortgage against the said G. K. Ryan, and that no plea of usury as a defense or counterclaim was interposed in said action to recover the principal sum out of which the claim for usury arose in this case."

The "case" contains the following relevant facts: "That at the time of the commencement of the suit and the date of the decree in the old suit of the association against Ryan, the said Ryan had not paid any usurious interest, but that said alleged illegal and usurious interest was collected in said suit. That the bonds and mortgages sued upon by said association in the case against Ryan were not upon their faces usurious contracts, but provided, inter alia, that in no event should more than the amount borrowed, together with the interest at the rate of eight per cent per annum be collected under said bonds. That Ryan, in attempting to defend in the said suit, put in an answer denying that he was indebted to the association in the amount claimed; that said answer was stricken out as frivolous, and judgment proceeded to be taken against him as by default."

At the close of plaintiff's testimony, defendant's counsel moved for a nonsuit, which was refused. The ground for the motion for nonsuit was, "that the record in the old case of the Southern Mutual Building and Loan Association [132] against Ryan showed that the cause of action of G. K. Ryan arose out of the transaction involved in that suit, and that Ryan should have set up in that action his plea of usury as a defense, or should have interposed a counterclaim for excessive interest, if any, and that he could not now maintain a separate action to recover said amount, as the same had become res judicata."

The exceptions are as follows: "1. Because his honor erred in refusing to grant the defendant's motion for a nonsuit herein, as it appeared in the record in the case of the Southern Mutual Building and Loan Association against G. K. Ryan, that the claim of the plaintiff in this action for the recovery of usury as a penalty of forfeiture originated in an action for the collection of the debt and interest in a foreclosure suit to which the said G. K. Ryan was a party defendant, and he is, therefore, estopped; 2. Because his honor should have granted the defendant's nonsuit upon the ground that when a party is a defendant in an action against him for the recovery of a debt and interest, that he is bound to set up such a claim of usury as a defense or counter-claim in that action, and cannot afterward maintain a separate action for the recovery of usury as a forfeiture when the same arose in such suit, as in this instance, where G. K. Ryan was a party defendant to said action of foreclosure."

The only evidence of the receipt of any money alleged to be for usurious interest by defendant from plaintiff was the money paid to defendant out of the proceeds of sale under decree in foreclosure in the case of said association against said Ryan. It is conceded that nothing was paid as usurious interest previous to the rendition of judgment. The question, then, is, Can a suit be maintained under section 1391 of the Revised Statutes, for double the sum of interest received in excess of lawful interest, where the only evidence of the receipt of usurious interest was the receipt of the proceeds of a judgment and sale in foreclosure, in a suit on a contract to which the defense of [188] usury might have been interposed. We think it clear that such a suit cannot be maintained. A judgment is the final determination of the rights of the parties in the action (Code, sec. 266), and is conclusive of all matter necessarily involved, whether raised or not, especially if the party denying the adjudication knew of the matter and could have interposed it at the previous trial, either in support of a claim or as a defense: Ruff v. Doty, 26 S. C. 178; 4 Am. St. Rep. 709. While it is true, as a general rule, that usury is not available as a defense unless pleaded (Loan etc. Bank v. Miller, 39 S. C. 193), yet since usury goes to defeat the recovery in whole or in part, and is necessarily based upon or connected with the contract sued upon, and in the affirmative proof upon the contract must be impliedly but necessarily negatived, a judgment defendant must be held estopped to affirm usury in the judgment debt, in any subsequent suit involving the existence of such usury as a fact. The law as to payment affords an illustration. The defense of payment is affirmative, and must be pleaded as a general rule, but if such plea is not made, and judgment is rendered for the whole debt, the judgment defendant is estopped to affirm payment in any subsequent suit based on the fact of payment. In 2 Black on Judgments, 759, the doctrine is laid down that "a judgment defendant is estopped from alleging that usurious interest was included in the judgment in a subsequent suit to recover treble the amount of such interest. For the usury, if in fact it existed, could have

been pleaded in defense to the former action, and whether it was
set up or not, the judgment is conclusive against that allegation."
This rule, of course, applies to judgments fairly obtained, for
if the judgment is a part of the scheme to evade the usury laws,
and is a device to cover the usurious transaction, it would not be
held conclusive on the question of usury.   In the case of Fowler
v. Henry, 2 Bailey, 54, the court held that, if a borrower, after a
loan made, and without any previous agreement to do so, confess
a judgment for money lent on usury, he is [189] forever concluded.
The court said: "There is no question that if a judgment be confessed or suffered in pursuance of an original corrupt and usurious agreement, that the borrower should so confess or suffer it,
it would be void under the statute [decision rendered in 1830];
but it is equally clear that if the defendant had an opportunity,
according to the ordinary forms of law, to make his defense, and
neglected to avail himself of it, that he is forever concluded."
This last-mentioned case also held that the indorser of a note,
made in consideration of such a judgment, could not avoid his
own liability by reason of usury in the original loan.   See, also,
Pickett v. Pickett, 2 Hill Eq. 363, *474, wherein the court said:
"That a judgment fairly obtained upon a usurious contract is
conclusive has been repeatedly held in this state.   As, for instance, in Fowler v. Stewart, where the suit was on a judgment
which had been rendered on usurious notes.   The defendant was
not allowed to go behind the judgment and examine the contract
on which it was founded.   Numberless cases of a similar character have occurred where a like decision was made."   Now we will
examine the statute under which the present action is brought,
and ascertain if such statute in anyway abrogates the above salutary rule as to the conclusiveness of a judgment to prevent the
affirmance of usury in the original debt in any subsequent proceeding between the same parties or their privies.   Section 1390
is as follows: "No greater rate of interest than seven per centum
per annum shall be charged, taken, agreed upon, or allowed upon
any contract arising in this state for the hiring, lending, or use of
money or other commodity, except upon written contract, wherein by express agreement a rate of interest not exceeding eight
per cent may be charged.   No person or corporation lending or
advancing money or other commodity upon a greater rate of interest shall be allowed to recover in any court in this state any
portion of the interest so unlawfully charged; and the principal
sum, amount, or value so lent or advanced, without any interest,
shall be [190] deemed and taken by the courts of this state to be

the true legal debt or measure of damages, to all intents and purposes whatsoever, to be recovered without costs; provided, that the provisions of this section shall not apply to contracts or agreements entered into, or discounts or arrangements made, prior to the 1st of March, 1890."

"Sec. 1391. Any person or corporation who shall receive as interest any greater amount than is provided for in the preceding section shall, in addition to the forfeiture herein provided for, forfeit also double the sum received, to be collected by a separate action, or allowed as a counterclaim to any action brought to recover the principal sum."

This action is brought under the last-quoted section, for "double the sum so received." It is manifest that section 1390 must be looked to for the purpose of ascertaining the meaning of "double the sum so received." Referring to that section, we find that the usurious interest must have been taken or received "upon any contract arising in this state for the hiring, etc., of money, etc." In this case the money received was the proceeds of the sale of land under a decree of foreclosure. The contract now said to be usurious had become merged into the judgment. The original contract was extinguished. The judgment became a new debt, and "is not infected by the usurious nature of the cause of action": Freeman on Judgments, 217; citing Thatcher v. Gammon, 12 Mass. 268. As said by Simpson, C. J., in Moore v. Holland, 16 S. C. 27, speaking of a judgment: "When it is granted upon a contract, it determines what the contract is, and closes it, giving the party in whose favor the judgment is rendered the means of enforcing the contract thus determined, or redress for its breach. A judgment of this sort involves two ideas, the contract upon which it is rendered and the judgment itself. The one is the act of the parties, the other is the act of the court. They are entirely separate and distinct." The statute nowhere speaks of the receipt of usurious interest included in a judgment, but merely speaks of the receipt of such interest [191] on a contract, and it cannot be doubted that if the legislature had intended to include judgments, it would have said so plainly. In the absence of a manifest intent to alter the wholesome rules as to the verity and conclusiveness of judgments, we will not strain an intent to include judgments in the term "contracts." It is the duty of the judgment debtor to pay the judgment, and it is the right of the judgment creditor to receive what the court has adjudged to be due him. Would it not be a very strange construction of this statute to hold under it what was rightfully paid upon a judgment was wrongfully received? Is it possible to specify the wrong or delict of the defendant in this case?

It is true that no right of action accrued under this statute until the payment of the usurious interest: Hardin v. Trimmier, 27 S. C. 111. Hence, it is argued that the right of action did not accrue until the payment of the judgment. But, as shown above, the statute only allows a separate action for the usurious interest received upon the contract. To make this statute apply, the usurious interest must have been received on the agreement before it merged into the judgment, and in that event, in a suit on the agreement or "for the principal sum," the debtor may plead usury, and set up the counterclaim as specified; or he may plead usury in the suit for the principal sum, and, if successful, he may, if he choose, instead of setting up the counterclaim in that action, bring a separate action for the specified sum; or he may bring a separate action before the action on the contract, or during the pendency of the action on the contract, provided he has not set up the counterclaim in said action on the contract. It is manifest, if the plea of usury is raised in the suit on the contract and is unsuccessful, that there can be neither any counterclaim in the suit on the contract nor a separate action, because the fundamental fact of usury is wanting, and there cannot be maintained either counterclaim or a separate action, except upon proof of usury; if one is estopped to [102] prove the fact of usury, he is in the same condition as if no usury in fact existed. The construction thus given is consistent with all former decisions of this court under this statute, is strictly in accordance with the terms and purpose of the act, and at the same time does not disturb the long-settled principles governing the conclusiveness of a judgment.

The motion for nonsuit should have been granted. The judgment of the circuit court is reversed, and the cause remanded for a new trial.

JUDGMENT—MERGER BY—DEFENSE OF USURY.—A domestic judgment merges and extinguishes the cause of action for which it was rendered in the courts of the same jurisdiction; consequently, no suit can be maintained upon the original cause of action but only upon the judgment: Bank of N. A. v. Wheeler, 28 Conn. 433; 73 Am. Dec. 683, and note. The effect of a judgment at common law is practically to destroy, so long as it exists, the ground upon which it rests: Barnes v. Gibbs, 31 N. J. L. 317; 86 Am. Dec. 210. Nor can it be shown in a subsequent action that there has been a mistake in the calculation of interest; that part of it has thus been left out of the judgment: Baker v. Baker, 28 N. J. L. 13; 75 Am. Dec. 243. Usury or other illegality in an obligation is no defense to a creditor's bill brought by a judgment creditor to enforce satisfaction of his judgment recovered upon such obligation. The judgment can only be impeached upon a direct proceeding brought to reverse or annul it: Bank of Wooster v. Stevens, 1 Ohio St. 233; 59 Am. Dec. 619. But it has been held that a bond given to secure a judgment on confession in an action on usurious notes is tainted with usury: Extended note to Sylvester v. Swan, 81 Am. Dec. 737, 738.

STATE *v.* DAVIS.

[50 SOUTH CAROLINA, 405.]

CRIMINAL LAW—MALICE.—An instruction that the law will imply malice from any wanton, thoughtless, cruel, or depraved act, any act going to show an intention on the part of the party, which shows a heart devoid of all social instincts and fatally bent on mischief, is correct, and proper to be given when the defendant is on trial for murder.

MURDER AND MANSLAUGHTER.—THE HEAT AND PASSION REQUISITE to reduce a homicide from murder to manslaughter must be based on a provocation which the law deems adequate, and must be such that, while it need not dethrone reason entirely, nor shut out knowledge and volition, would naturally destroy the sway of reason and render the mind of an ordinary person incapable of cool reflection and produce what, according to all human experience, may be called uncontrollable impulses to do violence.

MURDER AND MANSLAUGHTER, USE OF DEADLY WEAPON.—Where the death of a human being is caused by the intentional use of a deadly weapon, provocation by words only cannot reduce the killing to manslaughter.

MURDER—SELF-DEFENSE MADE NECESSARY BY THE SLAYER'S FAULT.—To instruct the jury that the defendant, on a trial for murder, must come into court with clean hands is not strictly appropriate, but does not entitle him to a new trial, if, from the whole evidence, it is clear that what the judge meant was that he who sets up the plea of self-defense must have been without fault in bringing on the necessity for taking human life.

JURY TRIAL—INSTRUCTIONS, REQUESTS FOR IN WRITING, WHAT ARE NOT.—A rule of court requiring counsel, before argument commences, to read and submit to the court in writing such propositions of law as they propose to rely upon, which shall constitute the request to charge, etc., is not complied with by reading certain sections of the criminal code and requesting the judge to charge as therein laid down.

ARREST, RIGHT TO MAKE, WITHOUT WARRANT.—At the common law, a private person had the right to arrest, without warrant, any person who committed, or attempted to commit, a felony in his view, but did not have such right where the offense was a misdemeanor only.

MURDER, ARREST, ERROR IN INSTRUCTION RESPECTING RIGHT OF.—It is error to instruct a jury that one who sees another stealing, or attempting to steal, his property, has the right to arrest him, where it does not appear that the value of such property was sufficient to make the offense a felony, and if the legality or illegality of the arrest is a vital question in the case, an error in so instructing entitles the defendant, if convicted, to a new trial.

MURDER—RIGHT OF PERSON TO REPOSSESS HIMSELF
OF PROPERTY.—It is error to instruct a jury in a trial for murder
that if the decedent had a piece of property which the defendant
took possession of in his presence, then the decedent had the right
to repossess himself of it, and if killed by the defendant with malice
aforethought while trying to so repossess himself, the killing was
murder, because such instruction is calculated to mislead the jury
into believing the deceased might lawfully exercise his right, though
in so doing he committed a breach of the peace.

Indictment for, and conviction of, murder. The instructions
of the trial judge which were complained of as erroneous are
sufficiently disclosed in the opinion of the court.

J. E. McDonald and James W. Hanahan, for the appellant.

J. K. Henry, contra.

[419] JONES, J. The appellant, under an indictment charging him with the murder of James E. Suber, was found guilty
and sentenced to be hanged. His grounds of appeal relate
wholly to the charge of the circuit judge. The charge and the
exceptions thereto appear in the official report. A general summary of the facts which the testimony offered by the state tended
to prove may make more clear the questions involved.

The deceased, James E. Suber, kept a store at Lyles [420] Ford,
in Fairfield county. About 7 o'clock P. M., August 10, 1896,
defendant was in the store. Deceased having gone out of the
store for a brief while, returning, saw defendant at his money
drawer, and hollered at him. Defendant ran out of the store.
One witness said that defendant, after taking his hand out of the
money drawer, attempted to put it in his pocket, and some money
fell on the floor. Deceased, after examining the drawer, followed defendant, and called out to him, "Hold on, Henry, you
have been in my money drawer and taken my money. You had
no business to do it, and I want it." Defendant walked on, and
deceased overtook him a short distance from the store, and laid
his hand on defendant's shoulder from behind. Defendant
turned, and deceased caught hold of the lapel of defendant's
coat, and demanded that he give up the money. Defendant denied having taken his money, and demanded to be turned loose.
Deceased refused to turn him loose unless he would give up the
money. They began to pull at each other, and in the scuffle deceased threw defendant down. They arose, and in the struggle
following, defendant fired his pistol and jerked loose. Deceased
attempted to seize defendant again, and defendant shot the second time. Deceased was told by a bystander to get his gun and
kill defendant. Deceased started to his store, when defendant

fired at him the third time, missing him. Defendant then moved
off rapidly. Deceased soon reappeared from his store with a gun
in his hand, but when told to pursue and shoot defendant, he
said, "No, I was not mad about his stealing my money; I only
wanted it, and he has taken my money and shot me, but I will
not shoot him now." Deceased was wounded in two places, one
ball entering the bowels from the right side, the other a little
below the left nipple, and died next day. In his dying declarations, admitted in evidence, he said he saw defendant in his
money drawer, and hollered at him; that defendant made one
more rake at the drawer, and ran out behind the counter and
jumped out of the door; that he (deceased) went to the drawer
and saw he had taken money; [421] that he followed him, put his
hand in the collar of defendant's coat, and told him to give him
his money; that he demanded the money two or three times;
that defendant wouldn't give it up, and that he tripped defendant; that he had no idea of hurting defendant; that he tripped
him up twice—that he didn't intend throwing him down, but intended to scare the money out of him; that as he rose the second
time, defendant shot him; that he took his hands off defendant,
being dazed, and attempted to change his position, but before he
could do it, defendant shot him again; that he went in the store
and got his gun and came to the side door, when defendant was
twenty-five yards off. He further said that defendant attempted
to bite him on the arm, and he told defendant if he did he would
maul him. He further said that he had done wrong in putting
his hands on defendant, but he had no idea defendant had a
pistol; that defendant shot him from under cover, and he did
not see the pistol.

1. It is urged as the first ground of appeal that the circuit
judge erred in charging that "the law will imply malice from any
wanton, thoughtless, cruel, or depraved act, any act going to
show an intention on the part of the party which shows a heart
devoid of all social instincts and fatally bent on mischief." It
was conceded in argument that this charge was theoretically correct, but it is claimed that it was inapplicable to the facts of the
case, and that he should have charged the jury that the law creates no presumption of malice when all the facts and circumstances attending the homicide have been developed in the testimony. This exception is not well taken. It was quite applicable and appropriate in this case for the judge in his charge to
explain the meaning of implied malice, the indictment being for
murder. The record further discloses that immediately after

explaining implied malice, he expressly charged precisely as it is claimed he should have charged.

2. It is contended that there was error in the following [422] charge: "Now, as I said before, if the testimony in this case, and you are the sole judges of that, satisfies you that the defendant here took the life of the deceased in sudden heat and passion, and upon sufficient legal provocation, and the deceased said anything or did anything to the defendant which was calculated to highly exasperate and inflame and arouse his passion, so that he had an uncontrollable impulse, and he was so inflamed with passion that he hardly knew what he was doing, and in that heat and passion he took the life of the deceased without malice, then you can find him guilty of manslaughter." It is objected that this charge: 1. Prescribed a stricter rule than that required by law as to the degree of heat and passion necessary to reduce the killing from murder to manslaughter; 2. Took from the jury the right to determine the degree of heat and passion necessary to reduce the killing from murder to manslaughter; and 3. Was in violation of article 5, section 26, of the constitution, forbidding judges from charging the jury in respect to matters of fact. Of the second and third grounds above, nothing more need be said than that they are not tenable. The first ground deserves more extended notice. The circuit judge correctly defined manslaughter as the killing of any human being, without malice, in sudden heat and passion, and upon sufficient legal provocation. It is contended, however, that he was not authorized to go further, and add words indicating that the heat and passion should amount to an "uncontrollable impulse," and that passion should so inflame that "he hardly knew what he was doing." In Desty's Criminal Law, section 128 d, it is stated that adequate provocation and ungovernable passion must concur—that to reduce murder to manslaughter a provocation must be established as sufficient to render the passion irresistible. In Clark's Criminal Law, 165, the doctrine is laid down, "that the provocation must be such as the law deems adequate to excite uncontrollable passion in the mind of a reasonable man." Mr. Bishop in his Criminal Law, volume 2, section 697, page 386, says: "The sufficiency of the [423] passion to take away malice and reduce what would be murder to manslaughter is so much a question of law that it is difficult to say on the authorities how intense in fact it must be. . . . . The passion must be such as is sometimes called irresistible, yet it is too strong to say that the reason of the party should be dethroned, or he should act in a whirlwind of passion."

So in Clark on Criminal Law, page 167, it is said: "The provocation must deprive one of the power of self-control, but it need not entirely dethrone reason." This is supported by the following citations: People v. Calton, 5 Utah, 451; Maher v. People, 10 Mich. 212; 81 Am. Dec. 781; Brooks v. Commonwealth, 61 Pa. St. 352; 100 Am. Dec. 645; Davis v. People, 114 Ill. 86. See, also, People v. Freeland, 6 Cal. 96. In the case of State v. Hill, 4 Dev. & B. 491, 34 Am. Dec. 396, relied on by appellant, Gaston, J., said: "We nowhere find that the passion, which in law rebuts the imputation of malice, must be so overpowering as for the time to shut out knowledge and destroy volition. All the writers concur in representing this indulgence of the law to be a condescension to the frailty of the human frame, which, during the furor brevis, renders a man deaf to the voice of reason, so that, although the act done was intentional of death, it was not the result of malignity of heart, but imputable to human infirmity."

"The provocation of the deceased must be the direct and controlling cause of the passion, and it must be such as naturally and instantly to produce in the minds of persons ordinarily constituted the highest degree of exasperation, rage, anger, sudden resentment, or terror, rendering the mind incapable of cool reflection": 9 Ency. of Law, 579. In State v. Smith, 10 Rich. 347, the passion which reduces a felonious killing to manslaughter is characterized as a "temporary frenzy excited by sufficient legal provocation"; and in State v. McCants, 1 Spear, *390, Judge Wardlaw speaks of this passion as "the violent impulse of anger outstripping the tardier operations of reason . . . . provoked by sufficient cause." It may be concluded, therefore, that "the sudden heat and passion upon sufficient legal provocation," [424] which mitigates a felonious killing to manslaughter, while it need not dethrone reason entirely, or shut out knowledge and volition, must be such as would naturally disturb the sway of reason and render the mind of an ordinary person incapable of cool reflection, and produce what, according to human experience, may be called an uncontrollable impulse to do violence. We do not think the charge of the judge went beyond the limits above prescribed, and was, therefore, not error, in so far as his charge relates to acts which the law deems adequate to provoke such passion. But it is well settled in this state that where death was caused by the use of a deadly weapon (as in this case), provocation by words only, no matter how opprobrious and hard to be borne, would not be sufficient to reduce the killing to man-

slaughter: State v. Jacobs, 28 S. C. 29; State v. Levelle, 34 S. C.
129; 27 Am. St. Rep. 799. Therefore, the judge erred in charging that "if the deceased said anything to the defendant which
was calculated to highly exasperate, etc." But, though erroneous in this respect, it was most favorable to the prisoner, in view
of the fact that deceased charged the defendant with stealing his
money just before the fatal shot. The error was harmless, and,
therefore, not reversible.

3. The third and fourth exceptions may be considered together. We think a reference to the charge as a whole on the
subject of self-defense will show that the judge committed no
error. The expression that the party who claims self-defense
must come into court with clean hands, while not strictly appropriate, was so explained by other language as to show the jury
clearly that the judge meant nothing more than the law required,
viz., that the party who sets up the plea of self-defense must be
without fault in bringing on the necessity to take human life,
for he said immediately afterward: "You cannot bring about a
state of affairs on your own part which necessitates your taking
the life of a human being, and then plead self-defense": [425] See
State v. Beckham, 24 S. C. 283. These exceptions are overruled.

4. The fifth exception is as follows: "5. For that his honor
erred in refusing and neglecting, when requested so to do by the
defendant's counsel, to charge the jury as to the right of private
persons to arrest without a warrant, as laid down in sections 1
and 2 of Criminal Code, volume 2, of the Revised Statutes of
1893." As to this fifth exception, perhaps it is too general to
require consideration; but, waiving this, does the record disclose
that the circuit judge refused or neglected to charge any request
presented to him in writing, as required by rule 11 of the circuit
court? It appears that at the beginning of the argument, counsel for defendant read to the court and requested the court to
charge as therein laid down sections 1 and 2 of the Criminal
Code, which are as follows: "Sec. 1. Upon view of a felony committed, or upon certain information that a felony has been committed, any person may arrest the felon and take him to a judge
or trial justice, to be dealt with according to law. Sec. 2. It
shall be lawful for any citizen to arrest any person in the night-
time, by such efficient means as the darkness and the probability
of his escape render necessary, even if his life should be thereby
taken, in cases where he has committed a felony, or has entered
a dwelling-house with evil intent, or has broken or is breaking
into an outhouse with a view to plunder, or has in his possession

stolen property, or being under circumstances which raise just
suspicion of his design to steal or to commit some felony, flees
when he is hailed." Rule 11 of the circuit court provides that:
"Before the argument of the case commences, the counsel on
either side shall read and submit to the court, in writing, such
propositions of law as they propose to rely on, which shall constitute the request to charge, etc." We do not think a request
to charge presented in the manner described is a substantial compliance with this rule: See Molair v. Railway Co., 31 S. C. 510.
The value of the rule requiring such requests [426] to be in writing, so as to promote accuracy and certainty, would be greatly
impaired by holding that the reading of extracts from statutes,
decisions, and text-books, with oral request that such be charged
to the jury, is a substantial compliance therewith. Justice and
its orderly administration will be promoted by insisting on compliance with the provisions of this rule. It may be that a case
might arise in which the court ex gratia would waive technical
compliance with a rule made merely for the orderly conduct of
the business of a court. But in this case such necessity does not
arise.

5. The sixth exception is as follows: "6. For that his honor
erred in charging the jury as follows: 'Now, gentlemen, I charge
you, as matter of law, that, if you see a party stealing your
property, or if you see a party committing a larceny, you
have a right to arrest that party,' when he should have
charged that a private individual could only make an arrest
in the cases mentioned and prescribed in sections 1 and 2 of the
Criminal Code, Revised Statutes of 1893." At common law, a private person had the right to arrest, without warrant, any person
who committed or attempted to commit a felony in his view. In
State v. Anderson, 1 Hill, 212, *327, the court said, that in order
to justify an arrest by private persons, the proof must show that a
felony was committed, and that the prisoner was the perpetrator. Section 1 of the Criminal Code, quoted above, allows any
person to arrest upon view of a felony committed, or upon certain information that a felony has been committed. In this case
the evidence tended to show that defendant had stolen some
money belonging to deceased, in his view, from a money drawer
in deceased's store, but no evidence was offered to show the
amount of the money stolen. If the amount stolen was less than
twenty dollars, then no felony was committed, unless the larceny was compound larceny. There was no evidence in the
case that the store was used as a dwelling. Hence the jury may

have concluded from the evidence that defendant had committed a simple petit larceny. [427] Such a larceny in this state is a
misdemeanor and not a felony. Section 2 of the Criminal Code
allows any citizen to arrest in the night-time under certain circumstances and for certain offenses, among others, when the
offender "has in his possession stolen property." The evidence
tended to show that the larceny took place a short while before
7:30 P. M., August 10, 1896, at which hour it appears deceased
was shot. From this evidence alone, it cannot be said with certainty that the alleged arrest was attempted in the night-time, so
as to make section 2 applicable. It seems clear, therefore, in
view of the evidence in the case, that the circuit judge erred in
instructing the jury, as he did, as to the right of any person to
arrest for larceny committed, in failing to distinguish between
larceny that is felony and a larceny that is misdemeanor. For a
simple petit larceny, a private person has no right to arrest without warrant. It may seem hard that one has no right to arrest
for a petit larceny of his own property, committed in his view,
but such is the law. Whether the alleged arrest was legal or illegal was a vital question in the case. From the charge of the
judge, the jury had a right to infer that deceased had the right
to arrest defendant, and, therefore, defendant had no right to
resist, and this may have controlled them in determining the
question whether the defendant killed in malice, or in sudden
heat and passion, upon the provocation of an unlawful arrest.
While it may be murder, under certain circumstances, to kill in
resisting an unlawful arrest, generally it is manslaughter only,
if done in heat and passion, provoked by the illegal arrest, and
not with malice.

 6. The seventh exception alleges error in the following charge:
"If you have a piece of property, Mr. Foreman, lying on that
table, and I walk up and take the property in your presence, you
have a right to repossess yourself of your property, and if I kill
you while you are trying to repossess yourself of your property—
if I kill you with malice aforethought, expressed or implied—
then I am guilty of murder." It is contended that the error here
[428] consists in not charging the jury that a person, in such circumstances, could only repossess himself of his property in an
orderly and quiet manner, and without a breach of the peace.
In so far as the judge instructed the jury that a killing with
malice aforethought is murder, the charge is unobjectionable;
but it was calculated to mislead the jury, to tell them that when
a person takes the property of another in his presence, that the

latter has the right to repossess himself of that property, without explanation that the exercise of such right must be without a breach of the peace. Under such circumstances, one could not lawfully resort to violence to regain his property. The law provides other adequate means to redress wrongs of that character more consistent with the peace and safety of society.

The remaining exceptions were not argued, and we content ourselves with overruling the same without extended consideration.

The judgment of the circuit court is reversed, and the case remanded for a new trial.

Pope, J., dissents.

___

HOMICIDE—UNCONTROLLABLE IMPULSE—WHAT IS.—An irresistible impulse to kill cannot be set up as a defense to murder so long as the accused knew that the act he was committing was a crime morally and punishable by the law of his country. Such knowledge makes it imperative that he shall control himself at his peril: State v. Alexander, 30 S. C. 74; 14 Am. St. Rep. 879, and note. See Genz v. State, 59 N. J. L. 488; 59 Am. St. Rep. 619, and note.

HOMICIDE—MALICE—WHEN INFERRED.—If the act which produced death be attended with such circumstances as indicate a wicked, depraved, and malignant spirit, the law will imply malice without reference to what was passing in the prisoner's mind at the time: State v. Levelle, 34 S. C. 120; 27 Am. St. Rep. 799, and note; Martinez v. State, 30 Tex. App. 129; 28 Am. St. Rep. 895, and note.

HOMICIDE—MANSLAUGHTER—KILLING WITH DEADLY WEAPON.—Where a homicide is committed with a deadly weapon, provocation by words only, no matter how opprobrious, is not sufficient to reduce the crime from murder to manslaughter: State v. Levelle, 34 S. C. 120; 27 Am. St. Rep. 799, and note. But see Evers v. State, 31 Tex. Crim. Rep. 318; 37 Am. St. Rep. 811.

HOMICIDE—KILLING BROUGHT ON BY FAULT OF ACCUSED—SELF-DEFENSE.—When the defendant provokes the occasion which produces the necessity to take the life of the deceased, he cannot rely upon self-defense, nor avail himself of threats made by deceased against his life: Levy v. State, 28 Tex. App. 203; 19 Am. St. Rep. 826, and note. See, however, People v. Button, 106 Cal. 628; 46 Am. St. Rep. 259, and note; and Shannon v. State, 35 Tex. Crim Rep. 2; 60 Am. St. Rep. 17, and note.

ARREST BY PRIVATE PERSON WITHOUT WARRANT.—Where a private person has arrested an innocent person, in an action brought against him for such arrest, he must prove to the entire satisfaction of the jury that a felony had actually been committed, and that the circumstances were such that they themselves, or any reasonable person, acting without passion or prejudice, would fairly have suspected the plaintiff of being the person who had committed it: Monographic note to Eanes v. State, 44 Am. Dec. 293. But if no felony has been committed, the arrest is illegal: Holley v. Mix, 3 Wend. 350; 20 Am. Dec. 702; Brooks v. Commonwealth, 61 Pa. St. 352; 100 Am. Dec. 645. See monographic note to Hawkins v. Commonwealth. 61 Am. Dec. 151-164, on arrest.

GREEN v. GREEN.
[50 SOUTH CAROLINA, 514.]

APPELLATE PROCEDURE—A DEMURRER CANNOT BE INTERPOSED IN THE SUPREME COURT WHILE A CAUSE IS THERE PENDING ON APPEAL.—That court does not undertake to review questions not presented to the trial court.

PRACTICE IN EQUITY—DEFENSES RESPECTING OTHER TRANSACTIONS.—In a suit by remaindermen against a life tenant to have certain property declared to be held by the latter as such life tenant, because it is the proceeds of the property the subject of the life estate, the defendant is not entitled to present and have litigated claims made by her that the plaintiffs have received more than their share of the property claimed under a will upon which the title and claims of all the parties are based.

LIFE TENANT AND REMAINDERMAN, PROCEEDS OF INSURED PROPERTY.—Moneys collected by a life tenant upon a loss by fire of a building subject to the tenancy, though the premiums have been paid with his personal funds, stand in place of the property destroyed, and should either be used in rebuilding it or should be held by the life tenant for the benefit of the remainderman after the tenant's death.

REAL ESTATE, CONVERSION OF INTO PERSONALTY.—If a building situate upon real estate is burned by an accidental fire, and such property was devised to one person for life with remainder to others. the proceeds of the insurance of such building do not become personal property, so as to pass as such under a residuary clause of the testator's will.

LIFE TENANT AND REMAINDERMAN—INSURANCE, ALLOWANCE FOR MONEYS PAID TO OBTAIN.—In a suit by remaindermen to have the proceeds of insurance effected by a life tenant declared to be held by her for life only, after which such proceeds shall belong to them, she is entitled to be credited with the amount paid by her to procure the policy under which the moneys were collected, but not for the amounts paid by her for prior policies on the same property under which no loss occurred.

Suits by certain persons as remaindermen and as heirs or representatives of deceased remaindermen against Lucy J. Green and others. From the complaint it appeared that certain real property situated in Columbia, South Carolina, had by its owner, Lucy P. Green, been devised to her daughter, Lucy J. Green, for life, and at her death was to go to testator's sons and the children of the daughter Lucy, if any she should have; that the life tenant effected insurance on a building, which being destroyed by fire, she collected the insurance and made sundry investments and reinvestments of its proceeds in other property; that she claimed these investments as her own property and intended to dispose of them as such; and the plaintiffs asked that it be adjudged that such investments and their proceeds were held by the defendant Lucy for life only, and that they be declared entitled thereto upon her death. The defendant, Lucy P. Green,

in her answer admitted the collecting of the insurance moneys
and their investment in other property, and alleged that the insurance was obtained by her with her own moneys, and that she
had effected and paid the insurance for several years prior to the
destruction of the property by fire, and she prayed that if she
should be adjudged not to be entitled to the money collected by
her, that she be credited with all amounts paid by her for Insurance. She also claimed that the proceeds of the insurance, if
not her property, must be deemed a part of the personal estate
of her deceased mother, and, as such, subject to a residuary
clause in the latter's will. Further answering, the defendant
Lucy alleged that certain of the plaintiffs had received sums from
the estate of the decedent, Lucy P. Green, largely in excess of
their shares, and she asked that an account be taken and a complete determination of the rights of all the parties made, and,
to that end, that certain other persons named in the answer be
made parties. Plaintiffs demurred to so much of the answer
as related to the claim that certain of the plaintiffs had received
more than their share of the estate of Lucy P. Green. An order
was entered sustaining this demurrer and refusing to bring in
the additional parties, as requested by the defendant. The defendants appealed on the following exceptions: "1· Because it appears from the pleadings that the foundation of the plaintiffs'
claim and that of the defendants to the relief sought by them is
one and the same, to wit, the will of Lucy P. Green, deceased,
and hence the defense or counterclaim is a proper one, under the
laws of this state, and the judge erred in not so holding. 2.
Because it appears from the complaint that the right of the
plaintiffs to maintain this action is derived by inheritance from
devisees under the will of Lucy P. Green, deceased; and it being admitted by the demurrer that the ancestors of the plaintiffs are indebted to the estate of Lucy P. Green, plaintiffs take
the assets descended, charged with the debt of their respective
ancestors, and must account for such debts before they can receive any portion of said estate, and the judge erred in not so
holding. And 3. Because one of said devisees, to wit, Allen J.
Green, being also one of the executors of the said Lucy P. Green,
the plaintiffs who inherit through him can take no assets of the
said estate until accounting is had of his executorship, and the
judge erred in not so holding. 4. Because the demurrer admitting that the contract of insurance only covered the interest of
the life tenant, the defendant, Lucy J. Green, as matter of law,
the remaindermen can have no interest in the insurance money,
and the judge erred in so holding. 5. Because, even if the con-

tract of insurance be held, as matter of public policy or law, to redound to the benefit of the remaindermen, the defendant, Lucy J. Green, must be reimbursed the insurance premiums and repairs made necessary by the casualties of war, the same having been paid out of her private funds, and the judge erred in not so holding. 6. Because the insurance money arising from the destruction of the dwelling-house by fire became personal property, and, if it passed at all under the will of Lucy P. Green, became a part of the residuary estate, and the answer alleging and the demurrer admitting an original failure of assets, the defense was proper either as a counterclaim or setoff, and the judge erred in not so holding. 7. That under section 292 of the code and the general principles of equity jurisprudence, all parties in interest being before the court (Halcott P. Green, one of the defendants, being admitted by the demurrer to be the administrator de bonis non of the estate of Lucy P. Green), the defendants have the right to have all matters arising under the will of Lucy P. Green, and germane to the settlement of her estate, adjusted in this action, even though the matter be subject for an independent cause of action, if for no other purpose to prevent circuity of action and multiplicity of suits, and the judge erred in not so holding. 8. Because his honor erred in referring all the issues of fact to the master, whereas it is submitted that the defendants not having consented to such order, it should have been referred only to take the testimony and report the same to the court." The defendants also served a demurrer to the complaint and moved to dismiss it on the ground that it did not state facts sufficient to constitute a cause of action for the following reasons: "1· It fails to allege facts sufficient to show any obligation on the part of the life tenant to keep the buildings insured, or that the insurance effected by life tenant was taken to protect the interest of the remaindermen; 2. It fails to allege that the amount received by the life tenant from the insurance company upon the burning of the dwelling exceeded the value of her interest therein; 3. That from the facts stated as matter of law, the money arising from the insurance is the sole property of the defendant, Lucy J. Green, and neither the plaintiffs nor their ancestors, who were remaindermen under the will of Lucy P. Green, deceased, have any interest therein; and, failing in this, 4. That if the remaindermen under the will of Lucy P. Green have any interest in the said money arising from the insurance, as matter of law, that interest is the right to receive, upon the death of the defendant, Lucy J. Green, the life tenant, only so much of the three thousand dollars insurance money as remains after deducting all premiums of insurance that have been paid, without any interest and without any profits or accretions that may have arisen from its use; and there being no allegation of insolvency, there is neither a resulting trust nor a case for equitable interference made by the complaint."

Greene & Greene and W. St. Julian Jervey, for the appellants.

Smythe, Lee & Prost and R. W. Shand, contra.

⁵²⁸ POPE, J. I will first consider the appellant's motion to dismiss the complaint on their demurrer against the complaint that it fails to set up facts sufficient to constitute a cause of action. It seems to me that the appellants are not entitled to any decision of their grounds upon which they base this demurrer, for the simple reason that there is no authority vested in this court to dispose of such a demurrer interposed for the first time in this court. The language of the constitution clothing this court with jurisdiction, except in certain cases falling within its original jurisdiction, is as follows, as set out in section 4 of article 5: "And said court shall have appellate jurisdiction only in cases of chancery, and in such appeal, they shall review the findings of fact as well as the law." Now ⁵²⁹ it appears to me that this language admits of but one construction, and that is that in cases of chancery the supreme court shall review the findings of fact as well as the law of the court below. It is no part of appellate, jurisdiction, under which a review of findings of fact as well as the law is made, to undertake to pass upon questions which were never passed upon by the circuit court. This case is one in chancery. While it is true the language of the code, as found in section 169, is broad, when it declares, "If no objection be taken either by demurrer or answer, the defendant shall be deemed to have waived the same, excepting only the objection to the jurisdiction of the court, and the objection that the complaint does not state facts sufficient to constitute a cause of action," still we think the meaning of the legislature must have been intended, in the light of the constitution, to be that in the circuit court alone there should be no waiver, either by not interposing a formal demurrer on this account or raising the same in the answer. But even if the legislature intended otherwise by this section 169 of the code, it was powerless to do so, for the constitution is the organic law, and all the departments of the government must uphold it. I so understand the previous decisions

of this court, as found in Miller v. George, 30 S. C. 526; Chafee
v. Postal Tel. Co., 35 S. C. 372. My conclusion is, that the four
grounds of appeal (the motion?) relating to the demurrer against
complaint must be dismissed.

I will next consider the grounds of appeal from Judge Buchanan's order. First, plaintiffs' demurrer to the second defense of
defendants, as set out in their answer. I cannot agree with the
appellants that the pleadings show that the foundation of the
plaintiffs' claim as well as those of the defendants is one and the
same, to wit, the will of Mrs. Lucy P. Green, deceased. It seems
to me that while the first clause of said will is that under which
both parties claim their rights as life tenant and remaindermen,
respectively, yet that no question is anywhere raised, by any
party to the action, that such rights as life tenant 630 and remaindermen, respectively, are created under said first clause of
Mrs. Green's will. The question presented by the plaintiffs is,
that after the entry upon the house and lot under this first clause
of Mrs. Lucy P. Green's will, the life tenant, after having procured an insurance of the dwelling-house thereon against loss by
fire, and after the same was accidentally destroyed by fire, and
the insurance money of three thousand dollars was paid to the
life tenant, she openly disavowed any trust relation by herself to
said money, but invested and reinvested the same as her own,
and has given a part of it away, and declared her purpose to treat
all of it as her own. I cannot see how what may be owing by
the remaindermen on account of excess of receipts over proper
shares, respectively, in the estate of Mrs. Lucy P. Green, can
have any relation to the relief sought against Miss Green. It is
not proposed to take from her control as life tenant one dollar
of all the life estate and its alleged investments by such life tenant. The issues are squarely made between the parties to the
action, on the one side by the plaintiffs and on the other side
by the defendants, as to the three thousand dollars insurance
money. It is in no wise pertinent to this question what may
be the condition of the accounts of the residuary legatees named
in Mrs. Lucy P. Green's will. The matter of such accounts does
not grow out of this devise under the first clause of Mrs. Green's
will. Such being my conclusion, I cannot sustain the first
ground of appeal.

A conclusive answer to the second ground of appeal is, that
the plaintiffs do not seek any judgment for their respective
shares of what they allege is an investment of a part of the life
estate arising from the three thousand dollars insurance money.

All that they ask is that such three thousand dollars and its investment in different property, some real and some personal property, may be impressed with the trust in favor of the remaindermen under the first clause of said will.

As to the third ground of appeal, which suggests that Allen J. Green, of Alabama, having been executor as well as one of the remaindermen, and having been paid in excess [531] of his share under the residuary clause of the will of Mrs. Lucy P. Green, that those of the plaintiffs who will take through him, as a devisee under the first clause, must first account for such excess before they are entitled to the relief prayed for, I must say I cannot see its force. Certainly a devisee in remainder is vested with title the moment the breath leaves the body of the testatrix, unless restrained by the terms of the will. No words of restraint appear here. Therefore, Allen J. Green, of Alabama, as one of the four sons of Mrs. Lucy P. Green, named in the first clause of her will, was vested at her death with title to this house and lot, with his right of possession and enjoyment postponed during the lifetime of his sister, Lucy J. Green. There is no question of vesting title to this property—I mean the house and lot. The question is confined to the three thousand dollars received by the life tenant as insurance on the dwelling-house destroyed by fire. It is quite true that if some of the assets of the residuary estate were about to be paid over to Allen J. Green's personal representative or heirs at law, the questions raised by the appellants would be proper, but such is not the case now before us. This exception is overruled.

As to the fourth ground of appeal. It is true that a demurrer admits, for the time being, the truth of the alleged facts in the answer, and that this answer does state that Miss Green did insure her life interest in the dwelling-house, and that having so insured only her life interest, she is entitled to the proceeds of such insurance, freed from any claims of any and all of the remaindermen, as her own property. It is also true that, as between insurance companies on the one side and of the insured on the other side, it has been repeatedly held in this state that fire insurance is intended to indemnify the person procuring the insurance, and also that anyone who has an insurable interest may effect an insurance against fire of that property in which he has such insurable interest, and that an "insurable interest" means that interest which, if the property be destroyed by fire, will cause a loss to the person insuring. [532] But still the question remains what, under the law, is the relation of a life tenant to the fund realized from the destruction of a dwelling-house in which she has only had a life estate, where the interests of the remaindermen in such property so destroyed by fire are concerned? Anyone who holds any character of trust toward the property insured, and who may effect a policy of insurance from loss by fire thereon, cannot claim such insurance money as his own. An executor of a will may effect insurance, and in the event of loss by fire, the proceeds of the policy belong to the estate confided to his care. So with an administrator of the estate of a deceased person who effects insurance on the property of his intestate's estate—the proceeds of such a policy would belong to the estate of his intestate. So with an agent who had an insurable interest and who effected a policy of insurance on property confided to his care—the proceeds of the policy belong to his principal. Such was the result in the case of Graham v. Fire Ins. Co., 48 S. C. 195; 59 Am. St. Rep. 707. Mr. Graham, as agent for one G. H. Tilton, who was the owner of property, had the property insured in his own name; the proceeds were paid to G. H. Tilton, though it is proper to state that in the policy, the loss, if any, was provided to be paid to G. H. Tilton, as his interest might appear.

It will be observed, too, that this was an action on the policy itself with the insurance company. Still, as between Tilton and J. M. Graham, Tilton would have been adjudged as entitled to the proceeds of the policy, even if the same had been paid to Graham by the insurance company, whenever it was made to appear that Tilton was the owner and Graham his agent. It is to be regretted that the decisions of the courts of the different states of this Union are not in accord as to the relation a life tenant bears to the real property which may be insured, so far as the remaindermen are concerned. All admit that if the will or deed which creates the life estate requires a policy of insurance to be effected by the life tenant, the proceeds of such insurance should be used in rebuilding the property destroyed by fire, or put at [533] interest, and that in the latter event all the interest earned is the property of the life tenant as long as such tenancy lasts, and after that the fund is paid over to the remaindermen. But in those instances where the will or deed creating the life estate is silent as to insurance, and the life tenant insures the property, the courts of some of the states decide that the proceeds of such a policy may be received by the life tenant as her own property in fee. Our own state along with others holds the doctrine that a life tenant holds the relation of an implied or quasi trustee to the remaindermen, and that any proceeds of a fire policy are subject to the laws regulating trusts: Clyburn v. Reynolds, 31

S. C. 118. This case evidently impressed appellants as an obstacle in their path.   Hence they first seek to differentiate their
case from Clyburn v. Reynolds, 31 S. C. 118, and, failing in that,
they ask this court to overrule that case as wrong in principle.
Looking to the differentiation of the one case from the other, it
is proper that I should briefly state what was decided in Clyburn
v. Reynolds, 31 S. C. 118.   It seems that James Chesnut, Jr.,
was both the life tenant in the tract of land known as Sandy Hill
plantation and also executor of the will under which he derived
his life estate in that plantation.   For several years he carried a
policy of insurance against fire on the dwelling-house situate on
said plantation.   Being in feeble health, he renewed the policy
in his name, as executor.   It was not certain whether he had
intended to have himself named as beneficiary of the policy in his
own name or in his name as executor.   The dwelling-house was
burned just before his death, and the proceeds of the policy were
paid, which proceeds were claimed by his personal representative
on the one hand and the remaindermen on the other.   This
court decided that it was unimportant whether he intended the
policy to be taken in his own name or as executor of his father's
will; and held that in case of the total destruction of the insured
property, the fund from the insurance policy thereon is substituted for the property, and the life tenant will be entitled to the
interest for life, and [534] the fund after life tenant's death be
payable to the remaindermen: Citing Haxall v. Shippen, 10
Leigh, 536; 34 Am. Dec. 745; Graham v. Roberts, 8 Ired. Eq.
99.   This court then proceeds to say: "In the case of Annely v.
De Saussure, 26 S. C. 505, 4 Am. St. Rep. 725, an insurance policy taken out by one tenant in common was held not to inure to
the benefit of the cotenant.   One tenant in common is not in
any sense a trustee for his cotenant, and has no insurable interest
in his share of the property.   A life tenant, on the other hand,
is a trustee for the remaindermen, and is certainly liable for loss
by fire caused by his negligence.   He ought not to be allowed to
put himself in a position in which he would have no motive for
proper care of the estate by having a policy of fire insurance by
which, in case of loss, he could substitute the full fee simple
value of the building in place of his interest for life.   We, therefore, think that a sound public policy requires that any money
collected by a life tenant on a total loss by fire should be used in
rebuilding or should go to the remaindermen, reserving the interest for life for the life tenant.   We quote as appropriate the
language from 4 Wait's Actions and Defenses, 22, in reference
to insurance beyond the value of the interest of the insured:

'And when the insurance is beyond the value of the interest at stake, the effect is the same; for, although the amount of the loss only can be properly recovered, there will be a hope of getting more.' It would be in the nature of 'gambling.' In accord with these views is the case of Parry v. Ashley, 3 Sim. 97, and our own case of Bath etc. Paper Co. v. Langley, 23 S. C. 129, in which the court uses these words: 'If . . . . the defendants stood in the relation of quasi trustees toward the plaintiffs, then the money received by them for the insurance on the house of the plaintiff belonged ex aequo et bona to the plaintiffs.' " The language used in this decision is plain and unmistakable. Evidently the judgment of the supreme court is bottomed upon the idea that the life tenant is an implied or quasi trustee for the remaindermen. Once you admit this trust relation between the life tenant and the remaindermen, [535] then the conclusion is inevitable that the life tenant cannot protect her own interest and disregard those of her quasi cestuis que trust. Strongly the court insists upon an opposite course being against a sound public policy. Once admit that a life tenant can claim as her own an insurance for the full value of the dwelling-house, in case the same shall be destroyed by fire, the rights of the remaindermen will be jeopardized. I have given days to the study of this case, and after that study I am forced to say that, notwithstanding the evident hardship to this very remarkable lady in the management of business requiring sagacity and patience as well as great faith in the future of her native city, I have been unable to see how the decision of Clyburn v. Reynolds, 31 S. C. 118, could be differentiated from the case at bar. Nor am I able to see why such a wise rule as is established by the decision in Clyburn v. Reynolds, 31 S. C. 118, should be overridden or modified. It is true some of the earlier cases do seem to limit the doctrine of quasi trustee in a life tenant for the remaindermen to perishable property, but as years advance the courts are gradually brought to the view that such a relation subsists between them in the case of life insurance, and I cannot say that reflection and a careful study of the authorities and arguments have changed my opinion that Clyburn v. Reynolds, 31 S. C. 118, embodies sound law.

As to the sixth ground of appeal, I cannot concur in the proposition of appellants, that when the dwelling-house devised for life to the appellant, Miss Lucy J. Green, was burned by accidental fire, the proceeds of insurance became personal property, so as to pass under the residuary clause of Mrs. Green's will, and should, therefore, be paid to her executors. The house and lot were devised. If the insurance money had been applied in rebuilding the dwelling-house, it would have remained real estate. Simply failing to do this does not change the ownership or the character of the estate. This exception is overruled.

[536] Nor, as to the seventh ground of appeal, can I agree with appellants, that as all parties interested in Mrs. Lucy P. Green's estate, which passed under her will, are now before the court, the character of the action be changed, as prayed for by appellants. I have already indicated my views on this point, and will not attempt to add to what I have already held.

As to the eighth ground of appeal, it seems to me that the circuit judge was correct in his order of reference to the master to take the testimony. Now that the pleadings have been construed as applicable to the case presented by the plaintiffs—which case is met squarely by the answers of the defendants—it will be necessary to take testimony on the issues raised by the pleadings. Circuit judges sitting as chancellors, when the pleadings are before them for construction, are fully competent under the law to order a reference to take the testimony. It is the better plan, it seems to me, to be pursued in cases like the present.

And now it remains for me to consider the fifth exception, which I intentionally postponed for consideration out of its numerical order. I am not willing to hold that Miss Green is not entitled to be reimbursed the money she paid for the policy of insurance upon the dwelling-house the year it was burned. It seems to me that she is not entitled to claim all the insurance fees she paid for ten years. Each policy, or the renewal thereof, is a separate and distinct contract. The only contract by and under which the three thousand dollars was paid her by the insurance companies was that of force during the year the fire occurred. In her second defense, she has put all the insurance premiums in an aggregate, and asks repayment thereof in case the three thousand dollars is held a trust in her hands. This was demurrable; but still I wished my views understood, for while I sustain the demurrer, yet it is with this in my mind. Amendments are readily obtained in the circuit courts, where good cause is shown therefor.

[537] It is the judgment of this court that the judgment of the circuit court be affirmed, that the demurrer attempted to be set up in this court be denied, and that the cause be remanded to the circuit court.

Jones, J., dissents.

LIFE TENANT AND REMAINDERMAN—INSURANCE.—A life tenant is not bound to keep the premises insured for the benefit of the remainderman. Each may insure his own interest, but, in the absence of any agreement, neither has any claim upon the proceeds of the other's policy. Therefore, a remainderman cannot compel a life tenant to place a sum received for insurance upon a building destroyed by fire, in trust so as to be turned over to the remainderman on the death of the life tenant, when the insurance was not effected for the benefit of the remainderman, though the moneys received therefrom may be equal to the whole value of the property destroyed: Harrison v. Pepper, 166 Mass. 288: 55 Am. St. Rep. 404, and note. As to the rights of reversioners and remaindermen generally, see monographic note to Allen v. De Groodt, 14 Am. St. Rep. 628-639.

WILLS — EQUITABLE CONVERSION —WHEN OCCURS. — Equitable conversion does not occur unless there is an imperative direction in the will that land shall be converted into money or money into land: Ducker v. Burnham, 146 Ill. 9; 37 Am. St. Rep. 135, and note. See monographic note to Ford v. Ford, 5 Am. St. Rep. 141-148.

APPEAL.—A question not raised at the trial will not be considered for the first time on appeal: Reich v. Cochran, 151 N. Y. 122; 56 Am. St. Rep. 607, and note.

CASES

IN THE

SUPREME COURT

OF

SOUTH DAKOTA.

JOHNSON *v.* BRAUCH.

[9 SOUTH DAKOTA, 116.]

HUSBAND AND WIFE—DEED FROM HIM TO HER—HOMESTEAD.—A conveyance from a husband to his wife of real property including their homestead is valid.

COTENANTS—TAX TITLE—PURCHASE BY ONE COTENANT.—One who is an administrator and also a joint owner and the father of the other cotenants of real property cannot by purchase at a tax sale or by a purchase made for his benefit, acquire any interest in the property. Such purchase inures to the benefit of the other owners as well as to himself.

CONSTITUTIONAL LAW. — A SPECIAL STATUTE AUTHORIZING AN ADMINISTRATOR TO SELL REAL PROPERTY, there being no necessity for such sale, and its only object being to convert the property into money for the purposes of distribution, is unconstitutional and void. Such a statute deprives the heirs of their property without due process of law.

ADMINISTRATOR'S DEED, WHEN CONVEYS A PERSONAL TITLE AND ALSO TITLE SUBSEQUENTLY ACQUIRED BY HIM.—If an administrator, purporting to act under a special statute authorizing him to sell and convey the property of his intestate, makes such a sale and executes a warranty deed, and he then has an interest in the property as an heir at law of the decedent, and subsequently acquires a further title therein by the death of another heir, his conveyance passes all the title which he held as heir at law and also all the title which he subsequently acquired.

French & Orvis and Gamble & Dillon, for the appellants.

E. C. Kennedy and N. J. Cramer, for the respondents.

116 FULLER, J. This action, to quiet the title to certain real property, was tried to the court without a jury, and from the

decree, based upon findings of fact and conclusions of law adverse to the claim of plaintiffs, and adjudging the defendants to
be indefeasible owners of a two-thirds interest in the property,
and from an order overruling a motion for a new trial, plaintiffs
appeal.   The title asserted by appellants Charles A. and Adelbert P. Johnson is evidenced by a warranty deed, dated February
26, 1890, executed and delivered to them by their coappellant,
Edward R. Houlton, who is the grantee named in a deed, with
the usual covenants of warranty, executed and delivered to him
on the eighth day of June, 1883, by Jacob Brauch, as administrator of the estate of Anna Brauch, deceased.   Briefly stated,
the essential facts are as follows: On the thirtieth day of May,
1874, while Jacob Brauch owned the real property in dispute,
and occupied the same with his family, consisting of Anna
Brauch, his wife, and their seven children, all of whom, so far as
they survive, are made parties defendant herein, he executed and
delivered to his wife Anna Brauch, a warranty deed of the premises, which was duly recorded in the office of register of deeds.
After the execution and delivery of the deed, Jacob Brauch filed
a declaration of homestead, covering the premises in dispute;
and the entire family continued, as formerly, to reside upon the
land until the month of August, 1877, when said Anna Brauch
died intestate, leaving her husband and children as sole surviving heirs at law, all of whom still continued to occupy and reside upon the premises until April, 1881, when a flood occurred,
and the buildings thereon were swept away, and the premises
rendered untenable.   On the thirty-first day of August, 1877,
Jacob Brauch, by regular appointment, [120] became the duly
qualified and acting administrator of the estate of Anna Brauch,
deceased, and so continued up to the time of his death, which
occurred on or about January 1, 1890.   Although the estate,
consisting of real and personal property, was perfectly solvent,
and all claims were promptly paid in full, in the due course of
administration, without the necessity of selling, or in any manner interfering with, any portion of the real property involved in
this suit, said Jacob Brauch, as administrator, acting under a
special legislative enactment—to be noticed later ou—sold and
conveyed the property on the eighth day of June, 1883, to the
appellant Edward R. Houlton, who is the grantor of his coplain-
tiffs and appellants, Charles A. and Adelbert P. Johnson, who,
in support of their title and claim of fee simple ownership, relied
upon their deed from Houlton, together with a certain tax deed
executed simultaneously by Henry B. Wynn to said Jacob

Brauch. Furthermore, it is confidently maintained that the deed from Jacob Brauch to Anna Brauch, purporting to convey the premises in dispute directly from the husband to the wife, is void in law, and not sustainable in equity. Certain subordinate facts, though carefully considered, will not be specifically stated; and others will be noticed in their proper relations, and with reference to rules of law by which the action of the trial court must be measured in order to correctly determine the rights of the parties.

The deed under which respondents, as surviving heirs, claim title, imports a valuable consideration, and was presumptively executed and delivered in good faith by Jacob Brauch to Anna Brauch, his wife, at a time when there were apparently no creditors to complain, and while a portion of the premises was being occupied as the homestead of the family. As statutes inhibiting the alienation or encumbrance of the homestead without the concurrent assent of the husband and wife, evidenced by an instrument in writing, executed by both, and duly acknowledged, emanate from a regardful consideration of reciprocal duties, and are designed only to protect the home [121] and family against the vicissitudes of fortune and the ravages of time and events, the spirit of such laws is not contravened by a conveyance direct from the husband to the wife, and it is useless for both husband and wife to join as grantors in such a deed: Comp. Laws, sec. 2590; Waples on Homesteads, sec. 9, p. 395; Furrow v. Athey, 21 Neb. 671; 59 Am. Rep. 867; Harsh v. Griffin, 72 Iowa, 608; Albright v. Albright, 70 Wis. 528; Dull v. Merrill, 69 Mich. 49; Wilder v. Brooks, 10 Minn. 50; 88 Am. Dec. 49. Subject merely to the temporary right of possession for the sole purposes of administration, under the statute the land in question, at the death of Mrs. Brauch, descended directly to her husband and children, who thereupon became tenants in common, and fee simple owners thereof, subservient only to the homestead right, so far as the same extended.

As disclosed by competent evidence, and found by the court, the tax deed executed to Henry B. Wynn on the twenty-first day of November, 1878, upon which appellants measurably rely, was obtained for, at the instance and request of, and solely with the money advanced by Jacob Brauch, for his own personal use and benefit, while a cotenant, and the duly appointed, qualified, and acting administrator of the estate of Anna Brauch, deceased. An administrator, joint owner, and father of dependent and helpless children is without power to thus appropriate to his own use and benefit their interest in property derived from a common source, and the tax title inured to the benefit of all: Weaver v. Wible, 25 Pa. St. 270; 64 Am. Dec. 696; 1 Washburn on Real Property, 689; Tiedeman on Real Property, 252; Brown v. Hogle, 30 Ill. 119; Bender v. Stewart, 75 Ind. 88; Lloyd v. Lynch, 28 Pa. St. 419; 70 Am. Dec. 137; Flinn v. McKinley, 44 Iowa, 68; Barker v. Jones, 62 N. H. 497; 13 Am. St. Rep. 586; Donnor v. Quartermas, 90 Ala. 164; 24 Am. St. Rep. 778; Carpenter v. Carpenter, 131 N. Y. 101; 27 Am. St. Rep. 569; Watkins v. Zwietusch, 47 Wis. 513.

When the deed to Edward R. Houlton, under which the Johnsons claimed title, was executed and delivered, and when [122] the special statute was passed, purporting to authorize Jacob Brauch, as the administrator of Anna Brauch, deceased, to "sell and convey, either at public or private sale," the property in dispute, there were no debts or claims of any kind against the estate, nor is there anything to indicate that the heirs and indefeasible owners of the property would derive any benefit from the transaction. Apparently, the only object sought to be attained was to enable an administrator to convert property owned jointly by himself and children, but two of whom were under disability, into money for the sole purpose of distribution. Special statutes authorizing a guardian to sell the estate of a decedent for the maintenance and education of minor heirs, or the payment of debts, subject to which they obtained title at the death of an ancestor, and with which the property is still burdened, have been sustained for the reason that the rights of creditors are paramount, and upon the theory that the legislature should, when necessary, protect the weak, and promote the welfare of persons incapacitated by some legal disability from disposing of their own estate. No necessity appears to have existed for a sale of the premises, and obviously the legislative act invades the functions of the judiciary. In contravention of the federal constitution, and the organic law then in force in this jurisdiction, tenants in common and the owners of private property were, without their consent, and in the absence of notice or an opportunity to be heard, divested of their estate without due process of law, and the act relied upon to justify the transaction is therefore unconstitutional and void: Brenham v. Story, 39 Cal. 179; Wilkinson v. Leland, 2 Pet. 627; Powers v. Bergen, 6 N. Y. 358; Lane v. Dorman, 3 Scam. 238; 36 Am. Dec. 543; Sohier v. Massachusetts General Hospital, 3 Cush. 483; 3 Washburn on Real Property, 227. The language of Mr. Justice Story in Wilkinson v. Leland, 2 Pet. 627,

is: "We know of no case in which a legislative act to transfer the
property of A to B without his consent has ever been held a constitutional exercise of legislative power in any state of the
Union."

[123] There being, under the circumstances of this case, no
merit in appellant's claim that relief should be denied respondents on account of their delay in asserting title, we will pass to a
consideration of the only remaining point requiring attention.
As an undivided one-third interest of the estate of Anna Brauch,
deceased, descended to, and by inheritance under the statute became the property of, her husband, Jacob Brauch, from whom
appellants' title was derived, the court decreed appellants Charles
A. and Adelbert P. Johnson, under their deed from Houlton, to
be the joint owners of said undivided one-third interest, and confirmed in respondents the remaining undivided two-thirds interest in and to the land in controversy. It is admitted in the pleadings, and upon the record, for the purposes of the trial, conceded,
that Adolph Brauch, one of the sons and heirs at law of Anna
Brauch, deceased, died intestate and without issue on or about
the twenty-ninth day of November, 1889, leaving his surviving
wife, the respondent Mary M. Brauch, and that Jacob Brauch,
the father of said Adolph, died on or about January 1, 1890. It
is provided in subdivision 2 of section 3401 of the Compiled
Laws that, "if the decedent leave no issue, the estate goes in
equal shares to the surviving husband or wife and to the decedent's father." Said Adolph Brauch having, without issue, died
scised of an undivided one-seventh of a two-thirds interest in his
mother's estate, one-half of said interest descended immediately
to his father Jacob Brauch; and counsel for appellants contend
that after said after-acquired title inured to the benefit of his
grantee, Edward R. Houlton, and passed to and became the joint
property of, appellants Charles A. and Adelbert P. Johnson, by
virtue of their warranty deed from said Houlton, the grantee of
Jacob Brauch. It is a well-settled principle of law that a title
subsequently acquired by one who has conveyed land by warranty
deed passes, by operation of law, immediately to his grantee;
and neither the character of Jacob Brauch's tenure, nor the capacity in which he attempted to convey the interest of his cotenants, is [124] sufficient to arrest the operation of the rule: Tiedeman on Real Property, enlarged ed., 253, and cases there collected. Under the foregoing rule, the deed from Jacob Brauch
to Edward R. Houlton—no equities intervening—in effect conveyed an undivided one-third interest in the premises in dispute,

together with an undivided one-half of one-seventh of the remaining two-thirds interest, inherited equally by the seven surviving children of Anna Brauch, deceased, and of which Adolph Brauch, at the death of his mother, became the absolute owner of an undivided one-seventh interest, which at his death descended in equal shares to his surviving wife and father: 4 Kent's Commentaries, 98; 1 Jones on Real Property, 990; Pillsbury v. Alexander, 40 Neb. 242; Flaniken v. Neal, 67 Tex. 629; Knight v. Thayer, 125 Mass. 25; Prewitt v. Ashford, 90 Ala. 294; Nicodemus v. Young, 90 Iowa, 424. While counsel for respondents do not seriously question the accuracy of the rule here applied, they insist that the death of Jacob Brauch occurred prior to that of his son, Adolph, and that the judgment and decree awarding to the Johnsons, as grantees of Houlton, an undivided one-third interest in the property which Jacob Brauch attempted to convey by warranty deed, cannot, for that reason, be disturbed. In the absence of any evidence, a finding of fact, or a reasonable inference to the contrary, the admission that the son died on or about the twenty-ninth day of November, 1889, and the father, on or about January 1, 1890, has been, for the purposes of this appeal, accepted as a verity.

Governed by the views herein expressed, the case is remanded to the court below with the direction that its decree be re-entered in conformity herewith; and, as thus modified the judgment appealed from is affirmed. Each party to pay one-half of the costs taxable in this court.

Haney, J., taking no part in the decision.

HOMESTEAD—CONVEYANCE BY HUSBAND TO WIFE.—A voluntary deed from a husband to his wife is not invalid because it conveys a homestead, a conveyance of which is required to be executed by both husband and wife: Furrow v. Athey, 21 Neb. 671; 59 Am. Rep. 867. See Turner v. Bernheimer, 95 Ala. 241; 36 Am. St. Rep. 207, and note. A statute requiring the husband to join in conveyances or encumbrances of the wife's separate estate applies only to conveyances by the wife to a third person other than her husband: Osborne v. Cooper, 113 Ala. 405; 59 Am. St. Rep. 117.

COTENANCY—PURCHASE BY ONE COTENANT AT TAX SALE. A cotenant in possession cannot acquire title against his cotenant by purchasing a tax title to the common property: Thompson v. McCorkle, 136 Ind. 484; 43 Am. St. Rep. 334, and note; Stevens v. Reynolds, 143 Ind. 467; 52 Am. St. Rep. 422, and note. See, contra, Bennett v. North Colorado Springs etc. Co., 23 Colo. 470; 58 Am. St. Rep. 281.

DEEDS — CONVEYANCE OF AFTER-ACQUIRED TITLE.— When a person conveys lands in which he has no interest at the time, but afterward acquires a title thereto, he will not be permitted to claim in opposition to his deed, from the grantee or any person claim-

Ing under him: Brown v. McCormick, 6 Watts, 60; 31 Am. Dec. 450;
extended note to Trull v. Eastman, 37 Am. Dec. 129, 130. Such after-
acquired title inures to the benefit of the first grantee: Morrison v.
Caldwell, 5 T. B. Mon. 426; 17 Am. Dec. 84.

MILLIRON v. MILLIRON.

[9 SOUTH DAKOTA, 181.]

HUSBAND AND WIFE—ALIMONY AND ATTORNEYS'
FEES.—In an action by a wife for separate maintenance, the court
may make an order requiring the husband to pay her a sum of money
with which to retain counsel and also to pay her a specified sum
monthly for the support of herself and children pending the suit,
though the husband has by answer denied all the allegations of the
complaint, and the statutes of the state contain no express grant of
authority to make such order, except in a suit for divorce.

S. H. Wright, for the appellant.

James Brown, for the respondent.

182 FULLER, J. Upon the application of plaintiff, supported by certain affidavits and her verified complaint in this action for separate maintenance, the court below made an order
requiring the defendant to pay plaintiff one hundred dollars,
with which to retain counsel, and twenty-five dollars per month
for the support of herself and her children pending the suit, and
from said order the defendant appeals to this court.

The marriage is admitted, and it appears from the complaint
and affidavits used upon the hearing of the motion for temporary
alimony and counsel fees that the defendant is a dentist by profession, and obtains for his services money amply sufficient to enable him to provide for his family and contribute to his wife,
who is entirely without means, the required maintenance, and
the amount found by the court to be necessary in order to enable
her to prosecute her cause, which, if proved as alleged, would
fully justify a decree granting the relief for which she prays.
Counsel for appellant maintains that in an action for separate
maintenance, when an answer places in issue the facts alleged in
the complaint, the court is without power to make the order complained of, or grant any relief, until the cause has been tried and
the facts determined by a jury; and to sustain such contention
he confidently relies upon section 6 of the bill of rights, in which
it is declared that "the right to trial by jury shall remain invio-
late and shall extend to all cases at law without regard to the
amount in controversy." In support of his position he also cites

section 5032 of the Compiled Laws, and further insists that in this state a court of equity has no jurisdiction to compel a husband to provide for the support [183] of his wife pending an action for separate maintenance. The statute expressly provides that while an action for divorce is pending the court may compel the husband to pay alimony for the support of his wife and children, or to enable her to prosecute or defend the action; and, although the divorce be denied, the court has power to require the husband to provide for the maintenance of the wife and her children or any of them: Comp. Laws, secs. 2581, 2582. That the court had jurisdiction of the party is apparent from an inspection of the record, and the facts stated in the complaint disclose subject matter clearly within equitable cognizance, and sufficient, if true, to justify a decree consistent with plaintiff's prayer for relief. While the statute makes no express provision for temporary alimony, except as an incident to an action in which the marriage relation is sought to be annulled or dissolved, a court of equity is not precluded from requiring the husband to pay suit money, and, in a proper case, support his wife during the pendency of an action to determine her right to permanent and separate maintenance. Independently of statute, the subject is inherently within the general jurisdiction of a court of equity, and our attention has been called to no act of the legislature designed to limit such courts to cases which include in the relief sought a prayer for an absolute divorce. The true rule is, that although the statute makes no provision for temporary alimony, as an incident to an action for separate maintenance, where no decree for a divorce is prayed for, a court of equity is not precluded, in a proper case, from compelling the husband to maintain his wife and provide suit money with which to enable her to prosecute or defend the action: Daniels v. Daniels, 9 Colo. 133; Verner v. Verner, 62 Miss. 260; Galland v. Galland, 38 Cal. 265; Simpson v. Simpson, 91 Iowa, 235; Miller v. Mill, 33 Fla. 453; Johnson v. Johnson, 125 Ill. 510; Harding v. Harding, 144 Ill. 588; Vreeland v. Vreeland, 18 N. J. Eq. 43; 2 Nelson on Divorce and Separation, 973, and cases there collected. In the case of Glover v. [184] Glover, 16 Ala. 440, the court says: "The broad ground upon which the jurisdiction is made to rest is the unquestioned duty of the husband to support the wife, and the inadequacy of legal remedies to enforce this duty." Plaintiff, if her complaint and affidavits used on the hearing of the motion are true, is without means with which to maintain herself and prosecute an action

rendered necessary by her husband's misconduct and wanton refusal to support her, and there is no valid reason why he should
not pay the amount awarded by the trial court. We have considered the facts disclosed by the record, upon which the order
complained of is based, sufficiently to justify the conclusion that
respondent is prosecuting her action in good faith, and that, in
view of all the circumstances, the trial court, in directing appellant to pay the amount specified, acted within its sound judicial
discretion; and the order appealed from is therefore affirmed.

Haney, J., taking no part in this action.

MARRIAGE AND DIVORCE—ALIMONY—ALLOWANCE OF
COUNSEL FEES.—Alimony and counsel fees cannot be decreed except in a case specified in the statutes: Kelley v. Kelley, 161 Mass.
111; 42 Am. St. Rep. 389. Temporary alimony and expense money
will not be allowed until the plaintiff makes out a reasonably plain
case as to the existence of the marriage: Bardin v. Bardin, 4 S. Dak.
305; 46 Am. St. Rep. 791. Compare Richardson v. Richardson, 4
Port. 467; 30 Am. Dec. 538.

LOWER *v.* WILSON.

[9 SOUTH DAKOTA, 252.]

JURISDICTION—SUMMONS, SERVICE OF ON A CLERK
OR AGENT.—Authority on the part of a clerk of an attorney at law
to accept service of papers in a case wherein the attorney had been
employed professionally does not authorize the clerk to accept service of summons in an action in which the attorney is a party defendant.

JURISDICTION, WAIVER OF WANT OF SERVICE OF
SUMMONS.—If the defendant moves to set aside the service of
summons and complaint upon a ground entitling him to the granting
of the motion, but it is, nevertheless, denied, he, by subsequently
answering the complaint and interposing a counterclaim and demanding affirmative judgment thereon in his favor, submits himself
to the jurisdiction of the court, and cannot thereafter avail himself
of its error in denying his motion to vacate the service of the summons. The result must have been different, if the defendant had
merely answered the complaint without seeking to assert an affirmative cause of action in his own favor.

H. E. Dewey, for the appellant.

Joseph B. Moore, for the respondent.

253 FULLER, J. The only service of the summons and complaint in this action upon the defendant James P. Wilson, a practicing attorney, was obtained on the first day of August, 1895, at
his office, and in his absence, by delivering to and leaving with

his clerk, Joseph W. Musgrave, copies thereof. After moving to vacate and set aside the summons and complaint upon the jurisdictional ground that the same had not been properly served, the defendants answered the complaint, and, for a cause of action against plaintiff, interposed a counterclaim, upon which an affirmative judgment for two hundred and thirty-five dollars was demanded. A trial to a jury resulted in a verdict and judgment against the defendants in plaintiff's favor, and the defendant Wilson, who alone appeals, assigns as error, and for a reversal relies solely upon, the ruling of the court upon the motion to vacate and set aside the service of the summons and complaint.

The indubitable purpose of a summons and statutory method of service is to personally apprise the defendant that an action has been commenced, and the nature thereof, so that, within a specified time, he may act advisedly with reference [254] thereto, and, as the statutory requirements were not observed, no legal service was had and the court acquired no jurisdiction. Mere authority upon the part of Mr. Musgrave to accept for appellant Wilson service of papers in cases where the former had been retained professionally, was wholly insufficient to authorize and render authentic the verbal acceptance of the service of the summons in an action in which said Wilson is sought to be made a party defendant: Comp. Laws, sec. 4898; Bulkley v. Bulkley, 6 Abb. Pr. 307; Knox v. Miller, 18 Wis. 397; Read v. French, 28 N. Y. 285; Litchfield v. Burwell, 5 How. Pr. 341. However, the failure to pursue any statutory mode of service was waived by appellant, who, by his counterclaim, subjected himself to, and invoked the jurisdiction of, the court by demanding an affirmative judgment, as well as by introducing evidence in support of the issues raised by his counterclaim and respondent's reply thereto. A different conclusion would enable a litigant, while insisting that he is not in court, to demand affirmative relief, which can only be granted upon the theory that the court has jurisdiction of the cause and of the parties thereto. It would be obviously unjust to permit a party who has interposed an objection to the jurisdiction of the court over his person to avail himself of the chance to obtain a favorable affirmative judgment against the plaintiff by voluntarily pleading a counterclaim, and by obtaining a trial upon its merits, and, at the same time, preserving his right to reverse any judgment which might be rendered against him. In order to be in a position to insist, in this court, upon his jurisdictional question, appellant should have kept out of the circuit court for all purposes other than to make the objection that the summons was not served upon him, and to resist the cause of action stated in plaintiff's complaint. While this court has held in Benedict v. Johnson, 4 S. Dak. 387, that one who has appeared specially for the sole purpose of objecting to the jurisdiction of the court over his person, may preserve an exception to an adverse ruling and answer the [255] complaint without waiving said objection, there is upon principle a clear distinction between that case and the one now under consideration. For the purpose of preventing the entry of a credit impairing, if not a cloud creating, judgment, because presumptively valid, he appears, and resists the cause of action stated in the complaint without asking for any affirmative relief. His answer, under such circumstances, is regarded compulsory to an extent that allows him to protect his immediate interests, and, at the same time, preserve his right to insist upon a jurisdictional objection that was good when made: Harkness v. Hyde, 98 U. S. 476. But when he voluntarily recognizes and invokes the jurisdiction of the court by stating an independent cause of action existing in his favor and against the plaintiff, and demands an affirmative judgment thereon, he brings himself clearly within the following wholesome rule of law: "Where a defendant becomes an actor in the suit, and institutes a proceeding which has for its basis the existence of an action to which he must be a party, he thereby submits himself to the jurisdiction of the court, and no disclaimer which he may make on the record that he does not intend to do so will be effectual to defeat the consequences of his act": 2 Ency. of Pl. & Pr. 626. Our conclusion, therefore, is that the objection to the jurisdiction of the court, good when made, was waived by appellant when he filed his counterclaim and went to trial upon the merits.

The judgment appealed from is affirmed.

JURISDICTION—WAIVER OF OBJECTION TO.—Waiver of objection to the validity or service of process does not result from going to trial on the merits after an objection has been properly made and overruled by the court: Jones v. Jones, 108 N. Y. 415; 2 Am. St. Rep. 447. General appearance, however, waives all questions as to service of process and is equivalent to a personal service, and any acknowledgment of a court's jurisdiction, when the party has entered his appearance voluntarily, waives his right to object to such jurisdiction: Note to Union Pac. Ry. Co. v. De Busk, 13 Am. St. Rep. 233. See monographic note to Alley v. Caspari, 6 Am. St. Rep. 180. But when want of jurisdiction over the subject matter appears from the record, the defect cannot be supplied by the submission: Perkins v. Perkins, 7 Conn. 558; 18 Am. Dec. 120.

PROCESS—PERSONAL SERVICE.—Personal service cannot be dispensed with except in cases distinctly provided for by statute: Frost v. Atwood, 73 Mich. 67; 16 Am. St. Rep. 560, and note. See Hobby v. Bunch, 83 Ga. 1; 20 Am. St. Rep. 301.

PLYMOUTH COUNTY BANK *v.* GILMAN.

[9 SOUTH DAKOTA, 278.]

ATTORNEYS AT LAW—PROOF OF PROFESSIONAL
STANDING OF.—Evidence of an attorney's negligence subsequent
to the receipt of business transmitted to him for his professional attention is no evidence that before that time he was not a lawyer
of reputed learning and ability.

COLLATERAL SECURITY, LIABILITY OF BANK FOR
NEGLIGENCE OF ATTORNEY EMPLOYED TO COLLECT.—If a
promissory note secured by a mortgage is transferred to a bank as
collateral security, which must be sent to a distant place for collection, it fulfills its implied requirement of reasonable diligence by
placing such note for collection in the hands of an attorney having
the reputation of being competent and reliable, and it is not answerable for the subsequent neglect of the attorney in the performance
of the duties intrusted to him.

DAMAGES, EVIDENCE IN MITIGATION OF.—In an action
to recover of the holder of collateral security damages resulting from
his alleged tardy foreclosure of a mortgage, evidence is properly admitted in mitigation of damages showing that the mortgaged
premises were conveyed to the plaintiff before foreclosure proceedings could have been completed by the exercise of ordinary care
and vigilance.

C. S. Palmer, for the appellant.

A. B. Kittredge, for the respondent.

²⁸⁰ FULLER, J. The defendant, for a complete defense
and counterclaim to this action, upon his overdue promissory
note for four hundred and twelve dollars, executed and delivered
to plaintiff on the eighteenth day of January, 1875, alleged in
his answer, and introduced evidence for the purpose of proving,
damages sustained largely in excess of plaintiff's claim, on account of the negligence of plaintiff in failing and neglecting to
enforce the collection of certain secured notes owned by the defendant, and indorsed over to, and left with, plaintiff for collection and collateral security. This appeal is by the defendant
from a judgment entered upon a verdict in favor of plaintiff for
the full amount remaining unpaid upon the principal note, according to its terms, and from an order overruling a motion for
a new trial.

The question not being raised in the additional abstract, respondent's motion to strike out appellant's bill of exceptions and
all the evidence contained in his abstract, because the particular
errors relied upon are not specified in said bill of exceptions, cannot be considered, for the reasons stated in Peart v. Chicago etc.
Ry Co., 8 S. Dak. 634, on appeal from the taxation of costs.
Concerning these collateral notes, aggregating eleven hundred

and fifty dollars, left with respondent when the note in suit
was executed, appellant testified, in effect, that it was agreed
between himself and respondent's cashier that in consideration
of a collection fee agreed upon, the bank would proceed at once
to collect said collateral notes, one of which was at the time past
due, and apply the proceeds, so far as necessary, to the satisfaction
of the four hundred and twelve dollar note, and pay the balance
over to appellant.   Respondent's cashier, with whom the business was transacted, testified that the notes in question were
merely transferred to the bank to secure the payment of appellant's four hundred and twelve dollar note, and that nothing [281]
was said about their collection, and no agreement was ever
made concerning a collection fee.   Under the court's charge, the
jury, by its general verdict, found, upon this conflicting testimony, that the secured notes in question were deposited merely
as collateral security, without any express agreement as to their
collection; and in this respect the case is materially different
from that disclosed by the record of the same case on a former
appeal to the territorial court, where it was clearly shown, by the
undisputed evidence, that an express contract was entered into
between the parties to the action, by which the bank agreed to
collect the notes for ten per cent, and turn the proceeds over to
defendant, Gilman, after deducting said collection fee and the
amount due upon the four hundred and twelve dollar note, including interest, according to its terms.   Furthermore, we find
from an examination of the abstract used on that appeal that
there was testimony introduced tending to establish the utmost
good faith and prudence on the part of the bank's officers in the
selection of suitable and competent attorneys to enforce the collection, which, of necessity must be intrusted by plaintiff, a nonresident corporation, to some one residing in this state where the
mortgaged premises were situated.   The case, as then made, involved the question of the liability of one who has, for a valuable
consideration, undertaken by an express contract to collect collateral notes, and turn the proceeds over to the owner, after deducting the amount secured thereby, together with a stipulated
fee for collection; and, although the notes were placed in the
hands of reputable attorneys for collection, the court held that
in view of the existence of an express agreement to collect, and
evidence tending to show a loss of the security by the negligence
of attorneys, it was error to direct a verdict in favor of plaintiff:
Bank v. Gillman, 6 Dak. 304.   From the evidence introduced by
appellant, and the admissions of respondent in its reply, it ap-

pears that a proceeding to foreclose the mortgage by which the collateral notes were at the time amply secured was instituted at the instance [282] of respondent, in the month of August, 1875; and that, owing to the carelessness or inability of the attorney to whom the business was intrusted, it became necessary to obtain an order vacating and setting aside, as invalid, the decree of foreclosure obtained in that action; and that no sale of the property, under a valid foreclosure, was had until the seventeenth day of October, 1881, when the property was sold on execution for but twenty-one dollars in excess of the legitimate costs and expenses of foreclosure.

In the present case, appellant introduced no evidence tending to support the allegations of negligence contained in his answer, and solely relied upon as a defense to the action, unless the attorney's failure to conduct a foreclosure suit in an orderly manner may be attributed to some act or omission on the part of respondent. Proof of an attorney's negligence occurring subsequently to the receipt of business transmitted to him for professional attention is no evidence that he was not formerly a lawyer of reputed learning and ability; and in this case there is no evidence to support an inference that respondent, a nonresident, without actual knowledge, was in any manner negligent or unjustified in placing confidence in the attorney selected, who was presumed to be reputable, in the absence of anything to the contrary. As the record stood, it was not error to instruct the jury that "the bank would fulfill its requirement of reasonable diligence if it placed these notes fairly, honorably and judiciously in the hands of reputable attorneys to collect, and they would not be responsible for any neglect of those attorneys, but responsible merely for their right and proper conduct and judicious management in the selection of those attorneys." Although the decisions are conflicting, we believe the true rule to be that where notes collectible through the agency of attorneys only, and by the foreclosure of a mortgage upon property at a distant point, are deposited in a bank as collateral security, with no instructions or express arrangement as to their collection, transmission, or proceedings to enforce [283] payment, the implied duty of the bank is discharged if such notes are duly forwarded to an attorney at law having the reputation of being competent and reliable, with the direction that a foreclosure suit be instituted, and the property be subjected to the payment of the amount due, according to the terms of said notes and mortgage, given to secure the same: Bank of Louisville **v.** First Nat. Bank, 8 Baxt. 101;

35 Am. Rep. 691; Guelick v. National State Bank, 56 Iowa, 434;
41 Am. Rep. 110; Fabens v. Merchants' Bank, 23 Pick. 330; 34
Am. Dec. 59; Aetna Ins. Co. v. Alton City Bank, 25 Ill. 243; 79
Am. Dec. 328; East-Haddam Bank v. Scovil, 12 Conn. 303.

Relying upon these collateral notes as security, the bank loaned
its money to appellant, who was charged with a knowledge that,
in case of default either on his part or on the part of the makers
of such notes, a foreclosure of the mortgage given to secure such
collaterals would require services which must be rendered by a
nonresident attorney at law personally unknown to the bank,
and in no manner connected with that institution; and to hold
it liable for more than a reasonable exercise of care and prudence
in the selection of attorneys of good repute would, without an
adequate consideration, subject respondent to all the liability of
a collection agency which advertises and undertakes, as a matter
of express contract, to collect in distant places, through its own
agents and attorneys there located, but as truly its representatives as the officials in charge of the home office.   The amount
due upon a promissory note dated Natchez, Mississippi, and
transmitted by the payee from Illinois to a bank at that point for
collection was lost by reason of the failure of a notary public, in
whose hands the same was placed by the bank for presentment,
demand, and notice to indorsers; and it was held in a suit against
the bank (Britton v. Niccolls, 104 U. S. 757) that the latter was
not liable for the manner in which the notary public performed
his duties.   That the court looks with disfavor upon decisions
that have enunciated a contrary doctrine is very evident from the
language employed by Mr. Justice Field, who, [284] in delivering
the opinion of the court, ably reviews numerous adjudications,
and concerning the notary, observes that "he was a public officer,
whose duties were prescribed by law; and, when the notes were
placed in his hands, in order that such steps should be taken by
him as would bind the indorsers if the notes were not paid, he
became the agent of the holder of the notes.   For any failure on
his part to perform his whole duty he alone was liable.   The
bankers were no more liable than they would have been for the
unskillfulness of a lawyer of reputed ability and learning, to
whom they might have handed the notes for collection, in the
conduct of a suit brought upon them."   To the effect that a bank
receiving a note as collateral security or for collection, which
must be transmitted to a distant place, has performed its entire
duty when a reputable agent or attorney has been selected for the
purpose of making or enforcing collection, see Fabens v. Mer-

chants' Bank, 23 Pick. 330; 34 Am. Dec. 59; Bank of Lindsborg
v. Ober, 31 Kan. 599; Stacy v. Dane Co. Bank, 12 Wis. 629;
Daly v. Butchers' etc. Bank, 56 Mo. 94; 17 Am. Rep. 663; Dar-
ling v. Stanwood, 14 Allen, 504; Bank v. Triplett, 1 Pet. 25
(Marshall, C. J., delivering the opinion of the court).   A careful
review of all the cases by Mr. Morse in his treatise on the Law of
Banks and Banking is concluded in part as follows: "Now, in
the case of collection, the usage to forward to a subagent is well
established, and the parties must be presumed to contract in reference to it.   The customer expects, or ought to expect, that the
bank will pursue the ordinary course of business in such matters.
This usual course is well known to be simply the transmission to
another agent in good repute, and this is all the bank or the customer can be supposed to contemplate as that duty of which the
accurate performance is guaranteed by the corporation.   Ordinarily, when there is any commission paid for collection, it is a
very small one. . . . . Such considerations may well be regarded
as sufficient for the mere task of transmission; but it is impossible that they should be sufficient to sustain an agreement to be
further responsible for the solvency and good [285] conduct and
thorough performance of their duties on behalf of all subsequent
banks and notaries, or other agents whom it may be necessary to
employ.   Such an insurance would call for a high premium.   It
is incredible to suppose that the bank, for a very small possible
remuneration, much more for a wholly contingent return in any
shape, assumes so great a risk": 1 Morse on Banks and Banking,
275.

That appellant was injured by the negligence of respondent,
occasioned by a tardy foreclosure of the mortgage given to secure
the collateral notes, was the theory of the defense; and, in mitigation of damages, respondent was very properly permitted to introduce in evidence certain deeds, by which the mortgaged premises were, together with other real property contiguous thereto,
conveyed to appellant, before a foreclosure of the mortgage could
have been completed by the exercise of ordinary care and vigilance upon the part of the attorney to whom the business was intrusted.   The court did not err in denying appellant's application to open and close the argument to the jury: Comp. Laws,
sec. 5047.

While every assignment of error has received regardful attention, the view we have taken renders unnecessary a consideration
of other questions discussed in the briefs of counsel.   The judgment appealed from is affirmed.

BANKS—LIABILITY FOR NEGLIGENCE OF COLLECTING AGENTS.—Considering the state courts alone, the weight of authority supports the principal case in holding that the liability of a bank to which a check or note payable at a distant place for collection has been consigned for collection extends merely to the exercise of due care in selecting a competent agent and the transmission of the paper to the latter with proper instructions, but the English courts and the supreme court of the United States, supported by a respectable number of state courts, adhere to the contrary rule, which is probably the best and most authoritative, that the bank is farther liable for any default or negligence of its collecting agent rendering collection of such paper impossible: Monographic note to Isham v. Post, 38 Am. St. Rep. 777. See Baille v. Augusta Sav. Bank, 95 Ga. 277; 51 Am. St. Rep. 74, and note. Contra, Waterloo Milling Co. v. Kuenster, 158 Ill. 259; 49 Am. St. Rep. 156. The holding in the principal case is opposed to the rule applied to attorneys, mercantile agencies, and the like: Monographic note to Allen v. Merchants' Bank, 34 Am. Dec. 315. See, however, Commercial Bank v. Martin, 1 La. Ann. 344; 45 Am. Dec. 87.

Safe Deposit and Trust Company *v.* Wickhem.

[9 South Dakota, 341.]

TAX TITLE ACQUIRED BY JUNIOR MORTGAGEE, RIGHT TO ASSERT AGAINST SENIOR MORTGAGEE.—If premises subject to a first and a second mortgage are permitted to become delinquent for taxes and to be sold and conveyed to a third person without any collusion with the junior mortgagee, he may afterward purchase the tax title and assert it against the senior mortgagee. Nor is it material that the junior mortgagee was a county treasurer, and as such, in his official capacity, made the tax sale in question.

MORTGAGEES, FIRST AND SECOND, DUTY RESPECTING THE PAYMENT OF TAXES.—A second mortgagee does not owe any duty to the first mortgagee to pay the taxes. If the title of both is extinguished by a tax sale, their prior relations cease, and the junior mortgagee may then purchase and assert the tax title, unless he is in possession under the foreclosure of his mortgage or has, in some manner, obligated himself to pay the taxes.

Aikens, Bailey & Voorhees, for the appellant.

J. L. Hannett, for respondent Wickham.

[342] FULLER, J. Plaintiff, the assignee of a senior mortgage upon the real property described in the complaint, brought this [343] action in foreclosure against the defendants named, and now prosecutes this appeal from a decree canceling said mortgage, and quieting title to the premises in the defendant Wickhem, who alone answered and defended in the action. The material facts are practically undisputed, and, in substance, as follows: On the eighth day of January, 1887, the defendant Crandall executed appellant's mortgage, to secure a loan of seven hundred

and fifty dollars, evidenced by a promissory note of even date, due in five years; and on the second day of March, 1889, they mortgaged the same property to respondent Wickhem to secure the payment of two hundred and forty-seven dollars, due in two years from that date. The Wickhem mortgage recited that it was taken subject to the mortgage in suit, and each of said instruments contained the usual stipulation on the part of the mortgagors to pay the taxes legally assessed against the property, in default of which the same might be paid by the mortgagees, and thereupon become a part of the mortgage indebtedness. During the life of these mortgages the property was legally sold for delinquent taxes, and regularly purchased at tax sale by the defendants Dillon & Preston, who upon the ninth day of October, 1889, received from respondent Wickhem, as county treasurer, a tax deed in the usual form; and upon the following day they duly conveyed said premises, by quitclaim deed, to respondent Wickhem, who relies wholly upon said instrument to defeat the lien of appellant's mortgage.

No question is raised as to the legality of any of the proceedings leading up to, and culminating in, a tax deed; and as the duty of the owner and the right of these mortgagees to pay the taxes had not been performed or exercised, and the time within which the premises could have been redeemed having expired, Dillon & Preston had a vested right to a treasurer's deed, the execution of which by respondent Wickhem, in his official capacity, might have been enforced by mandamus: 2 Blackwell on Tax Titles, 734. While the relation of respondent Wickhem to the property and to appellant should be considered with the fact that he was the officer who executed a tax [344] deed to Dillon & Preston, from whom he obtained title to the premises upon the following day, such circumstances are, in the absence of any collusion, insufficient to invalidate his deed, or justify the conclusion that the sale and transfer by Dillon & Preston to said Wickhem should be characterized as the mere payment of taxes inuring to the benefit of appellant, and wholly insufficient to divest the lien of his mortgage. Obviously, a junior mortgagee cannot, by purchase at a tax sale, acquire a title which shall defeat the lien of a senior encumbrancer: but appellant and respondent had ceased to be encumbrancers, as to one another, and had become strangers, by neglecting to pay the taxes, and by permitting an absolute and fee simple title to ripen and become fixed in Dillon & Preston before they sold and conveyed the premises, for a valuable consideration, to respondent. At the trial of the cause the defendant Wickhem was called as a witness, and testified explicitly that he had no arrangement or understanding with Dillon & Preston with reference to the tax certificate or purchase of the land until after the tax deed had issued and was delivered; and, upon all the evidence, the court so found the facts to be. Upon conclusions of law accordingly entered, appellant's complaint was dismissed as to respondent, and his mortgage was adjudged not to be a lien upon the premises in dispute. True, the conveyance from Dillon & Preston to Wickhem, being so nearly simultaneous with the execution and delivery of the tax deed, the transaction merits critical examination, and, in the absence of evidence to the contrary, might be sufficient in itself to justify an inference that an arrangement to purchase the land had been made between Wickhem, the junior mortgagee, and Dillon & Preston, prior to the execution and delivery of the tax deed, and in that event Wickhem would acquire no title which would defeat the lien of appellants' senior mortgage. A reversal of this case would be equivalent to a holding that the sale of land for delinquent taxes by a county treasurer, who is individually a junior mortgagee whose lien has been lost, and [345] the execution of a tax deed thereto, in his official capacity, to the holder of the certificate, after his title has fully matured and become absolutely vested, is, in the absence of any collusion, sufficient in law to incapacitate such treasurer and junior mortgagee from ever acquiring, as against a senior mortgagee, title thereto by deed from a stranger. In our opinion, the law and facts fully justify the judgment appealed from, and the same is therefore affirmed.

Haney, J., taking no part in the decision.

ON REHEARING.

[515] CORSON, P. J. This case comes before us upon a petition for a rehearing. The opinion is reported in Safe Deposit Co. v. Wickham, 9 S. Dak. 341, ante, p. 873, and the facts are fully stated in the opinion. The appellant, in its petition for a rehearing, so confidently insists that the court in its decision departed from the settled adjudications upon the questions discussed that we have re-examined the authorities with great care, and arrived at the conclusion that our decision is not only not against the weight of authority, but is fully sustained by it. The relation sustained by mortgagees to each other and the mortgagor, in regard to the payment of taxes on the mortgaged property, is thus stated by Mr. Justice Cooley in Connecticut Mut. etc. Ins. Co. v. Bulte, 45 Mich. 113. "It certainly cannot be said that

the second mortgagee owes any duty to the first mortgagee to protect his lien as against tax sales. Neither, on the other hand, does
the first mortgagee owe any such duty to the second mortgagee
or to the owner.   To the state each one of the three may be said
to owe the duty to pay the taxes, and the state will sell the interest of all, if none of the three shall pay.   As between themselves,
the primary duty is upon the mortgagor; but, if he makes default,
either of the mortgagees may pay, and one of the two must do so,
or the [516] land will be sold and his lien extinguished." It
would seem to logically follow that when the junior mortgagee's
lien is extinguished by the sale and conveyance of the mortgaged
property for a valid tax, the relation of the junior mortgagee to
a prior mortgagee and to the mortgagor ceases, and he may deal
with a tax title to the property as a stranger, unless he is in possession of the property under a foreclosure of his mortgage or
has in some manner obligated himself to pay the taxes.   The
law, as laid down upon this subject by Mr. Justice Dixon in his
concurring opinion in Smith v..Lewis, 20 Wis. 350, seems to be
fully sustained by the authorities.   That learned judge says: "It
will be found, on examination of the adjudged cases, that the
turning point in all of them was the obligation of the party setting up the tax title to pay the taxes.   If he was under such obligation, either from having been in possession and liable to pay
the taxes at the time of assessment, or from their having been
properly assessed against him, or by reason of any covenant or
promise to the party against whom he claimed the title, the deed
in such cases has been held unavailing.   It is void because it was
obtained in violation of the duty of the person claiming title under it. . . . . Lewis was under no obligation to pay the taxes.
He was not bound to keep them down, either for his own protection or that of the mortgagor, or of the first mortgagee: Williams
v. Townsend, 31 N. Y. 415; and consequently he might, under
a properly executed deed, have acquired a title valid both as
against the mortgagor and first mortgagee, unless there was something in the nature of his purchase at the foreclosure sale which
forbade it."   In that case, the junior mortgagee, being in possession, claiming the equity of redemption, the judge concludes he
could not set up his tax title as against the mortgagor.   In Wat-
erson v. Devoe, 18 Kan. 223, the supreme court of Kansas, in a
well-considered opinion by Mr. Justice Horton, in which Mr.
Justice Brewer concurred, takes the broad ground that a mortgagee, not being in possession of the mortgaged property, nor under
any special [517] obligation to pay the taxes, has the right to buy

the mortgaged property at tax sale, and assert such title as against
a prior mortgagee or the mortgagor; and cites and quotes from
Williams v. Townsend, 31 N. Y. 415; Smith v. Lewis, 20 Wis. 369,
*350; Chapman v. Mull, 7 Ired. Eq. 292; Walthall v. Rives, 34
Ala. 91; Harrison v. Roberts, 6 Fla. 711. That court bases its decision upon the fact that by the law of Kansas (which is the same
in this state) the mortgagee does not take the legal title, but only
acquires a lien upon the property, and hence is under no legal
obligation to pay the taxes. And that court calls attention to
the fact that, in states in which the legal title passes to the mortgagee, the duty is imposed upon such mortgagee, by virtue of his
legal ownership of the property, to pay the taxes. But we are
not inclined to go to the full extent of the Kansas case, and adhere to our former decision that had Wickhem, directly or indirectly, purchased the property at the tax sale, or purchased or contracted for the tax certificate, before his mortgaged lien was extinguished, he would have held his tax title subject to plaintiff's
equity. The evidence, however, was undisputed that Wickhem
did not, directly nor indirectly, purchase the property at the tax
sale, or make any contract in reference thereto, until the tax title
had vested in Dillon & Preston, and the mortgage liens were extinguished. The petitioner seems to rely very greatly upon the
cases of Horton v. Ingersoll, 13 Mich. 409, and Connecticut Mut.
etc. Ins. Co. v. Bulte, 45 Mich. 113, but in the view we take of
them, they do not support the petitioner's position. In the former case, the defendant had foreclosed his junior mortgage, and
bid in the property, and at the time he took the tax title he still
held the equity of redemption. In the latter case, the defendant
had not only foreclosed its junior mortgage, but was in possession
of the mortgaged premises when the tax title became vested in it.
Both cases come clearly within the rule laid down in Smith v.
Lewis, 20 Wis. 369, *350.

Rehearing denied.

Haney, J., took no part in the decision.

TAX SALES—WHO MAY PURCHASE AT—MORTGAGEES.—To
preclude a person from acquiring a tax title, he must be under some
legal or moral obligation to pay the tax, or there must be something
in his contract or fiduciary relation to the owner which renders it
inequitable, as between them, that he should acquire the title: Laton
v. Balcom, 64 N. H. 92; 10 Am. St. Rep. 381, and note. A purchase
by one whose duty it was to pay the taxes operates as payment only;
he can derive no benefit as against a third party by the neglect of the
duty he owed to such party: Monographic note to Blake v. Howe, 15
Am. Dec. 684, as to who may purchase at a tax sale. It is a general
rule that a mortgagee cannot purchase and assert a tax title against

his mortgagor to defeat the latter's equity of redemption: Eck v. Swennumson, 73 Iowa, 423; 5 Am. St. Rep. 690; Howze v. Dew, 90 Ala. 178; 24 Am. St. Rep. 783. And it has been held that a tax title cannot be acquired by a junior mortgagee to defeat a senior mortgage: Frank v. Arnold, 73 Iowa, 370.

SKINNER *v.* HOLT

[9 SOUTH DAKOTA, 427.]

APPEAL.—An undertaking on appeal, not in the statutory form, but good as a common-law bond, gives the appellate court jurisdiction, including the power to allow a new undertaking to be filed upon seasonable application by one who appears to have acted in good faith.

EXECUTIONS—EXEMPTIONS, LAW GRANTING UNLIMITED, WHEN UNREASONABLE AND VOID.—Under a state constitution declaring that the right of the debtor to enjoy the comforts and necessaries of life shall be recognized by wholesome laws exempting from forced sale a reasonable amount of personal property, the kind and value of which shall be fixed by general laws, a statute exempting from execution policies of insurance on the life of the debtor, irrespective of their amount, is void, because the exemption, being unlimited, is unreasonable.

INSURANCE, LIFE, EXEMPTION OF PROCEEDS OF.—A statute undertaking to exempt from execution the proceeds of life insurance policies irrespective of their amount is void, if the state constitution requires the exemption to be reasonable in amount and its value to be fixed by general laws.

JUDGMENTS — RETROSPECTIVE LAWS ATTEMPTING TO AVOID THE EFFECT OF.—If, after a judgment or decree has been entered declaring the proceeds of certain life insurance policies to be assets of the estate of a decedent and directing that they be applied to the satisfaction of his liabilities, a statute is enacted providing that the proceeds of such policies, whether heretofore or hereafter issued, shall be exempt from the claims of creditors, such statute cannot affect such judgment or decree.

CONSTITUTIONAL LAW, IMPAIRMENT OF THE OBLIGATION OF A CONTRACT, WHAT IS.—Any law of a state which so affects a pre-existing remedy as to substantially impair or lessen the value of a contract is forbidden by the national constitution, and is void as against contracts entered into before its passage.

EXEMPTION LAWS, CONSTITUTIONALITY OF.—A statute undertaking to exempt from execution the proceeds of life insurance policies is unconstitutional in so far as it applies to contracts existing prior to its enactment, because its application to such contracts would impair their obligation.

Wellington Brown, J. D. Elliott, and Warren Dimock, for the appellants.

Charles L. Brockway, for the respondent.

429 FULLER, J.   On the eleventh day of August, 1894, plaintiff, the surviving wife of John J. Skinner, deceased, appealed from an order of the county court, made and entered on the fourth day of that month, subjecting, in the due course of administration, the proceeds of a two thousand dollar life insurance policy to the payment of decedent's debts; and this appeal is from a judgment of the circuit court entered on the sixteenth day of July, 1895, reversing said order of distribution, and directing the administrator to pay over to plaintiff, for the separate use of herself and two minor children, the avails of said insurance policy, to the exclusion of defendants and appellants, who are general creditors of the estate.

The facts, so far as essential, may be stated briefly as follows: In the month of August, 1893, John J. Skinner died, intestate, leaving surviving him his wife, the respondent, Bertha R. Skinner, and their two minor children, as the sole heirs at law of his estate, which consisted wholly of the two thousand dollar policy of insurance upon his life, made payable to the insured, his executors, administrators, or assigns. After the demise of said John J. Skinner, the duly appointed and acting administrator of the estate collected from the insurer, and received into his possession as such administrator, and for the benefit of the estate, the two thousand dollar life insurance, and thereafter and in due form applied to and obtained from the county court, over respondent's objection, the order of distribution complained of and appealed from to the circuit court, and by which the avails of the said policy were subjected to the payment of certain claims existing in favor of defendants and appellants against said John 430 J. Skinner in his lifetime. When the cause was reached for trial, at the October, 1894, term of the circuit court, counsel, appearing for all the defendants, moved the court to dismiss the appeal, upon the ground that the undertaking on appeal did not run to the state, nor specify the place of residence of either of the persons executing the same as sureties thereto. During the pendency of this motion, opposing counsel applied for and obtained an order by which he was permitted to file a sufficient undertaking, and the motion to dismiss the appeal was overruled. The rulings of the court upon the motion to dismiss the appeal, and upon the application to substitute a sufficient undertaking are assigned as error, and present the first question for our consideration and review.

The conditions of the original undertaking, which was duly approved by the county judge, conform to and are expressed substantially in the language of section 5967 of the Compiled Laws, which specifies the requisite conditions of an undertaking on ap-

peal from the county court. Omitting formal recitals, and that
part of the undertaking which, in ordinary phraseology, describes
in clear and concise language the proceedings in and judgment
of the county court, by the rendition and entry of which plaintiff feels aggrieved and from which she appeals to the circuit
court, the conditions of said undertaking are as follows: "Now,
therefore, we, Bertha R. Skinner, as principal, and E. A. Sherman and R. G. Parmley, as sureties, do hereby undertake and
bind ourselves that the said Bertha R. Skinner will prosecute her
appeal with due diligence, and will abide, fulfill, and perform
whatever judgment, decree, or order may be rendered against her
by the circuit court, and that she will pay all damages which the
opposite parties may sustain by reason of such appeal, together
with all the costs that may be adjudged against her; and we
further undertake and bind ourselves that, if the judgment, decree, or order appealed from, or any part thereof, be affirmed, or
the appeal be dismissed, the appellant shall pay the sum directed
to be paid and distributed by the administrator [431] of the said
estate to the creditors of the same. Conditioned, however, that
our liability hereunder shall not exceed the sum of one thousand
dollars." In the affidavit attached to (and by section 5232 of the
Compiled Laws, made a part of) the foregoing instrument, each
surety for himself swears "that he is a resident of Minnehaha
county and state of South Dakota, and that he is worth the sum
of one thousand dollars over and above all his debts and liabilities, and exclusive of all property exempt from levy and sale on
execution." Though subject, perhaps, to the objections interposed, because defective and voidable as a statutory undertaking,
the instrument under consideration contains all the essential elements of a binding obligation at common law, and is amply sufficient to give the court jurisdiction to allow the new undertaking
to be filed upon the seasonable application of one who appears to
have taken her appeal in the utmost good faith: Towle v. Bradley,
2 S. Dak. 472; Woodman v. Calkins, 12 Mont. 456; Saterlee v. Stevens, 11 Ohio, 420; Pray v. Wasdell, 146 Mass. 324; Mix v. People, 86 Ill. 329; Field v. Schricher, 14 Iowa, 119. Section 5235
of the Compiled Laws is remedial in its character, and was designed to authorize an appellate tribunal having jurisdiction of
the subject matter to permit a new undertaking to be filed, in
order to stay proceedings, and make an appeal, which has been
taken in good faith, effectual, unless the defects or omissions are
such as render the original undertaking void, and vest no jurisdiction in the court to allow an amendment, or the performance

of an essential act omitted through mistake, accident, or inadvertence. A question measurably different is presented when there is no undertaking on appeal, or the defects therein or omissions therefrom render such instrument void, because, in that event, an appellate court acquires no jurisdiction to grant or refuse an amendment, or permit any act to be done, and the appeal, being ineffectual for every purpose, must be dismissed: Hazeltine v. Browne, 9 S. Dak. 351.

The policy of insurance was made payable to the executors, administrators, or assigns of John J. Skinner, the insured. [432] The estate was insolvent. The amount due appellants and allowed by the administrator aggregated about sixteen hundred dollars, and, after the payment of certain preferred claims, there remained of the two thousand dollars life insurance an amount sufficient to pay but sixty-three cents on each dollar of such indebtedness. The trial court concluded, as a matter of law, that the avails of said policy inured to the separate use and benefit of respondent and her two children, and were in no manner subject to the debts of the decedent. Section 21 of chapter 51 of the Laws of 1890, being entitled "An act to regulate and control life or accident insurance companies," is as follows: "A policy of insurance on the life of an individual, in the absence of an agreement or assignment to the contrary, shall inure to the separate use of the husband or wife and children of said individual, independently of his or her creditors; and an endowment policy, payable to the assured on attaining a certain age, shall be exempt from liabilities from any of his or her debts." Endowment life insurance partakes of the nature of an investment, and, like other insurance, is often obtained by and made payable to the assured, his executors, administrators, or assigns, for the sole purpose of creating a fund subject to the payment of his debts, and upon which his creditors may securely rely in case other resources fail. The clear intent of the legislature, as expressed in the foregoing enactment, was to defeat such purpose, and create a statute exempting from the payment of debts, without any limitation whatever, the total amount of life insurance which can be in any manner obtained on the life of the assured. A law which exempts to the debtor or his family all the money obtainable from the policies of all the life insurance companies in existence furnishes no basis for computation or measure of value, and is manifestly unreasonable, and clearly repugnant to the following provisions of the constitution of this state: "The right of the debtor to enjoy the comforts and necessaries of life shall be recognized by wholesome laws, exempting from forced sale a homestead, the value of which shall be limited and defined [433] by law, to all heads of families, and a reasonable amount of personal property, the kind and value of which to be fixed by general laws." A law which, without any limitation as to value, specifies a kind of property that a debtor, solvent or insolvent, may acquire, by investing therein or diverting thereto his entire estate, to the exclusion of bona fide creditors, is neither "wholesome" in character nor "reasonable" as to amount, and is by far too generous to be just: In re How, 59 Minn. 415. The view we have taken renders it unnecessary to determine whether the provisions under consideration contravene section 21, article 3, of the constitution, which provides that "no law shall embrace more than one subject, which shall be expressed in its title."

Subsequently to the decree of the county court, adjudging said insurance money to be lawful assets of the estate, and directing the administrator to apply the same to the payment of decedent's debts, the following statutory provision was enacted: "The avails of any policy or policies of insurance heretofore or hereafter issued upon the life of any person, and payable upon the death of such person to the order, assigns, estate, executors, or administrators of the insured, and not assigned to any other person, shall, if the insured in such policy at the time of death reside or resided in this state and leave or left surviving a widow or husband or any minor child, to an amount not exceeding in the aggregate the sum of five thousand dollars, inure to the separate use of such widow or husband or minor child or children or both, as the case may be, independently of the creditors of such deceased, and to such amount shall not in any action or proceeding legal or equitable be subject to the payment of any debt of such decedent." Unquestionably, the judgment of the county court, subjecting, in the order of distribution, the proceeds of the insurance policy, payable to the administrator, to the partial liquidation of the amount due appellants, was, when rendered, fully sustained by the law of this state, and should have been, on appeal, affirmed by the judgment [434] of the circuit court, made and entered on the sixteenth day of July, 1895, and from which this appeal was taken, unless the intervening enactment operates to invalidate said judgment and deprive appellants of every vested right therein established. Says Mr. Black: "It is generally held that the lien of a judgment is not discharged by an appeal being taken, but merely suspended": 1 Black on Judgments, 473. To hold that the judgment was good when entered, and so continued till the passage and approval of the law of 1895, when it became voidable, would deprive unreversed judgments of the element of conclusiveness, intrench upon the constitutional principle which separates the powers and functions of the three great departments of government, and in effect amount to a reversal of a judgment by the legislative power of a state. Moreover, section 10, article 1, of the federal constitution provides that "no state shall pass any law . . . . impairing the obligation of a contract," and section 12, article 6, of our constitution contains, in substance and effect, the same provision.

Respondent's husband died intestate, and the policy under consideration, which vested in him at the time of its delivery a tangible property right, fully matured at the time of his death, and became a part of his estate, subject to the payment of his debts in the due course of administration and was sufficient to pay sixty-three cents on each dollar due appellants according to the terms of their respective contracts. To give the statute under consideration any force retroactively not only impairs appellant's remedy, but effectually extinguishes their right by rendering their contracts totally worthless. In Planters' Bank v. Sharp, 6 How. 301, the United States supreme court said, touching the matter here under consideration: "One of the tests that a contract has been impaired is that its value has, by legislation, been diminished. It is not by the constitution to be impaired at all." Later the same court, speaking through Mr. Justice Swaine, say: "The remedy subsisting in a state when and where a contract is made and is to be performed is a part of its [435] obligation, and any subsequent law of the state which so affects that remedy as substantially to impair and lessen the value of the contract is forbidden by the constitution, and is, therefore, void": Edwards v. Kearzey, 96 U. S. 595. Appellants, as creditors of the estate, had in due form presented their claims to the administrator, who had allowed the same, and, by pursuing other remedies existing at the time, they had acquired vested property rights before the passage and approval of a statute by which such rights are divested and given to another without their consent, and without any compensation therefor. Upon the theory that such enactments are fundamentally unreasonable and contrary to the immutable principles of justice, courts have uniformly held that the legislative power is constitutionally incapable of making a valid law that will operate to impair existing contracts or defeat vested rights: Gunn v. Barry, 15 Wall. 610; Eidemiller v. Tacoma, 14 Wash. 376. In Guarantee etc. Trust Co. v. Fay, 14 Wash. 536, it was held by the

supreme court of Washington that an "act providing that the
proceeds of life insurance policies shall be exempt from all liability for any debt would be unconstitutional, as impairing the
obligation of contracts, if applied to antecedent policies and antecedent debts." Although a statute should be construed to operate prospectively only, unless its terms show clearly a legislative
intent that it should have a retroactive effect, it seems impossible to place that construction upon section 1 of chapter 89 of the
laws of 1895; and we find ourselves unable to avoid the inevitable deduction that it was the clearly expressed purpose of the
framers thereof to exempt from the payment of existing debts the
avails of all life insurance policies "heretofore or hereafter issued"
in all cases where the insured "at the time of death reside or resided in this state and leave or left surviving a widow or husband
or any minor child." Consequently, the conclusion follows that
said section, in so far as the same relates to antecedent contracts,
is inoperative, because in conflict with the constitution, **436** and
that the decision of the trial court based thereon is not sustainable. The judgment appealed from is therefore reversed, and the
case remanded for further proceedings not inconsistent herewith.

STATUTES IMPAIRING OBLIGATION OF CONTRACTS—EX-
EMPTION LAWS.—The law existing when a contract is made enters
into and forms a part of it; and this is applicable as well to the remedy as to the right, so that an impairment or taking away of the
remedy is an impairment of the obligation of the contract: Extended
note to Beverly v. Barnitz, 49 Am. St. Rep. 277, 278. The legislature
may change the formalities of legal procedure, but it cannot make
changes so as to impair the enforcement of rights: Brown v. Buck,
75 Mich. 274; 13 Am. St. Rep. 438. After a sale has been made under
execution, the rights of the judgment debtor are fixed as by contract:
Thresher v. Atchison, 117 Cal. 73; 59 Am. St. Rep. 159, and note.
The doctrine is now settled that laws creating exemptions where
none existed, or increasing the amount already exempted, whether
found in state constitutions or statutes, are unconstitutional in so far
as they apply to contracts entered into prior to the passage of the
statute or adoption of the constitution, because in contravention of
the constitution of the United States by impairing the obligation
of contracts: Monographic note to Rockwell v. Hubbell, 45 Am.
Dec. 252. Contra, Morse v. Gould, 11 N. Y. 281; 62 Am. Dec. 103,
and note.

SONNENBERG *v.* STEINBACH.

[9 SOUTH DAKOTA, 518.]

JUDGMENT AGAINST PARTY IN ONE CAPACITY DOES NOT AFFECT HIM IN ANOTHER.—A judgment against one as an individual, precluding him from claiming property, does not estop him from claiming it as a trustee for others.

EXECUTION, MOTION, RELIEF BY OF PERSON UNLAW-FULLY OUSTED UNDER A WRIT.—If, under a judgment against the defendants as individuals, they are wrongfully dispossessed of property which they hold as trustees for others, they may obtain re-lief by motion in the original action.

John Holman and R. B. Tripp, for the appellant.

French & Orvis, for the respondents.

[518] HANEY, J. Plaintiff appeals from an order of the cir-cuit court directing the sheriff to restore the possession of certain real property alleged to have been wrongfully taken from a church organization under and by virtue of an execution issued in this action upon a judgment adjudging plaintiff to be the owner, and excluding defendants and all others claiming through or under them from asserting any right thereto. The order was made upon the records of this action and an affidavit made by three of the defendants, wherein they affirm that the property is owned by a certain church organization; that they are, and were at all times mentioned in the pleadings, trustees of such organ-ization; that the other defendant is, and during said times has been, secretary and treasurer thereof; that such organization has for many years used the property for the purpose of holding re-ligious meetings in the church building situated thereon; that during all the times mentioned in the pleadings, [519] such organ-ization, through the defendants, as its officers, had possession, custody, and control of the property, but these defendants have not, during any of said times, and do not now claim, any right, title, or interest therein as individuals, and have not had posses-sion of the same as individuals; that the sheriff wrongfully took the property from the possession of the church, and delivered the same to the plaintiff. Plaintiff read an affidavit tending to show that the alleged church organization was never so incorporated or organized as to be capable of suing and being sued, or of hold-ing real property. In the main action, defendants answered dis-claiming any interest whatever in the property. They were sued only as individuals, and so answered.

It is unnecessary to decide whether the court was justified in finding or assuming that the church society was duly organized,

because it is uncontradicted that defendants held the property in
trust either for a duly incorporated religious society, or the members of and contributors to a religious society not so organized or
incorporated; and the substantial question arises in either case
whether, when a person is sued in his individual capacity, and
by the adjudication is precluded from claiming property as an individual, he is estopped from claiming it in the capacity of a
trustee of others, for whom he held the same when the suit
against him was commenced. Every person may at different
times, or at the same time, occupy different relations, act in different capacities and represent separate and perhaps antagonistic
interests. It is a rule of both the civil and the common law that
a party acting in one right can neither be benefited nor injured
by a judgment for or against him when acting in some other
right. Judgments are presumptively only conclusive against
parties in the character in which they are sued: Freeman on
Judgments, sec. 156; Erwin v. Garner, 108 Ind. 488; McBurnie
v. Seaton, 111 Ind. 56; Stockton etc. Association v. Chalmers, 75
Cal. 332; 7 Am. St. Rep. 173. Having been sued as individuals,
their individual right to the [520] property was alone involved,
and defendants were not required to voluntarily appear and answer in the capacity of trustees. We think defendants, as trustees, were wrongfully excluded from the property, and as such
are not estopped by the judgment against them from asking to
have it restored. This they could do by motion in the original
action: Freeman on Executions, sec. 476; Mayo v. Sprout, 45
Cal. 99; Smith v. Pretty, 22 Wis. 655; Howard v. Kennedy, 4 Ala.
592; 39 Am. Dec. 307.

The order of the circuit court is affirmed.

JUDGMENT AGAINST PARTY IN ONE CAPACITY DOES NOT
BIND HIM IN ANOTHER.—A judgment against one sued as an
individual does not bind him as a trustee or executor: First Nat.
Bank v. Shuler, 153 N. Y. 163; 60 Am. St. Rep. 601. To constitute
a decision in one cause an estoppel in another, the case adjudicated
must have been between the same parties in the same right or capacity: Nickum v. Burckhardt, 30 Or. 464; 60 Am. St. Rep. 822, and
note.

EXECUTION ISSUED AGAINST JUDGMENT DEBTOR IN AN-
OTHER CAPACITY.—Trust property is not subject to execution
under a judgment recovered against a trustee on his individual note:
Bostick v. Keizer, 4 J. J. Marsh, 597; 20 Am. Dec. 237. See Hazard
v. Israel, 1 Binney, 240; 2 Am. Dec. 438.

TROTTER v. MUTUAL RESERVE FUND LIFE ASSN.

[9 SOUTH DAKOTA, 596.]

EQUITY, PROBATE JURISDICTION OF COURTS OF.—
Courts of equity have concurrent jurisdiction with courts of probate
of all matters of guardianship and the settlement of estates of deceased persons, and will exercise such jurisdiction when the powers
of the probate courts are inadequate for the purposes of perfect
justice.

ESTATES OF DECEDENTS—HEIRS OF, WHEN MAY
MAINTAIN ACTIONS THOUGH THERE IS AN ADMINISTRA-
TOR.—When an administrator refuses to bring an action upon a
claim due the estate, the heirs, creditors, or any others interested in
its collection should have an adequate remedy, and hence may be
permitted to maintain such an action directly in their own names.

PLEADING—SURPLUSAGE, ALLEGATIONS WHICH MAY
BE TREATED AS.—If, in an action to recover upon a demand, the
complaint sets forth a release claimed to be inoperative for sufficient
reasons therein disclosed, the averment respecting such release may
be treated as surplusage, and certainly cannot preclude a recovery,
if they could not have had that effect if pleaded in an answer.

Aikens, Bailey & Voorhees, for the appellants.

R. B. Tripp, for the respondents.

[597] HANEY, J.   It is alleged in the complaint: "1. That the
defendant, the Mutual Reserve Fund Life Association at the
times herein stated was, and now is, a corporation duly created
and existing under and by virtue of the laws of the state of New
York; 2. That on or about the third day of October, 1893, at
Yankton, South Dakota, said defendant association, in [598] consideration of an application for insurance, payment of forty dollars, and the further payment of fifteen dollars within sixty days
from said date, received one Daniel L. Hadley, as one of its members, upon consideration of the payment of eleven dollars and
sixty cents, as a deposit in advance on account of mortuary premiums and dues, within thirty days from the first week day of
the months of February, April, June, August, October, and
December thereafter, and the payment of subsequent mortuary
premiums and dues, and made its policy of insurance whereby it
agrees that there should be payable to the executors or administrators of said member the sum of five thousand dollars within
ninety days after the acceptance of satisfactory evidence of said
member's death; 3. That on or about the fourth day of December, 1893, at Yankton, South Dakota, said member died; 4. That
on the thirteenth day of January, 1894, the county court of Yankton county, South Dakota, duly appointed the defendant Frank
E. J. Warrick as sole administrator of the estate of said member,
Daniel L. Hadley, deceased; that said Warrick thereafter duly
qualified, and is now administrator of said estate; 5. That on or

about the —— day of February, 1894, the said defendant association received and accepted satisfactory evidence of the death
of said member from said administrator, and said defendant association, prior to said date, also waived the acceptance of satisfactory evidence of the death of said member by denying liability
upon said policy of insurance, and other acts; that said administrator duly performed all of the conditions of said policy of insurance upon his part; 6. That the name of said member, Daniel
L. Hadley, deceased, was Daniel L. Trotter, and at the time of
his application for said insurance, the issuance of said policy, and
prior and subsequent thereto, he was more commonly known and
called by the name Hadley than Trotter; 7. That the said member died intestate, and these plaintiffs are his only next of kin and
heirs at law, to wit, mother, brothers, and sisters; that said member was never married, and had no wife or children; 8. That
⁶⁹⁹ these plaintiffs requested said administrator to bring this action; that he refused to do so and is therefore made a defendant,
and the suit is prosecuted by these plaintiffs; 9. That on or about
the tenth day of August, 1893, in consideration of three hundred
and twenty-five dollars and twenty-five cents, said administrator,
as such, by written indorsement upon said policy of insurance, undertook to, and in form did, release and discharge said defendant
association from all liability upon said policy of insurance; 10.
That said release was executed by said administrator without the
direction, authorization, or approval of said county court or judge
thereof, that the said administrator executed the same without
any authority whatever, and without the knowledge, consent, or
ratification of these plaintiffs, or any of them, and the same was
procured by the misrepresentation and fraud of said association
and misconduct of said administrator; that none of these plaintiffs have ever received any part of the consideration, or anything,
for said release, nor have they ever applied to the administrator
to account therefor, nor to the said county court, or the judge
thereof, to cause him to do so; 11. That the said association has
not paid the said five thousand dollars, and the same is now due
and payable." Appellants' demurrer to the complaint having
been overruled, they appealed to this court. The ground relied
upon is, that the complaint does not state facts sufficient to constitute a cause of action.

The county court has original, but not exclusive, jurisdiction
in all matters of probate guardianship and settlement of estates of
deceased persons. The circuit court has original jurisdiction
of all actions and causes both at law and in equity. It has, as a
court of equity, concurrent jurisdiction in matters of administra-

tion, and will exercise such jurisdiction when the powers of the
county court are inadequate to the purposes of perfect justice:
Story on the Constitution, art. 5, secs. 14, 20; Beach on Modern
Equity Jurisprudence, secs. 1033, 1034. As a rule actions to recover debts due an estate must be maintained by the executor or
administrator, and not by the heirs or creditors; but to this rule
there are exceptions, [600] as where there is collusion between the
debtor and personal representative or he is insolvent, or where the
circumstances are such that the reason of the rule ceases: Comp.
Laws, sec. 4697; Howes on Parties, sec. 72. When an administrator refuses to bring action upon a claim due the estate, heirs,
creditors, and others interested in its collection should have an
adequate remedy. Must they apply to the county court to have
the administrator removed, and one appointed who will perform
his duty? The order of removal may be appealed from, and
while the parties are engaged in this idle preliminary litigation
the debt may be lost. A new administrator would have to sue
in the circuit court. Why cannot those interested in the estate
do directly and at once what it is conceded may be done indirectly and after vexatious delays? The debtor cannot complain. It
matters not to him who is plaintiff, because the court will provide that the proceeds of the judgment shall be distributed according to law, and such judgment will be a bar to another
action for the same debt. It is in effect an action for the benefit
of the estate, brought in the name of heirs or creditors because
the personal representative has refused to bring it. Should the
action fail, the plaintiffs, and not the estate, will be liable for
the costs. We can discover no good reason why plaintiffs should
not be permitted to maintain this action. On the contrary, it
seems to be the only suitable method of attaining the ends of
substantial justice, the purpose for which courts are instituted.
Doubtless, all who are interested in the estate should be parties
to this action, but appellants have not demurred on the ground
that there is a defect of parties; and the demurrer would be bad
were that ground specified, because it does not appear on the face
of the complaint that there are any persons other than plaintiffs
interested in the result of the action. The objection that there
may be creditors who should be made parties must be taken, if
at all, by answer: Comp. Laws, sec. 4912.

The release is a matter of defense, which should not have been
mentioned in the complaint. The allegations relating [601] thereto must be construed together, and; if stated in an answer, would
certainly constitute no bar to plaintiffs' recovery. They do not
defeat plaintiffs' right of action. They are inoperative and use-

less, and should be disregarded as surplusage: Phillips on Code
Pleading, sec. 133. Without them we have a debt due the estate of five thousand dollars, upon which the administrator refuses to bring suit. We think the complaint states a cause of
action, and that the order overruling the demurrer should be
affirmed. It is so ordered.

JUDGE FULLER dissented on the ground that the averments
were not sufficient to create the presumption that the alleged compromise and release referred to in the complaint resulted from the
fraudulent and collusive conduct of the parties, and was, for that
reason, void in toto; that in order to avoid such release, it must be
presumed that the administrator violated his trust to the injury
of the plaintiffs, and that the association acted collusively and fraudulently. The judge claimed that under the statutes of that state
the administrator was bound to compromise and release claims in
favor of the estate when he was satisfied that its best interests justified such compromise, and he further said: "Assuming, but by no
means conceding, that any disgruntled distributee, legatee, or creditor of an estate may at pleasure supersede and take a personal representative out of the supervisory influence of the probate court, and
compel him to answer in a court of equity, merely because he declines to institute a suit when called upon, such suitors cannot prevail when their own pleading irresistibly sustains the inference that
the act complained of was performed in good faith, and strictly
within the line of duty. Neither will it do to disregard as mere surplusage allegations of the complaint which show that plaintiffs
have no cause of action." He further expressed the opinion that
the opinion reached by his associates sanctioned "a doctrine productive of endless litigation and confusion, by which any one interested in the estate of a decedent may, after requesting a personal
representative to institute a suit, make him a defendant in a court
of equity, and there call upon him to account at any time for every
act performed in the due course of administration."

EQUITY—PROBATE JURISDICTION OF.—Though the settle-
ment of estates of decedents is committed to probate courts by statute, equity has jurisdiction whenever its aid is required and the
powers of the probate courts are not sufficient to deal with the question at issue: Bailey v. Bailey, 67 Vt. 494; 48 Am. St. Rep. 826, and
note.

EXECUTORS AND ADMINISTRATORS—RIGHTS OF HEIRS
AND CREDITORS AS AGAINST.—It is a well-established general
rule that heirs, devisees, or legatees cannot sue in their own names
for the recovery of personal property of a decedent until after administration in probate, but to this general rule, the courts, and particularly courts of equity, have recognized various exceptions. Thus,
where there is collusion or insolvency on the part of the personal
representative, or some special case, the heir has been allowed to
sue: Extended note to Hubbard v. Ricart, 23 Am. Dec. 202; Johnston
v. Lewis, Rice Eq. 40; 33 Am. Dec. 74. One creditor of a decedent's
estate may interpose the plea of the statute of limitations to a claim
against the estate set up by another creditor, where the executor

or administrator fails or refuses to do so: Estate of Claghorn, **181 Pa. St. 600; 59 Am. St. Rep. 680.**

PLEADING—SURPLUSAGE—WHAT IS.—Surplusage consists in alleging other facts than those necessary, and may be entirely disregarded: Commonwealth v. Jeffries, 7 Allen, 548; 83 Am. Dec. 712. For examples of surplusage, see Freeland v. McCullough, 1 Denio, 414; 43 Am. Dec. 685, and note; Allemania etc. Ins. Co. v. Peck, 133 Ill. 220; 23 Am. St. Rep. 610; Chicago etc. R. R. Co. v. Dillon, 123 Ill. 570; 5 Am. St. Rep. 559.

CITIZEN'S BANK v. CORKINGS.

[9 SOUTH DAKOTA, 614.]

PARTIES TO ACTION—PLAINTIFF WHO IS A TRUSTEE FOR ANOTHER.—One to whom a cause of action has been assigned may maintain an action thereon whether he is interested in the proceeds or not. He is a trustee of an express trust, and as such is the only person who can prosecute the action.

PARTIES TO ACTION.—That a plaintiff suing upon a cause of action assigned to him is, by his agreement with the assignor, bound to turn over to the latter all the proceeds of the action, is a matter in which the defendant is not interested, and therefore it is not available to him as a defense.

ATTACHMENT, WHO MAY MOVE TO VACATE.—Under the statutes of South Dakota any person having a lien on the property of the defendant may move to discharge an attachment thereon upon the same grounds available to the defendant himself. Such motion may, therefore, be made by subsequently attaching creditors.

CORPORATION, CORPORATE CAPACITY OF, WHEN MUST APPEAR TO SUSTAIN AN ATTACHMENT.—If the plaintiff in the summons and the affidavit for attachment is designated by a name from which it appears not to be a natural person, and its corporate existence or capacity to sue is in no manner alleged, the attachment cannot be sustained and must be discharged on the motion of any person interested in, or having a lien upon, the property attached.

N. B. Reed and T. H. Null; for the appellant.

S. A. Ramsey and H. C. Preston, for the respondent.

[614] FULLER, J.   Upon the motion of Oscar Mohr, an intervenor in this action, and creditor subsequently attaching, the court made and entered an order dissolving a prior attachment levied by plaintiff, the Citizens' Bank, upon the property of the defendant, Corkings, and from said order vacating its attachment plaintiff appeals.

The property over which this contention arises was seized by appellant on the ninth day of December, 1895, and by respondent, [615] who levied, subject thereto, just one week thereafter. Without a specific recital of facts, we shall regardfully consider, so far as essential to a determination of this appeal, a certain other attachment proceeding instituted by appellant to subject the property in suit to the payment of its claim; also an action commenced against the defendant by respondent's assignor, which was dismissed prior to the assignment, but nevertheless considered by the trial court as an evidential circumstance at the hearing of the motion to vacate the attachments herein which resulted in the order appealed from as a final determination of the entire matter. Respondent's assignor, the Mohr-Holstein Commission Company, being a nonresident corporation, and not having complied with chapter 47 of the Laws of 1895, at the time of the assignment, prohibiting such a corporation from transacting business, acquiring property, instituting or maintaining any action in this state unless it has first filed with the secretary of state a copy of its articles and appointed a resident agent, etc., it is contended by counsel for appellant that respondent, who, prior to the commencement of his action, took a formal written assignment absolute in terms, but with the understanding that he would take the claim, collect what he could, and turn over to the company the proceeds thereof, less the expenses of collection, is not the real party in interest, and that he obtained the assignment for the sole purpose of avoiding the force and effect of the law of this state. Respondent's counsel contend that, as the indebtedness arose and was made payable in the state of Wisconsin, the case does not come within the prohibition, and confidently maintain that, in any event, the assignment is sufficient to constitute respondent a real party in interest. As the record stands, we are not called upon to determine whether a nonresident corporation may come into this state and transact business in violation of the statute, and subsequently evade the operation thereof by the assignment for collection of a cause of action arising therefrom.

[616] By the assignment in this case the corporation devested itself of every legal attribute of a party plaintiff, and invested respondent with a complete legal title to the property transferred, together with the exclusive right to collect and receive the entire proceeds thereof by suit or otherwise; and the fact that the consideration was made to depend upon the collection as a contingency is a matter between the immediate parties, and one with which strangers have not the slightest concern. Respondent is, in contemplation of the statute, not only the real party in interest, but, in a certain sense, the trustee of an express trust, and the only person in whose name the action could be prosecuted under sections 4870 or 4872 of the Compiled Laws: Hudson v. Archer, 4 S. Dak. 128; Cummings v. Morris, 25 N. Y.

625; Wetmore v. Hegeman, 88 N. Y. 69; Toby v. Oregon Pac. Ry. Co., 98 Cal.490; Arpin v. Burch, 68 Wis. 619. The debtor being fully protected, the rule is that a written or verbal assignment, absolute in terms, and vesting in the assignee the apparent legal title to a chose in action, is unaffected by a collateral contemporaneous agreement respecting the proceeds, even though the entire consideration for the assignment is made to depend upon the contingency of collection, and the assignee must sue in his own name as the real party in interest: Minnesota etc. Mfg. Co. v. Heipler, 49 Minn. 395; Allen v. Brown, 44 N. Y. 228; Pomeroy on Remedies and Remedial Rights, 132, and cases therein collated.

By section 5011 of the Compiled Laws, which provides that "in all cases the defendant or any person who has acquired a lien upon or interest in the defendant's property after it was attached may move to discharge the attachment," the legislature evidently intended to put subsequently attaching creditors or interested persons upon identically the same footing as the defendant, and authorize the application to be based upon the ground of fatal irregularities in, or the insufficiency of, the affidavit upon which the prior attachment issued: Deering v. Warren, 1 S. Dak. 35. Manifestly [617] respondent, who has acquired an attachment lien upon the property of the defendant since its seizure by appellant, has all the rights of the defendant to apply for a dissolution upon jurisdictional grounds, notwithstanding the fact of his being made a party to the action by the way of intervention: People's Bank v. Mechanics' Nat. Bank, 62 How. Pr. 422; Jacobs v. Hogan, 85 N. Y. 243. Respondent's attachment proceeding clearly appears from his moving papers and verified complaint in intervention, which is expressly made a part of the affidavit submitted to the court in support of the motion to discharge appellant's attachment, and in which it is alleged, in effect, that the summons in the case and the affidavit upon which said prior attachment issued are wholly insufficient to confer upon the court any jurisdiction of the subject matter or person of the defendant. As the motion to discharge appellant's attachment was made by respondent, a person who had acquired by attachment a subsequent lien upon the defendant's property, and the record discloses that vitally essential fact beyond all question, the court was fully justified in considering the application to vacate as made in that capacity, independently of the statutory right of intervention.

Appellant's summons and affidavit for an attachment are respectively entitled ·"The Citizens' Bank, Plaintiff, v. George W. Corkings, Defendant," and there is nothing in either tending to indicate the character of the Citizens' Bank other than that it is not a natural person, and its legal capacity to sue is in no manner made to appear. The affidavit for an attachment must show the existence of an action and specify the amount of the claim, and grounds thereof: Comp. Laws, sec. 4995. Unless it affirmatively appears from the affidavit for an attachment that there is an action pending between persons capable of becoming parties to an action, the court is without jurisdiction to issue an attachment, and must, upon proper application, discharge the same. No litigation can exist, and no facts sufficient to constitute a cause of action can be stated, in [618] favor of or against the Citizens' Bank, in the absence of the jurisdictional showing that it is a natural person, or an artificial being capable of suing and being sued: State v. Chicago etc. Ry. Co., 4 S. Dak. 261; 46 Am. St. Rep. 783; Deering v. Warren, 1 S. Dak. 35; Barbour v. Albany Lodge No. 24, 73 Ga. 474; Sims v. Jacobson, 51 Ala. 186; Proprietors Mexican Mill Co. v. Yellow Jacket S. M. Co., 4 Nev. 40; 97 Am. Dec. 510. There being no party plaintiff, it follows that there was no summons issued, no action pending, and, consequently, no attachment existing in favor of the Citizens' Bank, and it was the duty of the court charged with a knowledge of its own jurisdiction upon a cursory inspection of the record to declare the entire proceeding a mere nullity. The order appealed from is affirmed.

Haney, J., taking no part in this decision.

————

ACTIONS—ASSIGNMENT OF—EFFECT.—A right of action could not be assigned at common law. This rule has been very generally superseded at law, and never prevailed in equity: Thallheimer v. Brinckerhoff, 3 Cow. 623; 15 Am. Dec. 308. While the assignee cannot maintain an action which the assignor could not maintain: Hill v. McPherson, 15 Mo. 204; 55 Am. Dec. 142, he may generally sue upon the cause of action without joining the assignor as a party: Roberts v. Corbin, 26 Iowa, 315; 96 Am. Dec. 146, and note; Peterson v. Chemical Bank, 32 N. Y. 21; 88 Am. Dec. 298; Charles v. Haskin, 11 Iowa, 329; 77 Am. Dec. 148.

ATTACHMENT—VALIDITY OF—WHO MAY CONTEST.—A subsequent attaching creditor may intervene in an action for the recovery of money in which an attachment has been issued and levied upon property of the defendant, at any time before the entry of judgment, for the purpose of contesting the validity of the first attachment: Speyer v. Ihmels, 21 Cal. 280; 81 Am. Dec. 157. See Davis v. Eppinger, 18 Cal. 378; 79 Am. Dec. 184, and note.

CORPORATIONS—CORPORATE CAPACITY—WHEN MUST BE PLEADED.—The decided weight of authority sustains the proposition that in an action by or against a corporation in which it is designated by a corporate name, there is no necessity of alleging the creation or existence of the corporation: Note to Miller v. Pine Min. Co., 35 Am. St. Rep. 291, 292; Lake Erie etc. R. R. Co. v. Griffin, 8 Ind. App. 47; 52 Am. St. Rep. 465, and note.

ELDER v. HORSESHOE MINING AND MILLING COMPANY.

[9 South Dakota, 636.]

MINING LAWS.—A notice of forfeiture directed to R. W., his heirs, administrators, and to all whom it may concern, he being then deceased, and there being no administrator of his estate, is sufficient under section 2324 of the Revised Statutes of the United States, authorizing proceedings by a person claiming to be a co-owner of a mining claim to compel another co-owner to contribute his proportion of the expenses required to be made upon such claim, and, in default of such contribution within the time specified in such statute, that the interest of the non-contributing co-owner should vest in those who have made the required expenditures.

MINING LAWS.—The estate of the locator or owner of a mining claim before a patent is issued is a conditional estate, subject to be defeated by the failure to perform the required annual work upon the claim, and any qualified person may take advantage of the failure to perform the condition and relocate the claim.

MINING LAWS—EFFECT OF NOTICE TO CO-OWNER TO CONTRIBUTE HIS SHARE OF NECESSARY EXPENDITURES.— A notice published under section 2324 of the Revised Statutes of the United States calling upon co-owners in a mining claim to contribute their shares of the annual expenditures required to be made upon such claim, if such contribution is not made, cuts off the owner in default and all interests dependent upon his, whether the persons claiming are minors, heirs, or lienholders, though such persons are not expressly named in such notice.

MINING LAWS.—Notice calling upon co-owners in a mining claim to contribute their shares of necessary expenditures may include the expenditures for several years. It is not necessary to give a separate notice for each year.

Edwin Van Cise, for the appellants.

Martin & Mason and Frank McLaughlin, for the respondents.

637 CORSON, P. J. In January, 1878, Charles H. Havens and Rufus Wilsey located a mining claim in the Black Hills under the name of the "Golden Sand Lode." In June, 1878, Wilsey died, leaving a widow and several children, who then, and have ever since, resided in the state of Iowa. After the death of Wilsey, Havens continued to make the required annual expenditure upon the claim until 1892, when he sold the same to Thomas H. White, the managing agent of the defendant. At the time of his sale, Havens assumed to be the owner of the whole claim, by virtue of proceedings taken under the provisions of section 2324 of the United States Revised Statutes, by which he sought to transfer the interest of Wilsey to himself. The validity of these proceedings constitutes the principal question in this case. To fully comprehend the various questions arising out of these proceedings, it may be proper to state that, soon after the death of Wilsey, one John Stephens was appointed administrator of his estate by the probate court of Lawrence county. This administrator died in 1888, and there was no administrator of the estate of Wilsey after that time until 1893, when the plaintiff Elder was appointed. After Thomas H. White purchased the Golden Sand claim from Havens, he, through Joseph M. Thomas, a nephew, caused the said Golden Sand claim to be relocated under [638] the name of the "North Lode," and an application for a United States patent to be made therefor, which was issued to said Thomas, who in November, 1893, conveyed the patented claim to the defendant and appellant. The undisputed evidence shows that the expenses for work done upon the North claim after its location, and the expense of obtaining a patent therefor, were paid by the defendant, the Horseshoe Mining Company. In the summer of 1893, after the plaintiff Elder was appointed administrator of the estate of Wilsey, he, together with the heirs of the estate, tendered to said White, Thomas, and the defendant, one-half of the amount of the annual expenditure required to be made upon the Golden Sand claim from 1878 to 1893, and demanded a deed for one-half of the claim as patented by said Thomas, as the "North Lode." The parties refusing to make such conveyance, this action was instituted, in the name of the administrator and heirs, to recover one-half of the property. The case was tried by the court without a jury, and it found in favor of the plaintiffs, and the defendants have appealed.

It will be noticed that from 1888 to 1893 there was no administrator of the estate of Wilsey. The record discloses no transfer of the Golden Sand location by Thomas H. White to the defendant, and its title rests entirely upon the North Lode location. It will be observed that the Golden Sand lode was located in 1878 by Havens and Wilsey; that Wilsey died during the same year; that Havens did all the annual work required upon the claim from 1878 to 1892, and that in the latter year he transferred the whole claim to the agent of defendant; the Golden Sand lode was then relocated by the agent of the defendant as the North lode, and a patent issued therefor; and that the same was conveyed to the defendant the Horseshoe Mining Company. It is claimed by the plaintiffs that the relocation was a fraud upon them. But, in the view we take of the case, the only material question to be considered is as to the validity of Haven's proceedings in his attempt to acquire the [639] half interest of Wilsey to the Golden Sand lode; for, if he acquired a valid title to the Wilsey interest, then it was immaterial as to what disposition the defendant made of the claim subsequent to the transfer of the same by Havens, as it is not disputed that Havens' conveyance was, in form, a conveyance of the whole claim. For the purposes of this case, we shall assume, as found by the court, that the Golden Sand lode was properly located, and was a good and valid location at the time of the death of Wilsey, and that the annual assessment work was duly performed upon said claim up to the time it was transferred by Havens to White, in 1892. If, therefore, the proceedings taken by Havens devested the estate of Wilsey of its title, then the defendant obtained a good title to the whole claim under the North lode location.

In order to establish the fact that Havens had complied with the provisions of the United States statute, and had thereby acquired the Wilsey interest, defendant offered in evidence two published notices, published at the same time, and being substantially copies of each other, except that the first covered a period of eight years and the latter one year. The notice is as follows: "Notice of Forfeiture. To Rufus Wilsey, his heirs, administrators, and to all whom it may concern: You are hereby notified that I have expended $800 in labor and improvements upon the Golden Sand lode, ... as will appear by certificate filed on Jan. 2d, 1889, in the office of the register of deeds of said Lawrence county, in order to hold said premises under the provisions of the laws of the United States and of this territory; that being $100 per year, the amount required to hold the claim for the years ending December 31st, 1880, December 31st, 1881, December 31st, 1882, December 31st, 1883, December 31st, 1884, December 31st, 1885, December 31st, 1886, and December 31st, 1887. And if, within ninety days after this notice by publication, you fail or refuse to contribute your proportion ($400, being $50 for each of said years), your interests in said claim will become the property of the subscriber, under [640] section 2324 of the Revised Statutes of the United States." To the introduction of this notice the counsel for the plaintiffs interposed the following objections, among others: "5. Because the notice is itself a nullity, because it is shown in the record that Rufus Wilsey was at the time deceased, and a notice cannot run of forfeiture against a dead man or his estate. Neither is this notice addressed to the administrator of the estate, in name or by the proper designation, nor are the heirs enumerated in the notice; and a notice to the persons by description is in all cases invalid. The further objection is made to this notice of forfeiture that no sufficient pleading upon the subject is set out in the answer. Further objection is made to this one now offered, that the notice is further invalid because it undertakes to group the notice of the forfeiture for several years in one notice; also the further objection that no sufficient foundation for the publication of the notice, instead of the personal service of it, has been laid; and, further, that it is not shown that, if the publication were proper, the Lead Herald, the paper referred to, was the paper required by the statute in which it could be published." The court sustained the objection, stating that "the objection will be sustained on the ground that the evidence in this case shows that Rufus Wilsey was dead, and that there was no legal administrator; his administrator was also deceased at the time this notice of forfeiture was published; and that, therefore, his co-owner gained nothing by it." The second notice offered was for the year ending December 31, 1888, and the amount specified was fifty dollars. The same objection was taken and the same ruling made by the court.

Congress in 1872 enacted the present mining law, and therein provided that all valuable mineral deposits should be "free and open to exploration and purchase, and the lands in which they are found to occupation and purchase." The act prescribes the size of claims, manner of locating same, and that not less than one hundred dollars' "worth of labor shall be performed or improvements made during each year." The act also provides [641] that "the locators, ... their heirs and assigns, ... so long as they comply with the laws of the United States and with state, territorial, and local regulations . . . . shall have the exclusive right of possession and enjoyment" of the claim located. Section 2324, after prescribing the value of the work to be done or improvements made during each year, further provides that: "Upon a failure to comply with the foregoing conditions of annual expenditure, the claim or mine upon which such failure occurred shall be open to relocation in the same manner as if no location of the same had ever been made; provided, that the original locators, their heirs, assigns, or legal representatives have not resumed work upon the claim after failure and before such relocation. Upon the failure of any one of several co-owners to contribute his portion of the expenditures required thereby, the co-owners who have performed the labor or made the improve-

ments may, at the expiration of the year, give such delinquent
co-owners personal notice in writing or notice by publication in
the newspaper published nearest the claim, for at least once a
week for ninety days, and if at the expiration of ninety days after
such notice in writing or by publication such delinquent shall
fail or refuse to contribute his proportion of the expenditure required by this section, his interest in the claim shall become the
property of his co-owners who have made the required expenditures." It will thus be seen that the estate of the locator or
owner of a mining claim, before a patent is issued, is a conditional
estate, subject to be defeated by a failure to perform the required
annual work upon the claim, and that any qualified person may
take advantage of the failure to perform the condition and relocate the same. It follows, therefore, that the locator, his heirs
or assigns, must see that the condition is performed, in order
that their right to the possession may continue. When the location is made by two or more, they become co-owners, and one or
more of the co-owners may do the required work upon the claim,
and thus perform the condition, and thereby continue the right
of themselves [642] and co-owners to the exclusive possession of
the claim. But no duty is imposed upon any one co-owner to do
this. If the work is done, however, by one or more, the law requires the other co-owner or co-owners to contribute his or their
share of the required expense; and upon failure so to do, his or
their interest becomes the property of those performing the work,
upon compliance with the requirement of the statute, which is
the giving "such delinquent co-owner personal notice in writing
or notice by publication in the newspaper published nearest to
the claim." The statute makes no specific provision for any address or heading to the notice. As will have been observed, the
notice in the case at bar is addressed "to Rufus Wilsey, his heirs,
administrators, and to all whom it may concern." Wilsey having
died in 1878, the notice, as to him, was nugatory. It was also
addressed to the administrators. There being none then living,
it could have no effect in that respect. But it is also addressed
to the "heirs, and to all whom it may concern." At the time this
notice was published the title to a one-half interest in the claim
was in the heirs, subject to the lien of the administrator for administration purposes, and had been since the death of Wilsey:
Comp. Laws, secs. 3400, 5772, 5860, 5862; In re Woodworth's
Estate, 31 Cal. 595; Meeks v. Hahn, 20 Cal. 627; Brenham v.
Story, 39 Cal. 179; Janes v. Throckmorton, 57 Cal. 368; Beckett
v. Selover, 7 Cal. 238. It is said in the latter case "that both the

real and personal estate of the intestate vests in the heir subject to the lien of the administrator for the payment of debts and the expenses of administration and with the right of the administrator to present possession"; and this, says Mr. Justice Field in Meeks v. Hahn, 20 Cal. 627, "is the true rule." The provisions of our own statute upon the subject of succession, and the provisions of our Probate Code bearing upon this subject are substantially, if not identically, the same as the corresponding sections in the California code. If this view of the law is correct, the heirs of Wilsey were in fact co-owners with Havens in the Golden Sand claim from 1878 [643] to the time of the publication of the notice; and the notice directed to them as heirs would seem to be sufficient to charge them with notice, and require them to pay the estate's proportion of the expenses. If such was the position of the heirs, the existence or nonexistence of an administrator could not affect them. Having succeeded to the Wilsey interest, they took it burdened with the condition that their share of the annual expenditure must be provided for. It was their duty, therefore, to see that the work was done. The heirs are presumed to know the law, and to know that this work was required to be done annually. The fact, therefore, that there was no administrator when the notice was published, seems not to be very material.

But, in the view we take of the provisions of the United States statutes from which we have quoted, the question of the rights of heirs and of administrators over the real property of a deceased becomes unimportant. We are clearly of the opinion that Congress, by the provisions we are considering, intended that the notice published should have the effect of notice to all parties who might have any interest under the co-owner who is in default, and cut off all such interests, whether the parties claiming are minors, heirs, or lienholders, when, as in this case, the notice is so addressed as to include all parties. It is apparent that Congress, by the notice, intended to give to one or more co-owners who may cause the required work to be done upon the claim a summary remedy for collecting from a co-owner his proportionate share of the expense so necessarily incurred to protect the claim, either in money, or by taking the co-owner's interest in the claim. The evident purpose and object of the law of 1872 were to encourage the exploration and development of the mineral lands of the United States, and the sale of the same, and all the provisions of the law seem to have been framed with that object in view. This is apparent from that part of the act providing that,

unless the annual expenditure shall be made each year, the claim
shall be subject to relocation; [644] and no rights of heirs, minors,
widows, or lienholders are excepted or reserved, and no proceeding, judicial or otherwise, is required to devest the delinquent
locator or locators of his or their interest, or the interest of heirs
or lienholders in the claim. If the required work is not performed, and the claim is relocated after the expiration of the year,
the rights of all the parties are absolutely cut off, though the failure to do the work may have been caused by the death of the locator or locators during the year. Again, when an application for
patent is made, the land officers are required to publish a notice
—not addressed to anyone—that such application has been made.
If no adverse claim is filed within sixty days after the first publication of such notice, the rights of all parties holding adverse
claims are cut off, without regard to whether the parties claiming them are minors, heirs, lienholders, or otherwise. These illustrations sufficiently disclose the intention of Congress in the passage of the act of 1872. We feel justified in the conclusion that
Congress, in adopting the provisions in regard to the disposition
to be made of a defaulting co-owner's interest in the claim, acted
upon the same theory, and the published notice was intended to
accomplish the same result as the published notice of application
for a patent; that is, to cut off the claims of all persons, and vest
in the co-owner a clear title to his co-owner's interest, without
regard to the interest of minors, lienholders, or encumbrancers.
This, as I understand, is the view taken by the United States land
department of this provision. That department requires ab-
stracts of title, and, when it appears by the record that the proper
affidavits have been filed and the proper notice published, no further evidence is required. But if the construction contended for
by the learned counsel for the respondent is correct, then the department should require proof that the co-owner was living at
the time the notice was published, or, if dead, that there was an
administrator appointed and then performing the duties of his
office, and that the heirs were not minors, and possibly a number
[645] of other facts, in order that the applicant's title should be
regarded as sufficient to entitle him to his patent. With such a
construction as is contended for, the provision would be absolutely worthless, and, instead of conferring a benefit upon the
co-owner, would be a delusion and a snare. No person could
safely invest in a claim in the chain of title to which there was
such a notice, however regular it might appear to be by the record. It will be further observed on reading the provision that

the conditions under which the notice may be served personally
are not prescribed, thus leaving it optional to the party when and
under what circumstances he will serve the notice personally;
clearly indicating that, in the opinion of Congress, the notice
would ordinarily be published, and, as we reason, in order that
the liens of all parties might be cut off, and that the true owner
be vested with a clear title. This construction of the law renders
the notice, when rightfully published, effective in cutting off the
claims of all parties, and thus keeping the title clear and free from
uncertainty and doubt. It gives to the notice the effect usually
designed to be given to that class of notices when the claims of
all persons are intended to be cut off, as in the case of mortgages containing a power of sale (Reilly v. Phillips, 4 Dak. 604),
probate court proceedings, applications for patents, etc. The
court was in error in excluding the notice, and for this error the
judgment of the court below must be reversed.

The other objections made to the admission of the published
notice, it seems to us, do not merit very much consideration. The
objection that the heirs are not individually named in the notice
cannot be sustained. To require of a co-owner to ascertain, at
his peril, the names of all the heirs of delinquent co-owners,
would be to impose upon him a burden the law never intended
should be imposed, and one that could be of no possible benefit
to anyone, as the heirs, if personally named, would be no more
likely to obtain actual notice than when named simply as heirs.
Neither do we think there is any merit in the objection [646] that
in the one notice the expenditure for eight years is included.
Certainly, if the parties interested intended to pay, and thus protect their interest in the claim, they would be greatly benefited
by grouping them all in one notice. If they did not intend to
pay, the grouping would be immaterial to them. The law does
not prohibit it, and we can discover no valid reason why it may
not be done. The objection that the notice was fatally defective
because addressed to Rufus Wilsey and administrators, as well
as heirs, and to all whom it might concern, is not tenable. It was
one method of designating by whom the claim was located. Perhaps the notice addressed to the heirs of Rufus Wilsey, deceased,
would have been more technically correct; but we think the form
is not material, so long as the statute is substantially complied
with. The insertion of the administrator could do no harm, even
if there was none.

There are numerous other errors assigned in the record, but
we do not deem it necessary to discuss them at this time. The

judgment of the circuit court, and the order denying a new trial, are reversed.

MINES—FORFEITURE OR ABANDONMENT THROUGH FAILURE TO WORK—CO-OWNERS.—A claim may be relocated if either forfeited or abandoned: Russell v. Brosseau, 65 Cal. 605; Golden Fleece etc. Co. v. Cable Con. Min. Co., 15 Nev. 450. The proceedings necessary to effect such forfeiture are governed by section 2324 of the United States Revised Statutes, where the forfeiture is of one co-owner's share to another co-owner. It is provided that upon the failure of any one of several co-owners of a vein, lode, or ledge which has not been entered, to contribute his proportion of the expenditures necessary to hold the claim held in common ownership, any co-owner or co-owners who may have properly contributed the necessary labor and expense may at the expiration of the year give notice, either in writing or by publication in the newspaper published nearest the claim, to such defaulting co-owner, who by failure to contribute his share of labor and improvements in due time will be held to have forfeited his interest in the claim to the other co-owners. Such forfeiture can be effected only in favor of a co-owner: Turner v. Sawyer, 150 U. S. 578. And where the co-owner publishing the notice knew of the death of his co-owner to whom the notice was directed yet made no attempt to notify his heirs, no forfeiture was effected: Billings v. Aspen Min. etc. Co., 51 Fed. Rep. 338. In order that a forfeiture may be worked the facts upon which it is based must exist, and the statute must be strictly pursued: **Brundy v. Mayfield, 15 Mont. 201.**

CASES

SUPREME COURT

OF

UTAH.

EUREKA CITY *v.* WILSON.

[15 UTAH, 67.]

PRACTICE, JURISDICTION OF THE SUPREME COURT
OF UTAH WHERE THE ACTION WAS ORIGINALLY
BROUGHT BEFORE A JUSTICE OF THE PEACE.—Where an
action was brought before a justice of the peace and afterward appealed to the district court, its decision is final, and cannot be
reviewed by the supreme court, except in so far as it relates to the
validity or constitutionality of a statute or of a municipal ordinance.

LEGISLATIVE AUTHORITY, DELEGATION OF.—Where
the legislature has delegated its authority upon a subject to the
common council of a municipal corporation, that council cannot delegate such authority to a committee thereof.

CONSTITUTIONAL LAW—FIRE LIMITS.—A common coun-
cil of a municipal corporation may, by the legislature, be authorized to determine fire limits, and to provide that therein no building
shall be constructed except of brick, stone, or other incombustible
material without permission, and to cause the removal of any building constructed or repaired in violation of any ordinance.

CONSTITUTIONAL LAW, FIRE LIMITS, CONFERRING
ON COMMITTEE THE CONTROL OF.—A municipal corporation
which has, by ordinance, adopted fire limits and declared that combustible buildings shall not be constructed therein, cannot add a
proviso that a committee of its common council shall have power to
grant permission to erect buildings within such limits under such
regulations and restrictions as the committee may provide. This
proviso attempts to give the committee arbitrary discretion, under
which it might give permission to one person and refuse it to another in precisely the same circumstances.

MUNICIPAL ORDINANCE VALID IN PART AND VOID
IN PART.—If an ordinance is enacted defining the fire limits and
specifying buildings which may not be constructed therein, but with
a proviso that the building committee may grant permission, under
such regulations and restrictions as it may think proper, to con-

struct other classes of buildings within such limits, the proviso is
void and must be disregarded, and the balance of the ordinance
given the same effect as if the invalid proviso had not been attempted
to be inserted therein.

MUNICIPAL ORDINANCE, WHEN INVALID PARTS MAY
BE REJECTED AND THE RESIDUE ENFORCED.—An ordinance
may be good in part and bad in part. It is only necessary that the
good and bad parts be so distinct and independent that the invalid
parts may be eliminated and what remains contain the essential
elements of a complete ordinance.

MUNICIPAL ORDINANCE — FIRE LIMITS, WHEN AP-
PLIES TO REMOVAL OF BUILDINGS.—An ordinance prescribing
the fire limits of a municipality and forbidding the erection therein
of any building not of incombustible material is applicable to the removal of a combustible building from one part of the fire limits
to the other. The provisions of the ordinance extend to, and protect,
all vacant places within the fire limits.

J. W. N. Whitecotton, for the appellant.

B. N. C. Scott and Williams, Van Cott & Sutherland, for the
respondent.

⁶⁹ BARTCH, J. This case was commenced before a justice
of the peace, and the defendant, after having been convicted of
a violation of an ordinance of Eureka City which forbids the
⁷⁰ erection of wooden buildings, without permission, within
certain defined limits, appealed to the district court, and, upon
conviction and fine there, to this court.

The record presents several questions, raised on behalf of the
appellant, respecting the rulings of the district court as to the
sufficiency of the complaint before the justice of the peace, and
the allowance of amendments thereto. These questions simply
relate to the interpretation which the district court put upon
various provisions of statute, and do not affect the validity or
constitutionality of a statute. We have no power to consider
such questions in this class of cases, because, under section 9 of
article 8 of the constitution, the decision of a district court on all
questions except those affecting the validity or constitutionality
of a statute is final and conclusive. We so held in the case of
Eureka v. Wilson (decided at the present term), 15 Utah, 53, to
which we refer for our opinion on this point. In that case we
also discussed the question whether an appeal would lie in a case
like one where the validity of a city ordinance, and not of a statute, is involved; and on the authority of that case, and in conformity with it, we hold that the appeal herein was properly
taken, and that we have jurisdiction to determine the validity
of the ordinance under which the appellant was convicted, but
have no jurisdiction to determine any other question presented.

The principal question to be determined in this case, therefore, is whether the ordinance under which the appellant was convicted and fined is constitutional and valid. Counsel on behalf of the appellant insists that it conflicts with section 1 of article 14 of the amendments to the constitution of the United States, and that it delegates legislative power to a committee of the city council, and is therefore void. The provisions of the ordinance [71] in controversy here may be found in section 2, Ordinance No. 16 of Eureka City, and read as follows: "Every building hereafter erected within the fire limits of this city shall be of brick, stone, iron, or other substantial or incombustible material, and only the following wooden buildings shall be allowed to be erected, except as hereinafter provided, viz: Sheds to facilitate the erection of authorized buildings, coalsheds not exceeding ten feet in height, and not to exceed one hundred feet in area, and privies, not to exceed thirty-six feet in area and ten feet in height, and all such sheds and privies shall be separate structures; provided, that any person desiring to erect a building of other material than those above specified within said fire limits shall first apply to the committee on buildings within said fire limits of the city for permission so to do, and if the consent of the committee on building within said fire limits shall be given, they shall issue a permit, and it shall thereupon be lawful to erect such building under such regulations and restrictions as the committee on buildings within said fire limits may provide." The authority under which this ordinance was passed can be found in subdivision 54 of section 1755 of the Compiled Laws of Utah of 1888, which provides that the city council shall have power, among other things, as follows: "To define the fire limits and prescribe limits within which no building shall be constructed, except brick, stone, or other incombustible material, without permission, and to cause the destruction or removal of any building constructed or repaired in violation of any ordinance; and to cause all buildings and inclosures which may be in a dangerous state to be put in a safe condition." This provision of the statute confers upon the city council of any incorporated city in this state the power to establish fire limits, and to prohibit, within [72] such limits, without permission, the erection of any building with combustible material, leaving all persons free to erect buildings of brick, stone, or other incombustible material within such limits. The erection of buildings with combustible material may be prohibited by ordinance, and the granting of permission for the erection of such buildings may likewise, by ordinance, be regulated and restricted. Such was doubtless the intention of the legislature. The power thus conferred by the legislature upon the city council is, however, of a legislative character, and may not be delegated by the council to a committee. Such power being vested in the council, it must be exercised by it. If an ordinance specifies fire limits in a city in accordance with the statute, and prohibits the construction of buildings of wood or of any combustible material within such limits, without permission, and also prescribes proper regulations and restrictions under which such permission shall be granted to all applicants under like circumstances, it is valid, notwithstanding it confers power upon an officer or committee to grant permission to erect such buildings in conformity with its provisions. The power to grant the permission does not vest in the officer or committee an arbitrary discretion, but it vests in him or them merely a legal discretion, which must be exercised fairly, reasonably, and honestly. An ordinance of such a character is authorized by the statute, as well as by the police power of the state, and does not contravene section 1 of article 14 of the amendments to the constitution of the United States: Eureka v. Wilson, 15 Utah, 53.

Section 1 of the ordinance in question in this case defines the fire limits of Eureka City. Section 2, above quoted, in conformity with the statutes, prescribes the kind of material to be used in the construction of buildings [73] within the fire limits, which shall be brick, stone, iron, or other incombustible material. It also prescribes that certain classes of buildings, giving particular descriptions of the same, may be constructed with combustible material within such limits. Then follows a proviso wherein the "committee on building" is empowered, on application therefor by any person, to grant permission to erect any building with combustible material, under such "regulations and restrictions," as that committee may provide. All the provisions of section 2 not contained in the proviso appear to be authorized by the statute, and to conform to the principles hereinbefore stated, respecting ordinances. By adding the proviso, however, the council has attempted to confer upon a committee, not only an absolute power, which would enable it to defeat the very object of the ordinance at its mere will and pleasure, but also a legislative power, which would enable it to perform a duty imposed upon the council itself by the statute, and that is to provide regulations and restrictions to control the granting of permission according to the provisions of the ordinance. This the council had no power to do. The erection of a wooden building in any part of the city

is not in itself unlawful. It only becomes so when forbidden by
law, within the fire limits, for the security of persons and property, and the promotion of the interests and good order of the
city; and while a city council in this state may prohibit, by ordinance, the construction of buildings, within fire limits, of combustible material, still it cannot confer a power upon a committee,
such as is attempted to be conferred by the proviso, which may
be used as a means for unjust and arbitrary discrimination between citizens. If this proviso were valid, then, no matter what
regulations and restrictions the committee might adopt, it would
still be [74] within its power to grant permission to one person to
erect a wooden building, and refuse the privilege to another
under the same circumstances. The statute vested in the council
the exercise of powers of legislation respecting the establishing of
fire limits and the construction of buildings therein. This demands a discretion in the council itself, and cannot be delegated.
The proviso cannot be justified as a reasonable exercise of the authority conferred by the statute, and is void: Horr and Bemis'
Municipal Ordinances, sec. 10; Newton v. Belger, 143 Mass. 598.

The fact that the proviso is void, however, affords no sufficient
reason to declare the whole ordinance invalid.   The ordinance
is capable of enforcement independent of the proviso.   The provision defining the fire limits and the prohibition against the
erection therein of buildings of inflammable material, except certain described classes of buildings, are complete, distinct, absolute, and apparently in no essential manner dependent upon the
void provision. It is apparent from the valid portion of the ordinance that the council intend to prohibit the construction of
buildings of the objectionable material, so as to promote the security and protection of persons and property, and the good order
of the city; and the council itself doubtless has authority, under
the statute, to exercise the power, in a proper manner, which it
attempted to delegate to the committee. There is nothing apparent which would justify this court in holding that the city
council would not have enacted the ordinance except in connection with the proviso. The provisions contained in, and those
referring to, the proviso, must be stricken out as invalid and inoperative; and the remaining provisions of section 2 may stand
in connection with the other sections of the ordinance. It is a
well-settled rule that where the portion of a statute or ordinance
which is [75] invalid is distinctly separable from the remainder,
and the remainder in itself contains the essentials of a complete
enactment, the invalid portion may be rejected, and the remain-

der stand as valid and operative. In Detroit v. Fort Wayne etc.
Ry. Co., 95 Mich. 456, 35 Am. St. Rep. 580, Mr. Justice Mc-
Grath, speaking for the court, said: "It is well settled that an
ordinance may be good in part, although bad in part. It is only
necessary that the good and bad parts be so distinct and independent that the invalid parts may be eliminated, and that what
remains contains all the essentials of a complete ordinance." In
Fisher v. McGirr, 1 Gray, 1, 61 Am. Dec. 381, Mr. Chief Justice
Shaw, delivering the opinion of the court, said: "We suppose the
principle is now well understood that where a statute has been
passed by the legislature, under all the forms and sanctions
requisite to the making of laws, some part of which is not within
the competency of legislative power, or is repugnant to any provision of the constitution, such part thereof will be adjudged void,
and of no avail, while all other parts of the act, not obnoxious
to the same objection, will be held valid, and have the force of
law. There is nothing inconsistent, therefore, in declaring one
part of the same statute valid, and another part void": 1 Dillon
on Municipal Corporations, sec. 421; State v. Kantler, 33 Minn.
69; Ex parte Christensen, 85 Cal. 208; Indianapolis v. Bieler, 138
Ind. 30; Ritchie v. Richards, 14 Utah, 345; Santo v. State, 63
Am. Dec. 487; Railroad Co. v. Schutte, 103 U. S. 118; Jones v.
Robbins, 8 Gray, 329; Ingerman v. Noblesville Tp., 90 Ind. 393.

It follows that the erection, within the fire limits of Eureka
City, of buildings of combustible material other than such as are
provided for in the ordinance, was unlawful, and that the appellant, having erected and maintained a building of the class prohibited, was guilty of an [76] unlawful act, and amenable to the
punishment inflicted. The fact that the building in controversy
appears to have been moved from some other portion of the fire
limits to the place where it was erected, in violation of the ordinances, does not change the unlawful character of the act. The
ordinance did not interfere with the building where it stood before its removal, but prohibited new erections in the place of
such as were in existence, and its provisions extended to and
protected all vacant places within the fire limits. The ordinance
in question is a measure for general security, and the protection
of the inhabitants of the city, and was doubtless enacted to prevent the hazard of fire, incident to the continuing and placing
of combustible material in a dangerous position. This is but a
reasonable precaution, looking to the general welfare of the citizens; and we think it was the intention of the city council to
regard as within the operation of the ordinance all buildings of

the prohibited class placed where none existed before, whether by erection or removal from some other place. Such an interpretation seems to be warranted from the context, and to effect the salutary purposes for which the enactment was designed: Wadleigh v. Gilman, 12 Me. 403; 28 Am. Dec. 188.

There appears to be no reversible error in the record. The judgment is affirmed.

Zane, C. J., and Miner, J., concur.

———

JURISDICTION—CONFLICTS OF.—The subject of conflicts of jurisdiction is thoroughly considered in the monographic note to Plume etc. Mfg. Co. v. Caldwell, 29 Am. St. Rep. 310-318. See, also, Wyatt v. Larimer etc. Irr. Co., 18 Colo. 298; 36 Am. St. Rep. 280.

MUNICIPAL CORPORATIONS—DELEGATION OF POWERS OF.—Powers conferred upon a municipal corporation must be exercised by the municipality; and so far as they are legislative, cannot be delegated to others: Chicago v. Stratton, 162 Ill. 494; 53 Am. St. Rep. 325, and note; monographic note to Davis v. King, 50 Am. St. Rep. 118, 119.

MUNICIPAL CORPORATIONS — POWER TO FIX FIRE LIM-ITS — REGULATIONS CONCERNING. — Municipal corporations have the power, under the general welfare clauses commonly contained in their charters, to establish fire limits and forbid the erection or removal of wooden buildings within such limits: Kaufman v. Stein, 138 Ind. 49; 46 Am. St. Rep. 368, and note. See First Nat. Bank v. Sarlls, 129 Ind. 201; 28 Am. St. Rep. 185, and note. That such power is not inherent and independent of legislative grant: Pye v. Peterson, 45 Tex. 312; 23 Am. Rep. 608; Kneedler v. Norristown, 100 Pa. St. 368; 45 Am. Rep. 383. The removal of a building and placing it with proper supports and repairs upon another lot is an erection within the meaning of an ordinance regulating the fire limits of a municipality: Extended note to Mayor v. Hoffman, 29 Am. Rep. 349. Contra, Brown v. Hunn, 27 Conn. 332; 71 Am. Dec. 71. See Kaufman v. Stein, 138 Ind. 49; 46 Am. St. Rep. 368.

MUNICIPAL CORPORATIONS—ORDINANCES VOID IN PART —EFFECT.—When a municipal ordinance is good in part and bad in part, it is only necessary in order to maintain the ordinance, that the valid and invalid parts be so distinct and independent, that the invalid may be eliminated and what remains contain all the essentials of a complete ordinance: Detroit v. Fort Wayne etc. Ry. Co., 95 Mich. 456; 35 Am. St. Rep. 580, and note; Tarkio v. Cook, 120 Mo. 1; 41 Am. St. Rep. 678, and note. But such an ordinance is altogether void where all its parts are connected with and essential to one another; State v. Webber, 107 N. C. 962; 22 Am. St. Rep. 920, and note.

STATE *v.* KESSLER.

[15 UTAH, 142.]

CRIMINAL LAW—AUTREFOIS ACQUIT, PLEA OF AFTER A NEW TRIAL HAS BEEN GRANTED.—If, under an indictment for murder, the accused is convicted of murder in the second degree, and afterward he obtains a reversal of the judgment and the granting of a new trial, he thereby waives his right to rely upon his jeopardy in the former trial, and may be again put on trial for murder in the first degree, if the statutes of the state declare that the granting of a new trial places the parties in the same position as if no trial had been had, that all the testimony must be produced anew, and that the former verdict cannot be used or referred to either in evidence or argument or by plea in bar of any conviction which may have been had under the indictment. The court inclines to the view that such would be the effect of the granting of a new trial, if the statute were not taken into consideration.

DYING DECLARATIONS IDENTIFYING THE ACCUSED OR REFERRING TO PREVIOUS IDENTIFICATION are admissible in evidence against him on his trial for the murder of the person making the declarations.

JURY TRIAL, INSTRUCTIONS AFTER RETIRING.—If the jury, after retiring to consider their verdict, return to court and ask to be instructed as to the punishment for voluntary and involuntary manslaughter, it is not error for the court, in the presence of the accused and his counsel, to read to the jury the statute fixing the punishment of those offenses.

APPELLATE PROCEDURE, PRESUMPTION IN FAVOR OF REGULARITY OF PROCEEDINGS.—If the statute in force at the time of a trial for murder authorizes an oral charge to the jury, but requires the reporter to take it down, it will be presumed on appeal, in the absence of any statement in the record to the contrary, that the reporter did as the law directed.

Taylor & Root and Goodwin & Van Pelt, for the appellant.

A. C. Bishop, attorney general, and Benner X. Smith, for the state.

[143] ZANE, C. J. The defendant was tried on an indictment upon which he might have been convicted of murder in the first or second degree, or voluntary or involuntary manslaughter, and the jury found him guilty of murder in the second degree. He entered a motion for a new trial, which the trial court overruled, entered judgment on the verdict, and then sentenced him to imprisonment in the penitentiary for the term of fourteen years. From this judgment the defendant appealed, and this court reversed the judgment (People v. Kessler, 13 Utah, 69), and ordered the verdict set aside, [144] which was done. The defendant was then tried a second time on the same indictment and plea of not guilty, and on the further plea of former jeopardy of murder in the first degree, and former acquittal of that offense, and

the jury found him guilty of voluntary manslaughter. The court overruled his motion for a new trial, and sentenced him to confinement in the state prison for the term of six years. From this judgment he has appealed.

On the trial of persons charged with capital crime, the law permits fifteen peremptory challenges to each, and three to each in prosecutions for offenses of a lower grade. The court permitted the prosecution on the trial, over the objection of the defendant, to make more than three, and the defendant excepted. The court also sustained plaintiff's challenge to one juror, against the objection of the defendant, because he entertained conscientious scruples against the death penalty. To this ruling the defendant also excepted. The defendant offered in evidence the verdict returned on the first trial, and set aside by the court on plaintiff's motion. The court sustained the objection of the prosecution to its admission, and the defendant excepted. These rulings the defendant assigns as error. These errors raise the question, Could the defendant be tried again for murder in the first degree, after the verdict of guilty of murder in the second degree had been set aside on his motion? A description of murder in the first degree in the indictment upon which the defendant was tried included a description of murder in the second degree and the crime of manslaughter; and his plea of not guilty made an issue on all those charges. Upon his trial he was in jeopardy as to each offense. And the verdict of guilty of murder in the second degree, while allowed to stand, was [145] a bar to another prosecution on either charge, for the constitution of this state declares that "no person shall be twice put in jeopardy for the same offense." But the further question is, Did he, by obtaining a new trial on his own motion, waive his right to rely upon his jeopardy on the former trial or on the verdict of murder in the second degree, as a bar to a conviction of murder in the first degree upon his new or second trial? The statute declares that: "The granting of a new trial places the parties in the same position as if no trial had been had. All the testimony must be produced anew, and the former verdict cannot be used or referred to either in evidence or in argument, or be pleaded on the bar of any conviction which might have been had under the indictment": 2 Utah Comp. Laws, 1888, sec. 5093. This section declares: 1. That the granting of a new trial places the parties in the same position as if no trial had been had; 2. That all the testimony must be produced anew on the new trial; 3. That the former verdict cannot be used or referred to either in evidence or in argument, or be pleaded in bar of any conviction which might have been had under the indictment. Unless this section is repugnant to the state constitution adopted after its enactment, the defendant was rightly put upon his trial for all the óffenses charged in the indictment, and the jury had the right to convict of either offense, as the evidence might warrant. And as the constitution does not, in express terms or by reasonable implication, determine what the effect of a new trial on the defendant's motion shall be when the conviction was for an offense lower than the highest charged, we must hold that the statute is not repugnant to that instrument, and that it is therefore valid. But upon the general proposition, without taking into consideration the statute, [146] it appears more reasonable to hold, when a defendant is found guilty of a lower grade of crime than the highest charged in the indictment, and a new trial granted on his motion, that its effect is to set aside the whole verdict, and leave the case for trial upon the same issues as upon the first trial. On the first trial of this defendant the jury found that he shot Niebergall as charged, and thereby inflicted upon him a wound from which he died; that the shooting was unlawful, and with an intent to kill him, and that it was done with malice aforethought; but did not find the further fact that it was done with such deliberation as made it murder in the first degree. The jury did not actually find a want of deliberation. From the facts found by the jury a want of deliberation was inferred.

In legal effect, the verdict consisted of two parts: 1. An actual finding of murder in the second degree; and 2. By construction and inference, not guilty of murder in the first degree. But the defendant claimed that the finding of the jury was erroneous and illegal, and the court agreed with him, and set the verdict aside, and held that it should not be considered as a finding of the facts essential to guilt. That being so, how could the inferential finding of not guilty of murder in the first degree stand, after the finding of facts from which it was inferred, and upon which it depended, was set aside and vacated? To hold that a verdict of not guilty of murder in the first degree may be inferred from a verdict of guilty of murder in the second degree that has been set aside and remains to be found or not found on a new trial, is to declare that such inferences may be drawn from an unknown finding— from unknown facts. We are aware there is a great conflict in the authorities on this proposition [147] of law, and that the greater number of the authorities support the proposition that when a defendant has been found guilty of an offense of a lower grade than the highest charged in the indictment, and a new trial is granted on his motion, the verdict operates as an acquittal of the higher offense, and stands as such, notwithstanding the new trial. The weight of authority in support of or against a legal proposition does not always depend upon their number alone, but upon the reasoning by which their conclusions are reached as well. There are a large number of well-considered cases holding, if a verdict of guilty of a lower offense included in a higher described in the indictment is set aside on defendant's motion he may be retried for both offenses: Bohanan v. State, 18 Neb. 57; 53 Am. Rep. 791; State v. Behimer, 20 Ohio St. 572; State v. Bradley, 67 Vt. 465; Commonwealth v. Arnold, 83 Ky. 1; 4 Am. St. Rep. 114; Veatch v. State, 60 Ind. 291; People v. Keefer, 65 Cal. 232; People v. Palmer, 190 N. Y. 413; 4 Am. St. Rep. 477; United States v. Harding, 26 Fed. Cas. 139; 1 Wall. Jr. 127.

On the trial of this case the dying declaration of the deceased, Niebergall, was admitted in evidence, and the defendant moved the court to strike out the following language: "I met a gray-bearded man—the man I identified the other night, being with Chief Pratt, known as Dr. Kessler." At the time referred to Pratt had asked Niebergall this question: "Did you ever see this man before?" (pointing to the defendant), and the deceased said "Yes, sir; and he shot me down like a rabbit." Pratt, having the defendant in custody, had immediately before this told him to keep still when he shook his head. For that reason, under the attending circumstances, this court held on the former appeal that the defendant's silence, when charged with shooting Niebergall down like a rabbit, could not be used as [148] acquiescing in the truth of the statement, and as an admission by him that the statement was true. But the identification the defendant asks may be stricken out of the dying declaration was admitted because it was made by the deceased under a belief of impending death, after the deceased had lost all hope of life. The identification of the man who had inflicted the mortal wound upon him certainly related to the circumstances attending the fatal injury.

After the jury had retired to consider their verdict, they requested the court to inform them as to the punishment prescribed for voluntary and involuntary manslaughter, and they returned into court. The defendant and his counsel being present, the court read to them the statute fixing the punishment for those offenses. To this action of the court the defendant excepted. In this we find no error.

Finally, the defendant insists that his motion for a new trial should have been granted because the court gave an oral charge to the jury. When this case was tried, the statute authorized such a charge, but required the reporter to take it down. We must presume that was done, in the absence of any statement in the record to the contrary. We find no error in this record. The judgment of the court below is affirmed.

Hart, D. J., concurs.

Miner, J., dissents.

———

FORMER JEOPARDY — EFFECT OF OBTAINING A NEW TRIAL.—Where a person indicted for murder in the first degree was convicted of murder in the second degree and obtained a new trial, it was held that on the second trial he could not be tried for, or convicted of, a higher crime than murder in the second degree: Johnson v. State, 29 Ark. 31; 21 Am. Rep. 154. This holding is in accord with the weight of authority: Note to Conde v. State, 60 Am. St. Rep. 30. In states where statutes similar to that construed in the principal case exist, the decisions as to the effect of obtaining a new trial by the accused are not harmonious. In some of them the existence of the statutes has been held conclusive of the question, while the same doctrine has been adopted by the courts of Nebraska and Ohio where no such statutes have been enacted: Commonwealth v. Arnold, 83 Ky. 1; 4 Am. St. Rep. 114, and extended note, page 119. See People v. Palmer, 109 N. Y. 413; 4 Am. St. Rep. 477.

HOMICIDE—DYING DECLARATIONS—EVIDENCE AGAINST ACCUSED.—Dying declarations made under a belief of pending death are admissible, not only to designate the party who committed the crime, but also to detail the circumstances under which it was done: Moore v. State, 12 Ala. 764; 46 Am. Dec. 276; State v. Arnold, 47 S. C. 9; 58 Am. St. Rep. 867, and note. A dying declaration that "Jim Sullivan cut me; he cut me for nothing; I never did anything to him," is admissible in evidence: Sullivan v. State, 102 Ala. 135; 48 Am. St. Rep. 22. See extended note to Field v. State, 34 Am. Rep. 479-482.

TRIAL—FURTHER INSTRUCTIONS AT REQUEST OF JURY. A verdict will not be set aside where a court, in response to an inquiry propounded by a jury, correctly states the law: Perkins v. Commonwealth, 7 Gratt. 651; 56 Am. Dec. 123. See Collins v. State, 33 Ala. 434; 73 Am. Dec. 426. But proceedings of a court should be open and notorious, and in the presence of the parties: Crabtree v. Hagenbaugh, 23 Ill. 349; 76 Am. Dec. 694; State v. Patterson, 45 Vt. 308; 12 Am. Rep. 200.

HANDLEY *v.* DALY MINING CO.
[15 UTAH, 189.]

MASTER AND SERVANT—CARE TO BE EXERCISED IN THE SELECTION OF SERVANTS.—It is the duty of a master to exercise due and reasonable care in the selection of his servants with reference to their competency and fitness. He must also exercise the same degree of care in retaining his servants after such employment, for his responsibility is the same.

MASTER AND SERVANT.—The liability of a master for injuries caused by the incompetency of a fellow-servant depends upon such incompetency being established by affirmative proof and that it was known to the master, or that, if he had exercised due and proper diligence, he would have learned of such incompetency. The degree of supervising care which a master must exercise to ascertain whether his servant is competent depends on the nature of the service and the dangers attending it. A closer supervision is required over the habits and competency of an engineer than over those of a common laborer.

MASTER AND SERVANT—EVIDENCE TO CHARGE MASTER WITH KNOWLEDGE OF INCOMPETENCY OF SERVANT. Incompetency of a servant and negligence of the master in retaining him in his employment may be established by evidence of specific acts of incompetency, and that they were known to the master, or were of such a character and frequency that he, in the exercise of due and reasonable care, must have known of them. If repeated acts of carelessness are shown on the part of the servant, it is proper to leave the question to the jury to determine whether or not they came to the knowledge of the master, or would have come to his knowledge, had he used reasonable care.

NEGLIGENCE, INJURY RESULTING FROM AND FROM OTHER CAUSES.—If an injury is due to negligence for which the defendant is answerable, and also to a concurrent cause which would not have happened but for the negligence, he is answerable.

MASTER AND SERVANT.—If a servant is injured partly through the negligence or incompetency or carelessness of a fellow-servant, of whose incompetency or carelessness the master had notice, and partly through the negligence of another fellow-servant, the master is liable, if, but for the negligence of the incompetent fellow-servant, the injury would not have happened.

MASTER AND SERVANT.—A servant assumes the risk of the negligence of his fellow-servants, but not that of the master.

Action to recover for injuries sustained by the plaintiff while in the service of the defendant mining company. The injuries of the plaintiff were suffered while he was descending in a cage in the mine. In the first place, the station tender negligently left traps or chairs extending in to the mine so as to form an obstruction to the descent of the cage, and, in the second place, the injury, notwithstanding the first negligence, would not have happened but for the negligence of the engineer, named Adamson. It was claimed that the defendant had been guilty of negligence in retaining this engineer in its employment after knowl-

edge of his incompetency; and there was much evidence to show
repeated carelessness and negligence on the part of the engineer
and of injury to employés therefrom, and that the engineer had
the reputation of being incompetent and careless, and he had
that reputation for several years.   The trial court directed a verdict for the defendant, and the plaintiff appealed.

Brown, Henderson & King, for the appellant.

Bennett, Harkness, Howat & Bradley, and H. J. Dininny, for
the respondent.

[184] MINER, J. Plaintiff was a miner, taking out ore. Breen
was in the same department, loading ore on the cage, and had
no control of the plaintiff. Both were under the same foreman,
in the same department of labor. They were, therefore, fellow-
servants. It is the duty of a master to exercise due and reasonable care in the selection of his servants, with reference to their
competency and fitness. He must also exercise the same degree
of care in retaining his servants after such employment, for his
responsibility is the same. The employer's liability for injuries
caused by the incompetency of a fellow-servant depends upon
such incompetency being established by affirmative proof, and
that it was known to the master, or that, if he had exercised due
and proper diligence, he would have learned of such incompetency. In exercising this supervision by the master, to ascertain whether the servant is competent, the nature of the service
and the dangers attending it should be considered. A closer supervision over the habits, competency, and conduct of an engineer is required than over a common laborer, for the obvious reason that the dangerous consequences of neglect are likely to be
so much greater in the one case than in the other; the rule being,
the greater the danger, the greater the care. It is the duty of the
party charging incompetency and negligence to establish the fact
by proof. This may be done by showing specific acts of incompetency [185] and bringing them home to the knowledge of the
master, or by showing such acts of incompetency and negligence
of the servant to be of such a character and frequency that the
master, in the exercise of due and reasonable care, must have had
them brought to his notice. After proof of incompetency of the
servant is shown, the fact of incompetency may also be shown
by the general reputation; but, when reputation alone is relied
upon, it should be so generally known that inquiry would disclose it. When repeated acts of carelessness are shown on the
part of the servant, it then becomes proper to leave the question

to the jury to determine whether or not they did come to the
knowledge of the master, or would have come to his knowledge
had he used reasonable care: Bailey on Master's Liability, 47-C1;
Monahan v. Worcester, 150 Mass. 439; 15 Am. St. Rep. 226;
Hilts v. Chicago etc. Ry. Co., 55 Mich. 444; Laning v. New York
Cent. R. R. Co., 49 N. Y. 521; 10 Am. Rep. 417.

It is apparent from the facts above stated that the injury
would not have happened but for the negligence of the station
tender in leaving the chairs in the shaft, and of Adamson, the engineer, in not discovering the fact. These two acts contributed
to cause the accident. Without these two concurrent acts the accident would not have happened. The question now arises, Did
the incompetency of Adamson and his carelessness contribute, in
a legal sense, to the cause of the injury. Bailey on Master's Liability, page 433, states the rule to be: "When the injury is the
result of two concurrent causes, one party is not exempt from full
liability, although another party was equally culpable"; Wharton on Negligence, sec. 144, states the rule to be: "The fact that
another person contributed, either before the defendant's interposition, or concurrenty with such interposition, in producing
the damage, is no defense." Care must be taken in applying the
rule to distinguish [186] between concurring causes and intervening causes. "The negligence of each person is a proximate cause
where the injury would not have occurred but for that negligence; and it is no answer that the negligence or trespass of a
third person contributed to the injury. And this is true although
the party contributing by his negligence was acting without concert with, and entirely independent of, the party to whom the
cause is attributable in the first instance. The reason of the rule
lies in the fact that the effects produced by two or more concurrent
causes cannot be separated, and the damages apportioned; that,
because such may be the case, the injured party should not be
refused redress. The rule always has been, in case of joint tort
feasors, that either or all are liable." In case the injury is caused
by accident, and the defendant's negligence concurs to the extent that the accident would not have happened but for such
negligence, he is liable for the consequences. "The distinction
between concurring causes and intervening causes lies, not so
much in the character of the act done or omitted, but its effect
upon the result—the difference between contribution and cause
and effect; and to this it must be added that the concurrent or
succeeding negligence must break the sequence of events to make
the cause one of intervention. The only available test is, Did

the intervening cause, whether animate or inanimate, break the
sequence of events? If so, it is a case of intervening negligence;
otherwise, a case of co-operating, concurring, or contributory
negligence": Bailey on Master's Liability, 435, 436; Illidge v.
Goodwin, 5 Car. & P. 190; Cooley on Torts, 153; Eaton v. Boston etc. R. R. Co., 11 Allen, 500; 87 Am. Dec. 730; Milwaukee etc.
Ry. Co. v. Kellogg, 94 U. S. 474; Atkinson v. Goodrich Transp.
Co., 60 Wis. 141; 50 Am. Rep. 352; Grand Trunk Ry. Co. v. Cummings, 106 U. S. 700; Johnson v. Northwestern etc. Exchange
Co., 48 Minn. 433. In Wright v. Southern Pac. [187] Co., 14 Utah,
383, this court held "that, when the negligence of the employer
and that of a fellow-servant combine to produce an injury to a
servant, the employer will be liable in damages to the injured servant": Shearman and Redfield on Negligence, 187; Bailey on
Master's Liability, 439.

The facts found in the case on the part of the plaintiff must be
deemed to be admitted for the purpose of this discussion, as the
case was not submitted to the jury. The negligence complained
of in this respect was in keeping Adamson in the employ of the
defendant after it knew or was chargeable with notice that he
was an incompetent and careless engineer, and that his negligence and inefficiency contributed to cause the injury. The first
act of negligence was on the part of Breen, who left the chairs
in the shaft. The act of Adamson, the engineer, was subsequent
in point of time, yet his act of negligence, if it was such, was continuing negligence, which co-operated and acted with the negligent acts of Breen to produce the common result complained of.
Although Breen was negligent, yet if the defendant was chargeable with notice of Adamson's incompetency, and, through his
negligence was therefore wanting in ordinary care and prudence in discharging its duties, and such want of ordinary care
contributed to produce the injury in question, and the plaintiff
did not know of such want of ordinary care and prudence on the
part of the defendant, then the defendant would be liable. The
mere fact of the concurrence of one who stands in the relation of
a fellow-servant and the one receiving the injury does not excuse
the master from his contributory negligence. The injury was
the result of two concurring causes, and if the defendant is responsible for or contributed to one of these causes, he is not exempt from liability, because Breen, who is responsible for the
other cause, may have been [188] also culpable. The servant assumes the risk of the negligence of the fellow-servant, but not
that of the master: Union Pac. Ry. Co. v. Callaghan, 56 Fed.

Rep. 988; Lane v.. Atlantic Works, 111 Mass. 136; Lake v. Milliken, 62 Me. 240; 16 Am. Rep. 456; Grand Trunk Ry. Co. v. Cummings, 106 U. S. 700; Bailey on Master's Liability, 437.

There was some testimony in the case tending to show the incompetency of Adamson, the engineer, and that defendant was negligent in keeping him in its employ after it had knowledge of his incompetency. While we express no opinion upon the weight to be given to this testimony, yet we are of the opinion that, under all the facts shown, the case should have been submitted to the jury. The judgment of the court below is vacated and set aside, and a new trial granted.

Zane, C. J., and Bartch, J., concur.

MASTER AND SERVANT—CARE NECESSARY IN SELECTION OF SERVANTS.—A master owes to each of his servants the duty of using reasonable care and caution in the selection of competent fellow-servants, and in retaining only those who are. If he fails to perform this duty, and an injury is occasioned by the negligence of an incompetent or careless servant, the master is responsible to the injured employé, not for the mere negligent act or omission of the incompetent or careless servant, but for his own negligence in not discharging his own duty toward the injured servant: Norfolk etc. R. R. Co. v. Hoover, 79 Md. 253; 47 Am. St. Rep. 392, and note; Chicago etc. R. R. Co. v. Champion, 9 Ind. App. 510; 53 Am. St. Rep. 357. As to what will charge a master with knowledge of his servant's unfitness and render him responsible for his negligence: St. Louis Ry. Co. v. Hackett, 58 Ark. 381; 41 Am. St. Rep. 105; Campbell v. Cook, 86 Tex. 630; 40 Am. St. Rep. 878, and note.

NEGLIGENCE — LIABILITY FOR — PROXIMATE CAUSE.—A cause of action for negligence is not made out without proving that the negligence charged was the proximate cause of the injury: Brotherton v. Manhattan Beach Imp. Co., 48 Neb. 563; 58 Am. St. Rep. 709, and note. If the original act was wrongful, and would naturally, according to the ordinary course of events, prove injurious to others, and actually results in injury through the intervention of other causes not wrongful, the injury must be referred to the wrongful cause: Wood v. Pennsylvania R. R. Co., 177 Pa. St. 306; 55 Am. St. Rep. 728, and note.

MASTER AND SERVANT—CONCURRENT NEGLIGENCE OF MASTER AND FELLOW-SERVANT—LIABILITY OF MASTER. If the negligence of a master combines with that of a fellow-servant, and the two contribute to the injury of another servant, he may recover damages of the master: Railroad v. Spence, 93 Tenn. 173; 42 Am. St. Rep. 907; Bluedorn v. Missouri Pac. Ry. Co., 108 Mo. 439; 32 Am. St. Rep. 615, and note.

JUNGK v. HOLBROOK.

[15 UTAH, 198.]

SURETIES AND GUARANTORS, CONCEALMENT OF FACTS FROM.—If, on obtaining the signature of persons as sureties, guarantors, or indorsers, there is fraudulent concealment of any fact or circumstance materially affecting the liability of such surety, guarantor, or indorser, and operating to his prejudice, he is released from liability as against any creditor having knowledge of, or reasonably chargeable with notice of, such concealed fact or circumstance.

SURETY OR GUARANTOR, FAILURE TO DISCLOSE MATERIAL FACTS TO.—Noncommunication by a creditor to a surety of material facts within the knowledge of the former and which the latter should know, although not willful or intentional on the part of the creditor, discharges the surety.

SURETY OR GUARANTOR—FAILURE TO DISCLOSE FACTS.—The test as to whether a disclosure should be voluntarily made by a creditor of one who is about to become a surety for a debt is, whether there is a contract between the debtor and the creditor to the effect that the position of the surety shall be different from that which he might expect.

SURETY OR GUARANTOR, CONTRACTING WITHOUT NOTICE OF PARTNERSHIP BETWEEN THE DEBTORS AND CREDITORS, OR SOME OF THEM.—If a person is asked to become a surety on a contract for one firm in favor of another, and thereafter assents and becomes such surety, and it subsequently appears that the person thus asking and procuring him to become such surety was a silent partner in both firms and interested on both sides of the contract, and each of the firms had notice or knowledge sufficient to put them upon inquiry respecting this dual relation of their silent partner, the surety is released on the ground of the concealment from him of facts materially affecting the contract for the performance of which he became surety.

A CONSTITUTIONAL PROVISION SHOULD NOT BE CONSTRUED so as to have a retroactive operation, unless this is the unmistakable intention of the words used.

Bennett, Harkness, Howat & Bradley and Williams, Van Cott & Sutherland, for the appellants.

Brown, Henderson & King, for the respondents.

[205] MINER, J. This case was twice before the territorial court prior to this appeal. The cases are reported in Jungk v. Reed, 9 Utah, 49, and 12 Utah, 209. Upon each occasion the record discloses a somewhat dissimilar state of facts. The case now presents a somewhat different state of facts from those presented on the last appeal, so far as appears from the opinion rendered. The first question arises upon the charge of the court as given, and the refusal of [206] the court to charge as requested. In some respects the testimony bearing upon the question involved is somewhat indefinite and unsatisfactory. The jury were the judges of its weight and conclusiveness, and found against

the plaintiffs. There are sufficient facts and circumstances disclosed in the record from which the jury could infer or find that Jungk, Fabian, and Scott were partners for the purpose of purchasing sheep, and that Jungk and Fabian knew at the time, or were chargeable with notice, that Scott was a partner with Cropper and Reed, or at least interested with them in the contracts for the purchase and sale of sheep to them; that Cropper, Reed, and Scott were partners in the purchase and sale of sheep to Jungk and Fabian; that Cropper and Reed knew, or were chargeable with notice, that Scott was a partner or interested in the contract for the purchase of sheep with Jungk and Fabian; that defendants Holbrook and Duggins were wholly ignorant of the double relation existing between Scott and the two firms at the time they signed the guaranty contract and the notes given in pursuance of it, and would not have executed the contract or indorsed the notes had the true state of facts been made known to them by either firm; that the concealment of these facts and circumstances immediately affected the liability of the sureties; that Cropper and Reed and Jungk and Fabian fraudulently withheld from the sureties the true state of facts existing between them and Scott when the indorsements were made; that each of these firms knew that Scott was their partner in the transactions with the other firm, and that the sureties were making the indorsement in ignorance of the relation; that Jungk and Fabian sent Scott, as their agent and representative, to obtain the signatures of Holbrook and Duggins to [207] the contract; that Scott was their partner at the time; that Jungk and Fabian knew, or were chargeable with notice, that Cropper, Reed, and Scott owned sheep together at Oasis, and had them there when Fabian was present; that Reed and Cropper and Jungk and Fabian, knowing the facts, induced the sureties to sign the notes, and fraudulently withheld from them the double relation of Scott, as affecting their interest and liability.

If, in obtaining the signatures of these defendants to the contract of suretyship, or as indorsers of the notes made in continuation of their supposed liability, there was any fraudulent concealment on the part of Cropper and Reed and Jungk and Fabian, or either of said firms, of any fact or circumstance within their knowledge, or concerning which they were reasonably chargeable with notice, which materially affected and increased the liability and responsibility of Holbrook and Duggins as sureties or indorsers in those transactions in which they were sureties, and operated to their prejudice, then the sureties should be discharged. "It has been held that the mere noncommunication by the creditor to the surety of material facts within the knowledge of the creditor which the surety should know, although not willful or intentional on the part of the creditor, or with a view to advantage to himself, will discharge the surety." The fraud upon the sureties consists in the situation in which they were placed by the conduct of the other parties, and not on what was passing in their minds, not expressed, but concealed. Upon this subject, Brandt on Suretyship, section 420, says: "It has been held that 'one who becomes surety for another must ordinarily be presumed to do so upon the belief that the transaction between the principal parties is one occurring in the usual course of business of that description, subjecting ²⁰⁸ him only to the ordinary risks attending it; and the party to whom he becomes a surety must be presumed to know that such will be his understanding, and that he will act upon it unless he is informed that there are extraordinary circumstances affecting the risk. To receive a surety known to be acting upon the belief that there are no unusual circumstances by which his risks will be materially increased, well knowing that there are such circumstances, and having an opportunity to make them known, and withholding them, must be regarded as a legal fraud, by which the surety will be relieved from his contract.' " It is also held that, in order to discharge the surety, the undisclosed information should relate to business which is the subject of suretyship. Story says: "The contract of surety imports entire good faith and confidence between the parties in regard to the whole transaction. Any concealment of material facts, or any express or implied misrepresentation of such facts, or any undue advantage taken of the surety by the creditor, either by surprise or by withholding proper information, will undoubtedly furnish a sufficient ground to invalidate the contract. Upon the same ground, the creditor is, in all subsequent transactions with the debtor, bound to equal good faith to the surety": Story's Equity Jurisprudence, sec. 324; Franklin Bank v. Cooper, 36 Me. 179; Brandt on Suretyship, secs. 419-421; Comstock v. Gage, 91 Ill. 328; Franklin Bank v. Stevens, 39 Me. 532; Jungk v. Reed, 9 Utah, 49; Peck v. Durett, 9 Dana, 486; Pidcock v. Bishop, 3 Barn. & C. 605; 1 Law Lib. 87; Doughty v. Savage, 28 Conn. 146; Railton v. Mathews, 10 Clark & F. 934; Warren v. Branch, 15 W. Va. 21.

It is said that the "test as to whether the disclosure should be voluntarily made is whether there is a contract between the debtor and creditor to the effect that his position shall be a different one from that which [209] the surety might expect": Hamilton v. Watson, 12 Clark & F. 109.

These sureties did not know that Scott was a partner of each firm on the contract concerning which they were sureties, and did not indorse with the knowledge that they were becoming liable for the acts of Scott in the manipulation of the business of the several firms. They signed as sureties for Cropper and Reed, relying upon their integrity, and not as sureties for Cropper, Reed, and Scott. When they signed, they were not informed that a member of both firms had laid plans with each, by which the sureties should be robbed, and Cropper and Reed ruined, for the benefit of one member of the several firms. Nor did the sureties know that Cropper and Reed and Jungk and Fabian were either passive or active agents in such resulting dishonesty. Neither did the sureties know that Jungk and Fabian knew that Scott was interested with Cropper and Reed in the sale of sheep, nor that Cropper and Reed knew that Scott was interested with Jungk and Fabian in the purchase of sheep. If a material fact connected with the contract of suretyship, and directly affecting the sureties' liability, which might influence the sureties in entering into the contract, is concealed from the sureties, or, if knowing the fact, such information is purposely concealed from the sureties, in the interest of the creditor, such concealment, though no inquiry is made by the sureties, amounts to a fraud upon the sureties, and would discharge them from liability. Under all the facts and circumstances shown for the consideration of the jury, they have found the facts against the appellants. We find no reversible error in the instructions of the court, nor is there any error in refusing to give the instructions asked by the plaintiffs.

[210] Prior to the trial, plaintiffs moved the district court for Utah county for an order transferring said cause for trial to Salt Lake county. The motion was based upon an affidavit showing that plaintiffs owned the notes, and had resided in Salt Lake county since they were given, and that they were payable at Salt Lake. The motion was overruled, and an exception taken. The motion is based on section 7 of article 24, and section 5 of article 8, of the constitution. Plaintiffs resided in Salt Lake City when they commenced this action in the first district court in Utah county, January 10, 1891. This case had been tried in that county three times prior to the last trial, which occurred October 9, 1896. The defendants resided in Provo, Utah county. Section 5 of article 8 of the constitution provides, among other things,

that all civil and criminal business arising in any county must be tried in such county, unless a change of venue be taken, in such cases as may be provided by law. Section 7 of article 24 of the constitution provides, among other things, that all actions and cases pending in the district and supreme courts of the territory at the time the state is admitted into the Union shall, except as otherwise provided, be transferred to the supreme court and district courts of the state. Section 2 of article 24 of the constitution provides that all laws of the territory now in force, and not repugnant to the constitution, shall remain in force until they expire of their own limitation, or are altered or repealed by the legislature. Section 5 of article 8 of the constitution is only prospective in its operations, and therefore does not apply to actions which were commenced and pending in the territorial district courts when the constitution went into effect. A constitutional provision should not be construed with a retrospective operation, unless that is the unmistakable intention [211] of the words used: Black on Constitutional Law, 70; Endlich on Interpretation of Statutes, sec. 506; Watt v. Wright, 66 Cal. 202; Gurnee v. Superior Court, 58 Cal. 88; People v. County Commrs. of Grand Co., 6 Colo. 204; Lehigh Iron Co. v. Lower Macungie Tp., 81 Pa. St. 484.

Section 2 of article 24 of the constitution continues in force, under the state, such territorial laws as were not repugnant to it, and thereby makes them state laws. This court so held in Whipple v. Henderson, 13 Utah, 474; Pleasant Val. Coal Co. v. Board of Commrs., 15 Utah, 97. Among the laws of the territory then in force with reference to the place of trial were sections 3193 to 3201 of the Compiled Laws of Utah of 1888, which were amended (Sess. Laws 1896, p. 90) by making these sections conform to the new condition of things under the constitution. The territorial act was substantially re-enacted after striking out the words "judicial district," and substituting the word "county." The act was approved and took effect February 17, 1896, before this motion was made. This act provides where cases shall be commenced and tried, and when and where they may be removed for trial. Section 3196 provides that "in all other cases the action must be tried in the county in which the defendants, or some of them, reside at the commencement of the action." When this action was commenced, the plaintiffs resided in Salt Lake, and the defendants in Utah county. The first district formerly comprised Utah and several other counties. Under the new constitution, Utah county is made distinct by itself. The action was brought in pursuance of law in the proper county under the statute as it then existed. This statute was continued in force until changed by the act of 1896. We are of the opinion that the district court of Utah county properly assumed jurisdiction in this case. We [212] find no reversible error in the proceedings. The judgment of the district court is affirmed, with costs.

Zane, C. J., concurs.

Hart, D. J., concurs in the result.

SURETYSHIP — EXONERATION OF SURETY — CONCEALMENT.—Fraudulent concealment of facts from the principal will not discharge the surety necessarily; the concealment which entirely discharges a surety is one of facts not known to him, and known to the other party to be of a character to materially increase the risk beyond that assumed in the usual course of business of that kind, he having a suitable opportunity to make them known to the surety: Bryant v. Crosby, 36 Me. 562; 58 Am. Dec. 767. See Brown v. Wright, 7 T. B. Mon. 396; 18 Am. Dec. 190. As to what will release or discharge a surety, see extended note to Scott v. Fisher, 28 Am. St. Rep. 691, 692.

CONSTITUTIONS—RETROACTIVE EFFECT.—Neither constitutions nor statutes should be so construed as to have a retroactive effect, unless such intention is clearly expressed: Kirby v. Western Union Tel. Co., 4 S. Dak. 105; 46 Am. St. Rep. 765; Strickler v. Colorado Springs, 16 Colo. 61; 25 Am. St. Rep. 245, and note.

In re Handley's Estate.

[15 Utah, 212.]

CONSTITUTIONAL LAW — JUDGMENTS, POWER OF LEGISLATURE TO DIRECT A NEW TRIAL OR A REHEARING.—A statute declaring that the children of polygamous marriages are entitled to inherit as heirs of their father, and that in all cases ! heretofore determined adverse to such right, a motion for a new trial or a rehearing shall be entertained on application of such issue at any time within one year after the statute takes effect, is unconstitutional. After a court has rendered its judgment, the legislature cannot affect it by enacting a declaratory or explanatory law giving the law under which the judgment was rendered a different construction from that given it by the court.

CONSTITUTIONAL LAW—FORBIDDEN EXERCISE OF JUDICIAL POWERS BY THE LEGISLATURE.—A statute enacted after the parties to a judgment have lost the right to a rehearing or a new trial, in effect requiring the courts to grant a new trial or a rehearing, if applied for within one year after the passage of the statute, is an attempted exercise by the legislature of judicial powers, and is therefore void.

CONSTITUTIONAL LAW, LEGISLATIVE POWER TO DECLARE THE MEANING OF A STATUTE.—If the courts have construed a statute and declared its meaning, the legislature cannot thereafter, by a second statute, compel a different construction to be given to the first, so as to affect pre-existing judgments or rights dependent thereon.

Sutherland & Murphy and J. W. Judd, for the petitioners.

Dey & Street and W. H. Bramel, for the respondent.

[214] ZANE, C. J. It appears from this record that the late George Handley was a resident of Salt Lake City; that he died on the twenty-fifth day of May, 1874, leaving a lawful wife, Elizabeth Handley, and a polygamous wife, Sarah A. Chapman, and the following children: John Handley, William Handley, Charles J. Handley, and Emma N. Handley, of the lawful marriage, and Ruth A. Newson, Benjamin T. Handley, Mary F. Handley, and Harvey F. Handley, of the plural marriage; that both wives and all of the children [215] except Mary Handley are still living; that he died seised of real estate estimated to be of the value of twenty-five thousand nine hundred and sixteen dollars and ninety-two cents; that on April 12, 1888, his widow, Elizabeth Handley, was appointed administratrix of her husband's estate by the probate court; and that she filed an inventory and final account as such. It also appears that the surviving children of the plural wife, and their mother, as the heir of the deceased Mary, filed their petition in said court, asking that the children of the polygamous marriage be recognized as lawful heirs of their father, and that his estate be divided in equal parts among the children of both marriages. After hearing the evidence and proofs, the court made findings of fact and stated its conclusions of law to the effect that the petitioners were not entitled, under the law, to any part of the estate of the deceased father, and entered a decree accordingly, and for costs. It further appears that the petitioners appealed to the supreme court of the territory of Utah, and upon a hearing in that court the decision of the lower court was affirmed, with costs, on July 28, 1890 (In re Handley's Estate, 7 Utah, 49); that the petitioners then appealed to the supreme court of the United States, and the appeal was dismissed for the want of jurisdiction, and its mandate was sent down to the supreme court of the territory, and the latter issued its mittimus or mandate to the district court. After the lapse of six years from the expiration of the time within which a motion for a rehearing could be made under the rules of the supreme court of the territory or of this state, the legislature of the state of Utah passed the act in force March 9, 1896, in pursuance of which the petitioners present this motion for a rehearing. The statute is as follows:

"Section 1. That section 2742 of the Compiled Laws of the territory of Utah included when enacted and [216] effectually operated at all times thereafter and now operates to include the

issue of bigamous and polygamous marriages, and entitles all such
issue to inherit, as in said section provided, except such as are not
included in the provision in section 11, of the act of Congress
called the 'Edmunds-Tucker Act,' entitled 'An act to amend an
act entitled "An act to amend section 5352" of the Revised Statutes of the United States, in reference to bigamy and for other
purposes.'

"Sec. 2. That in all cases involving the rights of such issue to
so inherit, heretofore determined adversely to such issue in any
of the courts of the territory of Utah, a motion for a new trial or
rehearing shall be entertained, on application of such issue who
was or were parties at any time, within one year after this act
shall take effect; and the case or cases in which said motion is so
directed to be heard shall be deemed to be transferred to the
courts of the state of Utah corresponding to that of the territory
of Utah, in which such adverse decision was made, and the courts
shall thereupon proceed to hear and determine said motion, and,
if granted, to proceed to hear and determine said case or cases
without prejudice from lapse of time since the former hearing or
any prior determination of a like motion; provided, that this act
shall not be construed to affect the rights of bona fide purchasers
from any such parties before the approval of this act."

Handley, the ancestor, died in 1874, ten years before section
2742 mentioned in the act became a law, and its meaning, operation, and effect declared by the act quoted. An act of the territorial legislature of March 3, 1852, was in force when the father
and polygamous husband died. By that law the court determined the rights of the parties to his estate by the decree which
the petitioners seek to [217] set aside. This decree gave the entire estate to the children of the lawful wife, and it became final
after the time for filing a petition for rehearing had passed. If
it were conceded that the right of the children of the plural wife
to inherit a portion of their deceased father's estate should have
been determined by section 2742 of the Compiled Laws, and the
decree sought to be set aside had been rendered under it, section
1 of the act of March 9, 1896, could have no effect upon that decree, because it became final six years before that law took effect.
After the court has interpreted or construed a statute on the trial
of a case, and rendered judgment, the legislature cannot affect it
by a declaratory or explanatory law, giving the law under which
the decree was rendered a different construction. To hold that
the legislature can would recognize the law-making department
as a court of errors, with power to overturn all judgments and

decrees depending upon the interpretation or the construction of statutes. The purpose of separating and classifying the powers of government, and of intrusting the law-making power to the officers of one department and the right to execute laws to another, and the power to interpret and construe and apply laws to the conduct and contentions of mankind to another, was to prevent the evils that would arise if all were concentrated and held by the same hand. Such a concentration of power would give to the class of officers possessing it absolute power and that would amount to a despotism.

The second section of the act upon which the petitioners rely is subject to fatal objections. That section declares that in all cases involving the right of polygamous children to inherit, determined against them before the act in any of the courts of the territory, a motion for a new trial or rehearing shall be entertained on their application, [218] who were parties, at any time within one year after the act took effect. The court is required by it to entertain the motion for a new trial or rehearing regardless of when the judgment or decree became final. And the section further declares that such cases shall be deemed transferred from the territorial court to the state court. The state court is then directed to hear and determine the motion, and, if granted, to hear and determine the case without prejudice from the lapse of time since the former hearing, or any prior determination of a like motion. The court is peremptorily commanded by the legislature to entertain the motion for a new trial or rehearing upon the application of the polygamous issue, no matter what reasons may be brought to the attention of the court or may appear for not entertaining it. Though a final hearing may have been entered twenty-five years before, the motion must be entertained. If the right to inherit was decided against a polygamous issue, no matter for what reason, the legislature has decided the new trial must be entertained. The court is denied all discretion or right to judge for itself, as to its jurisdiction or otherwise. It is commanded to proceed at once, without first hearing any reasons or listening to any argument one way or the other. And, if a rehearing or new trial is granted, the court is directed to proceed to hear the case without prejudice from the lapse of time since the former hearing, or any prior determination, though the case may have been tried on such evidence, and a decree rendered a generation before. The court is forbidden by the act to take such matters into consideration; all laches and limitations must be disregarded. Under the territorial law, the right to a new trial was lost unless the motion was served and filed with the clerk of the court within ten days after the verdict, or, in case of a [219] trial by the court within ten days after notice of its decision; and the same rule exists under the state. And a right to a rehearing in the supreme court under the territory was lost unless the petition was filed within twenty days after the decision, and this is also a rule of the supreme court of the state. According to this act, any number of years may have intervened. The act in question appears to be a plain attempt on the part of the legislature to exercise judicial powers. Section 1 of article 5 of the state constitution declares: "The powers of the government of the state of Utah shall be divided into three distinct departments, the legislative, the executive, and the judicial; and no person charged with the exercise of powers properly belonging to one of these departments, shall exercise any functions appertaining to either of the others, except in the case herein expressly directed or permitted." Section 1 of article 8 of the same instrument is as follows: "The judicial powers of the state shall be vested in the senate, sitting as a court of impeachment, in a supreme court, in district courts, in justices of the peace, and such other courts inferior to the supreme court as may be established by law." The senate, while sitting as a court of impeachment, has judicial authority, so far as necessary, to try such issues. Otherwise the constitution has not intrusted any part of the judicial power of the state to the legislature. The petitioners claim that the provisions of the second section relate alone to the remedy. When the estate of the deceased, Handley, was ready for distribution, the four children of the lawful wife claimed all of it, while the four children of the plural marriage claimed the right to one-half of it. This made it the duty of the court to ascertain the heirs—the persons entitled to inherit. The remedy provided by law was employed, [220] and the issue was tried, and upon the evidence heard, and the law as interpreted, construed, and applied to the facts, the court found the entire estate to belong to the four children of the lawful wife, and entered a decree accordingly. That decree was affirmed by the court of last resort, and it became final when the twenty days given within which to file a petition for a rehearing expired—six years before the act of 1896 in question. That decree determined the interests of the children of the lawful wife to the estate in litigation, and gave them an immediate right to its possession. The remedy was exhausted, and the rights of the parties were established by that decree, and the title to the entire estate was vested in the four children of the lawful wife.

The right was a vested one.   It was finally ascertained and settled by the decree beyond the power of the court or the legislature to unsettle or divert it.   The remedy which the law afforded the petitioners was employed by them, and it had completed its work. It was exhausted six years before the legislative enactment upon which they rely.   After the decree became final, there remained no legal right to be enforced by the remedy which the act attempted to provide, or any legal wrong to be redressed.   The legislature attempted by a retrospective act to furnish a method by which vested rights could be devested, and to compel the courts to employ it.   The rights of the children of the lawful wife to the estate in question were ascertained and settled by the decree. Thereafter their rights were subject to no contingency.   They were completed and consummated.   They were vested, and beyond the reach of any remedy the court could employ or the legislature could invent.   No retroactive, explanatory, or declaratory enactment thereafter could have any effect upon them.   The court, having tried the case, construed the law in force [221] at the time; and, having applied it to the facts, and entered a final decree, the legislature could not afterward, by a declaratory or explanatory act as to that case, give to the law a different construction, requiring a different decree, and invent a new remedy or change the old one, and require the court to retry the case and enter a new decree according to its new construction, and new and changed remedy.

If we were to affirm the validity of the law in question, we would, in effect, say that the legislature may exercise judicial powers, authorize and require the courts to set aside final judgments and decrees, devest titles, and destroy and annihilate vested rights.   The people of the state have not intrusted such powers to the legislature: Cooley's Constitutional Limitations, 6th ed., 111; Merrill v. Sherburne, 1 N. H. 199; 8 Am. Dec. 52; De Chastellux v. Fairchild, 15 Pa. St. 18; 53 Am. Dec. 570; Reiser v. William Tell etc. Assn., 39 Pa. St. 137; Hooker v. Hooker, 10 Smedes & M. 599; Moser v. White, 29 Mich. 59; Gilman v. Tucker, 128 N. Y. 190; 26 Am. St. Rep. 464; People v. Board of Supervisors, 16 N. Y. 424.

Judge Cooley (Cooley's Constitutional Limitations, 111) says: "It is always competent to change an existing law by a declaratory statute, and, where the statute is only to operate upon future cases, it is no objection to its validity that it assumes the law to have been in the past what it is now declared that it shall be in the future.   But the legislative action cannot be made to retroact upon past controversies, and to reverse decisions which the courts, in the exercise of their undoubted authority, have made; for this would not only be the exercise of judicial power, but it would be its exercise in the most objectionable and offensive form, since the legislature would, in effect, sit as a court of review, to which parties might appeal when dissatisfied with the rulings of the courts." In Merrill v. [222] Sherburne, 1 N. H. 199, 8 Am. Dec. 52, the plaintiff claimed the estate of Nathaniel Ward by virtue of an instrument purporting to be his last will, which the heirs at law of Ward contested, and after a hearing the issues were found against Merrill, and in 1814, at the November term of the court, final judgment was rendered, disallowing the instrument. Merrill then petitioned the legislature for another trial, and they, at their June session, 1817, passed an act granting to the plaintiff, as administratrix of Merrill, then deceased, liberty to re-enter the cause in the superior court, and there have it tried like a common case for review; and upon due notice the case was entered upon the docket, and the heirs, appearing as defendants, moved the court to quash the proceedings on the ground that the act was unconstitutional. The court held the nature and effect of the act was judicial, that it was also retroactive, and that the legislature had no power to pass such an act, and quashed the proceedings. In a very learned opinion the court said, among other things: "Be that as it may, however, it is clearly unwarrantable thus to take from any citizen a vested right, a right 'to do certain actions, or possess certain things,' which he has already begun to exercise, or to the exercise of which no obstacle exists in the present laws of the land. . . . . But previous to the passage of the act granting a new trial to the plaintiff the defendant had become authorized by the laws of the land to possess all the estate of which Ward died seised. Every obstacle to the exercise of their rights had been removed or annulled; and whether their rights became vested by Ward's death, or by the final judgment in November, 1814, is immaterial, because both these events had happened before the passage of this act. . . . . The defendants being thus situated, the legislature interfered; not to enact what is in its nature and [223] effect a law, but to pass a decree; not to prescribe a rule for future cases, but to regulate a case which had already occurred; not to make a private statute by the consent of all concerned, but, at the request of one party to reverse and alter existing judgments; not to promulgate an ordinance for a whole class of rights in the community, but to make the action of a particular individual an exception to all standing laws on the subject in controversy. The expense and inconvenience of another trial were also imposed upon the defendants, and all their claims to the property in dispute, which had become indefeasible by the law then in being, were launched again upon the sea of litigation to be lost or saved, as accident and opinion might afterward happen to injure or befriend them. The misfortune of having vested rights thus disturbed is not small when we consider that on this principle no judgment whatever in a court of law is final."

In the case of Gilman v. Tucker, 128 N. Y. 190, 26 Am. St. Rep. 464, the court said: "We also think the act violated the constitutional guaranty, because it assumes to nullify a final and unimpeachable judgment, not only establishing the plaintiff's right to the premises in dispute, but also awarding him a sum of money as costs. After rendition, this judgment became an evidence of title, and could not be taken from the plaintiff without destroying one of the instrumentalities by which her title was manifested. A statute which assumes to destroy or nullify a party's muniments of title is just as effective in depriving him of his property as one which bestows it directly upon another. . . . . In the one case it despoils the owner directly, and in the other renders him defenseless against any assault upon his property. Authority which permits a party to be deprived of his property by indirection is as much within the meaning and spirit of the constitutional provision as [224] where it attempts to do the same thing directly. We are therefore of the opinion that the repugnancy between the law and the constitutional rights of the citizen is so irreconcilable that the law must fail."

The first section of the act of 1896 declared the operation and effect of section 2742 of the Compiled Laws of 1884, at the time it took effect, and at all times thereafter, included the issue of polygamous marriages, notwithstanding the court might have held in any given case it did not include such issue. The legislature assumed the right to declare the law had an operation and effect with respect to such cases, different from that which the court may have declared it had, and upon which it may have based its judgment. When the court construes the law, and holds it has a certain effect, and bases a judgment upon it, the legislature cannot declare that the law, as to that case, had any other effect than that declared by the court. By the second section of the act of 1896, the legislature decided and assumed that all judgments and decrees that had been entered involving the right of polygamous children to inherit were not final, and as-

sumed to direct the courts to disregard their effect as such, and
to entertain applications to set them aside, and assumed to command the state courts to deem such cases transferred, and to take
jurisdiction of them, to proceed to hear and determine such applications, and, if granted, to hear and determine the cases regardless of limitations or laches. In effect, the courts are required to disregard as final all judgments and decisions rendered
in such cases. We must hold the act of 1896 invalid, because in
its passage the legislature assumed to exercise judicial powers,
and also because they assumed the right to require the courts to
regard judgments as impeachable that were unimpeachable under
the laws in force at the time they [225] were rendered, and by
which vested rights were established and evidenced.

Miner, J., and Hart, D. J., concur.

LEGISLATURE—USURPING JUDICIAL POWER—ORDERING
NEW TRIAL.—The powers of the three departments of government
are not merely equal—they are exclusive in respect to the duties
assigned to each, and each is absolutely independent of the other:
State v. Noble, 118 Ind. 350; 10 Am. St. Rep. 143, and note. A legislature has no power to order a new trial, or to direct the court to
order it, either before or after judgment, such power being judicial:
De Chastellux v. Fairchild, 15 Pa. St. 18; 53 Am. Dec. 570, and note;
monographic note to State v. Hinman, 23 Am. St. Rep. 26. See
Gaines v. Gaines, 9 B. Mon. 295; 48 Am. Dec. 425. A statute awarding a new trial in an action already decided in a court of law is unconstitutional as an assumption of judicial power: Merrill v. Sherburne, 1 N. H. 199; 8 Am. Dec. 52. So with an act opening an existing judgment: Ratcliff v. Anderson, 31 Gratt. 105; 31 Am. Rep. 716.

STATUTES EXPOSITORY OF EXISTING STATUTES—RET-
ROACTIVE EFFECT.—A statute passed for the purpose of fixing
the interpretation to be given to an existing statute is unconstitutional if attempted to be applied retroactively to the peril of existing
vested rights: Haley v. Philadelphia, 68 Pa. St. 45; 8 Am. Rep. 153,
and note.

SALISBURY *v.* STEWART.

[15 Utah, 308.]

NEGOTIABLE INSTRUMENTS — ATTORNEYS' FEES,
STIPULATION FOR PAYMENT OF.—A note otherwise negotiable
in form, but containing a stipulation that, in the event of a suit to
enforce the collection of the note, or any part thereof, the maker will
pay an additional sum of ten per cent of the amount found to be due
as attorneys' fees in such suit, is not rendered non-negotiable by
such stipulation.

Young & Moyle and Rhodes & Tait, for the appellants.

Evans & Rogers and W. C. Hall, for the respondent.

[309] ZANE, C. J. This is an action upon a promissory note for three thousand five hundred dollars, [310] with interest at ten per cent per annum, executed by the defendants, and payable six months after its date to the order of John W. Taylor, the assignor of the plaintiff. It also contained the following stipulation: "And in the event of a suit to enforce the collection of this note, or any part thereof, we further agree to pay the additional sum of ten per cent upon the amount found due, as attorney's fees in said suit." Before its maturity the note was indorsed by the payee to the plaintiff. The defendants alleged in their answer, and offered to prove on the trial, that their signatures were obtained without consideration, by false statements of the payee, and promises which he did not perform, that would have been a defense to the collection of the note in his hands. The defendants assign as error the ruling of the court sustaining plaintiff's objection to their offer. The error alleged presents for our consideration and decision the question, Did the stipulation to pay ten per cent on the amount recovered, as an attorney's fee, in the event of a suit to collect it, included in the note, destroy its negotiability? While textwriters generally agree that such provisions do not affect the negotiability of notes, the question has given rise to much judicial controversy and difference of opinion, and it is impossible to reconcile the numerous decisions on the point. The question is new in this court, and we will endeavor to adopt the rule which our reason commends, and which we think is supported by the better line of authority. The makers of the note promised to pay the holders three thousand five hundred dollars, and interest thereon at ten per cent per annum. This payment was subject to no contingency. It was certain in every respect, and it remained so until a breach of the contract by the defendants. In case the makers should not keep their contract, and it should become necessary to institute suit upon the [311] note, the makers stipulated they would pay the necessary attorney's fee, and the law required them to pay the other costs. In that case the holder of the note would receive the three thousand five hundred dollars and the interest—precisely the amount the makers promised to pay him. In that event the holder would receive no more for his own use than he would have received had the makers paid according to their promise. It appears right that the parties whose default caused the expense should pay it; that it should not be imposed upon the party who kept his contract. The party who keeps a contract should receive from the one who breaks it compensation for his loss. If the defendants had kept

their contract, the holder would have received three thousand five hundred dollars and the interest. They not having done so, the stipulation and the law required the makers to pay him that amount, and no more, for his own use, and to pay the costs of the court and the attorney's fee. Only the costs of the court could have been charged against the defendants without the stipulation. The stipulation, in effect, also added the fee of the attorney, if one should be employed to bring the suit, to the costs imposed by the law upon the defendants. The fee is for the attorney. If the employment of an attorney does not become necessary, or if one is not employed, the court should not allow such a fee, and the allowance should not exceed the amount charged by the attorney. The allowance is not as a penalty, as interest, or as a bonus. It is simply to pay the costs of enforcing the collection of the note by suit. And, if none is charged, none should be allowed against the makers, and no more than is to be actually paid should be allowed against the makers. That is, in legal effect, the stipulation. The court should not allow the plaintiff, by deception, fraud, and false pretenses, to obtain money as an attorney's fee, and then appropriate [312] it to his own use. Plaintiff should not be allowed (as it is suggested they do sometimes) to call a penalty, additional interest, or a bonus, as an attorney's fee, and by such deception and fraud to induce the court to impose burdens on the makers of contracts—to oppress them in that way or any other. This reasoning proceeds on the presumption that the stipulation to pay the attorney's fee is not negotiable. In other words, the maker interposes the same defense to the attorney's fee when the note is in the hands of an indorsee who received it before due, for a valuable consideration, that he could have interposed if it had been sued upon by the payee. If the makers of the note in question had paid according to its terms, the stipulation for an attorney's fee would have been of no effect. A note becoming due in the hands of payee ceases to be negotiable in the sense that the indorsee takes it free from defenses before indorsement. The reason for the rule that the amount to be paid to the holder must be fixed and certain is that negotiable paper becomes a substitute for money, and for that reason it must indicate precisely how much money it represents. The note in question represented three thousand five hundred dollars and interest while it remained negotiable, and the stipulation further represented that, if suit should be brought, the costs of the remedy, including the attorney's fee, should be paid by its makers. The object óf this stipulation was to make the note represent to

the holder precisely the three thousand five hundred dollars and
interest. The amount of the court costs must depend upon the
services rendered by its officers, and the amount of the attorney's
fee must depend upon the amount to be paid him, or if suit is
brought without the employment of an attorney, as it may be,
no fees can be allowed. The amount to be recovered by the
holder of the note, which he may appropriate to his own use, is
more certain with [313] the stipulation than without it. Without
the stipulation the holder realizes the amount of the principal
and interest, less the attorney's fee, whatever that may be, when
the maker fails to comply with his contract, but with the stipulation he realizes the principal and interest named in the note.
The stipulation relates to the remedy, and not to the amount to
be recovered and appropriated by the holder to his own use.
The fact that the makers undertook to pay an attorney's fee if a
suit should be brought to enforce the collection of the note did
not render the note non-negotiable: 1 Daniel on Negotiable Instruments, sec. 62 a; Oppenheimer v. Bank, 87 Tenn. 19; 56 Am.
St. Rep. 778; Bank of Commerce v. Fuqua, 11 Mont. 285; 28
Am. St. Rep. 461; Gaar v. Louisville Banking Co., 11 Bush, 180;
21 Am. Rep. 209; Sperry v. Horr, 32 Iowa, 184; Second Nat.
Bank v. Anglin, 6 Wash. 403; Benn v. Kutzschan, 24 Or. 28.

In 1 Daniel on Negotiable Instruments, section 62 a, it is said:
"Such instruments should, we think, be upheld as negotiable.
They are not like contracts to pay money and do some other
thing. They are simply for the payment of a certain sum of
money at a certain time, and the additional stipulations as to
attorney's fees can never go into effect if the terms of the bill or
note are complied with. They are, therefore, incidental and
ancillary to the main engagement—intended to insure its performance, or to compensate for trouble and expense entailed by
its breach. At maturity negotiable paper ceases to be negotiable,
in the full commercial sense of the term, as heretofore explained,
though it still passes from hand to hand by the negotiable forms
of transfer; and it seems paradoxical to hold that instruments evidently framed as bills and notes are not negotiable during their
currency because when they cease to be current they contain a
stipulation to defray ·the expenses of collection." In Oppenheimer v. Bank, 87 Tenn. 19, 56 Am. St. Rep. 778; the following language is used: 'Upon a careful review [314] of the authorities, we can see no reason why a note otherwise imbued with
all the attributes of negotiability is rendered non-negotiable by
a stipulation which is entirely inoperative until after the maturity
of the note, and its dishonor by the maker. The amount to be

paid is certain during the currency of the note as a negotiable instrument, and it only becomes uncertain after it ceases to be negotiable by the default of the maker in its payment. It is eminently just that the creditor who has incurred an expense in the collection of the debt should be reimbursed by the debtor by whom the action was rendered necessary and the expense entailed." The judgment of the court below is affirmed.

Bartch and Miner, JJ., concur.

NEGOTIABLE INSTRUMENTS—EFFECT OF PROVISION TO PAY ATTORNEY'S FEES FOR COLLECTION.—A stipulation in a promissory note to pay all reasonable attorney's fees in case suit is brought to enforce payment does not destroy its negotiability: Oppenheimer v. Bank, 97 Tenn. 19; 56 Am. St. Rep. 778, and note; Nicely v. Commercial Bank, 15 Ind. App. 563; 57 Am. St. Rep. 245, and note. Upon this question, however, there is a difference of opinion, the principal case being opposed to Kendall v. Parker, 103 Cal. 319; 42 Am. St. Rep. 117; First Nat. Bank v. Babcock, 94 Cal. 96; 28 Am. St. Rep. 94, and note. See extended note to Witherspoon v. Musselman, 29 Am. Rep. 406.

McCLURE v. LITTLE.

[15 UTAH, 379.]

NEGOTIABLE INSTRUMENTS, ALTERATION OF WITHOUT AUTHORITY, WHEN DOES NOT MAKE VOID.—If there is a blank in a promissory note to be used for the purpose of naming the time when interest shall be payable, and it was the agreement of the parties that the words "semi-annually" should be inserted in such blank, but they were omitted by inadvertence, the act of the payee or his agent in subsequently filling out this blank to conform to such intention, though not authorized, is not fraudulent, and does not extinguish the debt nor estop the holder of the note from maintaining a suit to reform it so as to express the true intention of the parties.

ATTORNEYS' FEES ARE NOT RECOVERABLE under the statutes of Utah in favor of the plaintiff, unless they are shown to have been actually charged to, or paid by, him.

C. F. & F. C. Loofbourow, for the appellants.

Moyle, Zane & Costigan, for the respondent.

[382] MINER, J. Prior to 1890, defendant Smith and others owned Central Park, in Salt Lake, and sold it to one Andrews. In part payment Smith took two notes for twenty thousand dollars each secured by mortgage on the property. Plaintiff McClure bought the property subject to the mortgage. Negotiations afterward took place between Smith and McClure by which McClure agreed to give his notes, secured by trust deed on the prop-

erty, to Smith, and take up the encumbrance. The notes and trust deed were drawn up and delivered to McClure for him to take to Colorado for his wife's signature. They were afterward signed and returned to Smith by mail. The notes and trust deed were drawn upon printed blanks. The notes were all in the following form, except as to date of payment and amount:

"$16,250.00 gold.   Salt Lake City, Utah, October 1, 1891.

"One year after date, for value received, we, or either of us, promise to pay to the order of Elias A. Smith sixteen thousand two hundred fifty dollars negotiable and payable at the Deseret National Bank of Salt Lake City, [383] in U. S. gold coin, with interest at the rate of nine per cent per annum from date until paid. Interest payable ———.

"[Signed]   WILLIAM H. McCLURE.
                             "AMANDA M. McCLURE."

When the notes were delivered to Smith, the word "semi-annually" was left out of the blank following the words "interest payable." When Smith received the notes, October 21, 1891, he showed them to Mr. Young, who discovered that the word "semi-annually" was left out of the blank, and suggested the error. Smith remarked that it was a clerical error, and immediately wrote the word "semi-annually" in each note, so that they would read, "Interest payable semi-annually." Plaintiffs claim the word "semi-annually" was not in the trust deed when delivered to Smith, but the testimony is conflicting on this point. The notes and trust deed were made payable to Smith, with James T. Little as trustee, and contained the usual power. Smith was the indorser on the Andrews note. Smith and McClure were indorsing the new notes. Both were procuring the new loan for themselves as well as for the bank. While Smith was acting for the bank he had no authority from the bank officials to alter the notes. In July, 1893, proceedings were begun to foreclose this trust deed, by publication, on account of the nonpayment of the semi-annual interest falling due April 1, 1893. Thereupon plaintiffs brought this suit against Smith and Little, the trustee, to restrain the sale, and have the securities canceled and adjudged void on account of the alleged material and fraudulent alteration. Little and Smith answered, and admitted the alteration of the notes so as to conform to the agreement of the parties, by filling in the blank left, and that it was an immaterial alteration, done innocently with the plaintiffs' consent, and that the plaintiffs ratified the same. They denied any alteration in the deed. The Deseret Savings [384] Bank then filed its complaint in intervention, alleging that it became the owner of the notes after their execution, that at the time the notes were executed the makers agreed to pay interest at nine per cent per annum, payable semiannually, until paid, and set out therein the consideration therefor, but that by a clerical omission of the party making out said notes the word "semi-annually" was by mutual mistake and oversight left out of said notes from the blank left for that purpose; that other parties indorsed the notes as indorsers; that Smith was the cashier of the intervenor. Alleged that the notes had become due. Claimed one thousand dollars attorney's fees. Asked for a foreclosure of the trust deed; that the notes be reformed so as to include the words "semi-annually" in the blank left for that purpose in them, following the words "Interest payable"; for judgment, deficiency judgment, and for further relief. It appears from the proof that there was full value moving to the plaintiffs as a consideration for these notes. It clearly appears from the testimony that it was agreed between the parties at the time these notes and trust deed were drawn that they should draw interest at nine per cent per annum, payable semiannually, from date until paid, but by a clerical error of the draftsman, the word "semi-annually" was left out of the printed blank in the notes; that the notes were signed and returned to the payee, the mistake not being discovered until after they were signed and delivered by mail; when Smith saw the mistake, he said it was a mistake, and immediately filled the blank so as to have it conform to the agreement of the parties, supposing he had a right to do so. The change, however, was made without the consent of the makers, except that there was some slight testimony offered tending to show that plaintiffs afterward ratified the change by making payments of interest, [385] and offering to make part payment on one note. The testimony on all these questions was conflicting, but we are of the opinion that the contention on the part of the intervenor is sustained by a strong preponderance of the testimony. The alteration was made innocently, for the purpose of making the instrument conform to the understanding and agreement of the parties. It was not made fraudulently, for the purpose of injuring anyone. It does not sufficiently appear that the trust deed was altered in the respect mentioned. The alteration of the notes was a material alteration, but, as it was made under the circumstances mentioned, we are of the opinion that the prayer for reformation should be granted. A fraudulent alteration not only avoids the instrument itself, but also extinguishes the debt which constitutes the consideration for the instrument. But when the alteration was innocently made for the purpose of making the instrument conform to the agreement of the parties, without any fraudulent intent, and it appears that no one was injured by the filling of the blank left for that purpose, then the instrument is not annulled, nor the debt extinguished. We do not want it understood, however, that we approve of this method of tampering with written instruments for any purpose. This correction could more properly have been made by a court of equity. The alteration made was clearly improper, and should not have been made by Mr. Smith. In this case the intervenor sought to have the notes reformed in accordance with the understanding and agreement of the parties, and the word "semi-annually" inserted in the notes after the words "Interest payable," and the court so decreed. A court of equity has the power to so decree, and thereby restore the instrument to its original condition. We are of the opinion that under the statute the intervenor was entitled [883] to institute the proceedings in intervention, and that the court was correct in decreeing the relief asked, in reforming the notes so as to conform to the express agreement of the parties, and to grant a decree of foreclosure.

In this case the debtor seeks to avoid an honest debt because of the alteration, without offering to pay the same. It is a cardinal principle that equity will not aid a party in doing that which is not equitable. He who seeks equity must be prepared to do equity. A court of equity will hardly permit a debtor to get rid of a debt which he honestly owes, and which is based upon a valid consideration, because his creditor has innocently inserted a word in the contract that he had agreed should be inserted, even if the alteration was such as a court of law would not excuse: Taylor v. Adair, 22 Iowa, 279; Utah Comp. Laws 1888, sec. 3190; Nickerson v. Sweet, 135 Mass. 517; Tiedeman on Commercial Paper, secs. 392-395; McRaven v. Crisler, 53 Miss. 542; Boyd v. Brotherson, 10 Wend. 93; 2 Daniel on Negotiable Instruments, secs. 1403, 1404; Randolph on Commercial Paper, sec. 1765; Ball v. Stories, 1 Sim. & S. 210; Goodenow v. Curtis, 33 Mich. 505; First Nat. Bank v. Carson, 60 Mich. 432; Ames v. Colburn, 71 Am. Dec. 723; Duker v. Franz, 3 Am. Rep. 317; Ryan v. First Nat. Bank, 148 Ill. 349; Kountz v. Kennedy, 63 Pa. St. 187; 3 Am. Rep. 541; Seymour v. Mickey, 15 Ohio St. 515; 2 Parsons on Notes and Bills, 572.

Objection is made to the allowance of one thousand dollars attorney's fee. The note in suit did not provide for an attor-

ney's fee. The trust deed provides that the trustee may pay out
of the proceeds of sale the expenses of this trust, including a reasonable attorney and counsel fee, and compensation to said trustee, or his successor in trust, for his services. The proceeding
to foreclose the trust deed by advertisement was enjoined, and
the deed was foreclosed through these proceedings in intervention in equity. A witness was asked what a reasonable attorney's fee would [387] be in the case of McClure against Little and
Smith, with the bank as intervenor; such services being for the
filing of an answer to plaintiff's injunction in behalf of Little
and Smith, and hearing had on the motion to dissolve the injunction, lasting several days, and afterward a complaint in
intervention by the bank, asking reformation of the notes to the
original understanding, and foreclosure; involving about forty-
five thousand dollars, the hearing lasting several days; the question being what a reasonable attorney's or solicitor's fee would
be in both matters. The witness answered, "One thousand dollars." No other testimony was offered. No evidence was offered
on the subject of what was charged by or retained by the attorney. The objection to the question is that it comprehended
more than could be covered by attorney's fees. It included a
fee for the defense to the main injunction case, where no attorney's fee could be claimed, and attorney's fee as trustee, who had
claimed no fees; also attorney's fee for reformation of the notes
in the intervention proceedings by the bank, and is not a proper
basis for computation, and no attorney's fee should be charged.
The question comprehended more than could be legitimately
included in the foreclosure of the mortgage by the trustee. The
findings show that no attorney's fee was allowed in the original
proceeding, yet that proceeding was included as a basis for the
value of the services. The amount allowed was in excess of what
should have been allowed for attorney's fees in the case of intervention. Under the proof, much of the expense created is
the result of mistakes and errors of the intervenor or trustee.
Had the original proceedings been brought to reform and foreclose the notes and mortgage, only one proceeding would have
been necessary, with a consequent reduction of expense. There
is another reason why attorney's fees should not be allowed. [388]
Chapter 39, page 25, of the Session Laws of 1894 provides that,
when an attorney's or counsel fee is claimed by the plaintiff, no
greater amount should be allowed or decreed than the sum which
appears by the evidence to be actually charged by and paid to
the attorney for the plaintiff, and that only the amount to be

retained by the attorney shall be decreed. This statute was enacted to prevent a division of the fees provided for in the mortgage between the attorney and the mortgagee, and to allow only such reasonable attorney's fees to be taxed against the defendant as were actually agreed to be paid, or were paid, for his services. There was no proof showing what the attorney for plaintiffs actually charged, or what the agreement was he should receive from the plaintiffs. Consequently, no fees should have been allowed in the decree. No other construction can be placed upon the statute. Attorney's fees, when allowed, go to the mortgagee or trustee, and become a part of the judgment. The bank is responsible to the attorney for his fees, and will doubtless pay a sum equal to the amount it has asserted was a reasonable fee. We find no other error in the proceedings. The district court is instructed to modify the findings and decree, striking out the one thousand dollars attorney's fee. With this modification, the judgment and decree of the district court is affirmed, with costs.

Zane, C. J., concurs.

ALTERATION OF INSTRUMENTS — WHEN DOES NOT AVOID.—An alteration in a written contract, after its execution, though in a respect material to it, made in good faith, to correct it and to more nearly conform it to the agreement of the parties, and where such alteration could not possibly prejudice the other party, does not avoid the contract: Lee v. Butler, 167 Mass. 426; 57 Am. St. Rep. 466, and note; Foote v. Hambrick, 70 Miss. 157; 35 Am. St. Rep. 631, and note. But compare Otto v. Halff, 89 Tex. 384; 59 Am. St. Rep. 56, and note; Newman v. King, 54 Ohio St. 273; 56 Am. St. Rep. 705, and note.

COSTS—PROPER ITEMS IN ALLOWANCE OF ATTORNEY'S FEES.—Necessary costs and charges actually paid by a party in the course of a case are proper items of a cost bill: Cox v. Charleston etc. Ins. Co., 3 Rich. 331; 45 Am. Dec. 771. Under early statutes on the subject, costs mainly consisted of the fees allowed to attorneys and counsel for their services in the management of the proceeding. Nothing is recoverable as costs which has not been paid or liability for its payment actually incurred: Monographic note to Ela v. Knox, 88 Am. Dec. 181, 182.

SALT LAKE LITHOGRAPHING CO. *v.* IBEX MINE AND SMELTING CO.

[15 UTAH, 440.]

MECHANICS' LIEN — DISCONNECTED BUILDINGS.—A claim of lien can be filed and asserted upon several disconnected buildings without there being any account of the amount of materials furnished each, when they constitute part of a plant used in the business of smelting and are situated upon the same piece of ground.

MECHANICS' LIEN—BUILDING WHEN NOT COMPLETE. Though a smelter is otherwise completed, if there is afterward added to it a granulating flume which appears to have been necessary for the convenient and economical moving of slag, the time for the filing of the lien may be computed from the construction of such flume.

MECHANICS' LIEN, WAIVER OF.—The right to file and assert a mechanics' or attachment lien is not waived by obtaining and levying an attachment, if the lien of the attachment is not perfected and the action is subsequently dismissed.

Frank Pierce, for the appellant.

Frank B. Stephens, for the respondent.

[441] ZANE, C. J. This is an appeal by the defendant Mc-Cornick from so much of the decree entered by the trial court as adjudged that the lien set up in the cross-complaint of the Sierra Nevada Lumber Company was superior to the lien of the mortgage described in his complaint. The plaintiff, the Salt Lake Lithographing Company, filed its complaint against the defendants, in which it asked the court to appoint a receiver with authority to take possession of the property of the defendant, the Ibex Mine & Smelting Company, and convert it into money, and pay its debts according to their priority. The lumber company filed an answer and a cross-complaint in the cause, in which it alleged that it entered into a verbal contract with the Ibex Company on the fourteenth day of September, 1894, to furnish lumber and other building material, to be paid for as delivered, to be used in constructing a smelter, scales, assay office, flumes, ore bins, boardinghouse, and other appurtenances upon the land of the company—[442] describing it as one tract. It is also alleged that the smelter, scales, assay office, ore bins, boardinghouse, and other structures and appurtenances were to constitute, and did, when completed, constitute, one plant for smelting purposes; that in pursuance of the contract the lumber company furnished lumber and other material to the amount of six thousand seven hundred and twenty-eight dollars, used in the construction of the smelter and other parts of the plant on the piece of ground described; that the first material was delivered on September 14, 1894, and the last on March 27, 1895;

that notice of the lien was recorded May 25, 1895; that, after deducting all just credits, there still remained due two thousand six hundred and thirty-eight dollars, for which a first lien was alleged and claimed. The defendant McCornick also filed an answer and cross-complaint, in which he set up a mortgage executed to him by the Ibex Company on March 6, 1895, to secure a note of the mortgagor for sixty thousand dollars of the same date, recorded on the eleventh day of April of the same year. The lumber company denied that appellant had a lien superior to its own, and appellant denied that the lumber company had any lien; and if the court should find it had, he claimed his to be superior to it. It is conceded that the Ibex Company owned a mine for which the lumber company also delivered lumber, and the appellant claims that the accounts for material furnished for the respective plants were not kept separate, and that it cannot be ascertained how much should have been charged for materials furnished to each. While all the lumber and other material furnished to the Ibex Mining & Smelting Company to be used at the mine and at the smelter are contained in the same account, the items to be used at the mine and those to be used at the smelter are separate, and the charges for material to be used at each plant can be easily ascertained, and the court below found and allowed **443** only for that used in the construction of the smelter and other structures claimed to belong to that plant. The appellant also urges that the materials for which the lumber company claims its lien were used in several buildings, to wit, the smelter, the blowerhouse, the sampling mill, the ore bins, the boardinghouse, the superintendent's house, the blacksmith shop, the pug mill, the assay office, and the granulating flume; and that the charges for materials used in each structure should have been kept separately, and that they did not constitute a whole and that a lien could not be decreed on the entire premises for all. In effect, the appellant insists that a separate lien should have been decreed upon each structure, and the land occupied by it.

If each structure, and the land upon which it stands, could be used for separate purposes, and would be as valuable when so used as when used together as a smelting plant, there would be great force in the claim. But in view of the facts that the lumber was delivered under one contract, and the structures were all erected on the same piece of ground, and they were all to be used together in prosecuting the business of smelting—the same purpose, the same enterprise—we are of the opinion that a lien existed on the entire premises for the lumber used in each structure, and that one lien could be decreed thereon for the security of the entire bill, the aggregate: Phillips on Mechanics' Liens, 3d ed., sec. 229; Wall v. Robinson, 115 Mass. 429; Gilbert v. Fowler, 116 Mass. 375.

The appellant claims that the smelter was completed on January 29, 1895, and that the notice of the lien was not filed for record until May 25, 1895, and that the lumber company did not acquire a lien, because it did not file its notice within sixty days after completing the contract. The last item for material was delivered on March [444] 27, 1895, and was used in the construction of a granulating flume. The removal of the slag from the smelter was necessary, and it appears from the evidence that it could be most conveniently and economically done in the use of the flume. We are of the opinion that the court below did not err in allowing the item for lumber used in its construction, and that the lumber company had the notice recorded within the sixty days given by the statute after the completion of its contract.

It is also urged that the lumber company waived its right to the lien claimed by obtaining and levying an attachment upon the property of the Ibex Company for the same demand before filing its cross-complaint. It appears that the attachment lien was not perfected, and that it was dismissed. We are disposed to hold that the lien of the lumber company claimed in its cross-complaint was not waived by the institution of the attachment suit and levy of the writ: Brennan v. Swasey, 16 Cal. 141; 76 Am. Dec. 507; West v. Flemming, 18 Ill. 248; 68 Am. Dec. 539; Germania etc. Assn. v. Wagner, 61 Cal. 349. The decree appealed from is affirmed.

Bartch and Miner, JJ., concur.

MECHANICS' LIEN—DISCONNECTED BUILDINGS—ESSENTIALS OF CLAIM.—When materials have been furnished under a single and entire contract for a number of buildings erected on contiguous lots owned by the person to whom the material is furnished, a materialman's lien will attach to all the buildings and lots, and in an action to enforce such lien, it does not devolve upon the materialman to show how much of the material is placed in each building: Maryland Brick Co. v. Spilman, 76 Md. 337; 35 Am. St. Rep. 431, and note; Meek v. Parker, 63 Ark. 367; 58 Am. St. Rep. 119, and note. Contra, Wilcox v. Woodruff, 61 Conn. 578; 29 Am. St. Rep. 222; Chapin v. Persse etc. Paper Works, 30 Conn. 461; 79 Am. Dec. 263, and extended note.

MECHANICS' LIEN — ADDITIONS AND ENLARGEMENTS—WHEN LIEN FOR, ATTACHES.—Mechanics' liens for additions, enlargements, or alterations, made after a building is finished, do not attach from the commencement of the original building, but only from the commencement of such additions, enlargements, or alter-

ations: Haxtun Steam Heater Co. v. Gordon, 2 N. Dak. 246; 33 Am.
St. Rep. 776. See Montandon v. Deas, 14 Ala. 33; 48 Am. Dec. 84.

MECHANICS' LIEN — WAIVER OF — SUING OUT ATTACH-
MENT.—The lien is not waived nor forfeited by causing an attachment to be issued and levied upon the property of the debtor to secure the same demand, as the remedies are cumulative and may be
pursued at the same time. In case, however, of an attempt to pursue them in separate actions, the party might be put to his election,
but it is no defense to an action to enforce the lien that, in a previous suit for the same debt, an attachment was issued and levied
upon the property of the debtor, especially where such suit was dismissed and nothing realized by the attachment: Brennan v. Swasey,
16 Cal. 140; 76 Am. Dec. 507, and note. On the subject of waiver of
mechanics' liens, see extended note to Goble v. Gale, 41 Am. Dec.
221-224.

INDEX TO THE NOTES.

INDEX.

ACCORD AND SATISFACTION.

1. ACCORD AND SATISFACTION.—If there is a controversy between a debtor and creditor as to the amount due, and the debtor tenders the amount which he claims to be due on condition that the creditor accept it in discharge of the whole demand, and it is thereupon accepted, there is an accord and satisfaction, and the creditor cannot maintain a subsequent action to recover the difference between the amount received and that which he claimed to have been due. (Tanner v. Merrill, 687.)

2. PAYMENT OF PART OF A DEMAND, WHEN EXTINGUISHES THE WHOLE.—If there is a dispute between a debtor and creditor respecting the amount due, payment of the part admitted to be due and the taking of a receipt in full, accompanied with the refusal to pay more, discharges the whole debt, in the absence of mistake, fraud, or undue influence. (Tanner v. Merrill, 687.)

ACTIONS.

See Assignment, 5, 6.

ADMISSIONS.

See Pleading, 10.

ADOPTION.

1. PARENT AND CHILD.—ADOPTION IS purely a statutory matter and to give validity to proceedings relating thereto they must have been conducted in substantial conformity with the provisions of the statute; but the statute must be given a liberal construction in order to uphold the validity of proceedings under it. (Nugent v. Powell, 17.)

2. PARENT AND CHILD — ADOPTION — CONSTITUTIONAL LAW.—A statute which authorizes adoption without notice to, or the consent of, an abandoning parent of the child, and with the consent of the remaining parent only, is constitutional. (Nugent v. Powell, 17.)

3. PARENT AND CHILD—ADOPTION — CONCLUSIVENESS OF AFTER ABANDONMENT OF CHILD.—Adoption proceedings instituted upon application of the mother without notice to the absent father, in which it is found that such father has abandoned the child adopted, are not subject to collateral attack by collateral heirs of the party adopting such child on the ground of the absence of notice to such father. (Nugent v. Powell, 17.)

4. PARENT AND CHILD—ADOPTION.—ABANDONMENT OF A CHILD by its father constitutes a relinquishment on his part of his right to the custody and services of the child. Thereupon the mother becomes its natural guardian, and thereafter, in adoption proceedings, has the right to relinquish the custody and control of such child, and no rights of the father are affected thereby. (Nugent v. Powell, 17.)

5. PARENT AND CHILD—ADOPTION—CONSENT OF PARENT—NECESSITY FOR.—When, in adoption proceedings, a parent makes application to the court to relinquish all right to his or her child, the judge must make inquiry as to the right of the parent to make such relinquishment, and if, upon inquiry, it is ascertained that the other parent of the child is still living, and still possesses a right to the care, custody, or control of the child, the judge must refuse to approve such adoption unless the written consent of such absent parent is obtained and filed. But, if such parent, though living, has relinquished his or her right to the care, custody, or control of the child, his or her consent is not necessary to its adoption. (Nugent v. Powell, 17.)

6. PARENT AND CHILD—ADOPTION—PROCEEDINGS IN. A finding of fact by the district court in a case involving the validity of adoption proceedings, that a probate judge after full inquiry consented to the adoption, but did not enter the record thereof in the records of his office, but did write his consent and approval of the adoption upon a detached piece of paper and retained it among the papers in his office, is conclusive of the fact of application for, and consent to, the adoption and of an entry thereof upon the records, when it appears that such probate judge kept his records upon detached pieces of paper, and was not required by statute to keep them in any other manner. (Nugent v. Powell, 17.)

ADVERSE POSSESSION.

PRESCRIPTION.—ADVERSE POSSESSION PENDING AN ACTION OF EJECTMENT CANNOT CREATE A TITLE BY PRESCRIPTION in favor of the defendant, where judgment is rendered against him and a writ is issued thereon under which he is dispossessed, though before such writ is executed, he has been in the adverse possession of the property for a period sufficiently long to give him a prescriptive title but for the action against him. During the pendency of the action the defendant could not acquire any new right as against the plaintiff by merely remaining in possession. (Breon v. Robrecht, 247.)

AFFIDAVITS.

1. AN AFFIDAVIT IS a declaration on oath in writing, sworn to by a party before some person authorized to administer oaths. (Cox v. Stern, 385.)

2. AFFIDAVIT, VENUE OF.—IF THE PLACE where an affidavit was taken does not appear therefrom, but it does appear to have been made before a notary public, it will be presumed that he administered it in the county within which he was authorized to administer oaths. (Cox v. Stern, 385.)

3. AFFIDAVITS.—THE JURAT of an officer is not an affidavit, nor, strictly speaking, any part of it. The omission of such jurat is, therefore, not fatal to the affidavit, if it appears by extrinsic evidence that it was, in fact, sworn to by the parties named therein. (Cox v. Stern, 385.)

4. AFFIDAVIT—OATH WITHOUT AFFIANT'S SIGNATURE.— It seems that a statement made under oath may be an affidavit without the signature of the affiant. (Pittsburgh etc. Ry. Co. v. Mahoney, 503.)

See Chattel Mortgage, 2; Notaries Public, 3.

AGENCY.

1. PRINCIPAL AND AGENT—CONSTRUCTION OF CONTRACT.—If a contract made with a known agent, acting within the scope of his authority, is in writing, its construction and effect are ordinarily questions of law to be decided by the court, but, if the contract is verbal, the question whether credit was given to the agent alone is one of fact to be determined by the jury from a consideration of all the facts and circumstances attending the transaction. (Anderson v. Timberlake, 105.)

2. PRINCIPAL AND AGENT—LIABILITY TO THIRD PERSON.—If one known to be an agent deals or contracts within the scope of his authority, the presumption is, that credit is extended to the principal alone and that the act or contract is his engagement as if he were personally present and acting or contracting. This presumption prevails, in the absence of evidence that credit was given to the agent exclusively, and the burden of proof is upon the party seeking to charge such agent exclusively. (Anderson v. Timberlake, 105.)

3. PRINCIPAL AND AGENT—LIABILITY TO THIRD PERSON.—If a contract is made with a known agent acting within the scope of his authority for a disclosed principal, the contract is that of the principal alone, unless credit was given expressly and exclusively to the agent, and it appears that it was clearly his intention to assume the obligation as a personal liability and he was informed that credit was extended to him alone. (Anderson v. Timberlake, 105.)

4. PRINCIPAL AND AGENT—SUBSEQUENT PROMISE TO PAY BY AGENT—CONSIDERATION.—If a known agent contracts an account for his principal, a subsequent promise of payment by such agent is void for want of consideration. (Anderson v. Timberlake, 105.)

5. PRINCIPAL AND AGENT—LIABILITY TO THIRD PERSON—QUESTION FOR JURY.—If a known agent contracts an account within the scope of his authority, the fact that at the beginning of the transactions he directed the account to be charged to him is not conclusive that he intended to become sole debtor to the exclusion of all liability on the part of his principal, nor is it conclusive of the fact that credit was not extended to the principal. These questions are for the consideration and determination of the jury, to be taken in connection with all the circumstances attending the dealings between the parties in ascertaining whether exclusive credit was extended to the agent, and whether, with knowledge of that fact, he intended to assume individual responsibility. (Anderson v. Timberlake, 105.)

6. PRINCIPAL AND AGENT—PROMISE TO PAY BY AGENT. If a known agent, acting within the scope of his authority, contracts an account for his principal, his promise to pay, made at the time, is, prima facie, the promise of the principal, not involving the agent in personal liability, and, in an action to charge him therewith, evidence of such promise is admissible to show whether credit was extended to the agent solely, and whether it was his intention to bind himself and not his principal, and such evidence cannot be considered by the jury by itself, but may be considered in connection with all the circumstances attending the transactions between the parties. (Anderson v. Timberlake, 105.)

See Corporations, 2; Insurance, 8-10, 14.

ALIBI.

See Criminal Law, 6, 7.

ALIMONY.

See Marriage and Divorce, 3.

ALTERATION OF INSTRUMENTS.

NEGOTIABLE INSTRUMENTS, ALTERATION OF WITHOUT AUTHORITY, WHEN DOES NOT MAKE VOID.—If there is a blank in a promissory note to be used for the purpose of naming the time when interest shall be payable, and it was the agreement of the parties that the words "semi-annually" should be inserted in such blank, but they were omitted by inadvertence, the act of the payee or his agent in subsequently filling out this blank to conform to such intention, though not authorized, is not fraudulent, and does not extinguish the debt nor estop the holder of the note from maintaining a suit to reform it so as to express the true intention of the parties. (McClure v. Little, 938.)

AMENDMENT.

See Judgment, 11-14.

ANIMALS.

1. ANIMALS—DOGS—PROPERTY IN.—The owner of a dog has such a property right therein as enables him to maintain trover in case of its wrongful conversion. (Graham v. Smith, 323.)

2. ANIMALS, LIABILITY OF OWNER FOR INJURIES INFLICTED BY.—The owner of an animal not naturally vicious is not answerable for an injury done by it, unless it was in fact vicious, and the owner knew it. If an animal, being theretofore of a peaceable disposition, suddenly and unexpectedly, while in charge of its owner or of his servants, inflicts injury on another, neither is answerable, if at that time in the exercise of due care. If, on the other hand, the owner knew of the vicious propensity of the animal, he is answerable for injuries inflicted by it on the person or property of another who is free from fault. (Clowdis v. Fresno Flume etc. Co., 238.)

See Instructions, 6; Master and Servant, 17, 18.

APPEAL.

1. APPEAL.—ERROR NOT PRESENTED BY THE RECORD cannot be considered on appeal. (Townsend v. State, 477.)

2. APPELLATE PROCEDURE—PRESUMPTION IN FAVOR OF THE JUDGMENT.—If it appears by the record that the plaintiff took leave to amend his complaint in a respect indicated, it will be inferred that such amendment was made in the absence of any statement to the contrary and where the findings and evidence respond to the issues suggested by the proposed amendment. (Kellogg v. Douglas County Bank, 596.)

3. INSTRUCTIONS—PRESUMPTION ON APPEAL.—It will be presumed on appeal that the instructions given were applicable to the evidence, if it is expressly so stated in a bill of exceptions, although certain testimony set out therein tends to contradict such statement. (Adams v. Vanderbeck, 497.)

4. INSTRUCTIONS — APPEAL — STATUTE—PRESUMPTION.— A statute dispensing with the necessity of bringing up the evidence, on appeal, as to the question of the correctness of instructions, makes no change in the practice as to instructions given, for it must be presumed, in the absence of the evidence, that they were applicable to it. (Adams v. Vanderbeck, 497.)

5. IF INCOMPETENT EVIDENCE IS ADMITTED at a trial without objection, full weight must be given to it in considering whether the evidence is sufficient to sustain the findings. (Watt v. Nevada etc. R. R. Co., 772.)

6. EVIDENCE—IMPROPER QUESTION—ERROR.—The admission of improper evidence is not reversible error, if it is favorable to the party objecting. (Alabama etc. R. R. Co. v. Jones, 121.)

7. RAILWAY, NEGLIGENCE, WANT OF PROPER APPLIANCES.—A finding that the defendant railway corporation omitted to use proper appliances to prevent the emission of sparks, burning coals, and fire from its locomotives will not be disregarded, when the evidence upon the subject is conflicting. (Watt v. Nevada etc. R. R. Co., 772.)

8. APPEAL.—An undertaking on appeal, not in the statutory form, but good as a common-law bond, gives the appellate court jurisdiction, including the power to allow a new undertaking to be filed upon seasonable application by one who appears to have acted in good faith. (Skinner v. Holt, 878.)

9. APPELLATE PROCEDURE—A DEMURRER CANNOT BE INTERPOSED IN THE SUPREME COURT WHILE A CAUSE IS THERE PENDING ON APPEAL.—That court does not undertake to review questions not presented to the trial court. (Green v. Green, 846.)

10. APPELLATE PRACTICE—REVIEWABLE ORDERS.—An order setting aside a verdict and granting a new trial may be made the basis of a specification of error, and may be reviewed on appeal. (Kahn v. Traders' Ins. Co., 47.)

11. APPELLATE PRACTICE—FINAL ORDERS.—If, after an order is made by the district court vacating a verdict in favor of plaintiff and granting a new trial, the plaintiff elects to rely upon his exceptions thereto, and declines to further prosecute the action in that court, the court orders that the action be dismissed at plaintiff's costs, and that the defendant go hence without day and recover his costs from plaintiff, such order is final and may be reviewed on appeal. (Kahn v. Traders' Ins. Co., 47.)

12. APPEAL—REMITTING PART OF VERDICT—DISCRETION.—A ruling of the trial court, in an action for personal injuries, requiring the plaintiff to remit a part of the verdict, will not be disturbed where no abuse of discretion is shown. (Newbury v. Getchel & Martin etc. Mfg. Co., 582.)

13. APPEAL—REDUCING VERDICT—HARMLESS ERRORS.—Error in allowing a petition to be amended, after verdict, by stating an increased amount of damages, and error in instructing the jury as to the amount recoverable, are cured by the court's action in reducing the verdict to a less sum, and are, therefore, harmless. (Newbury v. Getchel & Martin etc. Mfg. Co., 582.)

14. APPEAL—ADMISSION OF EXHIBITS IN EVIDENCE—OBJECTIONS.—A specific objection to the admission of an exhibit is not available on appeal, where the only objection made in the court below was a general one. (State v. Brady, 560.)

15. APPELLATE PROCEDURE, DUTY TO REVIEW THE EVIDENCE.—A statute declaring where the evidence taken altogether does not support the verdict, decision, or judgment, the appellate court should grant a new trial, imposes on that court the duty of reviewing the evidence, and determining whether an assailed finding is supported by it. If there is a substantial conflict in the testimony, the verdict of the jury or the findings of the trial court should not be disturbed; but, on the other hand, the appellate court should in-

terpose when, upon all the evidence, it is clear that a wrong conclusion has been reached. (Watt v. Nevada etc. R. R. Co., 772.)

16. APPELLATE PROCEDURE, CONFLICT IN THE EVIDENCE, WHAT IS NOT.—Uncertain estimates and claims respecting the quantity of hay destroyed or produced cannot reach the rank of conflicting evidence as against testimony showing the total number of acres of hay as ascertained by a reliable survey on the ground and a fair average yield thereof, as admitted by the parties. (Watt v. Nevada etc. R. R. Co., 772.)

17. APPELLATE PROCEDURE, PRESUMPTION IN FAVOR OF REGULARITY OF PROCEEDINGS.—If the statute in force at the time of a trial for murder authorizes an oral charge to the jury, but requires the reporter to take it down, it will be presumed on appeal, in the absence of any statement in the record to the contrary, that the reporter did as the law directed. (State v. Kessler, 911.)

See Injunction, 3; Judgment, 5; Jurisdiction, 4; New Trial, 1, 2.

ARBITRATION.
See Insurance, 1-4.

ARREST.

1. ARREST, RIGHT TO MAKE, WITHOUT WARRANT.—At the common law, a private person had the right to arrest, without warrant, any person who committed, or attempted to commit, a felony in his view, but did not have such right where the offense was a misdemeanor only. (State v. Davis, 837.)

2. MURDER, ARREST, ERROR IN INSTRUCTION RESPECTING RIGHT OF.—It is error to instruct a jury that one who sees another stealing, or attempting to steal, his property, has the right to arrest him, where it does not appear that the value of such property was sufficient to make the offense a felony, and if the legality or illegality of the arrest is a vital question in the case, an error in so instructing entitles the defendant, if convicted, to a new trial. (State v. Davis, 837.)

ASSIGNMENT.

1. A JUDGMENT IS NOT ASSIGNABLE under the common law nor by the statutes of Illinois, so as to vest the legal title in the assignee. He obtains an equitable title only. (Yarnell v. Brown, 380.)

2. JUDGMENT.—THE ASSIGNEE OF A JUDGMENT TAKES IT SUBJECT to all equities existing between the parties thereto, but he is protected against the latent equities of third persons of which he had no notice. (Yarnel v. Brown 380.)

3. THE ASSIGNMENT OF A JUDGMENT necessarily carries with it the cause of action on which it is based, together with all the beneficial interest of the assignor in the judgment and all its incidents. (Citizens' Nat. Bank v. Loomis, 571.)

4. THE ASSIGNMENT OF A JUDGMENT in an action in which an attachment has been allowed and property seized thereunder, passes to the assignee the judgment creditor's right to recover damages of the sheriff for negligence in the care of the property seized by allowing a disposition to be made of it. (Citizens' Nat. Bank v. Loomis, 571.)

5. PARTIES TO ACTION—PLAINTIFF WHO IS A TRUSTEE FOR ANOTHER.—One to whom a cause of action has been assigned may maintain an action thereon whether he is interested in the pro-

coeds or not. He is a trustee of an express trust, and as such is the only person who can prosecute the action. (Citizens' Bank v. Corkings, 891.)

6. PARTIES TO ACTION.—That a plaintiff suing upon a cause of action assigned to him is, by his agreement with the assignor, bound to turn over to the latter all the proceeds of the action, is a matter in which the defendant is not interested, and therefore it is not available to him as a defense. (Citizens' Bank v. Corkings, 891.)

See License, 1; Mortgage, 7; Negotiable Instruments, 5, 8.

ASSIGNMENT FOR BENEFIT OF CREDITORS.
See Judgment, 18.

ATTACHMENT.

1. ATTACHMENT, WHO MAY MOVE TO VACATE.—Under the statutes of South Dakota any person having a lien on the property of the defendant may move to discharge an attachment thereon upon the same grounds available to the defendant himself. Such motion may, therefore, be made by subsequently attaching creditors. (Citizens' Bank v. Corkings, 891.)

2. ATTACHMENT—LEVY OF JUNIOR BEFORE SENIOR.— If several writs of attachment are placed in the hands of a sheriff, they are entitled to priority in the order in which they are received, and that officer cannot by levying the junior writ first give it precedence over the senior, nor can he by levying the senior writ first on certain property and subsequently levying the junior writ on other property restrict the right of the holder of the senior writ to the property actually levied upon under it. (Atchison etc. R. R. Co. v. Schwarzschild. 604.)

3. SHERIFFS — ATTACHMENT — RETURN — WHAT DOES NOT CONTRADICT.—The return of a sheriff is not contradicted by evidence of a fact that he is not required to state therein. Hence, if his return on a writ of attachment shows that he holds the property "subject to the order of the court," evidence, in an action against him for a negligent loss of the property, that it was delivered to a third person, as receiptor, by direction of the attorney for the plaintiff in the attachment. is admissible, because evidence that the property is held by a receiptor, under the direction of the judgment creditor, is not a contradiction of the return. (Citizens' Nat. Bank v. Loomis, 571.)

4. SHERIFFS — ATTACHMENT—RETURN—DISPOSITION OF PROPERTY.—Under a statute requiring a sheriff to show, by his return, what disposition he has made of attached property, it might be proper to show that he has turned it over to a receiptor, if such is the fact, but he is not required to show that such action was taken in pursuance of the plaintiff's directions. (Citizens' Nat. Bank v. Loomis, 571.)

5. SHERIFFS — ATTACHMENT — RETURN — WHAT IS SUF-FICIENT.—A sheriff's return of a levy upon property states all that the law requires when it shows that he has levied upon property, contains a description thereof, and shows what disposition had been made of it. (Citizens' Nat. Bank v. Loomis, 571.)

See Chattel Mortgage, 1; Corporations, 1; Judgment, 18; Mechanics' Lien, 3.

ATTORNEY AND CLIENT.

1. ATTORNEYS AT LAW—PROOF OF PROFESSIONAL STANDING OF.—Evidence of an attorney's negligence subsequent

to the receipt of business transmitted to him for his professional attention is no evidence that before that time he was not a lawyer of reputed learning and ability. (Plymouth County Bank v. Gilman, 868.)

2. DEFINITIONS—"AGREEMENT" BETWEEN ATTORNEY AND CLIENT.—An order or direction given by an attorney, to a sheriff, to turn over attached property to a third person, for safekeeping, is not an "agreement" within the meaning of a statute prescribing how an agreement between attorney and client shall be proved. (Citizens' Nat. Bank v. Loomis, 571.)

3. ATTORNEY FOR ADMINISTRATOR, WHEN NOT DISQUALIFIED TO ACT FOR AN HEIR.—An attorney for the administrator of the estate of a deceased person is not disqualified to act for one who claims to be entitled to a distributive share of the estate of the decedent, if such administrator does not claim to be an heir or otherwise entitled to any part of the estate. (Jones v. Lamont, 251.)

4. ATTORNEYS' FEES ARE NOT RECOVERABLE under the statutes of Utah in favor of the plaintiff, unless they are shown to have been actually charged to, or paid by, him. (McClure v. Little, 938.)

See Banks and Banking.

ATTORNEY'S FEES.

See Attorney and Client, 4; Negotiable Instruments, 2.

BANKS AND BANKING.

COLLATERAL SECURITY, LIABILITY OF BANK FOR NEGLIGENCE OF ATTORNEY EMPLOYED TO COLLECT.—If a promissory note secured by a mortgage is transferred to a bank as collateral security, which must be sent to a distant place for collection, it fulfills its implied requirement of reasonable diligence by placing such note for collection in the hands of an attorney having the reputation of being competent and reliable, and it is not answerable for the subsequent neglect of the attorney in the performance of the duties intrusted to him. (Plymouth County Bank v. Gilman, 868.)

See Checks; Negotiable Instruments, 10.

BIGAMY.

1. BIGAMY, ABSENCE OF CRIMINAL INTENT.—One who knowing his wife to be living, contracts a second marriage is guilty of bigamy, whether he intended to commit the crime or not. Hence a contract between him and his wife purporting to sever their marital relations is not admissible as evidence in his favor for the purpose of proving his want of criminal intent in contracting the second marriage. (State v. Zichfeld, 800.)

2. BIGAMY—EVIDENCE THAT THE PARTIES TO A MARRIAGE AGREED TO DISREGARD OR DISCONTINUE IT.—In a prosecution for bigamy where the first marriage was by a contract between the parties, without any solemnization, a subsequent agreement between them settling their property rights and purporting to sever their marital relations is not admissible in evidence, though offered, solely as tending to prove the absence of criminal intent in contracting the second marriage. (State v. Zichfeld, 800.)

BILLS OF LADING.

See Carriers, 2-5.

BILLS OF REVIEW.

1. BILLS OF REVIEW—NEWLY DISCOVERED EVIDENCE.—
To maintain a bill of review upon newly discovered evidence, the matter must not only be ascertained or discovered after the court has passed its decree, but it must also affirmatively appear, by appropriate averments and evidence, that the party complaining, by the use of reasonable diligence, could not, prior to the decree, have ascertained or discovered it. (Adler v. Van Kirk Land etc. Co., 133.)

2. BILLS OF REVIEW—NEWLY DISCOVERED EVIDENCE—MORTGAGE FORECLOSURE.—The relation between mortgagor and mortgagee is not confidential in character but simply that of debtor and creditor, and does not, of itself, relieve the mortgagor, in a settlement with the mortgagee and a consent to a decree foreclosing the mortgage, from his laches in failing to discover the falsity of facts inducing the settlement and subsequently relied upon by him as the basis for a bill of review of the foreclosure decree, on the ground of newly discovered evidence. (Adler v. Van Kirk Land etc. Co., 133.)

3. BILLS OF REVIEW—DECREE OF FORECLOSURE—NEWLY DISCOVERED EVIDENCE.—If a decree foreclosing a mortgage rendered by consent is based upon a settlement made by the parties eight months prior thereto, the mortgagor cannot, one year after the rendition of such decree, maintain a bill to review it upon the ground of newly discovered evidence, consisting in the fact that such settlement and consent to the decree were induced by false and fraudulent representations made by the mortgagee, the falsity of which was not known to the mortgagor until just prior to the filing of the bill, when it does not appear therefrom that the complainant, prior to the rendition of the decree made any effort to ascertain the truthfulness of the representations upon which the settlement was based or that such effort, if made, would have been unavailing, while it does appear from the bill that the falsity of such representations could have been ascertained by reasonable diligence at the time of the settlement, or at any time prior to the rendition of the decree, or thereafter. (Adler v. Van Kirk Land etc. Co., 133.)

4. JUDGMENTS BY CONSENT—BILL OF REVIEW.—To maintain a bill of review to impeach for fraud a decree rendered by consent, it must be averred and proved that the decree, or the consent upon which it was based, was procured by fraud practiced in the act of obtaining it, as distinguished from fraud which vitiates the cause of action and can be interposed only as a defense thereto. (Adler v. Van Kirk Land etc. Co., 133.)

See Judgment, 5.

BONA FIDE PURCHASERS.

See Vendor and Purchaser, 1-3.

BUILDING AND LOAN ASSOCIATIONS.

1. BUILDING AND LOAN ASSOCIATION—STOCK IN, WHEN NOT CANCELED.—If a member of a building and loan association notifies its secretary that he wishes to withdraw, and delivers his stock and pass-book for that purpose, but, before the stock is canceled, informs the secretary that he desires to remain in the association, who answers, "All right," and payments of dues are subsequently made as required, his stock is not canceled, though the secretary fraudulently issues a warrant for the amount of withdrawal, and, without knowledge of the member, induces the association to cash it. (Prairie State Loan Assn. v. Nubling, 377.)

2. BUILDING AND LOAN ASSOCIATIONS—LIABILITY OF FOR ACTS OF THEIR SECRETARY.—If payments of his dues are made by a member of a building and loan association to its secretary, who fraudulently fails to report them, the association is bound by such payments, and must give the member credit therefor. (Prairie State Loan etc. Assn. v. Nubling, 377.)

3. BUILDING AND LOAN ASSOCIATIONS—AUTHORITY OF SECRETARY.—Where the control and management of a building and loan association are vested, even tacitly, in its secretary, it is bound by his acts under such extended authority. If stock is handed in for cancellation, and the secretary procures a third person to purchase it and pay the amount due thereon, and the pass-book is delivered to him, and monthly payments are thereafter received from him by the secretary, who issues a warrant for the payment of such stock as canceled, and turns it over to the association as cash, the association, rather than the purchaser of the stock, must suffer from this fraud of the secretary. (Prairie State Loan etc. Assn. v. Nubling, 377.)

4. BUILDING AND LOAN ASSOCIATION—MEMBERS, WHEN ENTITLED TO EXECUTION AGAINST.—Though the statute provides that only one-half of the funds in the treasury shall be applicable to the demands of withdrawing stockholders, yet, if the association denies that a member is such or has any right to withdraw, and he maintains a suit to enforce his rights, execution may properly issue in his favor for the whole sum found to be due him. (Prairie State Loan etc. Assn. v. Nubling, 377.)

BURDEN OF PROOF.

See Agency, 2; Checks, 6; Constitutions, 2; Criminal Law, 7; Fraud, 2; Libel, 1.

BY-LAWS.

See Corporations, 3, 5; Insurance, 11.

CARRIERS.

1. CARRIERS—RAILWAY COMPANIES AS PRIVATE CARRIERS—EXEMPTION FROM NEGLIGENCE—EXPRESS MATTER.—A railway company, although it is a public or common carrier, may contract as a private carrier to transport express matter for express companies as such matter is usually carried, and in that capacity may properly require exemption from liability for negligence as a condition to he obligation to carry. (Pittsburgh etc. Ry. Co. v. Mahoney, 503.)

2. RAILWAYS—BILLS OF LADING, DELIVERY OF GOODS WITHOUT EXACTING SURRENDER OF, LIABILITY FOR.—A railway corporation delivering goods to the consignee in accordance with the terms of the bill of lading, but without requiring the presentation or surrender thereof, is not answerable to the consignor, though he had forwarded such bill with a draft attached thereto to a bank for collection, thus showing an intention that the consignee should not have the goods without first paying therefor, the corporation having no knowledge of such intention. (Nebraska Meal Mills v. St. Louis etc. Ry. Co., 183.)

3. CARRIERS—BILLS OF LADING—OPTION IN MODE OF SHIPMENT—HOW EXERCISED.—If a contract for the transportation of goods gives the carrier an option between modes of transpor

tation, this option must be exercised with regard to the interests of the shipper; and it is a breach of the contract to exercise it to his disadvantage, unless it is done in good faith and under circumstances which seem to demand it. The burden of proof is upon the carrier to show that it did exercise the option reasonably as demanded by the circumstances. (Stewart v. Comer, 353.)

4. CARRIERS—FREIGHT OVERCHARGES AND RECOVERY THEREOF.—If a bill of lading provides that if the goods shipped are transported in a box-car the rate shall be a certain amount per hundred pounds actual weight, and if transported on a flat-car, a certain rate per hundred pounds up to a certain limit, the goods shipped being far below this limit in weight, and the carrier transports part of the goods on flat-cars and part in box-cars, thus making the freight charges aggregate more than if the whole consignment had been transported on either kind of car alone, there is prima facie an overcharge, and the shipper having paid and the carrier having failed to show why the goods were so transported, the shipper is entitled to recover such overcharge, together with the penalty therefor prescribed by statute. (Stewart v. Comer, 353.

5. BILLS OF LADING AND WAREHOUSE RECEIPTS, EFFECT OF STATUTES CONCERNING NEGOTIABILITY OF.—A statute providing that warehouse receipts and bills of lading shall be negotiable by written indorsement, and that persons to whom they may be transferred shall be deemed to be the owners of the property therein described, so far as to give validity to any pledge, lien, or transfer, and that the property described in such bills of lading or receipts shall not be delivered except on surrender and cancellation thereof, does not affect the right of the carrier to deliver the property to the consignee, where the bill of lading has not been transferred, though it is held by the consignor who does not intend that the property shall be delivered until he has been paid therefor, the carrier having no notice of this intention. (Nebraska Meal Mills v. St. Louis etc. Ry. Co., 183.)

CERTIORARI.

1. CERTIORARI — EXTRINSIC EVIDENCE TO DISPROVE JURISDICTION.—Evidence dehors the record and contradicting it cannot be received in proceedings in certiorari for the purpose of proving that a statement made in a return or paper appearing by the record is false. (Los Angeles v. Young, 234.)

2. CERTIORARI—EXTRINSIC EVIDENCE.—Upon certiorari, if it becomes necessary for the court of review to be put in possession of facts upon which the court below acted and which are not technically of record, the lower court may be required to certify such facts in its return to the writ, and a statement so made would then become a part of the record; and where a notice is indorsed "Served, H. H. Y." it is perhaps proper to receive evidence from a constable showing that the indorsement was made by him and that he served the notice in question. (Los Angeles v. Young, 234.)

CHATTEL MORTGAGE.

1. MORTGAGE, WAIVER OF.—One who, having a mortgage on personal property, sues out an attachment against the mortgagor upon the mortgage debt and levies the writ upon the property mortgaged, thereby waives the mortgage lien thereon. This waiver cannot be avoided by proving that at the time of the attachment the plaintiffs therein were not able to discover whether the property attached was the same as that mortgaged, if they persisted in their

attachment until after the judgment therein, and desisted only when the property was declared to be exempt from execution. (Cox v. Harris, 187.)

2. CHATTEL MORTGAGE, AFFIDAVIT, DEFECTS IN.—The fact that an affidavit to a chattel mortgage does not show in what county it was taken, and the jurat is, as to some of the parties, not signed by the notary, does not invalidate the mortgage nor the record thereof, if, from the seal of the notary, the county in which he was authorized to act appears, and there is extrinsic evidence showing that the affidavit was made in that county by all the apparent parties thereto. (Cox v. Stern, 385.)

CHECKS.

1. BANKS AND BANKING — CHECKS — PRESENTMENT.—A' bank check is intended for payment, not circulation, and, as between the original parties, the time allowed for its presentation cannot be enlarged by successive transfers. (Watt v. Gans, 99.)

2. BANKS AND BANKING—CHECKS—PRESENTMENT.—The holder of a bank check must present it for payment within a reasonable time, depending upon the facts in each case. In the absence of exceptional circumstances, such reasonable time is the shortest period within which, consistently with the ordinary employments and duties of commercial business, the duty of presentment and demand can be performed. (Watt v. Gans, 99.)

3. BANKS AND BANKING—CHECKS—PRESENTMENT.—The payee who receives a check from the drawer in a place distant from the place of payment must, in the absence of exceptional circumstances, forward it by the post to some person at the latter place on the next secular day after it is received, and the person to whom it is forwarded is not bound to present it for payment until the day after it has reached him by due course of the post. If payment is not thus regularly demanded, and the bank should fail before the check is presented, the loss falls on the holder, who thus makes the check his own by his laches. (Watt v. Gans, 99.)

4. BANKS AND BANKING—CHECKS—DELAY IN PRESENTATION, WHEN OPERATES AS PAYMENT.—While, in the absence of agreement, a check received for a debt is merely conditional payment, its acceptance implies an undertaking of due diligence in presenting it for payment; and if the party from whom it is thus received sustains loss by want of such diligence, it must be held to operate as actual payment. (Watt v. Gans, 99.)

5. BANKS AND BANKING — CHECKS — DELAY IN PRESENTATION—PLEA OF PAYMENT.—In an action upon an original debt, in payment of which a check has been given, the failure of the plaintiff to present such check for payment within a reasonable time, resulting in loss to the drawer, is available as a defense under the plea of payment. (Watt v. Gans, 99.)

6. BANKS AND BANKING—CHECKS—DELAY IN PRESENTMENT—BURDEN OF PROOF.—Checks are presumably drawn upon or against a deposit of funds, and if the drawer establishes negligence or undue delay in the presentation of his check, and the failure of the drawee bank, after the expiration of the period within which, with due diligence, the check should have been presented for payment, the presumption of injury to the drawer arises, casting upon the holder the burden of proof to show that the drawer has suffered no loss or damage by the delay. (Watt v. Gans, 99.)

7. BANKS AND BANKING—CHECKS—DELAY IN PRESENTMENT—PRESUMPTION OF LOSS AND REBUTTAL THEREOF. The presumption of loss to the drawer arising out of want of dili-

gence in the presentation of his check and the intervening failure of the drawee may be rebutted by proof that the drawer had no available funds with the drawee to meet the check, or that he withdrew them before the failure, but, if such presumption remains unrebutted, the loss must fall upon the holder to whose want of diligence in presentation it is attributable. (Watt v. Gans, 99.)

COLLATERAL ATTACK.
See Adoption, 8; Guardian and Ward, 2; Injunction, 1; Judgment, 4.

COLLATERAL SECURITY.
See Banks and Banking; Damages 7.

COMMON LAW.
See Appeal, 8; Arrest, 2; Joint Liability, 1; Marriage and Divorce, 2.

CONFLICT OF LAWS.
See Descent; Distribution.

CONSIDERATION.
See Agency, 4; Fraudulent Conveyances, 8, 9; Mortgage, 12; Negotiable Instruments, 4.

CONSTITUTIONS.
1. CONSTITUTIONAL LAW—WASTE OF PROPERTY.—No one has an inalienable right to waste his property, such as natural gas, to the injury of the public. (Townsend v. State, 477.)

2. A CONSTITUTIONAL PROVISION SHOULD NOT BE CONSTRUED so as to have a retroactive operation, unless this is the unmistakable intention of the words used. (Jungk v. Holbrook, 921.)

3. CONSTITUTIONAL LAW.—THE POWER OF THE STATE TO FIX AND REGULATE RATES OF COMPENSATION to be charged by persons and corporations in charge of certain public utilities is so limited by the constitution of the United States that it cannot be so exercised as to require the furnishing of property or services without reward. (San Diego Water Co. v. San Diego, 261.)

4. CONSTITUTIONAL LAW — CONSTRUCTION OF STATE CONSTITUTION SO AS NOT TO CONFLICT WITH NATIONAL.—A provision of the constitution of a state requiring and authorizing the fixing by the board of supervisors of the county or the common council of a city of rates to be charged for water furnished to be used to the inhabitants thereof should so be construed as not to conflict with the constitution of the United States by depriving persons of property without compensation and without due process of law, and hence must be held to authorize the fixing of such rates by the exercise of judgment and discretion, and so as to allow just compensation. (San Diego Water Co. v. San Diego, 261.)

5. CONSTITUTIONAL LAW — WATER RATES, POWER TO FIX.—The people of the state have power in and by its constitution to declare that all water not then reduced to private ownership shall thereafter remain public, and that every person thereafter undertaking to supply cities, towns, or their inhabitants with water shall do so upon the condition that the rates to be charged therefor shall be annually fixed by the city. Such a business is so far public in its nature that the state may lawfully forbid its exercise by a private individual, and, a fortiori, may impose such conditions and re-

strictions upon its exercise as may be thought proper. (**San Diego Water Co. v. San Diego, 261.**)

6. CORPORATIONS, PROPERTY RIGHTS OF.—Though the constitution of a state declares that the legislature has power to alter, revoke, or amend any charter of incorporation, the property which corporations acquire in the exercise of the capacities conferred upon them they hold subject to the same guaranties which protect the property of individuals from spoliation. (St. Louis etc. Ry. Co. v. Paul, 154.)

See Elections, 1. 6; Highways, 5; Notaries Public, 1; Waterworks and Water Companies, 1.

CONSULS.

1. CONSULS ARE NOT PUBLIC MINISTERS, and are not entitled, by the general law of nations, to the peculiar immunities of ambassadors. In civil and criminal cases they are subject to the local law in the same manner with other foreign residents owing a temporary allegiance to the state. (Wilcox v. Luco, 305.)

2. CONSULS—JURISDICTION OF STATE COURTS OVER.—In the absence of any express declaration by Congress to the contrary, the state courts have jurisdiction over actions against consuls of foreign nations resident within the state, subject to the right of such consuls to have the judgment of the state tribunal reviewed by the supreme court of the United States, and the sufficiency of their defenses determined by that tribunal. (Wilcox v. Luco, 305.)

3. A JUDGMENT OF A STATE COURT AGAINST A FOREIGN CONSUL resident within the state, and served with process therein, is not void. (Wilcox v. Luco, 305.)

CONTEMPT.

CONTEMPT, JURISDICTION TO PUNISH.—To try the question of contempt and adjudge punishment is an exercise of judicial power. (In re Huron, 614.)

See Notaries Public, 2.

CONTRACTS.

1. CONTRACTS FOR REPURCHASE OF CORPORATION STOCK—REASONABLE TIME FOR PAYMENT.—A contract to repurchase capital stock in a corporation, and to pay therefor as soon and as fast as the purchasers are able financially to do so, without sacrificing their interests in, or the property of the corporation, does not contemplate that they can take all the time they may desire and that may be convenient for them to take, but implies that payment must be made within a reasonable time. The lapse of four years from the date of the contract is more than a reasonable time. (Chadwick v. Hopkins, 38.)

2. CONTRACTS FOR REPURCHASE OF CORPORATION STOCK—DEFENSES—BURDEN OF PROOF.—If, in an action to recover on a contract for the repurchase of capital stock in a corporation, the plaintiff alleges and proves a contract for repurchase, three years from the time of his original purchase of the stock, and denies a contract set up by the defendant to repurchase such stock and to pay therefor as soon and as fast as he was financially able to do so, financial ability to pay on the part of the defendant need not be shown by the plaintiff, and, if material, want of such ability must be shown as a defense. (Chadwick v. Hopkins, 38.)

3. STATUTE OF FRAUDS—PAROL EVIDENCE.—If two writings are relied upon to satisfy the statute of frauds, and parol evidence is necessary to connect them with each other, they must fail as a compliance with the statute, but if a writing refers to any other writing, which can be completely identified by this reference, without the aid of parol evidence, then the two writings may constitute a compliance with the statute. (Turner v. Lorillard Co., 345.)

See Agency, 1.

CORPORATIONS.

1. CORPORATION, CORPORATE CAPACITY OF, WHEN MUST APPEAR TO SUSTAIN AN ATTACHMENT.—If the plaintiff in the summons and the affidavit for attachment is designated by a name from which it appears not to be a natural person, and its corporate existence or capacity to sue is in no manner alleged, the attachment cannot be sustained and must be discharged on the motion of any person interested in, or having a lien upon, the property attached. (Citizens' Bank v. Corkings, 891.)

2. CORPORATIONS — POWER OF AGENT TO CHANGE CONTRACT.—An agent of an incorporated company may, if he has authority to do so, waive compliance with the conditions of a contract made between the company and a third person, although it contains a provision that no agent shall have power to bind the company by any change in the contract. (Robinson v. Berkey, 549.)

3. CORPORATIONS.—THE BY-LAWS OF A CORPORATION MUST BE reasonable and for a corporate purpose, and always within the charter limits. They must be in subordination to the constitution and laws of the state, and not interfere with its policy, nor be hostile to the general welfare. (People v. Chicago etc. Exchange, 404.)

4. CORPORATIONS, FORFEITURE OF CHARTER BY ACTS IN RESTRAINT OF TRADE.—Attempts to place restriction on trade and commerce and to fetter individual liberty of action by preventing competition are hostile to the public welfare and affect the interests of the people. Such attempts of a corporation are abuses of its franchise and warrant the filing of an information in the nature of a quo warranto against it for the forfeiture of its charter. (People v. Chicago etc. Exchange, 404.)

5. TRADE, REGULATIONS IN RESTRAINT OF.—A by-law of a stock exchange board limiting the number of solicitors which may be employed by any member within certain designated states, prohibiting the employment of any solicitors except upon a salary, and allowing a member to solicit only when counted as solicitors and while complying with the regulations of the by-laws, is in restraint of lawful trade, and therefore void. (People v. Chicago etc. Exchange, 404.)

6. CORPORATION—LIABILITY FOR SLANDER BY AGENT.—A corporation is not liable for a slander uttered by its agent or officer, even though he is acting honestly for the benefit of the company and within the scope of his authority, unless it is shown that the corporation expressly ordered and directed him to utter the very words in question. (Behre v. Nat. Cash Register Co., 320.)

7. CORPORATIONS, JUDGMENT AGAINST, EFFECT UPON STOCKHOLDERS.—If a judgment is rendered against a corporation, and proceedings are subsequently taken against its stockholders to enforce their liability, such judgment is conclusive against them of the liability of the corporation, and they cannot compel the creditor

to go behind it and relitigate the questions determined between the corporation and himself. (Ball v. Reese, 638.)

8. JUDGMENT AGAINST CORPORATIONS, WHETHER BINDING UPON STOCKHOLDERS.—A judgment against a corporation determining the amount of its indebtedness and of its assets, and directing an assessment upon its members or stockholders, for the purpose of paying its debts and expenses, is conclusive in a subsequent action brought in another state against one of such members, or stockholders, to collect his proportion of such assessment. (Mutual Fire Ins. Co. v. Phoenix etc. Co., 693.)

9. JUDGMENTS — CORPORATION AND STOCKHOLDERS, PRIVITY BETWEEN.—A stockholder is so far an integral part of the corporation that, in view of the law, he is privy to proceedings touching the body of which he is a member, and a judgment against it establishing the existence and amount of its liabilities is conclusive against him in proceedings to compel him to discharge his proportion thereof. (Mutual Fire Ins. Co., v. Phoenix etc. Co., 693.)
See Constitutions, 6; Contracts, 1, 2; Creditor's Bill, 1, 2; Fraudulent Conveyances, 3; Husband and Wife, 5.

COSTS.
See Partition, 3.

COTENANCY.

1. A TENANT IN COMMON IS, as to his individual share, to be deemed the owner of an entire and separate estate. (Madison v. Larmon, 356.)

2. COTENANTS—TAX TITLE—PURCHASE BY ONE COTENANT.—One who is an administrator and also a joint owner and the father of the other cotenants of real property cannot by purchase at a tax sale or by a purchase made for his benefit, acquire any interest in the property. Such purchase inures to the benefit of the other owners as well as to himself. (Johnson v. Branch, 857.)
See Estates, 6; Partition, 1.

COURTS OF PROBATE.
See Equity, 1; Judgment, 8.

CREDITOR'S BILL.

1. CORPORATIONS—CREDITOR'S BILLS AGAINST.—A judgment creditor of an insolvent corporation, with a return of execution "no property found," may maintain a bill in equity on behalf of himself alone, to subject the equitable assets of such corporation to the payment of his debt. (Hall v. Henderson, 141.)

2. CORPORATIONS—CREDITOR'S BILL AGAINST—MULTI-FARIOUSNESS.—A bill by a judgment creditor of an insolvent corporation, with a return of execution "no property found," against a stockholder in such corporation to reach his unpaid subscription to the extent of the judgment, is not multifarious or inconsistent because it seeks in the alternative, if the subscription has been paid, to reach for the same purpose property of the corporation which such subscriber has received from its officers with their knowledge that the corporation has received no consideration therefor. (Hall v. Henderson, 141.)

CRIMINAL LAW.

1. CRIMINAL LAW—WASTE OF NATURAL GAS.—The offense created by a statute which prohibits the burning of natural

gas in flambeau lights, thereby wasting it, is a continuous one, and a conviction therefor bars another prosecution for all violations of the statute by the defendant prior to the prosecution pending. Hence, evidence that he burnt natural gas, in a flambeau light, prior to the time charged is admissible. (Townsend v. State, 477.)

2. CRIMINAL INTENT, ABSENCE OF.—One who does a thing forbidden by statute is liable to the punishment there imposed, though in so doing it he had no evil intent, unless the statute makes such intent an element of the crime. If a statute has made it criminal to do an act under peculiar circumstances, one who voluntarily does it under those circumstances is charged with the criminal intent of doing it. (State v. Ziebfeld. 800.)

3. INSANITY AS A DEFENSE.—To render the distinctive defense of insanity available, the burden is on the accused to show affirmatively by a preponderance of the evidence that he was insane at the time the act for which he is indicted was committed. Though this burden may not be successfully carried so as to authorize a verdict of not guilty on this particular ground, it is nevertheless the duty of the jury to consider the evidence touching the alleged insanity in connection with the other evidence in the case, and then, in view of it all, to determine whether or not a reasonable doubt of the guilt of the accused exists in their minds. (Ryder v. State, 334.)

4. CRIMINAL LAW, DRUNKENNESS AS AN EXCUSE FOR CRIME.—Voluntary drunkenness ordinarily constitutes no excuse for a crime committed under its influence, even though the intoxication is so extreme as to make the person unconscious of what he is doing or as to create a temporary insanity. If, however, the habit of drunkenness has created a fixed frenzy or insanity, whether permanent or temporary, as, for instance, delirium tremens, such frenzy or insanity is not deemed voluntary, and he who acts under its influence is to be judged as if his condition had not been brought about by his bad habits. (State v. Kraemer, 664.)

5. CRIMINAL LAW — DRUNKENNESS — DELIRIUM TREMENS AS AN EXCUSE FOR CRIME.—One who was laboring under delirium tremens at the time of his commission of a criminal act, so that he did not know or realize what he was doing, is not excused, unless such delirium tremens antedated the fit of drunkenness during which such act was committed. (State v. Kraemer, 664.)

6. CRIMINAL LAW—ALIBI, PROOF OF.—Where alibi is a defense, the proper charge is, that the evidence in support of it should be considered in connection with all the other evidence in the case, and if, on the whole, there is reasonable doubt of the defendant's guilt, he should be acquitted. (State v. Ardoin, 678.)

7. EVIDENCE—ALIBI, BURDEN OF PROVING.—It is error to instruct the jury that the burden of proof is upon the accused to establish an alibi by a preponderance of the evidence. The setting up of the alibi does not change the presumptions nor the burden of proof, and if, because of it or anything else, the jury is not satisfied beyond a reasonable doubt of the guilt of the accused, he should be acquitted. (State v. Ardoin, 678.)

See Embezzlement; Jurisdiction, 5, 6; Robbery.

CRITICISM OF BOOK.
See Libel, 2, 3.

CURTESY.
See Husband and Wife, 2, 3.

DAMAGES.

1. DAMAGES FOR DESTROYING PROPERTY ARE GOV-ERNED BY ITS MARKET VALUE, rather than by any special value it has to its owner. (Watt v. Nevada etc. R. R. Co., 772.)

2. DAMAGES FOR DESTROYING PROPERTY.—If one has hay for which he has no use, and will have no use until a severe winter shall come, its value for which allowance must be made, on its destruction by the negligence of another, is the same as if it belonged to one at the same place having no stock. (Watt v. Nevada etc. R. R. Co., 772.)

3. DAMAGES FOR PROPERTY DESTROYED.—THE COST OF REPLACING PROPERTY destroyed by other property of like character is not the criterion of damages, but it is the actual value of the property at the time and place of its destruction. (Watt v. Nevada etc. R. R. Co., 772.)

4. DAMAGES—USE FOR WHICH PROPERTY WAS KEPT.— The fact that hay destroyed was put up and kept, because if ever there should come another winter like one which had occurred a few years before, the hay would be of very great value in preventing the starvation of stock, does not entitle its owner, on its destruction by the negligence of another, to recover a sum equivalent to the value of the stock which it might, at some future time, save from starvation, or any other than its market value at some place where it has such a value, less the expenses of transporting it there in a marketable condition. (Watt v. Nevada etc. R. R. Co., 772.)

5. DAMAGES FOR DESTROYING PROPERTY HAVING NO MARKET VALUE AT THE PLACE OF DESTRUCTION.—If property situated at a place where it has no market value is destroyed by the negligence of another, its owner having no immediate use for it, the damages for which the wrongdoer is answerable are to be ascertained by finding the value of the hay at the nearest place where it has a market value and deducting therefrom the cost of putting it in a marketable shape and transporting it to that place. This rule remains applicable though the owner did not intend to sell the hay, but to keep it for his own use in the future, and at the time of its destruction could not have replaced it, except by purchasing at such market place and paying the cost of transporting it thence to the place where it was destroyed and where, in the event of his ever having use for it, it would be used. (Watt v. Nevada etc. R. R. Co., 772.)

6. EVIDENCE OF VALUE.—WHAT THE OWNER WOULD TAKE FOR HIS PROPERTY cannot be shown as proof of its value; neither can the use to which he intended to put it in the future. The measure of damages or its destruction is its market value. (Watt v. Nevada etc. R. R. Co., 772.)

7. DAMAGES, EVIDENCE IN MITIGATION OF.—In an action to recover of the holder of collateral security damages resulting from his alleged tardy foreclosure of a mortgage, evidence is properly admitted in mitigation of damages showing that the mortgaged premises were conveyed to the plaintiff before foreclosure proceedings could have been completed by the exercise of ordinary care and vigilance. (Plymouth County Bank v. Gilman, 868.)

8. DAMAGES FOR THE DEATH OF A CHILD—OCCUPA-TION OF PARENT, WHEN MAY BE TAKEN INTO CONSIDERA-TION.—In determining what damages were sustained by a parent from the death of his minor child, it is most reasonable, in judging of the probable character of the occupation which the deceased would have pursued to regard, with other circumstances surrounding him, the calling of his father, since experience teaches that children do very frequently pursue the same general class of business as that of their parents. (Fox v. Oakland etc. Street Ry., 216.)

9. DAMAGES—INJURY TO CHILD.—Although a parent cannot recover damages for the death or injury of his child unless the child is capable of rendering services, he can recover against the person who inflicts the injury for his trouble and expense in caring for the child, and, if it dies from such injury, he can recover his necessary and reasonable expense in its burial, including compensation for his loss of time. (Southern Ry. Co. v. Covenia, 312.)

10. NEGLIGENCE CAUSING DEATH—MEASURE OF DAMAGES.—In an action to recover for a death caused by negligence, the recovery, if any may be had, may be for an amount equal to the decedent's pecuniary worth to his family, who were dependent upon him, from the time of his death to the time of the trial, added to the present cash value of his pecuniary aid to his family during the balance of his expectancy of life. (Alabama etc. R. R. Co. v. Jones, 121.)

11. NEGLIGENCE CAUSING DEATH—MEASURE OF DAMAGES.—In an action to recover for a death caused by negligence, recovery may be had in "an amount equal to the present cash value of the decedent's life to his family dependent upon him, during his expectancy of life." (Alabama etc. R. R. Co. v. Jones, 121.)

12. NEGLIGENCE CAUSING DEATH — EXPECTANCY OF LIFE—ERRONEOUS INSTRUCTIONS.—In an action to recover for death caused by negligence, the jury must, in assessing damages, take into consideration all the circumstances bearing upon the subject, as disclosed by the evidence, and ascertain what the duration of the party's natural life would have been. Hence, for the court to instruct as to the period of expectancy of life of the deceased as fixed by mortuary tables, is an invasion of the province of the jury and erroneous. (Alabama etc. R. R. Co. v. Jones, 121.)

13. NEGLIGENCE CAUSING DEATH—MEASURE OF DAMAGES.—In an action to recover for negligence causing the death of a person leaving a dependent family enjoying support from his earnings and also surplus accumulations, the recovery is not confined to the amount of injury sustained by the loss of such support, but the entire present value of the accumulations may be recovered as well. (Alabama etc. R. R. Co. v. Jones, 121.)

14. NEGLIGENCE CAUSING DEATH—MEASURE OF DAMAGES—EVIDENCE.—If, in an action to recover for the death of a railroad employé caused by negligence, the evidence is circumstantial as to what proportion of his earnings were consumed in his own support, and hence what amount of pecuniary benefit his dependents enjoyed from such earnings, evidence to show how many and what dependents there were is admissible to aid in determining the pecuniary loss sustained by his death. (Alabama etc. R. R. Co. v. Jones, 121.)

15. DAMAGES—DISFIGUREMENT AS ELEMENT OF—NEGLIGENCE.—In personal injury cases, the plaintiff's disfigurement of person may be considered as an element of damages. (Newbury v. Getchel & Martin etc. Mfg. Co., 582.)

16. DAMAGES—MEDICAL EXPENSES AS ELEMENT OF—MINORS—NEGLIGENCE.—In an action for personal injuries brought by a minor, he cannot, as an element of damages, recover the cost of medical services rendered, at least, until he has paid the bill, for his parents are primarily liable for it. (Newbury v. Getchel & Martin etc. Mfg. Co., 582.)

17. NEGLIGENCE CAUSING DEATH—PROOF AUTHORIZING RECOVERY.—In an action against a railroad company to re-

DANGEROUS PREMISES.

See Real Property.

DEEDS.

DEED, DELIVERY OF, WHAT SUFFICIENT.—If a deed is simply sealed and acknowledged and left with the officer taking the acknowledgment, with instructions to hold it until called for by the proper person, and the grantee knew of, and assented to, the conveyance, and took and retained possession of the land described therein, but the deed, when called for by him, could not be found, it is, nevertheless, well delivered. (Appleman v. Appleman, 732.)

See Executors and Administrators, 3.

DEFINITIONS.

Affidavit. (Cox v. Stern, 385.)
Agreement between Attorney and Client. (Citizens' Nat. Bank v. Loomis, 571.)
"Appropriate." (State v. La Grave, 764.)
Appropriation of Public Moneys. (State v. La Grave, 764.)
Avocation. (Starling v. Supreme Council, 709.)
Discount. (Anderson v. Timberlake, 105.)
False Swearing. (Kahn v. Traders' Ins. Co., 47.)
General Agent. (Kahn v. Traders' Ins. Co., 47.)
Lottery. (Loiseau v. State, 84.)
"Reckless." (Louisville etc. R. R. Co. v. Anchors, 116.)
Rule against Perpetuities. (Madison v. Larmon, 356.)
Uncontrollable Impulse. (State v. Davis, 837.)
Willful Injury. (Louisville etc. R. R. Co. v. Anchors, 116.)

DELIRIUM TREMENS.

See Criminal Law, 5.

DESCENT.

CONSTITUTIONAL LAW—NATURAL CHILD, RIGHT OF TO INHERIT.—If the father of a natural child is domiciled in France, where he dies, and by whose laws such child, being acknowledged by the father, has the right to inherit one-half of his estate, this right will not be enforced in Louisiana, even as to the personal estate of the decedent, if he left relatives residing in that state who, by its laws, are entitled to such property, or some portion thereof, as heirs of the decedent. The right of a natural child to inherit any portion of the estate of its father, when he leaves surviving any heirs at law, is repugnant to the policy of the state as expressed in its statutes. (Succession of Petit, 659.)

DISTRIBUTION.

CONFLICT OF LAWS.—THE DOMICILE OF THE OWNER governs his contracts as to personal property and the distribution of that property when he dies. This rule is subject to the exception that the law of the domicile of the owner of personal property will not be enforced in another country to the prejudice of its citizens or when utterly opposed to the spirit and policy of its legislature. (Succession of Petit, 659.)

DRUNKENNESS.

See Criminal Law, 4, 5; Homicide, 5.

DYING DECLARATIONS.

See Homicide, 6.

EJECTMENT.

1. HIGHWAYS.—EJECTMENT MAY BE MAINTAINED BY THE OWNER OF LAND over which there is a public highway against a telegraph corporation which has constructed and is maintaining its line upon such highway without his consent and without compensating him therefor. (Postal Tel. etc. Co. v. Eaton, 390.)

2. A JUDGMENT IN FAVOR OF THE PLAINTIFF IN EJECTMENT in which the title of the parties or their right to the possession of the demanded premises is put in issue, tried, and determined, is conclusive as an estoppel against, the defendant, to avoid which · he must show some title or right to possession other than that which was available to him in the former action. (Breon v. Robrecht, 247.)

See Adverse Possession.

ELECTIONS.

1. ELECTIONS—INMATES OF SOLDIERS' HOME, RIGHT OF TO VOTE.—Under a constitutional provision declaring that no person shall be deemed to have gained or lost a residence while kept in any almshouse or other asylum at the public expense, inmates of soldiers' homes by going to and residing in such home neither lose their old, nor gain a new, residence, though they intend to reside in the home permanently. Hence they are not entitled to vote except at their place of residence before becoming such inmates. Such home is an asylum within the meaning of the constitutional provision. (Lawrence v. Leidigh, 631.)

2. ELECTIONS—SUFFRAGE IS A STATE RIGHT.—Suffrage is not given by the federal constitution, but is a right of the states. (Gougar v. Timberlake, 487.)

3. ELECTIONS—SUFFRAGE—NATURE OF RIGHT—WHO ENTITLED TO.—Suffrage is not a natural right, but a political privilege, and is held only by those to whom it is granted, either by the constitution or written laws of the state. (Gougar v. Timberlake, 487.)

4. ELECTIONS — SUFFRAGE — QUALIFICATIONS UPON RIGHT OF—SEX.—Qualifications may be lawfully imposed upon the privilege of suffrage, and sex is made such a qualification by a constitution which gives to male citizens, in express terms, the right to vote, without mentioning female citizens. (Gougar v. Timberlake, 487.)

5. ELECTIONS—WOMEN SUFFRAGE.—The right to vote cannot be extended to women under a constitutional provision which expressly grants to male citizens, of the age of twenty-one years, the right of suffrage, but which is silent as to female citizens. (Gougar v. Timberlake, 487.)

6. ELECTIONS—CONSTRUCTION OF CONSTITUTION AND STATUTE.—The general rule of construction, that that which is expressed makes that which is silent cease, applies to a constitution and statute which give to male citizens, in express terms, the right to vote, but do not expressly negative the privilege to female citizens. (Gougar v. Timberlake, 487.)

EMBEZZLEMENT.

CRIMINAL LAW—PLACE OF CRIME OF EMBEZZLE-MENT.—If one is intrusted with property in one parish or county, and there forms the intention of fraudulently appropriating it to his own use, and, pursuant to such intention, goes with it to another parish or county, where he accomplishes his object by pawning it, his crime may be deemed committed in the place where he received the property and formed the criminal intent, and hence he may be convicted under an indictment charging him with committing the crime in the latter place. (State v. Sullivan, 644.)

EQUITY.

1. EQUITY, PROBATE JURISDICTION OF COURTS OF.—Courts of equity have concurrent jurisdiction with courts of probate of all matters of guardianship and the settlement of estates of deceased persons, and will exercise such jurisdiction when the powers of the probate courts are inadequate for the purposes of perfect justice. (Trotter v. Mutual Reserve etc. Assn., 887.)

2. PRACTICE IN EQUITY — DEFENSES RESPECTING OTHER TRANSACTIONS.—In a suit by remaindermen against a life tenant to have certain property declared to be held by the latter as such life tenant, because it is the proceeds of the property the subject of the life estate, the defendant is not entitled to present and have litigated claims made by her that the plaintiffs have received more than their share of the property claimed under a will upon which the title and claims of all the parties are based. (Green v. Green, 846.)

See Creditors' Bill, 2; Franchise; Injunction, 8; Judgment, 7, 16; Mechanic's Lien, 5; Pleading, 9.

ESTATES.

1. REMAINDERS. — WHERE A REMAINDER IS CONTINGENT, IT MUST VEST DURING the existence of the particular estate, or at the instant of its termination. (Madison v. Larmon, 356.)

2. REMAINDERS—CONTINGENT WHICH NEVER BECOME VESTED, WHO TAKES THE PROPERTY.—If a life estate terminates before the contingent remainder limited thereon becomes vested, the property passes in reversion to the heirs at law of the testator at the time of the termination of such estate. (Madison v. Larmon, 356.)

3. REMAINDERS—CONTINGENT AND VESTED.—If a testator devises real property to seventeen persons, constituting his children and grandchildren, for their lives, and declares that after they shall all be dead, he devises his property to his grandchildren then living, share and share alike, and if any grandchild shall then be dead leaving issue, such issue shall take the share the parent would take if living, the interest last devised is a contingent remainder which does not vest until the death of the last surviving life tenant. (Madison v. Larmon, 356.)

4. PERPETUITIES — CONTINGENT REMAINDERS. — If the event upon which a contingent remainder is limited must, happen, and the contingent become a vested remainder within the time allowed by the rule against perpetuities, the rule is not violated by the fact that the remainder so vested is not to be enjoyed until some future fixed time, or until the dropping out of an existing life estate. (Madison v. Larmon, 356.)

5. PERPETUITIES.—THE CONTINUANCE OF AN ESTATE FOR MORE THAN LIVES IN BEING AND TWENTY-ONE YEARS does not bring it within the rule against perpetuities, if it must all vest within that time. (Madison v. Larmon, 356.)

6. REMAINDERS—CONTINGENT WHERE THE PRECEDING ESTATE IS HELD IN COMMON.—Where the preceding estate upon which a contingent interest is limited is held in common, and as to each of the cotenants the particular estate terminates before the remainder can vest, it fails as to such share or shares and to that extent vests in the heirs at law of the testator. (Madison v. Larmon, 356.)

7. LIFE TENANT AND REMAINDERMAN, PROCEEDS OF INSURED PROPERTY.—Moneys collected by a life tenant upon a loss by fire of a building subject to the tenancy, though the premiums have been paid with his personal funds, stand in place of the property destroyed, and should either be used in rebuilding it or should be held by the life tenant for the benefit of the remainderman after the tenant's death. (Green v. Green, 846.)

8. LIFE TENANT AND REMAINDERMAN—INSURANCE, ALLOWANCE FOR MONEYS PAID TO OBTAIN.—In a suit by remaindermen to have the proceeds of insurance effected by a life tenant declared to be held by her for life only, after which such proceeds shall belong to them, she is entitled to be credited with the amount paid by her to procure the policy under which the moneys were collected, but not for the amounts paid by her for prior policies on the same property which no loss occurred. (Green v. Green, 846.

See Equity, 2; Mines, 2.

ESTATES OF DECEDENTS.

See Equity, 1; Executors and Administrators; Fraudulent Conveyances, 4; Taxes, 8.

ESTOPPEL.

1. AN ESTOPPEL IN PAIS MUST BE PLEADED. (State v. East Fifth St. Ry. Co., 742.)

2. ESTOPPEL.—STATEMENTS OR CONDUCT of a party do not operate as an estoppel in favor of another party, who was not influenced by them, and who would not suffer injury if there was a contradiction of them. (Boyeston v. Rankin, 111.)

See Ejectment, 2; Executions, 5, 6; Husband and Wife, 7, 8; Insurance, 9; Judgment, 19; Municipal Corporations, 16; Partition, 2; Wills, 16.

EVIDENCE.

1. JUDICIAL NOTICE—NOTARIES PUBLIC.—The courts of a county will take judicial notice of the notaries of such county. (Cox v. Stern, 385.)

2. EVIDENCE — JUDICIAL KNOWLEDGE — EARNING CAPACITY OF CHILD.—A court on demurrer, can take judicial cognizance of the fact that a child is of such tender years as to be incapable of rendering services authorizing the parent to recover for the loss thereof arising from its injury or death, and need not submit such question to the jury, although the declaration alleges an earning capacity on the part of the child. (Southern Ry. Co. v. Covenia, 312.)

3. EVIDENCE—PEDIGREE.—A case is not necessarily one of pedigree because it involves questions of birth, paternity, age, or relationship, if these questions are merely incidental, and the judgment will simply establish a debt, or a person's liability on a contract, or his proper settlement as a pauper, or the commission of a crime. (People v. Mayne, 256.)

4. EVIDENCE— SUPPORTING WITNESS BY HIS PRIOR DECLARATIONS.—A mother who has testified to the date of the birth of her child cannot be supported or corroborated by an entry of such date made by her in the family Bible. (People v. Mayne, 256.)

5. EVIDENCE.—AN ENTRY IN A FAMILY BIBLE is but a declaration made out of court, and not under the sanction of an oath. It is hearsay evidence, and is not admissible where the person making it is alive and capable of being examined as a witness in the cause. Hence, such an entry is not admissible in a prosecution for rape for the purpose of proving the age of the prosecutrix at the time of the alleged offense. (People v. Mayne, 256.)

6. EVIDENCE — COMPETENCY OF TABULATED STATEMENTS.—Tabulated statements, taken from voluminous and numerous claims and records already in evidence, and made by competent persons for the purpose of assisting the jury in arriving at their verdict, are competent evidence. (State v. Brady, 560.)

7. EVIDENCE — MEMORANDA — ADMISSIBILITY OF.—The record of a railroad ticket office, or memoranda showing the daily sales of tickets, is admissible in evidence, if the witness, who identifies the record, knows that it was correct when made, although he has no independent recollection, either before or after examining it, of the sales to which it refers. (State v. Brady, 560.)

8. EVIDENCE — EXPLAINING MARKS UPON PAPER OFFERED.—It is the duty of the state, in a criminal case, such as a prosecution for defrauding a county by filing fraudulent claims against it for the transportation of indigent poor persons, to explain marks upon a paper offered in evidence, and which were not upon it originally, in order to make it admissible, and such explanatory evidence, made by a county officer, as a witness, is not prejudicial, though the witness, in making the explanation, is compelled to impress the jury with the fact that the marks were made to check up fraudulent claims charged to have been made by the defendant. (State v. Brady, 560.)

9. EVIDENCE—OTHER DISTINCT OFFENSES.—In a criminal case, other distinct offenses cannot be proved for the purpose of raising an inference that the defendant committed the crime in question, or to show that he had a tendency to commit that crime; but evidence of such distinct offenses is admissible for the purpose of showing the knowledge, intention, and bad faith of the defendant. (State v. Brady, 560.)

10. EVIDENCE—OTHER DISTINCT OFFENSES.—Upon an indictment of an overseer of the poor, charged with defrauding a county by filing a fraudulent claim with the county auditor for the transportation of an indigent poor person, evidence of all claims of a like character, for the transportation of other indigent poor persons, filed by him with that officer, together with the records of the transportation companies, is, in connection with evidence tending to show their fraudulent character, admissible for the purpose of establishing the defendant's knowledge of the falsity of the claim in question. It is also admissible to show the existence of a systematic scheme or plan to defraud the county, and thus to negative the idea

that the filing of the claim in question was accidental, or made
through oversight or mistake. (State v. Brady, 560.)

See Affidavit, 3; Appeal, 5, 6, 16; Attorney and Client, 1; Certiorari,
1, 2; Damages, 14; Homicide, 6; Jurisdiction, 16, 17.

EXECUTION.

1. AN EXECUTION MAY BE QUASHED on the ground that the
amendment of the judgment by which the execution of the judgment was authorized was void. (Scamman v. Bonslett, 226.)

2. EXECUTION, MOTION, RELIEF BY OF PERSON UNLAW-
FULLY OUSTED UNDER A WRIT.—If, under a judgment against
the defendants as individuals, they are wrongfully dispossessed of
property which they hold as trustees for others, they may obtain relief by motion in the original action. (Sonnenberg v. Steinbach, 885.)

3. EXEMPTIONS—TIME FOR FILING CLAIM.—Under a stat-
ute providing that a claim of exemption must be filed after levy of
process upon the property claimed as exempt from sale, such claim
may be filed at any time before the sale under the levy. (Boylston
v. Rankin, 111.)

4. EXEMPTIONS.—RIGHT OF EXEMPTION OF PERSONAL
PROPERTY coexists and is coextensive with the right of the creditor to reach the subject, except in cases specially saved from the
operation of the exemption. (Boylston v. Rankin, 111.)

5. EXEMPTIONS—ESTOPPEL TO CLAIM—WHAT IS NOT.—
If, after levy of an execution upon property as that of the execution
defendant, a third party institutes a statutory trial of the right
thereto, and such defendant testifies therein that the property under
levy is not his, but belongs to such claimant, he is not thereby
estopped, upon judgment subjecting the property to the satisfaction of such execution, from claiming the property as exempt at
any time prior to the execution sale. (Boylston v. Rankin, 111.)

6. EXEMPTIONS — ESTOPPEL TO CLAIM — JUDGMENT,
WHEN IS NOT.—If, after levy of execution upon property as that
of the execution defendant, a third party institutes a statutory trial
of the right thereto, judgment therein subjecting the property to
the satisfaction of such execution is not conclusive upon, and does
not estop, the execution defendant, who is not a party to the claim
suit, to claim his right of exemption at any time before the execution sale. (Boylston v. Rankin, 111.)

See Building and Loan Associations, 4; Fraudulent Conveyances, 5.

EXECUTORS AND ADMINISTRATORS.

1. EXECUTORS, POWER OF TO ACT IN ANOTHER STATE.
So far as concerns realty, a will beyond the jurisdiction where it is
probated is inoperative and has no extraterritorial force, and the
executor cannot, because of his appointment in accordance with the
laws of one state, sell real property of his testator situated in another state, unless the will was there proved or the laws of that
state, dispensing with probate anew, confer the requisite permission. (Emmons v. Gordon, 734.)

2. EXECUTOR, WHETHER MUST ACCOUNT FOR PRO-
CEEDS OF LANDS SOLD IN ANOTHER STATE.—If an executor
sells lands of his testator situate in another state without the will
being there admitted to probate, such sales must be regarded as
made without authority and as passing no title. Hence an action

cannot be sustained against him or the sureties on his bond for the moneys received by him in consideration of such sales. (Emmons v. Gordon, 734.)

3. ADMINISTRATOR'S DEED, WHEN CONVEYS A PERSONAL TITLE AND ALSO TITLE SUBSEQUENTLY ACQUIRED BY HIM.—If an administrator, purporting to act under a special statute authorizing him to sell and convey the property of his intestate, makes such a sale and executes a warranty deed, and he then has an interest in the property as an heir at law of the decedent, and subsequently acquires a further title therein by the death of another heir, his conveyance passes all the title which he held as heir at law and also all the title which he subsequently acquired. (Johnson v. Brauch, 857.)

4. EXECUTORS AND ADMINISTRATORS — JUDGMENT AGAINST—FORM OF.—If the cause of action against administrators is a contract to which the decedent was a party, the judgment rendered against them should not be personal in its nature, but should be that they pay in due course of administration the amount ascertained to be due. (Chadwick v. Hopkins, 38.)

5. ESTATES OF DECEDENTS — HEIRS OF, WHEN MAY MAINTAIN ACTIONS THOUGH THERE IS AN ADMINISTRATOR.—When an administrator refuses to bring an action upon a claim due the estate, the heirs, creditors, or any others interested in its collection should have an adequate remedy, and hence may be permitted to maintain such an action directly in their own names. (Trotter v. Mutual Reserve etc. Assn., 887.)

6. EXECUTORS.—THE SURETIES ON THE BOND OF AN EXECUTOR who, by the will is given power to sell realty, are answerable for proceeds received by him from the sale or rent of lands situated within the state. (Emmons v. Gordon, 734.)

See Statutes, 16.

EXEMPTIONS.
See Executions; Fraudulent Conveyances, 5; Statutes, 10-12.

EXPRESS COMPANIES.
See Carriers, 1; Railroads, 3, 4.

FALSE PRETENSES.

FALSE PRETENSES—INSTRUCTIONS—"FALSELY."—In a prosecution for cheating by false pretenses, an instruction using the word "falsely," in connection with "representations" made, is not erroneous, if it manifestly means something more than "mistakenly," or "untruly," and must have been, in the light of other instructions, so understood by the jury. (State v. Brady, 560.)

FALSE SWEARING.
See Insurance, 5.

FIRE LIMITS.
See Legislature, 4; Municipal Corporations, 3, 4, 6.

FORMER ACQUITTAL.

1. CRIMINAL LAW—AUTREFOIS ACQUIT, PLEADING OF AS TO A HIGHER OFFENSE CHARGED.—If to an indictment of murder the defendant pleads autrefois acquit, and the plea is sus-

tained as to the charge of murder, he may be tried for the lesser offense of manslaughter, included within the indictment, if it is clear that the action of the court sustaining the plea was not intended to go any further than to protect the defendant from further prosecution for murder. (State v. Smith, 680.)

2. CRIMINAL LAW—AUTREFOIS ACQUIT, PLEA OF AFTER A NEW TRIAL HAS BEEN GRANTED.—If, under an indictment for murder, the accused is convicted of murder in the second degree, and afterward he obtains a reversal of the judgment and the granting of a new trial, he thereby waives his right to rely upon his jeopardy in the former trial, and may be again put on trial for murder in the first degree, if the statutes of the state declare that the granting of a new trial places the parties in the same position as it no trial had been had, that all the testimony must be produced anew, and that the former verdict cannot be used or referred to either in evidence or argument or by plea in bar of any conviction which may have been had under the indictment. The court inclines to the view that such would be the effect of the granting of a new trial, if the statute were not taken into consideration. (State v. Kessler, 911.)

FRANCHISES.

FRANCHISE, FORFEITURE OF.—A PROCEEDING IN EQUITY is not a proper remedy to enforce the forfeiture of a franchise (State v. East Fifth St. Ry. Co., 742.)

See Corporations, 4; Municipal Corporations, 15, 16; Quo Warranto; Railroads, 18-20.

FRAUD.

1. FRAUD, PROOF OF.—Evidence that merely excites suspicion that fraud may have existed is not sufficient. It must reasonably justify the inference of fraud. (Taylor v. Wands, 818.)

2. FRAUD—BURDEN OF PROOF.—One who alleges fraud must clearly and distinctly prove it so as to satisfy the ordinary mind and conscience of its existence as a fact. (Kahn v. Traders' Ins. Co., 47.)
See Bills of Review, 3, 4.

FRAUDULENT CONVEYANCES.

1. FRAUDULENT TRANSFER — WHO MAY ATTACK.—One holding a note made after a transfer may attack it as a fraud upon him if his note was a renewal of an obligation antedating such transfer. (Kellogg v. Douglas County Bank, 596.)

2. FRAUD, ON HUSBAND'S CREDITORS.—A GIFT BY A WIFE to her sons in her last illness, in anticipation of death, though suggested by her insolvent husband, cannot be regarded as a fraud upon his creditors. (Taylor v. Wands, 818.)

3. FRAUDULENT TRANSFER.—IF A DEBTOR ORGANIZES A CORPORATION and transfers his property to it for the purpose of shielding himself from his creditors, the property so transferred being the chief part of his assets, and the corporators being members of his family, the transfer is fraudulent, and may be avoided by his creditors. (Kellogg v. Douglas County Bank, 596.)

4. FRAUDULENT CONVEYANCES—COMPLAINT—ALLEGA. TION AS TO SUFFICIENCY OF ASSETS—DECEDENT'S ES. TATE.—In a suit by a creditor of a guardian, against the latter's ad. ministrator, to set aside a conveyance of real estate, made by the

guardian in his lifetime, as fraudulent, the primary object of the suit being to collect the amount due on the guardian's bond, the complaint must aver that assets of the estate in the hands of the administrator are not sufficient to pay decedent's debts, including the claim of the plaintiff. (State v. Parsons, 430.)

5. FRAUDULENT CONVEYANCES — COMPLAINT — EXEMPTION FROM EXECUTION.—A complaint to set aside a conveyance of real estate as fraudulent need not allege that the land conveyed was worth more than the amount allowed by law as exempt from execution. That is matter of defense. (State v. Parsons, 430.)

6. FRAUDULENT CONVEYANCES — COMPLAINT — GRANTEE'S KNOWLEDGE OF FRAUDULENT PURPOSE.—In a complaint to set aside a conveyance of real estate as fraudulent, an allegation that the grantee received the conveyance with knowledge of the fraudulent purpose of the grantor is sufficient, even if the complaint shows that a valuable consideration was paid. It is not necessary to aver that the grantor "had no property from the making of the conveyance until his death." (State v. Parsons, 430.)

7. FRAUDULENT CONVEYANCES—COMPLAINT—NO PROPERTY.—In a suit to set aside a conveyance of real estate as fraudulent, an allegation in the complaint that the grantor had no property subject to execution at the time of his death, and that his estate is wholly insolvent, is sufficient to show that there is no property of the estate with which to pay the claim except by setting aside the conveyance. (State v. Parsons, 430.)

8. FRAUDULENT CONVEYANCES — FUTURE SUPPORT — VALIDITY OF DEED.—If the consideration for a conveyance is an agreement for the future support of the grantor, the transaction is fraudulent in law as to the creditors, to the extent which the value of the property is in excess of the support furnished. (Harris v. Brink, 578.)

9. FRAUDULENT CONVEYANCES — FUTURE SUPPORT — LIEN OF CREDITORS.—If a debtor conveys his property, in consideration of his future support, an existing creditor, having no other means of enforcing his claim, is entitled, in equity, even after the grantor's death, to have his claim established as a lien against the property to the extent that the value of the property and of its use, exceeds the amount of the support actually furnished, in good faith, by the grantee. (Harris v. Brink, 578.)

10. FRAUDULENT CONVEYANCES — FUTURE SUPPORT — REMEDY OF EXISTING CREDITORS.—Existing creditors may avail themselves of property, conveyed for future support, for the payment of their claims, when the debtor has no other property out of which payment can be enforced. (Harris v. Brink, 578.)

11. FRAUDULENT CONVEYANCES — FUTURE SUPPORT — SUIT TO SET ASIDE.—If property is conveyed by a debtor for his future support, and the parties have acted in good faith, the conveyance may be sustained, so far as the consideration paid by the grantee, without notice, is involved, but will be set aside as to any value in the property in excess of the amount paid; and, in such a case, the grantee is chargeable with the value of the use of the property. (Harris v. Brink, 578.)

See Guardian and Ward, 4.

GAS-WELL.
See Injunction, 4, 5.

GUARANTY.
See Suretyship, 2-5.

GUARDIAN AND WARD.

1. GUARDIAN AND WARD—FINAL SETTLEMENT—WHAT IS NOT.—A final report made by a guardian who resigns and pays over a balance in his hands to his successor, is not a final settlement required by statute. (State v. Parsons, 430.)

2. GUARDIAN AND WARD—PARTIAL SETTLEMENT—COLLATERAL ATTACK.—A partial settlement, approved by the court, made by a guardian who resigns, cannot be attacked collaterally. It is binding as to all matters properly embraced therein until set aside, corrected, or modified in some direct proceeding brought for that purpose. (State v. Parsons, 430.)

3. GUARDIAN AND WARD—SUIT TO SET ASIDE FINAL SETTLEMENT.—A guardian's final settlement made by him with his ward, and approved by the court after the ward becomes twenty-one years of age, or if a female, after she marries a man of that age, cannot be set aside, modified, or corrected after the expiration of three years from the date of its approval; nor can it be set aside in an action brought within three years except for fraud or mistake. (State v. Parsons, 430.)

4. FRAUDULENT CONVEYANCES — SUIT BY WARD AGAINST GUARDIAN.—The solvency or insolvency of the sureties on a guardian's bond does not affect a ward's right to have his guardian's conveyance of real estate, made during the latter's lifetime, set aside as fraudulent, in order that it may be sold by the administrator for the payment of the debts of the decedent. (State v. Parsons, 430.)

5. GUARDIAN AND WARD—ACTION ON BOND—JOINDER.—An action on a guardian or administrator's bond, or against such guardian or administrator personally, and to set aside a final or partial settlement, may be joined if brought in the court having control of such settlements. (State v. Parsons, 430.)

6. GUARDIAN AND WARD — JOINT SUIT UPON TWO BONDS.—Under a statute providing that, if more than one bond is given for the performance of a duty, a joint suit may be brought, it is proper to sue upon two bonds of a guardian in the same action, although they were not signed by the same sureties. (State v. Parsons, 430.)

See Equity, 1; Limitations of Actions, **1.**

HIGHWAYS.

1. HIGHWAYS AND STREETS—DEDICATION—RIGHT TO CONTROL.—When part of a freehold becomes in fact a public highway or public street of a city, whether affected by dedication or conveyance of the owner, the state has full police power to regulate the actions of all persons in their use of it not inconsistent with its use as a street or highway, and to make such alterations from time to time as the state may deem proper. Subsequent to such dedication or conveyance, the dedicator or grantor has no greater right or interest in the use of such street or highway, as such, than any other person. (City Council v. Parker, 95.)

2. HIGHWAYS, RIGHTS OF LANDOWNER IN LANDS BENEATH.—Where a highway is laid out over lands outside of an incorporated city, town, or village, the public acquires only an easement of passage, with the rights and incidents thereto, while the owner of the land over which the road is laid out retains the fee and ownership of everything connected with the soil, for all purposes not incompatible with the right of the public to the free use of the road as a public highway. (Postal Tel. etc. Co. v. Eaton, 390.)

3. HIGHWAYS.—ONE WHO PURCHASES LAND, PART OF WHICH IS A PUBLIC HIGHWAY, upon which a line of telegraph has been constructed without the consent of the owner and without compensation to him, acquires the right which his grantor had to maintain ejectment against the telegraph corporation, unless duly compensated for the additional servitude which it imposes on the highway. (Postal Tel. etc. Co. v. Eaton, 390.)

4. HIGHWAYS, ADDITIONAL SERVITUDE.—A telegraph line constructed and maintained upon the public highway constitutes an additional servitude, and the owner of the land is entitled to compensation therefor. If not compensated, he may maintain an action to dispossess the telegraph corporation. (Postal Tel. etc. Co. v. Eaton, 390.)

5. HIGHWAYS, TELEGRAPH CORPORATIONS.—The consent of the proper officers of a county that a telegraph line be constructed and maintained upon a public highway is not binding on a landowner, who, if he be not properly compensated, may maintain an action against the corporation maintaining such line. The landowner is protected by the declaration of the constitution that private property shall not be taken or damaged without just compensation. (Postal Tel. etc. Co. v. Eaton, 390.)

See Ejectment, 1.

HOMESTEAD.

1. HOMESTEAD.—WHERE TWO PARCELS OF LAND CORNER WITH EACH OTHER, they are contiguous, and there is nothing unreasonable or unjust in holding that they may be selected and held as a homestead where they do not exceed the legal area or value. (Clements v. Crawford County Bank, 149.)

2. HOMESTEAD.—THE PLATTING OF PART OF A HOMESTEAD INTO LOTS and naming it as a village, and the filing of the plat and the selling of part of the lots do not create a town or village, so as to confine and limit a homestead to a village homestead, nor as to constitute an abandonment of the homestead right in the part so platted but remaining unsold. (Clements v. Crawford County Bank, 149.)

3. HUSBAND AND WIFE—DEED FROM HIM TO HER—HOMESTEAD.—A conveyance from a husband to his wife of real property including their homestead is valid. (Johnson v. Brauch, 857.)

HOMICIDE.

1. MURDER AND MANSLAUGHTER, USE OF DEADLY WEAPON.—Where the death of a human being is caused by the intentional use of a deadly weapon, provocation by words only cannot reduce the killing to manslaughter. (State v. Davis, 837.)

2. MURDER—SELF-DEFENSE MADE NECESSARY BY THE SLAYER'S FAULT.—To instruct the jury that the defendant, on a trial for murder, must come into court with clean hands is not strictly appropriate, but does not entitle him to a new trial, if, from the whole evidence, it is clear that what the judge meant was that he who sets up the plea of self-defense must have been without fault in bringing on the necessity for taking human life. (State v. Davis, 837.)

3. MURDER AND MANSLAUGHTER.—THE HEAT AND PAS-
SION REQUISITE to reduce a homicide from murder to manslaughter must be based on a provocation which the law deems adequate, and must be such that, while it need not dethrone reason entirely, nor shut out knowledge and volition, would naturally destroy
the sway of reason and render the mind of an ordinary person incapable of cool reflection and produce what, according to all human
experience, may be called uncontrollable impulses to do violence.
(State v. Davis, 837.)

4. MURDER—RIGHT OF PERSON TO REPOSSESS HIMSELF
OF PROPERTY.—It is error to instruct a jury in a trial for murder
that if the decedent had a piece of property which the defendant
took possession of in his presence, then the decedent had the right
to repossess himself of it, and if killed by the defendant with malice
aforethought while trying to so repossess himself, the killing was
murder, because such instruction is calculated to mislead the jury
into believing the deceased might lawfully exercise his right, though
though in so doing he committed a breach of the peace. (State v.
Davis, 837.)

5. CRIMINAL LAW—DRUNKENNESS, WHEN A CRIMINAL
INTENT IS ESSENTIAL TO A CRIME OR TO SOME GRADE
THEREOF.—If the law requires a special intent to exist as an element of a crime, one who, when he does the act, is so drunk that he
has not this intent, cannot be held guilty of a crime. Hence, if a
man while drunk kills another, and the statute divides murder into
two degrees, and to constitute the first a specific intent to take life
is required, the slayer should not be found guilty of this higher
degree of offense, if, at the time of his criminal act, his intoxication
was such that he could not have this intent, unless it further appeared that he first resolved to kill the decedent and afterward drank to
extreme intoxication and then carried out his former intention.
(State v. Kraemer, 664.)

6. DYING DECLARATIONS IDENTIFYING THE ACCUSED
OR REFERRING TO PREVIOUS IDENTIFICATION are admissible in evidence against him on his trial for the murder of the
person making the declarations. (State v. Kessler, 911.)

7. HOMICIDE. — INSTRUCTIONS IN A HOMICIDE CASE
which intimate an opinion that the killing was done by the accused,
when the latter has not distinctly admitted that he committed the
homicide, are erroneous. (Ryder v. State, 334.)

8. CRIMINAL LAW—MALICE.—An instruction that the law
will imply malice from any wanton, thoughtless, cruel, or depraved
act, any act going to show an intention on the part of the party.
which shows a heart devoid of all social instincts and fatally bent
on mischief, is correct, and proper to be given when the defendant
is on trial for murder. (State v. Davis, 837.)

See Former Acquittal, 1, 2; Indictment.

HUSBAND AND WIFE.

1. A HUSBAND'S LIABILITY FOR THE ANTENUPTIAL
DEBTS OF HIS WIFE is not affected by a statute providing that
a married woman may bargain, sell, assign, and transfer her separate personal property, and carry on any trade or business and
perform any labor or service on her sole and separate account, and
she may alone sue or be sued in the courts of this state upon account of such property, business, or service. (Kies v. Young, 198.)

2. HUSBAND AND WIFE—ESTATE BY CURTESY NOT SUB-
JECT TO WIFE'S LIABILITIES.—Though a judgment is recovered

against a wife. under which if a sale is made in her lifetime, the title in fee will vest in the purchaser, yet, upon her death without such sale, an estate vests in her husband as tenant by the curtesy free from the lieu of such judgment. (Hampton v. Cook, 194.)

3. HUSBAND AND WIFE—ESTATE BY THE CURTESY EXISTS NOTWITHSTANDING STATUTES CONFERRING ADDITIONAL RIGHTS ON MARRIED WOMEN.—A statute declaring that the real and personal property of every married woman in the state shall, so long as she may choose, be and remain her separate estate and property, and may be devised, bequeathed, or conveyed by her the same as if she were unmarried, and shall not be subject to the debts of her husband, does not, in the event of her death without conveying or making any other disposition of the property, defeat her husband's rights as tenant by the curtesy. (Hampton v. Cook, 194.)

4. HUSBAND AND WIFE—SEPARATION, AGREEMENT OF, WHEN DOES NOT AFFECT HIS INTEREST IN HER ESTATE.— An agreement between a husband and wife entered into pending a suit for divorce, and for the disposition of their property, by which each is to receive a specific sum from their homestead and one-half of the net proceeds of their personal property, and is released from all obligations of every character for the future acts and debts of the other, does not affect his right to share in her estate upon her death intestate. (Jones v. Lamont, 251.)

5. HUSBAND AND WIFE — SERVICES OF HUSBAND, RIGHTS OF HIS CREDITORS TO.—A married woman may employ her husband as her agent and make use of his business ability, experience, and energy in making her business successful. Earnings upon, or increase in, her capital in such business, though due in part to his services, belong to her, and are not liable to be seized by his creditors. Especially is this true when his services are rendered upon a compensation not shown to be an unusual compensation for such services. Instead of embarking in business in her own name, she may organize a corporation. supplying the capital, and the corporation may employ the husband in managing its business. (Taylor v. Wands, 818.)

6. MARRIED WOMEN—NOTE OF—PRESUMPTION.—If a married woman gives her individual note, it is presumed that she gives it on her own contract. for value, and to charge her separate estate. (Temples v. Equitable Mortgage Co., 326.)

7. MARRIED WOMEN—ESTOPPEL.—If a married woman borrows money, and by her conduct or representations induces the lender to suppose she is borrowing the money for her own use, when in fact her real purpose, unknown to him with whom she is dealing, is to obtain the money for her husband, she is estopped from denying that which she herself has induced the lender to believe. (Temples v. Equitable Mortgage Co., 326.)

8. MARRIED WOMEN—ESTOPPEL.—If a married woman gives her individual note and secures its payment by a mortgage on her separate estate. reciting that the loan received by her is for her sole use and benefit, and not to be used in the payment of any debt of her husband, nor in any manner for his use or benefit, she is estopped, in an action to recover on the note, from denying or contradicting the recitals contained in the mortgage. (Temples v. Equitable Mortgage Co., 326.)

9. MARRIED WOMEN—NOTE AND MORTGAGE OF—PLEA AND PROOF NECESSARY TO DEFEAT.—If a married woman gives her individual note and secures its payment by a mortgage on her separate estate, and attaches an affidavit to the mortgage

stating that the money received is for her sole use and benefit, and is not to be used in payment of any debt of her husband, nor in any manner for his use and benefit, she cannot, in an action to recover on the note. defend on the ground that it was given for a debt of her husband alone, unless she goes farther and alleges and proves that the holder of the note had notice of that fact. (Temple v. Equitable Mortgage Co., 326.)

See Fraudulent Conveyances, 2; Homestead, 8; Judgment, 1; Mechanic's Lien, 4.

INDICTMENT.

CRIMINAL LAW—REINDICTMENT NOT NECESSARY.—If an accused is tried under an indictment charging him with murder and found guilty of manslaughter, and, on moving for, obtains a new trial, he need not be reindicted before he can again be tried for the offense. (State v. Smith, 680.)

See Embezzlement.

INJUNCTION.

1. INJUNCTION AGAINST ENFORCEMENT OF JUDGMENT —COLLATERAL ATTACK.—A proceeding to enjoin the enforcement of a judgment or decree by execution or decretal order is a collateral attack upon the judgment, and cannot be maintained for mere errors or irregularities, but only by showing that the judgment or decree, or the part thereof, the enforcement of which is sought to be enjoined is void. (Davis v. Clements, 539.)

2. INJUNCTION AGAINST ENFORCEMENT OF JUDGMENT —COMPLAINT FOR, WHEN INSUFFICIENT.—A complaint in an action to enjoin the enforcement of a judgment ordering the foreclosure and sale of real estate is insufficient where it does not allege what the record of the case, in which the decree was rendered, shows on the subject. (Davis v. Clements, 539.)

3. INJUNCTION AGAINST ENFORCEMENT OF JUDGMENT —COMPLAINT FOR—DEMURRER.—A judgment of a court of general jurisdiction will be presumed, on appeal, to be valid. Hence, unless the facts stated, in a complaint in an action to enjoin the enforcement of such judgment, are sufficient to overcome or exclude this presumption, a demurrer to the complaint should be sustained. (Davis v. Clements, 539.)

4. INJUNCTION AGAINST NUISANCE — GASWELL NEAR DWELLING.—The mere drilling of a gaswell within about fifty yards of a dwelling will not be enjoined on the ground that if it is completed there will be a loud noise, pollution of the air, danger from fire or explosion, on account of the natural gas, or danger by reason of the. well overflowing with oil or water, thus causing great damage to, and depreciation of, property, if it is not shown that gas, water, or oil will be found, and that the well cannot be so operated as to avoid the apprehended injuries if such gas or liquids are found. (Windfall Mfg. Co. v. Patterson, 532.)

5. INJUNCTION AGAINST NUISANCE—GASWELL.—The sinking of a gaswell to supply fuel for a manufacturing plant is not a nuisance per se, and cannot be enjoined as such. (Windfall Mfg. Co. v. Patterson, 532.)

6. INJUNCTION AGAINST NUISANCE—BUSINESS.—A business which is a nuisance per se, as well as one that is so conducted as to become an actual nuisance, will be enjoined; but a business which merely threatens to become a nuisance will be enjoined only

where the court is satisfied that the threatened nuisance is inevitable. (Windfall Mfg. Co. v. Patterson, 532.)

7. TAXES — COLLECTION — INJUNCTION — SUFFICIENCY OF ALLEGATIONS IN COMPLAINT.—In applying for an injunction to restrain the collection of taxes, an allegation in the complaint that the owner of the property was a nonresident of the state is not equivalent to an averment that his personal property and business were not in the state. (Buck v. Miller, 436.)

8. STATUTE OF LIMITATIONS, INJUNCTION AGAINST PLEADING.—A court of equity may, by the use of its injunctive power, disarm the defendant from using the statute of limitations fraudulently in an action at law, as where there has been a fraudulent concealment by the defendant of the cause of action against him, or, whether the act was fraudulent or not, when the defendant has employed means to mislead the plaintiff or to hide from him the fact that a cause of action has arisen. Hence if one employs an attorney to perform services in collecting certain municipal bonds, agreeing to pay him therefor ten per cent of any amount which may be realized on such bonds, and afterward settles with his creditor, or sells the bonds to another person acting for the creditor, without disclosing these facts to the attorney, equity will enjoin the pleading of the statute of limitations against an action by the attorney to recover his compensation brought upon discovering the facts entitling him to maintain it. (Holloway v. Appleget, 827.)

See Municipal Corporations, 18; Taxes, 9.

INSANITY.
See Criminal Law, 2; Witnesses, 5.

INSOLVENCY.

1. INSOLVENCY—DEBTS DUE NONRESIDENTS, WHEN DISCHARGED BY.—If a debtor and creditor are residents of the same state at the date of a contract made and payable therein, a discharge granted under the insolvency law enacted before the making of the contract is a valid defense to an action thereon, notwithstanding the creditor subsequently and before the institution of the proceeding in insolvency became a resident of another state. (Scamman v. Bonslett, 226.)

2. INSOLVENT LAWS OF ONE STATE CANNOT DISCHARGE THE CONTRACTS OF CITIZENS OF OTHER STATES, because they have no extraterritorial operation, unless such citizens voluntarily appear in the insolvency proceedings and become parties thereto. (Scamman v. Bonslett, 226.)

See Guardian and Ward, 4; Judgment, 11; Railroads, 19.

INSTRUCTIONS.

1. INSTRUCTIONS—THEORY SUPPORTED BY SOME EVIDENCE.—It is proper to give an instruction on a theory which is supported by some evidence, although it may be opposed by a preponderance of evidence. (Newbury v. Getchel & Martin etc. Mfg. Co., 582.)

2. INSTRUCTIONS WITHDRAWING FROM CONSIDERATION BY THE JURY any evidence, however weak, tending to establish material facts, are calculated to mislead, and therefore improper. (Anderson v. Timberlake, 105.)

3. INSTRUCTIONS—QUESTIONS OF LAW.—If the evidence of a fact is positive, and not disputed or questioned, it ought to be taken as an established fact by the court and the jury instructed accordingly. (Kahn v. Traders' Ins. Co., 47.)

4. INSTRUCTIONS—PRESENTMENT OF ISSUES—APPROPRIATE LANGUAGE.—If the pleadings contain a plain statement of the matter in controversy, the court may use the language of the pleadings in presenting the issues to the jury, but if the language of the pleadings is technical, the issues should be presented in the language of the court. (Robinson v. Berkey, 549.)

5. JURY TRIAL.—AN INSTRUCTION SUMMING UP THE FACTS ASSUMED TO BE NECESSARY TO SUPPORT THE ACTION, and stating that if the jury find those facts to exist, their verdict should be for the plaintiff, is not the proper mode of instructing the jury, but if it omits no material fact essential to the right of recovery, a reversal will not be directed because of its having been given. (East St. Louis etc. Ry. Co. v. Eggmann, 400.)

6. JURY TRIAL—INSTRUCTIONS MINGLING TWO CAUSES OF ACTION.—If, in an action to recover for injuries received from the defendant's bull, the court instructs the jury in one instruction that the defendant is liable for injuries resulting from the negligence of the defendant's employés in the performance of a given duty, and in another, that before plaintiff can recover, he must establish the fact that the bull at the time he inflicted the injury was vicious, and that the defendant had knowledge of such viciousness, will not be regarded as prejudicial or erroneous, if the complaint, though in one count, charges the defendant with negligence and also with keeping a bull known to him to be vicious and dangerous, and alleges injuries resulting to the plaintiff. (Clowdis v. Fresno Flume etc. Co., 238.)

7. JURY TRIAL — INSTRUCTIONS, CORRECT MINGLED WITH INCORRECT.—While an inaccurate or incomplete instruction may be cured by subsequently supplying the defect or accurately stating the law, an absolute misstatement of the law is not cured by a correct statement elsewhere in the charge. (State v. Ardoin, 678.)

See Arrest, 2; Damages, 12, 19, 20; False Pretenses; Homicide, 2, 4, 7, 8; Trial.

INSURANCE.

1. INSURANCE—ARBITRATION AS COLLATERAL AGREEMENT.—If an insurance policy contains, first, an agreement to pay a loss within a certain time, and, secondly, an agreement to refer the loss to arbitration, the agreement to arbitrate is collateral to the agreement to pay. (Kahn v. Traders' Ins. Co., 47.)

2. INSURANCE—ARBITRATION CLAUSE AS A DEFENSE.—Breach of a condition for arbitration in a fire insurance policy is not effective as a defense when the insurer asserts that the policy has become absolutely void, or denies the general right of the insured to recover anything under the policy. (Kahn v. Traders' Ins. Co., 47.)

3. INSURANCE — ARBITRATION — NECESSITY OF PLEADING.—If a policy of fire insurance provides that the loss shall not be payable "until sixty days after the proofs, certificates, plans, and specifications, and award of appraisers herein required, shall have been rendered and examinations perfected by assured," an award by arbitrators or appraisers is not absolutely essential to a cause of action on the policy, nor is it necessary for the insured to plead either a submission of the amount of loss to appraisers and an award by them, or facts showing that the insurer has committed a breach of the agreement to arbitrate. (Kahn v. Traders' Ins. Co., 47.)

4. INSURANCE—ARBITRATION—INSTRUCTIONS.—If, in an action on a fire insurance policy, a defense based upon a failure to comply with an arbitration clause in the policy is not specially pleaded, it is error to submit to the jury an issue based upon such clause. (Kahn v. Traders' Ins. Co., 47.)

5. INSURANCE—CONDITION AGAINST FALSE SWEARING. To constitute fraud or false swearing under a condition in a policy of fire insurance avoiding it therefor, there must be false statements willfully made, with respect to a material matter, with the intention of thereby deceiving the insurer. An affidavit sent as proof of loss, stating that the insured goods "were burned up and destroyed by fire," when in fact most of them were destroyed by smoke and water, so as to constitute a total loss, is not false swearing within the meaning of such a policy. (Kahn v. Traders' Ins. Co., 47.)

6. INSURANCE, MORTGAGE CLAUSE—CONDITIONS AVOID-ING POLICY ON COMMENCEMENT OF SUIT TO FORECLOSE. Where a mortgage clause is attached to a policy making the loss payable to the mortgagee, as his interest may appear, and providing that, as to his interest, the policy shall not be invalidated by any act or neglect of the mortgagor, and the policy also contains a condition that, upon commencement of proceedings to foreclose or upon a sale under a deed of trust, or if any change takes place in the title or possession, whether by legal process, judicial decree, or voluntary transfer, the policy shall be void, such condition is to be construed as operating against the mortgagor only, and not as avoiding the policy as against the mortgagee on the commencement of a suit by him to foreclose his mortgage, nor by the appointment of a receiver in such suit to take possession of the mortgaged premises. (Lancashire Ins. Co. v. Boardman, 621.)

7. INSURANCE, ADDITIONAL—WHEN VOID.—If a policy of insurance, assented to by the insured, provides that it shall become void if the insured contracts other insurance on the property without the written consent of the company, indorsed on the policy, additional insurance, obtained without the required indorsement, renders the policy void, although the secretary of the company consents, by letter, to the additional insurance. (O'Leary & Bro. et al. v. Merchants' etc. Mut. Ins. Co., 555.)

8. INSURANCE, ADDITIONAL—WRITTEN CONSENT.—If a policy of insurance, assented to by the insured, provides that additional insurance shall be void, without the written consent of the company is indorsed on the policy, and that no agent shall have power to waive any provision of the policy, the written consent of the secretary and general agent of the company to additional insurance is not the consent of the company, and such additional insurance, so consented to by the secretary, is void, where there is no proof of his authority to give such consent, or to waive the indorsement. (O'Leary & Bro. et al. v. Merchants' etc. Mut. Ins. Co., 555.)

9. INSURANCE — ADDITIONAL INSURANCE—WAIVER OF CONDITION.—If a general insurance agent who issues the policy in suit has knowledge of, and consents to, additional insurance, but fails to indorse it thereon, and through neglect fails to notify his company thereof, and its adjuster, after the loss and with knowledge of such additional insurance, and without objection thereto, seeks to adjust the loss, the company is estopped from insisting on a forfeiture of the policy on the ground that such additional insurance was procured by the insured without the consent of the company thereto being indorsed on the policy as required therein. (Kahn v. Traders' Ins. Co., 47.)

10. INSURANCE—POWER OF AGENT—ADDITIONAL INSUR-ANCE.—An insurance agent clothed with authority to make con-

tracts of insurance, to issue policies and to receive premiums therefor, is the general agent of the insurer and authorized to consent to additional insurance. The insurer is bound not only by notice to such agent, but his knowledge of matters relating to the contract of insurance must be held to be the knowledge of the insurer. (Kahn v. Traders' Ins. Co., 47.)

11. MUTUAL BENEFIT ASSOCIATIONS, CHANGE OF BY-LAWS OF.—If a mutual benefit society issues to a member a certificate of insurance, it cannot, by the subsequent adoption of a by-law, modify or change the contract without the consent of the member. Hence, if when a certificate is issued, it defines what shall be deemed a total disability, and declares the member to be entitled to a sum specified on the suffering by him of such disability, the society cannot, without his consent, afterward reduce the classes of total disability. (Starling v. Supreme Council, 709.)

12. MUTUAL BENEFIT ASSOCIATIONS, LOSS OF MEMBERSHIP, WHEN DOES NOT BAR A RECOVERY.—If one was a member of a council of a mutual benefit association until that council broke up for want of members, and he then obtained a transfer card and deposited it within another council in the same city, which refused to accept him as a member, he cannot be compelled to apply for membership in a council in another city, and cannot be deprived of the benefit of the certificate issued to him on the ground that he had ceased to be a member, if he had paid to the supreme council all sums chargeable against him. (Starling v. Supreme Council, 709.)

13. JURY TRIAL—MUTUAL BENEFIT ASSOCIATIONS—INSTRUCTION AS TO WHAT IS AN AVOCATION.—If the jury is instructed that to entitle plaintiff to recover he must be totally disabled from following any avocation, and that it is for the jury to draw from the evidence the inference of fact upon this subject, the defendant cannot be regarded as prejudiced by the further statement on the part of the judge that the fact that a man may work for a few moments or perhaps for a few months, is not necessarily conclusive evidence that he can follow some avocation. (Starling v. Supreme Council, 709.)

14. INSURANCE—NOTICE OF LOSS.—If the general agent of the insurer on the day of a loss informs him by letter thereof, and within a few days thereafter the insurer sends an adjuster with power to investigate, adjust, and settle the loss, this is a compliance with the requirement of immediate notice of loss contained in the policy, and a waiver of proof of loss and magistrate's certificate. (Kahn v. Traders' Ins. Co., 47.)

15. INSURANCE—EVIDENCE OF LOSS.—In an action to recover on a fire insurance policy, a witness who was the bookkeeper for the insured up to the time of the fire is competent to enumerate and state the value of certain property destroyed by the fire, but not included in the proofs of loss. (Kahn v. Traders' Ins. Co., 47.)

16. INSURANCE—EVIDENCE OF PROOFS OF LOSS.—An affidavit of loss and schedule of goods in stock at the time thereof furnished by the insured to the insurer, are competent evidence, in an action to recover on a policy of fire insurance, to show a compliance, or attempted compliance, with the requirement of the policy that proofs of loss should be furnished. (Kahn v. Traders' Ins. Co., 47.)

17. INSURANCE—EVIDENCE OF OFFERS OF COMPROMISE. If a claim for loss under a fire insurance policy is admitted by all parties, and the only dispute between the adjuster of the insurer and the insured is the amount of his claim, offers of settlement made by such adjuster to the insured are admissible in evidence. They are

not only admissible, but they tend to show a waiver of additional insurance without the consent of the insurer, and also a waiver of proof of loss. (Kahn v. Traders' Ins. Co., 47.)

See Estates, 7, 8; Process, 2; Statutes, 11; Wills, 11; Witnesses, 11.

JOINT LIABILITY.

1. JOINT LIABILITY — DEATH OF OBLIGOR — PRACTICE AT COMMON LAW.—At common law the estate of a deceased joint contractor was not liable to the obligee in the joint contract except in case of the insolvency of the surviving joint obligor. In the latter case the obligee had the right to proceed in equity against the administrators of the deceased joint obligor. Otherwise, he must proceed against the solvent surviving obligor at law. (Chadwick v. Hopkins, 38.)

2. JOINT LIABILITY — DEATH OF ONE OBLIGOR—PARTIES—PRACTICE UNDER CODES.—Under codes removing any objection to joining causes of action formerly distinguished as legal and equitable, the administrator or executor of a deceased co-obligor in a joint contract may, in an action thereon, be joined with the surviving obligor whether he is insolvent or not, and separate judgment may be entered against such defendants in such action. (Chadwick v. Hopkins, 38.)

3. JOINT LIABILITY—DEATH OF ONE OBLIGOR—PROPER PARTIES DEFENDANT.—In an action to recover on a joint contract after the death of one of the co-obligors, the personal representative of the latter should be joined with the surviving obligor as parties defendant, and their rights and liabilities determined in one action, under a statute removing any objection to joining causes of action, legal and equitable, and providing that "any person may be made a defendant who has or claims an interest in the controversy adverse to the plaintiff, or who is a necessary party to a complete determination or settlement of a question involved therein." (Chadwick v. Hopkins, 38.)

JUDGMENT.

1. A JUDGMENT OUTSIDE THE ISSUES IS VOID.—Hence, if in an action to foreclose a mortgage made by a husband and wife to secure notes executed by him only, a personal judgment is entered against her, there being no allegation in the complaint respecting her personal liability, such judgment is void as against her. (Gille v. Emmons, 609.)

2. JUDGMENT. — THE AFFIRMANCE OF A VOID JUDGMENT does not give it any validity, nor deprive the defendant against whom it is void of the right to have it vacated on motion at any time. (Gille v. Emmons, 609.)

3. JUDGMENT OF SISTER STATE.—A judgment or decree of the courts of one state is conclusive in those of another, if the court pronouncing it had jurisdiction of the cause and the parties. (Mutual Fire Ins. Co. v. Phoenix etc. Co., 693.)

4. JUDGMENT AGAINST PARTY IN ONE CAPACITY DOES NOT AFFECT HIM IN ANOTHER.—A judgment against one as an individual, precluding him from claiming property, does not estop him from claiming it as a trustee for others. (Sonnenberg v. Steinbach, 885.)

5. JUDGMENTS AND DECREES CANNOT BE ATTACKED COLLATERALLY because they include items which courts other than those by whom they were rendered may hold to be illegal. (Mutual Fire Ins. Co. v. Phoenix etc. Co., 693.)

16. JUDGMENT, VACATING.—IF A JUDGMENT IS VOID as against a defendant, because outside of the issues, as where personal judgment is entered against a defendant in a foreclosure suit when the complaint does not show any personal liability, such judgment may be vacated on motion at any time. (Gille v. Emmons, 609.)

17. JUDGMENT—VACATING, IN EQUITY, AFTER TIME FIXED BY STATUTE.—Although a time is prescribed by statute, within which a judgment may be vacated for irregularity or fraud in obtaining it, yet a court of equity has power to vacate it, for such cause, after the time so fixed by statute, if proper reasons are shown for not making such application within the time, as where the person against whom it was pronounced did not learn of its rendition until after the expiration of the statutory time for setting it aside. (Larson v. Williams, 544.)

18. JUDGMENT, VACATION OF, WHO MAY COMPLAIN OF.— · If the only person whose rights are affected by the vacating of a judgment or decree does not complain thereof, a third person will not be heard to object that the method of obtaining relief was not proper. (Yarnell v. Brown, 380.)

19. RES JUDICATA.—THE DECISION OF A MOTION which must be tried and determined by the court, and from which decision no appeal can be taken, is not conclusive upon the parties in a subsequent action presenting the same issues, but in which they are entitled to a trial by jury. Hence, if an assignee for the benefit of creditors moves to discharge an attachment, and the court makes special findings declaring the assignment fraudulent and void, and for that reason refuses to discharge the attachment, and the assignee thereafter brings an action in replevin to recover the same property, the former findings and decision on the motion do not constitute such a trial of the questions involved as precludes the assignee or his successor in interest from trying the title to the property in the regular and formal action of replevin. (Blair v. Anderson, 606.)

20. RES JUDICATA—USURY.—One against whom a judgment has been recovered foreclosing a mortgage and whose property is sold under such judgment and the proceeds paid to the plaintiff therein, cannot maintain an action against such plaintiff on the ground that the judgment included usurious interest. Since usury goes to defeat a recovery in whole or in part and is necessarily connected with the contract sued upon, the recovery of a judgment thereon, whether the defense of usury was pleaded or not, negatives its existence and estops the defendant from subsequently alleging usury in the judgment. (Ryan v. Southern etc. Assn., 831.)

See Assignment, 1-4; Bills of Review, 4; Consuls, 3; Corporations, 7-9; Ejectment, 2; Execution, 5, 6; Executors and Administrators, 4; Injunction, 1, 3; Mechanic's Lien, 5; Merger, 2; Mortgage, 7; Statutes, 7-9.

JUDICIAL NOTICE.

See Evidence; Legislature, 2.

JURAT.

See Affidavit, 3; Chattel Mortgage, 2.

JURISDICTION.

1. JURISDICTION—NOTICE OF THE TIME WHEN A CAUSE IS SET FOR TRIAL is a prerequisite of the jurisdiction of a justice of the peace, if the statute requires such notice to be given. (Los Angeles v. Young, 234.)

2. JURISDICTION—STATE AND NATIONAL TRIBUNALS.—
Whenever judicial power is by the constitution of the United States
vested in its courts, the jurisdiction may by Congress be made exclusive of state authority, but if Congress does not provide that jurisdiction of the national courts shall be exclusive, the state courts
have concurrent jurisdiction. (Wilcox v. Luco, 305.)

3. JURISDICTION, WAIVER OF WANT OF SERVICE OF SUM-
MONS.—If the defendant moves to set aside the service of summons
and complaint upon a ground entitling him to the granting of the
motion, but it is, nevertheless, denied, he, by subsequently answering the complaint and interposing a counterclaim and demanding affirmative judgment thereon in his favor, submits himself to the jurisdiction of the court, and cannot thereafter avail himself of its error
in denying his motion to vacate the service of the summons. The
result must have been different, if the defendant had merely answered the complaint without seeking to assert an affirmative cause
of action in his own favor. (Lower v. Wilson, 865.)

4. JURISDICTION, LOSS OF BY APPEAL.—During the pendency
of an appeal in a criminal case from an order denying a new
trial, a motion to set aside such order cannot be heard in the trial
court. (People v. Mayne, 256.)

5. JURISDICTION OVER CRIMES COMMITTED ON LANDS
PURCHASED BY THE UNITED STATES WITH THE ASSENT
OF THE STATE.—If lands are purchased by the United States with
the consent of the state, for the erection thereon of forts, arsenals,
dockyards, or other needful buildings, the lands so purchased are
within the exclusive jurisdiction of the United States. Among such
needful buildings are courthouses and postoffices. (State v. Mack,
811.)

6. JURISDICTION OVER LANDS PURCHASED BY THE
UNITED STATES—ATTEMPT OF THE STATE TO RESERVE
JURISDICTION IN CRIMINAL CASES.—If a state consents to the
purchase by the United States of lands to be used as a courthouse
and postoffice, and assents to the exclusive jurisdiction of the United
States "except the administration of the criminal laws of the state,"
this reservation includes only the right of the state to execute valid
process upon the lands so purchased for the violation of state laws
committed within the state, but not upon the lands so purchased.
(State v. Mack, 811.)

7. PRACTICE, JURISDICTION OF THE SUPREME COURT
OF UTAH WHERE THE ACTION WAS ORIGINALLY
BROUGHT BEFORE A JUSTICE OF THE PEACE.—Where an
action was brought before a justice of the peace and afterward appealed to the district court, its decision is final, and cannot be
reviewed by the supreme court, except in so far as it relates to the
validity or constitutionality of a statute or of a municipal ordinance.
(Eureka City v. Wilson, 904.)

8. JURISDICTION OF A JUSTICE OF THE PEACE, WHEN
MUST APPEAR AFFIRMATIVELY.—If a statute requires a justice of the peace to give a party notice of the time when his cause
is set for trial, such notice must be in writing and, upon certiorari,
must appear by the return. Its existence is not proved by statements in the docket of the justice that the counsel for the adverse
party stated that the notice of trial had been served on counsel for
the defendant, and that he would produce the same. (Los Angeles
v. Young, 234.)

See Consuls, 2; Judgment, 8.

JUSTICES OF THE PEACE.
See Jurisdiction, 1, 7, 8,

LACHES.
See Negotiable Instruments, 8.

LEGISLATURE.

1. CONSTITUTIONAL LAW—LIMITATIONS UPON LEGISLATIVE POWER.—The only limitations upon the power of the legislature are those imposed by the state constitution, the federal constitution, and valid treaties and acts of Congress. (Townsend v. State, 477.)

2. CONSTITUTIONAL LAW, LEGISLATIVE POWER TO DECLARE THE MEANING OF A STATUTE.—If the courts have construed a statute and declared its meaning, the legislature cannot thereafter, by a second statute, compel a different construction to be given to the first, so as to affect pre-existing judgments or rights dependent thereon. (In re Handley's Estate, 926.)

3. CONSTITUTIONAL LAW—JUDICIAL ACTION BY LEGISLATURE.—The legislature does not exercise judicial functions by declaring that the use of natural gas in flambeau lights is a wasteful and extravagant use thereof. Such a declaration in a preamble would not invalidate an act, even if it were judicial action, as the preamble is not an essential part of the statute. (Townsend v. State, 477.)

4. CONSTITUTIONAL LAW—FIRE LIMITS.—A common council of a municipal corporation may, by the legislature, be authorized to determine fire limits, and to provide that therein no building shall be constructed except of brick, stone, or other incombustible material without permission, and to cause the removal of any building constructed or repaired in violation of any ordinance. (Eureka City v. Wilson, 904.)

5. TO CONSTITUTE AN APPROPRIATION OF PUBLIC MONEY there must be money placed in a fund applicable to a designated purpose. The word "appropriate" means to allot, assign, set apart, or apply to a particular use or purpose, and an appropriation in the sense of the constitution must set apart a portion of the public moneys for a public use. (State v. La Grave, 764.)

6. APPROPRIATION OF PUBLIC FUNDS, WHAT IS NOT.—A statute does not accomplish an appropriation of public moneys, though it declares it the duty of the county commissioners of every county in the state in which public arms, accouterments, or military stores are now, or at any time hereafter shall be received, for the use of any volunteer organized militia company, to provide a suitable armory for organized militia companies within such county; that all claims for the expense of procuring and maintaining armories shall be audited and approved by the board of military auditors, and, upon approval, shall be presented to the state controller, who shall draw his warrant upon the state treasury for the amount so approved, and the state treasurer shall pay the same, on presentation, out of the general fund, such expenses not to exceed seventy-five dollars per month for any company, except that companies drilling with field pieces or machine guns may be allowed an additional sum of twelve dollars per month for each piece or gun. (State v. La Grave, 764.)

7. CONSTITUTIONAL LAW—PRESUMPTION IN FAVOR OF LEGISLATIVE ACTION.—If the legislature has enacted a regulation for the benefit of the public or some general class thereof, and

the regulation is assailed as an unnecessary and unreasonable interference with property rights, or with the right to contract, the presumption is in favor of the validity of the legislative action, and unless some plain provision of the constitution has been violated or it can be said that the regulation is not within the rule of necessity in view of facts of which judicial notice may be taken, the statute must be sustained. (People v. Smith, 715.)

See Municipal Corporations, 2.

LIBEL.

1. LIBEL, PRIVILEGED COMMUNICATION.—A FATHER who honestly believes disparaging reports about a suitor of his daughter, and who repeats such reports to friends of the suitor in confidence, without intending to injure him, but to convey to him that his attentions to his daughter must cease, is not guilty of slander. His legal and moral duty as a father makes his communication privileged, if not prompted by malice, and before a recovery can be had against him by the suitor, he must assume the burden of proving that the father was actuated by malice. (Baysset v. Hire, 675.)

2. LIBEL—CRITICISM OF A BOOK.—When an author places his book before the public, he invites criticism, and however hostile the criticism may be and however much damage it may cause him by preventing sales, the critic is not liable to an action for libel, if he has made no misstatement of any material fact contained in the book and does not attack the character of the author. The propositions contained in the book the critic is at liberty to attack or denounce with sarcasm and ridicule. (Dowling v. Livingston, 702.)

3. LIBEL, CRITICISM OF A BOOK—UNDESERVED RIDICULE.—An instruction in an action brought by an author for the hostile criticism of his book, that the defendants had the right to ridicule it, if, in the candid judgment of any fair mind, it or any part thereof, deserved ridicule, is not sufficiently favorable to the defendant, because he had the right to use ridicule if he believed in good faith that the book deserved it, whether he is mistaken in his belief or not, and whether any fair mind would have agreed with his opinion or not. (Dowling v. Livingston, 702.)

4. LIBEL, CHARGE OF PLAGIARISM, WHAT IS NOT.—To charge one author with quoting from another without giving him credit is not libelous. It does not amount to an accusation of plagiarism. (Dowling v. Livingston, 702.)

5. LIBEL.—TO CALL A REMEDY PROPOSED BY AN AUTHOR A QUACK REMEDY is not libelous. (Dowling v. Livingston, 702.)

6. LIBEL—INCORRECT STATEMENT.—A statement in a review of a book that certain measures advocated therein had not the merit of originality, as Horace Greeley had advocated the same thing for fifty years, is not libelous, though, as a matter of fact, it is not true that Horace Greeley advocated the same thing for fifty years, or at all. (Dowling v. Livingston, 702.)

7. LIBEL—SUFFICIENCY OF COMPLAINT.—A declaration alleging that defendant, a corporation, has caused to be published in a certain newspaper a statement concerning the plaintiff, who had been the agent of such company, that he was no longer connected with it, and that any contracts made by him for such company would be void, and also alleging that such publication was maliciously made with the motive and for the purpose of falsely holding the plaintiff out to the world as an impostor, seeking and undertaking to act as an agent for such company without authority, when in

fact he was not so attempting. states a good cause of action for libel. (Behre v. National Cash Register Co., 320.)

LICENSE.

1. LICENSE TO USE REAL PROPERTY, WHEN NOT ASSIGNABLE.—One who, in consideration of moneys furnished with which to assist in the erection of a building, is given the right to use and occupy the second story thereof, acquires a mere license which he cannot assign to another, and his attempt to assign terminates his license. (Bates v. Duncan, 190.)

2. LICENSE TO USE ANOTHER'S LAND—REVOCABILITY OF.—A mere naked license to use the land of another is revocable at the pleasure of the licensor, but when the license has been acted upon and expense incurred in reliance thereon, it cannot be revoked without at least placing the licensee in statu quo. (Buck v. Foster, 427.)

3. LICENSE TO REMOVE STANDING TIMBER NOT EXERCISED IN THE TIME STIPULATED.—If a landowner sells the timber on his land, to be removed within a time specified, and the timber remains uncut after the expiration of that time, it reverts to the owner of the realty, but timber which is cut within that time becomes the personal property of the licensee and remains such, though it is not removed from the land within the time agreed upon. (Macomber v. Detroit etc. R. R. Co., 713.)

4. VENDOR AND PURCHASER—CONVEYANCE FREE OF IRREVOCABLE LICENSE—DRAINAGE THROUGH DITCH.—One who purchases land without notice of an adjoining owner's right of drainage through a ditch thereon, and without knowledge of such facts as would put a man of ordinary prudence upon inquiry, takes the land free of such right, although it is an irrevocable license, and his deed thereto, even to one who does have notice or knowledge of that right, conveys it free of the right. (Buck v. Foster, 427.)

LIENS.

See Judgment, 9; Taxes, 8.

LIMITATIONS OF ACTIONS.

1. GUARDIAN AND WARD—LIMITATION OF ACTION ON BOND.—An action for the breach of a guardian's bond, committed prior to the enactment of the Indiana civil procedure act of 1881, must be brought, under the present statute of that state, within twenty years after the cause of action has accrued. (State v. Parsons, 430.)

2. PLEADING—STATUTE OF LIMITATIONS—REPLY.—The plaintiff need not anticipate, and attempt to avoid, in his complaint, the defense of the statute of limitations. If it is pleaded as a defense, and the facts bring the case within any of the exceptions to the statute, the proper practice is to set them up in the reply. (State v. Parsons, 430.)

See Injunction, 8.

LITERARY CRITICISM.

See Libel, 2, 3.

LOTTERIES.

1. LOTTERIES.—TO CONSTITUTE A CRIMINAL lottery, there must be a consideration. When small amounts are hazarded to gain large amounts, the result of winning to be determined by the

use of a contrivance of chance, in which neither choice nor skill can exert any effect, it is gambling by lot, or a prohibited lottery. (Loiseau v. State, 84.)

2. LOTTERIES—SLOT MACHINES.—If an owner of a slot machine is a party to an agreement between others, that each of the latter shall drop nickels and play the machine, and that the one whose play shall indicate the highest card hand shall have all the cigars purchased by the nickels thus dropped, and the owner of the machine furnishes a cigar for each nickel dropped into the machine, and delivers all of them to the player, thus obtaining the high hand, such machine, thus used, is a lottery, within the meaning of a constitutional provision prohibiting lotteries; and neither a municipality nor the legislature of the state can authorize the licensing of slot machines to be thus used. (Loiseau v. State, 84.)

MARRIAGE AND DIVORCE.

1. MARRIAGE, FORM OF CONTRACT OF.—No particular form is required to constitute a contract of marriage. It is sufficient that the parties in some form declare that they take each other as husband and wife. Statutory provisions concerning the solemnization of marriage are generally deemed directory merely. (State v. Zichfeld, 800.)

2. MARRIAGE, COMMON LAW CONCERNING, WHEN NOT REPEALED BY STATUTES.—Statutory provisions requiring persons to take out a license for their marriage, and enacting how and by whom such persons may be joined in marriage, do not render a marriage contract without compliance therewith void. Hence the marriage of two persons effected by a written contract and without any other solemnization, but followed by the assumption of marital rights and obligations, is valid. (State v. Zichfeld, 800.)

3. HUSBAND AND WIFE—ALIMONY AND ATTORNEYS' FEES.—In an action by a wife for separate maintenance, the court may make an order requiring the husband to pay her a sum of money with which to retain counsel and also to pay her a specified sum monthly for the support of herself and children pending the suit, though the husband has by answer denied all the allegations of the complaint, and the statutes of the state contain no express grant of authority to make such order, except in a suit for divorce. (Milliron v. Milliron, 863.)

See Bigamy, 2.

MARRIED WOMEN STATUTES.

See Husband and Wife, 1, 3.

MASTER AND SERVANT.

1. MASTER AND SERVANT — ORDERS — PURPOSES.—An order to a servant designed for one purpose, and misunderstood by him for another, is not an order for the latter purpose. (Newbury v. Getchel & Martin etc. Mfg. Co., 582.)

2. MASTER AND SERVANT.—If a servant is injured partly through the negligence or incompetency or carelessness of a fellow-servant, of whose incompetency or carelessness the master had notice, and partly through the negligence of another fellow-servant, the master is liable, if, but for the negligence of the incompetent fellow-servant, the injury would not have happened. (Handley v. Daly Min. Co., 916.)

3. MASTER AND SERVANT.—The liability of a master for injuries caused by the incompetency of a fellow-servant depends upon

such incompetency being established by affirmative proof and that it was known to the master, or that, if he had exercised due and proper diligence, he would have learned of such incompetency. The degree of supervising care which a master must exercise to ascertain whether his servant is competent depends on the nature of the service and the dangers attending it. A closer supervision is required over the habits and competency of an engineer than over these of a common laborer. (Handley v. Daly Min. Co., 916.)

4. MASTER AND SERVANT—LIABILITY OF MASTER—TEST.—The liability of a master for injury to his servant depends upon the character of the act, in the performance of which the injury occurs, and not upon the rank of the employé who performs it. If it is one pertaining to a duty which the master owes to his servants, he is answerable to them for the manner of its performance; but if the act is one which pertains only to the duty of an operative, the employé performing it is a mere servant and the master is not answerable to a fellow-servant for its improper performance. (Newbury v. Getchel & Martin etc. Mfg. Co., 582.)

5. MASTER AND SERVANT—CARE TO BE EXERCISED IN THE SELECTION OF SERVANTS.—It is the duty of a master to exercise due and reasonable care in the selection of his servants with reference to their competency and fitness. He must also exercise the same degree of care in retaining his servants after such employment, for his responsibility is the same. (Handley v. Daly Min. Co., 916.)

6. MASTER AND SERVANT—EVIDENCE TO CHARGE MASTER WITH KNOWLEDGE OF INCOMPETENCY OF SERVANT. Incompetency of a servant and negligence of the master in retaining him in his employment may be established by evidence of specific acts of incompetency, and that they were known to the master, or were of such a character and frequency that he, in the exercise of due and reasonable care, must have known of them. If repeated acts of carelessness are shown on the part of the servant, it is proper to leave the question to the jury to determine whether or not they came to the knowledge of the master, or would have come to his knowledge, had used reasonable care. (Handley v. Daly Min. Co., 916.)

7. MASTER AND SERVANT—SAFE PLACE IN WHICH TO WORK.—A servant or other employé has the right to assume that his master or employer has discharged the duty of furnishing a safe place in which his employé is to work and to act upon such assumption in the absence of actual knowledge to the contrary. (Chicago etc. R. R. Co. v. Maroney, 396.)

8. MASTER AND SERVANT, SAFE PLACE IN WHICH TO WORK—DEFECTIVE SCAFFOLDING.—If a workman is employed to assist in the erection of a house, and scaffolding for his use is constructed by his employer, and as so constructed, is defective and unsafe, and hence gives way and injures such employé, his employer is answerable therefor, whether he knew that the scaffolding was unsafe or not, or the employé had equal opportunity with his employer to know that the scaffolding was unsafe and insufficient. The ruling would be different if the scaffolding had originally been properly constructed and had become unsafe by a defect subsequently arising. (Chicago etc. R. R. Co. v. Maroney, 396.)

9. MASTER AND SERVANT—WARNING TO SERVANTS—MASTER'S DUTY.—A master's duty to warn his servant of the dangers incident to his work, extends only to those dangers which the master knows, or has reason to believe, the servant is ignorant of. He is not required to give warning of dangers known to the

servant, or that are so open and obvious that, by the exercise of
care, he would know of them, and the jury should be so instructed.
Newbury v. Getchel & Martin etc. Mfg. Co., 582.)

10. MASTER AND SERVANT—A SERVANT ASSUMES THE
RISK OF DANGEROUS MACHINERY AND APPLIANCES,
WHEN.—If a servant discovers that the service has become more
dangerous than he anticipated, or that there are defects in machinery
or appliances making it unsafe for him to continue in his employment, and notifies the master thereof, he has a right to rely, for a reasonable time, on the promise of the master that the defect will be repaired and the machinery made safe. If, however, the master does
not repair the defect within a reasonable time, and the servant has
full knowledge thereof and of the consequent danger, it is his duty to
quit the service if he does not intend to take the risk, and if thereafter injured thereby, he cannot recover therefor of his master. (Illinois Steel Co. v. Mann, 370.)

11. MASTER AND SERVANT.—REASONABLE TIME FOR THE
SUPPLYING OF DEFECTS IN MACHINERY AND APPLIANCES
by an employer after being notified by his employé and promising the
latter to correct them is such time only as is reasonably necessary for
such repairs; and if the servant continues in his employment after
the lapse of that time, knowing that the defects have not been remedied, he assumes the risk of injury therefrom. (Illinois Steel Co.
v. Mann, 370.)

12. MASTER AND SERVANT—MINOR EMPLOYE—MASTER'S
DUTY—WARNING.—It is the duty of a master who knowingly employs a youthful, or inexperienced servant, and subjects him to the
control of others, to see that he is not employed in a more hazardous position than that for which he was employed, and to give
him such warning of his danger as his youth and inexperience demand; and the master cannot relieve himself of this duty by showing that he delegated its performance to another servant who was
at fault in performing it. (Newbury v. Getchel & Martin etc. Mfg.
Co., 582.)

13. MASTER AND SERVANT.—A servant assumes the risk of
the negligence of his fellow-servants, but not that of the master.
(Handley v. Daly Min. Co., 916.)

14. MASTER AND SERVANT—MINOR EMPLOYE—FELLOW-
SERVANT—VICE-PRINCIPAL.—The fact that a servant, injured by
the negligence of a fellow-servant, was a minor, does not make the
fellow-servant a vice-principal. (Newbury v. Getchel & Martin etc.
Mfg. Co., 582.)

15. MASTER AND SERVANT—MINOR EMPLOYE—RIGHTS
OF.—A master having furnished to his servant a proper machine with
which to work, is not answerable if it is used for an improper purpose; but this rule is not applicable to the case of a minor who obeys
the orders of his superiors and uses machines for the purpose of his
employment as directed by them, he having no knowledge as to
what machines he should use, except as he is informed by his superiors. He has a right to assume that they will subject him to no
greater risks than his contract of employment contemplated, and
that, on account of his age and inexperience, they will furnish him
proper machines, and give him the needed information as to how to
operate them. (Newbury v. Getchel & Martin etc. Mfg. Co., 582.)

16. MASTER AND SERVANT—MINOR EMPLOYE—CONTRIB-
UTORY NEGLIGENCE—CONSIDERATION OF MINORITY.—If a
minor is employed to cut wood into kindling by means of a "cut-
off" saw, and a fellow-servant sets him at such work with a rip-
saw, thus making the employment more hazardous, and he is injured,

It is proper, in an action by him against the master, to instruct the jury, upon the subject of contributory negligence, that they should consider the plaintiff's minority solely upon the question as to whether or not one of his years and experience and intelligence could, and did, know or appreciate the danger, if any, there was in operating the rip-saw. (Newbury v. Getchel & Martin etc. Mfg. Co., 582).

17. MASTER AND SERVANT, KNOWLEDGE OF THE LATTER, WHEN IMPUTED TO THE FORMER.—If servants in charge of an animal become aware that it is of a vicious disposition, such knowledge must be imputed to their master, though there has been no opportunity to communicate with him, and he, in truth, has no knowledge thereof. (Clowdis v. Fresno Flume etc. Co., 238.)

18. NEGLIGENCE OF SERVANT, WHEN IMPUTED TO HIS MASTER.—If servants are put in charge of a bull, to be driven from one place to another, and he develops a vicious disposition, attacking one or more human beings in their presence and to their knowledge, and they thereafter drive him along the public highway, where he attacks and injures another human being, it is a question of fact for the jury whether or not such servants exercised a proper degree of care in the management of the animal at the time of the last injury. (Clowdis v. Fresno Flume etc. Co., 238.)

19. MASTER AND SERVANT—EMPLOYE AS VICE-PRINCIPAL.—A servant, agent, or employé, while performing a duty required of the master, stands in the place of the master, and becomes a vice-principal. The master is, therefore, answerable for his negligence. (Newbury v. Getchel & Martin etc. Mfg. Co., 582.)

20. MASTER AND SERVANT—EMPLOYE AS VICE-PRINCIPAL.—The mere fact that one employé has authority over others does not make him a vice-principal, or superior, so as to charge the master with his negligence; but this rule relates to the negligence of the foreman, as such, and not to his want of care in doing those things which the master is obliged to perform by virtue of the relation existing between him and his servant. (Newbury v. Getchel & Martin etc. Mfg. Co., 582.)

21. MASTER AND SERVANT—FELLOW-SERVANTS.—If a servant is injured by the failure of the master to furnish him a safe place in which to work, the latter cannot escape liability on the ground that the injury was the result of the negligence of a fellow-servant in constructing an unsafe appliance, for the master owes a positive obligation to his servant which he cannot avoid by deputing its performance to another servant. (Chicago etc. R. R. Co. v. Maroney, 396.)

22. MASTER AND SERVANT—INJURY BY FELLOW-SERVANT—MASTER'S LIABILITY.—A master is not answerable for an injury to his servant occasioned by the negligence of a fellow-servant. (Newbury v. Getchel & Martin etc. Mfg. Co., 582.)

23. MASTER AND SERVANT—INJURY BY FELLOW-SERVANT—MASTER'S LIABILITY.—If a minor is employed to cut wood into kindling by means of a "cut-off" saw, but a fellow-servant sets him at such work with a rip-saw, thus putting him in a place of increased danger, and he is injured, he may, where he shows himself free from contributory negligence, recover of the master, if it is found that the fellow-servant had authority to direct him where and how he should work, especially if the fellow-servant ordered him into the more hazardous employment without giving him warning of the dangers incident to the use of the rip-saw, in such work, and that it was more dangerous to use than the "cut-off" saw. It is

otherwise, however, where the fellow servant is not shown to ha
had any such authority. (Newbury v. Getchel & Martin etc. M
Co., 582.)

See Railroads; Statutes, 14, 15, 17.

MECHANIC'S LIEN.

1. MECHANICS' LIEN — DISCONNECTED BUILDINGS. -
claim of lien can be filed and asserted upon several disconnect
buildings without there being any account of the amount of materi
furnished each, when they constitute part of a plant used in 1
business of smelting and are situated upon the same piece of grou
(Salt Lake etc. Co. v. Ibex Mine etc. Co., 944.)

2. MECHANICS' LIEN—BUILDING WHEN NOT COMPLE?
Though a smelter is otherwise completed, if there is afterward ad(
to it a granulating flume which appears to have been necessary
the convenient and economical moving of slag, the time for the fil
of the lien may be computed from the construction of such flu1
(Salt Lake etc. Co. v. Ibex Mine etc. Co., 944.)

3. MECHANICS' LIEN, WAIVER OF.—The right to file and
sert a mechanics' or attachment lien is not waived by obtain
and levying an attachment, if the lien of the attachment is not p
fected and the action is subsequently dismissed. (Salt Lake (
Co. v. Ibex Mine etc. Co., 944.)

4. JUDGMENT, PERSONAL, AGAINST WIFE, BY DEFAU
IS UNAUTHORIZED, WHEN.—If an unmarried man contracts
have a house built for himself, but he afterward marries, and p
ceedings are instituted against both husband and wife to forecl(
a mechanic's lien on the building, a personal judgment by defa1
against her is unauthorized, where there is no averment in the p(
tion which warrants it, although notice was served on both husba
and wife that a personal judgment would be taken as to both. (L
son v. Williams, 544.)

5. JUDGMENT—PROCUREMENT OF, BY FRAUD—VAC/
ING IN EQUITY.—In an action against a husband and wife to f(
close a mechanic's lien, it is an irregular and fraudulent practice
the successful party to procure a judgment by default against
wife, which judgment is not authorized by the petition, and wh
the plaintiff knows is not authorized by it. Hence, she may hav(
vacated, in equity, for "irregularity" and "fraud practiced in obta
ing it," after the time fixed by statute for setting it aside on th
grounds, where she did not know of its rendition until after
expiration of such time. (Larson v. Williams, 544.)

MERGER.

1. MERGER.—IF THE OWNER OF LANDS HAS EXECUT
A TRUST DEED THEREON AND A LEASE THEREOF to
same person, and the latter assigns the lease to a third person
whom the equity of redemption is also assigned by the landowr
the leasehold and the equity merge and become one estate, all
which is subject to the trust deed, and a sale thereunder passes t
paramount to that of the person claiming under the assignment
the lease. (Hudson Commission Co. v. Glencoe etc. Co., 722.)

2. JUDGMENT, ·MERGER, EFFECT OF UPON USURIO
CONTRACT.—If a contract claimed to be usurious becomes mer;
in a judgment, the original contract is extinguished. The judgm
is a new debt not infected with the usurious nature of the cause
action. (Ryan v. Southern etc. Assn., 831.)

MINES AND MINING.

1. MINING LAWS.—Notice calling upon co-owners in a mining claim to contribute their shares of necessary expenditures may include the expenditures for several years. It is not necessary to give a separate notice for each year. (Elder v. Horseshoe Mining etc. Co., 895.)

2. MINING LAWS.—The estate of the locator or owner of a mining claim before a patent is issued is a conditional estate, subject to be defeated by the failure to perform the required annual work upon the claim, and any qualified person may take advantage of the failure to perform the condition and relocate the claim. (Elder v. Horseshoe Min. etc. Co., 895.)

3. MINING LAWS.—A notice of forfeiture directed to R. W., his heirs, administrators, and to all whom it may concern, he being then deceased, and there being no administrator of his estate, is sufficient under section 2324 of the Revised Statutes of the United States, authorizing proceedings by a person claiming to be a co-owner of a mining claim to compel another co-owner to contribute his proportion of the expenses required to be made upon such claim, and, in default of such contribution within the time specified in such statute, that the interest of the non-contributing co-owner should vest in those who have made the required expenditures. (Elder v. Horseshoe Min. etc. Co., 895.)

4. MINING LAWS—EFFECT OF NOTICE TO CO-OWNERS TO CONTRIBUTE HIS SHARE OF NECESSARY EXPENDITURES.—A notice published under section 2324 of the Revised Statutes of the United States calling upon co-owners in a mining claim to contribute their shares of the annual expenditures required to be made upon such claim, if such contribution is not made, cuts off the owner in default and all interests dependent upon his, whether the persons claiming are minors, heirs, or lienholders, though such persons are not expressly named in such notice. (Elder v. Horsehoe Min. etc. Co., 895.)

MORTGAGE.

1. MORTGAGEES, FIRST AND SECOND, DUTY RESPECTING THE PAYMENT OF TAXES.—A second mortgagee does not owe any duty to the first mortgagee to pay the taxes. If the title of both is extinguished by a tax sale, their prior relations cease, and the junior mortgagee may then purchase and assert the tax title, unless he is in possession under the foreclosure of his mortgage or has, in some manner, obligated himself to pay the taxes. (Safe Deposit etc. Co. v. Wickhem, 873.)

2. TAX TITLE ACQUIRED BY JUNIOR MORTGAGEE, RIGHT TO ASSERT AGAINST SENIOR MORTGAGEE.—If premises subject to a first and a second mortgage are permitted to become delinquent for taxes and to be sold and conveyed to a third person without any collusion with the junior mortgagee, he may afterward purchase the tax title and assert it against the senior mortgagee. Nor is it material that the junior mortgagee was a county treasurer, and as such, in his official capacity, made the tax sale in question. (Safe Deposit etc. Co. v. Wickhem, 873.)

3. MORTGAGOR AND MORTGAGEE.—THE AGREEMENT OF THE PURCHASER TO PAY THE MORTGAGE DEBT as part of the purchase price does not, as between the mortgagor and mortgagee, convert the former into a surety, unless the latter had notice of the agreement. But if he has such notice, though he may treat both the purchaser and the mortgagor as debtors and enforce the liability against either, he is bound to recognize the condition of suretyship and to respect the rights of the sureties in all his subsequent dealings with them. If he releases the purchaser or makes a valid extension of the time of payment without the mortgagor's consent, he is thereby released. Should the mortgagor pay the debt, he is entitled to be subrogated to the rights and remedies of the mortgagee. (Nelson v. Brown, 755.)

4. STATUTE OF FRAUDS, AGREEMENT RESPECTING PURCHASE PRICE OF LAND, WHEN NEED NOT BE IN WRITING. If a purchaser of land agrees as part of the purchase price to pay certain indebtedness of the vendor secured by a mortgage thereon, and thereafter receives a conveyance of such land, this agreement is not within the statute of frauds and is enforceable though not in writing. (Nelson v. Brown, 755.)

5. MORTGAGES — FORECLOSURE — VALUE — SATISFACTION OF LIEN.—The value of land, for the purpose of satisfying a mortgage lien against it, is the amount for which it sold at a sheriff's sale, on a decree of foreclosure. (State v. Clapp, 415.)

6. MORTGAGES—FORECLOSURE BY SAME PERSON—SURPLUS—PRIORITY.—If two mortgages, of different dates, on the same land, against the same mortgagor, are foreclosed on the same day, but separate decrees are rendered, and the land is afterward sold under the junior mortgage, the junior mortgagee bidding it in for the amount of his decree, but there is subsequently another sale under the senior mortgage, at which the senior mortgagee bids in the land for a sum exceeding the amount of his decree, the surplus being paid to the clerk of the court, the junior mortgagee is entitled to such surplus to the amount of his mortgage. The mortgagor, as owner, is not entitled to such surplus until the junior mortgage debt has been satisfied. (State v. Clapp, 415.)

7. JUDGMENT, ASSIGNMENT, CONFLICT BETWEEN AND THE RIGHT TO REFORM A MORTGAGE.—If, after the levy of an attachment and the rendition of a judgment, it is assigned and an execution sale made to the assignee of the land which the judgment debtor had undertaken to mortgage, but which by mistake had not been included in that instrument, the mortgagee is entitled, by a suit in equity, to reform his mortgage so as to include all the property intended, after first paying such sums as had been advanced by the assignee and such charges as had been incurred in his favor up to the time when he had notice of the equities of the mortgagee. (Yarnell v. Brown, 380.)

8. MORTGAGES—POWER OF SALE—RIGHT OF MORTGAGEE TO PURCHASE.—A mortgagee may purchase the mortgaged property at a sale by him under a power of sale contained in the mortgage, if by the terms thereof he is expressly authorized to do so. Though no such authority is given expressly, the sale, if made fairly and without fraud, is not void, but merely voidable. (Mutual Loan etc. Co. v. Haas, 317.)

9. MORTGAGES—POWER OF SALE—EFFECT ON JUDGMENT CREDITOR.—A creditor of a mortgagor, who obtains a judgment subsequently to the execution of a mortgage which contains a power of sale and has been duly recorded, takes it subject to the rights of the mortgagee; and the power of sale being a part of the security, he takes it subject to the exercise of that power, and his judgment attaches merely to the equity of redemption. (Mutual Loan etc. Co. v. Haas, 317.)

10. MORTGAGES—POWER OF SALE—REVOCABILITY.—If a debtor executes a mortgage upon realty to secure a debt, the mortgage containing a power of sale to be exercised upon default of pay-

ment of the debt, such power becomes a part of the security, and is not revocable either by the mortgagor or by the rendition of a judgment against him in favor of another creditor, and if, on default in payment of the debt, the mortgagee exercises such power by selling the land, a bona fide purchaser at the sale obtains title free from the lien of judgments junior to the mortgage, though rendered before the exercise of the power. (Mutual Loan etc. Co. v. Haas, 317.)

11. A TENDER MADE AFTER THE MATURITY OF NOTES SECURED by a deed of trust or mortgage does not discharge its lien. It has no greater effect on the security than on the debt. Hence, if the tender is not kept good, the trustee or mortgagee may proceed to sell the property, and the purchaser will acquire a good title. (Hudson etc Co. v. Glencoe etc. Co., 722.)

12. MORTGAGE, RELEASE OF BY EXTENSION OF TIME FOR PAYMENT.—If a person intending to purchase real property calls on a mortgagee and notifies him of such intention and that he expects to assume the payment of the mortgage debt as part of the purchase price, and thereafter the mortgagee agrees to extend the time for payment in consideration of receiving certain interest in advance, this agreement is based upon a sufficient consideration, and, as the mortgagor is, under the circumstances, a mere surety, he is released by these extensions from all liability for the mortgage debt. (Nelson v. Brown, 755.)

See Bills of Review, 2, 3; Insurance, 6; Judgment, 1, 11; Negotiable Instruments, 9.

MULTIFARIOUSNESS.

See Creditor's Bill, 2; Pleading, 9.

MUNICIPAL CORPORATIONS.

1. MUNICIPAL CORPORATIONS — STREETS—DELEGATION OF RIGHT TO CONTROL.—A state may delegate the supervision and control over streets of a city to the municipality in which they are located. (City Council v. Parker, 95.)

2. LEGISLATIVE AUTHORITY, DELEGATION OF.—Where the legislature has delegated its authority upon a subject to the common council of a municipal corporation, that council cannot delegate such authority to a committee thereof. (Eureka City v. Wilson, 904.)

3. CONSTITUTIONAL LAW, FIRE LIMITS, CONFERRING ON COMMITTEE THE CONTROL OF.—A municipal corporation which has, by ordinance, adopted fire limits and declared that combustible buildings shall not be constructed therein, cannot add a proviso that a committee of its common council shall have power to grant permission to erect buildings within such limits under such regulations and restrictions as the committee may provide. This proviso attempts to give the committee arbitrary discretion, under which it might give permission to one person and refuse it to another in precisely the same circumstances. (Eureka City v. Wilson, 904.)

4. MUNICIPAL ORDINANCE—FIRE LIMITS, WHEN APPLIES TO REMOVAL OF BUILDINGS.—An ordinance prescribing the fire limits of a municipality and forbidding the erection therein of any building not of incombustible material is applicable to the removal of a combustible building from one part of the fire limits to the other. The provisions of the ordinance extend to, and protect, all vacant places within the fire limits. (Eureka City v. Wilson, 904.)

to employ in such lighting arc lamps of nominal two thousand candle power, to be suspended at least twenty-five feet above the tracks, is invalid, where no trains are run over the road through the city after 8 o'clock on any night. (Cleveland etc. Ry. Co. v. Connersville, 418.)

12. MUNICIPAL ORDINANCE MAKING CERTAIN ACTS EVIDENCE OF CRIME.—An ordinance providing that it shall not be necessary to prove the actual sale of lottery tickets in any place, house, office, or premises, but any sign, ticket, sheet, bulletin, or other device used to indicate that tickets are kept for sale or to give information as to the result of any drawing shall be taken and accepted as sufficient evidence of keeping a lottery house or shop, is valid. Such an ordinance does not justify a conviction unless there was guilty knowledge or intent. (State v. Voss, 653.)

13. MUNICIPAL ORDINANCE, CONSTRUCTION OF AS TO EXTENT OF PUNISHMENT.—An ordinance providing that, upon conviction, a person convicted shall be condemned to pay a fine not exceeding twenty-five dollars or imprisonment not exceeding twenty-five days, or both, on default of the payment of the fine, providing that the fine shall not exceed twenty-five dollars nor the imprisonment more than thirty days, does not authorize a fine of the amount named and an imprisonment of thirty days and a further imprisonment if the fine is not paid. In no event can the imprisonment exceed thirty days. (State v. Voss, 653.)

14. MUNICIPAL ORDINANCE REGULATING MARKETS.—An ordinance prohibiting all sales in the public markets after 12 o'clock noon, except fruits and vegetables in limited quantities, and forbidding the sale of fruits, vegetables, or other articles of food within six squares of the public markets by peddlers, is a valid exercise of the police power by a city. (State v. Namias, 657.)

15. QUO WARRANTO — FRANCHISE, FORFEITURE OF, WHETHER MAY BE WAIVED BY A CITY.—A municipality granting a franchise to a street railway corporation cannot waive the forfeiture thereof arising from nonuser. The streets of a municipality are for the use of the general public, and neither the city nor its officers can deprive the state of the right to proceed by quo warranto to enforce the forfeiture of the franchise. (State v. East Fifth St. Ry. Co., 742.)

16. QUO WARRANTO, ESTOPPEL TO MAINTAIN.—The fact that the municipality granting a street railway a franchise prevented it from laying its track at a designated place does not estop it as relator in a quo warranto proceeding from enforcing the forfeiture of the franchise for nonuser, if it appears that the acts of the municipality of which complaint is made by the corporation did not injure it. (State v. East Fifth St. Ry. Co., 742.)

17. MUNICIPAL ORDINANCES—STREETS—USE OF BY ADJOINING OWNER.—The proprietor of a hotel, who owns the fee in the street subject to the easement of the public, has no more right to permanently occupy the street adjacent to the sidewalk in front of the hotel with his hacks, in violation of a city ordinance, than has any other person, nor are his guests entitled to any greater consideration in the use of the sidewalks and streets of the city, because they are guests. (City Council v. Parker, 95.)

18. MUNICIPAL CORPORATIONS—STREETS—RIGHT OF ABUTTING OWNER TO INJUNCTION.—The proprietor of a hotel abutting on the street has the right to enjoin the use of the street in such manner as prevents and obstructs him and the guests of the hotel in the reasonable access to and egress therefrom and in the

transportation of baggage to their great inconvenience and his injury, and to restrain the occupancy of the street in front of his hotel in a manner prohibited by a city ordinance. (City Council v. Parker, 95.)

19. PUBLIC UTILITIES—RATES OF CHARGES.—The fact that some reward or compensation is allowed to a water company for water furnished a municipality is not conclusive of the power of the court. The question of just compensation is a judicial question, to be determined in the ordinary course of judicial proceedings, and whenever the rates fixed by the common council of a municipality are grossly and palpably insufficient to furnish such revenue as will afford compensation. redress may be had in the courts. [Per Van Fleet, Henshaw, and McFarland, JJ.] (San Diego Water Co. v. San Diego, 261.)

20. PUBLIC UTILITIES. RIGHT TO A HEARING WHEN CHARGES ARE TO BE FIXED.—The common council or other tribunal charged with the duty of fixing the rates to be charged by a corporation for water to be furnished to a municipality and its inhabitants should, if requested, give the corporation a reasonable opportunity to be heard, not merely for the purpose of presenting its own evidence, but also of explaining or overcoming, if it can, evidence presented by others. A refusal to permit it to be present when some of the evidence is given shows an unfairness in the investigation, and overcomes the presumption of the correctness of any decision which may be reached. (San Diego Water Co. v. San Diego, 261.)

21. PUBLIC UTILITIES — BASIS UPON WHICH RATES SHOULD BE FIXED.—In determining what a corporation furnishing water to a municipality and its inhabitants should be permitted to charge therefor, so as to realize a reasonable reward, the value of the plant is the basic element upon which the whole investigation rests. The original cost of construction is simply an item to be considered. [Per Garoutte, Temple, and Harrison, JJ.] (San Diego Water Co. v. San Diego, 261.)

22. PUBLIC UTILITIES, RATES WHICH SHOULD BE ALLOWED.—In fixing water rates the common council should provide for just and reasonable compensation to the water company. The rates ought to be adjusted to the value of the services rendered, and this means that the company should be allowed to collect only a gross income sufficient to pay current expenses, maintain the necessary plant in a state of efficiency, and declare a dividend to stockholders equal to at least the current rates of interest, not on the par value of the stock, but on the actual value of the property necessarily used in providing and distributing the water to consumers. [Per Beatty, C. J.] (San Diego Water Co. v. San Diego, 261.)

23. PUBLIC UTILITIES—RATES OF CHARGES, POWER OF COURTS TO REVIEW.—If the rates of charges fixed by a common council for the furnishing by a corporation of water to a municipality and its inhabitants are such as to give some compensation for the services rendered, the courts cannot inquire whether such compensation is proper or reasonable. That is a question of fact to be determined by such council, and is not subject to review by the courts. Rates which yield an income of more than three per cent of the value of the plant cannot be adjudged unreasonable by the courts. [Per Garoutte. Temple, and Harrison, JJ.] (San Diego Water Co. v. San Diego, 261.)

24. CONSTITUTIONAL LAW—COURTS. POWER OF TO REVIEW THE FIXING OF RATES.—If rates are fixed by legislative power or otherwise than by appropriate judicial proceedings, in

which full notice and an opportunity to be heard are given, it is within the province of the courts to review such action to the extent, at least, of determining whether the rates so fixed will furnish some reward for the property used and the services rendered. To fix rates which will not allow such reward is to take property for public use without compensation. (San Diego Water Co. v. San Diego, 261.)

25. CONSTITUTIONAL LAW—FIXING RATES, TO WHAT EXTENT REVIEWABLE IN THE COURTS.—When it is claimed that the rates fixed by the common council of a municipality for the furnishing of water will deprive the corporation furnishing it of all reward, the courts may ascertain whether the power has been carried beyond constitutional limits, and, if so, declare the action void. The court is not limited to the evidence produced before the common council, or other body authorized to fix the rates, and may act without knowing what such evidence was. Whether the action of the council or other body was beyond the constitutional limits is a mixed question of law and fact, to be determined by the courts upon evidence produced before them. (San Diego Water Co. v. San Diego, 261.)

26. CONSTITUTIONAL LAW—COMPENSATION TO BE PAID FOR WATER.—In determining the compensation to which a water company is entitled for supplying a municipality and its inhabitants with water, neither the sum for which the plant could be sold in the market, nor the cost of replacing it, is controlling. For the money which the company has reasonably expended for the public benefit in acquiring its property and constructing its works it is entitled to a reasonable reward. If the business appears to be honestly and prudently conducted, the rate which the company would be compelled to pay for borrowed money will furnish a safe, though not always a conclusive criterion of the rate of profit which will be deemed reasonable. [Per Van Fleet, Henshaw, and McFarland, JJ.] (San Diego Water Co. v. San Diego, 261.)

27. PUBLIC UTILITIES—RATES OF CHARGES—BONDED INDEBTEDNESS.—The existence of a bonded indebtedness cannot be regarded as a material element in fixing the charges to be paid for the furnishing of water to a municipality and its inhabitants. No distinction can be made between corporations which have completed their works with their own money and those which have borrowed money for that purpose from others. In either case the money actually and reasonably invested is the basic criterion of the revenue to be allowed. [Per Van Fleet, Henshaw, and McFarland, JJ.] (San Diego Water Co. v. San Diego, 261.)

See Legislature, 4; Quo Warranto, 1, 2.

MUTUAL BENEFIT ASSOCIATIONS.
See Insurance, 11, 13.

NATURAL CHILDREN.
See Descent.

NATURAL GAS.
See Constitutions, 1; Criminal Law, 1; Injunction, 4, 5; Legislature, 3; Police Power, 2; Statutes, 4, 5.

NEGLIGENCE.
1. NEGLIGENCE.--The word "reckless," when applied to negligence, has no legal significance per se which imports other than

simple negligence or a want of due care; but the use of the word "reckless," in connection with averments of facts to which it refers and explains, may imply more than mere heedlessness or negligence. (Louisville etc. R. R. Co. v. Anchors, 116.)

2. NEGLIGENCE, WANTON — WILLFUL INJURY, WHAT CONSTITUTES.—To constitute willful injury there must be design, purpose, and intent to do wrong and inflict the injury; while to constitute wanton negligence, the party doing the act or failing to act must be conscious of his conduct, and, though having no intent to injure, must be conscious, from his knowledge of surrounding circumstances and existing conditions, that his conduct will naturally or probably result in injury. (Louisville etc. R. R. Co. v. Anchors, 116.)

3. NEGLIGENCE.—CHILDREN OF TENDER YEARS are not held to the same degree of care as persons of mature age. Hence a child of eleven years of age, who is attracted to a dangerous reservoir maintained on the defendant's premises, and who falls in and is drowned, is not necessarily chargeable with contributory negligence precluding his father recovering for his death. (Price v. Atchison Water Co., 625.)

4. NEGLIGENCE, INJURY RESULTING FROM, AND FROM OTHER CAUSES.—If an injury is due to negligence for which the defendant is answerable, and also to a concurrent cause which would not have happened but for the negligence, he is answerable. (Handley v. Daly Mining Co., 916.)

5. NEGLIGENCE, CONTRIBUTORY, MUST BE NEGATIVED. One who seeks damages for an injury caused by another must, at least, prove some fact or circumstance showing that he was not himself guilty of negligence contributing to the injury. (Evansville Street R. R. Co. v. Gentry, 421.)

6. NEGLIGENCE, CONTRIBUTORY, POVERTY AS AN EXCUSE.—WHERE A CHILD has been injured upon a public street, and it is claimed that his parents were guilty of contributory negligence in permitting him to go there unattended, evidence of their poverty and consequent inability to employ servants is not admissible as tending to aid the jury in determining the issue respecting contributory negligence. The question of the parents' negligence in any given case cannot be made to turn on the state of their finances. (Fox v. Oakland etc. Street Ry., 216.)

7. NEGLIGENCE, GROSS AND CONTRIBUTORY.—Though a person injured by a street-car was guilty of contributory negligence in placing himself in a situation of danger, he may recover for injuries there sustained, if the person inflicting them, or his servant or agent, was guilty of gross negligence. (Fox v. Oakland etc. Street Ry., 216.)

8. NEGLIGENCE—QUESTION FOR JURY.—In an action to recover for a death caused by negligence in a collision of hand-cars, it is a question for the jury to determine whether it was negligence for the foreman of such cars to run them closely following each other at a high rate of speed over a river bridge. (Alabama Mineral R. R. Co. v. Jones, 121.)

9. NEGLIGENCE—QUESTION FOR THE JURY.—It is only where the deduction to be drawn is inevitable that the court is authorized to withdraw the question of negligence from the jury. The absence of conflict in the evidence is not controlling, if differences of opinion as to the conclusions and inferences to be drawn therefrom may reasonably arise. (Fox v. Oakland etc. Street Ry., 216.)

10. NEGLIGENCE IN LOOKING OUT FOR CHILDREN, WHEN A QUESTION FOR THE JURY.—Whether parents, in permitting

their child of tender years to be out of their sight for fifteen or twenty minutes, during which time it went upon a street and was injured by a street-car, was, under all the circumstances, a want of ordinary care, is a question for the jury. (Fox v. Oakland etc. Street Ry., 216.)

11. NEGLIGENCE, PLEADING, MOTION TO MAKE ANSWER MORE DEFINITE AND CERTAIN.—A complaint containing a general allegation of negligence is subject to a motion requiring it to be made more definite and certain. Therefore, if in an action to recover for the death of the plaintiff's child through falling into a dangerous reservoir on the defendant's premises, the latter pleads that if the plaintiff has suffered any damage, it is from his own negligence and that of such child, a motion on the part of the plaintiff to make the answer more definite and certain should be granted. (Price v. Atchison Water Co., C25.)

See Appeal, 7; Attachment, 3; Damages; Master and Servant; Railroads; Sheriffs, 2.

NEGOTIABLE INSTRUMENTS.

1. NEGOTIABLE INSTRUMENTS.—DISCOUNT signifies the interest allowed in advancing upon negotiable instruments, and is, in effect, buying such instruments for a less sum than that which upon their face is payable. (Anderson v. Timberlake, 105.)

2. NEGOTIABLE INSTRUMENTS — ATTORNEYS' FEES, STIPULATION FOR PAYMENT OF.—A note otherwise negotiable in form, but containing a stipulation that, in the event of a suit to enforce the collection of the note, or any part thereof, the maker will pay an additional sum of ten per cent of the amount found to be due as attorneys' fees in such suit, is not rendered non-negotiable by such stipulation. (Salisbury v. Stewart, 934.)

3. NEGOTIABLE INSTRUMENTS.—THE NEGOTIABILITY OF A PROMISSORY NOTE IS NOT DESTROYED by writing thereon a statement that it is given in accordance with the terms of a contract of even date between the same parties, though such contract, on being examined, shows that the note was one of three given at the same time, payable at different dates, and that in the contract the maker agreed that if any of them should not be paid within ninety days after becoming due, then the payee had the right to declare all the other notes to have become due and payable. (Markey v. Corey, 698.)

4. PAYMENT, CONSIDERATION FOR EXTENSION OF TIME FOR.—The payment of interest in advance is a sufficient consideration for the extension of a note for a definite and fixed time. (Nelson v. Brown, 755.)

5. NEGOTIABLE INSTRUMENTS—ASSIGNOR'S LIABILITY, ONE WHO WRITES AND SIGNS ON THE BACK of a negotiable instrument an assignment thereof is liable as an indorser to the same extent as if he had merely indorsed his name without any other words. (Markey v. Corey, 698.)

6. NEGOTIABLE INSTRUMENTS — INDORSEMENTS AND GUARANTY.—The writing on the back of a note, "For value received we hereby guarantee payment of within note at maturity, waiving demand, protest, and notice of protest," signed by the payee of the note, is both an indorsement and a guaranty, and hence passes the title thereto. (Kellogg v. Douglas Co. Bank, 596.)

7. COLLATERAL SECURITY.—An indorsement as collateral security for a debt contracted at the time of the indorsement protects

the indorsee to the extent of the debt the same as if the purchase were absolute. (Kellogg v. Douglas Co. Bank, 596.)

8. NEGOTIABLE INSTRUMENTS—ASSIGNMENT OF AS COLLATERAL—LACHES OF HOLDER—DISCHARGE OF ASSIGNOR. A creditor accepting a transfer of negotiable paper by mere delivery, and without indorsement, as a conditional payment or as collateral security, is bound to the use of due diligence in rendering it available, but his laches in this respect does not of itself operate to discharge the transferror, and to have this effect it must appear that such laches caused loss or damage to the latter. (Anderson v. Timberlake, 105.)

9. NEGOTIABLE INSTRUMENTS SECURED BY MORTGAGE, PURCHASER OF WITHOUT NOTICE.—One who becomes a bona fide purchaser of negotiable notes secured by mortgage before their maturity is not bound nor otherwise affected by an agreement between the mortgagor and a purchaser from him of the mortgaged premises whereby the latter assumes the payment of the mortgage debt. (Nelson v. Brown, 755.)

10. BANK, FAILURE OF TO COMPLY WITH THE LAW.—In a suit upon a promissory note made to, and negotiated by a bank, the maker cannot defend on the ground that such bank had not complied with the law in procuring the certificate authorizing it to transact business, nor in making a statement required to be made by the banking law of the state. (Kellogg v. Douglas Co. Bank, 596.)

See Alteration of Instruments; Bank and Banking; Carriers, 5.

NEW TRIAL.

1. NEW TRIAL—FINDING NOT SUSTAINED BY THE EVIDENCE.—If there is no substantial conflict in the evidence, and the verdict or decision is against such evidence, or the verdict or decision strikes the mind as manifestly and palpably contrary to the evidence, the supreme court will direct a new trial. (Watt v. Nevada etc. R. R. Co., 772.)

2. NEW TRIAL—ERROR IN RENDERING FINAL JUDGMENT.—If it appears from the record that the trial judge would not have abused his discretion in ordering a new trial, and that the final determination of the case does not necessarily depend upon a controlling question of law, while there are issues of fact in the case which make it necessary for a new trial to be had, it is error to render a final judgment in the case instead of sending it back for a new trial. (Rogers v. Georgia R. R. Co., 351.)

3. MOTIONS AND ORDERS — MODIFYING MANDATE — JUDGMENT—NEW TRIAL.—If a judgment is reversed because of the trial court's error in striking from answers certain contracts filed as exhibits thereto, which contracts were thereby taken out of the issues, a motion to modify the mandate of the supreme court so as to give the defendant a judgment instead of a new trial will not be sustained. (Pittsburgh etc. Ry. Co. v. Mahoney, 503.)

See Appeal, 10, 11, 15; Former Acquittal, 2; Homicide, 2; Jurisdiction, 4; Statutes, 8, 9.

NOTARIES PUBLIC.

1. NOTARIES PUBLIC, EXERCISE OF JUDICIAL POWER BY.—Under a constitution declaring that the judicial power of the state is vested in certain courts therein named and such other courts as may be prescribed by law, judicial power cannot be vested in a notary public. (In re Huron, 614.)

2. CONTEMPT, PUNISHMENT OF BY NOTARIES.—A statute authorizing notaries public to take depositions and issue subpoenas to compel the attendance of witnesses before them, and declaring that the disobedience of a subpoena, or the refusal to be sworn, or to answer as a witness, or to subscribe the deposition when legally ordered, may be punished as a contempt of the court or officer by whom the attendance or testimony is required, is unconstitutional in so far as it undertakes to authorize notaries public to punish witnesses for contempt, because the power to so punish is judicial and cannot be vested in a notary. (In re Huron, 614.)

3. NOTARIES PUBLIC, SEALS OF MAY AID AFFIDAVIT.—If, from the venue of an affidavit, it cannot be ascertained where the oath was administered nor for what county the notary who administered it was authorized to act, his seal may be looked at to ascertain of what county he was an officer. (Cox v. Stern, 385.)

See Affidavits, 2; Chattel Mortgage, 2; Evidence, 1; Records, 2.

NOTICE.

NOTICE.—A PARTY TO A WRITING, the genuineness of which is not disputed, is charged with notice of its contents and the effect thereof. (Anderson v. Timberlake, 105.)

See Jurisdiction, 1; Master and Servant, 6.

NUISANCE.
See Injunction, 5, 6.

OPTION.
See Carriers, 3.

PARENT AND CHILD.

1. PARENT AND CHILD—FATHER'S RIGHT TO CUSTODY OF CHILD.—The right of a father with respect to his child is not an absolute paramount proprietary right or interest in or to its custody, but is in the nature of a trust reposed in him, which imposes upon him the reciprocal obligation to maintain, care for, and protect the child. The law secures him this right so long as, and no longer than, he shall discharge the correlative duties and obligations. (Nugent v. Powell, 17.)

2. PARENT AND CHILD—RIGHT TO CUSTODY AND SERVICES OF CHILD.—All things being equal, the father has a better right to the custody and services of his child than has the mother, but he has no absolute vested right in such custody. (Nugent v. Powell, 17.)

See Adoption; Damages, 8, 9, 22.

PARTIES.
See Joint Liability, 8.

PARTITION.

1. PARTITION, RIGHT TO.—As a general rule an adult tenant in common may demand partition as a matter of right. (Martin v. Martin, 411.)

2. PARTITION, WAIVER OF RIGHT TO BY ORAL AGREEMENT.—An oral agreement between tenants in common in view of what they believe to be the temporary depreciation in the market value of their real property that they will not seek to divide their lands, but will jointly rent them and divide the rentals, that each will endeavor to obtain purchasers satisfactory to all, and then all will join in a conveyance, followed by their joint leasing of the property for a term of years, estops any of them, during the continuance of such lease, from maintaining a suit for the partition of their property. (Martin v. Martin, 411.)

3. COSTS IN PARTITION, WHEN PROPERLY AWARDED AGAINST PLAINTIFFS.—If plaintiffs sue in partition and their title is denied as to a portion of the lands, and they alone contest this issue and are defeated thereon, it is proper to charge the costs of the trial against them. (Appleman v. Appleman, 732.)

PART PAYMENT.

See Accord and Satisfaction.

PAYMENT.

See Accord and Satisfaction; Checks, 4, 5.

PERPETUITIES.

See Estates, 4, 5; Wills, 12-15.

PLAGIARISM.

See Libel, 4.

PLEADING.

1. PLEADING.—FACTS, NOT CONCLUSIONS should be stated in pleadings. (Davis v. Clements, 539.)

2. PLEADING—ULTIMATE FACTS—LEGAL CONCLUSIONS. A pleading should state the ultimate facts, and not the evidence of such facts. Legal conclusions are not to be pleaded. (Robinson v. Berkey, 549.)

3. PLEADINGS.—DEMURRERS DO NOT ADMIT OPINIONS OR CONCLUSIONS of the pleader, nor do they admit facts which are in their nature improbable or impossible. (Southern Ry. Co. v. Covenia, 312.)

4. PLEADINGS.—DEMURRER CANNOT BE HELD TO ADMIT impossible or improbable facts, so as to prevent the court from passing upon the allegations which in their nature are contrary to common experience and common knowledge as matter of law, and to compel their submission to the jury. (Southern Ry. Co. v. Covenia, 312.)

5. MOTIONS—REMEDY FOR INDEFINITENESS IN PLEADING.—If, in an allegation concerning the concealment of a cause of action, circumstances of discovery, and time when made, are not sufficiently certain and definite, the remedy is by a motion to make more specific. (State v. Parsons, 430.)

6. MOTIONS AND ORDERS—MODIFYING MANDATE.— A motion to modify a mandate of the supreme court is in the nature of a petition for a rehearing, and may be filed, during the time allowed for a rehearing, on behalf of a party who has not waived it, although the opinion has been certified to the court below. (Pittsburgh etc. Ry. Co. v. Mahoney, 503.)

7. MOTION AND ORDERS—PLEADINGS—STRIKING OUT. If averments in a pleading are in any way material, they ought not to be struck out on motion, and the test of materiality is whether

they tend to constitute a cause of action or defense; if they do, they are not irrelevant and ought not to be suppressed. (Pittsburgh etc. Ry. Co. v. Mahoney, 503.)

8. PLEADING—SURPLUSAGE, ALLEGATIONS WHICH MAY BE TREATED AS.—If, in an action to recover upon a demand, the complaint sets forth a release claimed to be inoperative for sufficient reasons therein disclosed, the averment respecting such release may be treated as surplusage, and certainly cannot preclude a recovery, if they could not have had that effect if pleaded in an answer. (Trotter v. Mutual Reserve etc. Assn., 887.)

9. EQUITY PLEADING — MULTIFARIOUSNESS.—A bill in equity may be framed in a double aspect, embracing alternative averments for relief, provided each aspect entitles the complainant to substantially the same relief, and the same defenses are applicable to each. (Hall v. Henderson, 141.)

10. EVIDENCE.—ADMISSIONS IN PLEADINGS are conclusive, even though evidence is admitted, and the court, jury, or referee finds otherwise. (Nugent v. Powell, 17.)

See Appeal, 9; Damages,18; Fraudulent Conveyances, 6, 7; Injunction, 2, 3, 7; Libel, 7; Railroads, 10, 12, 13.

POLICE POWER.

1. CONSTITUTIONAL LAW.—WHETHER THE POLICE POWER has been exercised within the proper limitations is a judicial question. (State v. Namias, 657.)

2. CONSTITUTIONAL LAW—WASTE OF NATURAL GAS.—A statute which prohibits the waste of natural gas is an exercise of the police power of the state, and the legislative determination that the burning of natural gas, in flambeau lights, is a wasteful use of it, is conclusive on the courts. (Townsend v. State, 477.)

See Highways, 1; Municipal Corporations, 10, 14; Statutes, 15.

PRESCRIPTION.

See Adverse Possession.

PRESUMPTIONS.

See Affidavits, 2; Agency, 2; Appeal, 2, 4, 17; Checks, 6, 7; Husband and Wife, 6; Injunction, 3; Legislature, 2; Notaries Public, 3; Taxes, 7.

PRIVITY.

See Corporations, 9.

PROCESS.

1. JURISDICTION—SUMMONS, SERVICE OF ON A CLERK OR AGENT.—Authority on the part of a clerk of an attorney at law to accept service of papers in a case wherein the attorney had been employed professionally does not authorize the clerk to accept service of summons in an action in which the attorney is a party defendant. (Lower v. Wilson, 865.)

2. FOREIGN INSURANCE CORPORATIONS—JURISDICTION OVER IN CAUSES OF ACTION ARISING WITHOUT THE STATE.—Under a statute providing that if the defendant be a foreign insurance corporation, an action may be brought against it in any county where the cause of action or some part thereof arose, and that if the defendant is an incorporated insurance corporation,

and the action is brought in a county in which there is an agency, the service may be made on the chief officer of such agency, such corporation may be sued and process served upon its agent, though the cause of action is not based on a contract of insurance and did not arise within the state. (German Ins. Co. v. First Nat. Bank, 601.)

PUBLIC UTILITIES.

See Constitutions, 3-5; Municipal Corporations, 19-27.

PUNISHMENT.

See Municipal Corporations, 13.

QUO WARRANTO.

1. QUO WARRANTO.—NONUSER OF A FRANCHISE cannot be justified in a proceeding to enforce a forfeiture because of such nonuser on the ground that the municipality granting the franchise had passed an ordinance repealing, or attempting to repeal, its grant. (State v. East Fifth St. Ry. Co., 742.)

2. QUO WARRANTO, RIGHT TO MAINTAIN FOR THE FOR-FEITURE OF THE FRANCHISE OF A STREET RAILWAY.—Though the franchise of a street railway corporation was granted by the common council of a municipality, and the ordinance making the grant provided that on failure of the corporation to comply with the conditions thereof, it should forfeit its rights and powers, and that a suit to enforce such forfeiture might be maintained by the municipality, and in its name, the state may maintain quo warranto to enforce such forfeiture. Its power to proceed by quo warranto cannot be contracted away or enlarged by the city. (State v. East Fifth St. Ry. Co., 742.)

See Corporations, 4; Municipal Corporations, 15, 16; Railroads, 20.

RAILROADS.

1. RAILROADS.—AN ELECTRIC CAR-LINE running within and beyond the limits of a city is a railroad within the meaning of a statute regulating the duties of railroads whose tracks cross each other and requiring them to observe precautionary measures at crossings. (Louisville etc. R. R. Co. v. Anchors, 116.)

2. RAILWAYS, ORDINANCE RESPECTING, WHEN MAY BE URGED BY EMPLOYES.—An ordinance limiting the speed of railway trains while running within a municipality and requiring the ringing of a bell is designed for the protection of employés, as well as of the general public. Hence one employed by a corporation and working upon or under its track may recover if injured through the negligence of its agent in not ringing the bell and in running more rapidly than permitted by such ordinance. (East St. Louis etc. Ry. Co. v. Eggmann, 400.)

3. MASTER AND SERVANT—EXEMPTION FROM LIABIL-ITY FOR NEGLIGENCE—EXPRESS AND RAILROAD COM-PANIES—NOTICE TO SERVANT.—If there is a contract between an express company and a railroad company to the effect that the former will hold the latter harmless against claims by employés of the express company for the negligence of the railroad company, an employé of the express company, performing duties for it in its relations to the railroad company, is chargeable with notice of such private contract, and is subject to it, especially where he has assumed all risks of the employment, including the assumption by the express company in favor of the railroad company. (Pittsburgh etc. Ry. Co. v. Mahoney, 503.)

4. MASTER AND SERVANT—EXEMPTION FROM NEGLI-GENCE IN CONTRACT BETWEEN EXPRESS COMPANY AND RAILROAD COMPANY—SERVANT'S RELEASE OF EXPRESS COMPANY.—If an employé of an express company, performing 'duties for it in its relations to a railroad company, releases the express company from all liability for injury sustained by the negligence of the express company "or otherwise," and there exists, at the time, a contract between the express company and the railroad company to the effect that the former will hold the latter harmless against claims by employés of the express company for the negligence of the railroad company, the administrator of such employé cannot maintain an action against the railroad company for negligently causing his death by suddenly closing the opening between parts of a train while he was passing through it in the discharge of his duty, as the word "otherwise" in the employé's contract with the express company covers all the risks involved, including liability for negligence on the part of the railway company. The employé did not stand independent of the contract between the two companies. (Pittsburgh etc. Ry. Co. v. Mahoney, 503.)

5. RAILROADS—KILLING LIVESTOCK—DUTY TO LOOK OUT FOR.—If, in an action against a railroad company to recover for the killing of livestock, it appears that the engineer was at the place on the engine where his duty required him to be, that he was looking ahead when the stock were first seen on the track in a curve, that because thereof, and other obstructions to the view, the stock could not have been sooner seen, and that it was impossible to stop the train before striking them, and the only circumstance from which negligence can be inferred was that the fireman, at the time of the killing of the stock, was engaged in firing his engine, and was not on the lookout, such absence of the fireman from a position to look out, and the failure of the railroad company to place a third man on the engine to keep a lookout when the fireman was firing his engine, do not authorize a recovery against the company. (Rogers v. Georgia R. R. Co., 351.)

6. RAILWAY CORPORATIONS—FIRE, LIABILITY FOR.—The finding that a fire was set by sparks which escaped from a railway locomotive is sustained by evidence that dry grass had been permitted to accumulate and remain upon the track and right of way, and that fire frequently sprang up among it after the passing of a locomotive, and that coals had been permitted to escape and remain on the track, and that many of the ties appeared to be burned. (Watt v. Nevada etc. R. R. Co., 772.)

7. RAILWAYS, COMBUSTIBLE MATERIALS UPON RIGHT OF WAY.—It is the duty of a railway corporation to keep its tracks and right of way free of such substances as are liable to be ignited by sparks or cinders from its engines. (Watt v. Nevada etc. R. R. Co., 772.)

8. RAILWAY CORPORATIONS—NEGLIGENCE IN PER-MITTING COMBUSTIBLE MATERIAL TO BE UPON THE RIGHT OF WAY.—A finding that a railway company negligently omitted to keep its right of way free and clear of dry and combustible material along and upon the plaintiff's land is sustained by testimony that dry grass grew along the track from eight inches to three feet in height, and more or less dry stubble grass had grown up in the center and on the edges of the track, and when the fire occurred, all this grass was as dry as could be. (Watt v. Nevada etc. R. R. Co., 772.)

9. RAILWAYS—FIRES, DUTY TO USE APPLIANCES TO AVOID SPREADING OF.—It is the duty of a railway corporation

to supply itself with such engines as will be least liable to set fire,
and be reasonably safe from destroying the property of others along
its line. (Watt v. Nevada etc. R. R. Co., 772.)

10. NEGLIGENCE, WANTON—WILLFUL INJURY.—In an ac-,
tion against a railroad company to recover for the death of an employé a count in the complaint averring that defendant's engineer
"wrongfully and willfully failed to blow the whistle or ring the bell,"
as required by law and "because of such willfulness or wantonness
the passenger train of the defendant ran into and against a passenger-car of" another road, thus causing the injury complained of,
is defective as a count charging willful injury, because it does not
show that the purpose of the defendant, in failing to ring the bell
or blow the whistle, was to run into or against such car, nor is such
count good as charging wanton negligence, because it does not aver
a state of facts from which knowledge can be imputed to the defendant that the natural and probable result of his conduct would
result in a collision and the injury complained of. (Louisville etc.
R. R. Co. v. Anchors, 116.)

11. NEGLIGENCE CAUSING DEATH—EVIDENCE OF COL-
LECTIVE FACT.—In an action to recover for the death of a railroad section hand, alleged to have been caused by negligence in the
sudden stopping, under direction of a foreman, of a hand-car immediately in front of another hand-car upon which the deceased was
riding, evidence that the place where the accident occurred was a
dangerous place to stop is a statement of a collective fact and admissible in evidence. (Alabama etc. R. R. Co. v. Jones, 121.)

12. NEGLIGENCE CAUSING DEATH—PLEADING.—In an ac-
tion against a railroad company to recover for the death of an employé, a count in the complaint averring that the "engineer negligently permitted and suffered the said locomotive and train to run
into and against a passenger-car," thus causing the injury, is sufficient as a count for simple negligence. (Louisville etc. R. R. Co. v.
Anchors, 116.)

13. NEGLIGENCE, WANTON—WILLFUL INJURY—INSUFFI-
CIENT PLEADING.—In an action against a railroad company to
recover for the death of an employé, a count in the complaint averring that the injury sued for resulted by reason of the willful running of the train at a high rate of speed, but not averring that the
intention or purpose of so running the train was to inflict the injury,
nor that the defendant knew that the probable result of his act
would be to inflict the injury, is insufficient as an averment of willful injury or wanton negligence, although it is also averred that
the defendant willfully caused the train to run into and against a
passenger-car, thus causing the injury complained of. (Louisville
etc. R. R. Co. v. Anchors, 116.)

14. STREET RAILWAYS—CROSSINGS—DUTY OF FOOT PAS-
SENGERS.—A person about to cross a street railway track in a city
is not required to stop, look, and listen, before he crosses, unless
there is some circumstance which would make it ordinarily prudent
to do so. (Evansville Street R. R. Co. v. Gentry, 421.)

15. STREET RAILWAYS—FOOT PASSENGERS—RELATIVE
RIGHTS AND DUTIES AT CROSSINGS.—A street-car has a right
to pass over a crossing, but foot passengers have special rights at
street crossings. They must, of course, use their sense of sight, hearing, and feeling to avoid injury; but it is also the duty of the motorman of an electric car to have it under full control as it passes over
such a crossing. (Evansville Street R. R. Co. v. Gentry, 421.)

16. STREET RAILWAYS—NEGLIGENCE AT CROSSINGS.—It
is negligence for the motorman of an electric car, on a double-track

road, especially after receiving orders to slow up his car at street crossings where a car is standing on the other track, taking on or letting off passengers, to run his car over such a crossing, at an unusual rate of speed, without slowing up; and, if death is thereby caused, without fault of the person killed, the street company is answerable therefor in damages. (Evansville Street R. R. Co. v. Gentry, 421.)

17. STREET RAILWAYS—ACCIDENT AT CROSSING—PROOF AS TO WANT OF CONTRIBUTORY NEGLIGENCE.—If a passenger on a street car, running on a double-track road, attempts, after alighting, to cross both tracks, but is struck and killed by a car coming from the opposite direction, it will not be presumed, in an action to recover for the death, that the decedent was free from contributory negligence, although the approaching car was being run in a reckless and negligent manner, if the evidence is silent as to the acts of the decedent from the time he stepped off the car until he was struck, and the interval was long enough to have permitted him to cross the tracks in safety. There can be no recovery without, at least, some slight proof of want of contributory negligence on the part of the decedent. (Evansville Street R. R. Co. v. Gentry, 421.)

18. STREET RAILWAYS, PRIVILEGES OF, WHETHER ARE FRANCHISES OR LICENSES.—The privilege granted to a street railway corporation of laying its tracks on designated streets and running cars thereon, and to charge and receive fares from persons riding upon such cars, is not a mere license. It is a franchise without which the corporate charter would be of no value. This remains true, though the privilege or franchise is granted by a municipality under authority conferred by the state legislature. In making the grant the state must be regarded as acting through the municipality as its agent. (State v. Kansas City etc. Ry. Co., 742.)

19. FRANCHISE, FORFEITURE OF. —THE INSOLVENCY of a street railway corporation constitutes no ground for forfeiting its franchise, if it continues to discharge its duties to the public. (State v. Kansas City etc. Ry. Co., 742.)

20. STREET RAILWAYS, FORFEITURE OF FRANCHISE OF. A street railway refusing or neglecting to run its cars for considerable periods of time when by its charter required to run them for sixteen hours each day, thereby forfeits its franchise, and such forfeiture may be enforced by quo warranto. (State v. Kansas City etc. Ry. Co., 742.)

See, Appeal, 7; Carriers; Damages, 17, 19; Municipal Corporations, 15, 16; Negligence, 7, 8, 10; Quo Warranto; Statutes, 17.

REAL PROPERTY.

DANGEROUS PREMISES ALLURING TO CHILDREN.—A landlord maintaining on his premises a reservoir filled with water to which children are attracted for the purpose of fishing and other sports, and who knows they frequent it for such purpose, and who takes no adequate means to exclude or warn them therefrom, is guilty of negligence, and hence answerable to the parents of a child who, being attracted there, falls in and is drowned. (Price v. Atchison Water Co., 625.)

REASONABLE TIME.

See Checks, 2; Contracts, 1; Master and Servant, 11.

RECORD.

1. RECORDING OF INSTRUMENTS.—If two instruments are executed on the same day and filed for record at substantially the

4. SALES OF ARTICLES FOR SPECIAL PURPOSE—IMPLIED WARRANTY.—A dealer in paints and oils, by virtue of the fact that he is a dealer, is held to an implied warranty of the quality of paints and oils sold, when he knows the purpose for which they are intended, and the purchaser relies upon his judgment and skill. (McCaa v. Elam Drug Co., 88.)

5. SALES OF ARTICLES FOR SPECIAL PURPOSE—IMPLIED WARRANTY.—If a manufacturer or a dealer contracts to supply an article he manufactures or produces or in which he deals, to be applied to a particular purpose, so that the buyer necessarily trusts to his judgment or skill, there is an implied warranty that the article sold and furnished shall be reasonably fit for the purpose to which it is to be applied. (McCaa v. Elam Drug Co, 88.)

6. SALES—SETTLEMENT UPON DELIVERY—WARRANTY WITH CONDITION—WAIVER.—If machinery is sold under a warranty which is not to take effect if the machinery is not settled for at the time and place of delivery, the failure to settle is a condition of the warranty, and, unless settlement is waived, the failure to settle is a waiver of the warranty, and, in the absence of any excuse, pleaded and established, for such failure, is a good answer to an alleged breach of warranty. (Robinson v. Berkey, 549.)

7. SALES—BREACH OF WARRANTY—PLEADING.—A warranty of quality by a vendor, whether expressed or implied, is collateral to the main contract of sale, and a cause of action based upon a breach of warranty is not the same as a cause of action based upon a breach of the contract itself. (McCaa v. Elam Drug Co., 88.)

8. SALES—PLEADINGS SHOWING BREACH OF CONTRACT AND NOT BREACH OF WARRANTY.—If, in an action by a buyer against a dealer in paints and oils, the complaint avers that such dealer agreed to furnish the plaintiff with paints and oils of a quality suitable to be used in painting his house, and this is followed by an averment of a breach of the agreement, stating wherein such paints and oils were defective, the complaint states a cause of action for a breach of the contract and not for a breach of an implied warranty, and an averment that the seller was a "dealer" in paints and oils adds nothing to the sufficiency of the complaint as an allegation of a breach of warranty, nor does it authorize a recovery on less evidence than if the seller had been other than a "dealer." (McCaa v. Elam Drug Co., 88.)

9. STATUTE OF FRAUDS—CONTRACT, WHEN WITHIN.—A contract for the purchase of goods "to the amount of fifty dollars or more," though in writing, is within the statute of frauds, if it appears therefrom that it was the intention of the parties to contract specifically as to the price to be paid, or if it appears from extrinsic evidence that such was the intention, and the writing neither designates what the price was to be, nor otherwise states the actual agreement of the parties with reference to the price in such manner as to render its amount properly ascertainable by the aid of extrinsic evidence. (Turner v. Lorillard Co., 345.)

10. STATUTE OF FRAUDS—STATEMENT OF PRICE WHEN NECESSARY.—If an intention to contract specifically as to the price to be paid for goods does not appear from the terms of the written contract of purchase, but parol evidence makes it certain that such intention existed at the time that the contract was made, the absence of the statement of price from the contract as written renders it nugatory and within the statute of frauds. (Turner v. Lorillard Co., 345.)

11. STATUTE OF FRAUDS—STATEMENT OF PRICE, WHEN NECESSARY.—If an intention is shown, either by the written contract itself or by extrinsic evidence, to agree specifically as to the

price to be paid for goods, the price becomes a part of the promise and must be embraced in the writing, to meet the requirements of the statute of frauds. (Turner v. Lorillard Co., 345.)

12. STATUTE OF FRAUDS—STATEMENT OF PRICE WHEN NOT NECESSARY.—If a verbal promise is made to pay what goods are reasonably worth, or simply to pay for them, no definite or fixed price need be stated in the subsequent written contract to satisfy the statute of frauds and parol evidence is admissible to fix the reasonable worth of the goods. (Turner v. Lorillard Co., 345.)

SEPARATE MAINTENANCE.
See Marriage and Divorce, 3.

SHERIFF.

1. SHERIFF — ATTACHMENT — RETURN — NOT CONCLUSIVE WHEN.—The return of a sheriff on a writ of attachment is not conclusive against him as to matters which he is not required to state. Hence, in an action against him for a negligent loss of the property, he may introduce parol evidence of such matters for this does not tend to contradict the return. (Citizens' Nat. Bank v. Loomis, 571.)

2. SHERIFFS—ATTACHMENT—LIABILITY FOR RECEIPTOR'S NEGLIGENCE.—A sheriff who levies a writ of attachment and delivers the property to a third person as receiptor, by direction of the plaintiff in the attachment, or his attorney, is not answerable for the receiptor's negligence whereby the property is lost. (Citizens' Nat. Bank v. Loomis, 571.)

See Attachment, 2-4.

SLANDER.
See Corporations, 6.

SLOT MACHINES.
See Lotteries, 2.

STATUTE OF FRAUDS.
See Contracts, 3; Mortgage, 4; Sales, 9-12.

STATUTES.

1. STATUTES—PASSING UPON CONSTITUTIONALITY OF.—Courts will not pass upon the constitutionality of an act of the legislature, if the merits of the case in hand may be fairly determined without doing so. (Cleveland etc. Ry. Co. v. Connersville, 418)

2. CONSTITUTIONAL LAW—USE OF PUBLIC PROPERTY.—A statute may regulate the use of public property when the health, morals, or welfare of the public demand it. (People v. Smith, 715.)

3. CONSTITUTIONAL LAW—WRONG AND UNJUST STATUTES.—Whether a statute encroaches upon the natural rights of the citizen is a legislative, and not a judicial, question, and courts cannot overthrow it upon that ground. They do not deal with the mere justice, propriety, or policy of a statute. (Townsend v. State, 477.)

4. CONSTITUTIONAL LAW—WASTE OF NATURAL GAS.—A statute which prohibits the burning of natural gas in flambeau lights, for illuminating purposes, does not contravene that clause of the bill of rights which guarantees to every person life, liberty, and the pursuit of happiness. (Townsend v. State, 477.)

5. CONSTITUTIONAL LAW—WASTE OF NATURAL GAS.—A statute which declares that it is a waste of natural gas to burn it in flambeau lights, and which forbids such use, under penalty of a fine, does not violate those provisions of the federal constitution providing that no person shall be deprived of his property without due process of law. (Townsend v. State, 477.)

6. CONSTITUTIONAL LAW—IMPAIRMENT OF THE OBLIGATION OF A CONTRACT, WHAT IS.—Any law of a state which so affects a pre-existing remedy as to substantially impair or lessen the value of a contract is forbidden by the national constitution, and is void as against contracts entered into before its passage. (Skinner v. Holt, 878.)

7. JUDGMENTS — RETROSPECTIVE LAWS ATTEMPTING TO AVOID THE EFFECT OF.—If, after a judgment or decree has been entered declaring the proceeds of certain life insurance policies to be assets of the estate of a decedent and directing that they be applied to the satisfaction of his liabilities, a statute is enacted providing that the proceeds of such policies, whether heretofore or hereafter issued, shall be exempt from the claims of creditors, such statute cannot affect such judgment or decree. (Skinner v. Holt, 878.

8. CONSTITUTIONAL LAW—FORBIDDEN EXERCISE OF JUDICIAL POWERS BY THE LEGISLATURE.—A statute enacted after the parties to a judgment have lost the right to a rehearing or a new trial, in effect requiring the courts to grant a new trial or a rehearing, if applied for within one year after the passage of the statute, is an attempted exercise by the legislature of judicial powers, and is therefore void. (In re Handley's Estate, 926.)

9. CONSTITUTIONAL LAW — JUDGMENTS, POWER OF LEGISLATURE TO DIRECT A NEW TRIAL OR A REHEARING.—A statute declaring that the children of polygamous marriages are entitled to inherit as heirs of their father, and that in all cases heretofore determined adverse to such right, a motion for a new trial or a rehearing shall be entertained on application of such issue at any time within one year after the statute takes effect, is unconstitutional. After a court has rendered its judgment, the legislature cannot affect it by enacting a declaratory or explanatory law giving the law under which the judgment was rendered a different construction from that given it by the court. (In re Handley's Estate, 926.)

10. EXECUTIONS—EXEMPTIONS, LAW GRANTING UNLIMITED, WHEN UNREASONABLE AND VOID.—Under a state constitution declaring that the right of the debtor to enjoy the comforts and necessaries of life shall be recognized by wholesome laws exempting from forced sale a reasonable amount of personal property, the kind and value of which shall be fixed by general laws, a statute exempting from execution policies of insurance on the life of the debtor, irrespective of their amount, is void, because the exemption, being unlimited, is unreasonable. (Skinner v. Holt, 878.)

11. INSURANCE, LIFE, EXEMPTION OF PROCEEDS OF.—A statute undertaking to exempt from execution the proceeds of life insurance policies irrespective of their amount is void, if the state constitution requires the exemption to be reasonable in amount and its value to be fixed by general laws. (Skinner v. Holt, 878.)

12. EXEMPTION LAWS, CONSTITUTIONALITY OF.—A statute undertaking to exempt from execution the proceeds of life insurance policies is unconstitutional in so far as it applies to contracts existing prior to its enactment, because its application to such contracts would impair their obligation. (Skinner v. Holt, 878.)

13. CONSTITUTIONAL LAW—CLASS LEGISLATION, WHEN NOT FORBIDDEN.—A statute for the protection of all persons who are given continuous employment over dry emery wheels is not forbidden class legislation. (People v. Smith, 715.)

14. EMPLOYERS AND EMPLOYES—CONSTITUTIONAL LAW. A state has the right to require employers to provide and employés to use appliances intended for the protection of the latter, and the requirement may be applicable, though an employer and employé may have contracted that the appliance need not be furnished, if the law has relation to the public welfare or health, and it is clear that the regulation is reasonable. (People v. Smith, 715.)

15. EMPLOYERS AND EMPLOYES, SPECIAL LAWS FOR THE PROTECTION OF THE LATTER.—A statute requiring emery wheels which are in continuous use to be provided with blowers to carry away the dust arising from their operation is a valid exercise of the police powers of the state. (People v. Smith, 715.)

16. CONSTITUTIONAL LAW — A SPECIAL STATUTE AUTHORIZING AN ADMINISTRATOR TO SELL REAL PROPERTY, there being no necessity for such sale, and its only object being to convert the property into money for the purposes of distribution, is unconstitutional and void. Such a statute deprives the heirs of their property without due process of law. (Johnson v. Branch, 857.)

17. CORPORATIONS—PENALTIES FOR NOT PAYING EMPLOYES WHEN DISCHARGED.—A statute requiring all railway corporations, upon discharging any employé, whether with or without cause, to on that day pay him his wages earned by him according to the contract rate, and, on default in such payment, that such wages shall continue at the same rate until paid, provided such wages shall not continue more than sixty days unless action therefor shall be commenced within that time, is not unconstitutional. The penalty thus imposed for the failure to discharge the obligation due to the employé is not unreasonable. (St. Louis etc. Ry. Co. v. Paul, 154.)

18. A STATUTE IS NOT REPEALED BY IMPLICATION, unthe later statute contains negative words, or an intention to repeal is made manifest by some intelligible form of expression. The legislature, in passing a statute, is not presumed to intend to interfere with a former statute relating to the same subject matter, unless the repugnancy between the two is irreconcilable. (State v. La Grave, 764.)

19. CONSTITUTIONAL LAW — STATUTES, REPEAL OR AMENDMENT WITHOUT RE-ENACTMENT AT LENGTH.—If a statute conflicts with a previously enacted statute, the latter is to that extent repealed or amended, whether expressly mentioned or not, although the constitution of the state declares that no law shall be revised, amended, or the provisions thereof extended or conferred by reference to its title only, but so much thereof as is revised, modified, extended, or conferred shall be enacted and published at length. (St. Louis etc. Ry. Co. v. Paul, 154.)

See, Adoption, 1, 2; Appeal, 4, 17; Carriers, 5; Criminal Law, 1, 2; Execution, 3; Executors and Administrators, 3; Former Acquittal, 2; Guardian and Ward, 6; Husband and Wife, 1, 3; Legislature, 2, 6, 7; Marriage and Divorce, 1, 2; Notaries Public, 2.

STATUTES OF LIMITATION.
See Limitations of Actions.

SUBROGATION.

See Mortgage, 3.

SUFFRAGE.

See Elections, 3.

SURETYSHIP.

1. PRINCIPAL AND SURETY — DEFAULT OF WHICH SURETY WAS NOT NOTIFIED.—The fact that an agent, for the performance of whose duties a bond with sureties was given, has, to the knowledge of his principal, been delinquent for more than three years in making payments of moneys collected by him, during which time he has been continued in his employment without notice to the surety of such delinquency, does not release the latter. The surety is bound to inquire for himself, and cannot complain that the creditor has not notified him of the state of the accounts for which he is answerable. (Wilkerson v. Crescent Ins. Co., 152.)

2. SURETIES AND GUARANTORS, CONCEALMENT OF FACTS FROM.—If, on obtaining the signature of persons as sureties, guarantors, or indorsers, there is fraudulent concealment of any fact or circumstance materially affecting the liability of such surety, guarantor, or indorser, and operating to his prejudice, he is released from liability as against any creditor having knowledge of, or reasonably chargeable with notice of, such concealed fact or circumstance. (Jungk v. Holbrook, 921.)

3. SURETY OR GUARANTOR, FAILURE TO DISCLOSE MATERIAL FACTS TO.—Noncommunication by a creditor to a surety of material facts within the knowledge of the former and which the latter should know, although not willful or intentional on the part of the creditor, discharges the surety. (Jungk v. Holbrook, 921.)

4. SURETY OR GUARANTOR, CONTRACTING WITHOUT NOTICE OF PARTNERSHIP BETWEEN THE DEBTORS AND CREDITORS, OR SOME OF THEM.—If a person is asked to become a surety on a contract for one firm in favor of another, and thereafter assents and becomes such surety, and it subsequently appears that the person thus asking and procuring him to become such surety was a silent partner in both firms and interested on both sides of the contract, and each of the firms had notice or knowledge sufficient to put them upon inquiry respecting this dual relation of their silent partner, the surety is released on the ground of the concealment from him of facts materially affecting the contract for the performance of which he became surety. (Jungk v. Holbrook, 921.)

5. SURETY OR GUARANTOR—FAILURE TO DISCLOSE FACTS.—The test as to whether a disclosure should be voluntarily made by a creditor of one who is about to become a surety for a debt is, whether there is a contract between the debtor and the creditor to the effect that the position of the surety shall be different from that which he might expect. (Jungk v. Holbrook, 921.)

See Executors and Administrators, 6; Guardian and Ward, 4; Mortgage, 3.

SURPLUSAGE.

See Pleading, 3.

TAXES.

1. TAX SALE.—A DESCRIPTION in an assessment and notice of sale for delinquent taxes of land as "NE. SE. sec. 24, township 13, R. 7, 40 acres," is sufficient. (Chestnut v. Harris, 213.)

2. TAXES—SITUS—TEST.—In determining the proper place to tax property, the test is to find its place of location and use, the place where, if a security or obligation, it is a credit, not where it is a debit. (Buck v. Miller, 436.)

3. TAXES—SITUS OF CHOSES IN ACTION FOR THE PURPOSE OF TAXATION.—In determining whether bonds, stocks, notes, and mortgages executed by nonresidents of the state, may be taxed, it is to be observed that it is the credit, and not the debt, to which value attaches, and which is, therefore, taxable. It makes no difference where the debtor lives, or where the debt was contracted, the chose in action, or credit, is taxable here, if the bond, note, or other evidence of the amount due the creditor is itself within the jurisdiction of this state. (Buck v. Miller, 436.)

4. TAXES—SITUS OF PERSONAL PROPERTY, GENERALLY, FOR THE PURPOSE OF TAXATION.—Personal property, in general, is taxable where its owner resides; but the situs of such property, for the purpose of taxation, does not always or necessarily follow the domicile of the owner. (Buck v. Miller, 436.)

5. TAXES—SITUS OF PERSONAL PROPERTY USED IN BUSINESS FOR THE PURPOSE OF TAXATION.—Personal property used in business in this state, either by the owner or his agent, is taxable here, although the owner may reside elsewhere; and this is true of credits and moneys, as well as of other forms of personal property. Hence, if money, notes, and mortgages are used in this state in the business of buying and selling property, and in making loans and investments, the money so used being collected and reloaned, such money, notes, and mortgages, if retained in this state, are taxable here. (Buck v. Miller, 436.)

6. TAXES—ASSESSMENT OF OMITTED PROPERTY.—Under a statute requiring a county auditor to give notice of his intention to assess omitted property, he is not required to go outside of his own county to give notice of his intention to assess such property. (Buck v. Miller, 436.)

7. TAXES—ASSESSMENT OF OMITTED PROPERTY.—ALL PRESUMPTIONS are in favor of the correctness of the proceedings of the county auditor in assessing omitted property, and those who question such proceedings must point out error if it exists. (Buck v Miller, 436.)

8. TAXES—OMITTED PROPERTY—DECEDENT'S ESTATE —LIEN.—Taxes assessed in pursuance of statutory provisions for the assessment of omitted property are a lien on all property in the county belonging to a decedent's estate. It is immaterial whether the property is found in the custody of executors, administrators, trustees, heirs, or devisees: and the lien can be released only by payment of the taxes. (Buck v. Miller, 436.)

9. TAXES — COLLECTION — INJUNCTION. — The collection of taxes cannot be enjoined, if any of the taxes against which the injunction is sought were legally assessed, where no payment of the valid taxes, or tender thereof, is shown to have been made. (Buck v. Miller, 436.)

See Injunction, 7; Mortgage, 1, 2.

TAX TITLE.

See Cotenancy, 2; Mortgage, **1, 2.**

would tend to incriminate or disgrace him. **The scope of such** quiry is largely within the discretion of the trial court. (Ryder State, 334.)

8. TRIAL—CHALLENGE FOR CAUSE—WHEN NOT GOOD A challenge of a juror, in a criminal case, should be overrule where he testifies that he can render a true and impartial verd upon the evidence and instructions of the court, and upon that alo1 without regard to what he may have heard and read about t case. (State v. Brady, 560.)

9. TRIAL—WAIVER OF SUBMISSION OF FACT—I STRUCTIONS.—Although a party's instructions, as asked, are bas on a claim, under the record of a right to a verdict as a matter law, that is no waiver of his right to have a question of fact subm ted to the jury if his instructions are refused. (Robinson v. Berke 549.)

10. JURY TRIAL—INSTRUCTIONS, REQUESTS FOR IN WRI ING, WHAT ARE NOT.—A rule of court requiring counsel, befo argument commences, to read and submit to the court in writing su propositions of law as they propose to rely upon, which shall co stitute the request to charge, etc., is not complied with by readi1 certain sections of the criminal code and requesting the judge charge as therein laid down. (State v. Davis, 837.)

11. JURY TRIAL, INSTRUCTIONS AFTER RETIRING.—If t' jury, after retiring to consider their verdict, return to court and a1 to be instructed as to the punishment for voluntary and involunta1 manslaughter, it is not error for the court, in the presence of t1 accused and his counsel, to read to the jury the statute fixing t1 punishment of those offenses. (State v. Kessler, 911.)

12. TRIAL—VERDICT.—When two contracts are in issue an action, and the amount of indebtedness is precisely the san under one as the other, it is immaterial upon which one the ju1 bases a verdict. (Chadwick v. Hopkins, 38.)

13. TRIAL—FINDING ON EACH OF SEPARATE COUNTS GENERAL VERDICT.—If a cause of action is presented in tw counts, each setting forth a cause of action, it is not error for tl court, although the plaintiff is entitled to a general verdict, to su1 mit the cause to the jury to find independently on each count, 1 separate findings on separate causes of action **are general, n(** special, verdicts. (Robinson v. Berkey, 549.)

TROVER.
See Animals, 1.

TRUST DEEDS.
See Merger, 1.

TRUSTS.
See Assignments, 5.

USURY.

1. USURY—WHO MAY PLEAD.—While titles to property ma(as part of a usurious contract are void, yet the right to have the1 so declared rests only with the borrower, his personal represent1 tives and privies, and a stranger to the transaction cannot set u the plea of usury in attacking such title. (Scott v. Williams, 340

2. USURY—WHO MAY NOT PLEAD.—If a borrower of mone exercises his personal privilege, and pays off a debt infected wit

usury without taking advantage of the plea of usury, neither his personal representatives nor privies can reopen the question or revise his act. (Scott v. Williams, 340.)

See Judgment, 19; Merger, 2; Vendor and Purchaser, 4.

VENDOR AND PURCHASER.

1. VENDOR AND PURCHASER — MORTGAGE — PRECEDENT DEBT—BONA FIDE PURCHASER.—It is proper to instruct the jury, in an action to quiet title to real estate, that the holder of a conveyance which is, in effect, a mortgage given to secure a precedent debt, is not a bona fide purchaser. (Adams v. Vanderbeck, 497.)

2. VENDOR AND PURCHASER — CONVEYANCE IN PAYMENT OF PRECEDENT DEBT—BONA FIDE PURCHASER.—An absolute conveyance of land by a debtor, in payment and satisfaction of a pre-existing debt owing by the grantor to the grantee, makes the grantee a bona fide purchaser, as against a prior equity in the land of which he had no notice. (Adams v. Vanderbeck, 497.)

3. VENDOR AND PURCHASER — CONVEYANCE IN PAYMENT OF PRECEDENT DEBT—BONA FIDE PURCHASER—ENFORCEMENT OF EQUITY.—If land is conveyed by the owner to another in payment and satisfaction of a debt due from the owner to that other who is ignorant of an equity in the land in favor of a third person, the enforcement of that equity against the land does not revive the indebtedness for the payment and satisfaction of which the land was conveyed. The grantee, in such a case, is as much a bona fide purchaser for value as if he had paid cash. (Adams v. Vanderbeck, 497.)

4. USURY—TITLE VOID FOR—WHO MAY PLEAD.—If a borrower of money makes an absolute deed to realty to secure the payment of a debt tainted with usury, and then upon sufficient consideration procures the grantee to execute a bond for title in favor of a third person conditioned to convey the land to the obligee on payment of the original debt, the borrower thereby deprives himself of the right to redeem the land or to avoid the deed for usury, and his personal representative has no greater rights than his intestate had. (Scott v. Willams, 340.)

See License, 4.

VICE-PRINCIPAL.

See Master and Servant, 14, 19, 20.

WAIVER.

See Chattel Mortgage, 1; Insurance, 9, 17; Judgment, 5; Jurisdiction, 3; Mechanic's Lien, 3; Municipal Corporations, 15; Sales, 6; Trial, 9.

WAREHOUSE RECEIPTS.

See Carriers, 5.

WARRANTY.

See Sales.

WATER RATES.

See Constitutions, 4, 5; Muncipal Corporations, 19-27; Waterworks and Water Companies, 1.

WATERWORKS AND WATER COMPANIES.

1. CONSTITUTIONAL LAW—RESTRICTIONS, DUTY TO SUB-MIT TO.—One engaged in the business of furnishing water to the inhabitants of towns or cities after the adoption of a constitution imposing certain restrictions upon such business is bound to submit to the restrictions so imposed. (San Diego Water Co. v. San Diego, 261.)

2. PUBLIC UTILITIES, RATES OF CHARGES—WHAT TO BE CHARGED AS EXPENSES.—In determining what a water company should be allowed as depreciation of its plant by use, ordinary repairs should be charged to current expenses, and substantial reconstruction or replacement should be charged to construction account, and depreciation should not be otherwise considered. (San Diego Water Co. v. San Diego, 261.)

See Municipal Corporations, 19-26.

·

WILLS.

1. WILLS, WHAT ARE NOT.—A paper cannot be regarded as a will, unless the intention of the decedent that it should stand for a last will and testament is clearly apparent. The heirs at law are not to be disinherited when such intention is not expressed with legal certainty. (Estate of Meade, 244.)

2. WILLS—TESTAMENTARY CHARACTER OF A PAPER, WHEN NOT APPARENT THEREFROM.—A letter directed to an undertaker, asking him, in the event of the writer's death, to cremate her body and to apprise her brother of such death, and adding that her brother would take charge of her estate and be sole administrator without bonds, to trade, sell, or occupy, as may seem fit to him, is not testamentary in character, and neither gives him her estate nor appoints him administrator thereof. (Estate of Meade, 244.)

3. WILLS—VALIDITY OF, WHERE BENEFICIARY IS NOT NAMED.—It is not essentially necessary that a testator, in his will, name the legatee or devisee, in order to give effect to the bequest. It is sufficient if he is so described therein as to be ascertained and identified. Hence, if a testatrix devises all of her property to whoever shall take care of her, at her request, providing that the person so selected shall have a written statement to that effect, the will is not invalid for the reason that no devisee is named. (Dennis v. Holsapple, 526.)

4. WILLS, OLOGRAPHIC.—FIGURES may be used in an olographic will for the purpose of expressing the amount of a legacy. (Succession of Vanhille, 642.)

5. WILLS—OLOGRAPHIC, PRINTED HEADING OR DATING.—If will is written on a printed heading, so that in dating it the writer uses the figures printed on the paper as a part of his dating, it is not wholly written, dated. and signed by his hand, and therefore is not a valid olographic will. (Succession of Robertson, 672.)

6. WILLS, OLOGRAPHIC.—THE COURT MAY DETERMINE FROM AN INSPECTION that part of a will was printed. Where the original will is before the court, it will look at it and take notice that a date thereon is partly printed and not wholly written by the testator, though the witness, whose attention was not directed to the printed heading. testified in general terms that the will was wholly in the handwriting of the testator. (Succession of Robertson, 672.)

7. WILLS—CONSTRUCTION OF WORDS IN.—If a testator uses the word "issue" in one part of his will as meaning children, it will be presumed that in using the same word in another part he intended it to have the same signification. (Madison v. Larmon, 356.)

8. EVIDENCE, EXTRINSIC, TO EXPLAIN WILL.—A will may be explained by extrinsic evidence as to the person intended, the thing intended, or the intention of the testator, as to each, when the employment of such evidence does not result in making more or less of the will than its terms import. (Dennis v. Holsapple, 526.)

9. EVIDENCE, EXTRINSIC, TO IDENTIFY DEVISEE.—If a testatrix devises all of her property to whoever shall take care of her, at her request, providing that the person so selected shall have a written statement to that effect signed by her, a letter written by her to her granddaughter after the execution of the will; informing the latter that the testatrix is sick and requesting her to come and take care of her, that she has made her will, and that she desires the granddaughter to have all of her estate, is admissible in evidence, in a controversy over the will, for the purpose of identifying the devisee. (Dennis v. Holsapple, 526.)

10. WILLS—BROTHERS AND SISTERS, WHO MAY TAKE AS.—If a testator devises certain property for his life to his children, C. S. and M., and after their death to their children, naming them, but, if any of such children shall die leaving no issue, then his share shall be equally divided among his brothers and sisters, the brothers and sisters who may thus take are not limited to those named in the will, but include all brothers and sisters of the child so deceased, whether born in the lifetime of the testator or not. (Madison v. Larmon, 356.)

11. REAL ESTATE, CONVERSION OF INTO PERSONALITY.— If a building situate upon real estate is burned by an accidental fire, and such property was devised to one person for life with remainder to others, the proceeds of the insurance of such building do not become personal property, so as to pass as such under a residuary clause of the testator's will. (Green v. Green, 846.)

12. THE RULE AGAINST PERPETUITIES IS, that no interest subject to a condition precedent is good, unless the condition must be fulfilled, if at all, within twenty-one years after some life in being at the creation of the interest. (Madison v. Larmon, 356.)

13. PERPETUITIES CREATED BY WILLS.—The time of the testator's death is the true period at which to judge of the remoteness of the provisions of his will. If it creates life estates and remainders, so that each remainder, however many estates there be, must take effect within twenty-one years after his death, it does not contravene the law against perpetuities. (Madison v. Larmon, 356.)

14. PERPETUITIES.—THERE MAY BE GIFTS FOR LIFE OF UNBORN PERSONS IN SUCCESSION, provided their estate must vest within twenty-one years after some life in being. (Madison v. Larmon, 356.)

15. PERPETUITIES.—A WILL GIVING LIFE ESTATES TO SEVENTEEN DEVISEES, constituting the children and grandchildren of the testator, with remainder over to the brothers and sisters, if any should die leaving no issue, is good. (Madison v. Larmon, 356.)

16. WILLS—ESTOPPEL TO CONTEST.—Persons who are beneficiaries in a will and who have received property thereunder cannot maintain a bill, as heirs at law of the testator, to have it declared invalid. (Madison v. Larmon, 356.)

WITNESSES.

1. WITNESSES—REFRESHING MEMORY.—In an action to recover on a fire insurance policy one year after the loss, a witness

who was the bookkeeper for the assured up to the time of the fire may refresh his memory from a schedule of the property destroyed, furnished by the insured to the insurer as a proof of loss and made up from duplicate invoices, from recollection of the stock on hand, from the insured's books and original invoices, and such witness may read the schedule to the jury in response to a question as to the amount of goods on hand at the time of the fire. (Kahn v. Traders' etc. Co., 147.)

2. WITNESSES—COMPLICATED AND VOLUMINOUS RECORDS AND CLAIMS—CLASSIFICATION AND TABULATION—TESTIFYING FROM PAPERS OFFERED IN EVIDENCE.—Upon the trial of an indictment of an overseer of the poor, charged with defrauding a county by filing a fraudulent claim against it for the transportation of an indigent poor person, where evidence of fraud as to other like claims, together with the records of transportation companies, is introduced in evidence, and the records are complicated, and the claims are numerous, it is not an abuse of discretion for the trial court to permit a witness to make a tabulated statement from the records, to classify the claims, and to testify from his examination of the various papers in evidence, especially where no prejudice is shown, and the purpose is to facilitate the trial and aid the jury in arriving at just results. (State v. Brady, 560.)

3. EVIDENCE—OPINIONS.—If the question under examination and to be decided by the jury is one of opinion, any witness, whether expert or nonexpert, may state his opinion or belief, giving his reasons therefor, when authorized so to do, by statute. (Ryder v. State, 334.)

4. EVIDENCE.—EXPERT TESTIMONY as to a matter within the common knowledge of the jury is inadmissible. (Alabama etc. R. R. Co. v. Jones, 121.)

5. INSANITY AS A DEFENSE—EXPERT AND NONEXPERT TESTIMONY—INSTRUCTIONS.—If the defense of insanity is relied upon, and there is evidence of expert and nonexpert witnesses who testify as to the insanity of the accused, and who were "parties who associated with the defendant, lived with him, lived in the same community," it is error to charge the jury that the testimony of expert witnesses is entitled to great weight, and that the testimony of intimate associates of the accused should be given similar weight. The jury are the sole judges, and should be left untrammeled to pass upon the credibility of all witnesses. (Ryder v. State, 334.)

WOMAN SUFFRAGE.

See Elections, 4-6.